LANDSCAPE DESIGN

LANDSCAPE DESIGN

A Cultural and Architectural History

ELIZABETH BARLOW ROGERS

HARRY N. ABRAMS, INC., PUBLISHERS

EDITORS: JULIA MOORE, ELAINE STAINTON, RICHARD A. GALLIN
DESIGNER: ANA ROGERS
PHOTO EDITOR AND PHOTO RESEARCH: JOHN K. CROWLEY
PHOTO RESEARCH: DIANA GONGORA

Endpapers: Embroidered parterre, Château de Vaux-le-Vicomte, France
p. 1: Water garden, Broadlands, England
pp. 2–3: Isola Bella, Lake Maggiore, northern Italy
pp. 4–5: Canopus at Hadrian's villa, near Tivoli, Italy
pp. 6–7: Gardens at Stourhead, England
pp. 8–9: Mossy garden at Saiho-ji, Kyoto, Japan
p. 11: Conservancy Garden, Central Park, New York City

Library of Congress Cataloging-in-Publication Data

Rogers, Elizabeth Barlow, 1936–
Landscape design : a history of cities, parks, and gardens / Elizabeth Barlow Rogers.
p. cm.
Includes bibliographical references (p.).
ISBN 0–8109–4253–4
1. Landscape architecture—History. 2. Landscape design—History. I. Title.
SB470.5 .R64 2001
712'.09–dc21   00–048480

Printed and bound in Japan
10 9 8 7 6 5 4 3 2 1

Harry N. Abrams, Inc.
100 Fifth Avenue
New York, N.Y. 10011
www.abramsbooks.com

THIS BOOK IS DEDICATED TO
TED ROGERS

AND THE MEN AND WOMEN
WHO BUILT AND REBUILT CENTRAL PARK.

TABLE OF CONTENTS

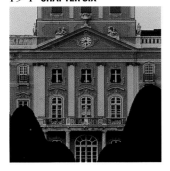

FOREWORD

The building of Central Park according to the vision of Frederick Law Olmsted and Calvert Vaux is one of the great political and cultural achievements of the American people. That the democratic experiment of a public park had succeeded so well and for so long seemed to constitute a mandate for its preservation and rebuilding in 1979 when Mayor Edward I. Koch appointed me to be the first Central Park administrator and Commissioner Gordon J. Davis helped me to found the Central Park Conservancy. As the studies of the Conservancy staff and consultants on the park's management and restoration plan went forward in the early 1980s, I wanted to understand better the landscape tradition of which Central Park is a part and to learn more about the history of landscape design that preceded and followed it.

During this period, I read books and articles that were beginning to appear in the area of garden history, thanks in part to the work of Elizabeth Blair MacDougall, former director of the program of landscape studies at Dumbarton Oaks in Washington, D.C., and her successor, John Dixon Hunt, who now serves as the chairman of the Department of Landscape Architecture and Regional Planning at the University of Pennsylvania. As editor of the international quarterly *Studies in the History of Gardens and Designed Landscapes, formerly the Journal of Garden History,* Professor Hunt has actively promoted the historiography of landscape design both through his own work and in the scholarship that he has encouraged with the symposia he has organized, the papers he has published, and the books he has encouraged and authored. Because of the work of MacDougall, Hunt, and several other contemporary landscape historians, including David Coffin, who pioneered the study of landscape design as a branch of art history at Princeton University, facile assumptions have been overturned and understanding deepened in a heretofore barely considered field of serious study. Further, archaeologists and historians have brought to light much new information that deserves to be synthesized in a comprehensive survey that will allow a comparative analysis of styles and periods and provide an understanding of the cultural values that have informed landscape design in different times and places.

As serious scholarship was emerging in the area of landscape studies, new works on urbanism were also being published. The late Spiro Kostof in particular stands out as a writer who stimulated understanding of the design of cities as large-scale, long-term landscape projects. Reading his works and those of other authors, I began to see a reciprocity of influence between cities, parks, and gardens and to understand that in addition to being part of a continuum of design sensibility, all three categories of landscape were almost always subject to a prevailing Zeitgeist.

Everywhere and always humanity's desire to reflect cosmological understanding, to perfect nature, and to order the physical circumstances of life is strong. To understand better the cultural ethos reflected in the landscapes I wished to describe I have read history, philosophy, science, and certain important works of literature. Readings in these areas, I believe, reinforce the assumption that everything we see reflecting human presence in nature has its origins in the mind and its cultural constructs. Whether reflecting deep religious convictions, economic motives, or passing fancies, art is always imbedded in the prevailing cultural values of a certain group of people at a particular period in history. Thus, ideological forces guide the minds and hands of those who shape space and, through design, give meaning to place. This representation of ideas in the built environment occurs sometimes with intent but often unconsciously. Thus, so-called vernacular landscapes have as much cultural significance as artfully contrived ones for those who care to observe and reflect upon the scenery of everyday life.

In making this intellectual journey I have had the encouragement of family members and the friends who have heard, read, and constructively criticized my thoughts and ideas. First and foremost, I wish to thank my husband, Ted, who has deferred alternative vacation itineraries in favor of travel excursions in the service of this book and who has listened to many groping ideas and glimmers of understanding along the way. In addition, I owe special thanks to four distinguished historians whose friendship and belief in my project's value have assisted me greatly. They are Frances H. Kennedy, Roger G. Kennedy, Helen Lefkowitz Horowitz, and Daniel Horowitz. In particular, Frances Kennedy, who is also a noted conservationist, gave me invaluable advice and introductions to others who were helpful. Helen Horowitz provided firm encouragement, insisting that I continue working toward publication at the point when the effort seemed most daunting. Then, as the book neared completion, she read the manuscript and made several helpful suggestions that improved its structure and narrative flow. I also thank my friend Ned O'Gorman for reading several chapters with a poet's ear for language and a gardener's eye for landscape.

Another friend, Carol Krinsky, professor of art history at New York University and author of several books on architecture, gave a close reading of the entire penultimate draft of my manuscript. By taking seriously my plea to be treated as a student, Carol served as an additional editor, penciling numerous marginal comments and queries that forced me to substantively rethink facts and points of view throughout. Reuben Rainey, professor of landscape architecture at the University of Virginia School of Architecture, also read the manuscript in its entirety and gave me several key suggestions for its improvement. I am particularly grateful for the kindness and generosity of these two important first readers and hasten to make the usual author's disclaimer on their behalf: They are entirely innocent of any errors that may remain in my text.

The same is true for the several other scholars who have read individual chapters in the areas of their expertise. Chapter One benefited from the eyes and mind of the Egyptologist Patrick Cardon. For another reading of that chapter I am indebted to David Hurst Thomas, curator of North American Archaeology at the American Museum of Natural History, and to his associate and wife, Lorann Pendleton, director of the Nels Nelson North American Archaeology Laboratory, for their invaluable knowledge of, and advice on other resources for, understanding the Native American landscape. I am further grateful to my friend Dave Warren, who is a member of the Santa Clara Pueblo, for also reading Chapter One and expanding my perception of the sensory dimensions and cosmological underpinnings of prehistoric, early ancient, and contemporary Native American place making and to Khristaan Villela, director of the Thaw Art History Center and assistant professor at the College of Santa Fe, for his thoughtful comments. Rina Swentzell, the Puebloan architectural historian, critiqued this chapter and made me understand more fully the sense she shares with many other Native Americans of the sacredness of *all* nature, not merely certain important sites. Further, I wish to thank Bradley T. Lepper, curator of archaeology at the Ohio Historical Center in Columbus, for introducing me to the Mound Builders of southern Ohio. Duane Anderson, director of the Museum of Indian Arts and Culture of the Museum of New Mexico in Santa Fe, gave my material on prehistoric and living Native American cultures a final, constructive reading, and Laura Hold, the librarian of the Laboratory of Anthropology at the Museum of New Mexico, guided me to relevant materials on the archaeology of the Americas. Writer, artist, and preservationist Nikos Stavroulakis was a most helpful host as I studied Minoan sites on his native island, Crete.

I thank Peter J. Holliday, professor of history of art and classical archaeology, California State University, Long Beach, for the careful and constructive reading he gave of Chapter Two. I first saw the Athenian Acropolis and Agora in the company of classical scholar Avi Sharon, who provided many useful insights into the history and cultural meaning of these important spaces. Chapter Three benefited from the scrutiny of Steven Murray, professor of art history and noted medieval architectural historian at Columbia University, as well as from the assistance of two Islamists, D. Fairchild Ruggles, visiting assistant professor in the departments of architecture and landscape architecture, Cornell University, and Behula Shah, the director of landscape studies at Chatham College. All of these specialists were generous with their time and advice, and I was educated by their patient coaching.

Guy Walton, professor of fine arts, New York University, and author and authority on French Renaissance and seventeenth-century gardens, read Chapters Four and Five, and his suggestions regarding their improvement were invaluable. Tracy Ehrlich, assistant professor of Art History at Colgate University, has particular expertise in the area of the Italian villa garden, and her reading of these same two chapters was equally helpful. Magnus Olausson, National Museum, Sweden, read the section on Drottningholm Palace gardens in Chapter Six and kindly met with me, enlarging my perspective on the relationship of Swedish garden design to that of the rest of Europe. I also thank Lena Löfgren Uppsäll and Marie Edman Franzen for sharing their knowledge of Swedish landscape design with me on our tour of Drottningholm Palace gardens.

Landscape architect Joseph Disponzio, a former colleague in the New York City Department of Parks and my teaching assistant in the course I taught in landscape design history at Columbia University in 1991, is a now an assistant professor of landscape architecture at Harvard Graduate School of Design. His knowledge of the French Picturesque style, the subject of his dissertation, and his critical reading of Chapter Seven were a great help. Peter Fergusson, professor of art history, Wellesley College, also gave me some eminently constructive suggestions on this chapter.

I wish to thank Kendall H. Brown, assistant professor in the Department of Art, California State University at Long Beach, and a former editor for the Macmillan *Dictionary of Art,* for reading Chapter Eight from the perspective of a East Asian specialist. John Major, East Asian scholar, author, anthologist, and coauthor of a guide to world literature also read Chapter Eight, and his knowledge of the Chinese and Japanese languages and cultures was for me an important asset. In addition, his suggestions regarding particular poems and novels have illuminated my understanding of some relationships between literature and landscape design while also giving me many hours of pleasurable reading. Kenji Wako, associate professor in the department of Environmental Planning at Osaka University, provided some pertinent corrections to my manuscript as did Yoshiko Nihei, who also did the excellent picture research responsible for many of the illustrations in Chapter Eight. Finally, I thank Stephanie Wada, associate curator with the Mary and Jackson Burke Foundation and a specialist in the art of Japan, for a final reading of this material.

Charles Beveridge, series editor of the Frederick Law Olmsted Papers and a professor in the department of history, American University, Washington, D.C., read Chapter Nine. This proved most helpful, as his intimate knowledge of the accomplishments of Olmsted and his partner Calvert Vaux surpasses my own long and appreciative familiarity with their work. David Schuyler, professor of American Studies at Franklin and Marshall College and also an editor of the Frederick Law Olmsted Papers, has special knowledge of the nineteenth-century American metropolitan landscape and is an authority on Andrew Jackson Downing, Frederick Law Olmsted, and Calvert Vaux. His reading of Chapter Nine and subsequent chapters also provided me with fresh insights on subjects with which I was familiar but lacked his nuanced understanding.

David Streatfield, professor of landscape architecture at the University of Washington and an authority on the gardens of California, gave me valuable insights into this region's role in the history of landscape design. I also offer thanks to Donald Brumder for hosting my tour of the gardens of Pasadena and arranging access to several private estates in Santa Barbara. Garden designer Willem Wirtz guided me around several private and public gardens in Palm Beach, Florida, and I am grateful for his impressive store of knowledge of that community's landscape history, past and present.

Lance Neckar, professor and associate dean of the College of Architecture and Landscape Architecture at the University of Minnesota, read Chapter Thirteen and provided constructive commentary on my treatment of modernist gardens in general. Elizabeth G Miller read part of this chapter as well, and Will Miller was a generous and thoughtful host on my tour of the J. Irwin Miller garden and related points of interest in Columbus, Indiana. George Waters, editor of *Pacific Horticulture* magazine was a similarly instructive guide to the Donell Garden in Sonoma, California, and other nearby landscapes of the modern era. I am indebted to Gordon and Carole Hyatt for their many kindnesses to me when I was visiting Naumkeag in the Berkshires. Because of the gracious assistance of Ronaldo Maia, I was accompanied by the knowledgeable Brazilian horticulturist Cynthia Zanotto Salvador on a tour of several of the modernist landscapes created by Roberto Burle Marx, which I also discuss in Chapter Thirteen. Chapter Fourteen benefited from an explanatory tour through the newly completed Animal Kingdom park in Walt Disney World in Orlando, Florida, with Paul Comstock, the head of landscape design within the Disney Company's Imagineering division.

When I was writing Chapter Fifteen, the artist Nancy Holt granted me an interview in which I learned a great deal about the process, both conceptual and technical, of producing art on a landscape scale. From her I also gained greater understanding of the role of her late husband, Robert Smithson, in the origins of the Earthworks movement. Charles Jencks was similarly kind in welcoming me to Portrack Garden in Dumfrieshire, Scotland, and I thank Alistair Clark, the head gardener there, for his discussion of this landscape work in progress. I am also grateful to Ian Hamilton Findlay for allowing me to spend a morning at Little Sparta, his poetical landscape creation in Lanarkshire, Scotland.

Henry J. Stern, commissioner of the New York City Department of Parks and Recreation, has instilled in the agency over which he has presided during two mayoral administrations a strong sense of its history. Jonathan Kuhn, the agency's director of art and antiquities, provided helpful answers to several questions regarding the department's past as well as access to the material in its archives. I am grateful as well to Jane Weissmann, former director of Operation Green Thumb, and to Andrew Stone, director of the New York City Land Project for the Trust for Public Land, who furnished me with materials and information relating to the community gardens movement discussed in Chapter Sixteen.

A book such as this one would be impossible without the patient research and insightful discoveries of these scholars, professional designers, and administrators as well as others listed in my bibliography. Their research, publications, and practice in the related fields of landscape design history and landscape restoration have made a fresh survey both necessary and possible. The lectures of my Yale professors, Vincent Scully and Christopher Tunnard, were, I am sure, partly responsible for my abiding enthusiasm for architecture, landscape, and urban design, an enthusiasm that was nourished by my friendship with the cultural geographer J. B. Jackson. Charles McLaughlin's loan of his thesis manuscript of *The Selected Letters of Frederick Law Olmsted* when I was doing research for *Frederick Law Olmsted's New York* in the days before photocopying machines, computers, or the subsequent publication of the multivolume Olmsted papers (an enterprise that he still supervises with fellow historian Charles Beveridge) stands out as an act of scholarly generosity and personal friendship for which I will always be grateful.

Other special friends include Sara Cedar Miller, the Central Park Conservancy historian and photographer, who gave me invaluable help when this book was still in its infancy, and Lane Addonizio, my Cityscape Institute colleague, who assisted in its final production. Without Sara's skills I could not have built the slide lectures from which the book germinated, and Lane's fine organizational ability kept both our office and this project on course. I also wish to thank Mary McCormick, president of the Fund for the City of New York and an original sponsor of the Cityscape Institute, together with Cityscape's funders, for understanding the importance of grounding our public-space education and improvement mission in a knowledge of past and present cultural values. I am particularly grateful to the LuEster Mertz Trust and to Furthermore, the arm of the J. M. Kaplan Fund that supports publications, for directly assisting the production of this book with foundation grants.

In Central Park I learned the value of collaboration and teamwork. That lesson has been reinforced by the people at Harry N. Abrams, Inc. Publisher and editor-in-chief Paul Gottlieb saw the need for a survey such as I proposed, and he allowed the book to grow beyond the specifications of our contract to its natural dimensions in terms of picture and word count. John Crowley, director of photographs and permissions, has been the most resourceful of picture editors, seeking out, with the help of Diana Gongora, images I was unable to provide and reading the manuscript carefully to assure the proper fit of pictures to text. Paulo Suzuki has brought his skills as an artist to our project and, basing his work upon earlier documents, has created a number of freshly drawn plans and perspectives to aid the reader's visualization of certain landscapes discussed in the text. Elaine Banks Stainton, senior editor, has overseen the difficult process of readying the book for production. Ana Rogers is the book's designer, and her fine work speaks for itself. Our team leader has been Julia Moore, executive editor and director of textbook publishing, the most astute and considerate of editors. She has assured the integrity of our project at every turn, always advocating what is in the best interest of the book's intent and content rather than what is merely expedient or least costly.

I would like to add a final additional word of gratitude to Ted, my husband, for encouraging me to undertake this broad-scale survey in the first place and to persist in bringing it to publication. I thank him especially for sharing with me a wonderful educational adventure as we have walked together in the cities, parks, and gardens described in the following chapters and talked about the civilizations, including our own, that are responsible for the impressions we have gathered and the knowledge of place-making we have gained together.

THE SHAPING OF SPACE;
THE MEANING OF PLACE

A history of landscape design is necessarily a history of human culture. It should be located in the broadest sense in relation to values of time and space, but also more specifically as an art-historical pursuit, seeking to demonstrate how philosophical concepts, and not only ideals of beauty, are expressed through art—in this case, an art that modifies and shapes nature. A history of landscape design is one way of writing the history of the human mind. Therefore, while this book seeks to provide a description of the designs of specific locales, the approach is contextual. It attempts to portray landscapes as products of attitudes toward the cosmos, nature, and humanity and to show how they share elements of form and meaning with artifacts from the disciplines with which they are most intimately, and often inextricably, allied—painting, sculpture, architecture, and the decorative arts—as well as with literature and other means of ideological expression. It is thus a narrative of a relationship between human beings and their world and of their attempts to invest nature with purposeful order and meaning and specific places with expressive form and heightened significance.

The mores that stem from people's attitudes in each age and geographical region are manifested in myths, rituals, social structures, and economic pursuits. These things affect the organization of space and the design of forms within it, which in turn rationalize and institutionalize patterns of cultural behavior. In speaking of a prevailing cultural consensus, however, one must offer qualifications. The decisions of governing elites, planners, architects, and landscape designers as well as those of the builders of vernacular structures for practical purposes and everyday use occur within social contexts in which there is often a historical lag between the articulation of philosophical ideas and the creation of forms that manifest those ideas. Contrarily, a philosophy yet to be expressed may be anticipated by a physical manifestation. In both cases, a gap between ideas and cultural expression is apparent. But whether it anticipates or confirms them, design does reflect certain normative cultural values, including those articulated by philosophers when they offer their particular intellectual lenses through which to perceive the cosmos and the place of human beings within it.

Many of the landscapes discussed in this book have now vanished. Others can be mentally or physically reconstructed only from the clues offered by archaeologists. Some are mere relics of their original designs. Certain landscapes, on the other hand, show an amazing persistence over time. Still others—the world's fair, the theme park, the shopping mall—are products of the present era. All can be interpreted as expressions of cultural values. Moreover, because landscapes have a temporal dimension, altering with time, they can be read as palimpsests, documents in which nature's own powerful dynamic and the changing intentions of human beings over the years inscribe a historical record.

Since culture is always both a cause and effect of particular political, economic, and technological circumstances as well as of cosmological and philosophical attitudes, each age and country leaves its own legacy, signifying in large measure its type of governance, degree of wealth, and level of construction skills, as well as its political character and religious beliefs. All of these things are given form through the tastes and talents of patrons and designers. Indeed, the tastes of patrons and the talents of designers could not be exercised in the same manner, nor would the style and iconographic content of their work be as it is, in the absence of particular combinations of governance, wealth, and technology as informed by philosophical thought. By way of example, one may say that work of the great seventeenth-century French landscape designer André Le Nôtre expresses the authoritarianism of Louis XIV's regime, the prosperity of the French economy under the management of the finance minister Jean-Baptiste Colbert, the development of new means of constructing earthworks by the military engineer Sébastien Le Prestre de Vauban, and the application of the mathematical philosophy of René Descartes to the art of landscape design. To say this does not diminish our estimation of Le Nôtre's genius; it merely furnishes the conditions and parameters of its flowering.

It should be stressed that to understand designed landscapes, as well as human attitudes toward natural ones, one must venture beyond the important areas of political, economic, and technological history into the realms of cosmology, religion, science, and metaphysics. The physical world, as shaped by thought and action, mirrors the human mind as a theater of myth, ritual, allegory, and reason. So, too, the mind's capacity for sensation and reflection finds expression in the shaping and furnishing of landscape space, as does the human desire for public ceremony and personal pleasure. This book traces the flow of these mental energies across time and space, examining the cultural matrices of various periods and places and the influence of these upon landscape design.

Landscape and religion bore a particularly close relationship to one another in prehistoric times and early antiquity, when people perceived nature and the cosmos to be pregnant with spirit forces, which they personified as gods governing the hunt and later the fertility of the soil and the harvest. Aware of the degree to which their lives were subject to the forces of nature, prehistoric and ancient societies developed rituals of propitiation to ensure seasonal benefits, such as bountiful game, adequate rainfall, and the warmth of the sun as well as the continuation of human life through successful reproduction. The spaces in which these ceremonies took place were theaters for religious expression within a larger landscape. This is the lesson of Paleolithic cave art and the astronomical alignments of the stones at Stonehenge and other megalithic circles (see figs. 1.2, 1.3). The cosmological orientation found in the archaeological remains of temples, platforms, and pyramids in Egypt, Mesopotamia, India, Crete, Greece, and the Americas implies a similar conclusion (see figs. 1.8, 1.9, 1.10, 1.24, 1.27, 1.28). In such ruins, one sees how human beings expressed in landscape terms their alliance with spirit forces within the earth and how they invoked the aid of cosmic powers. There is a reciprocity between the human and the natural that honors the notion of an inherent divinity in both. Sacred sites—mountains, lakes, and springs—called out to these early peoples. Pyramid, ziggurat, *kiva*, mound, and temple—these were ceremonial sites, as Puebloan plazas still are.

The transformation of religion from the worship of animal spirit, sun, and Earth Mother to that of a pantheon of deities presided over by Zeus and Apollo can be read in a selection of sacred landscapes. Ancient classical temples and their siting in the landscape reveal how Greek logic and mathematics began to transform the human bond with nature from one belief system to another. Blood sacrifice, ritual dancing, and oracular consultation as a means of invoking the cooperation of unseen forces in a precarious world did not disappear with the dawn of the Greek Classical age in the fifth century B.C.E. But alongside these practices, Greek philosophers proffered another means of shaping destiny. Reliance upon the powers of intellect in the affairs of humankind slowly assumed at least equal importance with dependence upon the forces of fate. Landscape, although still the province of propitiatory rites, was manipulated in ways that suggest a new sense of confidence in reason. This is evident on the Athenian Acropolis, where the defensible site of the earlier city, after being devastated by the Persians, was rebuilt in the fifth century B.C.E. as a religious precinct in which an architecture based upon exquisite mathematical proportions is worn like a proud crown (see fig. 2.1).

The power of empire and the pride of Caesars invested Hellenistic and Roman landscapes with characteristic forms of spatial composition, as well as with a more cosmopolitan and secular approach to design. Colonial cities were rationally laid out in grid plans, and in Roman ones aqueduct-fed baths and fountains as well as in basilicas, arenas, and theaters expressed imperial might and largesse. Unlike the modern city, which projected itself into the surrounding countryside, first as a centrifugal force of axes radiating outward, and later as a series of amorphous zones of expanded settlement, the ancient Roman city represented a centripetal gathering of energies into enclosed spaces: the town itself, the forum, and the inward-focused peristyle garden (see fig. 2.29). The ubiquitous reiteration of prototypical elements of Roman urbanism—forums, basilicas, baths, theaters, arenas, libraries, roads, triumphal arches, aqueducts—in cities linked by a vast road system throughout the Mediterranean world impressively demonstrated imperial might.

The elements of myth and ritual were elaborated as allegory in Roman times. For instance, the cave sanctuary in nature was symbolized in the artificial grotto where it served as a psychological echo chamber, a place where the human psyche found a physical link to the prehistoric world of the Earth Goddess and nature spirits. Grottoes with sculptural representations of nymphs and other subterranean spirits were installed in many villa gardens, one of the most spectacular of which was that built by the emperor Hadrian. Throughout its vast, now mostly vanished, decorative program of sculpture, wall painting, and mosaic, Hadrian's Villa also provides an early example of the associative garden, or the thematic treatment of landscape in which allegory plays a role.

Christians and Muslims appropriated allegory in the recurring metaphor of paradise as a garden in literature and art. The gardens of both cultures exploited the symbolic relationship of landscape and heavenly reward. Four watercourses in Islamic gardens and four paths leading from a central fountain in Christian ones represented the four paradisaical rivers mentioned in the Quran and the Bible (see figs. 3.10, 3.25). The cool, sparkling, reflective, murmurous qualities of water in these gardens were particularly conducive to otherworldly contemplation and well suited to the image of paradise as a place of tranquil refreshment and beauty.

Allegory also plays a strong role in Renaissance and Mannerist gardens, where the myths of antiquity were revived and reinterpreted by humanist scholars. At the Villa d'Este, for example, to manifest the beneficence of the owner, Cardinal d'Este, much of the garden's sculptural iconography was associated with the virtuous hero Hercules. Here and at the Villa Lante, the hunting park and country estate of Cardinal Gambara, are found symbols celebrating each cardinal's ability to fructify the land through a combination of art and nature (see figs. 4.18, 4.23). The use of allegory to glorify popes and princes can also be recognized in many seventeenth- and eighteenth-century gardens, as at Versailles, where the abundant symbols of Apollo, the sun god, refer to Louis XIV.

Along with this last, late use of allegory, another development was occurring that has affected the modern world view and, with it, the approach to landscape making: the birth of systematic science and the greatly increased reliance upon reason as a governing principle in the affairs of life. The shift from belief in an earth-centered, self-contained, closed universe to a boundless one, and the consequent opening of the human mind to new metaphysical possibilities, had a profound effect on philosophy. This unharnessing of the intellect from ancient constructs found parallel physical expression in the treatment of space in landscape design. The garden remained enclosed and by definition a place set apart from its cultivated rural surroundings and wild nature (the garden being characterized since the Renaissance as "third nature," as distinguished from the agrarian landscape—"second nature"—and wilderness—"first nature"), but it no longer represented itself as an enclosed space, and its axes were given apparent elongation, as if to join the actual horizon. Le Nôtre's plan of the Sun King's gardens at Versailles is thus as much an expression of the opening of the mind to a new heliocentric interpretation of the universe, which was then considered coterminous with our galaxy, as it is of the confidence, optimism, and pride of France during the first half of the reign of Louis XIV (see fig. 5.9).

Axial extension within the garden, in turn, provided a paradigm for city planning. This form of urbanization following the layout of the town and gardens of Versailles, the international model for new and modernizing cities, involved the construction of wide straight thoroughfares, often radiating from a prominent monument, prestigious structure, or central public space to the far reaches of the urbanized mass and even into the countryside (see figs. 6.44, 6.54). During the eighteenth, nineteenth, and early twentieth centuries, governments sponsored grand axial plans with broad avenues and magnificent architecture and sculpture as a means of expressing their power and authority, providing better police protection, and facilitating military control of rebellious mobs. In addition, the grand thoroughfares of the monumental city served the elite for whom the invention of the lightweight, spring-hung carriage had made vehicular promenading an important social pastime. Also toward these ends, ancient and medieval town walls were torn down and converted into boulevards. This occurred first in France, where the birth of the modern nation-state rendered obsolete the enclosed fortified city.

As Isaac Newton was solidifying the basis of the Enlightenment and confirming the role of reason in human thought, John Locke asserted that all knowledge of the world must rest on sensory awareness. This concept of the mind as an instrument for inductive reasoning and a theater for personal experience, rather than as a receptacle for revealed Truth and immutable law, helped change the character of landscape design in the eighteenth century. Respect for the potential of landscape to produce mental sensations through association caused garden designers to gather into their repertoire of effects images of a poetic and painterly nature, especially at first those that evoked the antique past through classical forms and pastoral Arcadian motifs. The garden became no longer a stage for the display of power, an arena of social interaction, but a place for solitary or companionable reflection and contemplation. Locke's philosophy thus provides a key for those who would ponder the meaning of miniature temples, sham ruins, grottoes, and grazing deer in an eighteenth-century English landscape park (see figs. 7.5, 7.6, 7.7, 7.9, 7.13).

Though much earlier in its origins, the East Asian garden was equally a place of poetic association and friendship. As in England, in China and Japan the associative potential of garden scenery was an important design consideration. In China, the talents of poet, painter, and garden designer were fused, often in the same persons. These artists enjoyed an especially close relationship with nature, and their compositions evoke the precipitous peaks of certain mountainous parts of their country (see fig. 8.3). Derived from China, Japanese garden design is also premised upon a great deal of naturalistic rockwork, although the carefully arranged, flatter, less contorted stones in Japanese gardens understandably reflect more that country's island scenery than the topography of its mainland neighbor. The rocks in both Chinese and Japanese gardens are replete with symbolical associations (see fig. 8.24). Plants, too, enjoy a symbolic function, and appreciation of selected species, such as peonies, chrysanthemums, plum trees, and bamboo is focused and intense.

In the late eighteenth century, pathos and memory came to play an important role in Western garden design as Romanticism replaced classical order as the dominant cultural impulse of Western civilization. Jean-Jacques Rousseau's belief in the importance of commonly accessible personal experience in nature and in the virtues of a democratically organized citizenry had important consequences for landscape design. Gradually, the focus of Lockean sensation was transferred from the literary and political to the patriotic and personal, and the Western garden became an arena in which to honor heroes of state and a place for the repose of the dead. This accounts for the affective and often elegiac character of the Picturesque style and why it made an appropriate design idiom for the nineteenth-century rural cemetery (see fig. 9.27). The popularity of Rousseau's philosophy, which gained strength through the several revolutionary movements that enfranchised a much larger segment of the general populace during this turbulent era, helps explain the origins of the public parks movement.

Concurrent with the birth of Romanticism and the revolutionary forces growing out of it and leading to the development of nationalistic capitalist democracies and communist states, the Industrial Revolution provided the cultural dynamic that made possible the accelerating advances in machine technology that continue to propel contemporary life. Over the past two hundred years, democracy's "right to life, liberty and happiness," including the enjoyment of private property, has promoted personal pleasure as a powerful principle in the field of landscape design, as in other areas of life. The advances of egalitarianism have caused the continued transformation of the pleasure garden, once the exclusive domain of the aristocracy, into a recreational preserve for the masses.

The Industrial Revolution profoundly altered the nature of urban life, especially as transportation advances induced a new mobility within and between cities, and time and distance assumed new meaning. Paris's radical reorganization in the second half of the nineteenth century reflects this Machine Age transformation (see fig. 10.7). The parks movement and the development of the residential suburb in America in the second half of the nineteenth century express a nostalgia for the agrarian past that was concomitant with industrialism and the growth of cities in the modern era. During this period and continuing to the present day, the market forces of a globalizing culture have promoted the eclectic character of landscape design in the West. In the absence of a general cultural consensus since at least the beginning of the nineteenth century, design has been increasingly viewed as a commodity, a mere matter of consumer taste, as expressed in the casual intermingling of various past styles (see fig. 11.4).

Twentieth-century modernism attempted a radical reinvention of architectural design, with landscape architecture, somewhat hesitantly at first, joining forces in forging a vocabulary that aimed to express rationality and function (see figs. 12.19, 13.23). But rational planning and functionalism were inadequate to suppress historical associations, and the result of the obsession with history that continues to the present time is reflected in stylistic multiplicity and eclectic design. In this context, Modernism, too, became a style, merely another design option.

Catering to popular taste, the creators of world's fairgrounds, theme parks, and shopping malls applied narratives of history and fantasy to landscape with the aid of media technology and mass-marketing techniques (see fig. 14.10). The modern self-theming of cities to attract tourists is a manifestation of this trend, one in which historic preservation, in traversing the distance between reverence for the past and profitability, sometimes takes a pratfall into the realm of parody. Nevertheless, some efforts to establish serious historical meaning within the contemporary designed landscape and to preserve nature and create psychologically resonant metaphorical representations of it still manage to heighten the spiritual bond between humanity and the built and natural environments (see figs. 15.28, 15.30).

A comprehensive survey such as this is necessarily a dialogue across the centuries and across the globe. In tracing patterns of influence, it is apparent that form follows culture, but, once developed, form often follows form. By example, the revival of the forms of Greek and Roman art and architecture during the Renaissance and later periods of Western history exemplifies the ways in which people of other eras and in other places have found in the forms forged in antiquity an expressive design vocabulary for their own particular societal aspirations. Transmission may also occur more directly, moving along the paths of military adventure and trade, as when the formal innovations of one country are exported to, or imported by, another through conquest and assimilation.

Such was the case from the fourth through the second centuries B.C.E. as Alexander the Great's far-flung Hellenistic empire carried Greek forms to the farthest reaches of the Mediterranean basin and beyond to Persia. Similarly, in early sixteenth-century France, the development of the French Renaissance garden was based upon direct imitation of Italian Renaissance garden principles and the immigration to France of Italian garden designers following the Neapolitan campaign of the French king, Charles VIII. But just as the Japanese assimilated Chinese garden concepts along with Buddhism beginning in the sixth century and then developed out of this beginning their own indigenous approach to garden making, so too did those who followed the French Renaissance garden designers evolve from their forms ones that were distinctive to French culture, which were subsequently adopted, adapted, and altered by others elsewhere.

Traditionalism, or historicization, for its own sake, as stylistic imitation of past forms simply for the period qualities they convey and aesthetic characteristics they display, can be explained as part of a widespread reactionary attitude toward the Industrial Age on the part of some since the beginning of the nineteenth century. The reverse of modernism, this attempt to cherish and derive emotional satisfaction from association with what is venerable and vanishing is a strategy for denying accelerating change and the Faustian transformation of the world through technology.

Following the currents of classicism and Neoclassicism, the growth of Romanticism and the dissemination of the Picturesque style, the development of various urban planning models from the Hellenistic grid to the contemporary edge city — these are some of the tasks of a broad-based landscape history. The pursuit of these landscape design developments will enable us to see, among other things, how the inherently autocratic style of city planning favored by European monarchs in the seventeenth century could be used in laying out Washington, D.C., the capital of a new democratic nation in the eighteenth, or how the adaptation of the English Picturesque style, developed by and for aristocratic estate owners in the eighteenth century, became the paradigm for the nineteenth-century public park.

Landscape design is fundamentally a relationship between people and place, a partnership between art and nature, and, increasingly, between art, nature, and technology. Art and technology have the power to modify nature, but landscape design operates within the laws of growth and decay that govern all animate life. The mystery of nature as an independent force—bounteous and generous, overpowering and destructive— makes the experience and practice of landscape design both spiritually rewarding and scientifically challenging. Its historiography is made especially difficult by the natural tendency to view past cultures through a contemporary cultural lens. Our attempt here is to penetrate, however imperfectly, the consciousness both of human beings who are like ourselves and of those who are mentally and spiritually very different from us.

In so doing, we must stress that the separation of myth, religion, philosophy, and science into independent modes of perception, inquiry, and belief is a product of the modern mind. The compartmentalization of knowledge and the promotion of scientific rationalism as the primary mode of investigating reality and constructing a world view in the West have devalued intimate experience and empirical knowledge.

Although psychology, especially the psychology of Carl Jung, has given us insight into the collective uncon-scious and the role of myth and archetypes as bearers of meaning, insight is not the same thing as the whole-hearted belief that integrates all social purpose—religious, political, economic, architectural—in a holistic way as it did for some prehistoric and ancient societies, as well as for later ones that subscribed to the ideals of Christianity, humanism, rationalism, or other widely shared systems of thought.

Today we are both exhilarated and disquieted. We thrill to the boons of technology and the adventure of the Information Age in which we are taking part, and yet we experience anomie and the psychological *dis-loca-tion* of an increasingly migratory way of life. The ease of replication within industrial capitalist economies fos-ters mimesis of time and space whether in the form of "historic" villages, theme parks, malls, restaurants, resorts, or museum reconstructions. These environmental simulations of the long ago and the far away, as well as the purely fantastic, aided by photography and cinema, are now universally marketed and displayed to mass audiences. A kaleidoscope of juxtaposed, heterogeneous images of place is also made accessible by the Inter-net. The ease with which images of period and place are now distributed has the effect of commercializing the original prototypes, turning them, where they still exist, into famous clichés and tourist icons.

The term *urban sprawl* has gained currency and disapprobation because we have invented a new kind of city, amorphous and without the mythic, religious, or even political foundations that cities have historically enjoyed. Business chains and franchise operations proliferate along commercial strips, transforming the locally particular into the repetitiously familiar. This may give the brand-name consumer and mobile traveler assur-ance, but the increasingly predictable, homogeneous, loosely urbanized environment equally induces bore-dom and—in a very prosaic and literal way—déjà vu.

As accelerating mobility and speed of communications continue to shrink distance and collapse time, place becomes increasingly provisional and temporary. Increasingly rootless, we articulate concepts valoriz-ing community. This is so because humans are in a fundamental way place-making animals, revealing in this act their individual and collective dreams (see figs. 16.3, 16.5). The landscapes that we create are combinations of artifice and nature, and in designing them people of every period have revealed a great deal about their cul-tural values while demonstrating the perennial exigencies of life and our universal need for water, food, and shelter. Perhaps as we reanimate our spiritual selves, develop new culturally sustaining myths, and reunite sci-ence with religion and philosophy, we will be able to create places that are life-sustaining in a truer sense than now. For, as the twentieth-century French philosopher Gaston Bachelard posited, when we examine space in terms of psychology and phenomenology we find that we are still place-bound creatures, carrying in the recesses of our memories personal histories of spaces we have inhabited and imagined. Further, we carry "placeness" in our genes and in our sensory apparatus as human animals, and because biological nature is still the matrix of our existence we long to feel at one with the natural world.

It is not surprising that the origins of the Romantic movement and the romanticization of nature and of prehistoric and aboriginal peoples as "noble savages" were concurrent with the Industrial Revolution. Machine technology has introduced into the world an enormously potent, self-referential set of systems that affect us in ways that are at the same time obvious and incomprehensible. "The machine in the garden," to borrow the metaphor of Leo Marx for the uneasy alliance of technology and nature, has taken up perma-nent residence in human consciousness, and perhaps without realizing that this is occurring, we may be wit-nessing the moment in Western history when industrial technology becomes affirmatively integrated with art and nature.

The alternative, unfortunately, is greater environmental degradation and planetary destruction, a possi-bility we have only recently taken seriously. Now, as the world becomes more populous and human life increas-ingly dependent upon the machine-built environment, we develop campaigns to protect wilderness. Our old relation to wilderness having been inverted, it is now at the mercy of human politics. Inseparable from the forces of energy that power our machines and the new reality we are creating, most of us desperately want to harmonize our fast-paced future with our past, enjoying the benefits of new sources of energy and the fruits of technology while honoring our own human nature and the longing for place and nature that is encoded into our beings. Our success in this endeavor will depend on many things, including an understanding of the rich psychological and mythopoeic relationship of human beings to landscape throughout history.

CHAPTER ONE

MAGIC, MYTH, AND NATURE: LANDSCAPES OF PREHISTORIC, EARLY ANCIENT, AND CONTEMPORARY PEOPLES

Throughout the ages landscapes have reflected cosmological notions underlying one of humanity's great imponderables: Where are we? How was the world created, and what is the place and fate of human beings within the contexts of space and time?

In this preliminary chapter our task is not to study, as we will later, the landscapes that express the creation stories of scripture-based religions such as Islam or Christianity, nor those that serve as paradigms of cosmological reason such as the gardens of seventeenth-century France, nor ones that reflect a contemporary cosmology based upon the science of physics and recent discoveries subsumed under the term chaos theory. Here we must examine something more basic, the rootedness in the human psyche of certain fundamental spatial constructs that relate to our upright posture, directional movement, desire to locate ourselves in space in ways that are charged with societal meaning, and our yearning for connection with the infinite and eternal.

Myth, religion, philosophy, and science are all rooted in cosmogony, the attempt to explain the creation of cosmos out of chaos—the transformation of primal disorder and confusion into a universe that is systematically arranged, harmonious, whole. By these means, human beings in all times and all places have sought to confer meaning and perceive structure within the natural world. Only through the human mind's dynamic transformation over the previous several centuries—a phenomenon of restless revisionism more characteristic of Western society than of other world cultures—have myth, religion, philosophy, and science been teased apart and made separate spheres of belief and knowledge. Here we must try to understand how non-Western peoples in widely separated parts of the earth and in periods of time both vastly removed and continuing to the present have created landscape forms of astonishing universality in cultures—both prehistoric and extant—where cosmology reflects a fusion of mythic, religious, philosophic, and scientific thought.

Over time, the development of geometry, surveying, and structural mechanics gave birth to the art of architecture. But here, too, we must be careful not to assign the technical specialization and the epistemological segmentation of modern Western culture to societies of the distant past who lived long before many of the practices and values of Western industrial society were established or to those that live today outside its precepts. Further, in considering our topic, the history of landscape design, it is especially important to understand that the perception of volumetric, terrestrial space—the foundation of our enterprise in both a practical and a theoretical sense—is hugely variable, altering with the cosmological and teleological understanding of each age.

To be more specific, since the Renaissance, the Western mind has presumed a spatial concept based upon perspective and a central vanishing point where all the lines of an imaginary horizontal planar grid converge. Particularly after the French mathematician and philosopher René Descartes (1596–1650) expounded his theory of spatial extension—*res extensa*—in the seventeenth century, this notion of value-neutral space as a universal proscenium theater in which objects are arrayed in accordance with the laws of perspective has governed landscape design theory and practice. Beginning in the second half of the eighteenth century, designed landscape space in the West became explicitly pictorial. It was consciously invested with the scenic values of landscape painting, which, though less obviously perspectival than the axially geometric gardens of the seventeenth century, nevertheless remained faithful, until the advent of twentieth-century modernism, to the same underlying principle of pictorial representation. However, the art of such societies as the Chinese, the Byzantine, or Inuit shows that participants in these cultures were uninterested in spatial perspective, not through ignorance, but because of an entirely different attitude toward the interpretation and construction of representational space.[1]

The belief in spatial hierophany—the notion that within the larger sanctity of nature some places are especially sacred—practically universal in prehistoric cultures and residual in some parts of the world today, militates against the assumption of a spatial continuum ordered purely by mathematics and Western theories of spatial perspective. Prehistoric and ancient peoples joined architecture and sacred forms in nature and in so doing invented, without naming it, the art of landscape design. In terms of three-dimensional planning employing axes and the measurement of form and spatial distance, the landscapes they created do not merely link or give scale to terrestrial monuments but have cosmological alignment and significance. To understand place-making as a human activity it is important for us to investigate—as best we can from contemporary Western society's vastly different, secularized, historicized point of view—the cultural values of the first shapers of space along with those who have continued to create landscapes that reflect a similar cosmology.

Early societies sought survival through rituals intended to propitiate the forces of nature. In their attempts to understand the cosmos and interpret the all-important seasonal rhythms of nature, these people became Earth's first astronomers. But to imply that they were scientists in the modern sense of the word is wrong; astronomy was indivisibly linked to religion. In contrast to the highly individual and personal nature of contemporary religious faith and the resolutely secular nature of modern science, the ritual and augural ceremonies of prehistoric and early ancient peoples were holistic societal practices, which took place in nature. Although quite probably they considered all of nature to be animated by spiritual forces, as members of human societies they experienced a psychological need to shape space in nature in spiritually significant ways. Almost universally, this meant establishing a relationship of form and alignment between built and natural features as well as an orientation to certain celestial reference points—the predictable and calendrically determined positions of sun, moon, stars. These cosmologically referential landscape constructions and ceremonies were considered vital to the continuance of the communities they served. In addition, in their search for harmony with the universe, prehistoric and ancient humans assigned a presiding spiritual force to certain mountains, springs, caves, trees, and animals, ascribing to them sacred meaning. Those who subscribe to similar belief systems today invest nature with sanctity and certain sites with religious significance, a concept quite alien to others who view land in secular and utilitarian terms, as a commodity serving economic rather than spiritual ends.

Paleolithic cave paintings, Neolithic stone circles, Mesopotamian ziggurats, Egyptian pyramids and obelisks, Hindu temples, Cretan nature sanctuaries, Mycenaean citadels, and the pyramids, mounds, and effigy earthworks of pre-Spanish-conquest Americans—these were all expressions of a partnership between human beings and unseen spiritual forces. The creators of these forms, who also invested their landscape settings with symbolical meaning and design intent, invoked the magical powers of spirits—those of the beasts whose flesh sustained them and of the gods and goddesses who controlled the cosmos and were responsible for human and animal fertility and the growth of crops. In a highly uncertain world, these creative people watched the skies, studying the rotations of celestial bodies, harbingers of the predictable annual cycle of rain and solar warmth and auguries of victory in battle. In the process, they created the first complex human societies, constructed important ceremonial centers, and evolved the world's earliest cities.

The built environments shaped by these early human cultures and many of those that succeeded them reflected their religious preoccupation with the cosmos. What is most striking about these very earliest societies is their fusion of myth-based religion and scientific observation. Limited but certain in their perception of the planet and the cosmos, they rooted themselves firmly and assigned religious meaning to place. When we understand how deeply embedded cosmology once was in religious mythos, we can comprehend cosmological landscape design—the shaping of the earth and the erection of monuments to reflect a cosmic paradigm. The universality of the axis, the pyramid, and the grotto in cultures as distant in space and time as those of the ancient Near East, prehistoric Europe, India, and the pre-Columbian Americas makes sense when we realize that these forms express cosmic concepts that owe their similarity to their origins in the human psyche. This, rather than certain theories of cultural transmission, seems to account for the similarity of landscape constructions as widely separated in site and date as the Egyptian and Mayan pyramids.

The cave, especially, as sanctuary, the womb of Earth, a place of cultic mystery and ritual revitalization, occupies a privileged place in the human imagination. Its many manifestations include the Egyptian tomb carved into the cliff face or nestled within the bowels of a pyramid, the subterranean sanctuaries of the Snake Goddess in prehistoric Greece, the cave beneath the Pyramid of the Sun at Teotihuacán, the Shiva cave-temples at Elephanta, Ellora, and Salsette in India, and the *kivas* of Puebloan cultures in the American Southwest. Associated with the cave is the rule of an earth goddess, which is rooted in universal myths that recognize the earth as a generative and procreative force, the fertile source of human and animal vitality. The cave, with its labyrinthine passages, suggests the intimacy of the mother's womb, the place from which life was observed to emerge. In addition, caves and crevices in the earth's surface are sources for springs, and shrines at caves or near springs are especially prevalent in dry lands. Understandably, a psychological attraction toward moist mysterious openings within the earth has persisted down through the millennia. The architectural grotto in ancient Roman villa gardens, which Renaissance garden-builders revived and passed on to subsequent eras and diverse cultures, is a sophisticated version of the cave sanctuaries in which prehistoric ancestors worshipped.

The work of Mircea Eliade, scholar of world religions and early myths, beliefs, and practices, confirms that among members of prehistoric and some contemporary cultures there exists the conviction that the natural world is imbued with divinity. Eliade points out that the most elemental sacred places constitute a microcosm, "a landscape of stones, water, and trees."[2] In this way humans evoke the durable potency of stone, the fertility associated with water, and the fecundity of nature as embodied in the living tree. The notion of an immanent sanctity within earth and sky is culturally pervasive, and from this is derived the concept of *genius loci,* spirit of place, and the idea of guardian deities of place.

One way to explain the similarity and universality of myths and the pictorial configurations and landscape constructs that reflect them is to study the psychological theories of Carl Jung (1875–1961).[3] According to Jung, archetypes—formal images that symbolically express quintessential meanings—cannot be directly identified and subjected to control by the conscious mind. Therefore, they find expression in myths. Just as Jung's own teaching is based upon four-bodiedness, or four states of perceiving (thinking, feeling, intuition, sensation), the archetype of quaternity as expressed in the four-part circle and the four cardinal points can be found in the landscape constructions of many cultures. In addition, the Great Mother, the Tree of the World, and Paradise are examples of Jungian archetypes, and the symbol of the snake, the sphinx, and various helpful animals are also symptoms of states within what Jung calls the collective unconscious. The metaphorical nature of landscape design and the prevalence of certain formal means of shaping space and expressing basic mythic concepts through architecture and decoration can thus be analyzed in Jungian terms as archetypal manifestations of primordial ideas that continue to resonate within the human imagination.

Creation myths deal with the evolution of cosmos out of chaos. Implicit in this is the act of giving form and place to objects and space. The positioning of Earth in the center of the universe and the centering of human societies within the world are fundamental constructs within many early cosmologies. Cosmic centering involves awareness of three vertical strata: above, below, and a terrestrial middle plane. It also involves cardinal directionality—the location of four principal axes along a 360° horizon line in accordance with the movement of the sun and various stars and planets. In diagrammatic terms, this basic image of the cosmos can be illustrated as in figure 1.1.

So firmly fixed is this cosmological model in the human consciousness that it appears not only in widely different parts of the world, but also in many eras, being appropriated through religious syncretism by people of different cultures, including those adhering to Buddhism, Islam, Hinduism, and Christianity. Its vertical dimension is an *axis mundi,* which acts like a center pole uniting heaven, Earth, and the underworld. Lakes are watery nether regions located just below the surface of the land, and, like caves, they are places of underworld entrance and exit. These are identified with female procreation and spirits that reside in darkness.

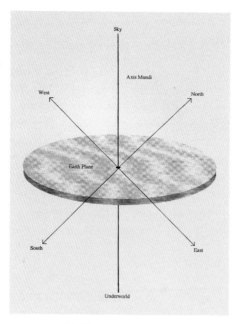

1.1. Diagram of *axis mundi*

The underworld is also the domain of serpent deities prevalent in several cultures. Mountains, the realm of air and celestial light, are identified with sky-dwelling gods who control cosmic order and thereby the welfare of human beings. They are sites of celestial communication between these gods and human beings occupying the intermediate terrestrial realm with its broad circular horizon.

The apparent east-west rotational movement of the sun across the heavens and the observation of its equinoctial position in relation to the horizon gave human beings their primary orientation on a horizontal plane. The bisection of this axis with a north-south one divided sky and Earth into quadrants, providing an elemental framework for celestial observation and terrestrial navigation. With these six cosmic coordinates—east, west, north, south, zenith, and nadir—embedded in consciousness, human societies formed settlements within the expansive earthly sphere through acts of centering.

The siting of places of habitation is governed by such practical considerations as the presence of water and the arability of land. But given these limitations, when Earth was relatively unpopulated and there was available a wide range of options, cultural groups also sought to settle themselves in places perceived to have a relationship to divine power, which generally meant in alignment with cosmic coordinates and landforms associated with mythic forces. Many were attracted to karstic formations—limestone strata riddled with caves and seeping with springs—and to arable valleys near mountains. Often, cultural groups expended enormous human resources constructing a mountain-mimicking pyramid, ziggurat, or temple in order to establish an *axis mundi* that would firmly relate it to a cosmic deity.

No one cared that there were many groups and multiple *axes mundi;* what mattered was a representation of the cosmic archetype, consecration rites surrounding the creation of a cosmic landscape, and sanctification of the site through worship. Thus centered symbolically in space, more than one city could imagine its cosmically connected, temple-crowned, human-made mountain as the navel of the earth. In a similar manner, through the repetition of cosmogonic rituals, temporality was displaced by timelessness.

Looking at archaeological sites of former cosmological landscapes today, we lack the ritual dimension that once gave them religious significance. Only in a few cultures where people still seek cosmic alignment within nature do we find ritual practices that link humans with the cosmos, as for example when dancers re-enact archetypal gestures and commemorate mythical moments through choreographed movement. We may surmise, however, that all sacred landscapes were once alive with dancing and other rituals in which music and chanting dramatized the myth-based cosmologies that sustained a sense of sacred order in the world.

I. CAVES AND CIRCLES:
SUSTAINING LIFE AND DISCERNING COSMIC ORDER

During the eons of Paleolithic habitation of Earth, when a shield of ice still covered parts of the globe that are temperate today, the cunning of a tool-making and weapon-wielding being was pitted against the speed and bulk of large roaming beasts. In this Old Stone Age, the virtually trackless steppes, savannas, and forests were home to small bands of hunter-gatherers who have left only slight evidence of their presence. Because there is no written record of this time, what we know of their customs, practices, and relationship to the land is based on the scattered and limited finds of archaeologists and paleontologists.

OLD WORLD CAVES

Such celebrated echoes from the last Ice Age as the caves at Lascaux in the Dordogne region of France, discovered in 1940, Cosquer Cave on the Mediterranean near Marseilles, discovered in 1991, and Chauvet Cave in the Ardèche region of the Rhône Valley, discovered in 1994, contain hundreds of images of large animals depicted in charcoal and vegetable colors on their walls (fig. 1.2). The vitality of the paintings may derive from their association with a propitiatory ritual to ensure the continued fertility of these beasts. One recent archaeological theory, however, explains them pragmatically, as instructional guides transmitted from one generation to the next. In this way, hunter-initiates might have been trained to track individual bison and other large beasts individually in times when animal populations waned and mass kills of entire herds were impossible.[4] The portrayal of hoofprints and other informational clues of particular importance to the hunter, such as large antler size, support the thesis of the paintings' didactic function. Some images indicate animals in a posture of bellowing or emitting their distinctive sounds, a reminder both of the importance of such auditory signals for prehistoric hunters and the degree to which they were responsively attuned to the aural dimensions of space.[5] Finger tracings and hand stencils, found in Cosquer and Chauvet, as well as in such widely separated sites as the Canyon de Chelly in Arizona and a cave in the Laura area of Australia, symbolize the taking possession of such spaces by humans.[6] The marking over of these nonartistic symbols at a subsequent period by others is an obvious indication of assertion of power by a later group.

Though we can never fully comprehend the mentality of the Paleolithic artists who created these paintings nor that of the hunters who derived meaning from them, we can surmise that whatever instructional purpose these images may have served, they were also allied with some kind of religious practice. The fact that they are within caves places them naturally in the rich realm of the human unconscious, with its well-established repertoire of archetypes. Like the later ancient Greek and Roman practitioners of the Eleusinian mysteries in which initiates were guided through a series of underground passages as part of a chthonic, or underworld, ritual based upon the legend of Demeter and Persephone, the prehistoric people who made the cave art appear to have been sensitive to the spatial aspects of the caves and to have taken into consideration the routes leading into them. Passage and chamber are integral parts of their planning, and an obvious concentration of art in an inner sanctum

1.2. Lion Panel, Chauvet Cave, southern Ardèche (Rhône Valley), France. c. 30,000 B.C.E.

1.3. Menhirs, Carnac, France. 3rd millennium B.C.E.

gives the impression of a corresponding intensity of experience and concentration of ritual there.[7]

The cave would surely have served as a sound chamber, and we may suppose that its resonant properties would have been exploited in ritual chants and perhaps also the beating of drums.[8] Further, it may be wrong to assume that prehistoric cave art is an objective representation of what the artists saw. Rather, we might think of it as animated line, a graphic expression of the life force inherent in nature. The way in which the figures are disposed to take advantage of certain plastic characteristics of walls of the cave is congruent with the notion of haptic, or tactile, rather than straightforward, optical perception, and the conception of space on the part of those who created these dynamic images was surely different from our sense of space as something defined, measurable, and emplaced.[9] Finally, the universality of religious practice among all societies, and especially, as we must imagine, prehistoric ones, makes it possible to suppose that the protein diet that the painted animals in the caves represented was obtained with some form of ceremonial enactment sanctifying the spirit embodied by the living creatures.

OLD WORLD MENHIRS AND CIRCLES OF STONE AND WOOD

The evolutionary development of agriculture and animal husbandry in the Neolithic, or New Stone Age, brought with it greater stability and confidence. Human beings formed more or less permanent settlements and imprinted the land by their occupancy. Boundary as a concept arrived when people began to circumscribe villages and subdivide land into fields. Megaliths, giant stones expelled from the maws of the retreating glaciers at the end of the last Ice Age, were upended, the world's first

monuments (fig. 1.3).[10] That these *menhirs,* as the huge markers found chiefly in Britain, Ireland, and northern France, are called, pointed a stony finger skyward was not accidental. Settlement within agricultural communities brought a new range of fears. Now it was not enough to ensure that animal spirits were propitiated and the lives of the beasts perpetuated. The cooperation of the cosmos itself was necessary if crops were not to fail and the now-cohesive and increasingly specialized social unit were to thrive. Humans were keenly aware of their dependence upon the sun and also upon the moon and stars. Diligent skywatchers, they associated the positions of various celestial bodies with recurring seasonal patterns.

The awe-inspiring megalithic forms of Stonehenge were erected upon the gently rolling grassland of the Salisbury Plain in southern England in a succession of construction campaigns between 2750 and 1500 B.C.E. They outline a ritual center that may have functioned as a religious festival space where celebrations relating to its function as an astronomical observatory were held (figs. 1.4, 1.5). This impressive work of architecture, sited at the confluence of several lines of hills, originated as an earthwork. The first builders of Stonehenge described a huge circle in the white chalky earth, which they then piled up in two banks broken only in one spot. They flanked this opening with two small upright stones. Beyond these, slightly off-axis with the break, they erected a 35-ton, roughly cylindrical, tapering megalith of sarsen, a gray sandstone from the nearby Marlborough Hills. Called variously the Friar's Heel, Hele Stone (perhaps from the Anglo-Saxon word *helan,* meaning "to conceal"), Heel Stone, Sun Stone, Index Stone, and Petrie's Stone 96, this marker was ascertained by eighteenth-century scientists to be aligned with an imaginary axis drawn between the rising sun and the center point of the circle on the day of the summer solstice. At least one modern archaeologist has pointed out that in the case of the many photographs depicting this phenomenon, the photographer has stood a few paces away from the center of the circle because the rising solstice sun is not concealed by the megalith but appears a foot and a half to the left.[11] This does not, however, negate an interpretation based upon archaeoastronomy, relating earthworks with the positions of heavenly bodies at certain important points in the calendrical cycle. The megalith does lie along an axis from the center of the circle to the horizon midway between the major northern moonrise and the minor northern moonrise, and it may have once aided observers of these lunar events.

Stonehenge served as a ritual center over

several centuries, and there was evidently enough social cohesion and sufficiently advanced technology for undertaking additional building programs. One generation of laborers constructed a 35-foot- (10.7-meter-) wide avenue, defined by chalk embankments like the original circle. It ran in a straight line along the axis of the megalithic outlier, bending somewhat as it approached the river Avon. The Stonehenge builders next erected monoliths of bluestone weighing up to 5 tons each in a double ring, open at the point of the axis. Although it has long been held that these were quarried from the distant Preseli Mountains in Wales and then transported some 300 miles (483 kilometers) by land, sea, and river to the site, an alternative, less heroic supposition holds that boulders plucked by the ice sheet that once moved ponderously across this part of the world carried enough Preseli bluestones as glacial erratics to furnish builders with the material they needed for their double ring of megaliths within much closer range.[12]

In any case, a subsequent generation of builders put these bluestones aside in favor of much larger megaliths of Marlborough sarsen quarried nearby, which they arranged as trilithons—two upright "columns" with a bridging lintel—in a horseshoe pattern with the open side facing the established axis of entry. Sometime prior to this construction campaign, which was probably executed by Breton immigrants—inasmuch as horseshoe arrangements of megaliths are found commonly in Brittany but only rarely in Britain—a rectangle with its sides aligned to

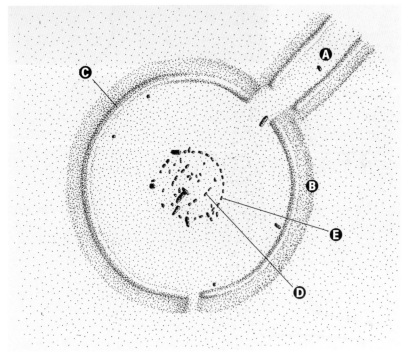

the cardinal points was carefully laid out within the circular chalk embankments. Its four corners were at the time marked by megaliths. Around the horseshoe, in a prodigious demonstration of structural sophistication, another building campaign resulted in the familiar ring of slightly tapering sarsens topped by lintels subtly curved and interlocked so as to form an integral circular architrave about 20 feet (6.1 meters) above the ground. A subsequent rearrangement of the bluestones to emphasize the sarsen

1.5. Plan of Stonehenge
Ⓐ Heel Stone
Ⓑ Ditch
Ⓒ Embankment
Ⓓ Bluestone Ring
Ⓔ Circle of Trilithons

1.6. Woodhenge, Cahokia, Illinois. 1100–1200 C.E. Painting by Lloyd K. Townsend

horseshoe and its surrounding sarsen circle completed the work on this mighty monument.

World-famous as an enigmatic relic of the Stone Age and unique for Britain in several respects, including its builders' use of lintels, Stonehenge is by no means an isolated example of Neolithic landscape architecture. There are many other stone circles in Britain and Ireland that also provide evidence of Neolithic astronomy, ritual need, and social congregation. Not surprisingly, over the centuries their mysterious presence in the countryside has engendered many legends regarding Druidical rites, fairy dances, and witches' sabbaths. The phallic shape of certain stones has encouraged their status as objects of fertility worship, and some New Age spiritualists today believe the stone circles to be cosmic power centers.

In addition to the megaliths arranged in circles, postholes indicating the arrangement of timbers as wooden rings have been found, and these, too, probably functioned, like the stones of Stonehenge, as astronomical markers and the architectural definition of ceremonial centers, often with funerary associations. Such a ring, or rather a series of concentric rings, is found a short distance to the northeast of Stonehenge, and archaeological evidence shows that it almost certainly served as both a place for astronomical observation and ritual burial.

NEW WORLD CIRCLES AND EARTHWORKS

Suggesting perhaps Jung's psychology of the collective unconscious—rather than astonishing coincidence—there exists an American timber post circle built around 1050 C.E. at Cahokia near present-day St. Louis by the mound-building people archaeologists call *Mississippian* (see fig. 1.29).[13] Here calendrically based religious rites reinforced the authority of the powerful elite over the commoners who tilled the fields and built the mounds. To the west of the most prominent earthwork, Monks Mound, archaeologists in the 1960s discovered four series of postholes forming rings (fig. 1.6). They found fragments of red-stained cedar posts in some of the holes. The first circle of this complex, dubbed the American Woodhenge, consists of twenty-four postholes. A second circle contained thirty-six posts, and a third, dated around 1000 C.E., sixty. The fourth circle, which was never completed, had holes for only twelve or thirteen of a planned seventy-two-post ring. The second circle of posts has been reconstructed to resemble the original forty-eight regularly spaced uprights marking various positions of the Sun including, most spectacularly, its rise directly over Monks Mound on the days of the spring and fall equinoxes.

Earthen circles similar to the one encompassing the megalithic monument at Stonehenge are also inscribed on the Ohio landscape. The Hopewell people, who occupied the Ohio Valley in the period between 100 B.C.E. and 400 C.E., mounded long ridges of earth to outline large circles, squares, pentagons, and octagons. The most monumental complex of these geometrical mounds is found at Newark, Ohio, where more than 7 million cubic feet (198,100 cubic meters) of earth were carried in baskets to create two large circles, an octagon, and an almost square enclosure, all connected by broad "avenues" extending over an area of 4 square miles (10.36 square kilometers) (fig. 1.7). The avenues are defined by two parallel walls of earth similar to the linear earthen ridges that define the mysterious "roads" emanating from Chaco Canyon in the American Southwest.

In recent years, the astronomer Ray Hively and philosopher Robert Horn have discovered a convincing rationale for the alignment of the roads and the large geometric forms at Newark and the High Bank works near Chillicothe by proving that the orientation of the earthworks in these places marks the maximum and minimum degrees north and south of true east of the moon's rising and setting on the horizon during an 18.6-year cycle. They also have shown how, in addition to giving physical expression to this impressive astronomical calculation, the builders of the Hopewell earthworks sited them in relationship to one another in ways that demonstrate their mathematical sophistication. It is likely that the geometric enclosures defined by the mounds were built to serve as spaces in which dancing, market fairs, and other ritual and social activities took place.

In addition to this kind of focused spatiality, which projected a relationship between earth and sky, there developed throughout the Neolithic Age a chthonic architecture of enclosure centered upon fertility, death, and the spirits of the underworld. Tombs—architectural versions of the cave, such as dolmens, simple chambers formed by two or more upright megaliths with a capstone, and other kinds of more elaborate stone-roofed structures—were built as sites for the care of the dead as reverence for ancestors increased. Rudimentary temples were also built as enclosures with shrines, altars for animal sacrifice, and spaces for public assembly.

Neolithic Urbanism

The evolution of Neolithic urban societies occurred during the millennium prior to the construction of Stonehenge. They flourished in the Nile Valley in Egypt and in the area known as the Fertile Crescent, a semicircle of arable land extending from the south-

east coast of the Mediterranean around the Syrian Desert north of the Arabian Peninsula to the Tigris and Euphrates river plain in Mesopotamia. There was as well a corresponding development in the Indus Valley. The accretion of power within the hands of a ruling elite, who used religious authority as a means of organizing administrative systems, made possible the division of labor. This led to more efficient agricultural production, the crafting of use-specific items and wares, the beginning of trade, the building of monuments, and the birth of cities. Important technological improvements and the administrative capacity to undertake enormous public works provided an unprecedented degree of control over nature, leading to the agricultural surpluses that made possible large urban settlements. Yet these prosperous societies adhered to religious cosmologies that made them obedient to priestly rulers who understood the movements of celestial bodies and who performed propitiatory rites to ensure fertility of crops and people. These practices are reflected in the ways these two mighty civilizations designed upon the land.

1.7. Newark Earthworks, Newark, Ohio. 100 B.C.E. and 400 C.E.

II. Architectural Mountains and Earth's First Cities: Landscape as Urban Power in Early Ancient Civilizations

In Mesopotamia, between the Tigris and the Euphrates Rivers, urbanism of a lasting kind began between 3500 and 3000 B.C.E. Shortly thereafter, another urban culture evolved within the Nile Valley of Egypt. Administrative structures capable of planning and controlling crops to sustain large populations were essential to the development of cities in these two areas. In both lands, rulers shared power with a priestly elite. In addition to furnishing the ritual structure that sanctified life and brought religious practice and protection to the city's inhabitants, priests administered a highly organized governing system. Government officials controlled grain storage and distribution, the division of lands, the construction of dikes, dams, and canals, the collection of taxes, and the fielding of armies and other means of organizing labor. They also defended the community and kept peace within an increasingly complicated economic and social sphere.

This methodical governance would have been impossible without the invention of writing and the development of a literate class. Literacy enabled communication and recordkeeping. Mathematical literacy enabled computation and measurement. The many portraits of scribes in Egyptian and Mesopotamian art attest to the important role of this official in society.

As the carrier of ideas and concepts, literacy had another important and far-reaching result beyond these necessary practical ones. The written word, whether pictographic or hieratic, is a symbol and, as such, is fundamental to the mental conception of other symbolical constructs, so it is safe to say that, for both practical and ideological reasons, the ziggurat, the pyramid, the temple, and the obelisk could not have existed in a preliterate world. And it is, of course, through writing as well as through painting, that we today are vouchsafed a glimpse of the relationship between ancient people and nature and of their esteem, and often reverence, for certain plants and animals.

Ziggurats

The association of mountaintops with divinity reflects a universal quest for cosmological meaning. This notion is embodied in the artificial ziggurat "mountain," the symbolical juncture of earth and sky deities. For peoples of the ancient Near East the ziggurat served as an earthly counterpart to the pole star, an axis around which the heavens were believed to revolve. It also manifested a cosmology that prevailed throughout the Mesopotamian region under the Sumerian (c. 3500–2030 B.C.E.), Akkadian (c. 2340–2180 B.C.E.), and Babylonian (c. 1750 and intermittently to 528 B.C.E.) cultures. This cosmology, which was first developed by the Sumerians, is later expressed in the Babylonian creation poem, the *Enuma Elish,* written sometime before the reign of Hammurabi (ruled c. 1792–1750 B.C.E.). In this cosmogonic account, the primal state of the universe consists of Tiamat and Apsu, two kinds of water, salt and fresh. Their commingling provides the matrix out of which the first places emerge, thus causing the primary scission that separates heaven from earth. This separation is enforced when Marduk, the Babylonian national god, does battle with Tiamat, utterly dominating and destroying her. From their struggle Marduk emerges as formgiver, architect, and master builder of the universe. He creates the line of horizon and asserts dominion over the fertile but formless primal matter represented by Tiamat. From Tiamat's dismembered but endlessly procreative body, he fashions the arc of the sky, personified by Anu, lord of heaven and the father of gods. He also sets the firm subterranean foundation that upholds the earth, embodied as Ea, god of waters and the netherworld. In the middle zone between these he stations Enlil, god of air and heaven, who is also identified with the wind. With this *axis mundi* set in place, Marduk bestows directionality, driving through Tiamat's ribs openings to the east and west and setting the zenith at the apex of her belly. Marduk, as architect-sculptor, then models the earth's topography, creating mountains and streams and making the great Tigris and Euphrates flow from Tiamat's eyes. By rearing a stepped platform into the sky, Mesopotamian priests could bring the presiding deity of the heavens, Anu (An in the Sumerian cosmos), into contact with Bel (Sumerian Enlil), the earth spirit sheltered within its sacred form, as well as with Ea (Enki in the pre-Babylonian mythology), the supernatural power in charge of the underworld and the subterranean waters that sprang forth, teeming with life, in the fecund marshes.

Mesopotamian religion was grounded in animism, the belief that such elements as wind and water had conscious life and that spirit forces dwelt within trees as well as in birds, fish, reptiles, and mammals. Plants and beasts were therefore believed to have an existence independent of their physical representations. That the ziggurat expressed the human desire to forge a connection between the various spheres of a magic-charged universe is evident from the names of some: Heaven and Storm, House

1.8. Nanna Ziggurat, Ur
(modern Muqaiyir, Iraq).
c. 2100–2050 B.C.E.

of the Mountain, Mountain of the Storm, Bond between Heaven and Earth.

The building of ziggurats and their attendant temple structures was reverently undertaken by the early kings of Sumer as a means of preserving the often fragile harmony with nature upon which depended the continued life of the community and state. Even as they were built, however, their demise was often foreseen in dedication inscriptions referring to a time when they would fall into ruin. Constructed with a central core of trodden clay and mud brick, which was then clad with baked brick, their inward-sloping walls and stepped terraces were created of brick courses interspersed at staged intervals with damp courses of reeds and bitumen. In spite of these damp courses and the presence of weepholes, ziggurats remained permeable to water. In time, this caused the interior core of mud brick to expand, forcing the exterior walls outward until they cracked and broke apart.

The biblical image of the collapsed Tower of Babel was probably based upon real examples of ruined ziggurats observed by captive Israelites. This image of cosmopolitan decadence has offered a compelling metaphor for allegorical storytellers and artists through the ages. Such mounds can still be seen today (fig. 1.8).

Pyramids

The Egyptian pyramid had a purpose altogether different from that of the ziggurat, for the pyramid was both the tomb of the king and the means of his posthumous daily ascension and unification with Re, the Sun God.[14] The cult of Re furnished the pyramid with its essential meaning. To understand its underlying theology, one must attempt to see the annual inundation of the Nile plain from the perspective of the early Egyptian. Each spring, as the flood waters rose and then began to subside, the mound of Elephantine—the island below the First Cataract of the Nile—appeared to come miraculously alive with vegetation, birds, fish, reptiles, and insects. This primal scene was enacted elsewhere as other rocky and sandy mounds within the river received a rich mantle of silt and sprang suddenly into fecund life. To the early Egyptian, the mound itself seemed to be the autonomous progenitor of this miracle, and thus it became revered as the elemental life force. Irrigation and the warming rays of the sun together were necessary to continue the earth's renewal and bring about growth. Thus, the creation mound was identified both with the phoenix, the mythological bird of light that dispelled the darkness over the waters, and the god Atum, the Egyptian form of the Demiurge, Plato's name for the force that fashions the material world.

The sun was believed to have emerged from the water to manifest itself first as the light of the sacred *ben-ben,* a pyramidal stone symbolizing both the life force inherent in the mound and the petrifaction of the sun's rays. In this manner, the imagery of Atum was conflated with that of Re, the sun god, and the *ben-ben* was expanded to monumental scale as the pyramid, the funerary home of Re's earthly representative, the all-powerful divine king, later called pharaoh. Thus did pyramids serve as supreme symbols of royal authority and power. When still covered with their gleaming casings of Tura limestone, their gold-capped tops sending forth rays like

1.9. Pyramids at Giza, Egypt.
Fourth dynasty, c. 2601–2515 B.C.E.

the sun itself, they broadcast to ancient Egyptians a magnificent promise of rebirth beyond the grave as well as annual renewal and earthly well-being through the rituals of divine kingship.

Grandeur on this scale was difficult to sustain, as is evident from the diminishing size of the Old Kingdom pyramids of the kings Khufu, Khafre, and Menkaure at Giza (fig. 1.9). Although monumental pyramids did not disappear all at once and some were still commissioned by later kings for their burials, none ever attained anything approaching the dimensions of the Giza group. The successors of the

pharaohs buried at Giza were laid to rest at Abusir in modest rock-hewn tombs dedicated to Re. Nevertheless, pyramids built at a miniature scale remained popular as funerary monuments well into the Christian era, and, as will become apparent, the form was revived in Europe and America in eighteenth-century gardens and nineteenth-century cemeteries, especially after archaeology brought neo-Egyptian features into vogue and nonsectarianism altered and augmented traditional grave symbolism with memorials associated with a vision of the afterlife even older than that of Christianity.

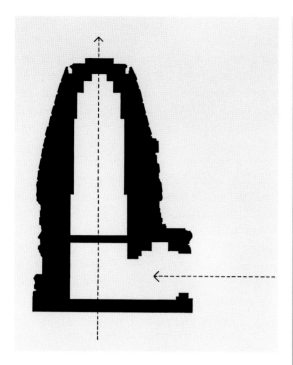

TEMPLES AS SACRED CAVES AND MOUNTAINS

In India and other lands where Hinduism is practiced, one can still encounter cosmologically sacred sites and structures—physical embodiments of places where gods are believed to dwell. Evolved from a very old, pre-Hindu tradition, Hindu cosmology associates caves and mountains as opposite poles of an *axis mundi* of sacred potency. In Hindu mythology Mount Meru is regarded as the navel of the universe, the cosmological center of a concentric arrangement of the continents, oceans, and celestial bodies. Temple architecture is correspondingly cosmological both in plan and elevation. Outwardly, the temple takes the shape of a mythological mountain, and temple worship is equated with a pilgrimage to a mountain sanctuary (fig. 1.11). In elevation, the temple conforms to the cosmic *axis mundi* running from the cave in the center of the earth to the celestial space above the mountain apex (fig. 1.10). The temple's dark interior sanctuary is a chthonic focal point, a simulation of the cavelike womb, source of life. It is there that the worshiper comes into the presence of the godhead. From this center, energy is believed to radiate upward along a cosmic axis through tiered vertical space composed of numerous concentric stories to a crowning circular finial that symbolizes the state of total enlightenment associated with spiritual perfection and the body's release from periodic reincarnation. This axis also symbolizes the pillar of heaven, identified as Meru, and the trunk of an immortal tree whose wide-spreading branches support the universe. In plan, a temple outlines a mandala, the cosmically

significant sacred geometric diagram that portrays the structure of the universe (fig. 1.12). The mandala plan of the temple is strictly oriented to the cardinal points of the compass, generally along an east-west axis, and astronomy and astrology play an important role in its siting and construction.

Above left: 1.10. Diagram of the cosmological elevation of a Hindu temple. Adapted from George Michell, *The Hindu Temple*

Above: 1.11. Hindu temple, Galaganatha temple, Pattadakal, Karnataka, India. 8th century C.E.

Right: 1.12. Diagram of one of the mandala forms that serve as the plans of Hindu temples. Mandalas, geometric designs symbolizing the universe, are used as aids to meditation in Hinduism and Buddhism. Hindu mandalas consist of squares arranged concentrically around a central square representing Brahman, the absolute being and sacred power pervading the universe. The surrounding squares are occupied by a hierarchy of lesser divinities.

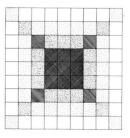

CITIES, PARKS, AND GARDENS

At the beginning of the third millennium B.C.E. in the Sumerian kingdom of lower Mesopotamia, and later, sometime in the early second millennium B.C.E., to the north in Babylonia, the antagonism between populations of nomadic animal herders and grain-growing peoples forced the latter to dwell in cities, which they fortified with stout double walls. In Egypt, on the other hand, it is uncertain to what extent large residential cities existed for any significant period of time. Each king would undertake vast building projects as a means of manifesting his divine kingship, and there were workers' and artisans' settlements adjacent to these. In addition, there were administrative centers with palace precincts and residential quarters for the members of the nobility who with scribes and other functionaries managed the government. The Egyptian temple complexes at Memphis, Heliopolis, and Thebes served as festival centers for important rituals. Yet it is still not clear whether the peasants who tilled the crops that provided food for the general populace and wealth for the temple administrations lived in cities or in village settlements in the fields.

Upper-class residential districts had the same amenities, including gardens, as do affluent suburbs today. Because funerary art represents many of the pleasant accouterments of life, it is from the wall paintings and excavated artifacts of despoiled tombs that one gains evidence of Egyptian garden design and horticultural practices. In a painting from a Theban tomb consecrated during the reign of Amenhotep III (ruled 1390–1352 B.C.E.), a house sits within a garden surrounded by a wall (fig. 1.13). The garden, which is laid out according to an orthogonal grid plan, could be entered through two gates, one cut into the wall facing a tree-lined path beside a canal, and the other through a porter's lodge. Once inside, the visitor was surrounded by date palms and sycamore trees. A large vineyard, orchards, and four ponds filled with lotus blossoms and ducks and fringed with clumps of papyrus formed part of the design. Two of the ponds have kiosks, or garden pavilions, beside them. These are set within a series of walled enclosures that divide the space into several garden "rooms" and segregate plantations of various tree species.

Floriculture was the source of a lively commerce. Flowers were fashioned into bouquets, garlands, and collars. At religious festivals and funerals, those attending brought floral arrangements as well as bundles and heaps of loose flowers. The dead were buried wearing intricately woven floral collars and shrouds decorated with garlands. Ramesses III helped make Thebes a garden city by planting trees and papyrus plants. In an urban center, which he founded in the Nile delta to the north, he is said to have created vineyards, laid out walks shaded by fruit trees, and planted flowers from many countries.

Ancient Near Eastern cities were for the most part hierarchical arrangements of space expressing class distinctions. Order, as reflected in geometric regularity, where it existed, was evidence of the authoritarian power of the ruler and the priesthood. This theocratic kingship defined ceremonial axes and controlled the distribution of lands, and there was segregation of specialized functions into defined districts. Cosmological considerations governed the organization of axes and the creation of temple precincts.

Sumerian cities took the shape of an organic hive of residential and artisan activity surrounding a religious and palace precinct. At Sumer and also at Akkad, the city founded by Sargon I (ruled 2332–2279 B.C.E.) after the Semitic Akkadians conquered Mesopotamia around 2340 B.C.E., temples and palaces stood near the center of the city. In these cities and at Ur, sited at the juncture of a large canal and the Euphrates, the principal temple was raised far above the ground atop a massive ziggurat, the pre-eminent image and cosmological symbol of the city (see fig. 1.8). The entire town rose above the surrounding plain on a base of debris from collapsed mud buildings that had accumulated over many generations. Massive gates punctuated the thick enclosing walls.

1.13. Wall painting of a garden from a tomb in Thebes, Egypt. c. 1400 B.C.E.

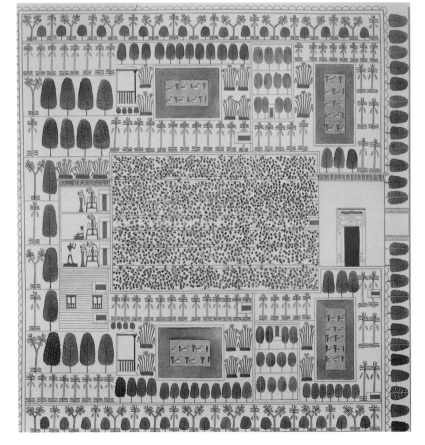

The Assyrian cities that subsequently rose in the area to the north of the Tigris-Euphrates plain were also impressive in their monumentality. A cuneiform map of the city of Nippur on the Euphrates in the center of Babylonia, dated about 1500 B.C.E., shows a city intersected by a canal, with moat- and river-bordered walls pierced by seven gates (fig. 1.14). No streets are shown, but its principal temples are depicted, together with a large park located in an acute angle formed by the walls at the southern end of the city. Parks, the pride of Sumerian and Babylonian kings, were the prototypes of the Persian *pairidaeza,* the walled hunting park. The *Epic of Gilgamesh* has a description of what may have been a hunting park in the southern Babylonian city of Erech (called Uruk during Akkadian times). Like their Persian successors, the ancient Near Eastern monarchs brought to their parks exotic trees, which they acquired from other lands by trade or conquest. Especially prized were the myrrh trees of the Hittites from the region that is Syria today. It was the idealized landscape of that hilly country that King Sargon II (ruled 721–705 B.C.E.) of ancient Assyria (a culture dominant in the region from about 1000 to 612 B.C.E.) and other rulers wished to recall with the simile "like the Amanus Mountains," which is frequently found in their boastful inscriptions proclaiming their park-building schemes.

In the exceedingly hot climate, the garden of shade trees was a much-appreciated luxury. From bas-reliefs and archaeological remains, it is evident that the Babylonians planted trees in rows and built intricate irrigation channels to water them. They created rush-bordered ponds to shelter wildlife and built pleasure houses on hills or terraces overlooking this panorama of garden scenery. A seventh-century B.C.E. Assyrian relief from Nineveh depicts a royal garden in which Assurbanipal and his queen are enjoying a feast beneath an arbor of grapes, celebrating his victory over the Elamite king whose severed head is hanging from a tree branch (fig. 1.15).

The regularly planted trees in this garden include the date palm, which was also grown along canal banks. Dates were cultivated in orchards as well, along with various fruit trees—apples, plums, peaches, cherries, figs, and pomegranates.

Later generations praised the fabled Hanging Gardens of Babylon as one of the wonders of the ancient world, and the search for them has occasioned much guesswork and patient excavation by several archaeologists. According to one of five accounts by ancient writers, they were built by King Nebuchadnezzar II (ruled 604–562 B.C.E.) for his queen, who was homesick for the mountain meadows of her native Media. Other descriptions speak of a series of descending terraces built on top of vaulted galleries. The suggestion has been discounted that trees and other vegetation growing in soil beds or tree pits upon the terraces of the ziggurat at Babylon could be what were referred to as the Hanging Gardens because of the insurmountable difficulty of bringing sufficient water in irrigation channels from the Euphrates River to this monument. Some

1.14. Cuneiform map of Nippur (Iraq). c. 1500 B.C.E.

Below: **1.15.** Assurbanipal and His Queen Feasting in a Garden, Relief from the Assyrian royal palace at Nineveh (modern Kuyunjik, Iraq). 668–627 B.C.E. Alabaster. The British Museum, London

1.16. Temples of Mentuhotep II (ruled 2009–1997 B.C.E.) and Queen Hatshepsut (ruled 1478–1458 B.C.E.), Deir el-Bahri, Egypt

archaeologists now surmise that raised gardens may have occupied superimposed terraces on what they call the Western Outwork structure between Nebuchadnezzar's palace and the Euphrates. Although their claim is not definitive, it is supported by the presence in this location of the kind of deep drains that would have been necessary for extensive irrigation.

PROCESSIONAL AXES

The processional axis, or ceremonial way, developed in conjunction with religious rituals in which priest and populace assembled in precincts before ziggurats, pyramids, and temples. A program of ritualistic approach and movement through a series of hieratic spaces necessitated axial arrangements, offering opportunities for kinetic drama. Thus we find the Giza pyramids of the Old Kingdom (2686–2181 B.C.E.) set in the desert verge and linked to riverside temples by long, sloping causeways—the pyramid and the mortuary temple at its base being the architectural climax of an axial route that began at a valley temple near the banks of the Nile.

At the beginning of the Middle Kingdom (2055–1650 B.C.E.), across the Nile from a temple complex at Karnak (near modern-day Luxor) and on axis with it, Mentuhotep II (ruled 2009–1997 B.C.E.) built into the monumental rock face of the cliff a

large temple-tomb (fig. 1.16). This funerary grouping had a large forecourt planted with tamarisks and sycamore fig trees. A high, square colonnaded platform supported a mortuary temple built in the form of a vestigial pyramid. Behind the mortuary temple, lodged in the cliff itself, stood another narrower court and hypostyle hall. This complex furnished a vocabulary of forms for the adjacent temple built five hundred years later by a remarkable monarch of the New Kingdom, Queen Hatshepsut, who reigned from about 1478 to 1458 B.C.E.

At this point in her long history, Egypt was experiencing a period of wealth and could, without any sacrifice of agricultural labor, build monumental works of architecture and landscape design by using its peacetime army. Like Mentuhotep II, Hatshepsut had her sepulcher carved within the cliff face at Deir el-Bahri. It formed the terminus of a grand axis that began at the temple complex of Karnak on the opposite bank of the Nile, continuing from a riverside temple on the west bank along an avenue of sphinxes, whence it ascended, first one, and then a second massive ramp, each flanked by long colonnades. This axis culminated at last in the great hall of Hatshepsut's temple. In the superb wedding of natural and architectural forms, the columns of the colonnade echoing the geological verticals behind them, Hatshepsut's architect Senenmut left his mark for posterity.

On the walls of the colonnade of the second of two large terraces, temple sculptors left a record of international trade as well as a fascinating footnote to the history of horticulture. Here reliefs depict an expedition to Punt, present-day Somalia, to procure the precious myrrh trees Queen Hatshepsut wished to plant beside her temple. The resin of this tree was dedicated in measured heaps to the sun god Amon. Scenes of this early botanical conquest show how roots were balled and held in place in baskets suspended by ropes tied to poles carried by groups of four or six men, depending upon the size of the tree (fig. 1.18).

Like the Egyptians, the Babylonians honored their deity and manifested their power and prosperity in axial arrangements of landscape space. Nebuchadnezzar II, who is remembered as the ruler who captured and destroyed Jerusalem and led the Jews into captivity, aggrandized Babylon through a lavish rebuilding program. His works included, in addition to the Hanging Gardens, the magnificent Ishtar Gate and a great processional way leading to the Temple of Marduk, which he had plated with gold.

Obelisks

During the Middle Kingdom, the life-giving, sun-blessed mound, the sacred *ben-ben,* which the pyramid had symbolized on a grand scale, assumed the form of a pyramidion, or pyramid in miniature. Ele-

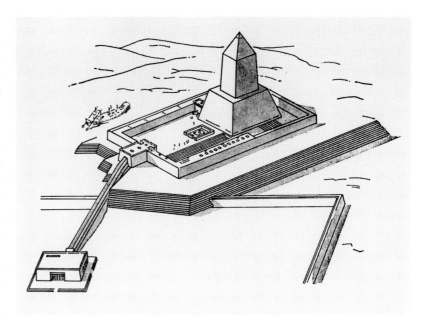

vated upon a tapering base, it became the top of an obelisk. Obelisks—more massive and squat than the New Kingdom "Cleopatra Needles" with which we are familiar—were placed upon high podiums within the open courts of the sun temples at Abusir (fig. 1.17).

Throughout the period of the New Kingdom (1550–1069 B.C.E.), monumental temples multiplied within the Nile Valley. Some were replacements or additions to earlier temples. Successive pharaohs extended axes, replicating the massive pylons guarding courts and adding new obelisks, which by this

1.17. Obelisk, Abusir, Egypt. This early version of the building-form obelisk is a limestone shaft 118 feet (36 meters) high, set upon a truncated pyramid that rises 65.5 feet (20 meters) from the ground.

Below: **1.18.** *Expedition to Punt.* Relief from the Temple of Queen Hatshepsut. Deir el-Bahri, Egypt

1.19. Obelisks erected by Ramesses II (ruled 1279–1212 B.C.E.) at temple of Amenhotep III (ruled 1390–1352 B.C.E.), Luxor, Egypt

Right: 1.20. Obelisk of Tuthmose III (ruled 1479–1425 B.C.E.), Central Park, New York City. Erected in present location west of The Metropolitan Museum of Art in 1880, this modest obelisk is known as Cleopatra's Needle.

time had assumed their elongated form. Thus dramatized by monuments and architecture, these axes organized spatial sequences of awe-inspiring ritual progression. For example, at the Temple at Luxor built by Amenhotep III (ruled 1390–1352 B.C.E.), Ramesses II (ruled 1279–1212 B.C.E.) erected a massive pylon before which he placed two colossal figures of himself and two obelisks (fig. 1.19). One of these was carried to Paris in the nineteenth century to become the focal point of the Place de la Concorde after these war trophies had become urban status symbols.

The quarrying, erection, subsequent transportation, and re-erection of obelisks in distant parts of the world provides a remarkable footnote in the history of world monuments and city planning. The first obelisks to be transported from Egypt were a pair appropriated in 671 B.C.E. as trophies of war by Assurbanipal I, the Assyrian conqueror of Thebes. Subsequently, Roman emperors garnered them in their Egyptian campaigns. Fifteen hundred years later, the papal planners of Baroque Rome repositioned them as focal points in the *piazze* of their rebuilt city.

Borrowing from this example, other countries transported Egyptian obelisks at great expense to distant cities where they became prestigious ornaments within the urban landscape, as the following bit of history makes clear. To celebrate one of the jubilees of his prosperous reign, Tuthmose III (ruled 1479–1425 B.C.E.) sent a crew of stonecutters to the quarries of Aswan for the purpose of extracting twin obelisks from the granite there. Workers chiseled and excavated the stone, carving the obelisks on the site. Other workers then dragged the obelisks by sledge to the river and floated them at flood time by barge to Heliopolis where they were placed in front of the Temple of the Sun. Nine hundred years later, in 525 B.C.E., the Persians burned and toppled the obelisks during their conquest of Egypt. After another five hundred years, when Egypt had declined to the status of a province of the Roman Empire, Augustus Caesar installed them in front of the Caesarium at Alexandria. In the nineteenth century C.E., a millennium and a half after Rome had fallen, the obelisks made their respective journeys as souvenirs of international diplomacy to the Thames embankment in London and New York City's Central Park (fig. 1.20).

These recycled obelisks illustrate how one civilization manifests its wealth and power by borrowing the forms (and in this case, actual objects) of another. For Assurbanipal I, the Theban obelisks symbolized the subjugation of a rival state. For Augustus Caesar, the obelisks of Tuthmose III were ready-made emblems of imperial glory. For nineteenth-century Parisians, the obelisk of Ramesses II served the same purpose the several obelisks brought to ancient

Rome had for Pope Sixtus V and his successors, ennobling the urban landscape and fixing space within an axial plan. For nineteenth-century Londoners, the second recycling of one of Tuthmose III's obelisks was, as it had been for Augustus Caesar, a symbol of imperial might. For New Yorkers, its twin was a means of ornamenting a picturesque landscape while proclaiming cosmopolitan civic status. Thus was a religious symbol of the sun, sacred to the Egyptians, turned into exotic treasure and appropriated as civic embellishment, while at the same time becoming a popular form for funerary monuments and architecture as discussed in Chapter Nine (see figs. 9.27, 9.28). We should not, however, lose sight of the fact that the obelisk in its original location was part of a complex, cosmologically focused landscape design. It is important to remember that, whether in the Old World or the New, the natural and cultural landscapes that gave sacred meaning to human life reflected the desire for predictable, life-sustaining order in the universe. This meant agricultural prosperity, dominance of elites over their subjects, and victory over enemies in war. The proper alignment with cosmic forces was therefore considered vital, and both practical and religious objectives furnished motives for the design of landscape space.

III. RITUAL AND LANDSCAPE IN PREHISTORIC GREECE: THE EARTH GODDESS AND THE MIGHTY LORDS

Unlike the topography of Egypt, which in ancient times consisted of a single ribbon supportive of human habitation in the cliff-walled, desert-bordered Nile Valley, that of Greece is made up of many broad, cradling, spring-fed valleys separated by mountains of impressive though not awesome size. The geologic forces that created the mountains are expressed in their southeastward orientation and their continuation as the Cyclades, Rhodes, and other islands—the higher elevations of a drowned mountain system. This orientation and the existence of such an array of island stepping-stones along the coast of Asia Minor gave the peoples who populated the Greek mainland, the Peloponnese, and Crete opportunities for interchange with the highly developed cultures to the east and south of the Aegean archipelago. At the same time, the sea preserved a strong degree of isolation, which allowed them to develop indigenous patterns of culture and religion.

As we have seen, Egypt's linear, riverine geography, because of its connectedness and the need for large-scale management of irrigation, encouraged the development of unified theocratic kingship. The fragmentation of the Greek landscape and the dependence of Greek settlements upon water from underground springs militated against autocracy and massive bureaucratic administration. Rather, it fostered the creation of several small tribal civilizations among whom hegemony was based upon successful warfare and maritime trade. A pastoral people who measured wealth in terms of livestock, the early Greeks lived in scattered settlements and did not need the mass organization of society necessary for the large-scale cultivation of grain.

In Egypt, the Nile landscape was a single mighty engine of fertility and life. Divinity resided at the desert verge in monumental pyramids and cliff-hewn temples. In Greece, the topographically diverse and dramatically beautiful landscape itself became invested with religious meaning. For ancient inhabitants it was the home of powerful goddesses and gods. Foremost among these deities in the remote centuries of prehistory was the Great Goddess, called Potnia in the Minoan culture of Crete.

CRETE

The importance of the earth goddess and animal spirit is apparent in sculpture and painting from the Minoan civilization that existed on the island of Crete from about 3000 B.C.E. until 1000 B.C.E.[15] This civilization was contemporaneous with that of Egypt and the Hittite Empire of Asia Minor. Although there is evidence of contact with these well-developed cultures, in its nonmilitaristic social values and goddess-worshipping religion, as well as in the sophisticated yet youthful ebullience manifested in its art, it demonstrates an independent development and autonomous nature.

After a millennium of evolution, Minoan civilization reached its zenith around 2000 B.C.E. and maintained this cultural high-water mark, in spite of massive destruction from earthquakes and fires about 1700 B.C.E. Subsequently, another, more horrendous episode of geophysical disturbance charted this culture's course toward collapse and extinction. This was the eruption of the Thera volcano about 1470 B.C.E., an event that toppled cities and set them ablaze, bringing in its wake tidal-wave inundation and a ruinous blanket of white ash over the island that made the soil impossible to cultivate. The disaster may have been compounded by subsequent Mycenaean invasions from the mainland. The principal architectural ruins and artifacts that define

1.21. Cave sacred to Zeus on the eastern face of Mount Ida, Crete. The cave plays a part in the Greek myth in which Gaia (Earth) and Uranos (Sky) gave birth to Kronos and Rhea, the parents of Zeus. Jealous to preserve his authority, Kronos devoured his offspring. Rhea's successful plot to hide the infant Zeus within the Idaian cave—there to be nursed by nymphs and fed goat's milk and honey—allowed him to survive, depose Kronos, and become the supreme male god and subsequent ruler of the Greek pantheon. That there was a shrine at this site in Minoan times, is attested by the many artifacts found there, including shields, spears, gold and ivory votive objects, figurines, and clay tablets, as well as deposits of ash and the bones of sacrificed animals.

Minoan culture therefore date from the period between around 2000 B.C.E. and 1470 B.C.E.

There is now considerable archaeological evidence showing that Minoans made ritual visits to hilltop sanctuaries and sacred caves. In addition to revering the earth goddess, they probably sought to propitiate the weather gods on high, a religious impulse not unlike that of the Mesopotamians and the pre-Columbian Americans. Public festivals brought congregations of worshipers to these dramatically situated, bare, and windswept peaks, where they found stone-paved terraces with altars placed before a *temenos,* or holy precinct, outlined by walls and balustrades crowned with sacral horns. Local pastoralists frequented these places, seeking protection for their cattle through votive offerings and propitiatory rites. The shrines themselves were well furnished with variously shaped altars, cult images, sacrificial tables, ladles, lamps, and libation vessels. Male and female clay figurines were left behind as surrogates for the worshipers, symbolizing their continuing devotional presence in the holy spot.

The hilly Cretan limestone terrain, a landscape type known to geologists as a karst formation and the source of the underground springs that sustained Minoan and later Greek communities, is riddled with some two thousand caves. A small number, perhaps thirty-five or so, had sacred status, probably because of their association with burial; among these an estimated sixteen were used for cult practices (fig. 1.21).

Right: 1.22. The Earth Goddess, Potnia, had a son and consort, Velchanos, or Kouros, a precursor of Zeus. His ritual death symbolized the annual death and rebirth of nature.

Votive gold double-axes and figurines of bronze have been found in sacred caves along with evidence of animal sacrifice and offerings of grain and other produce. There is evidence, too, of ritual dancing and feasting outside the caves. Funeral pyres burned at cave entrances before the performance of the chthonic rites within.

In addition to the peak and cave sanctuaries, walled enclosures guarded a sacred tree or perhaps marked the site of an epiphany. Some archaeologists surmise that worshipers tore branches or boughs from enshrined sacred trees and venerated them on altars or planted them in sockets between sacral horns. Scenes depicted on seals and other artifacts offer evidence of ecstatic dancing by priestesses in these locations.

Symbols of the Great Goddess, Potnia, were the double-axe, the stone pillar, and the snake. Perhaps it is she who is depicted as a bell-skirted, barebreasted, snake-wielding figure (fig. 1.22); in scenes on seals and wall paintings she is frequently symbolized by a pillar guarded by rampant lions, a form that clearly relates to that of the famous Lioness Gate, the principal entrance in the wall of the city-state of Mycenae on the Peloponnese (see fig. 1.25).

There were, in addition, other goddesses and gods. Britomartis, an early version of Artemis, the chaste mistress of the hunt and protector of animals, was worshiped in the mountain sanctuaries. Eleuthia, the Cave Goddess, protected women in childbirth; her special sanctuary was the Cave of Eileithyia at Amnisos. The Snake Goddess and the Dove Goddess were also part of the Minoan

pantheon, along with the Sea Goddess. Often, boundaries between these deities were blurred as they assumed one another's attributes. The most powerful and feared god for the Minoans was Potidas, or Poteidan, the sea god who prefigured the Greek Poseidon. His subterranean aspect was that of earth-shaker, lord of seismic tremors and tidal waves; his terrestrial form was that of a bull; and his celestial manifestation was as the sun and moon.

The civilization that emerged on Crete was sufficiently at peace and advanced enough in shipbuilding, maritime skills, and trade to exert commercial supremacy and nonmilitary dominance. Unlike the later fiercely warring city-states of the Greek mainland, which were heavily fortified with walls, Knossos and the other cities and towns of Crete were without walls. The Labyrinth, or ceremonial center at Knossos, was the most important religious complex on Crete, was a place of pilgrimage attracting worshipers from other parts of the island, and perhaps from other islands as well (fig. 1.23).

Minoans, like Greeks later, possessed a remarkable instinct for siting their religious centers and communities in relationship to natural topography. According to the controversial but here plausible interpretation of the architectural historian Vincent Scully, the builders of Knossos and Phaistos placed their centers within an enclosed valley, a "natural megaron," like a Minoan-palace great hall with its central hearth and columned porch, along a northsouth axis facing a gently mounded conical hill framed by the distant "horns" of a double-peaked or cleft mountain. These natural forms define landscape space and focus it. Further serving ritual needs and their symbolical expression were the labyrinthine passage, the long rectangular court, the columned pavilion, and the cavelike pillared hall. At Knossos, therefore, as one stands at the south propylaia, or gateway, one is facing a breast-shaped mound beyond which looms the cleft summit of Mount Juktas, site of a peak sanctuary and cave shrine where cult rituals were held. Similarly, at Phaistos, the central court is aligned along a north-south axis with twin-peaked Mount Ida, site of the cave sanctuary sacred to Zeus (fig. 1.24). Like the Puebloan plazas of the American Southwest, this central court with its enclosing architecture replicates at human scale the natural "megaron" that appears to contain it. Its alignment with a sacred form in nature, which also corresponds fairly closely to one of the cardinal directions, suggests that, like many Native American peoples, Cretan builders sited according to a combination of topographical foci and cosmological references.

Their axes were not inscribed *upon* nature, but existed rather as *orientation* lines connecting ritual

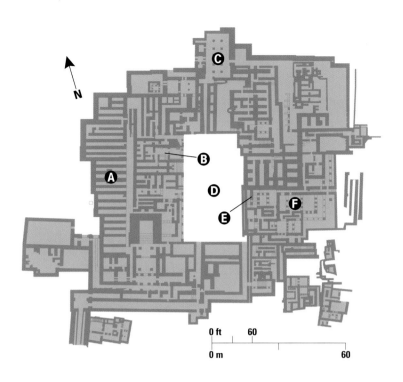

1.23. Plan of "Labyrinth" at Knossos, Crete, Greece. Minoan period, between 2000 B.C.E. and 1470 B.C.E. Ⓐ Storerooms. Ⓑ Throne Room. Ⓒ Pillar Hall. Ⓓ Central Court. Ⓔ Grand Staircase. Ⓕ Hall of the Double Axes

centers with shrines *in* nature. Thus, unlike the ceremonial axes the Egyptians and some Native Americans built for religious processionals, the axes of Greece were invisible lines. On Crete, these axes presumably tied the religious practices involving a Snake Goddess and her representatives in the sanctuaries at Knossos, Phaistos, and other Minoan settlements with the cultic practices of the mountain caves. The sacral horns surrounding the mountain altars were dramatically evoked by the dancers' daring somersaults through the horns of a living bull in a ritual ceremony that took place within the ceremonial court.

The intimate connection with local landscape and the desire to invest landscapes with religious

1.24. Central Court, Phaistos, Crete. Minoan period, between 2000 B.C.E. and 1470 B.C.E. On one side Phaistos faces the Libyan Sea and on the other, visible in the photograph, twin-peaked Mount Ida.

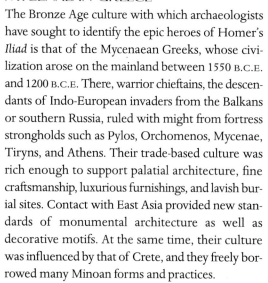

1.25. Lioness Gate entrance to the city of Mycenae, Greece. c. 1300–1200 B.C.E. Over the gate the huge stones are corbeled to relieve the weight upon the lintel. Into the triangular space so created was set a monumental tympanum with two rampant lionesses carved in high relief. These lionesses face an altar with a column set upon it; the column was probably an emblematic representation of the Earth Goddess.

1.26. Drawing of a seal impression from Knossos. Here the Earth Goddess, emblem of Minoan culture, is depicted as Mother of the Mountains and Mistress of the Animals.

meaning gradually weakened, and today human beings have, for the most part, discarded a propitiatory posture in their relationship with nature. So it is difficult for us to comprehend how deeply felt the connection with the earth goddess—Mother Earth—once was. Confidence and pride in human prowess caused a slow shift in values as a new godhead emerged, embodying the traits of the masculine hero. Nevertheless, a strong emotional link remained with a primary female goddess throughout antiquity as divinity split apart, becoming the pantheon of male and female deities made familiar by the literature of Homer.

MYCENAEAN GREECE

The Bronze Age culture with which archaeologists have sought to identify the epic heroes of Homer's *Iliad* is that of the Mycenaean Greeks, whose civilization arose on the mainland between 1550 B.C.E. and 1200 B.C.E. There, warrior chieftains, the descendants of Indo-European invaders from the Balkans or southern Russia, ruled with might from fortress strongholds such as Pylos, Orchomenos, Mycenae, Tiryns, and Athens. Their trade-based culture was rich enough to support palatial architecture, fine craftsmanship, luxurious furnishings, and lavish burial sites. Contact with East Asia provided new standards of monumental architecture as well as decorative motifs. At the same time, their culture was influenced by that of Crete, and they freely borrowed many Minoan forms and practices.

The same chthonic rites and worship of the earth goddess as occurred on Crete were practiced at Mycenaean sites. Apparent, however, in its warrior culture was an incipient challenge to the earth

goddess's supremacy, as Bronze Age men made military strength and protection of the clan through victory on the battlefield a recognizable benefit on a par with fertility and the protection of the crops. This is evident in a more defensively strategic occupancy of the land. Because of the existence of springs in limestone ridges and the extensive presence of such karstic formations in Greece, the Mycenaeans were able to site their cities on difficult-to-scale high points with long views of the surrounding valleys, plains, and sea. The Athenian Acropolis, which was occupied in Mycenaean times, was furnished with many such springs. Mycenae itself was situated on a hill above the plain of Argos. The population spread out upon the slopes below in convenient proximity to the fissures in the slope where springs were found, but close to the heavily fortified acropolis where they could seek safety from invaders. The approach to this stronghold was from the southwest along a path leading to the Lioness Gate within its cyclopean masonry walls (figs. 1.25; cf. 1.26).

In the turbulent period between 1200 and 1150 B.C.E., Mycenaean civilization was put to rout by invaders. Although they did not succeed in breaching the massive walls of the citadel, the Dorian newcomers from the north managed to topple the authority of the warrior kings there and in the other Mycenaean cities as they infiltrated the countryside, adding new traditions to the Helladic cultural base. Trading wealth vanished as did kingship, monumental architecture, and fine craftsmanship in gold and bronze. Mycenaean citadels became shells wherein a remnant population lived amid the ruins of vanished glory.

Geographical fragmentation abetted the general impoverishment in bringing about increased political fragmentation. Authoritarian-style rulership disappeared as society broke apart into tribal units. Common interests caused a collection of *phylai,* or tribes, to fuse as a *demos.* The members of a *demos* gradually formed a *polis,* a communal center for refuge and religious practice. During the four centuries of gestation and social transformation that constituted the so-called Dark Age in Greece, the *agora,* a public space for assembly and debate, and the *boule,* a council of nobles, became the seedbed of a radically new concept of governance. In this matrix, people cultivated a new respect for the individual. These were the forces at work as Greece, undisturbed by fresh invasions from the north or a resurgence of authoritarian influence from the east, moved toward the eighth-century social development that created new institutions capable of redirecting human destiny, the landscape expressions of which we shall examine in Chapter Two.

IV. COSMOLOGY IN THE LANDSCAPES OF THE AMERICAS: SPIRITS OF EARTH AND SKY

In looking at the landscapes of pre-Columbian archaeology and the remnant traditions of agricultural and pastoral peoples throughout the Americas, we can find enough parallels among disparate world cultures to support the notion of the universality of certain myths and religious practices. Such transcultural beliefs include the divinity ascribed to the sun, the importance of real and artificial mountains as sky platforms to bring a people into closer contact with their gods, particularly those associated with rain and fertility; the cave as the womb of the Earth Mother and a shrine in nature; the importance of both votive and sacrificial offerings; the portrayal of gods and spirits in animal form; the sense of human subservience to cosmological power, and the need—satisfied through drumbeat, communal chant, and dance in designated sacred spaces—to communicate with that power.

CULTURAL PARALLELS AND UNIVERSAL PATTERNS

The reverence for mountains and lakes, the belief that there is a numinous energy and life force animating stones and trees as well as living creatures is called *teotl* in the Nahuatl language of the Aztecs, *huaca* in the Andean tongue of Quechua, or *po-wa-ha* in Tewa, the speech of Santa Clara Pueblo and other pueblos near the Rio Grande in New Mexico. To ensure the flow of this positive energy through their settlements, the precolonial builders in the Americas did not lay out their towns haphazardly. The cardinal points of the compass figure in many creation stories.[16] Pueblo villages, for instance, are oriented with respect to four sacred mountains and, at closer range, four mesas and four village shrines. These have legendary associations with the explo-

ratory paths to the north and south, east and west, taken by four pairs of mythological twins as they emerged from a primal subterranean lake when Earth was still in formation.

Centeredness within this natural frame is important. The *nansipu,* or small hole in the middle of the Puebloan plaza, is an *axis mundi* uniting the upper world with the lower, the place whence life emerged and to which it returns. The circular *kiva* with its *sipapu,* another small hole like the *nansipu* of the plaza, reinforced the all-pervading theme of cosmic axiality. According to Puebloan belief, a sky-basket, identified with the male principle, overarches the bowl-earth, associated with the female. Within the earth part of this duality there are four concurrent planes of existence. Puebloan people emerged onto the fourth plane, the world of life and light, at the north opening of the Earth Mother.

Not surprisingly, lake bottoms and natural caves are associated with myths of human emergence into this world. For millennia, Native Americans in many localities have made pilgrimages to cave-shrines in their sacred mountains as well as to spirit-inhabited mountain lakes. Because the great Pyramid of the Sun at Teotihuacán was built sometime between 150 C.E. and 225 C.E. above a natural cave probably associated with an origin myth, it is now thought that the city itself was sited with regard to this important natural symbol as well as in relation to Cerro Gordo, the mountain to the north, the profile of which is echoed by the axially aligned Pyramid of the Moon (fig. 1.27).

Mimetic architecture—structures whose shapes imitate natural land forms—is apparent in the diverse cultures of the Americas. Although less predetermined in plan and form than Teotihuacán,

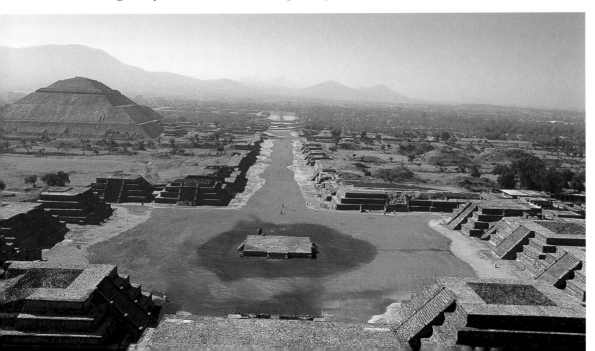

1.27. Pyramid of the Moon with Cerro Gordo, Teotihuacán, Mexico. c. 150–225 C.E.

Taos Pueblo, which is still occupied, bears a mimetic relationship to Taos Mountain like that of the Pyramid of the Moon to Cerro Gordo (fig. 1.28). But in neither case does the built environment dominate the natural one. The imitative forms are subservient to the natural ones. The former is the locus of human life and ritual ceremony; the latter is the residence of divinity.

Many of the great civilizations of the Americas vanished for reasons that can only be guessed. Without a literature such as the Homeric epics or the more factually based stories of Herodotus and other historians, the Aztecs were even more mystified than we about the fate of their predecessors in the Valley of Mexico, the builders of Teotihuacán. Although they set down their own oral traditions in hieroglyphic accounts, few survived the Spanish Conquest. Archaeology, too, was thwarted as the market value placed upon pre-Columbian artifacts made ancient centers vulnerable to the depredations of looters. Nevertheless, significant progress has been made by recent archaeology in decoding hieroglyphic symbols carved in stone and also in the field known as archaeoastronomy, the science that attempts to explain landscape constructions in cosmological terms. Archaeologists and archaeoastronomists have come to realize that by studying the siting of certain monuments and structures in relationship to the position of the stars, the course of the moon, or the position of the sun at the time of the spring and fall equinoxes, native peoples in the Americas were practicing what surely must have

been landscape design in the broadest possible sense—what we might call cosmological landscape architecture.

MOUNDS AND PLAZAS

Pre-Columbian architecture is essentially an architecture of mass and communal open space. Its construction was an administrative and technical feat of considerable magnitude. The scale of earth-moving operations undertaken by the people who built the first earthworks is indeed awe-inspiring, especially when one remembers that there existed no mechanized equipment such as that employed by the creators of the modern earthworks discussed in Chapter Twelve, nor did these builders use wheeled vehicles. Like the pyramidal masonry "skyscrapers" of the Maya in Mexico and Central America (250 C.E.–900 C.E.), the immense earthworks at Poverty Point, Louisiana (1800 B.C.E.–500 B.C.E.), the Hopewell Mounds in Ohio (100 B.C.E.–400 C.E.), and the monumental mounds of the Mississippian culture at Cahokia near present-day St. Louis (800–1350 C.E.) are meant to be ascended, descended, or walked around (fig. 1.29). Unlike Western architecture since Roman times, these structures do not provide widely vaulted, domed, volumetric interior space. As opposed to basilicas and cathedrals, they are not architectural shells in which to move about freely. Because this is true, landscape space—the space defined by both the architecture and the natural forms of the site—is fundamental in both a utilitarian and a religious sense.

1.28. Taos Pueblo with Taos Mountain behind it. Taos, New Mexico. Occupied continuously since c. 1200 C.E. Photographed in 1993

The earliest evidence in the Americas of a large-scale, well-planned, collaboratively constructed landscape space occurs in northeast Louisiana where approximately five thousand years ago several series of large earthen mounds were built. At Watson Brake, the builders of eleven of these early mounds linked them by earthen ridges to form an oval-shaped enclosure (fig. 1.30). Their purpose was probably to accommodate some funerary or other ceremonial practice. The persistence of this central space—or plaza, if we adopt the Spanish term—as a landscape form is evidenced, as we have seen, in the extant pueblos of northern New Mexico and Arizona, which have occupied their present locations since around 1300 C.E. The spectacular and well-preserved ruins within the sheltering cliff faces of Mesa Verde in the San Juan Basin of southern Colorado and Canyon de Chelly in northeastern Arizona, which was occupied as early as the fifth century C.E.

by people known as Basket Maker and then between 1100 and 1300 by the ancestral Puebloan people referred to as Anasazi, testify to the harmony between architecture and nature achieved by Native American builders. Even in these creviced locations they managed to fit miniature plazas with *kivas:* level, open ledges that served both sacred and quotidian functions (fig. 1.31). Thus, whether the Ciudadela at Teotihuacán, a 38-acre sunken plaza with the huge Temple of the Feathered Serpent at one end, a tiny platform in the wall of a Pueblo-occupied cliff, or a half acre of packed earth forming the *bupingeh* (middle-heart place) of contemporary Tewa people, plazas were and remain ceremonially important spaces, places of dance and priestly spectacle, including, in the Mesoamerica of pre-Columbian times, human sacrifice.

1.29. Monks Mound and the Great Plaza, Cahokia, Illinois. c. 800–1350 C.E. Entrance mural by Lloyd K. Thonsend, Cahokia Mounds State Historic Site, Collinsville, Illinois. Basing his work on extant remains and archaeological evidence, the artist has rendered central Cahokia around 1100 C.E., viewed from the south with the Twin Mounds in the foreground, the Grand Plaza, and Monks Mound in the distance.

1.30. Watson Brake, near Monroe, Louisiana. c. 3000 B.C.E On the Ouachita River to the southwest of Monroe a 3-foot-(approx. 0.9-meter-) high circular embankment studded with eleven roughly conical mounds embraces a plaza that measures approximately 920 feet (280 meters) by 650 feet (198 meters).

1.31. Cliff Palace, with apartments, *kivas,* and plazas set within the rock face, Mesa Verde National Park, Colorado. c. 5th century C.E., Basket Maker culture and c. 1100–1300 C.E., ancestral Puebloan culture

1.32. Pueblo Bonito, Chaco Canyon, Arizona. c. 860 C.E.–1130 C.E. The numerous large *kivas*, axially interconnected rooms, fine masonry workmanship, massive ceiling timbers imported from far away, and sheer scale of the D-shaped structure called Pueblo Bonito argue its possible function as a major ceremonial center.

ANCESTRAL PUEBLOAN SETTLEMENTS AROUND CHACO CANYON

In the Southwest, where the conditions for successful agriculture were especially demanding, native societies were more egalitarian and less hierarchical than those of the great Mississippian, Mesoamerican, and Aztec builders who erected the massive pyramids that arouse our awe today. The peoples of the Southwest fit these structures into their spectacular, dry environment with great ingenuity. In their landscape-conforming works, economy and beauty go hand in hand. The cavelike *kiva,* with its fire pit and *sipapu*—or emergence hole—indented in the floor, was the architectural descendant of the pit house. This barely visible structure was covered by the earthen floor of a plaza that served, as we have already noted, as a daily work space and, in some cases, as a ritual dancing ground.

Above all, the purpose of the *kiva* and the plaza above it is to provide a space in which humans can acknowledge and participate in the cosmic connection between the bowl-imaged earth and the basket-symbolized sky, affirm the orientation of their community with respect to the cardinal compass points and sacred mountains and mesas, and experience the life breath that flows throughout this universe. Larger pre-Columbian pueblos often had several functioning *kivas* to serve the various clans within them. Although built above ground, the *kivas* of today are still circular structures without any aspiration toward monumentality in the European sense.

Centering according to an *axis mundi* established at a place of community focus and cosmic ritual could assume vast regional dimensions as illustrated by the great ancestral Puebloan center at Chaco Canyon (fig. 1.32). Recent archaeological discoveries in the Four Corners area reveal a far-flung road system drawing many ancestral Pueblos, including those at Mesa Verde and Canyon de Chelly, into a spatial relationship with this important ceremonial nexus.[17] Archaeologists refer to this important urban complex as "the Chaco phenomenon." They face many unanswered questions as they continue to study Pueblo Bonito, Chetro Ketl, and other Great Houses in the center of the canyon along with the "outliers," ancestral Puebloan ruins with large ceremonial *kivas* and ancillary residential or storage chambers, such as are found at Aztec and Salmon. They have discerned at least seven sets of roads, which collectively comprise nearly 1,500 miles (2,414 kilometers), radiating from Chaco, and some suggest that at least one of the roads, which they call the Great North Road, because of its alignment within one-half degree of true north until it bends to a two° angle to focus upon an important cone-shaped mound, "is a cosmological expression of the Chaco culture."[18] The fact that this is a road lacking a clear practical destination supports such a conclusion.

Indifferent to topography, the Chacoan roads scale canyon walls by means of wooden stairs or steps carved into bedrock or built of masonry, but, where they change direction, they do so at an abrupt angle, usually at the site of a Great House or at a *herradura*—a low, horseshoe-shaped enclosure, frequently located at a high point where there is a distant view. Where they traverse slick rock, their course is sometimes etched by a single shallow groove. No one knows the exact function of these *herraduras*, but they may have been roadside shrines. There is little roadside debris or other evidence of overnight camps such as traders would have left and no evidence that the roads were used after the climax of Chacoan culture around 1140 C.E.[19] Like the Maya causeways and the Inka roads in Peru, the Chacoan roads were probably used for ceremonial purposes, and concentrations in various roadside locations of ceramic shards that appear to have been ritually broken suggest this possibility. Allied with the roads were mesa-top signaling stations, which may have been used to transmit practical messages, but which also probably functioned as observatories, thus serving a cosmological purpose.

Supporting the conclusion that Chaco was an important festival center in the ancient Southwest is the presence directly opposite Pueblo Bonito, on the south side of the Chaco Wash, of a *kiva* more than 63 feet (19.2 meters) in diameter called Casa Rinconada, possibly the largest *kiva* the ancestral Puebloans ever built (fig. 1.33). In its orientation and design, Casa Rinconada appears to symbolize the ancient Puebloan cosmos. The axis running through its north and south doorways is aligned within a fraction of a degree of true north, and the four sockets for the large timber roof supports form a perfect square, each side of which is also true to a cardinal

direction within a fraction of a degree. On the inside of its circular masonry wall were cut twenty-eight niches, with a possible additional one making twenty-nine. These may have had a relationship to the 29.5-day lunar month. Six larger, irregularly spaced niches were also cut into the wall. The northeastern roof support might have blocked its passage, but archaeologists have noted that a beam of light entering the *kiva* today on the day of the summer solstice illuminates one of the larger niches. Within Pueblo Bonito, window perforations appear to have been positioned to allow light to travel in a pattern across a wall surface in a manner that both predicts and marks the winter solstice. Whether or not Chacoan priests used these features in making their calendrical notations, it is certain that here, as elsewhere in the region of ancient habitation by Puebloan peoples, they studied the movement of celestial bodies and reflected their astronomical knowledge in their lives and in the landscape, timing their ritual and agricultural practices and aligning their buildings and roads with the positions of the Sun, stars, and planets in the sky.

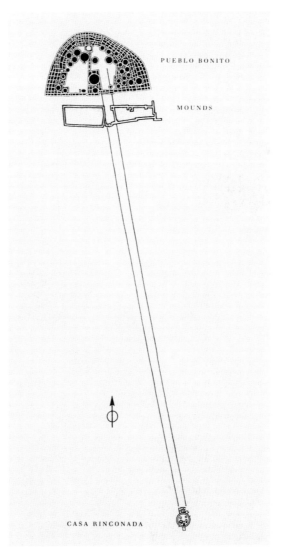

1.33. Casa Rinconada, Pueblo Bonito and its mounds, and the suggested axis linking these two ancestral Puebloan structures. Plan by Stephen H. Lekson, 1992. Unlike the *kivas* of unit houses or the *kivas* within a Great House such as Pueblo Bonito, Casa Rinconada stands in isolation. If, however, one takes into account an axis running from Casa Rinconada through the two large rectangular mounds at the southern edge of Pueblo Bonito in alignment with the wall that bisects it into an eastern and a western half, it is apparent that a linkage was intended. The mounds once had strong masonry retaining walls and a flat plastered surface on top, giving them greater architectural importance than that of a typical ancient unit house. Perhaps they were used ritually as ceremonial platforms. In any case, they are the vertical inverse of the sunken architecture within Pueblo Bonito. Not only do they heighten the feeling of its enclosure, but they also dramatize the approach from, and connection to, Casa Rinconada. Similar mounds, which are not typical midden or refuse mounds but often contain broken ceramics possibly associated with ritual ceremonies, are found at Pueblo Alto and at many outlier sites.

PUEBLO BONITO

MOUNDS

CASA RINCONADA

1.34. Aerial view of Lake Titicaca and the altiplano, Peru

At the beginning of the second third of the twelfth century, Chaco's importance as the area's controlling political force suddenly waned. By the middle of the twelfth century, the Chacoans had stopped all construction, and they no longer organized ceremonial festivals in the canyon. At Chaco and its outliers, by 1300 C.E., many roads had been ritually closed and the ceremonial rooms of Great Houses dismantled and burned. At the same time, new settlements appeared around Black Mesa in what is now northeastern Arizona and in the Rio Grande Valley, and these became the ancestral communities of the Hopi, Zuni, and Rio Grande pueblos of today.

INKA SHRINES

The Inka civilization that flourished in the fifteenth century C.E. revered as one of its sacred sites Tiwanaku, a cosmologically planned city built on the altiplano in the flat basin around Lake Titicaca between around 400 and 1100 C.E. Like other real and imaginary lakes of Native American mythology, Lake Titicaca played a significant role as the place of human origin. To the ancient inhabitants of the altiplano, its bowl shape and watery depths symbolized the feminine principle and embryonic gestation, whereas the rigid, dry, glaciated peaks around it had an obvious association with masculinity (fig. 1.34).[20] Lake Titicaca, in other words, was a natural form that perfectly represented the womb of earth and its center, while its jagged horizon line of mountains helped mark the cardinal points, pinning the sky with its beneficent sun and revolving stars and planets to the landscape plain around it.

Upon ascending the throne, each Inka ruler undertook a major building program as a means of asserting authority. Dynastic power and the cosmic connectedness of the empire, which extended 2,700 miles (4,345 kilometers) from north to south along the Pacific coast of South America, was evident in the four highways emanating from Cuzco's central plaza. From the consequent division of the surrounding countryside the empire took its name, Tahuantinsuyu, "Land of the Four Quarters." A network of highways covering approximately 19,000 miles (30,000 kilometers), over which teams of runners coursed on government business, allowed the Inkas to maintain their sway. Shrines in nature also helped weave the empire into a cultural unity. The ruined center of Tiwanaku on Lake Titicaca was one of these sacred sites, lending to the Inkas increased authority over the local population and linking them with that city's ancient builders. Here, on an island, Topa Inka (ruled 1471–1493 C.E.) enlarged a temple dedicated to the Sun and planted a grove of trees in the sacred precinct that enclosed a rock, believed to be the sun's place of origin and the spot where life began. Ritual processions to this mythologically designated origin rock passed through a series of ceremonial gateways.

Other nature shrines included springs, mountain peaks, and venerated stones called *pururuacas*, which were considered to be transformed warriors. Prominent and distinctively shaped rocks were often singled out within the landscape and given sacred status. A special boulder would receive an architectural enclosure, and a bedrock outcrop could be carved as a royal dais. Mimetic rocks, those whose outlines echoed distant mountains, might be assigned iconic status (fig. 1.36). Altogether, 328 *huacas,* or sacred places, were sited along forty-one sight lines, called *ceques,* which emanated like sun rays outward from Cuzco. At these shrines, travelers and pilgrims made votive offerings of beautifully woven cloth, figurines in stone and precious metals, and broken shells. They also deposited food and drink for the indwelling spirits of the *huacas.*

In some *huacas* sacrificed children were interred. They had served as participants in a ritual designed to bond the far-flung empire into a more secure religious union. The children, aged six to ten

1.35. Ritual lines with trapezoidal area, Nazca, Peru. c. 200 B.C.E.–600 C.E. The arrowlike triangles and trapezoids, which are visible around Nazca from the air, appear to be correlated with the flow of water, while the nexus of converging lines, called ray centers, are thought to be related to the river system. Geoglyphs—images etched by exposing the light soil below the oxidized gravel surface of the desert—can be interpreted in terms of a water-based religion. Remarkably, they were constructed by people who could only view their work piecemeal. Geoglyphs had to be conceived as scale models and then enlarged by a pointing technique as they were scratched onto the earth's surface.

Left: 1.36. Rock shrine within the sacred Inka landscape, Quenco, Peru

and chosen for their beauty and family status from villages throughout Tahuantinsuyu's four quarters, were consigned to the company of priests with whom they traveled the network of highways that led to Cuzco, where they were greeted with pomp. There boys and girls were paired in symbolic marriage ceremonies and paraded solemnly around the main plaza, the heart of the Inka universe. After the celebrations were over and the children had been properly feted, the traveling parties returned to their home villages. But this time they did not journey along the system of highways, but crossed the arduous terrain in straight paths following the sacred *ceque* lines. Each group was preceded by chanting Inka officials carrying statues and valuable offerings. Once they were received back home with honor, the children, dressed in finery and accompanied by figurines and other offerings, were placed in one of the local *huacas* and interred alive. In this way the Inka empire wove space into a fabric of power in which local places and Cuzco were tightly bound by ritual ceremony and pilgrimage along the *ceque* lines.

Nazca Lines and Effigy Earthworks

Like the wide Chacoan roads, the mysterious lines in Peru in the area embraced by the Nazca River system in South America, dating from 200 B.C.E. to 600 C.E., raise many unanswered questions, but we can surmise that they also had ceremonial and religious significance. Archaeoastronomers have discerned alignments of the Nazca lines corresponding to solar events on the horizon and the positions of certain important constellations in the sky (fig. 1.35). The delineation of what were probably long-distance pilgrimage ways that also functioned as cosmological reference points in two such widely separated desert

1.37. Serpent Mound, Locust Grove, Ohio. c. 1000–1140 C.E. The architects who laid out Great Serpent Mound fitted the writhing body of their nearly quarter-mile long reptile into the curve formed by the creek and its adjacent bluff. The oval form that appears to protrude from the snake's mouth can be read as an egg.

locations confirms the importance of astronomical observations and their calendrical correlations for ancient peoples.

But how do we attempt to explain the Nazca lines that are not straight: the geoglyphs—giant figures of birds, fish, mammals, insects, and even anthropomorphic creatures "drawn" on the hard desert surface as paths 4.5 feet (1.37 meters) to 9 feet (2.74 meters) wide, which were created by scraping away the darker oxidized surface soil and placing it in small outlining ridges while exposing the lighter soil below? Are they clan totems or etched forms with sacred meaning and ceremonial purpose to be traced with human footsteps as a means of absorbing their talismanic magic? It is easier to interpret the puma outline of the plan for Cuzco as a symbol of the Inka dynasty, but how can we explain the Great Serpent Mound in Ohio, now believed to date about 1000–1140 C.E., and the so-called effigy mounds of the Upper Mississippi Valley, which were built throughout the course of many centuries up until around 1300 C.E.? These giant earthworks—the Great Bear Mound in eastern Iowa measures 137 feet by 70 feet (41.8 meters by 21.3 meters)—are particularly astonishing when one remembers that they were achieved by a people who had no draft animals or carts with wheels and no power equipment other than human sinew (figs. 1.37, 1.38).

CONTEMPORARY PUEBLOS OF THE AMERICAN SOUTHWEST

The persistence of cultural memory and tradition is strong among Native Americans, and in parts of the American Southwest it is still possible to find landscapes where a potent residue of a once-pervasive ethos of place is discernible. A visitor gradually perceives that a pueblo—a settlement on tribal lands in northern and western New Mexico and northeast Arizona, consisting of multilevel adobe or stone dwellings built by the descendants of indigenous prehistoric peoples—is sited not by happenstance but in a particular way that acknowledges the cardinal directions and mesa and mountain forms in the near and far distance. Here on certain feast days dancers animate a "heart" place, a central plaza enclosed protectively by attached dwellings, with practiced movements meant to evoke the spirits of animals and the cosmological forces associated with fertility, procreation, and the continuance of life.

Acculturation and the psychological compartmentalization of two differing systems of belief are characteristic of extant Puebloan cultures, heirs to Catholicism by virtue of the Spanish Conquest. In Santa Clara Pueblo, as in San Ildefonso Pueblo, San Juan Pueblo, and Santo Domingo, the patron saint is honored with a mass on her or his feast day, but the more significant celebration from an ethnic perspective is the one that subsequently takes place in the pueblo's main and subsidiary plazas. Dances are performed first in one plaza and then another by men and women, old and young, in fine costumes and high headdresses decorated with symbolic representations of animals, birds, clouds, and mountains.

It is worth looking closely at one of the seemingly nondescript spaces where Native American dance ceremonies take place. Recalling her childhood at Santa Clara Pueblo, the architectural historian Rina Naranjo Swentzell has written:

As the pueblo, or human space, was encircled by high mountains, low hills and flat fields, the center point (*nansipu*), from which the people emerged out of the underworld, was also girdled by different spaces within the pueblo. The *nansipu*, marked by an inconspicuous stone, was located within the middle-heart place, or the plaza. The plaza was bounded by house structures, which in turn were encircled by the corrals or places where horses, pigs, and chickens lived. Beyond that, or sometimes overlapping, were the trash mounds. The trash mounds flowed into the fields, and from there the energy moved into the hills and mountains where it entered those far shrines, moved through the underworld levels or existences and re-emerged through the *nansipu*.

The stories of the old people told us that we came to live on this fourth level of existence with the help of plants, birds and other animals. Once we emerged out of the underworld, we continued to need those other living beings. In order to find the center point, or the *nansipu*, the water spider and the rainbow were consulted. Water Spider spread its legs to the north, west, south and east and determined the middle of this world. Then, to make sure that Water Spider was right, Rainbow spread its arch of many colors to the north, west, south and east and confirmed Water Spider's center point. There the people placed a stone, and around that stone was defined the middle-heart place. Next, the living and sleeping structures were built in terraced forms, like mountains, with stepped tiers which enclosed and protected the plaza, or the valley of the human place.

The house and kiva structures also emulated the low hills and mountains in their connectedness to the earth. The adobe structures flowed out of the earth, and it was often difficult to see where the ground stopped and where the structures began. The house struc-

1.38. Great Bear Mound, Effigy Mounds National Monument, Marquette, Iowa. c. 350 B.C.E. and 1300 C.E. The Great Bear Mound is one of several mound formations in the area that today comprises western Wisconsin, southwest Minnesota, and northeast Iowa. The few dozen that remain of what may have been as many as ten thousand before urbanization and agricultural operations eradicated them can be seen primarily in Lizard Mound County Park in Wisconsin and Effigy Mounds National Monument in Iowa. The Great Bear Mound in the latter is 137 feet (41.8 meters) in length and measures 70 feet wide (21.3 meters) at the bear's shoulders.

tures were, moreover, connected to each other, enclosing an outdoor space from which we could directly connect with the sky and focus on the moving clouds. Connectedness was primary. The symbolic flowed into the physical world as at the *nansipu* where the *po-wa-ha* (the breath of the cosmos) flowed out of the underworld into this world.

The kiva structure was totally symbolic. Its rooftop was like the pueblo plaza space from where we could connect with the sky, while the rooftop opening took us into the kiva structure which was like going back into the earth via the *nansipu* in the plaza. Within the feminine dark interior, the plaza-space configuration was repeated with the human activity around a *nansipu*, the earth floor under and the woven-basket roof above, representing the sky. The connecting ladder made of tall spruce or pine trees stood in the middle near the *nansipu*. Everything was organized to remind us constantly of the primary connections with the earth, sky, other forms of life and the cosmic movement. These primary connections were continually reiterated. . . .

Landscaping, or the beautification of outdoor spaces, was a foreign concept. The natural environment was primary, and the human structures were made to fit into the hills and around boulders and trees. In that setting, planting pretty flowers that need watering was ridiculous.[21]

Swentzell is telling us, as an aside, that in a landscape where the human connection to what has been called first nature (wilderness) and second nature (the agrarian landscape of fields and pastures) is paramount, a "third nature" as represented by the garden (an enclosed landscape space in which art and nature are conjoined) is irrelevant.[22] Similarly, in discussing the form and function of the *bupingeh,* as the plaza is called in the Tewa language, Swentzell remarks, "The emphasis of the *bupingeh* is not on the substance but rather on the emptiness—consequently, there are no statues, fountains, gazebos, park benches, grass, or flowers to enhance its appeal."[23] More than a void, however, the *bupingeh* is instinct with life; it is the space for ceremonial dance, "the connecting space between the cosmic energies of the Pueblo world which flow out of the *nansipu* through the physical space of the pueblo to the hills, far mountains, and clouds and back into the underworld."[24] Thus, the Puebloan today, perceiving symbolism directly in the built and natural forms of a perfectly centered, emotionally rich environment does not need to sustain his or her imagination with metaphorically suffused garden and park spaces or with ornamental structures and horticultural concerns.

As we have seen, over time, Native North American populations migrated from one site to another in response to climatic changes, resource depletion, war, or other territorial imperatives. Because of their nature-oriented religious views, wherever they established themselves, site planning centered the community with one or more sanctified central spaces, often the nexus of axial relationships with both celestial and terrestrial natural phenomena—equinoctial and solstitial positions of the sun, calendrical maximum and minimum rise and set points of the moon, the predictably timed appearance of certain auspicious constellations in the night sky, and mountain forms. Usually these directional lines of cosmological connectivity were implied, but in some places, such as the Four Corners areas of the Southwest or on the arid plains of Peru, Native Americans inscribed axes upon the land.

Prayer and propitiation were the necessary, available means with which agricultural people living within the bounds of limited systems of technology addressed uncertainty and the exigencies of their circumstances. Those architectural forms that brought them into closer contact with Sky Father, Sun, Rain God, Earth Mother, and Seed Goddess were the physical manifestation of a belief system that sought above all else fertility and the continuance of life. Eurocentric theorists once presumed that the Maya and the Teotihuacános were influenced in the construction of their great pyramids by Old World contact, which somehow seeded this building form in the New. A more convincing explanation is the cosmological one that the mountain-mimicking pyramid is a universal human phenomenon, a priestly platform for communication with sky-dwelling gods or a funerary monument for rulers whose divine status ensured the regular rotation of the sun in its diurnal and annual cycles. Circular forms echo the 360° horizon and are an important element of cosmic consciousness. Jung believed that circles are archetypal, magical rings drawn around that which would be protected as sacred. He pointed out that a mandala, or circle within a square, is like a *temenos,* or sacred enclosure, protecting what is magical and holy.

Jungian theory and the cosmological orientation of many early religions would help explain how axial lines, circles, pyramids, and other geometrical forms can be manifested in landscape design in widely divergent times and places. By acknowledging the widely shared need among societies to attune themselves to a religiously perceived cosmic power we can explain the correspondence between landscape forms employed for ritual purposes by prehistoric and early ancient peoples in Europe and Asia and their counterparts, including contemporary native peoples, in the Americas. The important fact to ponder with regard to Mesoamerican pyramids and the Mississippian mounds built by the well-organized culture that flourished in the region around St. Louis between about 750 C.E. and 1500 C.E. is not their coincidental similarity to Old World "prototypes," but their sheer size and the amount of human labor their construction entailed. As in Egypt and Mesopotamia, belief in a religion mediated by a priestly elite was absolute, and it effectively prevented the subservient populace who built these monumental earth and stone works from refusing to work.

Cave sanctuaries, real and artificial mountains, earthworks, circular definitions of space, and the alignment of axes with cardinal directions and the calendrical positions of celestial bodies constitute the primal components of landscape design dating from earliest times when humans perceived themselves to be embedded in nature and utterly dependent upon cosmic forces. Gradually, during the first millennium C.E., with the development of city-states, there emerged other ideals presupposing a more important role for humans in ordering life according to religious and ethical systems that placed them in fuller partnership with their gods. These values, too, dictated the shaping of space and the creation of places in which a newly minted vocabulary of classical forms that have remained influential throughout history was first manifested with great beauty.

1. See R. Murray Schafer, *The Tuning of the World* (Toronto: McClelland and Stewart, 1977), p. 157. Peripheral vision, rather than perspective focus, can be said to characterize the Chinese depiction of space, causing the eye to traverse from one viewpoint to another within the same work of art, with as much awareness of the peripheral areas as of the center; Byzantine art distorts scale and reverses perspective by increasing the size of distant objects; and Eskimo spatial representation, probably because their landscape is spatially more amorphous than elsewhere, is unfocused in the way that acoustic space is multidirectional and has no fixed boundaries. Besides being analogous to unfocused, nonoptical, aural space, Inuit space can be characterized as haptic—space that is perceived by our own bodily presence within it. Gilles Deleuze (1925–1995) and Félix Guattari (1930–1992), drawing on Edmund Carpenter's description of Inuit space as having "no middle distance, no perspective, no outline, nothing the eye can cling to except thousands of smokey plumes of snow . . . a land without bottom or edge . . . a labyrinth alive with the movements of crowded people," have characterized this type of landscape as "smooth" space in which "there is neither horizon nor background nor perspective nor limit nor outline or form nor center; there is no intermediary distance, or all distance is intermediary." See Gilles Deleuze and Félix Guattari, *A Thousand Plateaus: Capitalism and Schizophrenia*, trans. Brian Massumi (Minneapolis: University of Minnesota Press, 1987), p. 494. Deleuze and Guattari distinguish between smooth space—as for instance the open sea, arctic wastes, and deserts, the trackless realm of nomads—and "striated" optical space, where laws of perspective apply and distance is discernible and measurable. But in the two philosophers' view, much more than being categories of landscape analysis, smooth and striated space are cultural constructs. Because of the natural propensity of human beings to create order out of chaos, there is always a tendency to replicate cosmogenesis, to give smooth space a center and directional coordinates, thereby converting it into striated space. The reverse also can occur as when, for instance, we lose perspective in close distance or experience vision as a "sea" of impressions.

2. See Mircea Eliade, *Patterns in Comparative Religion*, trans. Rosemary Sheed (Cleveland: Meridian Books, 1963), chap. 8, sec. 97. This work provides a valuable introduction to the universal reverence among many world cultures and early human societies for such symbolically potent archetypal forms as monumental stones, sacred trees, Earth Mother, sky gods, water, the sun, and the moon.

3. Jolane Jacobi, *The Psychology of C.G. Jung* (New Haven: Yale University Press, 1973). This work provides a useful overview of Jung's thought and a clear introduction to the subject of archetypes and symbols, image carriers of psychological states, which Jung posits as residing in the collective unconscious of humankind.

4. See Steven J. Mithen, *Thoughtful Foragers: A Study of Prehistoric Decision Making* (Cambridge: Cambridge University Press, 1990), chap. 8.

5. See David Abram, *The Spell of the Sensuous: Perception and Language in the More-than-Human World* (New York: Pantheon Books, 1996), pp. 140–41. According to Abram, "Without guns or gunpowder, a native hunter must often come much closer to his wild prey if he is to take its life. Closer, that is, not just physically but emotionally, empathically entering into proximity with the other animal's ways of sensing and experiencing. The native hunter must *apprentice* himself to those animals that he would kill. Through long and careful observation, enhanced at times by ritual identification and mimesis, the hunter gradually develops an instinctive knowledge of the habits of his prey, of its fears and its pleasures, its preferred foods and favored haunts. Nothing is more integral to this practice than learning the communicative signs, gestures, and cries of the local animals."

6. See Jean Clottes and Jean Courtin, *The Cave Beneath the Sea: Paleolithic Images at Cosquer* (New York: Harry N. Abrams, Inc., 1996), pp. 59–79 and pp. 173–175. See also Jean-Marie Chauvet, Éliette Brunel Deschamps, and Christian Hillaire, *Dawn of Art: The Chauvet Cave* (New York: Harry N. Abrams, Inc., 1996), p. 110 and plates 25, 26, 28, and 91.

7. See John E. Pfeiffer, *The Creative Explosion: An Inquiry into the Origins of Art and Religion* (New York: Harper & Row, Publishers, 1982), pp. 102–18.

8. According to Schafer, there is a chamber in the Neolithic cave of Hypogeum on Malta (c. 2400 B.C.E.) that functions exactly like an artificial cavity-type resonator, producing an amplified, reverberating sound when activated by the low-frequency components of a deep male voice. See R. Murray Schafer, *The Tuning of the World*, pp. 217–18.

9. For a good discussion of the haptic nature of nomadic art and space, see Deleuze and Guattari, *A Thousand Plateaus*, pp. 492–500.

10. See Eliade, *Patterns in Comparative Religion*, chap. 6, sec. 74, for an interpretation of the archetypal significance of stones. Here he writes: "Above all, stone *is* . . . . Rock shows [the human being] something that transcends the precariousness of his humanity: an absolute mode of being . . . . Men have always adored stones simply in as much as they represent something *other* than themselves. They adored stones, or they used them as instruments of spiritual action, as centres of energy designed to defend them or their dead. And we may say from the start that most of the stones connected with worship were used as *instruments;* they helped towards getting something, towards ensuring possession of it."

11. To follow the several phases of the argument proposing and rebutting a solar alignment for this megalith, see Aubrey Burl, *Great Stone Circles* (New Haven: Yale University Press, 1999), pp. 130–134.

12. See Burl, op. cit., pp. 110–12.

13. For a detailed, recent archaeological record of this important urban center, see Timothy R. Pauketat and Thomas E. Emerson, eds., *Cahokia: Domination and Ideology in the Mississippian World* (Lincoln: University of Nebraska Press, 1997).

14. Eventually the god Re was absorbed into the powerful priestly religion of Amon, the sun god worshipped by the populations of the New Kingdom (1550–1069 B.C.E.).

15. The name *Minoan* derives from Sir Arthur Evans (1851–1941), the British archaeologist who unearthed the famous "Labyrinth" at Knossos. Evans, raised like the rest of his generation on the classics and influenced by Heinrich Schliemann, who had made similar assumptions in his work at Mycenae, looked to Homeric literature and ancient legend as well as to Thucydides and Herodotus for help in interpreting his astonishing discoveries. Thus, he assumed that the vast Labyrinth was the palace of the legendary King Minos and conferred the name "Minoan" on the prehistoric culture of Crete. Evans, however, correctly identified many chambers and the great central court as spaces dedicated to ritual use. Rodney Castleden's recent interpretation of the Knossos ruins sugggests that the entire Labyrinth was a temple under the auspices of a female priesthood serving the great Earth Goddess. See *Minoans: Life in Bronze Age Crete* (London: Routledge, 1990) and *The Knossos Labyrinth* (London: Routledge, 1990).

16. See Alfonso Ortiz, *The Tewa World: Space, Time, Being, and Becoming in a Pueblo Society* (Chicago: University of Chicago Press, 1969). A Native American anthropologist, Ortiz explains the siting of a group of Rio Grande pueblos including Santa Clara, San Ildefonso, and San Juan, in accordance with Tewa origin myths similar in content to the origin myths of other pueblo communities. The Tewa myths tell of the emergence of six pairs of brothers from an underworld lake when the earth was yet "half-cooked." Remaining below are the first mothers, Blue Corn Woman (the summer mother), White Corn Maiden (the winter mother), and the people awaiting release into the upper world. Each pair of brothers is associated with a particular color, which in turn is associated with north (blue), south (red), east (white), west (yellow), the zenith (dark), and the nadir (all-colored). Four of the pairs depart, each toward one of the cardinal directions, while the fifth and sixth head for the zenith and nadir. Before returning to the underworld to await the earth's readiness for the emergence of the people, the first four pairs of brothers throw some of the as-yet unbaked earth's mud at each of the four directions, creating the *tsin,* or flat-topped mesas. The mesas have caves or tunnels running through them where dwell the supernatural *Tsavejo,* or masked whippers. These are also the places where the *Towa é,* spiritual guardians of the pueblo, reside. Beyond the mesas lie the sacred mountains, prominent peaks, each associated with one of the four cardinal points. The zenith is associated with a large star, or perhaps Venus, in the eastern sky, and the nadir with the rainbow. Individual pueblos identify their communities with sacred mountains, and they continue to celebrate winter and summer with dances that honor White Corn Maiden and Blue Corn Mother.

17. See Stephen H. Lekson, John R. Stein, and Simon J. Ortiz, *Chaco Canyon: A Center and Its World* (Santa Fe: Museum of New Mexico, 1994). See also Stephen H. Lekson, *The Chaco Meridian: Centers of Political Power in the Ancient Southwest* (Walnut Creek, California: Altamira Press, 1999).

18. Anna Sofaer, Michael P. Marshall, and Rolf M. Sinclair, "The Great North Road: A cosmographic expression of the Chaco culture of New Mexico," in *World Archaeoastronomy* (Cambridge: Cambridge University Press, 1989), p. 365.

19. Ibid., p. 366.

20. Alan Kolata and Carlos Ponce Sangines call Lake Titicaca "the sacred locus for many indigenous myths of creation," in which "native Aymara Indians referred to the fertile axis formed by the lake as *taypi,* the essential conceptual and physical zone of convergence between the principles of *urco* (associated with the west, highlands, dryness, pastoralism, celestialness, and masculinity) and *uma* (associated with the east, lowlands, wetness, agriculture, underworld, and femininity). See "Tiwanaku: The City at the Center" in *The Ancient Americas: Art from Sacred Landscapes,* ed. Richard F. Townsend (Chicago: The Art Institute of Chicago, 1992), p. 317.

21. Rina Naranjo Swentzell, "Remembering Tewa Pueblo Houses and Spaces," in *Native Peoples* 3:2 (Winter 1990), pp. 6–12.

22. For a thorough discussion of how humans have invested landscape with meaning and how Renaissance humanists derived the concept of gardens as a "third nature," see John Dixon Hunt, *Greater Perfections* (Philadelphia: University of Pennsylvania Press, 1999), chap. 3.

23. Rina Naranjo Swentzell, "Bupingeh: The Pueblo Plaza," *El Palacio* 2 (1994), p. 16.

24. Ibid.

CHAPTER TWO

NATURE, ART, AND REASON:
LANDSCAPE DESIGN IN THE CLASSICAL WORLD

The term *classical* is important to our understanding of landscape history. As used here, it signifies the aesthetic values embodied in Greek and Roman art and architecture: simplicity of form, harmonious proportion, and ornament that draws attention to significant parts of structures. It usually affirms symmetry over eccentricity, seeks the normative, and avoids the florid. *Classicism* also embodies the notion of humanism, the system of thought that centers upon the capacities and values of human beings. Also inherent in the mentality of classicism is the ideal of the city as the locus for the good life, its citizens' beneficent mother, a landscape where the human and the natural are united in a bond sealed by divine visitation, bounty, and protection, a place from which exile was an extreme punishment.[1]

Humanism, in fact, is the term European Renaissance intellectuals applied to their rediscovery of Plato, Aristotle, and the literary heritage of ancient Greece, which had been preserved in certain Byzantine monasteries and the libraries of Arab scholars, and to the stylistic inspiration they derived both from ancient Latin authors and from Roman ruins and the works of ancient art and architecture. The rationality and order they found in classical architecture and planning expressed human values and human dignity to Renaissance societies. The same kind of regard accounts for the recurring appeal of the classical heritage of Greece and Rome, as witnessed in the Italian Renaissance, the French style of Louis XIV, eighteenth- and nineteenth-century Neoclassicism, and its twentieth-century variations, including the appropriation of the classical idiom by Postmodernists.

Although they are fused into a single legacy, we must not conflate Roman classicism and its Greek antecedents into a single style. They are, in fact, expressions of two separate cultures. Roman classicism is the product of a practical, pragmatic, and technologically advanced society. It is innovative within the bounds of a firmly established, large-scale cultural framework and, in spite of the persistence of cultic worship and superstition, confident of its ability to apply the forces of nature toward human ends.

In reconstructing the culture of Classical Greece, we are able to consult written sources. History, literature, and philosophy offer an enriched perspective not available for subjects yielding only an archaeological record. With the written word, we have evidence of a people who had a fundamental grasp of the tragic nature of human existence and an enduring, deep interest in the transforming power of art. In their culture, we find myth and magic being challenged by reason. In landscape terms, this is expressed through the balanced tension of geometric forms bound in partnership with nature. The proportions and arrangement of these geometric forms speak to the supremacy ancient Greeks accorded mathematics—the primary mode of reason—as a means of understanding the cosmos and the natural world.

Earlier cosmologies were compounded of astronomical observation fused with myth. The first Greek philosophers, such as Thales and Parmenides, who lived on the Aegean coast of Asia Minor in a period that spanned the late seventh, sixth, and early fifth centuries B.C.E., sought an underlying principle of rational unity governing all natural phenomena. Abstract rational logic—deduction—assumed value as a trustworthy means of apprehending the world and attaining cosmological understanding. As these Greeks developed a philosophical, rather than a mythological, approach to viewing the world and themselves, they did not attempt to drain nature of the inherent divinity accorded it by earlier and contemporary people. Instead, they sought divine principles at work in nature. At the same time, their rationalism began the process of transforming the gods into allegorical representations of various ideals—military prowess (Athena), reason (Apollo), fertility (Demeter), and family life (Hera)—to name certain prominent members of the Greek pantheon.

Pythagoras, the sixth century B.C.E. philosopher who created a settlement with his followers at Crotona in southern Italy, offered an approach to comprehending the world that was both intellectual and spiritual. Although Pythagoreans were sworn to secrecy, we believe that they combined the cultic rites of a mystery religion with the pursuit of truth through understanding mathematical forms, musical harmonies, and the motions of the planets. This pursuit of religious meaning and rational truth at the same time provided an important cornerstone for the development of Western culture. It also aids our understanding of the premium the Greeks put on geometry and harmonic proportion in architecture. Seen in this light, the Parthenon, constructed during the fifth century B.C.E. on the Athenian Acropolis, demonstrates how they employed rationality to serve an older myth-based religion that had been transformed to allegorize the virtues of the autochthonous, or indigenous, deity, Athena, the namesake city's patron goddess.

The *Dialogues* of Plato (c. 428–347 B.C.E.) and the *Physics* of Aristotle (384–322 B.C.E.) offer further understanding of how place was conceptualized in antiquity. They provide a philosophical substructure for the shaping of landscape space and the siting of architectural monuments within it. In the dialogue of the *Timaeus,* Plato outlines a cosmology in which a nonspecific force called the Demiurge—an invisible and all-encompassing God—replaces the anthropomorphic deities who create cosmos out of chaos in the mythologies of pre-historic Greece and the Ancient Near East. For material things to exist within the Platonic cosmos, there must be regions of occupancy—*chora*—within the Receptacle, the fertile primary ground for world-being, in which particular places—*topoi*—are located. According to Plato, the Demiurge's task is the fitting of forms, which are based upon abstract, geometrically determined, ideal Forms, into *topos*—in other words, the location of pattern-based matter *in place* within regional space, or *chora.*

Plato's pupil Aristotle discarded the concept of objects derived from pre-existing, geometrically based Forms. He sought instead to abstract idealized prototypical Forms from the manifestations of forms in nature. Further, he ignored *chora*, regional space, in his *Physics,* claiming that "place is coincident with the thing, for boundaries are coincident with the bounded" (Book IV, 30). For Aristotle, things may move from place to place, and place is continually being filled with things, but *topos* as the container of elemental form needs no regional context; place *is.* For Aristotle, the universe is finite, spherically bounded, and Earth-centered; the cosmos has been so ordered by a Prime Mover, or God conceived as *Nous,* pure mind. Aristotle's approach is empirical; observation and sensory perception are its basis. But Aristotelian thought, which, though elaborated by later philosophers, remained the primary Western intellectual framework until the sixteenth century, is not open-ended, inasmuch as it presupposes that sensory perceptions and observations can order knowledge within a comprehensive system.

While philosophical thought does not inevitably dictate landscape design form, we have already seen that the latter does express prevailing ideology, or cultural consensus. Forms may anticipate or follow ideas, but they almost always reflect the value systems that characterize a given society during the course of its existence. It is therefore possible to discern within the landscapes of classical antiquity as well as throughout the rest of landscape design history a substructure of philosophical thought. Myth still plays a role in the Greek landscape, which is everywhere touched by Homeric themes, but, if we choose also to read Greek landscapes as manifestations of the mathematically oriented and spatially descriptive cosmological view found in Plato's *Timaeus,* philosophy's importance as an intellectual force in shaping them is also apparent.

Plato's cosmology has a physical counterpart in the ordering of urban landscape space. This is evident from the earliest development of the Greek city-state beginning in the eighth century B.C.E. when the center and the outlying environs were conceived as the complementary components of *chora,* or regional space.[2] On the other hand, Aristotle, who tutored Alexander the Great, had a profound influence upon subsequent Western intellectual development as it was fostered within the crucible of Hellenism. His cosmic view of the inseparable nature of form and *topos* was manifested in rationally ordered, enclosed spaces. From late antiquity until the sixteenth century, Aristotle's belief in the unity of form and *topos*—of place as spatial containment—prevailed alongside his concept of knowledge as a comprehensive, circumscribed system. To chart the shift from an approach that can be described as the weaving of a loose fabric of regional landscape to Aristotelian place-making is to understand an important aspect of the difference between Greece and Rome.[3] In the former, temples were sited in nature and worshipers came to them in procession. In the latter, the relationship of architectural forms to nature was of less importance than readily replicated spatial arrangements that symbolically aggrandized rulers of the imperial state.

As we shall see, the Greek city, or *polis,* is bipolar. Important civic temples and monuments were located at or near a central gathering place, the *agora,* where political, judicial, and market activities occurred, and religious sanctuaries were located outside the town within the *chora,* the regional domain of the *polis.* Where Greeks established colonial cities, imposing their institutions on pre-existing populations, exurban sanctuaries served the purpose of fostering political and social cohesion among disparate peoples. Although a loose girdle of fortified walls protected the Greek city, it had a strong sense of its relationship to its *chora.* Enclosed, but not self-contained, the city sent out tentacles in several directions: to the sea as well as to the valley, plain, and hills, where were situated the *demes,* the politically affiliated regional villages or towns within the territorial framework of the *polis.* Here in the agrarian countryside were the sanctuaries of the cults that received the members of both the city and villages on the festival occasions. Devotees came in procession to the sacrificial altars where bonds between the civic core and the life-sustaining hinterland were implicitly renewed. In this fashion, the *polis* claimed and made manifest its occupation of an entire region of which the fortified city with its civic deities was simply one pole, while the outlying territory of the *chora* was the other. Further uniting the urban and the natural landscape were the nature shrines—sacred woods, springs, and mountain caves—where a *daemon,* or genius of the place, drew supplicants.

By contrast, Aristotle's philosophical notion of the particular emplacement of things within a specific locale (*topos*) that is strictly bounded, with exact limits, outlines, and surface planes, finds cultural expression in landscape design terms in the progressive enclosure and definition of urban space throughout the Hellenistic and Roman periods. The result was a multiplication of similarly planned, symmetrically arranged, inward-focused spaces, and the replication of the city itself as such a space through colonization. The Greek urban-exurban continuum, with loosely girdled cities connected to sanctuaries in nature by pilgrimage routes, was gradually abandoned in favor of precisely walled, institutionally self-contained urban centers, which were connected not to sacred sites in nature, but to one another and to the all-important capital of the empire, Rome, by a far-flung network of roads.

Aristotle's concept of physics, as well as his notion that all knowledge can be organized within an ultimately finite and therefore self-contained system, is an intellectual approach well suited to imperial objectives in which there is a strong penchant for order and administration. Inevitably, a good deal of the old awe and reverence for landscape forms bequeathed by earlier peoples became less compelling as urbanization and the political machinery for its maintenance assumed paramount value during the course of the empire. Roman urban plans, public spaces, and peristyle gardens evolved from models built in the Hellenistic period, dating roughly from the time of Alexander the Great (ruled 336–323 B.C.E.) to the accession of the emperor Augustus in 27 B.C.E. At these various scales, Roman landscape design expressed a sophisticated civilization's material wealth, imperial power, apparatus of systematic administration, and sensual enjoyment of plants, water, and open-air living.

New colonial towns, with their paved, sidewalk-bordered streets, demonstrated formulaic axial planning and advanced concepts of engineering. Rectangular and walled, these towns were directed inward toward a center: a forum sited at the intersection of the two principal crossroads. The forum itself was enclosed by a peristyle, a colonnaded, roofed walkway. Unlike the *agora* of Greek cities, the forum was not penetrated by through traffic. Roman houses, like their Hellenistic predecessors, had featureless street facades. Their rooms were organized around and faced on an atrium, or central court, which was partly open to the sky. Some affluent Romans also had peristyle gardens, that is, rear gardens surrounded by porticoes.

To emphasize the interiority of Roman planning is not to say that Romans were indifferent to landscape features or insensitive to natural beauty. Their appreciation of natural scenery can be seen in the siting of buildings, particularly the villas that multiplied as wealth increased in the imperial age, and in the wealth of images drawn from nature that are found in the fresco paintings that decorated Roman walls. For members of the leisure class, the concept of a view became what we think of when we use the term today: an agreeable prospect of local scenery. Superstitions persisted from the centuries when there was less technological skill available for shaping nature to serve human ends, but in this highly urbanized and secularized society, the profoundly felt spiritual link with nature of earlier cultures had been broken. The *nymphaeum,* a grotto designed to appear as the abode of nymphs, became the architectural substitute for the goddess-inhabited cave of old.

Everywhere throughout the Roman empire, the surveyor's line and rod superimposed a *human* order upon nature. One has only to think of their hydraulic engineering and aqueduct construction to realize the degree to which the Romans exercised unprecedented control over nature, enhanced the life of cities, and made possible the creation of the ornamental garden.

Worldly power and earthly pleasure — these are the twin messages encoded in Roman town planning and landscape design. But civilization has its price: longing for an imagined lost golden age of innocence in which the bond with nature is not yet broken. The distance between the eighth century B.C.E. of Homer and the first century B.C.E. of Virgil is the distance between a view of nature as an epic stage for the drama of gods and humans enacting their mutual fate and a view of nature as the idyllic counterpoint to civilization, the province of pastoral poetry. Not surprisingly, in this period, wealthy people developed an urbane appreciation of rural life. The villa, with its gardens and fountains, is an expression of that taste and a model for subsequent developments in landscape design.

The villa of the Roman Empire provides evidence of a new cultural role for landscape: the thematic one. Wealth and cosmopolitan urbanity bred the desire to create associational landscapes, places where allusion was made through place-names, architectural replication, and sculptural dramatization to other esteemed landscapes and landmarks or scenes from myth and literature. Thus, the grounds of opulent villas, notably Hadrian's at Tivoli outside Rome, became in effect theaters of the imagination. Although designed as a private retreat for the refined leisure of an emperor rather than as a commercial venture appealing to a mass audience, Hadrian's Villa can be compared to a contemporary theme park in this regard. In Roman times, as imagination began to operate in shaping programs of landscape design, the garden took on the character of an allegorical space. And, as we shall see, it eventually became a metaphor for both the Christian and Islamic visions of paradise, as the philosophy and practices of the antique world were replaced by different beliefs about the nature of creation and the organization of human life.

In this chapter, then, our task is to trace a course that takes us from a human association with the landscape that assigned divinity to certain sites in nature and placed built structures in relationship to these spirit-inhabited places, to one that created forms that in themselves confidently articulated human aspirations and power within a rapidly urbanizing world. We are thus traversing an important trajectory in the development of Western attitudes. It is one in which an ideology of subservience to nature begins to give way to one of dominance over nature. In this process, the magic once perceived in nature is replaced by confidence in human action. The Greek experience is remarkable for the development of many of the philosophical, social, and political ideas that still resonate within the cultures of contemporary societies as well as a vocabulary of building forms that has been re-employed throughout Western history. For us here, it is remarkable especially for the attitudinal equilibrium it achieved between religious awe in the face of the universe and proud trust in the powers of reason, a tension beautifully expressed in terms of landscape design.

I. Gods and Humans: The New Contract with Nature

Homer's great epic poems, the *Iliad* and the *Odyssey,* composed probably in the eighth century B.C.E., reveal to us a confident civilization of youthful promise, at a time when it was fashioning for itself a glorious narrative of its history as a diverse but culturally united people. Valor in war, accomplished horsemanship, and the consoling power of a well-developed sense of beauty are intrinsic to this worldview. The worship of trees and aniconic stones—nonrepresentational, non-symbolical forms—had been superseded by the personification of divinity. Although the powers and personalities of the gods and goddesses were still in the process of formation, it is clear that they populated the collective imagination not as representatives of an ethical system or figures commanding worshipful love, but rather as projections of the human psyche and personifications of various aspects of human life. As such, they acted as the idealized and worthy guardians of human society and served as socializing forces, bonding disparate peoples into larger territorial groups through common worship.

Greek Myth, Religion, and Culture

In fashioning their myths, the Greeks took their native inheritance, Minoan and Mycenaean religions—which are believed to have been centered upon worship of a Great Goddess or Earth Mother—and added to them divinities derived from Asia Minor. Thus, Athena, the majestic patron of the arts and the goddess of reason and justice, probably traced her origin to the Earth Mother in Minoan and Mycenaean cultures. However, Apollo, the god of light, order, and inspiration, was perhaps the descendant of a god worshiped in the region formerly called Anatolia, the large peninsula now occupied principally by Turkey. These gods can be seen as archetypes of emerging aspects of civilization at a period when primal beliefs were gradually being replaced by a more rational, ethical, and scientific outlook. Greek religion was nevertheless still firmly embedded in the matrix of nature. On the Athenian Acropolis, a shrine for the worship of the rustic god Pan is evidence of the duality implicit in Greek religion, which acknowledged the wild, irrational impulses associated with human sexuality alongside the civilized values personified by Athena.

There were numerous holidays in which procession, worshipful slaughter, and feasting helped forge the bonds of community and civic pride among all the inhabitants of the *polis* and sometimes between neighboring city-states (*poleis*), while placating the divinities that were believed to ensure cosmic order. With the notable exception of Athens, where the reverse was true in the case of its principal festival, the Panathenaia, these processions took the people from the city into the exurban landscape, where many of the important religious sanctuaries were located, thereby affirming the territorial dominance of the *polis* over its surrounding agrarian countryside. These ritual festivals held in nature also served as initiatory rites for adolescents as they became participants in civic life. In ancient Sparta, where the city-state played an especially strong role in the education of children and adolescents, the festivals were connected with the worship of Artemis Orthia.

The increasing power of the aristocracy spurred the creation of the arts and the organization of athletic competitions. The festivals were characterized by communal procession and sacrifice performed before the sanctuaries of the gods, as well as by dancing and athletic and dramatic competition performed in the gods' honor. Dionysus became the patron deity of the theatrical arts, and when the plays of Aeschylus, Sophocles, and Euripides were performed, it was at the Great Dionysia, the important dramatic festival competition held every four years at Athens. At Olympia, the Panhellenic (all-Greek) festival of games sacred to Zeus was begun in 776 B.C.E. and continued at four-year intervals for the next thousand years. Zeus also presided over the Nemean Games, while Apollo was honored in the athletic festival held at Delphi and Poseidon in the contests that took place at the Isthmus of Corinth. Truces among warring city-states were maintained to allow the contestants and spectators to arrive safely at these Panhellenic celebrations.

People also made pilgrimages to important shrines, particularly the one at Delphi, to find spiritual guidance. The desire to chart a safe course, whether through the perils of statecraft or one's own lifetime, made oracular consultation a popular religious exercise in a society that saw human activity as drama directed from on high, the plot of which could be discerned by the spirit forces of the earth.

The Greek political system, with its isolated city-states, accounted for the many festivals of various kinds held throughout the mainland and the Peloponnese, the large peninsula below the Gulf of Corinth that consitutes the southern part of Greece. Altars studded both the rural and urban landscapes, as animal sacrifice, an essential and integral part of every festival including those featuring athletic games, was necessarily performed out-of-doors. Ritual sacrifice was only one manifestation of the interrelationship of the human, animal, and divine in ancient Greece. There was considerable overlap between urban and agrarian spheres, and objects in nature

2.1. The Athenian Acropolis with the olive tree planted to commemorate the presence in antiquity of Athena's sacred tree. It stands in the courtyard of the Erechtheion where it is believed that a charred olive tree managed to sprout leaves, bringing hope of renewal and rebirth of the Athenian *polis* after the Persians had burned and razed the buildings of the Acropolis in 480 B.C.E. The Erechtheion housed a *xoanon,* the ancient cult statue of Athena. The caryatids that form the columns of its south porch overlook the fire-scarred foundation stones of the Old Temple of Athena. Although the Acropolis was rebuilt later in the fifth century B.C.E. by Pericles, and the Parthenon became the majestic replacement of the destroyed temple, its site was always considered by Athenians to be hallowed ground.

were everywhere charged with magical meaning. By roadsides, sacred stones glistened with oil where passersby offered libations. Caves and springs, often the sites of votive shrines, served as places of human purification. Frequently sanctuaries encompassed sacred springs, and often there were sacred groves nearby as well. Certain trees became identified with particular divinities: the olive tree was sacred to Athena, and a revered specimen grew on the Acropolis; at Samos, a willow's branches hung over Hera's sanctuary; on Delos, a palm tree commemorated a similar tree upon which Leto had leaned when giving birth to Artemis and Apollo; at Dodona, the oracle imparted wisdom through the rustling branches of an oak; at Didyma, Daphni, and Delphi grew the laurel tree sacred to Apollo (fig. 2.1).

The columned temples that began to appear from the eighth century onward throughout Greece were not houses of worship. Instead, they were conspicuous and worthy "residences" of large-scale sculptural representations of gods or goddesses associated with the sacred sites where they were built. These cult figures were occasionally carried in procession, but normally they remained within an interior chamber, or *cella,* facing east toward the altar, which was set up within the sacred temple precinct in front of them.

A *temenos,* a sacred landscape marked off by stones or encircled by a wall, might contain one or more temples. From a religious perspective, the motive for establishing a *temenos* was the epiphany of a god in a particular spot. It was the sense of the indwelling spirit of the god—the god or goddess manifesting himself or herself in a certain place—

that made that site holy. From a social and political perspective, the sacral landscape provided a means of asserting territorial dominance by a particular *polis,* which is why the destruction of important exurban sanctuaries in wartime was tantamount to destroying a city itself.

The sanctification of a particular spot was subject to various political considerations. At some sites, votaries of existing gods were reluctant to admit competition from a new deity. On the other hand, there were economic benefits to the communities where major deities were given residence, for pilgrims brought fees and a brisk production and sale of votive objects. A series of wars was actually fought to gain control of the Panhellenic sanctuary of Delphi.

Topography and a tendency for siting within a well-chosen frame of the spirit-charged natural world dictated the location of temples and altars. Axiality for its own sake did not govern the planning of pre-Hellenistic Greek temple precincts. Symmetrically laid-out terraces, colonnades, stairways, and altars were devices of the Hellenistic era; prior to the second third of the fourth century B.C.E., in the Archaic and Classical periods, the approach was less studied, and such axial relationships as existed were implied lines linking temples with particular distant mountains because of their associations of sanctity. The result was often a landscape "design" that we experience as dramatic and picturesque. These impressions, however, are informed by a modern sensibility. The Greeks did not see their temple precincts as we do—as an artistic arrangement of bleached ruins haunted by vanished time, with mountains and sea completing the romantic scene. In their ascendant centuries, the temples were brightly painted, and pilgrimages to them were not those of tourists, but of religious supplicants. Nature and divinity were inextricably fused; landscape was experienced religiously rather than aesthetically.

The visible echoes of previous ceremony and custom only deepened the sanctity and fame of certain sacred sites. Bloodstains on the altar, oil-anointed stones, accumulations of ash, bone, horns, and skulls—these signs of others' piety provided the weight of tradition. Votive offerings (the source of lively local industry), valuables of all kinds, including but not limited to the paraphernalia of sacrifice (vessels, axes, roasting spits, and especially, tripod cauldrons of metal) were contributed to the sanctuaries. Grateful victors donated shields and weapons of war. The victorious erected monuments and inscribed tablets proclaiming acts of glory. Various *poleis* built treasuries in the form of miniature temples, notably at Olympia and Delphi, to house valuable offerings and as further gifts to the presiding gods. *Stoas,* long colonnades, roofed and with walls and often a series of rooms on the back side, provided shelter from the sun and an opportunity for the placement of more sanctified objects. Wealthy individuals contributed to the construction of stadiums and the many monuments that adorned the site. In this manner, important sanctuaries became crowded with a host of structures, numerous memorial gifts, and votive offerings. Nowhere was this more evident than at Delphi.

DELPHI

The most dramatic synthesis of site and sanctuary is to be found at Delphi, the spiritual center sacred to all Greeks and a place where rivalries among *poleis* were superseded by bonds of Panhellenic identity (fig. 2.2). Some of the architectural forms found here have served as frequently imitated prototypes throughout the history of landscape design. The circular *tholos* in the sanctuary of Athena Pronaia at Delphi in the site called Marmaria (the Marbles) along the pilgrimage route to Apollo's sanctuary, is the model for innumerable later garden temples (fig. 2.3). The various

2.2. Reconstructed Plan of Sanctuary of Apollo, Delphi. c. 400 B.C.E.
Ⓐ Treasury of the Athenians
Ⓑ Rock of the Sibyl
Ⓒ Sphinx of the Naxians
Ⓓ Temple of Apollo
Ⓔ Theater

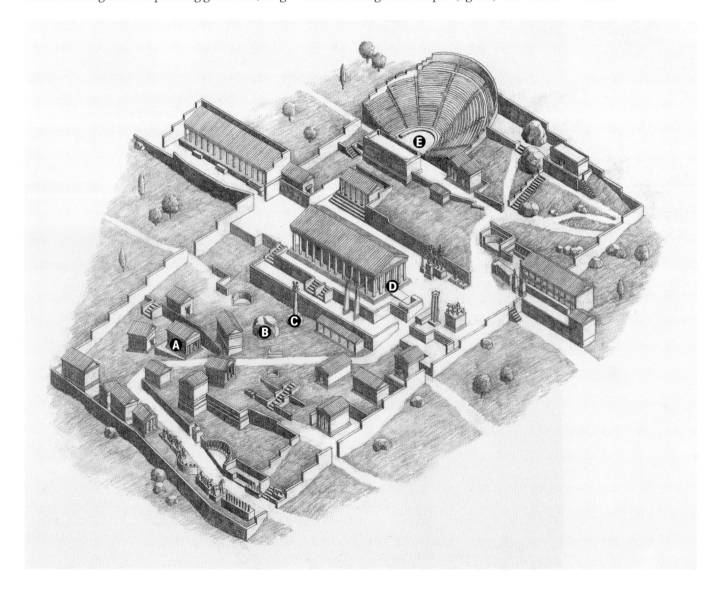

2.3. Tholos, Sanctuary of Athena Pronaia, Delphi, perched on a ridge at Marmaria along the approach to Apollo's sanctuary. 4th century B.C.E.

Below: **2.4. Rock of the Sibyl and Temple of Apollo, Delphi. 4th century B.C.E.**

passing the fourth century B.C.E. *tholos* and the fifth century B.C.E. Temple of Athena Pronaia, marking the sanctuary of the goddess at Delphi, one stopped at the Kastalian Spring, a long-established site of cult worship marking the place known as Pytho because here Apollo killed "the bloated, great she-monster wont to do great mischief to men upon earth," thereby becoming Pythian Apollo according to the Homeric hymn.[4] It was believed that here Apollo had planted a branch cut from his sacred laurel tree in the Vale of Tempe, and because he had assumed the shape of a dolphin in order to steer the ship of the men from Crete whom he had commandeered as keepers of his temple, he enjoined them to pray to him also as Apollo Delphinius. Pilgrims to his Delphinius altar and participants en route to the Pythian Games, as the Panhellenic athletic contests held in Apollo's honor at Delphi were called, purified themselves with a ritual bathing of their hair in the water of the spring.

Upon entering the *temenos* of the Pythian Sanctuary of Apollo, which is perched on a flank of Mount Parnassus beneath the sacred Korycian Cave and above a steep drop to the valley where the Pleistos River snakes to the sea, they embarked upon the Sacred Way, a switchback path leading to the Temple of Apollo (fig. 2.4). This circuitous approach made access to the temple indirect, and intensified the dynamic relationship of the visitor to it and its dramatic surrounding landscape. Above the temple to the god loom the twin peaks of the Phaedriades, the Brilliant Ones. Though unplanned, this long-established approach route operated as an organizing force in the placement of the many treasuries and

treasuries within the *temenos* of Apollo found infinite replication in mausoleums of later times (fig. 2.5). Delphi's influence, along with that of other important sanctuaries, is visible in our own stadiums and outdoor summer festival theaters.

Pilgrimage to Delphi was made both for the purpose of consulting the Delphic oracle on affairs of state and in order to participate in the sacred games. It was a journey of men rather than women, who lacked an official role in government and did not generally take part in athletic contests. After

monuments scattered about the site. The reservation of certain portions of the site for particular rituals also helped to create some sense of discipline within the array of monuments and structures.

At a point where the Sacred Way reversed its course and headed due north, it passed the Rock of the Sibyl. This was believed to be the precise spot where the female voice of Ge, or Gaia, the earth goddess, who had been worshiped here long before Apollo, originally offered oracular wisdom. Behind this boulder once stood the Archaic Sphinx of the Naxians: a crouched lion with eagle's wings and the visage of a woman held aloft on a tall Ionic column. With serene and enigmatic authority, it asserted the ancient rights of female prophecy within Apollo's sanctuary. Above the sphinx stood the peripteral colonnade of the temple, and soaring above these, hornlike, were the twin peaks of the Phaedriades. Upon the temple terrace, engraved marble *stelai* (of which one remains) and a fourth-century, 50-foot tall statue of Apollo gave majestic welcome to the pilgrim. Directly in front of the temple stood the Great Altar of Apollo, made of dark marble from the island of Chios, with white marble at its base and top.

In addition to a central hall, or *naos,* the Temple of Apollo contained an inner chamber, called the *adyton,* entered from above by steps. Beneath a stone canopy within the *adyton* was a round stone covered with fillets woven into a net. This was *omphalos,* the "navel" of the world and the "grave" of Dionysus, who was honored by an important biennial Delphic festival and was thus entitled to share with Apollo occupancy of the temple's most sacred area. A large tripod with a cauldron-shaped seat was placed next to the *omphalos.* Within the belly of this tripod-cauldron priests stored sacred objects. Upon it sat the Pythia, priestess of Apollo, freshly bathed in the Kastalian Spring, when it was time to utter prophecy. Beside her grew a sacred laurel tree.

Within the *hestia,* or sacred hearth, burned laurel leaves and barley. The fumes from these enhanced the mystical atmosphere of the *adyton* and presumably aided the prophetess in achieving a trancelike state known as *enthousiamos,* in which the spirit of the god entered into her mind and mouth. Her speech, which was often unintelligible, was "translated" into hexameter verse by priests standing nearby. Thus, this temple, which was holy to all Greeks, was the place where art joined with the old mystical powers of the earth, and Apollonian light fused with the dark impulses of Dionysian spirit.

Assisting in this process at Delphi was the theater, or rather a succession of theaters, the latest one, which seats five thousand people, dating from the time of imperial Rome (fig. 2.6). Behind a horseshoe-shaped orchestra, 60 feet in diameter, thirty-five rows of seats, broken at the twenty-eighth row by a *diazoma,* or inside circular aisle, are set within the contours of the steep hillside. Here choristers sang hymns to Apollo, and playwrights and musicians competed for honor during various festivals, including the Pythian Games.

After 450 B.C.E., a stadium occupied a site farther up the hillside above the sanctuary and theater. Musical contests and, later, games were held there. During Roman imperial times, an Athenian philanthropist gave the stadium its monumental entrance and stone seating for seven thousand spectators.

2.5. Treasury of the Athenians, Delphi. After 490 B.C.E., built following the Battle of Marathon

Below: 2.6. Theater, Delphi. 4th century B.C.E.

**2.7. Theater, Epidaurus.
c. 320–30 B.C.E.**

Epidaurus

Among the most important festival centers of ancient Greece is the sanctuary of Asclepius at Epidaurus, an ancient sanatorium where patients' dreams played a role in their diagnosis and where a special open-air sleeping area served as a therapeutic facility. According to the Greek lyric poet Pindar, Asclepius, the son of Apollo and his mortal lover, Coronis, was raised by the centaur Chiron, who taught him the healing arts. While dedicated to Apollonian harmony of mind, body, and spirit, Asclepius was linked to the remote Greek past, and he therefore shares with the Cretan goddess Potnia the symbol of the snake. It is for this reason that the modern physician's emblem, bequeathed to us from ancient Greece, is a *caduceus,* a staff intertwined with snakes.

To the powerful natural serenity of the site at Epidaurus, cradled in undulating hills, was added the harmony of architectural geometry. Polycleitus the Younger designed the theater there in the fourth century B.C.E; it was enlarged in the second century B.C.E. (fig. 2.7). The perfect circle of the orchestra is thought to be an outgrowth of the *halos,* the circular threshing floor upon which the first ritual dances and dramas of ancient Greece were performed. The ratio of its lower fan of thirty-four rows to its upper twenty-one (34:21), is 1.618, or that of the Golden Section.[5] The ratio of fifty-five total rows to its original thirty-four (55:34) is also close to 1.618. Further evidence of the use of the Golden Section as the underlying design principle by Polycleitus and his followers: the sum of the first ten numerical digits added together is fifty-five; the sum of the first six digits is twenty-one; and the sum of digits seven through ten is thirty-four. Even those unaware of Greek mathematics, however, feel intuitively the beauty derived from the combined power of site and geometry, of mountainous majesty and mathematical beauty.

In the process of enlarging both its form and its meaning, the Greek *polis* had incorporated and absorbed its ancient acropolis, the fortified citadel that had once been the home of both the people and their gods. Though, with the important exception of Athens, the residential and civic center was now separated from the outlying sanctuaries set in nature, both together constituted the regional space defined as *chora.* Cityscape, or the urbanized landscape, is an important part of our continuing story, and the Greek contribution to landscape design was certainly not confined to pilgrimage centers remote from the everyday haunts of humanity. Because the philosophical notion of *chora* was one in which the festival center in nature was perceived as one pole of a spatial continuum and the urban center the other—both together constituting the *polis,* or city-state, a regional polity—we must now look more closely at the civic component. Inevitably, the *polis* as a governmental institution gave rise to new ideas about urban layout and new urban institutions, enriching the concept of city with customs and structures that reflected an independent, collective society. And, as is common knowledge, the Greek political concept of self-governance and the planning and architectural forms that expressed it have been vastly influential in the West throughout history.

II. Polis and Acropolis:
City and Temple in the Greek Landscape

The Greek *polis* was a crucible for a new social order. Democracy, or government by the people, was first conceived in ancient Greece. Although the definition of citizenship was circumscribed and limited to property-owning males, the equality of this political system nevertheless carried with it respect for the individual and an ideal of justice according to stable, published laws. Democracy also embodied the notion of individual rights as well as that of individual responsibility for the collective good. More than simply the expression of a political system, the *polis* was first and foremost a concept of community. Its actual form of governance—monarchy, oligarchy, or democracy—was not its distinguishing characteristic so much as the fact that power was exercised responsibly on behalf of the community.

In the Greek *polis,* the notion of divine kingship was untenable; the *basileus,* or ruler, governed not as a god in the manner of an Egyptian pharaoh, but in partnership with the gods. He was, according to Aristotle, responsible for the conduct of religious rites and traditional sacrifices, athletic contests such as torch races, public lawsuits dealing with impiety, and private ones when the charge was an important crime such as homicide. In Athens, the title of *archon basileus* was not hereditary; the office depended upon election by the citizenry and service was for a prescribed annual term. Monuments of grandeur celebrating divine kingship such as are found in the Ancient Near East were therefore completely alien to Greek culture. Thus, it was the much-praised Greek genius for distributing and limiting power through a workable constitution, together with the democratization of education and culture within the relatively small circle of those who met the criteria for citizenship, that gave the *polis* its highest meaning and mature form. To understand that urban form and the institutions produced by this radical social change, a brief discussion of Greek philosophy and Greek polity as developed in Athens, the most celebrated Greek city-state, is in order.

The Athenian Acropolis was rebuilt by Pericles in the middle of the fifth century B.C.E., following a period in which its buildings lay in ruins after being burned in 480 B.C.E. by troops under the Persian king Xerxes. Its reconstruction was more than a manifestation of Athenian hegemony and Greek Classical grandeur. The monuments of the Acropolis, particularly the Parthenon, embodied a new philosophical understanding of the world. Although this building celebrated the great goddess Athena, who presided with serene dignity over the affairs of the *polis,*

another, more abstract idea of deity was here given architectural expression. Confidence in human reason was superseding blind oracular wisdom. Further, the manipulation of human affairs by the Homeric pantheon according to the particular dispositions of the various gods was now considered by many rational Greeks to be naive. The rule of Necessity (*ananke*) alone did not provide an adequate philosophical or spiritual foundation for those who believed that intelligence—reason itself—was a godlike human gift.

The Greeks' philosophical quest for a rational understanding of an underlying harmony in nature is epitomized in the spirit of empyrean intellect that infuses the stones of the Parthenon with timeless beauty. It also informs the political concept of the *polis*—the rational city-state—and the public spaces created for secular public life. Physically, according to Aristotle, the *polis* should consist of a population and territory large enough to suffice for the purposes of life, but not so large that the settled area could not be taken in in a single view. It should be defensible—"difficult of access to the enemy, and easy of egress to the inhabitants"—well situated with regard to the sea and the land, and "in size and extent it should be such as may enable the inhabitants to live at once temperately and liberally in the enjoyment of leisure."[6] It should have a natural abundance of springs and fountains in the town or, lacking these, a system of reservoirs to furnish ample pure drinking water. Straight streets "after the modern fashion which Hippodamus [fifth-century B.C.E. Greek city planner] introduced" should be laid out for the sake of beauty, but districts of these should be combined with quarters in which old-fashioned tortuous ways provided security because assailants would have difficulty in getting in and would also find themselves baffled in trying to get out. Further, cities should have walls as a precaution against siege, and "care should be taken to make them ornamental, as well as useful for warlike purposes, and adapted to resist modern inventions" with guardhouses and towers at suitable intervals.[7] In addition to the temples in the surrounding countryside where ritual participants went in procession on feast days, there should be temples and public dining halls for priests and magistrates in the upper "freemen's agora," a place of leisure in contrast to the lower "traders' agora."

The basic unit of the Greek *polis* was the *deme,* the regional village or town within the orbit of the *polis. Synoecism,* or the amalgamation of several *poleis* and *demes* into a political unit under the authority of a single *polis* gave certain cities broad regional authority. Athens thus subsumed all of the *demes* of Attica, and all property-owning males in Attica were considered Athenians. While the intensely competitive Hellenic spirit was responsible for constant rivalry and warfare among *poleis,* the security bred of *synoecism* made possible urban expansion beyond the high-walled citadels of Mycenaean times.

As the historian François de Polignac suggests, *synoecism* was facilitated by the religious cults that held festivals at sanctuaries set apart from the city.[8] Thus, in territory where the character of the god or goddess was not forcefully identified with the enfranchised elite of free, property-owning males within a particular *polis,* women, foreigners, local populations, and members of neighboring *poleis* participated in forms of pan-Greek culture that produced a commonality. Although there were festivals at nearby Eleusis and at Sounion, the Attic cape where Poseidon was worshiped, Athens was unique in focusing its spiritual life predominantly within its walls. This practice also helps explain why Athens effectively placed all its bets on its maritime empire, importing grain as tribute, rather than asserting firm control over its immediate agricultural hinterland. Other *poleis* also had civic deities, including Athena, who protected the city and resided in sanctuaries in the agora or upon an acropolis. But the exurban sanctuaries connected by processional routes to these cities, such as the Artemision of Ephesus or the Heraion of Argos, were of even greater significance to their inhabitants because they encompassed the agrarian sphere that was vital to the city's well-being (fig. 2.8).

A new urban nucleus, the agora, appeared as trade expanded and cities grew in population and size at the end of the Dark Age (c. 1100–c. 900 B.C.E.) that ensued after the collapse of Mycenaean civilization. This occurred as they began to spread beyond the zone of their original formation upon an acropolis, recentering themselves on the adjacent lower elevations. Eventually, as the evolving institutions of

the *polis* were given physical expression, those of law, justice, and civic ritual were positioned around the agora, which continued to assume importance as a public space. Market and trading functions clustered there. Further, it served as a communal meeting place where assemblies of various kinds could occur. Greek cities in general, but Athens especially, thus came to have two nuclei: the acropolis, the zone of religion and communal tradition, and the agora, the place of government, commerce, and community life. Other functions such as artisans' shops and housing were fitted in between and around these two important centers.

At Athens, as the residential population abandoned the Acropolis and spread out on the lower ground, temples were located in the vicinity of the Agora as well as in other places deemed appropriate to honor a god. As this occurred, the Acropolis became almost exclusively a religious precinct. The home of patron goddess Athena, whose temple, the Parthenon, was a lofty landmark visible from afar, the Acropolis profoundly embodied the city's commingled spiritual values and civic pride. The Propylon, the gateway separating the sacred space from the rest of the city, led through the entry building complex known as the Propylaia, which includes the beautiful small Temple of Athena Nike. Directly ahead is the ever-after-vacant space and foundation stones whose rosy discoloration is evidence still of the fiery destruction of the first temple to the goddess by the Persians. By contrast, when one is facing outward toward the Saronic Gulf, it becomes evident that the Propylon was sited to frame the view of the island of Salamis, where the Greeks decisively defeated the Persians, in 480 B.C.E.

Because Greek architects did not develop a method of building arched foundations and superstructures, the siting of their theaters and stadiums was dependent upon topography. The steep-pitched Greek theater especially needed to be fit within the contours of the terrain, and it is therefore frequently found on the slope of the old acropolis or nestled into a hillside near the edge of town.

Gymnasiums, although usually operated as private institutions, reflected the *polis'* mission of *paideia,* the education of its citizenry in body and mind. Gardens and *odeums,* small buildings for the performance of music or the recitation of poetry, were part of such important gymnasiums as the Academy in Athens, where Plato established his school. *Stoas,* handsome colonnaded structures serving multiple purposes, were often used for public discourse of a philosophical nature and were features of the gymnasiums as well. Because of their campuslike nature and consequent need for space, gymnasiums were usually

2.8. Argive Heraion, the remains of the Archaic and Classical sanctuary of Hera, the tutelary goddess of the Argolid. c. 420–410 B.C.E.

located on the edge of the city outside the town walls, often in association with a stadium and frequently in connection with a shrine dedicated to an appropriately vigorous deity, such as Hermes or Heracles, or some hero of local renown. Like the Persian hunting parks seen by Greek soldiers and described by the Greek historian Xenophon (c. 431–c. 352 B.C.E.), these were well-treed preserves set aside from the routine business of everyday life. The *palaestra,* or wrestling ground, was an essential feature of the larger and better-equipped gymnasiums, inasmuch as physical fitness was considered an indispensable part of education. Additional public *palaestras* ensured that this important aspect of Greek life was readily available to the male populace as a whole.

Housing for the populace reflected the emphasis upon public life in the Greek city. Since Greek males spent most of their waking hours engaged in pursuits that were conducted out-of-doors or in structures designed for societal purposes, dwellings were uniformly modest in size and completely lacking in the luxury that would later characterize upper-class Roman homes. Water provision was a critical consideration, and there developed, in addition to wells and cisterns, aqueduct-fed fountains, which were later housed in special structures. Because Greek women had much less access than men to other parts of the public realm, they no doubt used these as informal social centers when they gathered to fill their amphoras, or water jars.

Although Greek cities contained similar institutions and building types, they enjoyed a wide variation in design. The most important difference in urban planning was the one that existed between the relatively unplanned growth of such cities as Athens and the development by design of cities like Miletus in Asia Minor. Athens's resistance to grid regularization even after this type of planning had become common can be explained by the observation that historic circulation patterns are notably resistant to change. The unplanned aspect of a venerable urban center like Athens—or Rome itself, for that matter—where habitual land uses and hereditary property rights are firmly rooted, is valued above more rational geometric planning paradigms, even after these are routinely practiced elsewhere. For this reason and also because it was important to rebuild quickly in order to accommodate a large returning population, Athens (like London after the Great Fire of 1666) chose to reconstruct itself along irregular, "organic" lines following its destruction by the Persians at the beginning of the fifth century B.C.E.

Miletus, on the other hand, presented with the same task of rebuilding after being destroyed by the Persian invaders, faced less immediate population pres-

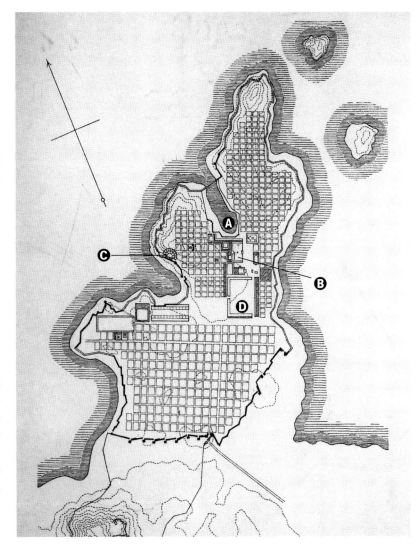

2.9. Plan of Miletus. Miletus was laid out in the 5th century B.C.E. as two grids, the more finely textured one with smaller street blocks to the north, and a looser-grained grid with two intersecting principal axes to the south. A band of public spaces containing various temples and a large agora traversed the town between the two grid sections. Descending from the Lion Harbor, which deeply penetrated the northern section of the city, was another arm of public space, and it, too, contained an agora. A long L-shaped *stoa* fronted impressively on the Lion Harbor. It was backed by another L-shaped *stoa* facing the town on the east. Additional *stoas* made this agora in effect a peristyle court. By the middle of the 2nd century B.C.E., the considerably larger southern agora of Miletus had been similarly formed by the conjunction of independent *stoas.* Ⓐ Lion Harbor. Ⓑ Northern Agora. Ⓒ Theater. Ⓓ Southern Agora

sure and adopted a grid plan of uniform blocks defined by regular streets of predetermined width crossing at right angles (fig. 2.9). Other Greek cities of Ionia had employed at least a rudimentary version of the grid layout as early as the seventh century B.C.E. In fact, the development of orthogonal planning—i.e., the laying out of streets at right angles—as a coordinated program in which the city itself was the focus and frame, not some pragmatic objective or ceremonial purpose, was a Greek achievement. Adopted by the Romans, who surveyed and divided land into squares according to a process called *centuriation,* and promoted by Thomas Jefferson as the method of giving spatial coordinates to the entire American continent, the grid has proved a convenient way of parceling both rural and urban land and a convenient means of enabling circulation in cities throughout history.

Although the invention of the grid was attributed by Aristotle and others to the planner and urban theorist Hippodamus, a native of the Ionian city of Miletus, he could not have originated its use. The logical means of subdividing land orthogonally that he employed in the fifth century B.C.E. had been used, at least for principal streets and temple complexes, by some earlier cultures, notably at Mohenjo-Daro and Harappa in the Indus River valley, in Mesopotamia where archaeologists have found traces of grid planning at Babylon and other ancient cities, as well as in some Assyrian, Egyptian, and Etruscan settlements. Hippodamus must have worked on the reconstruction of Miletus following the Persian devastation of that city before being called upon by the Athenians in the second quarter of the fifth century B.C.E. to lay out their port city of Piraeus.

Early colonial practice had placed the grid-divided land, with the exception of the agora and other public spaces, into the hands of a founding elite, with subsequent immigrants assigned the status of tenants. Hippodamian planning, by contrast, was based upon a political system in which the population of a town was divided into three classes—artisans, soldiers, and farmers—with three categories of land—sacred, public, and private—allocated either as general civic space or as real property. This early zoning code, as much as the physical layout of the grid, was an innovative concept that influenced later Greek city planning. As for the Hippodamian plan itself, the town was formed *per stringas,* a series of bands delineated by a few main east-west thoroughfares crossed by one or more major north-south arteries. Narrow lanes subdivided the rectangular units of land into blocks, which were then further subdivided into building lots. Because the blocks were more or less square, the resulting plan was that of a checkerboard.

According to Polignac, both civic cults and cults in nature were of particular importance in colonial cities.[9] Their establishment invariably necessitated the building of a sanctuary for the Hellenic god or goddess, most frequently Apollo the founder or Athena the protector, who served as the guardian of the *polis* and the symbol of Greek hegemony within the newly claimed territory. In addition to the temple or temples located in the center, sanctuaries and shrines, usually dedicated to Demeter, Artemis, and deities associated with fertility and nature, were built in the periurban *chora.* These served to claim the territory politically and also helped in the process of incorporating native residents into the culture of Hellenism. In some cases, native populations syncretized the worship of pre-existing native divinities with the imported Hellenic ones. Demeter and her daughter Kore

(Persephone) were universally popular because of their association with annual rebirth in nature, and the settlers usually located the shrines of chthonic deities like these where there were caves or springs, places that natives may have already adopted for their religious purposes. As was true in the mother *poleis* that founded these new cities, the civic shrines at the center were identified with the dominant ruling class, while the sanctuaries in the *chora* served to incorporate into membership within the community at large women, indigenous peoples, other non-Greeks, and the agrarian population in general. The religious access offered by these sanctuaries was an important means of conquest and an essential feature of colonization, serving to meld members of fragile heterogeneous societies into viable communities.

Heroic monuments also played a role in forging civic identity. Cults based on tombs helped legitimize claims to land, serving to symbolize group sovereignty in the same way as did the rural sanctuaries. Enshrined heroes were often founders of cities, their legendary kings, even though dynastic rulership was not a feature of the mature *polis.* Mythical founders were adopted as a means of adding heroic stature to the civic identity of a *polis,* as in the case of the Athenians, who incorporated the legendary hero Theseus into their urban mythology. In the fifth century, the ruler Cimon had Theseus's putative remains taken from his first *heroon,* or civic monument for the celebration of heroes, which stood sentinel at the city gates, and placed in a new *heroon* in the heart of the city. Later generations sometimes erected statuary within a rediscovered ancient necropolis, particularly when the site was conterminous with the agora, the city's principal political space. But even without funerary associations, monuments to heroes were placed in important parts of the city, protectively at its entrances or proudly in its center.

But monumentality as such was not a characteristic of the Greek city in the pre-Hellenistic period. Although the Greeks could achieve monumentality in architecture and sculpture, they did not consider either the organic or the gridded cityscape a planning means toward this end. The tools of urban monumentality—formal symmetry and axial layout—were not employed until Hellenistic and Roman times. Instead, a combination of forms was pleasingly disposed for convenience and commonsensical ends. The U-shaped arrangement of *stoas* did set up certain loose symmetries, but this was more the result of adaptation to the dictates of orthogonal planning in the grid cities than to an intentional desire for grandeur. Temples, agoras, gymnasiums, and other public or semipublic spaces were logically disposed within the frame of the grid, while theaters were placed according to the dictates of topography. Both "organic" and grid plans could produce aesthetically pleasing results.

Most apparent in the Greek city, whatever its form, is the primacy its population placed upon public space for public life. While public life in the form of ritual celebrations took place within the larger landscape outside the city, there were within the city temple sanctuaries, particularly those honoring Athena or Apollo—protectors of the *polis*—as well as other kinds of places for public assembly. As important carriers of public life, the agora, the most important civic space, and the Greek theater, the site where the community's self-image received fullest expression, deserve our attention.

The Athenian Agora

A closer understanding of the Greek urban landscape as an expression of culture necessarily requires a short account of the development of Athens and its civic core, the Agora. According to the archaeologists John Travlos[10] and John Camp,[11] at the end of the seventh century B.C.E., on a flat basin of land in the Kerameikos—the potters' quarter and cemetery district northwest of the Acropolis—a nucleus of eastward-facing public buildings began to take shape alongside the Panathenaic Way where it skirted the low hill of Kolonos (fig. 2.11). Although the Agora's boundaries were formally delimited by *horoi,* boundary stones marking the points of entry of the streets feeding into it and underscoring its character as a quasi-sacred space, axial organization and symmetry played no role in the disposition of structures around it. Conceived in piecemeal fashion, it suggested unity and coherence, but these characteristics came from a harmonious architectural design vocabulary, geometrically derived proportions, and similarity of building materials, rather than from an overall plan. Unlike the Roman forum, the Greek agora was not perceived by its builders as a self-contained space, but simply as the nexus of the urban organism.

Before the end of the sixth century B.C.E., when the Theater of Dionysus was built on the southeast slope of the Acropolis, the Agora served as an orchestral space where singing, dancing, and plays were performed in front of spectators seated in wooden grandstands. After the transfer of athletic and theatrical events to the Acropolis slope, the open space of the Agora became the site of important commemorative monuments. One of the most important of these was the *Tyrannicides,* a marble group by the fifth-century B.C.E. sculptors Kritios and Nesiotes depicting Harmodios and Aristogeiton, the heroes who killed Hipparchos, brother of the tyrant Hippias, at the end of the sixth century B.C.E. This work, a

2.10. *Tyrannicides,* 2nd century C.E. Roman copy after 5th-century B.C.E. bronze sculptures by Kritios and Nesiotes, reportedly from Hadrian's Villa. Museo Archeologico Nazionale, Naples

replacement for an earlier work by Antenor that was removed from the Agora in 480 B.C.E. when the Persian king Xerxes plundered Athens, can be seen in a Roman copy in the National Archaeological Museum in Naples. It is an early representation of contemporary heroes and, as such, a precedent for the commemorative monuments of heroic individuals found in public squares and parks to this day (fig. 2.10).

On the north side of the Agora, facing the Panathenaic Way as it led up to the Acropolis, the Stoa Poikile, or Painted Stoa, was built in the second quarter of the fifth century B.C.E. Its name derived from its function as an art gallery, its walls decorated with battle scenes painted by notable painters of the day. It was here, too, that bronze shields were taken to be displayed as trophies of war. The Stoa Poikile functioned as an important meeting place, one frequented by street performers and beggars as well as philosophers. Followers of the philosopher Zeno (c. 335–c. 263 B.C.E.), who met his pupils in this *stoa,* bequeathed to posterity the term *stoicism* for his teachings on freedom from passion and a calm acceptance of fate.

Herms—figures we will meet in other landscape settings as garden ornaments—were placed throughout Athens at the entrances to private homes, shrines, and important public spaces including the Agora (fig. 2.12). At the northwest corner of the Agora, at the point where it was intersected by the Panathenaic Way, a large concentration of these sculptures presided. A herm was a portrait bust of the god Hermes set upon a rectangular shaft from which protruded, halfway up, a representation of male genitalia. As symbols of male potency, herms were popular

2.11 a and b. Agora, Athens: (a) in the Archaic period. c. 500 B.C.E. and (b) c. 300 B.C.E.

Around 520 B.C.E., the citizens built the Enneakrounos, a large public fountain house, the terminus of one of two recently constructed pipelines carrying water from the slopes of the Acropolis. With the drainage of the ground to the east and the construction of other public buildings on the remaining three sides of the open space thus formed, the Agora assumed the general size (10 acres) and irregular square shape that it maintained over several centuries.

Between 415 and 406 B.C.E., a new Bouleuterion was built adjacent to the old one. The Old Bouleuterion probably continued its function as the city archive, and the building became known as the Metroon. As such it was considered the sanctuary of Rhea, the Mother of the Olympian gods under whose auspices the civic records were guarded and the city's laws protected.

The Skias, or Tholos, stood immediately to the south of the New Bouleuterion and the Metroon. Its name denoted its round shape, like a *skias,* or sun hat. Here the fifty *pryataneis,* those senators who were functioning as the executive committee of the Boule, or Council, were served their meals. Approximately one-third of these remained on duty as guardians of the city, sleeping there throughout the night.

In the southwestern corner of the Agora, in front of some small buildings below the Tholos, was the 4th-century-B.C.E. Monument of the Eponymous Heroes with ten bronze figuress flanked by ten bronze tripods (see 2.14). These represented each of the legendary figures selected by the Delphic Oracle as names for the ten "tribes" into which the people of Attica were divided. The tribes were created by the constitution drawn up by the statesman Cleisthenes at the end of the 6th century B.C.E. In front of the monument was a barrier of stone posts and wooden railings. Here a citizen could read the civic notices posted beneath the figure representing his tribe. Here also general announcements, including drafts of proposed legislation, were posted. The Monument of the Eponymous Heroes was thus an important information center in ancient Athens, functioning much like the modern press in focusing debate on public issues.

At the northwest corner of the Agora stood the Royal Stoa (Stoa Basileios) where magistrates swore their oaths of office. Sets of thrones, which originally stood in front of the *stoa,* attest to its function as a place of judicial review. Pottery fragments marked as the property of the state denote its use also as a site for official functions involving drinking and dining. It was to the Royal Stoa that Socrates was summoned in 399 B.C.E. to be indicted.

Directly to the south of the Royal Stoa was the larger Doric Stoa of Zeus, with two projecting wings and a façade of Pentelic marble, believed to have been built between 430 and 420 B.C.E. Sacred to the cult of Zeus Eleutherios (Freedom), the building was a monument to Greek freedom from Persian domination after 479 B.C.E. Like the Painted Stoa, it served as a communal memorial and was adorned with paintings and trophies of war. Here Socrates conversed with his pupils.

Some of the paraphernalia associated with trial by jury, such as the small bronze axles, which served as ballots, have been discovered in and around the Agora. The exact location of the prison has not been confirmed; however, in the ruins of a building at the southwest corner of the Agora, archaeologists have found a cache of small clay medicine bottles, such as were used to dispense the executioner's dose of hemlock, along with a small statuette of Socrates possibly left as a tribute.

On the south side of the Agora stood a long *stoa,* built during the decade of 430–420 B.C.E. and replaced by another double-colonnaded *stoa* in Hellenistic times. This structure housed the weights and measures that ensured honesty in market transactions. Sixteen private meeting chambers behind the colonnade were furnished with dining couches. Nearby was the Mint, a building with the remains of a foundry where official items of bronze, such as the ballots of jurors and the weights and measures of commerce, were fabricated from the 4th century B.C.E. on and where coins were struck in the third and second centuries B.C.E. Between the Mint and the South Stoa was the fountain house dating from the 6th century B.C.E.

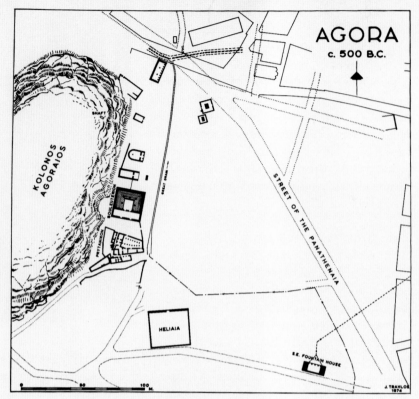

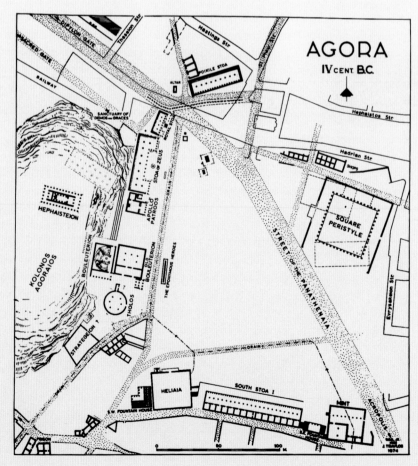

2.12. Marble herm from the Greek island of Siphnos. Height 26 inches. 520-510 B.C. E. **National Archaeological Museum, Athens**

when an aqueduct was built to carry water to this site next to the Agora, served as planting pockets for a tree-shaded promenade. These were replanted with myrtle and pomegranate during the horticultural restoration.

From literature, history, and archaeology, a portrait of the life of the Agora emerges. To the ancient fountain house in its southeast corner came the women of the city bearing their amphoras. Nearby were the open-air market stalls where farmers sold livestock and produce. Beneath the colonnades of the various stoas a lively crowd mingled, gossiping or engaging in philosophical discussion and doing business of all kinds. At the Monument of the Eponymous Heroes, knots of men gathered to read the latest news (figs. 2.13, 2.14). Within the Bouleuterion complex, lawmakers attended to affairs of state. Courts of law, or a jury assembled outdoors, tried

figures. They were often placed as talismans in front of homes as well as in public places and alongside important roads.

In the second quarter of the fifth century B.C.E., trees were planted in the Agora to provide shade. These were probably plane trees and, like the trees planted at the same time at the Academy, they lined principal walkways and defined an outdoor classroom in which Socrates and other philosophers walked and talked with their students. Under one plane tree hung the notice board listing fines for women who had behaved in a disorderly manner. Later, beneath another, the Athenians placed a statue of the orator and statesman Demosthenes (384–322 B.C.E.).

In the middle of the fifth century B.C.E., Pericles focused the wealth garnered from Athens's hegemony within the Delian League upon the construction of the Parthenon and other temples on the Acropolis. During the last third of the fifth century B.C.E., there was a burst of civic building activity around the Agora, so that, by the time the Athenian treasury was drained by Spartan victory at the end of the Peloponnesian Wars, its defining architecture had assumed the form that housed the city's important institutions throughout most of the fourth century B.C.E.

Today, the Agora functions as an archaeological park enjoyed by tourists and city residents, and a careful replanting plan undertaken in the 1950s using indigenous plant species common in ancient times provides an approximation of the welcome shade and greenery that this important public space had then. Now, as in antiquity, plants need irrigation to survive in the hot, dry Athenian climate, and the restored trees were planted along the same channels that originally furnished water to the Agora. Cavities excavated in bedrock around three sides of the Temple of Hephaistos, probably in the early third century B.C.E.

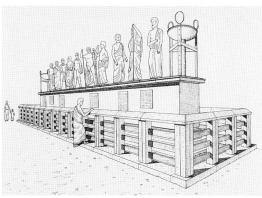

offenders. Upon occasion there would be functions of a sacro-civic nature with burnt offerings and contests performed before audiences seated in temporary grandstands. Among the many festival days of the year when the Agora was thronged with people celebrating or passing through en route to one of the sacred sites inside or outside the city, none was more important than the Great Panathenaia, which occurred in the middle of summer every fourth year.

2.13. The site of the Monument of the Eponymous Heroes today, with the Temple of Hephaistos in the background

Left: **2.14. Drawing of the restored Monument of the Eponymous Heroes. c. 330** B.C.E. **In front of the monument was a barrier of stone posts and wooden railings. Here a citizen could read the civic notices posted beneath the figure representing his tribe. Here also general announcements, including drafts of proposed legislation, were posted. The Monument of the Eponymous Heroes was thus an important information center in ancient Athens, functioning much like the modern press in focusing debate on public issues.**

Theater in Athens

Of scarcely less importance than the Great Panathenaia was the Great Dionysia, which took place annually. In the beginning, celebrants honored Dionysus, patron god of drama and of this festival, in the Agora; later, the Athenians built a theater held sacred to him on the southeastern flank of the Acropolis. It contained a circular orchestra, 66 feet in diameter, with a floor of smooth-packed dirt and an altar in the center. Wooden planks set into the terraced hillside accommodated the audience, and a modest wooden *skene,* or scene building, provided the necessary theatrical backdrop.

Pericles' fifth-century B.C.E. building program called for a new theater to accommodate the mature Greek drama that Aeschylus had pioneered in the Great Dionysias held in the 470s B.C.E. In order to make room for a larger *skene,* the theater was moved farther north to a position near the walls of the Acropolis. It is this theater, improved by the Athenian orator and financier Lycurgus in the fourth century B.C.E. and extensively remodeled in Roman times, that tourists visit today. To the east of the theater, above the auditorium, Pericles built a large square building called the Odeion to hold musical contests, which were also part of the Great Dionysia.

The Kerameikos Cemetery

Just outside the Dipylon, or double gateway that formed the principal entrance to the city, lay the Kerameikos Cemetery. Burial at this site dates from the twelfth century B.C.E., and archaeologists have discovered here enormous eighth-century-B.C.E. funerary kraters and amphorae decorated in the Geometric style. During the sixth century B.C.E., incised, painted, and bas-relief grave monuments, together with commemorative sculpture, began to adorn the landscape. By this time the city walls had been built. Athenian law restricted burial to the outer Kerameikos beyond them, while the inner Kerameikos became the district where potters clustered to make the distinctive red-and-black Attic pottery that was one of the city's most important commercial wares, thus giving its name to ceramic production ever after.

Large-scale, carved stone versions of *lekythoi*—small, slender, ceramic urns—became popular grave markers in the late fifth century B.C.E. along with memorial altars, inscribed stelai, and sculptures of lions. Plots lining the Academy road, which was especially scenic, became the final resting place of distinguished statesmen and Athenians and their allies fallen in war. In this way a necropolis took shape, becoming, as we shall see in Chapter Nine, an aesthetic inspiration for metropolitan suburban cemeteries in Paris, Boston, New York, and other rapidly expanding cities

of the industrial age. After the fourth century B.C.E., a law was issued forbidding costly sculptural works, and people honored the dead with simple round columns instead.

The Athenian Countryside

The vital sum of all these activities indicates an extraordinary spirit of cultural unity during the centuries of Athenian self-governance. Moreover, even though Athens was unique among Greek cities in the degree to which its religious life was focused inside the city, the connection between the city and its surrounding landscape was palpable and continuously experienced. To the northwest, the Sacred Way became the road to Eleusis, site of an important religious sanctuary. To the northeast lay the road to Mount Pentelicus, 10 miles distant, over which workmen hauled the thousands of tons of marble used to build the Parthenon and other important public buildings. To the southeast, reinforcing the Parthenon's lineage as a temple of the goddess Athena, Mount Hymettos, with its peak sanctuary to Zeus Ómvrios, provoker of rain, reared its twin horns in axial relationship to it. To the southwest lay Piraeus, connected to the city by parallel long walls protecting the transit of people and goods from the Spartan enemy. Between the road to Eleusis and the road to Thebes in the north was the road upon which Plato journeyed as he went from the city to the nearby shady groves of the Academy. The siting of the city thus, with mountains protectively encircling three sides, while the fourth faced the sea—a paradigm that was intuitively repeated by *poleis* elsewhere, notably in the plain of Argolis—gave the Athenians a much clearer sense of specific territoriality than did their fortifying walls. *Polis* and *chora* were an expression of both Mind (*Nous*) and Nature, an integrated whole in which a profound ideal of human existence was made manifest.

In addition to developing an architectural vocabulary of columned, pedimented structures that has remained a living language for builders for more than two millennia, the ancient Greeks enlarged the sense of urban life as a communal undertaking and created institutions such as the theater that expanded the human potential for self-awareness. Though their remarkable experiment in governance proved difficult to perpetuate and replicate, some of their cultural and educational institutions endured, and the language of Classical Greek architecture was expanded by Hellenistic and Roman architects.

With the Hellenistic Empire the *polis* as a self-governing civic and religious institution ceased to exist. In its place there arose a new cosmopolitan culture embracing the entire Mediterranean basin and extending as far east as Persia. Within this far-flung region composed of many interactive urban centers, designers manipulated the forms inherited from Greece in sophisticated ways, creating theatrical spatial compositions that gave a new dynamism to landscape design paralleled by the dynamic movement and high degree of emotionalism Hellenistic sculptors gave to their figural compositions. By Roman times, the relationship of such architectural ensembles to natural settings no longer mattered as much as their employment to frame and contain space. Further, the replication of Roman civic forms was seen as a means of asserting authority and inspiring allegiance in colonial cities throughout an empire of even vaster dimensions than the one created by Alexander the Great.

III. Empire: Hellenistic and Roman Urbanism

Weakened by the long years of warfare with Sparta and assailed by other centers of growing power during the fourth century B.C.E., Athens saw her hegemony among Aegean city states diminished and her own freedom threatened. Warfare was now a way of life throughout the Hellenic world, and although colonization was one solution to the problem of growing urban populations, within the context of the general Hellenic unrest, colonial outposts were vulnerable offshoots with an uncertain future.

It is a historical irony that Macedonia, a land power without a significant navy, should have been the engine that propelled Greece toward empire and the subjugation of Asia. Following the murder of Philip II of Macedon (382–336 B.C.E.), his brilliant son, Alexander (356–323 B.C.E.), assumed the throne at the age of twenty. Already an experienced campaigner, he found the battlefield his natural home and soon set about completing the Macedonian subjugation of Thessaly, Thrace, and Illyria. After securing lands all the way to the Danube and beyond, he ruthlessly crushed rebellious Thebes. The rest of the Greek city-states fell into line, including Athens, co-conspirator of Thebes, which Alexander could now afford to treat leniently.

Alexander the Great's thirteen-year reign was one of continued whirlwind conquest as his armies subdued the cities of Asia Minor, Syria, and Egypt. With the eastern Mediterranean under his control, he marched into Mesopotamia and, crossing the Caucasus, on into India. In the process of building an empire, he founded several cities, among them Alexandria in Egypt. Although his empire quickly fragmented following his death in 323 B.C.E., his great achievement was the creation of a Hellenistic culture and economy that stretched from Gibraltar to the Indus River.

In this vast matrix, art and trade flourished, and the advances in geography, natural history, and other aspects of science that Alexander had encouraged continued. In terms of art, Alexander had appropriated from his tutor Aristotle an ecumenical attitude, believing the world to be an *oikumene*, a place of eclectic exchange in which many cultures contributed form and style to the Greek base. Because of these circumstances, the Greek heritage, now infused with a broad array of disparate cultural influences, was both disseminated and developed, acquiring certain important features that became basic ingredients of much subsequent landscape design. These included axial organization and a new monumentality, potent tools for dramatizing urban power and making the appearance of cities more symbolically expressive.

In the Hellenistic world, there was a heightened sense of the drama of human affairs. The serene idealism of Classical Greek art was not compatible with the clamor of imperial armies. Power creates its own cultural imperatives: hagiography finds its counterpart in architectural monumentality and portraiture, while the tragedy of brutality and suffering often breeds melodrama. Hellenism's broad sweep across continents was paralleled by an extravagant treatment of space. Buildings were organized into elaborate complexes, and sculpture was no longer self-contained, but full of restless movement.

The vocabulary of design remained Classical, yet it was accented in new and theatrical ways. The manipulation of vertical space became an important aspect of landscape design as staircases and terraces took on new importance along with the organization of horizontal space through symmetry and axial alignment. Engaged columns, pilasters, and other means of surface articulation animated buildings and increased their dramatic presence. The prosperity engendered by trade and the continued growth and spread of populations through colonization meant that many opportunities existed for experimentation with these elements of urban form.

Hellenistic Urbanism
The Hellenistic city appropriated the Hippodamian grid as a planning device and exploited it architecturally. *Stoas* and, later, colonnades lining principal thoroughfares made the planar orthogonal lines of the city three-dimensional, turning agoras into architecturally defined spaces, and streets into rhythmically punctuated ways (fig. 2.15). Like those of

2.15. Curetes Street, Ephesus, Turkey. Principal thorough-fares in Hellenistic cities such as Ephesus were often colon-naded, providing visual unity to the streetscape and a precedent for later arcaded streets and squares (see figs. 4.48, 4.49, 6.45).

Below: 2.16. *Stoa* facing Lion Harbor, Miletus. 2nd century B.C.E.

Classical times, the Hellenistic agora functioned as a vital urban nexus open to all manner of through traffic and did not become a self-contained space segregated from its surrounding streets. Instead, it experienced a transformation akin to that of another important Hellenistic architectural form: the peristyle, or column-enclosed court, as can be seen in Miletus (see fig. 2.9; fig. 2.16).

Illustrating the versatility and theatrical planning principles that are also inherent in Hellenistic urban design, the second century B.C.E. city of Pergamum forsook the grid entirely for an essay in vertical composition (figs. 2.17, 2.18, 2.20). This suited its location on a narrow mountain ridge near what is

now the modern town of Bergama in Turkey. Pergamum under the Attalid dynasty sought to rival the Periclean splendor of the Athenian Acropolis. Athena was the city's patron deity, and its kings, Eumenes II (ruled 197–159 B.C.E.) and Attalos II (ruled 159–138 B.C.E.) oversaw a building program that honored both the goddess and themselves. Here, because of the topography of the site, the city's urban planners abandoned the grid and instead produced a fan-shaped layout as they built the city in successive stages over several generations. Their efforts resulted in an extraordinarily scenic composition in which architecture and landscape were fused into a unified dramatic experience.

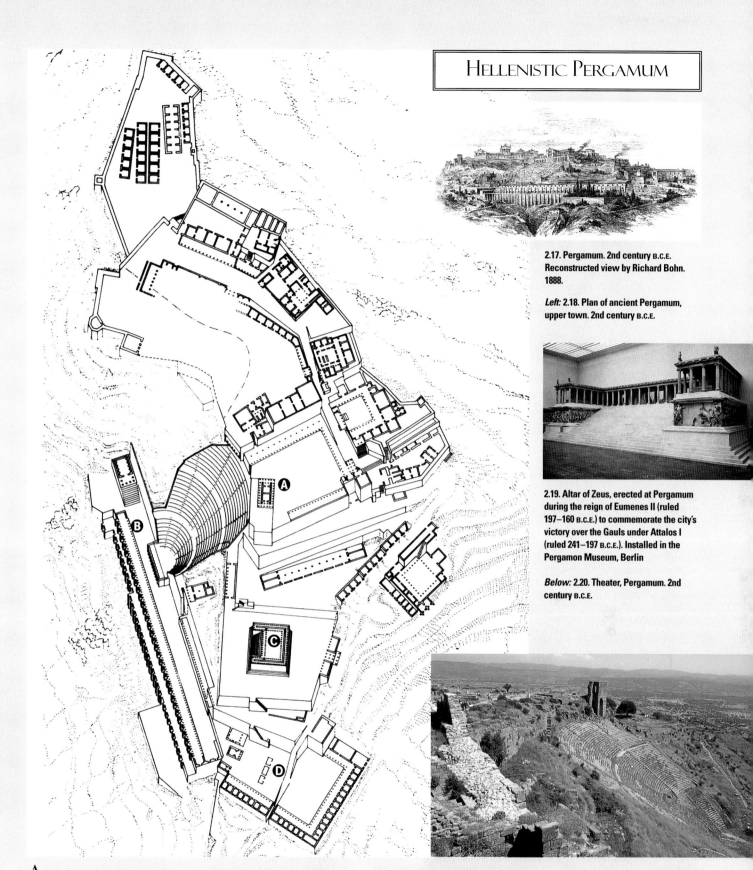

2.17. Pergamum. 2nd century B.C.E. Reconstructed view by Richard Bohn. 1888.

Left: 2.18. Plan of ancient Pergamum, upper town. 2nd century B.C.E.

2.19. Altar of Zeus, erected at Pergamum during the reign of Eumenes II (ruled 197–160 B.C.E.) to commemorate the city's victory over the Gauls under Attalos I (ruled 241–197 B.C.E.). Installed in the Pergamon Museum, Berlin

Below: 2.20. Theater, Pergamum. 2nd century B.C.E.

Acting as a pivot for the entire fan of stepped terraces and buildings that constituted the upper city, a large theater was set into the steeply pitched western face of the acropolis ridge (fig. 2.20). A long terrace with two levels of buttressed retaining walls anchored the theater into its hillside. The colonnade running the length of the terrace **B** established a rhythmical pattern that was echoed in the architecture above. From the theater one ascended into the colonnade-framed terrace that formed the precinct of the Temple of Athena **A**. On the terrace below this to the south stood the great Altar of Zeus **C**, which lends its name to the Pergamon Museum in Berlin where it can be seen today in its reconstructed form (fig. 2.19). Its grandiloquent frieze depicts the mythical battle between the Gods and the Giants with the thrusting diagonals and surging movement into space that are characteristic of Hellenistic sculpture.

Above the Athena terrace stood the library, the palace complex, barracks, and arsenal. The Temple of Trajan, a later Roman addition, occupied its own terrace to the north of the theater, making an effective counterpoint to the great altar and its terrace to the south. Beneath the monumental Altar of Zeus was the city's upper agora **D**; it was at this point that the road, which zigzagged along the hilly south-facing slope above the lower agora and extensive terraced gymnasium complex of the town below, entered the acropolis area and began its rise through the sequence of scenically arranged terraces.

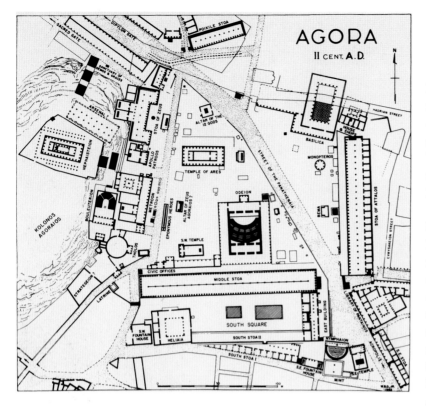

2.21. Athenian Agora, 1st century, C.E., at the period of its fullest development

Below: **2.22. Reconstruction of the Stoa of Attalos II of Pergamum (ruled 159–138 B.C.E.), Athenian Agora. The original *stoa* was destroyed in 267 C.E. The reconstruction was built in the 1950s to house the Agora Museum.**

FROM HELLENISTIC TO ROMAN URBANISM

To understand more fully the forces at work as the Classical heritage of Greece was transformed through Hellenistic culture into that of imperial Rome, it is worth revisiting the Athenian Agora. Although Athens did not offer the underlying organizing principle of a grid plan, which would have facilitated the kind of articulation of public space as is found at Miletus, the agora in its Hellenistic and Roman incarnations nevertheless manifests the trend toward the regularization and inward-focusing of open space (fig. 2.21).

By the second century B.C.E., Athens was a province of the Roman Empire, a renowned center of learning, revered as the fountainhead of Greek culture and home to the most eminent philosophers of the day. Cicero, Horace, and Ovid came there to study, and various Roman emperors bestowed their largesse upon the city's venerable civic core in the form of new buildings. Not surprisingly, the Agora's character as a civic space changed; it lost all remaining identity as a place of democratic assembly and became instead a receptacle for Greco-Roman culture and a repository of the glorious Classical past, which Rome now appropriated.

The integrity of the original Agora space had been breached by the construction of the Hellenistic Middle Stoa, but this had been done to achieve a more regular spatial definition and accommodate the city's continued commercial vitality. Now there no longer existed any prohibition against encroachment upon the remaining space. Vividly illustrating the Athenian loss of governmental autonomy and the Agora's transformation from civic core to cultural center was the construction of the Odeion in its center. This huge concert hall was probably built at the time of the emperor Augustus's visit to the city between 16 and 14 B.C.E.

Symptomatic of the decline of Greek power, moreover, was the memorializing of its past. The Agora played a large role in this effort as it became a virtual museum of architectural reconstruction in an early attempt at "heritage theming." Augustus's building program included the careful dismantling of the Temple of Ares, a marble structure of the Doric order that is believed to have stood several miles north of Athens somewhere in the foothills of Mount Parnes, and its reassembly in front of the Agora's western range of Classical and Hellenistic buildings. At this time, he had columns and other elements of neglected fifth- and fourth-century B.C.E. buildings in the depopulated countryside of Attica transported to the Agora for conservation and reuse. From Sounion, from Thorikos, and from elsewhere came handsomely carved building parts, and from other places came small temples and altars. Inscriptions were carved on these, honoring the deified emperor Augustus and his relatives.

In keeping with the continued exaltation of the Agora as a center of culture and learning, at the southeast corner along the Panathenaic Way, a private citizen, Titus Flavius Pantaenus, built a library at his expense in the second century C.E. Like many Roman buildings, it was given the interior focus of a peristyle courtyard, while Greek-style stoas stood along three sides of the exterior (fig. 2.22).

On the opposite side of the Panathenaic Way, on the site of the old Mint and next to one of the reconstructed Classical temples, the Nymphaeum, a fountain house in the shape of a large hemicycle, was built in the second century C.E. The curving wall that rose above a series of basins, pools, and fountains seems to have been carved with niches for statues. This elaborate fountain was connected to the great aqueduct that carried water to Athens from the Kephalari Springs on the lower slopes of Mount Pentelicus. The construction of the Athenian Nymphaeum illustrates the ancient Roman practice of celebrating an important public work through symbolic civic display. It was built in the second century C.E. during the reign of Hadrian, the emperor-architect who, more than all the others, identified with Greek culture and history. Besides the Nymphaeum, his legacy to the city included the monumental Temple of Olympian Zeus, a library, a gymnasium, a pantheon, and a shrine of Panhellenic Zeus and Hera.

ELEMENTS OF ROMAN URBANISM

Order was the hallmark of Roman urbanism. In its most utilitarian dimension, Roman order meant *centuriation,* the division of the territory surrounding a town into squares measuring 2400 feet (731.5 meters) per side. These *centuriae* were so named because Roman surveyors subdivided them into approximately one hundred oblong strips of land, arable fields for the most part, which were allocated as private property to the citizens of the town. A similarly utilitarian application of Roman order was to be found in the grid layout of military encampments that often served, as in the case of Florentia (Florence), as the future sites of colonial cities (fig. 2.23). The Roman grid, inherited from both Greek and Etruscan practice, was developed around a central cross axis, the street running north-south being the *cardo,* and the east-west one traversing it being the *decumanus.* The *insulae,* or blocks formed by the subsidiary orthogonal streets, formed a checkerboard pattern of squares, rather than the oblong units familiar in Hellenistic grid planning. In many cases the *cardo* and *decumanus* forming the town center would be identical with the intersection of two survey lines of *centuriation;* sometimes, however, a Roman town grid might respect the cardinal points of the compass in its orthogonal alignment while *centuriation* proceeded—as was the case with Florentia where the course of the Arno and the surrounding topography were taken into account—in accordance with certain practical considerations.

In addition to providing a formula for the establishment of a military settlement or a new town, Roman order prevailed in the predictable location of the forums and major civic structures of the town at the intersection of the *cardo* and *decumanus.* Further, planners subjugated all private building to a zoning code that decreed that no building could be higher

than twice the width of the street upon which it stood, an ordinance that was sometimes breached as a town became overcrowded and people needed to erect tall tenements for housing. The manufacture of standardized, kiln-fired bricks, roof tiles, and drainage pipes in many sizes and shapes and the mass production of metal pipes and fastening devices, together with the invention of concrete and the necessary timber-form technology for repetitive pouring of vaults, walls, foundations, and other building parts, made possible the organization of a construction industry capable of operating with military-style efficiency. Indeed, many construction workers were soldiers of the Roman Empire.

But there was a higher sense of order than that of the pragmatic grid honored by Roman urbanism, an order in which the grid played an ever-diminishing role until its use as a planning tool was virtually phased out in the second century C.E. This order might be called imperial order, for it was a means of making manifest—through planning and architecture employing common urban spatial arrangements and building types—the grandeur, beneficence, and ubiquity of empire. Throughout Asia Minor, North Africa, Iberia, Great Britain, Gaul, Italy, and all the islands of the Mediterranean, a uniform building technology and urban planning mentality provided hundreds of variants upon this theme. Imperial grandeur was bestowed upon cities as great basilicas and public baths were built. High-based temples and triumphal arches added more scenographic verticality, and theaters and

2.23. Aerial view of Florence, Italy. The original grid plan of Florentia, a Roman military encampment and colony, can be detected in the regular layout of the streets around the Piazza della Republica, the old Roman Forum.

amphitheaters provided both entertainment and landmark character. Paternalistically conceived, these Roman cities were designed through the machinery of imperial authority as livable habitats for their citizens. With running water, latrines, paved streets, and other amenities, they are the first cities in which modern urban dwellers could have felt at home. Collectively, along with the Roman roads and Roman aqueducts that served them, the cities proclaimed in physical terms the *Pax Romana* across the broad sphere of empire. More than anything else, the replication of this order over and over again throughout the Roman Empire's vast breadth manifested its wealth and the power of its highly centralized government.

What were the elements of the urban rhetoric that effectively and lastingly portrayed Roman imperial order? Although the grid was manipulated and even ignored, axiality itself was more firmly applied than ever before. Bilateral symmetry around strong axes governed the design of major public buildings and their attendant courts. The forum was a highly controlled space. Streets led to its entrances, but, unlike the Greek or Hellenistic agora, it was not traversed by thoroughfares. The Roman forum was thus at once integrated with, and separated from, the circulation system of the town, This street design, together with the firm architectural definition of borders, gave the forum—like the great buildings that, with it, constituted the civic core—an inward focus.

Roman architecture and planning were in this way informed by profound space-shaping and place-fixing impulses. As cultural heirs of the Greeks, Romans sometimes paid homage to a local "genius of the place," but the cultural matrix in which they built was one grounded in an Aristotelian worldview and imperial politics. The sense of self-containment, enclosure, and embrace that their buildings and cities displayed denied integration with the greater landscape and, instead, metaphorically proclaimed the values of the entire urbanized commonwealth. These building and urban forms, which were architecturally similar from place to place, were grounded not in their own locales, but rather in the concept of orderly imperial rule. It is thus understandable that the old shrines and sanctuaries in nature ceased to exert their pull, and communal processions to them stopped after the gods took up permanent residence in the cities. Roman temples, like Roman basilicas, were for the most part found in or beside the forum, in the civic centers of towns.

Unlike the architecturally elaborate Hellenistic shrines at Lindos and Kos, which enjoyed a natural setting, the Sanctuary of Fortuna Primigenia, begun in the second century B.C.E., was an urban shrine. Set into a hillside, it hovers above the town of Praeneste (modern Palestrina) outside Rome, offering a splendid example of the integration of site and architecture (fig. 2.24). It demonstrates, according to architectural historian Spiro Kostoff, "the cadenced climb in stages, with an artful use of landings, viewing points, and the alternating concealment and revelation of the terminal object, [that] was a special gift of Roman designers."[12] Behind the colonnades of its lower terraces were rows of shops. Lateral stairs ascend from the ground level to the first of seven terraces; to ascend from one terrace level to the next, one is forced to return to the central axis. Here there are steep stairs or, in the case of the third and fourth terraces, long ramps, which climb from each side and then connect in the center above large barrel-vaulted niches that emphasize the central axis. Shops were placed behind porticoes that run the length of the fifth and sixth terraces on either side of the central stairs. The deep sixth terrace had side porticoes as well. The small semicircular top terrace served as the orchestra for a theater and was therefore surrounded by stepped seating, above which stood as the climax to the whole soaring architectural composition a semicircular double portico and, rising behind it, a small round temple. The organization of the hillside into a series of terraces with stairs arranged to enforce axial movement and the resolution of axial thrust in a climactic semicircular embrace is considered a source of inspiration for Bramante's Belvedere Court at the Vatican, begun around 1505 (see Chapter Four, figs. 4.7, 4.8, 4.9), and subsequently through Bramante's example, the work of other Renaissance landscape designers.

2.24. Sanctuary of Fortuna Primigenia, Praeneste (Palestrina). Early 1st century B.C.E.

2.25. Triumphal Arch, Arausio (Orange), France. 21 C.E.

Below: 2.26. Arcadian Way, Ephesus, constructed during the reign of the Emperor Arcadius (395–408 C.E.). This marble-paved street leading from the middle harbor gate to the theater was lined with shops and had wide, covered, mosaic walkways on either side of it.

Most of the columns that once formed the colonnades of the stepped facades and projecting wings of the Sanctuary of Fortuna Primigenia have been removed, but the remaining structure bears witness to the Roman affinity for a construction technology and design vocabulary in which the arch played a dominant role. The arch has the ability to span distances with balletic grace; its analogue is the leap, whereas that of the seriate column is the measured step. For this reason, the arcaded porticoes of Roman streets provide an altogether different visual rhythm from that set up by the Greek stoa or Hellenistic colonnade. But, as is evident at Praeneste, Roman aptitude for arch construction did not mean forsaking the classical orders of Hellenistic architecture. On the contrary, columns and pediments were used extensively in both old and new ways as architects forged a specifically Roman architectural vocabulary. Peristyle courts increased in popularity, and colonnades were extensively employed to ennoble prominent thoroughfares. Most important, Roman designers applied columns and other sculptural elements decoratively to adorn and articulate the otherwise undifferentiated surfaces of freestanding arches as well as arched entrances and building façades like that of the Colosseum in Rome. The column-ornamented, freestanding triumphal arch erected to celebrate victory in battle became emblematic of Rome, a familiar image appearing on coins and in other ways symbolizing imperial rule (fig. 2.25).

These elements, which were often employed in conjunction with brick facing, constituted the architectural ingredients of Roman urbanism. Cities throughout the empire established a well-defined and predictable sequencing of commonly established urban forms. The spatial linking of these according to certain conventional formulae, as well as the overall familiarity of the forms themselves, gave the Roman urban landscape its essential character.

Principal thoroughfares were designed to visually link these forms and spaces. They were differentiated from the byways of the town by their sunken grading, additional width, and an abundance of special features including fountains and, in important cities, freestanding arches and other architectural incidents such as nymphaeums. Sometimes colonnades or arched porticoes extending for several blocks enhanced the streets' status as principal avenues (fig. 2.26).

2.27. Via di Stabia, Pompeii, Italy, with stepping stones and fountain at the intersection. Before 62 c.e.

Below: **2.28. Fountain, House of the Little Fountain, Pompeii. 1st century c.e. In order to enjoy the abundance of water available in the Imperial Age, Pompeians built showy mosaic fountains. These often took the form of a small pedimented structure containing a semicircular niche. Inside the niche, water cascaded down a miniature staircase or spouted from a jet held by, or contained within, a sculpture. The mosaics that decorated these fountains were formed of sea shells and brilliantly colored tiles.**

These aggrandized thoroughfares were often market streets, as they always led from a principal arched gate within the town wall to the central forum and were therefore arteries of traffic and foci of human activity. Because they were sunk slightly below the level of the buildings on either side, these streets formed curb-lined troughs. This facilitated the runoff of water and waste into drains like those that carry away rainwater and sewage in cities today. The street curbs also gave the roadbed linear definition, clearly marking its axial direction and imposing order upon the adjacent buildings. Although individualistic in their interior planning, these buildings almost invariably respected a uniform building line parallel to the street. Raised blocks at intersections facilitated pedestrian crossing (fig. 2.27).

The forum, normally at the nexus of the town's principal thoroughfares, might lie astride the street crossing. If that was the case, its sense of spatial enclosure would nevertheless be carefully maintained by its embracing porticoed architecture and the careful articulation of its entry points. More often, the forum lay beside a principal thoroughfare within the arms of one of the angles formed by the major crossing, its entrance prominently marked by architectural elements. Like the principal thoroughfares, it received special emphasis by being sunk slightly below the surrounding grade, with its edges outlined by a few shallow steps. Because the entrance portico was above the grade of the street, passage into the forum was marked by going first up, and then down, one or more stairs.

With great sophistication, urban planners employed steep flights of stairs within Roman cities to negotiate topographic changes in grade and to ascend the platforms on which Romans set their temples, basilicas, and other monumental structures. In addition to offering formal variety, these stairs and

ramps gave a degree of vertical drama. Some flights of stairs rose straight, others laterally from the ends of buildings, still others from the flanks of an axial element. In certain instances where there were several levels, these different methods of ascent were employed in combination, as at Praeneste. Steps could, of course, be used as seats and probably served, as they often do today, as places for informal gathering.

Noncommercial public space was plentiful in Roman cities. It was one of the hallmarks of imperial urbanism, and its daily use in a variety of instructive and pleasurable ways was a happy perquisite of Roman citizenship. As an institution of Roman life and as a statement of imperial largesse, the monumental public baths were important elements in the social fabric of cities. Their high, vaulted, axially planned and beautifully decorated interiors contained—in addition to hot, warm, and cold bathing rooms—well-stocked libraries. In addition to offering sensory, mental, and social stimulation, they were centers of physical fitness. Adjacent gardens and palaestrae for exercising were often planned as axially connected peristyle courts. The fusion of the gymnasium and the heated bath manifested the sophisticated cosmopolitanism of imperial times. When not erected by emperors as a means of demonstrating beneficence and gaining public approval, they were built by wealthy patrons. Many Roman baths are early examples of civic philanthropy and bear inscriptions recognizing the donor.

Although as populations grew and apartment dwellings replaced individual residences within Rome itself and in many other Roman cities, these structures did not make cities feel overcrowded or dis-

2.29. House of Pansa, Pompeii. 2nd century B.C. The rear peristyle garden significantly increased the size and amenity of the house, giving it several more well-lit rooms as well as a garden pool.

Below: 2.30. The House of the Vettii, Pompeii. Mid-1st century B.C.E. In this house of a well-to-do merchant, the peristyle garden has more sculptural fountains than any other discovered in Pompeii. The lead pipes that furnished the water for these fountains can still be seen.

agreeable. There was abundant public space, aqueduct-fed fountains and baths, and a sophisticated infrastructure for sewage disposal. Moreover, cities were beautified with sculptures and ornament. Roman architects became increasingly confident in the handling of light. Polished marble and glittering mosaics reflected light. Light also animated the surface of water. The continual motion and sound of water splashing in fountains and pools and gliding over water stairs set within the niches of *nymphaeums* added another important sensory dimension to imperial Roman cities (fig. 2.28). Patterns of light and shade—no longer legible because today colonnades and porticoes are bare, unroofed archaeological ruins—were also an important part of the sensory experience of street and plaza.

Urban Gardens

This growing design sophistication is apparent not only in the remains of Roman public buildings and public spaces, but also in the decoration and landscaping of the Roman homes and gardens unearthed by archaeologists. At Pompeii and Herculaneum, the houses of a prosperous merchant class reveal many fine wall paintings and the remains of once-beautiful gardens. The Hellenistic peristyle court provided the design prototype for these peristyle gardens, but whereas the former was surfaced with beaten earth or paving stones, the latter were lush with vegetation (fig. 2.29).

During the Roman imperial period, beginning with the reign of Augustus in the first century B.C.E.,

the construction of an aqueduct had an important effect on the standard of living in Campania, the land on the slopes of Mount Vesuvius. An ample water supply made possible the construction of large public baths as well as curbside fountains on the major streets of its cities, and pools and large gardens at its villas. Irrigation benefited the flower and perfume industry of Pompeii and allowed the planting of greater numbers of perennials and shrubs in gardens than heretofore, since these need more frequent watering than do deep-rooted trees (fig. 2.30). The small villa on the Via dell'Abbondanza, formerly referred to as the House of Loreius Tiburtinus and

A ROMAN GARDEN

2.31. Garden Canal (*Euripus*), House of Octavius Quartio, Pompeii

Right: 2.32. House and Garden of Octavius Quartio (formerly called the House of Loreius Tiburtinus), Via dell'Abbondanza, Pompeii. 3rd century B.C.E., remodeled with garden extension after earthquake in 62 C.E. This handsome house, with its large garden stretching the length of the block, was located near the amphitheater. It was converted into an inn, as were other fine old homes in the vicinity during the economically declining years preceding the catastrophe of 79 C.E. when Pompeii was buried under a rain of volcanic ash from the eruption of Mount Vesuvius. Besides serving as a hotel for the visitors who came to see the gladiatorial games at the amphitheater, it offered, as a modern hotel might, a hospitable place to give a party when one did not have a large enough house in which to entertain friends.

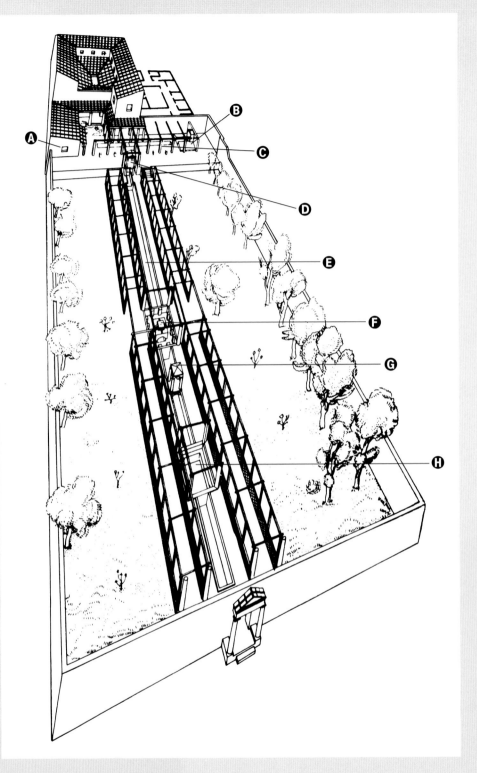

At the back of the house, built upon a porticoed terrace overlooking the garden, is a masonry *biclinium* **B** of two parallel couches, a less usual configuration than the U-shaped *triclinium,* or three-person couch arrangement, where upper-class adults typically took their meals. Here the terrace *biclinium* set under a vine-covered pergola, consists of a niche framed by two columns and decorated with rocks and seashells, and a small pool upon which servants floated food placed in ornamental dishes. The pool faces a *euripus,* a canal running the length of the terrace **C**, which was lined with sculptures. This canal may have received water from a fountain in the niche, although no pipes have yet been found.

The *euripus* is crossed in two places by footbridges, one in front of the *biclinium* where servants would have stood during meals, and another facing a large fresco-decorated room, which was probably a *triclinium.* This footbridge faces a small temple surmounting a *nymphaeum* **D** and connects the terrace with the garden. Jets of water poured from the stepped base of the temple onto an apron of random-cut paving stones in front of this footbridge, before draining into the *nymphaeum* below. At the west end of the terrace there was a *zoothecula* **A**, a pleasant retiring room where sated diners could nap or relax while looking back across the *euripus* and the landscaped terrace.

Below the temple, water spilled down three steps and flowed into another *euripus* **E** perpendicular to the one along the terrace and extending the entire length of the garden (see fig. 2.31). This stream is punctuated by a pergola-shaded pool containing an elaborate *nymphaeum*-fountain **F** designed to make the water falling into the pool **E** below ripple and shimmer. Farther along the *euripus* there is a second, smaller, temple **G**, the optical effect of which, when viewed from in front of the first, is to increase the impression of the garden's size. At the far end of the garden *euripus* is another pergola-shaded pool **H**.

2.33. Detail from a garden scene, wall painting from Villa of Livia at Prima Porta, near Rome. Late 1st century C.E.

Below: **2.34.** House of the Little Fountain, Pompeii. 1st century C.E.

more recently as the House of Octavius Quartio, provides an example of a Pompeian garden organized around a series of pools and fountains (figs. 2.31, 2.32).

Wall paintings and mosaics expressed the ancient Roman's love of nature. Few houses, even outside the apartment-filled metropolis, had extensive gardens like that of the one on the Via dell'Abbondanza, and *trompe-l'oeil* paintings of garden scenery were frequently used to extend the illusion of garden space. Though weather and the bombing of several Italian cities during World War II have taken a severe toll on many of these fragile frescoes, a number of tantalizing fragments remain. They show how in some cases an axial view from the atrium into the peristyle garden was prolonged by *trompe-l'oeil* paintings on a rear wall. Attached columns framing these delightful garden scenes made them appear to be natural views seen from a portico. The well-known fresco from the Villa of Livia at suburban Prima Porta was painted as a continuous mural on the four walls of a sunken chamber built as a retreat from the summer heat (fig. 2.33). Here an illusory garden, painted against an azure background, evokes the shrubs, flowers, fountains, birds, and white-painted lattice fencing found in actual Roman gardens of the period.

Garden paintings often decorated small courtyards and light wells. In addition to these straightforward representations of fountains, flora, and fauna, two other illusionistic subjects—the sacro-idyllic landscape and the villa landscape—were painted on the walls of Roman houses. The Roman architect and engineer Vitruvius (active 46–30 B.C.E.) writes of the "images of the gods, or the representations of legends" contained in sacro-idyllic paintings, that is, paintings of gods and other figures in an empyrean landscape. Somewhat more realistic, but closely related in spirit were paintings of villas and porticoes set within a landscape depicting "harbors, headlands, shores, rivers, springs, straits, temples, groves, hills,

cattle, shepherds."[13] These frequently contained figures engaged in rural pursuits such as fishing and hunting. A painting of this type is found on the south wall of the garden in the House of the Little Fountain at Pompeii (fig. 2.34).

From all this, we can see how, using a standardized architectural vocabulary, Roman builders composed their urban designs in predictable yet highly satisfying ways. The pleasing recombination of conventional geometric forms; the shaping of space around ritual activities and the concomitant use of axial composition and symmetry to enforce notions of order, stability, and place; a love of illusion and theatrical effects; and a sensory approach to physical comfort and aesthetic delight were the attributes of Roman urban design. Through *centuriation,* significant portions of nature had become firmly subjugated to Roman order, and now domesticated landscape was to be found within the peristyle garden as well as in the surrounding countryside. We can expect to find these same principles and practices in Roman villas of the Age of Augustus (27 B.C.E.–14 C.E.) and during the reigns of the emperors who succeeded him.

IV. Garden and Villa: The Art of Landscape in Ancient Rome

The ideal of a second home in the country, a retreat for what the Romans called *otium*—a kind of industrious leisure comprised of worthwhile mental and physical pursuits away from the distractions of urban business, politics, and society—has exerted a strong appeal in various cultures throughout history. While writers from Horace to Thomas Jefferson extolled rural values and the wholesome simplicity of rural life, their lives in the country did not require them to engage in rustic toil. Much as they admired the farmer, their affluence and broad intellectual horizons enabled them to adopt an aesthetic attitude different from that of the plowman with his hard daily labors performed under the hot sun.

Like the term *country house,* the word *villa* stands for a social ideal as well as an architectural form, connoting a vision of the good life, a life free of sordid care and pecuniary want. But in Republican times and also for those Romans who, like Virgil, romantically yearned for the imagined goodness and simplicity of a pre-Imperial age, the chief purpose of villa life was fruitful husbandry. The *villa rustica* is the earliest villa form, ideologically supported by Roman poets, including Virgil, who wrote the *Eclogues,* his great pastoral poem, and the *Georgics,* a poetic treatise on agriculture, in the second half of the first century B.C.E. For Virgil, the *villa rustica* connoted a Golden Age of peace and plenty, and in extolling the virtues of agrarian life, he promoted a kind of Jeffersonian ideal of the independent farmer whose industry can bring a return to simple ancient values.

This idealistic vision, however, did not match economic and social reality. Many small farmers never returned to the land after being driven away during the Punic Wars in the third and second centuries B.C.E. Pillaging armies and the competition of slave labor and cheap imported produce caused the collapse of the old agrarian way of life. The process was completed during the years of civil strife that occurred in the first century B.C.E. when victorious partisans confiscated the properties of the defeated. At the same time, landowners converted land from the cultivation of grain and other crops for domestic consumption to ranches for cattle and sheep grazing and to plantations for wine and oil production.

The owners of these *latifundia,* or large rural establishments, were for the most part city-bred, operating their landholdings for profit with slave labor. If the proprietor was in residence for part of the year, as was often the case, he built for his use a house similar to the ones found at Pompeii and Herculaneum. Because in plan it followed the form of city houses, it was classified a *villa urbana,* to distinguish it from the *villa rustica.* The two were, nevertheless, usually merged into a single block that was easier to fortify and defend than widely separated structures would have been. Security and practicality, as opposed to aesthetics, thus dominated the architectural character of such country villas as the one in Boscoreale near Pompeii, dating from the beginning of the first century B.C.E., where wine pressing and storage facilities, together with barns and stables, were united within the same walls as a commodious house for the proprietor (fig. 2.35).

A third villa type, the *villa suburbana,* was, as its name implies, one located on the outskirts of the city. In addition, there was the *villa marittima,* the seaside villa that became a popular pleasure resort for wealthy Romans in the Imperial Age. The entire area around the Bay of Naples was ringed with the kind of porticoed seaside villas seen in landscape paintings of the period (fig. 2.36).

Pliny's Villas

To understand better the villa as a building type during these times of Roman power and prosperity, generations of architectural historians have turned to the letters of Pliny the Younger, a wealthy landowner in the first century C.E. Pliny was the owner of both a

2.35. Villa at Boscoreale. 1st century B.C.E.

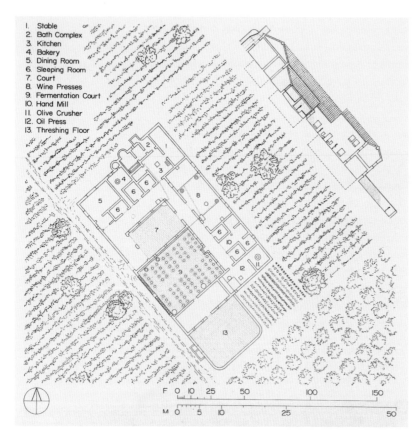

1. Stable
2. Bath Complex
3. Kitchen
4. Bakery
5. Dining Room
6. Sleeping Room
7. Court
8. Wine Presses
9. Fermentation Court
10. Hand Mill
11. Olive Crusher
12. Oil Press
13. Threshing Floor

2.36. Fresco painting of a harbor with seaside villas, from Stabiae, Italy

villa marittima and a *villa urbana*. Although Laurentinum, his maritime villa, was only seventeen miles outside of Rome at Vicus Augustanus, it offered the same kind of opulent and luxurious life many other members of the Roman aristocracy enjoyed along the beautiful Campanian shore around Naples. In his letter regarding it, he describes its axial sequence of rooms, framed by views of the sea on one end and mountains on the other:

> There is an atrium at the entrance, simple but not drab, then a *porticus* in the shape of the letter "D" which surrounds a small but cheerful court. This makes a fine retreat in bad weather, being protected by windows and still more by the overhanging roof. Opposite the center is the cheerful *cavaedium,* and then a rather lovely *triclinium,* which runs out toward the shore and, when the sea is whipped up by the southwest wind, is lightly washed by the breaking waves. It has folding doors and windows of equal width so that on the sides and front it seems to command, as it were, three seas. At the rear it looks back through the *cavaedium,* with its colonnade,

the portico behind, and the atrium onto the woods and distant mountains.[14]

In addition, this luxurious retreat had a series of steam-heated bedrooms off the large dining room where one could retire for a nap after dinner. There were also a gymnasium, two steam rooms, hot and cold baths, a large swimming pool overlooking the sea, and a ball court. In a separate part of the villa, a towered suite contained another dining room with a view of the shoreline and other villas to the north, as well as several more heated bedrooms, presumably for guests. Many windows overlooked a terrace garden on the seaward side, and perhaps half as many opposite faced a flower and vegetable garden. Pliny's own favorite spot at this villa was the *heliocaminus,* a small heated sunroom where, even on a winter day, he could sunbathe. Adjacent to this amenity was a small suite of private rooms to which he could retire and enjoy the spectacular view in all directions.

Like wealthy people who today have vacation homes both at the beach and in the mountains, Pliny had, in addition to Laurentinum, Tusci, a villa in Tuscany on the southern slopes of the Apennines overlooking the Tiber. It was to this *villa urbana* that he went in the summer to study and write and, with the labor of slaves, to tend his vineyards and other crops. Here he could gaze at an "immense amphitheatre which only nature could create." There, as he described it:

> The broad plain is ringed by mountains on the crown of which are ancient stands of tall trees, and various kinds of hunting may be found there. . . . It is a voluptuous experience to look down on this scene from the mountain. You seem to be seeing not real land but rather a painted scene of exceptional beauty, and wherever the eye turns it is refreshed by its variety and precision.[15]

In this spectacular landscape, Pliny created a setting of elegance and luxury akin to that of his seaside villa. There were baths with pools of varying temperatures, comfortable bedrooms, dining suites, peristyle gardens, and promenades. In addition, there was a large hippodrome-shaped garden filled with evergreen and deciduous trees, including various kinds of fruit trees and boxwood topiary in all manner of shapes, probably including the owner's monogram, a popular practice in Pliny's day. In his letter describing his Tusci villa, Pliny mentions other features of this garden: obelisks, roses, and green lawns as well as a central section designed to imitate wild nature. At the curved end of the "hippodrome," there was a *stibadium,* or semicircular dining couch with water flowing beneath it. It faced a small pool that served

as a basin upon which servants floated dishes toward Pliny and his guests. Behind this arrangement stood a pavilion with a fountain in the center and an alcove bedroom. This one, open to the garden, was entirely faced with marble. It must have been pleasant to lie there in the filtered green light listening to the sounds of birds and the murmurous waters of the fountain.

VILLAS OF THE CAMPANIAN PLAIN

Several architects and historians have given graphic representation to Pliny's descriptions of his two villas, but the archaeological remains have not been identified. At the archaeological site of Oplontis, near Herculaneum on the slopes of Mount Vesuvius, however, one can visit an excavated villa near the coast of Campania that was built and remodeled between the first century B.C.E. and the eruption of 79 C.E. (fig. 2.37). The villa may once have been owned by the emperor Nero's second wife Poppaea Sabina, hence its name, the Villa of Poppaea.

At one end, a monumental pedimented door overlooks a large exterior ornamental garden. Root cavities in the garden reveal hedges, likely of box. Four *herms* were placed among plants, probably oleanders. There were, in addition, four sculptural fountains in the shape of centaurs. The villa also has an east wing in which were located four small interior gardens. The apparent size of these charming gardens was increased by wall paintings of vines, fountains, flowers, and birds (fig. 2.38).

Another attractive garden lies to the south of a large swimming pool measuring 56 feet in width and,

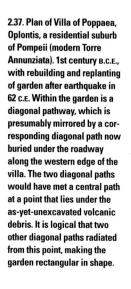

2.37. Plan of Villa of Poppaea, Oplontis, a residential suburb of Pompeii (modern Torre Annunziata). 1st century B.C.E., with rebuilding and replanting of garden after earthquake in 62 C.E. Within the garden is a diagonal pathway, which is presumably mirrored by a corresponding diagonal path now buried under the roadway along the western edge of the villa. The two diagonal paths would have met a central path at a point that lies under the as-yet-unexcavated volcanic debris. It is logical that two other diagonal paths radiated from this point, making the garden rectangular in shape.

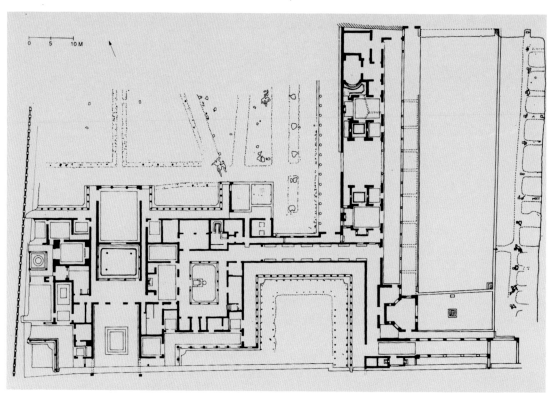

according to excavations to date, 165 feet in length (17 meters wide and more than 50 meters long). This garden could be enjoyed through the open windows of a *diaeta,* or livingroom, here designed specifically for enjoying framed views of horticultural or natural landscape vistas. To the east of the swimming pool, and a few feet below it, thirteen statuary bases have been discovered in a garden of uncertain extent. Root casts prove that some of the trees in this garden were lemon trees.

The Villa of Poppaea at Oplontis, like Pliny's Laurentinum and Tusci, shows that, by the first century C.E., the villa was less important as an agricultural establishment and instead was used increasingly as a place for *otium,* or refined leisure. In its extensive use of colonnaded porticoes on the outside and its opening of axes to embrace wide vistas beyond the villa itself, it demonstrates the same strong aesthetic appreciation of nature found in Pliny's letters.

Not far from Oplontis, still buried beneath the hard volcanic ash that covered Herculaneum and nearby parts of the Campanian plain, is the Villa of the Papyri, named for the more than two thousand charred scrolls that were discovered in 1754 in one part of its library. J. Paul Getty built his museum in Malibu, California, in the early 1970s using the plan drawn by Karl Weber, a Swiss engineer who oversaw the systematic excavation of the villa's rooms during the eighteenth century. For students of ancient gardens, this original Getty Museum provides an instructive modern replica of ancient villa design and gives one a feeling for the colorful ostentation of floors, walls, and ceilings of such villas before time and catastrophe took their toll. There is an inner peristyle gar-

den modeled after the one built in the first phase of the villa's construction during the second century B.C.E., as well as a much larger peristyle garden that copies the one added in the following century. Within the latter, set within the boxwood compartments surrounding a 218-foot- (66.5-meter-) long pool, are replicas of many of the statues that Weber found.

THE GROTTO OF TIBERIUS

Unfortunately for posterity, there are few other remains from the great villa-building period of the first century C.E., when the economic prosperity and security of the empire made this kind of construction possible. However, one such villa, a fascinating combination of water, sculpture, and outdoor entertaining, has come to light in recent years: the so-called Grotto of Tiberius at Sperlonga along the Via Flacca, the shore road between Terracina and Gaeta, famous for its villas. Uncovered around 1960 during the course of highway construction, the villa, which incorporates into its plan a natural seaside cave, provides a provocative glimpse of the pleasures enjoyed by wealthy Romans in imperial times.

It is also a testament to the fact that by this period the grotto's function as a holy place was only a dim legacy from the days when people made pilgrimages to cave sanctuaries to worship in nature. Sophisticated Romans now preferred to treat landscape in terms of a poetic and theatrical ideal. Why should not a real grotto serve as the setting for the enactment in sculpture of a favorite Homeric tale, Odysseus's visit to the cave of the one-eyed giant Polyphemus?

Odysseus and his men, imprisoned by the Cyclops in his cave, saved themselves by ramming a sharpened stake into the drunken monster's single eye. This part of the Odysseus legend formed the theme of an elaborate decoration of the Sperlonga grotto, whose builder is assumed, on the basis of a fragmentary inscription, to have been one Faustinus, a landowner and friend of the poet Martial who lived in the second half of the first century C.E. The cave and its adjacent *villa marittima* are close to the scarred cliff face where, according to the Roman historians Tacitus and Suetonius, a huge chunk of rock overhanging the entrance to the cave suddenly broke off and fell during a banquet, endangering the life of Tiberius (ruled 14–37 C.E.) and thereby conferring on posterity the association of this emperor's name with the grotto.

The grotto at Sperlonga is a purposeful extension of Hellenistic theatricality through a dramatic combination of landscape, architecture, and sculpture. The cave, hollowed from the cliff by wave action, has been extended architecturally into the landscape (fig. 2.39). Its mouth formerly originated on a spur of the rocky cliff into which was set a huge Hellenistic

2.39. Reconstructed plan, after Eugenia Salza Prina Ricotti. The outlines of the original overhanging entrance to the cave are defined by line **X**–**Y**. The Polyphemus sculptural group was set within the stony ledge of the back of the cave **A**. Ricotti has also deduced that the round pool **B** represented Charybdis, the eddy that helped Scylla destroy seafarers, and that a lateral grotto **C** was used alternatively as an additional triclinium, a stage upon which actors, dancers, and musicians could entertain the banqueters, and as a place where guests could assemble and refresh themselves before or after a party. There are, in addition, three alcoves **D** to which sated diners could retire for a nap.

Right: **2.40.** Polyphemus group, Sperlonga Museum. 1st century C.E. More than 7,000 marble fragments have been discovered at Sperlonga, the most important of which belong to several large sculptural compositions depicting various episodes from Homer's *Odyssey.* Four such groupings have been identified: *Odysseus Rescuing Achilles's Corpse,* placed at the mouth of the cave; *Odysseus with Diomedes and the Palladion,* to the right of this scene; the wreck of *Odysseus's Ship Encountering Scylla,* set in the circular pool; and the *Blinding of Polyphemus* (shown here), naturalistically positioned inside the grotto to the south of the pool.

Below: **2.41.** Island *triclinium,* Sperlonga. 1st century C.E.

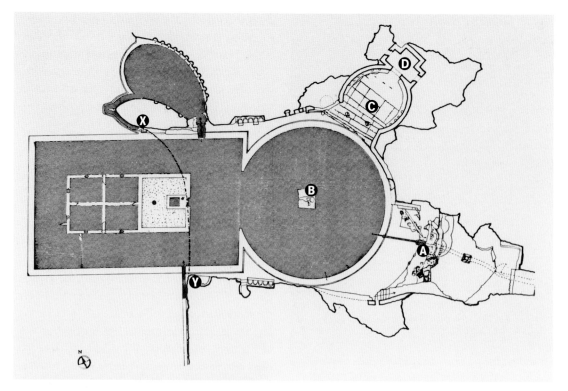

sculptural composition depicting Odysseus's ship trying to pass through the Strait of Messina, where the sea monster Scylla lay in wait to ensnare travelers in its snakelike coils. This work and others from the grotto have been attributed to Agesander, Athenodorus, and Polydorus, the three Rhodian sculptors who are believed to have created *Laocöon and His Sons,* that famous work of Hellenistic sculpture now in the Museo Pio Clementino, one of the Vatican museums. Stylistically, there is certainly a resemblance in the forceful bodies, violent movement, and anguished

expressions characteristic of these pieces. But whereas the *Laocöon* group is nearly intact, the Polyphemus sculptures were badly smashed by zealous Christians when they erected a medieval church on the site. A small museum now houses some of their fragments and several small, charming late Hellenistic sculptures of children that may have decorated the sides of fountains and pools (fig. 2.40).

A *triclinium* for outdoor banqueting stood in the center of a fish pond. The Romans were passionately fond of ornamental fish and, in addition to keeping fish as pets, they also had ponds that served as holding tanks for the table. Today the water level of the pond has lowered, and one can clearly see the holes for rock fish in its sides as well as the island *triclinium* where the dining couches were raised above the water upon which servants floated dishes to the recumbent guests (fig. 2.41). This luxurious resort gives one an idea of the wealth of the Roman Empire. But if we are impressed by Faustinus's standard of living and style of entertaining, we are awestruck when we contemplate the remains of the second-century C.E. villa at Tivoli.

HADRIAN'S VILLA

Since the sixteenth century, tourists, artists, architects, and archaeologists have been fascinated by the spectral ruins of Hadrian's Villa. Set where the hilly slopes and precipitous gorges cut by the river Aniene, the principal tributary of the Tiber, meet the rolling Campagna plain below the town of Tivoli (Tibur in Roman times), Hadrian's Villa is estimated to have been approximately 300 acres (120 hectares), or slightly more than one-third the size of New York City's Central Park. This sprawling complex of broken vaults, collapsed domes, crumbling mosaic pavements, and fractured columns, covers an undulating terrain defined by two valleys with a southeast-northwest orientation. It was built between 118 and 138 C.E., the year of Hadrian's death. Although he was abroad for several extended periods during its construction (a philhellene, he spent the winters of 124/125 C.E. and 131/132 C.E. in Athens), it may be assumed that Hadrian often thought about the project as he commissioned copies of ancient sculptures from Greek artists or corresponded with his architects on various aspects of the villa's design.

In plan and scale it suggests something far grander than the usual villa (fig. 2.42). The ruins are those of large banqueting halls and gardens, theaters and baths, grottoes and pools, private apartments, and quarters for many servants and guests. Hadrian's Villa has sometimes been compared with Louis XIV's seventeenth-century gardens at Versailles. Similarities include the grandeur and scale of each project, both rulers' desire for a court setting away from the capital, and their personal involvement in the design process. Both used the landscape as a lavish entertainment site and as a means of advertising the richness and depth of their respective cultures. There is, however, a notable design difference. Hierarchical axes order the composition of the gardens of Versailles; Hadrian's Villa, on the other hand, has no principal organizing axis, but rather a series of independent ones that sometimes collide obliquely. Its general plan comprises several independently organized building and garden complexes, each of which embodies the Aristotelian notion of place—*topos*—as defined and contained space. To infer that Hadrian's Villa is simply a series of discrete *topoi* and had no overall plan, however, is erroneous. Extensive terracing and a complex infrastructure of underground service routes extending over a large portion of the site indicate a comprehensive vision from the start.

Though heavily ransacked for building materials in the Middle Ages and robbed by Renaissance popes and connoisseurs of much of its opulent decoration of carved marble, gilded bronze, and ornamental fountains, the villa is nonetheless a text that, with the assistance of recent scholarship, can be read as the summation of imperial Roman architectural expression.[16] More than that, it can be understood as a brilliant essay in Greco-Roman bonding, for Hadrian, as we have seen, greatly admired Greek culture and was responsible for the civic revival of Athens.

Although it pays tribute to the greatness of the Classical past, the villa was for Hadrian a laboratory of architectural innovation. He had the educated eye of a well-traveled connoisseur and oversaw with great particularity the designs he commissioned. Like a present-day theme park, it was eclectically programmed. But unlike a theme park, which is designed to nourish the fantasies of popular culture, Hadrian's Villa was the product of intense personal passion and extensive scholarship. It was a vast and glittering private landscape of allusion filled with indirect references to other places and events in the panoramic sweep of empire as well as to the gods, goddesses, and heroes of the Greco-Roman pantheon. Because the emperor was under no constraint to conform to normative building conventions and was therefore able to push Roman design idioms to expressive heights, the villa should be read as his personal building project, one in which his taste and decisions governed even minute details of decoration as well as creative new spatial volumetrics.

Like his predecessor, Nero, Hadrian disliked the old imperial palaces on Rome's Palatine Hill. But whereas Nero had tried to build his fabulous Domus Aurea, or Golden House, in the center of Rome, causing the populace to revolt because of his indiscriminate expropriations of property, Hadrian chose to carry on his immense building project away from the public eye. Seventeen miles east of Rome, Tivoli was already populated with the kind of aristocratic villas described by Pliny. Most of these were located on the hilly slopes overlooking the Campagna plain, where the Aniene cut a steep gorge and dropped in a dramatic waterfall.

Hadrian did not, as might have been expected, choose a site for the villa on the wooded heights of Tivoli. Rather, he located it on the flat land 2½ miles below the town. This choice, less cool and less inherently scenic than such sites as that of the steeply pitched Renaissance Villa d'Este in the heart of Tivoli, can be explained by the fact that the finest land above was already occupied and a prior villa in the lower location may have been the property of Hadrian's wife, Sabina. The location may also be explained by the ease with which water could be furnished in copious amounts from one of the four aqueducts traversing this region en route to metropolitan Rome.

More than a country retreat, Hadrian's villa is a thematic summation of the philhellenic emperor's meditation upon the vast, rich, mature civilization over which he ruled. A feat of Roman engineering requiring monumental earth-moving, terracing, and the laying of water lines and other necessary elements of infrastructure, the villa admirably served Hadrian's objective: to create a park that was its own allusive, experiential place of history and cultural memory, an idealized statement of the Greco-Roman heritage. He achieved this through a series of loosely linked

HADRIAN'S VILLA

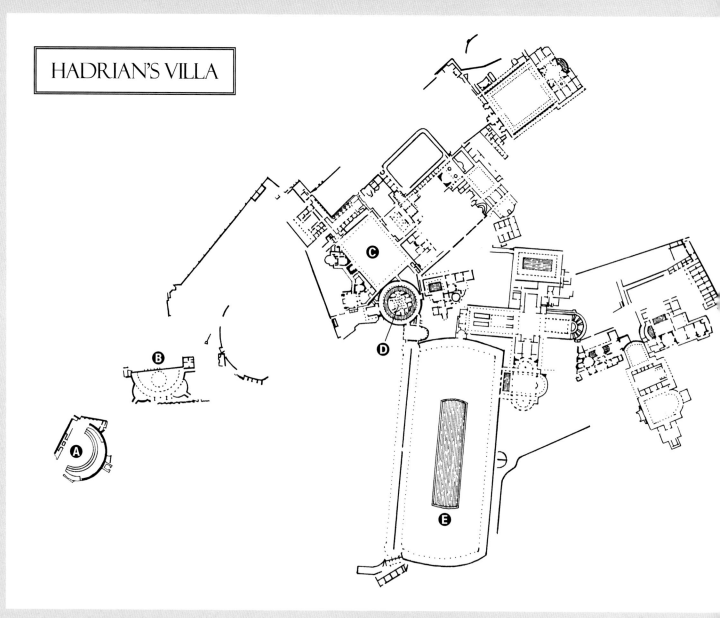

2.42. Plan of Hadrian's Villa, Tivoli. 118–138 c.e.
Ⓐ North Theater. Ⓑ Temple of Venus. Ⓒ Library Court. Ⓓ *Nymphaeum* (Marine Theater). Ⓔ Peristyle Pool. Ⓕ Canopus

2.43. Semi-circular Dining Couch (*stibadium*), Canopus, Hadrian's Villa

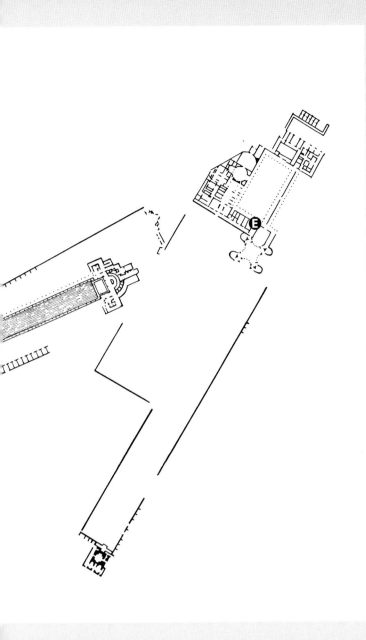

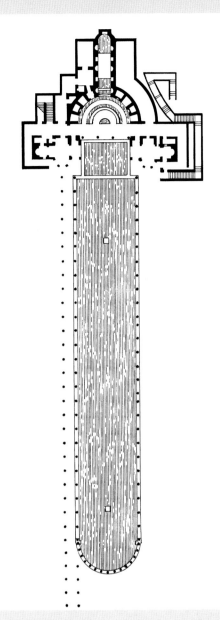

2.44. Plan of Scenic Canal and *Triclinium*, also called the Canopus. 118–138 C.E. The northwest end of the canal is semicircular. Sculptures placed between columns and pergolas lined the long sides of this canal set within a draw with steep terraced embankments. Its axis was terminated in the large half-dome at the southeast end. This impressive structure, its interior wall once encrusted with mosaic and undulating in a series of alternating radial gores, served as the backdrop for a *stibadium,* a semicircular dining couch (fig. 2.43). This *stibadium* was rimmed with water, and circular sockets near its base held bronze serving tables. In front of it was space for additional wooden dining couches; these faced a semicircular pool upon which servants floated banquet dishes.

A honeycomb of small chambers lightened the structure of the canopied vault. The eight at the lower level are faced on the inside of the vault with niches, four

for sculpture and four for sets of miniature stairs designed to animate the flow of small water cascades within them. These alternating pairs were interrupted in the center of the vault by an arched opening. Here, barely visible from a distance, the principal axis of the entire Canal-*Triclinium* landscape composition drives to its apsidal conclusion in the hillside in a brilliantly conceived grotto. A stone platform, accessible through a series of side chambers, carries one into this *nymphaeum,* the walls of which have niches for sculpture. Only the area above the platform is roofed with a barrel vault, leaving two large openings for light to enter this deeply recessed chamber.

Water channeled by twin aqueduct spurs flowed into the grotto, filling the pools beneath the stone platform. Distributed through a system of pipes, the water cascaded over marble and mosaic and into other channels and pools until it reached the canal.

2.45. "Marine Theater," Hadrian's Villa. 118–138 C.E.

architectural "events" in which experience was heightened by sequential discovery. These consisted of a number of centrally focused landscapes framed by spatially complex monumental architecture, such as that of the Scenic Canal and Triclinium, often called the Canopus,[17] a long, partially colonnaded canal terminated by a large hooded vault near the Vestibule, or main entrance hall, which served as a dramatic banqueting setting (figs. 2.45, 2.46). No certain assignment of function has been made for the Island Enclosure, a canal-and-column-encircled space of ingenious design that for many years bore the conventional label "Marine Theater," but its ornamentation, like that of the Canopus, was planned according to a program of allusion that exemplified cosmopolitan Roman culture and its Greek antecedents (fig. 2.44). While serving this thematic end, the villa was also the equivalent of a contemporary spa hotel. There were exercise facilities for both staff and guests, and two baths, similar in design to Roman metropolitan ones with their sequence of hot, warm, and cold pools and rooms for oiling and massage.

Many of the connective elements that knit these parts into a comprehensive framework—colonnades, pergolas, paths, and planting—can only be guessed at today. A wealth of ornament and decorative detail, also vanished, helped to unite the whole into an artistic harmony. There were shimmering mosaics and surfaces of richly inlaid marble and a host of sculptural figures in marble and bronze. Hadrian, in addition to being a creative architectural thinker, was a connoisseur and patron of artists, owning a vast number of ancient Greek marbles and Roman copies of famous Greek sculptures. Sculptures of reclining river gods adorned the villa's many water gardens, and there were statues depicting Diana as mythological huntress and as a fertility goddess. Images of Perseus, Bacchus, Orpheus, Apollo, and other figures from classical mythology joined representations of Hadrian's beloved Antinous, who was portrayed in various godlike guises. These, with portrait busts of Hadrian himself, were probably placed in niches or beside some of the numerous garden paths of the villa.

The most important unifying factor is the one we miss most today: water. Hydraulic engineers were responsible for the fountains, pools, and canals that animated space with sky-reflecting mirrors of light. Standing at the Canopus today, we can only imagine the spectacle this part of Hadrian's Villa presented when, with light playing on the curved and undulating surface of the moist, glittering, mosaic-covered half-dome and sparkling on the gently moving water of the canal, the most powerful ruler on earth looked out upon the proconsuls, ambassadors, and other dignitaries of the Roman Empire whose banqueting couches were arrayed before him.

Besides its function as place of entertainment, Hadrian's Villa served as a residence and place where the affairs of empire were dispatched. An original villa residence predating Hadrian's purchase of the property was extensively revised to serve as imperial living quarters, and, inasmuch as the business of government followed the emperor wherever he went, the imperial secretariat required offices. Viewing structures, an East Belvedere and a West Belvedere, which overlooked valleys on respective sides of the property, served as scenic observation points and may have been destinations for conversational strolling.

For our purposes here—the discussion of landscape as an expression of cultural values—attention should be drawn to two parts of the villa: the "Vale of Tempe" with its Doric Temple overlooking the eastern valley at the northern end of the property, and the incompletely excavated high ground that is in private ownership, where the South Theater and a network of underground tunnels exist. Modern scholars believe that the steep gorge in the eastern valley of the villa grounds, which was further deepened through quarrying operations, memorialized the Vale of Tempe near Mount Olympus in northeastern Greece.[18] Dramatically situated above this beautiful spot, overlooking the wider landscape framed by the Tiburtine Hills, stands a small, circular, open-sided Doric garden temple enclosing a Roman copy of Praxiteles' famous statue of Aphrodite of Knidos (fig. 2.46). It was not a temple in any religious sense, but rather an ornamental structure framed by a large *nymphaeum* (now vanished), the whole composition forming an architectural tribute to a poetically venerated Greek landscape.

At the opposite end of the villa grounds was the South Theater, which, according to a recent thesis advanced by William L. MacDonald and John A. Pinto, may have accommodated the Eleusinian rites based upon the legend of Demeter and Persephone.[19] These mysteries, symbolizing immortality of the human soul as well as the annual cycle of death and rebirth in nature, were performed at Eleusis near Athens and involved ritual descent into the Underworld domain of the god Hades. An elaborate network of tunnels connects with the theater, whose complicated infrastructure exceeds the needs of ordinary drama. MacDonald and Pinto have suggested that ritual participants may have descended from the stage into these subterranean passages in an initiation ceremony. If this is correct, we may conclude that the replication of the experience one had at a famous religious center outside Athens within an artfully contrived landscape of the Roman Campagna demonstrates that spiritual objectives previously met in unique natural environments to which one made pilgrimage could now be found in synthetic ones built to recall them.

The villa's role as a "themed" environment, one enriched by imaginative association with other renowned places, can best be understood in terms of a shift in the relationship between humans and landscape. In the cosmopolitan milieu of the Late Roman Empire it was natural that theatrical versions of earlier myth-impregnated environments should be constructed. Then, as later in history, the garden or park landscape provided an ideal setting for such imaginative re-creations.

We have seen how the concept of landscape was transformed in antiquity from one in which form directly referenced elements of Earth and sky in an expression of cosmological belief to one in which symbols and the mimesis of other locales set in motion within the human imagination certain ideas and associations. We have seen, too, how urban order came to assume a far greater importance relative to the natural order than was true in the centuries of prehistory and early antiquity.

The allegorization of landscape was perhaps the most important and lasting contribution that the Late Roman villa designers bequeathed to posterity. The "theming" of a passage from Homer, as at Sperlonga, wed landscape to literature in a striking tableau; here nature served as stage set, a theater for fantasy. The simulated Hades at Hadrian's Villa was a "virtual reality" experience of its day in which emotion was manipulated toward a religious end—if the subterranean galleries there were indeed used in celebrating the Eleusinian mysteries. Landscape had thus become something both more and less than nature. It now was space to be assigned programmatic content rather than place pregnant with intrinsic meaning. Henceforth, landscape design—though sometimes purely functional or aesthetic in intent or merely imitative of earlier models—was imbued with a narrative impulse. The narrative motive still prevails today in commercial theme parks and certain self-theming historic districts, villages, and old urban centers. Concepts of space and time are continually revised through the agencies of intellect and imagination. History has become a potent source of imagery as population growth and powerful Industrial Age technologies threaten both nature and the built past as never before. Hadrian's Villa is thus ancestor to numerous replications of geographically distant and temporally remote places in landscape design history, including the themed environments of today.

Ironically, at the same time that landscape was being domesticated and drained of the divinity that it had long embodied at various sacred sites in nature, allegory stood ready to put it into the service of two

religious movements: Christianity and Islam. The use of water, sculpture, mosaic, and plants to evoke a spiritual or poetic mood; the interpenetration of indoor and outdoor spaces; a growing interest in architectural siting; a sensuous appreciation of light, color, and sound; topiary design and practice—these are some of the things that Roman landscape designers bequeathed to future generations. Where they occupied former parts of the Roman Empire, Islamic garden designers incorporated some classical elements into their plans, blending them with their heritage from Persia. But in the Christian West, life was thoroughly transformed in the centuries following the fall of Rome and before the Renaissance. There no one any longer built villas with sybaritic bathing pools and gardens populated by mythological figures. Nor were there any luxurious town houses with indoor plumbing and gaily decorated fountains. *Triclinia* beneath vine-clad pergolas for long summer dinners disappeared.

Although luxury and license remained a prerogative of the aristocratic elite in Christian lands, people increasingly turned their eyes heavenward, and some exceptional monks even refused to eat the fruit they grew for fear of breaking their austere Christian vows. The worldly emphasis on three-dimensional space in architecture and painting was lost, but some of the old building forms, notably the peristyle garden, were too intrinsic a part of a basic building vocabulary to vanish completely. Most important, perhaps, the principal gardens after the fall of Rome were no longer gardens in reality, but images of the earthly paradise that existed before the biblical fall of humankind or of the heavenly kingdom where the blessed could attain fruitful ease after the travails of this life.

2.46. Doric Temple, "Vale of Tempe," Hadrian's Villa. 118–138 C.E. This temple and its picturesque landscape, which echoes in form the larger nearby Temple of Vesta overlooking the dramatic gorge of the river Aniene, was the ancestor of many similar garden temples. The *tholos*, or circular temple, became a standard feature in Western garden design of the eighteenth century and a common ornament in the nineteenth-century public park.

Notes for Chapter Two

1. The term *classicism* appears throughout this book. It refers to the human impulse in all the arts to create through a process of intellect—rather than by intuition, emotion, or sensory association—an ideal vision that by its nobility, authority, rationality, and harmonious order serves as a paradigm for imitation. These qualities are thought to have characterized the art and general culture of ancient Greece and much of ancient Rome, sources of inspiration to other cultures throughout history. Classicism thus respects tradition over innovation. In architecture and landscape architecture, classicism implies participation in a tradition of measurability and mathematical precision as expressed in balanced, geometrical lines and forms and symmetry, as opposed to irregularity and asymmetry. When the word is capitalized within a sentence, it refers to a specific period, seen by historians as mature and pivotal within a stylistic development. Examples include: the art of Greece in the last three-quarters of the fifth century B.C.E., or the art created in Renaissance Italy from about 1505 to about 1525. *Neoclassicism* refers to any of the many revival idioms that evoke the balance, order, symmetry, and stylistic simplicity of classicism, often imitating in period design or detail a style considered as Classical. For example, the Beaux-Arts style in American architecture and landscape design in the years around 1900 is neoclassical, being derived from the École des Beaux-Arts in Paris, which based its curriculum upon the principles of French seventeenth-century design; in turn, those traced their origin to the Italian Renaissance and to the Classical monuments in Roman architecture.

2. An excellent explication of this thesis is to be found in François de Polignac, *Cults, Territory, and the Origins of the Greek City-State,* trans. Janet Lloyd (Chicago: University of Chicago Press, 1995).

3. Indra Kagis McEwen draws upon Polignac's text, *La naissance de la cité greque* (Paris: 1984) in *Socrates' Ancestor: An Essay on Architectural Beginnings* (Cambridge, Massachusetts: MIT Press, 1993) to extrapolate the metaphor of the *polis* as "a surface woven by the activity of its inhabitants: the sequential building of sanctuaries over a period of time, which at times stretched over decades, and the subse-quent ritual processions from center to urban limit to territorial limit and back again, in what can be seen as a kind of Ariadne's dance, magnified to cover a territory that was not called *choros* but *chora,*" p. 81.

4. "To Pythian Apollo," *Hesiod: The Homeric Hymns and Homerica,* trans. H. G. Evelyn-White, Loeb Classical Library (Cambridge, Massachusetts: Harvard University Press, 1914), p. 345. Apollo's slaying of the snake may be read as symbolizing the supplanting of the powerful snake-wielding earth goddess with a male divinity associated with the sky. The god's association with light, and hence with human reason, is underlined by the fact that acccording to the hymn "on that spot the power of piercing Helios [the sun god] made the monster rot away." Thus, according to Vincent Scully, "Delphi must therefore have seemed to the Greeks the place where the conflict between the old way, that of the goddess of the earth, and the new way, that of men and their Olympian gods, was most violently manifest," an association he believes to be implied as well in the siting of the temple on a ledge beneath the horn-like, sky-piercing peaks of the Phaedriades, which tower over the temple and the adjacent the gorge from which flows the sacred Kastalian Spring. See Vincent Scully, *The Earth, the Temple, and the Gods: Greek Sacred Architecture* (New Haven: Yale University Press, rev. ed., 1979), p. 109.

5. The Golden Section is achieved by the division of a plane figure or a line in such a way that the smaller section or linear segment bears the same proportrate relationship to the larger as the larger does to the sum of the two, giving a ratio of approximately three to five. This ratio can also be expressed as a quotient of approximately 1.618 when the larger integer is divided by the smaller.

6. Aristotle, *Politics,* Book VII: 5. In *The Complete Works of Aristotle: The Revised Oxford Translation,* ed. Jonathan Barnes (Princeton: Princeton University Press, 1984), vol. 2, pp. 2105–06.

7. *Politics,* Book VII: 11, vol. 2, pp. 2111–12.

8. Polignac, *Cults, Territory, and the Origins of the Greek City-State,* p. 76.

9. Ibid., chap. 3.

10. See John Travlos, *Pictorial Dictionary of Ancient Athens* (New York: Praeger, 1971), pp. 1–29, for text and plates showing the evolution and transformations of the Athenian Agora from the sixth century B.C.E. to the fifth century C.E.

11. See John M. Camp, *The Athenian Agora: Excavations in the Heart of Classical Athens* (London: Thames and Hudson, 1986), pp. 35–38.

12. Spiro Kostoff, *The City Shaped: Urban Patterns and Meanings Through History* (Boston: Little, Brown and Company, 1991), p. 229.

13. Vitruvius, *De Architectura,* Book VII, Chapter V, sec. 2, trans. Frank Granger, Loeb Classical Library, *Vitruvius* Vol. II (Cambridge, Massachusetts: Harvard University Press, 1934), p. 103.

14. See *The Letters of Pliny,* A. N. Sherwin-White, trans. (Oxford: Oxford University Press, 1966), pp. 186–99. A *porticus* is a colonnaded gallery or portico. A *cavaedium* is an open quadrangular court formed by the inner walls of the house. The word *triclinium* is used to mean a U-shaped arrangement of three dining couches, a dining room, or garden area for outdoor dining.

15. Ibid., pp. 321–30.

16. As explained in Chapter Four, in the sixteenth century, Pirro Ligorio, architect to Pope Pius IV and Cardinal Ippolito d'Este, appreciated Hadrian's Villa as an archaeological site, excavating many works of art there, which he subsequently used to embellish villa gardens of his own design, including that of the nearby Villa d'Este.

17. The label Canopus for the Scenic Canal derives from the *Historia Augusta,* a none-too-reliable late-fourth-century collection of imperial biographies: "[Hadrian] fashioned the Tiburtine Villa marvelously, in such a way that he might inscribe there the names of provinces and places most famous and could call [certain parts], for instance, the Lyceum, the Academy, the Prytaneum, Canopus, the Poecile, the [Vale of] Tempe. And in order to omit nothing, he even made an underworld." For a comprehensive inquiry into the assignment of this name to the Scenic Canal and Triclinium see William L. MacDonald and John A. Pinto, *Hadrian's Villa and Its Legacy* (New Haven: Yale University Press, 1995), pp. 6–7 and pp. 108–11.

18. Ibid., p. 59.

19. Ibid., pp. 124–38.

VISIONS OF PARADISE:
LANDSCAPE DESIGN AS SYMBOL AND METAPHOR

Rooted in human responses to the environment in all historical cultures is a deep-seated recognition of the manifold imperfections of this world and a deep longing to re-create a lost place or time where and when life perpetually flourishes, death is unknown, there are no harsh extremes of climate, and no backbreaking toil to grow food and haul water, fear is replaced by law, chaos is vanquished by order, and warfare ceases forever in a perpetual reign of peace. Most of the world's myths—biblical, classical, Islamic, early Christian, medieval, Chinese—expound this theme.

The word *paradise* is derived from the Persian *pairidaeza,* signifying a royal hunting park or orchard enclosed by walls (fig. 3.1).[1] Paradise, both as a literary topos and as a realized garden, is ideologically divorced from the world and physically separated from it. It is not outwardly expansive and space-embracing, but rather spatially contained and inward-focused. This mythical paradise is, in the Judeo-Christian tradition, a place where humans and animals enjoy a vegetarian bounty and do not prey on one another. The Islamic tradition adds to this benign and secure environment, where the blessed enjoy fruitful ease, such sensory delights as delectable food, wine, music, fragrance, and erotic love.

It is important not to overemphasize the paradise metaphor at the expense of certain mundane considerations such as topography, climate, or the representation of the beneficent power of a ruler to fructify the local landscape. Nevertheless, the paradise image—a bountiful, geometrically ordered, enclosed space in which water is typically made to flow in four directions, emanating from and sometimes returning to a central source—is the common paradigm for expressing multiple associations, both religious and secular, in actual Islamic and Western medieval gardens. Such gardens can be found in Muslim lands extending from Mughal India to Moorish Spain and elsewhere in Europe as the *hortus conclusus,* the enclosed garden, depicted in Christian medieval manuscripts, tapestries, and woodcuts and exemplified in the cloister gardens of monasteries and churches. The visions of paradise as manifested both in actual gardens and in the art of these cultures all imply a reordering of the things of this world to create an idealized and rationally organized environment. Similarly, the notion of paradise as a systematic arrangement of all created plant species underlies the layouts of Renaissance botanical gardens.

It is difficult now to imagine how harsh and unfriendly the natural world once seemed and equally impossible to conceive the fear people once had of wilderness. The impulse to romanticize wild nature as expressed in a more naturalistic approach to garden-making—an approach that implies paradoxically a relatively high level of technological confidence and economic dominion over nature—was completely foreign to the cultural milieus in which true paradise gardens were created. Romanticism as an attitude and the design ideas that flow from it date only from the latter part of the eighteenth century. Although the word "paradise" is often used loosely to denote any garden that is in essence idyllic, the garden symbolizing paradise as it is described in the Quran and the Bible is almost always nature (including human nature) tamed, domesticated, and regulated. According to the Judaeo-Christian view, paradise is a paradigm not only for the garden but also for the just city and the holy man or woman whose well-ordered existence symbolizes obedience to the laws of God. Before examining some actual landscapes that were intended to portray the order, tranquillity, bounty, and freedom from want and care that two world religions, Islam and Christianity, associate with paradise, we should enrich our understanding of paradise as a literary topos. This will help us to understand the important new role that landscape design came to play as a means of creating representational space, places in which symbols evoked ideas and ideals other than those of a purely paradisiacal nature.

I. Paradise as a Literary Topos:
Gardens of God and Gardens of Love

3.1. Detail of *Bahram Gur Pins the Coupling Onagers,* miniature from Shah Tahmasp's *Shah-nama (Book of Kings),* folio 568 recto. Painted by Mir Sayyid Ali, c. 1533–35. Tabriz, Persia. Ink, opaque watercolor, and gold on paper. The Metropolitan Museum of Art, New York. Gift of Arthur A. Houghton, Jr., 1970 (1970.301.62)

Garden of Eden

The price of disobedience, as readers of Genesis know, is expulsion from paradise. In this account, the newly made Earth was devoid of all vegetation because there was no creature to till it and no rain, but rather a flood rising up out of the ground, irrigating its barren plains.

> Then the Lord God planted a garden in Eden away to the east, and there he put the man whom he had formed. The Lord God made trees spring from the ground, all trees pleasant to look at and good for food; and in the middle of the garden he set the tree of life and the tree of good and evil.[2]

This laconic account gives us very few visual details with which to flesh out this imaginary "first" garden. We are told, however, that "there was a river flowing from Eden to water the garden, and when it left the garden it branched into four streams."[3]

Of the Hebrew and Christian vision of heaven the Bible gives us even less scenic description, and

there have been but few representations in the rich inventory of Western religious art to suggest its physical attributes. The idea, however, of a middle place marked by the presence of the Tree of Life and the Tree of Good and Evil, with four streams flowing away from it, presumably in the four cardinal directions, echoes in biblical terms the cosmological diagram familiar to us from other prehistoric cultures of a vertical *axis mundi* with four horizontal axes extending to the east, west, north, and south points of the horizon. Irrigation runnels laid out according to a quadripartite pattern such as this must have occurred in some arid parts of the Ancient Near East where agriculture was first practiced.

Classical Paradises

The longevity and the universality of visions signified by the word *paradise* are evident from many descriptions in classical literature. Homer created an image of the garden as a paradisiacal reward for valor in his description of the Elysian Fields in the *Odyssey.* Here Menelaus receives the news that

> the gods intend you for Elysion
> with golden Rhadamanthos at the world's end,
> where all existence is a dream of ease.
> Snowfall is never known there, nor long
> frost of winter, nor torrential rain,
> but only mild and lulling airs from Ocean
> bearing refreshment for the souls of men—
> the West Wind always blowing.[4]

The *Odyssey* also contains Homer's famous description of the paradisiacal orchard of Alcinous, which "long-suffering Odysseus stood admiring" before entering the house of his host:

> There tall trees grow luxuriantly, pears
> and pomegranates, apples bright with fruit,
> delicious figs, and flowering olive trees.
> Their fruit can never fail nor ever perish,
> winter or summer, all year long, for always
> Zephyr blows, nurturing some and ripening others.
> Apple on apple, pear on pear matures,
> fig upon fig, and grape on clustered grape.
> A vineyard rich in fruit is rooted there:
> part is spread out on level ground to dry
> in sunlight, part is harvested at vintage,
> and part they trample. Unripe grapes in front
> shed flowers while the others slowly darken.
> By the last row, well-ordered garden plots

grow bountiful fresh greens of every kind.
Two springs flow, one dispersed throughout the
garden,
the other gushing from the courtyard, near
the towering house where townsfolk come for
water.[5]

Myths of Rhadamanthos, Elysion, the Blessed
Isles, the distant east (or west), and magical mountaintops—places impossibly remote for ordinary travelers to reach—were prevalent until the late fifteenth
century, when Europeans discovered and explored
vast areas of the planet that had long been *terra incog-
nita* in their minds. Before this time the hopeful belief
persisted that physical paradise was an actual faraway
realm where one might be transported under the
right conditions. Along with this ideal of a terrestrial
paradise, which might be discovered by far-voyaging
mariners, was the notion in classical literature, paralleling the story of the Fall of Man in Genesis, of the
lost paradise of a vanished Golden Age.

The Greek poet Hesiod's eighth-century B.C.E.
masterpiece, *Works and Days,* articulates both concepts. His version of the Prometheus and Pandora
myths helps explain the hard lot of humankind, condemned to wrestle with the obdurate earth to grow
the crops that sustain life, after having first known
freedom from want. *Works and Days* also gave Greeks
a sense of their descent from a race of heroes. It elab-
orates a series of ages of diminishing ease, physical
accomplishment, and nobility of heart and mind: a
Golden Age, a Silver Age, a Bronze Age, and a current Age of Iron, an age of warfare and unremitting
labor. Other cultures have mythologized similar
epochs of regressive human well-being. Hesiod,
however, honors the remembrance of Mycenaean
glory and the epic tradition of the Dark Age immor-
talized by Homer and inserts, between his Bronze
Age and the present difficult Iron Age, an Age of
Heroes, those legendary warrior kings who con-
sorted with the gods in the *Iliad* and the *Odyssey.*

War and carnage propelled many of these
heroes to their doom,
Yet others of them father Zeus, son of Kronos,
settled at earth's ends,
apart from men, and gave them shelter and
food.
They lived there with hearts unburdened by
cares
in the islands of the blessed, near stormy
Okeanos,
these blissful heroes for whom three times a year
the barley-giving land brings forth full grain
sweet as honey.[6]

The Greek lyric poet Pindar (c. 522–c. 443 B.C.E.)
later developed the theme of a vanished epoch when
people lived in innocence and knew no hardship or
sorrow. Among the Roman poets, Virgil (70–19 B.C.E.)
offered a prophetic vision of a new Golden Age under
Emperor Augustus, while Ovid (43 B.C.E.–17 C.E.)
looked back nostalgically on a bygone time of simple
rustic happiness.

In addition to their temporal images of a previous era of peace and plenty, the spatial concepts of
faraway Elysian Fields and Blessed Isles provided consoling visions of an afterlife for the deserving. These
two visions, one of an ancient time of bounteousness
and tranquillity, the other of a just reward after death,
are akin to the two Christian usages of the term *paradise* to signify a prelapsarian Garden of Eden and a
post-Resurrection home for the faithful in heaven.

By the fifth century, the Christian vision of paradise had been appropriated by the late classical
Carthaginian poet Blossius Aemilius Dracontius who
described it thus:

A place there is from which four rivers flow,
painted with jeweled turf and deathless flowers,
full of sweet-scented, never-fading herbs,
happiest garden in God's universe.[7]

Alcimus Ecdicius Avitus, bishop of Vienna from c. 490
to 518, draws on well-established tradition in his *De
Spiritalis Historiae Gestis,* locating paradise

East of the Indies, where the world begins,
where earth and sky are said to meet together.

Paradise for Avitus is a place where

temperate climes preserve eternal spring;
rough winds are absent, under sunny skies
clouds yield to unremittingly clear weather.
The nature of the place requires no rain,
for grasses thrive contentedly on dew.
The ground is always green, earth's smiling face
radiates warmth; plants grow on hills forever,
and leaves on trees: for though they burst in
flower often, swift sap invigorates their buds.[8]

Muslim Paradise

The Quran, the book of divine wisdom derived from
the Hebrew Bible and revealed to Muhammad by
God in the sixth century C.E., has four rivers emanating from paradise as in Genesis. Here, however,
the rivers are more metaphorical than geographical,
eternally flowing streams of milk and purified honey.
The Quran dwells on the luxury and opulence of paradise, the prize for the godly. There the blessed,

dressed in robes of silk, will be rewarded:

> Reclining upon soft couches, they shall feel neither the scorching heat nor the biting cold. Trees will spread their shade around them, and fruits will hang in clusters over them.
>
> They shall be served with silver dishes, and beakers as large as goblets; silver goblets which they themselves shall measure: the cups brimfull with ginger-flavored water from the Fount of Selsabil. They shall be attended by boys graced with eternal youth, who to the beholder's eyes will seem like sprinkled pearls. When you gaze upon that scene you will behold a kingdom blissful and glorious.[9]

There is an understandable emphasis upon cooling shade, clear running water, and refreshing beverages in a desert culture. The elite and affluent imagery of the Quranic paradise—a luxurious desert oasis with four watercourses streaming from it—has been metaphorically linked with the designs for Islamic royal gardens. Like the gardens of the Christian West, these invest the primal cosmological diagram with a specific symbolism and religious authority. This is evident in their spatial organization, with a central raised platform serving as the dais for an important structure, often a monarch's pavilion or tomb, and four water channels marking the principal compass directions. But, unlike the garden in the Christian West, the Islamic garden was a place where erotic love was given appropriate license.

ISLAMIC GARDENS OF DELIGHT

In the literature of Islam, the garden does double duty in a metaphorical sense, its attributes being assigned to God by the mystics and to the human lover by the poets. God's grace could be read in the springtime, which briefly colored and brightened the parched landscapes that constitute much of the Muslim world; there are paeans of praise to the coming of spring in Islamic writing. In all seasons, the oasislike paradise garden reflects the heavenly glory. There one finds the faithful personified as the gatekeeper of Paradise, and abundance in the form of a heavenly fountain. There in the Garden of Eden (the primordial garden and the eternal garden are synonymous in the Quran) stands the Tuba tree, furnishing a double image as it symbolizes both a state of blessedness and the slender grace of the beloved.

The opposition between divine and human love that permeates Christian texts is absent in Quranic mystical thought. Ruzbihan Baqli in the twelfth century advised spiritual recreation in the contemplation of three things: water, greenery, and a lovely face. All of the garden's flowers existed for the purpose of praising God, and each was assigned one or more divine attributes. Simultaneously, these same flowers stood for the beauty of various human body parts. Thus the tulip, which symbolizes the martyr, also represents the cheek (as do the hyacinth and the pomegranate flower), and the narcissus, whose white "blind" eye symbolizes the unenlightened, also furnishes an appropriate compliment to the real eyes of the lover. In describing a lovely woman in his *Shahnama* ("Book of Kings"), the Persian national epic, the eleventh-century poet Firdawsi, compiled a rich collection of garden-derived metaphors and similes:

> She was like ivory from head to toe, with a face like Paradise and a figure as graceful as a tree. Her cheeks were as red as pomegranate blossoms and her lips its seeds, while two pomegranates grew from her silver breast. Her eyes were like the narcissus in the garden, and her eyebrows stole the blackness from the crow's feathers. She is Paradise to look upon.[10]

The flower *par excellence* in the Islamic garden is the *gul,* or rose. So revered and admired is it that the very name of the garden, *gulshan* (also *gulzar*) embodies its name. According to Muslim mystics, the rose was created from a drop of perspiration that fell from Muhammad's forehead. The rose, which also provided the conventional analogy for the face of the Beloved, sometimes represented the beautiful *houri* who inhabited Paradise. In the mystic tradition, the rose also stands for the soul at peace, its evocative fragrance lingering after it has died. In addition, its many petals folded into one graceful flower symbolize union and harmony among humankind. These associations furnished the symbolic substance of the Islamic garden.

THE CHRISTIAN ALLEGORICAL EXEGESIS OF THE SONG OF SONGS

The most lyrically erotic book of the Old Testament is the biblical love poem known as The Song of Songs. Written as a dialogue between the bride and bridegroom (identified with Solomon), with a chorus of companions providing commentary, The Song of Songs is filled with erotic energy, as the bridal couple extol each other in the language of landscape with image after image of fragrance, fruit, gem, tree, monument, mountaintop, and comely animal. Nature, both wild and cultivated, is summoned forth in all its processes of dynamic change to evoke the alternating presence and absence of the loved one. Pomegranates, gazelles, asphodels, and lilies are pressed into literary service as similes to describe the beloved.

The interpretation put forward by Saint

Bernard, abbot of Clairvaux (1090–1153), transformed these images of the Garden of Love into symbols of divine communion by means of an elaborate exegesis in which the poem became an expression of the Virgin Mary's election as the Bride of God and Christ's mystical union with his Church. Given the extremely sensuous nature of the poem, it illustrates not only Christianity's ability to square Scripture with its strong bias in favor of chastity but also its tendency to see allegorical meaning in worldly phenomena.

The bridegroom's declaration,

My sister, my bride, is a garden close-locked,
a garden close-locked, a fountain sealed,[11]

is converted into a specific symbol of Mary's virginity, her womb being a metaphorical garden where the Christ, the Tree of Life, was planted by God.

The Christian interpretation of The Song of Songs as an allegory led to the depiction of the Virgin Mary in the *hortus conclusus,* or enclosed garden, conventionally shown as a flowery meadow inside high walls or encircled by a low wattle fence of the kind familiar all over Europe during the Middle Ages (fig. 3.2). Such fences were constructed to keep wild animals out of cultivated garden plots. One mythical beast, however, was permitted entrance: the unicorn. With its tireless speed and single invincible horn, this imaginary animal symbolizes Christ, who allows Himself to be caught in order to lie down in the Virgin's lap—that is, he allows himself to be born on Earth. The Marian garden that we most often see in medieval tapestries, miniatures, and prints is a flower-studded greensward in which the flowers all have allegorical attributes. The budding rose represents the Virgin's modesty and the lily her purity, while the iris, (the *fleur de lys*) stands both for the Kings of France and, by inference, for the line of David and Jesus. The garden's straight paths symbolize divine order, and its fountains refer to the sealed fountain in The Song of Songs. Wild landscape and wild animals (except for the mythical unicorn) are firmly excluded from the Marian *hortus conclusus* by a wattle fence, hedge of thorns, or high wall.

For some devout early Christians, the wilderness was emphatically not a place for Thoreau-like observation and self-knowledge, but rather a hostile and unfriendly locale, its scenery a metaphor for the rigor with which the saintly penitent must subdue the evil forces within his own breast. By making wild, uncultivated nature the domain of demons, Christian thought devalued nature and robbed it of its previous sanctity. Caves became the cells of hermits instead of the homes of oracles, and mountaintops were no longer the abodes of gods as they had been

3.2. *The Madonna in a Closed Garden,* a hand-colored woodcut by an anonymous Swabian or Franconian master. 1450–70. National Gallery of Art, Washington, D.C., Rosenwald Collection

in antiquity, but rather the setting for Christian trial and temptation. Because an apocalyptic ending of human history was predicted and all hope fastened on the afterlife, the beauty of Earth was devalued. Further, denial of the real world gave license to the exploitation of nature and its subjugation to human will. Humans, however, could not remain sensually indifferent to the world or their own sexuality. As will become apparent, the garden—controlled nature—would remain, as it was for the author of The Song of Songs the locus of an idealized approach to love.

THE GARDEN OF LOVE

For classical writers like the late-fourth-century C.E. Latin poet Claudian, who moved to Rome from Alexandria in 395 C.E., the garden was the obvious domain of Venus. The last major poet writing in the classical tradition, Claudian developed the imagery of the landscape of pleasure in his version of the familiar classical myth of Persephone's abduction by Hades, *De raptu Proserpinae.* In another poem, *Epithalamium de Nuptiis Honorii Augusti,* he painted a picture of a precinct sacred to Venus high on a mountaintop above the Ionian Sea. It overlooks a garden encircled by a golden hedge and filled with birdsong and aromatic plants. This is a garden of fantasy and allegory, a place of delectation and dalliance wherein are found such personifications as

License bound by no fetters, easily moved Anger,
Wakes dripping with wine, inexperienced Fears,

3.3. *The Lover and Dame Oyeuse,* a garden scene from an illuminated manuscript, *Roman de la Rose.* Ms. Harl. 4425 folio 12 verso. c. 1485, Flanders. The British Library, London

Pallor that lovers ever prize, Boldness trembling at his first thefts, happy fears, unstable Pleasure, and lovers' Oaths, the sport of every lightest breeze. Amid them all wanton Youth with haughty neck shuts out Age from the grove.[12]

Although Christianity firmly revoked the license that ancient peoples, such as the Hebrews, Persians, Greeks, and Romans, had accorded erotic love and condemned contemporary Islamic mores as sybaritic, the association between gardens and human love remained rooted in the Western imagination. The garden's function as an arena of allegory dealing with the trials and triumphs of young love was perpetuated in medieval and Renaissance literature. Around 1230, the French poet Guillaume de Lorris narrated his dream of romantic love in an epic poem, *The Romance of the Rose,* a work that was carried forward some forty years later by Jean de Meung, who provided it with an ending that is entirely different in meaning from that intended by its first author (fig. 3.3).

Drawing on the style of the troubadours, Guillaume de Lorris invests his portion of the poem with a delicate psychology that goes beyond the troubadours' usual one-sided treatment of love into an exploration of the heart and mind of the lady who is symbolized by the Rose. His part ends with the rejected Lover's realization that he cannot simply overcome all the barriers surrounding the object of his

desire. In order for him to possess the love of the Rose, she must also have her heart pierced by love's arrow.

In Jean de Meung's conclusion—a brief for the importance of procreation—the Lover persists in his quest and is encouraged to ravish the Rose. Venus leads the charge, and the Rose's guardian is persuaded to give her to the Lover who joyously proceeds to deflower her. However, the tone here is moral, not lewd. The Lover is not only rewarded with his true love but also with the prize of paradise. To achieve this happy ending, the author of the second part of the poem effectively exposes the earthly garden of courtly, romantic love as false, while building his case for the fruitful garden of procreation as the Christian pasture of the Good Shepherd.

In the hundred life-affirming stories of the *Decameron* by Giovanni Boccaccio (1313–1375), written in the middle of the fourteenth century when the Black Death ravaged the population, flesh and spirit are compatible; both are a natural, joyous part of existence. Choosing as a model the Villa Palmieri near Florence, Boccaccio describes an enclosed garden with its crisscross of wide rose- and jasmine-bordered paths "all straight as arrows and overhung by pergolas of vines," its orange and lemon trees and white marble fountain "covered with marvelous bas-reliefs." Here men and women could enjoy one another's company and praise the garden as a the very model of paradise:

> The sight of this garden, and the perfection of its arrangement, with its shrubs, its streamlets, and the fountain from which they originated, gave so much pleasure to each of the ladies and the three young men that they all began to maintain that if Paradise were constructed on earth, it was inconceivable that it could take any other form.[13]

The notion of the garden as an enclosed space, set apart, and infused with metaphorical meaning—a representation of nature perfected through human art in the service of an ideal—is fundamental to our understanding of the history of landscape design.[14] The literature of paradise gave rise to the notion of the garden as a symbolical space, and thus the written word helped landscape design assume a role beyond the one of prehistoric and classical times in which humans accorded divinity to actual sites in nature, shaping space and arranging architectural forms in relationship to the sky and certain features of Earth such as mountains and caves. The concept of landscape as symbolically divine, rather than actually divine space, derived particular strength from Islamic and Christian religious ideology as is evident in the way in which these world cultures translated the paradise ideal into the form of actual gardens.

II. PARADISE ON EARTH: THE ISLAMIC GARDEN

In desert lands, the oasis is typically viewed as a kind of paradise, a respite from the parched land and withering sun. Through conquest and a tolerant religion, the nation of Islam spread westward across North Africa to southern Spain and eastward into Central Asia and India, a territory composed principally of vast dry zones with extremes of heat and cold within which scattered green oases furnished a most precious element, water. In their migrations, Islamic peoples absorbed elements borrowed from other design traditions, which they synthesized into a distinctive style. In desert climates and also where water flowed seasonally, the four heavenly rivers of paradise described in the Quran and the refreshing fountains, as well as the shade and fruit trees to be found there, provided apt symbols for paradise in the oasislike Islamic garden.

Unlike Japanese or English gardens, Persian gardens and their Islamic successors were not constructed as spatial itineraries, places of sequential discovery; rather they were designed to serve the purposes of luxurious ease and sensory delight or, in the case of Mughal tomb gardens, as settings for monuments of commemoration. Water's soothing sound and mesmerizing reflectivity were essential to their ephemeral atmosphere and paradisiacal character. Built mostly in warm climates, they were exterior living spaces, often sumptuous, yet airy. The porticoed palace, the garden pavilion, and the kiosk opened up to the out-of-doors, and often their walls were pierced by grills to admit a filigree of fragmented light, dematerializing interior space. In these spaces, the distinction between inside and out, between architecture and landscape, between the material world and poetry, seems almost to dissolve.

Fruit trees and flowers, birds and animals, shimmering tiles, and the gleam and murmur of running water—these are the vibrant and delicate substances from which, like a beautiful carpet, the Islamic garden is woven. Indeed, Islamic carpet design and garden layout go hand in hand. Garden carpets depict in a stylized manner the *chahar bagh,* or fourfold garden with its intersecting axial watercourses surmounted by a central fountain (fig. 3.4). In addition, they depict symbolically the vegetation planted in actual gardens: the shade-giving plane tree, identified with the Tuba tree in the Quran; the cypress representing death and eternity; and fruit trees standing for life and fertility. The central cartouche can be interpreted as a platform, which in real gardens was often surmounted by a pavilion. These form the basic and timeless design formula of the Islamic garden—one or more quadripartite sections defined by narrow watercourses—which has its roots in ancient Persia where the archaeological remains of Achaemenid palaces trace the outlines of pavilions overlooking carved stone channels.

The paradigm of quadripartite landscape space with a defined center, from which energy flows outward in four directions and to which energy returns from the four corners of the cosmos, is a place-making practice rooted, as we have seen, in prehistoric tradition. But there is a distinction to be made between Islamic and prehistoric cosmological design. Prehistoric societies viewed landscape space in terms that charged *specific* local landscapes with intense religious meaning; their organization of space into quadripartite-center configurations was a declaration of the *actual* residence of divinity within a given landscape. Islamic garden design was rooted in a religion that was also impregnated with cosmological meaning, but because holy literature had begun to supplement and supplant oral tradition, thereby disseminating religion more broadly, a universal cosmological *symbolism* of sacred space, rather than the designation of certain spaces as cosmologically sacred, was now an operative cultural principle guiding landscape design. This observation is true for Hebrew-derived, Christian landscape design as well.

EARLY PERSIAN GARDENS

It will be recalled that the word *paradise* was originally used to denote a hunting park. Xenophon (c. 431–c. 352 B.C.E.), the soldier and writer who was a disciple of Socrates, reports on the beauty of the hunting

3.4. Garden carpet, 12'4" x 8'8" Persian. 18th century. Victoria & Albert Museum, London. The carpet is designed with a pattern that is intended to portray a *chahar bagh.*

park, the *pairidaeza* at Sardis, of the Achaemenid king Cyrus the Great (died c. 529 B.C.E.). From Xenophon's description we learn that this royal park was both a hunting park and a geometrically planted orchard. At Pasargadae, Cyrus the Great constructed a palace, a separate audience hall, and a garden pavilion overlooking a stone watercourse with square pools at regular intervals.

The shady porticoes of the palace and audience hall at Pasargadae, as well as the garden pavilion itself, overlooked the thin ribbon of water and the orchard-garden that surrounded it. Thus we find in the sixth century B.C.E. the two indispensable elements of Persian garden design: a straight, geometrically elaborated watercourse and a raised platform for garden viewing.

To supply such gardens as this with water, Achaemenid engineers constructed underground tunnels called *qanats* using a method developed as early as the sixth century B.C.E. and still in use today. These were laboriously dug by hand from the point of delivery to the base of a snow-capped mountain in a gentle ever-ascending grade. Shafts for debris removal and air supply created openings at intervals of approximately 50 feet, and these apertures still dot the vast Iranian plain.

After the conquest of Persia by Alexander the Great (356–323 B.C.E.), a century of Hellenizing influence preceded the re-establishment of a Persian empire and Persian design traditions under the Parthians (c. 240 B.C.E.–226 C.E.). Their capital was Ctesiphon. Between the third and seventh centuries C.E., the Sassanians, successors to Parthian rule, who also made Ctesiphon their capital, continued to express Persian influence in their gardens. As inferred from the design of a legendary Persian carpet measuring 450 feet by 90 feet, which was woven for King Khosrow I Anushirvan (ruled 531–579 C.E.), the imagery of the fourfold garden, divided by channels of running water, with a platform overlooking these watercourses, was an established idiom for actual garden construction. This Persian legacy accorded well with the Quranic concept of paradise, providing a readily accessible model for the Islamic garden.

ISLAMIC ORIGINS

In 610 C.E., the prophet Muhammed initiated the Muslim religion. It quickly spread through the Arabian peninsula and into the Middle East and Persia. In 766 C.E., the Abbasid caliphs, having asserted their political dominance, founded their capital of Baghdad on the Tigris River. During their rule between the eighth and the thirteenth century, horticulture and technology advanced rapidly. By the early tenth century, the city could boast twenty-three palaces with opulent gardens. One of these fabled, long-vanished

palaces was known as the House of the Tree. An artificial tree stood in the middle of a large round pond and had eighteen boughs made of gold and silver hung with precious gems in the form of fruits. This ingenious automata had gold and silver birds perched on its branches, and these emitted musical notes when stirred by the passing breeze.

Simultaneously, beginning in the eighth century, Islamic warriors carried their culture west to Spain. Here Muslim rulers synthesized Hellenistic, Roman, Early Christian, and Persian influences. As the power of the Abbasid caliphs declined, their role shifted from one of political power to one of religious leadership. Baghdad fell to Mongol invaders in 1258, following the campaigns of Genghis Khan and his heirs, but Islamic culture nonetheless remained a unifying force throughout much of Asia, North Africa, and Spain. Within this culture, the essential garden formula of a watercourse and raised platform for sedentary viewing was further developed as a quadripartite space in which the divisions were articulated by narrow water channels that could be thought of as symbolizing the four rivers of paradise.

ISLAMIC GARDENS OF SPAIN

The leaders of the Muslim army that invaded Spain in 711 C.E. were inspired by the hope of plunder as much as by religious enthusiasm. After defeating the Visigoths, the western Goths who had in the fourth century C.E. claimed the parts of the Roman Empire now occupied by France and Spain, the Arabs established themselves within the remains of their enemies' settlements and the extensive ruins of former Roman colonies. Then, in 750, after a palace revolution, a surviving member of the Umayyad caliphate, the first dynasty of Arab caliphs (661–750), fled Damascus to found the independent emirate of al-Andalus in the southern Spanish region that is known today as Andalusia. Geographically distant, therefore, from Islamic culture in the Middle East, the Arabs in Spain formed their own brilliant and erudite society. Here in Spain, Muslim, Christian, and Jewish communities coexisted under Arab rule. The Arabs had brought with them Persian artistic concepts along with Arabic science, and they married these with Greek philosophy. In this way, Córdoba became in the Middle Ages a center of learning, renowned for such philosophers as Ibn Rushd, known in the West as Averroës (1126–1198), a rationalist who translated Aristotle and anticipated Thomas Aquinas.

While southern Spain has the same hot climate as many other parts of the Islamic geographical sphere, its topography is for the most part more rugged and its land well watered and more fertile. Moorish engineers, rebuilding and extending the

remains of Roman aqueducts all around them, created intricate irrigation systems by introducing the *noria,* a bucket-scoop waterwheel that raised water into elevated canals. This greatly increased the amount of arable land and facilitated the construction of numerous gardens. Agriculture prospered, and famous treatises on the subject were written, such as the one by Abu Zakariya, a thirteenth-century agronomist and botanist in Seville. Farmers introduced sugarcane and brought into cultivation rice, cotton, flax, silkworms, and many kinds of fruit. Both the valley of the Guadalaquivir and the plain of Granada became densely settled zones with a rich tapestry of agriculture and gardening, their air fragrant with the scent of orange, lemon, and citron trees.[15]

Topography and contact with the abundant remains of Iberian Rome served to modify the conquerors' Syrian architectural heritage with its previously assimilated Roman and Persian forms. But Spanish Muslim architecture never aspired to the monumental three-dimensionality of architecture in the West. Instead, its aim was atmospheric, and its highest achievement lay in the interweaving of indoor and outdoor spaces in sensuous and sophisticated ways. Thus, in a typical Moorish house and garden, the patio and the structural spaces surrounding it interpenetrate one another in a casual yet studied congress of architecture and nature. Ceramic tiles, with their brightly glazed, reflective surfaces, produced an effect of cool airiness.

The spatial interpenetration of indoors and outdoors was not confined to fortress palaces or homes such as are found today in the Albaicín district of Granada, where the durable plan of the Roman peristyle was appropriated and reinterpreted as the *carmen,* the inward-focused house and garden of Arabic Spain (fig. 3.5). The same planning principle can be seen in the design of the Great Mosque at Córdoba, begun in 785–6. The mosque (now a cathedral), has a hypostyle interior in which the columns supporting a vast number of horseshoe-shaped double arches are evenly placed throughout like rows of trees in an orchard. Originally the wall on this side of the mosque opened via a façade of arches to a 3-acre courtyard planted in avenues of orange trees, which were aligned with the columns of the mosque's interior. An underground cistern supplied the fountains and irrigation channels in this court, called the Patio de los Naranjos, or Court of the Oranges (fig. 3.6). Unfortunately, the underground cistern has long since been converted into an ossuary, and Christian chapels have filled in the arches that once opened onto this patio.

The Alcázar[16] in Seville, which dates from about a hundred years after the Christian conquest of that city in 1248, exemplifies the extensive Islamic influence upon subsequent Spanish architecture (fig. 3.7). Using the considerable resources of Islamic craftsmanship, the king of Castile, Pedro the Cruel (ruled 1334–1369), built his fortified palace on the ruins of the former Islamic citadel. The Alcázar gardens consist of a series of enclosed patios. Though altered in

3.5. Carmen, Albaicín district, Granada. 16th century

Below: 3.6. Patio de los Naranjos (Court of the Oranges), Great Mosque, Córdoba. c. 9th century C.E.

of enclosed garden spaces, some of which were torn away in the sixteenth century when Charles V built a vast square palace with a huge circular interior court.

At the Alhambra, the planted areas of several of the enclosed gardens are defined by cross-axial paths. Soil beds were originally sunken well below these walkways and not as we see them today at almost the same grade. Planted with flowers, these garden courts would have been read by viewers sitting on carpets and low cushions placed in the surrounding porticoes as brightly colored tapestries. The fragrance of their orange trees, a unique garden design feature of Moorish Spain, would have also perfumed the air. Because one rarely enters directly from the outside into a Spanish-Moorish patio, but rather through a vestibule or twisting corridor, the sight of a beautiful interior garden is unexpected and therefore the impression it makes is powerful, relying as it does on one of the chief tricks of garden art: surprise. For instance, an undistinguished opening off the Court of the Myrtles turns into a small dark corridor leading to the most famous and complex space within the Alhambra, the Court of the Lions (fig. 3.8).

Here one finds a central fountain and a cruciform pattern of water channels. The fountain is supported by stylized lions with water flowing from their mouths into the basin below, which contemporaries may have linked symbolically with Solomon, or at least with the notion of wise royal rule associated

3.7. Garden of the Alcázar, the Mudéjar residence of Spanish royalty, Seville. Restored and rebuilt by Pedro the Cruel, beginning in 1366, but substantially altered in subsequent periods

Right: **3.8. The Court of the Lions, Alhambra, Granada. 1370–90**

subsequent centuries, the Moorish origins of these gardens are evident in their high enclosing walls, geometrical layout, raised paths, numerous fountains, brightly glazed tiles, and plantings of cypress, palm, orange, and lemon trees.

Granada was the last Arabic city recaptured by Christian monarchs, falling to Ferdinand and Isabel in 1492. Its remaining Arabic gardens—the Alhambra and the Generalife—which date from the thirteenth and fourteenth centuries, are among the oldest gardens in the world and enjoy legendary status. Sometime around 1250, Muhammad Ibn Ben Ahmar, the founder of the Nasrid dynasty, who took possession of Granada in 1238, climbed to the top of a bare red escarpment above the valley of the Darro with the spectacular Sierra Nevada rising behind it and laid claim to a site for his palace where there was already standing a building that probably served as a fortress in the late eleventh century. Here he ordered the construction of an aqueduct, the water from which has made possible the gardens of the Alhambra and the Generalife ever since. Built over a period of 250 years, principally during the reigns of Yusuf I (1333–1354) and Muhammad V (1354–1359; 1362–1391), the Alhambra, like the Alcázar in Seville, is an accretion

3.9. Acequia, Generalife, Granada. Original layout. c. 1250, with subsequent alterations

with the Hebrew king.[17] The basin is also fed by water that runs in a silver thread through the narrow white marble canals from the surrounding porticoed spaces. The most magnificent of these pavilionlike structures is the Hall of the Two Sisters flanking the Court of the Lions on the north. Its cupola of stucco blocks set over an octagon is formed into a honeycombed, sta-lactitelike ceiling of mesmerizing intricacy ascending as a symbolical representation of various levels of the heavens. Adding to the ethereal quality of the architecture are slender alabaster columns, brilliant gilding, and polychrome tiles designed in a rich array of abstract patterns. Here one finds the familiar avoidance of figural imagery and Islamic preference for geometrical forms, believed to embody the mathematical order underlying all creation. For the same reason, topiary was scrupulously avoided and plants in this and other Islamic gardens were allowed to assume their natural forms.

On a nearby hillside is the Generalife, or Jinnah al-'Arif, as the summer palace of the Spanish Arabic kings was known when it was begun in 1319. In addition to the quiet beauty of its secluded interior garden courts, with their lush vegetation and clear pools of water, the Generalife captures within its scenic embrace the magnificent snow-capped Sierra Nevada as well as the picturesque towers of the Alhambra silhouetted against the fertile valley of Granada below. As in other Islamic gardens, the designers here used the musicality, reflectivity, and cooling characteristics of water to enhance sensory experience. The most prominent of the gardens of the Generalife, the Patio de Acequia, or Patio of the Canal, has, instead of the usual water cross-axis dividing it into four quadrants, a long narrow pool, bridged in the center, into which jets of water fall in arcs (fig. 3.9). These water jets, like the floral borders lining the edges of the marble pavement beside this pool, were probably sixteenth-century additions and appear somewhat flamboyant in the context of an Islamic garden. At its northern end, the Patio de Acequia terminates in a pavilion, the delicacy of which has been compromised by the two stories added during the reign of Isabella I (ruled as queen of Castile, 1474–1504; with Ferdinand, joint sovereign of Aragon and Castile, 1479–1504).

There were no kitchens or residential quarters at the Generalife. Used overnight only in summer, sleepers found rest cushions or couches in alcoves off the porticoes. Cooking was done on braziers in the galleries of pavilions or out-of-doors. In spirit then, if not exactly in plan, this garden was, like the Timurid gardens far to the east at the other end of the Islamic world, a paradisiacal campground for a people whose way of life was as closely related to landscape as to buildings.

THE TIMURID EMPIRE

From the 1360s until his death in 1405, the Turkish military genius Timur, or Tamerlane as he is known by Westerners, extended his conquests from the Mediterranean on the west to India on the east and far into Russia. He soon filled his Central Asian capital at Samarkand in what is now modern Uzbekistan with huge tile-decorated mosques and other buildings crammed with the plunder of his conquests. He especially delighted in the creation of numerous pleasure gardens in the fertile valley around Samarkand. Irrigated by large water tanks, planted with fruit trees, sometimes furnished with dazzling tiled palace pavilions, and occupied by summer tent encampments, they were not so much tranquil refuges as magnificent places of pomp in which royal visitors were received and day-to-day business was conducted. Carpets and pillows were spread beneath embroidered silk canopies. At festivals, servants passed great leather trays heaped with roasted horsemeat, boiled mutton, spicy rice dishes, and fresh fruit among hundreds of richly dressed, bejeweled courtiers.[18]

The Timurid conquest of Central Asia was the foundation from which the Mughal Empire sprang. The high-walled gardens of Samarkand, filled with fruit trees and wild game, inspired Timur's descendant Babur (1483–1530), the founder of the Mughal dynasty, to build similar gardens at Kabul in what is now modern Afghanistan and at Agra in northern India. Also inspirational for Babur were the gardens at Herat in Afghanistan, which he visited in the autumn of 1506. There he experienced firsthand the pleasures of sophisticated courtly life in a garden setting. Recollecting Herat and the loveliness of the garden city of Samarkand, and understanding, too, the garden's political significance as a way of claiming territory, asserting legitimacy, and maintaining power,

he laid out numerous gardens high in the mountains at Kabul. There, well-watered hillsides were covered with bunch grasses and spotted with masses of wild native tulips in the spring. In this choice natural setting, Babur channeled natural springs into stone-lined reservoirs surmounted by platforms, and then planted many fruit trees. A typical Mughal garden can thus be envisioned in plan as an enclosed space divided into quarters, with a central water axis, a water-surrounded platform for one or more structures (palaces or pavilions) located in the center, and a mixture of vineyard, orchard, and flowers.

In the gardens of Kabul, Babur entertained his warrior-nobles, planned military campaigns, celebrated important events, held public audiences, composed music, and wrote poetry. The garden, in effect, became the royal court, not an adjunct to it. Although Babur's successors later built fortified palaces in various urban centers, the festive tents and light, airy pavilions that stood upon the geometrically designed, water-laced terraces of *chahar baghs,* as these quadripartite compartmentalized Timurid gardens were called, remained important venues of court life.[19]

Babur built the Bagh-i-Vafa, or Garden of Fidelity, on an elevated site overlooking the Sorkhrud river. This garden is depicted at a greatly compressed scale in the *Babur-Nama,* the illustrated manuscript of Babur's memoirs commissioned by his grandson, the emperor Akbar (ruled 1556–1605). These paintings show runnels carrying water from canals to irrigate fruit trees. Here Babur and his followers could walk among the flowering branches or sit beneath a silken tent or pavilion raised upon a *chabutra,* a central square stone platform, above the four symbolical "rivers" that flowed beneath it (fig. 3.10). Babur is known to have stopped and camped here frequently with his retinue, sometimes in autumn when the pomegranates ripened.

As Babur visited the various villages in the countryside around Kabul and the cities en route to it, such as Jalalabad, he frequently directed that his stopping places be laid out as gardens. Garden building and his constant movement from one garden encampment to another were important politically. His appearance in force with his armed retainers and the garden entertainments he organized helped him to assert his dominance as *Padshah,* or protecting overlord, among rebellious clans.

It was not an easy task. Babur was confronted by the growing power of the Uzbeks to the north. On the east he was hemmed in by the Himalayas and on the west by the emergent power of the Safavid dynasty in Persia. As Timurid refugees crowded into Kabul following the capture of Samarkand by the Uzbeks, there was only one direction in which Babur could turn: to the south and Hindustan, or northern India.

درختهای انار هم هست که داکرد حوض تمام سه بُرکه زار

3.10. *Babur Giving Instruction for the Layout of the Bagh-i-Vafa,* from a Mughal miniature, one side of a double page from the *Babur Nama,* c. 1590, Ms. I.M. 1913.276A, 276 Victoria & Albert Museum, London. Here the Mughal emperor is superintending the building of a garden at Kabul.

In 1526, after the Battle of Panipat, where he defeated the Delhi sultanate representing a collection of earlier Muslim dynasties that had consolidated power in northern India, he was able to proclaim himself *Padshah* there. To solidify his triumph, he claimed for his court the former capital of the Delhi sultanate at Agra on the Yamuna River. In spite—or perhaps because—of its dry climate and harsh scenery, which filled him with disgust, he immediately set about replicating the gardens he had left behind in Kabul.

Indeed, the riverside gardens he built at Agra were referred to as "Kabul." And it was from this garden setting, rather than from the fortress across the river, that Babur ruled, once more establishing the *chahar bagh* as a place of state.

Wherever possible, garden designers employed water in highly imaginative ways. On the plains of India, where there were fewer mountain cascades than in Kabul, they had to develop elaborate hydrological measures in order to furnish water channels

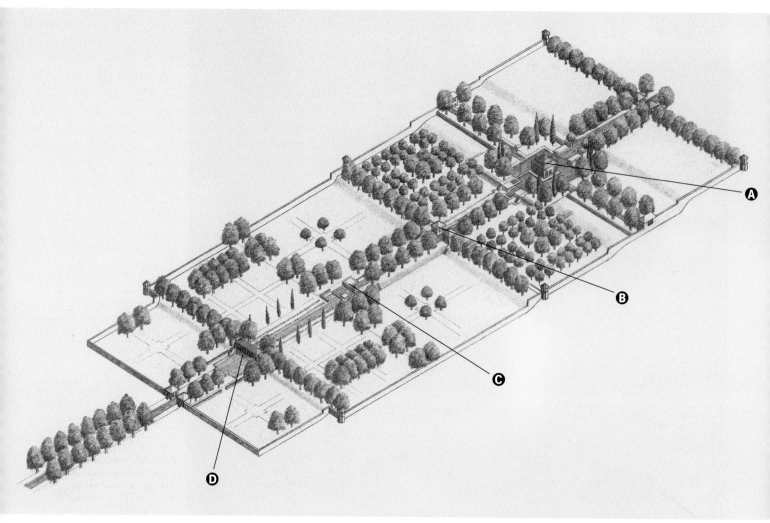

3.11. Shalamar (Abode of Love), overlooking Lake Dal, Kashmir, India. Garden layout from 1620. *Shalamar* is the name of an earlier garden in this location. The present garden, which was begun by Jahangir (ruled 1605–1627) and continued by his son, Shah Jahan (ruled 1627–1658), was called Farah-Baksh (Bestower of Joy).
Ⓐ Black Pavillion
Ⓑ Twin pavillions at Entrance to Harem Garden
Ⓒ Site of Diwan-i-Khas (Hall of Private Audience)
Ⓓ Diwan-i-Am (Hall of Public Audience)

and irrigate vegetation. Early Mughal gardens were supplied by ox-driven *norias*. A basin, often octagonal in shape, received water from the tank and distributed it into the channels of the garden as well as into cisterns and baths. Later, engineers were able to provide water more copiously by constructing canals that tapped major rivers. Then it was possible to widen narrow channels into true watercourses and install fountains and *chadars*—masonry ramps carved in a faceted pattern in order to enliven the movement of water and increase the sparkle of refracted light.

THE GARDENS OF KASHMIR

After 1586, when Babur's grandson Akbar conquered Kashmir in the well-watered foothills of the Himalayas, Mughal garden builders were able to freely exploit the sensuosity of water. To this favored locale of summer retreat, Akbar and his successors Jahangir (ruled 1605–1627) and Shah Jahan (ruled 1627–1658), with their vast retinues of soldiers, horses, mules, and royal ladies borne in litters on the backs of elephants, made epic journeys from the hot, dry northern plains of India. They traveled through hazardous mountain passes in late winter in order to arrive in time to enjoy the wildflower meadows of spring.

At least three of Jahangir's gardens in Kashmir still exist, the most important of which is Shalamar (the Abode of Love), a terraced garden he began laying out in 1619 in the foothills of the mountains overlooking Lake Dal (fig. 3.11). Here Jahangir's engineers diverted a stream and directed the water into a broad central canal running the length of the entire garden. Shalamar originally comprised three square terraces, each with a *baradari,* or open-sided pavilion placed on a stone platform set in the water at the point where the canal widens to form a square pool. In passing over the garden's succession of low terrace retaining walls before emptying in the lake, the canal forms a series of cascades. A line of water jets reinforces the principal axis of the canal, and in each pool more jets animate its surface. Regularly planted plane trees further emphasize Shalamar's geometrical *char-bagh* layout while providing welcome shade.

The lowest terrace (now truncated by a modern road) is a public space dominated by the *Diwan-i-Am,* or Hall of Public Audience, where the emperor received petitioners. Above it stands the emperor's garden; its central pavilion was the *Diwan-i-Khas,* or Hall of Private Audience (now vanished except for the low black marble throne), where members of the court were admitted (fig. 3.12). Above this is the harem garden. It is deeply shaded by two rows of plane trees, and its entrance is guarded by two small symmetrical pavilions. Where the harem garden meets the emperor's garden, horizontal slits in the stonework allow the water to flow into side pools and from these, through further slits, down into the canal in a shimmering veil over the side walls of the twin platforms flanking the cascade. In the center of a large square pool with fountain sprays, accessible only by two causeways, stands the open-sided Black Pavilion, believed to have been used as a banqueting hall (fig. 3.13). Here lateral canals create the cruciform plan of a true paradise garden, confirming the inscription on the pavilion: "If there is a paradise on the face of the earth, it is here, it is here, it is here."

Mughal garden designers were ingenious in devising ways to enhance the garden's paradisiacal atmosphere through the sensuous manipulation of water. For instance, where the water in the central canal at Shalamar drops over the retaining walls of the terraces, its force projects it beyond the coping; here in the face of the wall beneath the coping, stone carvers cut small niches resembling pigeonholes, and in these servants placed flowers on important occasions. Called *chini kanas,* they also contained oil lamps to illuminate the flowing water at night.

In other Kashmiri gardens such as Achbal and Nishat Bagh, also on Lake Dal, *chadars* enliven the passage of water wherever grade changes occur (fig. 3.14). Contrasting with the sparkle and roar of

chadars, there are serene pools. At Vernag, located near the Banihal Pass to the Indian plain, the beauty of the site was such that only a spring-fed octagonal basin was added. From its outfall, a 1,000-foot-long canal stretches through a meadow to empty in a mountain stream beside a cedar-clad slope.

3.12. View of pool and canal from the site of the vanished *Diwan-i-Khas,* Shalamar. In the distance is the *Diwan-i-Am,* beyond which lies Lake Dal.

Far left: **3.13.** Black Pavilion, Shalamar. Visible at the left, the pavilion is surrounded by a square pool filled with water jets.

Left: **3.14.** Nishat Bagh. First quarter of 17th century, period of Jahangir. To accommodate the abrupt grade as well as mystical numerology, twelve terraces symbolizing the twelve signs of the zodiac were built. Here the water of the principal canal is carried down successive changes of level via tall *chadars.* Their patterned surfaces animate the water, making it glisten and sparkle as it falls. These carved ramps also create a pleasing pattern of light and shade when dry. Stone thrones straddle the canal above the cascades, and pairs of stairways flank them.

MUGHAL TOMB GARDENS

The fourfold garden, elaborated by a grid of canals with *chabutras* at their intersections, remained a constant form during 150 years of Mughal garden development. In the great imperial tomb gardens of the sixteenth century the *chabutra* at the principal intersection was transformed from a mere platform into the base of a magnificent monument. Unlike the royal pleasure gardens at Kashmir, which were terraced, with social functions assigned to each ascending level, the tomb gardens are essentially flat with only the mildest grade change to permit the gravitational flow of water throughout a grid of narrow watercourses. Water collects in the square pools and octagonal basins placed at intersections within the subdivided square grid that surrounds a central square platform. This platform—or large-scale *chabutra*—serves as the base for an impressive mausoleum, which is often decorated with a colorful inlay of semiprecious stones.

The first departure from the relatively modest tombs of Islamic rulers, begun in 1564, was that of Babur's successor, his aesthetically sensitive, superstitious, and pleasure-loving eldest son Humayun, who assumed the throne at the age of twenty-two following the great emperor's death in 1530. The Islamic garden historian James L. Wescoat sums up his role as an urbanist:

> When Humayun built his palace in Agra Fort and his city in Delhi, he initiated a process of urbanization which radically altered the meaning and function of gardens in Mughal culture. Babur had shunned the citadels he conquered. For reasons unknown but perhaps harkening back to the Timurid ideal of Samarquand in the 14th century, Humayun began to recenter Mughal social life within citadels, ornamenting and surrounding them with gardens.[20]

His widow, Haji Begum, commissioned the construction of his mausoleum, which is characterized by another Mughal garden scholar, Elizabeth Moynihan, as being like a cosmic mountain above the four rivers of paradise represented by the garden's four water channels.[21]

Inlaid stone and marble were the materials with which Shah Jahan built the Taj Mahal in honor of his adored wife Mumtaz-i-Mahal (Chosen One of the Palace), who died in 1631 as she was bearing their fourteenth child (figs. 3.15, 3.16). Begun on the banks of the Jamuna in Agra the following year, construction continued for the next sixteen. Like other monumental Mughal mausoleums, the Taj Mahal is set within a *char bagh;* however, instead of occupying the

traditional space at the intersection of the garden's four principal canals, the extended *chabutra* supporting the mausoleum was placed at the far end following the pattern to be seen at other riverfront gardens at Agra, which has the effect of ensuring that the unforgettable lines of the remarkable structure are always seen against the sky. The tall minarets have been pulled away from the corners of the building and set at the edge of the terrace upon which the building rests, and this ingeniously enlarges the space occupied by the building, while at the same time lightening its apparent mass. Its sky-catching dome and minarets and the well-proportioned central canal mirroring it in the water dematerialize its obvious mass.

Considered by many as the apotheosis of Mughal culture, the Taj Mahal is also its last important creative achievement. Shah Jahan, who had killed his brother to secure the throne, was deposed in 1658 by his son Aurangzeb, who in turn had already killed his three brothers. Aurangzeb had his father imprisoned in the Red Fort on the other side of the river within sight of the Taj Mahal where, after his death in

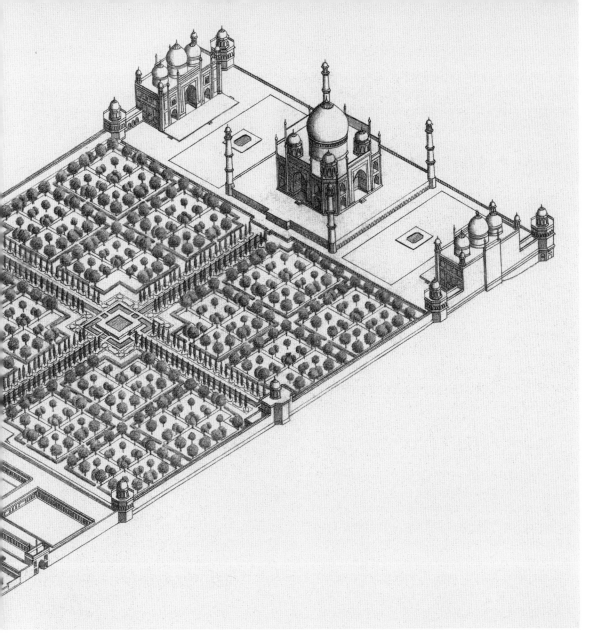

3.15. Taj Mahal, Agra, India.
1632–48

Below: 3.16. Taj Mahal

1666, he was laid to rest beside his wife. Although the Mughal dynasty, which had been founded by Babur and secured in power by Akbar, continued to exist until overthrown by British rule in the nineteenth century, Aurangzeb's religious fanaticism and subsequent wars of succession depleted the resources of empire beyond recovery. The great period of Mughal architecture and garden building was over. Islamic culture, however, continued to flourish elsewhere, notably in and around Constantinople after the conquest of the Byzantine Empire by the Ottoman Turks, and in Persia after the restoration of its autonomy in the sixteenth century.

TURKISH GARDENS

The Ottoman Turks, a tribal people of Central Asia, adopted Islam in the ninth century. They were used as mercenaries by both the Abbasid caliphs and the Saljuq Turks. One of the Ottoman warrior tribes that served the Saljuqs migrated into Asia Minor in the thirteenth century. As Mongol invaders undermined Saljuq authority in 1253, the Ottomans established autonomy and initiated their own program of conquest, eventually capturing Constantinople in 1453. Their victorious leader, Mehmed II (ruled 1444–1446; 1451–1481), renamed it Istanbul.

On the ancient Byzantine acropolis overlooking the Bosporus to the north and the Sea of Marmara to the south, Mehmed II built the Topkapi Saray, a vast palace and garden complex, the design of which expressed an elaborate code of Ottoman courtly ritual and protocol. Removed from the crowded center of the city and surrounded by water on two sides and a high wall on the third, it furnished the sultan with the necessary condition of seclusion within a sanctified paradisiacal enclosure.

Because the sultan's orbit was strictly limited by the mystique of his inaccessibility, he depended more than other rulers did on his palace and grounds for visual stimulation and entertainment. Most of his life was spent within an inner court in sumptuously furnished apartments, library, and delightful gardens. An outer garden was planned both as an important personal statement in which the themes of power, pleasure, and paradise were interwoven and to serve as a great amusement park containing multiple stratagems to combat the boredom of a circumscribed existence.

Life at Topkapi centered around courtyards and gardens, pools and fountains, orchards and vineyards, harem, mosques, baths, kitchens, stables, offices, barracks, schools, and armory. Within its precincts, which were divided into men's and women's quarters, a strictly organized social hierarchy prevailed. At the top, powerful viziers, representing the omnipresent but secluded sultan, conducted affairs of state and meted out justice in the name of the powerful ruler.

The Topkapi Saray, as it evolved in the fifteenth and sixteenth centuries, consisted of three large contiguous, but not axially arranged, courts outlined by functional groupings of buildings. In addition, there were appended to the third court a private hanging garden, sometimes referred to as a fourth court, and a large exterior garden with terraces spreading to the Bosporus and the Sea of Marmara. Within the exterior garden, various areas were set aside for such recreational pursuits as javelin throwing, polo, archery, hunting, and other royal pastimes. Here, too, were several kiosks for scenic viewing and other pastimes.

The first court at Topkapi Saray was known as the Court of Processions after the processional thoroughfare leading from the Hagia Sophia through its imposing arched Imperial Gate. It was an open, uncluttered ceremonial space, less distinguished by its loosely organized surrounding architecture than by the bejeweled pomp of finely decorated horses and cavalry and the spectacle of exotic animals exhibited there on occasion. At the second monumental gate, which stood at the far end of the first court, those mounted on horses, with the exception of the sultan, were forced to dismount, and protocol demanded silence upon passing through its vestibule into the second court.

Inside, the second court proved to be an idyllic garden surrounded by a stately marble colonnade. Birds sang in the tall cypresses and other trees, and ostriches, peacocks, deer, and gazelles wandered on lawns behind red-painted wooden fences. Paths fanned out to the gates of various functional quarters—commissary, kitchens, confectionery—as well as to a range of administrative chambers—Council Hall, chancery, archives, and treasury. At the far end of this court rose its architectural focus, the third gate, called the Gate of Felicity. Its domed canopy denoted the presence of the sultan just beyond within the third court, the private sanctum of the usually invisible ruler.

The third court, reserved for the royal family and inner household, as well as for the students who were being trained as the future Ottoman administrative elite, was sumptuously decorated. Ranging along its southwestern side was the harem where the sultan's female family members and children lived, as well as their women attendants, servants, and the distaff administrators of these quarters. Here, as elsewhere in the vast sprawling complex, there were gardens. These included a large pool overlooking a boxwood garden and another extensive garden for the exclusive use of the women and the sultan.

In the sultan's private garden the Islamic genius for interweaving architecture and garden space was given full play. Here, freed from the rules of ceremony and the protocol of aloof reserve demanded of him, the sultan could indulge the emotional side of his nature, writing poetry, enjoying music, reading, dining with male or female companions, or watching the sporting contests below in the outer garden.

There were alcoves furnished with low pillowed sofas in the large, airy, luxuriously decorated Revan and Baghdad kiosks (fig. 3.17). Placed under the domes of these pavilions and within window recesses, fountains added their agreeable murmur and sparkle to the luminous interiors. Bronze fireplaces provided comfort in winter, and canvas shades lowered by pulleys provided privacy as well as shade from the summer sun. Set upon a marble platform beside a large reflecting pool, such fantastical structures appeared to hover in space.

In such an environment it is not surprising that the most sensuously appealing flowers and fruits were planted. Sultan Süleyman's account book of 1564–65 refers to an orange grove, potted jasmine, and a field of carnations, while a later record speaks of renewing the jasmine pergolas near the terrace of the House of Felicity. Fruit trees of several varieties abounded, and according to the report of one foreign visitor, grapes were grown throughout the year.

Greco-Roman ruins were turned to good account. Many antique sarcophagi had been converted by Mehmed II into fountain basins, and the large Goth's Column commemorating a Roman victory against their ancient northern foes was left standing in the parklike outer garden a short distance from the gate that connected it with the hanging garden, or fourth court.

Extending to the shores of the triangular promontory, the outer garden consisted of a series of stepped terraces built over vaulted substructures, some of which incorporated the ruins of the Byzantine acropolis. With its flowing fountains, fertile vineyards, beds of flowers, domed pavilions, sparkling pools, comely pages, and beautiful concubines, it must have appeared as a physical manifestation of paradise as described in the Quran. In addition to serving as a botanical garden for a multitude of rare and delightful plants, the large outer garden also acted as a game preserve and zoological garden for many wild and domesticated animals, waterfowl, and songbirds.

Stretching outward from the medieval Byzantine seawall, four seaside kiosks embraced the extraordinary view and provided delightful haunts wherein successive sultans could indulge in courtly pastimes in the company of pages, dwarfs, concubines, and an occasional visiting scholar or potentate. There were other garden kiosks beside the Bosporus in addition to those of Topkapi. Much admired by travelers to Turkey in the eighteenth century for its curved dome, patterned tiles, and inlay work of marble, granite, and

3.17. Baghdad Kiosk, in the sultan's private quarters. 1639

porphyry, the Ottoman kiosk was often replicated, using less opulent materials, in later Western gardens.

Turkish gardens were also renowned for their extensive use of fountains. Some fountains were upright and meant to imitate the Fountain of Salsabil in the Quran, with water dripping as gently as tears from one scalloped cup into another in a series projecting from a carved marble slab. Others were noisier and provided a screen for confidential conversation. There were also, wherever necessary, ablution pools, which were usually square or rectangular basins. Thus was Ottoman wealth lavished upon garden art and the ideal of paradise made real.

Isfahan, A City of Gardens

In the century following the establishment of the Ottoman Empire at Istanbul, Shah Abbas (ruled 1587–1629) of the Safavid dynasty defeated the Central Asian warlords. Ten years after ascending the throne, he began to manifest Persia's re-established autonomy and wealth with the building of a new capital, Isfahan, adjacent to the site of an ancient Achaemenid city and eleventh-century capital of the Saljuq Turks. In March 1598, Shah Abbas traveled from his capital at Qazvin to his palace in the ancient city of Isfahan for the spring celebration of the Persian New Year when wildflowers briefly bloom on the high Iranian plain. With its views of lavender-colored mountains and green fields, gardens, and orchards running down to the Zaindeh River, Isfahan furnished a spectacular site in which Shah Abbas could create an imperial garden city. Construction began immediately to the south of the old town, and garden pavilions, shops, and caravansaries were erected along with public baths, schools, and mosques. An intricate terraced irrigation system was built to carry a canal the length of the 150-foot-wide (45.7-meter-wide) Chahar Bagh Avenue, so named because it served as

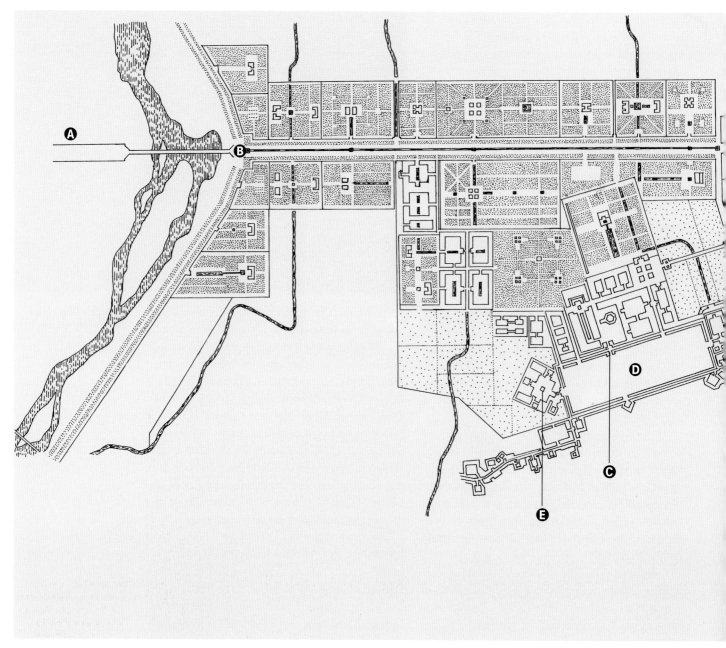

3.18. Isfahan, Iran. Built first quarter of the 17th century
Ⓐ Hezar Jarib
Ⓑ Chahar Bagh Avenue
Ⓒ Ali Qapu
Ⓓ Maydan-e-Shah
Ⓔ Mosque

the connecting spine and water distribution channel for the spectacular now-vanished gardens flanking this linear urban design project (fig. 3.18).

By the second half of the seventeenth century, Isfahan was at the height of its splendor, with a population numbering 600,000. Its plan from that period shows, to the south of the tangle of streets and welter of buildings in the old town, three main axial arrangements: the Maydan-e-Shah, or Imperial Square with its surrounding shops and royal palace on the west, the Chahar Bagh Avenue, and the mosques aligned to face Mecca in conformity with universal Islamic practice.

The chief public ground was the Maydan-e-Shah. Measuring approximately 1664 feet by 517 feet (507 meters by 158 meters), it served as a versatile recreational field and a place of pomp, pageantry, and public executions. This great Imperial Square was enclosed by a uniform two-story arcade housing the shops of merchants dealing in precious gems, gold, silk, and medicinal drugs. Within the square itself, tents and awnings were thrown up on weekly market days for dealers selling furs, jewelry, and pearls as well as for traders of cloth, spices, vegetables, and fruit. At such times, it was a place for prostitutes to solicit business and for jugglers, tightrope walkers, acrobats, magicians, and wrestlers to entertain crowds. Spectacular punishments took place there, providing whatever moral instruction was intended as well as satisfying the human appetite for cruelty. From a great platform supported by eighteen pillars behind the Ali Qapu, or Lofty Gateway, on the western side of the Maydan-e-Shah, the Shah and his retinue could watch polo, a game native to the Middle East, and many lively tournaments featuring feats of derring-do similar to the events of a contemporary rodeo.

rugs, illuminated manuscripts, jewelry, and other precious objects lay within the palace grounds. Instead of a single large palace, Shah Abbas built several garden pavilions and palaces, such as the Chehel Sotun, or Hall of Forty Columns, with its great open porch and easy interpenetration of outdoor and indoor living spaces (fig. 3.19). Two large square fountains guarded by four water-spouting lions were set into the floor of the great porch. The ethereal character of this structure was enhanced by brightly painted wood mosaic inlaid with mirrors as well as by its tranquil, reflective pools of water.

Anchored on the north by the palace grounds, the Chahar Bagh Avenue runs along a slightly sloping grade for nearly a mile to the river, then across a two-story arcaded bridge to terminate on the south in the huge royal estate known as the Hezar Jarib. One-hundred-eighty-feet (55-meters) wide, the Avenue was planted in Shah Abbas's time with eight

3.19. Chehel Sotun, Isfahan, with dome and minarets of the Royal Mosque in the distance. From *Voyage en Perse* by E. Flandin and P. Coste, 1851

The Imperial Mosque was built at the southern end of the Maydan-e-Shah in 1612. Because its plan was rotated to orient the mosque toward Mecca, Shah Abbas's architects had to resolve the structural transition between the Maydan and the mosque. This was done with the construction of a portal, an open vestibule, and two stories of *iwans,* the large niche-like vaults originally conceived by the Parthians, fully developed by Sasanian architects, and deployed here and elsewhere throughout the Islamic world. This mosque is a dazzling display of Persian architectural genius. Multicolored tiles, predominantly light and dark blue, cover interior walls as well as the exterior of the large dome in a richly interlacing pattern, their intricate reflective surfaces dematerializing the solid masonry beneath them.

Imperial storerooms and the workshops for artisans engaged in the production of fine embroideries,

rows of plane trees and poplars, with roses and jasmine growing in between them. Five runnels of water divided the avenue. The large central one was lined with onyx and punctuated at each change of water level with individually designed square or octagonal pools and fountains. Gardens built by courtiers and rich merchants bordered this promenade on either side. These were entered through small pavilions. Larger pavilions with such evocative names as Garden of the Vineyard, Mulberry Garden, and Garden of the Nightingale stood in the center of each. Passersby on the Chahar Bagh Avenue could glimpse these now mostly vanished gardens through latticework walls and, for a small price, gain entrance. Tantalizing descriptions of their contents come from visitors to the Safavid court.

Extending the Chahar-Bagh axis was the bridge with its thirty-three arches and, on the south side of the river, 3-mile-long garden-bordered avenue. It led to Shah Abbas's *pairidaeza,* the Bagh-e Hezar Jarib, which according to French jeweler Jean Chardin, who visited the city around 1670, was a mile square and laid out in twelve terraces. A tree-lined road to the west connected this garden with the Bagh-e Farahabad (Abode of Joy), built for Shah Sultan Husayn (ruled 1694–1722) around 1700. This garden contained large pools with islands supporting summer pavilions.

A teeming center of aristocratic privilege and commerce, Isfahan, with its extraordinary site and numerous gardens, combined secular commerce with the Muslim ideal of paradise, harnessing water to bring lushness to the high desert. Less overtly sensuous, but as culturally pervasive was the Christian manifestation of paradise in landscape terms as an enclosed, inward-focused realm informed with religious symbolism.

III. PARADISE CONTAINED: WALLED CITIES AND WALLED GARDENS OF THE EUROPEAN MIDDLE AGES

After the fall of the western provinces of the Roman Empire in the fifth century C.E., followed by the advance of Islam in the Mediterranean basin, civilization became more highly regionalized throughout Europe. Without centralized administration over these former imperial territories, the great road and aqueduct systems built by the ancient Romans fell into partial disuse and extensive disrepair, and as we shall see in Chapter Four, the capital itself shrank within its walls. The disruption caused by successive challenges to centralized power produced new kinds of reciprocal relationships in relation to land tenure, an economic and social system often characterized as "feudal."

Like Córdoba and the Islamic centers of learning, monasteries continued to serve as repositories of knowledge, and many ancient Roman towns were perpetuated as episcopal seats. The Carolingian period, lasting from the middle of the eighth century into the tenth century, helped to reanimate in a limited fashion some of the grandeur of ancient Roman cities, which now served as the fortified settlements and seats of bishops and counts. The Cistercian monastic revival of the eleventh century promoted agricultural improvements, which in turn stimulated the regrowth of cities. By the middle of the eleventh century, revived maritime trade boosted the fortunes of Genoa, Pisa, and Venice, which began its dazzling rise from watery refuge to immensely prosperous mercantile center. In the Low Countries and along the Baltic and North Sea coasts as well as in the valleys of the Rhône, Rhine, and Danube, conditions were also favorable for the rise of towns as centers of production and trade. Constantinople, capital of the Eastern Roman Empire, remained an important center for crafts manufacture and the international exchange of goods, and this was a stimulus to trade in the West.

In the late Middle Ages, beginning in the eleventh century and accelerating as Europe recovered from the effects of the Black Death in the middle of the fourteenth century, there was a revival of trade and the emergence of banking houses. This was coupled with a wary but growing conviction on the part of feudal lords that a stimulus to their own prosperity lay in franchises granted to independent towns from which they could obtain handsome revenues. Seeking greater independence from feudal lords, townspeople formed trade guilds and municipal councils. As a powerful merchant class came into being and cities became more prosperous through trade, their jealously guarded privileges exempted them from control by the Church or local barons. Our survey of European cities in the Middle Ages is necessarily limited to this last late flowering of urbanism during the period often termed *Gothic* and comprising roughly the late twelfth through the fifteenth centuries.

Like most cities heretofore throughout history, these medieval ones were necessarily walled for reasons of defense. Girdled towns stood in stony contrast to their surrounding fields. Towered castles and church spires etched their profiles on the otherwise unpunctuated skyline. The inward-focused peristyle garden of Rome became the medieval cloister garden, a paradisiacal jewel within the bosom of the monastic precinct. This stout containment of various units of the built environment, with some walled structures nesting within others, was obviously done for reasons of security. But such enclosure can also be read as an expression of the way in which medieval intellectuals sought to order knowledge within a self-contained framework.

The Dominican monk Thomas Aquinas (1225–1274), the most influential theologian and philosopher of the Late Middle Ages, brought Christian doctrine and Aristotelian logic into a syncretic intellectual system. By inquiring into the nature of nature, he laid the foundations of the scientific revolution. His approach to knowledge was not one of open-ended speculation, but rather one that attempted to order all knowledge into a comprehensive, God-ordained harmony of parts, or *summa.* Although it served as an expandable framework, Aquinas's system was, like that of Aristotle, a closed one based on the notion of an Aristotelian geocentric universe in which all matter was spherically contained within Earth and its surrounding atmosphere and all contents ultimately knowable.

The Late Middle Ages was a period in which religious allegory flourished and sharp distinctions were drawn between good and evil, heaven and hell, human and divine. Paradise was an ever present and almost palpable cultural concept. But the route to paradise lay through earthly travail and self-denial, and the blessed abode necessarily remained an invisible vision, a vividly imagined reward for faith and endurance of the trials of this life. Virtues and vices were personified and paired in opposition to one another. This Christian theology was illuminated in manuscripts, carved in the stones of cathedrals, fashioned into stained-glass windows, and depicted in fresco and mosaic on wall surfaces.

The great epic poem of the period, Dante's *The Divine Comedy* of 1321, joined Christian theology and classical astronomy into a vast symbolic structure. Dante's reordering of pagan cosmology into a moral drama was, like the system of Aquinas, both all-embracing and self-contained. Since Christian teaching encouraged the sublimation of sexual desire to religious belief, Dante's Beatrice is an ideal of virtuous womanhood, his virginal guide to paradise. As in the *Romance of the Rose,* physical love in *The Divine Comedy* is hedged in, contained, like a garden surrounded by a high wall or fence. The concept of enclosure was so inherent a part of the medieval garden that a gate and fence, with only a few rudimentary plants inside, became its convenient graphic symbol (see fig. 3.2).

Although the values that the late medieval world portrayed were decidedly spiritual, the period was remarkably full of worldly energy and new advances in technology. Entrepreneurial capitalism had begun to supersede feudalism. Human nature asserted itself lustfully as well as spiritually, and gardens served not only as symbolical representations of paradise but also as aristocratic preserves for love-making. Horticulture as a craft was re-established, and the foundations of Renaissance science and humanism were laid as this cultural era drew to its dynamic close.

WALLED CITIES

More than merely defensive units for the protection of local populations, the European walled cities of the Late Middle Ages were active centers to which the privilege of entry for the purpose of doing business was granted to outsiders. Toll revenues collected at their gates from peasant farmers coming to market or merchants from abroad formed a substantial part of their wealth. Their organic growth patterns along major

routes within and immediately outside their walls reflect the burgeoning medieval market economy.

Because the growing towns existed as islands within the uncertain seas of feudal combat and local rebellion, their safety depended upon high, thick walls with crenellations, which shielded the archers defending them (fig. 3.20). Round or square towers punctuated these walls at intervals of every hundred feet or so. Small openings cut into the towers permitted a wide range of crossfire when a town was under siege. Gates, the necessary portals of the city, were inevitably the weak points of a town wall. They were therefore doubly guarded by massive flanking towers. Because towns often grew on both sides of a river, the two ends where the river bisected the walls also received additional fortification in the form of strong towers, as did the ends of bridges leading to walled towns built on a single riverbank (fig. 3.21). Not all of the newly created towns that sprang up in the eleventh- and twelfth-century urban revolution were initially built with these walls. But for successful towns, particularly those that developed under royal or ecclesiastical aegis, investment in massive fortifications was imperative.

3.20. Plan of 17th-century Mainz, Germany, showing walls and fortifications. The military technology that occasioned the construction of walls as earthworks and bastions with arrowheadlike projections did not occur until the sixteenth century. At that time, cannon fire rendered obsolete high crenellated walls and machicolated towers with floor openings from which molten lead, boiling oil, or missiles could be dropped on attackers advancing with battering rams.

Below: 3.21. Bridge, walls, and towers of Toledo, Spain

3.22. Campo, Siena, Italy

salesroom combined within the same structure—there was considerable competition for space throughout. Streets could be narrow, and houses often encroached upon their boundaries or pushed upper stories into the space above them. The medieval street might thus acquire a highly irregular—and to later eyes picturesque—character.

In such notable instances as Florence and Siena, civic pride—the luxury of late medieval prosperity—began to assert itself. An urban aesthetics that was specific to individual cities became apparent. In Florence, where there already existed the example of a Roman orthogonal grid with its *cardo, decumanus,* and central forum, citizens sought beautiful, wide, straight streets. Streets received more sunlight after the imposition of building codes governing balconies and other projections. In Siena, hilly topography conspired with the elegant curvilinear Gothicism that remained a local ideal in art as well as town planning, with the result that building lines were made to conform to the gentle arcs of its principal thoroughfares and shell-shaped central Campo (fig. 3.22).

With prosperity, medieval towns became increasingly dense; however, there was still within their walls a good deal of green open space. Behind dwellings, yards contained animals, fruit trees, and kitchen gardens. In the wedge-shaped areas between the radial streets there was room, particularly near the periphery of the town, to site new abbeys and monasteries. As surging enterprise drew an illiterate and impoverished peasantry from the surrounding countryside, mendicant orders, such as those of the Franciscans and Dominicans, arose in response to the increasingly turbulent, uneasy, and afflicted life of medieval cities. These orders were dedicated to maintaining the social order, suppressing heresy, and ministering to the population through preaching and caring for the sick and the indigent. They formed hospices and hospitals on remaining open lands in the less trafficked zones between the major thoroughfares and near the peripheries of cities. Here another medieval innovation, the urban university, found similar accommodation. Although these institutions had long been considered the province of the Church, in the cities, where wealth was independent of ecclesiastical patronage, they soon acquired independent status. The public bath reappeared, becoming a late medieval center of relaxation and social intercourse.

The market forces governing the growth of cities in the eleventh and twelfth centuries were often dynamic enough to stimulate development outside the walls as well as within. Suburban settlements known as *faubourgs* sprang up in the zones immediately outside certain principal gates even before the towns became crowded inside.[22] Because the taxes imposed

Inasmuch as the construction of monumental walls and towers represented public works projects of considerable magnitude, medieval cities were usually made as compact as possible in order to minimize their circumference and hence the extent of their perimeter fortifications. This and the imperatives of the city's market economy dictated a rounded urban form with radial streets emanating from a central square and trading area to its several gates. In former Roman colonial cities, these radial thoroughfares simply surrounded and fed into the grid with its ancient *cardo* and *decumanus* and became organically integrated with its pre-existing street pattern (see fig. 2.23). Around the central market square, town halls were built when the administrative functions of increasingly complex urban units made civil governance a necessity. In the jockeying for position within the medieval city, in which site occupancy denoted relative degrees of urban power, the most powerful guild halls received greater centrality. The cloth hall wherein the wool trade—the mainstay of the medieval economy—was conducted, often boasted a pre-eminent location. If the town was an important episcopal seat, sometimes the main square was dominated by a cathedral; however, cathedrals were often sited a short distance away at the point where the old grid and the newer medieval urban fabric commingled. In such a location there would develop a cathedral square, and inevitably certain regional and temporary market functions would coalesce around and within it.

Additional market squares developed, some close to the center, some adjacent to parish churches, and others near the town's principal gates. The last came about because, once inside the walls, those granted the privilege of doing business in the town created a public trading area in the most immediately convenient location. Because the towns were, in effect, market organisms built for the production and trade of goods—with home, workshop, and

upon those doing business within the town walls could be avoided here, lively market squares formed within them. As the growing cities within the walls exerted pressure to expand, and as this need combined with their desire to annex the profitable *faubourgs,* a new band of walls was built enclosing the area occupied by one or, often, several *faubourgs.* This situation, from the point of view of the *faubourg* residents, was also desirable since, offsetting the burden of taxation, true citizenship brought with it various legal privileges, economic advantages, and greater physical security. With the creation of the new walls, the old inner circle of walls was usually, though not always, removed, and a new cycle of *faubourg* creation began near the gates along the redrawn town periphery.

Although enjoying a large degree of communal autonomy, medieval cities and towns were still embedded within the larger power structure in which the king and other great secular magnates held sway, retaining their holdings through military prowess. Living off revenues generated by the city as well as the countryside, feudal lords had interests that were fundamentally inimical to those of the townspeople. Nevertheless, they, along with the king, served as military protectors, a role that was effectively expressed in the defensive architecture of the castle and its protective siting on a hillside above the town. Alternatively, princes and bishops built residences in strategic locations at vulnerable positions within the fortified walls. Though situated within cities, these aristocratic compounds were not part of urban life, acting as barriers to public circulation and obstacles to the towns' natural development.

Most of the maps and views of medieval cities are not medieval; they are, as a rule, engravings of the sixteenth and seventeenth centuries. But, because street patterns are typically resistant to alteration and urban structural turnover in pre-industrial times was slow, these nevertheless serve as fairly accurate plans and perspectives of medieval towns (see fig. 3.20). Today the historic gates or portals depicted in these engravings survive only as monuments and place-names, commemorating former walls. Although a few walled medieval cities still exist, their walls are tourist attractions and no longer function as barriers to entry. In cities that have continued to experience periods of growth, such as Paris, Vienna, and Florence, former walls can be traced as boulevards and ring roads.

Beyond security and taxation—the primary functional reasons for urban enclosure—there were symbolical and psychological reasons for the inward focus of medieval cities and the institutions and structures within them. The cathedral itself was a sanctuary enclosing a sacred mystery. In this regard, it was not unlike the nature sanctuaries of antiquity; its cool,

dim interior was analogous to that of a cave or grotto. Outside many churches, behind the apse, there was often a space called "paradise" where flowers to decorate altars, statues, and shrines were grown. Within cloister gardens, in addition to the four paths emanating from a central fountain or well like the biblical rivers of the Garden of Eden, fruit trees and other plants symbolized the renewal of life in the green groves of heaven. Thus, like the *chahar bagh,* which was a physical and symbolical manifestation of the Islamic paradise described in the Quran, the quadripartite cloister garden was emblematic of the equally idyllic (if less sybaritic) paradise found in the Hebrew and Christian Bible.

WALLED GARDENS

In the medieval garden the best productions of wild nature were concentrated and enhanced through husbandry and horticulture. Game, fish, fruit, grapes for winemaking, and flowers were found there. The medieval garden was also meant to be a *locus amoenus,* an earthly paradise, a sanctified spot from which the wicked (or uninitiated) were excluded, the province of such deserving souls as princes, poets, and lovers as well as monks and gardeners (fig. 3.23).

In horticulture, as in so many other areas, European knowledge declined after the eclipse of Roman civilization. We have seen how Arabic scholarship at Córdoba kept alive ancient agricultural practices inherited from antiquity. A great boost to the revival of horticulture in the West occurred when the Bolognese lawyer Piero de' Crescenzi (1230–1305) wrote his *Liber ruralium commodorum* consisting of twelve books on the practical aspects of agriculture (fig. 3.24). Crescenzi was an early participant in the rediscovery of classical writing. His treatise relied substantially on the works of such ancients as Cato the Elder (234–149 B.C.E.), Marcus Terentius Varro (116–27 B.C.E.), and Lucius Columella (first century C.E.) as well as *De vegetabilibus* by Albertus Magnus (c. 1200–1280), written a half century earlier.

3.23. *Maugis & Orlande in a Garden.* Miniature from manuscript 5072, folio 71 of Renaud de Montauben, Bruges. 1462–70. Bibliothèque Nationale, Paris. Turf benches were common features in medieval gardens.

3.24. *Crescentius Discussing Herb Planting,* detail of a page from *"Le Livre des prouffis champestres et ruraux,"* a Bruges manuscript painted by the Master of Margaret of York, c. 1470. Ms. 232, folio 157. The Pierpont Morgan Library, New York

Below: 3.25. Schematic plan for the monastery at St. Gall, Switzerland, c. 819. Drawing after a 9th-century manuscript illustration. Near the lower right-hand corner is a vegetable garden with eighteen rectangular beds carefully labeled with the names of various types of produce. Next to this garden lay the cemetery, which was also the orchard. The herb garden in the upper right-hand corner of the plan is located logically next to the infirmary. Until the rise of medical schools in the late Middle Ages, when a new professional class tried to outlaw the practice of monastic medicine, monks acted as physicians not only within their own communities but also to patients from outside the monastery. The medicines that they and the trained doctors who were their successors used were herbal ones, and the pharmacopoeia they derived from plants was extensive.

Presented, like Columella's first-century treatise, as a series of books on the practical aspects of farming and estate management (including site selection and overall layout of domicile, farm buildings, orchards, and gardens), its value to us is twofold: first, as a description of medieval gardening practices and design and, second—because of the numerous illustrated manuscript and published editions—as a visual source of the ideal, if not the actual, appearance of many medieval gardens. It is primarily a "how-to" manual, detailing the proper ways of tilling the soil, sowing and reaping crops, growing fruit and shade trees, tending vines, making wine, and managing livestock, fish, and game. While Piero gives prescriptions, rather than descriptions, of actual gardens, it is fair to assume that the gated walls, square planting beds, vine-clad arbors and trellises, flowery turf benches, fountains and well-tended fruit trees that we see in illustrations of the *Liber ruralium commodorum* reflect the appearance of actual medieval gardens in his day and later. What is most apparent in studying these manuscript paintings and early book prints is the absence of spatial composition. The principle of subordinating the garden's parts to an overall plan in which spatial considerations are paramount does not

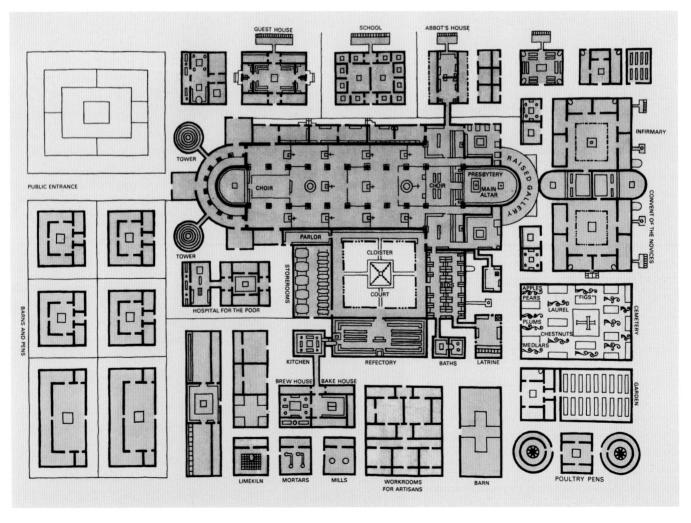

seem to govern their layout. These are gardens of objects—plants, walks, and structures—the arrangement of which is primarily for utility and the pleasure they afford in and of themselves.

Indeed, most medieval gardens were utilitarian arrangements designed to provide cooking and medicinal herbs, fruit, and vegetables. Although considerably earlier than the period we are examining here, the ninth-century Plan of St. Gall showing the ideal layout of a monastery was probably a valid prototype for similar Late Medieval communities (fig. 3.25). The St. Gall scheme is probably more orderly than the gardens in real monasteries, where vegetables were often grown in the random spaces around the various workshops and in individually tilled plots behind the monks' cells.

Most of the great rural monasteries have vanished, but there are still to be found within certain urban monasteries and convents, like carefully guarded jewels, old cloister gardens with the sanctified atmosphere of medieval times. Notable among these are three in Rome: that of the Basilica of SS. Quattro Coronati (Four Crowned Saints) (fig. 3.26), that of St. John in the Lateran, and that of St. Paul's Outside the Walls. The colonnettes framing the cloister garden are often twisted or braided and inlaid with glittering bits of mosaic in the decorative style known as Cosmatesque.

Between these and two other Roman cloister gardens—that of S. Giovanni Battista dei Genovesi and that of the Palazzetto Venezia—a profound

stylistic change is evident. Although the cloister's basic form and intended symbolism remain unaltered, one senses in these the influence of the theories of Leone Battista Alberti (1404–1472), the great humanist scholar, poet, mathematician, and architect, who promoted the development of an architectural style along principles derived from classical antiquity. In these early Renaissance examples, the decoratively conceived, comparatively insubstantial colonnettes of the earlier cloister gardens have given way to solid, unadorned columns with simple foliated capitals derived from ancient Roman architecture.

Even devout men like painter Fra Angelico found inspiration in the forms of pagan antiquity, as is evident in his contemporary panel of *The Annunciation* (c. 1440–50) (fig. 3.27). Like other painters of his day, Fra Angelico was influenced by the theory and practice of Alberti as he began to define three-dimensional spaces for his figures to inhabit. Mary is depicted in an enclosed convent garden, a symbol of her virginity and a paradisiacal space, or "third" nature, elevated in meaning above the cultivated fields of "second" nature and the fearful connotations of wilderness, or "first" nature. However, the architecture of the loggia where the heavenly visitation occurs is similar in style to that which we will examine in the next chapter in our discussion of the Renaissance villa and its interweaving of landscape and architectural space. To understand better the important changes that were occurring in the relationship between human beings and the landscape and the ways in which the concept of three natures was elaborated by allegory at this time, it will be necessary to look more closely at the cultural and intellectual movement called humanism.

3.26. Cloister Garden, SS. Quattro Coronati, Rome. Early 13th century, with a 12th-century fountain

Below: 3.27. Fra Angelico, *The Annunciation.* 1435-45. Tempera on panel. The Prado, Madrid

Notes for Chapter Three

1. According to Xenophon (c. 430–c. 355 B.C.E.), the Greek soldier, writer, and disciple of Socrates, Persian parks also served as open spaces for the purpose of flood control and as "parade grounds" in which to muster the army. In Hebrew, the word *pardes,* meaning also park or garden, became associated in apocalyptic and rabbinical tradition with a blessed place where the virtuous dead receive their reward. In the transformation of the Persian *pairidaeza* to the Greek *paradeisos,* the word gained the connotation of a garden or, rather, two specific gardens: the Abode of the Blessed Dead and, in the literature of postbiblical times, the Garden of Eden. The Latin *paradisus* appropriated the three meanings of the Greek *paradeisos:* garden or park (ordinary gardens for the practice of horticulture as well as enclosures for wild animals); celestial paradise (Heaven); and earthly paradise (the Garden of Eden).

2. *Genesis* 2: 8–10 (The New English Bible).

3. Ibid.

4. Homer, *The Odyssey,* trans. Robert Fitzgerald (Garden City, New York: Doubleday & Company, 1961), lines 561–68, p. 81.

5. Homer, *The Odyssey.* "The Garden of Alcinous," trans. Robert M. Torrance. *Encompassing Nature: A Sourcebook,* ed. Robert M. Torrance (Washington, D.C.: Counterpoint, 1998), p. 281.

6. Hesiod, *The Works and Days.* "The Five Ages," trans. Apostolos Athanassakis. In *The Norton Book of Classical Literature,* ed. Bernard Knox (New York: W.W. Norton & Company, 1993), p. 193.

7. Dracontius, *De Laudibus Dei,* Book I. "The Earthly Paradise," trans. Robert M. Torrance. In *Encompassing Nature: A Sourcebook* (Washington, D.C.: Counterpoint, 1998), p. 600.

8. Ibid., p. 601.

9. Sura 76. The Koran, trans. N. J. Dawood. (Harmondsworth, Middlesex, England: Penguin, 4th rev. ed., 1974), p. 18.

10. Firdausi, *Shahnamih,* I, 157. As quoted in William L. Hanaway, Jr., "Paradise on Earth" in *The Islamic Garden* (Washington, D.C.: Dumbarton Oaks and Trustees for Harvard University, 1976), p. 53.

11. The Song of Songs 4:12

12. Claudian, *Epithalamium de Nuptiis Honorii Augusti,* lines 78–85, trans. A. Bartlett Giamatti. In A. Bartlett Giamatti, *The Earthly Paradise and the Renaissance Epic* (New York: W.W. Norton & Company, 1966) Norton paperback edition, p. 51.

13. Giovanni Boccaccio, *The Decameron,* trans. G.H. McWilliam (Harmondsworth, Middlesex, England: Penguin, 1972), p. 233.

14. For a discussion of the etymology of the word *garden,* which represents the notion of separation from, and enhancement of, nature, see John Dixon Hunt, *Greater Perfections* (Philadelphia: University of Pennsylvania Press, 1999). Here, too, the reader will find treated the relationship between landscape design and literature in various cultures throughout history.

15. For an excellent discussion of gardens of Islamic Spain and their relationship to the surrounding landscape both literally and symbolically, see D. Fairchild Ruggles, *Gardens, Landscape, and Vision in the Palaces of Islamic Spain* (University Park, Pennsylvania: The Pennsylvania State University Press, 2000).

16. The word *alcázar* is derived from the Arabic word *al-qasr,* which means "fortress."

17. According to 1 Kings, 7:23–26, the temple of King Solomon had a large basin that rested on the backs of twelve oxen. Between 1056 and 1066, Yusuf, a Jewish vizier in Granada, which was then controlled by the Zirids, the Berber clan whose caliphs ruled from 1013 until they were conquered by the Almoravids in 1090, built a magnificent palace and garden with a fountain that was likened by a contemporary poet to that of Solomon, except that "...not on oxen it stands, / But there are lions, in phalanx by its rim... / Whose bellies are wellsprings that spout forth / through their mouths floods like streams." Although it is not possible to support with certainty the claim of one scholar (Frederick Bargebuhr) that the lions of this very fountain were reused to support the fourteenth-century, twelve-sided basin of the fountain in the Court of the Lions, the sophisticated Islamic and Jewish elite who saw the fountain in the Court of the Lions at that time would have readily associated with royal Solomonic imagery its inscription: "For truly, what else is this fountain but a beneficent cloud pouring out its abundant supplies over the lions underneath? / Like the hands of the Caliph when he rises in the morning to distribute plentiful rewards among his soldiers the lions of war." For a good discussion of the implied symbolism of the fountain in the Court of the Lions, see D. Fairchild Ruggles, *Gardens, Landscape, and Vision in the Palaces of Islamic Spain,* pp. 163–166, 199–200, 213.

18. The Spanish ambassador to the court of Tamerlane, Ruy Gonzélez de Clavijo (d. 1412), left a description of these festive gatherings and of the gardens in which they took place. See Ruy Gonzélez de Clavijo, *Embassy to Tamerlane, 1403–1406,* trans. Guy Le Strange (London: G. Routledge, 1928).

19. As this garden type moved from Central Asia into northern India, *chahar,* meaning "four," and *bagh,* meaning "garden" underwent a slight spelling change. Thus, the fourfold Mughal garden in India is known as a *char bagh.*

20. James L. Wescoat, "Gardens of invention and exile: The precarious context of Mughal garden design during the reign of Humayun (1530–1556)," *Journal of Garden History.* vol. 10, no. 2, p. 114.

21. Elizabeth B. Moynihan, *Paradise as a Garden in Persia and Mughal India* (New York: George Braziller, 1979), p. 112.

22. In France, these newly urbanized zones were called *faubourgs,* from the Old French *fors,* meaning "outside," and *borc,* the archaic "town." Hence, when we speak today of the districts of Paris known as Faubourg Saint-Germain or Faubourg Saint-Antoine, we are referring to parts of the city that were outside the old walls.

CLASSICISM REBORN: LANDSCAPE IDEALS OF THE RENAISSANCE IN ITALY AND FRANCE

The wall surrounding the Renaissance garden eventually became, metaphorically, a shell to be cracked open. The confidence in human reason, which is a lasting legacy of the Renaissance, profoundly changed humanity's view of nature. Throughout the period examined in this chapter, the garden remained visibly contained within walls. But the emphasis upon axial planning was a first step toward spatial thrust and the apparent extension of its boundaries to the horizon. Although the process of transformation into an outward-focused concept of landscape design was a slow one—it began to be obvious only in the seventeenth century—it had its origins in the cultural rebirth known as the Renaissance and the Neoplatonic separation of the real and the ideal, the world of humans and the world of God.

Dante Alighieri (1265–1321) prefigured a more expansive human view of landscape in *The Divine Comedy,* in which the narrator begins his pilgrimage in a dark wood, guided—significantly—by the ancient Roman poet Virgil through a metaphysical landscape, which ultimately offers, after an ascent of Mount Purgatory, the exhilaration of panoramic perspective. Petrarch, figuratively following in Dante's footsteps, attempted what was then unheard of, the actual ascent of Mont Ventoux, a hardship endured because, as he wrote to a friend, "My only motive was to see what so great an elevation had to offer." Here we have, quite literally, a new and much bolder human perspective of the terrestrial landscape than that of medieval individual who, with gaze turned inward, contemplated only the visionary landscape of paradise. Petrarch's view from Mont Ventoux prefigures a shift in attitude toward landscape as a response to a new confidence in human powers of reason. The resulting liberation of science and the fostering of a spirit of open-ended inquiry found an expressive analogue in the design of actual contemporary landscapes as the inwardly focused, self-contained paradise garden gradually gave way to an expansive, outwardly directed, more worldly garden.

More specifically, we can see in the evolution of Renaissance garden design a reflection of changing cosmological belief.[1] The humanist philosopher and mathematician Nicolaus of Cusa (1401–1464) posited the concept of spatial neutrality—that is, the notion that space is unbounded and the universe has no center—a century before Nicolaus Copernicus (1473–1543) developed his theory of planetary movement around the sun and two centuries before Galileo (1564–1642) improved the telescope for astronomical use. In the West, the trend toward landscape designs that portray seemingly unbounded garden space, tentative and partial at first but fully assured by the seventeenth century, mirrors the progress of cosmological thought from Cusa to René Descartes (1596–1650) as the old Aristotelian spatial paradigm was gradually abandoned and the foundations of modern physics were laid.

In addition to opening the door to modern science, Renaissance humanism revived the classical forms and practices of antiquity. The publication in 1499 of the immensely influential *Hypnerotomachia Poliphili,* believed to be the work of the archaeologically minded Francesco Colonna, provided numerous illustrations depicting arbors, pavilions, colonnades, fountains, grottoes, *parterres,* topiary, and other elements of a reinvented classical language specifically directed toward landscape design (fig. 4.1). *De re aedificatoria,* the influential treatise on architecture by Leon Battista Alberti (1404–1472), published in 1452, provided a ready reference for a new generation of architects. They turned, as Alberti did, with reverential enthusiasm to whatever could still be understood in the writings of the first-century B.C.E. Roman architect and engineer Vitruvius and the visible remains of classical architecture—the shells of old basilicas and baths, the broken columns of ancient temples and porticoes, the excavated decorative fragments of Nero's Golden House and Hadrian's Villa near Tivoli. Pliny the Younger's descriptions of his first-century C.E. Laurentinum and Tusci villas, available in manuscript form in the fifteenth century and published in 1506, promoted the Renaissance ideal of villa architecture as well as the general notion among great families of the *villeggiatura,* summer residence in the country (see Chapter Two).

Using ancient practice as a guide in codifying their own building principles, Renaissance princes revived the use of axial symmetry, and they put their own stylistic stamp on many decorative motifs borrowed from ancient classical structures. In the powerful proportions of old Roman forms as well as in the rich vocabulary of antique classical ornament they found a means to ennoble humanity and to glorify certain men—the princes of the Church as well as the secular rulers of the day. Like the ancient Romans, they built villas in the country as retreats from business life, places to cultivate the intellect and sometimes—especially in Tuscany and the Veneto, but also in Rome—the land.

Wealthy connoisseurs collected antiquities. Classical sculpture, which had lain buried in the ground, was avidly unearthed, and several Renaissance villa gardens were designed as showcases for these works of art. But as there were insufficient ancient works to furnish all the gardens that were being built, Renaissance artists emulated the norms of antiquity in new sculpture and decoration.

The resurrection of ancient sculpture and the revival of antique forms re-established interest in classical deities, making profane subjects as important as sacred ones and as useful for artistic purposes. Gods and goddesses took up residence in the human imagination once again. Embraced by popes and cardinals, who interpreted "pagan" mythology as prefiguring Christian religion, the ancient divinities provided garden designers with a reinvented antique imagery and classical design vocabulary that superseded the Christian paradise imagery of the Middle Ages. Often these mythological figures were symbolically allied with Christian ideals, as in the case of Hercules, a figure of virtuous strength and chastity. In landscape design, classical sculpture was arranged in groupings, or tableaux, to convey allegorical messages that flattered the patrons who commissioned them, and these were often linked as a series of iconographic statements within a planned garden itinerary.

Astronomy and astrology remained firmly intertwined, and Renaissance intellectuals were as fascinated with mystical symbols as their medieval forebears had been. Within the humanists' conceptual framework, classical myth came to take its place alongside Christian mystery. The arcane symbolism within the *Hypnerotomachia Poliphili* proved enormously appealing to Renaissance patrons and artists. Sculpture and water were used as elements in increasingly elaborate iconographic programs that celebrated the fruitful partnership humanity had achieved with nature through art and technology. Indeed, the message-laden garden programs Renaissance humanists developed for their noble patrons can be considered the theme parks

4.1. Colonnade with topiary forms, *Hypnerotomachia Poliphili (The Strife of Love in a Dream).* Text and illustrations probably by Francesco Colonna. Woodcut from the 1561 French edition

of their day. Although the garden still functioned as a metaphor of paradise, it now became something more: a theater for the initiated, those with sufficient humanist education to enable them to decode allegorical statements as they followed a garden itinerary in which fountains and sculptures told often complex stories that alluded to the patron as the author of a new Golden Age, a facilitator of a terrestrial paradise benefiting all humankind.

As in other branches of art, so too in landscape design the lofty serenity and stable balance of mature Renaissance composition soon gave way to the more complicated and dynamic spatial organization characteristic of the late Renaissance of the mid-sixteenth century. Iconography grew ever more allusive and personal. A similar stylistic development as is seen in painting, sculpture, and architecture can be found in the history of landscape design, as we trace its course from quattrocento humanism through a brief period of classical equipoise in the early years of the sixteenth century into the opulent age of the late Renaissance.

As the Renaissance emerged in Italy, the Reformation and the establishment of various Protestant denominations occurred in Northern Europe. Rome, as the seat of Catholicism, launched the Counter-Reformation in the mid-sixteenth century and, in the context of that movement, attempted to inspire faith through artistic means. Thus, in the late sixteenth century, Italy embarked upon a course of design that led to the robust plasticity and florid ornamentation of the Baroque style characterizing Italian art and architecture throughout the seventeenth century. Meanwhile, throughout the sixteenth century, Renaissance Italian artistic forms were absorbed in France. There an indigenous Renaissance style developed, which evolved into the grandeur of the French seventeenth-century version of the Baroque, a more austere form of neoclassicism than the highly theatrical Italian Baroque style. The manifestations of these respective developments in the evolution of Renaissance style in Italy and France will be examined in Chapter Five. Our task here is to trace the rise of Italian humanism and its contribution to the development of a Renaissance style that in Italy reached a climactic stage at the beginning of the sixteenth century, was brilliantly manipulated in a Mannerist mode and adopted by the French, who transformed it into an artistic idiom of their own, even as Renaissance thought was exerting an influence upon the landscapes of Germany, the Low Countries, and England. Although the process of cultural transmission to other lands was well established by the sixteenth century, we will reserve that discussion for Chapter Six. Because the Renaissance was initiated and carried forward by a small elite of royal and noble patrons influenced by ideas fostered by scholars and expressed by artists, our discussion is necessarily focused upon power centers, the courts of monarchs and princes, the villas and *châteaux* they commissioned, and the cities they sought to beautify.

I. Petrarch, Alberti, and Colonna: Humanism and the Landscape

Humanism and the Rebirth of the Villa

Petrarch (Francesco Petrarca, 1304–1374) fathered the intellectual movement known as humanism. Humanism to Petrarch meant the rediscovery of the writings of classical antiquity and the objective, inquiring attitude toward the natural world that informed those texts. He believed that Greek and Roman thought were the cornerstones upon which a new future would be built. He further believed in a new morality in which human will, though subservient to divine law, could exercise a greater degree of autonomy than it had during the Middle Ages, when an expansive curiosity was viewed as an affront to theological doctrine. The recovery and study of the classical past, coupled with the intellectual and moral energy released by the new spirit of scientific inquiry and respect for individual achievement, constituted in the minds of the historical protagonists an intellectual rebirth, which they called in Italian *rinàscita,* a term that became translated in French and English as *renaissance* in the nineteenth century when it gained currency among those examining the art of the sixteenth century. Everything that lay between the fall of Rome and the dawn of the exciting new age was to them an intermediate time, or Middle Age. Thus, these humanists bestowed the name by which we still know the interval of history between the sixth and the mid-fourteenth centuries.

Kept alive by priests and monks, Latin continued to serve as the international tongue of educated Europeans throughout this period. Now, however, the humanists wanted more than the continuation of medieval Latin as the language of the educated class. They actually wanted to write not in the Latin they had inherited from medieval scholastics but in the language and syntax of the Roman orator and statesman Marcus Tullius Cicero (106–43 B.C.E.) and the Roman poet Virgil (70–19 B.C.E.). Moreover, humanist scholars wanted not only to write in the tones and style of these eminent ancients, but they also wanted to think about the world in the same ways as they had, examining morality from the perspective of Plato (c. 427–c. 347 B.C.E.) or investigating the natural world in the manner of Pliny the Elder (23–79 C.E.). Ironically, success in reviving ancient Latin as a literary language had the effect of promoting vernacular tongues at the expense of medieval Latin, which fell into gradual disuse.

Petrarch and his followers drew no distinctions between the life of the mind and the life of the city; to serve his countrymen, the contemplative man was morally bound to also be a man of action. The humanism of Petrarch was disseminated by men of letters who saw themselves as statesmen along the lines of Cicero, men whose political programs were informed by intellectual discourse and promulgated with rhetoric. Cosimo de' Medici (1389–1464) captured political control of Florence in 1434, ruling as an enlightened humanist. In 1439, he brought the General Council of the Greek Orthodox and Roman Catholic churches to his city, hospitably subsidizing the gathered prelates who included among them Gemistos Plethon (c. 1355–1450/55), the most respected authority on Plato. The presence in the streets of so many distinguished guests provided the people of the city with a new sense of cosmopolitanism. Some of these ecclesiastics came from Constantinople, then the wealthiest and most sophisticated city in the world. Founded by Constantine as the new Rome in 330 C.E., Constantinople was both the principal seat of Christianity in the Byzantine Empire and the main repository of classical culture after the fall of the Western Roman Empire in 476 C.E. Some Greek Orthodox monasteries had managed to preserve, along with Early Christian manuscripts, copies of certain ancient classical texts. Because the Byzantine Empire endured until the Ottoman Turks overthrew Constantinople in 1453, the Greek Orthodox Church still served in Cosimo's day as a link in a long chain of scholarship reaching back through vanished Roman libraries to the ancient Greeks. Humanist scholar Marsilio Ficino (1433–1499) thought that Florence could perhaps replace this lost center for ancient Greek scholarship and perpetuate the intellectual conversations begun in his city following the 1439 gathering there of so many learned Greek scholars. Ficino is believed to have founded the Platonic Academy under the auspices of Cosimo around 1462 at the Medici patriarch's Villa Careggi near Florence. To this place Cosimo came "not to cultivate the fields, but my soul."[2]

The creation of this society of humanists, which lasted until 1494, signaled a moment of confident idealism in Western history. The tenets of humanism became the province of a small but influential group of intellectuals, including officers of the Church. These prelates were increasingly disposed toward its philosophy as well as its theories of beauty, which they nourished with their literary and artistic patronage. The garden assumed special status as a place of contemplation and learning, as well as an architectural space and opportunity for fresh artistic expression.

Ficino's Neo-Platonism drew on the works of Plotinus, the third century C.E. Alexandrian philosopher who posited a Godhead from which all creation emanates and with which the soul can be mystically united, as well as on the writings of Augustine and the twelfth-century Neoplatonists. His philosophy gave special status to the soul as the agent of the transcendent, cognitive, creative intellect standing at the midpoint between the earthly and the divine, mediating between the higher and lower worlds. For Ficino, mystical love as inspired by Plato's theory of love in the *Symposium* and *Phaedrus*—"divine madness"—is the source of poetic genius. Its goal is beauty, which is divisible into two oppositional realms: celestial and natural, as personified by the two Venuses often portrayed in Renaissance art—one symbolizing sacred love, the other profane. Ficino's philosophy gave new status to the artist, whose task it was to translate pure form—ideal beauty—into physical reality, a project assisted by mathematical concepts of proportion and harmony.

Ficino's disciple, Giovanni Pico della Mirandola (1463–1494), articulated the then-radical concept of individual free will, which granted the artist enormous creative potential and mimetic power to juxtapose and combine forms in new representations of nature with meanings derived not from doctrinal religion but from the human intellect. Increasingly, the natural sciences informed this enterprise. As the tenets of a static medieval scholasticism based on the concept of a closed, rather than an open, universe, were gradually overturned by this invigorating license to a more open-ended mode of inquiry, the *hortus conclusus* became the *giardino segreto,* or secret garden, a secluded and enclosed garden room, a place of intimate contact with nature within the larger Renaissance garden. As if in self-conscious recognition of the philosophical nature of this transaction, a principal theme often expressed in the iconography of the Renaissance garden is the syncretism of Art and Nature. Moreover, the *giardino segreto* anticipated the botanical garden in which exotic and native plants were collected and displayed in a systematic fashion.

Petrarch, a devout Christian, sought spiritual truth in nature as well as practical knowledge. Toward these ends, he created two gardens near his home at Fontaine-de-Vaucluse, collected rare plants, and conducted experiments in growing several plant varieties under varying geographic, seasonal, meteorological, and astrological conditions. One garden, situated on a slope, he referred to as his "transalpine Parnassus." The other, closer to his house and situated on an island in the middle of a fast-flowing river, was accessible "by a little bridge leading from a vaulted grotto where the sun never penetrates." Prefiguring by four

hundred years the form and function of Alexander Pope's famous grotto at Twickenham, which we will examine in Chapter Seven, Petrarch said that he believed his grotto "resembles that small room where Cicero sometimes went to recite; it is an invitation to study, to which I go at noon."

The several villas built by Cosimo and his Medici successors a century after Petrarch proved to be prudent investments in the rural economy and refuges in times of plague or political strife. They were also centers for intellectual recreation and conversation. For a time, in the buoyant atmosphere of the Renaissance, the Italian villa became once more, as it had been in antiquity for Pliny the Younger, a philosophical and literary retreat where the aristocracy celebrated the pleasures of rustic life.

THE THEORIES OF ALBERTI

Lorenzo the Magnificent (1449–1492), the grandson of Cosimo, did not enjoy the same degree of wealth and power as Cosimo had, conspicuous though he was as a benefactor of Florence. Occupying his time less fully with the banking activities of his family, Lorenzo threw himself even more energetically into statecraft and the pursuit of the arts. He liked to gather artists, musicians, and members of the Platonic Academy around him at his villas at Fiesole, Cafaggiolo, Careggi, and Poggio a Caiano. Although Leon Battista Alberti died soon after Lorenzo came to power, he was influential within this humanist circle, and his treatise on architecture, *De re aedificatoria,* was a constant reference work for Lorenzo.

Alberti was a versatile polymath, among other things a poet, a scholar of classical literature and philosophy, and an author of treatises on perspective and other aspects of painting as well as on sculpture and on villa design specifically. Although he later designed buildings, he avoided direct involvement in the construction process, setting himself apart from architects of humbler origins who usually served as both designers and supervisors of construction. Alberti advised Pope Nicholas V on various urban projects. His theories on architecture merged under one definition of beauty: "that reasoned harmony of all the parts within a body, so that nothing may be added or taken away, or altered, but for the worse," a state he called *cocinnitas.* He saw in geometry nature's order, advocating symmetry and the arrangement of various building parts according to symbolically significant ratios of proportion, thus translating Neoplatonic ideals of natural harmonic form into architectural reality.[3]

Alberti derived several of his architectural concepts from the principles of order and harmony found in nature and saw nature in its own right as a source

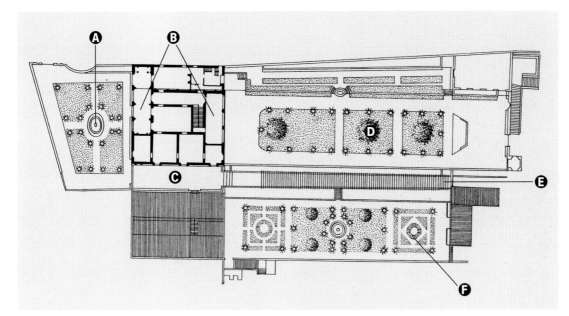

4.2. Plan of the Villa Medici,
Fiesole. Designed by Miche-
lozzo di Bartolommeo. Prior
to 1455
Ⓐ Giardino Segreto
Ⓑ Loggias
Ⓒ Terrace
Ⓓ Lemon Garden
Ⓔ Pergola
Ⓕ Lower Garden

4.3. Lemon garden, Villa
Medici. 20th-century
restoration

of pleasure. According to Alberti, villas should be sited on gentle elevations with a view of the surrounding countryside. Gardens should have porticoes that would afford both sun and shade and also serve as an architectonic link in making garden space continuous with that of the house. For large gatherings he prescribed a festive open space and for quiet pleasure the presence of springs of water. He advised planting boxwood hedges in sheltered locations and was not averse to arranging these in the form of the owner's monogram after the fashion of the ancient Romans. Nor did he disapprove of comic statues in the garden, "provided they are not obscene."[4]

The Villa Medici at Fiesole

Sometime prior to 1455, Cosimo commissioned Michelozzo di Bartolommeo (1396–1472) to design the Villa Medici at Fiesole for his son Giovanni (figs. 4.2, 4.3). Built between 1458 and 1461, the villa's primary function was not as a working farm, but as a setting for intellectual life and a demonstration of aesthetic and ideological values. As architectural historian James S. Ackerman points out, "Michelozzo's simple arcaded cube was the first modern villa designed without thought or possibility of material gain."[5] Judging from a contemporary fresco painted by Domenico del Ghirlandaio (1449–1494), it was covered in off-white stucco. Although devoid of Albertian classical details, it followed the prescription for siting set forth in *De re aedificatoria*. Conspicuous from afar, it rose from a terraced embankment in conscious imitation of Pliny's siting of his first-century-C.E. villas at Laurentinum and Tusci, where scenic perspective was an important consideration. The Medici villa at Fiesole with its commanding view of nearby Florence was the first since ancient times to consciously exploit the potential of its site in this way and was thus a prototype for the

Plinian view that would become a significant element in the location, orientation, and design of future Italian gardens, which for this and other reasons were situated on hillsides whenever possible.

The east front of the villa was an entirely open loggia before one of the bays was walled in. On the west front the loggia remains entirely open, and one can fully appreciate its spatial fusion with a lovely *giardino segreto,* or secret garden. This is an early example of the way Italian designers, who conceived of villa and garden as integral architectural components, created indoor and outdoor spaces that interpenetrated one another. Originally *giardini segreti* were small

4.4. Sandro Botticelli. *Primavera.* c. 1482. Galleria degli Uffizi, Florence

enclosed garden rooms, but here, where the scenic potential of the site was exploited, garden and loggia overlook a panoramic view of the Arno Valley and the city of Florence, with Filippo Brunelleschi's cathedral dome dominating the skyline.

A gate leads from this garden to a terrace running along the south side of the house. Beyond this terrace, a long pergola overlooks the lower terrace garden with its clipped, cone-shaped magnolia trees (*Magnolia grandiflora*) surrounded by lawn and hedges of box. Restored and planted in its current form at the beginning of the twentieth century by Cecil Pinsent for Lady Sybil Cutting, as noted in Chapter Ten, this garden and the grassy terrace above are decorated with lemon trees in terra-cotta pots. The grade change between the pergola and the lower terrace garden is not exploited as an opportunity for ornamental stairs, as similar slopes were to be in later Italian gardens. The lower garden is, however, cut into the hillside and is sufficiently lower than the upper garden so as not to intrude upon the panoramic view from the upper terrace.

Even though the Villa Medici at Fiesole was built simply as a country retreat rather than as working villa, agricultural scenery abruptly abuts it. This unselfconscious shift from garden formality to olive trees and fields, which had also characterized the ancient villa landscape as described by Pliny, can be seen in many other Tuscan gardens. Much as modern urbanites enjoy the apple orchards and potato fields around their country houses without themselves engaging in agricultural pursuits, Lorenzo's circle delighted in the bucolic landscape of Fiesole. There the scholar-poet

Angelo Poliziano (1454–1494) wrote his "Rusticus," a celebration of the pastoral poetry of such ancient writers as Horace, Hesiod, Columella, and Virgil. The poem is also a paean to the view of Florence with the silvery Arno in the distance and to Lorenzo's patronage and generosity of spirit. In this way, rural values and urban power were harmoniously aligned within the cultural matrix of humanism.

The humanist attitude toward nature implicit in the siting of the Villa Medici at Fiesole is also reflected in Florentine quattrocento painting. The artist's receptivity to natural beauty could not have occurred had not late medieval philosophy as well as the new humanism caused a profound shift in society's overall cultural perspective. Christian faith was not abandoned, but individual excellence and human achievement were increasingly valued. Scientific observation and humanistic aesthetics fostered an interest in nature and delight in the beauties of landscape. Classical mythology was incorporated into the education of the well-to-do, and allegory using classical themes and images was extensively employed in art and literature.

Sandro Botticelli's *Primavera,* a painting of about 1482, expresses both the naturalistic and arcane aspects of Renaissance humanism (fig. 4.4). Paintings such as this, as well as gardens of the period, were intended as both literal and metaphorical paradises. At the same time, they were presented as visual texts to be decoded, as bearers of messages to be deciphered, as stationary dramas for the discerning. While the key to its meaning has been much debated by scholars, it is clear that in the *Primavera* we have not only an image comparable to the medieval paintings of the Virgin Mary in a flowery mead, but, more important, a Renaissance interpretation of the paradise or Venus gardens of ancient literature. The garden over which Botticelli's Venus presides is clearly the garden of love. On the right we see Zephyr, the harbinger of Spring and ravisher of Chloris. The latter, as compensation for having been thus taken, is turned into the adjacent Flora. In the orange trees that form a bower for Venus, Cupid points his arrow toward one of the three Graces. Completing the scene is Mercury, a god associated with the month of May. The painting is thought by some authorities to commemorate the wedding, in May 1482, of a member of the Medici family.

It is apparent from this and other quattrocento paintings that allegory, for more than a thousand years pressed into the service of the Christian faith, has returned to its classical origins and that classical subjects are no longer prohibited by religious authorities intent upon stamping out "pagan" belief. Christian and classical themes now served in a syncretic manner as primary subjects for artists for the next three hundred years. Gardens were populated almost entirely by classical deities and mythological heroes, as Christian humanists read new meanings into ancient myths. One explanation for this lies in the extraordinary influence exerted by the *Hypnerotomachia Poliphili* on garden design.

HYPNEROTOMACHIA POLIPHILI

In 1499, the Venetian publisher Aldus Manutius brought forth an enigmatic and fascinating book with descriptions and woodcut illustrations that were to have a great influence upon garden design. Called *Hypnerotomachia Poliphili,* it is reputedly the work of a Dominican monk and nobleman, Francesco Colonna (1433–1527). At Palestrina, Colonna was engaged with his father, Stefano, in restoring the Temple of Fortuna Primigenia, a Greco-Roman goddess associated with Egyptian veneration of the Nile (see fig. 2.24). Colonna shared the interest of Pico and other Neoplatonists in mystery religions and their initiatory rituals. These involved the decoding of cabalistic messages, which were sometimes in the form of hieroglyphs. Such hieroglyphs were believed to represent the immaterial essence as well as the functional nature of the things they symbolized, the Idea, in Platonic terms, as well as its material form.

Translated by Jean Martin in 1546, the *Hypnerotomachia Poliphili* was published in France as *Discours du songe de Poliphile* with a new set of woodcut illustrations in the mannerist style associated with the School of Fontainebleau. When the English edition appeared in 1592, its title was rendered as "The Strife

of Love in a Dream."[6] The protagonist, Poliphilus, whose name means "Lover of Polia," is the narrator of a many-layered erotic dream in which his passion for architecture and gardens of great intricacy and decorative sumptuousness is fully indulged along with his extravagant devotion to his beloved. Poliphilus journeys to the gardens of Queen Eleuterilyda and, in the company of Polia, to the island of Cytherea, where he describes the "groves, meadows, gardens, streams and springs" in elaborate detail. In the middle of the island is "Venus's fountain with seven precious columns,"[7] the scene of the climax of Book One in which the naked Goddess of Love is described in delectable detail and Poliphilus is pierced by Cupid's arrow. Here and in the other imaginary locales visited by Poliphilus, Colonna displays his intense interest in ornamental architecture and ingenious devices.

The woodcut illustrations from Colonna's book, with their fanciful topiary and knot garden designs and images of grove, grotto, classical pergola, vine-clad arcade, and pseudo-Egyptian esoteric devices, including an elephant with an obelisk mounted in its back, became a source of inspiration for several generations of garden designers. The book was also an important means of disseminating Renaissance garden style, especially in the second half of the sixteenth century following the publication of the immensely popular French edition (fig. 4.5).

As in the Renaissance garden, water plays an especially important role in Poliphilus's pilgrimage as he progresses from a singing brook past gushing fountains, including one in the form of the streaming breasts of a sleeping nymph and another resembling harpies surmounted by Graces, also with water coming from their breasts in silver threads (fig. 4.6). According to the cultural historian Simon Schama, "the fountains of the *Hypnerotomachia Poliphili* con-

4.5. Topiary and knot forms, *Hypnerotomachia Poliphili (The Strife of Love in a Dream)* by Francesco Colonna. Woodcut probably from the 1561 French edition. Recommended by Alberti, topiary—shrubbery pruned into fanciful shapes—was an antique garden practice enthusiastically revived in the Renaissance.

4.6. Graces with water streaming from their breasts, *Hypnerotomachia Poliphili (The Strife of Love in a Dream)*. Text and illustrations probably by Francesco Colonna. Woodcut from the 1561 French edition

trived an effect that was somehow both erotic and philosophical, animal and ethereal. And it was this irresistible combination that cast a spell on the landscape architects of the Roman and Tuscan villas of the mid and late sixteenth century."[8]

Influenced by the nature of Colonna's book, although not by its specific text, in which a clear narrative line is difficult to follow, gardens became firmly associated with allegory as places of allusion and meaning. Their paths became prescribed routes through a series of theatrical stops where sculptural or architectural embellishments, often in association with water, posed intellectual riddles and provided answers of a symbolic nature. In attempting to understand their meaning in the Renaissance, it is important to recall not only the intellectual excitement generated by a renewed appreciation of classical mythology but also the interest among certain educated people in the arcanely symbolic imagery derived from Egyptian forms, Neoplatonism, and alchemy.

Poliphilus, like Dante's protagonist in *The Divine Comedy*, begins his journey in a dense grove of trees. This dark wood symbolizes the lack of certainty that confronts any pilgrim setting out upon a quest. The grove, which in antiquity was associated with sacred places as well as with Plato's Academy and Aristotle's

Lyceum, was revived in the Renaissance in the form of the *bosco*, a planting usually of evergreen ilex trees.[9] The *bosco* is the realm of nature and the representation of the Golden Age extolled by the ancient writers Ovid and Virgil, an earthly paradise evoking the time when people lived in a hospitable environment surrounded by nature's bounty of berries and nourishing acorns. Its natural forms and deep shade produced an air of wildness and mystery, serving as a foil to the otherwise geometrical garden. Pleasant refuges from the hot summer sun, *boschi* were integral to the iconographic programs of certain garden landscapes. They provided appropriate settings in which the visitor could encounter, with a degree of surprise, the symbolical features that had been strategically placed along a prescribed path.

The grotto, like the sacred grove, had ancient associations with mysterious life forces. The wellspring of streams, it was the home of river gods and nymphs. Grottoes such as the one described by Colonna became practically obligatory elements in sixteenth-century gardens, and their popularity continued far into the nineteenth century, when they served as Romantic features in many parks and gardens. In the period we are examining here, there were two kinds: those with artificial stalactites and encrustations of colored stones and shells and those of a more architectural character, nymphaeums with niched arcades for statuary.

The importance of the *Hypnerotomachia Poliphili* as a mirror of the Renaissance imagination stems from its fusion of the highly artificial and the natural into a "third nature"[10] embodying complex and interwoven sets of symbols that often convey polysemous mythic narratives, allegorical stories with several intended meanings. With its combination of eroticism and idealism, it profoundly expanded the garden's conceptual horizons, making it possible to read into its design multiple texts and individual expressions of imagination.

A new sense of the garden's expressive possibilities and a new vocabulary of garden design forms were now at hand. Albertian *cocinnitas,* or economically perfect harmony of parts, as manifested in the integration of the elements of the garden plan along clearly defined axes with compositional symmetry of parts, was now fused with Colonna's notion of the garden as an allegorical environment in which one could follow an itinerary of initiation and revelation.[11] Mathematics and mythology, geometry and allegory, were now firmly joined. To exploit this expressive potential in a grammar of landscape art—a design style—would take genius. Fortunately, genius was at hand in the person of the architect Bramante.

II. Bramante and the Rediscovery of Axial Planning: Gardens of Sixteenth-Century Italy

Establishing the Italian Renaissance Garden Paradigm: Belvedere Court and Villa Madama

Encouraged by his reading of Pliny the Younger, Petrarch's first somewhat tentative embrace of panoramic perspective on Mont Ventoux heralded the scenic appreciation that would later become a hallmark of Renaissance thought. The Italian word *belvedere,* meaning "beautiful view," is an important one in the history of landscape design because of its association with a particular type of garden structure. Built in various styles, depending upon time and place, a belvedere may be either an independent tower or part of the villa itself. A belvedere is, quite simply, a lookout whose purpose is the enjoyment of scenery. During the Renaissance, belvederes became an important means of enjoying the view of gardens and the surrounding landscape. The papal villa known as Belvedere, built by Innocent VIII (papacy 1484–1492) on a hill within the Vatican is important for our discussion here, however, not only because of its original siting with commanding views of the Roman countryside but also because the subsequent treatment of the ground that lay between it and the Vatican influenced the course of garden history.

Bisected in the late sixteenth century by a structural addition to the Vatican Palace, half of the Court of the Belvedere today serves as a parking lot for Vatican employees, while the remaining half is a pleasant sculpture garden where visitors can stroll (figs. 4.8, 4.9). Few today, therefore, comprehend its significance as a pivotal development in the history of landscape design. Perhaps because so much later Italian, and indeed European, landscape design was derived from Bramante's axial terraced composition here, this once-revolutionary garden seems only inevitable, not radical, to us.

The seed for a garden on this spot was sown in the quattrocento. The first humanist pope, Nicholas V (papacy 1447–1455) was deeply interested in architecture, and he employed Alberti as his consultant on such projects as the reconstruction of Old St. Peter's and the integration of this basilica with the Vatican Palace. The plan that Alberti conceived included a palace garden. Though considerably smaller in scale, in its ambitious program this garden harked back to Hadrian's Villa rather than to any immediate predecessor, for it was not conceived as a series of outdoor rooms where intimate conversation could take place, as were some of the new villa gardens near Florence, but rather as a space for public gathering and theatrical entertainment. This plan was abandoned at Nicholas's death in 1455, and not until a half century later was a garden program for the Vatican begun in earnest.

Immediately upon his election to the papacy, Pope Julius II (papacy 1503–1513) began implementing a plan for a Vatican garden that was part of a political agenda to increase the importance of the papacy as a power in Europe, with the Vatican serving as the seat of a new Roman empire. The revival of the ancient Roman villa tradition within the walls of the Vatican thus served as a symbolical link to imperial times. To perform this work, the pope chose as his architect Donato Bramante (1444–1514), who had recently completed the sophisticated *tempietto* adjacent to San Pietro in Montorio on the Janiculum Hill, and whom he would soon commission to design a new basilica for St. Peter's. Bramante's first commission from the pope was to provide a physical link between the Belvedere of Innocent VIII on its hill and the Vatican Palace below, creating sheltered communication between the two buildings. At the same time, he was to provide a setting for the pontiff's fine collection of antique sculpture and an outdoor theater to serve as a suitable space for papal pageantry. In addition, Julius II wanted to have a private garden retreat, a place where he could meet and converse with a circle of friends who shared his interest in the rediscovery of the classical world.

In developing his design, Bramante employed Alberti's principles of symmetry and proportion in an axial organization of forms and space that had not been seen since antiquity. He even set about resolving a problem that was generally left unresolved in ancient Roman landscape planning, the harmonization of two colliding axes.

On the uneven terrain between the Vatican Palace and the Belvedere, Bramante placed two parallel loggias, which were three stories on the lowest level adjacent to the palace, then two stories as the rising slope was transformed into an intermediate terrace, and finally one story where an upper terrace joined the villa (fig. 4.9). The steps necessitated by these grade changes in the terraced hillside became important design elements in their own right, their double staircases celebrations of ascent. Perpendicular to the broad terraces between the loggias (today's museum galleries) was a strong central axis terminating next to the villa in a raised niche—or exedra, so called because of its semicircular form. From the windows of the papal apartments the garden

4.7. Great Niche, north end of the Belvedere Court

Below, left: 4.8. The southern section of the Belvedere Court today

Below, right: 4.9. The Belvedere Court, designed in successive stages by Donato Bramante, Michelangelo Buonarroti, and Pirro Ligorio. 1503–1561.

appeared as a stage set or painting demonstrating the principles of single-point perspective, one of the technical discoveries of the Renaissance that theater designers and artists often virtuosically demonstrated in their work. Following Bramante, designers planned gardens with elevated terraces or balconies overlooking them in order that the viewer could readily grasp from this vantage point the axes that enabled and made manifest a perspectival treatment of space.

The elevated niche and its flanking wings screened the awkward juncture of two axes, that of the Belvedere Court and that of the villa. Bramante is believed to have modeled this architectural composition along the lines of the terraced Sanctuary of Fortuna Primigenia at Palestrina (see fig. 2.24). Around 1550, under Pope Julius III (papacy 1550–1555), Michelangelo Buonarroti (1475–1564) replaced Bramante's semicircular Praeneste-like steps with the double flight of stairs we see today. Paired staircases by then had become ubiquitous in Italian garden design as a means of reinforcing axial symmetry and dramatizing the transition from terrace to terrace. Hillsides were

therefore the most desirable sites for garden designers after Bramante showed at the Belvedere Court how designers could successfully exploit steep terrain.

The construction of the Belvedere Court did not occur all at once, but proceeded sporadically over half a century. In addition to replacing Bramante's unusual convex-concave stairs in front of the exedra, Michelangelo enclosed the arcade that formed its curving rear and raised the northern wall next to it an additional story. In 1561, Pius IV (papacy 1559–1565) summoned the architect Pirro Ligorio (c. 1510–1583) to finish the project. Ligorio vaulted the niche to create the Nicchione, or Great Niche, and built its surmounting semicircular loggia (figs. 4.7, 4.9). At the opposite end of the Court, he added a

semicircle of tiered stone seats resembling those of a Roman theater to facilitate viewing the tournaments and other spectacles that took place there (fig. 4.9).

In 1516, Cardinal Giulio de' Medici, later Pope Clement VII, commissioned Raphael (Raffaello Sanzio, 1483–1520) to design the Villa Madama on Monte Mario. Raphael's friend and collaborator Giulio Romano (1492/9–1546) helped with the realization of the design, and Antonio da Sangallo, the Younger (1485–1546), was probably also involved in the project. It was the first villa to be constructed on the outskirts of Rome. Like the Farnesina, the 1508–1511 villa designed by Baldassare Peruzzi (1481–1536) on the banks of the Tiber, it was intended for supper parties attended by popes and cardinals as well as by philosophical noblemen and witty courtesans. These entertainments were an important feature of Roman life during the papacy of Julius II and his successor, Leo X (papacy 1513–1521). Like the Farnesina, the Villa Madama has a beautifully frescoed loggia that serves as the nexus of interpenetrating indoor and outdoor spaces.

Designed in a halcyon era when humanist gatherings and summer entertainments were still the order of the day, the structures of the villa were subservient to the gardens, which stretched out along lengthy axes. From the entrance on the south, one passes into an entry court and beyond through an entry loggia into the large central court. This axis is projected through another loggia in which recessed niches seem to pull the outdoor space into the architecture of the building, while simultaneously pushing the fabric of the building into the adjacent garden. Giovanni da Udine (1487–1561/4), whose beautiful frescoes of garlands embellish the ceiling of the Farnesina, also worked at the Villa Madama, painting the frescoes that decorate the bays of this loggia in the antique style of those found in Nero's Golden House (fig. 4.10). Originally the loggia, which is now glassed in, opened directly onto the garden. Lofty loggias with the adjacent garden in axial relation to them, the successors of the Villa Medici at Fiesole, help to dissolve the visual separation between building and nature and are among the hallmarks of Italian villa design.

Curiously, the axial orientation of the Villa Madama, unlike that of the Villa d'Este at Tivoli, does not exploit the scenic potential of its lofty site on Monte Mario but runs laterally across the hillside instead of along its gradient. Raphael planned another perpendicular axis that would have accomplished this purpose, but his design for this extension of the garden was never executed. The garden's principal view therefore remains that from the loggia along the villa's main axis as it continues outdoors through a garden of boxwood compartments and a long terrace stretch-

4.10. Giovanni da Udine, Loggia fresco, Villa Madama

Left: 4.11. Fish pond, Villa Madama

ing across the flank of Monte Mario to the north. These two spaces are separated by a tall vine-clad wall pierced with a pedimented gate guarded by a pair of colossal male figures. Parallel to this garden at a lower level is a rectangular fish pond (fig. 4.11). Fish ponds were common in medieval gardens, but the architectural character of this one introduces us in a preliminary and rudimentary way to what would become one of the chief means of Italian Renaissance garden expression: the use of water as an important design element. Water was employed with great imagination in subsequent sixteenth-century Italian gardens, appearing in fountains, pools, water staircases, water *parterres,* and *giocchi d'acqua,* or droll water games that involved the spectator physically by providing surprise drenchings from concealed jets suddenly activated. Water in these gardens was a means of providing mesmerizing reflectivity, movement, and excitement. It was meant to connote evanescence, insubstantiality, and temporality, while implying the agrarian bounty achieved when humans harness this vital force of nature.

THE MANIPULATION OF GARDEN FORM AND SPACE IN THE MID-SIXTEENTH CENTURY: VILLA GIULIA

The mature Renaissance style of straightforward axial movement and calm, self-contained monumentality seen in the works of Bramante and Raphael at the beginning of the sixteenth century yielded to the mid-century manipulation of that style into an idiom of

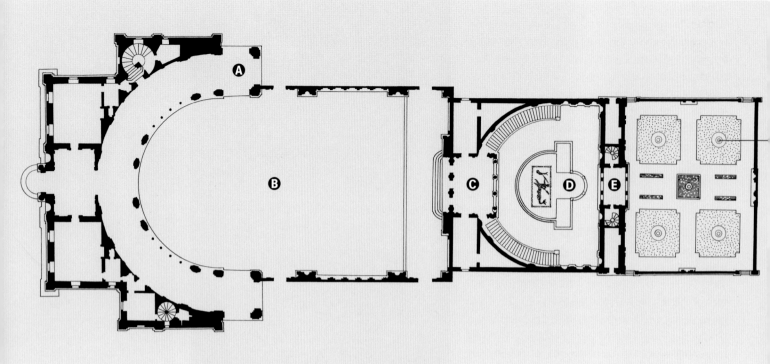

4.12. Plan of Villa Giulia, Rome.
Designed by Michelangelo
Buonarroti, Giorgio Vasari,
Bartolomeo Ammannati, and
Giacomo Barozzi da Vignola.
After 1550
Ⓐ Portico
Ⓑ Garden Court
Ⓒ Loggia
Ⓓ *Nymphaeum*
Ⓔ Rear Loggia
Ⓕ Rear Garden

Right: 4.13. Ceiling of portico,
Villa Giulia

sinuous elegance, spatial eccentricity, and compositional ambiguity and tension, as found in the art of
the painter, architect, and designer Giulio Romano
(1492?–1546) and the painter Parmigianino (Girolamo
Francesco Mazzola, 1503–1540). The same change
can be charted in garden design. Scale and perspective are distorted, and composition is purposely unbal-
anced, rather than centered.

The Villa Giulia, built for Pope Julius III shortly
after his ascent to the papacy in 1550, is a Renaissance
masterpiece. Michelangelo himself participated in its
plan as did the architects Giorgio Vasari (1511–1574),
Bartolommeo Ammannati (1511–1592), and Giacomo
Barozzi da Vignola (1507–1573). Though stripped of
much of its original rich sculptural décor, the villa is
nonetheless a remarkable sight, demonstrating a
sophisticated interlocking of interior and exterior space
and axial gamesmanship (fig. 4.12). Located in a valley to the west of Rome just outside its walls, it was
originally designed as a papal retreat and later served
as a stopover and staging area for formal processions

by foreign dignitaries approaching the Vatican. As at
the Villa Madama, the house was simply an accessory
to the garden and intended not as a residence but as a
place for papal entertainment.

One enters the vestibule and passes immediately
into a beautiful semicircular portico embracing a
horseshoe-shaped court. While the wall frescoes imitate the ancient Roman painting that antiquarians were
discovering at the time, the ceiling frescoes of this curving portico are painted as *trompe-l'oeil* flower- and vine-
covered trellises (fig. 4.13). These perhaps echo the real
arbor that sheltered papal dignitaries and other distinguished guests as they walked to and from the Tiber
through the once-extensive gardens. A massive, highly
polished, blood-purple porphyry fountain basin, recovered from the Baths of Titus, formerly stood in the
center of the garden court, catching the water that fell
from the mouth of a swan beside a figure of Venus.[12]

Beyond the garden court lies the *pièce de résis-
tance* of the entire design: the *nymphaeum,* which
Ammannati artfully screened from direct view, placing it behind a loggia (figs. 4.14 and 4.15). From the
back of the loggia a pair of curving staircases sweeps
down to Vignola's cool subterranean grotto. *Topia,*
landscape paintings reminiscent of the sacro-idyllic
landscapes that decorated ancient Roman villa walls
were placed along the sides of the court in front of
the *nymphaeum,* a grotto inhabited by sculptural representations of nymphs, here serving as caryatids. The
topia are now gone, and gone, too, is the romantic
mystery of the moss-padded grotto as it appeared to
the American author Edith Wharton, who wrote
about Italian villas and their gardens at the beginning

of the twentieth century when they were declining into antique picturesqueness. Using a modern algaecide, restorers have recently removed the greenish patina from the marble caryatids of the *nymphaeum,* returning them to their original whiteness.

Villa Giulia's spatial treatment compels the movement of the eye along a more tortuous route than does a High Renaissance garden with its clearer axial organization and more static spatial composition. Surprise—the unfolding of elements not seen or anticipated in advance—has become a device within the garden designer's means, one that assumes kinetic experience, movement through space, as an underlying principle. Here the garden has become an itinerary, a route that teases as it pulls one along a path. Along the central axis stretching between the entry vestibule and the garden behind the *nymphaeum,* space is subtly organized into a series of unexpected events. One passes from the narrow vestibule into the embrace of the horseshoe-shaped court and is drawn irresistibly toward the loggia at the rear. Because the bays on each side of the central portal of this loggia have been opened up, this axial tug is partially relaxed, but one is nevertheless propelled forward.

Inside the open loggia one is surprised to find the precipitous drop to the lower level court. The curvilinear staircases wrapping around the sides of this semicircular court echo the curving embrace of the entry court portico. But here is a visual puzzle, for while one can see through a rear loggia behind the *nymphaeum* into a garden, the strong axis has

become entirely imaginary at this point, and there is no immediately visible route leading from the first loggia to the second and out into that garden. To proceed, one must descend one of the curving staircases to the lower court where yet another puzzle presents itself, for here one sees the subterranean grotto with its caryatids supporting the terrace of the loggia above but finds no visible access to it. Like Poliphilus in *Hypnerotomachia* or Alice in Wonderland, one must, as in a dream, search for the door that opens to the delightful underground grotto where the buxom caryatids stand on their water-girt platform. Ammannati placed this secret entrance in the midlevel grotto located beneath the first loggia between the two curving staircases. A pair of staircases leading up to the rear garden hides within a second midlevel grotto beneath the rear loggia.

4.14. *Nymphaeum,* Villa Giulia, as seen in an engraving by Giovanni Francesco Venturini, plate 7 from *Le Fontane ne' Palazzi e ne' Giardini di Roma, con li loro prospetti et ornamenti, Parte Terza.* n.d.

Below: 4.15. The same view today

at this time, and to accommodate them the garden began to assume the role of outdoor museum. In addition to the Belvedere Court at the Vatican, Bramante built a *giardino segreto,* the so-called Statue Court, located between the upper court and the Belvedere, for Pope Julius II's collection of antique sculpture. In 1584, Cardinal Fernando de' Medici bought the collection amassed some sixty years earlier by Cardinal Andrea della Valle, sending the free-standing pieces to Florence to embellish the Boboli Gardens and keeping the reliefs to decorate the facade of his villa on the Pincian Hill in Rome.

Inspired by the discoveries of classical archaeology, patrons commissioned new sculpture. The notion became firmly established that the garden was a setting in which white marble figures should be seen against dark green foliage or framed by architectural niches within building facades and garden walls. The humanists' interest in classical mythology furnished artists with thematic material, which they wove into narrative itineraries. Familiar literary themes that found expression in the garden included those of the Golden Age, Elysium, rustic goodness, Venus presiding over the Garden of Love, Apollo, the Muses, Mount Parnassus, and the virtuous hero assigned near-impossible tasks or waylaid by treacherous enchantments.

An important element of Renaissance garden iconography was nature itself. One sees, for instance, in the *bosco* above the Belvedere Court and the Villa Pia in the Vatican Gardens, the desire for a wildwood, an evocation of the sacred grove in antiquity. Similarly, it is reported that Pope Julius III, with his taste for simple country food, peasant dances, and wine festivals, enjoyed strolling in the untamed parts of his *vigna* (literally vineyard, the term contemporaries used for a suburban villa retreat). These were abundant with wildlife, melodious with birdsong, and adorned with works of art. Like their ancient predecessors, Renaissance villa owners wanted their groves to be haunted by the sculptural representatives of river gods, nymphs, satyrs, Pan, Diana, and Venus.

Added to this literary agenda was another, more obvious, motive for the development of Renaissance garden iconography: the aggrandizement of the garden owners' reputations through symbols, with the implication that the patrons' power was being put to beneficent use for humankind. Increasingly, after the middle of the sixteenth century, Italian gardens became manifestations of princely power. This was true in Florence as well as in Rome, although such Tuscan gardens as the Medici villa at Castello remained much more conservative in design than did the dazzling villa creations of the popes and cardinals in and around Rome.

HUMANISM AND THE ROLE OF SCULPTURE, NATURE, AND SYMBOLS OF PRESTIGE IN GARDEN ICONOGRAPHY

4.16. Oval court, Villa Pia, Vatican Gardens, Rome. Designed by Pirro Ligorio. 1560

In G. B. Falda's engraving of the Vatican Gardens we see the Villa Pia, also called the Casino Pio, built by Pirro Ligorio for Pope Pius IV in 1560. Like the Villa Giulia it has a spatially ambiguous plan that visually pulls one in and through while making physical passage at first appear occluded. At the same time, it provides an example of another important Renaissance Italian contribution to the tradition of garden design: the *casino,* or summerhouse, built as a retreat from the bustle and ceremony of court life. Here the pope held soirées at which invited scholars sat around an oval court discussing philosophy, poetry, and religion. Discussion groups had become an important part of the intellectual life of Renaissance men of letters, and Ligorio's oval, which is embraced by exedras of carved stone seats, is an architectural expression of the humanists' pleasure in scholarly conversation (fig. 4.16).

The recovery of the art and architecture of antiquity provided villa designers with immediate sources of inspiration. As an archaeologist, Ligorio himself had thoroughly explored Hadrian's Villa on behalf of the Este family, and the mosaics that embellish the loggia of the Villa Pia and the arched portals entering the court reveal a renewed appreciation of ancient Roman decorative art. Low reliefs in stucco found on ancient Roman baths, palaces, and villas were echoed at the Villa Pia and elsewhere.[13]

Along with the wall frescoes and mosaics uncovered by sixteenth-century archaeologists, ancient marble sculptures were being excavated from the Roman soil. Several great collections were formed

Apotheoses of the Renaissance Villa Garden: Villa d'Este and Villa Lante

Although Castello and the Boboli Gardens contained water features symbolically associated with Duke Cosimo's reputation as a builder of aqueducts, it is to the Roman Campagna that we must turn to find gardens that apotheosize water and use it with the inventiveness of a choreographer directing the movements of the dance or the creativity of a sculptor exploring the plasticity of clay. These effects were accomplished through the ingenuity of sixteenth-century *fontanieri*, virtuosic hydraulic engineers with an understanding of metaphysics as well as physics and a reputation akin to that of magicians because of the ingenuity of their creations.[14] In the gardens of Villa d'Este water reaches a height of expressiveness that is analogous not only with dance and sculpture, but with music as well. For it is the drip and gurgle, the murmur and roar, the splash and tinkle, as well as the cooling spray, of water everywhere that has made this garden unforgettable to visitors through the centuries.

Like other superb gardens, Villa d'Este is the product of a passionate obsession on the part of an owner willing to spend extraordinary sums of money and with the taste to hire the best design talent available. In 1550, the cardinal of Ferrara, Ippolito D'Este (1509–1572), was appointed governor of Tivoli by Pope Julius III. Tivoli, an ancient Roman summer resort about twenty miles west of Rome, was not only the site of Hadrian's Villa, but of many other second century C.E. patrician villas. Its desirability then as later was due to the waters of the Aniene River, which came cascading dramatically down steep precipices; to its salubrious mineral springs; and to the excellent drinking water that was channeled from several sources along the riverbank to four major aqueducts serving the Roman metropolis. An aqueduct carrying water from the Rivellese Spring, the cost of which was borne by both the cardinal and the town of Tivoli, which also benefited, was built in 1561 after work on the garden had begun in earnest.

The governor's palace, a perquisite of the cardinal's appointment, was part of an old Franciscan monastery beside the Church of Santa Maria Maggiore at the top of a hill adjacent to the western town wall. Pirro Ligorio was commissioned to oversee the renovation of the palace into a summer residence suitable for Cardinal Ippolito, the son of Duke Alfonso I of Ferrara and Lucrezia Borgia. But the palace was to be a relatively minor element of the entire project; as the cardinal had already demonstrated at a villa he had rented on the Quirinal in Rome, gardens were his passion. In Ligorio he had not only a capable designer but also the foremost archaeologist of his day, the person

who was responsible for several excavations including that of nearby Hadrian's Villa and for the rediscovery of many antique marbles, mosaics, and other artifacts. Being a wealthy humanist collector, Ippolito had, in fact, put Ligorio on his payroll as his personal archaeologist in 1550, the year in which he had been appointed to the Tivoli post and had begun to dream of a great hillside garden below the palace. One part of Ligorio's job was undoubtedly to garner antique marbles to combine with contemporary sculpture in allegorical compositions throughout the garden.

Although Ligorio was himself a sufficiently accomplished classicist to develop the various iconographic themes that would portray the humanistic ideals of the cardinal, he was probably assisted by the cardinal's resident poet, Marc-Antoine Muret (1526–1585).[15] After 1560, Giovanni Alberti Galvani served as superintending architect in charge of overseeing the construction of masonry stairs, fountains, fish ponds, and other features. Professional *fontanieri* were hired to develop the water devices that operated the spectacular fountains.

The construction of the gardens of the Villa d'Este continued over a twenty-two-year period until the cardinal's death in 1572, when work stopped abruptly. Contemporary visitors, including the French essayist Montaigne (1533–1592), lamented their unfinished state, although in the seventeenth century, when inheritance problems engendered by Cardinal Ippolito's will were finally resolved, Cardinal Alessandro d'Este undertook some restoration and improvements. While vegetative growth, alterations, and periodic lack of maintenance have blurred some of the formality seen in a contemporary engraving, we can still discern Ligorio's design and, with the help of modern scholarship, decode the humanist themes that are woven into its fabric: Nature's abundance and generosity and the relationship between Art and Nature — one of the central preoccupations of the Renaissance (figs. 4.17–4.20). In parsing the humanist meaning of the garden, which besides expressing the Art–Nature duality has many references to the virtuous mythological hero Hercules, here identified with Cardinal d'Este, one should remember that the original public entry to the garden was not from the villa, but rather from a gate in the outer wall set in the hillside below.

Standing on the balcony of the villa today, the visitor looks beyond the verdant mature tree canopy of the gardens to the distant hills. Below is the Cardinal's Walk and the rainbow spray of Bernini's seventeenth-century Fountain of the Great Beaker, which mingles visually with the watery plume of the Fountain of the Dragons beneath it. The dragons symbolize the ones guarding the Garden of the Hesperides, which were slain by Hercules. Descending

VILLA D'ESTE

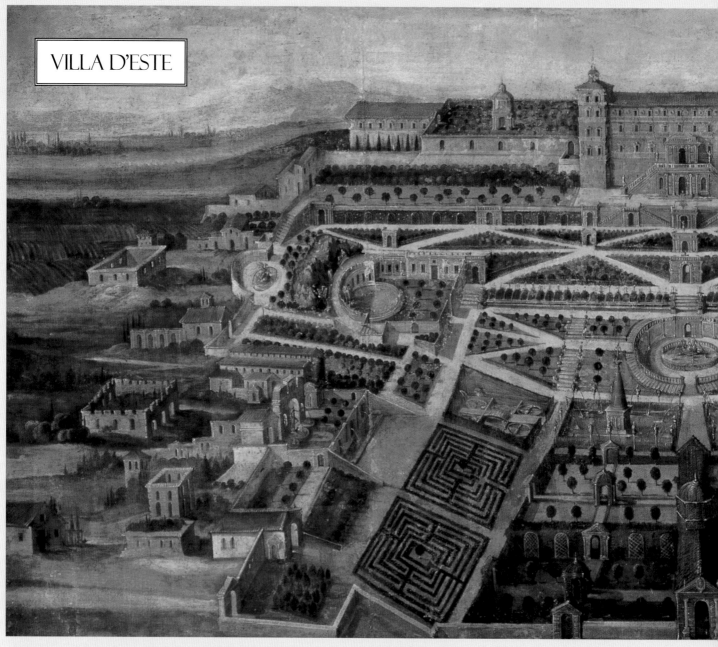

4.17. Villa d'Este, Tivoli. Designed by Pirro Ligorio. 1550–72. Panoramic view after an engraving by Étienne Dupérac. 1573

The traditional plan of most Italian Renaissance gardens—a plan in which there are compartmentalized beds near the villa and, as one approaches the outer limits of the property, a surrounding screen of trees—has been reversed here because of the nature of the site. A wooded slope with diagonal paths to accommodate the steep grade lies directly beneath the retaining wall supporting the villa terrace. Where the valley has been remodeled by an extensive process of cutting and filling to create an apron of level terrain and a geometrically pitched northeast side slope, cross-axes divide the garden into square compartments.

The relationship between Art and Nature constitutes the principal theme of the garden's iconography. Nature is dramatically manifested in the Fountain of Nature, also known as the Water Organ, culminating the water axis on the northeast (fig. 4.18). Following a "concert," which occurred when water pressure was manipulated to trap and release air in its pipes, a *fontaniere* would flush the vaulted chambers behind the elaborate facade, and a deluge would spill down the steep slope. This effect was made permanent in the twentieth-century Fountain of the Cascade, an enormous waterfall pouring into the pond below. An earlier cascade was created here by the seventeenth-century architect, sculptor, and fountain designer, Gianlorenzo Bernini (1598–1680); it fell in successive stages like a natural waterfall rather than

as the dramatic sheer spill we see today.

The human ability to employ the resources of nature toward fruitful ends constitutes Art, which is celebrated along the second major cross-axis, the Alley of the Hundred Fountains (fig. 4.20). The Alley itself is composed of three conduits symbolizing the three tributaries of the Tiber—the Albuneo, the Aniene, and the Erculaneo—which flow toward Rome. The art of channeling their waters into aqueducts was an important factor in the life of the recently reborn metropolis. Along the upper rim, water is channeled between carved obelisks, boats, eagles, and *fleurs de lys* (the last two forms being emblematic of the Este family).

At the northeast end of the Alley of the Hundred Fountains, within an

enclosed piazza, stands the principal fountain of the garden, the Fountain of Tivoli, or as it is now known, the Oval Fountain (fig. 4.19). A colossal statue of Albunea, the Tiburtine Sibyl, presides over the cascade, which is furnished by water from the River Aniene, which flows into an oval basin surmounted by a ball; its spurting jets delineate the Este *fleur de lys*. The sources of the Aniene and the Erculaneo are represented as reclining river gods set in naturalistic grottoes built into the surrounding slope. Crowning this artificial rock work is a statue of Pegasus, the magical horse whose hoofprints supposedly struck water out of Mount Parnassos, thereby creating the fountain of the Muses and proclaiming the power of Art.

4.19. Oval Fountain

4.18. Fountain of Nature, engraving by Giovanni Francesco Venturini, plate 13 from *Le Fontane del Giardino Estense in Tivoli, con li loro prospeti, e Vedute della Cascata del Fiume Aniene, Parte Quarta*. n.d.

4.20. Alley of the Hundred Fountains

one of the diagonal ramps, one comes to the Alley of the Hundred Fountains composed of three conduits symbolizing the three tributaries of the Tiber, which flow from the hills of Tivoli toward Rome. Here water is channeled between carved obelisks, boats, eagles, and *fleur de lys* (the last two forms being emblematic of the Este family) and pours from one basin into another through grotesque animal heads.

After visiting the Fountain of Tivoli and the Fountain of the Rometta, a water feature that was fashioned of stucco-covered brick to represent ancient Rome in miniature, one returns to descend one arm of the sweeping oval staircase and gaze back up at the villa through the spray of the Dragon Fountain. Taking the central staircase, which has channels of clear water running down its flanking walls, one arrives at the next level, that of the fish ponds. Here, looking back toward the villa, one realizes that Ligorio has repeated Bramante's design for the Belvedere Court as a series of descending terraces organized around a central axis. But there is an important difference: Bramante's Renaissance garden could be grasped in its entirety from a single vantage point within the Vatican Palace, but the Villa d'Este cannot be taken in altogether. Not only is it more spatially intricate than the Bramante prototype, but it is also a programmatic garden, one in which the separate parts are meant to be experienced sequentially as part of a humanist itinerary that celebrates the importance of Cardinal d'Este and the noble family of which he was the most conspicuous representative. Today, it is shorn of much of the sculptural decoration because the cardinal's fine collection of antique statuary was sold in the eighteenth century. While this loss deprives the villa of iconographic specificity and thematic continuity, the garden tour that was once enjoyed by the cardinal's guests and subsequent travelers nevertheless remains a memorable experience for modern visitors.

Contemporary with the Villa d'Este is Cardinal Giovanni Francesco Gambara's garden at Bagnaia, three miles east of the town of Viterbo. It is known today by the name of its seventeenth-century owners, the Lante family. Like the Villa d'Este, it offers a virtuosic expression of Bramantian axial planning combined with a highly imaginative use of water. Also like the Villa d'Este, the Villa Lante is filled with an allusive iconography wedding humanist learning to personal glory and family pride. It bears further similarity in being a garden that is meant not to be taken in all at once, but rather as sequential stops along a prescribed route that move the visitor off the central axis. Here, however, the garden itinerary has a prologue as one is meant to pass first through the kind of "dark wood" traversed by certain literary figures as they started out on their journeys of initiation, a

device with great appeal to the humanist imagination.

Cardinal Gambara was given the bishopric of Viterbo in 1566, and two years later received confirmation of one of the perquisites of his office, property rights in the old hunting park at Bagnaia. His predecessors had enclosed the park, which consisted of the wooded slope of Monte Sant'Angelo, and had built the aqueduct that brought water to the town as well as to the park. A small hunting lodge was the only structure on the property when the cardinal conceived the notion of building a great villa garden there. In place of the *barco,* or park for hunting, there would be a twenty-acre *bosco* with the kinds of messages of allusion that a humanist scholar steeped in the literature of antiquity would have sought. Continuing this iconographic narrative, there would be a formal garden in which Art gained the upper hand over Nature, in celebration of the cardinal's magnificence and benefactions to the people of Viterbo.

The designer of Villa Lante is almost universally believed to have been the architect Giacomo da Vignola, whose services Cardinal Gambara begged of his friend Cardinal Alessandro Farnese, as Vignola was then engaged upon another important garden commission at the Villa Farnese nearby at Caprarola. Construction proceeded over the next decade, and in August 1579, a lavish banquet was given there for Pope Gregory XIII (papacy 1572–1585), after which the pontiff promptly canceled Gambara's pension. Knowing that Gambara had been appointed by Pope Gregory's predecessor, the reform-minded Pius V (papacy 1566–1572), and that he was a prominent officer of the Inquisition, we may find it strange that he would build opulently, in a style derived from pagan art and literature. That, however, was the mentality of a proud and wealthy aristocrat whose appointment had as much to do with politics as with piety.

While the garden is the renowned part of Villa Lante and the park is often neglected by visitors, one should tour the *bosco* first in order to follow the itinerary planned by Cardinal Gambara. The *bosco* evokes the Golden Age myth, investing it with another, that of a punishing flood familiar to readers of the Old Testament. In the classical version, because of human wickedness, Jupiter, like Jehovah in the Hebrew scriptures, became angry and decided to destroy the earth with a flood so mighty that dolphins could be found swimming in the forest. Only two virtuous humans were left to repopulate, and their descendants were compelled to labor in order to make the earth fruitful.

The garden spells out the virtues of Cardinal Gambara, who made the surrounding land more bountiful and, in the tradition of classical civilization, was a patron of the arts enabling the human spirit to reach its highest potential. This, in brief, is the mes-

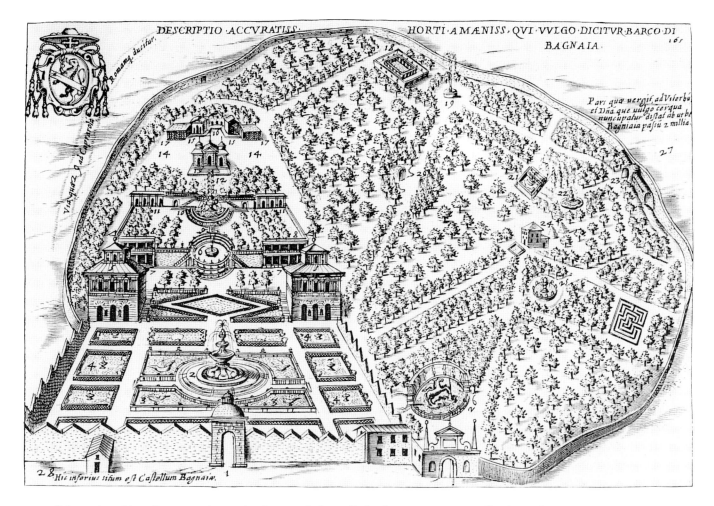

4.21. The Villa Lante, Viterbo. Designed probably by Giacomo Barozzi da Vignola. c. 1568–1579

sage of the park and its adjacent garden. It develops through design, as at the Villa d'Este, the age-old theme of relationship among humans, art, and nature, while symbolically portraying the heroic efforts of one man in bringing the three into such an enriching harmony as to constitute a second Golden Age (figs. 4.21–4.27).[16] Thus, the humanistic text encoded in its design program gives, as does that of the contemporary Villa d'Este, a literary dimension to the garden experience, and the presence throughout the garden of the cardinal's device in the form of a crayfish (a visual pun matching his family name, *Gambara,* with *gambero,* the word for "crayfish" in Italian) suggests his achievement.

Inspired by a sense of ancient geometry and proportion as well as by the iconographic program derived from antique themes, the Villa Lante can be seen in plan as a counterpoint of circles and squares. It is finally this balance and harmony of design, and not the messages of a new Golden Age under Pius V or Cardinal Gambara's prestige in the guise of humanism, that account for the deep pleasure that so many visitors have experienced in viewing it. In creating a hillside garden built upon a clear, strong axis, its several terraces linked by stairs, Vignola displayed a debt to Bramante. But he altered and expanded Bramante's design means. His axis is aquatic and can only be trav-

eled visually for the most part; one walks alongside it, perceiving it perhaps more powerfully for this very reason. And, instead of the architectural climax of the Belvedere exedra, here the central axis simply melts into nature as it ends in the Fountain of the Deluge.

Extravagant Epitome of Humanist Allegory: The Sacro Bosco at Bomarzo

We must turn to Bomarzo near Viterbo, the garden of Cardinal Gambara's friend Count Pier Francesco Orsini (1513?–1584), to see the arcane climax of humanism as a programmatic factor in garden design. The epic poem *Orlando Furioso,* completed in 1532 by Ludovico Ariosto (1473–1533), as well as Virgil's *Aeneid,* Dante's *Inferno,* and probably the writings of Petrarch, provided inspiration for this enigmatic landscape in which Count Orsini manipulated scale and perspective to create an itinerary of unusual scenes studded with bizarre sculpture and architectural monuments forming a series of tableaux, each serving as a riddle to be decoded by his guests.

It was only gradually that Bomarzo assumed its character as an enchanted forest, or *sacro bosco,* as the count developed one part after another into an itinerary of personal history and symbolical discovery. For instance, the gruesome tableau of a stone giant

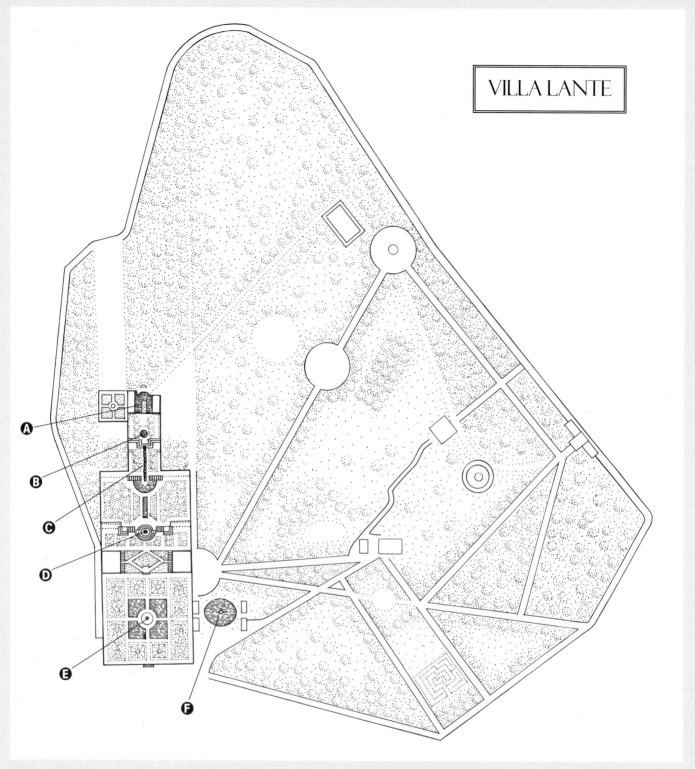

VILLA LANTE

4.22. Plan of the Villa Lante.

4.23. Fountain of Pegasus

4.24. Fountain of the Deluge

Upon entering the Villa Lante, one first encounters the Fountain of Pegasus surrounded by Muses **F**, perhaps derived from the Pegasus on the rock above the Oval Fountain at Villa d'Este. In both, the winged horse's hoof striking the earth generates the Spring of Hippocrene, symbol of the source of artistic creativity (fig. 4.23).

Along one of the diagonal paths through the park was the Fountain of the Acorns, now vanished, which linked the *bosco* with the Golden Age, since acorns were, according to Ovid, a staple in the diet of Arcadian man. Another vanished fountain, that of Bacchus, evokes Virgil's descriptions of the Golden Age when wine was believed to run freely in streams from the ground. Other trellis-surrounded fountains depicting unicorns and dragons symbolized the life of virtue and helped establish the identity of the park as the earthly paradise. High up the wooded slope there is a gate through which one can enter the garden at its top. There one is confronted by the Fountain of the Deluge **A**, a fern-encrusted grotto with six openings from which water drips and pours into a basin where two dolphins are swimming, their forms now almost obliterated by vegetation (fig. 4.24). This refers to Ovid's account of

the destruction of mankind by flood. Flanking the Fountain of the Deluge, twin dining pavilions, known as the Loggias of the Muses, bear the name and crayfish device of Cardinal Gambara. (The word for crayfish is *gambero* in Italian, and his crest is therefore a visual pun referring to his name.) Reinforcing the symbolism of the Deluge, small pipes installed beneath the eaves of the pavilions that frame the Fountain of the Deluge allowed water to rain from above. These also served a sportive function, permitting water tricks in which garden visitors were sometimes treated to an unexpected drenching in keeping with the humor of the day. Symmetrical colonnaded aviaries, modeled probably on descriptions of those in Varro's ancient garden, were designed as wings to the Loggias of the Muses, and within them berry-producing plants were grown to attract songbirds.

Around the octagonal Fountain of the Dolphins **B**, below some stairs, a stepped ramp leads down to the next terrace. A greatly elongated crawfish, its head and front claws emanating from the middle of the stairs at the top of the ramp and its rear claws hanging over top of the Fountain of the River Gods that stands on the terrace below, forms a *catena d'acqua*, or water chain (fig. 4.25; **C**). Its

linked curves both create and echo the movement of the swirling water that spills over the shallow shell-like basins set within it. Thus, out of the wreck of the Deluge, Cardinal Gambara can be seen to be harnessing water for human welfare. The water spilling through the beneficent crayfish's claws symbolically becomes the Tiber and the Arno as it falls into the basin flanked by the two great river gods (fig. 4.26). Their cornucopias denote the fertility that water brings to the land, a fertility that is emphasized by the statues of Flora and Pomona standing in niches within the retaining wall near the base of the steps leading from the terrace above. In the middle of this terrace, which is flanked by rows of plane trees, stands the Fountain of the Table. The stone table with its central water channel and bubbling jets provided Cardinal Gambara and his guests with an experience similar to that of ancient Romans whose banqueting arrangements sometimes included pools upon which servants floated food (see figs. 2.42, 2.46).

The Fountain of Lights **D** links the Cardinal's dining terrace with the water theater below, a concentric construction of upper concave and lower convex steps. One hundred sixty small jets shoot

upward from small lamps when the fountain is turned on; water pours from the sides of each step into a channel in the one below. From the terrace of the Fountain of Lights, one gazes down upon a series of garden compartments outlined in boxwood and a central water parterre. Within the water *parterre* **E** is a circular island, recalling perhaps the Marine Theater at Hadrian's Villa (fig. 4.27; see fig. 2.44). The loggias of the twin *palazzine* open onto the garden, and in them one finds frescoes depicting the Villa Farnese at Caprarola, the Villa d'Este at Tivoli, and the Villa Lante itself. In this part of the garden, wild nature has been thoroughly tamed by art, and Cardinal Gambara is seen as the patron of this transformation. Cardinal Gambara's original centerpiece of the island terrace, a water-oozing spire (*meta sudans*), was replaced in the seventeenth century by four bronze youths holding aloft Cardinal Alessandro Peretti Montalto's device of three mountains and a star. The surrounding water parterre was meant to evoke an ancient *naumachia*, a flooded theater where mock naval battles were held. In each of its four ponds is a small stone boat holding stone arquebusiers. These were engineered to fire jets of water toward the central fountain.

4.28. Sculpture of a giant tearing a young man apart, Sacro Bosco, Bomarzo. After 1542. Carved from the native rock, this ensemble represents a scene from *Orlando Furioso* and is believed to express Orsini's passionate despair over the rejection of his suit by a young woman with whom he had fallen in love some years after his wife's death.

4.29. Hell Mask, Sacro Bosco, Bomarzo. The legend above the Hell Mask, drawn from Dante, reads in translation: "Cast away every thought, you who enter here." But instead of embarking upon a terrifying journey into the underworld, Orsini's guests were actually being invited into a banquet pavilion. The huge stone tongue within the Hell Mask served as a table and its eyes as windows.

Hypnerotomachia Poliphili—indeed, the same kind of Renaissance appetite for marvels as is found in Shakespeare's *Tempest*.

Much of the garden's intended meaning is obviously lost upon the modern visitor who is directed to the garden of the Villa Orsini by signs pointing to the "Parco dei Mostri" (Park of Monsters), an invitation for tourists to stop and gawk at a collection of fantastic forms, some of which are carved out of the living rock, a soft tufa. Lacking familiarity with the literary symbolism that was the common currency of humanist intellectuals, one may at first wonder: Is this an exhibition showing the hallucinations of a deranged brain? Is it a sixteenth-century version of Coney Island with some of the twentieth-century amusement park's topsy-turvy atmosphere and penchant for the freakish, the magical, and the macabre.

Although now exploited commercially as a local wonder, the garden at Bomarzo, in fact, provides a fascinating window on the landscape of the Renaissance. Count Orsini, a renowned military captain and friend of several eminent men of letters, inherited the property at Bomarzo in 1542. Shortly thereafter he married Giulia Farnese to whom he was apparently deeply devoted, as evidenced by the small temple commemorating her, which is the culmination of the visitor's itinerary through the garden. Interrupted by the count's military campaigns, the building of the *sacro bosco* nevertheless became his obsession and occupied his imagination until his death in 1585.

Bomarzo's lack of a tautly geometric plan is explained by the fact that it was built by several different architects who attempted to express the owner's literary and personal passions over a long period of time. The result is a closer approximation in spirit to the multivalent, initiatory, and allegorical character of the *Hypnerotomachia Poliphili* than perhaps any other Renaissance garden. Its disorganized appearance and the discrepancies in scale among its monuments are further explained by the fact that these fantastic forms were carved from various natural boulders strewn about the site. There is even uncertainty as to the point of entry, although logic points to the northeast corner, where two sphinxes bear legends enjoining the visitor to discern with awe and amazement the marvelous character of the works that lie beyond.

Bomarzo is a unique expression of landscape art, and its inherent theatricality points the way to the dramatic character of seventeenth-century Baroque design, a stylistic development we will trace in the next chapter. Here we will turn our attention to villas of a different character in which abstract mathematical composition and architectural spatial configuration is much more important than humanist iconography.

tearing a young man apart is derived from a scene in *Orlando Furioso* and may refer to Orsini's grief after being rejected by a young woman; whereas the war elephant carrying a dead soldier with its trunk and other fantastical figures grouped around a gaping Hell Mouth bearing an inscription derived from Dante resemble the monsters at the entrance to the underworld in the *Aeneid* (figs. 4.28, 4.29). Like the Villa d'Este and Villa Lante, the *sacro bosco* of Bomarzo is a domain of allusions. Its architecture and sculpture represent various literary themes, not least of which is the theme of the sacred wood itself, a deity-haunted precinct, an Arcadia, or *locus amoenus* like those found in Ovid or Virgil. One may approach this curious place therefore with a disposition to look for humanistic literary themes, autobiographical and philosophical allusions, a great deal of epigrammatic didacticism, and a fascination with the antique and the exotic such as propels Colonna's narrative in the

PALLADIAN VILLAS OF THE VENETO

Andrea Palladio (1508–1580) is one of the most influential figures in the history of architecture because of his famous treatise *I quattro libri dell'architettura,* or *The Four Books of Architecture* (1570), and the Olympian beauty of his work. A stonemason by training, he became the protégé around 1537 of Giangiorgio Trissino, a Venetian humanist who had formed an academy in his villa near Vicenza where young nobles received a classical education. Vicenza is located in the Veneto, the mainland region in the alluvial plains at the foothills of the Alps that Venetians refer to as the *terraferma* where the city-state of Venice had established control beginning in the fourteenth century. Although still a thriving maritime republic, Venice needed a land base as a means of defense and to control its food supply, a prudent investment and sound economy, too, in an inflationary age. In addition, patrician Venetians were attracted to the charms of rural life, or the *villeggiatura,* as they, like other Italians who sojourned outside Rome and Florence, called their periodic residence at their country estates. Men such as Daniele Barbaro, another important patron of Palladio's, found precedent for involving themselves in agricultural affairs in the ancient Roman authors Cato, Varro, and Columella. Trissino was instrumental in helping Palladio initiate his career as an architect with commissions from the nobility of Vicenza for palaces and villas.

In publishing his *Quattro libri* Palladio had as precedent the books of Sebastiano Serlio (1475–1554), issued in six parts between 1537 and 1551. Collected and published posthumously in 1584 as *L'Architettura,* these treatises codified the five classical orders—Doric, Tuscan, Ionic, Corinthian, and Composite. Serlio's illustrations were a design resource for Palladio, and like Serlio, Palladio took advantage of Venice's leadership in the field of printing when he published his own well-illustrated, similarly formatted work. In addition, Palladio was introduced by Trissino to the architectural treatise of Vitruvius, *Ten Books of Architecture,* and Barbaro asked him to provide the illustrations for his commentary on this work, which appeared in 1556. Palladio was, of course, familiar with Alberti's treatise, *De re aedificatoria.* Alvise Cornaro, a humanist with an interest in architecture, whom Palladio met when he lived for a time in Padua, nourished in him a practical approach to design and a respect for *santa agricoltura,* blessed agriculture, and the farmers who cultivated the land.

Palladio's understanding of classical form was wedded to a profoundly architectural imagination. Adorned with pedimented facades like Roman temples, the villas he built in the Veneto dominate the landscape in a regal manner. Palladio considered carefully their position in relationship to the landscape. In Book Two of *I quattro libri,* he offered these siting instructions: "Don't build in valleys enclosed between hills because buildings in hidden valleys, apart from being invisible from a distance and having no view themselves, lack dignity and majesty."[17] As the architectural historian Caroline Constant explains, Palladio was interested in scenographic space, or space that is physically discontinuous, an assemblage on the ground plane that is perceptual and therefore unlike perspectival space, which is contained and defined by walls. She asserts that "for Palladio the ground plane was, conceptually, a surface of human manufacture rather than part of the natural world, and hence, a *tabula rasa.* It served—much as the picture plane did for Cubism—as a base on which to conduct various experiments into the nature of three-dimensional form. By elevating the central block of the villa, Palladio stressed the idealized nature of the ground plane, creating a new ground from which to survey the surrounding domain. Without the building, we would not see the landscape in the same terms; the architecture gathers the landscape into its domain and redimensions it."[18]

For the papal prelate Daniele Barbaro and his brother, Marc'Antonio Barbaro, an important Venetian statesman, Palladio built the Villa Barbaro at Maser (Treviso) in the Veneto on the plain below the Dolomite foothills during the decade of the 1550s (fig. 4.30). Built on the foundation of a medieval *castello,* the villa's projecting main building block has a stuccoed Roman-templelike facade and is flanked by service wings that end in dovecotes. These are elegant renditions of local vernacular architecture, as the *barchesse,* or utilitarian farm building, and the dovecote were typical constructions in the north Italian rural countryside. Unique among the works of Palladio, the *nymphaeum* here is a hemicycle with sculptural niches. Palladio may have been influenced in its design by such Roman models as the Villa Giulia and Pirro Ligorio's plans for Villa d'Este, both of which were roughly contemporary with the Villa Barbaro (fig. 4.31). However, the villa has an entirely different relationship to its landscape surroundings than do Roman or Tuscan villas where walls, rather than the ground plane, articulate and contain space. Placed near the juncture of the arable plain and the wooded hillside, the Villa Barbaro at Maser *presides* over its landscape, a beautiful object *in* space, with space having priority over object, which nonetheless aggrandizes and confers meaning upon its spatial surroundings. Complementing the Palladian architectural and landscape treatment of the Villa Barbaro are the magnificent frescoes by Veronese (Paolo Caliari, 1528–1588), which illusionistically amplify interior

4.30. Villa Barbaro, Maser (Treviso). Designed by Andrea Palladio. 1549–58

Below: 4.31. *Nymphaeum*, Villa Barbaro

Bottom: 4.32. Villa Rotonda, Vicenza. Designed by Andrea Palladio. 1565–69

something from and is enhanced by the other, is even more apparent at the Villa Almerico-Valmarana, called "La Rotonda" or Villa Rotonda, in the rural environs of Vicenza (fig. 4.32). Built between 1565/6 and 1569 for the recently returned papal prelate Paolo Almerico on property he owned outside the city, it may not have been conceived like other nearby villas as a working farm, but merely as a country retreat, although this is a subject of scholarly debate. Villa Rotonda is unusual also in having four pedimented facades, because as Palladio explained in *I quattro libri,* "it enjoys beautiful views on every side."[19] He described the site as a theater, and the villa on its slight hill is in its isolation and lack of ancillary structures like a solo performer within the ring of surrounding hills, the focal point of a larger landscape composition.

Because of his ability to scenographically unite serenely aloof, abstract classical forms and rustic surroundings, Palladio's villas have served as models from his time to the present for country villas where landscape statements harmonizing the inherent tension between human reason and nature have been honored within the imagination of a culture or an individual. Palladian influence was especially strong in eighteenth-century England where aristocrats such as Lord Burlington and Charles Howard, the third earl of Carlisle, among others, revered his architectural genius.[20] The American president Thomas Jefferson owned four copies of *I quattro libri,* and as an architect himself he appreciated and emulated Palladio when he built his own hilltop residence, Monticello.[21]

Palladio as well as his predecessors Colonna, Alberti, and Serlio grasped the importance of printing as a means of transmitting architectural ideas and visual information. As we shall see in this and subsequent chapters, both politics and the printing press carried the currents of humanism and architectural theory from Italy into France and then farther afield. At the same time, design ideas first propounded in garden settings soon influenced what we today call city planning, landscapes on an urban scale.

space with poetically classical landscapes and figures.

The reciprocal relationship between Palladian architecture and landscape found at the Villa Barbaro, in which neither gains the upper hand but each gains

III. Axial Planning on an Urban Scale: The Development of Renaissance Rome

The same popes who were adding verdant charm to the edges of the ancient city with the construction of gardens such as those of the Villa Giulia and the Villa Madama were simultaneously applying the principles of landscape design to the rebuilding of Rome itself. From its ancient imperial pre-eminence as a world capital, Rome had shrunk during the Middle Ages to a population of 17,000 housed in a tangle of small dwellings huddled in the elbow of the Tiber that lies opposite Castel Sant'Angelo and the Vatican (fig. 4.33). The third-century Aurelian walls outlined a much larger area. These contained the ruins of the Palatine, the Colosseum, the great imperial baths, triumphal arches, commemorative columns, and the moldering remains of the Forum where cattle grazed from late antiquity to the eighteenth century. Within this spectral setting of imperial glory several churches and monasteries had been built during the Middle Ages. Only footpaths connected them to one another and the urban core beside the Tiber.

After their return from exile in Avignon in 1377, and following the bull of 1439, which granted hierarchical authority to the bishop of Rome, the popes gradually gathered into their hands the reins of municipal power, wresting control over urban affairs from the commune and the warring factions of the nobility. The *maestri di strada,* equivalent to modern planning commissioners, were brought into the administrative apparatus of the Church. At the same time, the Church acquired the power of eminent domain and the ability to levy improvement taxes on property owners. Rome, already landmark-studded but with no regular street plan, offered a challenging opportunity for the application of the newly redeveloped principles of axial composition. Given the wealth of the Church and its desire to augment its international position during the Counter-Reformation, it is not surprising that a series of popes eagerly embraced this opportunity.

The Via Giulia, Piazza Sant'Angelo, and the Campidoglio

Julius II (papacy 1503–1513) wished to extend the papal administrative, judicial, and financial functions into the Banchi, the business district opposite the Ponte Sant' Angelo. He therefore commissioned Bramante (who was already employed on the construction of the Belvedere Court) to design a straight street with uniform building heights running to the Ponte Sisto. The Via Giulia, commemorating Pope Julius, thus opened up this labyrinthine medieval quarter.

Leo X (papacy 1513–1521), the Medici pope, and Paul III (papacy 1534–1549) further regularized the

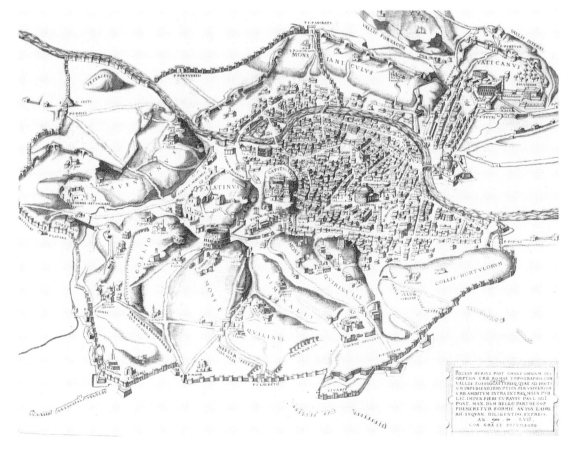

4.33. Engraving by N. Beatrizet showing medieval Rome, Aurelian walls, and ancient ruins. 1557

area with the construction of three more straight streets that radiated from the Piazza Sant'Angelo, thereby creating the first Roman example of a *trivio*, a place where three ways meet, a form later employed in laying out the Villa Montalto in Rome and the Villa Aldobrandini in Frascati. These same two popes were responsible for a second *trivio* with much longer streets beginning at the Piazza del Popolo. Subsequently the *trivio* was employed in France where a three-pronged set of radial avenues was called a *patte d'oie,* or goose foot.

The point of juncture between the city of the glorious imperial past and the modern city of the popes, the Capitoline Hill, one of the seven hills of Rome, was in the time of Paul III a muddy, forlorn open space. When the Holy Roman Emperor Charles V (ruled 1516–1556) planned to visit the papal city in triumph following his victory over the Turks in Tunisia in 1536, Michelangelo was summoned to turn it into a place of dramatic greeting and Roman pride. The genius with which he carried out his assignment, which was not completed until long after his death, provides us with an incomparable example of the theatrical imagination at its most sober and profound, for the spatial drama and urban scenography of his Campidoglio remain unrivaled in the history of urban planning (fig. 4.34).

Considered by ancients Romans to be the *caput mundi,* the center of the world, the Capitoline Hill,

site of the Palace of the Senator[22] and still the nominal home of Roman city government, was designated as a major point along the imperial route leading down the old Appian Way and through the Forum to the inhabited city, then across the river at the Ponte Sant'Angelo to St. Peter's and the Vatican. Michelangelo's commission was to create a dignified new hilltop piazza, despite the austere flank of Santa Maria in Aracoeli on the north and the old unprepossessing medieval guild hall to the south of the Palace of the Senator.

The great equestrian statue of the Roman emperor Marcus Aurelius, once thought to be a representation of Constantine, the first Christian emperor, and therefore saved from being melted down along with many monumental pagan bronzes, was transported to the Campidoglio from the Lateran Palace, its home throughout the Middle Ages. Set upon Michelangelo's modest yet authoritative pedestal in front of the Palace of the Senator, it served as the calm center and as a spring activating the dramatic tension and tremendous spatial energy of his design.

Michelangelo's solution to the incoherent space defined by the perimeter structures of the Campidoglio was one of camouflage through the design of a pair of opposing twin facades. On the south, that of the Palazzo dei Conservatori gave the old medieval guild hall the appearance of a Renaissance structure, and, on the north, that of the Palazzo Nuovo—not built until the papacy of Innocent X (1644–1655) and now known as the Palazzo del Museo Capitolino (Capitoline Museum)—successfully screened the awkward wedge of land beside Santa Maria in Aracoeli. Although only two stories in height, both façades are given monumentality by Michelangelo's inventive giant order of pilasters running from the porticoed ground floor to the cornice line. Because the existing guild hall was set at an 80° angle to the Palace of the Senator, he skewed both of his façades 10° from the 90° norm, thereby creating a trapezoidal piazza. The space, though contained, is thereby made dynamic and destabilized, and the eye is allowed to slide past the sides of the Palace of the Senator into the great field of ruins beyond, where the Campidoglio slopes down to the Forum.

The spatial dynamism is further increased by the paving pattern, a twentieth-century replica of the original one laid according to Michelangelo's design. The heroic sculpture sits within a slightly sunken oval and in the middle of a twelve-ray star, the points of which form the coordinates of a radiating design. When read from above, this design gives a spherical appearance to the oval, as if it were a dome and the sculpture its crowning ornament.

But the greatest element of this scenographic

4.34. Campidoglio, Rome. Designed by Michelangelo Buonarroti. 1536. The original bronze equestrian statue of Marcus Aurelius that was the focus of Michelangelo's design has been moved to the Capitoline Museum.

drama is not the piazza, but the ascent to it via the Cordonata, a broad stair ramp with wide treads that are as gently cadenced as the adjacent steps of Santa Maria in Aracoeli are penitentially steep (fig. 4.35). Over-lifesize ancient Roman statues of the horse tamers, the mythological twins Castor and Pollux, excavated in 1560 near the Capitoline, stand at the top, Olympian honor guards with the serene disinterested gaze of immortals, framing the perspective Michelangelo created.

In 1561, Pius IV (papacy 1559–1565) promoted the axial reordering of medieval Rome with the building of the Via Pia (now Via XX Settembre) from the papal palace on the Quirinal to the Porta Nomentana, the city's northeastern gate. Michelangelo was again summoned to produce an urban design. Here he gave a dignified focus to the palace approach with another monumental pair of sculptures of Castor and Pollux, turning their half-tamed horses to face the street near its entrance. At the opposite end, he screened the ancient fortifications of the Porta Nomentana with a purely scenic gate scaled to harmonize with the vista enclosed by the walls of the villa gardens on either side (fig. 4.36).

PLAN OF SIXTUS V

Although unsurpassed as urban scenography, the Campidoglio and the Via Pia, with their artfully framed vistas, represent a piecemeal approach to city planning. Uniting the city's streets into a well-articulated circulation system and composing its already extraordinary existing landmarks into a series of views worthy of Rome's growing reputation as a tourist destination, required a comprehensive vision and forceful leadership for its realization. A visionary leader presented himself in late-sixteenth-century Rome in the person of Sixtus V (papacy 1585–1590). Indeed, all previous efforts to improve the cityscape of Rome were but overtures to the great symphony

of urban improvements that was orchestrated during the short Sistine papal term.

Born of Dalmatian peasant stock, the great future pope of the Counter Reformation, Felice Peretti, rose through the ranks of the Church to become Cardinal Montalto, building the Villa Montalto with the revenues that went with his elevation to high office. There he nurtured his plans during the thirteen years of Gregory XIII's papacy. Located in the developing eastern suburb of the settled city at the base of the Esquiline Hill on the site of the present railway station, the Villa Montalto later became the hub of a bold urban design. This plan, which Felice commissioned from the architect and engineer Domenico Fontana (1543–1607) as soon as he was elevated to the papacy, carried the urbanization of Rome to the boundaries of its ancient walls and even, where possible, beyond. No contemporary drawing exists for Fontana's master plan of Rome, but a dramatic, if somewhat inaccurate, bird's-eye rendering of it in fresco decorates one of the walls of the Vatican Library (fig. 4.37). The web of long arrow-straight thoroughfares had important significance within the context of the Counter-Reformation: linking the Colosseum, the Pantheon, the Forum and other prominent monuments of ancient Rome and, more importantly, its seven major churches, with one

Left: 4.35. Cordonata leading to the Campidoglio

Above: 4.36. Via Pia (modern Via XX Settembre) with Porta Pia; *La Via Pia,* fresco painting by Cesare Nebbia, Salone dei Papi, Lateran Palace, Rome. c. 1588

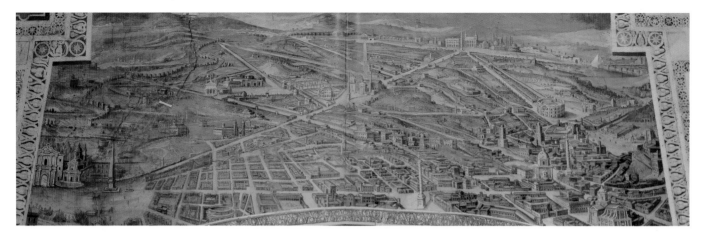

4.37. Perspective of Rome according to the Plan of Sixtus V. Vatican Library. Fresco. 1585–90

another, they inscribed on the face of the ancient city a highly visible itinerary of tourism and pilgrimage that served to enhance its prestige as the original and continuing center of the Catholic Church.

Not since the days of the Roman chariots had equally smooth, wide, and regular urban arteries been built. Moreover, they were to be paved in order to facilitate the movement of the newly invented spring-suspension carriage. As yet, there were no sidewalks, and pedestrians and vehicles occupied the same street space. The word *corso,* signifying a principal thoroughfare, assumed new meaning in Rome as carriage driving became a fashionable recreation for the upper echelon of society. The Via Pia, the longest straight road built to that date, bore daily witness to Rome's pre-eminence as the world's first city to accommodate these new vehicles in large numbers. Rome indeed was experiencing another modern urban "first": traffic congestion. The cardinals and their immense ecclesiastical retinues, the dignitaries of the embassies from other countries now posted to Rome, the courtesans, the tens of thousands of pilgrims who came every year, the tourist contingent newly awakened to the wonders of the classical past, the foreign artists and artisans—all these thronged the city, congesting its narrow medieval byways and crowding its new thoroughfares. The long-slumbering metropolis was once again lively as horses, carriages, cattle, and pedestrians jostled one another in the burgeoning cosmopolitan setting.

But more than roads were needed to facilitate transportation and stimulate the regrowth of Rome. It was necessary to reconstruct the ancient aqueducts if the untenanted, ruin-studded stretches of the city were to be repopulated. Other popes had begun this process, but none had solved the problem of carrying water to the heights of Rome's famed hills. That was the assignment Sixtus V set for himself, and within only eighteen months, the plan he had nurtured for the Acqua Felice (so named because of the pope's first name, Felice) came to fruition with the completion of a conduit spanning 7 miles of overhead arches and 7

miles of underground tunnels. Its successful opening brought water to the Villa Montalto in 1586 and three years later to twenty-seven public fountains located throughout Rome. Utilitarian at first, many of these were later transformed into the ornamental fountains for which Rome has remained famous.

The Acqua Felice also made possible the construction of a public laundry beside the Baths of Diocletian. And where the already reactivated Acqua Vergine brought water to the site of the present Fountain of Trevi, Sixtus V installed a basin for the washing of wool.[23] With the water problem solved and the nexus of the new street system located in the area where he owned property, he was in a position to gain financially from his program of public works.

As a landscape designer working at a city-planning scale with a visionary patron, Fontana proved his talent in engineering and urban scenography. Together pope and architect created the skeleton of modern Rome, a circulation network of interconnecting streets and focal points, the whole comprising a series of vista corridors punctuated with landmarks old and new. As with the Acqua Felice, Sixtus V bestowed his name on the longest and most important of these unifying thoroughfares, the Strada Felice. This avenue connected Santa Maria Maggiore with Santa Trinità dei Monti on the brow of the Pincio Hill. A final stretch downhill to the Piazza del Popolo was never constructed, and the Spanish Steps linking Santa Trinità with the Corso below were not built until the eighteenth century. But the Strada Felice's extension on the other side of Santa Maria Maggiore all the way to Santa Croce in Gerusalemme was carried out, thereby creating a straight span of about 2 miles across the breadth of Rome. Intersecting the Strada Felice at almost a right angle was Michelangelo's Via Pia, the two creating a symbolical cross, referred to as the *"bellissima croce."*

In the fresco of the Rome of Sixtus V one sees the impulse to untangle the tortuous labyrinth of medieval Rome with the Strada Felice and other roads slashing across the built and as-yet-unbuilt landscape.

One also sees the celebration of Rome's incomparable history through the new prominence given to its landmarks. In addition to the pilgrimage churches, the Colosseum and the Columns of Marcus Aurelius and Trajan are focal points of the plan. To set these off, Sixtus V removed the structures around them and regularized the building lines of those remaining to form squares. Elsewhere he created new squares. Fontana and his patron hit upon the happy idea of resurrecting several of the old Egyptian obelisks, exotic souvenirs of ancient campaigns, which had long ago toppled here and there about the city, and using them as markers to center space or temporarily arrest the eye and punctuate its journey along a vista corridor.

The 82-foot-tall obelisk marking Nero's racetrack near St. Peter's had, remarkably, remained standing throughout the Middle Ages next to the south side of the church. Fontana directed the feat of moving this 320-ton monument to its present position in front of St. Peter's, thus defining the center of the ovoid piazza, which Bernini later embraced with his great curving fourfold colonnades. Fontana had the obelisk lying in the Circus Maximus erected in the center of the space that became the Piazza del Popolo, giving focus to its converging trident of new streets (fig. 4.38). Two more obelisks were set up along the Strada Felice, one at its midpoint in front of Santa Maria Maggiore, the other at its southeastern terminus in front of Santa Croce in Gerusalemme. To incorporate them into the religious symbolism of the Counter-Reformation's triumphant Catholicism, the pope had each of the four Sistine obelisks surmounted with a globe bearing a cross. Thus, an ancient Egyptian form, developed to stand in sentinel pairs at tomb entrances, became an isolated freestanding object centering urban open space, a felicitous borrowing that would be copied in other times in other lands, often without the Church's triumphant cross.

Sixteenth-century Italian landscape design not only manifested the humanists' interest in reviving ancient forms and themes, but it also served as a means of asserting prestige and displaying wealth and power. The same humanist iconographies into which were encoded messages of family and personal pride within a garden setting could be applied on an urban scale to proclaim the power of the Church or of a ruler. The garden, in effect, served as a design studio wherein problems of axial layout and scenography were solved in ways that were simultaneously applied to city planning. For example, Fontana's development of the triangular piazza in front of Pope Sixtus V's Villa Montalto as a garden *trivio* with three avenues radiating outward from an open space near the Church of Santa Maria Maggiore, in a manner that

both ennobled the entrance to the *casino* and suggested the breadth of the gardens behind it, shows how closely connected were the principles of landscape design within and without the garden (fig. 4.39).

This means of stabilizing architectural forms in relationship to a particular setting and suggesting territorial possession through spatial extension, developed here as part of Fontana's plan for the villa, became a widely used device wherever monumental planning occurred. Fontana's role as city planner is thus pivotal. He conceived the design of the Villa Montalto's *trivio* within the comprehensive frame of cityscape. By linking it and other radial compositions of axes, such as those emanating from the *trivio* at the Piazza del Popolo, to form a transurban network, he created a plan for an entire city, something that had not occurred in the West since ancient Roman times and then only for colonial cities and not the capital.

As the unification of garden space through axial layout became increasingly the objective of garden designers in the seventeenth century, their royal employers saw the symbolic value of reordering old cities and building new ones according to the same principles. It is not surprising that these principles, which served effectively as a spatial metaphor for princely grandeur and dominion, were eagerly absorbed by ambitious monarchs elsewhere, notably in France. However, before the lessons of Sixtus V's plan were applied in an urban setting in that country in the early seventeenth century during the reign of Henry IV (ruled 1589–1610), a gradual process of replacing French medievalism with the new Renaissance style imported from Italy had necessarily ensued. This stylistic evolution, begun in the Loire Valley, reflected the political relations between the two countries over the course of the sixteenth century as Italian influence in France alternated with the development of an independent French Renaissance style.[24]

4.38. Egyptian obelisk, erected in the Circus Maximus during Roman imperial times and resurrected in the Piazza del Popolo, Rome. 1585–90

Below: 4.39. Villa Montalto, Rome. Designed by Domenico Fontana. Engraving by Giovanni Battista Falda, plate 14, *Li giardini di Roma con le loro Piante Alzate e Vedute in Prospettiva.* n.d.

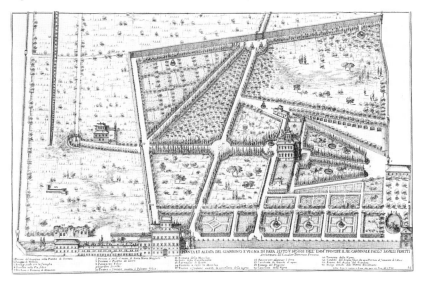

IV. CURRENTS OF FASHION: THE TRANSFORMATION OF THE ITALIAN GARDEN IN FRANCE

Italian humanism laid the groundwork for the development of French garden style in the sixteenth century. Alberti's treatise and the publication in 1546 of a French translation of Colonna's influential *Hypnerotomachia Poliphili,* carried certain currents of Renaissance thought northward. Equally important was the invasion of the kingdom of Naples in 1494 by the French king Charles VIII (ruled 1470–1498) in an attempt to reassert an old dynastic claim to the throne. Charles's occupation lasted only five months, but Alfonso II's state-of-the-art gardens at Poggio Reale, overlooking the Bay of Naples and with a view of Mount Vesuvius, made a lasting impression on him and on the nobles in his retinue.

Following the capture of Castel del Uovo, Charles took up residence there and had ample opportunity to marvel at the straight *allées* approaching the castle on all sides, the orange and other fruit trees surrounding it, its large walled garden, ingenious hydraulic system, fountains, ornamental fish ponds, canals, aviaries, and game-filled hunting park. Though it has long since disappeared and its design cannot be accurately reconstructed, we know that this pleasure palace was square with corner towers and had a sunken court that could be flooded for water spectacles. When Charles returned to his own palace at Amboise in October, he brought with him Italian artists and craftsmen, including, the Neapolitan priest-gardener Pacello de Mercogliano.

The appearance of the palace and garden at Amboise, as well as that of other great châteaux of the Loire Valley, was recorded between 1576 and 1579 by the architect Jacques Androuet du Cerceau (c. 1520–c. 1584) in a monumental series of engravings, which were published in several editions of *Les plus excellents Bastiments de France,* an invaluable reference work for garden historians inasmuch as almost all sixteenth-century French gardens have disappeared. The work is important, moreover, as a record of the French transformation of Italian Renaissance gardening principles into a unique design idiom. The châteaux engraved by du Cerceau were those that had been built during the several preceding decades of the sixteenth century when French designers were appropriating the lessons of Italy and refashioning them into expressions of their own aristocratic culture.

SIXTEENTH-CENTURY CHÂTEAUX: BLOIS, FONTAINEBLEAU, ANCY-LE-FRANC, ANET, CHENONCEAUX

Charles VIII died suddenly in 1498, but his nephew and successor Louis XII (ruled 1498–1515) was equally enthusiastic about the new princely pastime of garden-making. He continued to make improvements at Amboise and the other royal châteaux he had inherited. At Blois, he placed the garden outside the castle walls, and this permitted a considerable expansion in size over the one at Amboise (fig. 4.40). Its design, however, made no attempt to unite the château and garden visually by aligning them along a common axis as was being done in Italy.

4.40. Blois. Engraving by Jacques Androuet du Cerceau, *Le Second Volume des plus excellents Bastiments de France.* 1579. The main gate leading to the principal axis of the garden is approached through a dogleg passage connecting with a covered bridge that leads from the palace. The expert craftsmanship of the joiner is evident in the octagonal wooden pavilion with its tall domed lantern covering a marble fountain and in the galleries formed by wooden trellises. These galleries were high and wide enough to accommodate riders on horseback.

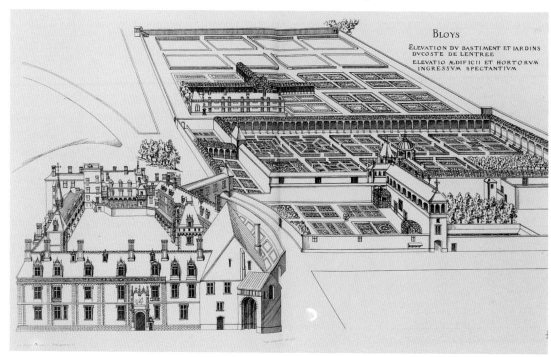

Louis XII was succeeded by his nephew Francis I (ruled 1515–1547). The sister-in-law of the new king became the duchess of Ferrara, which, as the home of the Este family's gardens and parks, was an important site of garden design. This connection with Italy perhaps, along with Francis's favorable disposition toward the new cultural developments there, fostered the burgeoning French Renaissance.

Francis sought to conquer Italy and become Holy Roman Emperor, but was checked by Emperor Charles V (who was also king of Spain) in 1525. Upon Francis I's return to France the next year, following imprisonment in Spain, he decided to abandon his Loire Valley *châteaux* and to establish the court in the environs of Paris as part of a political alliance he sought with the bourgeois class. In 1528, he began rebuilding the *château* at Fontainebleau (fig. 4.41). The master mason Gilles de Breton was put in charge of the work. He built a new triple-story entrance to the Court of Honor and a new courtyard with an Italian-style gallery overlooking a trapezoidal lake. On the shore opposite the elm-lined causeway leading to the main entrance of the *château*, the Jardin des Pins was laid out as a series of square beds with a pine-bordered central axis.

Francis imported Italian artists to assist in the decoration of Fontainebleau, and the presence of these talented men in France gave additional impetus to the spread of Renaissance art and humanism. Francesco Primaticcio (1504–1570), one of the Italian painters and architects summoned to France, is reputed to have designed the grotto at Fontainebleau. In this way, the development of the Renaissance landscape in France continued with direct assistance from designers trained in Italy during the generation in which a new artistic idiom was being forged and refashioned into a style that was identifiably French.

The Italian Renaissance architect Sebastiano Serlio was also invited to France by Francis I. Better known as a theoretician and architectural consultant, he is credited with the design of Ancy-le-Franc in Burgundy (fig. 4.42). The project, begun under his direc-

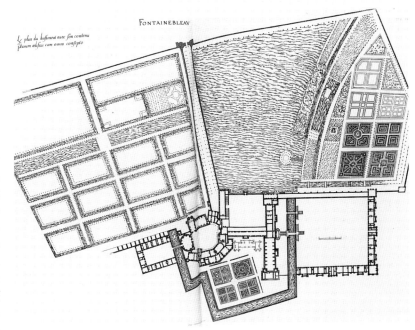

tion in 1546, firmly established axial symmetry and the unity between house and garden probably for the first time in France.

The preference for Italian architects and garden designers did not endure for long in France. French national pride was responsible for diverting commissions from Serlio and his compatriots as native designers grasped the principles of Renaissance architectural composition. Foremost among the first generation of such designers was Philibert de l'Orme (c. 1510–1570). De l'Orme went to Rome to study antiquities between 1533 and 1536. There he was introduced to the circle of humanists, collectors, and artists who were excavating Hadrian's Villa and beginning to build the new villas that were to exert a powerful influence on future generations of designers. Upon his return to France, he exercised his talent in the service of Cardinal Jean du Bellay, whom he had met while in Rome, and shortly after Henry II became king in 1547, de l'Orme was appointed superintendent of all royal buildings.

Henry's mistress, Diane de Poitiers, a widow eighteen years his senior, held sway over the king's

4.41. Fontainebleau. Engraving by Jacques Androuet du Cerceau, *Le Second Volume des plus excellents Bastiments de France.* **1579**

Below: **4.42. Ancy-le-Franc. Engraving by Jacques Androuet du Cerceau,** *Le Premier Volume des plus excellents Bastiments de France.* **1576. Serlio used the terrace of the medieval moat surrounding the** *château* **as an overlook from which to view the twelve compartments contained within the rectangular garden. A hedge and a canal both outline the garden. Beyond it is a** *bosquet* **similar to the** *boschi* **of contemporary Italian gardens. Within it, along an axis perpendicular to the main axis running through the** *château* **and the garden, a broad grassy swath has been carved. On either side of it are green byways and small secluded areas.**

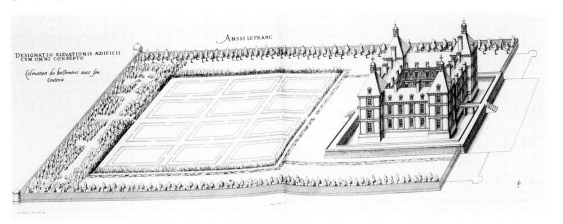

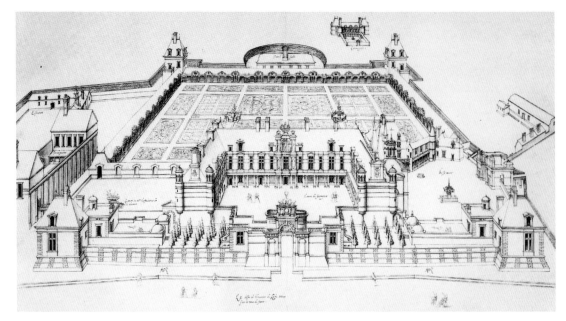

4.43. Anet, designed by Philibert de l'Orme. Engraving by Jacques Androuet du Cerceau, *Le Second Volume des plus excellents Bastiments de France*. 1579. The Court of Honor is enclosed by the U-shaped *château* and entrance structure, in this case an impressive gatehouse. Stretching on either side of this gatehouse, symmetrical small *bosquets* and terraces terminate in mirror-image pavilions. The moat surrounding Anet has been enlarged to form a semicircular pool encompassing a pavilion for theatrical spectacles. The crescent-shaped pool perhaps echoes the shape of the moon, the device of Diana the Huntress. Because this mythological goddess is also associated with the woods, the stands of trees on either side of the entrance may represent one of her groves.

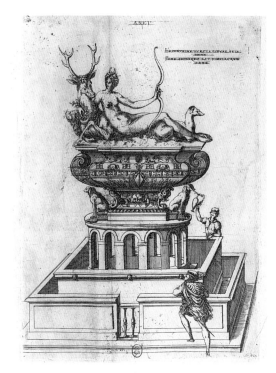

4.44. Diana Fountain, Anet. Engraving by Jacques Androuet du Cerceau, *Le Second Volume des plus excellents Bastiments de France*. 1579. This elegantly elongated image boldly portraying a nude Diane de Poitiers as Diana the Huntress can be found in the Louvre Museum today.

size and impressive surrounding gallery gave it a very modern appearance at the time. Twin pavilions overlooked its far end, and in these musicians played for the king, his mistress, and members of the court. Also at the far end of the garden stood a pavilion for theatrical entertainment, a new feature of French Renaissance garden design. As at nearby Gaillon, the *château* built in 1502 by Georges d'Amboise, archbishop of Rouen, the garden pavilion rose from a pool of water.

Ostensibly built as a memorial to Diane's late husband, Anet actually glorified Diane herself and celebrated her liaison with the king. Not only was this done in typical Renaissance style with monograms and coats of arms fashioned out of boxwood in the garden compartments but also with the kind of decorative program seen at the Villa d'Este and the Villa Lante. At Anet, the thematic program refers to Diana, goddess of the hunt, in such sculpture as the stag and hounds crowning the main entrance portal and in the elegant Mannerist fountain (now removed from the entry court) depicting a reclining, nude Diane de Poitiers in the guise of the mythological Diana (fig. 4.44).

In spite of Henry II's attachment to his mistress, he fathered ten children with Queen Catherine de Médicis, among them three future kings of France. The daughter of Lorenzo de' Medici, duke of Urbino, and Madeleine de La Tour d'Auvergne (a Bourbon princess), Catherine had been orphaned almost at birth. She was raised by nuns and married at the age of fourteen to Henry. When, after a few years, she began to bear royal children, she lived quietly and pri-

affections. Instead of allowing Anet, the *château* in which Diane's husband had held a lifetime interest, to revert to the crown as it was supposed to upon his death, Henry made a present of it to her. Philibert de l'Orme was immediately appointed architect of its reconstruction.

Although he had to preserve the existing house, de l'Orme incorporated it within a symmetrical plan as he applied the lessons he had learned in Italy in a rational, comprehensive ordering of space (fig. 4.43). The garden was enclosed and inward-focused, but its

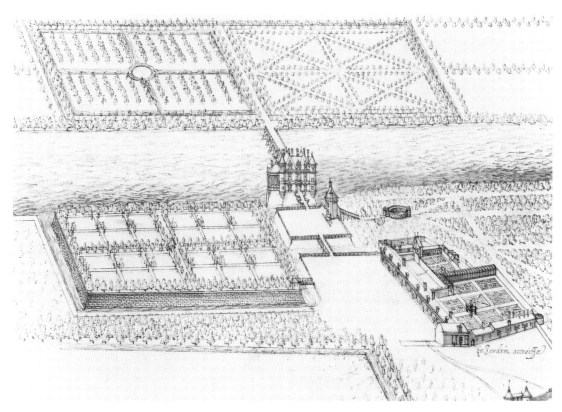

4.45. Chenonceaux. Drawing by Jacques Androuet du Cerceau. The original owner, Thomas Bohier, had built an enclosed garden with the trellised galleries and square compartments associated with the period of transition between medieval and Renaissance style. It can be seen in the right foreground of du Cerceau's engraving. To the left of the entrance, Diane of Poitiers ordered a high moat-surrounded terrace on which was laid out a considerably larger rectangular garden of twenty-four beds arranged around a principal cross-axis. Planted with the assistance of the archbishop of Tours, it contained many different kinds of fruit trees, musk roses, lilies, and vegetables. The axis of the bridge de l'Orme had built to span the river extended as a tree-lined *allée* to connect with a new garden commissioned by Catherine de Médicis. De l'Orme placed the bridge slightly to one side of the main axis of the *château,* thereby preserving the principal view of the river from the entrance corridor without forsaking an impression of axial linkage.

vately, supervising their education until, following Henry II's sudden death in 1559, she was catapulted onto the stage of history as regent and queen mother during the reigns of her sons Francis II, Charles IX, and Henry III. Well-read, politically astute, vivacious, artistic, and energetic, she was an enthusiastic participant in the new fashion for *château* remodeling and garden building that was gathering force in France during the second half of the sixteenth century.

During the King's lifetime, Diane de Poitiers was mistress of the royal *château* at Chenonceaux, dating from 1512 and defensively sited within the river Cher (figs. 4.45, 4.46). After the king's death, Catherine claimed this remarkable structure for her own. She took an interest in the garden that Diane had begun and directed the construction of a new south garden. She probably retained Philibert de l'Orme's services for this project.

Catherine used the enlarged gardens of Chenonceaux for political ends, staging elaborate pageants and festivals within them to celebrate the peace treaties that punctuated the bloody religious wars that raged during the reigns of her sons. There were festivals, too, at Fontainebleau and at the Tuileries. The use of these gardens as settings for various allegorical pageants

4.46. Chenonceaux

marked the beginning of an enduring tradition. As will become evident in the next chapter, the gardens of French monarchs increasingly assumed the role of theaters for court life, and certain spaces were built within them to accommodate the spectacles and plays that were regularly staged as entertainments for royalty and nobility. The politicization of the garden was paralleled by the design of cities as didactic expressions of royal prestige as Henry IV began the impressive transformation of Paris from a medieval to a modern city.

V. The Evolution of French Urbanization and Garden Style: Paris in the Time of Henry IV

Transformation of Paris

With the extinction of the Valois royal line following the death of Henry III, the complicated French laws of succession led to the selection of a distant cousin, the Bourbon king of Navarre, as king. The ascension of this Protestant soldier to the throne as Henry IV in 1589 eventually marked the end of the bloody religious wars of the second half of the sixteenth century, but his authority was established only after a struggle. Determined to quell the rebellious Catholics who denied his legitimacy, Henry IV first laid siege to their stronghold of Paris, and when this was unsuccessful, with his famous pronouncement that Paris was worth a mass, he converted to Catholicism and thereby gained the city. His peripatetic Valois predecessors had migrated from one to another of their Loire Valley and Île-de-France *châteaux,* chosen principally by individual royal preference for specific hunting parks. But Henry IV had to consolidate his victory and establish Paris as the indisputable royal capital. He turned his attention to projects that would improve the city's appearance, stimulate its economy, address its issues of public sanitation, and increase its opportunities for both ceremonial statement and residential amenity. His campaign to accomplish these objectives was based upon the creation of new architectural works and public spaces larger in scale than any hitherto seen in Europe outside of Italy — spaces that would glorify the institution of monarchy and the growing supremacy of France as the dominant social and political power in Europe. The origin of Paris as a modern city and France as a modern nation owes much to this energetic monarch whose list of urban and state achievements would have been even more impressive had his life not been cut short by an assassin in 1610.

The rebuilding of Paris's badly battered walls was not one of these achievements, nor was it to be counted among those of his successors. With the increasing security of French borders attained by the bastioned outpost citadels constructed first by Henry IV's engineers and much later by the brilliant Sébastien Le Prestre de Vauban (1633–1707), France was becoming territorially confirmed as a nation-state. This meant that Paris could dispense with its ancient fortifications and exist henceforth as an open city. To execute his building program for the capital as well as the border defense fortifications and to supervise the increasingly centralized administration of finances that made such large-scale, nationalistic projects possible in the first place, Henry IV appointed

as his chief minister the duke of Sully, Maximilien de Béthune (1560–1641). Among the several titles he held, Sully was invested with a newly created one, that of *Grand Voyer,* the officer who regulated transportation and integrated planning of all roads, bridges, canals, city streets, and public places. An astute politician and talented administrator, Sully created a revenue budget and organized a corps of engineers to design forts, maintain bridges and roads, and map territory. His road reports led to the building of a centralizing web of highways focused on Paris, while the maps he commissioned not only assisted in increasing royal control over taxation, commerce, and transportation, but also promoted a new cartographic image of the nation-state as a geographic unit with well-defined boundaries.

For Henry IV, Sully played the role that Colbert would later play for Louis XIV: that of supervising the works that would turn Paris into a dignified royal capital.[25] With Sully's assistance, Henry initiated a new urban scale, opened up the city both visually and spatially, and introduced significant preliminary improvements in its circulation. In this effort, monarch and minister were clearly inspired by Sixtus V's plan for Rome. The result was the reordering of parts of medieval Paris and the creation of new public spaces in conjunction with the development of their surrounding real estate.

The king's first step upon gaining control of Paris was to turn the old stronghold of the Louvre, the fortress castle that his predecessors had already begun to modernize, into a fitting royal residence and symbolically assertive seat of government. Noble architecture alone was not enough to accomplish this task; his plan, only partially fulfilled during his life, called for the integration of the space between Catherine de Médicis' Tuileries Palace and the Louvre into one vast courtyard, the largest open space ever before seen or planned in Paris and the precursor of an entirely new urban scale (fig. 4.47).[26]

In building the Grande Galerie connecting the two palaces on the south, Henry IV's architects removed part of the old fortification wall that ran along the Seine, thereby providing sweeping river views from the palace while simultaneously presenting it as an object of admiration from afar. Architectural improvements to the Tuileries and the removal of much of the medieval clutter of nonroyal structures between it and the Louvre provided the sought-for unity among the southern ranges of the palace complex. But the entire space did not begin to receive

4.47. Plan of Paris by Michel Turgot. 1734. Because of a drafting error that failed to account for a slight discrepancy in scale when earlier drawings of the Louvre and Tuileries were amalgamated into a new plan of spatial unification, the axes of the two palaces were misaligned. But this problem only became noticeable in the nineteenth century when the intervening structures remaining from medieval Paris were removed. If the axis of the Louvre had been congruent with that of the Tuileries, the Louvre's new entrance, the Pyramid designed by I. M. Pei, would be aligned with the Arc de Triomphe and other important monuments that punctuate the Champs Elysées.

Below: 4.48. Place des Vosges (formerly the Place Royale), Paris

its final form until the nineteenth century when Napoleon built the western half of the northern gallery of the Tuileries and transformed Henry IV's New Garden between the palace and the Renaissance-era Square Court into a new courtyard with its centerpiece, the Arc de Triomphe du Carrousel, placed on axis with that of the Tuileries. (Only with the completion of the rest of the north gallery in the mid-nineteenth century was the area between the two palaces finally cleared of the clutter of the remaining structures. Then, following a devastating fire in 1871, the Tuileries, with the exception of its end pavilions, was removed, thereby configuring the space as we know it today.)

Henry IV's urban planning aspirations went beyond royal aggrandizement. He wanted to stimulate the economy of Paris and stem the drain of capital to foreign lands by fostering native production of luxury goods, especially silk. Along the northern edge of the Tuileries Gardens he planted an *allée* of mulberry trees, and near the northeastern wall of the city on vacant crown land, the former site of the Hôtel Royale des Tournelles, he provided inducements to a group of investors to build a silkworks containing spinning mills and workers' housing.

Sully advanced the king's plan to build artisans' residences on the rest of the site, the whole complex forming a square known as the Place Royale (fig. 4.48). To finance the construction of houses on the remaining three sides of the square adjacent to the silkworks, the king donated building lots to his political allies. The lots were granted with the stipulation

4.49. Pont Neuf and Place Dauphine, Paris. Detail from Plan of Paris by Michel Turgot. 1734

became an enclave for the nobility, and much of the ground floor space, which had been planned as a shopping arcade, was closed in as new *hôtels* were fashioned from two or more units of the original scheme.

Upon discovering the profitability of the residential real estate, the investors in the silkworks requested the king's permission to relocate it and close in the north end of the square with another range of houses in keeping with those on the other three sides. However, because of its ambiguous social intent and in spite of the royal pageants and tournaments held within the square and the placement by Cardinal Richelieu of an equestrian statue of Louis XIII in its center, the Place Royale never became fully given over to the nobility, but remained instead a popular residence for an increasingly eclectic group of tenants.

The religious wars of the sixteenth century had deferred a long-cherished plan to span the Seine and provide a direct access to the western end of the Île de la Cité, home of the Parlement of Paris. To finance the completion of the Pont Neuf, as the new bridge has been called ever since, a tax was imposed on wine. As it was being constructed, the king put forth a scheme for the Place Dauphine, a square in the form of an irregular triangle conforming to the prowlike shape of the end of the island. Opposite the Place Dauphine, a buttressed platform juts westward like a balcony over the river to form a small square on the bridge itself (fig. 4.49).

In the cramped walled cities of the period, where land was scarce and the sides of new bridges offered prime building sites as well as a revenue source for their builders, this bridge was an anomaly. The Pont Neuf, like the slightly earlier Ponte Santa Trinità in Florence, was built without any structures on it, except for a pumping station designed to bring water to the Tuileries. By keeping the bridge clear of structures, the king promoted public appreciation of Paris's already considerable scenic potential. With its open views in all directions, the bridge offered those crossing it the spectacle of the river and its traffic, the Grande Galerie and other structures of the Louvre-Tuileries complex rising on its Right Bank, the buildings opposite giving the Left Bank its own architecturally significant character, and, in between, beyond the Palais de Justice where the courts and offices of the Parlement were housed, the spires of Notre Dame at the eastern end of the Île de la Cité.

As at the Place Royale, the houses at the Place Dauphine were intended for residents of the merchant and artisan classes. However, perhaps to avoid the situation that had occurred at the Place Royale with the amalgamation of the building lots by aristocrats into larger *hôtel*-size units, here the king had Sully convey the entire site to a single developer, his

that the owners build houses according to a predetermined uniform facade plan; they could later rent or sell them for a profit. The result was the city's first planned large open space, an early example of urban architectural uniformity. By rewarding his friends with the opportunity to become developers, the king also provided a model and catalyst for later speculation in Parisian real estate.

In addition to providing housing attractive to foreign artisans, the Place Royale (rechristened by Napoleon the Place des Vosges, as it is called today) was also planned with a recreational objective. It was to be a place for social promenading, an increasingly popular Parisian pastime with ritual implications that required an architecturally defined setting. Intended for the general populace, not merely for local residents, this new kind of urban space was also meant to be a stage for court ceremonies, jousting tournaments, and public celebrations. In permanent demonstration of this function, a royal pavilion was created in the center of the south side of the square with an arched portal opening from the rue de Birague, the axis of entry.

As it turned out, the investors built residences for themselves and their friends, rather than the housing intended for artisans. Although some artisans did take up residence in the Place Royale, it quickly

loyal follower Achille de Harlay, the seventy-one-year-old president of the Parlement, whose own house lay adjacent to the future square; Harlay was obligated to build the housing ensemble as designed for tradesmen within a period of three years or find others who would buy the lots and do so. Although not in strict alignment for reasons of geography, the ensemble — bridge, sculpture, and square — was conceived as an urbanistic unit, signifying a new integrative approach to the planning of cities, one that exploited the visual relationships of objects in space.

FRENCH GARDEN STYLE

The period of Henry II and Catherine de Médicis had been one in which French designers thoroughly assimilated the lessons of Italy. During the reign of Henry IV (1589–1610) and the lifetime of his queen and widow Marie de Médicis, they forged a distinctive garden style, one that nevertheless was firmly rooted in Italian precedent and developed as a translation of the basic vocabulary of Italian design into a native idiom. Because of the king's connection through marriage with the Medici family, the period of his reign marked another wave of Italian influence, sometimes referred to as the Second School of Fontainebleau in recollection of the designers brought north by Francis I in the 1530s. Beginning in 1598, members of the Francini family of hydraulic engineers, sent by Grand Duke Ferdinando de' Medici, came north bearing knowledge of contemporary Medici garden design at the Boboli Gardens where Marie de Médicis had spent her childhood and where there was a splendid grotto, at Castello where there was also a fanciful grotto, and at Pratolino where there was a long avenue lined with fountains leading to the villa. They were also familiar with the mechanical equipment needed to propel jets in the contrivances known as *giocchi d'aqua,* or water games, found in the gardens of the Medici, and to pump and manage the flow of water in the fountains and other aquatic features that adorned the Villa d'Este at Tivoli, the Villa Lante at Bagnaia, the Villa Farnese at Caprarola, and the Villa Aldobrandini at Frascati. In France, they created at Saint Germaine-en-Laye grottoes and automata modeled on those of the Villa Medici at Pratolino. These both frightened and intrigued the Dauphin, the future Louis XIII, when he was a child growing up at Saint Germaine-en-Laye. Alessandro (Alexandre) Francini is believed to have designed the ornamental grotto for Marie de Médicis in the Luxembourg Gardens, and his 1631 book of architectural drawings contains elaborate ornamental doorways that evidently served as models for several found on French architectural grottoes of the seventeenth century (fig. 4.50). A French Huguenot, Salomon de Caus (1576?–1626), who traveled extensively in Italy, published his treatise on garden hydraulics, *Les Raisons des forces mouvantes* in 1615, when the enthusiasm for automata had begun to wane.

Although the grotto, the ornamental cascade, the architectural fountain, and the fountain arrangement known as a *buffet d'eau* remained in vogue as French garden style matured under Louis XIV, the ingenious Italian-derived hydraulics that were fashionable in the time of Henry IV and Marie de Médicis fell into disuse. As France readied itself to become the supreme European power in the second half of the seventeenth century, French designers, having thoroughly incorporated Italian influence, codified — through treatises on garden theory and in engravings published in pattern books — their own distinctive and subsequently influential style of landscape design. Perhaps the most original feature of the new French garden was the *parterre de broderie,* an embroiderylike design of decorative scrolls, palmettes, and arabesques in herbs, boxwood, or clipped grass, often with the addition of a monogram, which replaced the geometrically configured beds in Italian gardens (fig. 4.51). Several *parterre* patterns are found in the *Traité du jardinage selon les raisons de la nature et de l'art* (1638) by Jacques Boyceau de la Baraudière, André Mollet's *Le Jardin de plaisir* (1651), and Claude Mollet's *Le Théatre des plans et jardinages* (1652).

The Mollets were royal gardeners residing and working in the Tuileries, along with members of the Le Nôtre and Desgots families, who also formed several generations of gardeners in the service of the crown. Under their care the Tuileries became a kind

4.50. Entrance to a grotto, from *Livre d'Architecture* by Alexandre Francini. 1631

4.51. Design for a *parterre de broderie* in the style of André Mollet. Engraving from *Traité du Jardinage* by Jacques Boyceau. 1638

Below: 4.52. *Palissades,* plates 4 and 6 from *Le Théatre des plans et jardinages* by Claude Mollet. 1652

Palissade de Trianon.

fig. 4.

Palissade du Théatre d'eau á Versailles.

fig. 6.

of laboratory in which the French garden style, with its axial *allées,* intricate *parterres de broderie,* clipped cone-shaped yews and space-defining tall hedges, called *palissades,* was matured and perfected (fig. 4.52).

Jacques Boyceau was not a gardener in the same practical mold as these. He was a Huguenot warrior and aristocratic intellectual who had been made an official of the king's chamber even before he was granted the position of *intendant-general* of the king's gardens, including those of the Luxembourg Palace (figs. 4.53, 4.54). A friend of some of the most notable intellectuals of his day, he aimed to produce in his *Traité* something more significant than a trade book. Like Alberti before him, he found in nature's forms the perfection and symmetries to guide human artistic creation. The mastery of these laws, or at least a thorough practical acquaintance with them, formed for him one of the essential ingredients of the gardener's education. Boyceau's chief importance to the history of landscape design is his role in articulating the principles governing a new landscape idiom and the influence he exerted in supervising such talented practitioners as the Mollets and Le Nôtres.

In addition to furnishing many elegant parterre patterns, Boyceau's *Traité du jardinage* enunciated

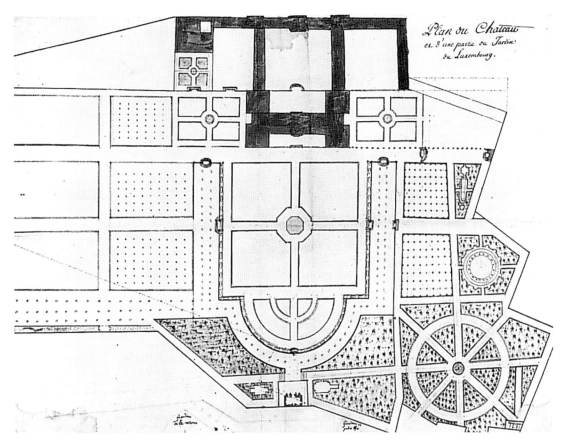

4.53. Plan of Luxembourg Gardens drawn before 1627. Though Jacques Boyceau's role in the creation of the Luxembourg Gardens for Marie de Médicis cannot be proved, a certain design maturity is evident here. There is a fine sense of proportion in the relationship of path width to *parterre* and *palissade,* a generosity of scale, the manipulation of the ground plane for optical effect, calculated diversity within a framework of carefully balanced symmetry, and the use of eye-catching features— fountains, sculpture, orange trees in boxes, balustrades, and stairs—to break up space with rhythmical accents, thereby creating measurability.

Below: 4.54. Luxembourg Gardens

what might be called the first professional curriculum of landscape design, thereby recognizing garden-making as a distinct profession. Trained gardeners, according to Boyceau, needed instruction in geometry, draftsmanship, architecture, and aesthetics besides learning practical horticulture through apprenticeship. He sought to instill in them through this curriculum a thorough understanding of perspective and proportion. His work both laid the groundwork for future developments in French landscape design and exemplified the developments that had taken place in France during the past century as the lessons of Italy were thoroughly absorbed. With its confident repertoire of patterns for elaborate *parterres* of boxwood "embroidery" and axial means of organizing landscape space, his treatise served Louis XIV's royal gardener André Le Nôtre so well that the latter never felt compelled to write a treatise of his own.

1. Dante's cosmology in *The Divine Comedy* was, like that of Aristotle, one of hierarchical space, Earth-centered and spherically bounded. Heaven was positioned somewhere within the luminous celestial ring that constitutes the upper "band" of Earth's ether, a place where physical laws governing the terrestrial world no longer apply. Here dwelled, according to the medieval Christian cosmology to which Dante was heir, the divinity of godhead, angels, saints, and beatified souls. Because of the doctrine of resurrection, those who were redeemed had a transcendent, yet corporeal, existence within this immaterial, yet real, realm. By contrast, Nicolaus of Cusa's treatise *On Learned Ignorance* posited a theory of limitless, uncentered space, which rendered Dante's concept of a hierarchy of spheres invalid. Cusa's discovery implied the idea of infinite axial extension that was later anticipated by René Descartes.

2. Quoted in James S. Ackerman, *The Villa: Form and Ideology of Country Houses* (Princeton, New Jersey: Princeton University Press, 1990), p. 73.

3. See Leon Battista Alberti, *De re aedificatoria,* trans. Joseph Rywert, Neil Leach, and Robert Tavernor (Cambridge, Massachusetts: MIT Press, 1988), p. 295.

4. Ibid., p. 300.

5. Ackerman, op. cit., p. 78.

6. The author of this edition is surmised to have been Sir Robert Dallington (1561–1637), a courtier and man of letters. His translation, which is incomplete and very inexact, has been superceded on the five-hundredth anniversary of the work's original publication by the Aldine Press in Venice by a thorough and highly readable translation by Joscelyn Godwin, Professor of Music at Colgate University. Now, at last, scholars of garden history who read English can not only admire the illustrations that inspired many aspects of Renaissance garden design but can also comprehend the pleasure Colonna and his contemporaries, many of whom were churchmen like him, felt in appropriating from antiquity the licence to celebrate eroticism in its many aspects, ranging from sexual love to love of beautiful art and architecture. See Francesco Colonna, *Hypnerotomachia Poliphili,* trans. Joscelyn Godwin (New York: Thames & Hudson, 1999).

7. Francesco Colonna, *Hypnerotomachia Poliphili,* trans. Joscelyn Godwin (New York: Thames & Hudson, 1999), p. 6.

8. Simon Schama, *Landscape and Memory* (New York: Alfred A. Knopf, 1995), p. 274.

9. For Colonna's description of the twenty groves of trees on the Isle of Cytherea, see Francesco Colonna, *Hypnerotomachia Poliphili,* trans. Joscelyn Godwin, pp. 294–99.

10. The concept of "third nature" is one of the constructs of the Renaissance mind. A complex topic, it may be explained in simplified terms as follows: "First nature," or *natura naturans* (nature's vital force), plus "second nature," or *natura naturata* (nature's created substance), when influenced by the human mind and hand, becomes "third nature," nature with the added component of design. For a good explanation of the Renaissance derivation of the concept of "third nature," see Claudia Lazzaro, *The Italian Renaissance Garden* (New Haven: Yale University Press, 1990), pp. 9–10.

11. As Professor Godwin points out in his introduction to his translation of *Hypnerotomachia Poliphili,* although Colonna was undoubtedly familiar with both Alberti's treatise and that of Vitruvius and appropriated Alberti's term *lineamenta* to signify architectural details, his cast of mind was scarcely mathematical, and "when he deals with dimensions or geometrical constructions, he is soon out of his depth." While Colonna's vivid, detailed, enthusiastic descriptions and graphic illustrations were obviously inspirational, the *Hypnerotomachia* was hardly "the manual of a practitioner." See Francesco Colonna, *Hypnerotomachia Poliphili,* trans. Joscelyn Godwin, pp. xi-xii.

12. This remarkable basin is now to be found in the Sala Rotondo of the Museo Pio Clementino within the Vatican Museums.

13. Here Ligorio's archaeology is evident in his use of antique coins and reliefs as inspiration for these stucco designs.

14. For a complete discussion of the role of these important *fontanieri* in creating and maintaining the fountains of the Villa d'Este, see David Coffin, *Gardens and Gardening in Papal Rome* (Princeton, New Jersey: Princeton University Press, 1991), pp. 54–55.

15. For instance, the central stairway in the garden is interrupted half-way up by the oval Dragon Fountain, framed by gracefully curving stairs. The four dragons within the fountain basin are doing double iconographic duty. Cardinal Ippolito identified himself with the virtues chosen by the mythological hero Hercules when he slew the dragon that was guarding the Garden of the Hesperides and then picked the three golden apples symbolizing temperance, prudence, and chastity. The dragon was also the crest of Pope Gregory XIII, and the fountain with its four dragon heads was hastily completed in honor of his visit to Tivoli on September 27, 1572, shortly before the Cardinal's death.

16. See David Coffin, *The Villa in the Life of Renaissance Rome* (Princeton, New Jersey: Princeton University Press, 1979), pp. 358–59 and Reuben M. Rainey, "The Garden as Myth: The Villa Lante at Bagnaia," in *Union Seminary Quarterly Review,* 33: 1 & 2, (Fall/Winter 1981–82), pp. 98–99.

17. Quoted in Ackerman, *The Villa,* p. 98.

18. Caroline Constant, *The Palladio Guide* (Princeton: Princeton Architectural Press, 1985), pp. 9–10.

19. Quoted in Ackerman, *The Villa,* p. 106.

20. Burlington built his villa at Chiswick as a scaled-down version of the Villa Rotonda (see fig. 7.1), and Howard commissioned the architect Sir John Vanbrugh to design the Temple of the Four Winds also in imitation of the Villa Rotonda (see fig. 7.11).

21. Jefferson borrowed ideas derived from English Palladianism at Monticello, and his work at his Poplar Forest estate is an exercise in geometrical form and mathematical harmony that owes a clear debt to Palladio (see figs. 7.43, 7.44).

22. This building was originally known as the Palazzo dei Senatori but renamed the Palazzo del Senatore, or Palace of the Senator, when after 1358 the papacy assumed control over civil Rome and the Senate was reduced to a single representative appointed by the pope.

23. To stimulate the Roman economy through the production of silk and woolen cloth, Sixtus V enacted a law commanding the widespread planting of mulberry trees and also established a wool-spinning factory within the Colosseum, a project that languished only because of his death.

24. See Kenneth Woodbridge, *Princely Gardens: The Origins and Development of the French Formal Style* (New York: Rizzoli, 1986), for an excellent discussion of this subject. I am indebted to this source for much of what follows in Section IV.

25. See Hilary Ballon, *The Paris of Henri IV: Architecture and Urbanism (The Paris of Henri IV: Architecture and Urbanism* (Cambridge, Massachusetts: The MIT Press, 1991), for a lucid, scholarly study that portrays the birth of modern Paris and explains Parisian land speculation in the early seventeenth century. Here, the reader will find a detailed narrative of the creation of various streets, squares, and buildings and watch, as it were, the Louvre, the Pont Neuf, and other now-familiar landmarks rising out of the ground.

26. See Ballon, op. cit., pp. 36–39.

POWER AND GLORY:
THE GENIUS OF LE NÔTRE AND
THE GRANDEUR OF THE BAROQUE

In seventeenth-century France, the nature of monarchy changed in a functional way. Feudal kings in the late Middle Ages had traveled with their retinues, holding court in castles scattered throughout their kingdoms or enjoying the hospitality of vassal lords. The Renaissance princes of the fifteenth and sixteenth centuries were peripatetic, enjoying the pleasures of the hunt in several royal forests and performing affairs of state while entertaining in the *châteaux* of the Loire Valley and the Île de France, some of which we examined in the previous chapter. It was not until the rule of Louis XIV (ruled 1643–1715) that this situation changed. Although the king and his retinue traveled to various royal seats—Fontainebleau, Saint-Germain-en-Laye, Chambord, and, later, Marly—residing in these for considerable periods of time, the court of France increasingly revolved in the orbit of Versailles, as Louis's attachment to his father's old hunting lodge and his determination to make it the radiant center and symbol of his reign grew. It was here that a distinctive style expressing authoritarian order and elegant rationality matured.

This style might never have gained pre-eminence as an international design idiom had not Louis XIV heeded Cardinal Jules Mazarin's deathbed recommendation and appointed Jean-Baptiste Colbert (1619–1683) as his finance minister. Colbert soon reformed the system of taxation, making it more honest, and during the first part of the king's long reign, Colbert's brilliant reorganization of finance and industry increased the prosperity of France. Louis was able during most of his reign to enjoy its benefits and turn them to both personal and national advantage.

Through the elevation of all the arts to new heights of excellence, as well as through astute political diplomacy, Louis XIV established France as the leading power in Europe, making it a great state and also the exemplar of style. Both Colbert and the king understood well the role that all the arts, especially the fine arts—architecture, painting, and sculpture—would play in that process.

Colbert belonged to the prestigious Académie Française, established by Cardinal Richelieu and incorporated in 1635, and was instrumental in founding several academies for the advancement of the arts and sciences. The establishment of these ushered in an era of important building projects sponsored by the king.[1]

The king gave dance, music, and theater new dignity and status. He founded the Académie Royale de Danse in 1661, and the Académie Royale de Musique (the Paris Opera) in 1669. Molière's troupe of actors was the precursor of the Comédie Française, which was officially chartered by the king in 1680. Louis himself was a dancer and performed in several ballets in his youth. Thus, Louis over the years, with the assistance of Colbert, supported and institutionalized the diverse talents that were responsible for forging a rich and sophisticated culture within which the French seventeenth-century style flourished as a powerful political and social statement and tangible manifestation of the power and glory of monarchy.

We have seen how readily the French appropriated the idiom of the Italian Renaissance and how thoroughly they transformed it into a style with a distinctly French inflection. Building upon this French Renaissance style, the architects and planners who served Louis XIV now took inspiration from contemporary Italian Baroque art and architecture, adapting it into yet another distinctive style. It is a style of sober grandeur, which is differentiated from the robust plasticity and exuberant theatricality of its Italian models by its linear elegance and by the application of mathematical principles to produce designs of eminent rationality.

There was a moment, however, at the beginning of the young king's reign when this outcome may have been in doubt. Colbert understood that work on the unfinished Louvre Palace should be recommenced as a first major building project of the new regime. In 1665, displeased with the plans submitted by French architects, he summoned to Paris the distinguished Italian architect and sculptor Gianlorenzo Bernini (1598–1680) in order to commission a design that would glorify the young king with the same kind of dynamic, robustly theatrical architecture that Bernini had brought to papal Rome. But the Italian's three proposals, vast in scale, would have demolished the existing palace. His solution, moreover, although also neoclassical in its inspiration, would have taken French architectural aesthetics in a dynamically Baroque direction rather than the more chaste one advocated by the king's advisors.

Louis, ceding to Colbert's counsel after several months of consideration, dismissed Bernini's proposals and put the problem in the hands of a committee consisting of Claude Perrault (1613–1688), an expert on the architecture of antiquity, the architect Louis Le Vau (1612–1670), and the painter Charles Le Brun (1619–1690). The East Front of the Louvre, which represents the solution their collaboration produced, has a central Roman-style pavilion, colonnaded wings with paired columns, and symmetrical pavilions at each end. The whole architectural composition is upheld by a ground-floor podium. In choosing an architectural vocabulary that directly linked Louis XIV symbolically with the might of imperial Rome, especially with the cool Olympian grandeur of the classicizing styles of emperors Augustus and Hadrian, the Louvre design committee substituted its own brand of neoclassicism for that of the Italian Baroque. Even though the architects who worked for Louis used such Italian Baroque forms as high domes and curving walls with verve and skill, the path of austere grandeur that is represented by the term *French classicism* is one that they never relinquished, and the Baroque elements that they did appropriate were submitted to its firm authority.

Except for the Louvre and a few other projects, Louis XIV, unlike Henry IV, took only a secondary interest in beautifying the capital, concentrating instead upon making the palace and gardens of Versailles into a cynosure of universal renown. That he was able to accomplish this astonishing feat is due not only to the circumstances of patronage that he and Colbert established but also to the presence of genius at his side. That genius belonged to a remarkable generation of French designers, in the front rank of whom stood André Le Nôtre (1613–1700), a man who throughout his long life was honored to bear the title of king's gardener.

In Le Nôtre's hands, Renaissance garden style—which we today frequently characterize as "formal"—assumed a new scale and, as it did so, forsook small-scale compartmentalization and intricate effects in favor of unified spatial composition and monumentality expressive of the evolving French style of regal grandeur in landscape terms. Formal order was made to merge with nature, and boundaries appeared to dissolve into distant prospects. The walled gardens of Catherine de Médicis, though large by Renaissance standards, were suddenly dwarfed by the dimensions of the new gardens. The former are composed of axially arranged, visibly contained spaces, inwardly focused and walled, whereas the latter are commensurate with their illusion of limitlessness—that is, large enough to have distant and generally imperceptible boundaries and axes that carry the eye to the horizon line.

This illusion of indeterminate axial extension provides a landscape analogue to the spatial concepts of René Descartes

(1596–1650), the French philosopher, mathematician, and founder of analytical geometry. Descartes believed that starting from skepticism the human intellect could comprehend the mathematical principles underlying God's creation. His rigorous methodology viewed the natural world in mechanistic terms, as objectively measurable. With Descartes, the scientific enterprise itself became boundless, and this new mode of open-ended inquiry helped establish fresh cosmological premises. The seventeenth-century cosmology, which Descartes's philosophy synthesized, provided the groundwork for modern physics. Descartes built his cosmology on that of the German astronomer, physicist, and mathematician Johannes Kepler (1571–1630), who explained how planets moved in eliptical orbits. To Kepler's theories Descartes added the concept of a heliocentric universe previously expounded by the Polish astronomer Nicolaus Copernicus (1473–1543). Because of the invention of the telescope by Galileo Galilei (1564–1642), the universe was now known to be much vaster than previously imagined. Descartes held that space was indefinitely divisible and that all movement is in a straight line. Accordingly, extension (*extensio*) is the essence of both space and matter, which are equated with each other and which determine the nature of quantity, dimension, and the measurement of distance. This meant in effect the abandonment of the Aristotelian notion of *topos,* the idea that place is coterminous with contained and defined space. Cartesian space, by contrast, is boundless and, with regard to the concept of place, value-neutral, since space could now be conceived as a universal grid of mathematical coordinates with places existing merely as locational points along its infinitely extensible planes.[2]

In this view, place is secondary to matter and space. Its nondistinctive status helps account for the abstract character of Le Nôtre's designs, which express Descartes's attempt to geometricize all nature rather than to explicate *topos.* The geometric formality of Le Nôtre's designs is also due to his employment of Cartesian analytic geometry as a practical compositional tool; the precisely calculated proportions of their component parts and his calculation of the effects of perspective on the viewer manifest an understanding of Cartesian mathematics. Although Le Nôtre may not have intended explicitly to portray the Cartesian vision of heliocentric cosmic space, an impossibility in any case, Cartesian philosophy is implicit in the indefinitely extended axes of the serenely grand gardens he designed for France's Sun King.

In addition to giving expression to a new cosmology, Descartes assisted in the overthrow of Aristotelian Scholasticism by espousing a philosophy based upon the belief that the human mind could, through deductive reasoning, grasp and control the world. The optimism inherent in the Cartesian belief that, through their own powers of intellect, human beings could master the inner workings of nature and direct these toward progressive ends is echoed by the confident grandeur of Le Nôtre's gardens. It was the Sun King's duty to symbolize in his divinely appointed person and to project through his royal authority France's position as the intellectual leader of the modern Western world, and it was Le Nôtre's job to portray this absolute power through landscape design. Both king and gardener realized, however, the difference between reality and suggestion. Le Nôtre created a garden that implied rationality yet was based on an illusion, human dominance over nature; for his part, the king realized the limits of rationalism as a tool of power and means to accomplish his political goals in a world filled with passion and intrigue.[3]

While it is often assumed that William Kent in eighteenth-century England was the first designer to "leap the wall" of the garden to embrace all of nature, Le Nôtre, operating under the cultural influence of Descartes, had performed this feat nearly a century earlier. But unlike the naturalistic style of the English garden formulated by Kent and his followers, the confident, world-embracing idiom of the French classical style with its extended axes and geometrically derived layouts celebrated absolute monarchy, not libertarian values.

The work of transforming ordinary countryside into stepped terraces, grand canals, artificial cascades, and axial promenades was accomplished at the price of villages and fields laid waste and peasants relocated. It was also achieved at a huge monetary cost, even at the low prevailing wage rates. It was certainly seen as impressive just for that reason; the enormous expenditure was an important aspect of the seventeenth-century French gardens' message, demonstrating the king's economic power and superior taste. Furthermore, these gardens were designed to serve as stages upon which the members of an aristocratic society played out the dramas of their lives with theatrical ritual as they met one another upon balustraded terraces, walked along sweeping *allées,* or trysted within the relative privacy of *bosquets.*

Theaters of social life, the gardens of seventeenth-century France often served as real stages for the performing arts. Within them, concerts, ballets, plays, fireworks, and banquets took place with increasing regularity. Theatrical entertainments were part of Louis XIV's means of keeping an otherwise bored nobility in check. Le Nôtre knew the composer Jean-Baptiste Lully (1632–1687) and the playwright Molière (Jean-Baptiste Poquelin, 1622–1675) and organized his spaces with their performance requirements in mind.

French classical gardens were theatrical in yet another sense. Had they been merely expositions of Cartesian logic, elegantly defined empty stages for aristocratic intercourse and entertainment, they would have been boring. But with their abundant water jets and populations of stone gods and goddesses, they provided the spectator with movement and a rich mythological companionship. Like the Renaissance villa gardens of Italy from which they are derived, they were programmatic texts in stone, water, and vegetation. Le Nôtre and his collaborators (notably Le Brun, whose express charge was the sculptural program of the gardens at Vaux-le-Vicomte and Versailles) had a sufficient humanistic education to continue the Renaissance practice of garden arrangement according to elaborate programs of allegorical allusion.

The elegant rationality of the style Le Nôtre forged in collaboration with the architects, artists, and artisans of his day influenced courts throughout Europe. Just as France under Louis XIV became the dominant military power in Europe, so the French classical landscape style became prevalent during and after his reign. Although inflected according to regional conditions of taste and topography, it rapidly spread to the Netherlands, England, Germany, and Russia.

The French classical garden was influential even in Italy, as is apparent a century later in the scale and plan of the royal gardens of Caserta near Naples. But Italian landscape design was so imbued with the robust theatricality of local taste that French classicism was never thoroughly integrated into it. Rather, the currents of Italian Baroque style continued to flow northward as various European monarchs and princes summoned artists and craftsmen to mingle their talents with those of French designers. In Italy itself, a wealthy clergy and its related aristocracy brought the art of villa garden building to a triumphant and spectacular close. Humanistic iconography, at first in the service of the princes of the church and state, was finally abandoned altogether and ornament became an end in its own right. Thus, the elaborate symbolical programs that informed such gardens as the Villa d'Este gave way to the kind of sculptural tableaux one finds at Caserta (see fig. 5.42).

Grand-scale geometrical landscape composition in the French manner initiated another tradition, that of monumental city planning, beginning already in the time of Louis XIV and carried forward in the eighteenth century in Washington, D.C. and St. Petersburg, as discussed in the next chapter, and in the nineteenth century, most spectacularly in Paris itself, as we shall see in Chapter Ten. And although they may work with an entirely contemporary sensibility and no longer have as their primary philosophical reference the Cartesian cosmological view that was a principal *raison d'être* for axial extension in the seventeenth century, many of today's French landscape designers stand squarely in Le Nôtre's long shadow as they rebuild the public spaces of Paris and other French cities. For all of these reasons it is worthwhile to examine more closely the career of this remarkable royal servant.

I. The Making of Vaux-le-Vicomte and Versailles: André Le Nôtre

By luck, André Le Nôtre was born at the moment when all the fashionable and newly wealthy men of seventeenth-century France, following Cardinal Richelieu's example, sought to display their taste and status in an increasingly grand manner and on an increasingly lavish scale by constructing new *hôtels* and *châteaux* or extensively remodeling old ones. As these city mansions and country estates were furnished with gardens, Le Nôtre obtained many commissions during his long professional life.

It was not only royalty and the nobility who were in a position to offer Le Nôtre commissions; the new financial elite, the *surintendants* and *intendants,* who were in charge of collecting taxes and maintaining the country's finances and administration, formed a class that rose to prominence during the decades when the old nobility's wealth was declining after prolonged religious and civil wars. The newly wealthy professional administrators were sufficiently enriched to own property of a scale to demand the services of architects and landscape designers, thus providing opportunities to consolidate the previous century's experiments.

André Le Nôtre's Predecessors and Teachers

François Mansart (1598–1666) was the most original architect and garden designer among André Le Nôtre's immediate predecessors, carrying Italian Renaissance axial planning to a new scale.[4] This design achievement had a cultural basis. As human confidence and the desire to dominate nature increased in the seventeenth century with the opening of new continents through exploration and the expansion of mental horizons through science, Mansart grasped the possibility of projecting the garden outward in an open-armed gesture of seemingly illimitable axial extension. He stretched axes in long perspective lines emanating from, and converging upon, the *château*. At Maisons, Berny, Balleroy, Fresnes, Petit Bourg, Gesvres, and elsewhere, he elaborated approaches and forecourts, running axial vistas through village and forest (fig. 5.1). He and his followers placed the *château* within a field of successive sight lines, dramatically revealing it along intersecting axes.

Jacques Lemercier (1585–1654), the architect employed by Cardinal Richelieu on several projects,

5.1 *Château* and gardens of Petit Bourg, Corbeil, France. Design attributed to François Mansart, ca. 1650. Engraving by Adam Pérelle, 1727

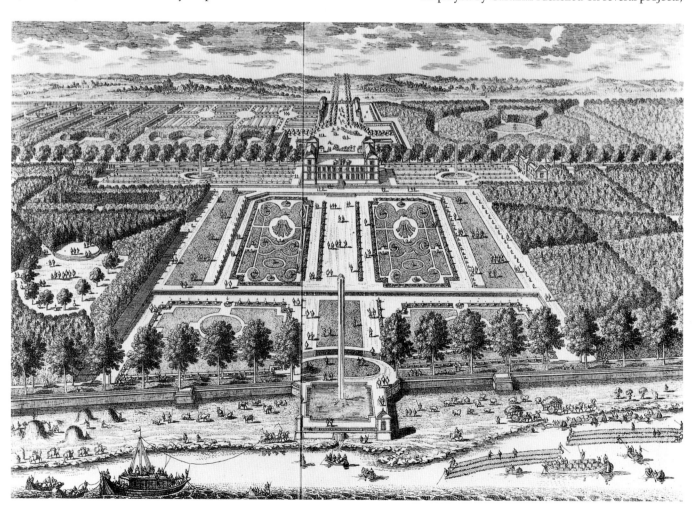

was also an important influence for the young Le Nôtre. Lemercier's commissions from the cardinal included his country retreat, Rueil, where he built an impressive architectural cascade, and the *château* and new town that bore the cardinal's name. At Richelieu, Lemercier laid out an abstract grid that encompassed the extensive grounds of the *château* and canalized the river Mable as an important cross axis (fig. 5.2). This early application of Cartesian geometry to landscape design helped set the course that Le Nôtre would follow and perfect.

In his youth, Le Nôtre may have worked with Mansart; it is clear that his genius owes a debt to that of this temperamental and arrogant master builder. But Le Nôtre's pivotal, enduring accomplishment had much deeper sources than this purported apprenticeship. Indeed, history offers few examples of the marriage of vocational destiny, natural genius, and opportunity more complete than that of André Le Nôtre. His grandfather, Pierre, had been *Maître Jardinier* in the service of Catherine de Médicis, and his father, Jean, held the title of *Premier Jardinier du Roi*. Born in the gardeners' quarters of the Tuileries Gardens in 1613, André grew up constantly exposed to his future profession. The companions of his infancy and childhood were members of the Mollet and Desgots families, gardeners who were also lodged in the Tuileries. Ties of closest friendship and even marriage knit their members into a solid professional clan.

Not only did Le Nôtre inherit his father's title upon the latter's retirement, but, more important, he displayed a quick intellect in receiving the education to which his father directed him. That education was the one prescribed by Jacques Boyceau in his treatise of 1638; it incorporated among other things the means to give physical form to Cartesian rationality through newly formulated laws of geometry, perspective, and optics.

Le Nôtre's education also included a sensory approach to, and appreciation of, line, proportion, and color, which he acquired during his apprenticeship in the studio of the painter Simon Vouet (1590–1649). The fact that Jean Le Nôtre, his father, placed him with Vouet in order to develop his draftsmanship and general aesthetic perceptions illustrates the position landscape gardening now occupied in relation to the fine arts. Later, Le Nôtre became a notable connoisseur and collector of works of art.[5]

In addition to his training with Vouet, Le Nôtre seems to have received a sound education in architecture. It is likely that he was instructed by both Mansart and Lemercier. Certainly, his gardens are so imbued with architectural principles and architectural intelligence that it would have been impossible for Le Nôtre to have designed them without a thorough aca-

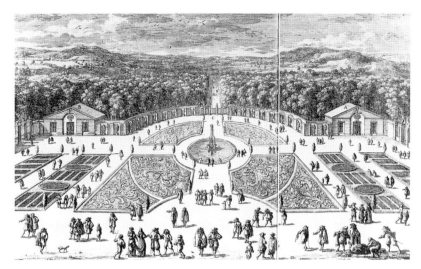

5.2. View of *Parterre* and *Demie Lune,* Richelieu, Touraine, France. Designed by Jacques Lemercier. 1631–39. Engraving by Pérelle, 1688

demic training in architecture. Endowed with practical experience from his earliest years as well as personal gifts and technical skills that enabled him to be more than a talented practitioner of a well-respected craft, Le Nôtre took on the task of transforming the tenets of French Renaissance garden design into a new idiom.

Shortly after Louis XIV took over the reins of government, Le Nôtre had the good fortune to have as a client the king's minister of finance, the ambitious and cultivated Nicolas Fouquet (1615–1680). Fouquet knew how to solicit from artists their best and most imaginative work and how to add an educated client's eye and discernment to the collaborative process necessary for realizing a notable design. Like other passionate builders, he was willing to spare no expense to achieve perfection. Thus equipped by taste and temperament and enriched by the emoluments of office, Fouquet approached, at the age of forty-one, the task of creating the monument of his brilliance and also of his doom, Vaux-le-Vicomte, the *château* and garden that epitomize the French classical style.[6]

VAUX-LE-VICOMTE

Lying within the broad agricultural plain that is the predominant landscape of the Île de France, Vaux-le-Vicomte was a small estate that Fouquet had inherited in 1640 from his father. It was an unremarkable piece of countryside, bereft of the topographical drama of contemporary villa gardens in Italy, where patrons and designers sought hillside sites because they considered them inherently salubrious and scenic. Such manipulations of topography as were necessary to realize the design of Vaux-le-Vicomte would have to be achieved by brute labor.

Expectation and surprise—or, put another way, rationality and mystery—are both present in a masterpiece of landscape architecture. Vaux-le-Vicomte is rich in both elements. It has a plan of complete

VAUX-LE-VICOMTE

5.3. Vaux-le-Vicomte, Melun, France. Designed by André Le Nôtre. 1656–61

Vaux-le-Vicomte opens up like a play in several acts. There is, first, the drama of entry that many visitors approaching from the modern parking lot are apt to miss. Approaching instead along the central axis, which runs through the middle of the *château* and the garden beyond it, one walks down a slight incline toward a beautiful grille punctuated at intervals with tall stone herms and terminated by symmetrical pedimented pseudoportals. The moat is sunk well below the balusters, and its sudden appearance produces the first of many grade-manipulated surprises. Only as one attempts to follow visually one of the arms of the moat around the *château* can one guess that the elaborate screen of grille, pseudoportals, and service buildings has been masking something magnificent beyond.

Standing at the entrance to the *château*, one now can see on either side verdant grass *parterres*, the edges of which are punctuated with yews clipped into precise identical cones, and, through the far windows of the central pavilion, one glimpses more manicured verdure. With the same anticipation that is to be felt upon the rising of the curtain in a theater, one walks through the central vestibule and oval salon out to the terrace. There lie the *parterres de broderie*, parallel beds of box and gravel patterned like brocade (fig. 5.4). Fountains, pools, sculpture, topiary, hedges, and trees are all laid out along a grand central axis that

finally turns from graveled promenade into a grassy ramp upon which stands a colossal gilded Hercules, symbol of virtuous strength and intended somewhat arrogantly by Fouquet as a reference to himself (fig. 5.7). Still this axis continues, banked by forest groves, until it seems to melt into the luminous sky.

Strolling along the central axis one finds changes in level that were not apparent at first. The axis, from successive vantage points, extending from the *château* all along the distance of the central promenade, deceptively appears to flow in one unbroken sweep to meet the grassy ramp and gilded Hercules; in fact, Le Nôtre has manipulated the ground plane to produce several surprising results.

A few feet beyond the circular pool at the end of the *parterre de broderie* just beyond the garden's first principal cross axis, which is emphasized by a pair of previously invisible long rectangular pools, there is a slight shift in the elevation. Descending, the visitor continues along the central promenade. Here one walks along a barely perceptible incline past flower-filled urns that today mark what was once the *Allée d'Eau*, so named for the evenly spaced low jets of water bordering it. The mild slope of this part of the garden allowed the runoff from the aqueous balustrade formed by the water jets to flow in two clear streams on either side of the central *allée*. This part of the garden terminates

in a large square pool.

Beyond the pool, and now suddenly visible, is one of the most impressive surprises in the entire garden. The elaborate architectural grotto, which from a distance appears to rise from the far end of the square pool, does not in reality do so. Here, the ground abruptly drops, revealing a huge chasm. This chasm contains the garden's second major cross axis in the form of a wide canal. As unexpected as this sight is, it is only half of the surprise, for at the bottom of the stairs to the canal, the entire supporting wall of the terrace above becomes a giant water feature, the Grandes Cascades (fig. 5.5), a mighty wall of water, commensurate in effect with the scale of the canal beside it and a dramatic counterpoint to the grotto opposite. Now dry, it must be imagined with the roar and gurgle of water spouting from grotesque masks into cupped bowls and upturned shells.

To approach the grotto one must walk to the far end of the canal and back along the opposite bank. Its architecture of rusticated stone forms a massive support for the terrace above. Beneath the flanking pair of broad stairs that rise to meet this terrace repose giant classical river gods, one symbolizing the Tiber, the other the local Anqueil, the river feeding the canal (fig. 5.6). The grotto steps contain a carved lion and squirrel. The agile high-vaulting squirrel was Fouquet's emblem, and the lion symbolized his protector, the king. Herms carved in bold

relief separate the grotto into seven niches containing artificial rockwork over which water was made to flow into a large rectangular basin. The balustrade of the terrace above the grotto was originally decorated with sculptures. Behind it a jet of water known as the Gerbe, was, according to contemporary accounts, as thick as a man's body and rose a lofty five meters (16'5") into the air.

The Gerbe, when operable, must have appeared as a shimmering base for the gilded Hercules. Modeled on the Farnese Hercules, the scale of this colossus is not apparent from the terrace of the *château*. When apprehended, it makes one aware of the great distance—half a mile (800 meters)—one has traveled in a straight line from the spot where it first appeared in view.

Beneath the towering base of the Hercules is an ordinary stone bench. From this vantage point one may gaze back at the *château* (fig. 5.7). Now all the games with geometry, perspective, and optics are played all over again in reverse. The canal and cascade are no longer visible; all the garden's cleverly interlocking parts are visually compressed into a single flattened plane. The garden presents itself once again as a unified image, the undisputed focus of which is the *château* with its swelling roof dome breasting the sky, the centerpiece of Le Nôtre's and Le Vau's collaboration, to which all its component parts now adhere.

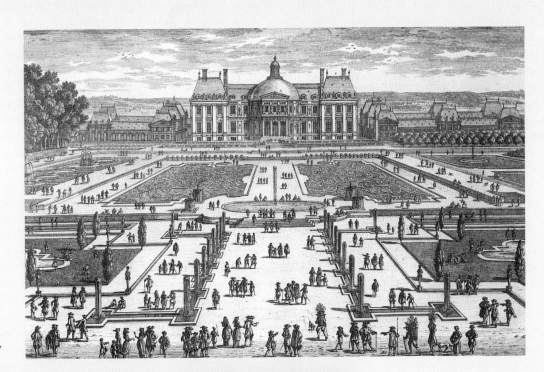

5.4. *Château* and Grand *Parterre,* Vaux-le-Vicomte. Engraving by Adam and Nicholas Pérelle, from *Recueil des Veues des Plus Beaux Lieux de France,* 1688

5.5. Grandes Cascades, Vaux-le-Vicomte. View by Israël Silvestre, engraving by Adam Pérelle, from *Recueil des Veues des Plus Beaux Lieux de France,* 1688

5.6. River god, Grotto, Vaux-le-Vicomte

5.7. View of the *château* of Vaux-le-Vicomte from the base of the Hercules sculpture

clarity, a design in which one may grasp the whole composition and from its organizing axes infer the principal spaces, a design in which there is a deft interlocking of parts and a logical progression from one to another. It also contains much more than meets the eye when the eye enjoys its first satisfying survey of the harmoniously proportioned whole. And even that whole is not revealed at first glance, but rather through a process of unexpected discovery.[7]

It is by the laws of geometry, perspective, and optics that Vaux achieves, within the framework of logic, a number of masterly surprises, an accomplishment belonging not only to Le Nôtre, but also to the architect Louis Le Vau and the painter Charles Le Brun with whom he worked in close collaboration. Le Nôtre had in all probability read the *Traité de la section perspective* (1636) by the mathematician and engineer-architect Girard Desargues (1591–1661), who attempted to modify Cartesian theory with the notion of a properly geometric infinity. The subtle alterations of grade and multiplicity of perspectives at Vaux dramatize and dignify the *château* and carry the eye along an axial progression to carefully established focal points within the garden, as well as to the remote horizon beyond. These effects are the result of precise mathematical calculation. The application of this mathematical knowledge allowed Le Nôtre to conceal certain elements of the garden until the visitor, progressing through its sequenced spaces, finds them revealed as if by some sort of legerdemain (figs. 5.3–5.7). In this orchestration of garden experience, Le Nôtre exhibits his kinship with the Renaissance designers responsible for hide-and-reveal tactics found at the Villa Giulia and elsewhere.

As is well known in the annals of garden history, Fouquet gave a party to celebrate his achievement on August 17, 1661. To it he invited the entire court and the young king. Not only had Fouquet naively deluded himself with regard to the effect that so much ostentation and fashionable display would have upon his master Louis XIV, but, ever confident of his ability to charm and flatter his way into power, he had been foolhardy in offering financial advice and credit to the king's mistress, Louise de La Vallière, offending her and enraging the king. In addition, he had as an enemy Jean-Baptiste Colbert, who, eager to succeed him, was able to persuade the dying Cardinal Mazarin to denounce Fouquet. Whether or not Fouquet actually did use public funds to build Vaux, its magnificence and size certainly suggest that this might have been the case.

The party itself lives on in history, not only because of its ironic, if predictable, outcome, but because it expanded the scale of garden festivities, just as Vaux had expanded the scale of the garden itself,

to unprecedented dimensions. First, there was a royal tour through the garden with its dancing waters and allusive sculptural program developed perhaps by the fabler La Fontaine.[8] Then a lavish banquet was held indoors, followed by a comedy and fireworks. The guests returned outside after the banquet to watch *Les Fâcheux,* written for the occasion by the young Molière, who was one of the actors. This was performed in front of the *Grille d'eau,* a beautiful tiered fountain at one end of the first cross axis. Molière begged the king to help him by commanding the garden itself to cooperate in producing the spectacle. Thereupon, statues appeared to come to life, trees to move, and rocks to open.[9] When night fell, the *château* was lit by hundreds of lanterns placed upon the cornices; the grotto, too, was illuminated. Elaborate fireworks rained down from above, some in the form of *fleurs de lys.* A mock whale swam the length of the canal discharging more fireworks. Then, as the king prepared to depart, rockets shot from the dome of the *château,* setting the whole sky ablaze.

On September 5, Fouquet was arrested on charges of high treason and embezzlement. Although judged innocent on counts that might have warranted the death penalty, Fouquet was imprisoned for life. Louis, having immediately appropriated much of the sculpture and new plantings he had seen at Vaux-le-Vicomte, as well as the services of its creators, began redesigning both the gardens of Fontainebleau and those his father had laid out at Versailles.[10]

VERSAILLES

Shortly after Fouquet's arrest, the three principal designers of Vaux-le-Vicomte—Le Vau, Le Brun, and Le Nôtre—were hard at work transforming Louis XIII's old hunting lodge at Versailles into a place for entertainment with a suitably grand suite of apartments for the young king and queen. Le Vau was in charge of remodeling the *château* without altering its basic lines; he was also asked to create an orangery. Le Brun was made responsible for the decoration of the *château.* To Le Nôtre fell the task of developing the plan that would enlarge the gardens to a monumental scale, defying both the site's marshy and highly irregular terrain and Colbert's assertion that Versailles was but meanly proportioned as a symbol of monarchical magnificence.[11]

As Superintendent of the King's Buildings, Colbert oversaw the financing and coordination of the entire construction process, a task in which he was assisted by Charles Perrault (1628–1703), First Clerk and later Comptroller of Buildings. Perrault, whose more enduring fame rests upon a much-loved collection of fairy tales, was probably responsible for the development and construction in the 1660s and 1670s

5.8. Apollo Fountain,
Versailles. Sculpture by
Jean-Baptiste Tuby. 1668–71

of the heliocentric iconography that celebrated the glory of the Sun King and the sun's—and therefore Louis's—mythological representative, Apollo, throughout the gardens of Versailles (fig. 5.8).

As the iconography of the Sun King became elaborated in several garden compositions, Versailles more and more became the center of court life. After 1678, when Jules Hardouin-Mansart (1645–1708), the grandnephew of François Mansart, had succeeded Le Vau as official architect to the king, Louis decided to make his favorite *château* the seat of government. Throughout the early building campaigns at Versailles, Le Nôtre guided the design of the gardens. In creating in the central *allée* the smooth greensward of the *tapis vert* and its flanking *bosquets* of geometrically arranged trees, in laying out the *parterres* beside Hardouin-Mansart's 1683 Orangerie, and in building the gardens of the Trianon and the long canal that extended the principal axis to the distant reach of the garden, he worked steadily with professional collaborators, workmen, and gardeners.

But because Versailles was not conceived as a single unified scheme, as was Vaux-le-Vicomte, it does not have the coherence of its predecessor. Its size is gargantuan, a mighty sprawl over hundreds of acres. And yet Le Nôtre maintained a rigorous logic in its design; its central axis and several transverse axes provide a strong framework around which various features were arranged and rearranged over the years. Within this framework, Le Nôtre and his collaborators contributed much pleasing incident in the form of fountains, pools, treillage, sculpture, and crisply geometric topiary. It was Le Nôtre's genius to substitute for the ordered intricacy of the older French Renaissance gardens a new clarity, simplicity, austerity, and refinement, creating a style of great architectonic strength. He drove his axes into the indefinite distance, erasing all visible garden boundaries, creating the paradigm of a world-embracing landscape. In so doing, he also laid down the premises for a new urban order.

It is a style in which monumentality is achieved not so much by architectural means as through spatial ones. Because of its role as a model for future garden and urban design, the plan for Versailles as it existed shortly before the king's death is worth studying in regard to its organization of space (figs. 5.9, 5.10). By the application of Cartesian mathematics, landscape is geometricized on a grand scale. Space is projected by axes and defined by cross axes. Radials converge as a *patte d'oie,* or goose foot, upon the palace; these are tree-lined boulevards, the principal avenues of the town of Versailles—a planned community of red brick and stone buildings of regulated height, which was laid out as a grid with public squares at certain intersections.

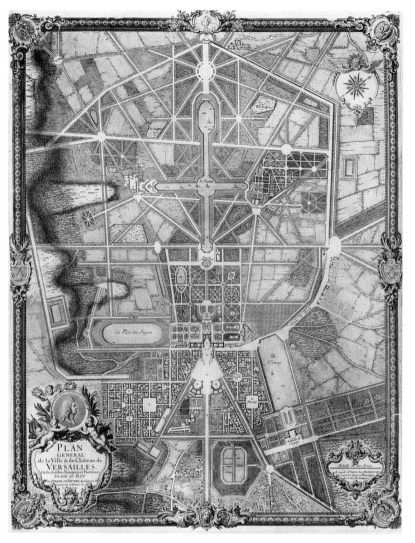

5.9. Plan of 1710 by Pierre Le Pautre of the palace, gardens, and town of Versailles

Below: **5.10. Aerial view, Versailles**

The gardens are elaborated within an overall structure and subdivisions that are inventively geometric, and the entire composition, which necessarily had to take its point of departure from Louis XIII's Versailles, is a remarkable demonstration of Le

Nôtre's genius for producing a sense of rational order under awkward conditions. The palace sits athwart the main axis. The first cross axis of the garden bisects *parterres de broderie,* embroiderylike designs in boxwood and colored gravel. Here, where it is seen from the palace windows at close range, the design is intricate and the scale compact. Several successive cross axes and axes paralleling the principal one create a grid within the old stand of forest trees. These are subdivided by paths forming geometric designs, each with a central feature, usually a fountain basin with sculpture. For instance, along the axis of the Parterre du Nord near the palace, the Allée d'Eau—twin rows of fountains supported by cherubs—leads to the circular Bassin du Dragon.[12]

The principal axis, which would be vapid if simply projected the length of the garden as an *allée* of uniform grade, width, and surface material, is enlivened by changes of level and dimension; alternations between gravel, grass, and water; and the addition of several important sculptural features celebrating the Sun King. The first of these, which is reached by a broad flight of stairs descending from a horseshoe-shaped terrace located just beyond the second cross axis of the garden, is the 1670 masterpiece of Jean-Baptiste Tuby (1630–1700), the Fountain of Latona, mother of Apollo. The sculptural grouping depicts Latona and her two children, Apollo and Diana, surrounded by the wicked Lycian peasants who had refused them water and who, as victims of divine retribution, are in the process of being metamorphosed into frogs (fig. 5.11).[13] This allegorical composition based on a story from Ovid's *Metamorphosis* refers to the Fronde, the civil war in which a rebellious faction representing the parliament of Paris opposed the crown during the minority of Louis XIV, a threat to royal power the king never forgot or forgave. Here the anti-authoritarian *frondeurs* are symbolized by the discomfited former peasants, now frogs.

Beyond the two mirror-image *parterres* adjacent to this fountain, the axis turns from gravel into grass, with side *allées* flanked by *bosquets.* This strip of lawn, or *tapis vert,* is terminated by another major sculptural feature punctuating the axis: the Basin of Apollo with Tuby's sculpture of the god rising as the morning sun from the water in a chariot drawn by splendid horses, his appearance heralded by horn-blowing tritons (see fig. 5.8). Cast of lead and then gilded, this group remains one of the principal sights of Versailles as the morning sun illuminates its frontal, east-facing side or the setting sun washes it from the rear. On the far side of the Basin of Apollo, the axis becomes a canal that appears to stretch in a watery line to the horizon, now marked by two giant poplars. It has an important cross axis, giving it a cruciform shape. The

5.11. Latona Fountain, Versailles

northern arm extends to an embankment beside the Trianon, the pavilion and gardens Louis built as a private retreat in 1671 and reconstructed in 1687.

An octagonal basin forms the head of the canal and the point of departure for a major cross axis and two pairs of diagonal axes. These diagonal axes set up a new series of alignments as they and other minor axes crisscrossing them project the garden's space outward in a dynamic fashion. Beyond the canal, a *rond-point* creates a starburst of axes, which is echoed elsewhere in the garden by other circles with axes radiating out from them. It is as if Le Nôtre were trying to demonstrate in a terrestrial manner Descartes's proposition of *extensio,* the indefinite extension of cosmic space. Practically, the plan of Versailles furnished the inspiration for thousands of landscape creations, serving as the wellspring for gardens and city plans throughout Europe and, later, all across the globe.

Over the years, Louis directed Le Nôtre to revise several parts of the gardens. He caused the fountains and *bosquets* containing sculpture illuminating the Apollonian theme to become the tourist attraction they have remained ever since. Because Louis's life was lived almost entirely in public amid the busy swarm of his ever-present court, there was an almost endless stream of visitors from home and abroad to admire the gardens. Madeleine de Scudéry, a contemporary to whom we owe a lively account of the unforgettable but unfortunate festivity at Vaux-le-Vicomte, in 1669 produced *La Promenade de Versailles,* an itinerary for visitors. In 1674, the artist and historiographer André Félibien published his guidebook entitled *Description sommaire du chasteau de Versailles.* The king often conducted tours and was the author of a periodically revised guide, first issued in 1689, which peremptorily advised one where to stand and what to notice.

The engravings of Israël Silvestre, Adam Pérelle, and Antoine Le Pautre are all animated by human fig-

ures in aristocratic dress, lending a measure of scale to buildings, *palissades,* and fountain jets and bringing the gardens to life with many telling social details. The gardens at Versailles were, moreover, not only intended as a stage for the pageantry of aristocracy; Le Nôtre and his collaborators created elaborate temporary stages and areas suitable as outdoor theaters for the actual dramas and other spectacles that soon became an indispensable part of court life (fig. 5.12). The composer Lully collaborated with Molière on several of the spectacles that were staged there. *Palissades* served as theatrical wings; similarly, arches of plaster, masonry, and greenery could be used as side

5.12. Israël Silvestre's suites of engravings of the memorable Fêtes de Versailles (Paris: *Les Plaisirs de L'Isle Enchantée,* 1673) provide a fine example of Versailles' ability to accommodate theatrical spectacle. The engravings depict the entertainments that both glorified the king and demonstrated his power. The first celebrated his alliance with his mistress, Louise de La Vallière, during five days at the beginning of May 1664, The marriage of nature and stagecraft is apparent in several tableaux of various events and is discernible even in a banqueting scene, where torchbearers form a line of "footlights" in front of the guests, while, behind them, costumed waiters hold aloft trays of mounded delicacies as they move with balletic grace and precision in front of the security guards that hold back the gathered spectators. In a similar fashion, a proscenium arch was erected to frame a garden perspective that served as the living backdrop for both a ballet and a play, which was given on the second day of the *fête.*

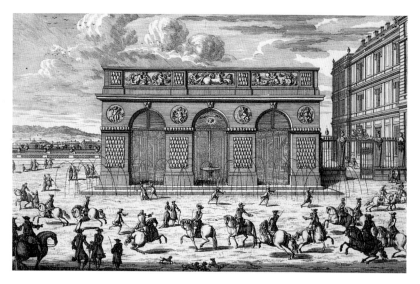

5.13. Grotto of Thetis. Engraving by Adam and Nicholas Pérelle, from *Recueil des Veues des Plus Beaux Lieux de France,* 1688

entrances. Sometimes these were enlarged to define a proscenium in the same way that the frame of a picture defines its illusionistic space and focuses the viewer upon its perspective lines.

In 1665, work was begun on the Grotto of Thetis, which had a reservoir on its roof to supply water for the gardens' numerous fountains (fig. 5.13). One of the last and most opulent of such architectural grottoes to be built, it stood on the upper terrace between the north side of the *château* and the Parterre du Nord. Charles Perrault developed the concept for the grotto, relying on Ovid's *Metamorphoses* for the story of Apollo driving his fiery steeds across the sky all day and then repairing at nightfall to the underwater palace of the sea goddess Thetis. Its three niches contained sculptural groups depicting the repose of Apollo, who is being bathed by the nymphs of Thetis, and the grooming of the horses of the Sun by Tritons. The interior walls were richly ornamented with shell mosaic, and the exterior of the grotto was equally decorative. Perrault credited his brother Claude, a physician-architect, with designing the gilded grilles forming a sunburst pattern in its three wrought-iron arched gates. When these gates were opened, the richly decorated facade and well-lit interior became the backdrop for theatrical productions, including that of Molière's *Le Malade imaginaire* in 1674. The descent of Apollo and his horses into the sea, which was expressed in the grotto's exterior frieze by Gérard van Opstal, was symbolically paired with Tuby's horses rising with the god in the Basin of Apollo.

The extensive building period to which the construction of the Grotto of Thetis, the decoration of the Basin of Apollo, and the installation of the Latona Fountain belong coincided with the king's taking the witty and accomplished Athénaïs Rochechouart de Mortemart, Marquise de Montespan, for his new mistress in 1668.[14] Her establishment was followed by the construction of Le Vau's Enveloppe, or the

Château Neuf, as it was also called. Because its broad façade destroyed the floral *parterre,* or queen's garden, on the south side of the old *château,* the king, who loved flowers, sought another part of Versailles where he could enjoy the fragrance and colorful display of exotic specimens in carefully arranged beds. He also wished to have a pleasant retreat where he could retire with Madame de Montespan and a few favorites, away from the public glare of the large, well-populated Château Neuf.

It was for these reasons that in 1671, on the site of the former village of Trianon, the Trianon de Porcelaine, so named for the Delft ceramic tiles that decorated its roof, was built. Throughout the long period in which the Trianon de Porcelaine was in use, Madame de Montespan remained the favorite; its demolition in 1687, when Hardouin-Mansart's Grand Trianon (the Trianon de Marbe) was built, marked her replacement by Françoise d'Aubigné, Madame de Maintenon. Michel Le Bouteux, the husband of Le Nôtre's niece, was in charge of the nurseries that supported the lavish floriculture of this section of Versailles. He was also responsible for ordering and planting many exotic flowers, such as tuberoses, which gardeners installed at every season of the year in floral *parterres.* The ability to procure these exceedingly rare treasures symbolized absolute monarchy as much as did Le Nôtre's commanding axes and Versailles's heliocentric iconography celebrating Louis XIV's role as Sun King.

During this period, by which time the main architectonics of Versailles were established, increasing attention was paid to the development of the *bosquets* (fig. 5.14). Le Nôtre created several of these green theaters within the Petit Parc, including Le Marais, a fanciful rectangular pond surrounded by metallic reeds and containing a tree, also of metal, in the *bosquet* just beneath the terrace sustaining the Parterre de Nord; L'Étoile, a starlike maze of tree-lined paths converging upon a central Montagne d'Eau formed of *rocaille* (rustic rockwork); and the Labyrinthe located to the west of the Orangerie on the south side of the Petit Parc where various turnings and cul-de-sacs were punctuated by fountains with sculptures depicting animals from the *Fables* of Aesop. The ground to the west of the Labyrinthe was low-lying and spongy. Here, in 1671–74, Le Nôtre used two units of his *allée*-gridded plan to form a large water feature consisting of a semicircular basin known as the Miroir and a larger basin containing the Isle Royale. He emphasized the garden's dominant theme by making the Isle Royale circular like the Sun and projecting sixteen raylike *allées* from the edges of the water basin in which it sat. The Enclade, the only remaining *bosquet* built before 1680, has in its center a round pool in which Gaspard Marsy's giant sprawls, felled in his hubris by the mountain he tried to erect to heaven. It is an arresting piece reminiscent of Giambologna's Appenino at Pratolino, less in keeping with the elegant classicism of Versailles than with the theatricality of Italian Baroque art.

The 1680s, which opened with Le Nôtre's return from Italy (where he had traveled only to learn that the most advanced concepts in landscape design were now originating in France), also constituted the period in which Jules Hardouin-Mansart was busy directing the last major building phase of Versailles. Louis, at the height of his power and passion for building, now sought a new retreat, one even more private than the Trianon. At Marly, overlooking the Seine and Saint-Germain in the distance, he commissioned Hardouin-Mansart to design a new small *château* with separate guest pavilions in order to ensure the king's privacy (fig. 5.15). By 1683, he was able to host entertainments in the unfinished gardens. Because Marly, unlike Versailles, enjoyed a hillside location, the king was eager to have Le Nôtre design for it a cascade such as the ones he had seen on his recent trip to Italy. However, it was not until 1697–99, just before Le Nôtre's death, that the project of building La Rivière on the slope behind the *château* was accomplished.

Today all but a few of the marble sculptures that once decorated Marly, together with an abundance of bronze and marble vases and statues, are displayed at the Louvre. The *château* and guest pavilions have vanished. Only a broad stripe of green turf marks the course of the king's cascade. This piece of grass symbolizes the chief problem that beset not only Marly, but also Versailles and the Trianon: an insufficiency of water for the more than 1,400 dazzling waterworks these gardens contained. The grotto, *parterres,* and *bosquets* of the Petit Parc at Versailles and the gardens of the Trianon were in the time of Louis XIV enlivened with water cascading, purling, leaping, or lying quietly in basins. Water served as one of the principal performers in the pageantry of these landscapes, mirroring their architecture of stone and verdure and animating perspectives. There was, in fact, an insatiable demand to furnish the ever-multiplying fountains, which constantly taxed the ingenuity of the *fontainiers,* plumbers, and engineers who worked to increase and maintain water supply and pressure.

To operate the fountains at Versailles required a corps of highly disciplined workers under a master-*fontainier.* Rarely was there adequate water to allow all of the fountains to play at once. Boys were commanded to serve as runners when the king or other important visitors toured the gardens, blowing whistles to alert plumbers to turn on valves as the royal entourage approached. The king's hydraulic engi-

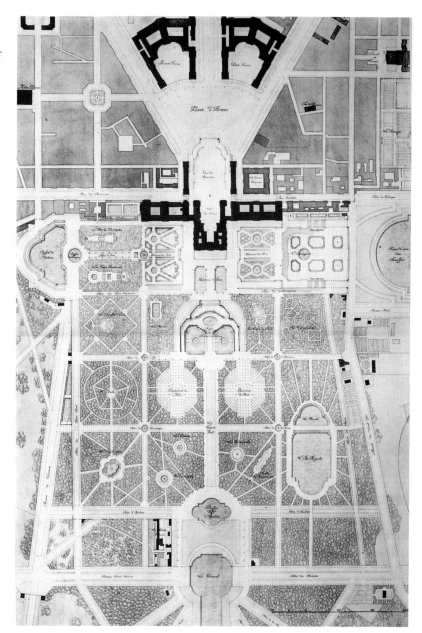

5.14. Plan of the *bosquets* **of Versailles. 1664–1713**

Below: **5.15. Château de Marly. Engraving from** *Recueil des Veues des Plus Beaux Lieux de France* **by Adam and Nicholas Pérelle, 1688**

5.16. Cascade, Sceaux

neers undertook many elaborate and costly schemes to increase the water supply. Between 1682 and 1688, they built a vast contraption known as the Machine de Marly. It was equipped with fourteen huge wheels that powered pumps conveying water from the Seine uphill to two reservoirs, whence it was distributed to the gardens of Marly, Versailles, and the Trianon, But even then the fountains could not all flow simultaneously. After 1684, the military engineer Sébastien Le Prestre de Vauban directed an ambitious scheme to divert the waters of the Eure River 28 miles (70 kilometers) distant; as many as 30,000 soldiers were set to work, and huge sums of money were spent. In the face of the War of the League of Augsburg, Louis abandoned the project.

The treatment of the royal gardens of Louis XIV as vast public works projects employing both military and civilian workers in the movement of earth on a scale hitherto unknown—leveling view-obstructing hills, excavating low-lying marshes to form canals, and filling in depressions to create enormous level terraces—is evident even in the Potager du Roi, the vegetable garden at Versailles. Here, between 1677 and 1683, Jean-Baptiste de la Quintinye (1626–1688), the king's head gardener for fruits and vegetables, oversaw the creation of a 20-acre walled enclosure on low-lying lands to the southeast of the palace with dredged spoil from the Pièce d'Eau des Suisses and topsoil from the Satory Hills. A statue of this highly respected man today presides over the extensive *potager* with its planting beds carefully delineated by many varieties of espaliered fruit trees.

It was Le Nôtre's genius to consolidate the work of such predecessors as Boyceau and Lemercier into a style of great architectonic strength, carrying their achievements to a logical conclusion and substituting for the ordered intricacy of the older Renaissance gardens a new clarity, simplicity, austerity, and refinement. Le Nôtre's legacy lies in his treatment of space as an abstract, geometrical entity, his understanding of spatial optics, and his expansion of landscape design to a monumental scale. This far-reaching legacy is expressed not only at Vaux-le-Vicomte and Versailles, but also in the gardens Le Nôtre designed at other royal and noble residences near Paris. He reorganized Fontainebleau according to a grandly simple plan. At Saint-Germain-en-Laye he laid out a new rectangular garden, which replaced that of Henri IV, and at Saint-Cloud, he employed the hilly terrain to good effect, creating a broad *allée* that dropped and then ascended to a high point, affording a fine view of Paris in the distance. He gave expression to the power and the optimism of the age at Colbert's *château* of Sceaux in the construction of a spectacular cascade and the digging of a 3,465-foot- (1056-meter-)

long canal that today, with its reflected border of tall swaying poplars, serves as a canyonlike cloud chamber (fig. 5.16). In another major feat of design and hydraulic engineering, he created the Grand Canal, a great circular basin, and magnificent oval pools at Chantilly between 1671 and 1681 (fig. 5.17).

In 1700, shortly before Le Nôtre's death, Louis and his gardener toured the gardens of Versailles for the last time. Because of his advanced years, Le Nôtre was invited to ride in a chair wheeled by a footman. With characteristic modesty and frank delight, Le Nôtre was heard to exclaim: "Alas! my poor father, had he been alive to see this poor gardener, his own son, riding in a chair beside the greatest king on earth, his happiness would have been complete."[15]

Between Le Nôtre's death in 1700 and his own in 1715, Louis faced family tragedy and became increasingly stoical as he anticipated his own approaching end amid disastrous military defeats and the declining economic power of France.[16] The vanished glory of his age was soon after captured by eighteenth-century painters such as Jean-Honoré Fragonard in scenes of figures disporting themselves in the now-derelict great gardens of the epoch of the Sun King, which they saw in their abandonment as sweetly picturesque (see fig. 7.41). A similar air of melancholy vacancy appears in the photographs Eugène Atget made of some of Le Nôtre's gardens at the beginning of the twentieth century.[17]

The reaction to a static and authoritarian order had already begun to set in as new ideas and voices challenged the spirit of the *ancien régime*. But Le Nôtre's influence remained strong. His practice was inherited and his style continued by his nephew Claude Desgots (d. 1732). In Antoine-Joseph Dezallier d'Argenville (1680–1765) Le Nôtre found an author who codified his design method in the treatise that he had never found time to write. Dezallier's book became a manual for designers commissioned by the courts of Europe to create gardens in the French classical style. As combined with the lingering influence of the Italian garden, it evolved through the first two-thirds of the eighteenth century into an international garden style, which was inflected according

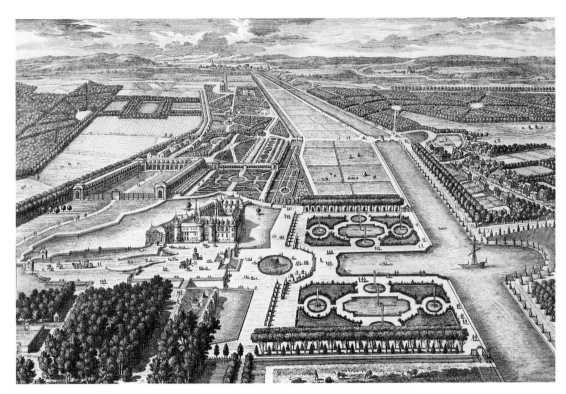

5.17. Chantilly. Engraving from *Recueil des Veues des Plus Beaux Lieux de France* by Adam and Nicholas Pérelle, 1688

to local conditions and taste. It is a style that is still influential, as can be seen in some of the gardens of the American landscape architects Dan Kiley and Peter Walker, for example. It can also be observed in France itself, where the recently built Parc Citroën in Paris shows how its enduring principles can be translated into a contemporary idiom.

II. THE GARDEN AS THEATER: ITALIAN BAROQUE AND ROCOCO GARDENS

The austere harmonies of French classicism never penetrated very deeply into the Italian design ethos. The seventeenth-century Italian style, like that of Le Nôtre, was an integrative one in which individual parts were organized into a unified composition. But instead of achieving compositional unity with authoritarian axes flung down along lines apparently extending into infinity, the builders of Italian gardens—often encouraged by topography—wove dramatic hanging terraces and ornamental flights of stairs into hillsides to produce theatrical arrangements of landscape. The dramatic potential of moving water continued to be exploited in the construction of elaborate sculptural cascades like the one at Villa Lante (see fig. 4.25). Unlike French garden designers, whose struggles to furnish water to their fountains, pools, and cascades were herculean and often intensely frustrating as well as wasteful both of capital and human lives, Italian architects were more fortunate in their ability to convey water to their sites in copious quantities, albeit also at the expense of much backbreaking labor and often intense politics. Their gardens were vehicles for princely pomp and display, and the glorification of their patrons became ever more explicit as

decorative coats of arms and other family emblems were prominently featured instead of being merely encoded symbolically into the landscape.[18]

Not only were dramatic astonishment and theatrical perspective effectively used in the layout of Italian Baroque gardens, but also many of the gardens of this period contained actual outdoor theaters with a grassy stage, hedges for wings, and sometimes, peeping forth from the greenery, terra-cotta figures representing stock characters of the *commedia dell'arte* tradition popularized by troupes of Italian actors since the second half of the sixteenth century (fig. 5.18). Pastoral drama was echoed in the sculptural Satyrs and Pans that populated garden woods or the edges of garden walks, as well as in the taste for genre figures of peasants engaged in a variety of tasks.

Italian designers probably found the Cartesian paradigm of non-place-specific axial planning less congenial than one that recognized place as particular and bounded. This may be explained by the fact that the topography throughout much of Italy is hilly, thereby promoting greater opportunity visually for spatial enclosure than for spatial extension. In

5.18. Green theater with *commedia dell'arte* terra-cotta figures, Villa Marlia, near Lucca, Italy

Below: 5.19. Water Theater with spiral pillars, and Cascade in the background, Villa Aldobrandini, Frascati, Italy. Designed by Giacomo della Porta, Carlo Maderno, and Giovanni Fontana. 1601–1621. Engraving by Giovanni Battista Falda, from *Le Fontane delle Ville di Frascati*. Atlas stands beneath the cascade carrying a celestial globe signifying divine wisdom. Originally a figure of Hercules (now gone) assisted Atlas. Similarly, Cardinal Aldobrandini wished to be seen as helping Pope Clement VIII to uphold Christian truth.

addition, Italian designers were more likely to retain, however unconsciously, the concept of *topos*—the philosophical notion of emplacement derived from Aristotle—because it was already abundantly manifested in the antique classical landscape tradition to which they were heirs. Although much larger than their Italian Renaissance counterparts, on the whole, Italian gardens in the seventeenth century were more intimately scaled than those of contemporary France, and though axes might dissolve into nature, they did not appear to extend into the indefinite distance as if to meet the line of the horizon. In conservative Tuscany, this observation holds true to an even greater degree. A predilection for comparatively simple famil-

ial pastimes resulted in relatively small gardens composed of well-proportioned "rooms" of greenery. One French feature, the *parterre de broderie,* did gain popularity. By the end of the seventeenth century, it had mostly replaced the geometric compartments of traditional *parterres.*

Villa Aldobrandini

By the mid-sixteenth century, nepotism had become thoroughly institutionalized within the Catholic Church, and it was common practice for a pope to appoint a nephew as cardinal to serve in the capacity of trusted assistant during his pontificate. The cardinal-nephew thereby became a strong candidate to suc-

Far left: 5.20. Polyphemus, Water Theater, Villa Aldobrandini. This figure and that of a centaur (fig. 5.21) illustrate a common humanist theme: the struggle of reason over bestiality.

Left: 5.21. Centaur figure, Water Theater, Villa Aldobrandini

ceed him at a later date. At the very least, the influence of this relative as a member of the Church establishment would perpetuate the prestige and wealth of the papal family. Papal villa gardens and those created by the cardinal-nephews were therefore opulent essays in power politics.

Frascati, a hillside town outside of Rome, was famed, like Tivoli, as a locale of the *villeggiatura,* the annual summertime retreat to the country from the heat of the city. It gained prominence after the election of Pope Clement VIII in 1592, when his nephew Cardinal Pietro Aldobrandini undertook at great expense the introduction of water from the Molara Springs on Monte Algido. The provision of a waterworks allowed the construction of an impressive cascade and magnificent water theater at the villa he built for himself and his uncle. The architect Carlo Maderno (c. 1556–1629), assisted by the fountain engineer Giovanni Fontana, was responsible for this impressive design.

The relaxed, ample, architectonic muscularity of this garden sequence epitomizes the Italian Baroque garden style. The architectural robustness and play of light and shade characteristic of the period are particularly evident in the semicircular arcaded water theater facing the ground floor of the villa (fig. 5.19). Its sculptural decor displays the naturalistic character, compositional arrangement into counterbalanced diagonals, and thrusting movement into space that we associate with Baroque art in general. The iconographic program, however, is still allusively symbolic—a late example of the humanistic message-garden (figs. 5.20–5.21).

THE FARNESE GARDENS AT CAPRAROLA AND ON THE PALATINE HILL, ROME

At Caprarola, near Viterbo, in the first third of the sixteenth century, Cardinal Alessandro Farnese had commissioned Antonio da Sangallo the Younger (1483–1546) to build a fortified palace, a huge pentagonal building with bastions. In 1556, with fear of renewed Spanish invasion diminishing, the cardinal commissioned the architect Vignola to transform his fortress into a summer villa. It has been saved for discussion here because the additions, which were made around 1620 by Girolamo Rainaldi (1570–1655), illustrate the evolution of Italian garden design from a metaphorical fusion of art and nature within the context of a carefully conceived humanistic iconography into a more purely aesthetic architectural statement.

Caprarola's significance in the history of landscape design lies in the creation of the Barchetto, a secluded retreat with a *casino* and herm-guarded *giardino segreto* approached by a quarter-mile-long path leading through the woods from the summer garden next to the palace (figs. 5.22–5.25). It was built five years after Vignola's death in 1573, probably according to the design of Giacomo del Duca. Its design as a series of descending terraces built into a hillside, its fountain flanked by reclining river gods, and its curvilinear *catena d'acqua,* or water cascade, imitate Vignola's achievement at Bagnaia.

The Barchetto at Caprarola, created in two epochs of garden building—with its original form echoing Vignola's design at the Villa Lante and its later additions by Rainaldi—provides a unique and

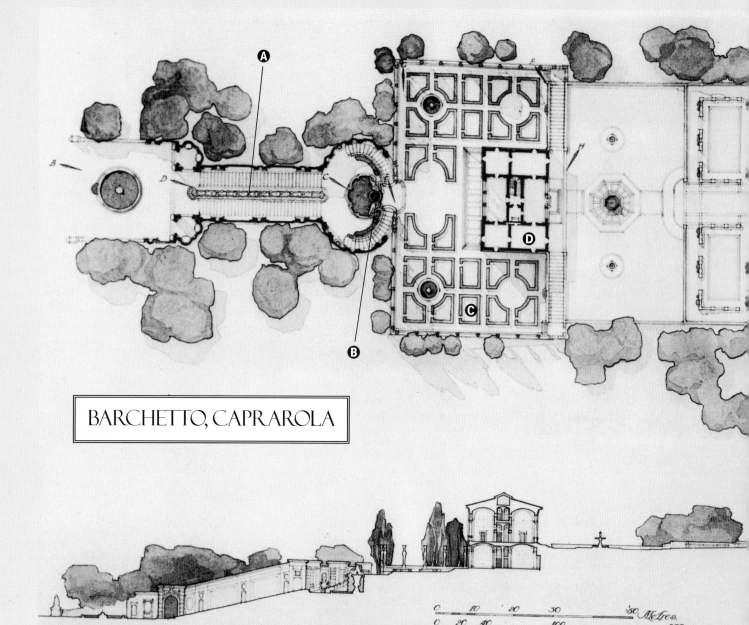

5.22. Plan of Barchetto, Caprarola. Designed by Giacomo Barozzi da Vignola, Giacomo del Duca, and Girolamo Rainaldi. 1556–1620. Drawing by J. C. Shepherd and G. A. Jellicoe, from *Italian Gardens of the Renaissance*, 1925

One approaches the Barchetto today on the same fir-lined path, passing through woods of chestnut, beech, ilex, and holm oak, as did Cardinal Farnese when he wished to enjoy the privacy of the *casino* he had built for summer dining. It is pleasantly surprising to encounter the first of a series of terraces carved into this woodland setting. Here one finds a circular fountain basin above which rises a beautiful water chain modeled on that at the Villa Lante (fig. 5.23; Ⓐ). This is composed of pairs of wriggling dolphins, and the playful effect of the water's undulations as it slips over the scalloped basins between the dolphins is similar to the shimmering flow between the curvilinear borders describing an elongated crayfish of Cardinal Gambara's water channel. Here the gentle cascade is bordered by ramps leading up to a piazza, where river gods recline

on either side of a huge vase-shaped fountain Ⓑ. From this, jets of water patterned to form the Farnese lily spill water into a basin below (fig. 5.25). Curving ramps lead up to the *giardino segreto* Ⓒ and the *casino* Ⓓ. The *casino* has a double loggia at its base and a single loggia above where the *piano nobile* opens onto an upper terrace. These are the main components of the sixteenth-century Barchetto.

The seventeenth-century additions by Rainaldi exploit the architectural character and dramatic potential of the original scheme. Large torsos of Prudence and Silence, as these figures are known, were mounted on grand carved double pedestals in front of the sixteenth-century walls outlining the sides of the first terrace, adding theatrical intensity and an augmented air of mystery to the space. Boldly scaled rusticated pavilions set

between the outer sloping walls on either side of the circular pool and the inner walls, which also slope upward as they define the edges of the twin ramps beside the water chain, give additional architectonic power to the composition. At the piazza of the Vase Fountain, along the curving wall embracing the stairs that lead to the terrace above, forcefully articulated rusticated pilasters framing niches of rough stonework have replaced the sixteenth-century surface, which was probably decorated with stucco reliefs. Also part of the seventeenth-century revision are copies of large antique heads set into the niches and upon the scrolling brackets that ornament the curving walls of rough, banded stonework.

Ascending the stairs one enters the *giardino segreto*. Here the seventeenth-century planners gave a more powerful spatial definition to the sixteenth-century

garden by substituting large herms with expressive faces and gestures for the globe finials that originally decorated the perimeter parapet (fig. 5.24). The vases on their heads give a uniform "cornice line" to the green room of box compartments they preside over, thereby increasing the architectural character of the space. In contrast to Vignola's summer and winter gardens adjacent to the palace below, where grottoes, fountains, and classical figures furnished a specific symbolism, there is no special iconographic message to decode here; the herms, believed to be the work of Pietro Bernini (1562–1629), are satyric gods gathered in an ordered clearing within the wild woodland, allusive only of the mysterious life forces present in an enchanted spot.

5.23. *Catena d'acqua,* Caprarola

Below: 5.24. *Giardino segreto* and stairway with a
water banister of stone dolphins, Caprarola

5.25. River gods and Vase
Fountain, Caprarola

5.26. Farnese Gardens, Palatine, Rome. Designed by Giacomo Barozzi da Vignola, Giacomo del Duca, and Girolamo Rainaldi. Late 1560s–1618. Engraving by Giovanni Battista Falda, from *Li Giardini di Roma*, c. 1670

Below: 5.27. Aviary, Farnese Gardens, Palatine, Rome. c. 1618–33. Engraving by Giovanni Battista Falda, from *Li Giardini di Roma*, c. 1670

beautiful example of the transformation of Italian Renaissance landscape design into innovative Baroque expression. Rainaldi's robust architecture and the use of high staircase walls and large-scale sculpture to control movement and shape space in a plastic and dynamic way constitute new developments in the course of landscape design history.

One thinks today of Italian gardens primarily in terms of architectural stone and greenery, forgetting the once-important role of flowers. The *giardino segreto* of the Farnese palace at Caprarola as well as the one in front of the *casino* and the large terrace garden behind it were originally filled with exotic flowers. From old records, we know that several kinds of roses, marigolds, violets, lilies, crocuses, hyacinths, and narcissi, as well as fruit trees—oranges, pomegranates, citrons—grew in these gardens.[19] The Farnese pope, Paul III (papacy 1534–1549), was avidly interested in botany, an enthusiasm that was continued by his grandson, Cardinal Alessandro Farnese, as well as by the cardinal's nephew and heir, Cardinal Odoardo Farnese. Indeed, the scientific interest in botany, a development of the

Renaissance, was given new impetus in the seventeenth century, an age of exploration and discovery, when plants from the Americas and Asia were eagerly sought by many wealthy collectors and by botanical gardens, such as those founded at Padua in 1545 and Leiden in 1587. It is not therefore surprising to find in Rome a famous early botanical collection of the wealthy Farnese family, begun in the sixteenth century and continued throughout the seventeenth.

The Farnese Gardens built atop the Palatine in Rome over the ruins of the palaces of the emperors Tiberius and Domitian were created by various members of the great Farnese family including Pope Paul III, Cardinal Alessandro,[20] and Cardinal Odoardo Farnese (fig. 5.26). They span the same period from the late Renaissance to the end of the seventeenth century as the successive stages of the Farnese gardens at Caprarola and were probably designed by the same architects—Giacomo Barozzi da Vignola, Giacomo del Duca, and Girolamo Rainaldi. They constituted a renowned center for plant propagation and exhibition until archaeologists digging the ruins of imperial Rome in the eighteenth century destroyed them.[21]

Several flights of stairs lead to an upper terrace where the main axis is punctuated by a fern-encrusted water theater set between the bases of twin aviaries and flanked by a pair of staircases leading up to gardens on the crest of the Palatine (fig. 5.27). The aviaries, which were completed in the first third of the seventeenth century, still stand, but the elaborate gardens that lay beyond them exist only as a partial, pleasing but not historical, twentieth-century design amid the archaeological excavations.

Country Retreats of the Roman Aristocracy: Villa Borghese and Villa Pamphili

Two of the great estates within Rome assembled by princes of the Church between the last years of the sixteenth century and the end of the seventeenth—Villa Borghese and Villa Pamphili—today serve as popular public parks. Two other important gardens, Villa Montalto and Villa Ludovisi, were destroyed in the nineteenth century, the former to accommodate the train terminal and rail yards next to the Baths of Diocletian and the latter to profit speculators in the new housing market that was created when Rome became a national capital following the reunification of Italy.

When Cardinal Camillo Borghese became Pope Paul V (papacy 1605–1621), he promptly conferred a cardinalate upon his nephew Scipione Caffarelli, thereafter known as Cardinal Borghese. The new cardinal and his relatives soon began amassing land for a large suburban estate, or *vigna,* on the Pincian Hill just outside the northern walls of the city. Family pride, sporting pleasure, and aesthetic delight motivated the design of their villa in the early years of the seventeenth century. Although suffering today from insufficient maintenance—like many Italian public parks—the gardens of the Villa Borghese remain a popular amenity for modern Romans, and its art galleries constitute a museum of international renown. The casino designed by Flaminio Ponzio (1560–1613), with its extensive decoration completed by the Flemish architect Jan van Santen (Giovanni Vasanzio), was conceived as a close cousin of the nearby Villa Medici both in plan and in the heavy ornamentation of its exterior walls (stripped of their sculpture by Napoleon).

When completed, the Borghese Gardens consisted of three separate enclosures, or *recinti* (fig. 5.28). The first *recinto* was a *bosco* of regular *boschetti* (compartments of trees) planted in the 1620s in front of the villa. This section was accessible to the public. A second *recinto,* which was reserved for the private use of the family, lay behind the villa. It was planted with groves of holm oak. The third *recinto* consisted of a well-stocked game park on the irregular lands to the north. Between the first and second *recinti,* the villa was constructed, with an intimately scaled private garden—*giardino segreto*—placed on either side of it. High walls surrounded the entire estate.

The wall that originally screened the two *giardini segreti* from the transverse avenue running in front of the villa was torn down during the nineteenth-century modernization in the English style. The condition of these small gardens today is considerably altered from that of the seventeenth century, when they were filled with espaliered citrus trees, freestanding orange trees, and, in the springtime, masses of exotic bulbs. Gone, too, are the birds that sang in copper-netted cages in the twin aviaries that still stand in the northern garden. Beyond the aviaries, which were probably inspired by those of the Farnese Gardens atop the Palatine, is the Meridiana, a sundial.

Aesthetic and sensual pleasures motivated the creation of the Villa Borghese. Art collecting, social entertainment, and hunting were the principal purposes it served. Sculpture was used decoratively in its application to the villa facades and throughout the garden. To understand the change that took place in Italian villa design between the sixteenth and seventeenth centuries, one can compare the siting of the Villa Borghese with that of the nearby Villa Giulia. As at the Villa Aldobrandini, the Villa Giulia and its garden are powerfully united through axial composition (see fig. 4.12). The Borghese Villa, on the other hand, is not the principal organizing force and focus of axial planning, but simply one element within a broader landscape composition. The landscape itself is treated

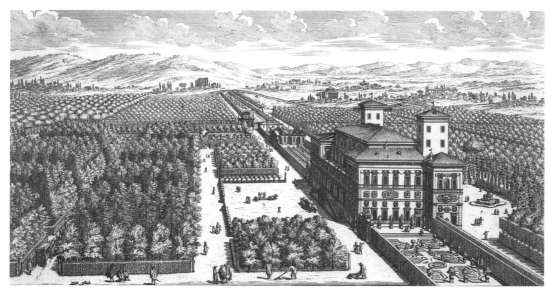

5.28. Villa Borghese, Rome, Italy. Main gateway and casino designed by Flaminio Ponzio. 1609–1617, with decoration by Giovanni Vasanzio. Gardens laid out beginning in 1608. Engraving by Simone Felice, from *Li Giardini di Roma,* c. 1670

5.29. Villa Pamphili, Rome, Italy. Casino designed by Alessandro Algardi. Casino and gardens built 1644–48. Engraving by Simone Felice, from *Li Giardini di Roma*, c. 1670

Below: 5.30. *Giardini segreti,* Villa Pamphili

in a less particular, more loosely articulated fashion than those of earlier gardens. In all these ways, the Villa Borghese announces its participation in a new era of Italian landscape design.

The tenets of this later style are further illustrated in the Villa Pamphili, atop the Janiculum Hill in Rome. In 1640, Camillo Pamphili increased the size of the *vigna* he had inherited from his father at that location by acquiring another one adjacent to it. Then, upon the election of his uncle as Pope Innocent X in 1644, Camillo was chosen to fill the cardinal-nephew position. Although in 1647 he was permitted to resign his cardinalate in order to perpetuate the Pamphili family by marrying Olimpia Aldobrandini, land purchases continued until 1673, when, under his son, the *vigna* reached its ultimate size of 240 acres.

Begun in 1644, the beautiful *casino,* tall, compact, and richly decorated with sculpture and frescoes in the manner of the Villa Borghese, was completed by 1648. Like the Villa Borghese, its primary function was as an art gallery and a place for social entertainment. There were no bedrooms, as the family residence lay a short distance to the west on the Via Aurelia. Although the plan of the *casino* was traversed by two of the several wide axes dividing the grounds into a notably regular composition, the elegant structure was not a focal point in the overall design of the gardens (fig. 5.29).

The low *parterres de broderie* of the *giardini segreti* next to the villa show French influence on later Italian garden design (fig. 5.30). The transformation of the original compartmentalized design of these *parterres* to an embroidered pattern probably did not occur until the eighteenth century, as Italian gardeners long resisted this style, although it had been popularized elsewhere in the mid-seventeenth century through French pattern book engravings.[22]

Like the Villa Borghese, the Villa Pamphili illustrates the grand scale and quasi-public character of the seventeenth-century Roman garden parks where some members of the populace were occasionally permitted entry. In their rich display of architecture and sculpture to ennoble and dramatize landscape, these great Roman villas memorialize the opulent lives of the princes of the Church in an age of proudly ambitious aristocracy.

Tuscan Garden Design: Villa Garzoni and La Gamberaia

In Tuscany, outside the Italian center of international power, the breadth of scale and architectural grandeur found in the Villa Borghese and the Villa Pamphili remained foreign. Although in villas around Florence and Lucca one finds Roman design idioms—for instance, hanging hillside terraces with vase-topped balustrades, cascades, and ornamental sculpture—these characteristics are manifested in a far less

extravagant manner. Most of the gardens of Tuscany built in the seventeenth century have an affinity with earlier gardens such as those of the Villa Medici at Fiesole. Their designs are conservative, usually composed as a series of outdoor rooms with views of the surrounding agricultural landscape of olive trees and vineyards. One of these is usually a *limonaia,* a walled garden filled with potted lemon trees, which were removed in the winter to an adjacent long, barnlike conservatory (fig. 5.31). But Tuscan gardens show innovative and evolutionary tendencies as well, first those characteristic of a Baroque sensibility, and later those of the graceful Rococo style of the eighteenth century, when many additions or remodelings of old gardens were made.

Where the nineteenth-century fashion for English-style gardens did not obliterate the original designs and restoration has been possible, present-day maintenance costs and a preference for abstraction have caused the planting schemes of these old gardens to be simplified. But in the best-preserved of them, we may still find the exuberant curvilinear movement and ornamentation characteristic of the Baroque style. It is to be seen in the black-and-white pebble-ornamented walls, the pebble mosaic paving, the sculptural hedges, the lavish use of ornamental statuary (much of it in terra-cotta), the water theaters, and the intimate green theaters in which *commedia dell'arte* performances were held—all of which are characteristic of this golden age of Tuscan garden design.

The outlying garden closest in spirit to the Roman Baroque models is that of the Villa Garzoni in Collodi, near Lucca, a composition of hillside ter-

races with robust balusters and lighthearted sculptural decoration, arabesque floral *parterres* with heraldic devices in colored pebble mosaic, and a water cascade issuing from a grotto, above which soars a figure of Fame trumpeting her horn (figs. 5.32, 5.33). The villa itself bears a curious relationship to the garden because of its origins as a defensive castle strategically sited with a ramp leading from the town below.[23] Purchased by the Garzoni family from the Republic of Lucca in the early years of the seventeenth century, it was transformed into a villa with gardens on the adjacent slope several decades later. Subsequent improvements, such as the addition of a bathhouse near the apex of the cascade, were made in the eighteenth century under the direction of the Lucchese architect Ottaviano Diodati.

Central niches reinforce the main axis between each set of double stairs. In keeping with the more frivolous spirit of the later age, these and various side niches are inhabited by a whimsical blend of genre figures and pagan deities. Here and elsewhere, in the company of Apollo, Diana, Pomona, Ceres, Bacchus, and other familiar mythological garden residents including fauns and herms, one finds sculpted peasants engaged in agricultural pursuits. Thus, the grotto with Neptune rising in his horse-drawn chariot from the sea occupies the niche on a middle terrace, while a peasant holding a cask is contained in the terrace below, and a peasant with a turkey stands in the one above. These three niches are heavily framed with rusticated stone set against walls of *rocaille*-work fashioned into black-and-white arabesques. Black-and-white pebble-mosaic paving ornaments the ground plane in

5.31. *Limonaia.* **Vicobella, Siena**

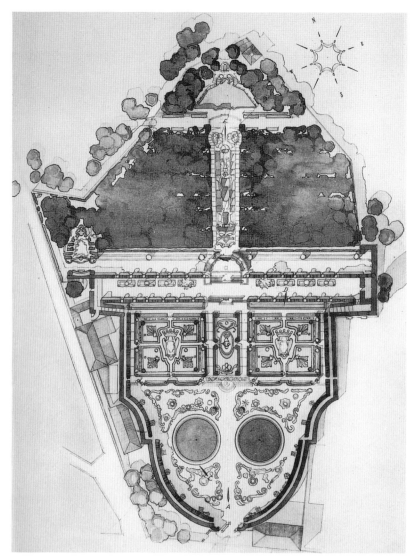

5.32. Plan of Villa Garzoni,
Collodi, near Lucca, Italy.
Drawing by J. C. Shepherd
and G. A. Jellicoe, from *Italian
Gardens of the Renaissance*,
1925

Below: 5.33. Villa Garzoni

5.34. Staircase with monkeys, Villa Garzoni

several places, continuing the characteristically Baroque curvilinear surface patterning. A terra-cotta band of twelve monkeys playing ball adds piquant charm to the balustrades of the upper terraces (fig. 5.34).

From here one can look down and appreciate the arabesques of box *broderie* surrounding twin circular pools, the elaborate floral and stone mosaic *parterre* with the Garzoni monogram and heraldic devices, and the curvilinear cresting of the sculptured yew hedge that contains the whole of the lower garden in a generous embrace. An outer hedge parallels this hedge, creating a shady walkway around the perimeter of the lower garden.

Close association of the garden with its agrarian environs; intimacy of scale and conservative retention of old forms such as lemon gardens; shady *allées* of ilex trees, terra-cotta figures, sculptured hedges, and pebble mosaic walks—all characteristic elements of the Tuscan garden—can be found at La Gamberaia in Settignano on the outskirts of Florence (figs. 5.35–5.38). The artful twentieth-century restoration of this garden forsakes historic accuracy, instead emphasizing the abstract geometries of its Baroque shapes and animating its period character in other ways that are pleasing to contemporary taste.

The place takes its name from that of the original owners of the property, the Gambarelli family. According to a plaque over the door, in 1610, Zanobi Lapi erected the handsome simple villa around a central court. The garden was laid out between 1624 and 1635 by his nephews and heirs. During the eighteenth century, the Capponi family owned the property, and they altered and embellished it with statuary, fountains,

and a long green bowling alley. A *giardino segreto* was set into the hillside beneath the lemon garden at this time. Seriously mutilated during World War II, La Gamberaia was subsequently acquired by Marcello Marchi, who restored it to its present excellent condition.

Extravagant End of an Era: Isola Bella and Caserta

Entirely different in spirit from the quiet conservatism and unassuming beauty of Tuscan gardens, Isola Bella, Count Carlo Borromeo's grandiose fantasy in Lake Maggiore in northern Italy, is unsurpassed as an illustration of the theatrical character of Italian Baroque design (fig. 5.39, see pp. 2–3). Today Isola Bella is more lush and romantically patinated by time than it was when, from 1630 to 1670, the Borromeos leveled an island off the coast of Stresa in Lake Maggiore and erected the great tiered galleon of a garden named in honor of Count Carlo's wife, Isabella. The fundamental theatricality of this unusual landscape comes from its phantasmagorical appearance, rising improbably like a ghostly vessel from the clear mountain-fringed waters of Lake Maggiore. Its wedding cake of terraces opens out to embrace the view, and its high cresting sculptures gesture into space (fig. 5.40).

Because of the shape of the island, the garden is not on axis with the palace; the relationship of the two is camouflaged by trees, and one does not realize that upon climbing the stairs of the interconnecting Courtyard of Diana, with its pebble-faced, arched niches and statue of the goddess, one has changed directions. The *parterres* above were originally laid out as *broderies* in the French fashion. Facing these is a

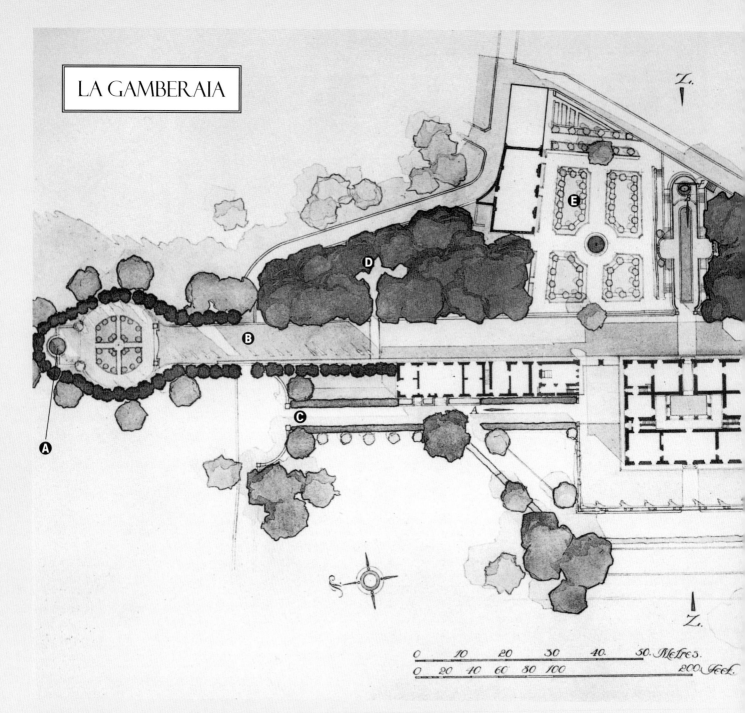

LA GAMBERAIA

5.35. Plan of La Gamberaia, Settignano, near Florence, Italy. Garden built 1624–35; altered and embellished by Capponi family after 1717; restored with water *parterres* by Princess Ghyka, early twentieth century. Drawing by J. C. Shepherd and G. A. Jellicoe, from *Italian Gardens of the Renaissance*, 1925. Ⓐ *Nymphaeum.* Ⓑ Bowling lawn. Ⓒ Entrance. Ⓓ Bosco. Ⓔ Lemonaia. Ⓕ Water *parterre*

Ⓞne enters La Gamberaia from a gate that leads up a long hedge-bordered drive to the principal portal of the villa. To the right, facing west, overlooking its immediate landscape of olive trees and, beyond this, the city of Florence, is a grassy terrace contained by a low parapet surmounted by Baroque finials and stone dogs. To the left of the villa entrance, extending all along its eastern side and beyond to the north and south, lies the turf bowling alley flanked by a high, urn-surmounted retaining wall of stucco. The long surface of this wall is broken by painted panels of geometric design and enlivened by a pattern of dark

stucco resembling a balustrade. Tall cypresses mark the northern end of the bowling green, and there one finds a *nymphaeum* of decorative black-and-white *rocaille*-work with reliefs of two musicians on the outside and Neptune flanked by lions on the inside. To the south, this avenue of grass ends in a balcony overlooking Tuscan vineyards and olive trees.

The retaining wall separates the bowling lawn from an elevated *bosco* of mature ilex and a fine lemon garden. This lemon garden overlooks the eighteenth-century *giardino segreto,* a narrow court of elaborate *rocaille*-work,

now filled with pots of hydrangeas (fig. 5.36). Surrounded by a balcony balustrade decorated with stone busts and urns as well as a figure of the god Pan at its eastern end, it is entered by ornamental staircases on either side. Light and shadow play over its wisteria-draped, fern-sprouting rustic walls and terra-cotta statues set within niches. La Gamberaia's *parterre* garden has well-proportioned pools of water instead of planting beds, a curving hedge with arched openings overlooking the Arno Valley, and stone putti peeping forth from immaculately clipped topiary (figs. 5.37, 5.38).

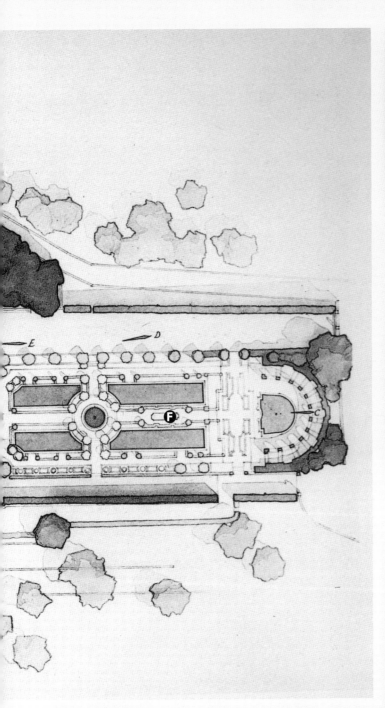

5.36. *Giardino segreto*, La Gamberaia

5.37. Villa La Gamberaia

5.38. Water *parterre*, La Gamberaia

a century earlier by Le Nôtre in France. At Caserta, near Naples, Charles III, the Bourbon king of Spain, Naples, and Sicily, hired Luigi Vanvitelli (1700–1773) to design the gardens of La Reggia in 1752 in a manner and on a scale clearly meant to rival Versailles. The immensely long canal axis, nearly 2 miles (5 kilometers), does not stretch illusionistically into the distance, however, but ends in an Italian-style hillside cascade (fig. 5.41). This monument to Bourbon grandeur is made vacuous by its sheer size, since it lacks the same understanding of optics based on laws of perspective, the same integration of parts into mathematical harmonies of scale, and the artful grade manipulations and incidents of intricacy that give variety and surprise to Le Nôtre's grand compositions. In short, the subtle intelligence that provided both grace and power in Le Nôtre's designs is largely absent in Vanvitelli's work, and Caserta remains interesting primarily for the ambition it displays.

The French classical style, as we have seen, was informed by Cartesian mathematics and the politics of authority. It was forged in the crucible of the post-Copernican view of the cosmos as not being Earth-centered and spherically contained, but heliocentric and open-ended. The Italian Baroque style, on the other hand, expresses a lofty confidence based less on science than upon its rich patrimony from the antique past. This confidence was combined with theatrical zest to produce bold architectural effects and grandiose sculptural compositions. Together, these two traditions were imitated in countless places, sometimes separately, sometimes in combination, often with modifications because of local culture and topographic conditions. Until revolution and Romanticism discredited the royal and aristocratic patronage that had created them, they constituted a formal design vocabulary that became the idiom of courts and cities throughout Europe.

water theater. One mounts a set of concave-convex stairs to arrive at the terrace upon which this extravagant confection, encrusted with pebbles and decorated with niches framing giant scallop shells and statuary, rears against the sky. Projecting into the blue Alpine backdrop is the family emblem—a prancing unicorn—and plume-capped obelisks, as well as several oversized statues. Behind the water theater, from another small *parterre* garden, one may look down upon other Borromean splendors: fountains, exotic plants, rare flowers, and a flock of white peacocks.

By the eighteenth century, courts all over Europe were imitating the design concepts developed

Top: 5.39. Isola Bella, Lake Maggiore, Italy. c. 1630–70

Above: 5.40. Gardens, Isola Bella

Right: 5.41. Cascade, La Reggia, Caserta, near Naples, Italy. Designed by Luigi Vanvitelli. 1752

1. See Robert W. Berger, *In the Garden of the Sun King: Studies on the Park of Versailles Under Louis XIV* (Washington, D.C.: Dumbarton Oaks, 1985), Chapter 2, for a good discussion of the role of Petite Académie (later renamed the Académie Royale des Inscriptions et Medailles) in determining the iconographic program at Versailles. The Petite Académie was an institution devoted to developing an iconography of royal glorification that could be applied to the creation of medals commemorating the deeds of the king as well as to the decoration of royal buildings. Richelieu by his own example was responsible for initiating a building craze among the aristocracy. During the first half of the seventeenth century more than three hundred new *hôtels* and gardens were built in Paris. French pride in their capital dates from this period, and although Louis XIV had no particular desire to live there, he was nonetheless supportive of the city's increasing beautification.

2. According to philosophy professor Edward Casey, for Descartes "the spatial world is to be grasped as a plenary, seamless realm of *res extensae*—of material things whose very nature consists in their extension." See Edward Casey, *The Fate of Place: A Philosophical History* (Berkeley: University of California Press, 1997), p. 154.

3. The king, fearing the political consequences of rationalism, forbade the teaching of Descartes's theories in French schools.

4. For my discussion of Mansart, I am indebted to Kenneth Woodbridge, *Princely Gardens: The Origins and Development of the French Formal Style* (New York: Rizzoli, 1986), pp. 166–78. Much of what follows in this chapter describing seventeenth-century French gardens and landscape designers is derived from my reading of this indispensable volume on the subject.

5. André Le Nôtre collected painting and sculpture, bequeathing near the end of his life to Louis XIV, the king whom he had served so long and so well, his fine collection of Poussins, Claude Lorrains, and other masters of the French School along with many fine antique marble and bronze sculptures.

6. Fouquet's device, appropriately enough, was the high-vaulting squirrel; his enemy and successor Colbert, with greater wisdom, chose as his symbol the lowly grass snake.

7. A useful guide for experiencing the unfolding perspectives of Vaux-le-Vicomte is that provided by the architectural historian Franklin Hamilton Hazelhurst, whose diagrams and sketches illustrate Le Nôtre's manipulations of grade and perspective to achieve a masterfully rational yet boldly dramatic design. See *Gardens of Illusion: The Genius of André Le Nostre* (Nashville, Tenn.: Vanderbilt University Press, 1980), pp. 17–45.

8. See Denise and Jean-Pierre Le Dantec, *Reading the French Garden: Story and History* (Cambridge, Mass.: MIT Press, 1990), pp. 116–17. The authors' assertion that La Fontaine was possibly associated in some way with Vaux is supported by the fact that he was a few years later directly responsible for the thematic development of the Labyrinthe at Versailles. For a complete discussion of his contributions to the iconographic program there, see Robert W. Berger, *In the Garden of the Sun King* (Washington, D.C.: Dumbarton Oaks, 1985), Chapter 4.

9. From an account by La Fontaine, *Oeuvres diverse,* La Pléiade, pp. 522–27, as quoted in Bernard Jeannel, *Le Nôtre* (Paris: Fernand Hazan, 1985), p. 42.

10. At the time of Fouquet's memorable party, Louis was deeply in love with Louise de La Vallière, his first publicly acknowledged mistress. And it was to honor his love for Louise, as well as to create the spaces for the delightful summer entertainments that would celebrate his reign, that he commissioned work to progress during the greater part of the 1660s. As the garden historian William Howard Adams has remarked, "The sequence of the development of the gardens at Versailles is intimately related to the emerging power of the King, his concept of the monarchy, and his love affairs. All three influences were at times entangled in the expansion and use of the gardens to further the King's policies or to celebrate an amorous conquest." See Howard Adams, *The French Garden 1500–1800,* (New York: George Braziller, 1979), p. 84.

11. Almost twenty years older than the king, Colbert tried to lecture the young monarch on the unsuitability of such a poor place as the symbolic representation of the greatest king in the world. But Louis was an absolute monarch firmly in command of his own will, and Colbert was forced to gracefully submit as he took on the job of overseeing Louis's ambitious building program at Versailles. See Jeannel, op. cit., p. 46.

12. Louis XIV had been king since the age of five. He had lived through the civil disturbances known as the Fronde, lasting from 1648 to 1653, during which time a rebellious Parlement in league with Louis II de Bourbon, prince of Condé, had attempted to wrest power from the Queen Mother, Anne of Austria, and her chief minister, Cardinal Mazarin. This left a lasting impression on the king, who was forever suspicious of any challenge to his supreme authority or the concentration of power, however slight, in any hands other than his own. The Dragon, like the Python, was used as a symbol of the rebellion of the Fronde, and, as the swans surrounding this figure were the attributes of Apollo, the putti riding the swans can be read as the youthful Louis resisting the plotters against the divine right of kings. See Berger, op. cit., p. 26.

13. Latona with her two children can be read as the mother of Louis XIV, who, with her sons, Louis and Philippe, suffered the indignities of the *frondeurs,* or rebels, whose representation here as frogs carries the explicit message of royal triumph. See Berger, op. cit., p. 26

14. Seeking the king's attentions, Athénaïs had become the friend and confidante of her predecessor, Louise de La Vallière; Madame de Montespan, in turn, was replaced in 1675, after she had borne the king several children, by their governess, Madame Scarron—or Madame de Maintenon as she had become known after the king, following Madame Montespan's pleas, bought for her the estate of Maintenon.

15. Louis, Duc de Saint-Simon, *Saint Simon at Versailles*, ed. Lucy Norton (New York: Harper Brothers, 1958), pp. 58–59.

16. The tragedies of the king's old age included the loss of the two heirs-apparent: his son, the Dauphin, in 1711, and his grandson, the duc de Bretagne, who along with his wife, the princess of Savoy, died of measles in 1712.

17. For an excellent discussion of Atget's work in the gardens of Le Nôtre, see William Howard Adams, *Atget's Gardens* (Garden City, New York: Doubleday & Company, Inc., 1979).

18. The Villa Lante provides a useful example illustrating this point: Cardinal Gambara's crayfish is cunningly woven into the fabric of the sixteenth-century garden, whereas Cardinal Montalto's device of three mountains surmounted by a star, which was added in the seventeenth century, is much more obviously and ostentatiously displayed in the central fountain of the *parterre* garden where it is held aloft by the figures of four youths with lions (see fig. 4.27).

19. See David Coffin, *Gardens and Gardening in Papal Rome* (Princeton, N. J.: Princeton University Press, 1991), p. 198; also Georgina Masson, *Italian Gardens* (Woodbridge, Suffolk: Antique Collector's Club, 1987), pp. 140–41.

20. The financial resources, opulent lifestyle, intellectual curiosity, and aesthetic sensibilities of this prince of the Church can be gauged by the fact that, in addition to the Orti Farnese and the villa at Caprarola, he purchased and enjoyed the old Chigi villa on the banks of the Tiber, designed by Baldassare Tommaso Peruzzi (1481–1536) and decorated by Raphael, which has since been known as the Farnesina.

21. See Coffin, op. cit., p. 208.

22. See Coffin, op. cit., pp. 160–62. Coffin suggests that, since the mid-seventeenth century engravings of Villa Pamphili that depict embroidered *parterres* were by a French engraver, they may have been represented according to the contemporary French convention well in advance of their actual conversion to this style.

23. The road actually passed through the villa until its most recent restoration and remodeling in the 1950s.

EXPANDING HORIZONS:
COURT AND CITY IN THE EUROPEAN GRAND MANNER

The seventeenth century saw the birth of scientific modernism in Western culture. A probing inquiry into the nature of nature, the growing reliance on inductive reasoning, and a new confidence based upon a continuously expanding understanding of the universe was paralleled in landscape design by the extension of axes beyond the boundaries of the garden. The universe and all nature were now perceived in dimensions far grander and more indeterminate than those imagined by the Christian theologians and Aristotelian scholastics of the Middle Ages, or even by the Renaissance humanists whose curiosity and methods of inquiry helped build a bridge between the medieval and modern worldviews.

As we saw in Chapter Five, confidence in human power and growing dominion over nature as well as celebration of the intelligible order of nature revealed by science infused the work of Le Nôtre and other seventeenth-century landscape designers. They had by this time completely abandoned the imagery inherent in the *hortus conclusus,* the garden as a sanctified precinct set apart from the world at large. Instead, they laid out long axes that stretched to the horizon and built monuments that celebrated human authority and achievement.

The increased power that human beings perceived themselves to hold over their own destiny grew in tandem with the power of nation-states and the institutionalization of monarchical government. Louis XIV created at Versailles the ultimate symbol of autocratic rule, and the value of that landscape in bolstering a royal reputation was not lost upon the other princes of Europe. The growing power of states necessitated a concomitant increase in the dignity and monumentality of capital cities, which now expanded their role in manifesting national cultural identity. The extension and protection of state boundaries through new developments in military engineering, first apparent in France under Louis XIV, rendered old city walls obsolete and made possible an expansion of urban territory that paralleled the outward extension of the gar-

den's axes. The axial plan of Versailles was applied to parts of the layout and redevelopment of the city itself as well as to the construction of many Versailles-inspired princely gardens.

The landscape formulas of French classicism thus provided an international style applicable to both the design of gardens and the building of cities, especially capitals. Although French-inspired, this style was never completely severed from its Italian roots, and the design influence of that country remained a potent one. Italy, with its heritage of antique architecture and artifacts, was the principal destination of travelers on the Grand Tour in the eighteenth century. Italian artists continued to find employment abroad in the construction of palaces, gardens, and theaters as well as in the decoration of public places with fountains and monuments. Indeed, it was in seventeenth- and eighteenth-century city planning that the decorative motifs and theatrical grandeur of the Italian Baroque style were combined with the geometries of French authoritarian classicism to create a new international vocabulary of urban design.

Where there was sufficient wealth and centralized governmental control to implement grand urban designs, the monumental cityscape of radiating axes emerged, as in Karlsruhe, Germany. Streets were no longer conceived as residual spaces between buildings but instead were consciously composed perspectives like those found in the theater. The city itself became a giant stage for the pageantry of church and state, with tree-lined streets punctuated by ceremonial arches. Some of these were temporary constructions for special occasions; others were permanent commemorations. Heroic sculptures formed the legendary *dramatis personae* of the urban scene. Along with columns and obelisks, they acted as focal points, terminating vistas. In this fashion, the modern city was created, a city with broad avenues suitable for regimented and rapid movement and with public places enlivened by appropriate symbols of national and local culture.

I. French and Italian Exports: The Application of Classical and Baroque Design Principles to Gardens in the Netherlands, England, Germany, and Beyond

The flow of ideas depends upon means of communication. Since antiquity, direct observation of foreign scenes by travelers had carried innovations in architecture and landscape design to new places. But beginning in the sixteenth century, the growth of printing and the publication of books and albums of engravings were responsible for the rapid spread of landscape design concepts. Architects, sculptors, and hydraulic engineers still responded to commissions from princes. But by the seventeenth and eighteenth centuries, stylistic imitation became far easier because engravings served not only as proud records of existing gardens but also as examples from which prospective garden makers derived inspiration.

Books and Prints

Leon Battista Alberti's *De re aedificatoria,* originally published around 1450, and Francesco Colonna's *Hypnerotomachia Poliphili* of 1499, were translated into French in the mid-sixteenth century, and these books retained a broad influence until well into the seventeenth century. While they could be mined for prototypical classical details, neither provided engraved plans of entire gardens. Similarly, Andrea Palladio's *I quattro libri dell'architettura* of 1570, was, like Alberti's work, primarily a book of architectural instruction rather than an illustrated catalog of designs.[1] Jacques Androuet du Cerceau, a French architect, published several books of his own engravings of designs for knot designs, fountains, and garden pavilions. His two-volume work, *Les plus excellents bastiments de France* (1576 and 1579), recorded and promoted the French Renaissance garden style.

The *Traité du jardinage* of Jacques Boyceau (1638) and André Mollet's *Le Jardin de plaisir* (1651), pioneered how-to books on the layout of ornamental pleasure gardens. Jean-Baptiste de la Quintinye's *Instruction pour les jardins fruitiers et potagers* (1690) was based on the author's experience as the head gardener of the *potager,* or kitchen garden, at Versailles.[2] This book, which carried the horticultural treatise to a new level of science, contained detailed instructions on planting, pruning, and espaliering of fruit trees and the cultivation of vegetables. As valuable as these texts were, they could not compensate for the serious lack of a text and illustrations detailing the achievements of André Le Nôtre over half a century.

In 1709, the publisher Pierre Mariette remedied this situation when he brought out *La Théorie et la pratique du jardinage* by Antoine-Joseph Dezallier d'Argenville (1680–1765), which, translated into three

6.1. An example of the illustrations from *La Théorie et la pratique du jardinage* by A.-J. Dezallier d'Argenville. As many of the book's engraved plates were drawn by Alexandre Le Blond (1679–1719), an architect and follower of Le Nôtre who also contributed several *parterre* designs to this work, the title page of the English editions published by John Johns bears Le Blond's name as author; this has confused some garden historians in the past.

languages and running to eleven editions, disseminated the French seventeenth-century style to an international audience (fig. 6.1). Dezallier's book was written as a manual for aristocrats wishing to lay out Le Nôtre–style gardens on plots ranging from 3 to 60 acres. In addition to furnishing numerous *parterre* and *bosquet* patterns, it articulates four maxims that codify the underlying principles of Le Nôtre's approach.

First, a garden designer should make art yield to nature. Dezallier did not mean by this what the English later would mean, that a garden should appear unstudied, an integral part of the larger natural scene, but rather that topographic and other characteristics of the site should be considered carefully. Further, ostentatious display of wealth through excessive ornament should be abandoned in favor of simple steps, turf banks, ramps, natural arbors, and hedges without trellises.

Nor did giving way to nature mean to Dezallier abandoning geometrical design and eliminating topiary and other regimented horticultural effects. Rather, for him it consisted of eradicating all Renaissance intricacy, which now appeared as mere fussiness, and clarifying and unifying all garden parts into a design that respected both the natural site conditions and the patron's purse. The French seventeenth-century garden had already chastened the intricacies of Renaissance style, but it was still elaborately ornamental and therefore exceedingly labor-intensive. Further simplification was needed if it was to be developed on a broad scale by aristocrats who did not possess the same resources as royalty.

Second, according to Dezallier, a designer should be careful never to cloud and darken gardens by making them dull and gloomy with thickets and excessive ground cover. He found openness desirable, especially around a building, inasmuch as a building needs its own envelope of space. But, as a third principle, he enjoined the designer from making the garden *too* open. He recommended "contrariety and change," a happy balance between openness and enclosure and, through the arrangement of sight lines, the possibility of mystery and surprise. As a final cardinal rule, the designer should manipulate the terrain and planting so as to conceal the garden's boundaries, thus making it appear larger than its actual size.[3]

The second part of Dezallier's book contains practical information on transcribing geometrical figures onto the ground plane as well as on methods of digging and dressing the ground, techniques for building terraces and stairs, and instructions for laying out *parterre* designs, planting trees, and building basins and fountains. Widely read, *La Théorie et pratique du jardinage* was instrumental in spreading French taste throughout Europe. The noted architect Nicodemus Tessin the Younger (1654–1728), who served the Swedish court, copied two sections of this important text verbatim for the instruction of his son, adding such comments as he found necessary to make it relevant to climatic and topographical conditions in Stockholm.

Dezallier wrote his book at the same time that Peter the Great was founding his new capital on the Neva and after the Holy Roman Empire had virtually dissolved into many Germanic principalities. Court architecture was experiencing its heyday, and there were many opportunities for applying Dezallier's landscape design precepts to the construction of princely gardens. From one perspective *La Théorie et pratique du jardinage* could be seen as a codification of the principles of French seventeenth-century landscape design at the very moment it was going out of fashion, particularly in England and soon in France itself. From another point of view, however, it provided a useful and popular guide for those who wanted to continue an important aspect of royal and aristocratic tradition almost until the time of the French Revolution. Consequently, its results are evident in many courtly gardens of the eighteenth century.

In another important pattern book, *De la distribution des maisons de plaisance* (1737) by Jacques-François Blondel, one finds architectural, landscape, and interior plans and elevations in the classical style. Blondel's garden plans display axial symmetry and other hallmarks of that style and include numerous illustrations of garden ornament: treillage, fountains, belvederes, embroidered *parterres,* grillwork, urns, trophies, sphinxes, herms, and more. His designs demonstrate how aristocrats without royal resources at their command can achieve on a modest scale effects similar to those at Versailles. Actually, Blondel stands at the juncture of what is often referred to as the French Classical style and that of the French Picturesque. In his *Cours d'architecture* (1773), he praises the beauties to be found in views of simple nature outside the garden bounds, and this, along with the Rococo delicacy of his designs, indicates the burgeoning picturesque taste and interest in pastoral themes.

DISSEMINATION OF FRENCH LANDSCAPE STYLE

Dezallier was well aware of the economies necessary if the French seventeenth-century style were to survive. His 3- and 6-acre gardens cleverly give an illusion of grandeur within a small compass, and he warns his readers that elaborate ornament demands a royal purse. Yet there were royal purses still to be found, as well as cheap labor for massive construction works.

Late in the reign of Louis XIV and for decades thereafter, the resident court and the court city became the pattern throughout Europe, from Hampton Court in England under William and Mary (ruled 1689–1702) to St. Petersburg in Russia, founded by Peter the Great (1682–1725) in 1703, to Drottningholm in Stockholm, commissioned by the dowager queen Hedvig Leonora and built between 1680 and 1700, to the Buen Retiro in Madrid, created during the reign of Philip IV (ruled 1621–1665). Central Europe offered many opportunities for absolute rule and its princely trappings. The Peace of Westphalia of 1648 concluding the Thirty Years' War had brought about the collapse of the Holy Roman Empire and the weakening of Hapsburg rule along with the concomitant empowerment of many German princes. As these wealthy men assumed an almost fully sovereign status, they inevitably sought to aggrandize their electorates, kingdoms, principalities, and dukedoms with palace gardens built according to French taste, some of which were actual copies of French designs.

There were, nevertheless, essential cultural and physical differences from country to country, which accounted for various vernacular design dialects in the language of the new international-style garden. A closer examination of the Netherlands and England in particular shows versions of the French theme at a time of self-conscious nationalism. Less secure in their boundaries than either the English or the French, German principalities showed the influence of new developments in military design in their treatment of the French landscape model.

The Netherlands

The Dutch did not create a wolly indigenous style but instead adapted the Renaissaie landscape idiom developed elsewhere to their count's geography of canalized land reclamation and its stroi tradition of urban bourgeois prosperity. Gradually recogzed as a nation in its own right after the expulsion of Spanish rule in the seventeenth century, the Netherlands exhibited the prosperity of its economic ruling class in many private gardens. Even monarchical ambitions were tempered by the circumstances of topography and the pragmatic values of a mercantile nation, making the Dutch and Anglo-Dutch gardens of William and Mary more intimate in scale, more compartmentalized, and less grandly unified than their French prototypes.

The Dutch designed compact gardens and substituted variety and intricacy for broad effects. The influence of the Mannerist designer and publisher of numerous architectural pattern books, Hans Vredeman de Vries (1527–1606), whose *Hortorum viridariorumque elegantes et multiplicis formae* of 1583 set the tone in this regard, was long-lasting. The engravings in this influential pattern book show many variations on the theme of the urban or suburban garden: gallery-surrounded *parterres* of *pièces coupées* (grass cutwork) divided by *berceaux* (arched trellises) and accented with topiary and fountains (figs. 6.2a and 6.2b). For de Vries, garden enlargement was additive, consisting of multiplied design units, or garden rooms, rather than the integrated expansion of the garden's parts to a new design scale. Like other designers from the Renaissance onward, he had enthusiastically studied the treatise of the ancient Roman architectural theorist Vitruvius Pollio (active 46–30 B.C.E.). He was also familiar with *Tutte l'opere d'architettura* by the Renaissance theorist Sebastiano Serlio (1475–1554). His own schemes, rendered with the exaggerated perspective characteristic of Mannerism,

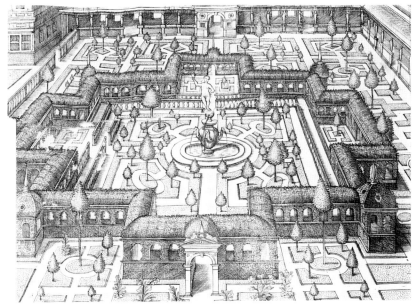

contain various forms derived from ancient and Renaissance architecture, such as obelisks and pyramids. Although de Vries gave his pattern gardens the names of the classical orders codified by Serlio, the terms—*Doric* for rectilinear geometric beds and *Ionic* and *Corinthian* for those of circular and labyrinthine construction—are more imaginative than apt.

Jan van der Groen (c. 1635–1672), gardener to the Prince of Orange (1650–1702) between 1659 and 1671, displayed a similar delight in intricacy in *Den Nederlandtsen Hovenier*, a popular gardening treatise first published in 1669 and nine times subsequently. Besides illustrating elaborate, compartmentalized gardens at Rijswijk and Honselaarsdijk, van der Groen's book contains numerous *parterre* patterns. These are in both the French manner of flowing arabesques and an indigenous style of interlaced geometric knots reminiscent of Islamic tiles and textiles (fig. 6.3). The illustrations for latticework have the same robust

Top: 6.2a. Engraving depicting the layout of an imaginary garden with fountain and surrounding *berceaux*. Designed by Hans Vredeman de Vries, *Hortorum viridariorumque elegantes et multiplicis formae.* 1583

Above: 6.2b. Engraving depicting imaginary layout of a garden *parterre* of *pièces coupées,* geometric pieces of cut grass. Designed by Hans Vredeman de Vries, *Hortorum viridariorumque elegantes et multiplicis formae.* 1583

Left: 6.3. Designs for Flower Beds, an engraving from *Den Nederlandtsen Hovenier* (The Netherlandish Gardener) by Jan van der Groen. 1659–71

6.4. The colonnade at Het Loo, originally designed in 1686 by Jacob Roman as two curving colonnades attached to the sides of the house. These were united and repositioned when the garden was redesigned and extended between 1695 and 1699 following the coronation of William and Mary.

Below: 6.5. Parterre at Het Loo. Although large by Dutch standards and developed in the style of French seventeenth-century gardens, Het Loo is more intimately scaled and more visibly contained by its boundary walls.

shapes found in the architectural detailing of many Dutch buildings and, like them, sport ball finials and pyramidal spires.

An exuberant use of topiary and a native taste for genre subjects in garden statuary characterized the many gardens that lined the banks of suburban rivers and canals, providing weekend retreats for wealthy merchants. These gardens afforded a two-way spectacle, since they provided an unfolding scene of great interest to boat passengers and, being furnished with pavilions and platforms overlooking the water, offered their owners the pleasure of observing the water parade.

Although the Dutch appropriated the seventeenth-century French landscape style, they reduced its grandeur and scale to suit the topography and social expectations of the Netherlands. We see this in the now impeccably restored royal gardens of Het Loo in the eastern part of the country, the Veluwe, a nonarable rolling landscape of low-growing brush and heather. This is excellent country for the pursuit of game, and like Versailles, Het Loo had its origin as a hunting lodge. As Stadholder of Gelderland after 1672, Prince William III of Orange had hunting rights to the Veluwe. Being a passionate sportsman, he purchased the old castle of Het Loo with the notion of building a more elegant and modern hunting establishment elsewhere on the property.

Work began in 1686 under the supervision of the Dutch architect Jacob Roman (1640–1716) according to designs thought to have been developed by the Academy of Architecture in Paris. Simultaneously, following the revocation of the 1685 Edict of Nantes, the French Huguenot designer Daniel Marot (1661–1752) moved to the Netherlands, and he was soon employed as the principal designer of the new palace's interiors and gardens. This fact accounts for the remarkable decorative unity between the two, with *parterres de broderie* echoing the arabesques of molded ceilings, damask wall coverings, and iron grillwork. Between 1695 and 1699, subsequent to the coronation of William and Mary as king and queen of England in 1689, their gardens at Het Loo were extensively remodeled by Roman, Marot, and Romeyn de Hooghe (1645–1708) to make them suitable for entertaining state visitors when the joint sovereigns were in residence in the Netherlands.

Het Loo displays its debt to Versailles in its strong central axis with ornamental *parterres* symmetrically arranged along it and its use of sculpture depicting classical subjects. But a closer look reveals important differences, the most pronounced being its relative modesty, intimacy of scale, sense of containment, and lack of transition between art and nature. Where Versailles virtually explodes into the surrounding space, Het Loo is strictly confined within its rectilinear enclosing walls like earlier gardens of the Renaissance. The principal axis of the Lower Garden extends beyond its boundary, but the twin arms of the curving colonnade at the far end of the Upper Garden hold it in a firm embrace, thereby vitiating its outward thrust (fig. 6.4). Nor has Het Loo major transverse axes like those that open Versailles and Vaux-le-Vicomte to distant prospects of rural countryside.

The Lower Garden near the palace is laid out in square compartments as in a Renaissance garden, and this is also true of the King's Garden and Queen's Garden on either side of it (figs. 6.5, 6.6). The French and Dutch designers of Het Loo employed none of the compensation for optical foreshortening one finds in Le Nôtre's more sophisticated designs, but they relied instead on the simpler geometries of an earlier period. The pair of elaborate trellis arbors in the Queen's Garden are similar to those of Renaissance gardens.

Besides the containment of Baroque ornamental elements within an enclosed orthogonal framework reminiscent of Renaissance gardens, the most significant difference between Dutch and French seventeenth-century gardens lies in the role played by the canal in each. At Versailles, Chantilly, and elsewhere in France, the canals that help drain the land are boldly scaled ornamental sheets of water used to create the principal axes of the garden. In the Netherlands, where

6.6. Queen's Garden at Het Loo

Below: 6.7. Canal dividing the Upper and Lower Gardens at Het Loo

Below left: 6.8. Cascade at Het Loo. Compare this cascade in scale to Le Nôtre's cascade at Sceaux (see fig. 5.16).

much of the country lies below sea level, a ubiquitous functional canal system actually creates much of the land. This system divides the Dutch landscape into rectilinear units, so that canals form transportation arteries and also mark property boundaries. Although purely ornamental canals were constructed in some of the larger aristocratic gardens, these never assumed the same importance as the broad water axes of French gardens. At Het Loo, for instance, a pair of narrow parallel canals divides the Upper Garden from the Lower Garden. These are bordered by tree-lined promenades similar to those flanking the canals of the countryside at large (fig. 6.7). In addition, because of the scarcity of stone, architectural cascades such as those at Het Loo were necessarily small in scale and the exception rather than the rule (fig. 6.8).

ENGLAND

The French landscape tradition had only a brief life in England, particularly after eighteenth-century Whig aristocrats, who represented the country's increasingly powerful antiroyalist commitment to par-

liamentary government, rejected Gallic influence on the grounds that it symbolized monarchical absolutism. Nor did the Counter-Reformation assert its Baroque splendor there as it did in the European Catholic monarchies. The Renaissance literature of Shakespeare and Bacon is filled with images indicating the delight in nature of a people blessed with a landscape already endowed with much gentle beauty. Shakespeare's plays and poems are filled with pastoral images and scenes of sylvan revels, in which he mentions numerous garden flowers and wildflowers. Bacon's essay "Of Gardens" (1625) points the way toward both the sensuous and the sensible in garden design. He lists all the flowers and fruits that provide horticultural pleasure at various seasons of the year, while disdaining knot gardens, which he characterizes as "toys" worthy only of a pastry chef.[4]

The pastoral literature of antiquity also played an important role in the English version of the Renaissance dialectic between art and nature. The vision of rural contentment conjured by Virgil, the most romantic of the ancient pastoralists, had an especially profound influence, inspiring poets and landscape designers alike. Ovid furnished a host of woodland deities with which to populate English groves. And not only the "saints" of Cromwell's Commonwealth, but many royalists, too, found ancient role models in Horace, who equated industrious husbandry with republican virtue. The treatises of Cato, Varro, and Columella were mined for practical information on agricultural practices. For the gentry as well as the aristocracy, Pliny the Younger's vision of *otium,* or intellectually productive exurban leisure, gave authority for the use of country houses and gardens as places to demonstrate an interest in both new and antiquarian knowledge.

In addition, late Renaissance architecture in England, thanks to Inigo Jones (1573–1652), rested on the pure geometries of Andrea Palladio's classical style. Even in the more robust grandeur of Jones's successors—Christopher Wren (1632–1723), Nicholas Hawksmoor (1661–1736), and John Vanbrugh (1664–1726)—English architecture shunned the absolutist overtones of the decoratively refined French style and avoided the flamboyance of the exuberantly ornamental Italian Baroque. This fact necessarily bore consequences for landscape design. Palladio's spare yet Olympian style was vigorously revived by Lord Burlington's circle in the eighteenth century, when architectural simplicity based upon ancient models gained even greater political connotations than in the seventeenth. The Palladian style helped place English landscape design upon an Italian foundation. Further,

the scale of English gardens remained closer to the relatively intimate scale of Italian ones, and English topography provided more opportunities for terracing in the Italian manner than did the plains of France or the lowlands of Northern Europe.[5]

The conflation of antiquarian interest with political values received a further boost from travel. English aristocrats, already steeped in Latin literature, formed strong direct associations with Italy in the seventeenth century, when taking the Grand Tour became practicable and fashionable. Thus, Italian garden influence unmediated by that of France played a greater role in England than on the Continent. Several garden patrons attempted to recapture the idyllic spirit of the ancient gardens of literature, as well as to imitate the poetic associations found in Italian Renaissance gardens such as that of the Villa d'Este through the use of statuary and grottoes in axial terraced compositions.

These English nobles had a strong interest in scientific discovery. This helps account for their fascination with the technological aspects of garden hydrology as embodied in the ingenious automata—*giocchi d'acqua*—they had seen in Italian gardens. A popular treatise by Salomon de Caus (c. 1577–1626), *Les Raisons des forces mouvantes* (1615), made the mechanics of automata familiar to them. De Caus, a French Huguenot, had spent three years in Italy as a young man and, upon coming to James I's court in 1610, introduced waterworks technology, terracing, and other Italian gardening concepts. The English aristocratic mania for grotto construction reflected a desire to emulate the grottoes of Italian gardens and to establish the grotto's status as a place for scientific study.[6] Like the popular contemporary cabinets of curiosities, these grottoes contained mineral and rock specimens as well as collections of marine shells. They also served as laboratories for a variety of experiments combining hydraulic machinery with natural forces.

Garden prospects, including the scenery beyond the garden boundaries, served the same function as perspective backdrops in the theater. "Prospect" was an early and often-cited value in the development of the English garden. By evoking ancient Roman forms and including real British ruins—mostly those of old monasteries, for which there was much antiquarian enthusiasm—these English gardens became memory theaters and palimpsests of an ennobled past. Stages for social intercourse and entertainment, they also became arenas of philosophical contemplation and dramatic meditation upon national and family history. At Wilton and other seventeenth-century gardens, the prospects contained elements of association with imperial Rome. In addition, the notion that the

6.9. Wilton House Gardens. Designed by Inigo Jones and Isaac de Caus. Engraving c. 1632. The garden proper consisted of three principal divisions built around the central axis. Near the house this avenue was flanked with square compartments of *broderie* overlooked by terraced walks. The middle section contained a pair of arbor-bracketed groves (counterparts of the French *berceaux* and *bosquets*) through which ran the Nadder. This stream was not canalized, as would have been the case in a French garden, but left to take a naturally irregular course traversing the symmetrical groves. At the far end, in front of Inigo Jones's fine architectural grotto, was a lawn divided by curving tree- and hedge-lined walks, in the center of which stood a bronze cast by Hubert Le Sueur of the antique sculpture known as the Borghese Gladiator. On either side of it were arbors for strolling on hot days.

ruins of medieval Britain could express England's own antique greatness was gaining currency.

Isaac de Caus (fl. 1612–1655), the son or nephew of Salomon de Caus, collaborated with Inigo Jones on the design of the most famous garden in England in its day, that of Wilton House (fig. 6.9). The visitor to Wilton today is scarcely aware of the buried splendor of the Renaissance garden because it has been revised several times over the years, most notably during the eighteenth century by the ninth Earl of Pembroke. His Palladian bridge of 1737 and towering cedars remain as relics of the eighteenth century, but they are only the most visible parts of the palimpsest. There are the remains of a splendid grotto (now a schoolhouse) and other scattered fragments of the garden that was the pride of Philip Herbert, fourth earl of Pembroke, in the 1630s. Then, Wilton's greatly admired garden offered hospitality to the fashionable and learned world.

The earl's gardeners laid out a symmetrical landscape along a central axis leading to Inigo Jones's porticoed structure and beyond to a green amphitheater and wooded grove. There the prospect culminated in a Roman-style triumphal arch topped by an equestrian statue. Behind the loggia of Jones's structure, which was decorated with marble bas-reliefs and may have served as a banqueting chamber, and beneath the terrace connecting the garden with the wooded slope beyond, was an extraordinary three-chambered grotto, a particular source of Wilton's fame.

Within it, automata, mechanically propelled waterworks, delighted the earl's guests. Le Nôtre's influence later demystified grottoes and made such mechanical marvels as the ones Isaac de Caus installed at Wilton seem puerile. But in early-seventeenth-century England, where there was little distinction between science and art, the two were combined in many ingenious experiments.

The pleasures represented by Wilton ceased and gardening on a grand scale was halted during the Commonwealth (1649–1660). Throughout these Puritan times, agricultural prosperity was encouraged, but ornamental horticulture was not. Several old gardens were intentionally destroyed, and in London some of the royal parks were actually put up for sale. Following the Restoration in 1660, however, royalty and aristocracy vigorously resumed their garden-building activities. The French garden designer André Mollet (d. c. 1665), who had introduced the *parterre de broderie* to England during the reign of Charles I, returned and took up the position of Royal Gardener at St. James and other royal palaces.

At Hampton Court, Charles II, following his exile in France, began building a garden in which a long canal served as the central axis of an extensive

patte d'oie inspired perhaps by the goose-foot radial avenues earlier introduced by Mollet (figs. 6.10a, 6.10b). With the death of André Mollet around 1665, John Rose (1629–1677), an accomplished horticulturist who had studied under Le Nôtre in France, became the royal gardener. He may have helped to

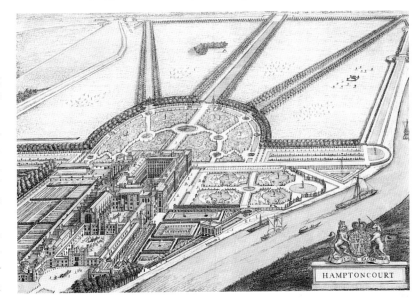

6.10a. Perspectival view of Hampton Court by Johannes Kip after a painting by Leonard Knyff. Engraving from *Britannia Illustrata (Le Nouveau Théâtre de la Grande Bretagne)*. André Mollet assisted Charles II in laying out the *patte d'oie* (goose-foot design) of three avenues radiating from the semicircular promenade enclosing the *parterre* beds designed by Daniel Marot.

6.10b. The gardens of Hampton Court are much simplified today. Marot's *parterres de broderie* have become grass lawn, the *patte d'oie* now emanates directly from Christopher Wren's palace front and terminates in the semicircular promenade rather than somewhere beyond, and the small clipped pyramidal yews seen in the engraving have assumed immense proportions in the photograph.

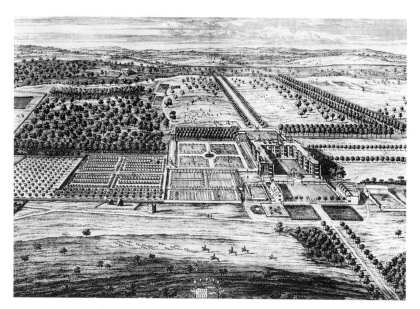

6.11. View of Temple Newsam House. Engraving by Johannes Kip, 1702. From *Britannia Illustrata (Le Nouveau Théatre de la Grande Bretagne)*.

Below: 6.12. The garden at Westbury Court in Gloucestershire, restored after its purchase by the National Trust in 1967, was the creation of Maynard Colchester beginning in 1696 and his son and namesake after 1715. It is a good example of an English gentleman's garden of the period of William and Mary.

those at Badminton in Gloucestershire, built by Henry, duke of Beaufort, in 1682, and Chatsworth in Derbyshire, seat of the dukes of Devonshire, laid out in 1685.

Although their many intricately designed sections were planned symmetrically, these gardens lack the cadenced thrust of strong principal axes and hence the controlling organization and compositional unity found in contemporary French examples (fig. 6.11). Indeed, the transverse axes in these gardens often gain as much as or more importance than the central one. They are Dutch-influenced, and relatively anti-authoritarian in spirit. Many were built following the Glorious Revolution of 1688 and during the constitutional monarchy of William and Mary. They perhaps also illustrate a characteristically British sense that reticence and understatement are nobler attributes of the great and wealthy than ostentatious display.

Dutch influence in British garden design, with its inference of decorous bourgeois prosperity, was carried to some parts of colonial America, notably Williamsburg, Virginia. In England, it was evident in the increased use of topiary and canals as garden features. These canals were not employed in the French manner as extensions of the principal axis; instead, as in the Netherlands, designers placed independent bodies of water at one side of the garden, often with one or more attendant pavilions, as at Westbury Court, begun at the end of the seventeenth century by Maynard Colchester on his ancestral estate in Gloucestershire (fig. 6.12).

Wishing to avoid the bad air of London and the importunate courtiers massed at the old ramshackle palace of Whitehall, King William, who was asthmatic, and Queen Mary, who was loath to re-enter

carry out this plan, which included, in addition to the long central canal, a narrower semicircular one containing a *parterre* within its curving embrace. Double rows of linden trees lined this canal as well as the three long axes of the *patte d'oie* radiating from it.

The royal gardens where Mollet worked are now urban parks, greatly altered through time, and most of the ones of the seventeenth-century nobility have vanished or, like Wilton, have been revised over the centuries in accordance with new styles and cultural values. But the forms of many of these survive in the engravings of Johannes Kip (1653–1722) and Leonard Knyff (1579–1649), whose topographical bird's-eye views were published in the early eighteenth century in both English and French: *Britannia Illustrata* and *Le Nouveau Théâtre de la Grande Bretagne*. Contemporary with Versailles and sometimes vast in scale, the gardens depicted by Kip and Knyff include

the atmosphere of court intrigue she had witnessed as the daughter of James II, chose Hampton Court as their principal residence. They incorporated Charles II's initial garden design into a new plan, summoning Daniel Marot to create the Great Parterre as a plant showcase similar to the one he had made at William and Mary's palace of Het Loo. Queen Mary's Glass Case Garden for tender exotic plants and elaborate topiary—pyramidal yews, clipped box, and globular mounds of bay and holly—recalled similar features of Het Loo. The monarchs also summoned Christopher Wren to build a large new palace adjacent to Thomas Cardinal Wolsey's Tudor one. Two impressive sides of the proposed square palace block were completed: the facade to the east facing the main garden, known as the Great Fountain garden for its large central fountain, and the one on the south looking out upon the Privy Garden.

In 1699, Henry Wise (1653–1738) lowered and lengthened the Privy Garden in order to provide a view of the river Thames and the Barge Walk. Wise was a partner with George London (d. 1714) in their recently formed Brompton Park Nurseries in Kensington, suppliers of much of the plant material in, as well as designers of, many of the gardens surrounding the great country seats depicted in the engravings of Kip and Knyff.

Today the enormous overgrown yews in the Great Fountain Garden at Hampton Court, their pyramidal outlines blurred after they were no longer clipped, serve as reminders of the disfavor into which the Anglo-Dutch garden fell in the eighteenth century. By contrast, within the principalities of Germany, where aristocratic authoritarianism still prevailed, the classical splendor of Versailles became an almost universal model for courtly gardens and urban planning, although, at least initially, some Italian currents ran northward as well.

Germany and Austria

Northern humanism, as developed by Erasmus, was more religious in nature than that of Italy, a cultural fact that influenced landscape design. Although the first Renaissance gardens to be observed and imitated in such prosperous cities as Augsburg, Nuremberg, and Frankfurt were those of Italy, German gardens did not readily incorporate the pagan images and erotically charged atmosphere of Italian models until the libertine atmosphere of the eighteenth century permitted such license. The vigorous new garden art that flourished in Germany combined French and Dutch influences with Italian ones. Not surprisingly in a country of so many regional power centers, these influences were never amalgamated into a distinctive national style. The many Renaissance gardens that were laid

out beside town houses, the residences of archbishops, and the castles of princes were enclosed, compartmentalized rectangular spaces, axially disconnected from the edifices to which they were attached, with intricately designed *parterres,* tunnel-like arbors, balustraded terraces, tubs of plants, sculptural fountains, aviaries, grottoes, and gazebos (fig. 6.13).

The most famous German garden in its day was the Hortus Palatinus in Heidelberg, begun in 1615 by Salomon de Caus for Elizabeth Stuart, daughter of King James I of England, and her husband, Elector Friedrich V of the Palatinate (fig. 6.14). The garden sits high above the Neckar Valley and consists of a series of L-shaped descending terraces, which were originally subdivided into squares outlined by pergolas and hedges and ornamented with gazebos, fountains, and statuary. De Caus, being a hydrological engineer and specialist in automata, built numerous grottoes and other water features, which when mechanically activated sounded musical notes and even in some cases played melodies

6.13. View of Joseph Futtenbach's garden in Ulm. 1641

Below: 6.14. Perspective view of Hortus Palatinus, Heidelberg, Germany. Designed by Salomon de Caus. 1615–20. Engraving by Matthäus Merian, the Elder

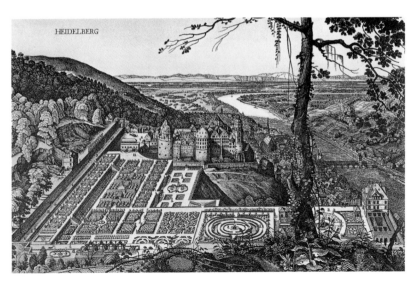

6.15. View of Grosser Garten, Herrenhausen. Engraving by J. van Sasse after J. J. Müller, c. 1720. Martin Charbonnier, the gardener to Sophie, wife of Elector Ernst August and the principal sponsor of the garden, was sent to the Netherlands to study the latest developments in landscape design. It is not surprising, therefore, to find this firmly rectangular garden surrounded by canals on three sides, its central axis culminating in a semicircular curve as at Het Loo.

Right: 6.16. Karlsruhe, palace, gardens, and hunting park of Margrave Karl Wilhelm of Baden-Durlach. 1715. Detail of an engraving by Johannes Mathaus Steidlin, 1739

Below: 6.17. Belvedere Gardens, Vienna. Designed by François Girard. 1693–1732

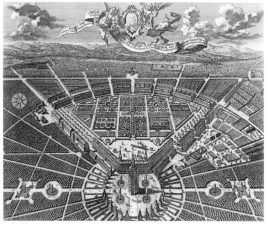

ent, particularly in Lower Saxony at Hanover, where Sophie, the daughter of Frederick V of the Palatinate, who had married Duke (later Elector) Ernst August, oversaw the creation of the Grosser Garten at Herrenhausen (fig. 6.15).

In the politically unstable atmosphere of seventeenth-century Germany, authority was fragile and transient, and the princely landscape was often constructed as a symbolic expression of absolutist power, an assertion of control over potentially fractious municipalities. Karlsruhe, the creation in 1715 of Margrave Karl Wilhelm of Baden-Durlach, makes this statement with its spiderweb of avenues radiating outward from the palace (fig. 6.16). Their indeterminate length made the entire surrounding countryside appear subservient to the margrave.

Vienna itself, the imperial capital, continually feared invasion by the Turks, and it was not until after the decisive victory of 1683 that garden building on a significant scale occurred there. In 1693, Prince Eugene of Savoy, a much-admired hero in the recent war, acquired land outside the southern wall of the city and set about building his Belvedere palace and gardens in the French style, a project not completed until 1732 (fig. 6.17). Designed by François Girard in collaboration with the architect Johann Lukas von Hildebrandt (1668–1745), the gardens, with their broad terraced *parterres,* fountain basins, cascades, clipped hedges, and boxlike pavilions facing the Orangery, contain faint but perceptible echoes of Vaux-le-Vicomte and Marly, evidence of Austrian acceptance of French influence with regard to landscape design. However, in Hildebrandt's architecture, which is strongly indebted to the Italian Baroque style of Francesco Borromini, an underlying Austrian anti-French sentiment is perhaps more evident. Other nobles also built luxurious palaces and gardens nearby as Vienna flourished in its status as a world capital.

In 1693, Emperor Leopold ordered the court architect Johann Bernhard Fischer von Erlach (1656–1723)[7] to convert the hunting lodge and park at Schönbrunn 6 miles (10 kilometers) from the center of the city into a palace and grounds that would symbolize in its grandeur and magnificence not only Hapsburg imperial power, but also the triumph of the Christian West over Ottoman rule. The original scheme, determinedly Italian rather than French, placed the palace like a beacon on a hill. This plan was too costly and impractical, however, even for an imperial purse, and a revised design located it on the plain below (fig. 6.18).

In 1770, Empress Maria Theresa commissioned the design services of Ferdinand Hetzendorf in preparing a final plan for the park. In keeping with

composed by de Caus himself. Damaged during the Thirty Years' War (1618–48) and devastated during the Palantine campaign of Louis XIV toward the end of the seventeenth century, the gardens fell into ruin and were never completed.

After the Thirty Years' War ended, garden patrons looked almost entirely to France for inspiration, as that country was increasingly the center of economic energy and artistic imagination. German princes imported gardeners and fountain engineers along with design theories as they modified French style to suit their tastes. Dutch influence was also pres-

the taste of the age, the architect added an obelisk and an artificial ruin at the terminus of a new diagonal avenue. At the base of the hill he constructed the Neptune pool, and, at the end of the long axis on top, he placed a handsome *gloriette,* a neoclassical eye-catcher, that brought the august composition to a fitting climax (fig. 6.19).

Near Munich, beginning in 1701, Max Emanuel, elector of Bavaria, began remodeling the Nymphenburg, the palace and garden built by his father, Elector Ferdinand Maria, as a present for his mother, Henriette Adelaide of Savoy, upon his birth. To accomplish this project he sent the architect Joseph Effner (1687–1745) to Paris to study the principles of French landscape design. But it was not only the lessons of Le Nôtre that Effner carried home from abroad; he also imbibed the more relaxed spirit of the Rococo, the lighthearted, intimately scaled ornamental style that originated in France in the early eighteenth century. In essence, the Rococo style constitutes a last phase of the Baroque, and it is not as robust in its forms or as sober in its iconography as the Baroque. Rococo designers especially prized elegant curvaceousness and delicacy of detail. They put a premium on naturalistic floral and rustic forms as well on the creation in gardens of highly picturesque rustic scenery. They extended the long popularity of the grotto, often incorporating into their plans *rocaille,* the amorphous, frequently shell-encrusted, artificial rockwork suggestive of coral reefs and caves.

In Rococo design, Baroque forms have been playfully recast to reflect the mores of the *ancien régime,* which was bored with the grandeur of authoritarian monarchy, even though most aristocrats still adhered to this collapsing political system. Because of increased Western contact with China and a growing

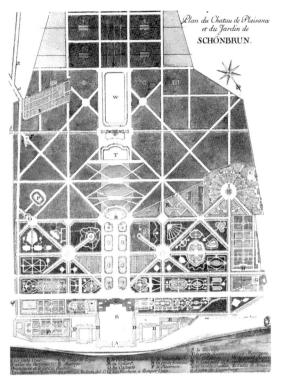

6.18. Plan of Schönbrunn, Vienna. Designed by Johann Bernhard Fischer von Erlach. After 1693. The palace as resited stands near the entrance gates, and behind it on the level ground *parterres* and *bosquets* were laid out. The hillside bore the extension of the central axis running from the palace to a loggia at its terminus. In plan, the garden formed a grid with intersecting diagonals built around this strong central axis.

Below: 6.19. *Gloriette,* Schönbrunn. Designed by Ferdinand Hetzendorf. 1770

enthusiasm for the decorative arts of that country among European aristocrats, the Rococo style also embodies elements of *chinoiserie,* the decorative reinterpretation of Chinese forms that first appeared in the seventeenth century and assumed its full proportions in the eighteenth century, when pagodas, "Chinese" bridges, and tea pavilions became popular features in Western gardens. Rococo designers put a premium on exoticism in general, incorporating into their landscape plans such ornamental structures as "Egyptian pyramids" and "Turkish tents," festively painted wooden pavilions built in imitation of the silk caravan tents of Islamic royalty.

In the park of Nymphenburg, Effner built the

Pagodenburg (1716–19) (fig. 6.20) and the Badenburg (1719–21), where there is a magnificently decorated room containing a bath and water-heating equipment, and the Magdalenenklause (1725), which he designed as a hermitage. The elements of escapist fantasy and hedonistic gaiety that are the essence of Rococo art and that continue to delight visitors to Nymphenburg can be seen in many other Bavarian gardens including the Hofgarten at Veitshöchheim near Munich (fig. 6.21). The sensual and amorous spirit of the Rococo even conquered Prussian Pots-

dam under Frederick II (ruled 1740–1786). At Sanssouci, Rococo lightheartedness was tempered somewhat by the regimental ranks of six long, steeply pitched parabolic vineyard terraces descending from Georg Wenzeslaus von Knobelsdorff's palace (1745–47), a grand but relatively intimately scaled essay in the popular new architectural style (fig. 6.22). In one of the *bosquets* beyond the canal that defined the boundary of the *parterre* terrace, frivolity and exoticism found full expression in Büring's Chinese Tea House (1754–57) (fig. 6.23).

EASTERN EUROPE

French landscape style, particularly after its development into an eighteenth-century Rococo design idiom, was adopted by princes in Hungary, Poland, and Bohemia. Here where the climate is drier than in France, designers omitted the long canals and ornamental lakes that helped drain French gardens and that were used to brilliant effect by Le Nôtre and his followers.

When the Hapsburgs expelled the Turks from Hungary in 1686, several Renaissance palaces, which had been neglected since the Ottoman occupation of 1541, began to be restored. The Austrian architect Johann Lukas van Hildebrandt, built a summer palace for Prince Eugene of Savoy on one of the islands in the Danube. It was surrounded by a garden that combined the French and Italian influences. Although this garden has now vanished, the one built somewhat later during the 1760s at Esterháza, the estate in Fertöd of Prince Miklós Esterházy, has been preserved and restored. Esterháza exemplifies the courtly style that prevailed throughout eastern Europe at this time when the Rococo taste was at its height (fig. 6.24). The layout of the *parterre* garden, with its flower-edged beds, sandstone urns, statuary, and fountains, was based upon an engraving in *Le Jardin de plaisir* (1651) by André Mollet. Garden temples, a pair of cascades, and a triumphal arch ornamented the *bosquets* surrounding this garden. A Chinese pavilion was built

in honor of Empress Maria Theresa's visit in 1773. In addition, Esterháza boasted an opera house, a music building, and a puppet theater. Upon the historic occasion of the empress's visit, the court composer, Franz Joseph Haydn, created two operas to entertain the royal guest. Beyond the ornamental gardens lay a deer park with crisscrossing *allées* and also a boar park with avenues radiating from a *rond-point*.

Although firmly reasserting European stylistic dominance, eighteenth-century Hungarian gardens maintained some of the horticultural elements bequeathed to them by the earlier period of the country's Turkish occupation. These included citrus plants, pomegranates, tulips, and other exotic species. The gardens of the nobility also became showcases for additional non-native species derived from botanical exploration, such as chestnut, catalpa, locust, and hornbeam trees. Like the Rococo follies nearby, exotic plants were prestigious symbols of the garden owners' cosmopolitan perspective and scientific interest.

At the same time, there was a reaction throughout Europe to the kind of landscapes that perpetuated an increasingly discredited authoritarian taste. As we shall see, beginning in the first third of the eighteenth century, the English began to produce gardens that were less regular and more naturalistic than those descended from Versailles and derived from the Dutch influence under William and Mary. As England's

6.24. Palace and garden, Esterháza, Hungary. Architect and garden designer unknown. 1766

Below: 6.25. Wilanów, Warsaw, Poland. Designed by Augostino Locci and Adolf Boy. Late 17th century. Gardens restored by Gerard Ciolek. 1955–65

power as a nation rose, English garden design influenced Continental taste to an increasing degree. Near the end of the eighteenth century, many European princes and other aristocrats adopted the style known as *jardin anglais*—and also as *jardin anglo-chinois*—for their garden-building projects. Further, many of their descendants tore out the garden designs they had inherited when the *jardin anglais* reached the height of fashion in the nineteenth century. The popularity of the new English landscape style in the latter part of the eighteenth century helps explain why the Rococo effects of this period, such as *chinoiserie,* were employed equally in both geometrically formal gardens and informal ones and also why the naturalization of exotic plants went on at the same time in the two kinds of landscape. By turning Baroque forms into whimsy, Rococo ornament became suitable within settings that relied on a naturalistic aesthetic as well as within those that still retained classical design principles of axiality and symmetry. Similarly, exotic plants complemented the penchant for the bizarre found in French Rococo gardens, but these could be also naturalized within a less contrived "English" landscape.

In Poland, King Jan Sobieski (ruled 1647–1696) introduced the Rococo-accented French-style garden after that country had been made safe from Turkish hegemony. At Wilanów, he hired the Dutch architect Tylman van Gameren (1652–1706) to build a palace. He then commissioned Agostino Locci and Adolf Boy to lay out a *patte d'oie* radiating from the palace and a *parterre de broderie* on the first of two terraces leading down to a lake (restored between 1955 and 1965 by Gerard Ciolek). Fountains, sculpture, and a row of *bosquets* were placed on a lower terrace (fig. 6.25). The retaining wall separating the upper and lower terraces was built as a *buffet d'eau* in which basins placed along its length collect water spilling from inset jets. The balustraded staircase between the

6.26. Garden with Neoclassical colonnade, Lançut, near Rzeszow, Poland. Designed by Izabelle Czartoryska in collaboration with architects Chrystian Piotr Aigner and Albert Pio and landscape designers Ignacy Simon and Franciszek Maxwald. Early 19th century

Below: **6.27.** Engraving of *parterre* gardens, Drottningholm, Stockholm, Sweden. 1692. From *Sweden Suecia Antiqua Hodierna,* artists' views commissioned by Eric Dahlberg of important residences and gardens of Sweden

two terraces was ornamented with stone figures representing the four stages of love as Apprehension, Consummation, Boredom, and Separation—a cynical iconography appropriate to a libertine age. The English-style park, added later, contains a *chinoiserie* temple of about 1805 based upon a design by William Chambers and a mock medieval castle disguising a pumping station that elevates water from the lake.

Another important garden, Bialystok, built between 1728 and 1758 as the residence of the Branicki family, was nicknamed the "Polish Versailles" because of its *parterres, bosquets,* and *allées,* as well as its abundance of ornamental pavilions, sculpture, fountains, pools, and cascades. Like Wilanów, Bialystok illustrates the way in which the seventeenth-century French style continued to serve as an international model for aristocratic gardens, even as it was being supplanted by other influences.

The stylistic transition is evident at Lançut where a noblewoman, Izabelle Czartoryska (1746–1835)—a talented garden designer and participant in the development of the park at Wilanów—planned the landscape around this seat of the Lubomirski family after she married the last member of that line.

Czartoryska directed her garden designers to tear out most of the site's original bastion fortifications to create the long views characteristic of English parks, and into this landscape she instructed her architects to build a neoclassical conservatory (1799–1802), a *gloriette* (c. 1820), and a semicircle of neoclassical columns embracing a statue of Venus (now missing), which served as a focal point, or eye-catcher (fig. 6.26).

SWEDEN

Following the end of the Thirty Years' War in 1648, Queen Christina of Sweden summoned André Mollet to Stockholm. During his five-year stay in Sweden, he published *Le jardin de plaisir* (1651), and through this influential work and by the example he offered in his redesign of the royal garden, where he installed a large *parterre de broderie,* the French landscape style became established in that country. Its most notable practitioners were Jean de la Vallée (1620–1696), the son of a French architect working in Sweden, and Nicodemus Tessin the Younger (1654–1728), the son of a German fortifications engineer and architect, Nicodemus Tessin the Elder (1615–1681), who was also employed there. These designers modified the

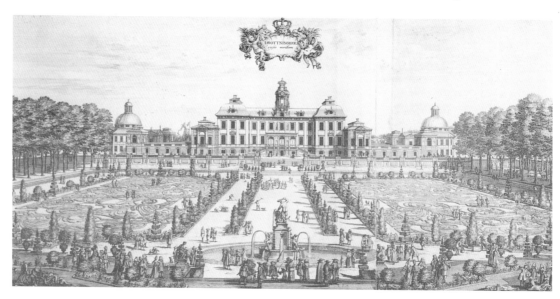

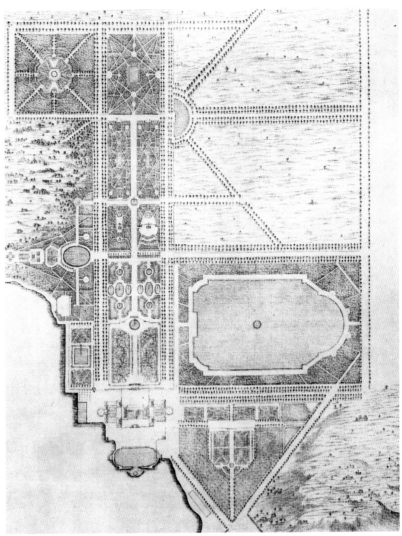

French style so that it became a national variant.

The gardens of the royal palace of Drottning-holm, which were commissioned by the dowager queen Hedvig Eleonora in 1681, constitute the masterwork of Tessin the Younger (figs. 6.27, 6.28). In the sections of Dezallier d'Argenville's *La Théorie et la practique du jardinage* that he later copied as an instructive text for his son, Carl Gustaf, Tessin appended commentaries relating to the adaptation of French landscape principles to Nordic conditions. At Drottningholm, he had the hard bedrock blasted away to create a flat plane for the *parterres* and *bosquets* that he adapted from his drawings of French examples. He organized these along a single longitudinal axis. Where he could not remove a particularly massive outcrop, he disguised it by building across its face an architectural cascade. To have excavated a canal like the one at Vaux-le-Vicomte would have been exceedingly difficult, and neither the transverse axes nor the large geometrical pond shown on the plan were built.

Instead, in the last quarter of the eighteenth century, when Fredrik Magnus Piper (1746–1824) introduced the *jardin anglais* into Sweden, Gustav III took an active role in designing the gardens surrounding the central axis in the English fashion, laying out a chain of meandering ponds, winding paths, and irregular clumps of trees. Gustav III had been tutored in garden design by Carl Gustaf Tessin, and as a seven-year-old boy he participated in the birthday fete for his mother the queen in 1753, presenting her with the keys to the Chinese Pavilion that King Adolf Fredrik had had secretly built and installed as a surprise for her. Demolished in 1763, it was replaced by a new Chinese Pavilion designed by the Director of Public Works, Carl Fredrik Adelcrantz. In 1779, the king commissioned Adelcrantz to design another Rococo garden feature, the blue-and-white striped Turkish Tent on the slope below the Chinese Pavilion (fig. 6.29). Thus, at Drottningholm one finds in one landscape a survey of one hundred years of European garden transformation, with Adelcrantz's eighteenth-

century Rococo features and the slightly later English-style garden of association designed by Gustav III existing side by side with Tessin's interpretation of Le Nôtre's seventeenth-century geometrical style.

Russia

In 1716 Peter the Great appointed Jean-Baptiste Alexandre Le Blond (1679–1719), an architect and the designer of the *parterres de broderie* in the influential *La Théorie et la practique du jardinage* by Antoine-Joseph Dezallier d'Argenville, as architect general. His commission was to build a summer palace called Peterhof on a high cliff beside the Gulf of Finland. Because of the imperial workforce of soldiers and peasant laborers at his disposal, Le Blond was able to lay out the principal lines of the gardens and install a large amount of planting before his death from smallpox in 1719.

Atop the ridge, Le Blond designed the Great Palace, which was extended by Bartolomeo Rastrelli (1700–1771), the foremost architect in Russia in the mid-eighteenth century, during the reign of Empress Elizabeth Petrovna (ruled 1741–1762). On its south side he placed a *parterre* garden and on its north an

6.28. Plan of Drottningholm palace and gardens, Stockholm, Sweden. Designed by Nicodemus Tessin the Younger. 1681

Left: **6.29. Turkish Tent, Drottningholm, Sweden**

6.30. Canal bordered by fountains, Peterhof, Russia

Below: 6.31. Coimbra, Portugal, Gate

Below right: 6.32. Palace of Queluz, near Lisbon, Portugal. Designed by Mateus Vicente de Oliveira. 1747–52. In addition to its elaborate *parterres* of box with Rococo fountains and statuary, the garden has a long Dutch-style canal. The Rococo *azulejo* panels lining it depict shipping scenes.

impressive double cascade and a long fountain-bordered canal (fig. 6.30). A Samson in strength, Peter sometimes felled with his own ax the trees that had to be cleared to create these long avenues and *allées.*

The landscape style carried out by Peter the Great was a highly cosmopolitan one. Although derived principally from France, it was also shaped by contributions from Italian and Dutch sources. The teams of foreign and native architects and the army of serf laborers who built it were part of an even greater enterprise begun by Peter in 1712: the construction of St. Petersburg, a capital, industrial city, and naval and mercantile port on the muddy banks of the Neva River. The story of its creation is in this chapter's discussion of the application of the principles of Baroque landscape design to urban planning.

By the time of Catherine the Great (ruled 1762–1796), English influence had superseded the French in Russia. The empress, who professed to Voltaire in 1772, "I now love to distraction gardens in the English style," hired the English-trained landscape gardener John Busch (fl. 1730s–1790s) to create a picturesque park with meandering water bodies at the summer palace of Tsarskoye Selo outside St. Petersburg. The plan for this landscape, which lies adjacent to the earlier Baroque *parterres* and *bosquets,* bears a superficial resemblance to that of the park that Gustav III and Piper built next to the French-inspired gardens at Drottningholm. Tsarskoye Selo, like the Swedish royal gardens, boasts several *chinoiserie*-style pavilions. But to appreciate the breadth of stylistic possibilities found in eighteenth-century landscape design, one must mentally traverse the European con-

tinent to its westernmost extremity where French and English influence remained slight, allowing a vigorous Iberian version of Baroque and Rococo garden art to flourish.

PORTUGAL

The Portuguese conquerors who garnered imperial wealth from the East Indies and Brazil built churches, palaces, and monasteries. They also ornamented their small, hilly country with many beautiful gardens that creatively amalgamated several foreign influences. Because of the country's favorable climate, they were able to naturalize many exotic plant species collected by Jesuit missionaries from abroad. The marquess of Pombal established a botanical garden at Coimbra, the seat of an important Portuguese university, in 1772, and a botanical garden was set up at the same time in Lisbon.

The Portuguese were the heirs of Islamic Spain. Glazed tiles—*azulejos*—painted with arabesque and geometric designs in tones of yellow, blue, and green, had long been manufactured there, and by the fifteenth century, these were being imported to Portugal where they were applied to many kinds of walls and floors, including those found in several gardens.

The Portuguese established their own tile factories as the craft waned in Spain. They expanded their palette of colors and substituted pictorial motifs for the abstract ones required by Islam. At the same time, they devised composite images by fitting together several square tiles. As Baroque and Rococo motifs gained artistic currency, the Portuguese became the undisputed masters of tile design, creating numerous exuberant patterns. This tilework constitutes an important element in their virtuosic blending of Islamic, Spanish, Italian, and French influences into an original national landscape style (figs. 6.31, 6.32).

Water tanks, an Islamic legacy, are particularly important features in Portuguese gardens. In sum-

mer droughts, they ensured both the residential water supply and the irrigation of the garden's plants. They were usually placed in a fairly elevated position to allow the water to be distributed by force of gravity. Here the reflectivity of both water and tile combine with the designer's imagination to make these utilitarian structures into delightfully decorative garden features, as at the Quinta da Balcalhoa and the Palácio dos Marqueses de Fronteira (figs. 6.33, 6.34).

Replete with ornament and sculpture, seventeenth- and eighteenth-century Portuguese gardens are nevertheless conservative in their overall design. Although some box parterres were laid out in *broderie* designs, the design of others, such as that at the Palácio Fronteira, where there is an intricate maze, harks back stylistically to the Renaissance. Decorative shellwork similar to that found in Italian Mannerist grottoes is abundant here. Even more important, these Portuguese gardens are spatially contained; they are old-fashioned for their day in having walls and also in their absence of strong axial organization. Garden designers adapted their schemes to existing topography and did not practice extensive regrading, as was the case in contemporary gardens elsewhere in Europe. Their loggia terraces were built for viewing *parterre* designs from above, but otherwise they have no connection with the plan of the garden. Although backward-looking in these ways, the gardens that were built in Portugal at this time are highly original. In their exuberant exploitation of the design opportunities inherent in a regional commodity—glazed tiles—the Portuguese confidently forged their own distinctive landscape idiom.

FRENCH ROCOCO INFLUENCE IN CHINA

By the eighteenth century, the Picturesque style had begun to establish a powerful counterinfluence to that of Versailles. Aristocrats felt increasing financial constraints, and a style that made a virtue of nature's serendipity was less costly than one that required meticulous maintenance. In France, the gaiety and hedonistic charms of picturesquely accented Rococo landscapes masked the anxieties of the *ancien régime* as it faced a turbulent future in which cultural forces would forever alter the premises of autocratic government and the nature of landscape design.

At the same time, Rococo-accented classicism remained a model for royal patrons, even appearing in a form that might ironically be dubbed *"franciserie"* in far-away China. There Emperor Qian Long (1736–1795) commissioned a Jesuit priest, Father Giuseppe Castiglione (1688–1766), and his colleagues

6.33. Quinta da Balcalhoa, Arrábida Peninsula south of Lisbon. 1528–54. This garden was built after the property was acquired by Braz de Albuquerque, the soldier and mariner who conquered Goa. It was restored in the middle of the twentieth century by its American owner, Mrs. Herbert Scoville and now offers the best example of a Portuguese Renaissance garden. The tiles decorating the pavilions beside the water tank encapsulate the early development of *azulejo* design in Portugal, showing the transition from abstract Islamic patterns to Spanish Renaissance pictorial ones.

Left: 6.34. Palácio dos Marqueses de Fronteira, Lisbon, Portugal. Built for the first marquess of Fronteira, João Mascarenhas, who freed Portugal from Spanish rule, the seventeenth-century palace garden is in the Mannerist syle of the preceding century. It has a box maze laid out according to a pattern of 1628 by the German garden designer Joseph Futtenbach. Within this maze are five octagonal water tanks. A long tank flanked by a 15-foot (4.6-meter) high wall inset with three grottoes and fifteen blind arches is decorated with blue-and-white tile panels depicting knights on prancing steeds.

五面正園花

6.35. The south side of the Great Fountain, Xi Yang Lou, or European sector, of the Chang Chun Yuan (Garden of Extended Spring) within the Yuan Ming Yuan (Garden of Perfect Brightness). Chinese copperplate engraving. 1786

to build in this style the Xi Yang Lou, a collection of Sino-European marble buildings and fountains, as well as a maze and water clock, within the Chang Chun Yuan, or Garden of Extended Spring, part of his Summer Palace of Yuan Ming Yuan, the Garden of Perfect Brightness described in Chapter Eight (fig. 6.35, see fig. 8.14).[8] The garden's buildings housed the gifts of foreign emissaries as well as the hydraulic machinery that operated its fountains. The sole remains of this extraordinary Chinese landscape after its destruction and looting by combined British and French forces in 1860, the Xi Yang Lou proves that the exchange between China and Europe was not one-sided, although Rococo *chinoiserie* was to play a much larger role in Western gardens than Western planning concepts and forms played in those of China.

Although many notable gardens were produced by the fusion in the eighteenth century of the predominant French influence with that of other traditions, of even greater consequence was the more far-reaching and long-lasting effect of landscape design from this era on the planning of cities. Increasingly, as monarchical authority sought to glorify itself on a public scale, not just the royal demesne but the entire capital city became the focus of monumental urbanism. The idea that cities could be planned according to Baroque and French seventeenth-century design principles was suited, moreover, to the rising tide of nationalism and the desire to find an urban form that was expressive of the power of the state.

II. The Heroic City: Expressions of Classical and Baroque Urbanism

By the beginning of the eighteenth century, the appearance of cityscapes owed much to the lessons landscape design professionals had learned in the seventeenth century. Axial extension, *allées* defined by ranks of trees, intersections marked with fountains or other central features, sculpture and monuments with programmatic content—these are, as we have seen, the basic ingredients of Le Nôtre's garden style. Le Nôtre had conceived the plan for the town of Versailles as integral with that of the gardens of the palace, and Margrave Karl Wilhelm had treated town and park in a similar fashion at Karlsruhe (see fig. 6.16). But royal patronage was not strictly necessary for the further development of this style of urbanism. Throughout the seventeenth century, with the rise of the middle class, cities gained increasing autonomy and became more than court appendages, episcopal seats, or mere trading centers. National governments and municipal corporations employed architects, engineers, and artists to revise and extend their layouts and to embellish them in a manner that promoted state and civic pride.

The resulting form of urbanism, which has remained a valid paradigm for planners down to modern times, was thus concomitant with the growth of nation-states and the status of the city as an expression of the wealth and virtue of its citizenry. The premise of infinitely extensible axes that is central to this manner of design foreshadowed the disappearance of city walls as nations came into existence and city-states ceased to function as independent and autonomous political units. In addition, with the seventeenth-century technical invention of spring suspension and the introduction of plate-glass windows, carriage travel became a sociable pastime as well as a comparatively efficient means of locomotion, and this fact had obvious consequences for the scale of streets and the design of cities.

THE PRINCIPAL ELEMENTS OF THE BAROQUE CITYSCAPE

The first step in the transformation from high-walled citadel to the modern city occurred when military engineers developed a new system of defense employing projecting bastions instead of battlements. With their "ears" and pointed triangular "demi-lunes," these strategic constructions were built to withstand cannon siege while allowing the defending artillery maximum protection as they fired back along a series of intersecting diagonal sight lines. In plan, they form starburst patterns. Like the gardens of Le Nôtre, they thrust outward, metaphorically invading space.[9] As interior cities became increasingly secure behind chains of fort cities constructed along their frontiers, their fortifications began to be eliminated, and even the new bulwarks in time gave way to boulevards, tree-planted ring roads that attracted recreational activity, notably carriage driving and promenading, which in turn gave rise to nineteenth-century shopping and café life.

Military engineers such as Le Nôtre's contemporary Sébastien Le Prestre de Vauban (1633–1707) were frequently called upon to lay out cities.[10] Their plans demanded the abandonment of the "organic" approach to urbanism characteristic of many older cities and the subordination of everyday life to a conceptual order based on symbolical intent as well as practical considerations. Even where the perennially useful grid was employed, the underlying symbolism of the Baroque cityscape, which pressed Renaissance humanism into the service of proclaiming princely power, demanded its ruthless interruption by radials emanating like the rays of the sun from the court or seat of government. It is because of its indifference to the requirements of the daily lives of ordinary individuals that urban historians—Lewis Mumford, for one—have judged this kind of authoritarian planning harshly. But its compensatory offering was theatricality and a new vision of the dignity of public space and public life in which a reciprocity of sight lines between civic institutions symbolically expressed the political and cultural aspirations of the society.

The *rond-point* with its long vistas along the straight diagonals of the hunting park provided a new model for radial thoroughfares emanating from a circle in a star pattern, facilitating both the movement of ordinary traffic and military troops in an emergency, while considerably increasing the dynamism and drama of city space. The tree-lined *allées* found in French gardens provided a model for street tree planting. They are the progenitors not only of broad avenues for pleasant strolling, but also of tree-lined processional and parade routes like the Champs Élysées in Paris and Pennsylvania Avenue in Washington, D.C. Embellished by obelisks, portals, arches, fountains, monuments, and sculptures that serve as place fixers for squares and circles that punctuate their length and provide a cadence to the movement along them, these ceremonial axes dramatize the city and articulate messages of civic pride and national power.

Urban squares were intentionally designed as stages for public life and heroic commemoration. Even without the foci of fountains and monuments, these architecturally conceived spaces conveyed a powerful sense of place and became elements of the imagery that gave each city its individual character in the minds of its citizens and visitors. In addition, the Baroque cityscape was one in which heights were dramatized; the lofty church or palace, the proud hilltop monument, the urban cascade, and the grand stairway provided urban distinction and sense of place.

The Baroque cityscape married the appreciation of real and symbolic order characteristic of French classicism to the instinct for dramatic siting and theatrical effects found in Italian landscape design. The combined genius of Michelangelo, Bernini, and Le Nôtre helped shape a new urban form that inspired plans for the layout of cities on a grand scale suitable to new modes of transportation. More orderly than any plans since the days of the Roman Empire, these also envisioned new standards of public sanitation and safety as well as new standards of public recreation and entertainment.

ROMAN FOUNTAINS AND BAROQUE URBANISM

As other ancient aqueducts were revived with the aid of the recently rediscovered document *De aquis urbis Romae* by the soldier, writer, and superintendent of Rome's water-supply system Sextus Julius Frontinus (c. 35–103 C.E.), seventeenth-century Rome lost no opportunity to celebrate the copious fresh water supply with the construction of fountains in its new squares. Waters from the underground Aqueduct of Trajan gushed into Fontana and Ponzio's Fontanone dell' Acqua Paola adjacent to San Pietro in Montorio on the Janiculum, a large architectural display fountain of the style known since antiquity as a *castellum*. A *castellum* typically signaled an aqueduct's formal point of entry into the city and commemorated the

6.36. Fountain of the Triton, Piazza Barberini, Rome. Designed by Gianlorenzo Bernini. 1642–43. Engraving by G. B. Falda

beneficence of the emperor who had constructed it. In this manner, papal and imperial prestige were conflated in the resurrected aqueduct system of Rome.

In Bernini, Rome had a sculptor capable of aggrandizing the urban plan of Sixtus V, which we examined in Chapter Four. He brought to the secular imagery of the city's public spaces the same powers of dramatic composition one finds in his commissions for the Counter-Reformation Church. In addition to remodeling the Acqua Vergine Antica,[11] he created two fountains at the Piazza Barberini—the Fountain of the Triton and the Fountain of the Bees from the Barberini pope's coat of arms (fig. 6.36). His masterpiece stands at the center of the Piazza Navona: the Fountain of the Four Rivers, with its four symbolic river gods. These figures are not self-contained and languidly at rest like the river gods of antiquity, but actively twist and gesture like actors in a dramatic tableau.

From today's vantage point, it is sometimes difficult to remember that even with the construction of new streets and significant works of architecture, seventeenth-century cities were far more rural in character than ours. Though some streets were paved, many were not, and we see with surprise in seventeenth- and eighteenth-century prints of Rome the still-rough, undressed character of the surrounding ground plane and the quasi-rustic character of the public life within the spaces that envelop these architectural and sculptural masterpieces. Nevertheless, at the beginning of the seventeenth century, Rome was the most sophisticated and urbane city in the Western world. With its numerous ruins as testaments of its historical greatness, it was a place in which one felt the poetics of the collapsed centuries. Added to this was the festive air of papal pomp and worldly pleasure made manifest in stone. These provided ample basis for Rome's growing international reputation as a place of unrivaled wonders.

With its new fountains and treasure trove of ancient artifacts ready-made for urban scenography, Rome provided a vocabulary of forms for cityscapes elsewhere. It also initiated the characteristically Baroque concept of dynamic movement through space, an idea that had its roots in the Mannerists' concern with perspective and that now made a sensual experience of the eye's journey through space. Baroque spatial organization was not merely horizontal; the architectural embellishment of heights with buildings, monuments, and grand stairs of ascent gave a vertical dimension to movement. The animated movement of water rising and falling into Roman fountains and, in addition, the gestural sculpture that ornamented them added further spatial drama to the urban scene.

Essentially plastic in their formal orientation and theatrical in their approach, Roman designers developed an urbanism that thrived on incident, creating a street network of interrelated points of interest rather than, as in France, an exploration of the possibilities of space for its own sake. Roman urbanism contained a celebratory message, one that sought to dazzle the senses and awe the mind with the reaffirmed glory of the Catholic Church and the resurrected splendor of the imperial past. French urbanists, on the other hand, with less emotional exuberance, greater reliance on intellect and reason, and a gift for centralized administration, dramatized the power of the modern state. The manifestation of this power in an overall plan for Paris in which Le Nôtre's seemingly infinite axes were applied on a civic scale would, given Louis XIV's preoccupation with Versailles, necessarily await a later age, that of Napoleon III in the nineteenth century (see Chapter Ten). As we saw in Chapter Four, the groundwork for that urbanistic feat had already been laid even before the time of Louis XIV and Le Nôtre in the series of projects undertaken in Paris during the rule of Henry IV at the dawn of the seventeenth century.

Paris after Henry IV

In Paris, as in Italy, the invention of the spring-suspension carriage had made straight avenue circulation a new priority in urban design. In 1616, in imitation of the Corso on the outskirts of her native Florence, Henry IV's widow, Marie de Médicis, had the Cours-la-Reine laid out for carriage promenaders on the outskirts of the city along the banks of the Seine to the west of the Tuileries (fig. 6.37). Quadruple rows of elms created three avenues almost a mile in length, bringing not only the amenity of the tree-lined street to Paris, but also the socialization of urban space. People had discovered, along with the visual and physical enjoyment of movement itself, the theatrical possibilities of street life with its daily spectacle of carriages and promenaders. Bewigged and dressed in silks and lace, the socially ambitious saw themselves as protagonists in the diurnal drama of meeting and greeting one another in public. The Cours-la-Reine was soon thronged with carriages, one more opulently appointed than the next, and its popularity was so great that on the opposite side of town the Cours St.-Antoine was inaugurated on the rue St.-Antoine, the main ceremonial entry to Paris from the east along the road from Vincennes. Here the trees were planted to form twin allées for promenading with a broad carriage drive in between. To extend it eastward, the Cours de Vincennes was built in the 1660s.

The most important *cours* of all was that initiated by Le Nôtre around 1670 when the axis of the Tuileries, called the Grand Cours, was extended approximately a mile into the open countryside to the Étoile, as the *rond-point* with its starburst of radiating avenues is called. Between this axis and the Cours-la-Reine beside the Seine, royal gardeners planted a stretch of ground as a quincunx—a regular arrangement of trees set in a pattern composed of multiple units of five, in which four trees comprise the angles of a square or rectangle, while the fifth serves to mark its center. The poetic name for this grove was Champs Élysées, meaning the Elysian Fields. Another short axis connected the Cours-la-Reine with the wide, tree-bordered carriage drive and promenade of the Grand Cours. Today the Grand Cours bears the name of the old grove beside it and is known as the Champs Élysées. Since Napoleon located his Arc de Triomphe in the center of Le Nôtre's Étoile, Paris has effectively faced west instead of east toward Vincennes, and while the recreational nature of the Grand Cours still lingers in the recently restored promenades and cafés lining the Champs Élysées, the route has also served for the last two hundred years as the city's principal ceremonial thoroughfare.

Under Louis XIV, military engineers began construction of a new system of *boulevarts* (bastions), and from the beginning these were designed to form a green girdle of wide tree-lined carriage drives and promenades, the forerunner of the circumferential modern boulevards built at grade level when the *boulevart* walls were at last removed. Since the construction of these new bastions stretched well into the eighteenth century, it became increasingly apparent that even their modest pretence at defense was both useless and unnecessary, and the city began to spread freely, incorporating into itself the surrounding *faubourgs*. Moreover, it probably became apparent to government authorities that, although they served as a convenient customs barrier and a good lookout for patrolling sentinels posted to keep the peace, the

6.37. View of the Cours-la-Reine, 1616. Engraved by Aveline

walls might even assist rebellion and mob usurpation of power within Paris if a revolutionary force gained control of them. Thus the primary function of the boulevards, or *remparts,* as they continued to be called, was one of recreational circulation, and cafes and other places of entertainment eventually sprang up along the more frequented ones such as the popular Boulevard du Nord.

One can only imagine what Paris might have looked like today had Louis XIV chosen to follow Colbert's advice and made it his capital. Since the king visited the city only four times during the last twenty-two years of his life, it is understandable that Paris received but two new squares during his reign: the Place des Victoires (1682–87) and the Place Louis XIV (1699, today the Place Vendôme). Both were built by Jules Hardouin-Mansart, the court architect, as squares defined by uniform architectural facades, spaces in which to place a statue of the king. Of greater consequence to the welfare of the city's population, Colbert had fifteen new public fountains built and torch lamps installed for nighttime illumination. Nevertheless, not having the king's firm backing for comprehensive urban planning, he left Paris a city better known abroad for its offal-filled streets than for this modicum of public health and security or its isolated architectural gems and new rampart boulevards.

Louis XV (1710–1774) left his mark on eighteenth-century Paris with the construction of several squares, of which the most notable is the Place Louis XV, renamed the Place de la Concorde (1763). Located at the junction of the Tuileries axis with that of the Champs Élysées, it was designed by Jacques-Ange Gabriel (1698–1782) with eight stone pavilions representing the provincial capitals of France. These framed the square; its centerpiece was a bronze sculpture of the king. Because of its prominence and asso-

6.38. Aerial view of the Place de la Concorde, Paris

Below: 6.39. Covent Garden, London. Designed by Inigo Jones. 1639. Painting by Samuel Scott. Mid-18th century

ciation with royalty, it became the site of many guillotine executions during the Revolution, including that of Louis XVI (1754–1792). To replace the central sculpture which had been destroyed during the Revolution, the Obelisk of Luxor, commemorating the deeds of Ramesses II and originally located in front of the Temple of Thebes in Upper Egypt, was presented by the viceroy of Egypt, Muhammad Áli, to the French king Louis-Philippe (ruled 1830–1848) in 1831. This valued gift enabled Paris to follow the example set by Sixtus V in Rome by establishing an Egyptian obelisk as the focus of an important urban square (fig. 6.38; see fig. 4.38).

LONDON'S SQUARES

The fixity of human settlement is such that, unless a powerful authoritarian will can exert control, patterns of land occupancy generally resist radical alteration. Even when opportunities to rebuild anew arise after such calamities as war and fire, in their efforts to re-establish property ownership and a sense of historical continuity and place, people prefer old circulation patterns and building lot configurations to new ones, although the new ones may be considerably more convenient and attractive. In such dire circumstances, people become instinctive preservationists. The urbanistic history of seventeenth-century London proves the point.

London's disastrous fire of 1666 destroyed almost 400 acres within its walls and an additional 60 outside, leaving a huge semicircle of smoldering ruins. In addition to eighty-seven parish churches and many other public buildings including those housing the entire financial and mercantile districts, 13,200 houses went up in flames leaving nearly a quarter million people homeless.[12] While this was a disaster of greater magnitude than the historic loss of the Vesuvian cities in 79 C.E. because of London's larger population, it also provided an opportunity to rebuild the urban core and its surrounding precincts. Following the fire, Christopher Wren, John Evelyn, and others presented plans that incorporated the lessons of both Versailles and Rome. But these were soon shelved, and London rebuilt itself not according to a grand plan, but piece-meal over the next fifty years along the lines of its old streets and lanes.

The walls of London, like those of Paris, gradually fell into disuse, and, with the city's continued residential growth as its population climbed to overtake that of any European city, a number of residential squares were laid out by developers. In Westminster and the West End, as well as in Bloomsbury east of those areas, leaseholds to great mansions and their gardens were sold to building developers, but the landowners' names and titles were commemorated in the new streets and squares that took their place. The notion of the symmetrical planned square with architecturally unified building facades and a ground-floor arcade had been borrowed from Italy by Inigo Jones (1573–1652) when he built Covent Garden as a speculation for the fourth earl of Bedford in 1639 (fig. 6.39). Specifically, the great neo-Palladian architect had modeled his plan for Covent Garden on that of the Piazza d'Arme built by the Medici dukes in the fortress and port town of Livorno at the end of the sixteenth century, a symmetrical square of arcaded buildings (fig. 6.40).[13] Initially an address for the well-born, Covent Garden became a market square in 1671 and,

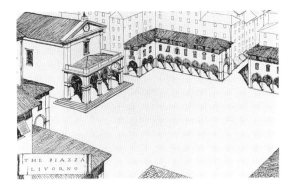

with the licensing of the nearby Drury Lane Theater, the nucleus of the performing arts district that flourished there in the eighteenth century.

At the same time that Covent Garden Piazza (as it was first called) was being built, the layout of another group of speculative houses around Lincoln's Inn Fields was under way. In the early 1660s at Bloomsbury Square, the fourth earl of Southampton set the pattern of residential development that became common in London after the Great Fire as land-owning aristocrats realized the profits to be made by turning landlord. Bloomsbury Square lots varied in size, and leases specified only that houses be reasonably large and of a suitably dignified character. From this point forward, the squares of London assumed a more heterogeneous, less authoritarian appearance than their Continental counterparts. They were greener, too, for, whereas Parisian squares had been planned as public spaces, in London, where there was no tradition of their public use as promenades or arenas for spectacles, they were often designed as fenced and locked gardens, with keys provided only to those whose houses fronted upon them. This difference between the squares of Paris and London was perpetuated in the nineteenth century when Baron Haussmann, Louis-Napoléon's Prefect of the Seine, built several new ones as landscaped islands within Paris's improved circulation system, whereas those of London continued to be planted as quasi-private gardens for adjacent residents.

In the busy building years following the Great Fire, many of the London squares that today contribute greatly to the city's green and pleasant character took shape. With the development of elegant Grosvenor Square between 1725 and 1731, London's largest square with the exception of Lincoln's Inn Fields, Mayfair became the district of choice for many titled people (fig. 6.41). On the neighboring estate to the east, Berkeley Square continued the now-familiar pattern of Georgian town houses facing a common green. With the exception of Covent Garden, which early assumed its character as a public space, most of these greens remained discreetly sequestered behind iron palings and off limits to passersby. It was not until

1832 with the creation of Trafalgar Square, where ten years later the naval victory of Lord Nelson was memorialized with a 145-foot- (44-meter-) high column, that London received a nonresidential public square and urban landmark similar in spirit to the piazzas of Rome.

LONDON PROMENADES

Seventeenth-century London offered other places in which the gregarious could congregate. The same cultural forces that were at work in Paris and elsewhere were at work in London, too, creating a new element of the population attached to the court yet flourishing with growing independence from it. With increased wealth derived from manufacturing and trade and the first wave of riches from overseas colonies, "society" had come into being. The growth of cities during this period was accompanied by a change in their character. They no longer functioned simply as fortified centers of production, exchange, and religious celebration. Cities in the seventeenth century, especially capital cities like London and Paris, became places of pleasure and, to a greater degree than was true of cities since antiquity, places where ideas as well as goods were traded, the wombs of intellectual discovery and ideology. The need of the new leisure class for entertainment as well as for intellectual and social stimulation brought into being new urban forms: the coffeehouse and its French variant the café, as well as the theater and the promenade.

6.40. Piazza d'Arme, Livorno, Italy. c. 1600. This arcaded square is thought to have inspired Henry IV's planned squares in Paris (see figs. 4.48, 4.49). However, the Piazza d'Arme and Covent Garden, which is modeled after it, each form the context of a major public building—Livorno's Duomo and St. Paul's Church—while the Place Royale and the Place Dauphine have no such "centerpiece."

Below: **6.41. Grosvenor Square, London**

6.42. View of St. James's Palace and Pall Mall, London. Painting by William James. c. 1770

6.43. Hyde Park, London. The park's continuing popularity as a place of fashionable parade, an arena for daily exercise and impromptu social encounter, is evident in "Hyde Park, near Grosvenor Gate," 1842, an engraving by Thomas Shotter Boys. Rotten Row, the park's famous equestrian course, is visible on the right.

To conduct business, to display status, to advertise marriageability (or availability if one was a courtesan)—for these and other reasons one needed a public sphere, a defined space where, with predictable regularity, one could be sure of meeting and greeting one's own kind. The promenade, or the parade as it was also called, served this function. In the same way that boulevards came to lose their association with fortifications and began to be built independent of the location of former city walls, malls for promenading—the descendants of the once-popular game of pall-mall, which originated in Italy—became urban features in their own right. Samuel Pepys's diary brings the public life of all these sociable public spaces vividly to life, coloring in their outlines with contemporary observation and anecdotal detail. Pepys and his fellow government servants, together with all elements of society could be seen parading whenever the weather was fine in St. James's Park along Charles II's pall-mall alley, which was surfaced with well-watered pulverized cockleshells. Nearby the king built Catherine Street, named for the queen. It soon assumed its popular name, Pall Mall, as it has been known ever since (fig. 6.42).

Although the royal parks belonged to the crown, it was customary by the seventeenth century for royalty to share them with the public. In Green Park, Charles II enjoyed fraternizing with his subjects as he took his daily stroll along Constitution Hill, as the broad walk at the southern end of the park is still called. In the eighteenth century, Queen Caroline, the wife of George II, had the Queen's Walk built along its less public eastern border, for by that time the park had become crowded with Londoners enjoying themselves as they strolled along its crisscrossing web of gravel paths set amid green grass. During its long history as an urban public space, Green Park also served as a place for military parades, public celebrations, duels, and in the nineteenth century, numerous hot-air balloon ascents.

Long popular as the scene of May Day celebrations, Hyde Park, which had been sold by Parliament in the time of Cromwell, was repossessed in 1660 by Charles II and turned into a resort of fashion (fig. 6.43). The park was enclosed by a brick wall and the Ring, first called the Tour, was laid out by the king as a carriage promenade for the *beau monde*. Rotten Row, a corruption of *route du roi*, the link between Kensington and St. James's Palaces, became the first illuminated thoroughfare in England when William III ascended the throne and, upon taking up residence in Kensington Palace, had some 300 lamps installed in the branches of the trees along its borders as a deterrent to the highwaymen who threatened nighttime security.

Like the gardens of Buckingham Palace today, Kensington Gardens was in the beginning reserved for the private enjoyment of the king and queen. William and Mary had the gardens laid out in the Dutch fashion by Henry Wise (1653–1738) and George London (d. 1714). Considerably altered by Queen Anne, they were not opened to the public until George II permitted "respectably dressed people" to frequent them on Saturdays. By granting this permission he turned the Broad Walk into a fashionable promenade running from north to south in front of the palace.

London, then, was throughout the seventeenth and eighteenth centuries a city growing piecemeal, district by district, as the properties of several noble families who had the good fortune to own land were turned into profitable real-estate speculations. It therefore had no sense of overall order based upon a comprehensive plan. Its character is limned by historical circumstance rather than by a grand design. As will become apparent from an examination of the history of St. Petersburg, bold urban design visions stand a greater chance of realization where there is no preexisting urban fabric and where there is sufficient centralized authority to ensure their construction in accordance with a master plan.

St. Petersburg

If London provides an early example of laissez-faire capitalism as one of the driving forces of city development, St. Petersburg provides its opposite: an autocratic city created by fiat and planned entirely by government decree. The story of its founding is legendary.

We may imagine Peter the Great, the imperious autocrat portayed in Étienne Maurice Falconet's bronze equestrian sculpture and Pushkin's sinister poem *The Bronze Horseman,* bestriding the banks of the Neva, commanding the waves to subside and an army of conscripted serfs to implement his vision of a mighty Baltic port, Russia's "window to the West." The historic decision was made in 1703 after his return from Holland and England where, traveling incognito, he had worked as a ship's carpenter and studied shipbuilding at the Royal Navy's impressive modern dockyard at Deptford. Determined to reconquer the Baltic provinces that had been lost to Sweden, he set about building the Fortress of St. Peter and St. Paul on an island at the mouth of the river. Here the Neva—named for its chief characteristic, mud— had formed a swampy delta. Its branches had created a series of islands that, together with the mainland on the left bank, became the site of the future capital. Only the mightiest act of will bolstered by supreme authority and supported by the callous consumption of virtually unlimited human resources could have turned this desolate northern outpost on a remote fringe of Russia, occupied by only a few rude cottages of Finnish fishermen, into one of the world's most beautiful cities.[14]

Peter's victory over the Swedes at Poltava in 1709 provided the necessary security for him to move the Russian capital from Moscow to St. Petersburg. In spite of uncontrolled periodic disastrous flooding, fires, and wolves roaming the streets, it was soon the home of the imperial family, and a decree of 1716 enjoined a hundred noble families to also take up residence in these Baltic wilds. Another edict that year conscripted 40,000 workers from the provinces. All stone construction was forbidden in Moscow in order to channel both masons and that scarce building material into St. Petersburg. Personally indifferent to luxury, Peter nevertheless imposed building regulations that dictated a standard of grandeur for the palaces that his reluctantly relocated nobles were forced to build.

The appearance of St. Petersburg was to be unequivocally Western. In 1703, Peter appointed the Italian architect Domenico Trezzini (1670–1734) as his first Master of Building, Construction, and Fortification. After 1713, Trezzini was succeeded by the German Andreas Schlüter (c. 1659–1714), who brought in his train several younger architects. These young

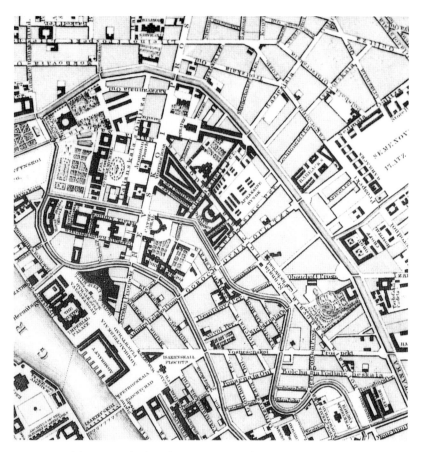

6.44. Plan of St. Petersburg

men were able to provide the talent necessary to keep up the frantic pace of building after Schlüter's death the following year. In 1716, Alexandre Le Blond signed a contract to serve as architect general of St. Petersburg for five years. To carry out his designs he brought with him several skilled artisans and workmen.

Le Blond laid out the Nevsky Prospekt, the northern arm of what was to become three radial avenues focused on the Admiralty, which was topped with a 235-foot- (71.6-meter-) tall spire that, like a magnet, drew the city toward its symbolic and actual *raison d'être,* the great docking facility beside the swift-flowing Neva (fig. 6.44). Stretching for 2.75 miles southeast, the Nevsky Prospekt crossed the Moika River and the Katherine and Fontanka Canals before bending and narrowing somewhat as it continued toward its conclusion at the Alexander Nevsky Monastery. At first it was simply a 115-foot- (35-meter-) wide, straight, stone-paved avenue lined with trees. Then, in the nineteenth century, it was developed into an arcaded shopping street offering English, French, and German luxury goods.

In building St. Petersburg, Peter the Great had envisioned not only a city with the grandeur of Versailles, but one also reminiscent of Amsterdam, another great commercial port. He had especially admired the Dutch city's new series of concentric canals bordered by tree-lined promenades and unbroken rows of town houses, and he had left orders in 1716 that, while he was away with the army, a similar series of canals was to be laid out on Vasilevsky Island. Upon his return two years later he found that the canals were too small to be navigable. They were therefore filled in, and this part of the city acquired instead a uniform grid of streets.

As St. Petersburg became more cosmopolitan, the aristocracy no longer came reluctantly, but gladly forsook their estates for this northern capital with its whirl of social life centered upon the court and the imperial family. A number of Italian architects were commissioned to work alongside the Russian architects to build palaces and otherwise embellish the city. Bartolomeo Rastrelli designed the Winter Palace, now part of the Hermitage Museum, and several other grandiose structures in the Rococo style. Later in the century, under Catherine the Great, the Neoclassicism associated with the French Enlightenment prevailed over this more flamboyant architectural idiom.

In her inaugural year of 1762, Catherine the Great, extolled for having found a city of wood and left one of stone, formed the Commission for the Masonry Construction of St. Petersburg. In keeping with the forceful role of government in controlling the development of St. Petersburg, rules were codified to ensure architectural conformity of building heights and facades.

The elegance of the Russian capital under Catherine the Great lay in the ordered grandeur that resulted from these controls as well as in the city's wide modern streets. It was also apparent in a host of decorative details: wrought-iron grilles and gates, railings and lampposts, trees and statues. Under Czars Alexander I and Nicholas I, the talented architect Carlo Rossi (1775–1849) built Palace Square in front of the Winter Palace, one of the world's largest squares and most impressive public spaces (fig. 6.45).

6.45. Palace Square with the Alexander Column, St. Petersburg

Defined by the curving arms of his General Staff Building, which forms a hemicycle on its southern side, the square is given a central focus by the 154-foot- (47-meter-) tall Alexander Column of polished red Finnish granite, believed to be the largest single stone ever cut.

By the nineteenth century, St. Petersburg had become a pleasure capital for the rich. With its university and Academies of Arts and Sciences, its daily spectacle of carriages and shoppers along Nevsky Prospekt, its theaters and ballet, its German private schools and French restaurants, it was, for those who could afford it, an extremely agreeable and cosmopolitan milieu. Although no one was more aware of the repressive terror that undergirded the city darkly, the poet Alexander Pushkin (1799–1837) gave delighted voice to its violent gaiety, its regimented design, and its military spectacle in *The Bronze Horseman*.

The masters of the modern socialist state who succeeded the czars who built St. Petersburg found its grand design congenial. The heroic scale of St. Petersburg's streets and squares, the regimentation of its architecture, the iconography of power conveyed by its public sculpture—all these brilliantly served as the model that Russia's twentieth-century Communist rulers appropriated in the planning of Moscow and other cities where they wished to proclaim both doctrinaire political authority and a conservative modernity.

By contrast, monumental planning in a symbolic sense held small appeal to the shapers of a democratic country whose fundamental goal was the pursuit of immediate wealth through free enterprise. The opportunities inherent in a seemingly limitless supply of land and the hardships attendant upon occupying it were such that practicality, not pomp, was the order of the day in colonial America. Only when freedom from British rule was achieved did the founders of the new United States, supported in their aesthetic ideals by the presence in their country of French allies following the war for independence, commission an architect from France, Pierre L'Enfant, to prepare a plan for its new capital of Washington, D.C. (see fig. 6.54). As we shall see, this initial exercise in American urban grandeur was confined to this one city and was only fully realized in the twentieth century. For the most part the serviceable grid employed by Spanish colonial settlers proved of equal merit to the British, whose cities became the models for the western expansion of the United States of America after independence was achieved.

III. Nature's Paradise:
America in the Colonial and Federal Periods

The European arrival in America had profound consequences for landscape design. Sixteenth- and seventeenth-century explorers and colonists, whose motives were primarily economic, sought wealth in the form of ore, minerals, timber, and other natural resources. In appropriating a new continent, they had scant regard for the customs, ritual centers, and attitudes toward nature of the native occupants, the traces of whose presence within the landscape were by and large effaced. Spanish, Dutch, French, and English traders and settlers came, some to build towns and farm the land, others to convert souls, trap animals, or mine gold and silver. Although all of these European cultures left their mark, the two principal ones to imprint the American landscape in design terms were the Spanish and the English.

Spanish Colonial Settlements

The first European power to establish settlements in the Americas, Spain began its colonizing activities immediately following Christopher Columbus's momentous discovery. At first, when it was still believed that Columbus's landfall had occurred in the Indies, government-sponsored expeditions were motivated purely by the desire for trade and the appropriation of riches. But the dimensions and natural resources of a vast continent gradually revealed themselves. By 1550, Spanish explorers had ventured from Cuba north to the peninsula they named La Florida, continuing west as far as present-day Arkansas and north along the eastern seaboard of what is now the United States. At the same time, adventurers departing from Mexico City traveled overland into the arid lands that became Texas, New Mexico, and Arizona and by sea up the Pacific coast to the more verdant region that is now California and Oregon. Tales of mythical cities and magical places like the Fountain of Youth and Diamond Mountain were discredited one by one, and by the first decade of the sixteenth century, it was clear that if wealth was to be gained, Spain would have to subjugate this vast territory and build an empire based not on fabulous finds, but rather on the hard work of farming, ranching, and mining. Laying claim to the entire North American continent, Spain began its colonization efforts.

The Spanish strategy of conquest was based upon three distinct types of settlement: the mission; the military *presidio,* or fort; and the civilian *pueblo* or *villa,* as towns were variously called depending upon their size and importance. The missionary spearheaded the campaign to convert native peoples to Catholicism and Spanish cultural mores. The soldier manned the *presidio* and served as the initial secular intermediary with native peoples, protecting the mission and settlement from hostile invasion while establishing contacts with friendly tribes. The colonist came in their wake, building the *pueblo,* establishing civil law, and developing the regional economy.

The Spanish government issued explicit instructions for the layout of these new towns, at first on a case-by-case basis. As settlements multiplied, however, colonial administrators found it necessary to codify their planning prescriptions in a royal ordinance called the *Recopilación de Leyes de los Reynos de las Indias,* or the *Laws of the Indies,* which Philip II promulgated in 1573. Pragmatic in its objectives and designed to create a simple paradigm that could be easily followed by architecturally inexperienced men in remote lands, the *Laws of the Indies* ignored the innovative urban schemes of contemporary late Renaissance planners, opting instead for the ancient Roman formula for military encampments and new towns as set forth by Vitruvius around 30 B.C.E. and summarized by Alberti in his fifteenth-century treatise *De re aedificatoria.* In this way, the orthogonal streets and central forum of the ancient colonial city became the plaza-centered grid settlement of Spanish America.[15]

After the colonists had selected an appropriately healthful site and performed the required rituals—usually the saying of mass—they marked off a rectangular area for the town and built the protective *presidio.* Their next task was to construct a water supply and irrigation system and to lay out and allot fields outside the town. Then they began filling in its outlines, first reserving a central space for a plaza of rectangular proportions, its recommended length, according to the *Laws,* being at least one and a half times its width inasmuch as "this proportion is the best for festivals in which horses are used." Whereas, as discussed in Chapter One, the plazas of the Native American pueblos were cosmologically aligned according to religious custom with each side facing one of the cardinal directions, Spanish colonial plazas had each corner pointing in a cardinal direction because the *Laws* proclaimed that this prevented undue exposure "to the four principal winds." Four main thoroughfares ran from the middle of each side of the plaza across the length and breadth of the town, and the borders of the plaza were defined by secondary streets. The *Laws* directed that other streets be laid out "consecutively around the plaza." This injunction almost invariably resulted in a checkerboard or grid pattern. This grid layout was useful for parceling real estate among the settlers of the *pueblo.* At the same time, it asserted symbolically the authority of the crown over both the settlers and the native population.

Building lots around the plaza were reserved for administrative and other public purposes as well as for shops and dwellings for merchants. The remaining lots in this location were to be distributed by lottery, and the crown held those not distributed for future allocation. It was recommended that the main church be freestanding, sited in an elevated location, and furnished with its own adjacent plaza. The *Laws* further enjoined those responsible for laying out the town to reserve outside the palisade a common large enough so that if the town grew "there would always be sufficient space for its inhabitants to find recreation and for cattle to pasture without encroaching upon private property."

The *Laws* instructed town planners to give the plaza and the four main streets diverging from it arcades "for these are a great convenience for those who resort thither for trade." In Santa Fe, New Mexico, and in other Spanish colonial settlements one may still find sidewalks around the plaza sheltered by *portales,* or porticoes, more rustic in character but nevertheless derived from those found along the principal thoroughfares of ancient Roman and Renaissance cities (see fig. 6.40). These *portales* sometimes extended along the four principal streets as well as along the eight streets running from the corners of the plaza. If the town planners followed the injunction set forth in the colonial ordinance, the *portales* at the corner streets would not obstruct the street crossing, being arranged so that "the sidewalks of the street can evenly join those of the plaza." Particularly after native uprisings made their overseers wary, settlers were directed to fortify the houses around the plaza.

In practice, there were deviations from the rules for town planning set forth in *Laws of the Indies,* but their intentions were honored widely throughout Spain's two hundred years of North American colonization. The Spanish "old towns" of several contemporary cities reflect this heritage, later emphasized by the neo-Spanish-Colonial architecture of many buildings in southern California and throughout the American Southwest. Thus we find at the beginning of the eighteenth century, when new forms of planning inspired by French practice and Italian precedents were changing the appearance of European cities, that such *pueblos* as San Antonio, Texas; Santa Fe, New Mexico; and Los Angeles, California, were being laid out as grid cities with a central plaza.

BRITISH COLONIAL SETTLEMENTS

England's two first American settlements—Jamestown, Virginia (1607), and Plymouth, Massachusetts (1620)—were laid out in a regular fashion as fortified villages within palisaded enclosures. Because of the extreme hardships their settlers endured in inhospitable locations, these villages did not develop into significant towns, much less cities. The colonial governors—or the proprietors in the case of the townships of New England—who laid out subsequent settlements acquired land-planning experience that enabled their communities to succeed better. This planning occurred on a regional scale inasmuch as lands granted by crown charter were distributed to colonists in the form of nucleated farming communities resembling European villages where farmers lived and went into the surrounding countryside to tend their fields.

However, in a land-rich country occupied by independent-minded people already of a migratory disposition, decentralizing forces were immediately at work. Plantation owners who grew tobacco in Virginia and Maryland succeeded in shipping it from their own wharves in spite of the protests of governors who wanted to consolidate colonial trade in port towns; the crown proclamations designating locations for these would-be towns were more than once repealed under pressure. In Massachusetts, following the pacification of the native inhabitants and the failure of the first efforts to perform the work of agriculture and animal husbandry in common, Governor William Bradford (1590–1657), the English Puritan who settled and guided the Plymouth Colony for thirty years, found that in order to tend their stocks of cattle the colonists were taking up residence upon their "great lots," the outlying fields allocated to them. He lamented their desertion of "the town, in which they lived compactly until now," and feared that this population dispersal "will be the ruine of New-England, at least of the Churches of God ther."[16]

NEW ENGLAND TOWNSHIPS

In spite of Bradford's fears, the settlement of the older parts of New England by groups of proprietors who were tied to one another by common religious belief, kinship, and economic interest did result in a village-centered occupancy of the land unlike that of the scattered farmsteads that later became the dominant pattern as the American frontier moved west. For these reasons as well as for security and adherence to tradition, most early New England settlers lived in distinctively defined communities, even as some were dispersing because their agricultural domains and greater opportunities lay at a distance.

Today many of these villages and the towns that grew from them constitute a cherished part of the American landscape. They vary in form but fall roughly into three basic types: "linear" towns such as Salem, Massachusetts; compact "square and gridded" communities such as Cambridge, Massachusetts, and New Haven, Connecticut; and "organic" settlements such as Exeter, New Hampshire; Woodstock, Vermont; and Boston, Massachusetts.

Historic Salem, or its Indian place name, Nehum-kek, by which it was known to Massachusetts Bay Colony settlers, consists of a single irregular street running along high ground between the North and South Rivers. Branching off at intervals on either side of this spine, short streets lead to one or the other river. Along its north side lies the town common, now lined with handsome brick houses.

New Haven was settled in 1638 as a nine-square grid—that is, a square composed of nine blocks, each measuring 825 feet (251.5 meters) square—fitted between two streams entering a harbor on the north shore of Long Island Sound (fig. 6.46). The central square, reserved as a green to be held in common, thus constitutes one-ninth of the town, an unusual amount of public space for that period, even in New England where commons were an important feature of town planning. The meetinghouse, the central institution of the religiously ruled New England community, was always given pride of place in any planning scheme, being located atop a prominent topographical elevation or, in the case of New Haven and many other towns, adjacent to, or within, the central common. Outside the town boundaries lay the fields, which were typically laid out as long narrow strips of land and parceled to proprietors by lottery or some other equitable means. In this suburban zone were additional common lands reserved as cattle pastures and timber lands. As New Haven's population expanded, its green was bisected, with three churches occupying one half, while the other half remained as open public space. In addition, each of its eight remaining blocks was subdivided into four smaller blocks as townsmen surrendered for houses the areas reserved for garden plots. Houses also lined the radial thoroughfares leading from the boundaries of the nine-square grid to the waterfront and to the fields, for at its inception New Haven had attracted more settlers from Massachusetts than the originally planned number of 250. The town's importance increased when, in 1717, the newly founded Yale College was moved from Saybrook to one of the blocks adjacent to the green.

The foresight demonstrated in New Haven's planning and that of other New England towns does not entirely account for their scenic character. The combination of site and architecture, the latter a product of several generations of thoughtfully erected buildings using a limited range of visually pleasing materials, produced the townscape that is admired today wherever it has not been sacrificed to meet the

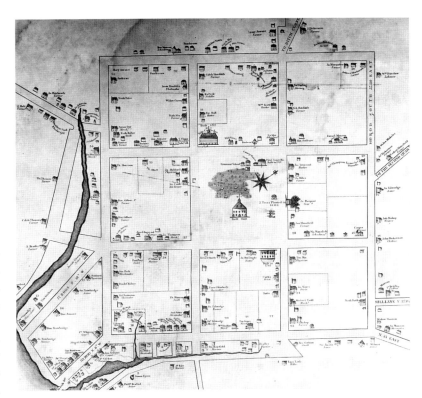

6.46. Plan of New Haven. 1748

needs of the automobile. The ordered serenity of these towns, which are often nestled in the folds of the glaciated New England landscape with its naturally picturesque ponds and hills, provides modern vacationers with a glimpse of an earlier America that is still capable of stirring emotions both patriotic and nostalgic. Save for a few well-tended historic sites, there is little evidence of the rude and cramped houses of the first settlers. Instead, especially in towns where historic preservation is fueled by sufficient affluence, one finds a harmony of later architectural styles. The Neoclassicism favored by the builders of the young republic is seen in columned porticoes and broad pediments, while nearby the turreted solidity of neo-Romanesque rusticated stone betokens the prosperity of the victorious Union after the Civil War when manufacturing wealth made possible the further architectural adornment of this part of the country. But sadly missing are most of the elms that, before the twentieth-century blight of Dutch elm disease, lifted their graceful canopies over village greens, college campuses, and roadways.

This generally satisfying townscape is the result of a consensual attitude on the part of the inhabitants regarding those elements that collectively portray community. Perhaps more than elsewhere in the United States, one apprehends in the physiognomy of the New England town American republican political values. Not surprisingly, the nineteenth-century French student of democracy Alexis de Tocqueville, in tracing the modern origins of this experiment in human governance, emphasized the formative influence of the colonial New England township. But underlying this expression of a democratic social structure was a basic Puritan one that had envisioned a controlled hierarchical ordering of the town.[17] If not prescribed in the manner of the Spanish *Laws of the Indies,* this paradigm did have an ex post facto codification in an anonymous and less detailed document entitled "The Ordering of Towns." It presupposed townships 6 square miles (9.7 square kilometers) in area, which were to be arranged in six concentric zones around a central meetinghouse, with outlying lands held as commons in the manner of English villages before the enclosure movement. The allotment was to be in accordance with "the condition of mankind," or according to social and economic status, with the fifth ring of settlement having the largest and most desirable parcels consisting of 30 to 40 acres of arable land, woodlot, and meadow.

In spite of the lament of Governor Bradford and sermons by divines such as Cotton Mather castigating land-hungry "outlivers," those who settled more than half a mile distant from the meetinghouse, this strongly nucleated ideal was destined to be modified as the first settlers began to produce surplus livestock for sale to newcomers and the need for additional lands grew apace. More and more outlying land became owner-occupied as the commodities it produced engendered trade, and convenience and security dictated that entrepreneurial settlers take up residence on their properties. Thus, from the beginning, commercial forces vied with those that promoted compact community settlement. The spatial configuration of the New England town was therefore the result of the modification of sectarian attitudes and the adaptation of the agrarian mores brought from Old England to a new physical, social, and economic environment.

6.47. Plan of Philadelphia, 1683. Engraved by Thomas Holme

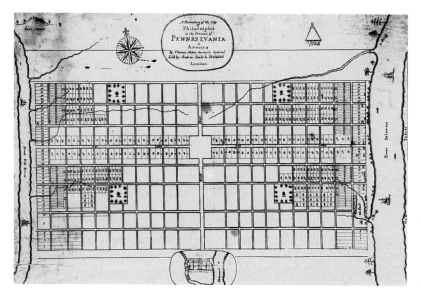

WILLIAM PENN'S "GREEN COUNTRY TOWN"

If sectarian fervor combined with an increasingly trade-oriented population characterized the early settlement of New England, a somewhat different set of values—religious tolerance and avowed commercial enterprise—set the tone of the settlement undertaken by the Quaker colonizer William Penn (1644–1718). Philadelphia remains a testament to his abilities and influence as an urban and regional planner.

As governor and proprietor of Pennsylvania under a charter granted by King Charles II in 1681, Penn approached the task of colonization as an administrator and businessman. He developed a land distribution program that granted city lots on a basis proportionate to the size of a purchaser's overall land holdings. He sent three commissioners with the first group of settlers, enjoining them to select a healthy and navigable site for the city, which they had located by the summer of 1682 on land midway between the Delaware and Schuylkill Rivers.

The plan Penn envisioned for his city was one in which uniform streets were to stretch from the country bounds to the water's edge. With London's Great Fire of 1666 still fresh in his memory, he wrote, "Let every house be placed, if the person pleases, in the middle of its plat, as to the breadth of it, that so there may be ground on each side for gardens or orchards, or fields, that it may be a green country town, which will never be burnt, and always be wholesome."[18] In this fashion did Penn enunciate the ideal that homeowning Americans have embraced over the course of three hundred years—a freestanding house surrounded by its own plot of land. To assist in the task of laying out the new city, he appointed Captain Thomas Holme as surveyor general.

With Penn's arrival in October 1682, the plan for the city began to take shape under his personal direction. He had Holme draw a gridiron bounded on the east by the Delaware and on the west by the Schuylkill, with a central square at the crossing of its two principal axes, Broad Street and High Street (fig. 6.47). Familiar with Lincoln's Inn Fields and Moorfields—open spaces accessible to the general public in London—the city's recently developed private residential squares, and probably at least one of the several post-Great Fire plans calling for urban green space, he directed Holme to place a square within each quadrant of the city. Penn was explicit that they be open to all members of the community, unlike the new London squares, which were reserved for the exclusive use of neighboring property owners.

The public square, along with the freestanding home with its adjacent garden, was Penn's important contribution to the future American cityscape, for the gridiron plan, punctuated with one or more of these green spaces, became the model that settlers applied almost ubiquitously to new communities as they moved westward. Sometimes occupied by courthouses or other public buildings, such squares everywhere denote civic intention and community focus.

As in New Haven, Penn's generously scaled blocks became subdivided as row houses were built along narrow streets inserted where gardens had been intended. This happened also in other cities as population growth accelerated and speculation in urban land increased. Where land speculators platted grids designed to realize a maximum profit from lot sales, the squares of Penn's "green country town" were often eliminated or reduced to a single token public space. There existed, however, another important example of American colonial planning in which a gracious and livable city—Savannah, Georgia—was built and maintained over a long period of time according to the intentions of its founder.

James Oglethorpe's Savannah

In 1732, James Oglethorpe (1696–1785), an English philanthropist and member of Parliament who was interested in prison reform, secured a charter from King George II for the founding of the colony of Georgia. Here he hoped, with a subscription of funds raised from a group of humane aristocrats, to transport incarcerated debtors who wished to seek a fresh start in life as well as persons experiencing religious persecution and others eager for economic opportunity. The following year found him working indefatigably alongside the 114 original colonists, supervising the clearing of a large rectangular area of the tall pine forest where his town was to be laid out along a crescent bend in the Savannah River 10 miles (16.1 kilometers) inland from the sea. A palisade was soon erected and the first houses built even as the terms of property deeds were being defined. These deeds demonstrate the regional scope of Oglethorpe's plan, which granted each settler a house lot measuring 60 by 90 feet (18.3 by 27.4 meters), a 5-acre garden plot, and a 44-acre farm, with the stipulation that he must construct a house within an eighteen-month period and cultivate at least 10 acres of his outlying farmland.

Like Penn, Oglethorpe was familiar with the pattern of residential development in London whereby groups of houses were being built speculatively around green squares, a process that the prosperity of Georgian England had accelerated. He was probably also familiar with the plans for Philadelphia and New Haven. But the original and ingenious feature of his plan for Savannah was the concept of the ward as a group of forty house lots laid out as four "tithings," or blocks of ten houses each, with the

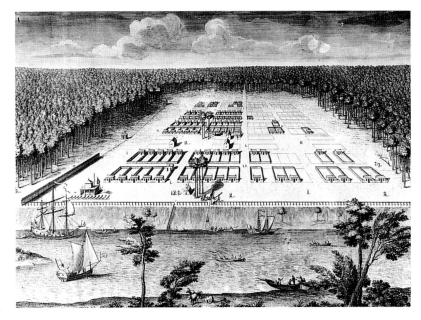

blocks ranged beside a central green, next to two sides of which two large lots were reserved for churches and other public and semipublic buildings such as stores. Savannah therefore was not to be laid out, like Philadelphia or New Haven, as an urban grid with one or more spaces exempted from development; rather the grid was to be formed additively by ward units, each with a green square in the center. This meant that, as the city grew, it could never become a solid urban mass because it would always have an open green square within each new ward (figs. 6.48, 6.49).

Oglethorpe's original vision fortunately remained in effect, determining the character of Savannah's development until the middle of the nineteenth century. A comparison of the town in 1734, when it was undergoing construction, and in its 1855 antebellum state of mature development, when the twenty-four squares had been built, shows how the determined impulse to carve out of the colonial

6.48. View of Savannah, Georgia, by Peter Gordon. Engraved by P. Fourdrinier, 1734

6.49. View of Savannah, Georgia. Lithograph after a painting by J. W. Hill, 1855

wilderness geometrically ordered space could produce within the confines of a purely formulaic plan a city that was unrivaled in its gracious greenness.

AMERICAN COLONIAL GARDENS

Because life for the first American colonists in New England was extremely harsh, such gardens as they made were purely utilitarian, providing food and medicinal herbs. While Puritans may have had little interest in ornamental horticulture, the settlers sent over by the Dutch West India Company remembered from their homeland such small intricate late Renaissance gardens with *parterre* beds, topiary, arbors, and fountains as are seen in the garden pattern books of Hans Vredeman de Vries and Jan van der Groen (see figs. 6.2 and 6.3). Peter Stuyvesant, the Director General of the Dutch West India Company in New Amsterdam between 1646 to 1664, had, for example, next to his residence on the Battery in Manhattan a garden with *parterres* and fruit trees arranged around a simple axis. Most of the Dutch colonists he oversaw, however, practiced a utilitarian horticulture, and early views of the island show several *bouweries,* as they called their small farms with orchards.

Promotional tracts aimed at recruiting colonists extolled the natural bounty of the land, making America sometimes appear as a second Eden. In Virginia and the Carolinas, where climate and soil were especially hospitable for gardening and novel specimens abundant, settlers combined in their gardens the plants grown in their native England with botanical discoveries from their new homeland. Like colonists elsewhere, their interest was primarily in plants that could nourish them or cure their ills. Williamsburg, the colonial capital Governor Francis Nicholson (1655–1738) and his successor Alexander Spotswood (1676–1740) planned with a degree of elegance beginning in 1699, became an important center for the development of gardening in America.

Nicholson, when he was governor of Maryland, had laid out Annapolis in a novel manner for colonial America. His plan for that city featured two large circles and radial steets intersecting grid blocks. Now he brought his planning experience to bear on Williamsburg, achieving a dignified urban design with the Capitol at the eastern end of its principal axis—Duke of Gloucester Street—and the newly founded College of William and Mary at the western. At a right angle to Duke of Gloucester Street, a broad grassy swath known as the palace green led to the site of the Governor's Palace.

When Spotswood came to occupy this mansion in 1710, he continued the axis of the palace green in the gardens he laid out behind it and encouraged as the mark of genteel civilization the planting of orchards and gardens here and at the college (fig. 6.50). An intelligent site planner, Spotswood also helped place several buildings in the new town in relationship to open spaces and view lines. Unfortunately, he abused an informal understanding he had with another prominent colonist, John Custis (1678–1749), when he cut down several more trees than anticipated on the latter's property in order to open up a "visto," probably that along the palace green. He also aroused the ire of the House of Burgesses when he transformed the ravine behind the Governor's Palace into a series of elaborate terraces and built a rectangular canal connected to a fish pond and a large park. The legislators balked at the earth-moving and excavation costs incurred in building "the Fish-Pond and Falling gardens," putting to an end Spotwood's landscaping efforts at Williamsburg, but not before he had set the tone for its future development.

In the affluent western half of the town, colonists laid out utilitarian gardens that were, nevertheless, modeled on those of the Governor's Palace, their straight gravel paths flanked by topiary after the fashion established a few years earlier in the royal gardens of William and Mary and those of the country estates designed during their English reign (see figs. 6.10–6.12). In his garden Custis displayed some of the botanical specimens that were then arousing scientific curiosity as a lively transatlantic seed exchange began to occur. Nearby plantation owners, notably William Byrd and his son, William Byrd II, both members of London's Royal Society, were active in recruiting such naturalists as William Banister (1654–1692) to come to Virginia to study the flora of the region, and their activities also promoted the use of native plants in town gardens. The Byrds' Westover plantation served as a laboratory for botanical experiments in which Banister, who also had his own botanical garden, assisted until his untimely death on a collecting expedition with the elder Byrd.

6.50. Governor's Palace and Gardens, Williamsburg, Virginia

By the middle of the eighteenth century, Williamsburg, like Charleston, had become an important center for the transmission of botanical knowledge among plantation owners, town gardeners, and interested parties back home in England. Many of Williamsburg's gardens were reconstructed by the Rockefeller Foundation beginning in 1926 (see Chapter Fifteen). The landscape architect in charge, Arthur Shurcliff, researched the Dutch-English landscape style of William and Mary prevailing at the time of the town's foundation, studying existing Virginia site plans and archaeological remains. He subsequently created geometric *parterres* and topiary as well as a holly maze in the same configuration as the one of yew at Hampton Court.

The most splendid gardens of the colonial period were those belonging to wealthy southern plantation owners who enjoyed the benefits of a mild climate and were able to employ a large workforce of slaves in garden construction. In the eighteenth century, as Virginia and the Carolinas became the locus of much botanical activity, these southern gardens displayed many plants new to horticulture.

Along the James River in Virginia, tobacco generated the wealth that enabled great estate holders to landscape their properties with graceful terraces leading to river landings, the usual means of approach to a plantation mansion, although they also dignified their inland entrance drives by planting long *allées* of trees on either side. Carter's Grove, the plantation begun in 1751 by Carter Burwell, was ambitiously landscaped in this fashion. Near Charleston, South Carolina, where rice and indigo were the basis of a prosperous colonial economy, the terraced slopes of the gardens above the Ashley and Cooper Rivers were called falls. Many of the once-great gardens that lined the banks of these two rivers succumbed to the American Revolution and the Civil War as well as to natural disasters and the misfortunes of time. There remains, however, one excellent representative example, Middleton Place, which is open to the public. Descendants of the original owner, Henry Middleton, have restored the gardens their ancestor laid out in 1741 beside the Ashley River (figs. 6.51, 6.52).

Although it is an eighteenth-century garden, Middleton Place does not stand within the tradition of contemporary English landscape design, but rather harks back to the earlier style of William and Mary exemplified at Williamsburg. From the Charleston Road on the inland side a long drive becomes a sweeping oval turnaround, carrying the visitor past the stables to the point where the main house once stood. This principal axis continues opposite the house site, becoming the spine of the gardens' most original feature, the falls, a series of five gracefully bowed grassy

6.51. Plan of Middleton Place, near Charleston, South Carolina. Plan drawn by A. T. S. Stoney. 1938

Below: 6.52. Aerial view of Middleton Place gardens

terraces, the curves of which are echoed in the pair of lakes that form the shape of a butterfly where the garden meets the plantation's low-lying rice fields and the causeway leading to the river landing.

Extending over 40 acres, the gardens at Middleton Place were laid out under the supervision of George Newman, a landscape gardener Henry Middleton brought from England. One hundred plantation slaves working for ten years in the nonagricultural season built the impressive green falls and the geometric gardens to the north of the entry lawn, as well as the drives, *allées,* ponds, and long rectangular canal. Newman fitted the gardens into a triangular

6.53. Plan of Mount Vernon by
Samuel Vaughan. 1787

space defined by the edge of the entry lawn, the canal, and the river; they originally contained box-bordered *parterres,* a bowling green, and a mount for viewing the elegantly ornamented landscape and surrounding marshland and rice paddies. A sophisticated means of controlling the alternating water levels required for rice culture also maintained the surface height of Middleton's Butterfly Ponds and tidal mill pond.

Another century was to pass before the descendants of the slaves who had built Middleton Place would be emancipated. It is sobering to remember that the nation's founding father and first president was also a plantation owner whose garden was created with slave labor.

Mount Vernon

George Washington (1732–1799) was a Virginia landowner whose prosperity depended upon revenues derived from agriculture and livestock. His home at Mount Vernon, high above the Potomac, was one of five farms he worked on the banks of the river. As a son of the Enlightenment, he followed with keen interest not only those developments in botanical science that were of benefit to agronomy but also the exciting discoveries that were enriching the palette of ornamental horticulture. Although he lacked Thomas Jefferson's firsthand knowledge of contemporary English and French landscape design, he owned engravings by Claude Lorrain and responded aesthetically to the Picturesque and sublime, which he found at hand in the unspoiled beauties of the American scene. With no more professional advice than that found in his garden books, including a copy of Batty Langley's *New Principles of Gardening,* he fashioned the grounds around his Mount Vernon residence and took considerable pleasure in growing his fruit trees, planting evergreen and flowering shrubs, and propagating plants in his greenhouse.

The drawing by Samuel Vaughan (1787) of Washington's plan for laying out the grounds at Mount Vernon shows the house with its broad veranda facing the river (fig. 6.53). To the rear of the house, a circular drive outlines a round lawn, and a pair of serpentine, symmetrical drives define a large pear- or bell-shaped bowling green before converging in the drive leading to the highway. Two "wildernesses" at its western end and a surrounding belt of trees, many of them native species—crab apple, poplar, locust, pine, maple, dogwood, black gum, ash, elm, holly, mulberry, hemlock, magnolia, laurel, willow, sassafras, linden, arbor vitae, aspen, pine—gave further definition and enclosure to the bowling green. A conservatory housed his collection of rare botanical specimens.

On opposite sides of the bowling green Wash-

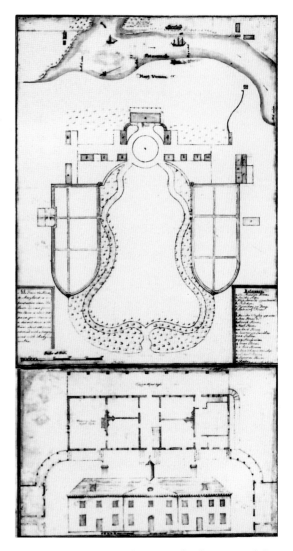

ington placed two gardens, one for flowers and the other for vegetables. He laid these out as geometric beds and screened them from the more informally composed adjacent grounds with walls, curving their ends in order to mediate the visual transition between their lines and those of the serpentine walks. In addition to planting thickly the space in between the garden walls and the bowling green, he constructed two earthen mounds next to the entrance drive, setting weeping willows beside them while leaving open a view of the distant woods.

Two groves of trees flanked the house on the east, and here he turned the sloping grounds into a deer park and planted low-growing shrubs so as not to interrupt the vista framed by his classical portico of rising hills ranging into the blue distance. A ha-ha, or continuous ditch, served as an invisible fence, thus preventing deer from grazing adjacent to the house. In keeping with contemporary practice for rural burial places, Washington set the family tomb on this elevated ground overlooking the river.

The elegance and originality of Washington's landscape design as well as the situation of the house with regard to the scenic beauty of Mount Vernon's eastern view drew rhapsodic praise from more than one visitor. The ornamental garden and its surrounding panoramic scenery were undoubtedly a source of contentment to both Martha and George Washington. At the same time, practical and scientific horticulture continued to be for him a lively passion. He corresponded with nurserymen and botanists in America and abroad and placed orders for trees, shrubs, and seeds. He visited the gardens of the Philadelphia plantsman John Bartram and the newly established Prince nursery in Flushing, Long Island.

Washington may perhaps be credited as being the father of that important national institution, the American lawn. Another contemporary visitor, Julian Niemcewicz, a Polish aristocrat, called Mount Vernon's grass "a green carpet of the most beautiful velvet." Niemcewicz also remarked on the beautiful tulip trees (*Liriodendron tulipfera*), magnolias (*Magnolia virginiana*), "the splendid catalpa not yet in flower" and "the New Scotland spruce of beautiful dark green, and many other trees and shrubs, covered with flowers of different hues, planted so as to produce the best of color-effects." He ended his encomium, written in 1798, by declaring that "the whole plantation, the garden, and the rest prove well that a man born with natural taste may guess a beauty without having ever seen its model."[19]

WASHINGTON, D.C.

Unable on political grounds to choose as a national capital one among the colonial cities of the thirteen states that formed the original federation, the founders of the new nation decided for reasons both practical and symbolical to create an entirely new city in the sparsely settled countryside bordering Maryland and Virginia. Shortly after Congress enacted the legislation that created a federal district in 1790, Washington

retained Pierre Charles L'Enfant (1754–1825) to prepare a plan for it (fig. 6.54). L'Enfant, a French artist and architect who had come to America as a volunteer in the cause of the Revolution, had risen to the rank of major in the Corps of Engineers. After the war, he stayed on to find work in the new United States. It was a time when other young French professionals, deprived of their former *ancien régime* patrons by the revolution in France, were emigrating to the burgeoning eastern seaboard cities in this country. Upon hearing of the decision to establish a new capital, L'Enfant, who was designing and remodeling mansions in New York City, wrote to Washington offering to draw up a plan for the new city. In accepting the French architect's offer, Washington, whether he realized this irony or not, was, in effect, importing a planning vision expressive of autocratic monarchy as the paradigm for a new kind of national grandeur based upon the principles of revolution and the Enlightenment.

L'Enfant had, in fact, spent eight of his boyhood years at Versailles where his father, Pierre L'Enfant, was employed in decorating the building of the Ministry of War. He had subsequently enrolled in the Royal Academy of Painting and Sculpture in Paris and was therefore aware of all the developments, both royal and private, to embellish that capital. His first assignment from Washington was to assess the topographic qualities of the site, and in accordance with the theory of Dezallier d'Argenville, the plan that he proposed did not imply the arbitrary imposition of a preconceived scheme upon nature, but rather used existing landforms as the basis of design. In particular, Jenkin's Hill, the area's highest eminence, was singled out as the "pedestal waiting for a superstructure," the suggested site for the United States Capitol in the memorandum that L'Enfant submitted with his final version of the plan in August 1791.[20]

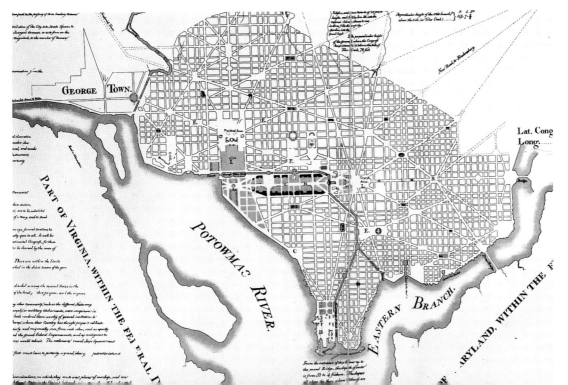

6.54. Plan of Washington, D.C. (detail). Designed by Pierre Charles L'Enfant. 1791

L'Enfant's plan disposed buildings and streets in a manner that brought the various elements of the union—executive and legislature as well as the several states—into a subtly conceived iconographic federation.[21] Like Thomas Jefferson, who had also drawn up a plan for the new capital in 1791, L'Enfant proposed a street grid. But instead of Jefferson's uniform grid, L'Enfant's was overlaid with another diagram consisting of squares and circles connected by diagonal avenues. The plan was comparable to that of L'Enfant's boyhood town of Versailles, a grid punctuated with squares and set within a framework of superimposed diagonal axes.

Although the urban scale fostered by an ambitious monarch at Versailles was expansive, that of Washington, D.C., was more so. The new capital city set at the edge of a vast continent was proportioned to reflect the the opportunity of abundant untenanted land as well as the ambitions of its founders. The major avenues were 160 feet (49 meters) wide, with 80 feet (24 meters) reserved for the roadbed and 30 feet (9 meters) for flanking walkways. These walkways were defined by double rows of trees, and there was an additional 10-foot strip separating the trees from the adjacent building lots on either side.

These great tree-lined avenues were named for the then-existing states and grouped roughly according to their geography with the northeastern states in the northern part of the district, the mid-Atlantic states in the center and the southern states in the southeastern section. Pennsylvania Avenue, the corridor linking the Capitol on Jenkin's Hill and the President's House, which was sited on an alluvial escarpment sloping up from the Potomac, was given pride of place, thereby honoring the importance of that state as host to the signing of the Declaration of Independence and the Constitutional Convention. Similarly, the intersection of New York Avenue with the square in which the President's House was located commemorated New York City's former status as the capital of the Continental Congress and the site where Washington took the presidential oath of office.

The Mall (abbreviated from Pall Mall) was described by L'Enfant as a "grand Avenue, 400 feet in breadth, and about a mile in length, bordered with gardens, ending in a slope from the houses on each side."[22] This Mall, which in L'Enfant's words would give Washington "a superiority of agreements" over most other cities, was to be the home of "theaters, assembly halls, academies"—purpose-built structures catering to the entertainment, social, and intellectual needs of a democratic society. L'Enfant's plan also included Judiciary Square, the site chosen for the Supreme Court, and fifteen other squares. These

were to be assigned to the then-existing states (Kentucky and Tennessee had recently joined the thirteen colonial states that formed the union) with the hope that their citizens would appropriate, through private subscription, funds for their improvement.

In brief, given the equivalent of a blank slate upon which to work, L'Enfant transcended the conjoined garden-town model of his native Versailles, creating in Washington, D.C., a city with many gardens within it. This combination of green openness and urban monumentality constitutes the American capital's uniqueness.

It is clear from the foregoing that cities were developing in a manner that made them physically and conceptually different from their predecessors. They were expanding and becoming ungirdled, their walls torn down, a physical metaphor perhaps for the way in which philosophers were embracing open-ended scientific inquiry. Furthermore, in the eighteenth century, their cultural contents were enlarged as new institutions were incorporated into the urban fabric. Formerly the province of princes or private universities, botanical and zoological gardens, libraries, museums, theaters, and opera houses were now considered the rightful legacy of the urban bourgeoisie. A fundamental result of the American and French Revolutions was the creation of a sense of popular entitlement. By the nineteenth century, cultural institutions were considered an essential part of the public domain. One institution, the public park, became an especially important element in the altered social structure of cities. From its inception, one American city, Washington, D.C., contained many parklike elements; in building Central Park a little over a half century later New York City spearheaded a movement for the creation of public parks throughout the nation, in which the notion of *rus en urbe,* an artful fusion of country and city, was promoted as an essential moral and public health benefit.

In summary, the urban fabric was becoming more loosely woven and of more generous dimensions. As cities grew, tore down their walls, and blurred the line between urban and rural, the human attitude toward nature was significantly transformed. The spreading city gradually engulfed the rural countryside, and nature became an increasingly important component within the urban framework. The creation of naturalistic parks, however, did not occur without a cultural shift. That change was becoming apparent in the relaxation of French landscape design norms at the end of the seventeenth century. But to grasp the character of this change more fully, we must turn to eighteenth-century England.

1. Its illustrations of plans for the design of palaces, bridges, and ornamental temples would, however, be wedded to landscape design in eighteenth-century England when these Palladian elements were incorporated into an Arcadian vision of perfected nature following the publication of the immensely influential translation, *The Four Books of Architecture,* in 1716.

2. John Evelyn, traveling abroad and deeply interested in horticulture and gardens, published an earlier translation of this work in 1643: *The Compleat Gard'ner, Fruit and Vegetable Gardens.*

3. In all these precepts Dezallier is echoed by Alexander Pope who in lines 50–56 of his *Epistle to Lord Burlington,* the creator of Stowe, entreated:

> In all, let Nature never be forgot.
>
> But treat the Goddess like a modest fair,
>
> Nor overdress, not leave her wholly bare;
>
> Let not each beauty ev'rywhere be spy'd,
>
> Where half the skill is decently to hide.
>
> He gains all points, who pleasingly confounds,
>
> Surprises, varies, and conceals the bounds.

In the English translation of Dezallier's work, he seems, in fact, almost to be advocating the style we associate with that country when he commends the siting of a garden so as to obtain "the pleasure of seeing, from the end of a walk, or off a terrace, for four or five leagues round, a vast number of villages, woods, rivers, hills and meadows, with a thousand other varieties that make a beautiful landscape." See John James edition (1728), p. 13.

4. The text of this essay can be found in John Dixon Hunt and Peter Willis, *The Genius of the Place: The English Landscape Garden 1620–1820* (New York: Harper & Row, 1975), pp. 51–56.

5. John Dixon Hunt gives scholarly and convincing explication of Italian influence upon the English landscape in *Garden and Grove: The Italian Renaissance Garden in the English Imagination: 1600–1750* (Princeton, New Jersey: Princeton University Press, 1986). This study demonstrates the assimilation of both Italian forms and Italian spirit into English garden style.

6. See John Dixon Hunt, *Garden and Grove,* p. 135.

7. Fischer von Erlach's *Entwurf einer historischen Architektur* (1721) was the first architectural treatise to depict exotic struc-

tures in the Egyptian, Chinese, and Islamic styles. Published in German and French and translated into English in 1730, it was influential in bringing about the taste for exoticism prevalent in rococo architecture. See Dora Wiebenson, *The Picturesque Garden in France* (Princeton, New Jersey: Princeton University Press, 1978), pp. 95–96.

8. See Victoria M. Siu, "China and Europe intertwined: a new view of the European sector of the Chang Chun Yuan," *Studies in the History of Gardens and Designed Landscapes,* 19:3/4 (July–December 1999), pp. 376–393.

9. See Vincent Scully, *Architecture: The Natural and Manmade* (New York: St. Martin's Press, 1991), Chapter 10, for a provocative discussion of this subject. See also Spiro Kostof, *The City Shaped: Urban Patterns and Meanings Through History* (Boston: Little, Brown and Company, 1991), Chapter 3.

10. Vauban was probably acquainted with Le Nôtre, having been assigned 30,000 soldiers in 1684 for the purpose of constructing a massive embankment and an aqueduct over 3 miles (5 kilometers) long to divert a stream from the Eure River to furnish the fountains at Versailles, which, even after the construction of the Machine of Marly, did not have sufficient water for their simultaneous operation. While Vauban preferred a conventional grid layout inside his citadels, radial streets such as those of Palmanova in Italy, the classic prototype of a polygonal fortress town, like the radial *allées* to be found in French seventeenth-century gardens, supplied a more effective means of ordering circulation for rapid defense and avoiding awkwardly shaped interior blocks.

11. Reconstructed several times, this fountain was transformed in the eighteenth century into the extravagantly baroque Fountain of Trevi.

12. Christopher Hibbert, *Cities and Civilization* (New York: Weidenfeld and Nicolson, 1986), p. 139

13. Livorno is thought to have also been the inspiration for Henri IV's planned squares in Paris. The Piazza d'Arme and Covent Garden, however, form the context of a major public building—Livorno's Duomo and St. Paul's Church—while the Place Royale and the Place Dauphine have no such monumental architectural focus.

14. St. Petersburg is often called "a city built

on bones." Estimates vary as to the exact number of ill-clad, ill-fed conscripted workers who died of cold, dysentery, malaria, scurvy, and other causes; the number may have been 25,000 to 30,000, although in Peter's day the figure was said to be 100,000.

15. For a good explanation of the *Laws of the Indies* and their Roman antecedents, see John W. Reps, *The Making of Urban America: A History of City Planning in the United States* (Princeton, N.J.: Princeton University Press, 1982), chap. 2, pp. 26–32. The quoted passages in my text derive from this source; see also Dora P. Crouch, "Roman Models for Spanish Colonization" in *Columbian Consequences, Volume 3, The Spanish Borderlands in Pan-American Perspective,* ed. David Hurst Thomas (Washington : Smithsonian Institution Press,1991), chap. 2, pp. 21–35.

16. William Bradford, *History of Plymouth Plantation,* as quoted in John Reps, *The Making of Urban America: A History of City Planning in the United States* (Princeton, New Jersey: Princeton University Press, 1965), p. 119.

17. See Stilgoe, *Common Landscape of America, 1580 to 1845* (New Haven: Yale University Press, 1982), p. 43 ff. for the development and transformation of the New England settlement pattern.

18. "Instructions Given by me, William Penn . . . to . . . my Commissioners for the Settling of the . . . Colony . . . ," Samuel Hazard, *Annals of Pennsylvania, from the Discovery of the Delaware, 1609–1682* (Philadelphia: Hazard and Mitchell, 1850), pp. 527–30.

19. Julian Ursyn Niemcewicz, *Under Their Vine and Fig Tree,* as quoted in Mac Griswold, *Washington's Gardens at Mount Vernon: Landscape of the Inner Man* (Boston: Houghton Mifflin Company, 1999), p. 32.

20. See John W. Reps, *Monumental Washington* (Princeton, New Jersey: Princeton University Press, 1967), p. 16, for this and other details of L'Enfant's memorandum.

21. For much of what follows I am indebted to the scholarship of Pamela Scott of Cornell University, whose essay "'This Vast Empire': The Iconography of the Mall, 1791–1848" is one of the Symposium Papers XIV of the Center for Advanced Study in the Visual Arts published in *The Mall in Washington 1791–1991,* ed. Richard Longstreth.

22. As quoted in Reps, op. cit., p. 21.

CHAPTER SEVEN

SENSE AND SENSIBILITY: LANDSCAPES OF THE AGE OF REASON, ROMANTICISM, AND REVOLUTION

The concept of landscape as varied and diverse scenery to be contemplated and appreciated rather than nature demanding to be tamed and ordered, was a novel one at the dawn of the eighteenth century. Both poetry and the development of landscape painting as a specific genre stimulated and influenced a growing taste for rural scenery and landscape designs that reflected the mind's sensations and moods.

With the couplet that serves as his memorable epitaph—"Nature and nature's laws lay hid in night,/God said, 'let Newton be,' and all was light"—poet, essayist, and garden enthusiast Alexander Pope (1688–1744) epitomized the place in history of the great English physicist and mathematician Sir Isaac Newton (1642–1727). With the discovery of the optical properties of light, definition of the laws of motion, development of an infinitesimal calculus, and formulation of the law of universal gravitation, Newton effectively laid the foundations of modern science. What followed was an unprecedented confidence in human reason. Newton fathered the Enlightenment and was a correspondent and later president of the Royal Society, which promoted open-ended scientific discovery in an era when the universities still taught according to an Aristotelian pedagogy that presupposed the systematization of scholarship within an all-encompassing, self-contained framework.

Newton's contemporary John Locke (1632–1704) was a philosopher whose vision of epistemology, politics, education, and medicine helped lay the groundwork for a new human psychology as well as for a new empirical approach to science. Taking issue with Descartes's belief in the mind as a repository of innate ideas, he declared that, to the contrary, all knowledge of the world must rest on sensory experience. This concept of the mind as an instrument for inductive reasoning and a theater for personal experience,

rather than as a receptacle for revealed Truth and immutable law, had an important effect on garden design in the eighteenth century as landscapes were contrived to furnish the sensate mind with specific mental associations and impressions.

As a physical manifestation of the intellectual philosophy laid out in Locke's *Essay Concerning Human Understanding* (1690), and the consequent authority granted to individual sensibility, the garden assumed a new character and function. Its role as a place of authoritarian power, display, and social entertainment was diminished as it became a place of meditation, reflection, and friendship. Locke provides the key to understanding the emphasis upon the associative potential of garden scenes in the eighteenth century. As the intellectual tradition of Neoplatonic classicism waned and landscape design based upon the notion of an underlying normative order of harmonic proportion ceased to be influential, the desire to produce stimuli for a wide range of mental experiences and emotions fostered a new kind of garden making. Its orientation toward sensibility, rather than abstract beauty, caused patrons and designers to value ancient architectural styles, ruins, commemorative monuments, and a richly varied natural scenery. These provoked admiration and reflection, induced moral instruction, and created pleasurable surprise.

The intellectual freedom engendered by Locke's fresh examination of the workings of the human mind fostered and supported the contemporary climate of political change. Locke was taken into the household of Baron Ashley (later the first earl of Shaftesbury) as a physician. He proved to be an influential confidant of that statesman as well, working toward the goals of increased civil liberty, constitutional monarchy, parliamentary rule, religious toleration, Protestant succession, and mercantile trade. Thus, although the actual gardens of his own day were the French-inspired ones of the Restoration and the Anglo-Dutch gardens of William and Mary, Locke's belief in political freedom, together with his seminal ideas on sensory awareness, provided the intellectual soil for the gardens of Georgian England. The result was a more naturalistic style, with architectural and ornamental elements used as images to stimulate ideas of a historical, ethical, partisan, or sentimental nature, thus promoting the proud ideal of the country itself as a kind of libertarian garden.

Jean-Jacques Rousseau (1712–1778), in his philosophical and political discourses on the importance of reverie and the power of the imagination, extended Locke's influence. The mind as a self-aware organ, capable of feats of intuition as well as reason, could produce visions of a more perfect human society. Inspired by images of ancient Sparta and republican Rome as well as of his native city of Geneva, he set forth in *The Social Contract* (1762) a doctrine of human equality and political democracy.

Believing in the innate goodness of "natural man" and in the inspirational character of nature, Rousseau became a prophet not only for the political revolutionaries who read in him their own social visions, but also of Romanticism. This movement, which gained force at the end of the eighteenth century and extends into our own day, posed a spiritual counterbalance to the scientific rationalism of the Enlightenment. Emotion and visionary intuition as a mode of human perception became as important as thought and rational calculation. Rousseau's philosophy, which enlarged the freedom Locke had granted the senses, was instrumental in reinvesting classicism with poetic visions of a lost Golden Age. It is understandable, therefore, that the eighteenth-century garden—a place particularly congenial to reverie, recollection, reflection, and imaginative participation in an ideal world beyond "corrupt" civilization—owed a debt to his theories. Appropriately, it was in the romantically conceived garden of the Marquis de Girardin at Ermenonville that Rousseau sought refuge at the end of his life.

Rousseau was the intellectual heir not only to Locke, but also to Anthony Ashley Cooper, third earl of Shaftesbury (1671–1713), an Enlightenment writer who, like Rousseau, believed in the innate goodness of natural man and of nature. Shaftesbury saw landscapes as having personality; he cried out to the "Genius of the Place,"[1] the spirit that interacts with the human mind, eliciting emotions, fostering perceptions, stimulating both memory and curiosity. Shaftesbury advocated grottoes, cascades, and other dramatically charged landscape forms as a means of stimulating mental associations with nature's mysteries. His thoughts influenced Addison and Pope, writers whose garden theories were influen-

tial at the time when a series of emblematically significant English gardens—including most notably Stowe and Castle Howard—were being created.

As the associative potential of gardens to thematically portray a particular ideology became less compelling and the enclosure movement gathered force, English landscape design tradition evolved into the abstractly expressive style of "Capability" Brown and, subsequently, into the Picturesque style with its Rococo inflection, which proved especially popular in France, where the style's variant of the *jardin anglais* was termed the *jardin anglo-chinois*. The Picturesque theorists who set themselves in opposition to Brown engendered a great deal of spirited debate because the eighteenth-century garden remained an arena of aesthetic idealism even after it had become less didactically explicit. The relationship between landscape and political and intellectual philosophy was important not only in Europe but also in the newly formed United States of America where Thomas Jefferson imaginatively took up the task of garden design while also shaping a vision for an agrarian nation of continental dimensions.

Perhaps the most important eighteenth-century minds besides Rousseau's to further the trend toward Romanticism in the West and to anticipate the coming age's commitment to industrial capitalism and democracy were those of the German polymath and poet Goethe and the seminal English poet Wordsworth. Although both had practical experience in garden design, their influence was more broadly cultural. Goethe saw nature as a source of experiential ecstasy that could, if carried to excess as was the tendency of his time, be debilitating as well as exhilarating. In *Faust Part II* he also anticipated the dark Romanticism implicit in Nietzsche's notion of a Superman. By portraying his famous protagonist in the guise of industrial developer—Faust's ultimate quest for experience and ascendance over nature and the rest of humankind—Goethe foresaw the exponential release of new sources of energy and capitalist power that would occur as the Industrial Revolution gained momentum. Wordsworth's poems also encouraged intense and intimate communion with and reflection upon nature. For Wordsworth, love of nature was inevitably conjoined with reverence for the human mind, the noble instrument of Lockean perception, without which nature's marvelous beauty would be as naught. In addition, Wordsworth fostered empathy for common humanity, finding simple, honest beauty in the quotidian experience of ordinary lives. Thus, Goethe and Wordsworth are pivotal, carrying forward into the nineteenth century the strikingly important eighteenth-century concept that "the genius of the place" and human genius, a gift to all mortals, are inextricably allied.

I. The Genius of the Place: Forging a New Landscape Style through Literature, Art, and Theory

Many advocates of the naturalistic garden read into John Milton's description of Eden in *Paradise Lost* a vision of a new style innocent of "nice Art / In Beds and curious Knots . . . . / A happy rural seat of various view . . . ."[2] But Alexander Pope was the poet most responsible for turning English garden design in a different direction. By his writing and example, Pope actively publicized the style of landscape design favored by the Whig aristocracy and gentry as well as their literary and artistic friends. These Whig landowners, often with Pope's advice, initiated projects that wed English taste for country houses in the architectural style of Andrea Palladio with English scenery, creating landscapes that attempted to evoke "the genius of the place."

Their creation of a new landscape style was less radical, and more evolutionary, than subsequent chauvinistic generations would like to believe. Le Nôtre's follower Antoine-Joseph Dezallier d'Argenville (1680–1765) published in 1712 an English edition of his 1709 influential treatise *La Théorie et la pratique du jardinage* in which he proposed that art give way to nature. The variety and irregularity he advocated within his otherwise geometrical plans showed the gradual relaxation of Louis XIV's authoritarian style around the time of the king's death when a more liberal culture began to be reflected in all the arts. While envisioning a different end from that which Pope had in mind when advising Lord Burlington to "Consult the Genius of the Place in all," it was Dezallier, not an Englishman, who first suggested the ha-ha, a continuous ditch that acted as a sunken fence permitting the visual unification of the garden and its surrounding countryside. But the naturalistic style soon became almost exclusively identified with England. This was due substantially to the pains Whig aristocrats took to express belief felt in their country's civil liberties.

Literary Proponents of a New Style

Joseph Addison (1672–1719) in his essays in *The Tatler* and *The Spectator* argued for a kind of landscape improvement that was anti-authoritarian and practical. He thought that "a Man might make a pretty Landskip of his own Possessions" merely by planting oaks on his hilltops, recognizing the beauty of his willow-filled marshes and fields of grain and improving these and his wildflower meadows by maintaining the paths between them. He scorned Dutch taste, deploring the fact that "Our Trees rise in Cones, Globes, and Pyramids . . . [with] the Marks of the Scissars on every Plant and Bush."[3] The liberation of the English garden from artifice and constraint in the eighteenth century mirrored, in Addison's mind, the country's freedom from autocratic rule.

Addison recommended to his readers the gardens of China, which "conceal the Art by which they direct themselves."[4] Chinese porcelains were beginning to appear in England with the burgeoning of the export trade, and Matteo Ripa's engraved landscape views, reputedly the first illustrations of Chinese gardens to reach the West, were in the hands of Lord Burlington after 1724. Addison's recommendation of the apparent artlessness of Chinese gardens as a stimulant to the "Imagination" prodded landowners to new possibilities. Like the "fantastical phenomenon" discussed by Locke in *Some Thoughts on the Conduct of the Understanding in the Search of Truth* (1690), they provided images and, thereby, a variety of sensory impressions that induced in the mind a state of reverie. Thus, the need arose for a shifting panorama of visual associations to feed the voracious human imagination.[5]

The ingredients for sensory entertainment of the imagination lay no farther away than the fields and libraries of the great country estates. In reading the ancient Greek and Roman poets, especially Virgil, a rusticating aristocrat could find support for delighting in simple rural scenes, for as Addison remarked, "Virgil has drawn together, into his *Aeneid*, all the pleasing Scenes [that] his Subject is capable of admitting, and in his *Georgics* has given us a Collection of the most delightful Landskips that can be made out of Fields and Woods, Herds of Cattle, and Swarms of Bees."[6]

The Whig landowner to whom Addison and Pope appealed liked to see himself as a Horace or a Pliny the Younger, a practitioner of an eighteenth-century version of *otium,* the use of rural leisure as an intellectual stimulus, when he returned to his estate after a term in Parliament. His sympathy with classical subjects and appreciation of the relaxed relationship that existed between art and nature in Roman times had been nourished by a receptive reading of the ancient poets and statesmen. The agricultural self-sufficiency of Pliny's villas, their function as places of private retirement and social entertainment, their attention to human comfort and scenic prospect—all these things inspired an agrarian emphasis in eighteenth-century English gardens. This, in turn, influenced the emblematic character of garden ornament as numerous statues of Ceres, Flora, and Bacchus took up residence in English fields along-side of those traditional garden deities, Pan and Venus. So compelling was the hold exerted by Rome on the eighteenth-century English imagination that Richard Boyle, third earl of Burlington (1695–1753) financed Robert Castell's publication in 1728 of *Villas of the Ancients,* a reconstruction in plan (somewhat mistakenly along symmetrical Palladian lines) of Pliny the Younger's two villas, Tusci and Laurentinum.

Because of this sympathy for the poets of the early Roman Empire, the first two decades of the eighteenth century in England are sometimes called an Augustan Age. In keeping with his self-image as a latter-day Augustan at the moment in history when England was on the verge of garnering an empire, the Whig lord's great house was frequently designed in the Palladian style. The simple dignity of this form of classical architecture and its relatively modest scale evoked more effectively the virtues of the antique world than did the more flamboyant and grandiose architecture of the contemporary Baroque style.

An amateur architect and the center of an influential artistic and literary coterie, Lord Burlington created his villa at Chiswick as a small-scale version of Palladio's Villa Rotonda (fig. 7.1). The landscape he created there over a twenty-year period beginning in 1725 pioneered the marriage of a symmetrical Palladian house with an artfully irregular landscape that nevertheless preserved elements of Continental classical order. Within the garden were winding paths and long perspectival corridors of greenery framing obelisks and several small Palladian temples and pavilions.

Other Whig lords were also amateurs in the original sense of the word: lovers of literature and the arts and sciences. They were students of the classics, travelers abroad and connoisseurs of painting, sculpture, and architecture. In addition, they were active on behalf of liberal reform and jealous guardians of recently granted political freedoms (including the freedom to disagree overtly with their government). Owners of large tracts of newly enclosed rural land, they solicited and implemented the advice of their literary mentors. Their patronage of a new generation of designers transformed garden design from an art based on architectural geometry to one based to a large degree on techniques of painterly composition. Their gardens were no longer created with "rule and line," but rather as a painter would compose a subject on a canvas. In them, poetry and history were employed as resources for various thematic itineraries.

As we walk today through some of these now-historic English gardens, it is difficult to remember how filled with associative meaning they were to their first visitors. Indeed, even by the middle of the eighteenth century, as we shall see, general acquaintance

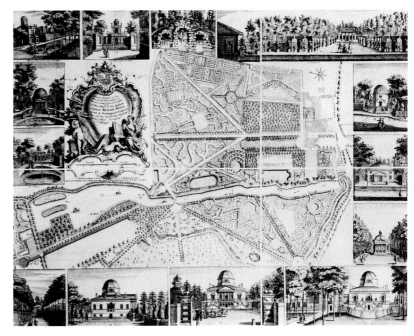

7.1. Plan and vignettes of Chiswick, London. Gardens developed by Richard Boyle, 3rd Earl of Burlington. 1718–35. Further developed with William Kent after 1735. Engraving by John Rocque, 1736

with old mythologies and their imagery was disappearing and the emblematic character of landscape was being replaced by a less didactic approach to design, one that the garden historian John Dixon Hunt calls "expressive." This type of garden relied less on such keys to understanding as Cesare Ripa's *Iconologia: or Moral Emblems* and more completely on nature unadorned, but carefully arranged, for its expressive effect.[7]

PAINTING AND POETRY AS INSPIRATION FOR LANDSCAPE DESIGN

Although we have used the term *landscape design* throughout this book to define the professional activity associated with the creation of gardens, parks, and urban plans, the word *landscape* as applied this way gained currency only in the eighteenth century. Addison led others in using it to imply the arrangement of landscape forms so that they resembled painting. The educated Whig aristocrats who spearheaded the evolution of a naturalistic idiom of gardening in the first decades of the eighteenth century did so in conscious imitation of the landscape paintings they collected. The French seventeenth-century painters Claude Lorrain (1600–1682) and Nicolas Poussin (1594–1665) were especially esteemed; Claude in particular embodied for these lords the spirit of Virgil and a vanished Golden Age, the aura of which they had experienced as travelers in the Roman Campagna (fig. 7.2).

Like Poussin, Claude had lived and painted in Rome. He painted figures in a half-wild bucolic landscape within which rose simple cubic peasant structures and imaginary temples based on ancient ruins. Mythological in subject matter, they exude the atmosphere of Arcadia and are reminiscent of the poetry

7.2. Claude Lorrain, *Landscape Near Rome with a View of the Ponte Molle.* 1645. City Museum and Art Gallery, Birmingham, England

of Virgil. Narrative association, as much as a new relationship between art and nature, would inspire the design of Stowe and Stourhead, Painshill and Esher Place. These gardens were arranged as theaters of meditation, a series of staged scenes where the human visitor was both spectator and actor. But unlike the theater, where pastoral dramas were enacted before the stationary spectator, here the viewer moved from scene to scene, and the scenes themselves were only allusive settings in which the dramatic action existed solely in the mind of each visitor. Indeed, the human mind itself was the protagonist in these green theaters.

Alexander Pope both promoted the new concept of gardening in print and demonstrated it in his own garden adjacent to his Thames-side villa at Twickenham. He compressed into pithy couplets in *An Epistle to Lord Burlington* his philosophy of garden composition, still perhaps the most succinct and forceful prescription for translating Lockean psychology, Virgilian poetry, and Claudian painting into landscape design:

> To build, to plant, whatever you intend,
> To rear the column, or the arch to bend,
> To swell the terrace, or to sink the grot;
> In all, let Nature never be forgot.
> But treat the goddess like a modest fair,
> Not over-dress, not leave her wholly bare;
> Let not each beauty every where be spied,
> Where half the skill is decently to hide.
> He gains all points, who pleasingly confounds,
> Surprises, varies, and conceals the bounds.
> Consult the genius of the place in all,
> That tells the waters or to rise, or fall,
> Or helps the ambitious hill the heavens to scale,
> Or scoops in circling theatres the vale;

> Calls in the country, catches opening glades,
> Joins willing woods, and varies shades from
>   shades,
> Now breaks, or now directs, the intending lines;
> Paints as you plant, and as you work, designs.
> Still follow sense, of every art the soul,
> Parts answering parts shall slide into a whole,
> Spontaneous beauties all around advance,
> Start, ev'n from difficulty, strike from chance;
> Nature shall join you; Time shall make it grow
> A work to wonder at—perhaps a Stowe.[8]

The English anecdotist Joseph Spence (1699–1768), in his *Observations, Anecdotes, and Characters of Books and Men,* quotes Pope as saying, "All gardening is landscape-painting. Just like a landscape hung up." Pope maintained this visual approach to poetry as well; his translation of Homer's *Iliad* shows a keen picturesque sensibility as he organizes several memorable scenes in the manner of *tableaux vivants.*

Although a Catholic Tory, Pope was a friend to the progressive Whigs whose interests he shared. Like other members of Lord Burlington's coterie, he admired Palladian architecture and was deeply committed to the classical traditions of ancient Rome. Like Addison, he scorned topiary and faulted symmetry because it produced monotony and lack of variety, well-ordered variety being perhaps the single most esteemed trait in Pope's theory of design.

His own garden at Twickenham was famed above all for its remarkable three-chambered grotto, the walls of which were studded with mineral specimens, shells, and mirrors to reflect and multiply the view, a place where Pope could engage in reverie, literary pursuit, or conversation with his constant stream of visitors. This grotto was conceived as a dream chamber, a place both to soothe and stimulate the mind. While this eighteenth-century version of a classical *nymphaeum,* with its artificial stalactites, imbedded minerals, and dripping water, was obviously the height of artifice, Pope was proud to boast that he had "strictly followed Nature" in creating it. And, from his perspective, he was correct. He had eschewed the elaborately artificial hydraulics and arcane mythological decorative programs of Renaissance grottoes in favor of a more naturalistic cave in which he had arranged his geological specimens so as to simulate a quarry or mine. Pope's grotto was, above all, a highly personal expression, containing associations with the many friends whom he had entertained there and reminding him through its numerous geologic specimens of the correspondents who had sent them to him.

Another popular and influential poet, James Thomson (1700–1748), saw the English garden as a metaphor for British freedoms. He is remembered for his long poem and life work *The Seasons,* a paean to British landscape that anticipates Romanticism in its religious attitude toward nature. His reverential awe for nature's bounty and beauty was coupled with the growing pride the English felt in the loveliness of their countryside, particularly as the wave of landscape improvement swept the nation. For Thomson the realm of imagination and the realm of landscape were intertwined. The mind itself was a kind of landscape: "the varied scene of quick-compounded thought," in which "visionary vales," "weeping grottoes," and "prophetic glooms" provoked reflection. It was "the mind's creative eye" that gave meaning to sensation.[9]

LANDSCAPE THEORISTS AND PRACTITIONERS

The philosophy that saw the mind as a theater of sensation and therefore landscape experience as a stimulus to reflection caused some landed Englishmen to think about their properties in a new way. Ordinary farmland could be ornamented with monuments that evoked sensations, heightening interest and stimulating emotion. A farm could therefore be both practical and poetic. The notion of the *ferme ornée,* or farm-as-landscape, was first proposed in England by the nurseryman and garden designer Stephen Switzer (c. 1682–1745).[10] His influential volume *The Nobleman, Gentleman, and Gardener's Recreation* of 1715 was expanded in 1718 into the three-volume *Iconographia Rustica.* It was again augmented in a 1742 edition with progressive ideas derived from two decades of landscape design development. It is against the background of the enclosure movement that Switzer's popularity and that of later garden theorists and practitioners can be best understood.

Since the waning of the Middle Ages, as Britain's population swelled and sheep and cattle grazing became a dominant agrarian activity, ancient forestland and inhospitable heath had been converted to hedged fields and pastures, notably in the southern counties. Around certain ancient villages, where there were additional grassy downs for grazing, some of the open fields, which had formerly been held as commons and tilled by allotment, were enclosed by contract agreement. This process of enclosure accelerated in the eighteenth century when more than 3 million acres of arable land were enclosed by acts of Parliament and private treaty as the economic value of improved turf for grazing transformed British agriculture from a community-based system of open-field cultivation and common pasturage to one of private ownership.

Simultaneously, in response to England's timber famine in the seventeenth century, John Evelyn's influential book *Sylva* had promoted a tree-planting program, and the reforestation of the countryside in order to increase the production of wood for fuel, shipbuilding, and other forms of construction was now fully under way. The enclosed lands, a combination of rectangular fields hedged with white hawthorn interspersed with ash and elm trees, were called parks. Where foxhunting was a sport, there were occasional copses between the fields. The increased control over water supplies by wealthy owners, who were able to impound it in ponds and pump it through pipes, made possible a far greater independence in the siting of houses than heretofore. This permitted a thorough consideration of the presentation of the residential seat and the views to be enjoyed from its windows. The vast amount of estate improvement attendant upon enclosure effectively transformed the English countryside into the landscape we know today. This tremendous beautification effort came at the price of a great deal of human suffering. Enclosure took pasturage rights away and forced the majority of rural people to become tenant farmers.

This is the context in which Switzer enthusiastically claimed the *ferme ornée* to be derived from "some of the best Genius's of France," as well as from Rome where it had been proved "the truest and best Way of Gardening in the World, and such as the politest and best Genius of all Antiquity delighted in." These were encouraging words for literary and aesthetically inclined landowners who wanted to incorporate poetic and painterly sensation into their recently enclosed utilitarian landscapes. But Switzer was, after all, a professional man dependent upon the favor of his clients. As many of these still owned the kind of gardens that had been laid out in the French classical tradition, he advanced his ideas more cautiously than did the literary advocates and their friends, the Whig landowners.

Batty Langley (1696–1751) represents to an even greater degree than Switzer the lingering influence of French classical tradition in England. Arguing for variety and respect for natural landscape features in his 1728 *New Principles of Gardening,* Langley nevertheless gives formulaic prescriptions, and his illustrations consist of ornate labyrinthine paths that twirl and squiggle like elegant Rococo exercises within highly regular garden plots. Geometric basins in the French manner form the centerpieces of these curious mazes, and elsewhere in his "grand, beautiful and natural" gardens he advocates broad, straight avenues and geometrically shaped lawns. Like Switzer's, his is a how-to book. In appealing to a clientele less educated than the artists, architects, and writers of the Burlington circle, he is concerned less with the poetical values and literary associations of classical sculpture than with the appropriateness (or lack thereof) of certain mythological figures in relationship to particular kinds of scenery—for instance, the correct placement of Pomona in the fruit garden, Ulysses near a body of water, Pan in the grove, Flora in the flower garden, and Bacchus in the vineyard.

By contrast to Langley's simplistic approach by rule rather than by inspiration, Thomas Whately (d. 1772), a government official writing as a landscape connoisseur in 1765, after landscape had been fully "released . . . from the restraints of regularity," provides both a valuable record of the appearance of some of the important gardens designed in the first half of the eighteenth century and an understanding of the transformation of landscape gardening aesthetics as the century continued. While gardening for the British Augustans was an art in which the emblems of classical literature, friendship, family, and nation were important, in Whately's day, the deities and heroes could quietly steal away as the expressive qualities of nature's own materials—"ground, wood, water, and rocks"—became the sole means of composing landscapes. Though shorn of temples and other symbolic structures, a well-designed landscape could, nonetheless, evoke a range of moods. Whately's *Observations on Modern Gardening* (1770) helped promote landscape design as one of the liberal arts. The naturalistic approach it recommended found a receptive audience in France, where this style was known as the *jardin anglais*. The book was so popular that a second edition was published the same year as the first.

The kind of gardening Whately advocated was based on the theories Edmund Burke (1729–1797) had expounded in 1757 in *A Philosophical Enquiry into the Origin of Our Ideas of the Sublime and Beautiful*. Burke, as a follower of Locke, strove to define the correspondences between certain human emotions and particular categories of sensory impression. Sublimity lay in those scenes that, because of their awesome size, sharp colors, loud sound, association with the unknown, and often abrupt irregularity, caused sensations best described as a kind of admiring terror or fearful wonder. Beauty, on the other hand excited "the passion of love, or some correspondent affection" and could be found not, as Descartes and Le Nôtre had found it, in mathematical proportion, but rather in such qualities as smallness, smoothness, delicacy, soft hues, melodious music, gently undulating surfaces, and curving lines. For gardeners, this last quality was of the greatest importance, accounting for the almost complete abandonment of straight lines in favor of the continuous S-curve known as Hogarth's line of beauty after William Hogarth (1697–1764), whose treatise on aesthetics, *The Analysis of Beauty* (1753),

held that wavy and serpentine lines were inherently pleasing to the eye

Whately's writing reflected the shift from emblematic to expressive means on the part of contemporary landscape designers. This was reinforced by a growing belief in the power of ruins to inspire a mood of elegiac melancholy, of dark-toned vegetation to turn the thoughts into paths of somber reflection, of bright green meadows to soothe the agitated soul, of sunny fields reminiscent of harvest revels to raise the spirits to the level of gaiety, of still brooks and placid lakes to speak of peace and serenity, of loud tumbling waterfalls to induce a thrilling fear. Water, in particular, was for Whately a practically indispensable element in the garden. Indeed, according to him, "So various are the characters which water can assume, that there is scarcely an idea in which it may not concur, or an impression which it cannot enforce."[11]

Whately's contemporary, Horace Walpole (1717–1797), like Pope, enjoyed the charms of a Thames-side villa. Like Whately, he used his pen to advance the fame of the English garden; between 1771 and 1780 he wrote the first history of the development of the new style.[12] Less theoretical and philosophical than Whately, Walpole chose to assign the chief credit for the landscape innovations he both practiced and witnessed all around him not to any general aesthetic evolution but to the imaginative genius of certain individuals, notably Charles Bridgeman (c. 1680–1738) and William Kent (1685–1748).

Bridgeman gave practical expression to the ideas of Pope and Addison, retaining some geometrical lines while banishing topiary, turning *parterres* into lawns, and opening views into the surrounding countryside. He also gave tangible form to the writings of Stephen Switzer, combining poetical allusions with practical landscapes in the "rural and farm-like way of gardening." Walpole credits Bridgeman with inventing the ha-ha and loosening up the garden's stiff formality. Kent, however, is his hero. Indeed, Kent's lasting renown is due in no small part to Walpole's characterization of him as "painter enough to taste the charms of landscape, bold and opinionative enough to dare and to dictate, and born with a genius to strike out a great system from the twilight of imperfect essays. He leaped the fence and saw that all nature was a garden."[13] Some garden authorities now interpret Walpole's assertions as British chauvinism, an attempt to discredit French seventeenth-century landscape style, which had, in fact, already "leaped the fence" when Le Nôtre flung axes toward the distant horizon.[14]

In addition to substituting techniques of painterly composition for those of architecture, the Whig patriots who championed the new garden style went beyond mere reverence for the classicism of ancient Rome to seek inspiration in their own native past, which they conceived as a conflation of Saxon and Gothic legend and history. Just as Pope had been praised for making Homer "speak good English," so the works of classical antiquity and the Renaissance were given a new grammar. While Palladio, in effect, was becoming an Englishman as architects gave his style a native inflection, the Society of Antiquaries, formed in 1718, gave new credibility to *local* antiquarian research. In this way such legendary native heroes as King Alfred acquired new dignity as "worthies" in the Whig political pantheon.

Kent's work during the 1730s significantly revised the designs of Charles Bridgeman, which had been considered progressive in the 1720s when his simplified and naturalized versions of the French classical garden were created to complement the boldly theatrical and allusive architecture of Sir John Vanbrugh (1664–1726). Vanbrugh's own importance in the evolving art of landscape design should not be underestimated. His background as a dramatist and his grasp of a site's scenic potential as a setting for works of architecture, together with his considerable talent as an architect, account for his legacy of impressive works. Vanbrugh realized the "romantick" qualities of Claremont, buying the property for his own country retreat and then, in 1711, selling it to Sir Thomas Pelham Holles, later earl of Clare, who subsequently employed him to design a striking belvedere as well as a garden, which he surrounded with high bastion walls. (In order to unite the garden and surrounding fields visually, Kent later removed and replaced these with a gently curving ha-ha.) Bridgeman's most striking contribution to Claremont was the construction of a large turf amphitheater of concave and convex tiers (fig. 7.3).

At Blenheim, Vanbrugh and Bridgeman collaborated in the creation of the original landscape. Van-

brugh built the palace and the exceptionally grand neoclassical bridge, and Bridgeman determined the axial lines and principal features of the landscape. At Blenheim, as at Claremont, Vanbrugh surrounded the garden with bastionlike walls, but Bridgeman later removed the section around the *parterre* beds. Bridgeman's greatest commission came when he was called, probably at Vanbrugh's suggestion, to design the gardens at Stowe.

Bridgeman's and Kent's careers were often intertwined as they worked together or in sequence. Bridgeman, who possessed a technical skill and horticultural knowledge Kent lacked, supplied the layout, and the more progressive Kent then revised it so that it became even more dramatic and more naturalistic than would have been the case if Bridgeman had been the sole designer. Their combined contributions to the art of landscape design can still be seen at Claremont, Stowe, and Rousham.

7.3. Claremont, turf amphitheater, designed by Charles Bridgeman. 1720s

II. Leaping the Fence: The Transformation of the English Landscape into a Pastoral Idyll with Political Meaning

The sober grandeur of Palladianism, the elevated moral tone of classical ornament, the fascination with real and fabricated ruins, the thematic itineraries of allegorical heroism: it was by these symbolic means that many eighteenth-century upper-class Englishmen invested their country estates with the ideal of their nation as a new Rome. These landscapes became through acts of imagination and arrangement emblematic of the Arcadian scenery associated with an ancient Golden Age or, more specifically, with the period when the Roman republic was turning toward imperial greatness. Their owners intended them to evoke the paintings by Claude and Poussin that hung in the galleries of their great houses. Thus was national ambition wedded to the serenely smiling, architecturally ornamented native landscape in a vision of nature as blessed, beautiful, and peculiarly English yet also Roman, an idyll with a political subtext.

STOWE

Stowe, the seat of Richard Temple (1675–1749), first viscount of Cobham, was an early and preeminent example of this ideal. Because Cobham was an influential and vocal Whig politician and hired landscape designers who mirrored his libertarian values in their transformation of Stowe's grounds from a plan of geometricized regularity to one of naturalistic free-flowing lines, it occupies a place of influence in garden history almost comparable to that of Versailles. Stowe was also a cultural mecca, as visits by the poets Pope and Thomson and the dramatist William Congreve (1670–1729) attest. As its pioneering position in the development of the new landscape style was quickly realized, Stowe became a favorite stop for eighteenth-century tourists.

With the passage of control of Parliament to the Tories in 1713, Lord Cobham was dismissed from government office. Already, like other rusticated Whigs, he had started to channel his energy into revising the old-fashioned terraced garden adjacent to the original seventeenth-century red-brick house of his ancestors into the most admired and progressively modern landscape garden in England as well as the center of Whig party politics. Bridgeman's work there, in association with Kent, continued until his death in 1738. It shows a masterly and flexible adaptation of axes, boundaries, and architectural features to the irregularities of the site. Kent, however, proved to be the bolder collaborator in developing the new direction in landscape design, successfully mediating between older and newer gardening styles. As has already been suggested, in his essay *On Modern Gardening,* Horace Walpole exaggerated in claiming that Kent "leaped the fence," thereby creating in one bold stroke the naturalistic garden style.[15]

An artisan of humble origins and a painter of modest talent, Kent had an engaging and witty personality, and this made him a likable protégé for Lord Burlington and Thomas Coke, earl of Leicester. It was as a traveling companion to them that Kent received his education in architecture and landscape as he visited Florence, Genoa, and the Palladian villas of the Veneto in 1709–19. He was familiar as well with Tivoli, Frascati, and Palestrina outside Rome where he saw such famous ruins as the Temple of Vesta, Hadrian's Villa, and Praeneste, as well as the Villa d'Este, Villa Aldobrandini, and other late-sixteenth- and early-seventeenth-century wonders. The villas of Rome itself, with their works of sculpture, paintings, objects of art, and large hunting parks, provided more stimuli for his impressionable senses. Kent was also a stage set designer, and as such he recognized and appreciated the theatrical aspects of Italian gardens and their function as places of luxury and sensory delight.

In 1733, Lord Cobham retired permanently from active political life. Kent was summoned to Stowe to begin its most innovative design phase. This consisted of creating the Elysian Fields in the valley through which had formerly run the road that approached the house from the east. With the road and the village clustered around Stowe Church removed, the valley could be incorporated into the garden as both a demonstration of the new naturalism and a thematic manifestation of political opinion and idealistic patriotism (figs. 7.4, 7.5, 7.6, 7.7, 7.8).

In 1740, young Lancelot "Capability" Brown found employment at Stowe. Brown, who soon became head gardener, is thought to have contributed some of his early-blooming talent to the last landscape completed in Cobham's lifetime: the Grecian Valley. The sinuous lines of the valley's tree border complement its gently undulating greensward, giving this part of Stowe a particularly Arcadian effect. The seeming simplicity of this design is, in fact, the result of the same extensive excavation and regrading that characterize Brown's later landscape compositions. It is in this impression of serenity and breadth that Brown's work is distinguished from Kent's, a fact that becomes apparent as we examine Rousham, Kent's finest work and an expression of his genius for compressing a great deal of poetic power into a small compass.

ROUSHAM

As a painter and theater set designer, Kent thought scenically, not architecturally. Attention to the tonality of vegetation and the effects of perspective achieved through contrasting light and dark foliage; expressive use of evergreens and other trees as screens and as a means of modulating otherwise vapid stretches of lawn; creation of both expectation and surprise by withholding choice prospects from immediate view; and the use of classical (and antique British) structures to enliven the distant scene; juxtaposition of the working landscape with the idyllic—these were Kent's techniques as a designer. At Rousham, in Oxfordshire, Kent gave full expression to these painterly concepts of landscape design.

Rousham, which is still owned by the Dormer family, was the eighteenth-century estate of Colonel Robert Dormer and his younger brother James, a lieutenant-general. Pope was a friend and correspondent of both brothers and a frequent visitor to Rousham. Kent, who was brought to Rousham by General Dormer following his brother's death in 1737, was commissioned to develop a garden within the framework of Bridgeman's plan of the 1720s. It is likely that Kent visited Rousham while he was working at Stowe, and he may have collaborated with Bridgeman, sketching some of the ideas that Bridgeman, with his superior technical ability, subsequently incorporated in the finished plan.

Because of its cramped and highly irregular site, everything depended upon enlarging the garden's apparent extent by, in Pope's words, "calling in the country" beyond the ha-ha. The river Cherwell, which traverses the property, serves in effect as part of the encompassing ha-ha system, and the bucolic views of the fields lying on its opposite bank were, even in Bridgeman's early plan, essential components of Rousham's landscape. To these Kent added a sham ruin, built to resemble a single gabled wall with arches, which rose at the top of a ridge about a mile from the river and was known simply as "the Eye-catcher." Near the river, he restyled an old mill, rechristened the Temple of the Mill, in the Gothic manner to add further picturesque interest to the scene. Bridgeman had already replaced the old terraced garden in front of the house with a large rectangular bowling green. Its raised borders are defined by ranks of trees channeling the view to the gently rolling fields beyond the Cherwell. Kent sited *Lion Attacking a Horse,* a copy of an antique sculpture, at the end of the bowling green in front of the open slope leading to the river.

The path from the bowling green leads to the narrowest part of the garden facing the river's sharp elbow-bend. Because of the angle cut by the river, the garden is severely pinched at this point, but Kent cleverly turned a defect into an asset, making this "hinge" the site of his Praeneste Terrace, so named because of his familiarity with the ruined arcades built in tiers on the hillside at Palestrina (ancient Praeneste) from which his design, abbreviated to a single arcade, took its inspiration. The visitor is invited to tarry here on an elegant stone settee sheltered within one of the niches of the arcade.

West of the Praeneste Terrace, the slope cradles a gentle valley. Bridgeman had remodeled a series of descending fishponds into a chain of ornamental basins. Kent reconfigured these when he formed the idyllic Vale of Venus (fig. 7.4). Beyond the Venus Vale, in a thickly planted grove of trees, he placed a sinuous rill. This narrow channel forms an elegant wavy line leading the eye from the Octagonal Pond beneath the arched cascade, over which Venus with her attendant swans and cupids presides, to the Cold Bath, a much smaller octagonal pool reflecting the dappled light of the small glade in which it is set.

From a lower path, there are uphill views of the Vale of Venus, where Pan emerges from the trees to spy on Venus. One can also see the Praeneste Terrace and, beyond the sharp bend in the river, Bacchus, Mercury, and Ceres assembled in a semicircular glade.

7.4. Vale of Venus, Rousham, Oxfordshire, designed by William Kent. Drawing by William Kent, c. 1738

Although these sculptures evoke the antique world, they do not furnish the garden with as explicit an iconography as that found at Stowe. This may be so because Kent, by temperament and because he lacked a classical education, hewed to a decorative and scenographic approach to landscape design.

By contrast, there were several aristocratic cognoscenti who wanted to infuse their landscape improvements with literary themes as well as painterly perspectives. Virgil, Ovid, and Milton were never far from their minds as they set about this task, nor were the sentiments expressed by their contemporary, Thomson, who wrote the ode "Rule, Britannia." It is not surprising therefore to see in the gardens of these British Augustans patriotic evocations of a new imperial Golden Age. In Alberti, whose *De re aedificatoria* was first published in English in 1726, they found a mentor on classical architecture and the amenities of country life. Likewise, they eagerly studied the letters of Pliny the Younger, who had divided his time between affairs of state and the pleasures of fruitful leisure at his country estates. Whether working as their own designers or with professionals to create gardens of heroic allusion—which were, in effect, statements of pride in England's own embarkation upon the course of empire—these garden owners took their place in the long tradition of Renaissance humanism.

Castle Howard

The most grandly heroic landscape conceived by an Augustan amateur was that of Castle Howard, the work of Charles Howard, the third earl of Carlisle. In contrast to Stowe, the garden with which it is most frequently compared, it did not develop from a garden and expand into a pictorial landscape; rather, Carlisle's intention was the creation of a landscape of serene and noble grandeur, whose principal motive was, like that of epic poetry, the celebration of

STOWE

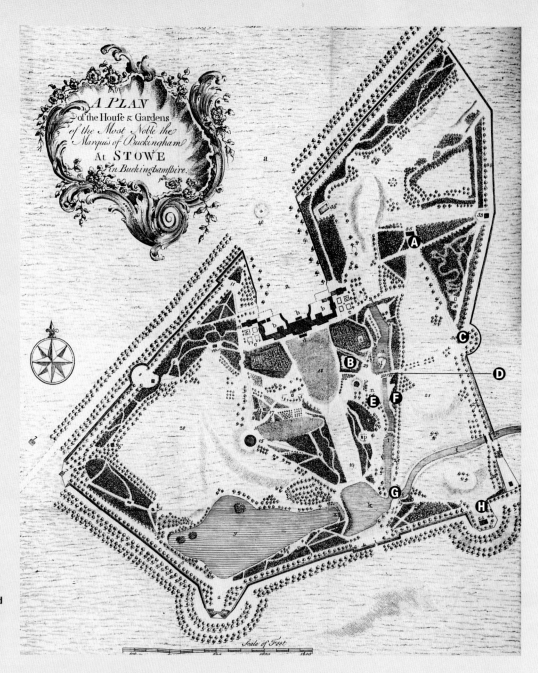

7.5. Stowe, Buckinghamshire, designed by Charles Bridgeman, William Kent, and Capability Brown. 1st half 18th century. Plan, engraving from *Stowe: A Description of the House and Gardens,* 1788 edition

The metaphorical program of the Elysian Fields resonates both with the satirical style of Alexander Pope and the passionately moral rhetoric of William Pitt the Elder (1708–1778), a relative of Lord Cobham's and a prominent figure among the young politicians who formed Stowe's band of ardent dissidents. Here the visitor was given an experience to inspire the noblest patriotic thoughts. As a terminus at the eastern end of the great Cross Walk, which symbolized the route into the imaginary Elysium, Kent erected the Temple of Ancient Virtue **B**, modeled after the Temple of Vesta at Tivoli (see fig. 7.6). Inside the circular temple were statues of Homer, Socrates, Epaminondas, and Lycurgus by the Belgian sculptor Peter Scheemakers (1691–1770), representing respectively poetry, philosophy, military genius, and law. Gazing from the

mound upon which it rested, one could see nearby the Temple of Modern Virtue, a sham ruin (now destroyed) bearing a sculpted headless torso, which supposedly represented Robert Walpole. (Understandably, Horace Walpole, his son, later deplored the use of satire as an iconographic device in garden architecture.)

On the opposite bank of a small stream named for the river Styx, Kent sited the Temple of British Worthies **F**, which featured pedimented niches containing busts of English heroes (see fig. 7.7). Significantly, the still-living Alexander Pope was afforded a place on the return elevation of the range containing Shakespeare, Milton, and Locke. Not without humor, another niche on the back of the temple was sacred to the memory of one Signor Fido, a lamented hunting dog. The bust of Mercury, which

adorns the central pyramid, symbolizes the messenger of the gods who will guide these and other worthies such as Lord Cobham across the river Styx to take their places in the Elysian Fields **E** among the exalted heroes within the Temple of Ancient Virtue. Thus through landscape Kent and his patron aligned an enlightened England and its noble past with the greatness of antiquity.

The river Styx itself is a small stream issuing from a once-elaborate grotto. Kent configured it into a chain of serpentine pools by means of a dam, which he disguised as the Shell Bridge **D**. Below the bridge, the stream widens into the Worthies River. It flows into the Lower River, a serpentine arm of Bridgeman's Octagon Pond. Here, at the bottom of the Elysian Fields, Cobham erected a monument to the playwright William

Congreve (1670–1729). This is a pyramid upon which sits a monkey surveying itself in a mirror, as Congreve held up a comic mirror to the foibles of society.

The Elysian Fields is a relatively intimate landscape into which Kent theatrically compressed a great deal of associative meaning. The continuation of Cobham's program of improvements to Stowe, and those of his heir and successor Richard Grenville, show a progressive broadening of views and expansion in the scale of both landscapes and buildings. Hawkwell Field, lying to the east of the Elysian Fields, had already been enclosed by Bridgeman's ha-ha, and Cobham developed it into a landscape composition based on Switzer's *ferme ornée* ideal. In the 1740s, James Gibbs ornamented this sloping pasture with three temples. Facing his Temple of

7.7. Temple of British Worthies. The members of the Protestant Whig pantheon are divided on either side of the central pyramid into patriots of action and figures of contemplation. The poet Alexander Pope was afforded a place on the back elevation (not visible) along with Signor Fido, a hunting dog.

7.6. Temple of Ancient Virtue, Stowe

Right: 7.8. The Queen's Temple in Hawkwell Field, Stowe

Friendship **H** he built the Queen's Temple **A**, where Lady Cobham entertained her friends on summer afternoons while Lord Cobham enjoyed the society of his Whig companions in the Temple of Friendship (see fig. 7.8) Halfway up the slope between these two buildings stands the Gothic Temple **G**, a highly original neomedieval structure of russet-toned ironstone, evoking by its alternative name—Temple of Liberty—a British past worthy of the patriotic aspirations of Lord Cobham's circle. A belt of trees screened from view the carriage road encircling Hawkwell Field. Projecting clumps of trees at various points directed the view toward significant eye-catchers. A Palladian Bridge **G** carried this road over the arm of the Octagon Pond that was known as the Upper River (see fig. 7.9).

7.9. Palladian Bridge, Stowe

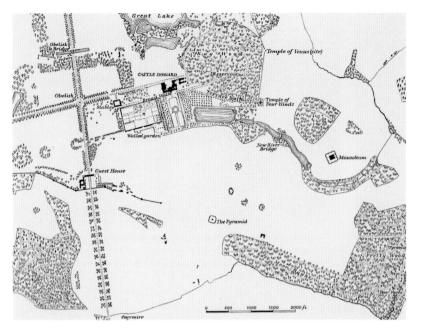

7.10. Plan of Castle Howard, Yorkshire, designed by John Vanbrugh and other advisers with the owner, Charles Howard, third earl of Carlisle. 1st half 18th century

Below: **7.11. Approach road to Castle Howard, North Yorkshire, with Pyramid Gate (1719) in background and Carrmire Gate (1730), designed by Nicholas Hawksmoor, in the foreground**

Right: **7.12. Temple of the Four Winds, Castle Howard, North Yorkshire, completed by Nicholas Hawksmoor following John Vanbrugh's death, as seen from Terrace Walk. 1728**

north-south approach road about 500 yards (457 meters) west of the house, a cross avenue carried one past the entrance court to a terminus at the edge of Wray Wood. At the intersection of these two straight avenues, an obelisk (1714) commemorates the duke of Marlborough; framing it, farther south, is the massive Pyramid Gate (1719) (fig. 7.11). Vanbrugh's park wall, with its castellated and proto-Romantic gothicism, reminds us of the medieval origins of this eighteenth-century country seat as *Castle* Howard. Farther south, at the entrance to the great avenue, Nicholas Hawksmoor's (1661–1736) Carrmire Gate (1730), with its crenellated extension ending in a turreted round tower, elaborated the medieval theme.

As at Stowe, where modified tradition leapt to pure innovation, here, too, a choice was made to abandon rectilinear design in favor of scenic composition. Carlisle turned the old lane below Wray Wood, which had led to the now-destroyed village of Henderskelf, into Terrace Walk, a broad grassy path with a scenic terminus in Vanbrugh's Temple of the Four Winds (fig. 7.12). This structure was modeled upon Palladio's Villa Rotonda. To the east of the Temple of the Four Winds, Hawksmoor's majestic Mausoleum, a domed rotunda with a Doric colonnade set upon a massive square platform surmounting a small knoll, gives solemn dignity to the landscape. In the middle distance, between the Temple of the Four Winds and the Mausoleum, a Palladian bridge of about 1744 spans the serpentine river whose bed had been excavated through the fields, giving additional classical character to the picturesque scene.

transcendent heroism. Rather than illustrating an allegorical epic through allusive ornament and architecture, Castle Howard achieves an Olympian mood through the serenity and grandeur of its scenery.

In 1699, at the age of twenty-three, Charles Howard became earl of Carlisle and took possession of his patrimony, a magnificent series of hills and vales surrounding old Henderskelf Castle in North Yorkshire. Discarding a conventional design by the nurseryman George London, Carlisle called in Vanbrugh whose robust and theatrical imagination matched his own aspirations. They took the then-radical step of conceiving of architecture in relationship to scenery, allowing the site to dictate the location of the new house parallel to, rather than on axis with, the approach road (fig. 7.10). As at Stowe, the creators of Castle Howard's landscape destroyed a village without apparent remorse as the Anglo-Palladian great house with its magnificent cupola, the first of its kind in England, took command of the sweeping view to the south.

Adjacent to the eastern flank of the house rose a dome-shaped hill known as Wray Wood where between 1718 and 1732, possibly with advice from Switzer, Carlisle boldly conceived a plan of meandering paths and various fountains set within a naturalistic plantation of trees. Bisecting a stately

7.13. Studley Royal, North Yorkshire, designed by John Aislabie. 1714–18. View of Moon Pond and Temple of Piety. c. 1728

Below: 7.14. Fountains Abbey, the monastic ruin that serves as the focal point of the vista from Studley Royal

OTHER AUGUSTAN AMATEURS

Although the breathtaking scope, scale, and expense of his enterprise set him apart and made Castle Howard unique among English landscapes, Carlisle represents the Augustan amateur landscape improvers in his single-minded pursuit of landscape perfection as his lifework and personal monument, as well as in the lofty idealism that allied his enterprise with national ambition. On a much smaller scale, though as absorbing to their owners, were The Leasowes, the *ferme ornée* of William Shenstone (1714–1763), and Woburn Farm, the estate of Philip Southcote (1698–1758). At other country seats, owners were stirred to a new appreciation of the moldering relics of England's abandoned monasteries, notably at Duncombe Park and Studley Royal. At Duncombe, a broad, gently curving grass terrace was built to capture the view of Rievaulx Abbey, whereas at Studley Royal, John Aislabie connected his geometrically arranged water garden by a wooded walk to a romantically contrived view of Fountains Abbey, where some parts of the buildings date from the twelfth century (figs. 7.13, 7.14).

At Painshill in Surrey, Charles Hamilton (1704–1786) proved to be another enthusiastic amateur caught up in the passion of landscape improvement. Between 1738, when he obtained a crown lease for the property, and 1773, when indebtedness forced him to sell it, he created an undulating circuit beside a fourteen-acre artificial lake. Visitors following it had views of Rococo features similar to those employed in contemporary French gardens: a Gothic-style "temple," a sham ruin of an abbey, an elaborate grotto, a rustic hermitage, a cascade, a Roman mausoleum, a Turkish tent, a Temple of Bacchus, and a Chinese bridge. Hamilton was responsible for importing many exotic plant species from North America and was one of the first Englishmen to use rhododendrons. After he went bankrupt, he took up residence in Bath, where he became a landscape consultant to other garden builders who valued his knowledge of plants and of how to build cascades.

STOURHEAD

Landscape building on the Augustan scale was expensive, and Hamilton was not the only amateur practitioner whose imagination outdistanced his purse. Like Hamilton, many other garden builders, including Lord Carlisle, called upon the London banker Henry Hoare to help finance their works. In this way, the fashion for estate improvement, which depleted the resources of others, made Hoare wealthy. This, in turn, allowed his son, Henry Hoare II (1705–1785), a Tory like his father, to create the landscape of Stourhead. Because of

7.15. Claude Lorrain, *Coast View of Delos with Aeneas*, 1672. National Gallery, London

Below: 7.16. Stourhead, Wiltshire, with Palladian bridge in the foreground and Pantheon (originally called the Temple of Hercules), in the back. Designed by Henry Hoare, owner, and Henry Flitcroft, architect. 1753–56

Hoare's own skill in making pictorial scenery and Stourhead's current excellent state of preservation by the National Trust, it evokes more completely the mood of an eighteenth-century Golden Age Elysium than any other garden in England.[16]

Henry Hoare II was only nineteen when he succeeded his father as the head of the family's Fleet Street bank. From 1738 until his mother's death in 1741, he traveled in Italy, educating himself in the scenery of antiquity and purchasing paintings by seventeenth- and early-eighteenth-century masters, including two by Poussin and one by Claude. When he returned, he took up residence as the master of Stourhead, and shortly after he became a widower in 1743, he began a program of garden improvements, an enterprise that lasted the rest of his life.

The garden historian Kenneth Woodbridge has made a convincing case for Hoare's use of the text of Virgil's *Aeneid* as the programmatic theme of Stourhead.[17] The circuit made by the visitor can be interpreted as a series of stations evoking Aeneas's journey from Troy to his founding of Rome, an odyssey that might have symbolized for Henry Hoare II his establishing a family seat at Stourhead. Whether or not a specific iconographic program was in his mind, Hoare clearly meant the landscape of Stourhead to be a dreamworld inhabited by the gods, goddesses, and heroes of antiquity.

Henry Flitcroft (1697–1769) was Hoare's architect for this and several other projects. He advised and helped Hoare plan the dam to flood the valley and enlarge its existing ponds into a lake. At the head of the lake, the Temple of Flora (1744; originally Ceres) bears over its portal the injunction of the Cumaean Sibyl in the *Aeneid* warning Aeneas as he prepares to

enter the underworld where his future as founder of Rome will be revealed to him. Other architectural features along the path leading counterclockwise around the lake had to be built before the dam could impound the waters at the head of the Stour and give them their intended setting. Shelving banks for the future lake had to be built as well, a task that continued until the dam's construction in 1753. At the same time, Hoare began planting contrasting masses of light- and dark-toned trees against each other in the manner of Pope and Kent. A wooden bridge, the design of which was derived from a drawing by Palladio, carried the circuit path around to the grotto over the northern arm of the lake.

Beyond the grotto, over the entrance to which is an inscription that alludes to the nymph-inhabited cave near Carthage where Aeneas sought refuge with his men, the path leads toward a visionary scene that bears an obvious relationship to *Coast View of Delos with Aeneas,* a painting by Claude Lorrain (fig. 7.15). This painting depicts Aeneas with his father, his son, and Anius the priest standing on a terrace in front of a Doric temple, gazing at a landscape containing a round temple modeled on Hadrian's Pantheon in Rome. In the Virgilian text upon which the painting is based, a travel-weary Aeneas has been praying to Apollo to grant him and his descendants a home by allowing him to fulfill his destiny by founding Rome. Hoare's Pantheon, built according to Flitcroft's design as a miniaturized version of the Roman one, is the visual and symbolical focus of the Stourhead landscape (fig. 7.16).

Across the lake, on axis with the Pantheon, Hoare built a stone bridge patterned after a design by Palladio. In the opposite direction, toward the village, was a view of the Bristol High Cross, which marked the principal intersection of that city before it was declared an obstruction and dismantled. In 1764, Hoare acquired its disassembled pieces from an English cathedral where they had been lying in a corner. This historic trophy blends with the mellow medievalism of the village and reinforces the garden's iconographic alliance between the glories of classical

antiquity and the British cultural heritage.

Henry Hoare's grandson, Richard Colt Hoare, the heir and master of Stourhead after 1780, broadened the garden's palette of plant material as an increasing number of exotic species began to be naturalized in England. He was an avid plantsman and a member of the Linnean Society, who planted many of the mature ornamental trees and some of the huge old rhododendrons one sees today. Like his forebears, he lived for a considerable time in Italy where his talents as a draftsman and watercolorist flourished and his purchases increased the number of fine paintings in the house. An antiquarian and therefore something of an architectural purist, he removed Stourhead's Turkish Tent, Venetian Seat, and Chinese Alcove, garden features his grandfather had added when such Rococo eclecticism was fashionable. At the same time, in 1806, he gave the small cottage between the grotto and the Pantheon a Picturesque Gothic porch.

In removing elements he considered extraneous and developing the garden at Stourhead no longer as a contrived sequence of emblematic associations but rather as an overall scenic idyll, Colt Hoare followed the taste of his time. The perception of the world in terms of Lockean sensibility was gradually giving way to the less intellectual set of values that

formed the seedbed of Romanticism. His broad simplification of his grandfather's original plan and the use of natural materials as the principal expressive force in landscape design paralleled the work at Stowe that was being carried out by Richard Grenville, Lord Cobham's nephew and heir.

Stowe, with Grenville's simplifications and noble additions, such as the Grecian Temple, modeled on the Maison Carrée, the Roman temple at Nîmes, long remained the epitome of English Augustan garden style, an international cynosure visited by the Empress Catherine the Great, Jean-Jacques Rousseau, Thomas Jefferson, and many others. But already the allusive garden of humanistic and heroic messages was a thing of the past, and although its style and features would be imitated on the Continent in years to come, in England its function as a model was over.

In the last third of the eighteenth century, when parliamentary acts of enclosure were creating a vast number of new estates, prosperous British landowners were less interested in making neoclassical Arcadias than in achieving a series of pleasing views as they toured their acres or gazed at them from their country houses.[18] Thus it was that the remaking of the rural landscape of England fell into the hands of the untraveled, relatively uneducated, yet immensely capable Lancelot Brown.

III. REMAKING ENGLAND: CAPABILITY BROWN, PROFESSIONAL IMPROVER

British mercantile policies in the middle of the eighteenth century regulated a vigorous commerce that worked in the country's favor, with trade doubling between 1750 and 1800. After 1780, the Industrial Revolution accelerated dramatically. This process was assisted both by the invention of new production machinery and by the availability of an industrial labor force following enclosure when many tenant farmers were uprooted from the land. While England felt the nascent surge of industrial capitalism, and its cities were beginning to increase significantly in population, it was still a preindustrial country. Its wealth was based upon a greatly expanded domestic and international trade, together with a more productive animal husbandry and agriculture than had heretofore been practiced. This wealth provided the substance with which to carry out the transformation of the eighteenth-century English countryside. By most accounts, the country was fortunate in having at hand a talented individual who felt himself capable of reshaping many estates so that they expressed the new agrarian prosperity in terms of an entirely "English" ideal.

"CAPABILITY" BROWN'S APPROACH TO LANDSCAPE DESIGN

The England into which Lancelot "Capability" Brown (1716–1783) was born grew with him into a confident, optimistic, and prosperous maturity. Brown's considerable achievement lay in his ability to create designs that were abstract and yet harmonious with the scenery of rural enclosure. His nickname Capability, from his frequent assurance to his clients that their properties had the *capability* of being rendered beautiful by their expenditures and his improving hand, expresses succinctly the flavor of the enterprise. Between the time he left his position as head gardener at Stowe in 1751 and his death in 1783, he had designed or redesigned nearly two hundred properties, and his advice had been sought on many others. He traveled tirelessly from one to another of his commissions. The often-narrated anecdote about Brown's turning down a job in Ireland with the excuse that he had not finished England yet is more than humorous: His vision was a grandly optimistic one in which he must have seen all of England re-created as idealized rural scenery. *Taste* and *imagination*—

operative words in the eighteenth century—were, along with the financial resources necessary to activate them, all that seemed required to achieve this desirable end. The garden, which since the seventeenth century had been expanding visually to embrace spaces beyond its borders, was, in Brown's terms, all of a piece with this larger landscape; a garden was simply a rural working landscape arranged so as to be at once productive and beautiful.

Brown's style, stripped of association, was in its own way as abstractly classical as that of Le Nôtre, and the volume of earth movement and topographical regrading required to achieve his seemingly naturalistic results was no less monumental than that required by the French master. Brown's eye was selective; it edited out the blemishes of nature, smoothing away abrupt contours and camouflaging its "accidents" with screening foliage. He was often referred to as a "landscape improver,"[19] and with the unconscious presumption of a deity he set about *correcting* nature to conform with an aesthetic ideal, which the poet Thomson hailed as "purest truth." Although Brown left no written theory, he undoubtedly believed that through rational science landscape could be perfected to a state wherein human beings and nature could meet on equal terms, in fruitful partnership.

From a technical point of view, other things were necessary as well, and in this regard Brown came to his profession far better prepared than Kent. Although Brown spent his youth in the small Northumberland village of Kirkharle where he was born, he was able to observe the estate improvement occurring in the immediate vicinity. His walk to school in Cambo took him past Wallington Park, which, after enclosure, was enjoying various improving alterations to its previously barren and degraded landscape. These included the kind of large-scale reforestation and hedgerow planting ubiquitous in England at the time. In 1732, after leaving school, he became a gardener at Kirkharle Hall where Sir William Loraine was creating a similar working landscape. Here Brown learned to drain swamps and acquired a practical knowledge of horticulture. It was with these skills that he left home, in 1739, for Oxfordshire in the south, finding employment first at Kiddington Hall and then, two years later, at Stowe.

It was Brown's lucky exposure to Kent's recent work in the Elysian Fields at Stowe that broadened his aesthetic horizons, while his employment by Lord Cobham allowed him to expand his professional abilities. Surveying, hydraulic engineering, and architecture were skills he readily acquired. He became sufficiently competent as a draftsman to develop plans for various neighboring estates, whose owners soon sought his services. Site planning came easily to him,

and he quickly found himself not only recommending the placement of various manor houses but designing them as well. Within the bounds of a conventional Palladianism, he provided his clients with mansions and garden buildings that were remarkable for their sound construction, comfort, and convenience.

Brown was probably familiar with the aesthetics of landscape from an intellectual perspective and referred to his design activity as "Place-making."[20] In 1753, William Hogarth (1697–1764) published *An Analysis of Beauty,* a book devoted to a minute analysis of the way in which that quality is to be found in the sinuous, rather than the straight, line. The first of several editions of Edmund Burke's treatise *A Philosophical Enquiry into the Origin of our Ideas of the Sublime and Beautiful* appeared in 1757. In it Burke set forth his concept of beauty as a "feminine" ideal composed of smoothness and softly rounded contours. He elaborated this definition in sensuous terms, likening beauty to the charm "of being swiftly drawn in an easy coach on a smooth turf, with gradual ascents and declivities,"[21] the intention thus being to produce a pleasing and harmoniously varied experience.

Whether or not Brown was a student of Burke and Hogarth in a conscious sense, their ideas were part of a Rococo aesthetic found in mid-eighteenth-century Georgian design, as characterized by the flowing lines and naturalistic forms of Thomas Chippendale's furniture. It is not surprising, therefore, that Brown's style was based upon an undulating linearity of ground plane edges, combined with rounded topographic modeling. Southern England naturally offers just such gentle and varied beauty as that recommended by Burke's definition, making the improver's art there merely one of emphasis. Thus, by rearranging certain landscape elements, Brown was readily able to achieve compositions that met Burke's criteria for the beautiful.

Brown, having discarded the emblematic garden, expressed mood through more abstract means than temples, monuments, and inscriptions. "Solemn" groves provided variety and contrast to "cheerful" fields. Placid sky-reflecting water was used almost invariably to bring an air of tranquil repose to the scene. Although he was described as working with "the Poet's feeling" and "the Painter's eye," Brown attempted neither to evoke Virgil nor render a three-dimensional painting by Claude. By contrast, the very Englishness of his landscapes inspired poetry and themselves became the subjects of paintings by such British artists as John Constable (1776–1837) and John Mallord William Turner (1775–1851).

Brown's work displays a strong plastic sensibility. He achieved the smoothness that Burke prized by extensive regrading and by removing all rough obstacles and "accidental" defects from the terrain. The resulting topography is never flat nor monotonously sloping in one direction, but shaped to form a series of gentle convex and concave curves. Where a slope meets a level plane of lawn or water, Brown created a soft tangential curve called a "concave scoop," and many of his finest views appear as long dells with higher ground softly swelling on either side (fig. 7.17). Trees are never planted in ranks, but rather in clumps, belts, and screens that partially reveal more distant prospects. He used both deciduous and evergreen native species for the most part, following Kent's practice of contrasting light and dark foliage in order to realize effects of perspective. The curving lines of his drives, tree belts, and lake edges never run along parallel courses, but in harmonious naturalistic configurations.

His ha-has, placed at right angles to the line of vision, ensure that these sunk fences are imperceptible to the eye traveling to the fields beyond, and their sides slope gradually so as to permit cattle to browse at their edges, thereby eliminating obtrusive tufts of spiky vegetation. Deer still graze in several of his parks, cropping the grass, and by clearing the lower branches of the trees up to a uniform line, they make possible long views through the woods.

A necessary component of Brown's landscapes was an element of suspense. The same kind of hide-and-reveal tactics that we will discern when we examine Japanese gardens can also be recognized in his. The belts of trees, designed to screen his circuit drives, some working fields, and other "eyesores" were planned with gaps to expose those aspects of the agricultural landscape that harmonized with his designs. His walks and drives were designed to entice carriage rides and perambulation, and his broad lakes invited visual exploration, but he never allowed eye and body to traverse the same route. Straight lines do not exist in Brown's compositions, and it is only by means of a leisurely circuitous amble that one gains the object in view. As at Stourhead, his parks are meant to be traveled on foot or, more likely, considering their scale, by carriage, but unlike Hoare's lakeside route at Stourhead with its Virgilian features, Brown's tours are not thematic; they attempt merely to stir human emotions rather than the intellect.

Capability Brown demonstrated his greatest skill in his thorough knowledge of drainage techniques and handling of water (fig. 7.18). The gentle transition between ground plane and water surface ensured an effect of maximum reflectivity, as one does not look down into his water from above, but rather across it. By making the contours of his lakes irregular and obscuring their curving ends in the shadows of dense plantings, or screening them with fore-

ground islands, he was able to add an air of mystery to his scenery. Brown also was a master builder of naturalistic cascades, and these provided additional variety and something approaching Romantic excitement within his otherwise tranquil compositions.

Brown allowed no ornamental planting to mediate between the house and its surrounding landscape, and he eradicated many fine old *parterre* gardens. Nevertheless, extensive human labor was still necessary to maintain his landscapes, and heirs to those that still exist no longer find it possible to afford all the scything, brushing, sweeping, and rolling once considered essential to sustain the beauty of his flowing lawns.

Brown's landscapes were ones in which the marriage between house and surroundings was all-important. It was necessary that the view from the house be a controlled one, extending all the way to the horizon. If this was not possible, anything extraneous was excluded from sight by screens of trees. The siting of the house to best advantage and its status as the

7.17. Petworth, West Sussex. Original layout by George London, ca. 1690; redesigned by Capability Brown, ca. 1750

Below: 7.18. The grounds of Broadlands, Hampshire, a typical landscape design by Capability Brown. 1767–68

7.19. Blenheim, Oxfordshire, designed by Henry Wise (1705–16) and Capability Brown (after 1764). Center, Wise's straight approach road to palace with bridge over the River Glyme (later dammed by Brown to form the lake). Bridge and palace designed by Sir John Vanbrugh. 1705–24

Below: 7.20. Lake created by Capability Brown with bridge designed by Vanbrugh, Blenheim, Oxfordshire

pre-eminent object in the landscape were paramount considerations. Thus, the separation of the house from the principal scenery of the garden, as at Stourhead, does not occur in Brown's designs.

Like Le Nôtre, Brown was blessed with a pleasing personality, and from his home at Hammersmith, a center of the nursery trade outside London, he traveled throughout the countryside, particularly in the counties of Wiltshire and Hampshire, to undertake commissions both large and small. He could not have done all this without a strong administrative ability, which enabled him to subcontract work, perform on time and within budget, and obtain critical decisions from clients whom he visited personally during the course of a job.

His genius and ability to implement a bold vision were nowhere better expressed than at Blenheim, where his landscape plan was allied with Sir John Vanbrugh's robustly masculine, dramatic architecture (fig. 7.19). A gift to the duke of Marlborough after his victory against the French at the 1704 Battle of Blenheim, Blenheim Palace was built

to serve both as a country seat and national monument. Its bastion-shaped gardens, with *parterres* by Henry Wise and a mile-long triumphal avenue from the Column of Victory to the palace—which was carried over the river Glyme by Vanbrugh's massive bridge—provided the canvas for Brown's artistic labors when he was summoned there by the fourth duke in 1764.

The *parterres* were soon swept away, but Brown retained the great triumphal avenue. His master stroke was to dam the Glyme, thereby flooding the lower piers of Vanbrugh's bridge. This brought the water into scale with the bridge, lessening the bridge's impact as an isolated and somewhat pompous artifact in relation to the meager Glyme. Brown demonstrated as well his considerable hydrological skill in being able to assess and control its exact level. The upper parts of the bridge's arches, which remain above the level of the water, unite with their reflections in the lake to form pleasing geometries, and the bridge itself is perfectly proportioned to the lake (fig. 7.20). Upon entering Blenheim Park from the village of Woodstock, the visitor sees this dreamlike vision: the land sloping more steeply than usual in Brown's landscapes down to the lake, the lovely bridge made poetic by the addition of a small island in front of it, and on axis with the bridge, the palace set upon its commanding plateau.

WILLIAM CHAMBERS VERSUS CAPABILITY BROWN

Success breeds enmity, and Brown had his detractors, the most virulent of whom was Sir William Chambers. Chambers, who had visited China in 1744 and 1748, set himself up as an authority on what he declared to be, quite fancifully, the Chinese taste in gardening. His appointment as Garden Adviser to the Princess of Wales at Kew, the royal estate adjacent to Richmond and the other half of what is today the Royal Botanical Gardens, put him on a collision course with Brown, who held the title of Surveyor to His Majesty's Gardens and Waters at Hampton Court. The eighteenth-century equivalent of a theme park "imagineer," Chambers pitched a wild battle on behalf of the kind of "pleasing, horrid and enchanted"[22] effects he claimed to have seen in Chinese gardens. His Gothic imagination assigned to them such things as "temples dedicated to the king of vengeance, deep caverns in the rocks, and descents to subterraneous habitations, overgrown with brushwood and brambles; near which are placed pillars of stone, with pathetic descriptions of tragical events, and many horrid acts of cruelty, perpetrated there by robbers and outlaws of former times."[23] While variety was also the hallmark of Brown's landscapes, abrupt transitions and the frissons of excitement at which Chambers aimed were alien to Brown's style.

Chambers's implementation of his notions of Chinese taste at Kew resulted in unbridled eclecticism. There he built a menagerie, an aviary, a "mosque," more than twenty classical temples, a Palladian bridge, a Chinese temple, a ten-story pagoda, and a Roman triumphal arch in ruins (fig. 7.21). Of this array, only the last two features remain. Notwithstanding royal patronage, Chambers's ideas found a more congenial soil in which to germinate in France and elsewhere on the Continent than at home. By contrast, Brown's less theatrical landscape style gained fewer adherents abroad than in his native England where an aesthetic appreciation of tranquil agrarian beauty was well established. As we shall see, enthusiasm for Chambers's writings guided the course of the Rococo garden abroad, where it was known as the *jardin anglo-chinois.*

At Claremont, Brown and Chambers met as rivals when Lord Clive, who had recently bought the estate, invited both men to submit designs for a new mansion. Clive's choice of Brown to work in collaboration with his son-in-law Henry Holland (1745–1806) in 1771 sparked such enmity in Chambers that his attacks on Brown's style assumed a tone of personal animus. *A Dissertation on Oriental Gardening,* published the following year, contains several thinly veiled barbs aimed at Brown. But Brown promptly found a champion in William Mason, a poet and landscape gardener. *An Heroic Epistle to Sir William Chambers* (1773) is a blistering burlesque in the style of Pope, written in mock praise of Chambers's "scatter'd glories of Chinese Virtù, which teach the muse of landscape

7.21. Pagoda, Royal Botanic Gardens, Kew, London, designed by William Chambers. 1761

Like thee to scorn Dame Nature's simple fence; Leap each Ha Ha of truth and common sense....[24]

Brown's abstract and nonliterary approach to landscape was fundamentally contrary to that of such scene makers as Henry Hoare, who worked as a latter-day humanist, and Chambers, who, with his taste for the anecdotally bizarre, aimed at a thrill-inducing version of Burke's sublime. Brown's landscapes are beautiful according to the definition of Burke, but some of his contemporaries found their gentle curvilinearity and rolling smoothness to be bland and boring. These critics articulated a new style, one intermediate between the beautiful and the sublime as defined by Burke, which they christened the *Picturesque.*

IV. NATURE'S CANVAS: ENGLISH PHILOSOPHERS AND PRACTITIONERS OF THE PICTURESQUE

In our age of adventure travel, packaged sight-seeing, and resort vacations, it is difficult to comprehend the seriousness of eighteenth-century tourists, their careful characterization of different categories of scenery, and the finely wrought discriminations they made among them. Readers of Jane Austen's novels can appreciate the intensity of the aesthetic debate within polite society during this period of active transformation of the English landscape. The fervor with which this discussion of the appropriateness of a particular landscape style was conducted at that time appears comically quaint in our own when design diversity has itself become a cultural value. Vast social changes, carried by swift currents of history even as these debates occurred, soon made the practice of landscape design

a public responsibility rather than a private entertainment, and the arguments over the respective merits of the Picturesque style versus the smoothly undulating landscapes of Brown came to seem no more consequential than a spirited difference of opinion within a gentlemen's club. But club arguments can assume a degree of rancor that divides people into ardent factions, and the charges and countercharges that are hurled in the heat of battle sometimes echo for years after their participants are gone.

The Picturesque controversy was taken up by the periodicals of the day, after which it became table talk in country houses throughout the land. This was so because people had begun to regard sight-seeing as a delightful form of recreation. Carriage travel had become relatively convenient and safe, but revolution in France and other political disturbances made tourist excursions on the Continent difficult. Many people were therefore eager to have their eyes opened to the charms of native scenery. Instructing them in this regard and instilling in them a new concept of regionalism and a new approach to the aesthetics of the natural landscape were the works of William Gilpin.

WILLIAM GILPIN, VICAR OF BOLDRE

William Gilpin (1724–1804), who was brought up in the north of England beside the Scottish border, was an early admirer of wilder and more rugged landscapes than those of southern England. Tutored by his father in painting and sketching, he instinctively viewed landscape as artistic subject matter wherein craggy topography and a certain roughness of objects provided greater variety and visual interest than smooth and flowing perfection. His discriminating eye led him to an appreciation of the different varieties of natural scenery as one traveled from one section of England to another. As developed by Gilpin, the term *Picturesque* did not apply to gardens, which "want the bold roughness of nature," and were therefore uninteresting subjects for painters. For him, *Picturesque* meant scenery that because of its boldly projecting outcrops of rock, contrasts of dark and light, compositional grouping of trees, and other such attributes was either naturally suitable for picture making or, with some compositional correction to foreground, background, or middle ground, could be made so. His appreciation of scenery was as a two-dimensional framed view of a three-dimensional scene, and his visual satisfaction depended on a correspondence between the works of nature and the animated "roughness" of elements and the atmospheric light and shade that give pleasure in a painting. Gilpin's imagination, therefore, was not excited by wild nature as such, but rather by nature as seen through the filter of art.

His own talent as a sketchbook artist admirably served his purposes as a travel writer and illustrator of a new and popular way of looking at landscape.

As a young clergyman living in London, he visited Stowe, and in 1748, he published anonymously *A Dialogue upon the Gardens of the Right Honourable the Lord Viscount Cobham, at Stow in Buckinghamshire.* In this "conversation" between Callophilus, a lover of beauty, and Polython, a man of sensitivity and imagination from the north of England, he analyzed the famous landscape as if it were a painting. Stowe's deficiency in Gilpin's nonetheless admiring eye was its want of Picturesque scenery such as one found in the northern counties where craggy precipices, foaming waterfalls, hanging woods, and other scenes of rough natural beauty abounded. He held that "Regularity and Exactness excite no manner of Pleasure in the Imagination. The fancy is struck by *Nature* alone; and if *Art* does any thing more than just decently improve her, we think she grows impertinent. Thus a regular ragged ruin, beautifully set off with Light and Shade, and garnished with flourishing bushes, Ivy, and dead Branches, may afford a great deal."[25]

The growing appreciation of wild scenery, as well as the currency that the word *picturesque* gained and continued to enjoy for a century or more as part of the vocabulary of landscape viewing, was due in no small measure to Gilpin's influence. Yet, his career as an artist-tourist was, in fact, written in the margins of his life as a busy schoolmaster and vicar attending his needy rural parishioners.

Like Pope, who had employed his summers in traveling for scenic enjoyment, Gilpin toured the countryside during his vacations as headmaster of Cheam School. He revisited those wild landscapes that had thrilled him as a youth, and he happily spent his days sketching and his evenings writing up his "observations," which were based on an analysis, according to his developing theories of Picturesque beauty, of the scenery he had drawn. He circulated these observations along with sketches from his travels in Wales, the Lake District, and elsewhere in northern England to a growing band of admirers.

In 1776, he left Cheam School to become the vicar of Boldre, a parish in Hampshire on the border of the New Forest beside the southern coast of England. There he deepened his appreciation of forest scenery and accumulated sketches and remarks on the diverse qualities of picturesqueness to be found in various species of trees (fig. 7.22). Gilpin realized at this time that he would be able to derive income beyond that of his clerical living from the publication of the observations and sketches made on his tours. Horace Walpole helped him find a way to mitigate the financial risk of publishing a book in which several illustrations were a necessity by introducing him to the newly developed aquatint method of printmaking.

In 1782, Gilpin decided to publish one of his

7.22. William Gilpin, aquatint engraving from *Remarks on Forest Scenery,* 1791. According to Gilpin, "The *blasted tree* has often a fine effect both in natural, and in artificial landscape. In some scenes it is almost essential. When the dreary heath is spread before the eye, and ideas of wildness and desolation are required, what more suitable accompaniment can be imagined, than the blasted oak, ragged, scathed and leafless; shooting its peeded, white branches athwart the gathering blackness of some rising storm?"

shorter accounts, *Observations on the River Wye,* with aquatints made by his nephew William Sawrey Gilpin (1762–1843). Following the success of this book, he decided to bring out in two volumes his *Observations on the Mountains and Lakes of Cumberland and West-moreland* in 1786. This was followed three years later with another two-volume work, *Observations . . . on several Parts of Great Britain; particularly the High-Lands of Scotland,* and, in 1791, with *Remarks on Forest Scenery,* also in two volumes.

These books enjoyed a huge popular success and saw a heavy circulation from lending libraries for many years following their publication. "And when was the public eye ever instructed by the pen and pencil at once, with equal excellence in the style of both, but by Mr. Gilpin?" asked Walpole rhetorically. Both poets and prose writers began analyzing scenery in terms of the Picturesque, so much so that the excesses of the fashion were soon being satirized by some, including Jane Austen, who, nevertheless, was a confirmed Gilpinite (fig. 7.23).[26]

Gilpin's writings, which were translated into French and German, became revered texts both for scenic tourists and landscape gardeners. Frederick Law Olmsted (1822–1903), the future designer of Central Park, remembered that the extended carriage tours he took through the Connecticut countryside with his father and stepmother as a boy were "really tours in search of the picturesque." He had read *Remarks on Forest Scenery* in the Hartford Public Library, and it later served him as a professional tool. He put the book in the hands of his pupils, along with Sir Uvedale Price's *On the Picturesque,* with the instruction "to read these seriously, as a student of law would read Blackstone." Henry Thoreau and Oliver Wendell Holmes also counted themselves among Gilpin's American admirers.

With regard to landscape design, Gilpin felt that roughness, or ruggedness, "observable in the smaller, as well as in the larger parts of nature—in the outline, and bark of a tree, as in the rude summit, and craggy sides of a mountain"[27] provided sufficient visual interest to serve the painter and that these qualities should be prized by the landscape improver as well. Polished surfaces and carefully articulated masonry joints were tributes to good craftsmanship, but these were hardly as Picturesque as a rubbly ruin, stained by weather, encrusted with moss and sprouting wildflowers.

According to Gilpin, nature was an admirable colorist but deficient in terms of Picturesque composition, and the estate improver's art therefore, like the painter's, was to take little liberties, particularly with regard to the foreground, adding here and there a few trees and in other ways giving an air of wild-

ness to the place. "Turn the lawn into a piece of broken ground: plant rugged oaks instead of flowering shrubs: break the edges of the walk: give it the rudeness of a road: mark it with wheel tracks; and scatter around a few stones, and brush-wood; and in a word, instead of making the whole *smooth,* make it *rough;* and you also make it *picturesque.*"[28] Similarly, grazing sheep with their rough woolly coats of "just that dingy hue, which contrasts with the verdure of the ground"[29] were highly desirable in a park.

RICHARD PAYNE KNIGHT AND UVEDALE PRICE

Gilpin's fellow enthusiasts for the Picturesque, Richard Payne Knight (1750–1824) and Uvedale Price (1747–1829), on the other hand, were less charitable in their attitude toward Brown. Their views were doctrinaire and uncompromising, and to their eyes, Brown's work was insipid. In *The Landscape, A Didactic Poem* of 1794, Knight uses Pope's heroic couplets in a diatribe against the "fav'rite Brown whose innovating hand / First dealt thy curses o'er this fertile land." Knight held an almost sentimental affection for the few remaining seventeenth-century gardens of Wise and London with their "kings of yew, and goddesses of lead," for by his time these had the virtue of having grown picturesquely decrepit with age. An old-fashioned garden of this kind, in addition, encompassed merely the immediate environs of the house where "Inclos'd by walls, and terraces, and mounds / Its mischiefs were confin'd to narrow bounds." In the same way that the eighteenth-century painter or sketch artist avoided a linear style and crisp outline in favor of chiaroscuro effects of light and shade, so according to proponents of the Picturesque, the landscape improver should avoid neat definitions of forms in favor of hazier, less distinct shapes that produced a more "artistic" appearance. Knight's friend Uvedale Price also deplored the sacrifice of the old hunting parks to the improver's hand, and his work

On the Picturesque (1784), which enjoyed several editions and was extensively read for the better part of a century, inquires "whether the present system of improving . . . is founded on any just principles of taste."[30] Like Knight, he believed that a knowledge of the works of the great masters, particularly those of Claude Lorrain, Poussin, Salvator Rosa, and the Dutch school, and an understanding of the *principles* of painting—"general composition—grouping the separate parts—harmony of tints—unity of character"[31]—should inform the minds of those who would be improvers.

According to Price, in studying painting one readily observes that two interrelated qualities constitute the essence of the Picturesque: *intricacy* and *variety*. He defines intricacy as "that disposition of objects, which, by a partial and uncertain concealment, excites and nourishes curiosity," while variety in scenery is defined as that which is in opposition to the formulaic perfection of Brown. Monotony is the enemy of the Picturesque, and Price deplores that once the "mechanical and commonplace operation, by which Mr. Brown and his followers have gained so much credit," is begun, one is forced to bid "adieu to all that the painter admires—to all intricacies—to all the beautiful varieties of form, tint, and light and shade; every deep recess—every bold projection—the fantastic roots of trees—the winding paths of sheep" together with "what time only, and a thousand lucky accidents can mature, so as to make [the landscape] become the admiration and study of a Ruysdael or a Gainsborough."[32]

Though both were united in their intense opposition to Brown, there are distinctions between Knight's version of Picturesque theory and that of Price. For Knight, picturesqueness resides within the eye of the beholder who, by "having his mind enriched with the embellishments of the painter and the poet," invests natural objects with "ideal and imaginary beauties; that is, beauties, which are not felt by the organic sense of vision; but by the intellect and imagination through that sense."[33] Price, on the other hand, tries to objectify the Picturesque, making it a separate category alongside Burke's categories of the beautiful and the sublime.

While critical of the serpentine outlines of Brown's bodies of water, Price reserves his greatest scorn for the improver's method of planting trees in clumps. Brown's clumps appear to him variously as regimental soldiers on parade or as so many puddings turned out of a mold. He finds even the old arrow-straight approach avenues of an earlier generation preferable to the narrow winding belts of newly planted trees beside Brown's drives. In this vein of contrariety, he romantically admires such entrance roads

as those leading to Stowe and Castle Howard for their solemnity and grandeur, especially at night when a few gleams of moonlight pierce the deep gloom of their dense foliage.

Practical minds took with a grain of salt Price's prescription of negligence as a means toward art. Even his admiring mid-nineteenth-century editor inserted into Price's reprinted text a note of warning regarding the advantages of smooth, well-graded carriage roads over picturesquely rough ones. While the Picturesque theorists greatly stimulated a new appetite for travel into the wilder parts of the British Isles, estate improvement, with some increased picturesqueness in the park, continued to develop in a manner derived from Kent and Brown. That an intermediate position between two perceived polarities prevailed as the English countryside continued to be coaxed into new patterns of domestic felicity was due in large measure to the practice and writings of Humphry Repton.

HUMPHRY REPTON

Humphry Repton (1752–1818), Brown's self-appointed successor and the inheritor of his practice, felt obliged to seize the gauntlet thrown down by Knight and Price. He therefore took up his pen to defend the great Brown, attempting to show how the principles of painting and landscaping were not, in fact, one and the same as the Picturesque theorists maintained. According to Repton, the landscape subject matter suitable for painting was that which could be contained within the representational confines of the artist's canvas, whereas the beauties of real landscape encompassed those of prospect—panoramic views obtained from a lofty ridge or belvedere. He maintained that "the good sense and good taste of this country will never be led to despise the comfort of a gravel walk, the delicious fragrance of a shrubbery, the soul-expanding delight of a wide extended prospect, or a view down a steep hill, because they are all subjects incapable of being painted."[34]

Repton, as a professional landscape gardener, had thought it important to discourage amateur improvers who were, in his opinion, in the same position as a patient "quacking himself." Unlike Brown, whose schooling was essentially vocational, Repton had, in fact, received a gentleman's education and had been led to his professional practice by his own enthusiasm as an amateur improver and the realization that, with Brown's death, a vacuum had been created, which a man with small means and a growing family could hope to fill.

Like his American successor, Frederick Law Olmsted, another amateur-turned-landscape-professional, Repton found his way to his vocational calling by a circuitous route; both were financially unsuccessful in business and as gentleman farmers. Repton decided to adopt a new vocation in 1788. Having moved into a cottage on Hare Street in the Essex village of Romford in order to accommodate his reduced financial circumstances, Repton, after a restless night pondering his future, arose, christened himself a "landscape gardener," and had cards printed, which, with the help of his friends, soon brought this new professional nomenclature into currency in the best drawing rooms of England. In order to fulfill his intention of becoming the successor to Brown, who had died five years earlier, he set out to see many recently improved estates, including such famous ones as Blenheim and Stowe and, following the new fashion for Picturesque travel initiated by Gilpin, he made a sketching tour in 1789 of the Essex forests.

Repton's almost immediate success was due to an idea he hit upon at the outset. A talented watercolorist, he would do more than assure his clients of their properties' capabilities; he would demonstrate with his facile pen and brush a series of "before and after" effects. In his Red Books, so named for their red morocco leather bindings, he made watercolor renderings with fold-over flaps. The scene depicted when the flaps were closed was one of rural scenery awaiting landscape improvement. When opened, the part of the image that had been formerly concealed was seen to portray the same landscape as it would appear when transformed by Repton's planned improvements. This "existing-and-proposed" format constituted an irresistible ploy, and Repton's clients were happy to pay his charge for producing a Red Book in addition to his usual fee for his survey work and recommendations on property improvement (figs. 7.24a, 7.24b). The volumes became proud tokens of their possessing that characteristic most prized by eighteenth-century polite society: good taste. They served, of course, in addition, as discreet advertisements of Repton's work, helping to attract future clients.

In Repton, Brown, who had left no written record of his principles of design, found a proponent in much the same way as Le Nôtre gained influence through the influential treatise of Dezallier d'Argenville. But, although Brown's professed heir and the grateful recipient, from Brown's son, of maps of the estates where his father had worked, Repton had imbibed the Picturesque sensibility of his time. In subtle ways, he distanced himself increasingly over the years from the system devised by the famous improver. Indeed, he advocated no system at all, but rather *good taste* based on certain principles first developed in the Red Books and later articulated in printed books after he realized that he could broaden the audience for his ideas, increase the reputation of his work,

and supplement his income through publication. *Sketches and Hints on Landscape Gardening* (1795) was followed by other works, including *Observations on the Theory and Practice of Landscape Gardening* (1803), and a final collection of thoughts gathered from a busy lifetime, *Fragments on the Theory and Practice of Landscape Gardening* (1816).

Like Kent, Repton conceived his landscape ideas pictorially. Perspectives, rather than plans, were his chief means of expression (although, unlike Kent, he did produce plans for his clients). As painting was his stock-in-trade and he was responsible for more than three thousand sketches and the multiplication of some of these many times over through published engravings, he was particularly stung when Richard Payne Knight in his essay *An Analytical Inquiry into the Principles of Taste* (1805) took exception to the term *landscape gardening* and attacked Repton personally by suggesting that "he who gave it the title may explain [why a practice that had produced] not one complete painter's composition [in many of the] beautiful and picturesque spots" of England should be so called.[35]

Repton felt compelled to mount a defense, and his rebuttal, *An Inquiry into the Changes of Taste in Land-*

7.24a and b. Humphry Repton, hand-colored aquatint of Water at Wentworth, Yorkshire, depicting existing and proposed landscapes, from Repton's *Observations on the Theory and Practice of Landscape Gardening*, 1803

7.25. Endsleigh, Devonshire, where Repton effected an architectural transition between house and garden, bringing into favor ornamental horticulture in the environs of the house. Hand-colored aquatint from Repton's *Fragments on the Theory and Practice of Landscape Gardening*, 1816

Below: **7.26. Repton's own cottage overlooking others, Hare Street, Essex, from *Fragments on the Theory and Practice of Landscape Gardening*, 1816**

scape Gardening (1806), once again exonerated Brown, blaming his uninspired followers for those crimes of clumping too tightly and belting too narrowly that were abhorrent to the warriors of the wild Picturesque. At the same time, he tactfully described concessions that he deemed appropriate for the sake of convenience and comfort, such as the reunification of the kitchen garden with the house or the design of the drive leading to the house not as a circuitous excursion but as a more direct route, though these things were in contradiction to Brown's practice. Attending to the practical needs of his clients, he made the *porte cochère* a regular feature in his plans.

The conservatism and respect for tradition that induced Repton to align himself with Brown in the first place, together with the fight he was forced to wage against the Picturesque critics throughout his career, do not obscure his steady advance toward an eclectic style that may be called the *ornamental Picturesque*. In Repton's plans, the balustraded terrace that Brown had banned found its way back to the house where it served as a zone of transition between architecture and landscape. Participating in the explosion of interest in botany occurring in his day, he incorporated exotic shrubs and trees in his plans and even allowed the flower garden, which had been categorically banished by Brown and despised by the advocates of the wild Picturesque, to exist once more in the vicinity of the house (fig. 7.25). He grasped the benefits to horticulture as well as the decorative possibilities inherent in industrial technology and found many uses for a new material, cast iron, both as ornament and as *treillage*. His pergolas and trellis arches, of both cast iron and wood, diminished the classicism of the landscape and soon became mainstays of the Victorian garden. The cast-iron-and-glass conservatories for tender plants he introduced as gardenlike extensions of the house had a similar result.

Although horrified at the excesses committed in France in the name of equality, Repton had a sharper social conscience than had Brown. Villages were no longer swept away because they marred a view; now their inherent picturesqueness served to complement the landscapes of great houses (fig. 7.26). Such ordinary landscapes are the domain of cultural geographers today and were, as we shall read in Chapter Eleven, also appreciated by the Edwardian garden designer Gertrude Jekyll (1843–1932), who lovingly photographed the cottages, gardens, and farmsteads of rural Surrey at the time when these components of the rural English scene were rapidly disappearing. If we were to chart the general attitude toward the vernacular environment among people of social influence, we might say that Repton points the way toward a more democratic and all-encompassing view of landscape and of the place-making achievements of common folk. In any case, by the end of his career, the era of great estate landscaping was effectively over, and the challenge that those who came after Repton addressed was one of inculcating the principles of taste within the ranks of a prosperous and expanding middle class.

John Nash, John Wood, and the Regency Townscape

Unlike Brown, who practiced architecture himself, Humphrey Repton associated with professional architects in the execution of his commissions. His eldest son, John Adey Repton (1775–1860), became an enthusiastic antiquarian and architect, apprenticing first in his father's office and later working in that of John Nash (1752–1835). Humphrey Repton and John Nash enjoyed a profitable professional association for a few years beginning in 1796. Both John Repton and his brother, George Stanley Repton (1786–1858), worked in Nash's office, and the stylistic union between the Reptonian Picturesque landscape and Nash's Regency Neoclassicism provided the model for a *rus in urbe,* or country-in-the-city, ideal of urban planning in which landscape was employed to soften and relieve the oppressive hardness of pavements and buildings.

Bath, the Regency spa built on the site of a hot spring and ancient Roman resort by the architects John Wood the Elder (1704–1754) and his son, John Wood the younger (1728–1781), is important as an early example of this *rus in urbe* approach to planning. Here, promenades were created as bands of greenery, and housing blocks were built around landscaped squares and on terraces with broad views of open countryside (fig. 7.27). These urban design amenities made Bath a new kind of city, one that married genteel architecture with natural scenery. Immediately popular, the town became in the eighteenth century a favorite locale for members of the aristocracy and gentry seeking to improve their health. It was moreover a place of amusement and social diversion. The atmosphere of friendliness and mild license, restrained by rules of social etiquette, provided opportunities for encounters among members of the opposite sex, creating the town's reputation of being a marriage market.

First, Wood the Elder laid out Queen Square (1729–36) in the trim Regency architectural style. He next developed the Grand Parade (1740–43), with green vistas beyond the river Avon. Another residential grouping, the Circus (1754–58) followed, in which a unified ring of houses was built around a central open space. Wood the Younger built the Royal Crescent (1767–75), and John Palmer established the Lansdown Crescent (1794) on the slope above it (1789–94). With its rolling greensward upon which sheep grazed and lovely views of the surrounding Avon Valley

7.27. Aerial view of Bath, "a new kind of city, one that married polished urbanity with pastoral scenery"

countryside, the Royal Crescent soon superseded the Grand Parade as the city's most popular promenade. The public's enthusiasm for this kind of plan—in origin, an example of enlightened real-estate development—led to a comparable effort in London around Regent's Park.

Regent's Park's beginnings are much the same as those of Hyde Park, as both were manor properties assigned to monastic orders and then appropriated as hunting parks by Henry VIII upon the dissolution of the monasteries in 1536. The Marylebone Park Crown Estate, as Regent's Park was originally known, was, like Hyde Park, subsequently put up for sale by Cromwell's Puritanical Parliament. Before it was repossessed by the crown, its purchasers cut down its venerable forest for lumber in order to realize a profit on their investment. As London's growth pushed northward throughout the eighteenth century, it became apparent to John Fordyce, the Surveyor General of Crown Lands, that, when the lease on the property held by the duke of Portland expired in 1811, the park (then occupied by the cottages of agricultural laborers and gentlemen seeking a rural retreat)

7.28. Park Crescent and the south end of Regent's Park, London, designed by John Nash. 1811

Below: 7.29. Orangery at Sezincote, Gloucestershire, designed by Samuel Pepys Cockerell for his brother Sir Charles Cockerell. c. 1800

would become prime real estate from which the royal family could realize an enormous financial gain if the land was developed judiciously.

Instead of recommending that it be divided like the neighboring Portland estate into a checkerboard of housing blocks built around a square, Fordyce held a design competition from which emerged Nash's concept of a ring of independent villas within the park and a crescent of town houses at its southern end (fig. 7.28). The plan for Marylebone, which was at that time renamed Regent's Park for Nash's patron, the Prince Regent (later George IV), following that of Bath, weds Regency Neoclassical architecture to Reptonian principles of landscape design. After some financial and practical difficulties were overcome, a crescent of stuccoed houses with uniform facades was built along the outer perimeter of the southern part of the park. Only eight of Nash's originally planned fifty-six independent villas were built, nor was the interior ring of row houses realized, and the park gradually began to accommodate other uses.[36] In spite of the lack of demand for its proposed villas, Regent's Park provided an influential example for future suburban-style development in London and elsewhere, and many later speculations in real estate bore the word "Park" as part of their name.

While most squares in London, unlike those in Paris, had been conceived as patches of greenery, they could hardly be called Picturesque. But such was the popularity of this style that, by the early nineteenth century, sheep were allowed to strike a pastoral note in Cavendish Square, and Grosvenor and Portman Squares were given more naturalistic treatment. Repton himself was commissioned to redesign Cadogan and Russell Squares in a Picturesque manner. With these and other similar developments, burgeoning London gave the newer parts of its urban fabric a looser weave. The greenery thus inserted into the metropolis remains one of the most appreciated contributions of this era to urban planning.

In 1804, Repton was called by Sir Charles Cockerell, who had recently returned from India, to advise on the landscaping of a property in Gloucestershire where he was building a house in the supposed Hindu style according to plans prepared by his younger brother Samuel Pepys Cockerell (fig. 7.29). After his visit to Sezincote, as Cockerell had christened his estate, Repton pronounced himself "pleased at having discovered new sources of beauty and variety," and when he was summoned two years later by the Prince Regent to prepare plans for a new Brighton Pavilion, the Prince Regent's summer home, he introduced his design proposal with an elaborate explanation of the suitability of such Sezincote-style Hindu architecture for the project. Ten years passed before the Prince Regent could assemble the funds to build the Pavilion, at which time he commissioned Nash to follow the exotic "Hinduism" of Repton's original inspiration.

REPTON'S INFLUENCE IN GERMANY

Hermann Ludwig Heinrich, prince of Pückler-Muskau (1785–1871), who did not admire the landscapes of Brown but considered Repton to be his mentor, was an amateur in the tradition of Henry Hoare, a man with a vision for transforming his own property into an Elysium. The 1,350-acre park he created, however, had no underlying iconographic program as did Hoare's Stourhead but was built according to a vision in which the eye's movement through landscape space was reckoned according to Picturesque principles guided by existing natural conditions. He was able to conceive landscape as a continuum of broad and varied spatial effects, and his work transforming a large stretch of the Neisse River Valley, including its industrial, agricultural, and urban scenery as well as the immediate grounds around his castle, into a unified environmental composition put him in the vanguard of nineteenth- and early-twentieth-century regional planning.[37]

A regimental officer with a well-developed taste for travel, Prince Pückler turned down an ambassadorship in order to manage his ancestral estates in old Silesia, approximately 100 miles (161 kilometers) southeast of Berlin straddling what is now the German-Polish border. Encouraged by Goethe, whom he met in Weimer in 1812, he believed that exemplary land improvement could contribute to the welfare of Prussia as much as diplomatic and political service. Energetic, athletic, and a lover of nature, he began transforming his estate of Muskau into an idealized version of nature in 1816, with an abiding passion that ultimately brought him financial ruin. In 1828, he made an extended trip to England and Ireland, ostensibly to improve his fortunes but in fact to steep himself in the scenery of the country he considered most conducive to "a gentlemanly (*gentlemanartigen*) enjoyment of life" in which comfort was combined with "the fullest appreciation of a noble sense of beauty" and "landscape gardening has also developed to an extent that no period and no other country seem to have known."[38] Although he invited Humphrey Repton's son John to Muskau to advise him, he was too assured and avid a connoisseur of landscape not to remain personally in charge of designing Muskau's park according to a unified scheme "thoroughly thought out from the first, and guided all the way through by one controlling mind, a mind that should

make use of the thoughts of many others, welding them into an organic whole so that the stamp of individuality and unity shall never be lost."[39]

To build his park, it was necessary to purchase some 2,000 acres of property, including the houses of townsmen and villagers and to demolish in the country town of Muskau an entire street adjacent to his castle, the site of the large lake made by damming the river Neisse. Still, Pückler-Muskau expressed a sense of duty and responsibility toward his vassals, the inhabitants over whom he exercised sovereign rights until that prerogative was assigned to the state alone as the European political climate was liberalized in the wake of the French Revolution. He left the gates of his park open, and it was used regularly by the townspeople as a local pleasure ground.

The remaining town lying against the side of a mountain formed a collection of architecturally Picturesque structures, which he included in the naturalistically Picturesque landscape he formed by draining marshes and creating lakes and waterfalls and building ornamental pavilions. Although confessing to "qualms of conscience that half a dozen trees murdered without reason" continued to cause him, he nevertheless advocated such tree removal in the interest of opening views and "making so many others visible which had previously been quite obscured."[40] He further recommended "that graceful negligence, so difficult to emulate, in which Nature remains ever the mistress, by the plantation of single shrubs and trees scattered freely over the grass."[41] The result of this design approach, evident in the distant views across the tree-fringed meadows of the park at Muskau, is remarkably similar to the kind of park scenery that Olmsted and Vaux strove to achieve (fig. 7.30; see fig. 9.44). Yet even Prince Pückler-Muskau fell victim to the fashion for ornamental horticulture and carpet bedding, which enjoyed perhaps greater

7.30. Long view over Meadow in the Park, Muskau, photography by Henry Vincent Hubbard, from Hubbard and Kimball, *An Introduction to Landscape Design* (1917)

popularity in his country than in Victorian England. But the ornate flower beds he placed near the palace at Muskau should not prevent us from realizing that his foremost gift as a designer lay in his ability to conceive of landscape in spatial terms.

Elsewhere in Germany, Peter Joseph Lenné (1789–1866) also brought Reptonian Picturesque planning principles to the work he undertook in association with the Neoclassical architect Karl Friedrich Schinkel (1781–1841). Lenné was responsible for designing the gardens at Sanssouci for the Prussian king beginning in 1816 and the grounds adjacent to Charlottenhof, the palace Schinkel designed in Potsdam (1826–28). He also designed the royal landscape park at Charlottenburg in Berlin, and in 1833, he began the transformation of the Tiergarten from game preserve and royal hunting park into a naturalistic park, which was opened to the public in 1840 and subsequently enlarged by Lenné to encompass a zoological garden. At a time when the international parks movement was gaining force, Lenné received commissions to design other German public parks at Magdeburg (1824), Frankfurt an der Oder (1835), and Dresden (1859). His private commissions included the grounds around Schinkel's castle at Babelsberg in Potsdam (1832–42), where Prince Pückler subsequently consulted, Klein Glienicke, Wannsee, Berlin (1824–50), and Schloss Pfaueninsel (Peacock Island), Wannsee (1824). Several of these landscapes can be visited today, and in some one sees the same breadth of perspective Prince Pückler gained in Muskau's sweeping vistas.

CHANGING TIMES, CHANGING VALUES

Humphry Repton lived in an age of political revolution, which saw the birth of republican government in France and the establishment of Britain's American colonies as an independent republic. In addition, the effects of the Industrial Revolution were beginning to transform both urban and rural life. These cultural currents profoundly altered the enterprise of landscape design, making it only marginally the prerogative of princes and the pastime of the landed gentry. The values of a prosperous aristocracy would soon be superseded by the commercialism of a new manufacturing class.

Repton, who had a normally cheerful disposition, was disturbed by the social dislocations of the Napoleonic wars and the consequent heartless life of mercenary opportunists; Becky Sharp, the protagonist of *Vanity Fair* (1847–48) by William Makepeace Thackeray, is a fictional portrayal of such a type. The superficial life of fashionable Bath was as alien to Repton's temperament as it was to Jane Austen's. Like William Wordsworth and Jean-Jacques Rousseau, Repton recognized that sensibility was the common property of the human soul rather than merely the province of an educated upper class. He was able to embrace the view of nature as a *moral* good and of landscape design as a *social* responsibility. His was a liberal-minded paternalism that was still tied to the old agrarian society, now in transition. Dorothea Brooke in *Middlemarch* (1871–72) by George Eliot, with her plans for improving tenant cottages, would have been a heroine after his heart. Although lamenting that gentlemen farmers no longer took care of the parish poor, for his son Edward, the vicar at Crayford in Kent, Repton prepared plans for a workhouse for paupers, which he saw as a humane model of that type of institution (fig. 7.31). Perhaps his greatest gift to posterity was the good sense he conferred upon the Picturesque style, modifying it and making it a practicable idiom for the design of the public park, the landscape institution *par excellence* of the coming democratic age. Yet even as the forces of revolutionary republicanism were gathering momentum, *ancien régime* aristocrats in France put their own particular stamp on the Picturesque style, which was quite different from that of Repton.

7.31. Illustration of a Workhouse, designed by Humphry Repton. Hand-colored aquatint from *Fragments on the Theory and Practice of Landscape Gardening*, 1816

V. Landscapes of Moral Virtue and Exotic Fantasy: The French Picturesque

The French never attempted to substitute the curvilinear landscape abstractions of Capability Brown for their own geometric ones. Their notion of the *jardin anglais* was that of an earlier period associated with the emblematic temples and monuments of the Augustan amateurs and the creators of the *ferme ornée*—Stephen Switzer, writer and garden designer; William Shenstone, the proprietor of The Leasowes; and Philip Southcote, the owner of Woburn Farm. Although they are called *jardins anglais,* the Picturesque gardens of France are independent phenomena, influenced by, yet philosophically and stylistically separate from, contemporary English gardens.[42]

While Turkish tents and Chinese bridges are also found in eighteenth-century English gardens, these picturesquely Rococo features are more prevalent in French ones. French eighteenth-century gardens were consciously conceived as stage sets by designers who often also worked in the theater. This aspect of French gardens of the *ancien régime* is perhaps also explained by the fact that they spring out of the dramatic tradition of French pastoral romance, which is filled with bucolic sentiment, rather than from a literary tradition of poetry imbued with moral philosophy, as was the case with the English eighteenth-century garden.

The structures that ornamented these gardens, called *fabriques,* were like theatrical scenery, usually rustic in style. The enthusiasm for *fabriques* was such that in the eighteenth-century French gardens that go by the name *jardin anglo-chinois* they became the whole point, more than was the case in England where the balance between ornamental structures and landscape still favored landscape. Some of these gardens were as full of theatrical set pieces as Disneyland.

While this type of garden was built for the amusement of aristocrats in the years immediately preceding the French Revolution, there were other gardens, also of a Picturesque character, in which *fabriques* did not overwhelm nature, where solitary contemplation and quiet friendship were the goal. These were directly influenced by Jean-Jacques Rousseau (1712–1778), a principal progenitor of the Romantic movement, whose writings awakened faculties of perception and an intuitive mode of thought in which sentiment, more than reason, was the governing principle. The French Picturesque garden can thus be characterized as falling into two basic types: those of a theatrical, exotic, and libertine *anglo-chinois* character on the one hand, and those of a moral and sentimental Rousseauesque character on the other. The former

is epitomized by the Parc Monceau, Carmontelle's bizarre fantasy creation for the duc de Chartres, a tame remnant of which survives today as a pleasant green oasis in the sixteenth *arrondissement* of Paris. Examples of the latter are Moulin Jolie, the garden designed by the artist Claude-Henri Watelet, and Ermenonville, the estate of the marquis de Girardin.

The Anglo-chinois Style

The publication in 1743 of a description of Chinese gardens by the French Jesuit missionary-artist Jean-Denis Attiret (1707–1768) helped bring into vogue a taste for irregular garden layouts and Rococo *chinoiserie.* Subsequently, François-de-Paule Latapie (1739–1823), the translator into French of Whately's *Observations on Modern Gardening,* declared that the English garden, with its lack of geometric formality, was derived from the Chinese. Between 1776 and 1787, George-Louis Le Rouge published twenty-one books of engravings titled *Détails des nouveaux jardins à la mode: jardins anglo-chinois,* which also promoted acceptance of the term *anglo-chinois* and the notion that the English garden was influenced by the Chinese. This apparent attempt to deprive the English of the distinction of having originated their own garden style, and the resentment of this on the part of the English, illustrates the historic rivalry between the two countries. But it was nonetheless true that an Englishman, William Chambers, was the principal advocate for designing in the Chinese manner. His *Design of Chinese Buildings* was published in both French and English in 1757. Le Rouge devotes an entire book, *Cahier V,* to reproducing this treatise by Chambers. With its illustrations in the hands of Continental garden designers, pagodas and other similarly exotic *fabriques* became even more popular in France and Germany than in Chambers's native England.

Innocent of the underlying design principles of the Chinese garden, Chambers saw Chinese structures "as toys in architecture," colorful bits of exotica to borrow for their superficial charm. These were but the decorative spice for his recipe of sensational effects. The production of sensations—particularly those of thrilling fear, amazed delight, and awed surprise—was the purpose of a Chambers garden. On these terms, a gardener should be a master of artifice and stagecraft, the provider of theatrical marvels. Helped by the technology of the age, landscape designers of the Chambers school could produce mock thunder and lightning and experiment with the newly released power of electricity.

7.32a and b. Two engraved views of Parc Monceau, Paris, designed by Carmontelle. 1773

Right: 7.33. Naumachia, Parc Monceau. This relic of the fantastic *anglo-chinois* garden designed by Carmontelle for the duc de Chartres (later duc d'Orléans) is now part of a public park in the sixteenth *arrondissement* of Paris.

PARC MONCEAU

It was with Chambers firmly in mind that Louis Carrogis (1717–1806), known as Carmontelle, set about designing in 1773 the 44-acre Jardin de Monceau in suburban Paris for the anglophile duc de Chartres (Louis-Philippe-Joseph, 1747–1793; later duc d'Orléans and called Philippe Egalité). Along with Chambers's *Design of Chinese Buildings,* Fischer von Erlach's *Entwurff einer historischen Architectur* (1721) furnished illustrations of Chinese, Egyptian, and other exotic architectural styles, and in designing Monceau, Carmontelle was probably inspired by engravings in both of these works.[43] In his prospectus for the garden, Carmontelle, who also served as a playwright, set designer, and master of ceremonies for the duke, stated that he wished to create a garden "based on fantasy, . . . the extraordinary, and the amusing, and not on the desire to imitate Nature." An ancestor of the modern theme park, Parc Monceau was built as an elaborate entertainment facility, a magical place evoking other lands and other periods in history (figs. 7.32a, 7.32b, 7.33).

An enclosed Winter Garden introduced the visitor to the marvels of the park. It had *trompe l'oeil* trees for walls, crystal lanterns, an illuminated waterfall, a grotto, and an overhead room from which musicians entertained those dining below. Passing outdoors, one wandered through a charming rustic farm, past a cabaret and an ornamental dairy, to the romantically Picturesque Ruins of the Temple of Mars. Beyond these stretched the Island of Rocks set in a winding stream overlooked by a Dutch Mill. There was a Flower Marsh and a garden mount, its base on one side constructed as a cave giving entry to the ice house, and its top crowned by a belvedere (alternatively described as a Turkish "minaret" and a Gothic pavilion). Past the Flower Marsh, one came to the Wood of Tombs, which contained, in addition to its romantically suggestive mock tombs, a pyramid, an urn, and a fountain.

Classical motifs predominated in the next sections of the garden with, first, an Italian Vineyard presided over by Bacchus and, beyond that, the *Bois irrégulier* with more ruined monuments, a statue of Mercury, a bell tower, and Houdon's Fountain of the Bathers. A ruined gate led from here to the Naumachia, built in imitation of those ancient and Renaissance ponds in which mock naval battles were fought. This oval pool featured an obelisk situated on an island of rock and a ruined Corinthian peristyle at one end (fig. 7.33; see fig. 7.32b).

Still the catalogue of tourist sights continued. The rest of the visitor's itinerary included the Military Column, a small botanical garden, the Fountain of the Nymph, a sculpture of Paris, a Turkish tent, a circular temple of marble, a Chinese bridge, the *Bois régulier,* a ruined castle that served as another belvedere, a water mill, a rustic cascade spanned by a stone bridge, and an island of sheep, which was next to the pretty little farm where one's itinerary through Carmontelle's sequence of scenes came full circle. But here there was still more for the busy eye to behold: a *parterre* garden in front of the main pavilion, beside which stood a maypole-carousel, called a *jeu de bague,* and two more Turkish tents.

These were the fantastic pleasures of Parc Monceau, a place where the display of objects, rather than

the plastic modeling of garden space, constituted the landscape designer's principal objective. In its mélange of exotic styles it provided a more catholic and international perspective than the gardens of Brown and Repton, which were, above all, celebrations of the Englishness of England. Here one sought the genie of the Arabian Nights rather than the genius of the place. Perhaps the principal legacy of this and other so-called *anglo-chinois* gardens was as a catalogue of ornamental features for the eclectic designers of parks and gardens throughout the nineteenth century.

BAGATELLES

In his novel *Bijoux indiscrets* (1748), Denis Diderot wrote of the mania for follies, or *bagatelles,* small exquisite houses built for the mistresses of the nobility and the *nouveaux riches* industrialists, where dalliance and seduction, given an appropriately elegant architecture, became almost a form of art. The most famous of these is the Folie d'Artois, known today simply as the Bagatelle, in the Bois de Boulogne (fig. 7.35). It was built by the comte d'Artois, according to plans by François-Joseph Bélanger (1744–1818), in 1777. Thomas Blaikie (1717–1806), a Scot who had also worked at the Parc Monceau, laid out the surrounding grounds as a *jardin anglo-chinois,* complete with a Philosopher's House, a Chinese Bridge, a Palladian Bridge, a Palladian Tower, a Temple of Love, and a Temple of the Pharaohs. These airy structures, built for the most part of wood and stucco and adorned with fragile *treillage,* have long since disappeared, but the lake and *rocher,* a massive construction of natural rock by the landscape painter and garden designer Hubert Robert (1733–1808), which was meant to resemble a Chinese mountain, remain (fig. 7.34).

ROUSSEAU AND THE MORAL LANDSCAPE

With the increasing secularization of society, as anticlericalism and the growing desire for a new, more democratic social order eroded the authority of the Church, monumental tombs, particularly those of national heroes, assumed a sentimental significance, replacing for many the shrines of saints. Rousseau, in particular, was adopted by French republicans as their patron. Ermenonville, the site of his burial in a handsome Roman-style tomb, was a pilgrimage spot visited by thousands until his body was disinterred and reconsecrated at the Panthéon in 1794 (fig. 7.36). After the removal of Rousseau's remains, the vacated tomb continued to act as a memorial. In other European gardens where his memory was also revered, such as the one at Wörlitz, copies of the tomb were placed on poplar-planted islands similar to the original grave site at Ermenonville (fig. 7.37). This much-copied garden

7.34. Lake and *rocher* bagatelle, designed by Hubert Robert

Left: 7.35. Bagatelle, Bois de Boulogne, Paris, designed by François-Joseph Bélanger. 1777

feature illustrates the elegiac character of Romanticism and also reminds us of Rousseau's fundamental importance to the history of landscape design.

Rousseau, in working out his democratic theories, had idealized his native Geneva as a paradigm of good government and social justice. Here citizens lived in close harmony with nature, for their autonomous dwellings amid urban greenery and their frequent forays into the categorically *sublime* (as opposed to *Picturesque*) Alpine countryside provided them with optimal circumstances for engaging in reverie. Reverie, according to Rousseau, was the foundation for the empire of the imagination—the life of the mind in which instructive contemplation gave birth not to idle fantasy, but rather to dreamlike images. From these, one comprehended the true and just order of things and learned to act in harmony with one's fellow creatures, who were similarly inspired by their own reflective experiences.

7.36. Ermenonville, Oise, France. Rousseau's Tomb designed by Louis-René, Vicomte d'Ermenonville, Marquis de Girardin. After 1766. The philosopher's body was reconsecrated in Paris at the Panthéon in 1794, but the tomb at Ermenonville remained an important memorial, continuing to draw visitors.

Right: 7.37. Throughout Europe where the tenets of Romanticism were embraced, similar funerary memorials to Rousseau, such as the one on the Isle of Rousseau at Wörlitz (1782), were constructed. From A. de Laborde, *Nouveaux jardins de la France,* 1808

Imagination—the faculty for creating images based upon intuitive perception—was an essential ingredient in Rousseau's idealism. His vision of Geneva as a Golden Age community was one such imaginary ideal, composed of images of natural man, refreshed and inspired by frequent contact with the outdoors and uncorrupted by the passions of an artificial society. This ideal being would live in simple dignity within the amiable bosom of his family, patriotically participating in the civic weal. Rousseau's immensely popular novel *Julie, ou la Nouvelle Héloïse* (1761), thematically prefigured, and probably helped inspire, Thomas Jefferson's antiurban vision of the virtuous republic composed of yeoman farmers.[44] There, as elsewhere in Rousseau's writings, images are employed to "lead all back to nature; to give men a love for a simple and egalitarian life; to cure them of the whims of opinion, restoring to them a taste for real pleasures; to make them love solitude and peace; to hold them at some distance from one another; and, in place of arousing them to crowd into towns, to incline them to spread themselves equally over the land, to vitalize it from all sides."[45]

ERMENONVILLE

In 1763, following service as an officer in the Seven Years' War, Louis-René, vicomte d'Ermenonville, marquis de Girardin (1735–1808), visited England, where he was impressed by the *ferme ornée* as a model of estate design and management. The garden as a privileged space for enlightened reverie, nature as imagination's muse, rustic simplicity as a means to virtue—these Rousseauesque principles also inspired the marquis when he built Ermenonville, beginning in the early 1770s. French Romanticism and the example of the English *ferme ornée* underlie his treatise *De la Composition des paysages, ou, des moyens d'embellir la nature autour des habitations, en y joignant l'agréable à l'utile* (1777), the only such French treatise to receive a contemporary translation into English.

Just as the images of Claude Lorrain had influenced the development of the English garden, so did this artist and such seventeenth-century Dutch landscape painters as Jacob van Ruisdael (1628/9–1682) and Meindert Hobbema (1638–1709) figure in the evolution of the French garden in the eighteenth century. In addition, three contemporary French painters, well known to the marquis, offered assistance both by the images they depicted on canvas and through their personal involvement in garden design. They were Claude-Henri Watelet (1718–1786), François Boucher (1703–1770), and Hubert Robert.

Watelet, like the marquis, was acquainted with Rousseau and was, like the nobleman, the author of a treatise on garden design.[46] His own garden, Moulin Joli, built on an island, incorporated various *fabriques* into its essentially geometrical plan, in addition to the picturesque old mill from which it derived its name. In basic sympathy with the prevailing social system of the *ancien régime* and lacking a principled opposition to geometric planning—unlike the Whig landowners in England who saw in regularity an implied challenge to their libertarian values—designers like Watelet were more disposed to harmonize geometric regularity and rusticity. His scenes of venerably decrepit rustic picturesqueness were therefore conceived as sophisticated Rococo perspectives within the garden's web of straight *allées.* Watelet's house, a simple bourgeois dwelling remodeled by his friend Boucher in the *style champêtre,* stood opposite the mill.

Initially, Girardin worked to develop Ermenonville with Jean-Marie Morel (1728–1810), author of *Théorie des jardins* (1776), who was later employed by Napoleon as his landscape designer. According to the landscape historian Joseph Disponzio, Morel is the French equivalent of Capability Brown in terms of landscape style.[47] Because Morel, like Brown, saw little value in monuments and structures designed primarily for their associative potential rather than their utilitarian function, he and Giradin argued. This led to Morel's retiring from the project and Giradin's proceeding as his own designer as he conceived of how to turn his 2,100-acre estate, which consisted of four sections—woods, forest, meadow, and farm—into a Picturesque landscape composition.

Girardin had visited The Leasowes, William Shenstone's English *ferme ornée,* and like Shenstone, he and other practitioners of the French Picturesque style preferred close-up views and more intimate effects to the broad panoramas often found in English gardens, a preference espoused by Rousseau in *Julie, ou La Nouvelle Héloïse.* Although loyal to the seigneurial system of property rights and his status as a member of the nobility, in laying out Ermenonville, Girardin also honored Rousseau's prejudice against straight lines, which were symbolical of authoritarian rule.[48] Imbued with the philosopher's ideals, he tried to increase agricultural productivity and paternalistically to improve the living conditions of his tenants. He engaged in agricultural experimentation, built cottages for his workers, and organized harvest festivals. He had the walls surrounding the old château pulled down, exposing the public road in order to bring into view the daily movements of ordinary men and women.

Both the north and south views from the *château* were composed in the manner of paintings; the view to the south was an Arcadian scene with a lake cradled by wooded hills such as might have come from the brush of Claude, while the view to the north was a quiet rural view of a flat field with a gently curving stream winding through it (fig. 7.38). The southern perspective was framed by a grotto and cascade, and in the lake stood two islands. The smaller one, ringed with poplars, contained Rousseau's tomb (see fig. 7.36).

The End of an Era

Although Rousseau was forced into exile with the publication of *Emile, ou Traité de l'education* (1762), his influence continued as subsequent editions of *La Nouvelle Héloïse* gained a broad readership among the rich and well-born. *Fabriques* in the form of various Picturesque hamlets began to portray his rustic taste, if not the substance of his ideas. In 1772 the prince de Condé had a portion of his extensive hunting forest at Chantilly redesigned by Julien-David LeRoy as a Norman farm village (fig. 7.39).

The fad for rustic gardens soon spread. At Versailles, Marie-Antoinette had her chief architect, Richard Mique (1728–1794), assisted by the comte de Caraman, build the Petit Trianon. The circular Temple d'Amour there became a celebrated site for entertaining visiting royalty, and, in 1781, Hubert Robert was called in to create a *rocher,* which is the source of the stream that meanders through the grounds (fig. 7.40). In the following year, Mique and Robert designed the pretty "farm" where, on the curving arm

7.38. Ermenonville, from A. de Laborde, *Nouveaux jardins de la France,* 1808

Below: 7.39. *Jardin anglais,* Chantilly, Oise, designed by Jean-François LeRoy. 1774, from *Promenades ou Itinéraire des Jardins de Chantilly,* 1791

Bottom: 7.40. Temple d'Amour and Hubert Robert's rocher of 1781, Petit Trianon, Versailles

7.41. Broken Column, Désert de Retz, Chambourcy, Yvelines, from A. de Laborde, *Nouveaux jardins de la France*, 1808

Below: **7.42. Jean-Honoré Fragonard, *The Fête at Rambouillet*, c. 1775. Museu Calouste Gulbenkian, Lisbon**

his heated greenhouses (the plants were taken to the Jardin des Plantes during the Revolution) and performed agricultural experiments on his model farm. Monville abandoned his original house on the property, the first actual dwelling in the Chinese style in Europe, for an even stranger abode: a colossal broken column (fig. 7.41). Recently restored, this structure has the surreal quality of a painting by Giorgio de Chirico. Like the work of the twentieth-century artist, it may have been intended as a metaphor portending the loss of classical civilization, as France stood on the brink of upheaval.

In the amorous libertinism and sweet licentiousness of the youthful figures disporting themselves in the now half-decayed parks of the Age of Louis XVI, Jean-Honoré Fragonard (1732–1806) is perhaps our best guide to a true appreciation of the spirit of the French Picturesque. He captures the haunting, dreamlike quality of the relics of French seventeenth-century gardens, now lapsed into picturesque decrepitude, in such masterpieces as *The Swing, The Fête at Saint-Cloud,* and *Blindman's Buff. The Island of Love* (also known as *The Fête at Rambouillet*), with its blasted tree, theatrically lit background, and party of merrymakers in a Venetian gondola that is being propelled into the turbulent rock-strewn current, has a special poignancy in the light of history (fig. 7.42).

of a lake, a *petite maison rustique* is surrounded by a mill, dairy, aviary, barn, and farmhouse.

One of the most eccentric gardens of the French Picturesque style is that of the Désert de Retz, which was built in Yvelines outside Paris by François Nicolas Henry Racine, baron de Monville (1734–1797). More personal than a *jardin anglo-chinois,* this garden, begun in 1774, contained Gothic ruins from the village church, a weed-clad pyramid (which functioned as an ice house), a Temple of Pan, an open-air theater, and various exotic *fabriques.* An expert botanist, de Monville cultivated rare plants in

VI. Designing Nature's Garden: The Landscapes of Thomas Jefferson

Although Thomas Jefferson (1743–1825) did not initiate the picturesque taste in America, he was certainly its most informed and original practitioner in the eighteenth century. With a keen intellect well furnished by a good education in classical literature and mathematics, modern science, and English law, he set about improving the estate he had inherited in Albemarle County, Virginia, shortly after completing his studies at the College of William and Mary and the commencement of his law practice. He chose for his residence the summit of a hill not far from his father's Shadwell Farm. He called the site Monticello, or "little mountain," a name that is aptly resonant when we recall the hilly landscape of parts of the Veneto where Palladio, one source of his architectural inspiration, built several villas. Jefferson adamantly spurned the vernacular Georgian-style architecture of the Tidewater Virginia plantations, turning to the late Renaissance architect, like the liberty-loving Whig aristocrats in England, for a neoclassical style that expressed the idealism of the Enlightenment and optimistically linked the new republic with the imagined political virtues of ancient Rome.

While Jefferson appropriated the union of Palladian architecture and naturalistic landscape, as well as the country estate life of husbandry, hunting, and hospitality enjoyed by the Whig peers of England, Monticello symbolized a much vaster and peculiarly American dream. They inhabited a small island; he, by contrast, had before him an immensity of sparsely tenanted lands and the new nation's self-granted franchise and growing power to lay claim to them. Set upon its eminence, Monticello offered spectacular views of forested mountain ridges growing blue in the distance. They were, in the Burkean sense, sublime. "Where has nature spread so rich a mantle under the eye?" Jefferson asked rhetorically. "Mountains, forests, rocks, rivers. With what majesty do we ride above the storms! How sublime to look down into the workhouse of nature, to see her clouds, hail, snow, thunder, all fabricated at our feet! And the glorious sun when rising as if out of distant water, just gilding the tops of the mountains and giving life to all nature."[49]

But, in spite of this paean to the American wilderness, Jefferson's agenda was fundamentally pastoral; his vision of the unfolding landscape was as an unimaginably rich resource, a bounty for future generations. He promoted agriculture as the basis of the young nation's economy, strongly preferring a land of farmers to one in which manufacturing drew people into cities. Whereas Rousseau had romanticized Geneva as an ideal arena of citizenship, Jefferson, who had witnessed the woes of crowded industrial society in England and mob behavior in Paris, saw the town as a necessary evil at best. The virtuous *nation*-state, rather than the virtuous *city*-state, was his ideal, an ideal made possible by historic circumstance, especially after the Louisiana Purchase of 1803 gave the country legal claim to an even greater abundance of sparsely settled land. The agreeable vision of Virginia as a kind of paradise and continental America as fulfilling in reality the antique myth of a pastoral Golden Age encouraged his dream of a society of "genuine virtue" in which men preserved their freedom by turning the immense and potentially fruitful wilderness into independently owned farms.

The National Grid

Monticello, with its large workforce of slaves, was the patrician exemplar of rural life. Although Jefferson might conceive of its landscape as a Picturesque *ferme ornée,* his practical mind—furnished with the precedent of his father, Peter, a colonial surveyor, and the knowledge imparted by Dr. William Small, a mathematics professor and his mentor at William and Mary—saw the national landscape in Cartesian terms, as susceptible to geometrical planning, subdivision, and valorization. In "An Essay Concerning the True Original, Extent, and End of Civil Government" (1690), John Locke had queried, "What would a man value ten thousand or a hundred thousand acres of excellent land, ready cultivated in the middle of the inland parts of America, where he had no hopes of commerce with other parts of the world, to draw money to him by the sale of the product?" But now the American land had both utilitarian economic potential as well as aesthetic importance for those who, like Jefferson, could indulge in an appreciation of the beautiful, picturesque, and sublime. In either case, this view of it as a commodity—real estate—to be bought, cultivated, and sometimes designed for delectation ignored the cosmological meaning of certain American landscapes in Native American eyes.

Twenty years before Jefferson advanced his ideal of a nation of continental proportions with the Louisiana Purchase, he had chaired the committee of Congress that prepared a plan for the Northwest Territory. With Hugh Williamson, a member from North Carolina, he developed an American version of Roman centuriation in the Land Ordinance of 1785. Instead of allowing settlement as heretofore according to natural topography, the committee set forth a purely mathematical system that would ensure an

7.43. Roads defining Jefferson's national grid dividing the United States into mile-square (640-acre) units

Clark (1770–1838) to make the first overland continental expedition to the Pacific coast and back, which they carried out between 1804 and 1806. Although neither man was a naturalist, they received sufficient instruction in botanical observation and plant collecting to enable them to acquaint the president and other men of science and horticulture with many new species.

Jefferson exchanged seeds and plants with gardening friends at home and abroad. He maintained a lively correspondence over many years with André Thouin, the director of the Jardin des Plantes in Paris, receiving and sending many specimens. He also sent to Lafayette's aunt, the countess of Noailles de Tessé, large quantities of beautiful native American plants, including mountain laurel as well as magnolia, dogwood, and pecan trees. After the return of Lewis and Clark in 1806, he directed the distribution of seeds from their expedition to nurserymen, fellow gardeners, and botanical gardens. Dr. David Hosack of the Elgin Botanical Garden in New York (now the site of Rockefeller Center) was among those who received some expedition seeds. In 1813, Jefferson asked Bernard McMahon, a Philadelphia seed grower and plant propagator with whom he maintained an extensive correspondence and from whom he ordered many seeds, bulbs, and plants for Monticello, to return Thouin's many favors to him by preparing for shipment to Paris a collection of the seeds and plants from beyond the Mississippi. Thus, in a period of intense botanical exploration and horticultural experiment, were friendships compounded from favors extended and information shared.

MONTICELLO

Although Jefferson found great personal stimulus in cosmopolitan social intercourse and sometimes grew melancholy from a superabundance of unrelieved solitude, and although he was experimental rather than managerial by nature and too involved in statecraft and public duties to make a financial success of his own agricultural enterprises, his devotion to Monticello, and later to his other estate, Poplar Forest, was vital and constant. Before it became a magnet for visitors after his retirement from public life, Monticello was his retreat where he could pursue his interest in science and philosophy, thanks to his superb library. It was also his agricultural and horticultural experimental station and the place where he first exercised his talents as an architect and landscape designer.

Methodical by nature, Jefferson faithfully kept a Garden Book in which he noted the planting, bloom, and harvest times of various fruits, flowers, and vegetables. Through this as well as from various architectural diagrams and sketches and from the

orderly, nondisputatious parceling of land. They established a national grid of 36-mile- (57.9-kilometer-) square townships formed by north-south meridian lines, which were periodically inflected to account for polar convergence, and "range" lines running east-west. The committee further prescribed that the townships be subdivided into 1-mile-square (640-acre) parcels. Surveying according to this Land Ordinance began along the Ohio River the following year.

After the Louisiana Purchase, it was necessary to account for previous French and Spanish land grants and the presence of certain rivers. Nevertheless, the relentless march of the national grid continued westward. The government at this time began to subdivide sale parcels into quarter sections of 160 acres, then into half-quarter sections of 80 acres, and finally, after 1832, into quarter-quarter sections of 40 acres. One only has to fly across the United States to see from the air how, with only a few surveying eccentricities and exemptions for reasons of prior settlement, topography, or local supremacy, road alignments following the national grid have etched a pattern resembling a giant piece of graph paper onto most of the landscape west of the Ohio (fig. 7.43).

THE AGE OF BOTANICAL EXPLORATION

Jefferson, whose Age of Enlightenment interest in natural history was as keen as his desire to understand more about the vast unexplored regions of the Louisiana Purchase, commissioned Captain Meriwether Lewis (1774–1809) and Lieutenant William

lively correspondence he carried on with nurserymen and gardening friends at home and abroad, there emerges not merely the chronicle of the creation of a famous landscape, but also the personality of an eighteenth-century polymath, self-taught architect, and natural scientist. From the Garden Book and his also reliably kept Account Book we learn that, in 1767, Jefferson supervised the sawing of lumber and the planting of fruit trees at the Monticello site; in the following year, he let a contract to level the summit; and in the year after that, he had the foundations dug for his new house. A brick kiln was put in operation and hardware ordered from England.

Jefferson owned four editions of Palladio's *Quattro libri dell'architettura* (1570) in which the Venetian architect illustrated the elements of his style. He also owned *Select Architecture* by the eighteenth-century Palladian and classical theorist Robert Morris. But he did not adhere to Palladio's or to any other architectural book in an academic fashion. Guided by the already derivative and much-altered Palladianism of England, he chose to combine ideas and adapt design forms drawn from several sources to his own sense of utility and comfort. These included the saucer dome over Monticello's parlor, derived from the Hôtel de Salm in Paris, the construction of which he had watched with lively interest in 1796 during the period he served as minister to France. However, lacking stone and sculptors to carve it, Jefferson eschewed French ornamental elegance; Monticello, with its simple native brick and chaste classical detailing in white-painted wood carved by master joiners brought from Philadelphia, retains an original *American*-Palladian flavor (fig. 7.44). The service basement was screened by a long arcaded portico similar to those found in the courtyards of Palladio's villas; however, the one at Monticello was partially buried in the hillside in order to make the movement of many household slaves and other menials as inconspicuous as possible.

Even before the house was built, Jefferson began collecting trees and shrubs and sowing seed for vegetables and flowers. He embellished the area in front of the entrance on the east with a hemicycle of flowering shrubs. In addition to planting the orchard and a kitchen garden on the southern slope, he laid out a horseshoe-shaped lawn to the west along the flattened top of the hill. Though clearly of a rationalistic, scientific, and utilitarian bent, his mind was also inclined toward the Romanticism of Rousseau. The melancholy potential of the rural cemetery with monuments and elegiac inscriptions gripped his imagination, and he understood from his reading about English gardens the associative value of temples, grottoes, urns, and texts in stone. Thus, in 1771, he thought about choosing for "a Burying place some unfrequented vale in the park . . . among antient and venerable oaks." He planned to erect in the center of this grove "a small Gothic temple of antique appearance, into which would be admitted very little light, perhaps none at all, save only the feeble ray of an half extinguished lamp."[50] He also envisioned channeling a stream into a cistern, which might serve as a pool for bathing. At the mouth of the spring he would carve a grotto, to be decorated with translucent pebbles and beautiful shells and in which a sculpture of a sleeping nymph, like the one to be found at Henry Hoare's Stourhead, would rest on a couch of moss. Other projects engrossed his imagination, including a cascade and various eye-catchers on Mount Alto across from Monticello. But while it was in his nature to fantasize architecture and daydream about Picturesque garden scenes, these projects inevitably took a back seat to his more pragmatic horticultural interests. No temple ever rose at Monticello, no grotto was built to adorn a spring, and instead of the Romantic burial ground, a simple square graveyard enclosed by a fence was established in 1773. Being both practical and artistic, the *ferme ornée* offered him a more pragmatic landscape paradigm for his improvement of Monticello's grounds. As might be expected, he possessed a copy of William Shenstone's *Works* (1764), which he had purchased a year after its publication when he was only twenty-two.

7.44. Monticello, near Charlottesville, Virginia

In 1786, he acquired the second (1770) edition of Whately's *Observations on Modern Gardening,* and it was with a copy of this book in hand that he set forth during the months of March and April with fellow American John Adams, on a systematic tour of English landscape gardens. For Jefferson the purpose of the tour was to inquire into "such practical things as might enable me to estimate the expense of making and maintaining a garden in that style."[51] Throughout his travels, he displayed his independence of taste and bias in favor of natural simplicity, criticizing Chiswick for its "useless" obelisks and for showing "still too much of art," characterizing Stowe's straight approach as "very ill," and faulting Blenheim's thin scattering of trees and "small thickets of shrubs, in oval raised beds" where there should have been "fine lawn and woods." However, he liked the way the sight line between the Temple of Friendship and the Temple of Venus at Stowe passed "not through the garden, but through the country parallel to the line of the garden" and how "the Grecian valley being clear of trees, while the hill on each side is covered with them, is much deepened to appearance." And at Blenheim he had to admit that, in spite of his judgment that "this garden has no great beauties," he was impressed with the cascade and the lake, finding "the water here is very beautiful, very grand."[52] With an abundance of fine native plants, the creation of American gardens was, he thought optimistically, more a matter of pruning and editing out what was unwanted.

On his retirement from public life in 1809, Jefferson set in motion a final campaign of landscaping at Monticello. He enlarged the terraced vegetable garden south of the central lawn to a length 1,000 feet (304.8 meters), beautified it with a small garden pavilion, and rearranged its beds so as to make it more agreeable for viewing from above. He laid out a serpentine path within the horseshoe-shaped lawn and created oval beds where he could display the many species of bulbs and flowers that he continually collected. He built a ha-ha to separate the lawn and pleasure grounds from the agricultural landscape. He constructed three circular drives, or roundabouts, each one progressively larger in circumference, for touring the property. Between the second and third he planted various experimental crops.

To his gardening friend William Hamilton, the owner of The Woodlands in Philadelphia, Jefferson wrote in 1806 near the end of his second presidential term and in anticipation of his resumption of active gardening at Monticello, speculating upon how, in the climate of Virginia, which was benign and favorable to horticulture but yet too warm in summer to be as comfortable as the "sunless climate" of England, one could achieve some of the same effects. Whereas in England, "they need no more of wood than will serve to embrace a lawn or glade . . . under the beaming, constant and almost vertical sun of Virginia, shade is our Elysium."[53] He proposed removing as many of the lower limbs of trees as possible without harming or marring the appearance of the tree in order to have simultaneously an appearance of open lawn and a shady canopy. At the same time, he was shaping Poplar Forest—a separate farm where he raised merino sheep, dairy cattle, and pigs and grew tobacco as a cash crop—into a refuge from the steady stream of visitors that now flowed through the doors of Monticello.

POPLAR FOREST

Like Pliny the Younger savoring the bucolic atmosphere of his Tusci villa in the first century or the heads of noble Venetian families spending the *villeggiatura* in their Palladian mansions in the agricultural Veneto in the sixteenth, Jefferson viewed Poplar Forest idyllically. In 1811, writing from there to the portrait painter Charles Willson Peale, he affirmed his continuing enthusiasm for his lifelong avocation:

> I have often thought that if heaven had given me choice of my position and calling, it should have been on a rich spot of earth, well watered, and near a good market for the productions of the garden. No occupation is so delightful to me as the culture of the earth, and no culture comparable to that of the garden. . . . But though an old man, I am but a young gardener.[54]

In truth, mathematics and architecture—his other lifelong avocations—focused his imagination and talent as a designer on the opportunity represented by Poplar Forest even more than his delight in gardening. In his political and social theory, Jefferson embraced a wide intellectual range, sometimes encompassing contradictory perspectives. His pastoralism and antiurbanism, for instance, were inconsistent with the growth of an independent manufacturing economy in America, which he advanced as a matter of national expedience. When compared with Monticello, Poplar Forest, a project of mathematically derived proportions and geometrical forms, demonstrates that as a landscape designer he was equally capable of pursuing divergent ends. In his library was a copy of Dezallier d'Argenville's *La Théorie et la pratique du jardinage,* and in 1805, at the time he was planning the Poplar Forest villa, he purchased Wilhelm Gottlieb Becker's *Neue Garten-und Landschafts-Gebäude* (1798) in which there is a plate illustrating an octagonal garden pavilion with a central space that is 20 feet (6.1 meters) square, a plan that also calls to mind in its symmetry and four equally

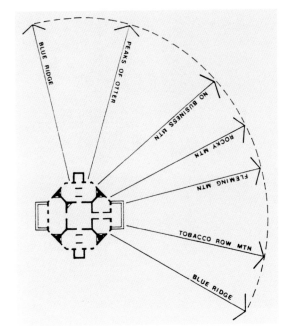

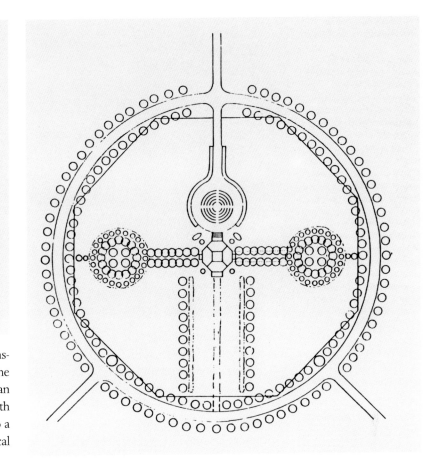

prominent facades Palladio's Villa Rotonda. Transforming the villa's measurements to a ratio of 2:5 (the obverse of the Golden Section), Jefferson designed an octagonal house 50 feet (15.2 meters) in diameter with a central room measuring 20 feet (6.1 meters) to a side, which serves as the linchpin of his geometrical landscape design (figs. 7.45a, 7.45b).

Although Jefferson was familiar with Dézallier, Poplar Forest's landscape was no formulaic application of French garden theory and practice. His interests in mathematics and classical history became increasingly important pastimes in his retirement, for as he confided to John Adams in 1812, "I have given up newspapers in exchange for Tacitus and Thucydides, for Newton and Euclid; and I find myself much the happier." At Poplar Forest, interlocking mathematical shapes—circles, squares, and squared circles, or octagons—are composed within the framework of a 100-foot (30.5-meter) modular system. Its design has cosmological overtones, the mandala-like image of its landscape plan coincidentally echoing forms and alignments found in prehistoric cultures. Its principal entrance faces due north, and its octagonal shape allows for fenestration that is oriented to the Blue Ridge, the Peaks of Otter, and other important local mountains. The entry drive has a circular terminus like that at Mount Vernon, but here its circularity is made emphatic by an outer ring of boxwood trees and an inner concentric ring of five dwarf boxwood hedges, which are divided into four sections by being broken at the cardinal points. Jefferson had the south lawn graded to form a grass *parterre,* or bowling green. It, too, is more mathematically pronounced than the one at Mount Vernon, being exactly 100 feet (30.5 meters) wide by 200 feet (61 meters) long.

Poplar Forest's most unusual design feature, two circular 12-foot- (3.7-meter-) high mounds placed 100 feet equidistant from the east and west fronts of the house, had four willows planted on their tops. These formed a 20-foot (6.1-meter) square—the same dimension and shape as the central room of the octagon. More willows encircled the mounds at their midpoint, and at their bases, which are 100 feet (30.5 meters) in diameter, Jefferson planted an outer ring of aspens. The entire composition of house, dependencies, and garden was encompassed by a circular ring road 500 feet (152.4 meters) in diameter. This road was lined with paper mulberries, prized by Jefferson for the regularity of their form. Thus, in the end, did Jefferson's penchant for mathematical relationships and classical geometries prevail over the tendency toward the Picturesque as expressed in his daydream of a dimly lit Gothic temple as his burial chamber on the grounds of Monticello. This affinity for rational form and proportion is apparent not only at Poplar Forest but also in his last great building project, the University of Virginia.

University of Virginia

Jefferson's plan for the University of Virginia demonstrates a rare level of spatial imagination and his ability to plan in a manner uniting architecture, land, and sky in a single composition. Jefferson intended this feat of landscape design to manifest his ideal of the University as a center of liberal education. The idea

7.45a and b. Poplar Forest, diagrams by Allan Brown, based on documentary analysis and Jefferson's survey of "Mountains in the order in which they are seen from Poplar Forest." From Brown, figs. 3 and 10, "Thomas Jefferson's Poplar Forest: the mathematics of an ideal villa" in *Journal of Garden History* (1990), vol. 10, no. 2, 117–139

7.46. University of Virginia, engraving by B. Tanner. 1828

Below: 7.47. Jefferson's plan for the University of Virginia as drawn by John Neilson, engraving by Peter Maverick, 1822. This document depicts Jefferson's original interior of the Rotunda as three oval chambers. It also shows the progressively increasing width of the gardens outlined by serpentine walls running between the pavilions and the dormitories. This resulted from Jefferson's desire to counteract optical foreshortening by incrementally lengthening the distance between the pavilions on either side of the lawn to accommodate the perspective along the central axis from the vantage point of the Rotunda.

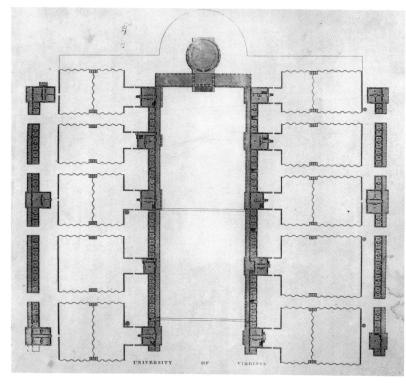

to found this institution had long germinated in his mind. He felt that his alma mater, the College of William and Mary, was moribund and poorly situated in comparison to the healthful hilltop that was chosen near Charlottesville after the Virginia legislature enacted the bill in 1819 to create the university that Jefferson had envisioned. It would not be, like William and Mary or other colleges and universities, housed in a large individual building; instead, it would be "an academical village" with "a small separate lodge for each separate professorship . . . the whole of these arranged around an open square of grass and trees."[55] Scholars have speculated upon where Jefferson may have gotten the idea of separate pavilions lining either side of an axial greensward, which is closed at one end by a central dominant structure. It is known that during the time he was living in Paris he visited Louis XIV's Château de Marly, where such an arrangement exists, and he may have retained an image of this landscape in his mind's eye as he set about planning the university and its grounds (see fig. 5.15).

Although Jefferson was clear in regard to his design intentions, he consulted with William Thornton (1759–1828), the architect of the United States Capitol, and Benjamin Henry Latrobe (1764–1820), who also worked on this project and many other important public buildings in the young republic. Latrobe confirmed Jefferson in his predilection for a rotunda at the end of the axis framed by the pavilions, and Jefferson decided to use as his model the Pantheon in Rome (fig. 7.46). He deftly employed false perspective in placing the pavilions at increasing intervals to counteract the appearance of spatial compression that occurs when one views aligned objects that are equidistant from one another. Further defining the axis and providing a covered walkway for faculty and students in inclement weather, he decided to connect the five pavilions on either side with a colonnade. Although Jefferson could not have been familiar with the stoas found in ancient Greek agoras and gymnasiums, in both form and function this pair of colonnades, which are linked with the colonnaded wings of the Rotunda, may be considered a distant cousin to the stoas where Plato, Aristotle, and other peripatetic teachers met their pupils.

Behind the academic pavilions were the dormitories. Between each pavilion and dormitory Jefferson defined a garden space by means of serpentine walls (fig. 7.47). He also established a botanical garden, which was later replaced by Cabell Hall. That one end of the axis was open was an important element of Jefferson's landscape composition at the University of Virginia. He wished to project the view in this direction to the distant mountains. This scenic gesture was, however, subsequently destroyed by a Neoclassical building built by the Beaux-Arts architect Stanford White (1853–1906) athwart the axis, thereby closing it at both ends.

That Jefferson practiced within the Picturesque design tradition of England and simultaneously employed the Cartesian geometries of France shows the breadth of his intellect and the depth of his interest in nature, landscape, and design. His essays at Monticello, Poplar Forest, and the University of Virginia belong to a long aristocratic tradition of garden design. It is significant in this regard that Jefferson was a man much at home in the French court, an Enlightenment rationalist whose fundamental design preference was for Neo-

classical forms. It is important to remember also that he was a slave owner as well as the author of the Declaration of Independence. In assessing his importance to the landscape of America, we must not forget that he expressed the country's future as a democratic (and commercial) society in his deployment of the non-hierarchical national grid as a means of subdividing the continent and selling its land. Of particular importance to his nineteenth-century successors, including especially Andrew Jackson Downing and Frederick Law Olmsted, was his pastoral vision of an agricultural society and a nation vast enough to accommodate those aspects of the nascent industrial technology as would benefit it but still leave it unscarred, unpolluted, and un-urban. This was his hopeful, and, in retrospect, poignant legacy to the American landscape.

VII. THE LANDSCAPE OF MIND AND SOUL: GOETHE AND WORDSWORTH

At the same time that Jefferson was attempting to craft a rational vision for the supremely Romantic challenge of settling a nation of continental proportions, European intellectuals grappled with the revolutionary forces that were beginning to unsettle old concepts of order. The ideals of political revolution were inherent in Romanticism's allegiance to the innate worth of the individual. The old order was fading; aristocratic privilege was gradually being supplanted by notions of equality. Increasingly, entitlement would have less to do with hereditary titles than with the concept of life, liberty, and happiness as the birthright of all human beings. Even in countries that were still monarchies, political systems were evolving that would support in a greater degree than heretofore this ideal of individual rights and, with the advent of industrial capitalism, the ability of many individuals besides members of the landholding class to affect the order of society and the condition and appearance of their surroundings. Two towering late eighteenth-century figures who were contemporaries of Jefferson, Goethe and Wordsworth, stood squarely in the currents of societal transition. Both sought to understand nature as well as humanity in deeply imaginative ways. Pivotal figures in a turbulent period of world change, they radiated their profound and lasting influence from remote corners of their native lands, Goethe from the small provincial court at Weimar and Wordsworth from the Lake District of England.

JOHANN WOLFGANG VON GOETHE
Johann Wolfgang von Goethe (1749–1832), like a proverbial Renaissance man, spread his boundless cre-

ativity into the realm of garden design as into many other realms of art and science. His influence in this area, however, was less as a designer than as a shaper of the cultural matrix within which the associative potential of nature was directed toward sentimental ends and landscape employed as a theater to enrapture the human mind.

His first novel, *Die Leiden des jungen Werthers* (The Sorrows of Young Werther, 1774), had an even more profound effect on his contemporaries than had Rousseau's immensely popular *Julie, ou la Nouvelle Héloïse* when published a few years earlier. *Werther* turned Goethe overnight into a figure of international renown, and served as a catalyst for the new *Sturm und Drang* (Storm and Stress) literary movement, which emphasized the validity of human emotion, impulse, instinct, intuition, and feeling. In this epistolary novel, sensibility is everything; for Werther, a life committed entirely to sentiment is the only one worth living, even if the consequences prove tragic.

Goethe's philosophical mentor, Johann Gottfried von Herder (1744–1803), advocated intuition over rationality and prompted Goethe's interest in Pietism and primeval legends, including the purportedly Gaelic poems of Ossian, James Macpherson's imaginary bard. It was in this period of his life that Goethe embraced German Gothicism, the epic power of Homer, and the raw grandeur of Shakespeare. Against Herder's Nordic wildness, Goethe's intellect sustained a countervailing tendency toward classicism. The introduction given German intellectuals to the systematic study of Greek art by Johann Winckelmann (1717–1768) with the publication of *Geschichte der Kunst des*

Altertums (History of the Art of Antiquity, 1764), helped Goethe to discriminate among ancient periods and styles. Winckelmann taught his readers to prefer the cool Olympian grandeur and humanism of Athens to the more worldly and materialistic power of Rome, and it was probably through Winckelmann's influence that Goethe came to cherish the temple-studded landscape of Magna Graecia, the ancient Greek colonies in southern Italy and Sicily.

In 1775, having completed his law studies at Leipzig and Strasburg and embarked upon a life of literature and intellectual achievement, Goethe took up permanent residence at the court of the provincial duchy of Weimar, where he had gone on a visit to the reigning duke, Carl August. Here his protean talents propelled him into a multiplicity of projects as he performed various political and administrative duties, oversaw mining operations, chaired commissions on war and highways, wrote and directed plays, composed poetry, accompanied the duke on military forays and diplomatic errands, pursued botany and other natural sciences, and even found time to design gardens.

In May 1778, in order to assess the political implications of the threatened war between Prussia and Austria, Carl August took Goethe with him to Berlin, and both on the way to and from the Prussian capital they stopped at Wörlitz, the park of Prince Franz of Anhalt-Dessau (1740–1817) and one of the first landscapes to be created in Germany in the English style (fig. 7.48). The prince was a talented amateur and, with professional assistance from the landscape gardeners Johann George Schoch (1758–1826) and Johann Friedrich Eyserbeck (1734–1818), was in the process of creating a garden of some 58 square miles (150 square kilometers) within his extensive properties along the Elbe.

Although the prince, Schoch, and Eyserbeck all traveled to England to study the latest trends in gar-dens there, they eschewed the design formulas of Capability Brown and Repton's version of the Picturesque in favor of the greater associative potential of sham ruins and inscribed monuments, as found in earlier English gardens such as Stowe and Stourhead. Nor was there at Wörlitz the desire to unite the palace visually with its surrounding landscape as Brown had done at Blenheim. Within Wörlitz's *ferme-ornée* landscape, many structures were given classical facades, even including some farm buildings and the observation stations on the dikes that controlled the flow of the Elbe into the long Wörlitz lake. Goethe found the scene enchanting.

Because of Chambers's influence and also that of the British volcanologist and ambassador to Naples, William Hamilton, who through his publications on Mount Vesuvius had stimulated a Romantic taste for volcanoes, Wörlitz boasts the Stein, Schoch's simulation of one at garden scale. The Stein, a hollow rock construction rising some 80 feet (24.4 meters) high and situated on an island within a branch of the lake, was built between 1788 and 1790. Goethe therefore could not have seen it when he made his first trip to Wörlitz, but the prince's guest book attests to another visit paid on July 27, 1794, and Goethe is reported to have made one or more sketches of it then as it "erupted." This theatrical event was usually accomplished at night by pumping fire and smoke out of its crater while pouring water over the lip of the cone into which were set pieces of red-tinted glass illumined from the inside. The eerie glow of the reddish light beneath the tumbling water thus gave the impression of molten lava.

Contemporary philosophy provides a key to our understanding of the appeal of this and other similar tricks. In its exposition of the soul's function as a perceiving organ, the seat of all ideas and emotions, a passive receptacle of impressions as well as an active

7.48. Wörlitz, Dessau, Germany, designed by Prince Franz of Anhalt-Dessau with Johann George Schoch and Johann Friedrich Eyserbeck. 1765–1817

force, Johann Georg Sulzer's treatise, translated as *Enquiry into the Origin of Pleasant and Unpleasant Sensations* in 1752, codified the principles inherent in the *Sturm und Drang* movement and provided the theoretical basis for the psychology underlying German sentimentalism. In 1762, the Scottish theoretician Henry Home, Lord Kames (1696–1782) published his *Elements of Criticism,* which treated gardening as a branch of the fine arts. According to Kames, through the consideration of the specific sentimental values adhering to particular scenes and their arrangement within the landscape, designers could make the garden a source of emotional inspiration.

The writings of Christian Lorenz Hirschfeld (1742–1792), the Danish professor of aesthetics at Kiel University in Schleswig-Holstein, were also important to the development of the sentimentalist garden and to the course of landscape design in Germany. Between 1779 and 1785, he produced his five-volume *Theorie der Gartenkunst* (Theory of Garden Art). Published simultaneously in German and French, this work attempted to explicate the evolution of landscape design while articulating a specifically German point of view toward it. Hirschfeld saw prehistoric antiquity as a time of felicity and oneness with nature. Subsequently, although the ancient Greeks were not garden designers, the manner in which their temples were situated in nature illustrates the harmony that existed between human beings and landscape in antiquity. Hirschfeld valued the virtues of the villa tradition of republican Rome, with its fruitful husbandry combined with scholarly leisure, and he lamented its degeneration, as illustrated by the excessive grandeur and too lavish use of ornament in the gardens of imperial Rome. Similarly, he held that the aggrandizement of the garden by Le Nôtre and his followers was inimical to the happiness of the individual, for the French gardens, intended primarily as social settings, defeated the need of the individual to disengage from society for self-renewal and self-discovery in nature.

The English garden, in Hirschfeld's opinion, thus offered a positive antidote to the French-style gardens that then prevailed in the German principalities because the English garden was more conducive to reflection and provided a relaxed setting for personal spontaneity and simple, unaffected behavior. He saw the garden as a zone of mediation between art and nature, society and solitude, a prescriptive force for entering a state of civilized innocence and socialized freedom.

Underlying Hirschfeld's work was another motive, that of nationalism. Whereas in England the nationalism espoused by Whig liberals found direct *political* expression (as well as symbolic expression in the garden), in Germany, which was fragmented into principalities, the forging of national identity was necessarily through *culture.* The *Volk,* the German people, were sustained by a venerable racial mythology, which was later dramatized in the operas of the nineteenth-century composer Richard Wagner. German utopianism, as found in Friedrich Schiller's poem "An die Freude" (1785) and Ludwig van Beethoven's Ninth Symphony (1824), was infused with joy in nature, and this joy in nature—the nature of dark forests and great rivers and green fields—could help to form a new national character, one that in Hirschfeld's view should be tempered with art. Affect—feeling and emotion as opposed to cognition and reason—was for him the guiding principle in garden design. Taste, a prized eighteenth-century virtue, had a moral dimension. In the same way as the ancient Greeks had both humanized and deified the larger landscape with their significantly sited temples and shrines, the contemporary German garden designer could uplift the spirit through the embellished natural landscape. The viewer could then create his own mental garden of noble associations and lofty ideals.

Hirschfeld's "German" garden style provided the soil in which to cultivate the seeds of nationalism and regional pride. Patriotism and community spirit were to be instilled through "portraits of those men . . . to whom we owe enlightenment, freedom, prosperity, pleasure."[56] Classical temples, even devoid of any contemporary reference, would give the landscape "useful, instructive truth," but those dedicated to Peace, Love, or some similar desideratum, or to a particular individual's valor or contribution to humanity, would be even more desirable. The "borrowed scenery" of village church spires and other distant views would remind onlookers of the reciprocal relationship between nature and humanity and of the garden's place in the larger realm of society. Real heroes were to be preferred to mythological ones, and vernacular, rather than classical, inscriptions were recommended. Hirschfeld is the father of the *Volksgarten,* in which monuments commemorating a shared history and common cultural values fostered national identity.

The *Volksgarten* was intended as a place where people of all classes could congregate in an atmosphere that combined the cultural influence of architectural features, statues, and inscriptions with the beauty of nature. Enlightened aristocrats eagerly appropriated Hirschfeld's concepts. In Munich, in 1789, Elector Karl Theodor commissioned Friedrich Ludwig von Sckell (1750–1823) and the American expatriate Benjamin Thompson (1753–1814) to lay out the Englischer Garten where native tree species and natural water courses form the scenic backdrop for various architectural features of a classical and exotic nature. More didactic by its greater inclusion

7.49. Tiergarten, Berlin, designed by Peter Joseph Lenné. 1818. Lenné applied Hirschfeld's ideas to his plan to transform Berlin's Tiergarten into a *Volksgarten*.

of statues of royal personages and cultural and military heroes was Peter Joseph Lenné's redesign in 1818 of Berlin's Tiergarten as a *Volksgarten* (fig. 7.49). The two popular public parks exemplify the transition going on in Germany as an aristocratic perspective with its lingering fancy for temples and *chinoiserie* gave way under changing circumstances to the values of a bourgeois society that desired a conservative imagery expressing the authority of the state.

Hirschfeld's influence presided over the way this cultural shift was translated into the designed landscape. He saw the necessity for certain modifications to the sentimentalist garden ideal in such public spaces as these. In the interests of accommodating crowds of promenaders and of increasing security, he recommended broad straight paths in some areas rather than winding, irregular ones. He felt that "comfort and security demand that the roads for wagons and horseback riders be kept separate from the paths of the pedestrians."[57] In addition to "good lessons . . . scattered along a path followed for entertainment,"[58] there should be places for group assembly and amusement as well as such practical amenities as rain shelters, rowboat concessions, and refreshment stands. Hirschfeld's *Volksgarten* is a forerunner of the public park as developed a few years later by John Claudius Loudon, Andrew Jackson Downing, Calvert Vaux, and Frederick Law Olmsted (see Chapter Nine).

In 1784, with Hirschfeld's *Theorie der Gartenkunst* as a guide and advice from the prince of Anhalt-Dessau, Goethe helped Duke Karl August undertake certain improvements in the valley of the Ilm where they hoped to create a park in the Romantic style, following the one at Wörlitz. He and the duke planned a riverbank grotto, and he oversaw in an ash grove in the most secluded part of the valley the construction of the Luisenkloster, a wooden "hermitage" with a thatched roof and moss-lined walls.

But for Goethe's capacious and restless intellect, the limitations of the sentimentalist garden and exces-

sive worship at the altar of nature were becoming apparent. The extraordinary popularity of *Werther* had become an embarrassment to him; Werther's tragic ending, to say nothing of the youthful suicides made fashionable by its apparent advocacy of emotional excess, was now for Goethe an implicit indictment of the *Sturm und Drang* movement. Indeed, within the novel the seeds of revulsion against excessive Romanticism had already been sown. Nature—sublime and infinite nature—"which overwhelmed [Werther] with so great a joy and made the world . . . a very paradise" could also be a torturing demon, "a monster forever devouring, regurgitating, chewing and gorging."[59] For all its intricate and miraculous diversity, its capacity to stir the senses, excite the imagination and move the soul, nature was a sublimely indifferent force, not the philosophical key to life's meaning.

Moreover, it was *feeling* itself, the Romanticist's means of experiencing life, that Werther's predicament brought into question. Even reason failed to provide a refuge for the restless spirit's quest for ultimate meaning. Goethe tried and failed to find in botanical science a fundamental unity that would bespeak a purpose analogous to divine purpose, now discredited by Deism. Yet in the end his search for the *Urpflanze,* or primal plant from which all others were but derivations, proved unsuccessful as did his efforts to supplant Linnaeus's system with his attempted *Harmonia plantarum.* It had become increasingly clear that science and religion could no longer be unified in a single philosophical framework; the human mind would henceforth find meaning in its own lifetime journey, taking such consolation as could be found from the realm of art.

Goethe explored the dilemma of modern humanity in which the comforts of religion diminish as the dogmas of the Church are devalued and science—however cleverly constructed and beautifully patterned its productions might be—merely underscores the randomness of all life and the indifference of the universe. His masterpiece, *Faust,* can be read as the clarion call of modernity and as the text that spells the end of the Enlightenment. Pope's confident assertion that after Newton "all was light," is countered in *Faust* not by a "devil's advocate," but by the devil himself, that agent of Darkness, Mephistopheles, who mocks Faust's mystical yearning for oneness with nature.

Goethe, while pointing the way to the future, was one of the last exponents of a cosmopolitan humanism in which classical culture could still provide a working vocabulary for artists. Like Hirschfeld, he sought the *Mittelweg,* or middle way, a compromise between classicism and Romanticism, reason and emotion, sense and sensibility. In *Die Wahlverwandtschaften*

("Elective Affinities," 1809), the garden becomes a metaphor for the tension created by these polarities within the fabric of society and within the marriage contract. The old gardener regrets that the geometrical garden of former days is now unused and no longer appreciated, while the newly created Romantic garden with its moss hut and sweeping views of picturesque village and countryside becomes the locus of tragedy. Excessive sentiment and unheeded wisdom provide Goethe's recipe for doom. This tale of unchecked extramarital passion is interwoven with the narrative of the garden-building project, which the aristocratic owners find to be merely a palliative for the boredom of an otherwise idle existence.

But the forces of cultural as well as political revolution had been unleashed, and these proved far too powerful to be restrained. The seeds of German nationalism that had been sown by German Romanticism would flower satanically in the evils of the twentieth century. But Romanticism's legacy has another side. One might say that, by questioning the existence of God and looking for higher meaning in nature, the human race had discovered the true measure of the soul or, put another way—Wordsworth's in his autobiographical poem *The Prelude*—

> . . . how the mind of man becomes
> A thousand times more beautiful than the earth
> On which he dwells, above this Frame of things
> (Which, 'mid all revolutions in the hopes
> And fears of men doth still remain unchanged)
> In beauty exalted, as it is itself
> Of substance and of fabric more divine.[60]

WILLIAM WORDSWORTH

William Wordsworth (1770–1850) embraced the Romantic movement in all its radical and revolutionary dimensions, celebrating as did his fellow poets Blake, Coleridge, Keats, Shelley, and Byron, the tremendous political, sexual, imaginative, and spiritual energy that it released precisely when the Industrial Revolution was unleashing unprecedented forces of mechanical energy. Written in the wake of the French and American Revolutions, Wordsworth's poetry is one of affirmation in which egalitarianism is eagerly endorsed, both politically and in terms of the rights of the human mind (*all* human minds) to gain access to emotion and experience. For Wordsworth, the human heart is the common property of humanity, and the poet's task is to reveal, through imagination and language, images and ideas that will cause people to exercise this emotional birthright.

Simplicity, purity of response, and the innocent wonder of childhood are more important to Wordsworth than elegant expression and enlightened discourse. Naïveté has its own profundity, and *feeling* is all. Nature unadorned, shorn of ornament and allusion, is capable of inspiring the loftiest thoughts. The rainbow, much cherished by Wordsworth as a symbol, stands for our covenant with nature, a covenant in which our own infinitely renewable imaginative resources are assured by nature's own numinous being.

He knows that there is pathos in the yearning for unity and wholeness, as the moments in which one experiences a sense of divine totality are elusive and transitory. Yet Wordsworth finds in our wonderment in the face of nature and in the contentment afforded by "spots of time"—the renewal of self through stored recollections of sublimity—the apparatus of faith. His poem *Lines Written a Few Miles Above Tintern Abbey*, composed on July 13, 1798, while revisiting the "sylvan Wye" with its picturesque scenery and poetic ruins—the scenery popularized by Gilpin—is an embodiment of the faith whereby the human mind can achieve, not through reason, but by some innate and incomprehensible power

> —that serene and blessed mood
> In which affections gently lead us on,
> Until, the breath of this corporeal frame
> And even the motion of our human blood
> Almost suspended, we are laid asleep
> In body and become a living soul,
> While, with an eye made quiet by the power
> Of harmony and the deep power of joy,
> We see into the life of things . . .[61]

Wordsworth did not need temples, statues, or inscriptions to excite this mood. His poetry gives sanction to landscapes without any associations other than those of one's own recollected experiences of nature rapturously imbibed in youth:

> The sounding cataract
> Haunted me like a passion: the tall rock,
> The mountain, and the deep and gloomy wood,
> Their colours and their forms, were then to me
> An appetite: a feeling and a love,
> That had no need of a remoter charm,
> By thought supplied, or any interest
> Unborrowed from the eye.[62]

The same scenes of natural unadorned landscape can serve as a source of wisdom in maturity when

> . . . That time is past,
> And all its aching joys are now no more,
> And all its dizzy raptures. . . .
> . . . For I have learned
> To look on Nature not as in the hour

Of thoughtless youth, but hearing oftentimes
The still, sad music of humanity,
Nor harsh, nor grating, though of ample power
To chasten and subdue.[63]

Nature is thus for Wordsworth a powerful moral force, teacher, and guide. In Locke's philosophy, the senses gave rise to ideas; in Wordsworth's Romantic vision, the transaction that occurs between the human mind and nature awakens a spiritual sense, and this engenders feelings of reverence and awe. In "The Ascent of Snowdon," with which he concludes *The Prelude,* Wordsworth narrates an epiphany:

A meditation rose in me that night
Upon the lonely Mountain when the scene
Had passed away, and it appeared to me
The perfect image of a mighty Mind,
Of one that feeds upon infinity,
That is exalted by an underpresence,
The sense of God, or whatsoe'er is dim
Or vast in its own being. . . .[64]

With this spiritual legacy, it is understandable that Romanticism became a dominant cultural force in the nineteenth century. The paintings of Turner, the music of Wagner, the criticism of Ruskin, the acting of Bernhardt—all attest to the vigorous long life of Romanticism, a movement whose echoes still resonate in our own day.

Wordsworth's work is pivotal. His is a revolutionary voice championing common humanity. He sings the heroes heretofore unsung; common folk, not legendary heroes, populate his poems. "The Old Cumberland Beggar," "The Idle Shepherd Boys," "The Sailor's Mother," and "The Tinker" exist amid the picturesqueness of "The Ruined Cottage," "Hart-

Leap Well," and "The Waterfall and the Eglantine." For Wordsworth, beauty lies not in a some remote Golden Age, but is "a living Presence of the earth." In "Home at Grasmere" ("The Recluse") he queries:

. . . Paradise, and groves
Elysian, fortunate islands, fields like those of old
In the deep ocean, wherefore should they be
A History, or but a dream, when minds
Once wedded to this outward frame of things,
In love, find these the growth of common day?[65]

For him, the union of mind and universe is a boundless one; it implies individuation and seeks the sublime in the quotidian. Court and city were corrupt institutions in Wordsworth's opinion, the breeding grounds of inequality and misery. It is in the haunts of nature that the mind can itself become a kind of paradise, the place where idealized moral beings like Rousseau's citizen of Geneva or Jefferson's yeoman farmer can experience joy and know self-worth. Solitude was for him a condition to be prized, a necessary means of developing the spiritual within oneself.

Although he did not align himself in the Picturesque controversy that had recently raged between Knight, Price, and Repton, he held definite views regarding landscape design, as was evident at Dove Cottage and Rhydal Mount, his Lake District villa near Grasmere, where his own gardens displayed his fine color sense and knowledge of botany (fig. 7.50). Rustic summerhouses, rock walls encrusted with moss and covered with vines, and steps with flowers squeezing through the paving stones were to be found in both. In 1806, at the request of his friends, Sir George and Lady Beaumont, he sketched a plan that would convert an abandoned quarry at their country seat, Coleorton Hall, Leicestershire, into a one-acre win-

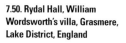

7.50. Rydal Hall, William Wordsworth's villa, Grasmere, Lake District, England

ter garden planted with evergreen shrubs, cypresses, and firs. A pool at the quarry's edge reflected its craggy side walls and the tall spires of the conifers. A single basin for goldfish set in a lawn spangled with a few wildflowers completed Wordsworth's design of this intimate and secluded retreat where one could experience the joys of solitude.

Glimpses of two ivy-clad cottages were allowed to intrude upon this Romantic scene, for Wordsworth subscribed to the utilitarianism that would increasingly dominate nineteenth-century culture, believing that these signs of productive husbandry were compatible with the poetic mood of his landscape composition. He felt that the landscape designer should respect the "sentiment of the place," the term he substituted for Pope's "Genius of the Place." Just as he banished the old classical deities of aristocratic humanism from his poetry, so, too, he wanted in the designed landscape no allusions other than those inherent in natural and rural scenery. He wished to raise aesthetics above the dictates of taste to the realm where the mind, informed by culture, could engage actively and imaginatively with landscape in all its aspects, including the vernacular.

The revolutionary era that informed Wordsworth's intellect and to which he gave voice had important consequences for landscape design. Hence-forth, Bacchus and Pan would absent themselves from the garden. With them, too, would disappear an international vocabulary of landscape ornament as cosmopolitan culture gave way to the ideals of Romantic nationalism. Thus, in an extension of the *Volksgarten* concept, folk heroes and other emblems of a political and secular order would take the place of antique divinities.

In the dawning Industrial Age, many people left the villages that were at last being considered picturesque adornments to the country seat, aggregating in cities larger than any built before. It would henceforth be the task of democratic humanitarianism to ameliorate the conditions of urban life through the institution of the public park, the Romantic landscape of the common man. But before examining the further manifestations of Romanticism in nineteenth-century landscape design and the corresponding continuation and modification of the picturesque as a viable style for private pleasure grounds and public parks alike, it is necessary to look at two other approaches to the spiritual in nature, those of China and Japan. As we have seen, the taste for Rococo *chinoiserie* in the eighteenth century brought but a facile interpretation of Chinese garden style into Western currency. We must therefore ask the question: What is the nature of Chinese and Japanese landscape design?

Notes for Chapter Seven

1. Shaftesbury's use of this phrase prefigures Pope's advice to Lord Burlington (and all gardeners) to "Consult the Genius of the Place in all . . . "

2. As anthologized in *The Genius of the Place: The English Landscape Garden 1620–1820*, ed. John Dixon Hunt and Peter Willis (New York: Harper & Row, 1975), p. 81.

3. Ibid., p. 142.

4. Ibid.

5. See John Dixon Hunt, *The Figure in the Landscape: Poetry, Painting, and Gardening in the Eighteenth Century* (Baltimore: Johns Hopkins Press, 1976), pp. 63–64, for a good discussion of the relationship between Locke's epistemology and Addison's advocacy of naturalism as the appropriate matrix for imagination.

6. Ibid., p. 144.

7. For a good discussion of this subject, see John Dixon Hunt, "Emblem and Expression in the Eighteenth-Century Landscape Garden," *Gardens and the Picturesque* (Cambridge, Mass.: The MIT Press, 1992), chap. 3.

8. "An Epistle to Richard Boyle, Earl of Burlington," *Alexander Pope*, ed. Pat Rogers (Oxford: Oxford University Press, 1993), lines 47–70.

9. See James Thomson, "Autumn," *The Seasons* (London: Longman, Brown, Green, and Longmans, third ed., 1852), lines 1361–66.

10. Switzer first used the term in the 1742 edition of *Iconographia Rustica*, where he spoke of the style that had become "the Practice of the best Genius's of France, under the Title of la Ferme Ornée." In a letter of 1748 to a friend, William Shenstone said of the Leasowes, "I give my place the title of a *ferme ornée*." In France, however, the term was not found until 1774, when used by Claude-Henri Watelet in *Essai sur les jardins*. See Patrick Goode and Michael Lancaster, eds., *The Oxford Companion to Gardens* (Oxford: Oxford University Press, 1986), p. 186.

11. Thomas Whately, *Observations on Modern Gardening* (London: T. Payne, 1770), Sect. XXVI, p. 61.

12. Horace Walpole's *The History of the Modern Taste in Gardening* and Thomas Whately's *Observations on Modern Gardening* stimulate reflection upon what the word *modern* meant for the garden theorist or historian of the second half of the eighteenth century. The eighteenth-century use of the word *modern* implied the abandonment of iconographic programs with metaphors drawn from classical literature, sculpture, or architecture in favor of an art in which the Burkean beauty of the remod-eled English landscape could stimulate the senses and imagination. Walpole, wishing to create the impression of a dramatic design coup in which the British substituted a naturalistic style for a geometrically ordered, French-derived one, failed to draw any significant distinctions between the Augustan gardens of the first half of the eighteenth century and the more naturalistically designed landscapes of the second half.

13. Horace Walpole, "The History of the Modern Taste in Gardening 1771–80" in *The Genius of the Place*, ed. Hunt and Willis, p. 313.

14. See John Dixon Hunt, *Garden and Grove: The Italian Renaissance Garden in the English Imagination: 1600–1750* (Princeton, New Jersey: Princeton University Press, 1986), pp. 180–84, for a good discussion of British political mythology following the Glorious Revolution and evidence of the evolutionary, rather than revolutionary, history of the English garden. Hunt points out the Italian antecedents that influenced Kent and other eighteenth-century designers.

15. In saying this, Horace Walpole was devising a worthy ancestry for his own contemporary, Lancelot "Capability" Brown, who was busy revising old estate gardens and creating new ones in the naturalistic style throughout the English countryside. Walpole's endorsement of Kent can be read as a chauvinistic claim to England's primacy in developing that style at an early date. Because of French-English rivalry, Walpole was reluctant to recognize, as more disinterested garden historians do today, that André Le Nôtre had in the seventeenth century visually extended the garden beyond its actual boundaries.

16. Debate continues over the value of its nineteenth-century overlay of rhododendrons and other exotic plants.

17. Kenneth Woodbridge, *Landscape and Antiquity: Aspects of English Culture at Stourhead* (Oxford: Oxford University Press, 1970).

18. For a comprehensive discussion of the enclosure movement and the physical changes it brought about, see W. G. Hoskins, *The Making of the English Landscape* (Harmondsworth, Middlesex, England: Penguin Books, 1970), chaps. 5 and 6. It should be noted that the bulk of land enclosure forced by numerous enactments by Parliament occurred between 1750 and 1860. These nonconsensual enclosures of the old open fields caused a great deal of social dislocation and left, in addition to a legacy of bitterness, regret for old beauties now vanished.

19. Enclosure led to "improvement," meaning the amelioration of the land to make it more comely and productive. In this sense, much of the eighteenth-century English countryside was in a state of improvement. But Brown, whose initial apprenticeship was in effecting estate improvements following enclosure, became an improver in the more daring sense of being one who sought to perfect nature by correcting its "flaws."

20. As quoted in Edward Hyams, *Capability Brown & Humphrey Repton* (New York: Charles Scribner's Sons, 1971), p. 77.

21. Edmund Burke, *A Philosophical Enquiry into the Origin of our Ideas of the Sublime and Beautiful,* 7th ed. (London: J. Dodsley, 1773), p. 300.

22. See William Chambers, "Designs of Chinese Buildings, Furniture, Dresses, Machines, and Utensils (1757), "in *The Genius of the Place,* ed. Hunt and Willis, p. 284.

23. William Chambers, "A Dissertation on Oriental Gardening (1772)," in *The Genius of the Place,* ed. Hunt and Willis, p. 321.

24. William Mason, "An Heroic Epistle to Sir William Chambers (1773)," in *The Genius of the Place,* ed. Hunt and Willis, p. 323.

25. As quoted in William D. Templeman, *The*

Life and Work of William Gilpin (1724–1804): Master of the Picturesque (Urbana: University of Illinois Press, 1939), p. 120.

26. Gilpin's biographer, William Templeman, quotes Austen's brother in saying that "She was a warm and judicious admirer of landscape, both in nature and on canvass. At a very early age she was enamoured of Gilpin on the Picturesque, and she seldom changed her opinions either on books or men." See Templeman, op. cit., p. 295.

27. Ibid., p. 137.

28. Ibid.

29. See Gilpin, "Remarks on Forest Scenery" in *The Genius of the Place,* ed. Hunt and Willis, p. 341.

30. Uvedale Price, *On the Picturesque* (1784), Sir Thomas Dick Lauder, ed. (Edinburgh: Caldwell, Lloyd, & Co., 1842), p. 59.

31. Ibid., p. 64.

32. Ibid., p. 73.

33. Richard Payne Knight, *An Analytical Inquiry into the Principles of Taste* (1805) in *The Genius of the Place,* ed. Hunt and Willis, p. 350.

34. Ibid., p. 416.

35. Richard Payne Knight, *An Analytical Inquiry into the Principles of Taste* (London: T. Payne, Mews Gate and J. White, Fleet Street, 1805), p. 214.

36. Part of the northeastern edge of Regent's Park was assigned to the Zoological Society of London in 1826 as the home of the London zoo, and eighteen acres of the Inner Circle were rented by the Royal Botanical Society from 1839 until 1932 when they were taken over by the Royal Parks Department and turned into a rose garden named for Queen Mary, wife of George V.

37. In a foreword to *Hints on Landscape Gardening,* John Nolen, an early-twentieth-century regional planner, hailed Prince Pückler as "a prophet of city-planning." Nolan wrote that "[m]ore than a hundred years ago he dwelt upon the necessity for natural and picturesque beauty in great cities, giving as an example the open parks and irregular streets of London." Prince Pückler's landscape theories also had a direct effect upon American cemetery design. His pupil Adolph Strauch immigrated to the United States, and as the superintendent of Spring Grove Cemetery in Cincinnati after 1855, he planned the cemetery's lawns and artificial lakes according to the principles the prince had enunciated in *Hints on Landscape Gardening.* By eliminating fenced burial plots and substituting grade-level grave markers for headstones, Strauch was able to create a flowing naturalistic landscape that influ-

enced the layout and style of other cemeteries in the country.

38. Pückler-Muskau, *Hints on Landscape Gardening,* p. 4. Pückler-Muskau's epistolary account, *Tour in England, Ireland, and France in the Years 1828 and 1829; In a Series of Letters by a German Prince* (Philadelphia: Carey & Lea, 1833), is more highly colored by personal sentiment but nevertheless similar to Frederick Law Olmsted's *Walks and Talks of an American Farmer in England* (New York: George P. Putnam, 1852), both being conversationally rendered accounts of the authors' daily impressions of people and places as they traveled through Britain, observing manners, mores, monuments, and landscapes.

39. Pückler-Muskau, *Hints on Landscape Gardening,* p. 13.

40. Ibid., p. 59.

41. Ibid., p. 68.

42. For a comprehensive and authoritative discussion of this subject, see Dora Wiebenson, *The Picturesque Garden in France* (Princeton, New Jersey: Princeton University Press, 1978).

43. See Dora Wiebenson, *The Picturesque Garden in France,* pp. 95–96. Carmontelle was known as an author of *proverbes dramatiques,* or dramatic proverbs. The dramatic proverb was a society theatrical piece, meant as an amusement for the court.

44. In her essay "Luxury in the garden: *La Nouvelle Héloïse* reconsidered," Susan Taylor-Leduc maintains that Rousseau's "allusions to 'Republican virtues' may be considered as a call to maintain a paternalistic feudal order" based upon the seigneurial land organization system and a corresponding *idéologie nobiliaire* prevalent in France before the Revolution. See *Studies in the History of Gardens & Designed Landscapes* 19:1 (January–March 1999), p. 75.

45. As quoted in James Miller, *Rousseau, Dreamer of Democracy* (New Haven: Yale University Press, 1984), p. 11.

46. Claude-Henri Watelet, *Essai sur jardins* (1774). (In his earlier *Encyclopédie* of 1756, Watelet coined the term *fabrique.*)

47. Joseph Disponzio, "Jean-Marie Morel: Portrait of a Landscape Architect," *1999 ASLA Annual Meeting Proceedings,* compiled by Dianne L. Scheu (Washington, D.C.: American Society of Landscape Architects, 1999), p. 4.

48. In describing the imaginary estate in *Julie, ou La Nouvelle Héloïse* called Clarence, Rousseau has the owner Monsieur de Wolmar point out the following:

"You see nothing laid out in a line, nothing made level. The carpenter's line never entered this place. Nature plants nothing by the line. The simulated irregularities of the winding paths are artfully managed in order to prolong the walk, hide the edges of the island, and enlarge its apparent size, without creating inconvenient and excessively frequent turnings." To this description, the author appends the following footnote: "Thus these are not like those of these small, fashionable groves, so ridiculously planned that one walks in zig-zag manner in them and at each step must make a pirouette." See *Julie, ou La Nouvelle Héloïse* (Julie, or the New Heloise), trans. Judith H. McDowell (University Park: The Pennsylvania University Press, 1968), p. 311.

49. Letter to Maria Cosway, 1786. As quoted in Merrill D. Peterson, *Thomas Jefferson and the New Nation* (Oxford: Oxford University Press, 1970), p. 24.

50. From Jefferson's Account Book and included in the meticulously annotated *Thomas Jefferson's Garden Book,* ed. Edwin Morris Betts (Philadelphia: The American Philosophical Society, 1944), p. 25.

51. As quoted in Peter Martin, *The Pleasure Gardens of Virginia* (Princeton, N.J.: Princeton University Press, 1991), p. 111.

52. Ibid., pp. 111–14 *passim.*

53. As quoted in Martin, op. cit., p. 147.

54. Andrew A. Lipscomb and Albert E. Bergh, *The Writings of Thomas Jefferson* (Washington, D.C.: Thomas Jefferson Memorial Association, 1903), vol. 13, pp. 78–79.

55. Lipscomb and Bergh, *The Writings of Thomas Jefferson,* vol. 12, p. 387.

56. As quoted in Linda Parshall, "C. C. L. Hirschfeld's Concept of the Garden in the German Enlightenment," *Journal of Garden History,* 13:3, p. 149.

57. Ibid., p. 157.

58. Ibid., p. 158.

59. *The Sorrows of Young Werther (Die Lieden des jungen Werthers,* 1774), trans. Michael Hulse (Harmondsworth, Middlesex, England: Penguin Books, 1989), p. 66.

60. William Wordsworth, "The Prelude" in *William Wordsworth,* ed. Stephen Gill (Oxford: Oxford University Press, 1984), Book XIII, lines 446–452.

61. Wordsworth, "Lines written a few miles above Tintern Abbey," Lines 42–50.

62. Ibid., Lines 77–84.

63. Ibid., Lines 84–94.

64. Book XIII, lines 66–73.

65. "Home at Grasmere," Lines 996–1001.

NATURE AS MUSE:
THE GARDENS OF CHINA AND JAPAN

The notion of landscape as a text with encoded meaning, a place of memory and association, an experiential space in which to stroll and enjoy the unfolding of sequential views or to sit quietly and ponder the thoughts prompted by the impressions of scenery upon the senses—these fundamentals were common to both East Asian gardens and the gardens developed in England in the eighteenth century. The reciprocal association between landscape design and painting that was first developed in China and then later adopted in Japan is similar to the eighteenth-century English sensibility that found in Claude Lorrain's seventeenth-century paintings an appropriate idiom for the layout of the parks of great estates. Similarly, an affinity for landscape themes, prevalent in eighteenth- and nineteenth-century English literature, is especially common in the poetry of China and Japan. The Romantic appreciation for the sublime in nature, which caused William Wordsworth to attune his soul to "the sounding cataract . . . the tall rock, the mountain, and the deep and gloomy wood," was akin to the reverence for nature of Chinese scholars and mystics many centuries before.

But in spite of this apparent similarity between East and West, at a certain point in time with regard to each culture's philosophical attitude toward landscape, the underlying differences between the historic gardens of Asia and those formed in Europe and America are fundamental and profound. Western environmentalists attempting to reforge the broken human contract with nature, who try to reason the causes for its rupture in the first place, must reckon with the Judeo-Christian tradition of a jealous God who tolerates no rivals and is situated in a remote Heaven, the true paradise as compared to the "false" paradise of this world. The ancient Greeks, who had dreamed their gods out of the ground and placed them in the sky upon Olympus, did not so thoroughly depopulate the earth of its divinities as did the monotheistic cultures of Judaism and Christianity. They journeyed to sacred places in nature, seeking oracular wisdom at Delphi and spiritual initiation at Eleusis. But it is to nature-oriented religions like Daoism and Shinto that one must

look to find a more direct bond between people and Earth. In China and Japan, although nature was as thoroughly harnessed to serve human economic ends as in the West, the scholarly and ruling elites espoused and expressed through landscape design Buddhist precepts informed by Daoist and Shinto ideals emphasizing life lived in spiritual harmony with nature.[1] Chinese Daoist thought fostered perceptions of *qi,* the "breath," or inherent energy, possessed by all phenomena. In Japan, Shinto religion led participants to reverence *kami,* the spirits found in nature.[2] Garden design in both countries reflected and nourished these ideals.

Rocks—the mineral substance of nature—had as strong an aesthetic and associative value in East Asian gardens as representational sculpture in carved stone and cast bronze did in Western ones. In China, garden designers employed carefully selected, waterworn rocks with clefts and fissures. These spatially intricate rocks were usually intended to evoke the mist-shrouded mountain ranges of the larger landscape, for the Chinese attributed to their country's peaks the same in-dwelling mystery and connection with the divine as did other early civilizations. Such scenery might be termed *sublime* according to the aesthetics of the West.

In Japan, where mountains are less dramatically formed, designers sometimes employed rocks in compositions that intentionally evoked scenes from Chinese painting, but more often rocks were placed in water or gravel "streams" as metaphorical islands. Japanese garden designers also displayed particular ingenuity in their selection of beautifully shaped flat stepping stones, positioning them so as to form, in conjunction with moss, ground-plane patterns of highly pleasing pattern and texture. Like the rocks in Chinese gardens and their somewhat smaller counterparts displayed in the studies of Chinese scholars, Japanese garden rocks were often associated with mythical or real animals of symbolical import. In both cultures, the viewer was encouraged to enjoy the abstract beauty of these mineral forms while also imagining their resemblance to other things.

I. Mountains, Lakes, and Islands:
Intimations of Immortality in the Chinese Garden

As in other parts of the ancient world, the practice of landscape design in China originated within a cultural matrix of mythology and imperial authority. In 219 B.C.E., the first emperor of the Qin dynasty, Qin Shihuangdi (ruled 221–206 B.C.E.), sent an expedition of young men and women to the eastern edge of the known world, where the immortals, known as *xian,* were believed to dwell on enchanted islands upheld by giant tortoises.[3] The emperor charged their leader with the impossible task of discovering the sacred substance that prolonged the lives of the *xian.* Although the expedition failed in its purpose, the notion of a paradisiacal quartet of islands—Penglai, Yingzhou, Fangzhang, and Huliang—remained embedded in Chinese mythology. The association of mountains and rocks that mimic mountains with immortality

furnished the paradisiacal theme that runs throughout Chinese garden history, and the faraway *xian*-inhabited islands were sometimes explicitly evoked in garden design as well as in poetry, painting, and the decorative arts.[4]

The Han emperor Wudi (Liu Che, ruled 140–87 B.C.E.) built a lake garden in which rock constructions simulating the four island peaks of the immortals rose from the water, and later emperors, notably Song Huizong and Khubilai Khan, built imitations of these *xian*-inhabited islands in their gardens. But even without the allusion to immortality, the premise that nature's own forms serve as a primary source of inspiration is a central principle of Chinese garden aesthetics. The combination of mountains (*shan*) and water (*shui*) (together meaning "landscape") furnished generations of garden builders with imagery for their compositions. These attempted to assemble in three dimensions the scenes found in Chinese landscape painting.

Although the Chinese practiced agriculture and horticulture in sophisticated ways within the larger agrarian landscape, designed gardens (as opposed to vernacular gardens) were the exclusive preserves of an aristocratic elite. Like almost all designed gardens until relatively recent times, they were created by rulers and nobles. Many members of the Chinese nobility were mandarins, high officials within the nine ranks of the imperial bureaucracy. A rigorous examination system admitted young men into this government service, and although the sons of the nobility had certain obvious advantages of birth and education, diligent commoners whose families could finance the rote education in Confucian classics necessary to pass the examination could attain mandarin status. Scholarship was therefore highly prized among those Chinese families who sought or wished to maintain social standing through connection with the court. Furthermore, scholarship was closely allied with connoisseurship and practice of the arts.

The Chinese scholar was adept at calligraphy, painting, or poetry, and often all three. These were the expected accomplishments of the usually well-born and always well-educated class that governed China. Thus, power—which always implied both imperial favor and personal merit based on scholarship—and aesthetics went hand in hand. Even when favor was withdrawn because of political circumstances, the Chinese gentleman scholar was not without financial or intellectual resources, and with the increased leisure brought about by retirement from government service he would often turn to the enter-

8.1. "Early Spring," a hanging scroll painting on silk, by Guo Hsi. 1072, Northern Song Dynasty. Taipei, Palace Museums

prise of garden building. Understandably therefore, garden-making in China was closely allied with the other arts practiced by the Chinese scholar. The mountainous landscapes of painting, the riverine scenery described in poems, and inscriptions whereby calligraphy glossed the meaning of both natural and constructed landscapes—these three already intimately interconnected arts furnished both the imaginative resources and instruments of Chinese garden design (fig. 8.1). However, before the intricate artifice of the mature Chinese garden, with its compression of seas into island-studded lakes and mountains into hillocks of fantastically shaped rocks was achieved in the Southern Song (1127–1279) and later periods, there was already a venerable history of garden-making. Not surprisingly, as in Persia, where the first known garden "paradise" was a royal hunting park, the Chinese garden had similar origins, as an imperial game reservation.

Qin and Han Landscapes

With the subjugation of all rival states in 221 B.C.E., emperor Qin Shihuangdi established his capital city of Chang'an (modern Xi'an) on the banks of the Wei River. Here he built his lofty and magnificent palace and a vast hunting preserve known as Shanglin Park.[5] Shanglin Park was encircled with stout walls, just as the empire itself was protected with stupendous fortifications. More than an imperial pleasure ground, this huge park, with its collected botanical and zoological riches, was perceived as a symbol of the empire's worldly supremacy and cosmic grandeur. Even when the empire of Qin Shihuangdi was overthrown, Shanglin Park was not destroyed, and the court poets of his Han successors extolled its size and magnificence as well as the abundance of its wildlife, no doubt seeing in its preservation a statement of their own masters' far-flung imperial power.

The relationship between gardens and the natural scenery of mountains and water was given further impetus when in 311 C.E. barbarian invaders breached the Great Wall, and the convulsions of political power that followed gave China a second imperial center south of the Chang Jiang (Yangzi River) near present-day Nanjing. Here were found precipitous, mist-enshrouded mountains, smooth lakes, and meandering rivers. With the North under foreign control, the governing elite composed of highly educated imperial civil servants built country estates in the lush countryside outside their reestablished capital. This relocation in the scenic South fostered receptivity to Daoism, the nature-mysticism espoused by the legendary Laozi (b. 604 B.C.E.). As the old Confucian order continued to disintegrate, nature appreciation offered sensitive imperial bureaucrats an escape from the harsh political realities of the times.

With the growth of Buddhism, which had been introduced via the Silk Route sometime between 50 C.E. and 150 C.E., the Chinese gained a religion in which quiet meditation was a means toward spiritual awareness. Contemplative religious practice reinforced a Chinese proclivity for wilderness retreat, and many scholar poets and landscape artists joined Buddhist monks in seeking spiritual fulfillment in nature. In the extraordinarily beautiful Lushan Range appeared the soaring rooftops of the famous monastery founded by the Buddhist monk Huiyuan (c. 334–416 C.E.), and here and there other Buddhist temples accented the lofty scenery. This scenery, which became virtually paradigmatic in Chinese landscape painting, expresses the ideal of complete human integration with nature. It is an ideal nourished not only by Buddhist thought but also by Daoism and the Daoist concept of transcendental *qi*, the "breath" that animates all things, giving them their own inherent nature. Through syncretism Daoism became fused to some extent with the teachings of Buddhism and Confucianism, and the Daoist notion of a spiritual energy composed of the complementary Yin and Yang forces that pervade the universe became commonplace in Chinese thought. The grandeur of towering peaks and the misty vastness of successive ranges, with tiny figures defining the scale of human activity within their majestic presence, evoke the Daoist belief in the eternal unity of all things in nature. It is this illusion of total immersion in the infinitude of nature that distinguishes Chinese art from the more obviously homocentric, individualistic, and spatially explicit art of the West.

Paintings and poetic descriptions of the naturally scenic Lushan landscape furnished the ideal that underlies much subsequent Chinese garden design. Huiyuan's followers, among whom were several painters and poets, carried the inspiration of mountain scenery of mossy paths, pine groves, steep cliffs, and precipitous waterfalls into the creation of their own Lushan "parks," private rustic retreats. These were not so much designed gardens as carefully selected spots in nature that could be enhanced with such things as a bamboo grove, a thatched hut, a flowering plum or peach tree. The poets Xie Lingyun (385–433 C.E.) and Tao Qian (365–427 C.E.) found beauty in the marriage of the sublime with the humble, "borrowing" the nearby Lushan mountain scenery while taking pleasure in fields, orchards, willow trees, and the sounds of barnyard animals. The rustication of gentleman scholars and their assumption of a quasi-hermitic way of life, often after a period of service in the imperial bureaucracy, became a fairly common phenomenon by the beginning of the Tang dynasty (618–907 C.E.). Their economic and social standing permitted them to retire from worldly affairs when the situation at court or personal preference made this desirable.

In the Tang era China's population reached 160 million. Ancient forests were felled as new lands were put into rice production. A vast system of canals connected the populous Yangzi River valley with the cities of the Yellow River plain to the north and Hangzhou to the south. In addition, a system of roads converged like the spokes of a wheel upon the Tang capital at Chang'an, a teeming cosmopolitan trading center at the end of the Silk Road in the western province of Shaanxi. It was a period of commercial and urban growth, massive irrigation systems, and other public works projects. Although a powerful aristocracy governed the country, its systematic education in preparation for government service ensured homogeneous cultural values within a unified ideological framework and created an ingrained conservative political orientation.

The imperial administrative apparatus helped sustain Chinese civilization through periods of invasion and internal upheaval for the next thousand years. Those who became civil servants received extensive privileges and perquisites. They were not, however, allowed to serve in their home provinces nor to own land in those to which they were sent. Some were assigned to the court, where eunuchs and favorite concubines contributed to an atmosphere of political intrigue. In court, a scholar-administrator could easily fall into disfavor, or he could find himself on the wrong side of changing imperial policy and thus experience disgrace. Serving in a province remote from his homeland, he would often long to return to his family, friends, and property. Beset by these complexities, the scholar-administrators who constituted China's literate and affluent mandarin class, found escape from doctrinaire administration and factional politics in a life of refined retirement, pursuing Daoist philosophy and Buddhist study. Able to indulge in wilderness travel, urban culture, and rural ease, they became China's great calligraphers, poets, painters, musicians, and garden makers.

WANG WEI

In the front rank among Tang officials who were accomplished practitioners of the arts was Wang Wei (699–759 C.E.). Having passed the civil service examination when he was twenty, he was appointed Assistant Secretary for Music at the court in Chang'an because of his musical abilities. Probably for some minor offense he was transferred to an insignificant provincial post where he served for several years before returning to the capital. He bought an estate 30 miles (48.3 kilometers) outside of Chang'an on the Wang River and in his retirement from public service flourished as an artist, combining his talents as calligrapher, painter, and poet.

Wang Wei was a devout lay Buddhist, and his poetry and, no doubt, his paintings—which survive only as copies—demonstrate his sensory appreciation of such things as the tender green of willow trees by a stream, the moon's silver disk mirrored in water or shedding its white light on night-stilled nature, the blush of peach blossoms in springtime, the fragrance and gnarled beauty of pine trees, the pliancy of bamboo stirring in the breeze, the oriole's chirp, the peaks of distant mountains wreathed in mist, and tiny boatmen glimpsed from afar. His "broken ink" technique and special brushstroke for expressively rendering the rocky faces of old eroded mountains enriched the painter's vocabulary and probably promoted the appreciation of weathered rocks themselves, a significant fact for the subsequent development of the Chinese garden. Wang Wei's most famous painting was that of Wangchuan Villa, his riverside estate, a scroll containing twenty scenes depicting several pavilions along a rocky riverbank and the views from them. The scroll, which no longer exists, was copied by later painters, and garden builders evoked its subject in their creations.

While solitary meditation beside a stream or in the mountains could deepen the spirit, scenes of nature were often enjoyed in company, and for China's literary and artistic intelligentsia, the garden became a favored locale for cherishing friendship and remembering particular friends. Wine was both a solace for worldly disappointment and a means of attaining a sense of oneness with the spirit of nature. In their gardens, many scholar-poets eluded the pain of living and achieved a state of ecstasy under the influence of alcohol, a condition that they often celebrated in literature.

Nor was drinking merely a solitary and escapist pleasure. The association of wine drinking, friendship, and nature appreciation through poetry in fact goes back at least to 353 C.E. when Wang Xizhi composed a famous calligraphy scroll celebrating a springtime gathering of poets at the Orchid Pavilion near present-day Shaoxing in the province of Zhejiang. Upon that and many similar occasions over the centuries cups of wine would be sent downstream by servants as each literary gentleman raced to compose verses, or cap another poet's lines, before his cup arrived at the spot where he sat upon the banks writing. By the Tang era, the literary drinking party was an established form of entertainment in Chinese gardens, and pavilions were built with meandering stream courses incised into their floor paving to accommodate this garden game (fig. 8.2).

Several other scholar-officials besides Wang Wei fused their literary and artistic talents, becoming noted calligraphers and painters as well as poets. For the Chinese gentleman-scholar-poet-artist, calligraphy and painting were often one, sharing not only the common use of a brush, but also the same fundamental commitment to the expression of *qi*. One aspect of Chinese painting is to be possessed of *qi* in order to constitute a graphic expression of this invisible energy source. In a similar fashion, the Chinese garden designer selected rocks whose forms and surfaces were animated by *qi* so that they became presences that were alive to eye, hand, and mind that viewed, touched, and contemplated them. Evocative of the mountains depicted in Chinese landscape painting and their association with immortality, these rocks furnished the garden with its paradisiacal iconography.

NORTHERN SONG GARDENS

Cosmic landscape paintings—silk wall hangings depicting mist-shrouded mountains within whose temple-studded vastness small figures beneath gnarled pines communed philosophically—reached their epitome during the Northern Song period (960–1127 C.E.), when the capital was at Bienjing, present-day Kaifeng. The Song emperor Huizong (ruled 1100–1125 C.E.), an accomplished painter, also patronized and thereby promoted a more intimate style of painting depicting jewel-like renderings of birds, blossoming fruit trees, and individual flower forms. From the contents of these paintings and from information about constructed landscapes of the period, we know that artists found inspiration in gardens, and the subject matter of their paintings in turn suggested forms and motifs for the creators of gardens.

Song Huizong was as interested in his imperial gardens as he was in painting. Assisted by practitioners of *feng shui* ("wind" and "water"), professional geomancers (diviners of favorable sites and alignments who procured for human constructions the most beneficial influences of the local landscape's spiritual forces), he established his pleasure park of Genyou in the northwestern quarter of Kaifeng. There he collected a large number of fantastical rocks—water-sculpted stones—and many choice botanical specimens. By creating an artificial mountain called Wanshou Shan (Mountain of Numberless Years), Song Huizong followed the recommendation of his geomancers that he build a tall landmass as a means of blocking evil forces and concentrating good ones.

During the Song period, individual rocks became "collectibles" in their own right. Their shapes were akin to the tall, vertical "Emperor Mountain" of paintings, and they were frequently displayed with

arrangements of subsidiary rocks representing lesser peaks. Their fissured and mottled surfaces were intended to evoke wild precipices, both real ones and those depicted by the painter's brushwork (fig. 8.3). Collectors especially prized fantastically shaped stones, hollowed in places, with light and shadow playing across their irregular surfaces. Song Huizong was a passionate collector, and the canals of Kaifeng were sometimes blocked for days to ordinary commerce

8.2. Detail of *ru yi* **at Pavilion of Ceremonial Purification, Forbidden City, Beijing.** Testimony to the enduring popularity of the poetry contest as a garden pastime is found in the floors of certain garden pavilions. The imperial Pavilion of Ceremonial Purification within the Palace Garden of Peaceful Longevity inside Beijing's Forbidden City has a floor where the stone is channeled in a meandering pattern called *ru yi* ("whatsoever you desire") to create a winding stream course.

Left: **8.3.** *Travelers Among Mountains and Streams,* hanging scroll by Fan Kuan. The tradition of placing mountain-mimicking stones of great sculptural interest in Chinese gardens dates from at least the tenth century, Taipei, Palace Museums

8.4. Xi Hu (West Lake),
Hangzhou

and the delivery of food as his stones were transported to Genyou Park. His enthusiasm was shared by Zhu Mian, the commissioner he put in charge of procuring stones as well as rare plants from the southern provinces. Zhu Mian's own garden, the Garden of Green Water, had a remarkable collection of both.

Song Huizong fulfilled his overweening passion for garden building at the expense of the protection of the empire at large. His extravagance and that of Zhu Mian weakened the treasury and left the borders vulnerable to invasion by the Jurchen Tartars. In 1125, his beautiful garden was destroyed in the sack of the city as warriors from the north cut down trees, tore out bamboos, trampled flowers, and demolished rockwork except for the formidable peak of Wanshou Shan. Zhu Mian was beheaded and his property confiscated, but, because of family skill and reputation, his sons continued to engage in garden building.

SOUTHERN SONG GARDENS

With the invasion that unseated Song Huizong, foreign rule was established over China's northern provinces. Its lords, the Jin dynasty, chose Beijing for their capital. In 1138, after twelve years during which the Song court and the many ethnic Chinese attached to it lived in a series of temporary capitals, they relocated to Hangzhou in the south. There a brilliant epoch of artistic and literary accomplishment ensued. The beautiful lakes and hills around Hangzhou became an inspiration to painters and provided a more picturesque setting for palaces and gardens than the plains of Kaifeng.

In the century and a half that constitutes the Southern Song period (1127–1279), the time of the Song court's transfer to Hangzhou, technical innovations, a money economy, and the expansion in agricultural productivity brought the country to a level

of prosperity well in advance of the rest of the world at that time. Commerce and trade stimulated the growth of cities. Movable type, which the Chinese had invented in the eleventh century, encouraged a book publishing industry and stimulated literacy. The arts flourished, and many wealthy landowners built gardens. The tourist visiting West Lake today can see "fairy-tale" scenery picturesquely accented by waterside pavilions, which are part of famous views with names like those of poems or paintings: "Listening to Orioles Singing in the Waving Willows," "Autumn Moon over the Calm Lake," "Lotus Flowers Swaying in Quyuan Garden" and "Three Pools Mirroring the Moon." Today's versions of these pavilions and their surrounding scenery preserve only faint echoes of the intricately constructed poetic landscapes built there in Song times (fig. 8.4).

Many private residences in Hangzhou had fine gardens, and Suzhou, a center of the silk industry and also an important cultural center, was the site of many more. In addition to numerous small, beautifully crafted urban gardens, aristocratic garden estates were built in the hills on the outskirts of the city. Suzhou's fame as a garden mecca was further enhanced by its location near Lake Tai, source of the water-modeled garden stones that are as highly prized in Chinese gardens as important works of sculpture might be in Western ones. The West Dongting Hill furnished an especially fine multicolored stone full of creases and cavities, and the Lingyan Hill yielded yellowish rocks, the hard, veined surfaces of which are streaked with white, red, and purple.

The Song official who had literary and artistic gifts liked to build a garden that reminded him and his visitors of the wild scenery sought by mountain recluses. Like the monochromatic landscape paintings that inspired his design, this garden prized line, form, and composition over color. Its elements were symbolical "mountains" of carefully selected and artistically positioned stones and arrangements of pine, bamboo, and plum—"the three friends of winter." The names of some of the scholar-gardens of Suzhou—Wang Shi Yuan (Garden of the Master of the Fishing Nets), Liu Yuan (Garden to Linger In), Zhuo Zheng Yuan (Garden of the Unsuccessful Politician)—evoke the idylls of a leisure class.

JI CHENG'S GARDEN MANUAL: THE YUAN YE

By the end of the Song period, the conventions of Chinese garden design were well established. As Chinese merchants prospered during the Ming dynasty, they, like the emperor himself, emulated the cultural elite, the mandarin class of scholar-officials. To help these arrivistes avoid the aesthetic blunders of the uneducated, garden designers began to write treatises that codified garden style and served as manuals for landscape builders.

Foremost among these was the *Yuan ye*, or *The Craft of Gardens*, by Ji Cheng (b. 1582) of Wujiang in the province of Jiangsu.[6] A noted garden builder himself, as well as a poet and painter, he completed his comprehensive three-volume classic on landscape theory and practice in 1634.

Ji Cheng's book is unusual, and perhaps unique, among garden manuals in its blend of practical advice and pattern-book instruction with poetic visualization and mood painting. Although specific in discussing the appearance of various kinds of stones and offering abundant diagrams for window and railing lattices, together with numerous door shapes and paving designs, the *Yuan ye* offers no static prescription for garden planning. The author firmly states that "there is no definite way of making scenery; you know it is right when it stirs your emotions," stressing that it is *qi*, the pulsating breath of life that must be the result of the designer's efforts.

Good siting is a primary ingredient of Ji Cheng's prescription for garden making. A garden designer must screen out what is ugly and offensive and make use of "borrowed scenery" (*jie jing*), whether a distant view of misty mountains, the rooflines of a nearby monastery, or the flowers of a neighbor's garden. A small piece of ground beside a dwelling can be turned into a garden by digging a pond, collecting stones with which to build up a "mountain," and making a welcoming gate for guests. Willows, a stand of bamboos, and some luxuriant trees and flowers are all that are needed to complete the picture and set the mood for poetry-writing parties and sitting in the company of one's favorite concubine melting snow water for tea.

In Ji Cheng's manual, in the chapter "The Selection of Stones," he discusses in reverent detail the highly prized Lake Tai stones with their hollows and holes. He recommends that these be given pride of place like fine sculpture in front of big halls, within large pavilions, or beneath a stately pine tree. It is clear from the *Yuan ye* that stone selection was a highly developed skill limited to a small number of individuals who could successfully quarry fine specimens from the mountains or find them in river and lake beds. Sometimes to be found in museum collections of Chinese art today, these prize stones, with light and shade directing the eye as it travels in and out of their folds and hollows and up the flanks of an imagined mountain precipice, do appear to possess *qi;* their vibrancy is akin to that found in works of painting and calligraphy in the same galleries.

Ji Cheng also writes about wall design. The walls in Chinese gardens provide an important means of segregating space, screening from sight the mundane workaday reality of city streets while making the garden invisible to passersby, except for glimpses gained through latticed openings composed of thin tiles or cast bricks. The walls of Chinese gardens often rise and fall according to the elevation of the ground. Curved roof tiles, sometimes following a wavy line, produce a sense of animated movement, while bas-relief friezes frequently add ornamental interest.

Walls outline various courts and corridors within the garden, subdividing it into discrete though linked scenic units. These are often pierced by windows with tracery, for which Ji Cheng provided many patterns (figs. 8.5, 8.6). Carefully placed windows and circular "moon gates" and vase- or gourd-shaped doors frame views of adjacent garden spaces (fig. 8.7). The whitewashed surfaces of these walls are often brush-rubbed with ground yellow river sand mixed with a small amount of chalk to give them a lustrous

8.5. Bamboo Hat Pavilion seen through window with blue glass in Thirty-six Mandarin Ducks Hall, Zhuo Zheng Yuan (Garden of the Unsuccessful Politician), Suzhou. This 10-acre garden originated in the Ming Dynasty and was extensively repaired and expanded in the 1950s.

8.6. Lattice window in gallery of Liu Yuan (Garden to Linger In), Suzhou. The garden originated in the Ming Dynasty from two gardens: Dong Yuan (East Garden) and Xi Yuan (West Garden). The East Garden was rebuilt with Taihu stones arranged as twelve peaks during the Qing Dynasty. After being deserted for a period, it was rebuilt during the reign of Emperor Gunagxu, at which time it acquired its present name.

Top: 8.7. Wall with Moon Gate, Yi-Yuan (Garden of Ease), Suzhou, founded by a high government official near the end of the Qing Dynasty

waxy polish. The function of a Chinese garden wall is not, however, ornamental; rather, it is meant to serve, like the neutral silk or paper of a painting, as a background, capturing shadows in calligraphic patterns and acting as a foil for the rocks and plants in front of it.

In plan, a typical Southern Chinese scholar-garden, built in the manner codified by Ji Cheng, arranges the functional parts of the mansion and its adjacent series of courts around the edges of the site. The principal hall faces a central pond, which occupies approximately three-tenths of the site (see fig. 8.9). Like the arms of a lake in nature, the ends of the pond are made to disappear from sight, in winding coves, behind bridges, or beyond covered walkways. Buildings, rocks, water, paths, and plants are parts of a harmonious whole, the intent of which is to frame compositions of scenery and furnish various vantage points from which to enjoy a sequence of views. These views are intended to remind one of the kind of journey in nature that one experiences when looking at a Chinese landscape painting, mentally climbing up tortuous mountain paths or following the indented shoreline of a lake.

LANDSCAPES OF LITERATURE: THE STORY OF THE STONE

Much of the story in the great eighteenth-century novel by Cao Xueqin (c. 1724–1764), *The Story of the Stone,* also known as *The Dream of the Red Chamber,* takes place within the Jia family's aristocratic com-

pound, which includes a scholar-garden called the All-scents Garden.[7] Almost an entire chapter is devoted to a detailed description of the annexation of additional family property to expand it into a new garden wherein the family can receive visits from a daughter who has just been elevated to the position of Imperial Concubine. We are told that "the digging of pools, the raising of hills, the siting and erection of lodges and pavilions, the planting of bamboos and flowers— in a word, all matters pertaining to the landscaping and layout of the gardens, were planned and supervised by Horticultural Hu," an eminent landscape gardener.

We are then invited on a tour of the new garden as it is nearing completion. The reader-visitor enters through "a five-frame gate-building with a hump-backed roof of half-cylinder tiles," admiring the beautifully patterned latticework of the wooden doors, simple whitewashed walls, and fine, unostentatious craftsmanship. Directly the tourist of this imaginary landscape encounters a miniature mountain formed of "large white rocks in all kinds of grotesque and monstrous shapes, rising course upon course up one of its sides, some recumbent, some upright or leaning at angles, their surfaces streaked and spotted with moss and lichen or half-concealed by creepers, and with a narrow zig-zag path only barely discernible to the eye winding up between them." A tunnel through a shoulder of this rock deposits the supposed wanderer in a lush artificial ravine. Below, through the trees, a clear rushing stream broadens into a wide pool edged by a marble baluster and spanned by a beautiful triple-arched marble bridge. Brightly painted, fancifully decorated, luxuriously furnished pavilions ascend the slopes of the ravine. Another pavilion is poised over the center of the bridge.

On the far side of the pool, a path threads its way between rocks and flowers and trees before suddenly coming upon whitewashed walls enclosing a dense thicket of bamboo. In the middle of this bamboo grove stands a small scholarly retreat. At the rear, this structure opens onto "a garden of broad-leaved plantains dominated by a large flowering pear tree." A stream gushes through an opening in the back wall into a narrow channel, which runs around one side of the house and then meanders through the bamboos before disappearing through another opening in the wall.

A climb around the base of a steeply sloping hill brings into view a mud-walled compound tucked into a fold halfway up the hillside. It contains an apricot orchard and a cluster of rustic cottages with thatched roofs. An irregularly shaped hedge formed by loosely interweaving the young shoots of mulberry, elm, hibiscus, and silkworm thorn trees stands outside the orchard wall, and below it a rustic well overlooks miniature fields of vegetables and flowers, the equivalent of a Western kitchen garden. The reader's tour through it engenders a lively discussion on the distinction between utilitarian landscapes such as this, which have obviously been planted by the human hand, and ones that presume to imitate nature with little appearance of artifice.

To manifest the difference, beyond the rustic village, the author takes us to a spot where we can hear the musical sound of water issuing from a vine-fringed cave in the rock. The "mountainous" topography of the garden is again evident as we scramble over this grotto, up a steep path, and then back down to the banks of the winding stream fringed with willows interspersed with "peach and apricot trees whose interlacing branches made little worlds of stillness and serenity beneath them. Blossoms float on the surface of the water."

The scarlet balustrade of a wooden bridge glimpsed through the screen of pendant willow branches beckons us to cross, whereupon we discover diverging paths leading to other parts of the garden. Ahead, an elegant pavilion stands in a courtyard containing a remarkable rock, with light and shade playing over its delicate surface of fissures and hollows. This miniature mountain—a collector's specimen—is surrounded by smaller rocks, but the courtyard is otherwise bare except for some vines and flowering plants of exquisite fragrance. Beyond this summerhouse stands the magnificent residence hall, from which "gold-glinting cat-faces, rainbow-hued serpents' snouts peered out or snarled down from cornice and finial."

In the eighteenth century, aristocratic families preserved the landscape design traditions formulated centuries before in the Song period. The new garden described by Cao Xueqin is an exceptionally large one, covering one-quarter square mile (.65 square kilometers) of the Jia family estate. Typically, the scholar-garden in an urban locale compressed a great deal of scenery of a similarly associative nature into a much smaller frame, as we shall see below when we examine an actual garden, contemporary with that of the novel.

In *The Story of the Stone,* the characters are examining the newly built garden for the purpose of naming its different parts, inasmuch as Chinese garden makers considered a garden without calligraphy denoting the names of various rock and plant groupings, water scenery, viewing pavilions, and scholarly retreats to be incomplete. Inscriptions are an important part of a Chinese garden, and the carving of names and descriptive verse onto rocks and stone plaques is a time-honored custom. In this case, provisional inscriptions

were to be painted on rectangular paper lanterns, pending approval by Yuan-chun, the young woman who had been promoted to the Imperial Bedchamber and for whom the garden was being readied in anticipation of her occasional visits to her family.

The act of naming and the fusion of literary tradition with scenic appreciation are a venerable Chinese practice that goes beyond garden inscriptions to include actual scenes in nature. In China, where the distinction between travel literature and the literature of landscape hardly exists, the descriptions of scenes along the traveler's route, like the scenes depicted on a landscape scroll, are more important than the personal adventures of the protagonist or the final goal of his journey. Travel writing as a genre has ancient roots in China, and poetical inscriptions recording the sensations and impressions of earlier visitors were carved into rocks (fig. 8.8). Inscriptions were not seen as defacing nature, but rather as enhancing it through literary commentary.

Many famous views have accretions of rock-carved inscriptions around them. A very early example is found in *The Chronicle of Mu,* probably written sometime during the fifth to fourth century B.C.E., in which Emperor Mu, who reigned six hundred years earlier, is described as having recorded his journey into the Xi Mountains with a rock inscription, after having planted a tree and named the spot Mountain of the Queen Mother of the West.[8]

Matching name and reality was, according to Confucian ideology, a fundamental means of estab-

8.8. Forest Rock inscription, Stone, Suzhou Yunnan Province

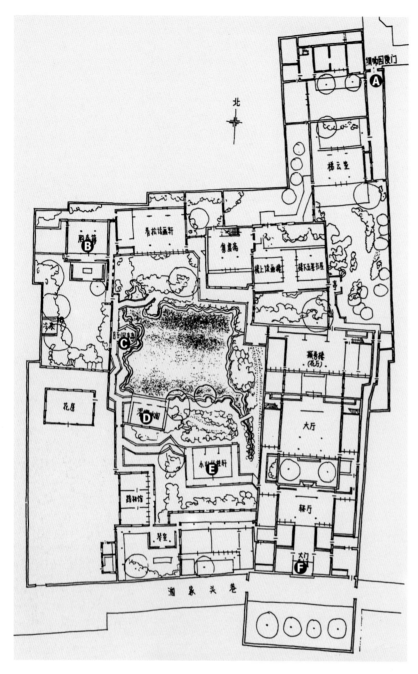

8.9. Plan of Wang Shi Yuan (Garden of the Master of the Fishing Nets), Suzhou. Qing Dynasty
Ⓐ Visitors' Entrance
Ⓑ Cottage to Accompany Spring
Ⓒ Pavillion of the Arriving Moon and Wind
Ⓓ Waterside Hall for Washing the Tassels of One's Hat
Ⓔ Hall of Small Mountains and Osmanthus Spring
Ⓕ Main Entrance

Right: 8.10. Pavilion of the Arriving Moon and Wind, Wang Shi Yuan, Suzhou

lishing moral order. The naming of famous scenes and places was a function of the ruling class, a way of asserting cultural identity over the breadth of the empire. Inscribing nature was rooted as well in Daoist philosophy, as scenic appreciation was a means of achieving transcendental harmony with the universe. By the end of the Song period, when landscape connoisseurship was well established, there was an extensive canon of Chinese travel literature, and the major sites of literary pilgrimage had received inscriptions and been marked on maps.

WANG SHI YUAN (GARDEN OF THE MASTER OF THE FISHING NETS)

The Wang Shi Yuan, or the Garden of the Master of the Fishing Nets, is one of several remaining scholar-gardens in Suzhou that give some impression of the lives led by the educated and bureaucratic elite in imperial China. Much literary meaning is packed into this one-and-a-half-acre garden of idyllically arranged scenery, and the spaces within it bear the kinds of poetical names that Jia Zheng's son Bao-yu was summoned to provide in *The Story of the Stone*. First laid out in 1140, in early Southern Song times by a high court official, it was restored in 1770 by another official, Song Zongyuan, as his retirement retreat. Though altered both before and after its appropriation by the municipal government in 1958, its outlines and principal features remain the same as in the Qing period (1644–1911). Like other scholar-gardens, it is highly compartmentalized, with courtyards and roofed structures interlocking like pieces of a puzzle (fig. 8.9).

In former times, visitors arriving by palanquin would have entered the Wang Shi Yuan through the main entrance on the south where the residential quarters are. Today access is through a narrow passageway from a side alley into the northern end of the complex, which leads more directly into the garden. In either case, the route into the Place for Gathering Breezes—the central garden space, dominated by a lake—is a circuitous one. Its chief focal point, as seen from the Duck Shooting Corridor adjacent to the family halls, is the Pavilion of the Arriving Moon and Wind, a delicate, six-sided structure with soaring rooflines collected in a high finial (fig. 8.10). Poised on its appropriately scaled rockery above the surface of the lake, it is a resting place where one can gaze dreamily at the reflections in the water. A mirror inside increases the sparkling play of light on its surfaces.

The visitor does not arrive by an obvious path to this spot but is diverted along the way by other pavilions and their adjacent courtyards. The Hall of Small Mountains and Osmanthus Spring is completely screened from the lake by a tall mountain of earth and rockwork. From inside, one views this composition through windows framed with lacy fretwork. On the south side of this structure lies a small courtyard containing many fine specimens of Lake Tai rocks placed in an undulating composition. The bright white wall of this courtyard constitutes the pictorial ground upon which the shadows of the fragrant osmanthus trees are cast, forming a tracery pattern that complements the fretwork of the small openings in it as well as that of the windows of the pavilion.

The Waterside Hall for Washing the Tassels of One's Hat sits at the water's edge on the south side of the lake opposite the Veranda for Viewing Pines and Looking at Paintings. The latter pavilion has a lake view seen through old pines and cypresses, which are set in a rockery. Besides these lakeside summerhouses, there are other garden pavilions, several of which serve the needs of the scholar. The Five Peaks Study, for instance, is a library. Since interior stairs are not favored in ornamental Chinese architecture, access to its second story was gained via steps set into a rockery next to its east wall. Adjacent to it is the House of Concentrated Study. Another study, the Cottage to Accompany Spring, had its own private pebble-paved courtyard garden to the south as well as another tiny courtyard on the north. The latter, which is framed from inside by beautifully carved window surrounds, contains a delicate composition of bamboo, rocks, and flowering plants.

IMPERIAL BEIJING

By 1279, Khubilai Khan, the grandson of Genghis Khan, had toppled the Jin dynasty in the northern part of China, captured Hangzhou, and gained control of the entire country at an estimated cost of 30 million lives. Khubilai moved the capital of his Mongol empire to Beijing and assimilated the more sophisticated culture of the people he had conquered. The Yuan dynasty, as the Mongol rulership was styled, lasted until 1368. Like other disaffected Chinese civil servants before them, a number of the mandarin elite went into permanent retirement rather than serve the foreign conqueror, some finding careers as artists whose works were in demand by the growing merchant class. Others went north to carry on their traditional duties, including artistic ones, at court.

The Jin emperors, whose occupancy of Beijing preceded that of the Mongols, had excavated a canal and a marshy lake, the nucleus of the three contemporary lakes around which "sea palaces" and pleasure parks were built. Khubilai Khan further excavated this lake, which is known as Bei Hai, or Northern Sea, setting up hunting preserves around it and embellishing its shores with many trees and costly buildings. At its southern end he formed an island from the

dredged spoil upon which he erected a "mountain" studded with rocks of lapis lazuli. To Marco Polo, this Green Hill presented a wondrous sight. According to him, the trees planted upon it were transported there by elephants.[9]

The first emperor of the Ming dynasty (1368–1644) located the capital at Nanjing where it remained until the third emperor, Yongle (ruled 1403–1424), reestablished the court at Beijing. For fourteen years Yongle's builders labored to erect a city modeled on the previous Ming emperor's capital at Nanjing. Guided by geomancy, Confucian symbolism, and cosmology, they gave physical representation to the emperor's rule under the "mandate of heaven." This was expressed as a hierarchical ordering of space in which were nested three rectangular walled enclosures containing the Inner City, the Imperial City, and the Forbidden City, all of which were centered on a great north-south axis punctuated by ceremonial gates (fig. 8.11).

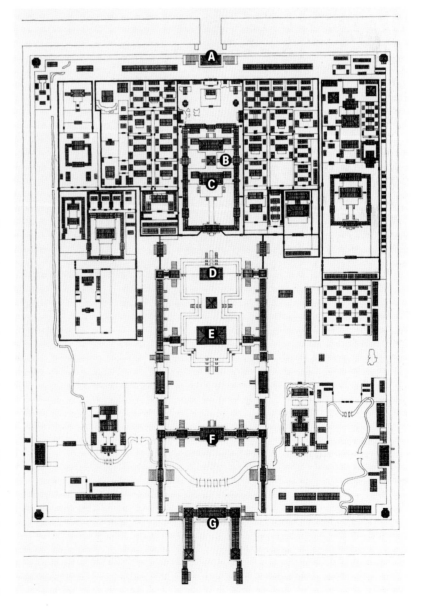

8.11. Plan of the Forbidden City, Beijing, Suzhou
Ⓐ North Gate
Ⓑ Palaces
Ⓒ Hall of Supreme Harmony
Ⓓ Wu Men (Meridian Gate)
Ⓔ Tuan Men
Ⓕ Tian 'an Men (Gate of Heavenly Peace)
Ⓖ Qian Qing Men (Gate of August Purity)

8.12. View from Bao He Dien (Hall for the Preservation of Harmony) toward Qian Qing Men (Gate of August Purity), Forbidden City, Beijing

Below 8.13. Gate at Palace Museum, Forbidden City, Beijing

In 1420, Yongle's vast complex of walled enclosures and palatial buildings was ready for occupancy, and Beijing officially became the Ming capital. The Altar of Heaven was also built in the reign of Yongle to the south of Qian Qing Men (Gate of August Purity), the great Front Gate of the Inner City. It was flanked by two circular temples, the Temple of Heaven and the Hall of Prayer for Good Harvests. During the reign of Jiajing (ruled 1522–1566) in the next century at the cardinal points just outside the Inner City additional magnificent altars were raised to the Earth, Sun, Moon, and Agriculture. At that time, about 1550, another walled rectangle was constructed, enclosing the district to the south of the

Inner City. Called the Outer City, it encompassed the Altar of Heaven and the Altar of Agriculture (replaced by a Worker's Stadium in the 1950s).

Because of fires and other mishaps, the imperial buildings that one sees today are almost all reconstructions of the Qing dynasty, but Chinese conservatism has nonetheless ensured continuity of form, making it possible at least to imagine the appearance of the ancient Ming capital of the fifteenth century. In spite of the degradation of much of its elegant imperial architectural heritage under Communist rule, Beijing still offers an unrivaled ceremonial progression along a central axis that thrusts northward through a hierarchical series of magnificent gates, symmetrically arranged courts, and majestic halls, passing first through the Outer City and then into the precincts of the Forbidden City (figs. 8.12, 8.13). Continuing through the Shen Wu Men—the Gate of the Martial Spirit built to guard the Forbidden City from northern invaders—and crossing a moat, the axis continues to Jing Shan, or Prospect Hill, also known as Mei Shan, Coal Hill.

Constructed in the fifteenth century with erosion material dredged from the moat that encircles the Forbidden City, Coal Hill is now a public park and the highest point in Beijing. The siting of the Forbidden City in its lea, where it was sheltered from northerly winds and unfriendly spirits, is in accordance with the Chinese geomantic practice of *feng shui*. In imperial times this eminence was planted with fruit trees and served as a bird sanctuary and place of retreat for the emperor and members of the court. During his long reign, the Qianlong emperor (ruled 1736–1795) built upon each of its five low peaks an open-framed pavilion housing a bronze statue of a deity. With their variously shaped roofs, these acted as "borrowed" scenery for the gardens within the Forbidden City.

YUAN MING YUAN

While vowing simplicity and professing the modest ideals of a scholar-poet, the Qianlong emperor who built the pavilions on Coal Hill proved to be a lavish creator of landscapes. His vast project, the Yuan Ming Yuan, or the Garden of Perfect Brightness, gave Europeans—thanks to the publication of letters of the Jesuit missionary Father Attiret (1702–1738) in the middle of the eighteenth century—their first real knowledge of the Chinese garden.

One of five imperial parks created in the northwestern hills outside the city during the Qing dynasty, the Yuan Ming Yuan was given its basic form by the Yongzheng emperor, who reigned between 1723 and 1735. His son, the Qianlong emperor, made a pledge to practice restraint in regard to imperial works, but he soon broke it, setting a force of a thousand men to work on the Yuan Ming Yuan (fig. 8.14). Lakes were dug, hillocks thrown up, fantastic rocks positioned in eye-catching arrangements, trees and flowers planted, and many pavilions, zigzag bridges, and other architectural features erected. The emperor then went on to embellish the Chang Chun (Garden of Everlasting Spring), which had been his grandfather's old retreat, in the same fashion. He also developed the Garden of Joyous Spring (Ji Chun Yuan), fusing it and the Chang Chun with the Yuan Ming Yuan as a complex of three separate but linked gardens.

By this time the Chinese scholar-gardens of southern China had a long and prestigious history, and this northern imperial garden was conceived somewhat as an eclectic "collection" of many famous southern garden scenes. For the pleasure of court ladies whose lives were narrowly circumscribed by palace garden walls, the emperor had a true-to-life shopping street created. On the northeast boundary of the Yuan Ming Yuan he commissioned Father Attiret's fellow Jesuit missionary Father Giuseppe Castiglione to design and construct a collection of structures built in a curious pseudo-Baroque style that mingled European and Chinese elements (see fig. 6.35).

In 1860, Yuan Ming Yuan was completely destroyed by the British and French as the last vengeful act in a war in which Great Britain and France

8.14. Perspective view of Yuan Ming Yuan (Garden of Perfect Brightness), painting by Tang Dai and Shen Yuan. Bibliothèque Nationale, Paris

forced the Chinese to grant additional trade privileges to Western countries. On October 18, a British corps invaded the garden grounds, ransacked its buildings, and then set fire to the entire complex. The flames consumed not only the Yuan Ming Yuan, but also several other adjacent pleasure palaces and their parks.

YI HE YUAN

Among the parks burned by the British and French in 1860 was the Yi He Yuan, the Garden of Ease and Harmony, one of the five major parks, including the Yuan Ming Yuan, that once adorned the Western Hills. This park, also the creation of Qianlong, who built it in honor of his mother's sixtieth birthday, was rebuilt by the Dowager Empress Cixi in celebration of *her* sixtieth birthday in 1894. Once more put to the torch by Europeans in the Boxer Rebellion of 1900, it was restored again by the empress in 1902.

In the center of the Yi He Yuan there is a sheet of light-reflecting, lotus-blooming water called Kunming Lake. It has a circumference of 4 miles (6.4 kilometers) and occupies approximately 500 of the park's 725 acres. Originally no more than a marshy pond, it was dredged and enlarged by the Qianlong emperor, who built an aqueduct system to feed it and other imperial lakes.

Stretching for almost half a mile (.8 kilometers) along the north side of Kunming Lake is the remarkable Long Gallery (Chang Lang), giving architectural definition to the gentle curves of the shoreline and providing, through ornamental frames of wooden latticework panels, picturesque views of the lake and its surrounding scenery (fig. 8.15). The Long Gallery's architecture and its function as a viewing

Top: **8.15. Long Gallery (Chang Lang) and view of Kunming Lake, Yi He Yuan (Garden of Ease and Harmony). Garden built in Qing Dynasty by Emperor Qianlong; rebuilt by Dowager Empress Cixi, 1894; restored again by the empress, 1902, following the Boxer Rebellion**

Above: **8.16. *Shu shi*-style painted panels from the Long Gallery (Chang Lang), Yi He Yuan**

Right: **8.17. Yu Dai Qiao (Jade Belt Bridge), Yi He Yuan (Garden of Ease and Harmony), Summer Palace**

platform are enhanced by the pavilions that punctuate it at particularly scenic points. Designed as small rooms, these offer privacy if desired, having doors that can shut off the main covered walkway. This remarkable waterfront promenade also functions as a gallery for the more than 14,000 painted panels that decorate the cross beams (fig. 8.16). These depict birds, animals, flowers, landscape scenes, and other graceful motifs.

The views looking west from the eastern shore of the lake are enriched by a series of bridges, each unique in its design. The causeway that traverses the lake, dividing it into one large lake and two smaller ones, incorporates six bridges. The most notable of these is the Jade Belt Bridge (Yu Dai Qiao), also called the Camel's Hump Bridge, which leaps with balletic grace over an inlet at the lake's western edge (fig. 8.17).

PLANT MATERIAL

Throughout its long history, the plants of the Chinese garden design remained those traditional ones celebrated in poetry and painting, which were derived from conventional symbolical association. Certain favorite flowers, such as peonies, were cultivated in masses, and their springtime bloom in the garden was the occasion for entertaining friends. Chrysanthemums, which like pines were revered as long-lived survivors, were the focus of special vantage points designed for fall viewing.

Indeed, consideration of the Chinese garden's movement through the cycle of the seasons counted as much for garden designers as its careful sequencing in spatial terms. It was thought that a light dusting of snow in the winter best revealed its essential architecture and the lines of force and mass that constituted a well-designed "mountain." Most apparent in that season are the "three friends of winter"—pine, bamboo, and plum, with their respective symbolical associations of longevity, hardiness, and strength of character; pliable and supple nature capable of lasting friendship; and delicate beauty even in old age. In summer the mirrorlike surface of the pond traded its cloud reflections and reverse shoreline imagery for an efflorescence of lotuses. Lifting their stalks out of the mud, they formed a verdant mat of waxy leaves dotted with pale flowers, a symbol of the purity and victory of the spirit over the senses. Thus, change itself and the anticipation of change, with all the associations of life, death, and renewal implied by seasonal transformation, are a conscious dimension of Chinese garden design.

Today the perpetuation of this style of garden-making is more a matter of replication of historic models than one of authentic landscape creation inspired by poetry and painting. Its influence can be traced in other lands in gardens that also aspired to capture the spirit-force of nature through landscape art. Among these are the Chinese garden's direct descendants, which are found within the precincts of the temples and palaces of Japan.

II. TEA, MOSS, AND STONES: TEMPLE AND PALACE GARDENS OF JAPAN

Chinese garden concepts arrived in Japan along with Buddhism in the sixth century. Although sharing a similar aesthetic approach, the gardens built in the small, well-watered island nation of Japan would ultimately differ from those of China, a country of vastly greater dimensions, a land of contrasting wide plains and mountainous precipices. After appropriating Chinese garden concepts, instead of continuing to create "recollections" of famous scenes in nature in the Chinese manner, Japanese garden designers increasingly sought a generic ideal of nature in conformity with the scale and topography of their own natural landscape.

The eleventh-century treatise known as the *Sakuteiki*, presumably written by Tachibana no Toshitsuna (1028–1084), is Japan's earliest known manual of garden rules.[10] In it one finds prescriptions for the handling of stones set within moving water in the so-called "large river style." The *Sakuteiki* counsels that, in order to make a proper garden, one should travel widely and become acquainted with beautiful scenes in nature, indicating that by this time the Japanese had singled out various famous views as prized components of their country's natural landscape. Besides giving precise instructions for building waterfalls and other garden features, the author encourages gardeners to orient their buildings to the south according to the principles of geomancy. Logically, streams should be placed on this, their most open, side. He prescribed that these flow from east to west in order to cleanse the evil air emanating from the northeast and ward off demons. In addition to following these prescriptions of the *Sakuteiki*, Japanese garden designers often incorporated a distant vista in their designs in order to enlarge the visual sphere of the usually quite small garden and to reinforce its connection with the natural world. They referred to this technique of borrowing scenery as *shakkei*.

Buddhist creation mythology and Daoist belief in the paradisaical Isles of the Blest furnished the lake-and-islands motif that underlies the composition of many Japanese gardens, even those compressed visions of a Zen Buddhist universe known as *kare sansui*, or dry landscapes. Beginning in the thirteenth century, members of the newly imported Zen sect designed these spare, almost austere, gardens as aids to meditation. These are minimalist compositions of carefully positioned stones, which are meant to be read as islands in a dry "river" of carefully raked gravel or sand or as mountains in a landscape of mosses. Such Zen-inspired gardens played an important role among members of the ruling classes; certain emperors and even some shoguns—powerful military dictators who ruled under the nominal authority of the emperor—found garden-making to be a satisfying escape from court politics and civil strife. The tea ceremony, developed in the late fifteenth century, was not a religious exercise, but it nevertheless provided a disciplined experience of concentration and aesthetic and spiritual refreshment for which passage along a garden path of moss and stones offered a prescribed prelude and conclusion.

The Japanese combined their penchant for cultural appropriation with a talent for reinvention. Japan's island geography and a semi-isolationist policy during much of its history fostered the assimilation and transformation of those ideas and forms that were adopted from the outside into a vigorous native expression. The arrival of Commodore Matthew Perry's American ships in Tokyo Bay in 1853–54 ended the country's previous two centuries of closure to all but Dutch and Chinese traders, whose access was strictly limited. Increasing transactions with the West started Japan on a path of profound change. Without some degree of cultural isolation and the focused aestheticism that matured the Japanese garden into a great art form, the slow but creative evolution that counts as development within a traditional artistic idiom came to a standstill. Its assimilative energies directed toward building a powerful economy and its political life reshaped since 1945 as a capitalist democracy, Japan has become today a conservator of its cultural heritage. As in other countries where the government and cultural institutions protect a "golden age" of previous artistic accomplishment, in Japan the state and the religious establishments of Kyoto maintain the incomparable imperial and Buddhist temple gardens as much-appreciated heritage icons and tourist attractions.

The talents of Japanese landscape designers today contribute to the pluralistic internationalism of garden art rather than to the continued development of a specifically indigenous style. The *vocabulary* of Japanese garden design—its abstract compositional harmonies, its elegant rusticity, its "borrowed" views, its asymmetrical configuration of design elements, its attention to ground plane patterns and textures in the arrangement of moss and stones—has furnished inspiration to modern garden designers in other countries. To appreciate more fully the richness of simplicity in this carefully matured language of landscape, we must now review the history of Japanese gardens.

SHINTO SANCTUARIES

The Japanese word for garden, *niwa*, was first used to denote a sanctified space in nature set apart for the worship of Shinto gods. A sacred rock (*iwakura*), rock

8.18. *Iwakura* (sacred rock). Aichi Shrine, Okayama Prefecture. The purified area around these sacred stones, believed to be inhabited by *kami,* or spirits, is marked by straw ropes (*shime-nawa*).

Below: 8.19. Sacred rocks at Ise

Right: 8.20. Ise Shrine, Ise City, Mie Prefecture, Japan

grouping, tree, or other natural object might be revered for its indwelling spirit (fig. 8.18). Like the *temenos,* the sacred precinct of ancient Greek religion, the Shinto shrine exists as a clearly marked space within a natural setting of assigned spiritual power. But unlike the *temenos,* an enclosed space, the Shinto shrine exists merely as a marked place, its boundaries set not by walls, but rather implied by a *torii* gate framing a sacred object or space in nature (fig. 8.19). Where greater architectural definition is sought, an apron of white gravel may isolate the revered place or object. Ropes, straw fencing, and sometimes cloth banners may also be used as means of demarcation.

The holiest spot in Japan is considered to be the Shinto shrine at Ise in Mie Prefecture. The shrine enclave includes the Geku, or Outer Shrine, which is dedicated to the provider of grain, and the Naiku, or Inner Shrine, sacred to the heaven-illuminating sun goddess Amaterasu, from whom Japan's imperial clan once claimed descent. The Inner Shrine is set within a clearing within a cryptomeria forest and is reached by a ceremonial path that passes through *torii,* over

the Isuzu River, and through the forest to the clearing (fig. 8.20).

The Inner Shrine precinct contains the *honden,* the main hall of the Inner Shrine, and two treasure houses. All are enclosed within three concentric fences and accessible only through gates on the short ends of the rectangular plot of white gravel on which they sit; adjacent and sharing common fencing within the clearing is an identical rectangular plot of gravel that serves as the alternate building site. The active shrine consists of a group of simple unpainted wooden structures roofed with the bark of cyprus trees. Every twenty years — most recently in 1993 — the *honden,* whose simple form is derived from Yayoi-period (c. 300 B.C.E.–c. 300 C.E.) raised rice granaries, is rebuilt and rededicated. Only a small structure in the middle of the otherwise empty plain of gravel protects the *shin no mihashira,* or heart post, a structural member of the previous shrine, which is left standing.

Historians believe that white gravel aprons such as this are predecessors of the *yuniwa,* the entry court of palaces and other monumental structures, a purified space that is empty or contains at most a pair of symbolic trees. The more worldly culture of a later period turned the *yuniwa* of noble residences into a secular, landscaped space, but those relating to shrines remained as religiously austere as the one at Ise. The majesty of the towering cryptomeria trees constitutes the more grand architectural expression of the Ise

shrine site, but the humble structures of ancient origin, the fenced compound containing them, and the adjacent cleared space create a moving statement of the desire for human order within the greater order of the cosmos.

THE NARA AND HEIAN COURTS

Buddhism was introduced from China into Japan in 552. Under the regent, Prince Shotoku (573–621), who promoted it and built temples, it gained the kind of institutional status enjoyed by Christianity in the West after the reign of Constantine the Great. The acceptance of Buddhism, together with contacts with Korea and the first official Japanese embassy to China in the early seventh century, stimulated the adoption of Chinese artistic and architectural forms. Formerly, rulers had constructed their dwellings in the vernacular style of the structures at the Ise Shrine. Moreover, because of the premium put upon spatial purification and ritual rebuilding, the capital was moved at the beginning of each new reign. In 710, however, the court was established at Nara, and there it remained for the next seventy-five years through several reigns.

The plan of the city, with its hierarchical ordering of space within a grid layout, was, at a lesser scale, a conscious imitation of that of Chang'an, the Chinese Tang dynasty capital. The temples constructed to house large images of Buddha were unlike any previous Japanese architectural forms. The spatial layout of their surrounding compounds also followed Chinese models.

Korean craftsmen were brought to Nara to help develop imperial gardens in the Chinese manner, with lakes and rock arrangements forming islands. From archaeological excavations, as well as from paintings and poetry of this period, we surmise that these were similar to the Tang models they sought to imitate, being *yarimizu,* or river-style gardens. Their meandering streams furnished the opportunity to organize poetry competitions like the ones popular in contemporary Chinese gardens.

Upon ascending the throne in 781, Emperor Kammu decided to move the capital once more, probably in order to separate the government from the influence of priests at Nara, who, to his distress, had amassed considerable political power. After ten years of building this new capital, Nagaoka-kyō, the not-yet-finished city was abandoned in favor of another site nearby, Heian-kyō, meaning the Capital of Peace and Tranquility, the original name of Kyoto. Once established, Kyoto became the imperial capital of Japan for more than a thousand years until the Meiji Restoration in 1868, when Tokyo was made the capital.

In Kyoto, as at Nara, the gridiron plan of

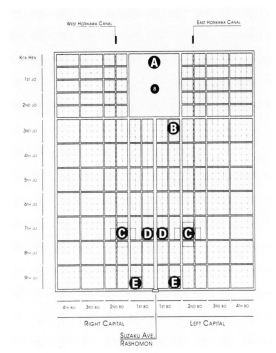

8.21. Plan of Heian-kyō (Kyoto), Japan
Ⓐ Imperial Court and Residence
Ⓑ Imperial Garden
Ⓒ Markets
Ⓓ Diplomatic Reception Courts
Ⓔ Temples

Chang'an formed the model for a new city roughly half Nara's size, or 3.5 miles (5.6 kilometers) north to south by 3 miles (4.8 kilometers) east to west (fig. 8.21).[11] Also, as at Nara, the imperial enclosure, known as the Daidairi, was placed at the end of a broad axis at the city's northern end. The surrounding city was subdivided into 76 large squares, measuring approximately 400 feet (122 meters) to a side. The eastern half of this residential grid became the location of choice for the nobility; however, the western half was never developed in accordance with its original outlines. In an attempt to avoid the political tensions that had existed at Nara, the emperor mandated that new temples be sited outside the city, and these were therefore built on the lower slopes of the surrounding hills, as were estates of the powerful nobility.

In the Heian period (781–1185), a golden age for Kyoto, all the arts, including landscape design, were held in high esteem. Gardens in this period were ampler than later ones, and the lakes in them were generous in size. Fortunately for posterity, Murasaki Shikibu (970?–1026?), a lady of the court, chronicled the aesthetic pursuits of the elite during the Heian era in *The Tale of Genji,* a novel written around the year 1000.[12] In it we read of Prince Genji in many beautiful garden settings as he enjoys such pastimes as rowing in Chinese-style boats around the islands in the lake or going on an outing to admire the fall foliage (fig. 8.22). Inspired by Chinese models, these islands consisted of arrangements of rocks, some intended to suggest the form of a symbolically meaningful tortoise or crane. Pavilions in the style known as *shinden-zukuri* stood at the edge of the water. These structures, derived from Chinese architectural norms, were ele-

8.22. Kochō ("Butterflies") from *The Tale of Genji,* Mary and Jackson Burke Collection. The elite pleasures of Heian court life are evident in this scene depicting a boating party held in Lady Murasaki's section of Genji's estate, with musicians and costumed dancers entertaining the imperial consort who has returned home for a visit. This six-fold screen is attributed to Tosa Mitsuyoshi (1539–1613).

Below: 8.23. Phoenix Hall of the Byōdō-in, Uji, Japan

gant in their lines but rustic in character, with reticulated two-part shutters that could be raised in summer. Their floors were polished wood, as tatami mats and other specifically Japanese conventions had not yet become established. These viewing platforms were actually projecting wings of a large central pavilion, or *shinden,* that faced the lake. A swath of white sand at the lake's edge served as a stage for mime and dance performances, which could be enjoyed from a *shinden-zukuri* pavilion. Raised covered passages linked the separate pavilions with each other and with the *shinden.*

Within Japan's feudal social structure, the powerful Fujiwara clan had gained supremacy by 850, and in their role as regents for emperors in their minority, members of this family gradually appropriated much of the imperial power and married into the imperial family. Their chief, Fujiwara no Michinaga (966–1027), held the title of *kampaku,* a high governmental position in which he mediated between the emperor and court officials in affairs of state. As respected but powerless figureheads, emperors typically spent their lives engaged in cultural pursuits. Making a virtue of their relatively reduced circumstances, they refined their chosen style, which was derived from rustic vernacular architecture, into a vocabulary of elegantly crafted details and beautifully proportioned parts. By contrast, the Fujiwara, like the shoguns who followed them, liked to display their power in works of magnificence. The splendor of the Heian period is found in the Byōdō-in, built as a villa by the *kampaku* Fujiwara Yorimichi (992–1074) on his estate south of Kyoto and converted into a temple in 1052 (fig. 8.23).

The pond garden (now severely compromised in size) and serene *shinden*-style Phoenix Hall (Hōō-dō) of 1053 at Byōdō-in—so named because its soaring wings evoke those of the mythical bird as it alights—were meant to depict Amida Buddha's Paradise. It is the sole remaining structure of the twenty-six halls and seven pagodas that were once grouped around the pond at the Byōdō-in.

As they became increasingly interested in cultural rather than military pursuits, the Fujiwara regents were challenged by other powerful clans, the Taira and Minamoto, and the emperor now more than ever governed in name only. Power first fell to the Taira, but their authority was upset by the Minamoto clan and their *samurai* army. The Minamoto established headquarters at the town of Kamakura, which gave its name to the period of their ascendancy. Shoguns, in whom hereditary military command rested, continued to exert authority more or less continuously from the late twelfth century until the Meiji Restoration of 1868.

Kamakura Gardens

The Kamakura period (1185–1333) is notable for the widespread adoption of the Chinese sect of Chan Buddhism, known in Japan as Zen Buddhism. Introduced as early as the seventh century by the priest Dōshō (629–700) following his return from China, Zen Buddhism was long overshadowed in Japan by the powerful Tendai and Shingon sects. But the austerity and simplicity of Zen religion as professed by the monk Eisai (1141–1215) upon his return from China in 1192, appealed to the warrior class. As it prospered under their sponsorship, its reductive aesthetic guided the design of certain temple gardens.

Equally important for designed landscapes at this time were the currents of aesthetic thought emanating from the Southern Song dynasty (1127–1279) in China. The vertical positioning of carefully selected rocks, typical of Song gardens, can be found in Japanese gardens of this era, whereas later stonework emphasized a horizontality that is less dramatic and more in keeping with the inherent quietude of Japan's natural landscape forms. More important than this, however, was the poetic idealization of landscape and the relationship between landscape design and painting found in Song garden art, qualities that exerted a strong influence on the development of the Japanese garden.

The Kamakura era and the subsequent Muromachi period effected a transition in landscape design from the great Heian residential lake gardens of the nobility to the Zen minimalism represented by the monastic garden of Ryōan-ji, built between 1500 and 1700. In the beautiful river district of Arashiyama in

8.24. Garden of Tenryū-ji Temple, Kyoto, rock arrangement suggesting Penglai (pronounced Hōrai in Japanese), one of the Islands of the Immortals, according to Chinese legend. Kamakura Period

northwestern Kyoto, Tenryū-ji, an estate garden built around 1256 and later converted into a monastery, exhibits the Song influence in its boldly conceived dry cascade and vertical rock arrangements. From a bridge made of three natural stone slabs, there is a view of a harmoniously balanced composition of seven rocks set in the water so as to suggest one of the Mystic Isles of the Immortals in Chinese legend (fig. 8.24). In 1339, the estate was converted into a Zen Buddhist foundation by Musō Soseki (also known as Musō Kokushi, 1275–1351), one of Japan's most significant religious figures and a gifted garden designer. Some garden historians believe that this serene and paradisaical garden, which today is operated by the Rinzai sect of Zen Buddhism, was reworked by Musō Soseki and is an example of his artistry. Though less than an acre in size and containing a pond that is only 100 by 200 feet (30.5 by 61 meters), it has something of the atmosphere of the old Heian *shinden* lake garden. Its surrounding views are now obscured by vegetation, but it originally drew into its small compass the distant crowns of Arashiyama and Kameyama mountains, providing what is possibly the earliest Japanese example we have of the technique of borrowed scenery.

Nearby, at Saihō-ji, another temple of the Rinzai Zen Buddhist sect, Musō Soseki began in 1339 to reconstruct an existing garden after it had been practically destroyed during the civil wars that had recently wracked the country. Comprising an upper and a lower garden totaling 4.5 acres, it, too, has a lake, this one considerably larger than that of Tenryū-ji. In the

8.25. Garden of Saihō-ji Temple, Kyoto, lake and mossy embankments. Kamakura Period

Right: 8.26. Garden of Saihō-ji Temple, dry cascade with flat-topped rocks

lower garden surrounding the lake, the atmosphere of the Heian pleasure garden has given way completely to a deeply spiritual environment derived from Jōdo (Pure Land) Buddhism and intended as a metaphor for Amida's Paradise. The light-reflecting water, verdant moss, and the deep shade cast by lichen-covered trees induce a meditative mood that is an essential part of Zen practice (fig. 8.25).

The upper garden on the hillside extends the Zen experience. Here one finds a dry cascade, thought to be the first example of a *kare sansui* composition in a Japanese garden. Its absence of water suggests *mu*, or "no-thing-ness," which is emblematic of Zen teaching. Its flat-topped rocks, perfectly arranged so as to suggest a waterfall in nature, are unlike the vertically positioned rocks at Tenryū-ji and mark the beginning in Japanese stone compositions of a preference for horizontal lines. These rocks are more sympathetically allied with the native landscape than upthrust ones, which were originally intended to evoke Chinese mountain scenery. As rock artistry continued to develop in Japan, vertical stones were still used as accents, but handsome flat stones became increasingly prized by garden designers as an important means of creating effects of tranquil beauty (fig. 8.26). In other words, in Japanese garden design, as in painting, the influence of Chinese models remained present as a continuing source of inspiration, but local traditions and local imagery modified received forms into an indigenous cultural expression. The oxymoronic notion of a *dry cascade* is like a Zen *kōan,* puzzling and without apparent logic, a means of frustrating rational thought and pushing the acolyte toward a deeper, more intuitive understanding.

The transcendent quality of this garden derives

in part from Musō Soseki's rockwork and in part from the patina of age. For the last hundred years or so, many varieties of moss have been encouraged to grow into a thick velvety tapestry that now covers the entire ground plane. Meticulously groomed, this soft blanket of gleaming green moss accounts for the garden's alternate name, Kokedera, or Moss Temple. Vigorous restraint, rich economy, and tradition-fed originality remained characteristic of Japanese gardens even as they continued to incorporate Chinese forms into a new idiom of elegant austerity.

MUROMACHI GARDENS

Kamakura rule was superseded by that of the Ashikaga shogunate in what is referred to as the Muromachi period (1333–1573), named after the northeastern section of Kyoto, where the third shogun, Ashikaga Yoshimitsu (1358–1408), built his palace. Called Hana no Gosho, or Flowery Palace, it had a beautiful lake garden. Active trade with China had brought renewed enthusiasm for Chinese Song arts to Japan. Antique Song paintings and porcelains and Ming works in the Song style were eagerly sought, and in spite of famine, plague, and a series of earthquakes, connoisseurship flourished among the ruling elite.

Yoshimitsu, a Zen follower, left his office nominally in the hands of his nine-year-old son, and retired to a private estate outside the city where a fine old garden from the early thirteenth century already existed. He renamed the place Kitayama (North Hill) Villa. Here, around 1397, he set about building Kinkaku, or Golden Pavilion, as his private chapel (fig. 8.27). In the Golden Pavilion and its successor, the Silver Pavilion, we see the effects of patronage by wealthy shoguns: garden designs derived from a fusion of Chinese Song and Japanese Zen aesthetics. The villa was converted to a Zen temple and renamed Rokuon-ji in 1408 upon Yoshimitsu's death. Popularly known as Kinkaku-ji (Temple of the Golden Pavilion) by later generations, this remarkable three-storied structure (actually a mid-twentieth-century replica of the only remaining part of Yoshimitsu's original *shinden*-style mansion) is perched over the water of the lake.[13] The lower floor, Amida Hall, was used as a reception room; the second, Kannon Hall, as a place for conversation and connoisseurship; while the third story, with its bell-shaped windows, probably functioned as a Zen meditation room. The gold-leafed ceiling of this room as well as its gold-lacquered exterior furnished the pavilion with its name. The Golden Pavilion is a delicately poetic structure, especially when its soaring eaves are dusted with snow and the pines and pond beside it are similarly whitened.

Although converted into a temple foundation following Yoshimitsu's death, Kinkaku-ji was first and foremost a princely pleasure ground. Its lake may inspire a state of spiritual reverie, but it was also used for boating parties, and the proudest event of Yoshimitsu's life occurred when he entertained the emperor and members of the court at a house party upon the garden's completion in 1408.

Kinkaku-ji's garden of only four-and-one-half acres was composed (it is thought by Yoshimitsu himself) in two parts—a lower lake garden and and upper "mountain" garden with tea houses—with such artistry that it augments itself through illusion. The lake, which covers a third of the garden surface, is divided by a peninsula and related central island into a heart-character shape (*kokoro*). Its waters reflect the Silk Hat Hill (Kinugasa-yama) that lies beyond its encircling pines. Song influence and Japanese aesthetics are evident in the careful selection and the placement of rocks into studied arrangements within the lake. Some of these are meant to evoke the nine mountains and eight seas in the Buddhist myth of creation. In addition, other interestingly formed rocks were placed as elements of islands. Several rock compositions take the shape of tortoises. The crane, another longevity symbol, is the motif for an island in front of the pavilion. Many of these beautifully arranged rocks were gifts to Yoshimitsu; often they have flat tops, a form that was increasingly admired among Japanese garden rock collectors.

In subsequent periods of Japanese garden history, fine stones were frequently carted from a ruined or impoverished garden to a new one. For instance, in 1474, following his retirement from the shogunate, Yoshimasa (1436–1490), grandson of Yoshimitsu, had some of the stones and pine trees of the Flowery Palace and Muromachi Hall, both of which had been devastated by civil warfare, removed to his villa retreat at the base of Higashiyama (the Eastern Hills). There he lived from 1483 until his death, when the villa was converted to a Zen temple, Jishō-ji, or Ginkaku-ji (the Temple of the Silver Pavilion), as it is better known. Rockwork became a professional occupation for a certain outcast segment of society, men who engaged in various kinds of necessary "dirty work." Some of these, such as Zen'ami (d. 1482), who worked at several of the great Muromachi estates, were talented garden craftsmen and much in demand.

The culture of Zen is perhaps more completely expressed in those gardens that were designed by and for the use of monks, practitioners of *zazen*, or seated

8.27. Kinkaku-ji (Golden Pavilion), Rokuon-ji Temple, Kyoto. Kamakura Period, Pavilion rebuilt in the middle of the 20th century after the original of the 1390s

8.28. Daisen-in, Kyoto, *kare sansui* garden with bridge with bell-shaped Zen window. Garden built by Kogaku, the founder of the temple, perhaps with the help of the artist Sōami. c. 1513

Below: 8.29. Garden of Ryōan-ji Temple, Kyoto, a *kare sansui* garden. Muromachi Period

meditation, than in such opulent, shogunate-financed retreats as Kinkaku-ji and and Ginkaku-ji. Carefully controlled compositions in small defined spaces, these gardens were meant to serve as an aid in altering consciousness so as to encourage a state of enlightenment. They are therefore different in character from the shogunal estate gardens like Kinkaku-ji and Ginkaku-ji whose primary end was aesthetic enjoyment.

Daisen-in is one of the subsidiary temple gardens in the great Zen monastery of Daitoku-ji built around 1513 by Kogaku (or Sōkō, 1464–1548), the founder of the temple, perhaps with the help of the artist Sōami (1485–1525), whose landscape paintings adorn the interior walls. This small garden, only 12 feet (3.7 meters) wide and 47 feet (14.3 meters) long, is an exquisite rendition of the kind of mountain scenery found in Song painting (fig. 8.28). It is built in the *kare sansui,* or dry garden style, which was perfected in the Muromachi period. Read as intended from left to right, it offers the viewer a "waterfall" of white gravel that comes spilling and pooling between a series of vertically placed rocks, to flow under a small

stone "bridge" and then fan out into a beautiful raked gravel "river" where a stone "boat" is seen floating. The remarkable boat-shaped rock once belonged to the shogun-aesthete Yoshimasa, builder of the Silver Pavilion. A curious divider, a narrow roofed bridge, bisects the garden. It is a twentieth-century reconstruction based upon architectural and graphic evidence of a bridge that was in place during the Edo period (1603–1868). From the side where the raked gravel river flows around rock islands toward an implied ocean beyond the garden wall, a bell-shaped window frames a view of the miniature mountains and waterfall where the "river" has its source.

Just as Western art at the beginning of the twentieth century transcended representation to achieve abstraction, a similar change occurred in Japan at the beginning of the sixteenth century. This transition to a more reductive expression is evidenced by the creation of the Zen garden at Ryōan-ji (Subdued Dragon Temple), which consists of nothing more than fifteen moss-fringed stones placed in a bed of white quartz gravel evenly scored with the long continuous marks of a rake (fig. 8.29).

Ryōan-ji's minimalist *kare sansui* garden has held great fascination for Western architects and garden historians since the 1930s when, conditioned by modernism, they began to understand its formal principles. Some have sought to understand it in metaphysical terms as well. For these reasons it has been extensively analyzed both allegorically and as a set of mathematical relationships in which five groupings of stones are held within their gravel bed in an arrangement of perfectly balanced tension. Viewed from left to right, this arrangement reads as follows: five stones, then two, next three, again two, and finally three stones. Sitting at any point on the veranda, the viewer will always find one stone is hidden from sight. Like that of a painting by the Dutch artist Piet Mondrian (1872–1944), the compositional balance of this garden can only be grasped intuitively, not analyzed logically. Neither mathematical explanation nor allegorical meaning can be attached to it. To achieve either would rob it of its enigmatic quality and thereby make it less satisfying from a Zen perspective, as the inexplicability it offers is fundamental to Zen experience and an intrinsic factor in its design. Its true power can only be felt if one is able to experience it over an extended period of quiet meditation and without the distraction of tourists. To appreciate fully its power as a work of art, one must suspend thought and enjoy not only the dynamic stasis of the rocks and the rhythmic lines running through the white gravel, but also the warm buff tones of the unassuming earthen wall with its tile roof and the borrowed scenery beyond it.

OPULENCE AND RESTRAINT: HIDEYOSHI AND SEN NO RIKYŪ

Japanese art, including garden art, demonstrates the richness of restraint and the power of understatement. But Japanese cultural history is not one unbroken chain of aesthetic refinement in which the modernist dictum of "less is more" is made continually manifest. At the opposite end of the spectrum from the austerity of Ryōan-ji are the gardens such as the one at Sambō-in, created during the rule of Toyotomi Hideyoshi (1536–1598), the second of three generals who united Japan in the late sixteenth century after a prolonged period of civil war. Hideyoshi quickly maneuvered himself into the title of *kampaku*. From that position as intermediary between the emperor and court officials, he brazenly reduced them to impotence and dependency and made himself dictator. His alliances with, and dominance over, Japan's other feudal warlords concentrated much of the country's wealth in his hands. Of plebian birth rather than part of the samurai aristocracy, he lacked early training in Zen aesthetics, and it is thus not surprising that he often used this wealth to indulge his desire for opulence.

Architectural gilding was the order of the day in the huge buildings Hideyoshi erected. On the site of the old Imperial Palace, he put up the Jurakutei, his moat-surrounded Kyoto castle. There he amassed a huge collection of specimen rocks, gifts from his subject lords. But by 1588 he had the Jurakutei dismantled and some of its buildings moved to his residence, Osaka Castle, and to the new palace he had built at Fushimi. The latter was located in the southern Kyoto suburb known as the Momoyama district; from it comes the name of the Momoyama period (1573–1603), which is synchronous with the hegemony of Hideyoshi and the rulers immediately preceding and following him. After Hideyoshi's death, Fushimi Castle and its exotic gardens containing sago palm trees were also dismantled. The stones from his lavish Tiger Glen, or Kokei Garden, were transferred to the temple of Nishi Hongan-ji, and the impressive ceremonial architecture of Fushimi was disassembled and redistributed to this and other temples in and around Kyoto.

In the Eastern Hills, not far from the site of Fushimi Castle, Hideyoshi decided to refurbish the garden of Sambō-in, a subtemple of Daigo-ji, in preparation for a massive spring outing to view cherry blossoms. Although Hideyoshi died before the garden could be finished, the abbot Gien of Daigo-ji supervised the completion of this richly conceived garden (fig. 8.30). Many of the choice rocks from Hideyoshi's garden at the Jurakutei were transferred to Sambō-in, including a highly prized rectangular

8.30. Garden of Sambō-in, Daigo-ji Temple, Kyoto. Momoyama Period

pale-colored one called the Fujito Stone, which had acquired a certain fame before Hideyoshi bought it for five thousand bushels of rice.

By this time, rock craftsmen, were employed in the selection and positioning of garden stones. Yoshirō, known as Kentei, or Excellent Gardener, worked for twenty years, until 1618, arranging the nearly eight hundred rocks found at Sambō-in into a composition that, if somewhat restless, is nevertheless a boldly dynamic expression of the energy invested in garden design in the Momoyama period.

Hideyoshi's taste, though opulent, was also broad, and he was interested in the development of the Japanese tea ceremony, *cha no yu*, by Sen no Rikyū (1521–1591), who made this secular, aesthetic pursuit into a spiritual experience as well. Originated in Song China and developed in Japan at the Silver Pavilion by the Zen monk Murata Jukō (1423–1502) during the Muromachi era, the tea ceremony became one of the most important and lasting developments of the Momoyama period, deepening the ingrained aestheticism of Japanese culture and giving a new dimension to the refined rusticity of the Japanese garden in which *sabi*—the mellow agedness produced by weathered stone, mosses, and lichens—is highly valued.

The ritual of the tea ceremony as formulated by Sen no Rikyū requires for its enactment a pattern of precise movements, a particular kind of setting, and certain elegantly simple utensils. It is conducted in a small, thatch-roofed hut with wattle-and-daub walls, the rustic simplicity of which is meant to induce a mood of *wabi*, refined austerity. Only a small upper window covered with bamboo lattice admits light to the tearoom. Guests must stoop to enter. Inside the tea house, the garden view is intentionally blocked from sight, leaving the focus of the tearoom, which is commonly four-and-a-half tatami mats in size,[14] upon the *tokonoma*, a small alcove wherein a particularly fine scroll and elegantly simple flower arrange-

ment may be displayed. The host enters and begins to prepare tea, as the three or four guests attune their senses to the gentle hissing of the steam kettle. The host places the tea in a ceramic tea bowl and, with a bamboo whisk, stirs it with precise and practiced motions into a light green foam, then hands the bowl to the most important guest. The tea bowl itself, like every other carefully positioned object in the room, is a focus of aesthetic admiration. After the tea has been drunk, the beauty of the bowl's form and glaze is silently admired. It is then returned to the host, who wipes it clean and prepares tea for the next guest.

The secluded intimacy of the tea ceremony did not require the same kind of well-composed garden space as that of a temple. What was sought was a means of separation from the busy surrounding world and a way of declaring entry into another realm. This was accomplished by the *cha niwa,* or tea garden path, sometimes called *roji,* meaning "dewy path." Typically, this is a narrow corridor leading from the street, through a gate made of open-weave bamboo, into a small area where a natural stone basin invites the guest to bend down and wash his hands before stooping again to pass through the small door of the tea house. A fence of bamboo twigs encloses this small garden. Understandably, azaleas or other showy plants are not grown in such a place; a tea garden's most notable aspect is the ground plane itself. Here flat stepping-stones are set within moss. These differ from the stones carefully selected for color, shape, surface modeling, and patina, which are found in other types of Japanese gardens. Strictly utilitarian, stones for the *cha niwa* are usually rounded river-washed stones, which speak the language of nature and enhance the atmosphere of rusticity and mood of quiet expectation one experiences upon approaching the tea house.

The stepping-stone path of the small tea garden actually plays an important role in the development of the Japanese garden overall, being the precursor of the paths of the much larger stroll garden, such as those in the imperial garden of Katsura Rikyū. The laying of these and other kinds of stones in the ground, with attention paid to size, texture, form, and line, is an art form in itself. This accounts for much of the pleasure one experiences in viewing the ground plane of Japanese gardens.

Another important feature contributed by the tea garden to other kinds of Japanese gardens is the stone lantern (fig. 8.32). Originally found in Buddhist temples, where they were lit for votive offerings, these lanterns were appropriated by the tea garden in order to illuminate at night the path and the stone hand-washing laver near the tea house (fig. 8.31). They became admired objects in their own right and were

soon being copied and then designed by tea masters in a manner that was different from that of their temple prototypes.

Today the separate schools for tea instruction begun by Sen no Rikyū's three great-grandsons—Ura Senke, Omote Senke, and Mushanōkoji Senke—still exist with their own tea gardens in Kyoto. Although many old tea gardens have vanished, the popularity of the tea ceremony is such that many new ones can be found both in Japan and abroad.

THE EDO PERIOD: KATSURA RIKYŪ

Following Hideyoshi's death, his five-year-old son Hideyori inherited his authority. The samurai leader Tokugawa Ieyasu (1542–1616), who had been appointed as one of the boy's five guardians, soon maneuvered himself into a position of supremacy. This provoked other barons into a power struggle against him, leading to civil conflict, a situation always imminent in Japan's feudal society. Ieyasu triumphed over his opponents in 1600, assuming for himself the role of all-powerful shogun in 1603. He moved to Edo, now Tokyo, and from his castle there, he systematically circumscribed the actions of the country's other strong families.

The Edo period (1603–1867), as the two-and-one-half-century era of Tokugawa rule is called, was characterized by rigid control of every aspect of Japanese life. Whatever power remained to the emasculated emperor and court was further curtailed by official rules that limited their role exclusively to scholarship and the arts. As such, they were seen as respected custodians of Japanese aesthetics, nothing more. Furthermore, in the the Tokugawa shoguns' zeal for absolutist control over all aspects of Japanese life, they expelled all Christian missionaries and most foreign traders.

It is understandable that, under such circumstances, escapist impulses would drive the alienated aristocracy to new aesthetic enterprise. Kobori Enshū (1579–1647), although himself a *daimyo,* or feudal lord, was a student of Sen no Rikyū's leading disciple, the tea master Furuta Oribe (1544–1615). As a tea master himself, Kobori Enshū took a natural interest in ceramics, sponsoring the work of various kilns in his province, and as a student of poetry, a noted calligrapher and a garden designer, he was a leading figure in this chapter of Japan's cultural life.

Kirei sabi (elegant beauty infused with a weathered rustic quality) is the name that attempts to capture the aesthetic ideal promoted by Kobori Enshū. It is "beautiful" in that it harks back to the graceful grandeur of the Heian period and expresses an understandable longing on the part of the court in the Edo era for the days of Heian glory, before the emperor had been robbed of his power. It is "rustic" in that it expresses the pastoral simplicity and closeness to nature advocated by Sen no Rikyū.

Although as aristocratic in origin as the Italian and French gardens with which it is contemporary, the air of understatement in *kirei sabi* is at the opposite extreme from the energetic grandeur of their related styles. In his garden designs, Kobori Enshū substituted a diagonal approach for the axial thrust found in Italian villa gardens and at Versailles. This promotes a zigzag movement, creating scenic "surprises" as one travels along a prescribed garden route. The technique of hide-and-reveal is, in fact, the essence of the stroll garden, a concept that substitutes movement through a sequence of garden spaces for the stationary viewing mandated by the designs of most *shinden*-style gardens and Zen temple gardens. Within the stroll garden, the stepping-stone path of the tea garden is therefore employed for a new purpose: the kinetic experience of landscape.

Because the spirit of Katsura Villa epitomizes Kobori Enshū's style of *kirei sabi* so perfectly, he has been frequently credited as its designer, although there is no record of his actual participation. Widely regarded as a paragon among gardens, Katsura demonstrates the flowering of aesthetic refinement that occurred when, deprived of all involvement in affairs of state, a member of the imperial family, handsomely supported by gifts from the shogun, devoted his life to building a private never-never land.

Katsura's origins as a garden derive from a problem presented by Imperial Prince Toshihito (1571–1629), whom Hideyoshi adopted before the latter's own son and heir was born. When Hideyoshi finally produced a biological heir in 1590, he established Toshihito as the head of a collateral imperial line. In addition, he gave him a sizable grant of land, which was exchanged for another on the banks of the Katsura River to the west of the city around 1605. A few years later, Prince Toshihito began building a modest country retreat there, and in the summer of 1616, he invited a group of nobles, poets, and dancers to a festive outing in his "little tea house in the Melon Patch." Prince Toshihito enjoyed good relations with the shogun as well as a generous income. Thus secure, he was able to expand his building program on his Katsura estate, and by the time of his death in 1629, the place had become a cultural mecca for poets, artists, and garden lovers.

Although the country house at Katsura was allowed to deteriorate immediately following Prince Toshihito's death, its fortunes were soon revived by his son, young Prince Toshitada (1619–1662). In 1632, the thirteen-year-old boy was part of a delegation visiting Iemitsu, the third and most powerful shogun of the Tokugawa line, from which he came away with a farewell gift of a thousand pieces of silver and thirty kimonos. Apparently the young man continued to enjoy the shogun's largesse, and he was able during his lifetime to bring the estate to its full glory as an important cultural center and shining example of the *shoin,* or *shoin zukuri,* style of architecture and the *kirei sabi* aesthetic in garden art (fig. 8.33).

Almost from the beginning, Prince Toshitada conceived of the garden as a setting for a series of tea houses. The first, the Geppa-rō, or Moon Wave Tower, was built close to the main house. Not far from this tea house, one of the villa's several rustic earth-covered bridges carries the visitor to the Inner Gate. The gate's quiet beauty resides in its harmonious proportions and the carefully crafted details of

8.33. Aerial view of Katsura Villa, Kyoto. Early Edo Period

Right: 8.34. Paving patterns, Inner Gate and courtyard, Katsura

Far right: 8.35. Two earthen bridges, Katsura, Kyoto

Below: 8.36. Shōka-tei, Katsura, Kyoto, with ascending stepping stones

Bottom: 8.37. Katsura Villa Garden, from a room of the Old Shoin, looking across moon-viewing platform

its simple bamboo-and-thatch roof. The design of the paths and the varied patterns of the stone paving around this gate and in the courtyard create a subtly textured ground plane (fig. 8.34).

In 1645, Prince Toshitada journeyed to Edo to request further financial aid from the shogun and during his travels studied the architecture of several notable tea houses. Soon he was hosting tea parties as well as nocturnal moon-viewing and boating parties at Katsura, and by 1649, documents record that there were, in addition to the Geppa-rō, four more tea houses. Three of these can still be seen today: the Shōkin-tei, or Pine Lute Pavilion; the Shōka-tei, or Flower Appreciation Pavilion; and the Shōi-ken, or Laughing Thoughts Pavilion. Katsura's tea house architecture derives from that of rustic farm buildings; the elegance and simplicity with which this vernacular style has been adapted to a refined purpose lies at the heart of the *kirei sabi* aesthetic.

Stroll gardens like that of Katsura suggest prescribed routes. Stepping-stone paths direct the visitor's footsteps from one to another of these tea houses, each exquisitely sited as a feature within the larger landscape. The experience is delightfully disorienting as one repeatedly changes direction and appreciates each new and skillfully arranged view. Like the tea houses, the paths have poetic names such as Maple Riding Lane and Plum Riding Lane. Some of the villa's landscapes evoke such famous Japanese scenes as the Bridge of Heaven, here abstracted and depicted at a reduced scale. The topography is graded to produce "mountains," and the stepping stones, like those approaching the Shōka-tei, are set into these hillsides so skillfully that one has the sensation of real ascent although the gentle topography rises only slightly (fig. 8.36). Where the grade is depressed, as

in the Valley of Fireflies, wood and earthen bridges or stone slab bridges ease the way (fig. 8.35).

The same hide-and-reveal tactics, which pleasantly surprise with views that are unexpected, are employed within the house itself. One always approaches a house obliquely and, once inside, never approaches the main room axially, so that a view may be withheld until one comes upon it, perceiving it within a frame of *shoji* (fig. 8.37). Elevated on a high foundation, the house loses connection with the ground plane; the sense of spatial interpenetration between interior and exterior is absent; and the framed garden views seem to be courtly paintings of nature, rather than the reality of nature apprehended at close range.

While the dreamworld of Katsura can be appreciated for its intrinsic qualities and without association, much of the scenery of this famous garden is probably based upon literary models, such as Lady

Murasaki's descriptions of Heian gardens in *The Tale of Genji*. We may assume that, while Kobori Enshū may have advised Prince Toshitada from time to time, this great stroll garden, with its echoes of Heian beauty interwoven with rustic quietude, was the work of the scholarly prince himself, who, disenfranchised from affairs of state, found in the creation of Katsura a deeply engrossing pastime. In the 1930s, Katsura was belatedly recognized by the Japanese as a national treasure. Preserved and maintained, it stands today as a monument to the prince and the triumph, in the long term, of art over the politics of power.

The Edo Period: Shugakuin Rikyū

Kyoto boasts one other perfectly preserved imperial garden in the *kirei sabi* style of Kobori Enshū: Shugakuin Rikyū. Here, in the scenic northeastern hills, an idyllic stroll garden with scattered tea houses incorporates to an even greater degree than Katsura does, the design technique of *shakkei,* or borrowed scenery. This landscape with its carefully wrought views beyond the limits of the garden was created under similar circumstances and at approximately the same time as Katsura by Prince Toshitada's uncle, the retired emperor Go-Mizunoo (1596–1680).

Angered by the shogun's heavy-handed supervision of imperial affairs, Go-Mizunoo abruptly resigned in favor of his daughter in 1629. Freed from ceremonial responsibility, he first turned his attentions to Sentō Gosho, meaning "Retired Emperor's Villa," the palace and garden he planned with Kobori Enshū. After this project was completed, Go-Mizunoo was ready to search for a site for a country retreat. This was undertaken with the encouragement of Tokugawa Iemitsu, who, in an effort to ingratiate himself with the imperial court in Kyoto and appease Go-Mizunoo's smoldering frustrations, had increased his income more than threefold.

Thus furnished with a generous stipend, Go-Mizunoo selected a site of seventy-three acres in the beautiful Mount Hiei foothills, approximately 450 feet (137 meters) above sea level, near Shugakuin Temple, and there, by the early 1650s, he was at work creating a landscape garden. Kobori Enshū was dead by this time, but like Henry Hoare, the owner-creator of Stourhead—the English garden that is most similar to Shugakuin—Go-Mizunoo was a sufficient artist in his own right to apply the lessons of Enshū in a wholly original manner. Relying on the site's superior inherent scenic potential, he created a design that is more relaxed and natural than that of Katsura.

Shugakuin now comprises three separate villa gardens. Placed at different elevations among terraced rice fields, these were connected by simple trails, replaced at the end of the nineteenth century by the tree-bordered gravel paths we find today. The garden surrounding the Lower Villa contains a small pond and three carved stone lanterns. The Middle Villa was used by one of Go-Mizunoo's daughters as an abbess's residence when she became a nun in 1680 and founded a temple nearby. Its garden also contains a pond, as well as a lawn and a wide-spreading umbrella pine. But the full range of Go-Mizunoo's genius is not apparent until one passes through cultivated rice fields and ascends the slope to the Upper Villa.

The passage upward from the Imperial Gate, the point of entry to this part of Shugakuin, is a narrow set of stairs constricted by tall hedges on either side. It is only after emerging into the sunlight at the top of the slope that one sees the panorama of the lake, called Yokuryū-chi, or Bathing Dragon Pond, and the borrowed scenery of the gently undulating mountains to the northwest (fig. 8.38). The lake is supported by a massive terraced dam on its west bank, which is concealed by a long, flat-topped, stepped hedge composed of approximately forty

8.38. Upper Garden, view of borrowed scenery from Ryū'untei Tea House to Yokoryū-chi Pond, Shugakuin, Kyoto. Late Momoyama / Early Edo Period

8.39. Stone paving, Senshi-dai, or Poem-Washing Platform, in front of the Rin'un-tei Tea House, Shugakuin, Upper Villa

Below: 8.40. Aerial view of Shugakuin Villa Garden's lake with its circuit path and surrounding agricultural landscape

Right: 8.41. Rock arrangement (called Kamejima, or Tortoise Island) and clipped shrubbery, Garden of Konchi-in Temple, Kyoto. Early Edo Period

kinds of shrubs, with an occasional tree growing in it. The vantage point for this sight is a delicate tea house, the Rin'un-tei, or Pavilion in the Clouds.

Even here, where the technique of borrowed scenery reaches its consummate expression, the designer paid great attention to the texture of the ground plane. For instance, in front of the tea house at the Senshi-dai, or Poem-Washing Platform, built to offer the magnificent view, there is a paved apron embedded with stones set singly and in groups of two and three. It illustrates, like so many other design details, the casual-seeming, but carefully considered, artistry we have come to expect in Japanese gardens where almost nothing is left to chance (fig. 8.39).

A path descends from the hill of the Rin'un-tei to make a counterclockwise circuit around the lake. The lake was used for pleasure boating, and its islands, one of which has a small pavilion, could be visited. The bridges that connect them to one another and the shore are scenic elements in a series of continually shifting views as one continues around the lake (fig. 8.40). On the north shore, on the site of the present boathouse, stood the Shishi-sai, a summerhouse where guests might be carried upon arrival to refresh themselves before proceeding clockwise around the lake and up a circuitous path to the Rin'un-tei. Once arrived, they could enjoy, as a sudden surprise, the view of the scenic panorama that unfolds beyond the confines of the garden.

OTHER EDO AND MODERN GARDENS

Increasingly, garden design became less the realm of Zen priests and gifted aristocratic amateurs and more the province of professional gardeners, whose guiding influence remained Kobori Enshū. *Hōjō* gardens (gardens designed in conjunction with the main build-

ing of a temple, often called the Abbot's Quarters) increased during the seventeenth century. This is due in part to the priest Ishin-Sūden (1564–1632), who served as an intermediary between the Tokugawa shogunate and the temple administrators, securing support for the latter's construction projects. Often these were *kare sansui,* or dry gardens, although they might contain rock arrangements, frequently ones suggesting the legendary crane or tortoise. The designs of these Edo period gardens were therefore less austere and ethereal than those of earlier Zen gardens such as Ryōan-ji.

Kobori Enshū himself designed the gardens at Konchi-in, a subtemple of Nanzen-ji where Ishin-Suden had his headquarters, after one of the fine buildings from Hideyoshi's Fushimi Castle in Kyoto was moved there in 1611. His vigorous *kare sansui* design employs rock arrangements that include crane and tortoise imagery. In addition to its rock compositions and bed of raked white gravel, the garden of Konchi-in contains a backdrop of carefully pruned shrubs (fig. 8.41). Clipped shrubbery, the massive stepped hedge of Shugakuin, and the extraordinary continuously curving one at Daichi-ji—an undulating, pulsating animal-like mass, which is the entire focus of the garden—are additional hallmarks of Enshū's boldly original style (fig. 8.42). The use of meticulously clipped shrubs, rather than rocks, as the principal elements in garden design is also found at Shisendō (Hall of the Immortal Poets), the garden retreat built by Ishikawa Jōzan (1583–1672), a Tokugawa dissident who retired here to a life of scholarship in 1636 (fig. 8.43). This garden contrasts with the lofty remoteness of the framed views seen from the interior of the *shoin* at Katsura; at Konchi-in, interior and garden space interpenetrate in delightful intimacy by way of the intermediate space of the wooden veranda.

Other characteristic features of Edo period gardens are the sand mounds with surfaces raked by Japanese priests into abstract designs that anticipate

8.42. Garden of Daichi-ji Temple, Shiga Prefecture. These undulating, rounded, closely clipped shrubs represent the Seven Lucky Gods.

Below: 8.43. Gardener pruning azalea, Shisendō (Hall of Immortal Poets), Kyoto, garden built by Ishikawa Jōzan. Early Edo Period

Bottom: 8.44. View from Ginkaku Pavilion of Ginshadan (white sand in a waved design) and Kogetsudai (mountain shape) in front of main hall, Ginkaku-ji Temple, Kyoto. Pavilion, Muromachi Period; sand garden, Edo Period

by nearly four centuries the patterned landscape scarification one observes in the earth art of our own time. One enters Hōnen-in, a temple of the Jōdo sect of Buddhism, from a roofed gate that provides a platform for viewing a pair of mounds, the surfaces of which are raked with subtle delicacy. Nearby, at the Muromachi period villa-turned-temple garden of Ginkaku-ji, there is a pair of sand mounds dating from the Edo era. One of these takes the form of a truncated cone, thought to recall Mount Fuji or the central mountain of Buddhist myth, and the other, a horizontal rectangle, is known as the "Sea of Silver Sand" because its reflective white surface provided an added attraction during moon-viewing parties (fig. 8.44).

By the eighteenth century, the tradition of Japanese garden art was becoming devitalized. Many gardens were built, but their designers substituted a more formulaic approach for the deeply felt spiritual and aesthetic impulses that had nourished the tradition in earlier times. The rise of Japan's prosperous merchant class created a large number of property owners, and this stimulated the demand for interior courtyard gardens. Nurseries and stone yards were established where plants, rocks, and lanterns could be purchased.

The appearance of the American naval commander Commodore Perry in Tokyo Bay in 1853 brought about a decisive change in Japanese government and culture. Powerless in the face of this challenge to Japan's long-standing isolationist policy, the Tokugawa shogunate, whose iron grip depended upon military might, was unable to maintain its control. Thus ended two-and-a-half centuries of seclusion from the rest of the world. In 1868, the emperor was restored to power and took up residence in Edo, which was renamed Tokyo, meaning "Eastern Capi-

tal." The Meiji Restoration—the remolding of Japanese culture during the last half of the nineteenth century—instituted constitutional government, did away with many complex rules of social stratification, and brought about other changes.

Rapid Westernization transformed the Japanese garden. In Tokyo, an English-style lawn was installed at the Shinjuku Imperial Garden, and businessmen and financiers built similarly hybrid landscapes. But a more profound design integration of two such opposite traditions would necessarily await a later day when the modernist movement made the West ready to receive inspiration from the spare and elegant compositional devices found in Japanese gardens—a sympathetic alliance with nature, borrowed scenery, hide-and-reveal compositional technique, rock artistry, and focus upon ground-plane patterns and textures.

1. Although the Chinese garden had in common with the Western Picturesque garden a penchant for irregularity and naturalistic effects, it was much more compressed and tightly coiled as a work of art, acting as a symbolic representation of the entire natural world. This aesthetic in turn provided the impetus for the creation of the Japanese garden, in which the nexus between art and nature was bolstered by the tradition of Shinto religion and by the further development of Buddhist philosophy after its importation from China. That Buddhism coexisted with, rather than destroyed, Shinto religion only strengthened the Japanese bond with nature. This development, which began toward the end of the sixth century C.E., displays a consistent Japanese ability consciously to assimilate foreign influences into its cultural core, in the process re-forming them into an authentically indigenous expression.

2. *Kami,* discernible only through faith, exert a mysterious creative and harmonizing influence (*musubi*) on human life. Tutelary *kami,* which are associated with individual clans, are revered at shrines. They reveal to worshipers the truthful way or will (*makoto*).

3. *Xian* were also believed to inhabit the Kunlun Mountains in the distant west.

4. See Claudia Brown, "Chinese Scholars' Rocks and the Land of Immortals: Some Insights from Painting," *Worlds Within Worlds: The Richard Rosenblum Collection of Chinese Scholars' Rocks,* ed. Robert D. Mowry (Cambridge, Mass.: Harvard University Art Museums, 1997), pp. 57–83.

5. For a description of Shanglin Park and several other Chinese landscapes subsequently discussed in this chapter I am indebted especially to Maggie Keswick, *The Chinese Garden: History, Art & Architecture* (New York: Rizzoli, 1978).

6. The following encapsulated discussion and quotations are derived from Ji Cheng, *Yuan Ye,* trans. Alison Hardie, *The Craft of Gardens* (New Haven: Yale University Press, 1988).

7. For the best contemporary English translation of this literary masterpiece, see Cao Xueqin, *The Story of the Stone* (Harmondsworth, Middlesex, England: Penguin Books, vols. 1–3, trans. David Hawkes, 1973–80; vols. 4–5, trans. John Minford, 1982–86). The following quotations describing the building of the garden and the naming of its various parts are found in vol. 1, chap. 17.

8. See Richard E. Strassberg, trans., *Inscribed Landscapes: Travel Writing from Imperial China* (Berkeley: University of California Press, 1994), p. 15.

9. The many pleasure pavilions built by Khubilai Khan and subsequent emperors around these lakes have fallen into ruin over the centuries. Fortunately for posterity, the Chinese garden scholar Osvald Sirén was given permission in the 1920s to wander at his pleasure within the precincts of the tea palaces before they had become accessible to the general public, and his beautiful photographs preserve for us at least an evocation of their haunting poetry. See Osvald Sirén, *Gardens of China* (New York: The Ronald Tree Press Company, 1949), pl. 145–76.

10. For an excellent summary of the *Sakuteiki* or *Treatise on Garden Making,* see Loraine Kuck, *The World of the Japanese Garden: From Chinese Origins to Modern Landscape Art* (New York: Weatherhill, 1968), pp. 91–93. Kuck's history of the Japanese garden is an invaluable reference work.

11. Chang'an was approximately 6 miles (9.7 kilometers) from east to west and 5.25 miles (8.5 kilometers) north to south. Kyoto, hemmed in by hills, could only expand to the south.

12. See Murasaki Shikibu, *The Tale of Genji,* trans. Edward G. Seidensticker (New York: Alfred A. Knopf, 1985).

13. The Golden Pavilion that one sees today is a generally faithful copy of the original, which was destroyed in 1950 by an arsonist protesting the post–World War II commercialization of the Buddhist Church.

14. A tatami mat measures approximately 3 by 6 feet (.9 by 1.8 meters).

CHAPTER NINE

EXPANDING CITIES AND NEW SOCIAL INSTITUTIONS: THE DEMOCRATIZATION OF LANDSCAPE DESIGN

The designs of many of the landscapes studied thus far derive—sometimes overtly, sometimes implicitly—from cosmological beliefs. The desire to perceive order and meaning in the universe is pervasive throughout human history and continues to govern some of our most deep-seated psychological and religious attitudes. In the West, however, as the Scientific Revolution gained momentum through the eighteenth century and political revolutions discredited entrenched power structures, the impulse to reflect in landscape terms a cosmological paradigm proclaiming divine order and elite authority diminished. As the theories of Newton were proved and extended by later scientific endeavor and became incorporated into the general cultural consciousness, intellectuals increasingly abandoned the quest for teleological meaning, concentrating instead on empirical explanations of the material world. Faith in reason and individual human action resulted in the substitution of personal judgment for blind obedience to authority, with significant political consequences as monarchies were toppled or their powers severely curtailed in favor of republican forms of government. For some people, faith in scientific progress displaced faith in supernatural powers and divine intervention in earthly affairs. For them, and for those who reconciled science with faith, the betterment of the conditions of life on Earth, not preparation for the hereafter, became the business of humankind.

Science assumed the authority previously enjoyed by religion and philosophy, which were demoted from their position as all-encompassing, culture-defining thought systems to being spiritual and intellectual disciplines. The unprecedented knowledge and technological results achieved by the Western pursuit of science, voyages of global exploration, and colonial expansion made Europeans, though arrogant in their presumption of world hegemony, at least more cognizant of other cultural perspectives. Travel also furthered the growing interest in natural science, and with the philosophical shift from teleology to scientific materialism, chemistry, biology, geology, and botany began to be pursued with the same fervor as the study of celestial bodies had been in former centuries when astrology was believed to govern human fate.

This pursuit of natural science had profound consequences for religion and philosophy, especially after Charles Darwin (1809–1882) published *The Origin of Species* in 1859. Galileo had long ago made it clear that Earth was no longer the center of the universe, but it now became apparent that humans were products of an evolutionary biology that linked them with the rest of the animal kingdom. Though bitterly resisted in some quarters, the same science that had caused human beings to modify their notions of their own nature and that of the cosmos also held the promise of untold material benefits.

But the power of people acting on their own behalf was often limited by their mistakes and misbegotten ideologies. In addition, humanity's growing power to control its destiny sometimes produced results that were not necessarily beneficial to Earth or even humankind in the long term. Darwin's theories necessarily took into account geological time and a dynamics of Earth in which forces of crustal uplift and erosion shaped the land, which was continually being recarved by wind, rain, and ice. Circumstances of geography and climate created ecological niches for species.[1] Now, in the nineteenth century, it became apparent to a few that the human species was capable of destroying other species and limiting its own future welfare as it continued to modify the environment by felling trees and clearing land for agriculture. This removal of native vegetation destroyed natural drainage systems, accelerated erosion, and altered climate.

George Perkins Marsh (1801–1882), American diplomat and early environmentalist, wrote *Man and Nature* (1864) as a stern warning against this calamitous course of unchecked abuse of nature. Just as Darwin's theories made some people revise their understanding of the Biblical creation story and regard it as myth and metaphor instead of gospel, so Marsh's views made unworkable the notion of the Creator making Earth solely for humanity's exploitation. For Western Christian societies, to look at landscape in ecological and conservationist terms as Marsh did was to question the wisdom of the scriptural injunction in Genesis 1:28 to "fill the earth and subdue it." Dominion without enlightened husbandry, according to Marsh, spelled destruction.

The difficulty that practicing Christians and Jews in the nineteenth century had reconciling their beliefs with the challenging new theories of science and humanity's role as God's partner and steward of Earth rather than His mere ward should not be minimized. Intellectually and morally, the late eighteenth century had in the nations of the West consolidated the Scientific Revolution that had begun in the sixteenth, while at the same time giving birth to the Industrial Revolution. Now, in the nineteenth century, the unsettling vision Goethe had limned in *Faust Part II* of nature overmastered by humanity in the form of the engineer and the developer was becoming a palpable reality. Romantics, following Rousseau and Wordsworth, found in wild nature the scenery of the sublime, a source of spiritual solace no longer available to those who had begun to question the premises of inherited religion. At the same time, the longing for the promise of redemptive salvation offered the faithful in earlier Christian centuries continued, and churchgoing remained a strongly rooted social convention and religious belief a personal need and cultural habit for many in the West.

The English writer and pioneer art critic John Ruskin (1819–1900) promoted an aesthetics that was rooted in the study of nature, which he equated with Truth. By preaching a philosophy of Beauty with the same fervor as ministers of the Evangelical tradition in which he had been raised, Ruskin furthered the modern notion that the appreciation and practice of art could serve as a source of spiritual life rather than simply as a manifestation of it. Like others of his generation, Ruskin was appalled by the dehumanization he perceived to be a result of industrial capitalism's advance, and he sought to revive the artisanship associated with the medieval period, a time when craft guilds flourished and Gothic stone carvers' close observation of nature resulted in a vigorously vital style of ornamentation. The American writers Ralph Waldo Emerson (1803–1882) and Henry David Thoreau (1817–1862) met science's challenge to religion with transcendentalism, the literary and philosophical movement that advocated intuition as a mode of perception transcending empiricism.

Whether reacting against or incorporating the implications of modern science and Darwinism, few in the nineteenth century reckoned that further blows to humanity's self-esteem and relationship with past tradition had yet to be assimilated. But the insights of Friedrich Nietzsche (1844–1900) and Sigmund Freud (1856–1939) established the intellectual climate of much of the twentieth century, a radical modernity in which people no longer looked to past traditions for inspiration and a sense of continuity with history; instead, they looked to the present and future as the only reliable basis for knowledge and human advancement. Even those who remained religious in outlook increasingly considered themselves their own best earthly guides. Humanitarian social consciousness

thus pervaded Western ideology, and utopian schemes flourished. This, abetted by widespread religious skepticism and atheism, helped create a cultural climate that gradually became receptive to, and more tolerant of, religious and social pluralism.

The consequences for landscape within the secular, highly energetic, increasingly cosmopolitan framework of nineteenth-century Western culture were enormous. In terms of landscape history, the public parks movement is a signal contribution of the nineteenth century to modern urbanism. As more purely aesthetic values supplanted ideological ones in landscape design, the eighteenth-century Picturesque idiom remained viable for the creation of nineteenth-century parks and gardens. Many aristocrats destroyed the geometrical gardens of their ancestral seats as the *jardin anglais* continued to be popular throughout nineteenth-century Europe, an emblem of the social progressiveness of their owners. At the same time, theorists and practitioners adopted a more catholic approach to landscape aesthetics, and the doctrinal fervor and invective that had characterized the design disputes of the eighteenth century were replaced by an eclecticism in which individual taste was given increasingly broad license. History as a cultural value in its own right and an intellectual framework for preserving and imitating past styles replaced commitment to a single style reflecting a consensual ideology. Geometrical design was allowed back into English gardens, and the display of exotic plant material became a mark of the Victorian style called *Gardenesque.*

From our own historical vantage point, the nineteenth century's faith in scientific progress and planning as a means toward utopian human fulfillment seems overconfident, a heady and overweening attitude that produced unforeseen consequences. The hypocrisies and inequalities of this extraordinary age are all too glaring. Although the Industrial Revolution fostered capitalist economies in the West, which produced a broad middle class and brought a cornucopia of goods and comforts to many, it was wrenching for others, causing large-scale migrations that tore people away from their homes and homelands. Those dispossessed from an immediate connection with landscapes of important sentimental and psychological value often endured, in addition, squalid living conditions in rapidly growing cities. Republican governments proved no more immune to corruption and class distinctions than those based upon aristocratic privilege and social hierarchy. Colonialism, which reached its zenith in the nineteenth century, was generally callous in its disregard of native cultural values, attempting to establish Western mores as universal while relegating non-European races to inferior status. Even after it became a sovereign nation, the United States accomplished the settlement of its continental territory under a similar cultural imperative.

At the same time, this period in Western history demonstrated the benefits of science as the foundations for modern medicine were laid, public sanitation victories achieved, better living conditions established, and faster means of transportation and communication developed. Scientific technology fostered an abundance of new inventions, constantly improving the processes of industrial production and accelerating its pace, making goods cheap and readily available. The potential danger to all human life consequent upon the splitting of the atom and widespread industrial degradation of the environment still lay in the future. In the nineteenth century, the energies of humanitarian reformers were focused on the unprecedented problems that attended the birth of mass society rather than on such global issues as these. Cholera, caused by contaminated drinking water, and other illnesses were associated with overcrowding. The use of industrial technology to build aqueducts, sewers, and other important elements of a new urban infrastructure was essential if populations were to survive in cities grown to a metropolitan scale. Further, parks and transportation lines connecting the commercial center with outlying residential suburbs needed to be built in order to maintain contact with nature otherwise lost to large-scale urban growth. The new immigrants pouring into cities in search of better lives posed special problems in terms of housing, education, and medical services. Responses to their suffering illuminated religion's revised role for many as an ethical, rather than a metaphysical, system.

Industrial capitalism and humane practicality went hand-in-hand. Jeremy Bentham (1748–1832) and James Mill (1773–1836) enunciated the doctrine of utilitarianism, the ethical theory that sees utility as a measure of economic and social value, directing all action toward the goal of achieving the greatest happiness for the greatest number of people. Imbued with democratic principles and utilitarian concepts of social justice, civic and political leaders undertook prison and burial reform, established public education, and created cultural institutions and large municipal parks for the social improvement and recreation of the population at large.

The creation of public parks and rural cemeteries were linked nineteenth-century phenomena. The rise in the numbers of dead in growing municipalities forced speedy disinterment of bodies in order to make room for new burials. Sectarian minorities without burial grounds advocated nondenominational public cemeteries. They were joined by sanitary reformers who saw urban churchyards as a source of groundwater contamination, fostering the spread of cholera and other infectious diseases. Père-Lachaise Cemetery in Paris, established in 1804, became an international model for municipal cemeteries elsewhere. In America, the first public cemeteries, Boston's Mount Auburn and Brooklyn's Green-Wood, served the function of public pleasure grounds in advance of the establishment of public parks, and their popularity did much to promote the municipal parks movement.

Within a repertoire of inherited design idioms featuring geometric, Picturesque, and gridiron layouts, which they often employed in combination, nineteenth-century designers strove to incorporate the newly discovered plants made available through expeditions of botanical discovery and the establishment of commercial nurseries. Through the publication of books and journals and as designers, such horticultural and landscape writers, editors, and practitioners as the Scot John Claudius Loudon (1782–1843) and the American Andrew Jackson Downing (1815–1852) democratized culture. They accomplished this by showing the aspiring members of the newly wealthy middle class how to attain the trappings of gentility, including homes and gardens similar, although on a smaller scale, to those of the aristocracy. The operative word in their works was *taste,* a discerning sense of what was excellent, harmonious, and beautiful—the quality that gave gentility visible form.

Increasingly, as living standards rose, commercial nurseries catering to the needs of the head gardeners on large estates were also able to bring horticulture within reach of other social strata. With the growth in home ownership, domesticity became a significant cultural value. The ornamental garden assumed new importance as an adjunct to the house, and even the humble cottage garden came to be regarded as an aesthetic object, rather than simply a utilitarian one. On great estates, owners ceased to remove cottages and sometimes whole villages, previously thought to blight the view of naturalistically arranged scenery. Increasingly toward the end of his career, Repton had found room for vernacular architecture in his designs, and Loudon now displayed the conscience of the times by illustrating his text on agrarian structures with sketches of cottages that provided both warmth and comfort for those who dwelt within and scenic charm for those who viewed them from without.

The nineteenth century signaled the separation of living space from the workplace as cottage manufacturing was replaced by industrial production in large factories. The middle-class interest in the private realm of house and garden could not have occurred without new, efficient means of public transportation after the invention of macadam paving and the railroad steam engine. These made possible the creation of residential suburbs, and landscape planners exploited this opportunity with considerable ingenuity. As the nineteenth-century metropolis became a regional-scale municipality, it encompassed its former rural environs, thereby accomplishing the ultimate ungirdling of cities and the final removal of old fortification walls.

Encouraged by Mill, Bentham, and the generally enterprising and practical temper of the times, people in the nineteenth century were disposed to admire utility. Although conservatives such as Ruskin found the new industrial building materials hideous, others equated the useful with the beautiful. While there was debate about the siting of the new-style conservatory at the Royal Botanic Gardens at Kew within the principal line of view, the technological ingenuity of its architecture was in fact a source of pride, and its immediate popularity justified its conspicuous location (see fig. 9.4). People soon attuned their eyes to the novel form and materials of such great glass structures, engineered to span unprecedented widths, and they became architectural icons of the age, employed in the construction of railroad stations and in the Crystal Palace of the Great Exposition held in London in 1851, followed by one built in New York City two years later.

In other ways, technology played an important role in landscape design. The lawn mower was patented by Edwin Budding in 1830. This efficient machine made possible a landscape aesthetic that put a premium upon the smooth, evenly sheared lawn as scythe mowing was abandoned (see fig. 9.6). The coming of railroads not only created the planned suburb, but brought quickly and cheaply nonlocal building materials and horticultural plants to urban centers. Innovations multiplied as inventors took out patents on a host of new materials: portland cement, asphalt paving, the wrought-iron sash bar for conservatory panes, sheet glass. Cast-iron construction, the revival of terra-cotta casting, and the manufacture of encaustic tiles increased the range of opportunity for ornamental expression. Steam, hot-water, and eventually gas heating systems provided comfort and convenience to people and protected tender plants. Applications of technology to the built environment had important effects on landscape design and the appearance of cities.

Increasingly, the garden became the laboratory of horticultural science. Not only were exotic species displayed as choice specimens of garden art, but also grafting, training, and hybridization produced plants in new forms, shapes, and colors. Competitive exhibitions such as the Chiswick Show were organized to judge their merits. Commercial nurseries thrived as botanical interest became widespread.

Garden encyclopedias replaced treatises on aesthetics. Numerous periodicals sprang up to serve an audience eager for advice on the practical aspects of landscape design and information about the latest developments in botany and horticulture. Horticultural societies, botanical gardens, and certain wealthy persons continued to send plant explorers to remote parts of the globe in search of uncatalogued species. Botanical illustration reached its apogee as an art form, and many beautiful colored engravings by such talented artists as Pierre-Joseph Redouté (1759–1841), Francis Bauer (1758–1840) and Ferdinand Bauer (1760–1826), and James Sowerby (1757–1822) were reproduced in the proliferating horticultural magazines (see fig. 9.1). Some of their names — *The Botanic Garden, Botanical Magazine or Flower-Garden Displayed, Gardeners' Magazine of Botany, Paxton's Magazine of Botany and Register of Flowering Plants, Horticultural Journal and Florists' Register of Useful Information Connected with Floriculture, The Floricultural Cabinet, Florists' Magazine* — suggest the nineteenth century's fascination with flowers newly available to gardeners through the efforts of ingenious hybridizers and intrepid explorers.

The competition among these periodicals in a time when literary piracy and plagiarism were common generated considerable editorial invective. The passions that ran high in their pages were symptomatic of an intense and broadening interest in horticulture and landscape design. In *Gardener's Magazine, and Register of Rural and Domestic Improvement,* the earliest general horticultural publication, Loudon forthrightly delivered his candid opinions between 1826 and 1844. As we shall see in Chapter Eleven, by the end of the century, after the Victorian garden had incorporated the botanical riches of the age, new design wars erupted in England, pitting advocates of informal impressionistic arrangement of herbaceous borders, such as the horticultural writer and editor William Robinson and the Arts and Crafts gardener, photographer, and author Gertrude Jekyll, against those who practiced "bedding out," the arrangement of plants according to precise patterns for seasonal display. At the same time, Sir Reginald Blomfield championed Italianate geometrical style in *The Formal Garden in England* (1892), fiercely opposing Robinson's naturalistic approach. Thus was the debate between Art and Nature once again joined within the context of landscape design.

The rapidly industrializing cities of the northeastern United States looked to England for landscape design models at the same time as the American frontier was being pushed westward. The street grid proved the most practical means for parceling and conveying real estate in new cities, but preceptors such as Andrew Jackson Downing, who instructed the growing middle class in the principles of horticultural management and Picturesque landscape design, began to pose an alternative. Downing gave the term *rural* new meaning by creating a middle landscape of suburban "villa" and cottage architecture—a built landscape that was neither wholly agrarian nor wholly urban.

Frederick Law Olmsted (1822–1903), in partnership with the English-born architect Calvert Vaux (1824–1895), directed the Picturesque idiom toward democratic ends in creating America's first public parks. The parks that Olmsted and Vaux designed, first in New York and then in other cities, were mostly naturalistic essays in which they replicated rural and wilderness scenery in order to create a poetic mood that would lift the spirits of careworn city dwellers. Olmsted and Vaux also became the country's first urban planners on a metropolitan scale, conceiving of parkways as a means of linking parks together into a citywide system and providing carriage drives to America's first suburbs. The curvilinear layout of the suburbs they designed posed a Picturesque alternative to the grid, heretofore the standard plan for new streets. Still other forces at the end of the nineteenth century set the country on a different course, as the designers for a Gilded Age imitated the historic architecture and planning forms of Renaissance and seventeenth-century France and Italy.

Indefatigable and *industrious* are adjectives often connected with the names of many nineteenth-century figures. Herculean were the labors of those who created the botanical gardens and other scientific and cultural institutions, meticulously recorded the observations of their difficult voyages to distant parts, built the parks and park systems that we still enjoy, and conceived and built the transportation and sanitary engineering infrastructure to support large cities—all the while corresponding voluminously and publishing profusely without the convenience of present-day communications technology. Our chronicle of the period begins with a discussion of the careers of several important figures who personify the human energy that flourished spectacularly at this time.

I. Botanical Science, the Gardenesque Style, and People's Parks: Landscape Design in Victorian England

Eighteenth-century Enlightenment science opened the door to the passionate pursuit of natural history in the nineteenth century. The real "discovery" of America had been the discovery by Europeans of unbounded economic opportunity, a good deal of which was based at first on a single plant, tobacco. A happy bonus had been the introduction to botanical science of a wealth of hitherto unknown ornamental species. The plant exchanges that occurred first in the colonial era and then in the federal period prepared the way for the explosion of horticultural activity in the nineteenth century. The taxonomic classification system developed by Linnaeus, in which Latin provided a universal language of binomial references for individual plant species, made it possible for members of a growing international scientific community to develop a common knowledge base and communicate intelligibly with one another.

The Royal Botanic Gardens at Kew

At the center of much of this botanical activity and forming the bridge between the eighteenth and nineteenth centuries stood Sir Joseph Banks (1743–1820), the president of the Royal Society from 1778 until his death and, as botanical advisor to George III, de facto director of the Royal Gardens at Kew. Wealthy, politically well-connected, and with three years of experience collecting plants on the *Endeavour* voyage as credentials for projects of this nature, Banks was able to attract royal and aristocratic patronage for naturalists attached to ships bound for distant lands. He assessed the professional skills and industriousness of young men in training at Kew, and from their ranks selected candidates such as Allan Cunningham and James Bowie for the arduous work of plant hunting in the wilds of South Africa, Australia, the Americas, and China. Banks enjoined these and other explorers to keep journals recording the climatic conditions and soil quality of native plant habitats. The greatest difficulty occurred in transporting seeds and specimens on long ocean voyages where cold, mildew, sea spray, vermin, and natural disaster took a significant toll.

It was not until 1838 that Nathaniel Ward (1791–1868) of London, a doctor and naturalist, stumbled upon an invention that proved of great utility to future plant collectors. After burying a chrysalis in soil placed in the bottom of a covered glass jar, he soon discovered that the seeds in the soil began to germinate because condensation produced by plant respiration within the jar created a moist, self-sustaining environment. He published his discovery in a treatise titled *On the Growth of Plants in Closely Glazed Cases* (1842), and the Wardian case—in effect a miniature greenhouse—soon became part of the standard equipment of all plant hunters. Meanwhile, collectors in the field, whose passage and pay were funded by the Horticultural Society of London—founded in 1804 to advance botanical science and garner foreign plant material for English gardens—ingeniously devised new methods and materials for packing their precious cargoes, albeit with statistically disappointing results. Nevertheless, enough plants survived, and England's ambitions as a colonial power assured continuing opportunities for botanists to attach themselves to vessels bound for exotic locales. To Banks belongs credit for establishing the eminence of the Royal Gardens at Kew as a repository for dried specimens and botanical data, a center for the global transfer of plant material, and the imperial nexus of a growing number of colonial botanical gardens.

William Townsend Aiton (1766–1849), the superintendent of Kew after 1793 and one of the founders of the Horticultural Society of London (later the Royal Horticultural Society), assisted Banks in ensuring that specimens of plants collected from various sources were sent to Kew. Banks's visionary leadership, combined with his ardent imperialism, set the agenda. He requested diplomats, army and navy officers, captains of merchant vessels, foreign missionaries, and colonial correspondents to foster Kew's botanical collections. As a result, in 1789, Aiton published *Hortus Kewensis,* a three-volume catalogue of the plants at Kew, prepared with the help of Daniel Solander, a former pupil of Linnaeus, and Jonas Dryander, another professional botanist from Sweden. Engravings from watercolors by James Sowerby (1757–1822) illustrate this handsome and monumental work (fig. 9.1).

By the 1820s, Kew's preeminence was being eclipsed by more progressive and active botanical organizations, notably the Horticultural Society of London, which in that decade was sponsoring plant-collecting expeditions to China, Africa, Mexico, parts of South America, and the Pacific coast of the United States. As botanical gardens proliferated at universities and in the newly wealthy manufacturing cities, Kew stagnated. Visitors noticed its decline, and John Claudius Loudon's *Gardener's Magazine* commented with asperity on the situation. However, in 1841, the British Treasury assumed support of Kew, renaming it the Royal Botanic Gardens. William Jackson

9.1. *Phaius tankervilleae,* a tropical orchid introduced into England in 1778. Engraving after a watercolor by James Sowerby. Plate 12, Volume 3, of the 1789 edition of *Hortus Kewensis,* published by William Townsend Aiton

**9.2. "East Front of Tew Lodge,"
from Loudon's _Designs for
Laying Out Farms,_ 1812**

Hooker (1785–1865) was appointed director. By then, Loudon had traveled extensively, visited botanical gardens in England and abroad, and was well established as the country's leading spokesperson on horticulture. His remarkable career as a scientific farmer, landscape gardener, inventor, writer, and editor epitomizes the creative energy, scientific appetite, technological aptitude, encyclopedic knowledge, and humanitarian conscience that fueled the cultural developments of the nineteenth century in general and the field of landscape design in particular.

John Claudius Loudon

John Claudius Loudon (1783–1843),[2] typified his age in his sympathy for the mass of humanity, his idealism, his ability to give physical expression to the conceptual, and his propensity for thinking in long-range and large-scale terms. He was in effect a metropolitan planner several decades before London and other British cities were organized governmentally to accept this kind of vision. An admirer of Thomas Jefferson whose term _self-government_ he borrowed upon occasion, he looked forward to the day when public improvements were undertaken by general consensus and in a comprehensive and rational manner, not piecemeal at the behest of the wealthy and powerful. He felt that tunnels, bridges, and other works of utilitarian engineering were nobler monuments to a society's genius than the grandest examples of purely heroic architecture and sculpture. Sanitary engineering and the conquest of distance by rail transport excited his imagination as he dreamed of livable cities and the measures that would enable the worker to be more conveniently united with a job and the middle-class homeowner with a plot of suburban greenery. He had the idea of shaping metropolitan growth and relieving congestion with a series of concentric greenbelts long before Ebenezer Howard (1850–1928) and subsequent plan-

ners proposed this type of controlled urbanism.

Loudon, the eldest son of a Scottish farmer, arrived in London in 1803 at the age of twenty, well educated and with practical experience in hothouse design and embankment construction for land reclamation. A letter of introduction from a former professor introduced him to Sir Joseph Banks, who generously befriended him. He also became acquainted with the botanical artist James Sowerby and with Jeremy Bentham, whose theory of utilitarianism and whose ideological range and systematic intellectual approach had a lasting influence upon him.

Loudon's first literary effort in London was a proposal to apply Picturesque principles to the planting of hardy trees and flowering shrubs within the city's squares. He followed this essay with _Observations on Landscape Gardening_ (1804), which helped him attract clients seeking his professional advice. Between 1808 and 1811, he resided at Tew Lodge Farm, Oxfordshire, where, in addition to proving to the landowner and his client, General George Frederick Stratton, the profitability of a new system of leasehold arrangements, Loudon directed numerous improvements paid for by the general, aspiring here to create England's premier _ferme ornée._ He removed some hedgerows in order to plant new ones as shelters against the prevailing winds, had rough fields regraded and installed with drains, and built a farmhouse in an innovative design that emphasized practicality, comfort, and technology over ornament and style; yet he made these elements of economy and convenience compatible with elegance and refinement (fig. 9.2). His farm roads followed the contours of the land in a Picturesque manner, and around his new house he planted shrubs and trees in irregular masses, once again according to the system of Jussieu. Although he did not coin the term _Gardenesque_ until twenty years later, here he put into practice the principles of his later definition by incorporating exotic species into his landscape design and displaying all plants, whether foreign or native, in such a way that each could reveal itself to advantage. Botanical display was a central focus for Loudon, and his intention at Tew Lodge Farm and elsewhere was to acknowledge landscape as nature, art, _and_ science.

From the beginning of his career, Loudon saw education as one of his missions. At Tew Lodge Farm he established an agricultural college to teach the sons of the landed gentry and prospective estate agents his new methods of scientific farming. Moreover, he was progressive in his concern for farm laborers, paying particular attention to the quality of their housing and food. But being not yet thirty, Loudon was more interested in demonstrating a successful experiment than in settling permanently at Tew Lodge Farm. However

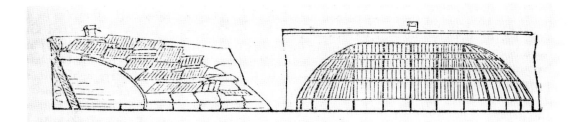

9.3. "The Polyprosopic Hot-house," one of the sketches by John Claudius Loudon of various methods of designing glasshouses, from *A Treatise on the Theory and Practice of Landscape Gardening*. According to Loudon, "The Polyprosopic Hot-house resembles a curvilinear house, but differs in having the surface thrown into a number of faces, the chief advantages of which are, that by hinging all the different faces at their upper angles, and by having rods connecting the lower outside corners of the faces terminating in chains, which go over pulleys in the top or above the back wall, the whole roof, including the ends, may be opened or raised sympathetically, like Venetian blinds, either so as each sash or face may be placed in the plane of the angle of the sun's rays at the time, or to the perpendicular, to admit a shower of rain."

Below: 9.4. Palm House, Kew, Richmond, designed by Decimus Burton and Richard Turner. 1844–48

challenging the life of a scientific farmer and educator might have been, his phenomenal energies and intellectual curiosity required a larger sphere of activity. After two and a half years, when General Stratton offered to buy back his lease, Loudon accepted.

With the Napoleonic wars in Europe drawing to a close, he now seized the opportunity to travel abroad, journeying across northern Europe during a nineteen-month period in 1813 and 1814. Letters of introduction from Sir Joseph Banks gained him access to aristocratic estates and professional societies where his knowledge of French, German, and Italian made it possible for him to speak fluently with head gardeners, architects, and others. In Russia, he was impressed with the pineapples, cherries, peaches, plums, apples, pears, and grapes that were being grown under glass on noblemen's estates. It was with a technical eye that he studied the construction of greenhouses or remarked on the heat-retention capabilities of the Russian stove. These observations served him well when, upon returning to London, he turned his thoughts toward an examination of how the construction of greenhouses could be improved through technology.

In this effort he was not alone. In 1812, Thomas Andrew Knight (1759–1838), the younger brother of Richard Payne Knight and a member of the Horticultural Society of London, published a paper in which he suggested that a purely functional hothouse in which the greatest amount of light could be admitted through the least expanse of glass, one that in addition could be efficiently heated, would offer horticultural and economic advantages over hothouses designed in the conventional manner. Conservatories at this time were still being designed in the tradition represented by Chambers's Orangery at Kew, with large arched windows set into masonry walls. Experimenting with different shapes and structural techniques in his Bayswater garden, in 1816 Loudon invented a curvilinear sash bar of wrought iron. His experiments also led him to propose a "ridge and furrow," or double-meridian, glazing system in which the glass panes of the conservatory were angled so as best to catch morning and afternoon light while preventing the scorching of leaves by the direct rays of the noonday sun. He also conceived a "polyprosopic" design of hinged surfaces that could be adjusted by

chains and pulleys in the manner of Venetian blinds to gain a more desirable angle in relation to the sun or to let in fresh air and summer rain showers (fig. 9.3). As curved-glass conservatories for tender plants became common on estates after the lifting of the British tax on glass in 1845, their juxtaposition with the eclectic neotraditional architecture of the Victorian mansion was sometimes ridiculed, but following Loudon (see fig. 9.2), these popular status symbols were given pride of place in Victorian landscaping schemes.

Joseph Paxton's ridge-and-furrow-style conservatory at Chatsworth, the great Palm House at Kew designed by architect Decimus Burton (1800–1881), with ironmaster Richard Turner, as a series of sheer, taut-skinned agglomerated hemispheres, and Paxton's iconic Crystal Palace built for the Great Exposition of 1851 in Hyde Park—all owe a debt to Loudon's pioneering work in glasshouse construction (fig. 9.4). Now Loudon's fertile genius, excited by technology, projected other innovations as well, including schemes for industrial workers' housing and a solar heating system, which he published in 1822 in his comprehensive, detailed, and well-organized *Encyclopaedia of Gardening*.

The *Encyclopaedia*, which ran to several editions and revisions over the course of fifty years, and the widely read *Gardener's Magazine* gave Loudon a forum for his progressive, reform-minded ideas. In 1825 at the age of forty-two, he lost his right arm and the ability to write and draw, but this did not deter him from

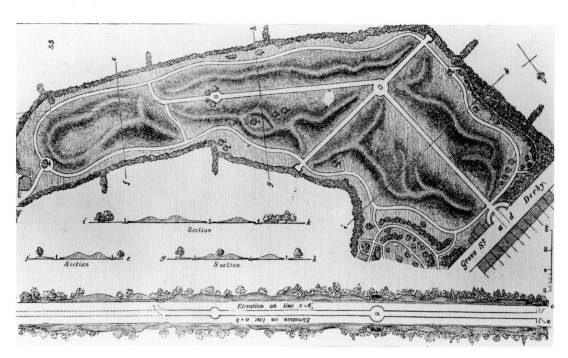

9.5. Plan, Derby Arboretum, 1839, by John Claudius Loudon

focusing his career primarily upon these and other important subsequent literary endeavors. With the help of contributors, draftsmen, relatives, and his wife, who served as his amanuensis and editorial assistant, he produced *The Green-House Companion* (1824), *An Encyclopaedia of Agriculture* (1825), *An Encyclopaedia of Plants* (1829), *Loudon's Hortus Britannicus* (1830), *Encyclopaedia of Cottage, Farm and Villa Architecture and Furniture* (1833), *Arboretum et Fruticetum Britannicum; or the Trees and Shrubs of Britain, Native and Foreign* (1838), and *Self-instruction for Young Gardeners, Foresters, Bailiffs, Land-Stewards, and Farmers* (1845).

In all these works he combined an ardent humanitarian interest in improved working conditions and educational opportunities for gardeners with matters of scientific and technological interest, practical horticultural advice, aesthetic theories, and critical descriptions of gardens, which he visited regularly on his travels through England and Europe. His audience consisted of Oxford and Cambridge dons, country vicars, doctors, directors of botanical gardens, architects, engineers, landscape designers, and head gardeners on the estates of the nobility. Lords and ladies read his works, too, as did, he hoped, his target audience: young gardeners who, not being able to afford the two-shilling cost of a copy of *The Gardener's Magazine,* had to borrow it.

Although as a young man eager to establish his own reputation, Loudon had taken issue with some of the design principles of the doyen of landscape gardeners, Humphry Repton, in 1840 he served as the editor of a new edition of Repton's collected works. Loudon realized, as had Repton, that publication was a surer route to far-reaching professional influence than commissions to landscape the properties of the

wealthy. But commissions, especially those that served a public interest, were an important means of demonstrating the principles and practices he advocated in his books and magazines. He was therefore delighted to be summoned to the industrial town of Derby in the spring of 1839 to lay out an 11-acre arboretum, the gift to the town from its former mayor, Joseph Strutt. Here, in the smoky Midlands, thanks to Strutt's philanthropy, Loudon had an opportunity to demonstrate his belief that a landscape containing the most beautiful specimens of nature could edify the general populace, relieve the misery of the working poor, and produce among the mingled classes sentiments of mutual respect and civic pride.

Although Loudon had integrated the awkwardly shaped parcel with an efficient circulation system, concealed its boundaries with dense planting, and made less apparent its cramped dimensions with a series of linear mounds that focused the view on the immediate surroundings and screened people and objects elsewhere on the grounds, as a design, the Derby Arboretum drew mixed reviews (fig. 9.5). But as a social experiment, it was an unqualified success. Three days of public revels attended its opening, and according to contemporary reports not a single plant was harmed. It remained a popular attraction, drawing on Sundays throngs of working-class people, some of whom traveled in the third-class railway carriages from as far away as Sheffield, Birmingham, and Leeds. When they arrived, they could refresh themselves at the entry lodge, where there were toilet facilities and hot water for tea. Then they were free to stroll along serpentine paths, admiring the shrubs and trees arranged according to the Jussieu system,[3] which were identified by labels giving botanical and common names, country of origin, mature height, and the date of introduction into Britain. Loudon also had the specimens of the Derby Arboretum numbered, and these numbers were keyed to information in a pamphlet he produced containing much scientific and anecdotal information, which visitors could purchase at the lodge. Those who preferred simple relaxation to botanical edification could walk on one of the two broad, straight gravel paths that constituted the Arboretum's cross axis. Pavilions at the ends of the crosswalks provided shade or shelter from a shower. Benches, with footboards as an accommodation to the aged and infirm, offered seating along the paths. Altogether, the Derby Arboretum was an impressive and progressive accomplishment in 1840, a forerunner of the work of Joseph Paxton, Frederick Law Olmsted, and other later park builders.

Loudon's marriage at the age of forty-seven to Jane Webb (1807–1858) was rewarding for both partners. Her kind spirit and literary abilities were tested to the utmost as she set about helping him write and publish his lifework, the handsomely illustrated, vast, and taxing *Arboretum et Fruticetum Britannicum*. Later, as a widow, she undertook to pay off the remaining debt that this immense and costly endeavor had imposed on them. Her reward was pride in his place in history and lasting renown in her own right. Loudon, who advocated the pursuit of horticulture by women, had encouraged her activities as a practical gardener as well as a writer, and she was instrumental in turning other women's time and physical energies to this healthful employment. Her *Gardening for Ladies* ran to several editions and was edited for American publication by Andrew Jackson Downing. With her last book, *My Own Garden; or The Young Gardener's Year Book* (1855), she introduced children to the pleasures that she and Loudon had shared with their daughter Agnes or observed on their travels as a family.

The Victorian Garden

Under the influence of the Loudons, the Victorian garden perpetuated the Picturesque tradition while also displaying the results of botanical science. Combined with expression of the Romantic spirit of the age was a bent toward practicality and desire to employ industrial materials that anticipated the functional landscape aesthetic of twentieth-century modernism (see Chapter Thirteen). But unlike modernist designers who sought to elevate functionalism to the status of aesthetic principle, Victorian landscape gardeners were unreservedly eclectic. They cloaked their functionalism in period costume—"the Styles" that Le Corbusier as a polemical modernist would famously rail against. The search for cultural coherence where none could be found in the face of soci-

ety's growing secularism and rapid technological change fostered this historicism. People who cared about such things looked nostalgically to the architectural vocabularies of other times and places as embodiments of various truer meanings than what they believed existed in nineteenth-century England. Followers of John Ruskin, for instance, developed the Victorian Gothic style with its evocation of medieval Christian values. Other Victorians, ambitious for Britain's growing imperial power, favored Neoclassical design idioms based on French and Italian models as appropriate means of advertising wealth and status. Imitations of the *parterre* beds found in seventeenth-century *châteaux* gardens proved admirably suited to their lavish, patterned floral displays.

Even such a prominent practitioner of the Picturesque as Repton modified his style at the end of his career to reflect a greater tolerance for period elements, such as terraces with balustrades. With practical considerations in mind, he abandoned the illusionary technique of the ha-ha with which he had, following Brown, fostered an impression of unbroken rural scenery extending from distant pastures to the walls of the mansion. He even designed Gardenesque flower beds in its immediate environs (see fig. 7.25). Repton's collected works, thanks to the 1840 edition edited by Loudon, were now a ready reference for those who came to feel that the eighteenth-century approach to the Picturesque had been overly zealous in its eradication of traditional forms. Even Price regretted having removed the terraces of his country house, Foxley, in his youth. People now saw that terraces offered foreground interest and a pleasing transitional element between the necessary geometry of the house and the carefully contrived naturalistic character of its grounds.

Efficiency, a virtue of the new industrial age, was a demonstrable value in the landscape as well, with new attention being given to maintenance. The invention of the lawn mower made hand-cut grass and the bucolic lawn cropped by cattle things of the past (fig. 9.6). Scythes were laid aside, and large swards

9.6. Lawn-mowing machine as illustrated in Loudon's *Gardener's Magazine,* 8 (1832)

9.7. Terrace knot garden, Hatfield House, Hertfordshire, original restoration design by the second Marquess of Salisbury. 1840s. Restored again by the Marchioness of Salisbury in the early 1980s

Below: 9.8. Levens Hall, Westmorland, Topiary Garden, created c. 1700; restored and maintained by head gardener Alexander Forbes, active 1810–62

of closely mowed green turf became highly desirable. Macadam paving now smoothed formerly rutted roads, which no longer meandered needlessly, if picturesquely, to their destination. The general air of neglect that had overtaken estates during the turmoil of the Napoleonic wars was erased as owners instituted modern maintenance practices and employed technology to improve their land.

Although there were periods of economic distress in the nineteenth century, on the whole English prosperity was such that, at the prevailing low wages, small armies of gardeners could be put to work on the great estates. The head gardeners, who commanded these workers while attending and informing the landscaping tastes of their lordly masters, became important purveyors of the several Victorian garden styles as the trend toward imaginative historicizing brought several older design vocabularies—Jacobean English, Renaissance Italian, and seventeenth-century French and Dutch—back into vogue. With this labor force and with railroad transportation to deliver materials from afar, including huge boulders for the rock gardens that became fashionable at this time, dukes and earls vied in the creation of gardens where spectacular effects and horticultural virtuosity were important ends.

William Barron (1801–1891), the head gardener to the earls of Harrington at Elvaston Castle in Derbyshire, achieved renown for his tree-transplanting expertise and for creating a famous topiary garden. In assembling the unusual mature specimen trees and already shaped tall topiary shrubs for Elvaston's landscape, he introduced the technique of moving plants with a large ball of earth still attached to their roots. Grafting, too, was a specialty at Elvaston and other gardens where composite trees assumed forms and vegetal characteristics never before seen in nature.

Landscape restoration often went well beyond what archaeology might have dictated in cases of period reconstructions in the Elizabethan and Jacobean manner, such as the one at Hatfield House, where the second marquess of Salisbury had knot gardens and a maze constructed (fig. 9.7). At Levens Hall in Westmorland, Alexander Forbes, the head gardener, set about restoring the topiary garden of around 1700, and the apparent antiquity of this reconstruction may have persuaded even such an astute observer as Loudon of its being the original one rather than its re-creation (fig. 9.8).

Italianate gardens swept back into vogue as broad terraces and staircases with balusters and urn-shaped finials spilled gracefully down to English lawns dotted with floral beds. Besides this use of stepped terraces as transitional elements in the intermediate zone between the house and the extensive landscape beyond, there was with the work of William Andrews Nesfield (1793–1881) a revival of the French *parterre de broderie.* Nesfield often based his designs on those provided in the pattern book of Dezallier d'Argenville, but he was versatile and enjoyed experimenting with Tudor knot gardens as well. He worked at Kew between 1844 and 1848 in association with Decimus Burton. For this important commission, Nesfield adopted a style reminiscent of the period of William and Mary as he created a *parterre* terrace platform for the Palm House, laid out a *patte d'oie* radiating from it into a new Pinetum, or arboretum of coniferous evergreens, reconfigured the pond, and redesigned the Broad Walk (fig. 9.9).

Display fountains had long ago ceased to play in English gardens. To bring the delight of animated water back into the landscape, Capability Brown had created the woodland cascade, one of the few Brownian elements not attacked by the proponents of the Picturesque. Now, with industrial technology at hand, there was renewed interest in fountain construction,

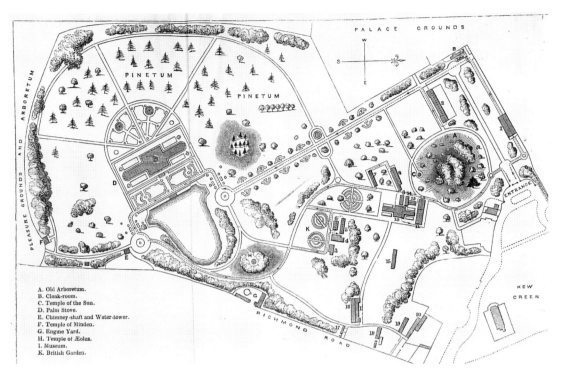

A. Old Arboretum.
B. Cloak-room.
C. Temple of the Sun.
D. Palm Stove.
E. Chimney-shaft and Water-tower.
F. Temple of Minden.
G. Engine Yard.
H. Temple of Æolus.
I. Museum.
K. British Garden.

9.9. Plan of Kew Gardens from the 1850s, showing Nesfield's alterations

Below: 9.10. Carpet bed, Kew Gardens. 1870

and some remarkable waterworks were created, such as Joseph Paxton's Emperor Fountain at Chatsworth (see fig. 9.11).

The green landscape took on myriad hues as brightly colored flowers from countries such as Mexico made their spectacular appearance in Victorian gardens. Color theory became one of the head gardener's job requirements. Not only did carpet beds—mosaiclike seasonal display beds—have to be designed for similarity of flower height and simultaneity of bloom, but they also had to be laid out according to artistic principles dictating the juxtaposition of solid floral masses of contrasting and complementary rather than similar tones.

The challenge facing nineteenth-century designers was how to assemble all of these interesting, useful, and charming objects—botanical specimens, historical ruins, glasshouses and summerhouses, rock gardens and kitchen gardens, flowers and fountains—within a coherent framework. Loudon's designs owed their coherence to what he called the axis of symmetry. As he explained it:

> In the simplest kind of symmetry, the two sides are equal and alike, and the axis is, of course, easily discovered; but in cultivated and refined symmetry, the sides are unequal, and so combined and varied with the centre, that it requires the eye of a philosophical artist to detect the axis.[4]

Thus, Loudon sought a sense of balance, not a mirror imaging of parts, and his axes were not necessarily visible, but sometimes merely implied. With the axis of symmetry as an organizing principle, he

arranged garden features and vegetation in various ways to produce a balanced effect.

Design harmony could also be achieved through congruity. Congruity meant respecting the character of the existing landscape as much as the abilities of the gardener, choosing local stones for boulders in rock gardens, placing water bodies in low-lying areas where they would naturally be found, banning sculpture and architecture of a purely associative nature, avoiding discordant juxtapositions in the arrangement of exotic plants, and developing zones of transition between distinctly different parts of the garden, as for instance the area between a smooth lawn and a rock garden.

Except in cases where the intent was a historicizing one, Victorian designers usually avoided straight lines. They were inspired by the curvaceous Rococo lines of Batty Langley. The circle was a much favored form and one advocated by both Repton and Loudon. Planting beds were frequently mounded in order to eliminate difficulties in viewing them from a ground-level perspective and to display their intri-

cate carpetlike designs to better advantage (fig. 9.10).

But rules are made to be broken, and contrast, rather than congruity, was the aim in some cases. In the hands of Joseph Paxton, some startlingly imaginative effects were achieved through unexpected juxtapositions of the seemingly natural and the highly artificial. Though not a landscape theorist and social philosopher like Loudon and with a practical man's distrust of intellectuals, Paxton more than any other immediate successor developed Loudon's vision in wedding technology to horticulture by designing one of England's earliest municipally funded public parks, Liverpool's Birkenhead Park.

JOSEPH PAXTON

The life of Joseph Paxton (1801–1865) illustrates how technological aptitude, design creativity, and energetic industriousness offered upward mobility in the increasingly prestigious field of horticulture. The son of a farmer, Paxton worked as a gardening hand in his youth before going to London at the age of twenty. Employed in the Horticultural Society's demonstration garden at Chiswick, located on property leased from the sixth duke of Devonshire, he impressed the duke, a frequent visitor, with his intelligence and abilities. In 1826, the duke offered him the position of head gardener at Chatsworth, his Derbyshire estate. The subsequent flowering of Paxton's genius, combined with the duke's largess, soon made Chatsworth a seat of horticultural renown. Ignoring Loudon's advice to restore the grounds—a Capability Brown landscape with surviving seventeenth-century features—to a more naturalistic appearance, young Paxton set about repairing and improving the garden's original waterworks. He quickly met the challenge of reactivating the "Weeping Willow," an artificial tree and joke fountain that sprayed the unwary from eight hundred miniature jets of water. He did not, however, re-create the setting of the orig-

inal as it appeared in the late seventeenth century, designing instead a woodland glen and rockworks as a naturalistic environment for this surprising hydrological feature. Paxton's mature landscape style continued to be characterized by the same independence from aesthetic theory and easy synthesis of artificial and natural.

His on-site education in landscape design history occurred in the 1830s as he accompanied the duke of Devonshire on tours of Versailles and other gardens near Paris, the gardens of England, and Italian villa gardens. Studying the waterworks in these places, he perfected his hydrological skills, becoming the foremost English fountain engineer of the day after the creation of the Emperor Fountain at Chatsworth—then the world's tallest (fig. 9.11). In Paxton's fountain designs, technology and art were one. Unlike earlier fountains, these did not usually include sculpture; the rainbow effect of light-struck spray and the choreographic pattern of multiple dancing jets created interest enough for Paxton and his patrons. His reputation ultimately rested on an even more spectacular demonstration of technology's uses in the garden, for his Great Stove at Chatsworth, an enormous greenhouse, won him international renown. This huge conservatory was built between 1836 and 1840 following Loudon's ridge-and-furrow design principle but using wood instead of wrought iron for the framing of its glass panes.

Paxton's growing reputation put him in the front rank of landscape designers receiving commissions from two sources. The first was private developers who saw the relationship between communal pleasure grounds and the surrounding real estate in economic terms; the second was sanitary officials and humanitarians who saw the benefits of parks from public health and recreational perspectives. Nash's design for Regent's Park in London had set a precedent for the former type of park development, and in 1842 a member of the Yates family, which had large landholdings in Liverpool, asked Paxton to come there to design Prince's Park, a speculative amenity that Yates hoped would make the adjacent house lots attractive to middle-class residents. Here Paxton created rows of terrace housing facing a curvilinear belt drive encircling a meadow with scattered clumps of trees and a serpentine lake (fig. 9.12).

Prince's Park remained in private ownership until 1908 and therefore was of little consequence in the growing parks movement as reformers in city after city, particularly in England's industrial Midlands, advocated "green lungs" within the swelling urban mass.[5] Paxton's next park, in Birkenhead on the opposite side of the Mersey River from Liverpool, was also undertaken with the hope of attracting members of

9.11. Emperor Fountain, Chatsworth, Derbyshire, designed by Joseph Paxton. 1843

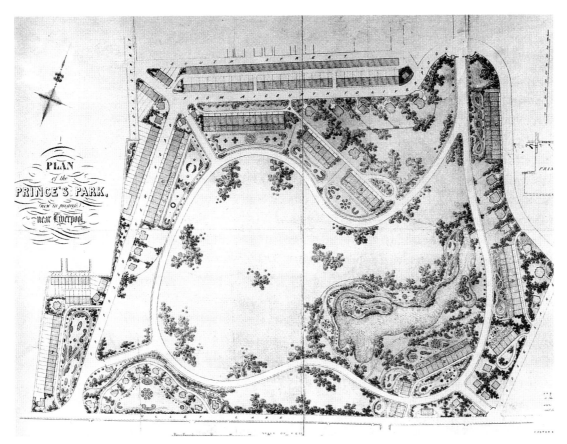

9.12. Plan for Prince's Park, Liverpool, designed by Joseph Paxton. c. 1842

the merchant class, but because of the circumstances of its creation, its accessibility to the general public, and the publicity that it received, it provided a far more influential model for future parks.

Municipalities had not yet been granted broad authority to acquire land, but citizen action to create public parks was nevertheless under way. In 1842, a group of businessmen constituting Birkenhead's Improvement Commission lobbied for a parliamentary bill that would allow them to purchase 70 acres of land "for the Recreation of the inhabitants."[6] In the event, they purchased more than 200 acres, of which approximately 124 were designated parkland, with the remainder reserved for building sites. Although not, strictly speaking, the first public park, Birkenhead, which opened in 1847, was the first to use public funds for parkland acquisition and development and to pay back this cost with the proceeds from the sale of the adjacent building lots. In addition, the municipality assumed responsibility for its maintenance, establishing the precedent of using for this purpose earned income derived from grazing rights and the auctioning of hay.

As at Prince's Park in nearby Liverpool, at Birkenhead Paxton arranged blocks of terraces around the sinuous loop of a circuit drive embracing a large meadow, the outlines of which were defined by scattered groups of trees. Here the meadow was bisected by a principal artery, Ashfield Road. Paxton placed an irregularly shaped lake in each half, and in

order to make it impossible to see the boundaries of the entire shoreline in a single view, he introduced islands in the lakes. Their dredging spoil was used to construct rocky berms that varied the topography and restricted the view lines, thereby creating a more intimate lakeside environment. Further, Paxton designed an independent path system for strolling through this landscape separate from that of the macadamized circuit drive, which was intended for carriages.

From their inception, parks were popular venues for sports as well as places for leisurely strolling in scenic surroundings. This caused difficulty for landscape designers like Paxton, whose bias was to exploit the scenic potential of the site, as well as for administrators and park managers, who were often forced to modify original designs to accept a variety of play facilities and who had to write regulations and deal with the consequences of sports use on the landscape. Sponsors sometimes even gave the active recreational motive primacy. In the case of two parks planned and built simultaneously in Manchester in the 1840s, Philips Park and Queen's Park, the entrants in the design competition had to include gymnasiums, grounds for archery, and alleys for skittles and quoits. Further, they were instructed to remember the *public* nature of the commission and the need to accommodate large gatherings of promenaders. Refreshment rooms, numerous park benches, drinking fountains, and lodges for caretakers were also part of the design program. Ball-playing and shuttlecock

9.13. Main entrance, Birkenhead Park, Liverpool, designed by Lewis Hornblower and John Robertson. 1847. This gate is a Victorian version of a Roman triumphal arch with massively scaled Ionic columns commemorating not military victory but civic pride in the park's construction.

Below: 9.14. The Victoria Drinking Fountain, Victoria Park, London. 1862

grounds and playgrounds with rope swings were included in the final designs. By contrast, James Pennethorne, the original designer, and John Gibson, a former Paxton employee at Chatsworth and superintendent after 1849, developed London's Victoria Park along scenic principles, using a rich palette of horticultural materials. But it, too, had to incorporate seesaws, climbing bars, and other play equipment and to permit, or at least tolerate, the use of its lakes for bathing, skating, boating, and dog washing.

As at Stowe, Stourhead, and other eighteenth-century models, the architects at Birkenhead incorporated historic English features and Palladian influences into the park's design vocabulary. Their versatility was apparent in their eclecticism, producing lodges in the castellated Gothic, Tudor, and Italian

styles, in addition to the Greek Revival "Norman" ones set into the entrance gate (fig. 9.13). Here as elsewhere, the influence of William Chambers lingered, and both Birkenhead and Victoria Parks had pagodas. Even as the popularity of pagodas faded, nineteenth-century building technology produced a cast-iron version, one example of which was shown at the Paris and Philadelphia Exhibitions of 1876 before being permanently installed at Chapel Field Gardens in Norwich.

The Turkish kiosk, combined with elements derived from the Chinese pagoda, furnished a distinctive architectural idiom for the bandstand made of wood or cast iron and set on a tall masonry base. This type of raised, open, ornamental pavilion became a feature of many parks. Musicians played mostly classical music, which was enthusiastically promoted by reformers as a civilizing influence and means of elevating mass culture, although Sabbatarians tried to proscribe concerts and other forms of recreation by having parks closed on Sundays. Temperance societies sponsored drinking fountains, and elaborate ones such as the Victoria Fountain in Victoria Park bore biblical and moral inscriptions implying the superiority of water over stronger drink (fig. 9.14).

As part of the reformers' agenda to wean the working class away from gin parlors, gaming, and other unedifying forms of recreation, sponsors deemed parks appropriate places for libraries and museums of art and natural history, and these were often combined with refreshment rooms. As more parks were created, commemorative monuments celebrating local benefactors, national leaders, and victory at war found a natural home amid their greenery, often serving as centerpieces of floral beds. Notables, royalty, and military heroes usurped the pedestals once graced by classical sculptures not only in England where the parks movement originated, but elsewhere as it rapidly spread (see fig. 7.48). Public toilets, a much-debated amenity, were installed in several parks, and once this practice was established, manufacturers began to produce cast-iron urinals. Winter gardens, or palm houses, modeled on the one at Kew and Paxton's Crystal Palace, provided microclimates for the palms, bromeliads, and other tropical plants that drew swarms of nineteenth-century park patrons. These also served, to the dismay of superintendents, as warm places where the homeless sought shelter in cold weather.

The mid-nineteenth century ushered in an era of international expositions, at which the increasingly mobile and educated middle class enjoyed displays of scientific technology and industrial arts. Steam and rail transportation made these events accessible for large numbers of people and therefore financially feasible. Leading the parade was London's Great Exhibition of 1851, for which Paxton built the world's most modern exhibition hall, the Crystal Palace, in Hyde Park. As New York attempted to emulate London with a Crystal Palace of its own in 1853, Paxton set about transferring his hugely popular building, for which he received a knighthood, to a new site in London at Sydenham. Conceived as a refined version of the pleasure ground, with operating costs paid from admission fees, Crystal Palace Park showed a different side of Paxton the park designer from the one demonstrated at Birkenhead. Here, instead of treating the landscape in a naturalistic manner, he chose a plan of neo-Rococo geometric formality with a Picturesque fringe around the edges (fig. 9.15).

Paxton's place in landscape design history is an important one, linking the inventiveness, horticultural interest, and humanitarian social vision of Loudon

with the growing parks movement in rapidly industrializing countries. With its republican government founded on the principle of social equality, America was the ideal testing ground for municipal parks and other kinds of democratic institutions.

9.15. Crystal Palace Park, Sydenham, London, designed by Joseph Paxton. 1856. Watercolor by James Duffield Harding

II. REDEFINING RURAL AMERICA: THE INFLUENCE OF ANDREW JACKSON DOWNING

Much of the American landscape design vocabulary applied to parks and private estates in the early decades of the nineteenth century was derived from England. There were, however, important differences in both the natural and the social climates of the two countries as well as the vastly disparate geographic scales of the island and the continental nation, one with a centuries-old habit of land husbandry and the other with a vast expanse of sparsely occupied prairie and woodland. These factors help account for the gradual evolution of an independent approach to landscape on the part of nineteenth-century Anglo-Americans.

THE BOTANICAL DISCOVERY OF AMERICA

North America remained a fertile ground for British-based botanical exploration during the first half of the nineteenth century. Thomas Nuttall (1786–1859), a printer from Liverpool, immigrated to Philadelphia where he became interested in botany and plant collecting. Following the routes of fur traders and other explorers of the American wilderness, he traversed the northern region of the Missouri River between 1810 and 1812. He published the results of his botanical labors in this region in *Genera of North American Plants* in 1818 before turning south to collect plants in Arkansas. In 1822, he accepted an appointment as curator of the botanical garden at Harvard and remained in this post until 1834, finding it possible, however, in 1833 to join an expedition to the Rocky Mountains.

In 1823, David Douglas (1798–1834), a Scottish

botanist trained by William Jackson Hooker at the University of Glasgow, visited Nuttall at Harvard and William Bartram in Philadephia under the sponsorship of the Horticultural Society of London. The following year, under the aegis of the Hudson's Bay Company, he sailed to the West Coast, and at Fort Vancouver established a base of operations for his exploration of parts of Oregon and British Columbia. He spent the next three years in the evergreen forest that blanketed this region, discovering the Douglas fir (*Pseudotsuga menziesii*) and many other coniferous and deciduous trees, flowering shrubs, and perennials. A return trip between 1830 and 1834 took him back and forth between California and Hawaii, where he met his untimely death in the field.

American botanists as well as those in Britain and other European countries were eager recipients of the seeds and cuttings that came from these sources as well as from the plant hunters foraging in other parts of the globe. Bartram's Nurseries in Philadelphia continued to offer for sale species collected by an earlier generation of plant hunters represented by John Bartram and his son William as well as the new varieties explorers were introducing to horticulture. In 1801, a New York physician, David Hosack, established the Elgin Botanic Garden on the site of present-day Rockefeller Center, then the property of Columbia University. The garden was intended as a teaching resource for Columbia medical students since botany and its sister course, *materia medica,* were still closely allied. It also contained a glasshouse for tender exotic plants, and many ornamental shrubs were propagated there as well. Thomas Jefferson often sent Hosack some of the seeds he regularly received from the Jardin des Plantes in Paris, and plant hunters such as François André Michaux (1770–1855) frequented the Elgin Botanic Garden. Unable to support its upkeep, Hosack closed the garden in 1811, but he continued to collect plants at his Hyde Park, New York, estate overlooking the Hudson River, where he employed the landscaping talents of André Parmentier (1780–1830), whose brothers were distinguished professional gardeners in Belgium.

Parmentier had emigrated to America in 1824 to become a nurseryman in Brooklyn. On a site overlooking New York Harbor, he established an ornamental garden with rustic seats and arbors, which he called the Linnaean Botanic Garden, as a showcase for his own plant collection. Although, as we have seen, Jefferson and Washington were both familiar with Picturesque principles of landscape design, Parmentier gained wide recognition as the originator of this style in America when he published an article describing naturalistic gardening in the *New England Farmer* magazine. Andrew Jackson Downing, who amply earned his biographer's epithet, "apostle of taste,"[7] said that he considered "Parmentier's labors and examples as having effected, directly, far more for landscape gardening in America, than those of any other individual whatever."[8] Downing, in turn, through his books and magazine indirectly effected far more change in landscape gardening in America during the middle decades of the nineteenth century than any other individual.

ANDREW JACKSON DOWNING: TASTEMAKER FOR A YOUNG NATION

The generation to which Andrew Jackson Downing (1815–1852) belonged was astutely observed by his contemporary Alexis de Tocqueville (1805–1859), who covered 7,000 miles of the settled and wilderness portions of the United States and Canada by steamer and stagecoach and on horseback during a nine-month period beginning in May 1831. Tocqueville's *Democracy in America* is much more than a traveler's description of the physical characteristics of the country with its settled colonial villages, burgeoning new cities, and frontier outposts. Although there are trenchant observations of all these things, his work is, as its title suggests, a political treatise. As such, it was not designed merely to limn the national character of the Americans as a simple narrative of their manners, mores, and economic circumstances would have done. Instead, its purpose was to foretell the consequences of the profound social transformation then in progress as the nations of Europe passed from aristocratic to democratic governance.

Downing had read the second volume of *Democracy in America* as it rolled off the presses in 1840. His job, as he saw it, was to counter the restless instability of his fellow citizens that Tocqueville had noted with visions of home as a cherished domain and place of charm. He wished to educate their taste, which would then make manifest republican virtue in the nation's landscape. He hoped that through a new vision of domestic comfort and refinement the "moderate amount of happiness" available to all men in a democratic society might be attained. His idealistic prescriptions were overrun during the post–Civil War transformation of American capitalist culture into something that more closely resembled the class stratification evident in the nations of Europe. But during his lifetime, he securely occupied the middle ground between Jefferson's Federalist generation—whose democratic principles were compromised by patrician values—and the generation of opulent materialistic display that gave the "villas" and "cottages" he promoted a new scale and meaning. Downing was, in short, a champion of the middle class, and he held a strong faith in the ability of education to raise people, if not to economic equality, at least to a sentimental equality in their appreciation and enjoyment of beauty.

Downing occupied the middle ground in a literal sense. Deploring both the rude, ax-scarred utilitarian landscapes that were a product of a frontier mentality and the cramped insalubrious atmosphere of the noisy commercial and industrial cities, he implied in his use of the word *rural* the concept of the suburb. To the freestanding middle-class dwelling and its adjacent grounds, and even the humble working-class dwelling with its surrounding small plot of land, Downing directed owners and landlords to pay the same prideful attention as that lavished by the wealthy on their country seats. He saw these homes, outside but accessible to urban centers by new means of transportation, as part of a larger, inherently Picturesque American landscape, and he believed that if his architectural and landscaping recommendations were followed, residents of this middle ground would be making a patriotic contribution to the nation's overall beauty while increasing their own personal comfort and enjoyment.

His congenial mind did not reckon that rural privacy might become retreat from community. A product of the American rural town, as a professional horticulturist and citizen, Downing promoted village beautification by tree planting. More important, he did not ignore the city. His reformer's cry, more ardent than any other's, championed the public park as the fundamental civilizing institution of American democracy in the 1840s.

Downing illustrated an aspect of American life shrewdly observed by Tocqueville: citizen initiative. There was no higher authority than the people in a democracy, so there were no *royal* academies. Public libraries, colleges, lyceums, museums of art and natural history, botanical gardens, horticultural societies, rural cemeteries, and public parks—all these educational and cultural institutions were founded by the vision of individuals, the action of community organizers, and the will of legislators who were elected by the people. Downing's role as citizen advocate and spokesman within this context was an especially important one.

Downing, the youngest son of a nurseryman in Newburgh, New York, was a self-taught botanist and student of the Picturesque. After his marriage at age twenty-three to Caroline DeWint of Fishkill Landing, he designed and built a home on the family property in Newburgh (fig. 9.16). This house and its grounds epitomized the life of rural refinement he wished for all Americans of moderate affluence. It represented as well his belief that as America came of age, its rootless, restlessly moving people should sink down roots, beautify their properties, and build communities that were more than commercial crossroads. Although similar to buildings in the "pointed" style recommended by Loudon, Downing's home had a particularly American feature—the veranda, or piazza, as contemporaries called it—which Downing promoted throughout his career in even his humblest samples of domestic architecture.

Thus situated, Downing could enjoy the commercial advantages of bustling Newburgh and the lively social intercourse made possible by the arrival at the town landing of friends traveling by river sloop and steamboat or at his door via train and carriage. He was within an easy three-hour train ride to New York City, where he met with his publisher or conducted other business. At the same time, he could preserve the illusion of living in nature, never having to see town or road, only foliage-framed views of Hudson River scenery. In attempting to come to terms with the nineteenth-century phenomenon of rapid metropolitan growth, Downing was perhaps unwilling to admit the degree to which the agricultural economy of the young republic was being rapidly superseded by an industrial one. For this reason he used the word *rural* to denote his vision of the *suburban* landscape that constituted the middle ground between city dwelling, with its noise, congestion, and extremes of wealth and poverty, and the equally unappealing alternative of hardscrabble farm life.

Downing's vision for a new American scenery to overlay the rough, agrarian landscape of frontier farms hacked from the wilderness was in the time-honored pastoral mode in which art and nature were held in perfect balance. He dreamed of an American Arcadia, for, like Thomas Jefferson, he saw the oppor-

9.16. Residence of Andrew Jackson Downing in Newburgh, New York, as it appeared shortly after it was built in 1838–39

9.17 and 9.18. "Example of the Beautiful in Landscape Gardening" and "Example of the Picturesque in Landscape Gardening," as portrayed in Andrew Jackson Downing's *Treatise on the Theory and Practice of Landscape Gardening, Adapted to North America,* 1841

ism focused its energies on enterprises that would eventually destroy much of the picturesque character of aspiring rural towns, elm-canopied village greens, well-tended fields, and rich pastures fringed with woods. Nevertheless, as a reformer, a republican idealist, and a progressive Anglophile, he necessarily accepted both the democratic, technological future and the tradition-rooted, agrarian past. Whatever fears he may have harbored, he did not reveal them but optimistically projected a vision of universal betterment through the agency of good design.

In 1841, while still running his nursery business, Downing published his first major work, *A Treatise on the Theory and Practice of Landscape Gardening.* Its clear prose and conversational tone soon gained him widespread public recognition and reputation as a horticultural authority and tastemaker. The first sections of the book demonstrate the breadth of his reading, particularly of works by Loudon and Repton. His knowledge of such landscape theoreticians as Whately, Price, and Gilpin is apparent in the contrast he draws between the beautiful and the Picturesque. In the second edition of the *Treatise* (1844), he had his engraver depict the beautiful, or "graceful" as he alternatively calls it, as a female-inhabited environment with gently curving paths, softly rounded tree forms, and gracious Neoclassical architectural details, while directing him to portray the Picturesque with spirelike conifers, steeply pitched eaves, and other signs of spirited irregularity, ruggedness, and angularity that presumably accord with the masculinity of the huntsman and his dog who complete the scene (figs. 9.17, 9.18).

The architecture compatible with the beautiful was "Italian, Tuscan, or Venetian," whereas builders in the Picturesque style had as appropriate models "the Gothic mansion, the old English or the Swiss cottage" and were free to incorporate in their schemes various rustic features. Downing reiterated Repton's three underlying principles of good design—"UNITY, HARMONY, AND VARIETY"—*unity* being a controlling idea based on the nature of the site and "some grand or leading features to which the others should be merely subordinate,"[9] *variety* the development of spectator interest through intricacy and ornamental details, and *harmony* the principle that ordered variety and made it subservient to the overall unity of the composition. Further, he tempered picturesqueness with practicality, declaring that "[f]irm gravel walks near the house, and a general air of neatness in that quarter, are indispensable to the fitness of the scene in all modes."[10] Concurring with Loudon, he maintained that "the *recognition of art*" was "a first principle of Landscape Gardening . . . and those of its professors have erred, who supposed that the object of this art is merely to produce a fac-simile of nature."[11]

tunities inherent in the country's immense and immensely fruitful natural landscape. Husbandry combined with taste could capitalize upon America's natural beauty, turning the countryside into a collage of Picturesque scenery. But opposing forces were at work, and the discordant aspects of the American dream—the industrial smokestacks of the city and the train tracks running beside the river—had to be screened from view, if the pastoral imagery of the garden were to appear intact. In nineteenth-century America, as in England, ambivalence about the Industrial Age was expressed by placing utilitarian technology and a highly eclectic architectural vocabulary of period styles within the same cultural embrace. Downing may have shared with others of his generation a sense of anxiety as the machinery of capital-

A large section of the *Treatise* comprises a descriptive catalogue of deciduous and evergreen ornamental trees. Here Downing does more than display his impressive store of botanical knowledge, dwelling upon aesthetic, rather than scientific, characteristics such as "the lights and shadows reflected and embosomed in [the oak's] foliage" and the "pleasing richness and intricacy in its huge ramification of branch and limb"[12] in the manner of Gilpin, whose works he had studied well.

In 1846, when Luther Tucker of Albany invited Downing to become editor of *The Horticulturist,* this new journal of "Rural Art and Rural Taste," Downing gained a platform for his expanding ideas. Here, in an editorial he wrote each month, he propounded his landscape theories; shared observations gleaned from his travels; gave advice on rural architecture, transplanting trees, growing hedges, enriching soil, manuring orchards, improving vegetables, and producing wine; mingled poetry and instruction in a rhapsody on roses; provided detailed instruction on the building of greenhouses and ice houses; argued the case—exercise, fresh air, health—for women to garden; and sermonized on the mistakes of city folk new to country life—all in a conversational voice and anecdotal style that endeared him to his readers. *The Horticulturist* reached a large audience. In it he promoted the planting of shade trees in villages, towns, and cities; lobbied for an agricultural college in New York State; and drew the attentions of his fellow citizens to such public parks as Munich's Englischer Garten.

In his column of August 1851, Downing warmed to the subject of a mayoral proposal for a 160-acre park in New York, arguing that the city had "until lately, contented itself with the little door-yards of space—mere grass-plats of verdure" and concluding that a park of even 160 acres was too small, that at least 500 acres were needed to serve the city's fast-growing population, which then stood at half a million. His vision for the new park was equally bold in its outlines. Not only would it have carriage drives, bridle trails, secluded walks, and "a real feeling of the breadth and beauty of green fields," but it would also be a place for commemorative statues, a winter garden like the Crystal Palace "where the whole people could luxuriate in groves of the palms and spice trees of the tropics, at the same moment that sleighing parties glided swiftly and noiselessly over the snow-covered surface of the country-like avenues of the wintry park without." Zoological gardens would also find a home there, as would spacious buildings for expositions of the arts. Above all, Downing extolled the social implications of the proposal. The park would be a republican institution, "a broad ground

of popular refinement," raising "the working-man to the same level of enjoyment with the man of leisure and accomplishment."[13]

The summer before, Downing had gone to England, delighted that his reputation had preceded him and that he was welcome at Chatsworth and many other great estates. His purpose in traveling there was not merely to tour the English countryside and visit the Royal Botanic Gardens at Kew. In *The Horticulturist* and in the books that followed his *Treatise*—*Cottage Residences* (1842), *Fruits and Fruit Trees of America* (1845), and *The Architecture of Country Houses* (1850)—architectural illustrations played an important role. He had sold his nursery business as his focus centered more and more upon the literary efforts that were turning him into a tastemaker to the nation. The people who now sought him out wanted plans as well as advice, and with these prospective clients in mind and having failed to interest the American architect Alexander Jackson Davis (1803–1892) in entering into a professional partnership with him, he wished to find a young English architect with whom he could open a design firm. In London, he observed the drawings of Calvert Vaux at an exhibition of the Architectural Association and asked to meet him. The immediate impression of both men was such that a week later Vaux had wound up his affairs in England, said good-bye to friends, and boarded ship for New York with Downing.

The new firm immediately began to receive commissions, including one from the brewer Matthew Vassar to improve the grounds of his 40-acre farm, Springside, near Poughkeepsie, New York. There was a subsequent important commission from Daniel Parish to build a "marine villa" in Newport, Rhode Island, and other domestic projects. In the Newburgh office, which Downing and Vaux built as an addition to the Downing residence, Vaux translated the Gothic Revival style he had learned in England into a more distinctly American idiom, often using board-and-batten construction and wooden verge boards and designing deeply hooded windows, covered entrance porches, and broad verandas. From Downing he must have also learned to appreciate the Picturesque possibilities of the American landscape.

In the fall following the return of the two men from England, Downing was invited by President Millard Fillmore to prepare a plan for the improvement of the public grounds around the Capitol in Washington, where L'Enfant's intentions for a grand avenue had never materialized. Downing eagerly seized this commission as an opportunity to demonstrate the first "*real* park in the United States."[14] Although vexed by congressional infighting, the project received initial funding. On the L-shaped site encompassing the present-day Mall and grounds of the White House, Downing developed an extensive pleasure ground and botanical showcase, a series of six Picturesque and Gardenesque episodes linked by curvilinear carriage drives and paths. Directly behind the White House, the plan called for a President's Park, entered through a marble triumphal arch. Also called the Parade, this was where various public and military functions would take place. Surrounding the Washington Monument, still in construction, Downing envisioned a meadow-like park of American specimen trees and grass. The Tiber Canal flowed between these two parks. The plan proposes to connect them by means of a suspension bridge. It also calls for an Evergreen Garden, a showcase for such nondeciduous species as rhododendrons, laurels, and magnolias. Smithsonian Park is a naturalistic campuslike space, with evergreens complementing James Renwick's neomedieval building. To the east, is Fountain Park containing both a fountain and a small artificial lake.

In 1852, Downing was commuting to Washington, D.C., on a monthly basis when his life was suddenly cut short as the *Henry Clay,* a Hudson River steamboat on which he was traveling, caught fire, causing the passengers to jump overboard and many, including him, to drown. Without his periodic on-site supervision and advocacy of the plan's construction, party politics, exacerbated by the impending crisis of the Civil War, mired the project.

Extensively eulogized, Downing nevertheless died encumbered with debt. The house he had built—for fourteen years a center of hospitable friendship, his office, and a manifestation of the Picturesque and Gardenesque taste he advocated—had been mortgaged and was soon sold. His books, however, continued to be published into the twentieth century, and the editorials he had written for *The Horticulturist* were collected in a volume entitled *Rural Essays,* which also enjoyed wide readership.

Downing's position in landscape history is a pivotal one. He was both an imitator of the styles developed by Repton and Loudon and an innovator, translating their Picturesque vocabulary, particularly in architecture, into a new American idiom. But his influence was more as an "apostle of taste" than as a designer, rhetorically setting the course that others would follow. The term *landscape architect* had not yet been adopted by Calvert Vaux and Vaux's future partner, Frederick Law Olmsted as a professional title.[15] Neither of these men ever forgot his debt to Downing as together they forged a landscape style in which broad passages of pastoral and woodland scenery gave the beautiful and the picturesque a more thoroughly American dimension than had Downing's transitional style with its Loudon-derived emphasis on horticulture and architecture. The park that they designed for New York was essentially different from the image Downing had painted for his readers in his essay in *The Horticulturist,* but his prescience in promoting it as a vital democratic institution was one that they fully embraced as they in turn developed a new vision for the nineteenth-century city.

III. Honoring History and Repose for the Dead: Commemorative Landscapes and Rural Cemeteries

The taste that Downing had promoted and the humanitarian consciousness he had displayed in championing the public park were, as we have seen, manifestations of the cultural shift that Tocqueville observed not only in his own country and the United States where there had been revolutions abolishing rule by monarchy, but also throughout Europe where court-dominated aristocratic culture was being superseded by more broadly based, egalitarian forms of governance. Socially conscious tastemakers such as Loudon and Downing were important precisely because the city itself was becoming a far-flung middle-class institution. As London had already demonstrated a century earlier, the city and the private estates that were its rural outposts, not the court, determined culture, and the bourgeoisie who were now primary cultural consumers welcomed the reformers' advice that refined them and elevated them above those less fortunate.

Although Italy and Germany were slow to become unified states, the trend toward nationalism had been set in motion, and bonds of cultural commonalty among their respective principalities, dukedoms, and city-states were reinforced through language, art, trade, and travel as well as by military alliance. The growth in nationalistic spirit paralleled the growth in importance and size of urban centers. With the diminution of the power of kingship, of the prestige of the Church, and of the wealth of aristocracy, the monuments that had once broadcast the supremacy of these institutions lost meaning. As societies rebuilt themselves along more democratic and sectarian lines, they felt compelled to create images of *constitutional* monarchs, revolutionary heroes, and the honored dead as icons of national status and civic pride, replacing older monuments of kings and religious figures.

THE COMMEMORATIVE LANDSCAPE

Commemorating national heroes assumed importance as nineteenth-century nations sought to institutionalize recently formed governments or cloak their military adventures abroad in a mantle of imperial glory by celebrating them in a public and permanent manner. This patriotic agenda called for the renaming of important urban places and the erection of monuments within them. For this reason, in 1841, the English raised a 185-foot high column by William Railton in London's Trafalgar Square to honor Admiral Horatio Nelson, the hero of the 1805 Battle of Trafalgar. In a similar fashion, the French commemorated Napoleon's campaigns of 1805–07 with a bas-relief column modeled after Emperor Trajan's column in Rome. It was erected in Paris in the Place Vendôme, formerly the Place Royale, where the equestrian statue of Louis XIV had long since been toppled by a revolutionary mob (fig. 9.19).

In Germany, as we have seen, the *Volksgarten* was an expression of cultural pride, and the sculptures there were intended to foster patriotic sentiment. We have noted as well how Rousseau's remains, at first entombed on the estate of an *ancien régime* liberal aristocrat, were removed to the Church of Saint Geneviève, which was deconsecrated and rechristened the Panthéon when it became a hall of fame for French national heroes. Many objected to the transfer of the great man's bones to the Panthéon in Paris, preferring instead the notion of pilgrimage to the tomb designed for him by Hubert Robert on the Isle of Poplars at Ermenonville (see fig. 7.36). The Enlightenment had bred a new secular spirit, and the French Revolution had seriously undermined the authority of the Catholic Church, making rural, rather than churchyard, burial an appealing alternative, especially given the Romantic sentimentalism of the day in which many found in deified Nature a spiritual substitute for Church dogma.[16] In the same spirit as that of the Europeans who turned the grave site at Ermenonville into a shrine and even replicated Rousseau's tomb in numerous other Picturesque gardens, Americans patriotically sought remembrance of George Washington. Many made pilgrimages to his rural tomb at Mount Vernon (fig. 9.20). Citizens in both Baltimore and Washington, D.C., commissioned Robert Mills (1781–1855) to design impressive monuments in Washington's memory (fig. 9.21).

Although the Federalist generation in America had eschewed large-scale public works because of their cost and association with European authoritarian pomp, which they felt to be inappropriate in a republic, the generation that prospered in the first decades of the nineteenth century sought to employ its wealth for public ends, ennobling their country's brief history with public monuments to the Revolution that had turned former colonies into a nation. In Boston, Henry Dearborn, a notably public-spirited citizen and the first president of the Massachusetts Horticultural Society, formed the Bunker Hill Mon-

9.19. Napoleonic Victory Column, Place Vêndome, Paris, constructed by Denon, Gonduin, and Lepère. 1806–10

Below left: 9.20. George Washington's grave as redesigned in the Gothic revival style by William Yeaton in 1835. Engraving by W. Woodruff, c. 1839

Below right: 9.21. Washington Monument in Baltimore, designed by Robert Mills, who also designed the Washington Monument in Washington, D.C. 1829. Engraving by W. H. Bartlett, 1835

9.22. Bird's-eye view of Boston by John Bachman, 1850, with Bunker Hill Monument near the left edge of the lithograph. The domed building to the left of center is Charles Bulfinch's State House on Beacon Hill of 1795. The process of filling in the Back Bay has begun, and the city's aspirations to elegance are apparent in the planting of trees lining the paths and perimeter of the Common and in the artist's projection of an ornamental landscape on the ground reserved for the Public Garden, which was not built until 1857.

Right: 9.23. Baltimore Battle monument, by Maximilien Godefroy. 1835. Engraving by W. H. Bartlett

Below: 9.24. Mourning picture for Captain John Williams, aged 36 (d. April 1, 1825). Pen and watercolor drawing by an anonymous artist

ument Association, which led to a subscription campaign to purchase the Revolutionary War battlefield site and underwrite "a simple, majestic, lofty, and permanent monument,"[17] an obelisk of Quincy granite, which was erected between 1825 and 1843 (fig. 9.22).[18] No small amount of municipal and state rivalry was involved as Boston competed with Baltimore, the southern city that had assumed the lead in the race for monumental magnificence by adding to its landscape — already adorned with Mills's Washington Monument — Maximilien Godefroy's 1835 Battle Monument, a column resting on a pyramidal Egyptian Revival base and topped with a statue of a female figure symbolizing the city (fig. 9.23).

BIRTH OF THE RURAL CEMETERY

The waning of ecclesiastical authority and the growth of Romantic sentiment among a rapidly broadening middle class brought new attitudes toward death and the desire to commemorate upstanding community members and loved ones as well as heroes. Added to this cultural imperative was the public health motive, about which there was much debate, for the crowding that accompanied population increases in nineteenth-century cities was noticeable not only in the festering urban slums, but also in the churchyard cemeteries that were filled to capacity so that corpses

were periodically exhumed to make room for new ones. The resulting stench of putrefying flesh caused passersby to hold their noses as physicians argued inconclusively over whether "miasmas" from decaying animal matter bred disease.

The notion of a permanent resting place where the dead could be visited by the living and remembered individually did not accord with either Catholic or Calvinist belief. Both held that mortal flesh, even in life, was corrupt and an encumbrance to the spirit, which, freed of mortality, could join God. Viewed in this light, the collective sight of the dead served as a reminder of the transitory nature of earthly life and a warning against vanity and pride. The equation of the afterlife with an Edenic gardenlike paradise did not figure in pre-nineteenth-century Western theology, and tree planting in cemeteries was considered an encouragement of latent tendencies toward pantheism, which priests and ministers wanted to stamp out. Not the living tree but the death mask was depicted on Puritan tombstones in New England graveyards: this *memento mori* was meant to discourage worldly ambition and individualism. Only with the decline of Puritanism did the symbolism of vegetative endurance and cyclical rebirth manifest itself in the substitution of the sweetly melancholy willow-tree-and-urn motif, also found in mourning pictures, for the death mask on some slab gravestones (fig. 9.24).

The creation of the extramural "rural" cemetery demanded a significant change in societal values involving the secularization of death and the granting of dignity to the individual life as well as the right to associative sentiment on the part of families and friends. In the aftermath of London's Great Fire of 1666, both John Evelyn and Christopher Wren had urged the discontinuance of churchyard burial, and the eighteenth-century Whig garden, replete with emblems of commemoration, offered an important prototype for the cemetery amid shady groves. Wordsworth's Romantic poetry evoked a mood of elegiac remembrance in images of country graveyards, while in a prose essay he instructed that "when

death is in our thoughts, nothing can make amends for the want of the soothing influences of nature, and for the absence of those types of renovation and decay, which the fields and woods offer to the notice of the serious and contemplative mind."[19]

It was not in England but in France, however, that the first metropolitan rural cemetery came into being. There, the post-Revolutionary invention of new institutions to replace discredited old ones and the growing fashion (initiated by Rousseau's tomb at Ermenonville) for memorials set in nature provided the impetus for a change in burial customs. In addition, new scientific theories of photosynthesis supported the practice of tree planting as conducive to urban health, and people began to desire the sight of cemeteries with grass lawns rather than bare earth. Historic preservation also played a role in those turbulent times when many royal monuments had been recently removed from churches and public places. Preservationists such as Antoine-Chrysostome Quatremère de Quincy argued for incorporating the salvage into cemeteries as proud relics of French cultural heritage. In 1796, the National Institute of Sciences and Arts called for papers on new customs and sites for burying the dead. In his prizewinning essay, the classical scholar Amaury Duval evoked the custom of antiquity as precedent for extramural burial, for in ancient Athens burial of notables took place in the Kerameikos, the pottery-making district outside the Dipylon Gate, and in ancient Rome the dead of prominent families were laid to rest in tombs along the Appian Way. He declared that for himself, he wished a grave in nature like Rousseau's.

The argument was echoed by others. There were proposals for the burial on private property of those, such as farmers, who owned land, and for those who did not, the authorities were encouraged to set aside dignified public burial grounds outside the city where family tombs would receive the remains of the departed, which would no longer be placed anonymously in common graves. In 1801, legislation was passed authorizing the communes of France to purchase land outside their boundaries for public cemeteries, and two years later the Department of the Seine created the first one on a high escarpment near the eastern edge of Paris. Known as the Cemetery of the East but called Père-Lachaise after the Jesuit priest Père François de La Chaise, Louix XIV's confessor, who had once owned the land, it was laid out according to a plan developed by the architect Alexandre-Théodore Brongniart (1739–1813) in a manner that combined axial geometry and monumental focal points with the picturesqueness of a serpentine circuit path and naturalistic plantings. A central *tapis vert* led the visitor to the site of a chapel, designed as an

Egyptian pyramid, which was never built because work was halted by the Napoleonic wars. To the left of this greensward axis were the plots reserved as grave sites for the masses, where five-year and ten-year leaseholds replaced the common burial pits of former times. On the higher terrain was institutionalized the concept of freehold ownership in perpetuity for families who wished to purchase plots.

Although common folk immediately began to bury their dead in the leasehold area, the sale of the perpetual plots was slow at first, gathering momentum after monuments purporting to be the tombs of Abélard and Héloise, Molière, and La Fontaine were installed and then joined by the actual ones of such contemporary celebrities as Frédéric Chopin. Civic pride rose with the burial of other cultural and political heroes, and by the 1820s, as they laid departed family members to rest, many denizens of the fashionable world sought the services of the funerary architects, stonecutters, iron-fence makers, and florists who had set up shop nearby. Mausoleums occupying entire plots soon gave Père-Lachaise the appearance of a miniature city of handsome stone dwellings, rather than that of a pastoral landscape of memory, as it was intended to be. Nevertheless, because of the famous names on many of the tombs and in spite of its overbuilt appearance, Père-Lachaise continues to be both a mecca for tourists and a tranquil refuge for contemporary Parisians (figs. 9.25, 9.26).

9.25 and 9.26. Père-Lachaise Cemetery

Americans, like the French at this time, were developing civic institutions that accorded with their republican ideals. They, too, wanted to create cemeteries that honored their brief national history, dignified the dead, and consoled the living. Their means of achieving this end was not by government decree as in France but, in a tradition Tocqueville recognized, through voluntary associations of citizen-reformers, who in this case developed a vision, enlisted support, formed a corporation, and sold burial plots.

Many people at the time resisted the placement of the dead outside town boundaries, inasmuch as marauding wolves were a still-recent menace and burial within insecure extramural precincts would facilitate the work of "resurrection men" who harvested corpses for medical dissection. However, as early as 1796, James Hillhouse persuaded his fellow citizens to subscribe to a burial ground on Grove Street immediately north of New Haven's original nine-square grid. Connecticut passed legislation establishing the first private corporation in America for that purpose, and under Hillhouse's direction, poplars were planted and freehold plots sold in perpetuity. Unlike the rural cemeteries that followed a generation later, the New Burying Ground in New Haven was remarkable for the precedent it set rather than for its design, which was, like the rest of the town, a straightforward grid plan offering convenient circulation for hearses and visiting families but little in the way of Romantic picturesqueness.

Mount Auburn Cemetery

Such was not the case in Boston, where the builders of Mount Auburn Cemetery exploited the potential of a naturally picturesque site across the Charles River on the border between Cambridge and Watertown. Here again, an energetic and visionary individual spearheaded the citizen effort responsible for launching the cemetery project in 1825. Botanist, physician, and community leader Dr. Jacob Bigelow interested the Massachusetts Horticultural Society in sponsoring the project. Earlier, Mayor Josiah Quincy had been a vocal proponent of a public cemetery somewhere on the outskirts of the city, but it took Bigelow's advocacy of the cause, combined with the enthusiastic participation of Henry Dearborn, the president of the Massachusetts Horticultural Society, to bring the concept to fruition.

The cultural climate of Boston provided strong impetus to the cemetery movement in America. There patriotic sentiment was strong, voluntary associations numerous, and religion liberalized through the agency of the Unitarian pulpit. Boston was, moreover, within the intellectual orbit of Concord where Thoreau and Emerson projected the phi-

losophy of transcendentalism and preached as well as practiced communion with nature. The American poet William Cullen Bryant (1794–1878), along with Wordsworth, touched a responsive chord in the breasts of New Englanders such as Bigelow and Dearborn, for whom the word *sentimental* denoted the manly emotion of remembrance with pleasurable melancholy, not maudlin excess, in a period when many fathers mourned the death of young wives and children. Bryant's most famous poem, "Thanatopsis" (1817), gave voice to Bigelow's medically and horticulturally informed opinion that the rapid dissolution of the uncoffined body laid to rest in nature constituted a sweet surrender of individual existence. At the same time, memory of the individual life lived within the bosom of family and community would be honored in epitaphs inscribed on monuments, and these would inspire others to lives of goodness and achievement.

The site for the new cemetery was secured in 1830 when another proponent, George Watson Brimmer, sold to the Massachusetts Horticultural Society a particularly beautiful piece of property consisting of 72 acres of heavily wooded, hilly terrain, the characteristic New England landscape of drumlins—ridges deposited by successive epochs of glaciation—and bogs, and ponds left in the wake of the retreating ice. Poetically inclined Harvard students, who liked to frequent this naturally picturesque spot of bosky dells, grassy knolls, and an abandoned colonial farmstead, called it Sweet Auburn after a vanished English hamlet destroyed by the enclosure movement, which Oliver Goldsmith had lamented in his poem "The Deserted Village" (1770). Like Père Lachaise, it had a high point or mount from which a panoramic prospect unfolded—hence Mount Auburn—but unlike the French cemetery where there was no stream or pond, it had a deep enfolding small valley into which water gushed and pooled. The tide of sentiment ran high as Joseph Story, associate justice of the United States Supreme Court, delivered his consecration oration to an estimated audience of two to three thousand Bostonians gathered in this natural amphitheater on September 24, 1831.

For the next three years, the society's president, Dearborn, masterminded the project, serving as the cemetery's landscape designer. Like others of his generation, Dearborn was a man of multiple talents and capable of practicing them at a professional level. To ready himself for the task at hand, he sent to London and Paris for books and engravings dealing with landscape theory and design, including an account of the creation of Père-Lachaise, which he translated for the benefit of his fellow citizens. He also steeped himself in the works of Repton and Price as he thought about how to turn the naturally Picturesque cemetery site into both a commemorative landscape and an experimental garden. This horticultural component was integral to his broad vision, as was the notion of creating a studio school on the premises for the instruction of professional landscape designers.

The author of a two-volume treatise on Greek architecture, Dearborn now sought to develop siting opportunities for the monuments that would make Mount Auburn an American version of Stowe or Stourhead (see Chapter Seven). His plan provided a circulation system that looped around the hilly topography in parabolic curves, providing efficient access for hearses to all parts of the grounds and, supplemented by additional paths, a means of strolling through the delectable scenery (fig. 9.27).

Although the two men never admitted a breach, a rift between Dearborn's and Bigelow's supporters was soon apparent. The horticultural faction sided with Dearborn's more inclusive vision of Mount Auburn as a broad-based landscape institution, with an active program of practical instruction like that of the London Horticultural Society where Paxton had apprenticed, while others supported Bigelow's more focused one of a cemetery alone. This resulted in an official separation in 1834, with the reincorporation of the Cemetery Proprietors of Mount Auburn as an independent entity.[20] As head of the trustees of the ten-member board governing Mount Auburn, Bigelow exerted a strong influence on the rules and regulations governing the cemetery's administration and visitation policies, at the same time exercising his considerable talents as an architect by designing several of its monuments.

Policy forbade slab tombstones like those found in the old New England churchyards where the forebears of the Mount Auburn trustees were buried. Bigelow and others looked to Classical Greece and ancient Egypt for a symbolism that reflected the liberal Unitarian and Universalist spirit preaching salvation for all and the heavenly reunion of families, which now prevailed over the stern philosophy of Calvinist predestination whereby only a tiny minority—the elect—were deemed eligible for reward after death. The obelisk, appropriated by ancient Rome as a trophy of conquest and converted by Renaissance city planners and garden builders into a widely copied landscape feature, connoted both timelessness and the death-embracing culture of ancient Egypt. Somewhat miniaturized, obelisks were frequently employed in eighteenth-century English gardens as memorials to cultural and political heroes. Just as an obelisk memorialized George Washington, now scaled-down versions in white marble marked the resting place of prominent Boston families who purchased plots in

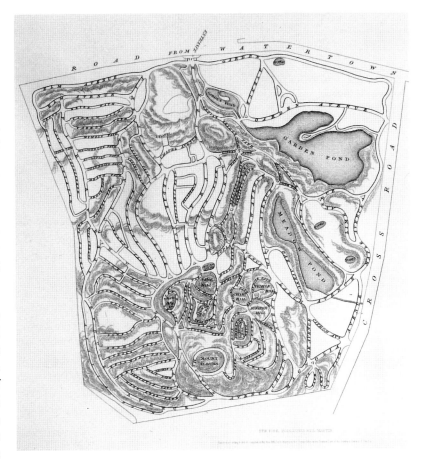

Mount Auburn. In addition, Bigelow used a pair of obelisks decoratively to frame the imposing neo-Egyptian style gate he designed for entrance to Mount Auburn, which bore the inscription: "Then shall the Dust return to the Earth as it was, and the Spirit shall return unto God who gave it"[21] (fig. 9.28). Pillars and pedestals surmounted by urns and sarcophagi resembling Rousseau's tomb were also popular among the first proprietors (fig. 9.29).

In James Smillie's 1847 engravings, the white marble monuments that had superseded the Puritans' gray slate tombstones gleam brightly against the dark foliage in the still heavily forested cemetery (fig. 9.30). Within the romantically Picturesque landscape, they act as poetic accents. The atmosphere of

9.27. Plan of Mount Auburn Cemetery, Cambridge, Massachusetts, designed by Jacob Bigelow. 1831. Engraving by James Smillie, from J. and C. Smillie, *Mount Auburn Illustrated,*1851

Below: 9.28. Entrance to Mount Auburn Cemetery. Engraving by James Smillie, from J. and C. Smillie, *Mount Auburn Illustrated,* 1851

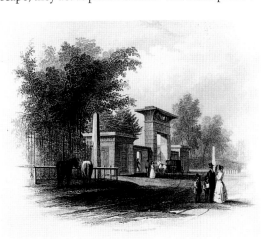

a forest glen is intentional. In the early years of the cemetery's existence, in keeping with the founders' desires to retain as much as possible the inherent charms of the site, maintenance was limited to keeping gravel paths accessible; only in the second half of the nineteenth century did the cemetery assume a parklike aspect. Also evident is Mount Auburn's intended function as a didactic landscape, a place of moral instruction, for the engravings show parents with young children in tow as well as solitary figures meditating in its sweetly melancholy gloom. The cemetery's purpose as a contemplative landscape was underlined by the publication of visitors' guides with brief, inspiring biographies of the distinguished dead. In spite of its role in expressing community values and community pride, the plots were private property, and the proprietors not only erected monuments—often in anticipation of their deaths—to function as future genealogies in stone, but they also fenced their places of perpetual rest with handsome cast-iron fences.

Although Bigelow promoted interment directly in the ground, many plot owners constructed chamber tombs similar to those at Père-Lachaise. Some chamber tombs were nestled into hillsides and faced with granite after stonecutters perfected techniques for carving and incising this durable material (fig. 9.31). As the cemetery began to acquire more burial plots, memorial sculpture, and works of architecture, notably Bigelow's Gothic Revival chapel and his George Washington Tower, it also acquired a greater degree of horticultural ornamentation. New trustees exercised keen fiduciary oversight and were careful to set aside funds from the proceeds of lot sales for landscape maintenance. Gradually Mount Auburn became, as it remains today, a memorial garden enriched by the mixture of many exotic and native plant species.

Bigelow designed and donated the cemetery's last major embellishment, a monumental female Sphinx, dedicated in 1871 to the Union dead (fig. 9.32). By this time, mnemonic devices and landscapes evoking the past were less compelling to a new generation

of Americans more interested in progress than in the past. Idealization of republican virtue and the domestication of death seemed less important after the Civil War than materialistic success and optimistic faith in the future. The notion of history as continuous linear improvement that many Americans came to identify with their nation's peculiar destiny fostered an attitude of denial toward death and an aversion to reminders of human mortality and the decline of civilizations. By contrast, the founders of Mount Auburn held that history was cyclical, believing that the young republic they were shaping would one day, like Rome, fall into ruin. Their elegiac monuments were meant for future generations to read as a testament to the greatness of the republican experiment in America, the solidarity of families, and the virtue and industry of the men and women commemorated within its idyllic precincts.

Mount Auburn served as the progenitor of rural cemeteries in other cities: Laurel Hill in Philadelphia (1836), Green Wood in Brooklyn (1838), Spring Grove in Cincinnati (1845), and Cave Hill in Louisville (1848). In addition, it exerted an influence over the old barren burial grounds in cities, and these, now no longer in active use, were given iron fences, grass, trees, and shrubs, becoming the pleasant green urban oases they are today.

Although there were plenty who left written records demonstrating that the didacticism of Mount

Auburn effectively touched them much as Bigelow and the other founders had hoped, even in the early years of its existence, people did not necessarily go there for moral uplift. From its inception, the cemetery was an immensely popular place for an outing, so much so that superintendents issued admittance passes and enforced rules restricting certain types of recreation. The same was true at Green-Wood, the Brooklyn cemetery where Manhattan residents flocked on Sundays for a holiday in scenic surroundings. Their evident enjoyment of this form of recreation caused some civic-minded New Yorkers to ask the question: why not a people's park devoid of reminders of mortality?

9.32. Sphinx, Mount Auburn Cemetery, designed by Jacob Bigelow and sculpted by Martin Milmore. 1871

IV. The New Metropolis: Frederick Law Olmsted and Calvert Vaux as Park Builders and City Planners

When Mount Auburn and Green-Wood were created, the country had not yet developed any public parks, museums, or other large-scale cultural institutions. Soon, however, voluntary associations of citizens began to found these, diminishing the cemetery's role as moral landscape and repository for monuments. Not surprisingly, Andrew Jackson Downing saw the rural cemetery as a transitional institution. In 1849, he editorialized in *The Horticulturist:* "The great attraction of these cemeteries . . . lies in the natural beauty of the sites, and in the tasteful and harmonious embellishment of these sites by art. . . . Does not this general interest, manifested in these cemeteries, prove that public gardens, established in a liberal and suitable manner, near our large cities, would be equally successful?"[22] His tragic death three years later prevented him from advancing the park cause. But by this time, politicians had embraced it thanks to the well-reasoned passion with which he and others, such as the poet William Cullen Bryant, who served as editor of the *New York Evening Post* from 1829 to 1878, had advocated establishing public parks for the people. Calvert Vaux (1824–1895) stood ready to put his talent and training with Downing into the creation of America's first large-scale public park, Central Park, and luckily he found in Frederick Law Olmsted (1822–1903), erstwhile farmer, journalist, and editor, a collaborator capable of helping him found both the parks movement and the profession of landscape architecture in America.

New York's Campaign for a Park

Vaux left Newburgh and moved to New York in 1856 at a time when the city was beginning to develop a lively artistic culture. In addition to theaters and music halls, department stores had opened their doors on Broadway, and shopping and promenading to enjoy both the commercial and the social spectacle had become a pleasurable routine for many New Yorkers. At the same time, the city's thriving port and commercial enterprises attracted a swelling volume of immigrants, particularly after the potato famine of the 1840s in Ireland and political turbulence in the wake of several failed revolutionary movements in Europe in 1848 stimulated mass exodus from countries abroad. New York reformers organized societies to minister to the needy, and although public health had been greatly improved after the Croton Aqueduct brought pure drinking water to the city in 1842, crowding now fostered both disease and vice. With few exceptions, New York had little to offer in the way of publicly accessible greenery. There was the Battery, the city's historic waterfront promenade at the foot of Manhattan Island; City Hall Park; Jones's Wood, an informal 160-acre picnic grove beside the East River between Sixty-sixth and Seventy-fifth Streets; and Green-Wood, the immensely popular rural cemetery in Brooklyn. The city's residential squares—St. John's Park, Gramercy Park, Union Square, Washington Square—were mostly fenced, with access restricted to neighboring property holders. Well-to-do New York businessmen—the city's civic leaders—traveling abroad noticed the parks in England, France, and Germany, which had been opened to the general populace as a matter of royal favor or *noblesse oblige.* It was obvious to them that to satisfy their recreational needs and especially those of their wives and children, as well as to establish their city competitively as a pleasant and civilized urban center of international importance, they should take responsible action to improve it by constructing a public park. In this they were urged forward by women whose work in various charitable associations made them conscious of the importance of this type of environmental and humanitarian improvement for the poor and whose burgeoning cosmopolitanism made them long as well for an American version of Hyde Park or the Champs-Elysées where they could readily socialize in public. Uptown landowners stood to gain from the improvement a park would bring to surrounding real estate, so they were natural proponents in bringing the plan forward.

After much contentious debate, the state legislature passed a bill in 1853, authorizing the acquisition of land below the existing Croton Reservoir in the center of the island between Seventy-ninth and Eighty-sixth Streets and north of it where the large New Reservoir was being built between Eighty-sixth and Ninety-sixth Streets. Fernando Wood (1812–1881), New York's Democratic mayor after 1854, saw that a large public works project could assist immigrant laborers and, incidentally, his own bank account, inasmuch as he was heavily invested in parkside real estate. In what later historians would cite as his single heroic act, he exerted his leadership in favor of proceeding with the construction of Central Park between Fifth and Eighth Avenues and 59th and 106th Streets.

THE DESIGN AND BUILDING OF CENTRAL PARK

It was now necessary to acquire the land. Beginning in the fall of 1853, a commission surveyed and estimated the value of the building lots and improvements on the site of the future park, meeting numerous futile complaints, particularly from landowners within the park who felt they had invested more capital and labor in improving their holdings than the price they were being awarded. Even so, the $5 million land acquisition cost far exceeded the cost that had been projected for the *built* park. As the parkland was exempted from the market, the surrounding property automatically went up in value. Regulations to curb certain activities considered to be nuisances such as piggeries and bone-boiling works were enacted, making the area surrounding the park desirable for the future as a place of fashionable residence. By October 1, 1857, with considerable hardship on the part of many former residents, including those clustered in an active African-American community known as Seneca Village on the west side of the park, the park site was cleared of inhabitants.

Anxious to wrest power from Mayor Wood, the legislature in Albany, which was dominated by the newly formed Republican Party, removed authority over Central Park from the city and placed it under a state-appointed, eleven-member commission. Egbert Viele (1825–1902), the engineer Wood had appointed to survey the park, was reappointed by the newly formed Board of Commissioners. Vaux had seen the plan Viele had prepared in 1856 for the park, which Wood had approved, and he realized how inferior it was with respect to the opportunity at hand. Vaux had recently acted as a founding member of the American Institute of Architects, and he now organized a successful lobbying effort for a design competition in order to achieve a plan that, according to him, would not disgrace the city or the memory of Downing. On October 13, 1857, the commission announced the terms of the public competition, and Vaux now became instrumental on the first of two significant occasions in directing the talents of Frederick Law Olmsted into the service of landscape design.

Olmsted had previously met Vaux once when he called upon Downing in Newburgh. But at that time he had no idea that he would pursue landscape as a career. Having first established himself with his father's financial help on Staten Island as a gentleman farmer employing the scientific principles similar to those pioneered by Loudon, he had felt impelled to travel abroad in 1850 to study English agricultural practices at firsthand, recording his observations in a book, *Walks and Talks of an American Farmer in England*. Its critical success led him to pursue further journalistic endeavors based upon travel. Choosing the pen name "Yeoman," he dispatched a series of letters to the newly formed *New York Daily Times*, from various points along the routes he took through the American South and the frontier states as far west as Texas. His constant theme was the superiority of free labor over slave agriculture, but interwoven into his text were passionately vivid descriptions of the countryside. Self-taught in his uncle's library where he may

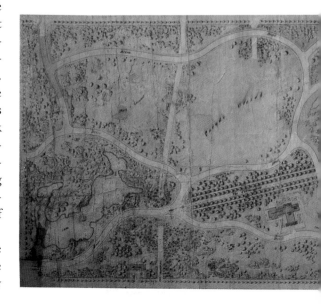

have first encountered the writings of Price and Gilpin, he was, like his father who had taken him on carriage rides as a boy in search of the Picturesque, a discriminating connoisseur of natural scenery. Now, however, the Panic of 1857 had forced the publishing house for which he worked to close. Being prevented from pursuing his literary career as a publisher and the editor of *Putnam's Monthly Magazine,* Olmsted was grateful to receive the job of superintendent of the clearing operations for Central Park under the supervision of Viele, the engineer-in-chief.

Vaux had learned a good deal about landscape design as he worked with Downing on the improvement of the public grounds in Washington, D.C., as well as on the private estates where they collaborated, but he realized that Olmsted's daily familiarity with the park landscape and his stature as an author and person of moral influence would make him an ideal partner in the design competition. Thus began the friendship of the architect and literary-man-turned-administrator as they paced together over the park's terrain and formed the vision embodied in the competition entry they labeled the Greensward Plan (fig. 9.33). By judiciously clearing away here and planting there, by moving earth to rearrange the land into gently rolling contours, by laying drains and converting swamps into ponds, there would emerge a landscape that was both pastoral and Picturesque.

To understand the Greensward Plan and the subsequent work of the two men after they became professional partners, one must attempt to enter the mind of Olmsted as fully as possible, for however much intelligence and design ability Vaux contributed, Olmsted's brand of nineteenth-century spirituality and democratic humanitarianism supplied something fundamentally philosophic to their common vision of the designed landscape. This vision was akin to Downing's in that it was rooted in a belief that parks

in cities and the domesticated middle landscape of freestanding homes set in parklike surroundings away from the crowded urban workplace would act as a civilizing force in society. But Olmsted's more comprehensive view of landscape was not derived from Downing or from Loudon, Downing's preceptor.

Downing had recast Loudon's concepts to suit the conditions of American society and the country's natural landscape, recommending a Picturesque and sometimes rustic architectural vocabulary to harmonize with and accent picturesque scenery. But, like Loudon, he was a horticulturist who valued plant display for its own sake. Olmsted—"Yeoman"—found the Gardenesque style a fussy distraction from the park's real purpose, which was the creation of rural scenery that evoked a poetic mood lifting one out of everyday care and ennobling the spirit with intimations of the divine. This kind of scenic contemplation was therapy for the overworked paterfamilias, a healthful occupation for women, a positive educational influence upon children, and a means of acculturation for the masses. Olmsted never presented himself as having botanical expertise, preferring plants arranged for their overall artistic effect to those presented as individual scientific specimens.[23] The task of incorporating the recently enriched botanical palette into garden compositions in which specimen trees or beds of flowers were objects of attention was for him irrelevant to the business of park making.

For the same reason, Olmsted held that architecture and sculpture should be subservient to landscape. Utilitarian and decorative elements should be placed within an overall impression of tranquilly beautiful and ruggedly Picturesque rural scenery. In later years, when he served as mentor to aspiring young landscape architects, he did not direct them to the works of the prominent nineteenth-century authors, Loudon and Downing, but rather to those of Price

9.33. Greensward Plan, Central Park design competition entry of Frederick Law Olmsted and Calvert Vaux. 1857

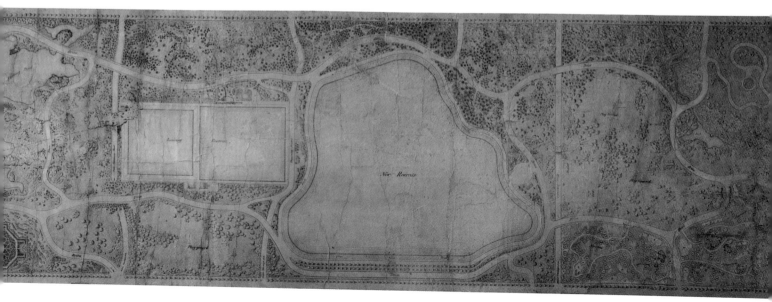

9.34. Sheep Meadow, Central Park, New York City

9.35. Sheep Meadow, Central Park, contemporary view. In keeping with the pastoral ideal embodied in this landscape, the sight of the surrounding city was screened from view by the park's topographic modeling and umbrageous border plantings. Olmsted and Vaux wanted to imply the nonexistence of the park's rectangular boundaries and the indefinite continuation of pastoral scenery, a successful strategy before the age of skyscrapers, which now loom dramatically along its borders, providing perhaps a new scenic category: the urban sublime.

and Repton. Like these eighteenth-century writers, he saw landscape not as a collection of features artistically arranged for display, but rather as a shifting panorama, a sequence of views and vistas that opened up harmoniously as one moved through the countryside or city park. His own deepest religious experiences were, like those of his father, Wordsworthian and transcendentalist—rapt responses to the beautiful and sublime in nature. He also loved the rich, picturesque mystery of things half-concealed by overhanging vines. His keen emotional response to lush tropical effects caused him to attempt to simulate the scenery he had seen in the Louisiana bayous and on the Isthmus of Panama in an American-inflected version of the eighteenth-century English Picturesque. By exploiting such optical characteristics as the play of light and shade in the shadows cast by trees across a sunlit meadow, the atmospheric haze of

a distant umbrageous horizon line, and the mystery suggested by an intricate fringe of vines screening a shadowy entrance to a grotto, he created a design idiom that was both naturalistic and Romantic.

His immersion as a young man in the "green, dripping, glistening, gorgeous!" landscape of rural England—"enchantment indeed, we gazed upon it and breathed it—never to be forgotten"[24]—had imprinted his mind with an imagery of pastoral beauty that served him as lasting inspiration, but the English class system that achieved this beauty for the advantage of a few aristocrats through the enclosure movement and the hard labor of the poor offended his sense of social responsibility. The sight in England that had impressed him most happily from a democratic standpoint was Paxton's Birkenhead Park: "Five minutes of admiration, and a few more spent in studying the manner in which art had been employed to obtain from nature so much beauty, and I was ready to admit that in democratic America, there was nothing to be thought of as comparable with this People's Garden."[25] Now, thanks to Vaux's invitation to join him in the design competition for Central Park, he had the chance to work on a far grander scale to create a "People's Garden" in New York.

Because of Olmsted's daytime duties as superintendent and the many interruptions by an incessant stream of job seekers, he and Vaux did much of their collaboration on moonlit nights as they paced the future park, appreciating the scenic potential of its bold outcroppings of Manhattan schist, proposing certain topographical alterations in order to deepen swamps into lakes and mound soil into rolling meadows. They studied where to place drainage lines and discussed the configuration of carriage drives and the

best vantage points for vistas. Friends gathered in the evenings at Vaux's house on Eighteenth Street to assist in the preparation of the pen-and-ink drawing. On March 31, 1858, the deadline for the competition, Olmsted and Vaux submitted their Greensward Plan, which now hangs in the Arsenal, the New York City Department of Parks headquarters in Central Park. On April 28, the commissioners announced their decision to award first prize and the announced premium of $2,000 to the Vaux-Olmsted team.

The element that more than any other defines an Olmsted-Vaux landscape is a spacious meadow with gentle rises and scattered clumps of trees arranged about its periphery so as to lead the eye beyond its indeterminate boundaries into an illusionistic distance of seemingly unending rural scenery. It was difficult to achieve in Central Park because of its broken topography and narrow rectangular shape. Above Ninety-eighth Street, however, there was a piece of tableland that lent itself to becoming the North and East Meadows, while below the Sixty-Fifth Street Transverse Road the designers proposed blasting away bedrock in order to fill and level the surface for a Ball Ground. Because the transverse road's

below-grade level made it inconspicuous, the Ball Ground was visually united with the 14-acre Sheep Meadow immediately north of it (figs. 9.34, 9.35). Together these two green areas served to portray as best possible the designers' scenic desideratum in the park's south end. To nourish a thick mat of turf for the grazing flock that would enhance the park's pastoral appearance they covered the Sheep Meadow with 2 feet (.6 meters) of topsoil. Grading the park's borders into low berms and planting trees "to insure an umbrageous horizon line"[26] was another feat of landscape legerdemain the designers employed in order to screen from view the future four-story houses that would rise along the suddenly valuable frontage lots.

The most ingenious aspect of the Greensward Plan was the engineering of four east-west crossings to carry workaday city traffic through the park along below-grade transverse roads (fig. 9.36). Here, too, low berms with plantings screened from park visitors' sight the carts and draft animals moving on these roads. In executing the Greensward Plan, Olmsted and Vaux carried the principle of grade separation of traffic one step further by segregating pedestrians from carriage traffic and riders on horseback. This gave Vaux, often in association with Jacob Wrey Mould, the opportunity to design a number of stone arches for paths and bridle trails carrying pedestrians and horseback riders beneath carriage drives as well as a handful of ornamental cast-iron bridges for paths spanning bridle trails (figs. 9.37, 9.38). Bow Bridge, at the narrow neck between the two lobes of the Lake, allowed pedestrians to cross from the foot of Cherry Hill to the Ramble, an intricately designed woodland for strolling. It constitutes Vaux's masterwork in this mid-nineteenth-century building material (fig. 9.39).

9.40. Bethesda Terrace, Central Park. The carved panels encasing the grand double stairs descending to the Bethesda Fountain and the lakeshore depict a rich profusion of animal and vegetal forms symbolizing the seasons of the year. Ornamentation like this, using images depicting nature's abundance in a manner similar to that of medieval stonecarvers, owes a debt to the writings of John Ruskin, an important influence on the intellectual and artistic culture of Victorian England and its counterpart in nineteenth-century America.

Today Olmsted and Vaux are sometimes criticized as being the carriers of patrician values and the agents of elitist objectives because they created a park for scenic viewing by carriage and on horseback—as well as on foot—and did not cater to a greater degree to more populist pastimes involving games and sports. This viewpoint imposes a later value system on their objectives and ignores the fact that, at the time they designed Central Park, the physical recreational movement still lay in the future. For their romantically inclined generation, scenic strolling was a healthful pastime much enjoyed by all classes. They were sincere in their belief that this pleasure, which Olmsted deemed to be akin to being moved by poetry, would soften the lives of the less fortunate members of society, which included many newcomers from other countries. They were convinced that the park's pastoral and Picturesque scenery would serve as an informal public school, instructing immigrants through an unconscious process of scenic enjoyment in the shared values, which were still predominantly agrarian, of the new democratic society-in-formation.

It is undeniable that there were certain prospective users who felt few transcendental stirrings in the presence of scenery and who saw the park merely as a social arena, a place to parade their wealth and marriageable daughters, often exercising ill-disguised class prejudice. But this did not mean that the idealism expressed in the vision of Olmsted and Vaux was not genuine. They did not discourage such immediately popular activities as ice-skating and boating on the Lake, and the rules Olmsted promulgated as superintendent were designed to protect the park from overuse and abuse rather than to discriminate against a class of users. Most important, the Greensward Plan was supple in its ability to absorb new uses over the years. Unlike many of the landscapes presented to the public by the twentieth-century park builder Robert Moses, which typically consist of single-purpose recreation facilities, the spaces Olmsted and Vaux created are able to serve a variety of purposes. In his writings, Olmsted divided the park's landscape into two kinds of space: "neighborly" and "gregarious," the former being for small groups consisting of families and friends who came to the park to picnic and enjoy scenery, while the latter was designed to serve the parade of strangers who congregated in the manner of Parisians on boulevards to enjoy the spectacle of one another. The park was thus intended as a place in which to delight in both nature and one's common humanity.

Absent from the Greensward Plan were Downing's proposed "noble works of art, statues, monuments and buildings," although in 1880 Vaux built the first structure housing the Metropolitan Museum inside the park near Fifth Avenue and East Eighty-second Street. In addition, a conservatory originally planned near Fifth Avenue and East Seventy-fourth Street was constructed in 1899 in the north end of the park near Fifth Avenue and East 105th Street on the site where Olmsted had set up a temporary nursery and botanic garden. Throughout the park, the rural motif ruled in the predominant interest of "neighborly" recreation, but an important area was reserved for "gregarious" purposes: the elm-arcaded Mall, a straight concourse extending from Sixty-fifth to Seventy-second Street, which was set on a diagonal axis to detract attention from the park's rectilinear boundaries. Focused upon Vista Rock in the distance, which Vaux later crowned with the neo-Gothic, castlelike Belvedere, this grand promenade, designed for sociable congregation, leads strollers to a broad stairway and through the Arcade beneath the Seventy-second Street Cross Drive to the lakeside Terrace, Vaux's architectural masterpiece (fig. 9.40).

Here, with his collaborator Mould, Vaux designed a pair of monumental staircases carved with ornamental panels, profuse with motifs of vegetation and wildlife representing the four seasons. These grand stairs provided an alternative means of reaching the Terrace, useful for those alighting from carriages parked on the Cross Drive rather than passing on foot from the Mall through the Arcade. In the center of the circular Terrace, a jet sent a plume of water into the air until it was replaced in the 1870s by a fountain surmounted by a sculpture representing the angel that bestowed healing power upon the pool of Bethesda in Jerusalem.[27] This work by Emma Stebbins (1815–1882) celebrated the public health benefits brought to the city a generation earlier by the Croton Aqueduct, and the figures at the fountain's base symbolize the blessings of Temperance, Purity, Health, and Peace. Two tall poles with ornamental bases and crossbars for long vertical fishtail banners stand next to the Lake where the designers effected a seemingly effortless transition from modest grandeur to Picturesque simplicity. This achievement is evident also in the way the designers made the geometric lines of the Mall and Terrace merge gracefully with the curving paths and naturalistic scenery alongside them.

In the south end of the park, the designers paid particular attention to the needs of women and children, visitors who might not wish to wander far from its principal entrance at Fifty-ninth Street and Fifth Avenue. Immediately south of the Sixty-fifth Street Transverse Road and serviceable from it, Vaux constructed the Dairy, a small building of rusticated stone with an ample wooden loggia providing shelter from the sun and inclement weather. Here children could play with toys furnished by a park attendant or drink fresh cow's milk. The designers christened a large nearby outcrop of Manhattan schist the Kinderberg. Polished by glacial scouring to form a natural slide, it had broad steps carved into its base and a rustic shelter crowning its top. The fenced playgrounds that are popular attractions in today's park were added after 1934 by Moses, but in the nineteenth century, park workers set up portable swings and seesaws in season.

In the original Greensward Plan, the northern border of the park is at 106th Street where an arboretum was specified but never built on the east side, while on the west side there was nothing beyond the Great Hill, which Olmsted and Vaux encircled with an appendage to the West Drive to afford carriage riders panoramic prospects from this high point in the park. The commissioners soon realized that the topography between 106th and 110th Streets would not readily permit urban development because it was both too elevated by bedrock protrusions and too swampy where the resistant Manhattan schist gives way to the easily erodible Inwood marble that underlies the Harlem plain. They wisely acquired this additional land in 1863, increasing the park's size from 750 acres to 843 acres. This allowed Olmsted and Vaux to save the sites of several fortifications left from the Revolution and the War of 1812, to promote as a forest of native American trees an already wooded area, and to create the Harlem Meer in the park's new northeast corner, a much larger water body than the Pond in the southeast (fig. 9.41).

An army of a thousand workers, directed at first by Olmsted, moved nearly 5 million cubic yards, or approximately 10 million one-horse cartloads of stone, earth, and topsoil out of or into the park between 1858 and 1873. In addition, Olmsted supervised chief landscape gardener Ignaz Anton Pilat in planting a rich variety of trees, shrubs, and vines. Moreover, he promulgated park rules and oversaw the training of a cadre of park keepers responsible for maintaining order and educating the public to respect the landscape. All the while, to his intense irritation, he was subjected to the oversight and penny-pinching curtailments imposed by the park commission's comptroller, Andrew Haswell Green.

In 1861, the Civil War interrupted the partners' collaboration on the ongoing creation of Central Park. Olmsted, who prided himself on his administrative abilities more than his landscape artistry, accepted a position as the executive secretary of the U.S. Sanitary Commission, the forerunner of the

9.41. Harlem Meer and the Charles A. Dana Center, Central Park

American Red Cross. He desired to serve the Union cause, and reasoning that moving nurses and supplies to the front was a managerial task similar to moving men and materials in the park, he departed for Washington, leaving Vaux in charge of the work in the park, which continued throughout the war.

Olmsted in Transition

Until 1863, when he accepted a position as the resident manager of the Mariposa Mines in California, Olmsted helped reorganize the Army's Medical Bureau, took charge of distributing food and goods collected from branches of the Sanitary Commission in the North, and oversaw the evacuation of wounded Union soldiers on hospital transport ships. In California, while supervising the Mariposa operations, he served as the head of a commission to make recommendations on the management of the Yosemite Valley as a public preserve. Although Anglo-Americans had discovered its spectacular scenery only sixteen years before, Yosemite was already a tourist attraction. Congress had the previous year withdrawn it from the public domain and deeded it to the state of California "for public use, resort, and recreation," the first area in the nation to be set aside for this purpose. Olmsted's preliminary report on *The Yosemite Valley and the Mariposa Big Trees* is a landmark enunciating the individual's right to enjoy public scenery and the government's obligation to protect citizens' exercise of that right.

At this period in his life, Olmsted still considered landscape design merely as a sideline. As the fortunes of the Mariposa mining venture sank, he considered returning to a career in journalism. At the same time, Vaux, who had been forced by political pressure to resign his Central Park position, wrote Olmsted saying that they had been offered reappointment as landscape architects—the title they chose for their profession—in Central Park and that there was another important commission awaiting collaboration: Prospect Park in Brooklyn, named for the ele-

9.42. Long Meadow, Prospect Park, Brooklyn. The Long Meadow illustrates the kind of scenic unfolding of pastoral landscape that constitutes the essence of Olmsted and Vaux's park ideal. The eye threads a passage through clumps of trees, passing over a series of gentle undulations to a hazy horizon line that appears to extend beyond the park's confines.

vation known as Mount Prospect.

Olmsted, loath to subject himself again to the kind of "squabbles with the Commission and the politicians" he had experienced in Central Park, was reluctant to accept Vaux's second entreaty to enter into collaboration. Vaux, however, urged him as persuasively as possible: "I am perhaps deficient in personal ambition—but I can feel for it in others. If you do not see that you are honored by developing this fitness for art work of course—don't come. It must be the art of landscape architecture and the art of administration combined. Think this over. We are neither of us old men you know. To me it seems & always has seemed a magnificent opening. Possible together, impossible to either alone."[28] Olmsted was still reluctant to consider himself an artist but thought that he could "do anything with proper assistants, or money enough—anything any man can do. I can combine means to ends better than most, and I love beautiful landscapes and rural recreations and people in rural recreations—better than anybody else I know."[29] Still uncertain that he could make a living in this line of work, he nevertheless decided to return to New York and join Vaux in the continuing construction of Central Park and the design of the park that Brooklyn's civic leaders wanted to build in emulation of it.

Creating Prospect Park

Vaux had already convinced James Stranahan, the president of the park board, that the original site authorized by the state legislature—350 acres straddling Flatbush Avenue—was less desirable than the western portion of this site plus a large tract of adjoining farmland where there existed the opportunity to create an illusion of infinitely extensive rural space and a large lake. The popularity of ice-skating in Central Park made an even larger Prospect Park lake competitively attractive, and the park commissioners agreed to divest themselves of the portion of their original site east of Flatbush Avenue—land now occupied by the Brooklyn Museum of Art and Brooklyn Botanic Garden—and to purchase the site recommended by Vaux, bringing the park's total acreage to 526.

The park did not have prominent, ice-polished rock outcrops like the ones that picturesquely accented the scenery in Central Park, but it was situated on a glacial moraine. This provided a naturally rich soil and a gently rolling terrain as well as glacial erratics—large boulders left after the ice melted. The designers artfully employed these as compositional elements when they built the Ravine between the Long Meadow and the Lake (figs. 9.42, 9.43). In creating the 75-acre Long Meadow, they were not constrained by the disposition of the park's boundaries

9.43. Plan of Prospect Park, Brooklyn, by Frederick Law Olmsted and Calvert Vaux. 1871

Below: 9.44. The Ravine, Prospect Park, Brooklyn. c. 1870

as they had been in Central Park where they were hampered by the firmly rectilinear shape dictated by the 1811 grid plan for Manhattan. Also, in Prospect Park they were free of the necessity of providing transverse roads for nonpark traffic. Thus they were able "to connect a series of dissevered and isolated patches of comparatively level ground, into one sweep of grass-land that is extensive enough, to make a really permanent impression on the mind."[30] On the perimeter of the Long Meadow—considered by many as the quintessential Olmstedian landscape—they mounded earth into berms and then created spacious vaulted tunnels, a design master stroke that orchestrates the passage of visitors in a manner that induces surprise and heightens sensory awareness and appreciation of the long vista of gently undulating rural scenery. The pleasure of the experience is heightened by the park's urban context.[31]

As in Central Park, the designers created a space for "gregarious" recreation in the elegant concert grove with ornamental stonework by Vaux similar to that which distinguished Bethesda Terrace in Central Park. The concert grove is flanked by an upper and a lower carriage concourse accessible from the park's sinuous circuit drive, and the whole ensemble constituted an informal amphitheater oriented to face the small Music Pavilion located on an island in Prospect Lake, now covered over by the Wollman Rink. The Ravine's stream with waterfalls spilling over rocks and profusely planted slopes, which has recently been restored, simulated the rugged picturesqueness one might find on an outing in the Catskill Mountains (fig. 9.44).

THE EXPLODING METROPOLIS

As walled cities became things of the past after the formation of nation-states and as industrial technology provided means of transportation that effectively shrank distance, making it possible to commute between widely separated places of work and home, the spatial envelope of cities became greatly enlarged. In spite of a lingering Jeffersonian bias in favor of a predominantly agrarian destiny for America, manufacturing and commerce were breeding increasingly large urban populations, and this fostered an unprecedented growth in the size of cities. Public sanitation victories through the kind of engineering technology represented by New York's Croton Aqueduct system and other Industrial-Age improvements such as smooth macadam roadbeds instead of cobblestone paving made large cities more livable than before.

But they still presented many difficulties for their inhabitants, the most notable being deprivation of contact with nature as the countryside became increasingly distant from the city. Olmsted and Vaux felt that a single park's role as a civilizing influence, ameliorating the noise and hectic pace of the metropolis, was still somewhat limited. They envisioned the carriage drives within parks being extended to become parkways, tree-canopied transportation corridors connected to other parks, the whole forming a new framework superimposed over the grid, a green skeleton guiding the city's expansion. They saw, moreover, that roadway layout necessarily dictated the pattern and nature of urban growth, with residential development of a more elegant nature being spawned by a circulation system that segregated private estates from commercial through traffic. In their grasp of the city as an evolving regional organism they were the country's first urban planners.

The parity implied by the 1811 grid plan for New York City was congenial to the expressed democratic values of the new republic. Moreover, it was a practical convenience for developers. Nevertheless, Olmsted wrote scathingly about its disadvantages. He felt the New York grid to be especially uncongenial to the needs of people because the block sizes dictated by its street layout forced property to be divided into deep lots, usually no wider than 25 feet (7.6 meters). This resulted in rows of cramped narrow houses with poor light and ventilation. He wished to remedy this condition by carrying the park influence to the level of a system, with greenery easily accessible throughout the metropolitan area. Where land had not yet been platted, lots for homes could be created that would permit healthful cross ventilation, penetration by sunlight, and a green lawn. Unlike the grid with its straight streets intersecting at right angles and static perspectives, the parkway system would

conform to topography and scenic opportunity, which could be captured by the kind of curving alignments that allowed the landscape to unfold from a series of ever-changing vantage points.

THE FIRST PARKWAYS

The creation of the Brooklyn park offered Olmsted and Vaux the opportunity to advocate a more comprehensive vision for the metropolitan landscape. In their preliminary report to the commissioners dated January 24, 1866, they articulated under the heading "Suburban Connections" the desirability of a pleasure drive connecting Prospect Park with the beach on the Atlantic Ocean. Imaginatively, they saw how another drive could run east along the beach, then pass through undeveloped countryside, continuing parallel with the East River until it touched the shore at Ravenswood, Queens, where either by ferry or high bridges as yet unbuilt it would connect with one of the wide crosstown Manhattan streets leading to Central Park. Further, they envisioned this extensive greenway dedicated to pleasure driving extending west from Central Park to the Hudson River, where it could run for a distance parallel to that river with views of the Palisades on the opposite shore and, in the distance, the blue outline of the Shawangunk Mountains.

Two years later after work on the park had begun, Olmsted and Vaux used the report they delivered to the board as an opportunity to expound this metropolitan-scale planning concept. They now proposed a scheme, which went beyond their original one of a recreational parkway linking two major parks with the region's ocean beaches and extensive river waterfront, to encompass the notion of Brooklyn's destiny as an ideal residential community. Even allowing for shipping and commercial activity equal to that of Manhattan across the river, much of the city—although it had not yet become a borough of Greater New York—could function as a bedroom suburb. "Brooklyn is New York outside the walls,"[32] they wrote, an implied reference to the faubourgs that had earlier sprung up outside the walls of Paris and other walled cities in Europe.

In their report Olmsted and Vaux detailed the history of urban street plans from medieval times to the present, citing the missed opportunity when Wren's plan was ignored in the rebuilding of London after the Great Fire of 1666. They proposed for Brooklyn the first elements of a major arterial system that took into account the need for smooth roadbeds for the increasingly numerous light spring-suspension carriages, which were "quite unfit to be used in streets adapted to the heavy wagons employed in commercial traffic."[33] At the same time, they realized that

9.45. Plan of a portion of Eastern Parkway, Brooklyn, New York. 1868. Six rows of trees were to be planted along the length of the parkway, dividing the 260-foot (79-meter) right-of-way into a center drive for carriages, with two lanes on each side, one of which was designated a pedestrian walk, while the other served as a side road for the approach of vehicles to the adjoining house lots. These were to be 100 feet (30.4 meters) in width, allowing for the construction of freestanding "villa" residences with private gardens. Service lanes where horses could be stabled, goods delivered, and garbage removed were to be located in back of the house lots.

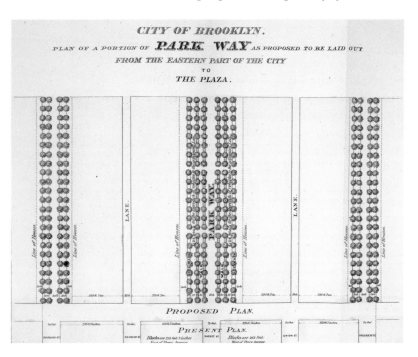

delivery carts and other kinds of commercial traffic could not be banned from abutting residential property altogether.

Taking inspiration from the new avenue de l'Impératrice (now avenue Foch), which Olmsted had seen on a trip to Paris in 1859, and Berlin's great tree-lined avenue, Unter den Linden, each of which was connected to a large park while simultaneously serving as "an intermediate pleasure-ground [rather] than a part of the general street system,"[34] the designers sketched the route of Ocean Parkway leading from Prospect Park to the beach at Coney Island and that of Eastern Parkway running from the park toward the Williamsburg section of Brooklyn (fig. 9.45). A third parkway was proposed to link the park with Fort Hamilton and the site of the future Marine Park overlooking the Verrazano Narrows to the south.

The designers further remarked that new public transportation improvements made possible the occupation of a much larger urban area at lower densities than heretofore. Separation of residence and workplace was a corollary of this enlargement of towns. Brooklyn, "set apart and guarded by nature as a place for the tranquil habitation of those whom the business of the world requires should reside within convenient access of the waters of New York harbor"[35] was ideally situated to become a pleasant residential suburb. Olmsted and Vaux hoped that with its domestic character established by the parkway and street system recommended in their report, the kind of energetic self-made young men who had left their leafy country towns for the commercial opportunities of the city would be drawn to purchase property in Brooklyn's new middle landscape. It was a model that could be replicated as Brooklyn and other cities grew, extending themselves to encompass their surrounding rural countryside. The loss of that countryside to urbanization was compensated for by the abundant greenery of the now more loosely woven fabric of the metropolitan landscape with its parkways connecting city dwellers to the generously scaled new urban parks filled with rural scenery.

Buffalo's Park System

The firm that Olmsted and Vaux had formed was now called upon to consult in other cities. Even as they were writing their report to the Brooklyn commissioners outlining their parkway concept, they were advising the city of Newark, New Jersey, that large cultural institutions such as museums were extraneous to rural parks and should be built outside them and that, in considering the acquisition of land for a public park, the town fathers should also consider purchasing strips of land for future construction of pleasure drives and walks. They gave similar advice to

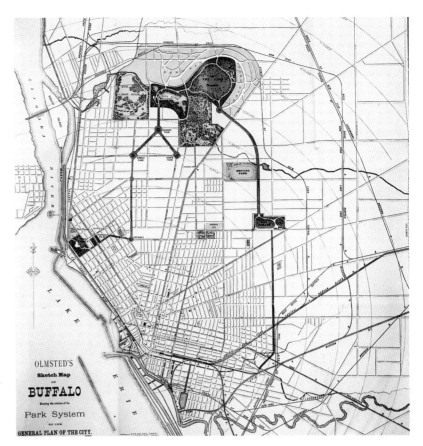

9.46. 1868 Plan of Buffalo Park System, 1876 map

clients in Philadelphia and Albany. It was in Buffalo, however, that the partners got to implement an entire park-and-parkway system. There, in 1804, Joseph Ellicott, brother of Andrew Ellicott, Pierre L'Enfant's chief surveyor for Washington, D.C., had laid out a city where a radial street plan was focused upon a central square.

A group of citizens in Buffalo, New York, summoned Olmsted in the fall of 1868 to examine three sites under consideration for a park. He traveled to the city for a site meeting and admired its departure from the grid in its layout. He then proceeded to sketch a plan that grafted onto this street pattern a system of parkway-linked parks. The new plan thus consisted of not one, but all three park sites with parkways connecting them to one another (fig. 9.46). The 350-acre Delaware Park gave the designers an opportunity to create a large meadow and a 46-acre lake and to provide an extensive circuit drive with grade separation of intersecting pedestrian paths as in Central and Prospect Parks. A second park, the Front, occupied 36 acres overlooking the Niagara River near its entry into Lake Erie and was designed as a viewing terrace, which could also accommodate large gatherings. The Parade, a 56-acre tract on elevated land near the eastern edge of the city, where military functions took place, included children's play equipment and Vaux's large refectory. The parkways, 200-foot-wide (61-meter-wide) landscaped boulevards, now lined with handsome residences, remain a much-

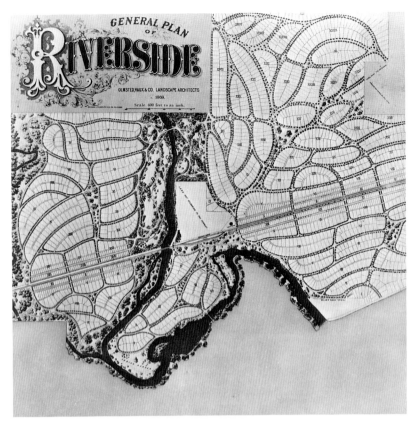

9.47. Plan for Riverside, Illinois, 1869

they specified to be 30 feet (9.1 meters) deep and planted with at least two trees. Like a New England town, Riverside had its common. There were, moreover, because of the configuration of the road system, many triangular pieces of land that were intentionally exempted from the process of parceling house lots, and these served as additional public green space. But the largest reservation of land for common recreational enjoyment was the 160-acre stretch of land paralleling the Des Plaines River, envisioned as a waterfront park.

Management difficulties and financial problems made the partners resign their commission in 1870. A thousand acres east of the river and a small piece of land to the west were eventually developed according to their plan, but many half-acre lots were divided into two lots, and the large park remained unbuilt. Today, however, this leafy suburb, which is now surrounded by ordinary grid-style urbanization, stands out as an example of the intelligent approach to the design of the new American metropolitan landscape in the middle of the nineteenth century when Olmsted and Vaux infused the process of real-estate development with social and recreational considerations of lasting consequence.

CHICAGO PARKS

At the same time that the partners were working on Riverside, Chicago was becoming a commercial dynamo vigorously seeking the civic symbolism that would assert its supremacy within the Union. The state legislature had recently passed a bill authorizing the creation of three large parks, two of which had received approval in a voters' referendum. Separate commissions were created to oversee each park, a fact that served to prevent the comprehensive urban planning approach taken in Buffalo.

William LeBaron Jenny, a French-trained architect, was chosen to design the western recreational complex consisting of Douglas Park and Garfield (originally Central) Park, while Olmsted and Vaux were hired to design the united Washington Park and Jackson Park for the South Park Commission (fig. 9.48). Unfortunately, the fire of 1871, which destroyed much of Chicago, prevented the construction of these parks from moving forward at the time. Even if begun, the parks on the South Park Commission's flat, unpromising site adjacent to Lake Michigan offered little opportunity for realizing Olmsted and Vaux's ideal scenery of rolling meadowland. In addition, because Chicago had a district-based rather than a city-wide park system, the designers were called upon to fit more elements into their plan for the two parks than would have been the case had they been able to adopt an integrated metropolitan approach,

appreciated Buffalo amenity. In 1874, on land contiguous to Delaware Park, Olmsted prepared a plan for "Parkside," the city's first residential suburb, which had curving streets lined with trees and large lots for fine homes with landscaped grounds.

RIVERSIDE, ILLINOIS

Almost simultaneously, in Riverside, Illinois, on the Des Plaines River 9 miles (14.5 kilometers) west of Chicago and accessible to commuters by train, Olmsted and Vaux had the chance to employ their principles for laying out residential communities (fig. 9.47). Here was an opportunity to demonstrate on 1,600 acres of farmland the truly metropolitan character of their vision, which was far different from Downing's merely suburban ideal. In doing so, they went beyond the explicit commission of the Riverside Improvement Company to design a parkway connecting city and suburb. They wanted to create a transportation alternative to the railroad, providing a recreational amenity not only for Riverside families, but also for carriage-owning Chicago residents who wanted a pleasant outing in the countryside. Like the Brooklyn parkways, the Chicago parkway—several miles of which were constructed—had segregated lanes, with pedestrians and horseback riders occupying the lane next to the central roadway and carts and wagons the outside utility lane.

For the circulation system within the community, the designers created curving, well-drained, tree-lined roads with sidewalks bordering lawns, which

assigning different recreational functions more broadly to a greater number of parks.

But Lake Michigan itself in their opinion compensated "for the absence of sublime or picturesque elevations of the land."[36] To extend its scenic influence and also to provide good drainage of the Midway and Washington Park, they planned a 165-acre lagoon in Jackson Park. Because the designers thought that most park visitors would arrive by boat on the lakeside, an inlet and adjacent 200-foot (61-meter) pier formed the principal entrance to South Park. In inland Washington Park, they found an opportunity for the creation of a large open meadow, which they called Southopen Green. The two parks were united by the Midway Plaisance,[37] a linear band of lawns and shrubbery with a central canal that connected the water from the "mere" in Washington Park with that of the Lagoon in Jackson Park. Defying the harsh lakefront climate, Olmsted saw the Lagoon as an opportunity to create an approximation of the tropical scenery he had admired on his travels in Louisana, thus combining "the fresh and healthy nature of the North with the restful, dreamy nature of the South."[38] Not until twenty years later, when he was summoned to be the landscape design member of the planning team for the Chicago World's Fair of 1893 on the site of Jackson and Washington parks, did he have a chance to implement this and other elements of the design he had produced with Vaux.

This project was the last the two men designed together, for in 1872, for reasons of mutual convenience, they dissolved their partnership. Vaux continued his career as a gifted practitioner of Romantic Ruskinian architecture until the vogue for Beaux-Arts Neoclassicism eclipsed the Picturesque style toward the end of the century. Olmsted, now fully confirmed in his own mind as a landscape architect, created a

new firm in which he was joined first by his adopted stepson, John Charles Olmsted, and later by his son, Frederick Law Olmsted, Jr.

BOSTON'S EMERALD NECKLACE

As in other cities, citizen action in Boston stimulated government response, and in 1869 the Massachusetts General Court passed an act authorizing one large or several small parks. Some Bostonians spearheading

9.48. Plan for the Chicago South Park Commission, by Frederick Law Olmsted and Calvert Vaux, 1871

Below: **9.49. Park System from the Boston Common to Franklin Park—Boston's Emerald Necklace—by Frederick Law Olmsted, Olmsted & Eliot, Landscape Architects. 1894**

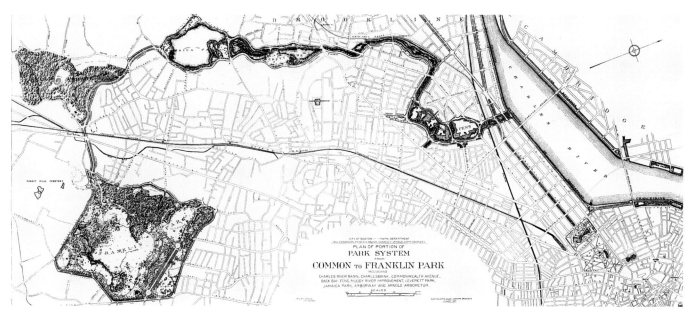

9.50. Meadow with School-master Hill, Franklin Park, West Roxbury, c. 1900, an example of the type of gently undulating rural scenery that Olmsted sought to provide as a means of preserving pastoral ideals within rapidly growing nineteenth-century industrial cities

Right: 9.51. Ellicott Arch, Franklin Park, 1892

Below: 9.52. Moraine Farm, Beverly, Massachusetts, open field, designed by Frederick Law Olmsted

the parks effort were impressed by comments made by landscape architect Horace William Shaler Cleveland (1814–1900) of Chicago to the effect that what Boston needed was not a "central" park, but rather a surrounding greenbelt including drives and scenic areas for public use. On February 25, 1870, Olmsted lectured at the Lowell Institute on "Public Parks and the Enlargement of Towns," presciently anticipating large-scale urban growth and advocating a similar metropolitan vision. Five years of often heated public debate and several planning proposals ensued. A commission set up in 1875 solicited Olmsted's advice on site selection. From this beginning, which led to a series of commissions lasting the rest of his professional life, he was able to project a bold planning vision of parkway-linked parks: a metropolitan-scale "Emerald Necklace" (fig. 9.49).[39]

Working with Charles Sprague Sargent, the director of the Arnold Arboretum, Olmsted was able to effect the transfer and leaseback arrangements between Harvard University, the owner of the Arboretum, and the city, which allowed jointly funded improvements and operations on the 120-acre site, one of the gemstones of the necklace. The two men disagreed about ways to plant the public parkland next to the Arboretum in Brookline. Sargent, the botanist, favored a taxonomic approach and the use of native plants only, while Olmsted, the artist, felt that including exotic plants would enhance the effects of light and shade, gradations of color, contrasts in texture, and compositional arrangement of forms he envisioned. Olmsted, who saw botanical display as a

perversion of the principles of park making, which he felt should always be directed toward creating broad stretches of naturalistic scenery, ironically found himself advocating a more diverse botanical palette than that of the professional botanist.

In 500-acre Franklin Park, considered by Olmsted to be the principal jewel, where the natural terrain of West Roxbury gave him the opportunity to create a broad rolling meadow and a grade-separated circulation system that allowed pedestrians to approach it through handsome rustic arches, he achieved a good approximation of his scenic park ideal (figs. 9.50, 9.51). Now, in 1884, with Vaux no longer at his side, he built these of natural stone boulders instead of the dressed and carved stone that made his former partner's arches in Central Park and Prospect Park works of ornamental architecture. Here the meadow was also conceived as a baseball field, with boulders for bleachers and a rustic changing area nearby. This is an early instance of sports permitted on an Olmsted park meadow, a harbinger of the future transformation by others in much less sensitive design terms of many existing Olmsted lawns and meadows into spaces for organized recreation.

OLMSTED, RICHARDSON, AND ELIOT

While Olmsted still nominally held the title of consulting landscape architect to the Parks Department, he was thoroughly disgusted by New York's political milieu, so in 1881, he transferred his office and home to Brookline, Massachusetts. His friend and neighbor there was the noted architect Henry Hobson Richardson (1838–1886), and during the five years before Richardson's death, the two had several opportunities for intensely sympathetic collaboration, in which Richardson's neo-Romanesque yet original style encouraged Olmsted's increasing boldness in the use of boulders and rough fieldstone. Olmsted still harbored a penchant for trailing vines and found the combination of these and massive rustic stone walls pleasing.

9.53. East Terrace, Moraine Farm, Beverly, Massachusetts, estate of John C. Phillips, designed by Frederick Law Olmsted. c. 1880

At Moraine Farm, the estate of John C. Phillips in Beverly, Massachusetts, on the banks of Wenham Great Pond, he had the opportunity to design a 275-acre American version of a *ferme ornée* where a beautiful hayfield with clumps of deciduous and evergreen trees at the edges performed the same aesthetic function as the Long Meadow in Prospect Park (fig. 9.52). Here, on the east side of the house designed by the Bostonian architects Peabody and Stearns and overlooking the pond, he built a long sinuous terrace banked by a retaining wall of natural boulders, beneath which masses of laurel and rhododendron cascade down to the edge of the water (fig. 9.53).

Olmsted was now the undisputed leader in the profession of landscape architecture in America. His services were heavily in demand, and he found himself traveling back and forth across the country by train to serve a wide clientele, designing park systems for Rochester, New York, and Louisville, Kentucky. In 1879, he assisted in preparing the report that led in 1885 to the scenic preservation of Niagara and of the abundant botanical diversity of Goat Island between the American and Canadian Falls. He and Vaux teamed up again to develop an environmentally sensitive plan that would allow visitors to fully appreciate this scenic wonder without the distraction of tawdry commercial development.

With his young partner, Charles Eliot, Olmsted was able to extend the concept of Boston's municipal park system to a broad metropolitan scale. Eliot, the son of the president of Harvard, was instrumental in forming the Trustees of Public Reservations (now known as the Trustees of Reservations), an early example of a conservation organization dedicated to preserving wilderness areas in New England. In addition to small publicly accessible properties held by the Trustees, Eliot envisioned large reservations in the public domain, for which a metropolitan commission was needed. He worked tirelessly with Sylvester Baxter, a writer turned regional planner, to develop political consensus among the communities within and

the jurisdictions outside the boundaries of the municipality of Boston for a Metropolitan District to acquire and improve parkland within a 10-mile (16.1-kilometer) radius of the city. Their survey of the area took in the islands in the harbor, beaches, forests, three river basins, several hills, five ponds, and other sites they found desirable as nature preserves or suitable for public recreation.

The Board of Metropolitan Park Commissioners appointed under the 1892 act was created to a large degree as a result of their work. This Board read the Eliot-Baxter report and plan, which was published the following year. In it, Baxter outlined their recommendations for restoring tree cover, guiding real-estate development, reducing water pollution, making transportation accessible, and designing small local community playgrounds. Eliot's report, with accompanying maps and diagrams, summarized the area's physical and historical geography and described the opportunities awaiting the commission's subsequent actions in the well-watered and hilly glaciated terrain of metropolitan Boston. Thus, as he neared the end of his active professional career, Olmsted was able to rejoice in the success of his young protégé in carrying forward his own peculiarly American mission of promoting civilization through landscape preservation. Tragically, Eliot's life was cut short by death only four years later. In addition, there were new forces at work in American society, seeking to promote civilization in more conspicuous ways.

OLMSTED IN A NEOCLASSICAL CONTEXT

The movement to shape cities according to the monumental model provided by Paris and other European capitals emerged from the generation of architects after Vaux, who trained abroad in a variety of Neoclassical styles derived from the French Renaissance and its Italian models. These younger men converted some of the nation's growing industrial wealth into mansions for the wealthy and civic grandeur for the public at large. Among these was Richard Morris Hunt (1828–1895), the first American of renown to design in the style called Beaux-Arts after the École des Beaux-Arts in Paris where a number of aspiring architects from the United States went to study in the second half of the nineteenth century. Olmsted and Vaux were not happy when a newly formed Committee on Statuary, Fountains and Architectural Structures invited Hunt to propose alterations to the Arsenal in Central Park in 1860; the Civil War caused these plans to be shelved for the duration. More upsetting was Hunt's proposal, drawn up at the committee's request, for a series of monumental Neoclassical gateways at the park's four southern entrances. Vaux's

9.54. U.S. Capitol, Terrace on the west front, designed by Frederick Law Olmsted. 1873

opposition persuaded the park commissioners not to construct these monumental entrances.

Olmsted felt that statuary in the park should be confined to the Mall and Bethesda Terrace, and he expressed his fear of other monumental Beaux-Arts architectural encroachments by Hunt on the park's pastoral landscape. Nevertheless, Olmsted was able to work within the context of a Neoclassical design vocabulary when necessary. In 1873, he accepted the commission of the Senate Committee on Buildings and Grounds to design the 46 acres around the United States Capitol in Washington, D.C. In this case, it was obviously necessary to ignore his precept of fitting buildings inconspicuously into the landscape, as the chief purpose of the project was to heighten the monumentality and dignity of the nation's most important public building. In addition to banning Gardenesque effects, which he considered fussy distractions from this principal object, he built the massive terrace that forms a podium along the Capitol's north, south, and west sides and unifies the building with its surroundings (fig. 9.54).

In the two final commissions of his career, Olmsted worked directly with Beaux-Arts architects. In 1888, twenty-five-year-old George Washington Vanderbilt commissioned him to design the grounds at Biltmore, his estate near Asheville, North Carolina. Here Hunt was the architect of a palatial mansion resembling a French Renaissance *château*. Olmsted's plan encompassed 2,000 acres of mountainous landscape. Inasmuch as the site did not lend itself to becoming a park in the pastoral and Picturesque tradition, Olmsted recommended that Vanderbilt should devote most of it to scientific forestry. The millionaire eventually increased his holdings to 120,000 acres and hired America's first professional forester, Gifford

Pinchot, who later became the founding head of the United States Forest Service. Olmsted also convinced Vanderbilt to create an arboretum.

At Biltmore, Olmsted's particular genius as a landscape designer expressed itself in the estate's road system: a 3-mile (4.8-kilometer) approach road, the borders of which he enhanced with "varied forms of vegetation . . . all consistent with the sensation of passing through the remote depths of a natural forest."[40] Here, as in Central Park and elsewhere, he wanted to plant lush masses of many species of rhododendron and a rich variety of other woodland shrubs in order to create the "sense of the superabundant creative power, infinite resource, and liberality of Nature"[41] that tropical scenery had always evoked in him. The long approach road at last brings the visitor, who has had no anticipatory view of what lies ahead, to a rectangular grassy esplanade, beyond which Hunt's immense *château* of Indiana limestone looms suddenly into view. At Moraine Farm, the view of the lake was not revealed until one passed through the house onto the terrace overlooking it; so, too, at Biltmore, Olmsted withheld the panoramic scenery of the Great Smokies with Mount Pisgah in the distance until one had passed through the house onto the terrace there. Thus, although more architecturally elaborate than the rustic terrace built earlier in Massachusetts, the terrace at Biltmore serves the same purpose as a viewing platform for a heretofore concealed spectacle of nature at its most glorious.

At the same time that he worked at Biltmore, Olmsted became a member of the design team, headed by the architect Daniel H. Burnham, that was planning the World's Columbian Exposition of 1893 for Chicago. This World's Fair, like the expositions organized first in England and then in Paris in the second half of the nineteenth century, was intended as an international showcase of the products of industry. But unlike the earlier fairs, which had produced technologically innovative structures—notably the Crystal Palace and the Eiffel Tower—Burnham and his Beaux-Arts-trained colleagues wished to put the architectural stamp of Neoclassical grandeur, rather than of modernity, upon this one. Olmsted was consulted on site selection and, with the assistance of his talented young protégé and partner Henry Sargent Codman, chose the still-unimproved site of Jackson Park. This gave him an opportunity to revisit the 1871 design he had prepared in partnership with Vaux. Now, however, it was necessary to adopt a much more pronounced orientation toward "gregarious" recreation, with the further understanding that, as at the United States Capitol, the grounds would showcase the buildings. The large lagoon he had planned twenty years earlier was still possible and desirable if

9.55. Central Basin (Court of Honor), World's Columbian Exposition, Chicago, designed by Frederick Law Olmsted in collaboration with Daniel Burnham. 1893

Below: 9.56. Lagoon and Island, World's Columbian Exposition, Chicago, designed by Frederick Law Olmsted. 1893

it were treated as a series of waterbodies, some of which were to be given a geometric architectural treatment to complement the buildings. With their uniform cornice lines and white color, the largest of these made an impressive grouping around Olmsted's most conspicuous water feature, a long central basin with a canal leading to other parts of the lagoon system, each of which served as a watery foreground for another composition of fair buildings (fig. 9.55).

Still, Olmsted found an opportunity to provide relief from the noisy crowds and architectural grandiloquence of the fair in the wooded island in the center of the lagoon. There he tried within the short growing period before opening day to create an air of poetic mystery and the appearance of a natural bayou by establishing a rich aquatic vegetation and dense shoreline growth (fig. 9.56). Here, fair visitors could find a ramble of sinuous paths and the illusion of nature in the midst of the hubbub and excitement of the fair. Olmsted wished to keep the island free of structures, protesting when a music hall was contemplated in that location. Praising the achievement of the Chicago World's Fair as the grounds were being completed, the writer on architecture, gardens, and landscape design, Mariana Griswold Van Rensselaer, told future visitors, "You will already know that much of the ground immediately beneath you was not even solid, ugly prairie, but treacherous marsh. And looking over this ground now—here with its straight, stately, wide canals and architectonic terraces, and there with its irregularly-shaped lagoons and islands—you will understand how a great artist like

Mr. Olmsted can absolutely create in a way which almost equals Nature's own."[42]

Olmsted, overworked and ailing, was now called upon to add his influential voice to those opposing a speedway in Central Park, one of many proposed encroachments over the years. A six-month holiday abroad with his daughter and son for the purpose of regaining his health gave him the opportunity to revisit with renewed delight the English countryside he had first admired as a young man. At the same time, he deplored the contemporary Victorian obsession with horticulture. As we shall read in Chapter Eleven, a controversy was raging between Sir Reginald Blomfield, author of *The Formal Garden in England* and proponent of a return to geometrical

9.57. Boathouse, Prospect Park, Brooklyn, New York, designed by Stanford White and Frank J. Helmle. 1905

planning principles, and William Robinson, the ardent foe of topiary and ornamental floral bedding-out and prolific author of *The English Flower Garden, The Wild Garden,* and other books and articles championing herbaceous borders artfully composed of casually intermingled perennial plants. Although the trailing vines recommended by Robinson exactly suited Olmsted's taste and he found *The Wild Garden* useful in selecting plants for such places as the Ramble in Central Park, he was now more convinced than ever that he had been right to take what was useful from the writings of Gilpin and Price and to have developed an American landscape style emphasizing broad, overarching scenic themes. He even made a pilgrimage to the church at Boldre where Gilpin had been vicar, and he traveled along the route beside the river Wye that Gilpin had described in one of his books. Visiting Paris, where he examined the grounds of the exposition of 1889, he hoped that in Chicago the "petty effects and frippery" of ornamental floral display would be avoided. He admired, however, the "fitness for their purposes" of the buildings left in the wake of the Paris fair and expressed reservation about those of the White City, as people called the collection of temporary buildings made of staff—plaster and fiber laid over timber forms—then rising on the shores of Lake Michigan. He hoped that the Chicago buildings were "not going to look too assuming of architectural stateliness and to be overloaded with sculptural and other efforts for grandeur and grandiloquent pomp."[43]

But for now, thanks to the influence of the Chicago World's Fair, the field belonged to Daniel Burnham and other Beaux-Arts practitioners. The achievements of Calvert Vaux were overshadowed by these architects, and the former partners' belief in the overriding therapeutic and spiritual values of naturalistic landscapes in an urban setting was denied by the Gilded Age's desire for monumental grandeur. While he still held the position of landscape architect to the board in charge of New York City parks, Vaux had protested against the design of a speedway planned now for the edge of the Harlem River, but his objections were high-handedly brushed aside, and he died under mysterious circumstances in 1895. Olmsted fell victim to dementia, retired from public life, and was confined during the five years preceding his death in 1903 in the McLean Hospital at Waverly, Massachusetts, where he had designed the grounds. But before his intellectual powers were eclipsed, he had seen clearly that the Beaux-Arts architects' appetite for monumentality was antithetical to the older ideal of a republican America that he and Vaux had tried to embody in their parks.

In 1894, Stanford White (1853–1906), the most fashionable Beaux Arts architect in the generation after Hunt, was approached to build a tennis house in Prospect Park. It was not constructed until 1909 by his former associate, Frank J. Helmle (1868–1939), also the architect in 1905 of the Prospect Park Boathouse (fig. 9.57). Designed after the Library of St. Mark in Venice by Jacopo d'Antonio Tatti, called Sansovino (1486–1570), the Boathouse, though handsome in its own right like the Tennis House, is alien to the spirit of the park's rustic and rural-seeming landscape. Further aggrandizing what was intended to be a pastoral refuge from city life, the firm of McKim, Mead and White carried out in Prospect Park what Hunt had failed to do in Central Park. Here they erected three monumental Neoclassical entrances (fig. 9.58). Not unreasonably, Olmsted felt that White and his Beaux Arts colleagues were "trying to establish the rule of motives that are at war with those that ruled in the original laying out of Brooklyn Park."[44] All the same, instructed by France, American tastemakers of the time were committed to the values of opulence expressed by the later term denoting the period as the Gilded Age, and the emulation of Europen urban grandeur was well established as a dominant motive underlying civic beautification. Instructed by France in another regard as well, they were also embarked on a course of Industrial Age urban modernity.

9.58. The Soldiers' and Sailors' Memorial Arch, Grand Army Plaza, Brooklyn, New York, designed by John H. Duncan, architect, with architectural embellishment by McKim, Mead and White and sculpture by Frederick MacMonnies, Thomas Eakins, and William O'Donovan. 1889–1901

Notes for Chapter Nine

1. The term *ecological* as used to describe the relationship between organisms and their respective environments was coined in 1866 by Ernst Haeckel, a German zoologist, in *Generelle Morphologie der Organismen*. See David Lowenthal, *George Perkins Marsh: Prophet of Conservation* (Seattle: University of Washington Press, 2000), ch. 13, p. 283, and footnote 41.

2. I am indebted to Melanie Louise Simo for her good analysis of Loudon's career and influence. See Melanie Simo, *Loudon and the Landscape: From Country Seat to Metropolis* (New Haven: Yale University Press, 1988).

3. Bernard de Jussieu (1699–1777) and his nephew Antoine-Laurent de Jussieu (1748–1836), the principal competitors of Linnaeus, based their system of plant classification on the physical forms of plants rather than on their reproductive structures.

4. *Gardener's Magazine,* vol. XVI (1840), p. 620. As discussed in Chapter Thirteen, Christopher Tunnard, champion of the modern garden, developed a similar theory whereby elements were to be composed asymmetrically along an invisible axis so as to achieve "occult balance." See Christopher Tunnard, *Gardens in the Modern Landscape* (London: The Architectural Press, 1938), p.92.

5. See Hazel Conway, *People's Parks: The Design and Development of Victorian Parks in Britain* (Cambridge: Cambridge University Press, 1991), p. 229. I am indebted to this excellent source for this and much other valuable information regarding the early public parks movement in Great Britain.

6. Ibid., p. 48.

7. David Schuyler, *Apostle of Taste: Andrew Jackson Downing 1815–1852* (Baltimore: The Johns Hopkins Press, 1996). I am indebted to this historian's intimate knowledge of nineteenth-century landscape design and designers in the following discussion of Downing and the development of the "middle landscape," the extension of the metropolis into rural areas with the creation of the first suburbs, and a new architectural vocabulary of suburban villa design. See also Judith K. Major, *To Live in the New World: A. J. Downing and American Landscape Gardening* (Cambridge, Mass.: The MIT Press, 1997) for a good discussion of how Downing adapted contemporary English design principles and horticultural practices to the conditions of American society and the character of its natural landscape in the first half of the nineteenth century.

8. Andrew Jackson Downing, *A Treatise on the Theory and Practice of Landscape Gardening,* 6th ed. (New York: A. O. Moore & Co., 1859), p. 25.

9. *Treatise on the Theory and Practice of Landscape Gardening,* p. 65.

10. Ibid., p. 59.

11. Ibid., p. 60.

12. Ibid., p. 120.

13. *Rural Essays* (New York: Levitt and Allen, 1856), pp. 147–53 *passim.*

14. As quoted in Schuyler, *Apostle of Taste,* p. 192.

15. As the garden historian John Dixon Hunt points out, John Claudius Loudon was the first to apply the term *landscape architecture* to the work of landscape designers. In 1840, Loudon republished Repton's *Observations on the Theory and Practice of Landscape Gardening* (1803) under the title *The Landscape Gardening and Landscape Architecture of the Late Humphrey Repton.* See Hunt, *Greater Perfections* (Philadelphia: University of Pennsylvania Press, 1999), p. 217. But neither Repton nor Loudon after him seems to have employed the term in presenting themselves to clients. Repton had christened himself "Landscape Gardener" upon entering professional practice, and Loudon considered himself to be primarily an agronomist, botanist, horticulturalist, and author. Olmsted and Vaux wished to distinguish between their kind of work — which often involved extensive engineering and significant reformation of the land to produce a naturalistic effect akin to that of rural scenery — and Loudon's kind of ornamental horticulture and that of Repton late in his career when he deemed appropriate a Gardenesque treatment in areas adjacent to the house. Nevertheless, the notion that they were *artists*, not simply engineers or administrators, was important to them. In discussing the use of the title with Olmsted, who apparently objected to it as being too vague, Vaux said as they were about to reenter partnership in 1865, "I have always liked the title Landscape Architect because — the specialty was fairly embodied. A title that could as easily be transferred to an inartistic public work is not as satisfactory. . . . The term Landscape Architect does not suit you, well I am sorry for it. I think it is *the* title. We want to set art ahead and make it *command* its position, administration, management, funds, commission, popularity and everything else — then we have a tangible something to stand on." (See Charles C. McLaughlin *et al. The Papers of Frederick Law Olmsted,* vol. V, pp.

363, 373–74.) The earliest instance of their use of *landscape architect* as a professional title came in 1860 when they were so described in their appointment to advise on laying out streets in northern Manhattan. (See *The Papers of Frederick Law Olmsted,* vol. III, p. 267, note 1.) Olmsted deferred to Vaux's preference for the term when they reestablished their partnership in 1865 as Olmsted, Vaux, & Company, Landscape Architects. At this time, they were reappointed by the Executive Committee of Central Park to serve as "Landscape Architects to the Board."

16. For the following discussion of landscapes of memory, those containing monuments and memorial grave sites, and of the movement from burying ground to rural cemetery I am particularly indebted to Blanche Linden-Ward, *Silent City on a Hill: Landscapes of Memory and Boston's Mount Auburn Cemetery* (Columbus: Ohio State University Press, 1989).

17. Circular letter, July 1823, as quoted in Linden-Ward, *Silent City on a Hill,* p. 124.

18. The developer of the Quincy granite quarries, Gridley Bryant, was instrumental in building the first railway in America in 1827 in order to transport the blocks of stone to the shore for transport to the monument site in Charlestown near Boston

19. William Wordsworth, "Essay upon Epitaphs." *Friend 25* (Feb. 1810): 408. Reprinted in *The Excursion: A Poem* (New York: C. S. Francis, 1850). Quoted in Linden-Ward, *Silent City on a Hill,* p. 61.

20. Dearborn, who had no further direct involvement at Mount Auburn, went on to help found and design in 1846 another rural burial ground in the Boston area, the Forest Hills Cemetery in Roxbury.

21. James Smillie, drawings, and Cornelia W. Walter, description, *Mount Auburn* (New York: R. Martin, 1851), p. 18.

22. Andrew Jackson Downing, "Public Cemeteries and Public Gardens" (July 1848) in *Rural Essays,* p. 157.

23. When Olmsted visited England for the second time in 1859, he corresponded with William Jackson Hooker (1785–1865), botanist and director of the Royal Botanical Gardens at Kew, deploring how "the old simple formal fashion of gardening . . . [and] the peculiar landscape beauty of old English places . . . is sacrificed to botanic beauty and variety and the interest of frequent contrasts & surprises." (Letter, c. November 29, 1859, in *The Papers of Frederick Law Olmsted,* vol. III, ed.) Charles C. McLaughlin, Charles E. Beveridge and David Schuyler (Baltimore: The Johns Hopkins University Press, 1983). In the essay "The Spoils of the Park," written in February, 1882, after he had left New York, Olmsted expressed in even stronger terms his aversion to the Gardenesque: "During the last twenty years Europe has been swept by a mania for sacrificing natural scenery to coarse manu-

factures of brilliant and gaudy decoration under the name of specimen gardening; bedding, carpet, embroider, and ribbon gardening, or other terms suitable to the housefurnishing and millinery trades. It was a far madder contagion than the tulip-mania, or the morus-multicaulis fever of our youth." In *Forty Years of Landscape Architecture: Being the Professional Papers of Frederick Law Olmsted, Senior,* ed. Frederick Law Olmsted, Jr., and Theodora Kimball (1922; reissued 1970, Bronx, New York: Benjamin Blom, Inc.), p. 143.

24. Frederick Law Olmsted, *Walks and Talks of an American Farmer in England* (New York: George P. Putnam, 1852), p. 87. As an Anglo-American experiencing a sense almost of homecoming, Olmsted is rhapsodic about his first encounter with the English landscape. He continues, with details of sensory appreciation, describing a scene that might have been a painting by Constable: "We stood dumb-stricken by its loveliness, as, from the bleak April and bare boughs we had left at home, broke upon us that English May—sunny, leafy, blooming May—in an English lane; with hedges, English hedges, hawthorn hedges, all in blossom; homely old farm-houses, quaint stables, and haystacks; the old church spire over the distant trees; the mild sun beaming through the watery atmosphere, and all so quiet—the only sounds the hum of bees and the crisp grass-tearing of a silken-skinned, real (unimported) Herford cow over the hedge."

25. Ibid., p. 79.

26. Frederick Law Olmsted and Calvert Vaux, *Description of a Plan for the Improvement of the Central Park: "Greensward"* in *Landscape into Cityscape: Frederick Law Olmsted's Plans for a Greater New York City,* ed. Albert Fein (Ithaca, New York: Cornell University Press, 1967), p. 71.

27. According to Scripture, "Now there is at Jerusalem by the sheep market a pool, which is called in the Hebrew tongue Bethesda, having five porches. In these lay a great multitude of impotent folk of blind, halt, withered, waiting for the moving of the water. For an angel went down at a certain season into the pool, and troubled the water: whosoever then first after the troubling of the water stepped in was made whole of whatsoever disease he had." John 5:2–4, *The Holy Bible,* Authorized (King James) Version.

28. Letter from Calvert Vaux to Frederick Law Olmsted, May 12, 1865, in *The Papers of Frederick Law Olmsted,* vol. V, ed. Charles C. McLaughlin, Victoria Post Ranney (Baltimore: The Johns Hopkins Press, 1990), p. 364.

29. Letter from Frederick Law Olmsted to Calvert Vaux, June 8, 1865, in *The Papers of Frederick Law Olmsted,* vol. V, p. 390.

30. "Report of the Landscape Architects and Superintendents" (January 1870), *The*

Papers of Frederick Law Olmsted: vol. VI, ed. Charles C. McLaughlin, David Schuyler and Jane Turner Censer, p. 357.

31. For a detailed description of the sensory experience of entering the Long Meadow through the Endale Arch, see Tony Hiss, *The Experience of Place* (New York: Alfred A. Knopf, 1990), pp. 28–36.

32. Frederick Law Olmsted and Calvert Vaux, "Report of the Landscape Architects and Superintendents to the President of the Board of Commissioners of Prospect Park, Brooklyn (1868)" in Fein, *Landscape into Cityscape,* p. 153.

33. Ibid., p. 151.

34. Ibid., p. 158.

35. Ibid., p. 155.

36. Quoted without citation in Victoria Post Ranney, "Olmsted in Chicago" (Chicago: The Open Lands Project, 1972), p. 27.

37. The term *plaisance* was used by Olmsted to denote a landscape with paths and grassy areas defined by shrub-planted borders, a part of a park intended for picnicking and strolling during daylight hours but one that, because of security issues posed by its dense plantings, was fenced and closed at night. See *Frederick Law Olmsted Papers, Supplementary Series,* vol. 1, p. 218.

38. Ibid., p. 28

39. Cynthia Zaitzevsky is the author of the definitive study of Olmsted's creation of the Boston park system. See Cynthia Zaitzevsky, *Frederick Law Olmsted and the Boston Park System* (Cambridge, Mass.: The Belknap Press of Harvard University Press, 1982).

40. Frederick Law Olmsted to George W. Vanderbilt, July 12, 1889, as quoted in Charles E. Beveridge and Paul Rocheleau, *Frederick Law Olmsted: Designing the American Landscape* (New York: Rizzoli, 1995), p. 226.

41. Letter to Ignaz Anton Pilat (1820–1870), head gardener of Central Park, September 26, 1863, in McLaughlin *et al. The Papers of Frederick Law Olmsted,* vol. V, p. 85.

42. Mariana Griswold Van Rensselaer, "The Artistic Triumph of the Fair-Builders" in *Accents as Well as Broad Effects: Writings on Architecture, Landscape, and the Environment, 1876–1925,* ed. David Gebhard (Berkeley: University of California Press, 1996), p. 71.

43. According to Charles E. Beveridge, editor of Olmsted's papers, this quotation comes from a "letter with no salutation or date, but internal evidence indicates that Olmsted wrote it to his partners John Charles Olmsted and Henry Sargent Codman in April of 1892." Letter to the author, January 17, 2000.

44. Letter from Frederick Law Olmsted to William A. Stiles, March 10, 1895. Citation courtesy of Charles E. Beveridge, letter to the author, January 17, 2000.

CHAPTER TEN

INDUSTRIAL AGE CIVILIZATION: BIRTH OF THE MODERN CITY, BEAUX-ARTS AMERICA, AND NATIONAL PARKS

The force that has driven modernism and postmodernism as much as the cultural currents and countercurrents running through them—the force that has informed all philosophy, politics, economics, sociology, and art since the last half of the nineteenth century—is machine technology.[1] It has injected into human culture unprecedented elements of power and speed, which have greatly accelerated the pace of change as well as the pace of life. Machine technology has offered innumerable benefits, and it has also focused attention on the processes of production rather than on its ends.

In examining designed landscapes of the past 150 years, we must continually reckon with their technological infrastructures and the extent to which they are informed by a machine-age mentality. This is true even when they were created to express opposition to the Industrial Age. Machine technology and human attitudes toward the machine—whether celebratory, ambivalent, or condemnatory—provide an ineluctable cultural context that has powerfully shaped landscape design in modern times.

The nineteenth century was, generally speaking, an optimistic age. It is true that the enormous stresses associated with accelerating scientific discovery, which increasingly undermined religious conviction, and even faith, in the purpose of the rationalist scientific enterprise itself, created a sense of unease. Emerson may have darkly intuited the consequences of runaway technology when he complained that "things are in the saddle and ride mankind," but his transcendentalist philosophy nevertheless envisioned nature as a positive, spiritually nourishing force, and he shared with other early witnesses to the Industrial Age the sanguine hope that modernity would prove beneficial to humankind.

In our discussion of Goethe's important insights into the dynamics of Romantic culture in the eighteenth century, we saw his attempt to reconcile its tenets with those of classicism as well as his conviction, caustically expressed by Mephistopheles, that pantheistic worship of nature and spiritual seduction by its idyllic charms deflected human potential from its full expression. In *Faust: Part II,* written between 1825 and 1831, Goethe sensed the new sources of physical and human energy that were being released by the Industrial Revolution. Ties with history, both personal and societal, had to be severed if *progress*—the watchword of industrial capitalism—was to occur. Faust, having destroyed his love, Gretchen, in Part I because he could no longer inhabit the traditional society she represents, is offered in Part II an intoxicant more potent than sex or even love: power. This is not the power of kings, but rather the power of industrial progress. It implies the right to challenge nature and alter culture for socially beneficial ends.

In Part II, Faust assumes the role of Nietzsche's Superman, becoming a developer capable of confronting mighty natural forces and traditional folkways and settlement patterns in the act of building and destroying. His vision is that of the engineer; he will harness capital and labor for a giant coastal reclamation project, erecting dams and digging canals, "To hold the lordly ocean from the shore / To set the watery waste new boundary lines," in order to create a dynamic new economy for the ultimate benefit of humankind. As in the American myth of Paul Bunyan, the intrepid pioneers who assist Faust in this mighty work are emigrants from Gretchen's Old World of familiar and constrained village life. In the process of their labor, they are enlarged; they become bold actors in the heroic drama of conquering and subduing nature.

Goethe foresaw the Industrial Age and the social freedom it would engender, but he also saw the tragic implications of its often inhuman disregard of people's lives. There was a price to be paid for economic efficiency in terms of physical and emotional dislocation. Not only did human life become less laborious with the advent of industrialization, it also became more impersonal. The rural round gave way to urbanism and a culture based on new concepts of time and space. People were no longer tied to the pastoral rhythms of the seasons or boundaries of daily movement circumscribed by wind-filled sails, the stamina of horses, and human walking distances. Movement is one of the imperatives of power. Machine-facilitated personal mobility and speed are among modernism's premier values. There is a hurried character to modern times that distinguishes them from any other age.

Rapid change is another hallmark of modernity. Faust can no longer go back to the wellspring of childhood but is doomed to restless forward motion, forever set upon the course of modernity with its unending cycles of change in which only novelty and invention hold meaning. The paradox of power is that everything is provisional, in flux; progress depends upon the willing and unsentimental sacrifice of what has gone before, for each new development will inevitably be discredited.

Cities, especially, became increasingly machinelike in appearance, and the nature of everyday life was irreversibly altered as easily purchased, mass-produced commodities and new building technologies made it possible to discard, replace, and improve the old or obsolete. No longer was the built environment the result of the muscular labor of humans and animals, and no longer were the articles of daily life—pots and pans, tools and utensils, carriages and wagons, clothing and furniture—crafted by hand. More people now lived in structures erected with the aid of machinery and consisting of many machine-made parts, cooked with factory-built appliances, ate their meals on factory wares, dressed in industrially produced clothing, and purchased inexpensive mass-produced clocks to help them fit their daily routine to industrial work hours and transportation schedules. A new temporal commodity, leisure, one of the outcomes of the regimented industrial work week, made possible new forms of recreation with important consequences for landscape design.

To accommodate large-scale population growth in the second half of the nineteenth century, major cities—notably, Paris, London, and Vienna—began to alter urban form through industrial technology, creating new transportation arteries to accelerate vehicular movement and employing new kinds of materials and engineering solutions to increase building scale and extend the range of construction possibilities. Old royal parks were opened to the public, and new people's parks were created as recreational leisure became for middle and working classes alike an antidote to machine-age urban stress and as increased leisure became one of the fruits of mechanization. Because military tactics now rendered such urban defenses completely obsolete, ancient walls continued to be torn down and the land they had occupied turned into wide boulevards. Thus ungirdled, the growing city also became more porous; dense old neighborhoods were now penetrated by the straight new thoroughfares designed to facilitate movement and commerce.

The changes revealed different classes of people to one another as enigmatic, but interesting, strangers. The curious tried to imagine these others' lives. Baudelaire, the poet supremely aware of Paris in transition, writes of the "ant-seething city, city full of dreams," affirming a new and terrible kind of beauty found "in sinuous folds of cities old and grim, where all things, even horror, turn to grace" as he observed the perplexed valor of the denizens of Old

Paris in the face of so much tremendous change. The epitome of the *flâneur,* he wrote poems about crones and coquettes, the soul-penetrating glances of strangers, the lives hitherto hidden from view and now exposed, all simultaneously occurring as rich and poor moved and mingled anonymously in the new urban milieu. There was something both frightening and thrilling in the possibility of these fleeting encounters.

Cosmopolitan urbanism implied a rejection of tradition. Like Faust, one was prepared to sacrifice past attachments and even moral scruples for technique, expediency, and efficiency as well as for intellectual adventure, sensory experience, and artistic self-expression. Personal experience came to be seen as a form of wealth, encouraging people to push to the limits of their abilities, energy, capital resources, and available time as they attempted to turn the material world to increasing advantage. Thus had the forces of Romanticism, nurtured by Rousseau's philosophy, proclaimed new moral autonomy for the individual.

The philosopher Immanuel Kant (1724–1804), though certainly no Romantic of the *Sturm und Drang* school, had above his desk a picture of Rousseau. Kant believed passionately in the unfettered human will and the individual's right to choose a personal course of moral action. He was therefore sympathetic to the tenets of the American and French Revolutions—at least before the Reign of Terror repressively stifled diversity of political opinion in France—because these great public manifestations of Romanticism vested authority not in a monarch, however benevolent, but in the people. Human beings, in Kant's view, were not to be considered as passive creatures in a world where everything was pre-ordained by God, natural science, and inherited systems of government. Kant took the position that the human mind bestows upon the universe a sense of order. This was quite different from the attitude of earlier philosophers such as Descartes or Aristotle, who thought of the mind as an instrument for discerning the established order of the universe by empirical means. The powerful intellectual and moral freedom granted individuals by Kantian philosophy was paralleled by the rising tide of democratization among nation-states and the attempt to create human environments through political processes involving governmental machinery designed for collective decision making.

In this light we may observe how, beginning in the eighteenth century and accelerating with the French Revolution, cities became increasingly the domain of the people, their form no longer dictated by royal policy and aristocratic privilege even when, as in the case of Second Empire Paris, their transformation was accomplished by imperial fiat and state authority. As old cities were being torn apart and their social contents rendered visible, there arose a new political awareness, which was nourished by broad readership of daily newspapers sold on the street. The streets that were designed as a deterrent to revolutionary mobs and as parade routes where marching bands elicited emotions of patriotic pride were also upon occasion the arenas of violent social protest. Ordinarily, however, they served as the lively theater of daily life as increasing numbers of people perambulated and an ever-growing segment of society was able to purchase the growing quantities of factory-produced merchandise appearing in shop windows.

Paris, the first avowedly modern city, not only stimulated a great surge of strolling in its new boulevards but also provided parks as special places where leisure could be spent. In the works of the Impressionists when the city is their subject we may observe the pleased wonder with which Parisians embraced the transformations that were occurring (fig. 10.1). Intimate emotions were no longer veiled from view; in the industrial city personal and public life had become fused into one. The constant movement in the streets, with the opportunities for people-watching and serendipitous sociability thus provided, and the display of commodities and luxury goods in sidewalk stalls and behind plate glass windows made them intensely interesting. Suddenly all was in motion, and all had become a source of spectacle and excitement. Everything, even—or perhaps especially—oneself, was on display.

10.1. Jean Béraud, *Outside the Vaudeville Theater, Paris*. c. 1885. Private collection. Here the raised sidewalk is the domain of the boulevardier, the *flâneur*, the shopper, and the theater goer. New features of the Paris urban scene are the columnar kiosks for posters advertising cultural attractions, the numerous street and building lights, and the plate-glass windows.

The notion of the city as an object of formal presentation and symbolical representation, an architectural artifact enjoying the prestige formerly accorded the court, an urban organism to be conceptualized in its entirety and ornamented proudly was an eighteenth-century phenomenon. The St. Petersburg of Peter the Great and Washington, D.C., the federal capital Pierre L'Enfant planned for the new United States, were monumental cities built according to these intentions (see figs. 6.44, 6.54). The intentions of founders, however, are often disregarded by subsequent generations and most cities in any case are conceived pragmatically rather than grandly, as serviceable places for conducting business and meeting the needs of daily life. Nevertheless, prosperity breeds philanthropy, civic pride, and the desire to emulate what is deemed best. Such was the case in Gilded Age America, the period following the Civil War when most cities built their major cultural institutions and parks. The "White City" that rose on the banks of Lake Michigan in 1893 set the course of architecture and urban planning firmly in the direction of monumental grandeur. Like Haussmann's Paris, which covered its new Industrial Age infrastructure with a neoclassical architectural veneer, the American city with which it was contemporary now sought to cloak itself with monumental dignity. Not surprisingly, the model for this effort was Paris itself. Architects and landscape architects trained at the École des Beaux-Arts carried forward the tenets of the City Beautiful Movement, a two-decade campaign to aggrandize American cities with heroic sculpture, noble architecture, spacious boulevards, and handsome public spaces. Without the backing of a monarchical regime like that of Napoleon III or a powerful public servant such as Haussmann to finance and forcefully administer a large array of coordinated capital construction projects, most City Beautiful plans were only fragmentarily realized. In Washington, D.C., which enjoyed special status as

the nation's capital, however, a congressional commission was formed to oversee a comprehensive plan, resulting in the clearance of obstructions from the Mall and its realignment and extension, the construction of the Lincoln and Jefferson Memorials, and the building, after much debate, of a scenic parkway for motorists in the Rock Creek valley.

Machine mobility, which first made cities such as Paris tourist meccas, created new accessibility to sparsely tenanted wild landscapes as well. In America, where transcendentalism had been an important philosophy in the nineteenth century, the concept of the nation as an Arcadia persisted even as it continued to be mechanically divided according to the Jeffersonian grid. This ideal was promoted by the United States Congress when, beginning in 1872, it created national parks in areas where there was spectacular natural scenery. These were soon equated in the eyes of many Americans with the cathedrals and other important historic monuments of Europe as icons of national identity. First railroads and later interstate highways brought vacationers in increasing numbers to these natural sites, now legislatively certified as sacrosanct. Railroad interests were, in fact, deeply and profitably involved in promoting the creation of national parks. Without Industrial Age modes of transportation as a stimulus to mass tourism, there would have been little reason to create the parks in the first place. If the scenic lands encompassed by the parks had remained inaccessible, there would have been no need to protect them from industrial or commercial exploitation, and without means of transportation, their acquisition with tax dollars could not have been justified by a corresponding benefit to the citizenry of the United States. During the first half of the twentieth century, when driving for pleasure was perceived as an important form of recreation, additional public dollars were spent on the creation of parkways and state park systems that permitted urban dwellers to spend a day in the country and enjoy the trip as well.

To understand how the revolution in transportation made the landscape at large accessible and how the modern city became a completely ungirdled entity—a phenomenon of motion, an arena of pleasure, and the nexus of a much larger region made accessible both for recreation and residential settlement—we must go back 150 years in time to examine the transformation of Paris during the Second Empire of Napoleon III. Haussmann's Paris, however authoritarian in concept and harsh in displacing the poor, was progressive in its attention to middle-class needs. With its consideration of transportation, recreation, and sanitation, and the atmosphere of widely shared urban pleasure it produced—as glimpsed in the paintings of the Impressionists and through the eyes of the novelist Marcel Proust (1871–1922)—it ushered in the era of modern urbanism.

I. Haussmann's Paris: Birth of the Modern City

Elected president of the Second Republic in the wake of the defeat of the republican revolutionaries of 1848, Napoleon Bonaparte's nephew, Louis-Napoleon Bonaparte—known as Napoleon III after he became emperor by a coup d'état in 1851—returned from exile in England to assume the reins of government. To forestall further revolutionary uprisings, he wanted to tear apart the dense fabric of Paris by creating new avenues. These would divide the city into sectors and isolate the potentially treacherous neighborhoods, making it more difficult for a mob to erect barricades and seize control of the capital in the future. But to think of his twenty-year transformation of Paris simply in political and tactical terms is a mistake. It was primarily a skillful reinvention of the urban form itself through comprehensive city planning and the application of Industrial Age technology to solving the problems of several types of circulation: water, sewage, trains, carriages, and pedestrians. By this time mass societies had come into existence, and the notion had become prevalent that government bore a fundamental responsibility for public sanitation, transportation routes, and the physical form and condition of the urban framework in general. *Urbanisme,* "city planning" in French, was a term coined in the second half of the nineteenth century to denote a technocratic approach to shaping cities by regularizing their form and ministering to the needs of their populations through the provision and maintenance of such basic infrastructure systems as streets and street lights, aqueducts, drainage lines, and sewers. The term also encompasses the concept of regulatory administration, that is, planning by means of building codes and land use regulations governing the safety and welfare of the city's inhabitants as well as the aesthetics of the urban ensemble. Because facilitation of movement is a primary objective of the modern city, the measurement of transportation volumes and flows and the development of terminals, roadbeds, and tracks to accommodate interurban and intraurban modes of travel are central to the planning process.

Paris: 1850–1870

The accomplishment of rebuilding Paris, which occurred despite deep misgivings and suffering on the part of many, must be measured in terms of the problems faced by the old urban order. Nineteen thousand residents had died in the cholera epidemic of 1848–49. In 1850, the population had grown to 1.3 million; over the next twenty years it continued climbing another 25 percent to reach 1.65 million. There was rampant unemployment and extreme overcrowding. Most of the city was a dense tangle of residential and manufacturing quarters, unfathomable except to those with long familiarity with its narrow, tortuous medieval streets. Historically redolent and venerably picturesque, Old Paris nonetheless glowed in the memories of many Parisians and tourists who continued to mourn, long after they had disappeared, cherished bits and pieces of its vanished cityscape.

The real impetus for reordering the street pattern came not from military motives so much as from the impulse of the rapidly expanding industrial capitalist society to have the mobility it needed to conduct business. Specifically, the premier machine of the Industrial Age, the steam-powered railroad train, propelled Paris and other cities into the modern age. Tracks penetrated several quarters along the city's urban periphery, large shedlike industrial buildings of steel and glass were built as terminals, and the volume of traffic generated by travelers coming and going necessitated replacing some of the city's welter of crooked streets with broad, straight thoroughfares to connect with destinations in the center.

During the years of his exile in England, Louis-Napoleon had seen some of the developments in transportation, sanitation, and parks that made London the leader in modernization among European cities. Fortunately for him, he was able to find in France a state administrator precisely suited to carry out an ambitious agenda of public improvements in Paris. Baron Georges-Eugène Haussmann (1809–1891), whom he appointed prefect of the Department of the Seine, was a government official skilled at manipulating tools that were new at the time, but which are common today: laws enabling the condemnation and appropriation of private property and debt financing. To justify their actions, the emperor and Haussmann reasoned that improvements in the city's infrastructure and the creation of new and improved public spaces would raise real-estate values and bring higher tax returns with which to pay off the debts incurred. Although Haussmann's financing schemes ran into trouble, leading to his downfall in 1870, the city's course of modernization was by then irrevocably set in the direction in which it continued until World War I.

Haussmann was able to conceptualize the entire city in technological, mechanistic terms as an entity, and although the Second Empire architecture that lined his new boulevards borrowed such time-honored motifs as mansard roofs and sculptural details derived from Baroque classicism, these were merely the decorative trappings of a resolutely technological approach to construction. Bourgeois financiers provided the money that built the buildings and many of the public improvements, and Haussmann's radical transformation of Paris was aimed at making the city not only efficient but also agreeable for this middle class. Before, there had been large *hôtels* for aristocrats and crowded lodgings for artisans and shopkeepers. Now, with regulations creating uniform cornice lines and roof heights, there were blocks of buildings with spacious apartments for bankers, merchants, manufacturers, lawyers, physicians, politicians, and other members of the bourgeoisie. There were also grand new hotels serving a new and transient segment of the population, the tourists who came in increasing numbers. Haussmann's urban framework, moreover, accommodated another invention of capitalist-consumer society: the department store, an airy palace with an interior skylighted courtyard constructed of cast iron and glass like the huge sheds built as train depots and like the new wholesale meat and produce market, Les Halles Centrales.

Circulation is the operative word in understanding Haussmann's program for rebuilding Paris. Not only did the growing commercial city need to move people and goods in and out by rail, but it also had to accommodate the many carriages owned by its prosperous bourgeoisie. In addition, omnibuses began operation in 1855, preceding the *Métro,* built in 1900, as a means of mass transit. Furthermore, if it was to remain healthy, the city needed to transport wastes more efficiently. The recent invention of ferroconcrete—concrete reinforced with metal—facilitated the construction of large collector tunnels that were part of a network of sewers planned by Haussmann. These carried the city's drainage northwest away from the built-up urban area to Asnières, where it was released into the Seine. Because of population growth and pollution of the Seine, Parisians' traditional source of potable water, Haussmann's engineers designed aqueducts to draw copious amounts from the Yonne, Vanne, and Dhuis River valleys.

The character of the city was changed in profound ways. Houses formerly faced interior courtyards, but now new block and building plans allowed tall windows to open onto the street. From their balconies residents gazed upon the spectacle of carriages and people moving below (fig. 10.2). Large shop windows of plate glass created a thin membrane between interior and exterior space; the display of merchandise stimulated pedestrian traffic as browsing and buying became popular pastimes, giving birth to the consumer society with its endless dreams of material goods as a basis of the good life. Cafés catered to the increased movement of people in the new streets, serving as outdoor living rooms where social life became a daily ritual in a city increasingly attracted to pleasure. Gaslight—soon to be replaced by elec-

10.2. Gustave Caillebotte, *The Man at the Window.* 1876. Private collection. From the window of the artist's family's apartment on the third floor of an outward-facing building of the 1860s on the rue de Lisbonne, the figure in the painting (the artist's brother René) is gazing down the rue Miromesnil toward its intersection with George-Eugène Haussmann's tree-lined boulevard Malesherbes, where the figure of a woman stands upon a raised sidewalk, ready to cross the street.

tric lighting—illuminated streets and the inside of shops and cafés, while increasing nighttime security and extending the hours people moved abroad in public. The *promeneur* walked the new boulevards for pleasure, while the *flâneur* idled away the hours, observing the quotidian dramas that often served as fodder for journalism.

The channels Haussmann cut through the city—his *percements*—and the public buildings erected by the talented architects employed by his Service des Bâtiments Civils became the *mise-en-scène* for a new kind of public pageantry. The cafés he planned for every major boulevard intersection were eddies in the current of humanity that flowed through them. The Opéra, the cultural institution claimed by bourgeois society more completely than any other, assumed the role of social stage played by Versailles two hundred years before. In 1860, Jean-Louis-Charles Garnier (1825–1898) won the competition to design a magnificent new opera house. The architect conceived its grand staircase as a spreading fan of steps to display the train of the Empress Eugénie's gown, but its real function, as it turned out when the building was completed in 1875 during the Third Republic (four years after the fall of Napoleon III), was to display the members of the fashionable world to one another against a backdrop of ruby and gold neo-Baroque splendor. Borrowing here as elsewhere the design vocabulary Le Nôtre had developed for the seventeenth-century French garden, Haussmann placed this opulent landmark as the focal point of one

10.3. Camille Pissarro, *Place du Théâtre Français, Paris, in the Rain (Avenue de l'Opéra).* 1898. The Minneapolis Institute of Arts

Below: 10.4. Paris, Artists' Plan. 1793

vicinity of important buildings, such as the city's palaces and Notre-Dame. Haussmann wished to make these monuments more visible and to create open spaces for public celebrations, while also making the city more defensible in times of riot. To contemporary Parisians, it seemed that Haussmann's urban surgery had suddenly revealed hidden areas of their city as obscure, unvisited side streets were made busy and prosperous by their proximity to new boulevards. Although thousands of people were evicted and demolition sites sold to developers, the commercial and real-estate boom of the period drowned out the voices of protest against this wholesale destruction.

In addition to creating the great boulevards, Haussmann realigned many ordinary streets, regulated the appearance of building facades, planted miles of street trees, landscaped new public squares at important intersections, installed lights, benches, and other sidewalk amenities, and enlisted the support of building owners in public-space cleaning procedures that made the city a cynosure of municipal housekeeping.

To assign the emperor and Haussmann entire credit for the transformation of Paris in the nineteenth century is erroneous. The sovereign provided the conceptual support and the technocrat the financial acumen and administrative zeal to achieve amazingly speedy results, but neither projected an entirely original vision. Together they effected a canny marriage of French monumentalism and industrial capitalism by energizing a planning process that had already begun.

Planning and historic preservation were born in Paris in the wake of the French Revolution, when the state confiscated Church property and evaluated monuments of the *ancien régime* for conservation purposes. The Convention of 1793 commissioned a group of artists to prepare the so-called Artists' Plan in which individual districts were studied with a view toward the development of appropriated land and with the idea of displaying within a nexus of radiating avenues buildings deemed of particular architectural importance (fig. 10.4). The Artists' Plan projected the creation and extension of long straight axes, notably in the densely clotted eastern part of the city, and it forecast one of the fundamental planning strategies of Haussmann's New Paris: that based on an analysis of the city as stagecraft, with historic monuments and landmark buildings as well as important edifices of state symbolically embodying the new French polity displayed like set pieces. But this plan did not comprehend Paris, as Haussmann's would, as an integer in which the city, not the sector, was the planning unit.

At the beginning of the nineteenth century,

of his arrow-straight avenues lined with uniform blocks of new buildings. The whole architectural ensemble served as an ordered and stable counterpoint to the surge of movement along the grand, wide thoroughfare. The flow of traffic and the lively character of public life in this new urban space were evident even on a rainy day in 1898 when the scene was painted by the Impressionist artist Camille Pissarro (fig. 10.3).

Movement in, around, and through architectural space was Haussmann's primary goal, and the sculptural facades, bell towers, spires, domes, triumphal arches, and statues of an earlier age, as well as those of his own, were merely the ornamental and symbolically necessary props for the much grander spectacle of his resolutely modern city. This involved the eradication of much ad hoc urbanization in the

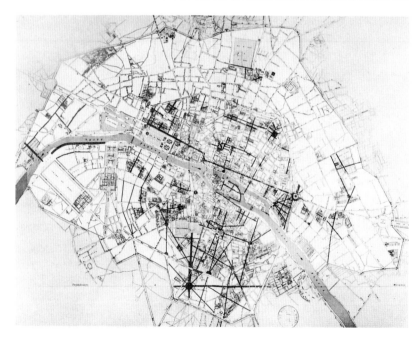

Napoleon I had pledged to make Paris the most beautiful city in Europe. He was also aware of the need to modernize the city with projects that would improve public health, outdoor food markets, and traffic flow. Although his reign was too brief and the shortage of development capital too severe to initiate the kind of large-scale transformations that his nephew undertook a half century later, he effectively set the Neoclassical tone for most subsequent city planning. Renaming the place Louis XV the place de la Concorde, he created an important cross axis running through it, emphasized by the construction of certain iconic monuments. A mile distant along the tree-lined axis of the Champs-Élysées at the summit of Chaillot Hill, he constructed the largest triumphal arch ever built, the Arc de Triomphe (1806–36), a potent symbol and grandiose climax to one of the world's most important urban perspectives.

With the help of his favorite Neoclassical architects, Charles Percier (1764–1838) and Pierre-François-Léonard Fontaine (1762–1853), Napoleon established the beginning of an axis into the densely built quarters of eastern Paris by transforming the northern edge of the Tuileries Gardens into the rue de Rivoli (fig. 10.5). Employing the traditional formula of the sidewalk arcade that we have observed in Henri IV's place Royale (place des Vosges), they built the first segment of massive buildings with horizontal bands of uniform balconies and stringcourses reinforcing the perspective line of the axis (see fig. 4.48). The continuous balconies on the *piano nobile,* third, and attic floors opened the spectacle of the street to those inside, suggesting its function as a parade route, while the extended ground-floor arcade made an elegant shoppers' promenade.

Louis-Philippe (ruled 1830–1848) as a constitutional monarch lacked the resources for large-scale urban embellishment available to earlier kings, but he nevertheless continued the concept set forth in the Artists' Plan of emphasizing individual public spaces by erecting the July Column on the place de la Bastille and the Egyptian obelisk at the place de la Concorde (fig. 10.6; see fig. 6.38). In the 1840s, he built the first railroad stations, including the Gare de l'Est, which was linked to the center of the city by the wide boulevard de Strasbourg.

An especially important development that affected the future of city planning was the establishment in 1819 of the École des Beaux-Arts with its rigorously Neoclassical program of architectural education. As mentioned in Chapter Nine, it was here that the American architects responsible for the City Beautiful movement received their training beginning in the second half of the nineteenth century. The French winners of its prestigious Prix de Rome almost invariably received important government building commissions when they returned from their advanced classical studies in Italy as *pensionnaires* at the French Academy, which is housed in the Villa Medici on the Pincian Hill in Rome. Thus, from the ranks of the École des Beaux-Arts came the architects who designed the monuments and blocks of new

10.5. Rue de Rivoli, Paris, begun in 1806 under Napoleon I. Photograph by Adolphe Braun. c. 1855

Below: 10.6. July Column, place de la Bastille, Paris

10.7. Paris map showing Haussmann's new boulevards, engraving from Jean-Charles-Adolphe Alphand, *Les Promenades de Paris.* 1867–73

Below: 10.8. Paris street furniture, engraving from Jean-Charles-Adolphe Alphand, *Les Promenades de Paris.* 1867–73

apartment buildings in Haussmann's New Paris. Their Neoclassical vocabulary and its application as a masonry and sculptural veneer over industrial materials in many of these structures help explain the stylistic consistency and apparent continuity with tradition of the rapidly modernizing city.

Napoleon III, having lived in London, where architects and engineers were applying new forms of industrial technology to construction and urban problem solving, desired to bring an even greater degree of modernity to the French capital. Even before appointing Haussmann prefect of the Department of the Seine, Napoleon III began extending the Rue de Rivoli east toward the Hôtel de Ville; refashioning Louis XIV's old hunting park, the Bois de Boulogne, into an English-style public pleasure ground; removing the slum that had grown up between the Tuileries and the Louvre; restoring the cathedral of Notre-Dame; and planning a new food market, Les Halles Centrales. Napoleon III had, moreover, prepared a map of the city that showed an arterial network of *percements* knifing through the older fabric of narrow short streets, and it was this graphic representation of his urban renewal proposals that he handed Haussmann upon his appointment. Even though this plan changed, particularly after 1861 when the annexation of the outlying *faubourgs* created the need for new arterial connections, municipal buildings, and public services, Haussmann always viewed this imperial document as his charter, considering himself to be merely the emperor's servant and agent in transforming Paris.

Haussmann had been prefect of Bordeaux before becoming prefect of the Department of the Seine in 1853, a position that can be roughly characterized as city manager of Paris. He was responsible for overseeing the planning, design, financing, and construction of all capital improvements as well as the daily operations of municipal management. To provide the necessary base maps for their work, Haussmann had thorough planimetric and topographic surveys made of the city and its recently annexed suburbs. The resulting Plan of Paris configured the city-in-transformation, plotting the *percements,* for which condemnation and demolition of property were necessary, as well as the new building alignments where existing streets were to be widened by the Service de la Voirie, or Bureau of Roads (fig. 10.7). Thoroughly technocratic in his approach to his job, he had as his chief associates engineers such as Eugène Belgrand (1810–1878), who conceived and managed the construction of the vast new aqueduct and sewer systems, and the landscape designer Jean-Charles-Adolphe Alphand (1817–1891), whom he put in charge of constructing new parks, promenades, and city squares.

Squares such as the place du Châtelet sacrificed their status as *places,* becoming instead vehicular traffic circles and pedestrian traffic islands, a function that distinguished the Parisian squares from the ones in London, which continued to serve as quiet urban oases even after that city's modernization. They were given attractive but standardized street furniture, which in its ubiquity served informally to symbolize the city's distinctive new appearance (fig. 10.8). In developing these nodes of relation, as Haussmann termed them, for the boulevard systems, Le Nôtre's paradigm of avenues radiating from *rond-points* served him well, allowing the city both fluidity of motion and monumental axiality.

The Champs-Élysées was redefined with new *allées* of trees and lined with gaslights designed by Jakob Ignaz (Jacques-Ignace) Hittorff (1792–1867), the city architect. In the eastern sector of the city, the southern part of the Canal Saint-Martin was decked over to become the boulevard Richard-Lenoir in 1861. The same kinds of trees, flowers, news kiosks, concession stands, and gaslights that made western Paris attractive to the rich also appeared in this less affluent part of the city.

Just beyond the outer ring of boulevards, which had replaced the customs wall of 1786–88, lay two large royal hunting parks: the Bois de Boulogne in the west was approached by Haussmann's new, wide avenue de l'Impératrice (avenue Foch), and the Bois de Vincennes was situated in the east to the south of the porte de Vincennes and the existing ceremonial thoroughfare, the cours de Vincennes. To serve the recreational needs of high society in *le West End,* Alphand was charged with continuing the conversion of the Bois de Boulogne into an elegant pleasure ground with passages of Picturesque scenery interspersed with a race track and restaurants (figs. 10.9a, 10.9b).

Because it is a collection of unrelated facilities as well as a palimpsest inscribed with traces of past uses, the Bois de Boulogne park complex does not have the unified planning vision characteristic of Olmsted's parks in America, with which it is contemporary. While developed in the English style with undulating paths replacing all but two of the former straight *allées* and an irregular-shaped lake reminiscent of the Serpentine in London's Hyde Park, it is more a collection of heterogeneous amusements. Lovely as it is in some of its parts, particularly the Bagatelle and the Shakespeare Garden, these were not developed as part of a comprehensive landscape design. Nor is there, as in Central Park, an overriding note of moral purpose; the Bois de Boulogne was intended more as a fashionable resort than as a pastoral antidote to urban stress.

Although intended for the working class, the Bois de Vincennes was treated to a similar degree of Picturesque detail as the Bois de Boulogne. In addition to these two large parks, Haussmann created the Parc Montsouris along the city's southern edge between the Porte d'Orléans and the Porte d'Italie and refashioned the Parc Monceau, the duc de Chartres's eighteenth-century *jardin anglo-chinois* at the northwestern edge of the city, into a Picturesque nineteenth-century park containing several of Louis de Carmontelle's remaining *follies.* In the northeastern quadrant of the city, between 1864 and 1867, he transformed the vermin-infested Buttes-Chaumont, an abandoned rock quarry where squatters lived, into a romantically Picturesque 55-acre park (fig. 10.10).

The spirit that informs all of these Parisian parks is highly theatrical. Resembling elaborate stage sets, many passages of their scenery are composed of rock-

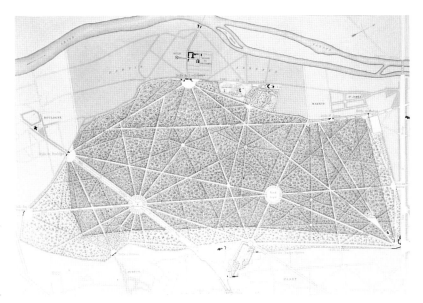

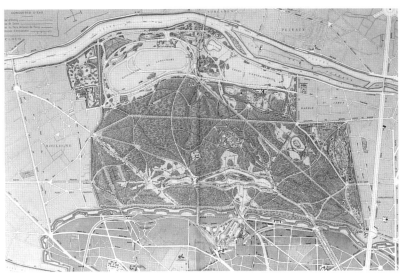

10.9a and 10.9b. Bois de Boulogne, before and after its transformation by Jean-Charles-Adolphe Alphand. Engraving from Alphand, *Les Promenades de Paris.* 1867–73

Below: 10.10. Plan of Parc des Buttes-Chaumont, designed by Jean-Charles-Adolphe Alphand. Engraving from Alphand, *Les Promenades de Paris.* 1867–73

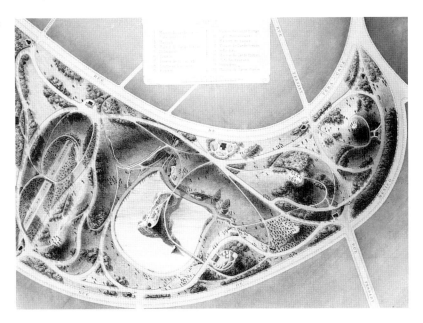

10.11. Pont des Suicides, Parc des Buttes-Chaumont, designed by Jean-Charles-Adolphe Alphand. Engraving from Alphand, *Les Promenades de Paris.* 1867–73

Below: 10.12. Square des Innocents, designed by Jean-Charles-Adolphe Alphand. Engraving from Alphand, *Les Promenades de Paris.* 1867–73

work combining natural and simulated stones. At the Parc des Buttes-Chaumont, Alphand's Picturesque genius was given full rein, and at *twice* the cost of redesigning the much larger Bois de Boulogne, he added huge quantities of artificial rockwork to the existing old quarry faces, thereby creating a romantic pseudomountainous landscape rising out of an artificial lake.[2] Two streams, one containing a waterfall that spilled into a grotto with artificial stalactites and stalagmites, are fed by water from one of the canals of Paris. Crowning the promontory that forms the park's central feature, a small replica of the Temple of Vesta at Tivoli serves as a belvedere from which to view the panorama of Paris. Leading to the temple is a high suspended bridge called, melodramatically, the Bridge of Suicides; an alternative, longer route provides sinuously curving paths to the top. This scene was meant to induce a *grand frisson,* or thrill of amazement, a sensation different from the tranquil mood of poetic reverie Olmsted attempted to produce in viewers of his scenery (fig. 10.11).

Haussmann's parks are not, like those of Olmsted and Vaux, a reaction to the industrial city, a rural vision of pastoral peace offered to counteract urban stress; rather they present themselves as additional pleasures in a city of many pleasures, a city already comfortable in its progressive modernity. Although these French parks partake of the same Picturesque style as the American parks, they are not naturalistic in the way Olmsted's parks are. The French parks incorporate plantings of lush, high-maintenance, subtropical vegetation, and their path systems do not conform to the dictates of topography, but assume the lines of the French curve, a drafting instrument with scroll-shaped cutouts. Regarding the latter, the garden writer and editor William Robinson penned these caustic words: "In the plans of the best French landscape-gardeners it is quite ridiculous to see the way the walks wind about in symmetrical twirlings, and,

when they have entwined themselves through every sweep of turf in the place, seem to long for more spaces to writhe about in."[3] The sinuosity that was an end in itself as well as the concentration on effects that the French term *féerique,* enchanting and fairy-like, bespeak an underlying cultural attitude that has more in common with Disney's Magic Kingdom than with the pastoral simplicity of Central Park where all adornment—botanical, sculptural, or architectural—was clearly subservient to a landscape composition designed to carry the visitor through a chain of scenes in which the experience is primarily *spatial.*

Several illustrations in Alphand's book, *Les Promenades de Paris* (1867–73), an important record of Haussmann's transformation of the city, depict the characteristic treatment of the new streets and their related green spaces (fig. 10.12). Maintenance codes governed the appearance of private frontages, ensuring the cleanliness of facades and their scraping and painting or whitewashing at intervals of ten years or less.

In making Paris both progressive and pleasurable, Haussmann also changed its scale. The city grew in size by one half with the addition of the new *arrondissements.* The unprecedented length of Haussmann's wide, straight boulevards—their perspective views emphasized by even building walls with uniform roof, cornice, and balcony lines—made the extent of the urban mass more readily apparent. In addition, wider streets made taller buildings possible and even desirable as a matter of proportionate relationship, a fact recognized in the 1859 building code, which decreed that on streets 65 feet (20 meters) or more wide, buildings could gain 8 feet (2.5 meters)—amounting to an additional story—in height.

Haussmann's boulevard openings were the

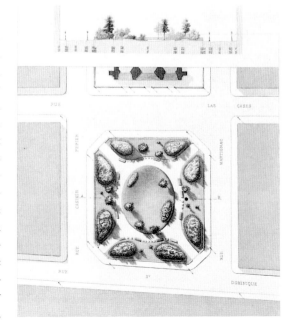

occasions for triumphal public celebration presided over by the emperor. With their Venetian banners and gold curtains decorated with stars and garlands, these unveilings memorialized not only the grandeur of the remade city, but also the power of government, municipal and state. Perhaps the emperor risked too much politically in allowing Haussmann to lavish resources to such an extent upon the capital and, at least during the first decade of his administration, to publicize them so conspicuously. Eventually, opposition within the Chamber of Deputies caused an investigation into the prefect's methods of financing, and the discovery of certain irregularities brought about his dismissal in 1870.

That same year Napoleon III capitulated to the Germans at Sedan during the Franco-Prussian War. A republic was proclaimed, bringing about the fall of the Second Empire and the end of Napoleon's reign. The war continued as Paris underwent a four months' seige and then German occupation before surrendering. Within weeks, revolutionary forces were elected to the Paris municipal council, and these radical members of the Commune seized control of the city. Their revolt against the national government, however, was quickly crushed by the troops of the new republic.

These events did not put an end to Paris's continued modernization in the Haussmannian manner. The Communards' damage to the city was severe, but after their brief time in power, the Third Republic set about repairing the destruction, extending more avenues, and refurbishing the Luxembourg Gardens. Gabriel-Jean-Antoine Davioud, a park designer in the Haussmann administration, designed the grandiose Trocadéro Palace in a pseudo–Spanish Moorish style as Paris prepared to host the International Exhibition of 1878, an opportunity to reassert its industrial modernity and cultural advancement.

Paris had already hosted two international fairs to showcase industrial technology in 1855 and 1867. Beginning in 1867, the Champs-de-Mars, which had been laid out as a parade ground in 1765 between the École Militaire and the Seine, became the site of these expositions. The huge vaulted spaces of the Paris exhibition halls experimentally employed the new building materials of iron and glass, the engineering potential of which was first demonstrated by Loudon's greenhouse constructions and then by Paxton's Crystal Palace in London. Just as the city was being opened up and made porous, so these new Industrial Age structures, which seemed startlingly light and lacking in *gravitas* at the time, posited an architectural idiom that no longer walled in volumetric space but dematerialized mass, transforming buildings into airy cages in which the interpenetra-

tion of indoors and outdoors became the dominant theme. The structure containing the exhibition halls for the 1867 fair was an enormous ellipse of seven concentric galleries featuring a garden with statues and palm trees in the center oval.

Gustave Eiffel (1832–1923) was at the time of the 1867 exposition a young engineer who had founded a factory capable of producing the iron skeleton of the vast gallery on the outer edge of the ellipse, the Galerie des Machines, which had a height of 82 feet (25 meters) and a span of 115 feet (35 meters). Eiffel was also responsible for the hydraulic lifts that introduced the public to a new means of vertical movement.

The Centennial Exposition of 1889, which followed the International Exhibition that had been staged in 1878 to prove that Paris had recovered from the effects of the Communard rebellion and the Franco-Prussian War, pushed French technological experimentation and search for new building forms to new heights, both figuratively and literally. The structure that most impressed visitors to the 1889 fair was Eiffel's 984-foot (300-meter) tower of open-lattice wrought iron. Eiffel, who had also distinguished himself as a bridge builder, designed it as a demonstration in structural aerodynamics and load-bearing engineering. Twice as high as the dome of St. Peter's or the Great Pyramid of Khufu at Giza and, unlike these monuments, a labor of mere months, not decades, this icon of early modernity has remained, above all other features within that heavily ornamented city, the instantly recognizable symbol of Paris.[4] It was the tallest structure in the world until the Chrysler Building in New York was built in 1930.

Elevators manufactured by the Otis Elevator Company ascend on a curve, carrying visitors to the successive platforms. Suddenly, it was possible to have a panoramic vision not merely of landscape, such as Alpinists could experience by ascending high peaks, but of urban form and history. The Eiffel Tower made available to millions of visitors the city's structure as concrete abstraction, giving each the ability to decipher in a single reading all known landmarks, topographical and structural, and to discern in this act the story of the city's earliest formation and growth through the centuries. Thus equipped with panoramic vision, one could also profoundly imagine the human dimension of the metropolis, the multitude of individual lives of the teeming population below. Yet, in the vertiginous descent, structure seems to fragment, and the scenery of the city below appears to spin in kaleidoscopic fashion. The ebullient Cubism of Robert Delaunay (1885–1941), who painted many versions of the Eiffel Tower beginning in 1910, captures the exhilaration of this quintessentially modern experience of space and landscape (fig. 10.13).

10.13. Robert Delaunay, *Eiffel Tower*. 1911. The Guggenheim Museum, New York

II. The City Beautiful:
Monumental Urbanism in Beaux-Arts America

It would be difficult to exaggerate the effect of Haussmann's Paris on other cities of the world. It is fair to say that, even within the context of modernism and postmodernism, designers have continued to employ some of the devices of monumental urban planning, of which mid-nineteenth-century Paris remains the primary example, especially in capital cities where the building program has called for a symbolical display of government power through architecture and landscape. Even without such an agenda, modernism's imperative to enable vehicular movement and to assist the forces of capitalist industry and commerce was strong, and practically everywhere old streets were widened, fortifications gave way to new boulevards, and rail transportation systems were built as city after city was opened up both to new possibilities of urban life and to a radically new urban form.

Ironically, in democratic America the desire for civic monumentality was such that Gilded Age magnates and political leaders overlooked the authoritarianism implicit in this style of city planning, adopting

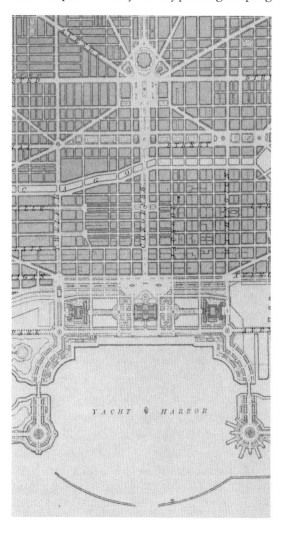

10.14. Plan for Chicago, Illinois, proposed by Daniel Burnham. 1909

its forms to express the lofty ideals of the republic rather than the power of monarchy. It was a time when newly made American millionaires looked to Europe for role models in the mores of aristocracy. It was a time when Americans sought to emulate Europe's impressive legacy of heritage buildings and monuments in the mansions of the rich and in the public art and architecture that proclaimed the prosperity and dignity of their cities. In this they were helped by the training undertaken by design professionals. The aesthetics of several generations of American architects and landscape architects was forged in Haussman's Paris under the influence of the École des Beaux-Arts where they studied beginning in the last third of the nineteenth century.

By the beginning of the twentieth century, in the wake of the 1893 Chicago World's Fair, the neo-classicism they imbibed there was being vigorously promoted by Charles Mulford Robinson, a Rochester, New York, journalist and the author of *The Improvement of Towns and Cities, or the Practical Basis of Civic Aesthetics* (1901) and *Modern Civic Art, or The City Made Beautiful* (1903). The City Beautiful movement aimed at ennobling American cities and European colonial capitals through monumental planning, and Daniel Burnham, fresh from his triumph as principal planner of the 1893 World's Columbian Fair in Chicago, was commissioned to develop new layouts for Cleveland, San Francisco, Manila, and Chicago (fig. 10.14). Where there were existing gridiron street patterns, these plans attempted to impose upon them grand diagonal boulevards whose intersections formed magnificent plazas and whose vistas terminated in monumental public works.

Frederick Law Olmsted had spent a good deal of time during his last productive years mentoring his son and namesake who became his professional heir and the future head of the firm. It is ironic in light of Olmsted, Sr.'s, antipathy toward the heroic style of the Gilded Age that one of the first commissions Olmsted, Jr., assumed upon entering practice was in collaboration with Burnham. Following the Chicago World's Fair, Senator James McMillan's Committee on the District of Columbia appointed him landscape architect on the team under Burnham's leadership to carry L'Enfant's original plan for the nation's capital to a new level of monumental grandeur. The other members were Stanford White's partner, Charles McKim (1847–1909), and the Beaux-Arts sculptor Augustus Saint-Gaudens (1848–1907).

In order to prepare themselves for this chal-

lenging assignment to give Washington, D.C., an image that not only glorified the founders of the republic and the president who saved the Union but also one that suited America's newly assumed identity as a world power, Burnham, McKim, Olmsted, and the secretary to Senator McMillan, Charles Moore, sailed for Europe in the summer of 1901 to study architecture, parks, and urban design in several cities. For seven weeks they sketched and discussed ideas stimulated by their travels to Paris, Rome, Venice, Budapest, Frankfurt, Berlin, and London.

Washington's layout had become muddled by later nonconforming elements, such as a train station athwart the Mall, but the outlines of its grand plan, derived from that of Versailles, were partially realized and called for further development. Not surprisingly, the members of the team returned on the first of August determined to clarify, reinforce, and extend L'Enfant's axial plan (fig. 10.15). Within the contentious atmosphere of Washington politics, they were fortunate to win critical support from President Theodore Roosevelt and, after his election in 1909, from President William Howard Taft. Thus, congressional opponents did not manage to derail the McMillan team's intentions, and the head of the Pennsylvania Railroad acceded to its recommendation that Union Station be placed north of the Capitol. Construction of a new station according to Burnham's plans was completed in 1907, and the old train tracks were removed from the Mall once it was made operational. Adjacent to the station on the northwest a similarly monumental new Post Office, also designed by Burnham, was built. The proposal to realign the Mall on axis with the Washington Monument and plant the remainder as a simple grass *parterre* bordered by quadruple rows of elms was also carried out after much debate and furor in the press.

As his final act of office before leaving the presidency, Theodore Roosevelt appointed a Council of Fine Arts composed of architects, painters, sculptors, and a landscape architect—Frederick Law Olmsted, Jr. Approved in a bill passed by the House of Representatives and Senate in 1910, the seven-member commission appointed by Taft continued to include Olmsted. The Mall axis was extended according to the McMillan Plan beyond L'Enfant's original plan, and a canal-like reflecting basin was built between the Washington Monument and Henry Bacon's new Grecian-style temple housing the monumental statue of President Abraham Lincoln by Daniel Chester French in Potomac Park. This impressive memorial to the nation's sixteenth president, the subject of controversy like other elements of the plan, was not completed until 1922.

The McMillan plan had called for a national cemetery on the opposite bank of the Potomac with "white stones, inconspicuous in themselves, covering the gentle, wooded slopes, and producing the desired effect of a vast army in its last resting place."[5] In 1925, Congress authorized construction of the Arlington Memorial Bridge according to designs prepared by the firm of McKim, Mead, and White. The bridge, a bridge plaza, and Water Gate between the bridge and the parkway proposed along the edge of Rock Creek were completed by 1932. Another important monument, one honoring the third president, Thomas Jefferson, was located at the end of the plan's great cross axis extending from Lafayette Square in front of the White House to a terminus in the Tidal Basin of the Potomac River. Plans inspired by the Pantheon in Rome were prepared for the Jefferson Memorial Commission by John Russell Pope, also the architect of the National Gallery of Art, and submitted shortly before his death in 1937. These were subjected to much wrangling, but after they had been somewhat modified, reduced in scale, and approved by the Senate in spite of objections from the Fine Arts Commission, the monument was put into construction in 1938. The

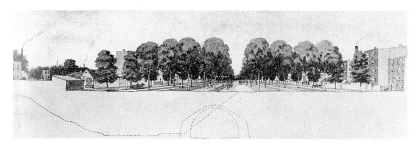

10.16a and 10.16b. Senate Park Commission renderings of alternative closed and open valley plans for Rock Creek and Potomac Parkway, Washington, D.C. 1902

Below: 10.17. Plan for Rock Creek and Potomac Parkway, prepared by James G. Langdon, Office of Public Buildings and Grounds, 1916

McMillan Plan's proposal for a dignified treatment of the grounds immediately surrounding the Washington Monument, the linchpin of the entire National Capital redevelopment plan, was never carried out.

As with other elements of the plan, politics and professional rivalries plagued the development of Rock Creek and Potomac Parkway, a 2-and-½-mile (4-kilometer) scenic road connecting the Potomac waterfront near the Lincoln Memorial with Rock Creek Park north of the National Zoo at the northern boundary of the District of Columbia.[6] It is sometimes forgotten that the City Beautiful movement, while advocating neoclassical monuments, axial planning, and geometrical landscape design, also propounded the need for park systems in which naturalistic landscaping complemented Beaux-Arts architectural grandeur. While Senator James McMillan chaired the Senate Committee on the District of Columbia, the official name of the 1901 McMillan Commission charged with detailing the plan for monumental Washington was the Senate Park Commission, and its 1902 report is titled *The Improvement of the Park System of the District of Columbia.* Frederick Law Olmsted, Jr., the author of the park and parkway sections of the report, sought to furnish the nation's capital with the same type of parks and park-connecting parkways that had recently been created in New York, Boston, and Buffalo and were

being developed for Cincinnati, Milwaukee, Minneapolis, and other American cities.

Seen as a means of curing an environmental problem and an eyesore (industrial wastes were dumped along the lower portions of Rock Creek), as well as a way to eliminate the topographical barrier between Georgetown and Washington proper, the project was delayed by debate, continuing for several years, over whether it should be an open-valley scenic parkway or a boulevard-type "closed" parkway covering a conduit (figs. 10.16a, 10.16b). Finally, on March 14, 1913, Congress passed a bill authorizing the open-valley concept. Olmsted continued to maintain his involvement as a consultant to the project and was disappointed when aspects of his advice, such as the perimeter roadways and some of the Picturesque effects seen in the 1916 plan, were ignored (fig. 10.17). Other aesthetically desirable elements were eliminated in the interests of economy and traffic engineering, but finally, in 1923, ten years after its authorization, the parkway was under construction. With the impetus gained from federal work programs in the 1930s, it was almost completed by the end of that decade.

The fulfillment of many of the objectives of the McMillan report remained the most realized achievement of the City Beautiful movement in America. Nowhere except in Washington, D.C., were the results of this effort accomplished on an urban scale, but several civic centers and many banks, libraries, museums, train stations, bridges, and monuments were added to the American cityscape as a result of this impulse (see fig. 9.59). Typically, municipal government followed, rather than led, the efforts that were organized by groups of public-spirited citizens and journalists as city after city in the United States followed the lead of Burnham and Robinson, seeking to counteract the ugliness of their earlier rapid commercial and industrial growth with Neoclassical urban monumentalism.

As we shall see in the next chapter, the rich vocabulary of forms inherited from France and Italy furnished British and American garden designers with many motifs, which they borrowed freely. The stu-

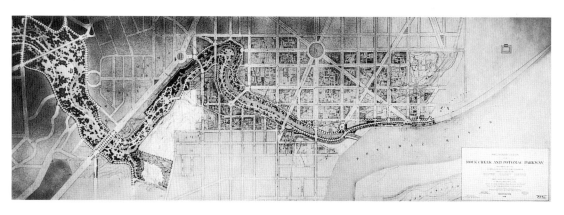

dents at the École des Beaux-Arts and the Rome Prize winners at the American Academy did not ponder deeply the humanist iconography informing these now agreeably mellow garden landscapes, but sought instead to appropriate their aura of venerability along with their undeniably fine compositional elements. They looked to these antique landscapes for inspiration because, like the characters in the novels of Henry James, they were subject to a peculiarly American sense of cultural inferiority. Regular transatlantic travel by steamship, another Industrial Age transportation advancement, made them acutely aware of their own country's narrow history and thin civilization when compared with the many centuries of human artistic endeavor recorded in the stones of Europe's ancient ruins, medieval cathedrals, and Renaissance villas and châteaux. Others of their countrymen saw American civilization in somewhat different terms, as an opportunity to forge a new kind of national identity, one that celebrated the country's uniqueness in occupying almost an entire continent that was by nature endowed with scenery in all three traditional categories—beautiful, picturesque, and sublime. Surely, they reasoned with transcendentalist conviction, that very scenery, particularly in its sublime dimension, was a natural resource even more fundamental to the ethos of their freshly evolving civilization than any replication of European monumental grandeur on native soil could ever be. By conserving significant lands within the public domain through the creation of a national park system, they would vouchsafe for future generations this wonderful patrimony, which also constituted a newly available stimulus to tourism and recreation.

III. America the Beautiful: The National Park System

In 1851, a U.S. Army party known as the Mariposa Battalion pursued a band of Miwok-Paiute Indians into the Yosemite Valley of California. Although prospectors had come upon it earlier, it was the Mariposa Battalion's report of Yosemite's stunning scenery that aroused the interest of entrepreneurs eager to exploit natural wonders as tourist attractions. We may recall that journalists had played an important role in the creation of Central Park. Similarly, writers and publishers took up the Yosemite cause. In this they were aided by the emerging art of photography. Stereographs for the armchair traveler spread the fame of the sheer granite walls rising 3,000 feet (914 meters) from the valley floor, but the real power and majesty of the scenery was better conveyed by the prints made from large glass plate negatives by Carleton E. Watkins (1829–1916) and other photographers.

Wordsworthian Romanticism and the desire to celebrate an American equivalent to the Alps—which John Ruskin had brought into focus as scenery of the sublime category capable of inspiring emotion in cultivated breasts—as well as the delight American chauvinists found in appropriating a "sacred place" that was equivalent to a Gothic cathedral or a Greek temple soon led to the proposal to set aside the Yosemite and the nearby Mariposa Grove of giant sequoia trees (Sequoia gigantea) as an inalienable part of the public domain. A bill was introduced in the United States Senate in 1864 to cede these lands to the state of California "for public use, resort and recreation," and when it was passed and signed into law by President Abraham Lincoln, the first step had been taken toward preserving portions of the national scenic patrimony for popular enjoyment. At this time, environmentalism and preserving wilderness to protect select ecosystems was not part of the public consciousness; the new park was regarded rather as a tourist commodity to be appreciated for its sublime scenery in the same manner as one would admire a noble work of art.

As discussed in Chapter Nine, at the time of Yosemite's acquisition by the state of California (it would later become part of the national park system), Frederick Law Olmsted, Sr., was in California as the director of the Mariposa Mines, and because of his reputation as a park administrator, was appointed by the governor to oversee the development of design and management policies for Yosemite Park and the Mariposa Big Tree Grove. In a letter to his wife, Olmsted shared his first impression of this fine stand of California giant sequoia trees: "You recognize them as soon as your eye falls on them, far away, not merely from the unusual size of the trunk but its remarkable color—a cinnamon color, very elegant. You feel that they are distinguished strangers [who] have come down to us from another world,—but the whole forest is wonderful."[7]

Olmsted, like almost everyone else at the time, realized the opportunity Yosemite presented for the burgeoning tourist industry and remarked in the report that he wrote in 1865 that Yosemite should "prove an attraction of similar character and a similar source of wealth to the whole community, not only of California but of the United States"[8] as the natural scenery of Switzerland. The nineteenth-century appetite for scenic wonders was tremendous, as the popularity of Niagara Falls had proved. Here, on an even grander scale than Niagara, was an example of scenery that could be characterized as sublime. Already painters and lithographers as well as photographers and writers were making a living depicting it, and hotel developers and souvenir vendors were busy with schemes to exploit it.

The first object of any plan for Yosemite would necessarily be to protect its scenic integrity and to prevent the kind of commercial exploitation that marred the landscape around Niagara in the nineteenth century. Fortunately nature had accomplished at Yosemite what extensive grading and planting had done in Central Park: the visual exclusion of the rest of the world from an idyllic landscape. Lofty walls enclosed the valley and helped the visitor experience the exhilarating sense of spatial completeness and sanctity as in a majestic cathedral. For Olmsted, Yosemite represented "the union of the deepest sublimity with the deepest beauty of nature, not in one feature or another, not in one part or one scene or another, not any landscape that can be framed by itself, but all around and wherever the visitor goes."[9] It had taken him some months to appreciate the beauty of California's dry-climate vegetation, but now in his Yosemite report, he could rhapsodize: "Cliffs of awful height and rocks of vast magnitude . . . are banked and fringed and draped and shadowed by the tender foliage of noble and lovely trees and bushes, reflected from the most placid pools, and associated with the most tranquil meadows, the most playful streams, and every variety of soft and peaceful pastoral beauty."[10] The plan that he proposed was one with as few "artificial constructions" as possible and a circular carriage drive with turnouts placed to present the best opportunities for scenic viewing.

Today we think of Yosemite as simply one park within a magnificent system of national parks, and

we therefore perhaps underestimate the powerful place it occupied in the nineteenth-century imagination. The geologist Clarence King must have felt, like Olmsted, that Yosemite presented a synthesis of the sublime and the beautiful when he spoke of "a soft aerial depth of purple tone . . . hiding details, veiling with its soft amethystine obscurity all that hard, broken roughness of the Sentinel cliffs."[11] The inclination toward the reverential was greatly enhanced by the atmospheric qualities of Albert Bierstadt's large and immensely popular paintings that cast religious light and color over the scene rather than emphasizing Yosemite's sculptural qualities as Carleton Watkins's photographs did (fig. 10.18).

Perhaps the Sierra Nevada and Yosemite found their true prophet in the naturalist John Muir (1838–1914). What Ruskin had been to the Alps, Muir was to the Sierra. Ruskin saw the mountains as the "schools and cathedrals" of the human race, "full of treasures of illuminated manuscript for the scholar, kindly in simple lessons to the worker, quiet in pale cloisters for the thinker, glorious in holiness for the worshipper."[12] Muir found holy inspiration in trying to fathom the geologic history of the mountains that had been shaped by almost unimaginably powerful forces, including the passage of mighty glaciers.

The poet Wordsworth, whose lasting influence pervaded, however unconsciously, the attitude of wilderness lovers such as Muir, had conceived of "spots in time," vivid scenes of nature that became imprinted on the mind. Like funds in the bank available for withdrawal at a later date, these scenes provided capital for recollection and contemplation in the future. Muir's impressions perhaps went further; he believed that the sights of nature reveal the majesty of God and leave a permanent mark upon our souls. To Ralph Waldo Emerson, he extended an invitation to experience the exaltation of a journey with him in the high Sierras. The transcendentalist and author of the famous essay "On Nature" answered the call and, in 1871, at the age of sixty-seven, made the arduous and rewarding journey.

Unknown except to Native Americans, trappers, and a few intrepid frontiersmen whose accounts of its seemingly fantastic, cosmically disordered scenery of spluttering mud volcanoes, shooting geysers, and boiling sulfur springs was often discounted, Yellowstone did not enter the public consciousness until around 1870. Again, it was journalists, artists, and photographers who stimulated appreciation of this collection of natural wonders. Ferdinand V. Hayden, director of the U.S. Geological Survey, sought funds for a scientific exploration of the area, and his expedition party included the photographer William H. Jackson (1843–1942) and the painter Thomas Moran

10.18. Carleton E. Watkins, *Cathedral Rock, 2,600 Feet, Yosemite.* c. 1866. The Metropolitan Museum of Art, New York. Elisha Whittelsey Collection

(1837–1926). Not only were the national parks to be objects of national pride and cultural icons themselves, but also the depiction of them set new standards of taste in landscape art and scenic appreciation. The work of Moran and Jackson was instrumental in the campaign that resulted in the passage in 1872 of a bill in Congress to establish Yellowstone as the country's first national park (fig. 10.19).

Proponents, many of whom were railroad magnates and businessmen, deemed the benefits of the proposed park to be considerable: It would stimulate tourism and passenger railroads. For many tourists, of course, it was not the sublimity of the Yellowstone Canyon that attracted them as much as the weird, infernal performances of the mud pots, hot springs, and geysers. They came primarily to be entertained by these phenomenal features. John Muir, however, could be depended on to read into the phantasmagorical Yellowstone landscape lessons both divine and Darwinian as he reminded his readers of the creative power of geologic forces embodying "creation, progress in the march of beauty through death."[13] To his spiritual passion Muir wedded a practical sense, and through his efforts the Sierra Club was founded as an organization advocating public ownership of wilderness lands and, later, environmental protection in more general ways.

In 1890, the Yosemite area (minus the Yosemite Valley) was transferred from the state of California to the national government, and, in 1899, Mount Rainier

National Park was created. Other parks were acquired not only for scenic, but also for scientific and historical reasons, especially after Theodore Roosevelt, encouraged through his association with John Muir, became an early proponent of conservation. The administration of these parks was haphazard, for there was as yet no National Park Service. Then, in 1914, Stephen Mather (1867–1930), an industrialist in Chicago and an ardent hiker and member of the Sierra Club, wrote to Secretary of the Interior Franklin K. Lane, complaining of the condition of the parks. Lane, well aware of the problem, had already employed a young lawyer in California, Horace M. Albright, to study ways to improve the administration of the national parks. Recognizing that, as a businessman, Mather possessed considerable organizational and administrative talents, Lane promptly invited him to come to Washington, D.C., and take charge of the situation. Mather accepted the challenge, and he and Albright became a formidable team. Their combination of idealism and pragmatism forged the National Parks Act, creating the National Park Service, which President Woodrow Wilson signed into law in 1916. The national park system that was forged in the ensuing years—as many more national parks were created, historic sites designated, and large tracts of unspoiled coastline legislated into national seashores—is a proud achievement of the American people and has been a potent instrument in shaping the nation's image of itself.

10.19. Thomas Moran, *The Grand Canyon of the Yellowstone*. 1872. National Museum of American Art. Lent by the U. S. Department of the Interior, National Park Service

1. *Modernism* is the movement that responded optimistically to machine technology and the speeded-up tempo of twentieth-century machine-age civilization. It is expressed in several arts: in painting and sculpture as Cubism, Futurism, and other styles that fragment form and generally value its abstract character more than any remaining narrative content; in music as jazz, a fluid, improvisational medium that captures the syncopated tempo and erotic energy pulsing through urban life; in architecture as design that honors industrial technology and materials by divesting itself of the proportions and ornament of classical humanism and the structural means and decorative vocabulary inherited from the medieval and Renaissance past; in literature as poems and novels that portray the transactions between the human soul and societies in which the security of community has been superseded by personal anonymity and an intoxicating sense of possibility derived from new means of physical mobility and a new sense of social freedom. Modernism is fundamentally a state of culture that romanticizes reason, believing that rational application of science and technology combined with egalitarian politics will create a better world. *Postmodernism* questions modernism's attempted radical break with history and, because many modernist ideals have been discredited, sees its utopian articles of faith as naive. Being reactive, it is stylistically reiterative, re-presenting historical styles in quotation form, as echoes of earlier forms within a contemporary culture that is philosophically groundless and therefore without a special formal vocabulary of its own. Ironically, postmodern culture is vastly more machine-driven than the culture of modernism that preceded it.

2. During his visit to Paris in 1859, Olmsted noted the essential character of this aspect of French park construction, remarking that "The principal rock-work is much more like an operatic fairy scene than any thing in nature; and as its great size prevents it from being regarded as puerile or grotesque, like Chinese garden scenes, it may be considered to have been conceived in an original style to which the term romantic may be rightly applied." Essay on "Parks at Home and Abroad" (1861); see Charles Capen McLaughlin, ed.-in-chief, *The Papers of Frederick Law Olmsted, Volume III: Creating Central Park,* ed. Charles E. Beveridge and David Schuyler (Baltimore: The Johns Hopkins University Press, 1983), p. 349.

3. William Robinson, *The Parks, Promenades & Gardens of Paris* (London: John Murray, 1869), p. 64.

4. For a brilliant meditation upon the meaning of the Eiffel Tower, see Roland Barthes, *The Eiffel Tower and Other Mythologies,* trans. Richard Howard (New York: Farrar, Straus and Giroux, Inc., 1979). Here Barthes writes, "The Tower attracts meaning, the way a lightning rod attracts thunderbolts; for all lovers of signification, it plays a glamorous part, that of pure signifier, i.e., of a form in which men unceasingly put *meaning* (which they extract at will from their knowledge, their dreams, their history), without this meaning thereby ever being finite and fixed: who can say what the Tower will be for humanity tomorrow? But there can be no doubt it will always be something other and something much more than the Eiffel Tower" (University of California Press ed., 1997, p. 5).

5. Report of the Senate Committee on the District of Columbia on the Improvement of the Park System of the District of Columbia, *The Improvement of the Park System of the District of Columbia* (Washington: 1902) as quoted in John W. Reps, *Monumental Washington: The Planning and Development of the Capital Center* (Princeton: Princeton University Press), p. 131.

6. I am indebted to Timothy Davis, "Rock Creek and Potomac Parkway, Washington, DC: The Evolution of a contested urban landscape," *Studies in the History of Gardens & Designed Landscapes* 19:2 (April–June 1999) for the excellent research upon which the following narrative is drawn.

7. "Letter to Mary Perkins Olmsted, Bear Valley, November 20, 1863," in *The Papers of Frederick Law Olmsted, Volume V,* ed. Victoria Post Ranney (Baltimore: The Johns Hopkins University Press, 1990), pp. 136–37.

8. "Preliminary Report upon the Yosemite and Big Tree Grove," in *The Papers of Frederick Law Olmsted, Volume V,* ed. Victoria Post Ranney, p. 501.

9. Ibid., p. 500.

10. Ibid.

11. John Muir, *Mountaineering in the Sierra Nevada,* as quoted in Sears, *Sacred Places: American Tourist Attractions in the Nineteenth Century* (New York: Oxford University Press, 1989), p. 134.

12. John Ruskin, *Modern Painters* (Boston: Dana Estes, 1880), vol. IV, p. 217.

13. "The Yellowstone National Park," *Our National Parks* (1901), as quoted in Sears, op. cit., p. 177.

CHAPTER ELEVEN

LANDSCAPE AND CITYSCAPE AS AESTHETIC EXPERIENCE: THE ARTS AND CRAFTS MOVEMENT AND THE REVIVAL OF THE FORMAL GARDEN

The unease and anomie that people experience when familiar social structures have collapsed created a conservative reaction to machine-age modernity: Historicism, a mentality that values particular cultures and vanished epochs. Giambattista Vico (1668–1744) was a progenitor of the idea that there is no universal, timeless human culture, that remote cultures are entirely different from current ones, and that it is the task of the historian to reconstruct a view of other times and other places with deep, sympathetic imagination. Johann Gottfried von Herder (1744–1803) propounded this thesis, which became one of the several strands of Romantic thought. His views helped establish a deeper and more discriminating appreciation of the particular artistic expressions of various cultures, both ones that were remote in time and place and others nearer at hand. The search for roots, for history, so prevalent today even as the entire world streams toward globalization, the latest and most advanced form of cosmopolitanism, is symptomatic of the continuing hold Herder's Romantic thesis has upon our minds.

John Ruskin (1819–1900) was the principal contemporary spokesman for the viewpoint that denied the beneficence of Victorian industrial progress as it was reaching its apogee in late nineteenth-century England. As the precursor of the Arts and Crafts movement, Ruskin articulated its fundamental principles in *The Seven Lamps of Architecture* (1848). These included architecture for the sake of beauty rather than mere function, honesty of materials, power of impression, inspiration from nature, virile liveliness, commemorative quality, and accordance with universally accepted styles. Ruskin found in medieval styles and their several period and regional inflections an architecture that accorded with these concepts. His influence was strong and long-lasting, helping to account for the naturalistic exuberance of nineteenth-century architectural ornament and the extensive use of animal and vegetable forms in the decorative arts.

Leaders of the Arts and Crafts movement expressed a similar reaction to machine technology. Perhaps the most articulate and angry among them was the English poet, designer, and socialist lecturer William Morris (1834–1896), who wrote extensively on the problems associated with industrialization, gave practical application to Ruskin's philosophy, and was closely allied with the group of painters who called themselves the Pre-Raphaelites. Like Ruskin, Morris was a strong proponent of medievalism because of the artisan traditions represented by the craft guilds in the Middle Ages. In 1861, he opened a firm, Morris, Marshall, Faulkner & Company— "Fine Art Workmen in Painting, Carving, Furniture and the Metals"—for the production of handcrafted home furnishings. For Morris, an imaginary sojourn in the Middle Ages provided a mental escape from the fast-changing landscape of the nineteenth century. His own highly organic but stylized designs for wallpaper and furniture ornament are akin to medieval patterns. In 1877—several years before he published *News from Nowhere* (1891), his utopian guide to the future—Morris founded the Society for the Protection of Ancient Buildings, which focused on the simple beauty of vernacular architecture. Historic preservation remained an important component of the Arts and Crafts movement.

The Viennese architect and city planner Camillo Sitte was perhaps the most influential opponent of the international urban planning movement that was gathering momentum in the wake of Haussmann's transformation of Paris. Sitte saw emulation of the medieval town square as a place-fixing remedy for the spatially diffuse modern city with its new wide, straight thoroughfares designed for rapid vehicular movement. Arts and Crafts aesthetics, later mingled with a painterly approach borrowed from the Impressionists, had an important influence on architecture in the second half of the nineteenth century, especially in Great Britain. Its Picturesque principles of design called for a continuation of handcrafted ornamentation of buildings, and this ran counter to the machine-age trend toward a faceless, abstract architecture based on the use of such new building materials as cast iron and glass.

Inevitably, Ruskin's towering influence was felt in the garden as well. Paxton's Crystal Palace in London, which had so impressed the public in 1851, conspicuously symbolized not only the Industrial Age architecture that Ruskin despised but also the Victorian enthusiasm for showy hybridized plants made possible by glasshouse horticulture. The Arts and Crafts movement that the followers of Ruskin and Morris carried forward numbered among its ranks several landscape professionals who saw the carpet-bedding practices of contemporary gardeners as vulgar rote exercises. William Robinson and Gertrude Jekyll were the foremost apostles of a new form of planting, which substituted a more casual and painterly approach employing naturalized shrubs, wildflowers, and perennials for the Victorian gardener's formulaic flower beds. In fractious opposition to Robinson's advocacy of a naturalistic, picturesque style of gardening, the architect Reginald Blomfield set forth an approach oriented more toward architecture than painterly composition, which Blomfield labeled "formal."

The Edwardian Age now appears as the halcyon twilight of aristocratic pleasures—garden parties, croquet games, lawn tennis—in verdant settings beautifully maintained by large staffs of gardeners. In the pre-income-tax United States, industrial wealth generated fortunes that Beaux-Arts-trained designers displayed in Italianate gardens of the Country Place Era. The gardens commissioned by latter-day British aristocrats and wealthy Americans for their country estates or the venerable European *châteaux* and villas they and others restored were highly eclectic. Overall, they displayed their owners' and designers' appreciation of historic gardens, reintroduction of intimate scale and spatial enclosure, use of topiary and other "old-fashioned" forms, and loose, naturalistic planting composition in which color plays an important role. Whether derived from Arts and Crafts principles, Italianate and Beaux-Arts formality, or a combination of the naturalistic and the formal, the principal design premise of the Edwardian garden was one of sheer aestheticism; it was an expression of art for art's sake. As such, it represented no ideological set of values and existed only in the context of *style*. It was, like the current obsession with expressing history in the landscape, a consumer's option in which period style became itself a dominant cultural value. No longer bound to representation—the re-presentation of ideas and beliefs through art—design had become a matter of mere choice involving selection among several available historical styles. As such, it no longer expressed the philosophical or literary values of its own age, being instead a graceful echo of forms whose original meaning was now lost.

11.1. Kate Greenaway, watercolor illustration for the poem "Mary, Mary, quite contrary, how does your garden grow?"

Thus, by the end of the nineteenth century, the result of Herder's Romantic thesis a century earlier, with its emphasis on historical appreciation as a source of heightened meaning in contemporary life, was firmly rooted. Whether accomplished by talented amateurs or by the emerging professionals who called themselves landscape architects, garden design had become almost entirely self-referential. Landscape designs bore no messages other than those of a sentimental nature—remembrances of flowers in Shakespeare's plays; charming evocations of "bygoneness," as in "Queen Anne" period gardens; or images evoking Kate Greenaway's illustrations for children's books (fig. 11.1).

Because of its association with domesticity, the landscape design field was open earlier than others to women practitioners. In the estate gardens she designed, Beatrix Jones Farrand, one of the founders of the American Society of Landscape Architects, drew upon the Arts and Crafts legacy of Jekyll; the work of Thomas Mawson, who combined Arts and Crafts garden style with Beaux-Arts planning principles; and a traveler's first-hand acquaintance with Italian villa gardens. Farrand's contemporary, Ellen Biddle Shipman, who had less opportunity to journey abroad and study examples of European landscape design, created original gardens that complemented the American Colonial Revival architecture then fashionable. In California and Florida, landscape designers were especially eclectic, borrowing inspiration from Italian villas and harking to distant echoes of Islamic Spain as they sought to forge regional idioms based upon the sunny Mediterranean-type climate and Hispanic heritage found in these states. In both, a vegetal palette incorporating many species of semitropical plants made gardens exceptionally lush. California designers also looked west across the Pacific, especially to Japan, for inspiration.

Whether continuing the eclectic tradition of the Edwardians or subscribing to the tenets of modernism, landscape design was now a much more individualistic enterprise than before. Gardening was seen as an expression of personality, the domain of private dreams, and such it remains today, especially in those highly personal landscapes often referred to as "vernacular." The Edwardian landscape's purposes were those of idyllic retreat or recreational refuge from the increasing freneticism of modern life. Being essentially a place of play, it had little concern for representing broadly shared philosophical perspectives or displaying emblems of power. Moreover, Edwardian croquet lawns and tennis courts were but a foretaste of the garden's expanding role as a place of physical recreation, one that was to be extended to society at large by the many new public parks built in the twentieth century. Henceforth, as the old order of social hierarchy faded, its purpose was to serve the general welfare and become a commodity for mass consumption.

I. Modernity Challenged: Ruskin's Influence, the Past Revalued, and Italy's Long Shadow

Baron Haussmann's modernization of the city of Paris during the reign of Napoleon III was but the first example of thorough urban reconfiguration to accommodate the new forces of accelerated movement brought about by the Industrial Age. Elsewhere in the second half of the nineteenth century cities were being similarly transformed. Vienna acquired a belt of fluid urban motion and monumental modern urbanism beginning in 1857 when Emperor Franz Josef I ordered the demolition of the fortifications walling the old city. The area of the glacis, the sloped terrain extending in front of the walls, which had long been controlled by the military, became a belt of open space available for new uses. The city, which was then administered by the liberal element of the bourgeoisie, employed the best Viennese architects of the second half of the nineteenth century to create the broad, landscaped Ringstrasse, a beltway with public green spaces and sites for important ecclesiastical, civic, and educational institutions and also for new residential buildings.

Though employing modern methods of construction, the architects of the Ringstrasse built in a medley of borrowed styles. They applied the Gothic style in designing the Rathaus, an attempt to associate this seat of municipal government with the pre-imperial medieval commune governed by burghers. By contrast, they deemed an early Baroque idiom appropriate for the state theater, the Burgtheater, perhaps because it spoke of the time when commoners were first able to join courtiers in the enjoyment of the dramatic arts. These structures, together with the neo-Renaissance university and the Neoclassical Parliament buildings, the latter built as a gargantuan Greek temple with vastly extended wings, were oriented to the broad expanse of the Ringstrasse. Contrary to the historic models they evoked, these works of architecture stood isolated, lacking the frame of well-defined public space. No medieval or Renaissance squares gave spatial enclosure and foreground perspective to the Rathaus or the university, and no monumental axes found their terminal points in the Burgtheater or the Parliament. Although the buildings were set in generously landscaped space, this further emphasized their isolation, heterogeneousness, and lack of visible containment. It was this loss of urban spatial coherence—buildings and public spaces defined and visually enhanced by one another—that disturbed Camillo Sitte, the Austrian architect and city planner who sought to stem the tide of cultural disintegration and loss of community as the rich texture of old cities and towns built by human hands began

to be superseded by impersonal urban environments created by machine technology.

Camillo Sitte and the Art of Building Cities

Camillo Sitte (1843–1903) maintained a historicist vision that was embodied in Picturesque architectural principles, and he sought to stabilize urban space by replicating the square of the medieval and Renaissance townscape. In 1889, he published *Der Städtebau nach seinen kunstlerischen Grundsätzen*—in its English translation, *The Art of Building Cities*. This remarkable essay continues still to speak to those who address their attention to cityscapes and who, like Sitte, regret the sacrifice of urban design to traffic engineering and the substitution of technocratic utilitarian planning for artistic principles of urban composition. In forming his critique, Sitte did not quarrel with eclectic architecture, as modernist architects soon would. Instead, he based his argument on an analysis of public spaces in classical and more recent historic times, before planning had been entrusted to government agency officials who had inevitably developed a systematic, formulaic approach to urban design. The Greek agora and the Roman forum had been vital centers of community life, and many of the Italian piazzas had evolved as satisfying assemblages of architecture, sculpture, and open space through an instinctive artistry spanning several generations. Closer to home, the close-knit town life in the time of craft guilds evoked in *The Mastersingers* by Richard Wagner, a composer whom Sitte greatly admired, provided an image of artisan values and community. Sitte included in his book several instructive diagrams analyzing the configurations of cathedral squares in Nuremberg and other German and Austrian communities (fig. 11.2).

One of the first to recognize and articulate the more open character of cities in the modern age as

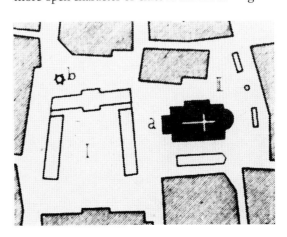

11.2. Diagram of the town of Nuremberg, by Camillo Sitte, from *The Art of Building Cities*. 1889

well as their enlarged size and building scale, Sitte pointed out the failure of rational planning to provide a suitable urban habitat, citing Vienna's wide, windswept thoroughfares furnished with tiny islands for crossing pedestrians, its unenclosed new parks that lacked the feeling of tranquillity and protection found in old palace gardens, its division into blocks that emphasized street frontage at the expense of interior courtyard space, and the design of public squares as reservoirs of traffic, rather than as places for public life. Although he realized that the publication of newspapers diminished one of the functions of the square—that of exchanging information—and that market stalls had been supplanted by indoor shops, Sitte still believed that artistically arranged public squares were essential elements of community, necessary both visually and spiritually. Like Frederick Law Olmsted, he disliked the relentless grid that ignored topographic considerations and that failed to capture scenic opportunities. Haussmann's Paris, though technocratic in its approach to planning and therefore conducive to the same monotonous banality that was beginning to afflict Vienna and other modernizing cities, was improved in Sitte's eyes by its continuation of the Baroque tradition of terminating axes with monumental buildings, showing that "perspective effects are possible even within the limitations imposed by practical considerations."[1]

Sitte was willing to make concessions to utility, and he knew that modern cities needed systematic planning with regard to transportation and sanitation. But he deplored the division of the unbuilt city into uniform blocks of land for real-estate speculation. Regarding the composition of public squares, he despised as dull the convention of centering monuments and applying symmetry as a uniform design principle. In short, the formulaic plan was his bête noire. "Whoever is to succeed in upholding esthetic considerations in urban development must," he declared, "first, realize that practical solutions to traffic problems are not necessarily rigid, unalterable remedies; and secondly, he must be prepared to demonstrate that practical requirements of modern living need not necessarily obstruct artful development."[2]

In a final chapter, Sitte offered diagrammatic suggestions to enhance the existing Ringstrasse buildings through the reconfiguration of their surroundings as enclosed plazas. But his attempts to define a psychology of place—like the opposite approach of his Viennese contemporary the architect Otto Wagner to aggrandize and regularize urban space—remained a utopian vision influential only in academic and intellectual circles. As the head of the State Trade School, Sitte advanced his Arts and Crafts ideals from

within the government bureaucracy, writing on bookbinding, ceramics, fountain restoration, and other subjects that combined his love of the past with his sense of urgent need for the aesthetic imagination to serve as a redemptive social force within the framework of contemporary capitalism.

THE VICTORIAN WAR OF STYLES: WILLIAM ROBINSON AND REGINALD BLOMFIELD

In the realm of the English garden, William Robinson (1838–1935) promoted an Arts and Crafts aesthetic at odds with the forces of scientific horticulture driving much of the landscape design in his day. Like Capability Brown, Robinson was a working gardener who rose to a position of exceptional influence. Like John Claudius Loudon, he was effective in reaching a broad audience through the pages of his garden periodicals and books. But although Robinson shared Loudon's encyclopedic botanical knowledge, he saw plants more in artistic than in scientific terms, and he abhorred the Victorian style of carefully displayed specimen plants Loudon had championed and christened the Gardenesque. For Loudon, admiration of an individual plant's form was a consideration equal in importance to its effect with other plants in the landscape, and for flower beds or groupings of trees and shrubs he urged that each be planted near to, but not touching, its neighbor. Robinson, to the contrary, envisioned garden compositions with plants intermingled and sometimes intertwined as in wild nature. His style was within the Picturesque tradition at the time when the Picturesque's potential to create rich and varied scenes had been greatly expanded by the introduction of many new species of flowering plants.

Robinson's firm opinions on horticultural matters, fluently expressed in peppery prose, soon led him to write for the *Gardeners' Chronicle*. He was fortunate in being able to communicate his ideas to an expanding and congenial audience. The tremendous suburban growth around London and other British cities at the end of the nineteenth century took the form of many hundreds of thousands of middle- and working-class homes with garden plots.[3] With a climate moist and temperate enough to grow a wide range of plant material, with long hours of summer daylight, and with sufficient money in the pockets of enough of its citizens to support a flourishing nursery trade, late Victorian and Edwardian England became a nation of gardeners. Poor cottagers living in old rural villages obtained gifts of cuttings for their gardens, which they arranged randomly with little design forethought. There was, however, considerable charm in the vernacular landscape of cottagers' gardens, and Robinson saw them as a rich source of ideas that suburban gardeners could use, particularly after he became acquainted with the garden-artist and craftswoman Gertrude Jekyll, who appreciated cottage gardens as much as he did. The native landscape of fields, hedgerows, and woodland dells offered further inspiration (fig. 11.3). The growing number of field clubs and local scientific societies and the publication of handbooks on wildflowers testified to a broad general interest in nature among the British. Robinson incorporated into his recommendations many ideas gleaned from these sources as well as from his own rambles. Ruskin's view of nature as the root of truth and beauty and his belief in honorable craft as an antidote to crude mechanization added support for Robinson's and Jekyll's Arts and Crafts approach to garden design.

Alpine Flowers for English Gardens, published in 1870, the same year as *The Wild Garden,* told readers that the plants Robinson had seen growing in rocky crevices in the Alps could also flourish in English gardens. The continuing popularity of rock gardens was due in no small part to Robinson's persuasiveness in promoting Alpine horticulture. Other writers had criticized bedding out of plants, promoted a floral version of the Picturesque, and urged gardeners to study wildflowers and to emulate the effects of field and forest, but none had Robinson's flair as a publicist and none was as prolific as he. In 1871, to further his views, he began publishing *The Garden,* a long-lived weekly journal to which both Ruskin and Gertrude Jekyll contributed. This was followed by other periodicals: *Gardening Illustrated,* begun in 1879; *Cottage Gardening,* started in 1892; and *Flora and Sylva,* published from 1903 until 1905. Graphically well designed and featuring handsome engravings, these magazines provided a platform from which Robinson promoted rock gardens, wild gardening, and herbaceous borders. They provided a forum where he could fulminate against aspects of garden taste that he despised. One was the fashion for topiary, which had been revived in High Victorian gardens, notably Levens Hall and Elvaston Castle, and which was later advocated by Robinson's contemporary, the Ruskinian ecclesiastical architect-turned-gardener John Dando Sedding (1838–1891), in *Garden-Craft Old and New* (1891) (fig. 11.4). Contentious and opinionated, Robinson continued to advance his ideas in his magnum opus, *The English Flower Garden* (1883). Through his conversational, commonsensical style and the vivid pictures he painted with words he won many readers, and the book ran to sixteen editions.

Robinson was as zealous in his attack upon Reginald Blomfield (1856–1942), an architect and the author of *The Formal Garden in England* (1892), as in his crusade against carpet bedding. Although Blomfield championed a return to the design formality of the English garden in pre-Georgian times, he did not feel that designing in the manner of these old gardens was incompatible with Arts and Crafts principles. His principal argument rested upon the belief that house and garden should be united in a single plan in which landscape space was treated as an extension of the architecture of the house. Robinson, for his part, did not object to geometrical lines in the garden. For him, a rectangular flower bed was, like the rectangular stretcher supporting the canvas on which an artist paints a free-flowing landscape, a convenient shape wherein the gardener's naturalistic effects could be displayed. Both men despised William Andrew Nesfield's revival of the *parterre* and the Italianate grandeur of the Crystal Palace Park at Sydenham. Blomfield, however, wanted to revive the classicism of Christopher Wren—so much so that his style was jokingly called "Wrenaissance"—and to return to the garden a sense of enclosure, making it an architectural arrangement of outdoor rooms partitioned by walls and hedges, proportioned in relation to the house, and employing the principles of symmetry in its layout. He perceived the unstructured naturalistic garden as an obstacle to this end. As bluntly opinionated as Robinson, he asserted dogmatically that "to suppose that love of nature is shown by trying to produce the effects of wild nature on a small scale in a garden is clearly absurd; anyone who loves natural scenery will want the real thing; he will hardly be content to sit in his rockery and suppose himself to be among the mountains."[4]

To the author of *The Wild Garden* and *Flowers for English Alpine Gardens* these were fighting words. Heirs to a now well-established tradition of British literary invective in books and articles on landscape design, Blomfield and Robinson were well matched in the passion with which they espoused their respective views. The word *formal,* with its connotation of the geometric style, was the source of some confusion. To Robinson the horticulturist it should apply only "where the plants of a garden are rigidly set out

11.3. "Wild Rose growing on a Pollard Ash in Orchardleigh Park, Somerset," an engraving after a watercolor by Alfred Parsons

Below: 11.4. W. R. Lethaby, "A Garden Enclosed," from *Garden-Craft Old and New* by J. D. Sedding. Imbued with a medievalizing Arts and Crafts aestheticism, this hedge-enclosed garden displays topiary forms and a central pillar with an armillary sphere, a feature possibly inspired by Francesco Colonna's *Hypnerotomachia Poliphili.*

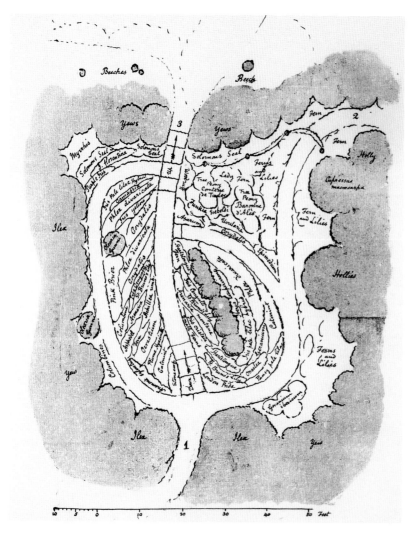

11.5. Plan of the Hidden Garden, Munstead Wood, Surrey, designed by Gertrude Jekyll

in geometrical design as in carpet-gardening and bedding-out." It was also for him, as for Blomfield, a synonym for *architectural,* and he would confine the architect solely to designing houses and some necessary grading around them. Everything else was to be left to the discretion of the garden designer with his superior knowledge of horticulture and claim to artistic plantsmanship. Eventually the acrimony subsided, and each side could claim victory as Edwardian gardens became alternatively formal and revivalistic or informal and naturalistic. Increasingly, they were places where both geometrical lines and painterly flower borders were at home.

Painterly Plantsmanship with Architectural Structure: Gertrude Jekyll and Edwin Lutyens

The Edwardian garden designer whose reputation has endured longest is Gertrude Jekyll (1843–1932), the first woman to act as a professional practitioner in the field. By good fortune, a young architect, Edwin Landseer Lutyens (1869–1944), lived near her village of Godalming, just north of Munstead Heath in Surrey, the then-rural southern county that is now a heavily suburbanized part of metropolitan London. Their friendship flourished on both a personal level and as a fruitful collaboration over several years. It was one that embodied both designers' deep respect for rural English vernacular building and gardening idioms. At the heart of their achievement was the conviction Jekyll undoubtedly conveyed to Lutyens regarding the importance of sensitive site planning.

As a girl, Jekyll read Ruskin's works avidly. Ruskin's deep respect for handicrafts and the artisan worker would remain a chief influence and moral guide for Jekyll the rest of her life. In 1861, the same year William Morris started his crafts firm and a time when higher education was gradually opening to women, Jekyll enrolled in the South Kensington School of Art. Here she learned drawing and color theory and experienced the influence of Owen Jones, a crafts designer and student of Moorish, Italian, and Chinese ornament who had served as superintendent of the Great Exhibition of 1851 as well as joint director of decoration for the Crystal Palace at Sydenham. Introductions to both Ruskin and Morris, whose International Exhibition of his firm's craft products she had probably visited in 1862, confirmed her in her course as an artist. She chose to be both a painter and a craftswoman, accepting many commissions for silver jewelry, embroideries, and inlaid woodwork, although, as a well-to-do woman from a prominent family, she could not defy social convention by formally establishing herself in business. In 1876, after her father's death, she went to live with her mother in Munstead House, where, with a nature that craved a large degree of privacy and tranquillity, she was happy to continue her arts and crafts pursuits in the rural quietude of Surrey.

In 1883, Jekyll purchased a 15-acre triangular plot of land opposite Munstead House, "fifteen acres of the poorest possible soil," the site of her garden and future home, Munstead Wood. Here she began developing a garden of woodland walks. She was severely afflicted by myopia—nearsightedness—and as this condition progressed, she was forced to abandon even close work. By 1891, her physician's prognosis of further deterioration caused her to throw more of her considerable artistic energy into gardening, which she was already pursuing with passionate interest. With the help of her brother she had taken up photography a few years earlier, and this gave her another visual medium of expression.

The hyphenated appellation *artist-gardener* perfectly suits Jekyll. Her blurry distance vision may possibly have assisted her in conceiving garden schemes less in terms of individual plants than as shapes, textures, and broad masses of color with single varieties often arranged to maximum optical advantage in long drifts along a diagonal to the path (fig. 11.5). Like the Impressionist Claude Monet (1840–1926), who was simultaneously creating his garden at Giverny both as a painterly expression in horticulture and a subject to be painted, Jekyll saw her garden as a series of seasonal scenes, appearing like pictures in a gallery with different exhibitions planned throughout the year. Not for her were Loudon's botanically ordered plant specimens. Glass houses, pridefully displayed in Victorian gardens, were removed in hers to hidden corners to serve purely practical ends. Her gardener's credo, expressed in *Colour Schemes for the Flower Garden* (1914), was deceptively simple:

> I am strongly of the opinion that the possession of a quantity of plants, however good the plants may be themselves and however ample their number, does not make a garden; it only makes a *collection*. Having got the plants, the great thing is to use them with careful selection and definite intention. . . . it seems to me that the duty we owe to our gardens and to our own bettering in our gardens is so to use the plants that they shall form beautiful pictures.[5]

Her easy and engaging style of writing was nurtured by her career as a garden columnist, first with the *Guardian Newspaper* and later as a contributor to William Robinson's magazine *The Garden,* which she coedited for a brief period following his retirement in 1899. She wrote the section on color for *The English Flower Garden,* which was republished in several subsequent editions of Robinson's popular book, and she contributed photographs of plants to serve as the basis of engravings in all editions after the second. In 1899, drawing material from her *Guardian* columns, she published a book of her own, *Wood and Garden*. She illustrated it with sixty-five of her own photographs, including many she had taken of cottagers at work in their gardens and woodmen competently felling trees with the time-honored tools she admired. Her prose is sensuous and vivid, and seasonal change, with the rhythm of the agrarian calendar dictating the gardener's rounds, remains a theme in all her books.

Book publication brought Jekyll increased celebrity and assisted her in building a design practice with her architect, friend, and protégé, Edwin Lutyens. Their common aesthetic grew as he rode with her in a pony cart through the byways of Surrey admiring vernacular architecture. In Lutyens, Jekyll felt she had found someone whom she could trust to provide the elements of architectonic structure and domestic comfort needed to complement her visions of nature perfected. He, in turn, was grateful to his sometimes overbearing, but immensely

helpful mentor, who imparted to him her Ruskinian sympathies, Arts and Crafts ideals, and deep appreciation of a vanishing England. His genius lay in his ability to fuse these elements with an architectural style that embodied many of the formal principles enunciated by Blomfield.

Socially conservative, Jekyll wanted to preserve the old class structure of masters and servants. But far from wishing to make the humble cottages of rural villages disappear from the improved landscape, as had been the case in the eighteenth century when lands were enclosed and great estate gardens such as Stowe created, she was in the vanguard of British heritage preservation. Even as an ancient way of life was succumbing to the modern age of industrialization, she wanted to save its building and craft traditions and to incorporate their techniques of brick, stone, and ironwork, along with the rustic charm of cottage gardens, into the style she and Lutyens were forging together. She also wanted to record the folkways and old agricultural methods that represented a venerable craft tradition even as new farm machinery and aspirations to transcend village poverty were causing these to vanish.

In much the same way as the French photographer Eugène Atget portrayed the still-vulnerable remnants of old Paris not already eradicated by Haussmann, Jekyll photographed the architectural fabric as well as the faces and handcrafted artifacts of her part of southern England. In 1904, she published *Old West Surrey,* which contains her photographs of rural subjects, including half-timbered cottages of mellow, well-laid brick with mullioned and diamond-pane windows and steeply pitched shingled roofs, and cottage gardens (fig. 11.6). These vernacular gardens were for her an important source of inspiration, and she planted many of the old roses and other traditional plants that bloomed in them at Munstead

11.6. Gertrude Jekyll, "Cluster Rose in a Cottage Garden." Photograph from Jekyll's book *Old West Surrey,* 1904

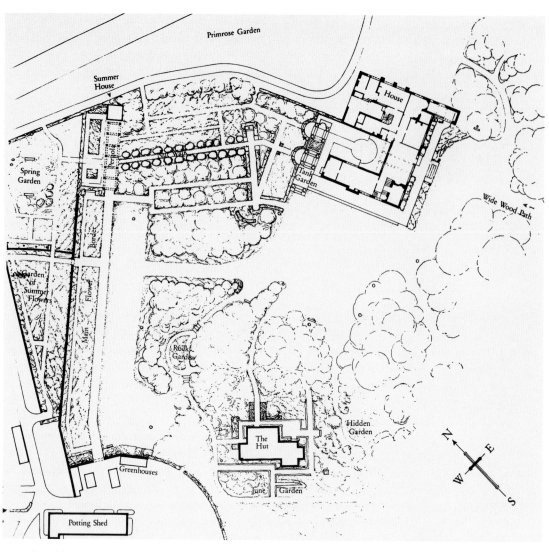

11.7. Plan of Munstead Wood (detail) after garden design by Gertrude Jekyll

Wood and in the gardens of the well-to-do clients who later called on her and Lutyens to design their country places.

In 1895, following her mother's death when Munstead House became home to her brother and his family, and thirteen years after Jekyll had begun to garden on her adjacent property, she was ready to build a house, Munstead Wood, on the site she had reserved for it (fig. 11.7). In *Gardens for Small Country Houses* (1912) Jekyll and her coauthor Lawrence Weaver wrote of the "right relation of the garden to the house," stating that "the connection must be intimate, and the access not only convenient but inviting."[6] At Munstead Wood, house and garden join in a mutual embrace. The house opens itself to the garden and incorporates the garden into its Paved Court, which is constructed of the same local stone as the house and edged with low boxwood hedges. At the north end of the Paved Court is the Tank Garden, where a rectangular pool is framed by stepped paving and lush plantings of ferns and canna lilies. Semicircular aprons of paving on either side of the pool mark the end of this formal construction where two garden paths, the Nut Walk and the path beside the Octo-

ber Michaelmas daisy border, lead to a Pergola and Summerhouse, beyond which lies Jekyll's 180-foot- (54.9-meter) long Main Flower Border, Garden of Summer Flowers, and Spring Garden.

The south and west sides of the house face a lawn and the adjoining woodland where, according to Jekyll, "much care has been given to the regions where the one melts into the other."[7] The principal path on the south is a wide grassy way, which Jekyll constructed to have as its focal point a handsome Scotch fir that, being double-stemmed, had not been cut when the property was a woodlot. Masses of rhododendrons carefully selected for their floral color were underplanted with hardy ferns, small andromedas, wild heaths, and the blue-flowered *Lithospermum prostratum*. Lesser paths formed a series of woodland walks, along which patches of trillium, drifts of Solomon's seal, and spires of white foxglove enhanced the impression of wild nature in its most generous state.

Jekyll's camera recorded many beautiful garden pictures at Munstead Wood over the years. Because of her growing reputation as a garden writer and photographer, she met Edward Hudson, the publisher, who, in 1897, launched *Country Life,* the first garden

magazine to feature coated paper to enhance the imagery of half-tone photographs. Jekyll began writing for *Country Life* in 1901, and her subsequent books were published under the *Country Life* imprint. Although the magazine showcased many great estates, Jekyll's participation added greater horticultural content and a focus upon small country houses, domestic establishments like her own Munstead Wood where the owner substituted for a head gardener in directing the work of a small gardening staff. Her first article described Orchards, the house and garden that she and Lutyens were then completing for her neighbors William and Julia Chance, a virtuosic combination of Lutyens's architectural imagination and Jekyll's painterly sensibility (fig. 11.8).

In 1898, following the Orchards commission, Lutyens crossed the English Channel to design Les Bois des Moutiers at Varengeville on the Normandy coast for the Anglophile banker Guillaume Mallet (fig. 11.9).[8] Imbued, like Jekyll, with the aesthetics of the Arts and Crafts movement, Mallet sought inspiration for the exquisitely harmonized floral tones of his superb collection of rhododendrons from medieval stained glass as well as from his collection of old embroidered fabrics, mostly clerical vestments. From Jekyll's *Wood and Garden* he derived the idea of introducing into the park Chinese azaleas (*Azalea mollis*) in a succession of carefully graded tones ranging from pale yellow to bright orangy red.

The Jekyll-Lutyens collaboration continued until her advancing age and his rise to professional prominence, culminating in a knighthood, brought it to a gradual halt. Increasingly, Lutyens moved toward formality while still maintaining his originality as an architect. Although conceived in the so-called Anglo-Indian style, his plan for New Delhi, the government capital the British built south of Delhi between 1912 and 1931, was akin in its Beaux-Arts classicism to the contemporary planning in America that was being promoted as the City Beautiful.

THE FORMAL GARDEN IN FRANCE: REVIVAL OF FRENCH RENAISSANCE AND SEVENTEENTH-CENTURY TRADITION

Contemporary with Blomfield's revaluation of seventeenth-century British gardens was the practice in France of Henri Duchêne (1841–1902) and his son Achille Duchêne (1866–1947), which drew upon that nation's immense seventeenth-century patrimony as defined by Le Nôtre. The restored *parterre* designs that we see today at Vaux-le-Vicomte are the work of Henri Duchêne (1897) and Achille Duchêne (1910) (see fig. 5.4). At Champs-sur-Marne the father and son erased the *jardin anglais* that had been superimposed upon a seventeenth-century plan, reestablishing the *parterre de broderie* as two fine panels of flowing arabesques. Recognizing the Duchênes' expertise in resurrecting this lost art with a particular crispness of line, the ninth duke of Marlborough (1892–1934) commissioned Achille to restore the north forecourt at Blenheim as a *parterre* garden. Duchêne then went on to design formal gardens to the east and west of the palace, the latter with two water terraces. Perhaps his most successful design was the beautiful restoration of the park surrounding the *château* of Courances in Essonne, France, in the years prior to World War I as a small *parterre* and series of spring-fed canals and pools framed by *palissades* and noble trees, with a small cascade rippling from the base of a sculpture of a reclining nymph (fig. 11.10). Although Duchêne, an arch-conservative French nationalist, deplored the Industrial Age and the democratization of culture that spelled an end to the aristocratic tradition of garden

11.8. Orchards, Surrey, with the "Dutch Garden" in the foreground. Photograph illustrating Jekyll's article in *Country Life.* 1901

Left: 11.9. Les Bois des Moutiers, Varengeville, France, showing the 1898 house designed by Edwin Landseer Lutyens as seen through the park, which has an extensive collection of azaleas, rhododendrons, and other flowering shrubs, all carefully chosen for pictorial effect.

Below: 11.10. Courances, Essonne, garden restoration by Achille Duchêne for the marquise de Ganay prior to World War I

11.11. *Potager* with *berceaux,* or trelliswork arbors, Lower Garden, Villandry. This twentieth-century garden was designed according to the sixteenth-century *château* garden layouts of Jacques Androuet du Cerceau.

Below: **11.12.** Jardin d'Ornement, topiary, Villandry

he associated with cultural democratization, with a Renaissance-evoking design that upheld his own belief in class hierarchy and social order. This three-level garden, a popular stop on the Loire Valley tourist circuit, manages to convey the intricate compartmentalization, meticulous order, and sense of containment within well-defined boundaries that are characteristic of Renaissance design.

Its *potager* is a geometrical *parterre* composed of nine large squares filled with lettuces and other vegetables of varied hues, arranged in a pattern derived from studying the sixteenth-century *château* garden layouts of Jacques Androuet du Cerceau (fig. 11.11, see figs. 4.40, 4.41, 4.42, 4.43, 4.44). The corners of each square are punctuated with the style of trelliswork arbors characteristic of Renaissance gardens, and today these are covered with roses.

The iconography of Villandry's noteworthy Jardin d'Ornement has more to do with late-nineteenth-century opera or nascent twentieth-century Surrealism than with the themes of Renaissance humanism (fig. 11.12). In one of its four compartments the topiary box represent hearts, flames, and masks symbolizing *l'amour tendre,* or tender love; in another butterflies and fans hint of *l'amour volage,* fickle love; a third is a labyrinth of hearts denoting *l'amour folie,* blind passion; and the last contains sword

making he had sought to reestablish among a waning nobility, he nonetheless tried to fit his talent to the demands of the twentieth century with its smaller properties, mastering an idiom of carefully scaled, finely detailed forms he termed *jardin d'architecture.*

At Villandry, a moated sixteenth-century *château* overlooking the river Cher within the Loire Valley a few miles west of Tours, its twentieth-century owner Dr. Joachim de Carvallo (1869–1936) undertook a garden construction project between 1906 and 1924 to replace the nineteenth-century *jardin anglais,* which

and dagger blades characterizing *l'amour tragique,* tragic love. In spite of this amusingly original interpretation of Renaissance garden design and perhaps because of a level of maintenance comparable to the time when battalions of gardeners were commonplace, the visitor almost feels transported to a distant age. An *allée* of lime trees defines the garden's main axis, which separates the two gardens just described from the Jardin d'Eau above with its verdant lawns, ornamental pool, fountain basins, and canal.

Jean-Claude-Nicolas Forestier (1861–1930), Achille Duchêne's and Dr. Joachim de Carvallo's contemporary, had a less reactionary temperament and restorationist bent. His was a flexible style that mediated between several trends: a return to Neoclassical formality, the legacy of the *jardin anglais,* an Arts and Crafts aesthetic, and the innovations of modernism. As an employee of the Paris Parks and Promenades administration after 1887, Forestier restored Thomas Blaikie's late-eighteenth-century *jardin-anglais* on the grounds of Bagatelle as a public park, leaving in place some of the garden's remaining *fabriques* and reintroducing French formality in the more architectonic lines of the new perennial and rose gardens (fig. 11.13). Forestier was also responsible for restoring Sceaux, the masterful landscape Le Nôtre had created for Colbert (see fig. 5.16). But his style ranged beyond that of French and English inspiration, incorporating such Islamic and Mediterranean features as patios and patterned tiles. This eclecticism was nourished by Forestier's international landscape practice. Like Duchêne, Forestier grappled with the challenge of designing gardens for the relatively small-scale private properties of a still wealthy but less landed clientele. His ability to amalgamate an Arts and Crafts horticultural palette, formal elements derived from Renaissance garden tradition, and Mediterranean and Islamic motifs in an original manner can be seen in the garden he designed for the Parque de Montjuich (Montjuïc) in Barcelona in 1918 (fig. 11.14).

THE INFLUENCE OF RENAISSANCE ITALY IN ENGLAND AND AMERICA

The merger of an Arts and Crafts aesthetic with Neoclassicism, eclectic creativity, and respect for regional materials and local scenery was part of a general stylistic trend adopted by various architects, landscape designers, and aesthetes well into the twentieth century. In addition to countering industrialization and mass production with artisan workmanship, the Arts and Crafts movement in Great Britain was, as we have seen, nationalistic, a preservationist effort to uphold English vernacular traditions. Even so, this commitment to "Englishness" was being undermined by Beaux-Arts influence in much the same way as the American style of Olmsted and Vaux was being challenged by Daniel Burnham and the Neoclassical architects who projected a new monumentalism and rectilinear axiality in American architecture and city planning.

The thatched cottages of the Cotswolds and the gardens of Surrey, with their hollyhocks and roses, seemed excessively quaint to some Englishmen like Harold Ainsworth Peto (1854–1933) who sought statelier Continental examples as inspiration for a landscape style that expressed their art-for-art's-sake philosophy in different terms from those of the English vernacular tradition. They saw the sixteenth-century and early-seventeenth-century villas of Italy as models to emulate. Peto developed Italian themes in his own garden at Ilford Manor, near Bradford-on-Avon, Wiltshire, gaining the admiration of Jekyll, who included some of his design details in her book *Garden Ornament* (1918). At Ilford Manor and in the gardens he designed for clients, Peto terraced slopes, marked grade changes with balustrades atop retaining walls, created graceful staircases with side walls terminating in finial-topped pillars or columns holding antique statuary, and built casinos and colonnades overlooking tanks of water lilies (fig. 11.15). In their sensitive use of native stone; in their employment of a subdued floral palette as a complement to evergreen

11.13. Perennial garden, Bagatelle, Paris, designed by Jean-Claude-Nicolas Forestier. Early 20th century

Left: **11.14. Corner pavillion designed by Jean-Claude-Nicolas Forestier for the Parque de Montjuich (Montjuïc), Barcelona. 1918.**

Below: **11.15. Ilford Manor, Wiltshire, garden designed by owner, Harold Ainsworth Peto. From 1899**

11.16. Gardens designed by Harold Ainsworth Peto for John Annan Bryce, Ilnacullin (Garinish Island), Glengarriff, Republic of Ireland. Begun 1910

11.17. Villa I Tatti, Ponte a Ménsola, Settignano. Gardens designed by Cecil Ross Pinsent for Bernard Berenson. 1909

shrubs and trees; and in their siting with respect to their surroundings, Peto's gardens demonstrate a discriminating assimilation of Italian themes to English landscape tradition. In several gardens he showed that he could manipulate water, one of the principal ingredients of Italian gardens, with considerable originality. At Hartham Park in Wiltshire, around 1903, he built a long canal and a casino modeled on one of the pair next to the Fountain of the Deluge at the sixteenth-century Villa Lante. At Garinish Island at the head of Bantry Bay in County Cork, Ireland, against the scenic backdrop of Sugarloaf Mountain, he brought the lush vegetation within the sunken garden and its Villa Lante–style pavilion into focus with a rectangular lily pool (fig. 11.16).

Americans, too, including the artist Charles Platt (1861–1933), saw Italian villas as a source of inspiration for the country houses their affluent countrymen were building on the North Shore of Long Island, in the Berkshires in Massachusetts, and at Newport, Rhode Island. In this period, which has come to be known as the Country Place Era, American heirs to large fortunes were marrying British aristocrats with some regularity, and there was a great deal of cultural correspondence between the members of high society in both countries. The American and English love

affair with Italy was such that many expatriates took up residence in Tuscany and elsewhere in Italy. These included Arthur Acton, owner of La Pietra in Florence; Lady Sybil Cutting, who presided over the Villa Medici in Fiesole; and Gertrude Jekyll's older sister Caroline, who married Frederic Eden and with him and advice from Gertrude created an English-inflected Italian garden behind the high walls surrounding their palazzina on the Giudecca in Venice.

Beginning with *Roderick Hudson* (1875), the novelist Henry James wrote about the expatriate life of this generation, its high ideals of beauty, and its determination to grasp artistic experience and live a life of connoisseurship. In 1900, James's fellow American, the art historian Bernard Berenson (1865–1959), took up residence at the Villa I Tatti near Settignano, a village close to Florence. While serving as agent to Isabella Stewart Gardner in assembling her Venetian palazzo and art collection in Boston, Berenson commissioned the English architect Cecil Ross Pinsent (1884–1963) to design at I Tatti an Italian-style garden with a *limonaia* and clipped box hedges (fig. 11.17). Pinsent was also responsible for modifying the seventeenth-century gardens for Acton at La Pietra and the fifteenth-century gardens for Lady Sybil at the Villa Medici (see figs. 4.2, 4.3). Later, between 1924 and 1939, he worked with Lady Sybil's daughter, writer Iris Origo, on the design of the gardens of La Foce, her estate south of Siena.

The English and American interest in old Italian villa gardens was reflected in several books on the subject. H. Inigo Triggs (1876–1923), a Neoclassical architect and garden historian, followed his *Formal Gardens in England and Scotland* (1902) with *The Art of Garden Design in Italy* (1906), a handsome folio volume of measured drawings of more than eighty gardens. Sir George Reresby Sitwell (1860–1943) in *An Essay on the Making of Gardens, A Study of Old Italian Gardens, of the Nature of Beauty, and the Principles Involved in Garden Design* (1909) wrote lyrically about the more than 200 Italian gardens he had visited and of his application of the lessons they offered to the gardens at Renishaw, his ancestral Derbyshire estate.

In much the way that Jekyll had become a photographer in order to develop an archive of scenic and horticultural effects and design details for the Arts and Crafts garden, the American artist Charles Platt supplemented his sketches of Italian gardens with photographs, publishing his work in *Italian Gardens* (1894). He particularly admired the tall green walls that compartmentalized garden space in the Quirinal Gardens in Rome and elsewhere (fig. 11.18).[9] Like Jekyll's, Platt's eye as a painter was attuned to floral color, and though his primary interest was in the architectural unity of villa and garden and their relationship to the

surrounding landscape, he noted flowers wherever these appeared in Italian gardens.

Novelist Edith Wharton (1862–1937) also fostered an American appreciation of Italian gardens. Commissioned by the *Century* magazine to write a series of articles titled *Italian Villas and Their Gardens,* she published these as a book with illustrations by the popular American artist Maxfield Parrish (1870–1966) in 1904. In this volume she deftly recorded the appearance of several of the Italian gardens described here in Chapters Four and Five. Their lines softened by lichened stone and overgrown vegetation in a way that was agreeable to eyes trained to appreciate the Picturesque, these venerable landscapes still offered Wharton much inspiration regarding the fundamentals of landscape composition.

Both Platt and Wharton understood that compartmentalized gardens—and the opportunities for concealment, surprise, and spatial intimacy they offered—constituted the essence of Italian garden design. At The Mount, her summer home on a knoll overlooking Laurel Lake in Lenox, Massachusetts, Wharton set about designing a New England version of an Italian garden (fig. 11.19). Her niece, the landscape designer Beatrix Farrand (1872–1959), prepared plans for the entrance drive and kitchen garden. Drawing on her intimate knowledge of Italian gardens but wishing to establish an American version appropriate to the topography and traditions of New England, Wharton laid out a series of grassy terraces bordered with hemlock hedges, which she linked axially to the house. She connected these to a long cross axis, a 300-foot-long (91.4-meter-long) walk bordered by linden trees with a *parterre* garden at either end, one of which was a large red flower garden with a dolphin fountain in the center and the other a sunken *giardino segreto* built with the proceeds of Wharton's successful novel *The House of Mirth* (1905). Heir to Robinson and Jekyll as well as the idylls of Italy, she also planted an Alpine garden on a slope studded with natural outcrops of limestone.

The garden's real beauty lay not so much in

these elements as in the overall impression it achieved in unison with its surroundings. Wharton may have been describing The Mount with its broad views of Laurel Lake and the Tyringham Hills when her heroine in *The House of Mirth*, Lily Bart, leans pensively against a terrace balustrade gazing at

a landscape tutored to the last degree of rural elegance. In the foreground glowed the warm tints of the gardens. Beyond the lawn, with its pyramidal pale-gold maples and velvety firs, sloped pastures dotted with cattle; and through a long glade the river widened like a lake under the silver light of September.[10]

Like Blomfield, Platt was interested in uniting architectural and landscape space. This was what the Italian villa designers, who conceived of house and garden as integral parts of a single plan, had done. In Cornish, New Hampshire, the summer art colony of which Platt was a member, he developed on five properties, including his own, an American version of the Italian villa, in which he created axial alignments, descending terraced slopes, and garden spaces shaped by architectural greenery as outdoor living rooms.

Between 1896 and 1901, at Faulkner Farm in Brookline, Massachusetts, Platt designed a garden for

11.18. Photograph of Quirinal Gardens in Rome by Charles Platt, *Italian Gardens,* 1894

Below: 11.19. Plan of The Mount, Lenox, Massachusetts, designed by the owner, Edith Wharton. From 1902
Ⓐ Drive
Ⓑ Kitchen Garden
Ⓒ Red Flower Garden
Ⓓ House
Ⓔ Giardino Segreto (Secret Garden)

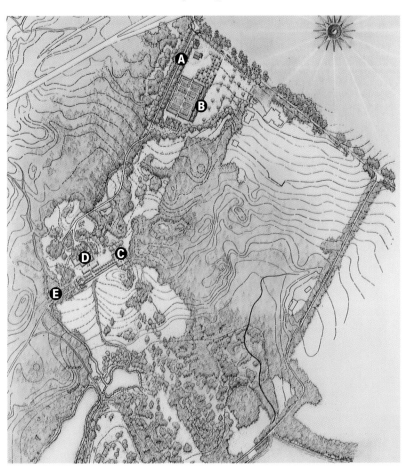

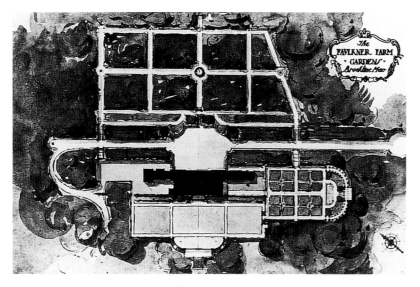

Top: **11.20. Plan of Faulkner Farm, garden designed by Charles Platt for Charles Sprague and Mary Pratt Sprague in Brookline, Massachusetts. 1896–1901**

Above: **11.21. View of the *parterre* garden at Faulkner Farm**

Charles Sprague and Mary Pratt Sprague (fig. 11.20). The steep grade of the site was conducive to creating a gridded *bosco* with a circular temple in the center on the hillside above the entry court and on axis with the principal entrance to the house. Below the house, Platt designed the spacious lawn as a transition between garden and forest, taking advantage of the

slope to create a series of descending grass terraces overlooking the western range of hills. As Olmsted had done at Biltmore and Moraine Farm, Platt withheld this panoramic view from immediate sight by placing a screen of densely planted trees alongside the long entrance drive on both sides of the entry court. He had lamented the decay of many of the flower-filled *giardini segreti* that had once vivified Italian gardens, and now at Faulkner Farm he laid out a large rectangular flower garden terminating at the far end in a horseshoe-shaped pergola and pavilion modeled, like those designed by Peto, on one of Cardinal Gambera's at Villa Lante (fig. 11.21).

Much admired and extensively published, Faulkner Farm launched Platt's career as a designer of houses and gardens that met the demand for what was hailed at the time as a new American landscape architecture. Italian-inspired, enriched by Arts and Crafts plantsmanship, the relaxed, historically evocative style that Platt helped create adapted a borrowed idiom to the American scene. As the republican values of the generation of Downing and Olmsted were replaced by those of the Gilded Age, the Italianate style became an expression of the cultural status of the successful industrialists and financiers who saw themselves as the successors of the Italian princes of the Renaissance, the collectors of artworks commissioned by the Medicis. Now, in democratic America, these latter-day Medicis had become builders of city palaces and country villas. Beaux-Arts training and Rome prize fellowships at the American Academy continued to be the primary path of career preparation for architects and landscape architects in the United States until World War II. For this reason one finds both in the planning of public parks and in the gardens of private estates a long-lingering debt to the principles of this style of neoclassical design.

II. The Edwardian and Post-Edwardian English Garden: Aristocracy's Golden Afternoon and Twilight

The incomprehensibility of vast social change as the entire religious and cultural underpinnings of a once-stable society is swept away by great tidal forces in the history of human affairs and the life of the human mind is the subject of Matthew Arnold's great, sad poem "Dover Beach" (1867). Its intimation of Western civilization's confusion and disarray was hardly heeded by Arnold's countrymen, the prosperous British aristocrats and industrialists who felt secure in the glory of their nation's empire over which a never-setting sun still shone.

But the Faustian power unleashed by the Industrial Revolution, the source of much economic pros-

perity, was demoniacally driving the science of war toward new and hideous ends of destruction while also propelling the great social transformations foreseen by Karl Marx. Nevertheless, from the perspective of those living at the turn of the twentieth century, the tragic upheaval of World War I and the Russian Revolution still lay a few years in the future, and even as these came to pass there were those whose fortunes survived. Before turning in Chapter Twelve to examine the landscapes of a visionary modernity as Western societies became more broadly democratic in the wake of their social transformations, we will examine a few more of the estate gardens of this lingering aristocracy. Reduced in scale as new taxes eroded many old fortunes and rising labor costs curtailed maintenance budgets, these early-twentieth-century landscapes were still gracious if no longer grand.

World War I brought the era of country-house building to a halt in England and ended what has been called the Edwardian Golden Afternoon—a time when a privileged segment of society enjoyed garden teas, lawn tennis, and touring quiet country roads by bicycle and another new machine of the Industrial Age, the motor car. Still, Lutyens and Jekyll continued to collaborate. Now, however, when the two old friends worked together, it was on plans for soldiers' cemeteries, as the Imperial War Graves Commission had appointed Lutyens, along with Blomfield, principal architect for the ones in France. But the domestic garden design idiom Jekyll and Lutyens had earlier forged was one that would serve well the postwar generation of estate owners, whose smaller properties and budgets did not allow the large-scale efforts of prior periods. The Arts and Crafts tradition pioneered by Robinson and the Jekyll-Lutyens partnership as it was fused with the Beaux-Arts style and the influence of Italian gardens found many notable expressions in the first half of the twentieth century. The style extends to the present day, and many of its finest practitioners were and are women. In part this was because the association of landscape architecture with the domestic realm made it seem more socially acceptable than female employment in some other professions.

With the writings of Robinson, Jekyll, and Blomfield and the lessons of Italian villa garden designers thoroughly assimilated and harmonized, the character of the early-twentieth-century English garden was now an agreeable stylistic amalgam of influences in which abundant, painterly herbaceous borders were happily incorporated into plans disciplined by architectonic principles. With unbounded prospect no longer necessarily possible or desirable as privacy and enclosure became design objectives once more, the eighteenth century's premium on unbroken openness was thoroughly invalidated. Although some naturalistic planting was found useful in blending the edges of the garden with the larger landscape beyond, Capability Brown, who had served before as a target of criticism for those advocating a different landscape style, came in for censure once again. It was a backward-looking time in which innovation lay in cherishing the British medieval and Tudor past and harmonizing this native heritage in an aesthetically agreeable manner with elements borrowed from the historic period styles of other countries.

EARLY TWENTIETH-CENTURY ENGLISH GARDEN DESIGN

In his influential book *The Art and Craft of Garden Making* (1900), Thomas Hayton Mawson (1861–1933) professed the notion of landscape design as a careful selection from a menu of styles. Mawson, the first Englishman to style himself a "landscape architect," championed the "idealists," that is "old garden designers [who created] many stately avenues, grand parterres, quiet alleys, shady walks, sparking fountains, quaint hedges, architectural ponds and broad unbroken lawns, which in many cases are wedded together in such a masterly way, as to impress the spectator with the grandeur and transparent honesty of the whole scheme."[11] Brown, on the other hand, was chief among the "realists," who tried to imitate nature but came to rely on serpentine lines to the point where "undulation became a stock accomplishment." Mawson admired Repton, however—not the earlier Picturesque landscape gardener, but rather the later advocate of the "Gardenesque."

Mawson promoted a return to the "truthful simplicity" of old gardens. He acknowledged, however, that "naturalism has, under certain conditions, its legitimate use and place in the creation of garden and park effects; and that a compromise between these two opposites or a combination of the two is at times the only method by which we can obtain anything like an effective whole."[12] Mawson's illustrations were more eclectic than Italianate. His style can best be summarized as a combination of Arts and Crafts flowers and topiary, Beaux-Arts unification of house and garden through axial planning, and the merging of these two influences with the curvilinear "naturalesque," as he called the informal style of garden design (fig. 11.22).

The early years of the twentieth century saw the rise of professional associations and accredited programs for training landscape design and horticultural practitioners. When the Institute of Landscape

11.22. "Terrace and Pavillion Designed for a Staffordshire Garden," from Thomas Mawson, *The Art and Craft of Garden Making*, 1900

Architects was founded in 1929, Mawson became its first president. A designer of public parks as well as many private gardens, he entered the emerging profession of town planning, participating in the garden cities movement and becoming, in 1923, the president of the Town Planning Institute. In 1904, Frances Garnet Wolseley (1872–1936) founded the Glynde School for Lady Gardeners near Lewes in East Sussex, and as a named patron, Gertrude Jekyll lent her considerable reputation to this enterprise. Soon after, Frances Elelyn "Daisy" Maynard (1861–1938), countess of Warwick, founded Studley College, another training center for women gardeners.

Another creator of the romantically expressive Edwardian garden was Norah Lindsay (1873–1948), whose flair for creating "pictures" was akin to Jekyll's. At Sutton Courtenay, Berkshire, her home after 1895, she created a series of garden compartments divided by stone walls and yew hedges. There was a Hornbeam Alley, a Persian Garden, and a Long Garden filled with topiary. Lindsay, who valued serendipity, admitted into her gardens a good deal of volunteer vegetation—attractive weeds—because they added an element of charming surprise (fig. 11.23). In the tradition of Robinson and Jekyll, she also created a wild garden, and, like Jekyll, served as a garden consultant to friends. She belongs to a special class of gardener whose passionate attachment to a particular place and to garden art amounts to a source of ecstasy. Writing in *Country Life* in 1931, Lindsay rhapsodized

about Sutton Courtenay's "old sun-burnt walls. . . wreathed in wistaria tassels; the moonlit evenings when the turf is dry and warm, covered in rose petals like strange exotic shells; and the scent of syringa and honeysuckle weaves invisible webs of sweetness across one's dreaming face."[13]

Although the garden at Sutton Courtenay did not survive, Lindsay's advice left an imprint on several extant gardens, including the deeply imaginative garden by Lawrence Johnston at Hidcote Manor, Gloucestershire. In 1907, Johnston, an American educated at Oxford, became the proprietor of Hidcote Bartrin, a 280-acre property in Chipping Campden. Here he proceeded to create a series of beautifully articulated architectural spaces, eschewing the quaintness of his Cotswolds milieu in favor of a plan that was both boldly original and highly fastidious

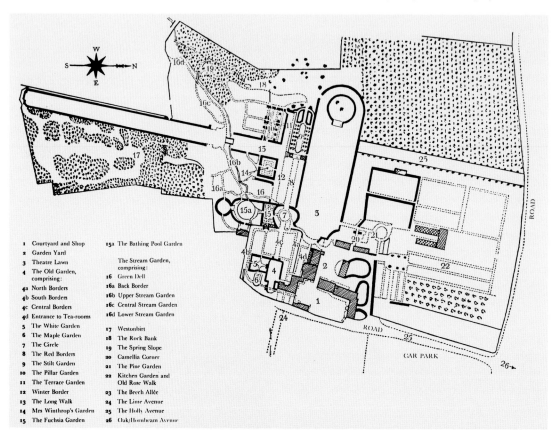

1 Courtyard and Shop
2 Garden Yard
3 Theatre Lawn
4 The Old Garden, comprising:
4a North Borders
4b South Borders
4c Central Borders
4d Entrance to Tea-rooms
5 The White Garden
6 The Maple Garden
7 The Circle
8 The Red Borders
9 The Stilt Garden
10 The Pillar Garden
11 The Terrace Garden
12 Winter Border
13 The Long Walk
14 Mrs Winthrop's Garden
15 The Fuchsia Garden

15a The Bathing Pool Garden

The Stream Garden, comprising:
16 Green Dell
16a Back Border
16b Upper Stream Garden
16c Central Stream Garden
16d Lower Stream Garden

17 Westonbirt
18 The Rock Bank
19 The Spring Slope
20 Camellia Corner
21 The Pine Garden
22 Kitchen Garden and Old Rose Walk
23 The Beech Allée
24 The Lime Avenue
25 The Holly Avenue
26 Oak/Hornbeam Avenue

(fig. 11.24). With the instincts of a Le Nôtre for optical perspective and proportional geometries, he used farm machinery to grade the land, manipulating the topography to achieve different ground levels and to play tricks of foreshortening by creating barely perceptible slopes, as in the case of the grassy walk through the Red Borders to the twin pavilions guarding the entrance to the Stilt Garden (fig. 11.25). Spatial definition is one of the chief assets of Hidcote, and the pleasurable scale of the garden is enhanced by the way in which Johnston formed "walls" with hedges of yew, holly, box, and beech, interweaving them to provide different textures and shades of green.

The architectural lines of the garden form a foil for the perennial plants, which Johnston, benefiting from Norah Lindsay's counsel, arranged in unusual and effective combinations, allowing his garden some of the same careless luxuriance and surprising juxtapositions as hers. He became an avid botanist, traveling to Africa and China to garner rarities that he could naturalize at Hidcote. Color was an important consideration. In Mrs. Winthrop's Garden, named in honor of his mother, he planted only yellow-flowered plants and those with golden-hued leaves (fig. 11.26).

Victoria "Vita" Sackville-West (1892–1962) and her husband, Sir Harold Nicholson (1886–1968) employed the same combination of classically derived architectural lines and romantically artistic planting beds as those at Hidcote in the garden they created beginning in 1930 at Sissinghurst, their estate in Kent (fig. 11.27).

Various published accounts have generated considerable fascination with the story of the Nicholsons' transformation of a derelict Tudor manor with its half-ruined cottages and forlorn agricultural landscape into a private dream world and refuge. It is the story of two survivors of a vanished culture of landed aristocracy, latter-day nobility whose thoughts were deeply imbued with English history. Their salvaging of a remnant of this heritage during the Great Depression and World War II constitutes a remarkable

achievement in the realm of preservation.

In *The Land,* a long pastoral poem that owes a debt to Virgil's *Georgics* and Thomson's *The Seasons,* Sackville-West created a portrait of the not-quite-vanished tradition of agrarian life of the south of England. Through her garden, she preserved and embellished this mellow English scene. She was acquainted with both Jekyll and Robinson, and her inspired planting schemes can be traced to their influence. On the first of two visits to Persia, where Harold Nicholson was posted in 1926 and 1927, she appreciated in the gardens of Isfahan the vital role of water and saw how the Islamic garden's fourfold geometric order could encompass and enhance the lushness of the vegetation. Her firsthand experience of Persian gardens was, according to her biographer, Jane Brown, "the baccalaureate of Vita the gardener."[14]

Harold Nicholson deemed himself a classicist, and although his cast of mind was not as fervently romantic as his wife's, he may have yearned as deeply as she did for an older, preurban England. In his subtle discrimination between these two modes of thought, there was room for reconciliation: "It would seem indeed as if the misunderstanding that arises between the romantic and the classical temperament is due, not so much to any conflict between the imagination and reason, as to the fact that whereas the classic finds pleasure in recognition, the romantic derives his own greatest stimulus from surprise."[15] The tension between the opposing but complementary poles of classicism and romanticism is a major factor in Sissinghurst's success as a work of landscape design.

Nicholson faced considerable difficulty in developing axes and classical geometries within the old manor's footprint. The spaces formed by old walls and structures, including a moat, contained many obtuse angles. In compromising his penchant for the classical in order to harmonize an abstract ideal with the reality of the ground, Nicholson arrived at something more akin to the plan of Hadrian's Villa, with its independent, impinging axes, than that of an Italianate or Beaux-Arts-style garden where axial coherence and geometric regularity predominate (see fig.

11.25. Red Borders, Hidcote Manor

Below: **11.26. Mrs. Winthrop's Garden, Hidcote Manor**

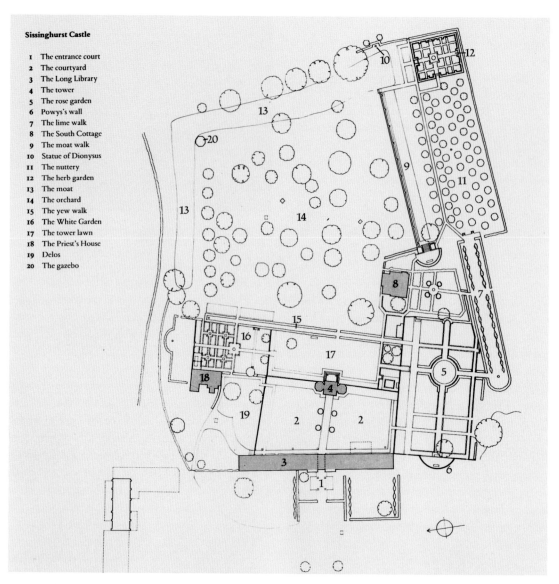

Sissinghurst Castle

1   The entrance court
2   The courtyard
3   The Long Library
4   The tower
5   The rose garden
6   Powys's wall
7   The lime walk
8   The South Cottage
9   The moat walk
10 Statue of Dionysus
11 The nuttery
12 The herb garden
13 The moat
14 The orchard
15 The yew walk
16 The White Garden
17 The tower lawn
18 The Priest's House
19 Delos
20 The gazebo

11.27. Plan of Sissinghurst, Kent, designed by Harold Nicholson and Victoria Mary Nicholson (Vita Sackville-West). From 1930

11.28. White Garden, Sissinghurst, arbor with climbing rose, box hedging, and large containers

2.43). Within its separate parts, however, he paid close attention to sight lines, scale, and proportion. The garden beds within these spaces constituted the loom upon which Vita Sackville-West wove a brocade of floral pictures in subtle textures and sophisticated color harmonies. Her most celebrated inspiration was the creation of the White Garden, where white flowers and silvery leaves catch the lingering daylight and shine forth in moonlight (fig. 11.28).

The garden as private Elysium, a refuge from

twentieth-century civilization and its discontents, has continued to offer emotional satisfaction to those who can afford a country retreat. Borrowing from the fused tradition of Jekyll, Peto, and their contemporaries, British gardeners such as Penelope Hobhouse and Rosemary Veery perpetuate the Arts and Crafts *cum* Neoclassical heritage in garden design. Theirs is a preservationist style that evokes a bygone England of old manor houses, embowered cottages, and the long dream of Italy. At the same time, practitioners in this vein are extremely sophisticated, combining in original and often stunning ways newer hybrids with simple native varieties and plants with venerable horticultural histories, such as old-fashioned roses. In spite of this stylistic continuity lasting to the present day, Sissinghurst, created on the eve of World War II, symbolizes the end of an era. The postwar social agenda in England and the rest of Europe, as well as the high taxes that support it, made the lavish private gardens built by the Edwardians and their Victorian predecessors impossible to sustain. Generally speaking, the same thing was true in the United States.

III. DESIGN SYNTHESIS:
THE END OF THE AMERICAN COUNTRY PLACE ERA

Less scarred by World War I than their British cousins, rich Americans until the Great Depression in the 1930s built large estate gardens in fashionable rural surroundings from Long Island to California. In addition, the fortunes of American Anglophiles continued to fertilize English soil; some still sought the expatriate life of landed "English" gentlemen, though not as spectacularly as had William Waldorf Astor (1848–1919), whose grandiose gardens at Cliveden and Hever Castle have never been surpassed as reflections of wealth and social status. Those who, like Lawrence Johnson, were less inclined toward opulence took up residence in the Cotswolds in the west of England or in the counties of Surrey and Sussex in the south, centers of the Arts and Crafts aesthetic and rural village preservationism.

The accumulated fortunes of the Gilded Age passed down to the high-living generation that, basking for a while in America's pre–Great Depression prosperity, built some of the country's finest gardens. Although concessions to climate, topography, and native scenery continued to be relevant concerns, the emulation of European examples and the perfection of European styles became for a time more important than the search for an original American landscape design idiom.

As we have seen, artistically inclined people and writers such as Henry James and Edith Wharton, with sufficient leisure and income to make regular extensive trips to Europe or take up residence abroad, sought escape as tourists and expatriates from what they perceived to be American philistinism. Architects continued to train in Paris and at the American Academy in Rome, established in 1894 as the intended counterpart to the French Academy founded by Louis XIV. At home, wealthy capitalists may have been despised by aesthetes and intellectuals for their crass commercialism, but they nevertheless funded the continuation of large country estates. World War II would bring this way of life to an end, just as World War I had brought near-closure to the privileged life of the aristocracy in England and Europe.

AMERICAN ELEGANCE: THE GARDENS
OF BEATRIX JONES FARRAND
AND ELLEN BIDDLE SHIPMAN

In the rarefied realm of estate design where social connections gave one a distinct advantage, Edith Wharton's niece, Beatrix Cadwalader Jones Farrand, became a prominent member of the second generation of American landscape architects. Long sojourns at Reef Point, the family summer home in Bar Harbor, Maine,

had nourished Farrand's love of gardens and plants and fostered her desire to become a landscape gardener, the term she preferred to that of landscape architect, although she was a charter member of the American Society of Landscape Architects.

Farrand's route to a career was an improvised tutorial in which she experimented with planting plans for the family garden at Reef Point and arranged to study for a time with Charles Sprague Sargent, professor of horticulture at the Bussey Institute of Harvard and founding director of the Arnold Arboretum. In 1895, after an extensive European tour during which she visited more than twenty notable landscapes, including several of the ones described in Wharton's *Italian Villas and Their Gardens,* she enrolled in Professor William Ware's course at Columbia University's School of Mines in order to learn drafting to scale, elevation rendering, and such aspects of surveying and engineering as she would need to grade slopes, lay drives, and provide proper drainage systems for designed landscapes. Equipped with these technical skills and her notes, photographs, and the prints of European gardens she had collected, the twenty-five-year-old, self-taught landscape architect was ready to begin professional practice.

Her first clients, whom she served from the office she established on an upper floor of her mother's brownstone home on east Eleventh Street in New York, included several fellow Bar Harbor summer residents; Pierre Lorillard, for whom she prepared a planting plan for the area around the entrance lodges of his suburban development, Tuxedo Park, New York; William R. Garrison, a leading resident of Tuxedo Park, for whom she designed a garden; Clement B. Newbold, owner of Crosswicks in Jenkintown, Pennsylvania; and Anson Phelps Stokes, the proprietor of Brick House at Noroton Point, Darien, Connecticut. Her mother and aunt, both socially well-connected, facilitated introductions and made her feel at ease with such powerful men as J. P. Morgan, John D. Rockefeller, and Theodore Roosevelt, all of whom were to become clients. Her avuncular friend Henry James, who resided in England, helped her meet the coterie of gardeners in the Cotswolds. The founding of the Garden Club of America in 1913 offered her another network at home.

Throughout her long career, Reef Point remained Farrand's laboratory for plant experimentation. Periods of residence on the coast of Maine with its mats of rock-hugging vegetation and dense forests of spruce, maple, and birch trees fostered her sensitivity to native scenery. She became an accom-

LEGEND

1. COPSE
2. NORTH SECTION
3. CEDAR TERRACE
4. FRENCH STEPS
5. NORTH COURT
6. HORNBEAM ELLIPSE
7. CAMELLIA CIRCLE
8. KITCHEN GARDEN
9. FLOWER GARDEN
10. SWIMMING POOL
11. CRABAPPLE HILL
12. PLUM WALK
13. PEBBLE GARDEN
14. BOX WALK
15. HERBACEOUS BORDER
16. ORCHARD
17. GOAT TRAIL
18. BEECH TERRACE
19. STAR
20. GREEN GARDEN
21. URN TERRACE
22. ROSE TERRACE
23. WISTERIA ARBOR
24. HERB TERRACE
25. FOUNTAIN TERRACE
26. MELISANDE'S ALLEE
27. THE TERRIER
28. LOVERS' LANE POOL
29. LOVERS' LANE SCREEN PLANTING

11.29. Plan of Dumbarton Oaks, Washington, D.C., designed by Beatrix Cadwalader Jones Farrand. The wooded site—with its mature oaks and other native trees, high elevation, and steep slopes dramatically descending to the valley threaded by Rock Creek—was one of extraordinary potential. Farrand exploited it ingeniously with a series of descending terraces whose formal symmetries and ornamental details merge gracefully with the natural surroundings.

Right: **11.30. Stairs leading from Rose Terrace to Fountain Terrace, with Herb Garden beyond, Dumbarton Oaks**

11.31. Urn Terrace, Dumbarton Oaks

Shrub plantings along the R Street frontage partially screen the lawn sweeping up to the front of the house, ensuring a degree of privacy. A large orangery off the east wing provides an effective transition between the house and the first of a series of outdoor rooms, the Beech Terrace, named for its central feature, a massive purple beech tree. As one descends to the Urn Terrace and, below it, to the Rose Terrace, then drops yet another level to the Fountain Terrace, one appreciates Farrand's eye for proportion, line, and detail (figs. 11.30, 11.31, 11.32). Her artistry appears in the scale of stairs and their finial and urn-punctuated piers, the deft interplay between straight and curving elements, and the contrasting textures of the carefully articulated ground plane with its finely crafted paving materials, grass, and planting beds (fig. 11.33). Below the Fountain Terrace, hidden from view, is one of Farrand's most charming conceits, a small outdoor amphitheater and Lover's Lane Pool.

The elegant simplicity and restraint inherent in Farrand's work, as well as her ability to amalgamate her European and Arts and Crafts sources into an original design, is also apparent as one follows the garden's gently spiraling plan through the orchard and herbaceous border, enters the Box Walk leading to the Ellipse, then returns on this straight path past the Tennis Court and Swimming Pool to the North Court. Here her skill in orchestrating garden space is seen once more in the series of grassy terraces leading to an overlook revealing the wild natural scenery of Rock Creek below (fig. 11.34). Now a public park, this section was planted by Farrand to enhance its character as a nature preserve. Steps, paths, benches, and a stone bridge facilitated and poeticized excursions into this section of the garden.

11.33. The Box Walk, an ivy- and boxwood-bordered brick path, Dumbarton Oaks

11.32. Rose Terrace bench, Dumbarton Oaks

11.34. Railing designed by Farrand, Rock Creek Park overlook, Dumbarton Oaks

plished designer of rock gardens, using indigenous plant material, and her mature work was marked by an intelligent search for an American garden design idiom. In this, she translated the inspiration she derived from Italian, Chinese, and other landscape traditions into an elegant and original style, which is exemplified in her two finest surviving gardens. Dumbarton Oaks in Washington, D.C., the estate of Mildred and Robert Woods Bliss, her masterpiece, demonstrates her confident originality in synthesizing the Arts and Crafts and Italianate landscape idioms of her time (figs. 11.29–11.34).

The Eyrie Garden, designed for Abby Aldrich Rockefeller, at Seal Harbor, Maine, has a large rectangular sunken garden, the walls of which are topped with imported Chinese tiles. This garden is entered on the north through a moon gate modeled on one Mrs. Rockefeller had admired in Beijing (fig. 11.35). Inside, Farrand planted annuals to maximize floral display during the short Maine summer, and surrounding the garden on the outside she created beds of perennials in a palette composed predominantly of lavender, blue, and white.

For Abby Rockefeller's husband, John D. Rockefeller, Jr., Farrand became a valued pro bono consultant on the planting plans for the carriage roads that Rockefeller conceived and funded at Acadia National Park on Mount Desert Island, Maine. Here, near her own summer home, at the dawn of the age of the automobile, she applied the principles learned from Olmsted's design of the drives at Biltmore and the Arnold Arboretum to enhance with native material—spruce, pitch pine, sweet fern, wild roses, sumac, goldenrod, and bush blueberry—Rockefeller's vision of scenic revelation through an artful arrangement of the motorist's serial vantage points.

Although women practitioners did not yet receive commissions for parks or other public works, landscape design was one of a limited number of professions open to them at the beginning of the twentieth century. The founding of the Lowthorpe School of Landscape Architecture for Women in 1901 in Groton, Massachusetts, the Pennsylvania School of Horticulture for Women in 1910, and the Cambridge School of Landscape Architecture for Women in 1916 helped open a career path to women wishing to enter the field. Like Beatrice Farrand, Ellen Biddle Shipman (1869–1950), who received her training in the office of Charles Platt, ran an all-woman landscape architectural firm. As in the case of Farrand, Shipman's entry into the field was facilitated by her horticultural knowledge and an ability to provide planting plans for Platt and other landscape designers such as Warren Manning. Because she did not travel to Europe until 1929, when she was sixty years old, her independent work was less influenced by foreign examples than that of Farrand or the Rome prizewinners, who were her contemporaries. It can best be characterized as an application of Jekyll's lessons to a traditional Colonial-revival style—a marriage of Arts and Crafts planting principles with the geometrical layout of old-fashioned American gardens—or, put another way, a translation of formal design into a more relaxed, domestic vernacular. It was a style that was both sophisticated and unpretentious.

Shipman and her husband, Louis, were part of the artists' colony in Cornish, New Hampshire, which included Charles Platt. Although she had learned basic drafting skills in Platt's office, she lacked Farrand's rigorous professional training, including the requisite engineering skills to develop extensive grading and drainage plans. Nevertheless, in 1920, she opened an office in New York City. Because her work was almost exclusively residential, she did not seek membership in the recently formed, male-dominated American Society of Landscape Architects. Nevertheless, she found a substantial niche within the profession. The young Garden Club of America—a national organization supporting the work of many local garden clubs throughout the country—had stimulated an interest in horticulture among affluent women. They provided Shipman with a natural client base and network of referrals for commissions—more than six hundred during her years of professional practice. Many of her jobs were undertaken in collaboration with other landscape architects, including Charles Platt, Warren Manning, and Fletcher Steele.

Able landscape photographers such as Mattie Edwards Hewitt recorded the appearance of many of Shipman's gardens (fig. 11.36). Publication of photographs of Shipman gardens in contemporary periodicals—*The Garden, House and Garden,* and *House Beautiful*—together with her skills as a public lecturer and her congenial personality, contributed to her success. Her clients tended to favor an atmosphere of

11.35. Sketch for Moon Gate, North Wall, Eyrie Garden, Seal Harbor, Maine, designed by Beatrix Jones Farrand. 1929.

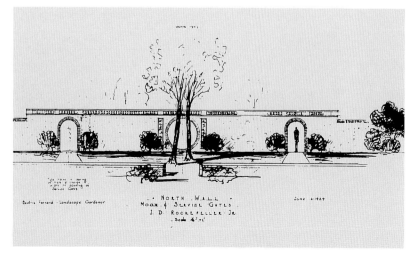

idyllic seclusion and well-guarded privacy. As a rule, Shipman screened the borders of her gardens with heavy plantings. Her "secret" gardens were spaces for dreamy contemplation as well as for intimate socializing with family and friends. Small-scale works of sculpture inject notes of fancy and function as pleasing garden decor. Their meaning is secondary, for by the twentieth century mythology no longer had allegorical significance for designer or client but served as a branch of storytelling, providing a genteel foretaste of the role of fantasy in the thematic landscapes of the present day.

Shipman's planting schemes were typically accompanied by detailed horticultural instructions intended to ensure proper maintenance by clients and their gardeners. In addition, she made regular visits to estates where her designs were installed, and some clients put her in charge of administering annual discretionary funds for plant purchases. Her practice was far-flung, and she spent a great deal of time traveling by train and later by plane to job sites all over the United States. The Sarah P. Duke Memorial Gardens at Duke University in North Carolina was one of her most significant designs. Because she socialized with her clients, who introduced her to their friends, many of whom also hired her, she had clusters of commissions in such places as Cleveland, Ohio; Grosse Point, Michigan; the North Shore of Long Island; and Mount Kisco, New York. In these pockets of affluence, until the exigencies of World War II brought commissions to a virtual halt, Shipman designed idyllic gardens, historically inflected refuges from the modern industrial scene—ironically, the source of wealth that enabled many of the gardens to exist in the first place.

Eclecticism and the Invention of a Historic Past in California and Florida

California proved an ideal place for experimentation and the transformation of older forms of landscape design into a distinctive, if eclectic, regional style. Because the state enjoys some spectacular hilly and mountainous scenery and has along its coast what is known as a Mediterranean climate, it was especially congenial to the creation of Italianate and Spanish-style gardens. Although the Anglo-American railroad barons and other capitalists who first settled the state created gardens within the prevailing nineteenth-century Picturesque tradition, they soon began to capture the opportunities inherent in the mild climate, which, combined with irrigation technology, permitted the introduction of species of eucalyptus and other semitropical plants from Australia and South Africa. Nurserymen in San Francisco, Oakland, San Jose, Santa Barbara, and the Los Angeles area realized the profitability of stocking exotic vegetation as well as the many kinds of fruit trees that thrived in this sun-drenched land. Palm trees propagated from imported stock contributed to California's growing palette of Mediterranean plants, which, given water, grew as lushly as those on the Riviera. Cacti and other plants from arid parts of the United States and Mexico found a natural home in the Desert Garden, begun in 1905 at the Huntington Gardens at San Marino, California's foremost assemblage of exotic plants. There, Henry Huntington's head gardener, William Hertrich, installed a number of botanical collections through massive transplanting and propagation in the estate's nurseries (fig. 11.37).

The climate of California encouraged the design of outdoor living spaces and a greater stylistic

11.36. Henry Croft Garden, Greenwich, Connecticut, designed by Ellen Biddle Shipman. The hallmarks of Shipman's style are evident in the sense of spatial enclosure, axial organization along a grassy path, sensuous softening of formal lines with luxuriant plant material, homespun elegance of the brick and stone masonry, and air of sprightly whimsy provided by the figure of Diana and other pieces of sculpture. Photograph by Mattie Edwards Hewitt, c. 1928

Below: 11.37. Desert Garden, Huntington Gardens, San Marino, California

11.38. Green Gables, Wood-side, California, water garden designed by Charles Sumner Greene, 1926–28

Below: **11.39. Filoli, Woodside, California, garden layout by Bruce Porter. 1915–17**

informality than elsewhere. Remoteness and a frontier spirit also served to foster a lifestyle less circumscribed by social convention than that of the Eastern seaboard. Helen Hunt Jackson's popular novel *Ramona* (1884), written to call attention to federal policy injustices toward Native Americans and Hispanics, drew a romantic portrait of California's pre-Anglo way of life with its Franciscan missions and Spanish haciendas. This stimulated some highly imaginative reconstructions of actual missions and their gardens and gave birth to the Mission Revival style and other design interpretations of a mythical regional past, notably the somewhat later Spanish Colonial style. In this attempt to forge a regional identity and to project an architecture compatible with the newly enriched vegetal repertory, designers appropriated various Mediterranean styles, with principal emphasis on that of Andalusian Spain. In urban design terms, this is best seen in Santa Barbara where, after the earthquake of 1925, the city set about rebuilding itself almost entirely in terms of a remarkably inventive pseudo-Spanish style, best illustrated by its grandly scaled centerpiece, architect William Mooser's courthouse. Unlike a traditionally inward-focused Spanish building, the Santa Barbara Courthouse has a colossal entry arch that frames a view of the beautiful mountainous landscape in which the city sits.[16]

Farther north, in the Bay area, to harmonize with the surrounding scenery, Bernard Maybeck (1862–1957) created a landscape idiom of mixed native and exotic vegetation, uncut local stone, and rough-dressed rockwork for the residential developments undertaken by the Hillside Club, an improvement society in Berkeley. In the first decade of the twentieth century, Japanese influence combined with that of the prevailing Arts and Crafts movement to produce the sensitive siting, fine hand detailing, and imaginative use of natural materials by Charles Sum-

ner Greene (1868–1957) and Henry Mather Greene (1870–1954), architects in Pasadena. In 1921, Charles Greene demonstrated in the David L. James house in the Carmel Highlands his complete mastery of an original design vocabulary in which local rock walls, the result of meticulous, painstaking craftsmanship, appear to emerge organically from the geological structure of the hillside. In 1911 and 1926–28, he performed an equal but different tour de force at Green Gables, the Mortimer and Bella Fleishacker estate overlooking the Santa Cruz Mountains in Woodside. In the monumental staircase and arcade of the beautiful water garden, Greene executed his Beaux-Arts design in a rustic, regional manner using uncut native stones (fig. 11.38).

Not all wealthy Californians pursued the path of stylistic experimentation opened up by these original designers. One of the most renowned of the remaining gardens from this period is Filoli, nestled into the exceptionally scenic landscape of Woodside, 30 miles south of San Francisco. The Georgian-style house, designed by Willis Polk (1870–1924) of San Francisco, was built between 1916 and 1919 for William Bowers Bourn II, owner of a hard-rock gold mine and a local water company, after Bourn purchased his 654-acre estate. Bourn's friend and hunting companion Bruce Porter (1865–1955), a poet, painter, and artist in stained glass as well as a landscape designer, was responsible for the layout of the garden, and Isabella Worn, a San Francisco floral designer, for the planting plans. Her work continued after new owners purchased the property in 1936. Neither Porter nor Worn had a talent approaching Farrand's, but, aided by the spectacular site, excellent climate, and good current management by the Filoli Center, their work resulted in a garden of considerable charm (fig. 11.39).

Sometimes the California Mediterranean expression was carried to theatrical heights, as at San Simeon, the estate of William Randolph Hearst. An amalgam of stage-set effects, San Simeon evokes

styles as diverse as those of ancient Egypt and contemporary Art Moderne. Julia Morgan (1872–1957), the first woman to be enrolled in the architecture program of the École des Beaux-Arts and the first to obtain a license from the State of California to practice architecture, designed the palatial house and exotic guest houses. Charles Gibbs Adams was the landscape architect who responded to Hearst's grandiose ideas as the gardens took shape around the vast collections of exotic animals, specimen trees, sculpture, and decorative artifacts that Hearst amassed at this private fantasy weekend "resort."

Although eastern architects such as Bertram Grosvenor Goodhue (1869–1924) joined the handful of resident professionals who received commissions to design houses and gardens on California estates in the 1920s, amateurs and nurserymen were responsible for laying out some of the most notable ones. Goodhue was the architect in charge of the 1915 Panama-California Exposition held in San Diego. In opposition to Irving Gill and others who saw this as an opportunity to forge a simpler, more modern regional idiom, Goodhue deemed a neo-traditional Spanish Colonial Baroque style to be the most desirable one for the fair's buildings. The landscape designers matched its architectural flamboyance with a riot of lush semitropical vegetation arranged in extravagant floral displays. The fair gave license to an unbridled eclecticism, and the opulent tone it set was highly influential. Not only did various forms of Spanish and Mexican architecture become popular, but direct imitation of Italian villa architecture and gardens was widely practiced.

A nurseryman, A. E. Hanson, was inspired by the fair to seek his living as a designer of great estates. With entrepreneurial energy and a flair for salesmanship, Hanson became a landscape contractor, hiring the design and horticultural talent he needed to fulfill his commissions. In his breezy memoir, he tells how he succeeded in getting the job to design Greenacres, movie millionaire Harold Lloyd's 16-acre estate in Beverly Hills. Working with golf course designer Billy Bell and architect Sumner Spaulding, he created between 1925 and 1929 a grandiose scheme that included a 100-foot (30.5-meter) waterfall spilling into a canoe course that also served as a water hazard for the golf course, a fairy-tale English village play yard with a thatched roof cottage and pony stable for Lloyd's three-year-old daughter, a "Villa Lante" cascade, a "Villa Medici" fountain, and a "Villa d'Este" pool. The house was modeled on the Villa Gamberaia (fig. 11.40).

Architect George Washington Smith (1876–1930), was instrumental in forging the Santa Barbara style of Spanish Colonial domestic architecture with

gardens featuring well-shaded patios with tiled fountain basins, also employed the villas of Italy as models. Casa del Herrero (House of the Blacksmith), the 11-acre estate that Washington designed for George Fox Steedman in 1922–25, is perhaps the architect's masterpiece. Here he worked first with landscape architect Ralph Stevens and then with Lockwood deForest (1896–1949) to create by 1933 a series of axially related garden spaces with tiled water channels and low, Spanish-style fountains (fig. 11.41).

Not only did some of the estates of southern California appear as stage sets, they were employed as such by the flourishing movie industry, which was unaffected by the Great Depression. Florence Yoch (1890–1972), assisted by her partner, Lucille Council, designed gardens specifically for movie sets, including the one for *Gone With the Wind*. In the 1930s, Yoch

11.40. Garden, Greenacres, Beverly Hills, California, designed by A. E. Hanson with Billy Bell and Sumner Spalding for Harold Lloyd, showing the water cascade with the "Villa Gamberaia" house in the background. 1925–29

Below: **11.41.** Garden, Casa del Herrero, Santa Barbara, California, designed by Ralph Stevens and Lockwood deForest, with house designed by George Washington Smith. 1922–25

11.42. Garden, Il Brolino, Montecito, California, designed by Florence Yoch, with house designed by George Washington Smith. 1923

11.43. Gardens, Vizcaya, Florida, designed by Diego Suarez and F. Burrall Hoffman, Jr., with house designed by George Washington Smith. 1912–16

was hired to create gardens for such Hollywood executives as director George Cukor and producer Jack Warner. She was given a budget of $100,000, a lavish sum at the time, for landscaping Warner's 18-acre Southern-plantation-style estate, located near Harold Lloyd's and those of several other famous movie stars in Beverly Hills' Benedict Canyon. But, like Hanson, Yoch found in Montecito the conditions that inspired what is perhaps her finest creation, Il Brolino, the fey topiary garden she designed on the 7-acre estate of lumber heiress Mary Stewart to complement George Washington Smith's handsome Italian-villa-style house (fig. 11.42). Here one sees the flexibility of her imagination in the way she softened the garden's geometrical lines with the fat, rounded, whimsical forms of animals and playing-card symbols in clipped boxwood, artfully juxtaposed against the background

trees and mountains beyond. This quality is also apparent in her habit of modifying symmetry with adjustments to site conditions and the occasional eccentric placement of a tree or other object within an otherwise formal space.

Like California, Florida was originally a Spanish colonial borderland with a climate that became a lure for resort builders and affluent escapees from the northern winter. Some built great estates, employing design idioms similar to those used in California. One of the most extravagantly spectacular Italianate gardens of the Gilded Age is Vizcaya, built between 1912 and 1916 on Biscayne Bay in Florida by James Deering, heir of the harvesting machinery manufacturer. F. Burrall Hoffman, Jr., designed the house as a boldly eclectic pastiche, with each facade portraying a different era of Italian villa architecture. Hoffman's artistically inclined friend, Paul Chalfin, helped him garner the tapestries and furniture to create the grand decorative effects that lend the interior its air of opulence. Diego Suarez, a Colombian who was tutored in landscape design at La Pietra by Arthur Acton, created the elaborate gardens, which combine echoes of Spain, France, and Venice, and serve as a reminder of Isola Bella, the Borromeo family villa whose terraces rise like the decks of a galleon from the waters of Lake Maggiore (fig. 11.43; see figs. 5.40–5.41).

Vizcaya was a bellwether, stimulating rich Easterners and eventually the European Riviera set to come to Florida. Promoted by the entrepreneur Henry Flagler, Palm Beach became a fashionable resort in large measure due to Addison Mizner (1872–1933). Mizner was a society architect practicing first in Philadelphia and then in New York. His career was given a tremendous boost after 1918 when he discovered Palm Beach and its potential as an American Riviera. With some of the same eclectic imagination and flair for client relations as A. E. Hanson, Mizner, who was widely traveled and a collector of antiques and architectural artifacts from all over the world, invented virtually single-handedly the Palm Beach style, a pseudo-Hispanic amalgam of dramatic decorative effects. Mizner took complete charge of his clients' projects, serving as architect, interior decorator, and landscape designer.

Though physically distant, as resort communities with a similar ethos of self-invented domestic and urbanistic stagecraft and a common Hispanic-Italianate-Mediterranean appearance, Santa Barbara and Palm Beach were close cousins. Mizner, in fact, took the skills he perfected in Florida to Parklane, an estate in Santa Barbara where he combined Venetian Gothic elements with images derived from the Villa Lante. Thus did wealthy Americans of this period commis-sion designers to take recipes from the European banquet and concoct architectural menus of cribbed grandeur intended to surpass the original models. Sometimes blatantly, as in the gardens of A. E. Hanson and elsewhere more subtly, as in the gardens of Platt, Farrand, and Shipman, we find evidence of the transformation of garden art into garden style.

Resort communities such as Santa Barbara and Palm Beach are phenomena of machine-age technology—beautiful and remote places made accessible by private railroad car (later by private jet). The cost of transportation for their temporary residents, among other factors, ensured their status as exclusive enclaves, especially in their early years. Commercial rail and aviation and, more significant, mass production of the twentieth-century machine par excellence, the private automobile, has democratized the landscape, making many beautiful places accessible to the masses. The implications of these technological developments for city planners and landscape designers is a major theme in the subsequent chapters of this book.

Notes for Chapter Eleven

1. Camillo Sitte, *The Art of Building Cities,* trans. Charles T. Stewart (New York: Reinhold Publishing Corporation, 1945), p. 76.
2. Ibid., p. 60.
3. During Queen Victoria's reign, London's population grew from 2 million to 4.5 million, while Glasgow tripled and Liverpool doubled in size. By the time of the queen's death in 1901, only one out of eleven people was still employed in agriculture.
4. Reginald Blomfield, *The Formal Garden in England* (London: Macmillan & Co., 1892), p. 15.
5. Gertrude Jekyll, *Colour Schemes for the Flower Garden* (1914) (Boston: Little Brown and Company, illustrated ed., 1988), pp. 17–18.
6. Gertrude Jekyll and Lawrence Weaver, *Arts & Crafts Gardens: Gardens for Small Country Houses,* (1912) (Antique Collector's Club, 1981 and 1997), p. 13.
7. Ibid., p. 70.
8. Largely destroyed during World War II when Nazi forces invaded Normandy, this extraordinary garden has been restored through the efforts of André Mallet, the son of Guillaume Mallet, and his wife Mary who made it available to the public, an enterprise that continues through the work of their son, Robert Mallet, who shares his grandfather's flair for sensitive horticultural artistry and a thorough understanding of Arts and Crafts stylistic principles.
9. Charles Platt, *Italian Gardens* (1894) (Portland, Oreg.: Sagapress/Timber Press, 1993), p. 37.
10. Edith Wharton, *The House of Mirth,* Book I, from *The Edith Wharton Reader,* ed. Louis Auchincloss (New York: Charles Scribner's Sons, 1965), p. 90.
11. Thomas H. Mawson, *The Art and Craft of Garden Making* (London: B. T. Batsford, 1900), p. 1.
12. Ibid., p. 5.
13. As quoted in Jane Brown, *The English Garden in Our Time: From Gertrude Jekyll to Geoffrey Jellicoe* (Woodbridge, Suffolk: Antique Collectors' Club, 1986), pp. 162–163.
14. Jane Brown, *Vita's Other World: A Gardening Biography of V. Sackville-West* (New York: Viking, 1985), p. 84.
15. Harold Nicholson, *Helen's Tower* (New York: Harcourt Brace, 1938), p. 41, as quoted in Brown, *Vita's Other World,* p. 56.
16. For a good discussion of the architecture of Santa Barbara and its courthouse, see Charles Moore and Gerald Allen, *Dimensions: Space, Shape & Scale in Architecture* (New York: Architectural Record Books, 1976), pp. 41–48.

SOCIAL UTOPIAS:
MODERNISM AND CITY PLANNING

By 1900, industrial power had vastly multiplied the products of human manufacture and consumption and greatly increased the speed with which goods and people were transported to both near and distant parts. Consequent social transformations accelerated the uprooting of age-old agrarian traditions, emptying villages of their young people and causing the continued exponential growth of cities beyond all previous conceptions of normative urban size. In spite of these dislocations and changes, a widely shared optimism and a broad belief in the possibilities for universal progress in the material conditions of human life prevailed. Many people had begun to fully comprehend the capability of Machine Age means of production to radically expand economies as industrial capitalism opened new markets for a growing abundance of low-cost goods. The ease of production had the obvious potential of raising the living standards of a broad spectrum of humanity, making the producers of wealth consumers as well. The rapid advances in industrial technology that added to individual well-being and made the domestic realm more comfortable also made possible the great public works projects that are the signal manifestations of the modern industrial city. Indeed, modern urbanism and industrial capitalism are inextricably allied, as we saw in our discussion of Haussmann's transformation of Paris between 1850 and 1870.

A growing democratic spirit and the moral purpose this implied inspired many visionary attempts to redress inequalities within existing and developing capitalist societies. Reformers wished to remedy the ills of poverty and plan optimal environments for all classes of humanity. Romanticism and its concomitant impulse toward revolution had already laid the cultural groundwork for respect of individual rights. Enlightenment rationalism—now a broadly shared attitude toward scientific inquiry and technical problem solving—assumed that reason could readily dictate remedies for the wants and injustices that had heretofore been the lot of humankind.

Although proponents of bourgeois capitalist culture—the economic engine that propelled the Industrial Revolution—refuted the theories of Karl Marx (1818–1883), they were nonetheless seminal to the ethos of modern Western society. Marx proclaimed that the aspirations of civilization cloaked a class struggle for material power. He saw how industrialization had attracted workers from the land, forcing them into slums within hugely distended metropolitan areas. He conceived socialist communism as a comprehensive political system to replace capitalism and redistribute wealth so that working-class people would enjoy the fruits of their labor. Although he had nothing to say about urban planning, the movement to improve urban living conditions gained momentum through Marx's critique, and a spirit of Marxist progressive reform prevailed even among those who did not seek to radically alter the premises of capitalist societies and their governments.

The American economist Henry George (1839–1897) had argued in *Progress and Poverty* (1879) that the abolition of other taxes in favor of a single tax on the appreciation in value of unimproved real estate would transfer this unearned wealth to the government for redistribution in the form of public works. Although not supported by many political leaders or economists, George exerted a strong influence among reformers in Britain and America, among whom Ebenezer Howard, father of the Garden City movement, figured prominently. Another American, Thorstein Veblen (1857–1929), a radical economist, teacher, and author, examined economic history through an evolutionary lens in his trenchant critique, *The Theory of the Leisure Class* (1899). He coined the term "conspicuous consumption" to describe manifestations of nonproductive leisure as a means of displaying wealth. The individual breadwinner with a nonworking wife was the most obvious example of what Veblen meant by conspicuous consumption.

These arguments those put forth by Peter Kropotkin (1842–1921), a Russian nobleman who advocated a protocommunist philosophy of social cooperation, and by British playwright

George Bernard Shaw (1856–1950) and his fellow members of the Fabian Society,[1] an organization promoting evolutionary socialism, provided the fertile ground that nurtured utopian visions as social thinkers focused their attention upon the problems of the recently formed mass society living in big cities. Middle-class mores still confined women's roles to the domestic sphere, although rates of labor-force participation for women grew steadily throughout the twentieth century. Of great importance in terms of urbanism, many women were active as professional volunteers in the reforms of the Progressive Era—the period beginning in the early part of the twentieth century in which a number of social improvements in the areas of housing, education, parks, social welfare, and civil service were initiated. Jane Addams (1860–1935), social worker, founder of the Hull House—the model for other settlement houses in America—feminist, and winner of the Nobel Peace Prize in 1931, was perhaps the most notable among the numerous dedicated women reformers ministering to the urban masses.

As advocates of the potential benefits of technology and engineering—provided these were applied to a broad social agenda rather than merely to amassing spectacular profits for capitalists—Progressive Era social reformers did not recoil from the Machine Age. They viewed it hopefully as the long-awaited instrument of relief from human misery. They were confident that the forces of industrial progress, when applied rationally to the problems of urban development, could improve the human condition by offering wholesome housing alternatives to the immigrant hordes in crowded slums and by providing the swelling ranks of urban dwellers with ready contact with nature. Although private capital was essential, they saw municipal and state governments or special-purpose public corporations as the logical sponsors of large-scale, urban projects because these legally chartered bodies had the power necessary to assemble large parcels of land and undertake the construction of roads, rail lines, and utilities. Thus, their social agenda went hand in hand with enlargement of the responsibilities of government and the establishment of quasi-governmental authorities.

Transportation technologies have been hugely influential in fostering the process of metropolitan growth, which has often been guided by the agendas of corporations as much as by regional planners. Although railroads greatly altered cities, making possible the growth of suburbs and interurban transportation networks, the automobile has had even greater consequences, especially in the United States. Of particular significance to the subject of landscape design, automobile mass production after 1913 led to the multiplication of nonurban recreational parks and the creation of exurban automobile parkways of a different scale and design configuration than the intra-urban boulevardlike ones planned in an era of carriage transportation. In addition to opening the countryside to vacationers, the automobile expanded urban form beyond its previous enlargement by rail lines. The driver's ability to steer the car along routes of individual choice stimulated the infilling of open lands between previously established corridors of rail-related metropolitan settlement with new roadways and networks of local streets. With the spread of suburbs, which were no longer tethered to rail lines, the urban fabric was loosened to the point where, at least in the land-rich United States, freestanding dwellings surrounded by lawns became the norm, particularly after New Deal government-sponsored home mortgage programs and post–World War II mortgage loans for veterans stimulated mass-produced tract housing. Cities as visibly discrete entities ceased to exist, becoming instead conurbations, or Standard Metropolitan Areas as census statisticians now refer to them.

Haussmann and Olmsted had demonstrated ways to conceptualize the city in technical and recreational terms. Now, at the beginning of the twentieth century, a second generation of urban planners applied this process to a more-than-metropolitan scale that encompassed the surrounding region. These planners went beyond the notion of greening the urban mass with landscaped squares and parks connected by intra-urban parkways. They envisioned the dispersal of industry and populations into the countryside, where living conditions could be made more humane and healthy than in the increasingly congested cities. Conceptual planning such as this was a first step toward zoning regulations and governmental policies affecting both public and private development.

While demonstrating an expanding social consciousness among industrial nations and the necessity to consider the needs of large, heterogeneous populations, the schemes presented by early-twentieth-century planners demonstrate significant differences in approach. On the one hand were the committed modernists, notably the architects Otto Wagner, Tony Garnier, and Le Corbusier, who approached the urban future with wholehearted optimism, untroubled by the transformation of the city's appearance into an expression of functional, machinelike order and practicality. On the other, there were urban theoreticians such as Ebenezer Howard and his disciples who tried to preserve some imagery from the preindustrial past. Thus, they retained picturesqueness in the form of individuated architectural elements and spatial configurations while fully embracing new engineering and industrial processes. They took as their mandate John Ruskin's words calling for "no festering and wretched suburb anywhere, but clean and busy street within, and open country without, with a [surrounding] belt of beautiful garden and orchard, so that from any part of the city perfectly fresh air and grass and sight of far horizon might be reachable in a few minutes' walk."[2]

The nostalgic impulses of Camillo Sitte and his followers, which we examined in Chapter Eleven, tempered some of modernity's zeal, giving birth to preservationism and the protection not only of monuments, but also of historic building ensembles and street patterns. But even the most committed preservationists of craft traditions and earlier design styles did not want to be deprived of such mechanical conveniences as central heating and indoor plumbing. Both progressive and historicist social utopians hoped that machine technology could help build a better world. This ambivalence about modernity and the desire to have both the fruits of technology and a sense of connection with the historical past continue to be reflected in the contemporary landscape, a subject we will consider in Chapter Fifteen. Here our task is to discuss the proposals and projects of the optimistic theorists and planners who sought to guide urbanism in the first half of the twentieth century.

I. Urban Expansion: Town Planning for the Machine Age in Britain and Continental Europe

With the rise of industrialization in the nineteenth century, some humanitarian capitalists built factories and workers' housing in new towns—model communities in the countryside outside large cities—thereby substituting sunlight, clean air, and greenery for the sooty congestion of the urban slum. These early planned communities with their individual houses, gardens, central parks, and local schools, all carefully separated from the industrial districts that were their raison d'être, provide a preview of later zoning practices. What is most apparent about several of these planned communities is the premium put on openness. The father of the garden city movement, Ebenezer Howard (1850–1928), followed these forceful opponents of metropolitan gigantism, turning their impulse toward reform into an influential philosophy of decentralized planning. Regionalism became a new framework within which rural and urban space could be organized so as to create greenbelt-encircled new towns, thus providing the advantages of both the city and the countryside. The city as an expanding and loosening, but still discrete, entity would, if developed as Howard prescribed, henceforth become no longer a solid urban mass, but rather a constellation of population clusters.

British Social Visionaries and Industrial Philanthropists

While furthering the agenda of proletarian egalitarianism and denouncing the noisome squalor of the industrial city, Marx and his socialist collaborator Friedrich Engels (1820–1895) paid no attention to urban form, believing that revolution must sweep away the old order before their utopian goals could be achieved. Without governmental means to foster the development of new towns, factory owners initially undertook to reform the living conditions of the

industrial workforce. The light from Ruskin's *Seven Lamps* illumined the path of many of these Victorian reformers, and their idealism reflected the influence of William Morris as they attempted to ameliorate and beautify the Industrial Age city through the application of an Arts and Crafts aesthetic rooted in the tradition of medieval artisans' guilds. Like Sitte, they focused on preserving past forms, and like him they codified what had been the organic growth patterns of an earlier time, thus creating a modern version of the Picturesque.

In 1853, Sir Titus Salt (1803–1876), a textile manufacturer, built Saltaire on the banks of the river Aire outside the city of Bradford in the Midlands of England. About a quarter of a century later, George and Richard Cadbury, owners of Cadbury Brothers, manufacturers of chocolate, created Bournville, a workers' community, in conjunction with the construction of new plant facilities near Birmingham. The Cadburys designed Bournville as a town of spacious greenery; they gave all of its 313 cottages gardens and allocated a generous portion of the 330-acre site to parkland. Curving streets and variously styled houses contributed picturesqueness. Nonemployees were allowed to take up residence in Bournville, and in 1900 George Cadbury established the Bournville Village Trust, which subsequently turned the revenues from the cooperatively administered estate into further improvements, resulting in the addition of schools, churches, shops, and other amenities.

In 1888, another philanthropically inclined industrialist, William Hesketh Lever (1851–1925), founded Port Sunlight near Liverpool as a company town for the employees of Lever Brothers, manufacturers of soap (fig. 12.1). Lever's humanitarian impulse to improve the living conditions of his industrial workforce and to bestow upon it the amenities of the countryside resulted in tree-lined streets, a network of pedestrian paths, allotment gardens, a central park and sports fields, and community buildings and houses designed in the English vernacular style of older country villages. Sunlight and fresh air were obvious antidotes to the grimy, tubercular conditions of the great coal-burning cities such as Birmingham, Manchester, Liverpool, and London.

Turning the palliatives of philanthropic industrialists into a more general and broad-scale prescription, the English reformer Ebenezer Howard promoted a vision of population dispersal into a series of planned communities in his influential book *Tomorrow: A Peaceful Path to Social Reform* (1898), republished as *Garden Cities of To-morrow* (1902). Considered

12.1. Port Sunlight, England, the model town built by Lever Brothers. 1888. The community occupies 140 acres of the 230-acre site. The central green spaces comprise ravines, which have been filled to stem tidal flooding. The road system follows the dictates of topography, curving in a picturesque manner, and the houses are placed with their backs to the railway line.

the father of the garden city movement, Howard saw how, thanks to the proliferating network of railroads, it was possible to leap over the city's no-longer-fixed boundaries and systematically create within the larger regional framework communities that combined the natural advantages of the country with the amenities of urban life.[3]

As a young man Howard earned his living as a stenographer in Chicago, which then enjoyed the Latin epithet *Urbs in Hortus* (the City in a Garden). He was probably familiar with Riverside, the garden suburb designed by Olmsted and Vaux. This hugely influential British social thinker went to great pains to prove that within the current capitalist system both social benefit and sound economic return could be gained through community ownership of land. Though not a designer, his diagrammatic model for a garden city became the schematic basis for the layout of actual new towns (fig. 12.2). Autonomous urban entities—full-scale communities with industrial and commercial employment—not suburbs, Howard's garden cities were conceived as an interconnected network of population centers linked by electric rail to one another and to a larger central garden city. He envisioned each satellite town as having a 1,000-acre core and a 5,000-acre rural belt, with a population of 30,000 living in the center and 2,000 in the agricultural surroundings. Each town was to be divided into wards containing 5,000 inhabitants, and each ward was to contain a school. In the heart of the town, civic and cultural institutions would ring a green open space, and between these and the inner ring of houses and gardens was to be a spacious Central Park. A second ring of houses and gardens lay beyond a wide Grand Avenue. Conveniently encircling these was a local railway looping off the main line. Factories were to be placed adjacent to this railway spur, with agricultural allotments, pastures, orchards, woodlots, and institutions for orphans,

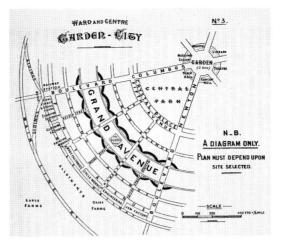

12.2. Diagram of one ward of the Garden City by Ebenezer Howard and sector of Howard's schematic plan. 1898

Below left: 12.3a. Plan of Letchworth Garden City, England, designed by Raymond Unwin. 1903

Below right: 12.3b. A group of massed cottages, Letchworth Garden City

epileptics, and convalescents located in the greenbelt beyond it.

In 1899, Howard founded the Garden City Association, the organization that fostered the two primary manifestations of his ideal: Letchworth (1903) and Welwyn Garden City (1919). To launch Letchworth, Howard obtained the assistance of George Cadbury and William Lever. The Garden City Pioneer Company Limited, which they incorporated, acquired 4,000 acres of land 35 miles north of London and created a subsidiary joint stock company to raise capital for construction. Sir Barry Parker and Sir Raymond Unwin, who were half cousins, brothers-in-law, Fabians, and devoted followers of Howard, planned the town, adapting Howard's diagram to the conditions of the site (figs. 12.3a, 12.3b). Because the land was to be transferred to the community at a future date, the restricted dividend stock was not secured with equity and therefore sold sluggishly. But with the establishment of industry, the town did get under way, and its sponsors were able to withstand pressure to sell off parcels of property and to develop Howard's experiment much as originally envisioned until World War I curtailed their efforts.

Unwin, an architect much concerned with establishing optimal density ratios, championed codes setting a maximum of twelve houses per acre. These were designed as attached units, with steep-pitched

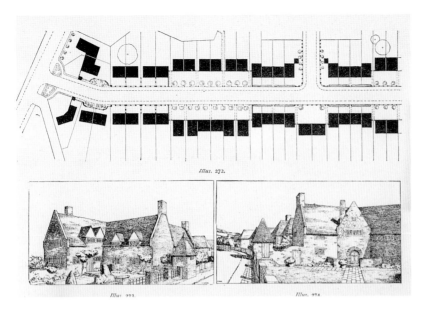

Illus. 272.

Illus. 273. *Illus. 274.*

12.4. Hampstead Garden Suburb, London, England, designed by Raymond Unwin. 1909. A street and its picturesque alignment of cottages, which have been massed in order that they may resemble larger-scale houses built in the Arts and Crafts style.

Below: **12.5. Proposal for Vienna's urban center, by Otto Wagner. 1911**

rooflines and structural massing reminiscent of the Arts and Crafts style of Edwin Lutyens or Charles Francis Annesley Voysey (1857–1941), a British architect expert in attractive, functional design for the modest home. Unwin's illustrations for his book *Town Planning in Practice* (1909) demonstrate his meticulous attention to various planning schemes and the details of design at Letchworth. He worked also in Hampstead Garden Suburb, which he designed within the confines of metropolitan London in 1907 as a corollary to the effort local citizens mounted to extend Hampstead Heath and to frustrate the construction of a planned underground city railway station. Borrowing from the German and English vernacular traditions, he employed irregular and nonuniform street alignments and an Arts and Crafts architectural vocabulary for his building blocks in order to create a richly picturesque environment for the working- and middle-class small-home leaseholder (fig. 12.4). The garden city ideal upheld by Unwin placed a premium upon clearly articulated pedestrian and vehicular cir-

culation, street and building composition, and the provision of ample and carefully arranged greenery and recreational facilities. His circulation plan reduced the amount of land occupied by roads from a typical 40 percent to 17 percent. Hampstead Garden Suburb reinforced a British preference for living at low densities and at ground level within metropolitan areas rather than in high-rise apartment blocks, as was the practice on the Continent. It did not, however, serve the varied classes for whom it was intended, as its attractiveness soon caused it to be occupied more or less exclusively by the well-to-do.

Urban Planning in Austria and France

Like the fathers of the garden city movement in Britain, Camillo Sitte had sought in Austria to preserve the flavor of a cozier, older way of life by applying the aesthetic of the Picturesque to the modern industrial city. Others, however, equated beauty with Machine Age functionality. Among these were Sitte's Viennese contemporary Otto Wagner (1841–1918). Wagner envisioned the modern metropolis in terms of highly systematized regimental order, with uniform building blocks, wide transportation corridors, and spacious greenery arranged according to a Neoclassical monumental planning paradigm (fig. 12.5). Thus, within an apparently similar design framework, Wagner's proposal for the new metropolis was even more resolutely modern in orientation than Baron Haussmann's radical reinvention of Paris.

Showing greater sensitivity to the texture of everyday life than did Wagner, the Beaux-Arts-trained, protofunctionalist French architect Tony Garnier (1869–1948) made an important contribution to the development of visionary urban planning. In 1899, Garnier won the Prix de Rome, the prestigious fellowship to study at the French Academy in Rome where he was a *pensionnaire* until 1904. Rather than following the prescribed didactic program of classical architectural study, however, Garnier, who was attracted to the growing liberalism of the times, used his stay in Rome to work on a plan for "Une Cité Industrielle." This would be located in southeastern France, the region of his native Lyons, a center for textile manufacturing, metallurgy, and the nascent automobile industry. In design terms, Garnier's plan expressed his belief that the past was morally bankrupt and that historicizing architecture was an affectation and therefore suspect, a premise shared by others who also were attempting to develop the building forms of a new democratic age. These architects postulated a radical break with history, eschewing design continuity with the past.

Although Garnier's architecture boldly embraced modern construction technology, relying especially upon reinforced concrete as a building material, as an urban planner he was far less polemical and doctrinaire than several architectural modernists of the succeeding generation. Conceptually, he was closer in spirit to the proponents of the garden city movement. Its tenets were undoubtedly familiar to him, for in 1902, Howard's *Garden Cities of To-Morrow* was published in a French translation. Garnier's classical training at the École des Beaux-Arts ensured a more geometrically ordered approach than that of his British contemporaries with their lingering taste for the irregularities of the Picturesque. While he lacked their proclivity for vernacular architectural style, the problem he wished to solve—that of building economically sound, livable communities—was the same.

Garnier's Cité Industrielle was oriented to the natural landscape as well as to a social ideal. Although its site was not specific, he imagined a particular topography, locating his imaginary town on hilly terrain overlooking a valley formed by the Rhône and one of its tributaries. Industry would guarantee it a viable economic foundation, and common ownership of land and intelligent planning, including the provision of educational, civic, cultural, athletic, and medical facilities, would offer the intellectual and physical amenities appropriate to the democratic social values of a new age. Designed for a population of 35,000, it was to have no defined perimeter boundaries and ample amounts of unbuilt land between functionally separate areas. These reservations of open space would allow for some necessary expansion. This type of zoning according to land use, now commonplace in cities, was innovative in the early twentieth century. Innovative, too, were the proposed sanitary and traffic standards, regulations providing for eminent domain, and controls over the supply of water, bread, milk, and medicines.

Garnier drew voluminous plans and produced numerous perspective drawings that have an engaging quotidian specificity (fig. 12.6). His laconic text is explanatory, not hortatory. In proposing a site, he considered the availability of hydroelectric power to generate electricity for the factories and the town and the presence of minerals and other raw materials for manufacturing. He then arranged the town in three well-spaced tiers: its industrial zone containing blast furnaces, steel mills, assembly plants, engineering laboratories, and workshops in the plain beside the river and the railway line; residential blocks and the town center on a plateau above these; and, higher still, hospital buildings arranged on a series of sloping terraces. Like the houses of the town, these would have southern exposures and be shielded from the wind. Over-

all, Garnier's plan called for construction to occupy less than half the site with the remainder devoted to landscaping and a public pedestrian way.

With its places of public assembly, Greek-style open-air theater, gymnasiums, fields for sports, running and cycling tracks, areas for discus throwing and high jumping, and other athletic facilities, the Cité Industrielle illustrated both a spiritual and physical kinship with the ancient Greek city. There is, moreover, a pleasing Mediterranean-style modernity to Garnier's cubelike, unornamented buildings of reinforced concrete. In addition to the primary schools planned for each of the town's neighborhoods, there were to be secondary schools for industrial, administrative, and professional trade studies. One professional school was intended to train those seeking careers in the fine and commercial arts—architecture, painting, sculpture, and related areas of design, including decorative and practical work in fabric, ceramic, glass, and metal.

Unlike later radical modernists who saw the destruction of historical building fabric and artifacts as liberating, Garnier's vision made room for the old town, and his cultural quarter was to contain in addition to a botanical garden, greenhouse, library, and exhibition hall, a museum for "historical collections and important archaeological, artistic, industrial and commercial documents relating to the town." Moreover, Garnier decreed that "monuments will be erected in the park surrounding the rooms containing the archives." For the secular and peaceful society he envisioned, there was no need to provide churches or military barracks.

Garnier's plan languished, although he managed to get it published twice—in 1914 when he was director of the International Urban Exhibition in Lyons and again in 1931. As a practicing architect in Lyons with strong ties to the socialist mayor Édouard Herriot (1872–1957), Garnier obtained commissions to build some of the components envisioned in his

12.6. Domestic quarter, *Une Cité Industrielle.* The stripped-down appearance of Garnier's houses did not mean a banishment of ornament and color, only a more neutral background to heighten the expressive potential of freestanding works of art than was the case when decoration was conceived as integral with architecture. Garnier felt that the use of poured concrete and cement resulted in "large horizontal and vertical surfaces, endowing the buildings with a sense of calm and balance in harmony with the natural contours of the landscape." He established a web of connecting footpaths independent of the street system throughout the entire town so as to create "a huge park, free of enclosures and barriers delimiting individual plots of land."

12.7. Ildefons Cerdà's Plan for the expansion of Barcelona, Spain. 1859. The tangled web of pedestrian-scale streets of the old city, the Barri Gotic, is axially penetrated in only a few places by the new street pattern. Traversing the entire city, now greatly increased in size, are two intersecting diagonal boulevards.

Below: **12.8. Linear City, proposal by Arturo Soria y Mata. 1882**

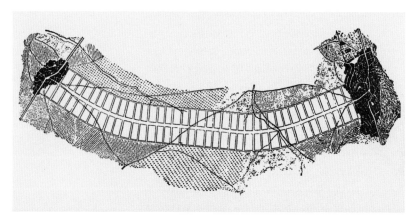

Cité Industrielle. These included a hospital, sanitarium, sports stadium, post office and telecommunications headquarters, art college, weaving school, employment exchange, the États Unis residential district, and memorials to war victims. Although he never saw his comprehensive plan for a parklike town realized, it nonetheless became a landmark in the history of twentieth-century city planning. Garnier's pioneering concept of low-rise housing, separate systems of vehicular and pedestrian circulation, and an array of facilities addressing the diverse needs of people for environmental safety, health, education, employment, recreation, entertainment, and politics remains a notable expression of the belief in rational, comprehensive, socially oriented planning that characterized the architectural profession in the first half of the twentieth century.

Urban Planning in Spain

In Spain, Ildefons Cerdà (1816–1876), an engineer and the author of *Teoría General de Urbanización* (1867), saw circulation as the primary definer of city form. He grasped how predominant modes of locomotion catalyzed urban transformations as cities built with narrow ways for foot traffic changed their street patterns and widths to accommodate equestrians and later wheeled vehicles. In 1859, Cerdà designed the Eixample, the planned extension of the city all around medieval Barcelona, as checkerboard blocks with each square having chamfered corners to accommodate better the turning radii of carriages (fig. 12.7).

In Madrid, a generation later Arturo Soria y Mata (1844–1920) carried Cerdà's interest in locomotion a step further. Realizing that the rapid-transit line linking city and suburb could establish yet another urban form, Soria proposed in 1882 *La ciudad lineal,* a linear city with a single 1640-foot-wide (500-meter-wide) street of indeterminate length (fig. 12.8). Boldly, Soria envisioned this artery not only as a transportation corridor but also as an immense belt of utilities and services including water, gas, and electric lines, reservoirs and public gardens, and stations for various municipal services. Settlement was to occur in orthogonal blocks along secondary streets perpendicular to the central spine, with houses occupying only one-fifth of each building lot. A small piece of Soria's scheme was realized: 13 miles (22 kilometers) of a 34-mile (55-kilometer) planned linear city outside Madrid.

In contrast to the purely technological approach of Soria, the Catalan industrialist Eusebi Güell (1846–1918) and his architect Antonio Gaudí (1852–1926) attempted in the construction of Park Güell between 1900 and 1914 to express Barcelona's transformation into a modern industrial city still tied to its indigenous cultural, spiritual, and technological heritage (figs. 12.11–12.15). Park Güell was originally intended as a suburban alternative to the increasingly crowded city that the magnate saw filling the blocks outlined by Cerdà's Eixample. Güell had already exhibited a concern similar to Lever's at Port Sunlight in the construction of Colònia Güell to house his textile workers. His new project would allow middle-class Barcelonans to escape the city's growing clamor and congestion. Perhaps more important, it would encode into its architectural fabric emblems of the Catalan "regional soul" as promoted by the Catholic revival in which both Güell and Gaudí were active participants.

Park Güell's creation occurred within the period of the *Renaixença*, the renascence of Catalan traditions, including that of religious pilgrimage and penitential piety, led by Barcelona's cultural elite. Neither this movement nor the park is as anomalous as one might imagine at first. They sprang from a regional variant of the impulse to revalidate folkways, ancient rituals, craft traditions, and vernacular idioms of language, architecture, ornament, and dress that was occurring simultaneously in other places. Not unexpectedly, given the rapidly changing, increasingly rootless, secular nature of the times, conservative men such as Güell and Gaudí sought to reconnect their society with history, as powerfully represented by the Catholic Church. Religious societies planned excursions by rail into the surrounding countryside where members visited thousand-year-old Romanesque churches, cave shrines, and mountain sanctuaries. Barcelonans revived the *sardana,* a regional folk dance still performed in the city's cathedral square. The Joc Florals, a poetry and rhetoric festival established in 1859, celebrated the Catalan language and the tradition of Provençal troubadours. The architect Lluís Doménech y Montaner (1850–1923) led a crafts revival that successfully integrated craft technologies—particularly those of ceramics and metalwork—with the industrial arts, resulting in the robust ornamental plasticity that characterizes many of Barcelona's buildings today (fig. 12.9). That Gaudí was a scion of coppersmiths was an important factor in his development as an architect.

Park Güell occupies an especially interesting position in the history of landscape design because of Güell and Gaudí's attempt to synthesize cosmopolitan progress and ethnic conservatism. Gaudí combined modern industrial technologies and ancient craft tra-

12.9. Passeig de Gracia, Barcelona, with lamp standard and seat designed by Gaudí and, in the backgound, his Casa Milá

ditions to create forms that are both witty and soberly pious. He built upon the symbolical identification of the steep site—located on the southeast side of Muntanya Pelada (Bald Mountain), also referred to as Mount Carmel—with the sacred mountain of Montserrat. After the fortuitous discovery of a cave and mineral spring on the property, he used the natural materials of the site to fashion other forms suggestive of an antediluvian holy landscape. Elevated to greatness by Gaudí's genius and the superbly imaginative craftsmanship of Catalan artisans, Park Güell is a landscape curiosity, a failed utopian experiment and Industrial Age vision of paradise. It is also a more elegant and refined, but not-too-distant, cousin to the midway plaisances of the world's fairs—low-brow amusement areas such as the one that provided a piquant counterpoint to the elevated cultural ambience of the 1893 Chicago World's Fair—and the delightfully garish amusement parks such as Luna Park and Steeplechase at Coney Island with which it is contemporary. Like these, it sought to imbue landscape with evocations of the fantastic and supernatural.

Without the appropriate frame of cultural reference and knowledge of Park Güell's historical background, the visitor will find it inexplicably bizarre in much the same way as the untutored tourist finds bafflingly enigmatic the sixteenth-century park of Count Orsini at Bomarzo with its riddling allusions to Ariosto's *Orlando furioso,* Dante's *Inferno,* and Virgil's *Aeneid.* In Barcelona, patron and architect attempted to combine the social program of the garden suburb with the symbolical and thematic allusions of the pleasure garden. To achieve their objective Güell and Gaudí drew upon the architecture of the late-nineteenth-century international expositions in which they had played significant roles, including the one held in 1888 in Barcelona's Ciutadella Park. Increasingly, these

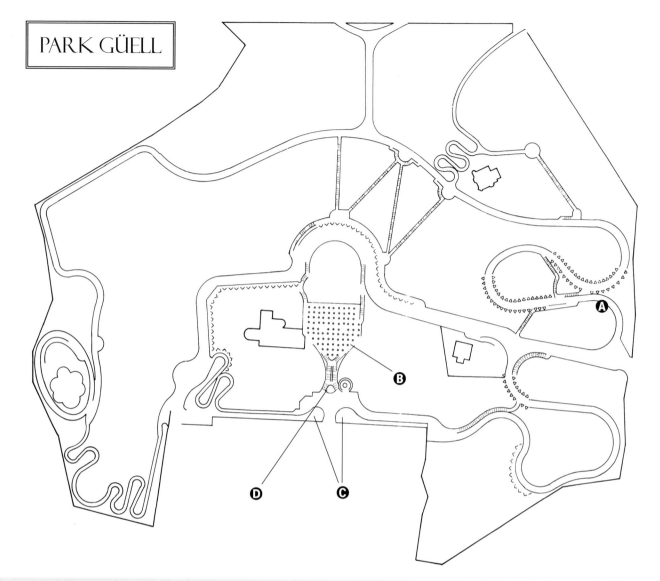

PARK GÜELL

12.10. Plan of Park Güell, Barcelona, designed by Antonio Gaudí. 1900–14

12.11. Tile mosaic in *trencadís* pattern on the walls of Gaudí's grand stairway, Park Güell

Upon entering the park, one passes between two gatehouses **G**. Designed practically to accommodate residents, arriving guests, and concierge, they nevertheless have a fairy-tale aspect with their candylike encrusted surfaces. Gaudí created the fluid parabolic curves of their surging roof lines using the traditional Catalan masonry called *bóveda tabicada* in which thin bricks or flat rectangular tiles are laminated to form vaulting.

Beyond the gatehouses lies the entry vestibule with its enigmatic clues and teasing symbols. As festive and welcoming as a contemporary theme park, like Disney World's Magic Kingdom, this space is replete with pseudo-Gothic heraldic motifs. A grand stairway **D**, which splits in two halfway down, is encased by low walls embellished with reassembled pieces of broken tile in a pattern called

trencadís, a traditional Catalan mosaic technique (fig. 12.11). It is framed by tall side walls with overhanging crenelated parapets and decorated with a bold checkerboard design using the same mosaic technique. Gaudí's deliberate smashing of newly fired tile and its application to curving surfaces exemplifies his creativity in adapting traditional craft forms to new and original artistic ends.

This space, while essentially cheerful, is also vaguely disquieting. It is made ambiguous by the presence of a shadowy grotto in the triangle created by the bifurcation of the grand stairs, a bronze ceramic serpent head protruding from a round shield adorned with the colors of the Catalan flag, and a brilliant mosaic-covered, water-spouting dragon (fig. 12.12. Artificial caves on either side of the ceremonial stairs serve the practical functions of stor-

12.12. Dragon, Grand stairway and entrance grotto, Park Güell

Above: 12.13. Upper Bridge, Park Güell

12.14. Greek Theater, Park Güell

age, shelter, and carriage turnaround, but the rough masonry of these vaulted recesses gives them the appearance of geologic wonders. They constitute, it turns out, a prelude to the architectural and symbolical double entendres one encounters in moving through Park Güell's richly programmed landscape.

The grand stairs Ⓓ ascend to the imposing Market Hall Ⓔ with its forest of columns. If the sixty families projected to take up residence there had done so, this hypostyle hall might have functioned as intended. It remains, instead, a curious and impressive untenanted space, a demonstration of Gaudí's virtuosic technical skills and protean imagination as an architect. Monumental Doric columns rise to support a massive roof platform. This acts as the floor surface of the Greek Theater Ⓑ, a large elevated plaza intended for civic and

religious rituals and such expressions of Catalan folk culture as the popular *sardana* dances. Like a Mannerist conceit, a wide, high-backed, curving bench blocks immediate entrance from the stairs into this open hall, and the architect has provided no visible clue as to any means of entry into it. Once the visitor has found the route inside, the powerful fluted columns, the pearly-toned *trencadís* work in the ceiling's multiple shallow domes, and the great round ceiling medallions by the artist Josep María Jujol vie for primacy in producing the strongest impression.

The wavy entablature of the Market Hall is surmounted by a serpentine bench, added after 1909 when Park Güell's construction program was coming to a close. Here, surrounding the entire perimeter of the Greek Theater, Jujol created a ceramic masterpiece, sheathing Gaudí's

gently undulating, biomorphic balcony and continuous seat with a boldly brilliant mosaic containing numerous liturgically symbolic colors, emblems, and inscriptions (fig. 12.14).

Adapted to the steep topography of the site, the circulation system consists of gently inclined promenades or principal avenues 33 feet (10 meters) wide; somewhat steeper carriage roads having a width of 16.5 feet (5 meters); 10-foot- (3-meter-) wide connector paths for pedestrians; and *dreceras,* or narrow ways with steps to facilitate climbing, in areas too steep for conventional pedestrian paths.

While Gaudí's circulation system conformed generally to the dictates of topography, to avoid narrow switchbacks and hairpin turns he made the roads loop broadly, creating the need for structural support where there was no ground plane

beneath them. He treated the undersides of the bridges that carry these sections of the roadbed as vaulted porticos dressed with rough-hewn masonry, making them appear as cavelike chambers, integral parts of the surrounding stony landscape. Here he employed the same Catalan *bóveda tabicada* system used in the gatehouses, canting support columns and splaying their capitals so that they merge with the portico ceiling, dressing the whole in rough-hewn native stone and creating in this fluid parabolic interior an impression that is almost geological, rather than architectonic (fig. 12.13). In the upper bridge/portico Ⓐ, spiky agave plants grow from the tops of the capitals of the columns, which here function as large rustic jardinieres.

had become showcases for fanciful kiosks and other exotic structures outside the architectural mainstream as well as a means of demonstrating innovations in industrial technology.

The fact that Güell anglicized the name of his real-estate development, spelling it "park" instead of *parc* (Catalan) or *parque* (Spanish), indicated a conscious association with the English landscape tradition, both in its eighteenth-century manifestation in such gardens as Stowe and Stourhead and in its contemporary garden city one, as at Letchworth. Gaudí used an indigenous symbolism to create a twentieth-century sacralized Catalan version of the *jardin anglais*. Here, instead of valorizing the industrial present with evocations of a classical Arcadia, he dramatized the sacredness of the rough prehistoric Catalan landscape with emblems of a pilgrim's progress toward Paradise combined with a vividly organic imagery derived from regional nature.

In planning their residential refuge, Güell and Gaudí rejected the orthogonal lines of Cerdà's Eixample in much the way that Olmsted and Vaux rejected the grid in their plans for Central Park and the suburb of Riverside, Illinois (fig. 12.10; see figs. 9.34, 9.48). Not only did they follow the dictates of topography in the Park Güell's curvilinear road system, but because it represented a paradisiacal place, they also demarcated the development with walls and an elaborate entrance gate to set it apart from the rest of the city.[4] They made the experience of coming into the park akin to participating in a mystical pageant by furnishing its entrance with an elaborate set of symbols appropriate to the as yet uninitiated pilgrim embarking on a journey of pious discovery—Poliphilus in Colonna's *Hypnerotomachia Poliphili,* Dante in *The Divine Comedy,* and Prince Tamino in Mozart's *The Magic Flute* come to mind. These are embodied in several original and highly plastic forms (fig. 12.12). In designing them Gaudí did not rely on blueprints. Instead, he was there, on the job, sketching, directing, and continually innovating—creatively marrying ancient craft with contemporary industrial technology.

Park Güell's functionally segregated circulation system, like that of Central Park, was an object of considerable attention, also providing the opportunity for a series of bridges of great originality and design distinction. While the spiritual benefits intended to be derived from passage through Central Park on foot, horseback, or carriage were characterized by Olmsted as being of a "poetic" nature—the benign influence of nature operating on the senses and the soul— Gaudí's system of roads and paths had a more specifically religious intent and program. All routes wound upward to a stone cairn surmounted by three stone crosses symbolizing Calvary, or Golgotha, the hill of Jesus' Crucifixion. Gaudí intended the climb to this highest point in the park, an energetic Sunday promenade, to recall the famous pilgrimage routes in the Pyrenees, particularly the one leading to Montserrat, Catalonia's holy mountain and refuge of monks and martyrs. Visible from this high point are the spires of Gaudí's Church of the Sacred Family and much of the rest of Barcelona's urban landscape.

For the mystically inclined architect as well as for the proprietor of Park Güell, the site was *both* allegorical and invested with its own sacred significance. The bishop of Vic actively encouraged the spread into Catalonia of the nineteenth-century cult of grotto sanctuaries that originated in France and was conspicuously manifested at Lourdes. The network of caves within Muntanya Pelada, discovered shortly after Güell had ordered work to begin on the site, validated his belief in a thematic treatment and gave Gaudí's improvisatory genius the opportunity for fresh flights of architectural fantasy. Not only was Gaudí cooperating in the creation of a hieratic landscape, he was also countering Enlightenment rationalism and its corollary, modern industrial engineering, with a seemingly organic architecture that used local craft technique to fashion indigenous building materials into an expression that appeared to be deeply rooted in the land. Inventively seeking ways of making architecture appear organic, Gaudí employed the helix in his spiral ramp for the portico adjacent to the Greek Theater. Here, one of nature's most elegant and prevalent patterns is used to ingenious effect.

Although Gaudí's style is sometimes associated with the curvilinear forms and vegetal motifs of the Art Nouveau movement, his goals were different. Perhaps the greatest and certainly the most ardent practitioner of Expressionism, the architectural style that flourished during the first quarter of the twentieth century, Gaudí sought to find an idiom outside of any cultural conventions or historical references, to evoke sensations from free-form sculptural elements. Because he mystically associated nature with the symbolism of a Catalonian nationalism deeply rooted in Roman Catholicism, the existence of real caves on the site merely impelled him further in a direction prompted by religion. Taking his cues from the "book of nature," which he believed was the creation of God, he intended to deny Darwin and scientific rationalism and to substantiate creationism through a biomorphic and geomorphic architectural imagery expressive of the prebiblical, prehistoric landscape. At the same time, though laden with this symbolic intent, the structures attached to the roads and other cavelike recesses served quite practical, nonmetaphorical ends, providing sheltered seating, storage space, and other amenities.

Inherent problems thwarted the complete realization of Güell and Gaudí's visionary plan. Title to the parcels Güell planned to sell was hedged with regulations stating that only one-sixth of a lot could be covered with buildings, that building height and location be set according to a formula that ensured the view lines of all other residences, that walls along property lines be no higher than 32 inches (80 centimeters) from the ground, that no trees over six inches in diameter be removed. Unlike Howard, Güell did not set up a corporation to administer his proposed community in perpetuity. Rather, he left vague his commitment to the future provision of services and maintenance, inserting in his proposed contract of sale an escape clause for the proprietor, specifying that the residents were to form an association for such purposes. As a result, the lots remained unsold, and the estate became the private refuge of Güell, Gaudí, and another family closely related to Güell. In 1923, five years after Güell's death, his heirs transferred the property to the municipality of Barcelona to administer as a public park. Today it is one of the most visited parks in the city.

European Modernism

Though secular rather than religious in their outlook, European radical modernists possessed a fervor equal to that of the Catalonian *Renaixença* leaders in their attempts to create new human environments appropriate to the Industrial Age. They romanticized the speeded-up future enabled by machine technology. The Futurists, as a group of young Milanese artists and intellectuals called themselves, were particularly enamored of high-speed motion and mechanized power. Among their ranks was the architect Antonio Sant'Elia (1888–1916) whose *Città Nuova* proposal abandoned Haussmannesque urban retrofitting for the modern age in favor of a clean start. All traces of the past are swept away to allow skyscrapers to rise boldly above circulation corridors arranged on multiple levels (fig. 12.15). Engineering, rather than social concern, characterizes Sant'Elia's proposal: intersecting layers of underground railways, highways, pedestrian skyways, and even an airport runway passing above and below one another by means of great viaducts and bridges. Elevators provide vertical access between levels and within the tall buildings.

At the same time, in 1903, Austrian architect Josef Hoffmann (1870–1956) founded the Wiener Werkstätte with painter and furniture designer Koloman Moser (1868–1918). This studio of collaborative architects and artisans offered an Arts and Crafts alternative to Machine Age modernity. In Germany, early modernism united the Arts and Crafts tradition as practiced by architect Peter Behrens (1868–1940)—

12.15. Proposal for a skyscraper city with grade-separated transportation channels, by Antonio Sant'Elia. 1914

a follower of William Morris and one of the founders in 1907 of the Deutscher Werkbund in Munich—with a the Machine Age aesthetic and a purely functionalist approach.

Walter Gropius (1883–1969), a student in Behrens's office, followed the Belgian architect and designer Henry van de Velde (1863–1957) as director of the arts and crafts school founded in Weimar by the grand duke of Saxe-Weimar in 1906. Gropius premised the curriculum of the Bauhaus, as he named the school, upon the Werkbund's ethos of developing an indigenous German art based on sound construction and the collaborative effort of architects, artists, and artisans. Students were trained to respect the particular characteristics of wood and other natural materials. By 1923, however, Gropius had abandoned the Expressionist mood that had infused early Bauhaus instruction in architecture and had turned away from the Werkbund's belief that craft ideals should influence industrial design toward an emphasis upon machine technology. The functional design and industrial materials of the school's new quarters that Gropius built in Dessau (1925–26) became a visible manifesto of the Bauhaus's evolved mission to promote new building methods. Socialism was implicit, too, in Gropius's architecture. He saw machine technology as the carrier of a different kind of design beauty from that of the more labor-intensive, and thereby more expensive, Arts and Crafts aesthetic. By abandoning handiwork ornament in favor of a more abstract architectural aesthetic based on composition alone, architects could bring a more commodious life to more people than ever before. Industrial building parts were relatively inexpensive, especially compared with ornamental, hand-carved stone, and less-skilled architects than Gropius could achieve satisfactory, if not particularly inspired, results employing them in modular designs.[5]

Subsequently characterized as one of the progenitors of a new International Style, Bauhaus architecture and that of kindred designers now discarded regional design vocabularies and traditional building materials in favor of steel-frame construction, curtain walls, open floor plans, and asymmetrical planar elevations.[6] The early practitioners of this classless and often rigorously utilitarian architecture were polemical in their anti-authoritarianism. For them, ornament—the carrier of iconographies of power and of symbolism associated with aristocratic grandeur and monarchical rule—appeared superfluous and possibly even immoral.

Their avant-garde cosmopolitanism was anathema to political conservatives, particularly to nationalists, and to members of Adolf Hitler's Nazi (National Socialist) Party, who preferred a traditional style rooted in the German Picturesque and, in the case of monumental public buildings, a sober classicism that glorified the power of the State. Gropius's new Bauhaus in Dessau existed barely a decade before he and his colleagues became part of the diaspora of German intellectuals who left Europe after 1933 when Hitler came to power. Gropius became the head of the architectural program at Harvard, and this, along with the exodus of many other German and Austrian modernists, hastened the acceptance of the International Style as an architectural idiom in the United States.

Gropius's contemporary, the Swiss-born architect Charles Édouard Jeanneret, known as Le Corbusier (1887–1965), extended the premises of the International Style to the most traditional of human structures, the home, which he memorably defined as "a machine for living." He shared with the Futurists an enthusiasm for dynamic motion and boldness of scale, which he manifested in city-planning schemes that welcomed the automobile with wider roadways, while expanding traditional city blocks into a superblock grid scaled to provide abundant light and air around tall residential towers.

12.16. Le Corbusier's sketch plans for Rio de Janeiro, Brazil. 1929

While his indifference to specific economic, political, and social realities ensured that his plans remained largely on paper, Le Corbusier's Olympian pronouncements and his tireless program of publication assured lasting and far-reaching influence for his planning paradigms and proposals. Like Sant'Elia, he saw that the city might be more dense and also more open if motorized transportation systems operated both vertically and horizontally, and, like Soria, he appreciated the linear spine as a means of planned decentralization and industrial dispersal. He held in contempt Sitte and other practitioners of the Picturesque style in architecture, and he deplored New York's skyscrapers because these were placed cheek by jowl within a preexisting street pattern rather than set upon a much more loosely woven grid of spacious superblocks filled with sunlight and greenery.

Without subscribing to its proponents' density ratios or proposed satellite clusters, Le Corbusier appropriated the virtues of the garden city—plentiful sunlight, abundant recreational open space, and ease of movement—as his principal objectives. Biology furnished him with numerous images—"BIOLOGY! The great new word in architecture and planning," he once declared—but his idea of organic planning was metaphorical and, above all, architectural rather than environmental. The stunning setting of Rio de Janeiro, for instance, provoked in him "the strong desire, a bit mad perhaps, to attempt here a human adventure—the desire to set up a duality, to create 'the affirmation of man' against or with 'the presence of nature.'"[7] He then sketched a 328-foot-(100-meter-) high motorway looping the city in an arc around its beautiful harbor, the upper deck a continuous structure containing apartments, the lower band of which would begin almost 100 feet (30 meters) from the ground, presumably clearing the tops of any existing buildings (fig. 12.16).

But this modernist, romantically homocentric response to setting characterized only Le Corbusier's encounters with real sites such as that of the Villa Savoye (1929–31) at Poissy, where he designed a structure raised on pilotis with views across a broad meadow, an intended evocation of the Latin poet Virgil's urbane pastoralism. His theoretical plans, on the other hand, envisioned flat, featureless plains upon which to inscribe rationalistic architectonics. Classicism, Cartesian geometry, and admiration for authoritarian leaders—exemplified in his respect for the achievements of Louis XIV (Place Vêndome, Invalides, Versailles), Louis XV (Place de la Concorde) and Napoléon I (Champ de Mars, L'Étoile)—underlie his bold proposal for a Contemporary City for Three Million Inhabitants (fig. 12.17). Exhibited at the Salon d'Automne in 1922, it envisioned a grid of

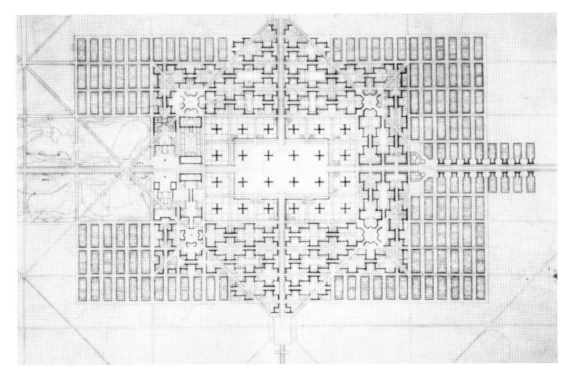

12.17. Plan and perspectives of a Contemporary City for Three Million Inhabitants, by Le Corbusier. 1922

Below: 12.18. Facade of a residential unit with a two-story maisonette with terrace in the Contemporary City for Three Million Inhabitants.

superblocks occupied by tall, freestanding, slablike buildings where people would live in practically identical two-story "freehold maisonettes" furnished with terraces (fig. 12.18). Employing one of his favorite biological metaphors, Le Corbusier, who felt that the highly mobile population of the modern age need no longer harbor sentimental notions of home and hearth, called these residential units "cells." Industry was to be located outside the city proper, and workers, comprising two million of the three million inhabitants, would be located in "garden cities" nearby.

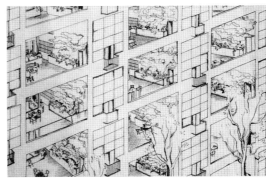

Besides providing a paradigm for the contemporary servantless apartment dwelling, Le Corbusier's plan of a City for Three Million Inhabitants anticipated the fitness culture of today with its plethora of athletic facilities: tennis courts, swimming pools, soccer fields, and rooftop running tracks and sunbathing areas. As the buildings were raised on pilotis, paths could pass beneath them, forming a network of pedestrian ways independent of the arteries for vehicular circulation. An underground commuter railroad linking the center with the industrial suburbs and a metropolitan subway would provide mass transit. Like Sant'Elia, Le Corbusier was fascinated with the idea of landing airplanes in the middle of the city and designed a platform for this purpose on the upper level of his multilevel transportation center.

In 1923 he published *Vers une architecture* (translated in 1927 as *Towards a New Architecture*) in which he enunciated "three reminders to architects." These principles exerted a profound influence on modernist landscape architects, some of whose work we will examine in Chapter Thirteen. Here Le Corbusier maintained that architecture is an art of mass based on cubes, spheres, cones, cylinders, or pyramids—forms revealed to our eyes by light; that surfaces should be modulated to accentuate these simple forms; and that architecture should have nothing to do with "the styles" but allow the plan, an abstraction based on mathematics, to serve as a generator of design, a harmonizing force, and the carrier of sensation.

In 1930, at the third Congrès Internationaux d'Architecture Moderne (CIAM) congress in Brussels where the theme was "Rational Methods of Site Planning," Le Corbusier exhibited a plan that he called *The Radiant City* (fig. 12.19). Originally conceived as a response to Soviet officials in Moscow who wanted to reorganize the capital, the plan elaborated and refined the repetitive cellular structure within a geometric superblock grid that he had previously developed for the City for Three Million Inhabitants. Here Le Corbusier created a plan that was capable of expansion on either side of its axial spine. He placed the towers of the administrative and business district on this axis but away from the urban center in much the same position that the corporate office buildings of the La Défense district occupy in relation to Paris today.

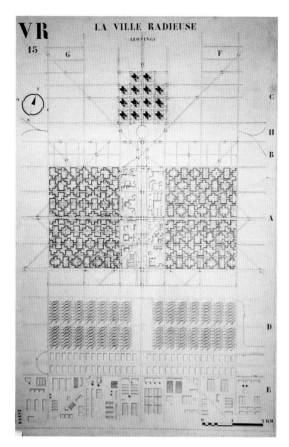

12.19. Plan for The Radiant City, by Le Corbusier. 1930

With the exception of the new capital cities of Chandigarh in the Punjab province of India, begun in 1950, and Brasília, where in 1956 Le Corbusier's disciples Lúcio Costa (1902–1998) and Oscar Niemeyer (b. 1907) began erecting a South American version of the Radiant City, the CIAM planners did not see their visionary urbanism come to fruition. In Chandigarh, Le Corbusier assigned to his cousin Pierre Jeanneret responsibility for planning the layout of the city. In a country that had scarcely begun to industrialize, Jeanneret conceived a sophisticated road system far in advance of the demands of actual motorized traffic. In the end, the city's achievements were not those of planning but rather of architecture, notably the capitol complex of monumental government buildings Le Corbusier designed around a vast pedestrian plaza. These include the High Court and the Legislative Assembly with its monumental portico and massive flaring roof, which demonstrate the architect's movement away from the International Style toward a new definition of modernism based on bold experimentation with the sculptural potential of exposed concrete. In Brasília, although Niemeyer brought a similar dramatic verve to the major buildings, the geometric regularity underlying Costa's plan imposed a sense of artificiality on the city. Moreover, the prestigious monumental architecture of the civic centers in these cities was counterbalanced by the autocratically planned

residential areas where people tried with much inconvenience to accommodate their daily movements and living patterns to the monotonously repetitive housing and windswept emptiness of the superblock scale.

In spite of such evident disjunction between the ideal and everyday reality in these early examples of modernist planning, Le Corbusier's reputation and influence upon the contemporary city remained potent. The years following World War II saw the rapid dissemination of the International Style[8] throughout the capitalist world as the bomb-ravaged cities of Europe and Japan rebuilt themselves and as rapidly urbanizing nations elsewhere appropriated its aesthetics and architectural forms as the most economical means of building on a large scale within a compressed time frame. Among the generation of architects who came of age in this period, Le Corbusier was revered as one of the principal progenitors of the modernist movement they now carried forward. As industrial cities from New York City to Toyko, from Stockholm to Madrid, continued to attract huge populations, increasing numbers of people lived in high-rise slabs modeled superficially on Le Corbusier's Unité d'Habitation in Marseilles, which was one residential block of a proposed "vertical garden city" for local industrial workers, or in cruciform towers like those of his Radiant City.

No one, certainly not Le Corbusier and the other leaders of the modernist movement, understood the full dimensions of the role of the automobile in transforming cities and the effect that highways and superhighways would have on cities and countryside alike. The scale of the superblock facilitated motor age traffic, but, because the open space that was to become a network of greenways in the Radiant City usually became parking lots instead, the pedestrian was thwarted. Instead of strengthening the social bond, this loosened the communal fabric and diminished personal security. Born of the twentieth century's enthusiasm for personal mobility and automobile transportation, the highways carrying cars into the hearts of cities made old urban centers very different kinds of places from what they had been previously, raising the question of how much besides a lengthy commute had been gained. Nowhere was the effect of modernism's failed promises more evident than in the United States. There, tremendous industrial growth, much of it stimulated by consumer demand for automobiles, accelerated the impact of the machine on the landscape, though at first there was an era of promise as planners and landscape architects sought to design better communities for a new age.

II. Greenbelt Towns or Suburbs?: Creating the American Metropolis

In America, urban planning, which had first been conceptualized and practiced by Frederick Law Olmsted and Calvert Vaux as a means of guiding and shaping metropolitan growth around a green armature of parks and parkways, had become by the end of the nineteenth century an exercise in Beaux-Arts Neoclassical monumentalism. As we saw in the previous chapter, only Washington, D.C., which already had in place its Neoclassical urban framework, achieved a comprehensive urban redesign at this time. Elsewhere pragmatic city leaders settled for a few Beaux-Arts monuments, buildings, and squares. The second generation of urban planners in America, which included Frederick Law Olmsted, Jr., who had been a major participant in the McMillan Commission's report outlining Washington's aggrandizement as a monumental city, gradually abandoned the ideals of the City Beautiful for what has been termed the City Functional, the City Practical, and sometimes the City Social. Although socialism never became as strong a force in America as in Europe, there were some who hoped to place the values of society as a whole above those of Darwinian capitalist competition. Ebenezer Howard's influential garden cities movement helped define economic well-being in social, rather than mere monetary, terms. But any broadening of its aims would require large-scale social and economic reform backed by political policy.

American Visionaries

The generation of visionary reformers that came of age during World War I in America grasped just how profoundly industrialization was transforming society. The economic theories of Henry George and Thorstein Veblen influenced and supported their belief that land profits should be directed toward the common good and that land planning should rationally partner nature with engineering and technology to provide livable communities. Some recoiled from the impending future of vastly enlarged cities and were uneasy with the purely architectural solutions of European modernists like Le Corbusier, while others embraced skyscraper-scale metropolitanism. Both decentralists and metropolitanists felt that regional planning involving vast engineering projects was now a necessity and that industrial technology provided the means of harnessing nature's resources for human ends. As planners conceived the new towns and suburbs, the highways and bridges, and the hydroelectric dams and transmission lines that would create an entirely new urban scale, social reformers drew up

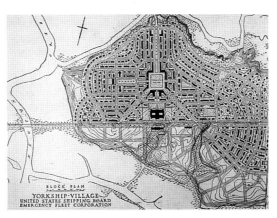

their plans for remedying the ills of existing cities. Recreation as a means of acculturation for immigrant groups gave birth to the playground movement, and in the early years of the twentieth century the recreation director became a certified professional along with the social worker.

World War I provided urban planners with a convenient link to the social reform agenda of the Progressive Era as well as a means of transferring British garden city and regional planning ideals to the United States, where the federal government sponsored villages to house war-industry workers during World War I. Frederick Law Olmsted, Jr., served as chief of design for the United States Housing Corporation, and architect and planner Henry Wright (1878–1936) was one of three designers hired by the government-sponsored Emergency Fleet Corporation headed by architect Frederick Lee Ackerman (1878–1950), to plan Yorkship Village (1918), now Fairview, New Jersey (fig. 12.20). The plan was based upon the neighborhood-unit outlined of Clarence Perry (1872–1944), a sociologist-planner who learned the values of good community design firsthand as a resident of Forest Hills Gardens.

Partly inspired by examples of German garden cities, such as Krupp and Essen, Forest Hills Gardens in Queens, New York, was a garden suburb in the Picturesque tradition. The Russell Sage Foundation, the project's sponsor, intended it to be a cozy domestic landscape built according to the latest "scientific principles" of town planning, an educational demonstration to developers of the profitability of an architecturally integrated, exclusively residential community built for middle-class homeowners. Here, in 1909, Olmsted, Jr., laid out three wide principal roads for through traffic and a series of gently winding, narrow residential streets (fig. 12.21). By paying close attention to the smallest details of design, including the mellow reddish tint of stucco and sidewalk cement,

12.20. Plan for Yorkship Village, now Fairview, Camden, New Jersey, by Frederick Lee Ackerman. 1918. Ackerman, who was assisted by Henry Wright, focused his plan with Beaux-Arts radials and Picturesque curvilinear roads upon a village green. A system of footpaths separated pedestrian from vehicular traffic, and varied setbacks for the neo-Georgian two- and three-story row, twin, and triplex houses illustrate the designers' attention to streetscape.

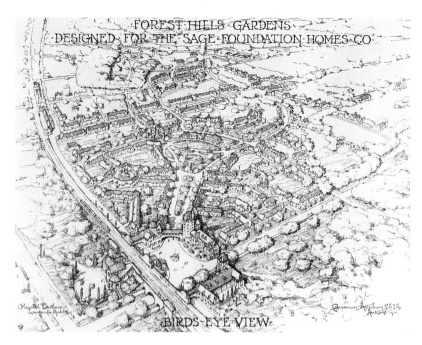

FOREST·HILLS·GARDENS·
DESIGNED·FOR·THE·SAGE·FOUNDATION·HOMES·CO·

BIRDS·EYE·VIEW·

12.21. Bird's-Eye View of Forest Hills Gardens, Queens, New York, designed by Frederick Law Olmsted, Jr., and Grosvenor Atterbury. 1909

the color and size of brick, which looked aged, not new, and the contrasting effect of white trim and dark, creosote-coated oak timbers, architect Grosvenor Atterbury gave the community's structures a harmonious Gothic-Tudor or German-Tudor, pseudo-medieval appearance. Though quaintly styled, the planned community was innovative in promoting neighborly living in attached row and two-family houses. These were grouped together so that residents shared front lawns and backyards. There were conventional single-family houses as well. Although Olmsted's design failed to account for the growing trend in automobile ownership, the generously planted curving streets and the attractively landscaped common ground—including a central mall leading to Flagpole Green—and the mellow picturesqueness of Atterbury's architecture made this rail- and, later, subway-served garden suburb an especially desirable place to live.

Perry saw the neighborhood unit as a means of re-creating the kind of environment conducive to the face-to-face relationships that impersonal big cities were perceived to be destroying. From his Forest Hills Gardens experience he developed a demographic-based formula that provided necessary educational, recreational, and service facilities based on convenient walking radii. Using this model for Yorkship Village, he specified that houses were to be located within a half mile of the local elementary school and its playground and no more than a quarter mile distant from local shops, which would be at the juncture of contiguous neighborhood units. A landscaped village-green-type square, complete with flagpole such as the one found in Forest Hills Gardens, would serve as the focal point for community institutions.

The neighborly, greenbelt-buffered community

of low-cost housing approximating Perry's ideal at Yorkship Village was sufficiently attractive to disturb some congressmen who felt that this government-sponsored development reflected badly upon the nation's private housing industry. As a result, Congress passed legislation mandating that wartime workers' villages be auctioned for sale after the emergency was over, thus curtailing the experiment in public ownership, in the manner of Howard's garden city, based on financial management structured to maintain low rents and turn profits back into community improvements.

THE REGIONAL PLANNING ASSOCIATION OF AMERICA

Throughout the first half of the twentieth century, social philosopher, architectural critic, and urban historian Lewis Mumford (1915–1990) was America's most passionate and articulate proponent of metropolitan decentralization and the creation of new towns. To understand Mumford's planning philosophy and that of his friends and colleagues who formed the Regional Planning Association of America, we must first examine the life and work of Mumford's adopted mentor, Patrick Geddes (1854–1932). The Scottish biologist, sociologist, professor, and pioneer of regional-scale urban planning was the author of *Cities in Evolution* (1915). Geddes's views were influenced by the science of geography, the study of the earth's topography and resources in relation to human settlement and economic activity. He read the work of pioneers in this field: Élisée Reclus (1830–1905), the French anarchist, geographer, and author of the nineteen-volume *La Nouvelle Géographie universelle, la terre et les hommes* (1875–94), and Paul Vidal de la Blache (1845–1918), professor of geography in Paris, editor of the periodical *Annales de géographie,* and author of *Atlas général; histoire et géographie,* (1894). Geddes was also indebted to the ideas of Frédéric Le Play (1806–1882), the French mining engineer, sociologist, and author of *La Réforme sociale en France* (1887). Le Play placed the family rather than the state at the center of the social structure.

Geddes realized that aerial perspective—a prerogative that tall buildings and later airplanes conferred on twentieth-century denizens—was a boon for planners in a mass society in which large industrial cities were becoming the norm. Aerial views allowed one to conceive cities whole and to more easily envision urbanism at a metropolitan scale. To see far and wide from on high the shapes of Earth—its mountains, valleys, winding river courses, and coastlines, as well as the houses, roads, bridges, and other works of human beings—fostered regionalism. The panoramas thus offered were an enormous aid to the geographer, demographer, and urban reformer. As we saw in Chapter Ten, the meaning of the Eiffel Tower lay both in its demonstration of the engineering and building technologies of structural steel and in the fact that it allowed visitors to grasp Paris entire, while on their vertiginous descent the city was turned into a kaleidoscope of striking new perspectives.[9]

For Geddes, historical information about a city's past could also become comprehensible as, from an elevated perspective, streets and buildings coalesced into patterns describing its habitation in different periods of time. To translate the concept of planning at a regional scale into a graphic plan, Geddes set up his Outlook Tower, equipped with a camera obscura, on the roof of a building at the end of the Royal Mile in Edinburgh, where he could physically survey the town and its surrounding river basin. He urged what he termed *synoptic* vision, "a seeing of the city, and this as a whole; like Athens from its Acropolis, like city and Acropolis together . . . from hill-top and from sea."[10] Obviously, more was needed than an overview from an aerie such as the Outlook Tower in order to understand Edinburgh or any other city or region. Geddes advocated what he termed the "Valley Survey" and the "City Survey" to study local landscapes in all their physical, social, economic, and historical dimensions. He aimed to eliminate the artificial separation between town and country.

Geddes thought in temporal as well as spatial terms. Evolutionary biology provided a popular nineteenth-century metaphor for cultural transit, and like others of his day, he adopted the notion of cities and civilizations going from dawn to noon to sunset, or from birth to maturity to decline. He saw urbanism as a socially organic process associated with increasing occupational specialization and organizational complexity. In this fashion he charted the growth of cities in successive stages, from "polis" to "metropolis" to "megalopolis" and, finally, to "necropolis." He also drew a distinction between "paleotechnic" and "neotechnic" societies. The former denoted the early Industrial Age with its workers living in polluted, crowded, coal-burning towns, their lives directed "toward money wages instead of Vital Budget."[11] The latter possessed new sources of power, including hydroelectricity, which would make possible decentralization of populations and the decongestion of existing industrial centers. The cities that were already spreading and coalescing into conurbations were prime candidates for Geddes's recommended "Regional Survey." At the very least, on sanitary grounds and to assure a pure water supply, sensible planning was mandated.

Geddes called the paleotechnic economic order "Kakotopia," a market-driven heedless scramble for profits, whereas the neotechnic order he labeled

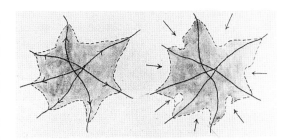

12.22. Diagram by Patrick Geddes from *Cities in Evolution* (1915) showing the desirability of reversing unchecked growth and infilling of green space as cities spread outward along the lines of transportation corridors

"Eutopia, . . . a place of effective health and well-being, even of glorious and in its way unprecedented beauty, renewing and rivaling the best achievements of the past."[12] Geddes clearly had in mind the new garden cities and planned communities then being built in England, which, following Howard's prescription, extended industrial prosperity to working-class families. He also wanted to reverse the dynamic of the metropolitan organism so that instead of the city's spreading into the country along rail and highway lines and then amorphously infilling the land in between, the country could gain on the city by wedging itself inward in the form of nature preserves (fig. 12.22). Geddes admired the urban parks that had made the nineteenth-century city a greener place, but he saw the need for forestry—"no mere tree-cropping, but sylviculture, arboriculture too, and park-making at its greatest and best"[13]—as creating opportunities for real freedom in nature unavailable in the metropolitan parks with their fences and palings and their rules designed to maintain decorum befitting the grounds of a mansion.

The concept of the city as a complex and evolving social organism captivated the imagination of the young Mumford, who, with his superior and more disciplined literary gifts, elaborated Geddes's message and carried his ideological influence to an American audience in tones that echoed the Scot's fervently moral voice. Geddes's evolutionary categorization prompted Mumford in his prejudice against "megalopolis," the city grown gargantuan or what we today call "Spread City." In adopting Geddes as his mentor, Mumford distanced himself from European modernism, promoting instead planning concepts derived from Howard and the village-inspired British new towns. On the whole, architects and planners in America aimed to give homeowners and tenants a more personal experience of nature and a more community-focused environment than that provided by Le Corbusier's broad, geometric grid of superblocks with regularly spaced, identical towers. Their site planning bore traces of both the Picturesque and Beaux-Arts styles in which they had been trained, although they eschewed Neoclassical architecture with its costly materials and ornament in favor of a simpler building vocabulary more suited to their aim of providing affordable housing and functional communities. Thus, they usually employed brick with white trim and often evoked American Colonial vernacular forms in their neo-Georgian buildings and village greens.

In 1922, Mumford met the Beaux-Arts-trained architect Clarence Stein (1882–1975), who shared his ideal of planning according to Geddes's regional survey methods. With the moral and financial support of developer Alexander Bing (1878–1959), who added business sense to this agenda, they hoped to demonstrate the concept and means of providing better living conditions for a wider social range than had been possible previously. For Stein, this meant improved housing for modest-income families in environmentally sound communities in which schools, shops, and parks were within the easy walking radii recommended by Perry.

Charles Harris Whitaker (1872–1938), editor of the *Journal of the American Institute of Architects* (JAIA), shared the Progressive Era reform agenda of these two men. He sought to expand the public concerns of architects beyond the City Beautiful movement toward a social-service orientation that addressed more fundamental needs than ennobling the urban landscape with monuments symbolizing civic pride. Benton MacKaye (1879–1975), a trained forester, an environmentalist, and the father of the Appalachian Trail, reinforced the group's regional and conservationist perspectives. In 1923, with a handful of others, they formed the Regional Planning Association of America (RPAA).

A native of Shirley, Massachusetts, MacKaye felt that the New England town with its compact settlement around a village green and proximity to rural nature offered the best possible model for regional urbanism. He viewed with horror the side effects of the new automobile culture on the landscape, as tacky roadside stands, billboards, and filling stations sprang up along rural highways, blighting the natural scenery as well as graceful old towns. He conceived the creation of the "townless highway," his term for the limited-access throughway that bypassed urban centers and eliminated grade crossings with underpasses. New towns, too, would benefit from being constructed away from, yet in reasonable proximity to, this special-purpose artery. Further, the visionary MacKaye was a proponent of Giant Power, as he and other regionalists called their idea for transmitting electricity via high-voltage lines from coal- and water-powered stations located at mines and dams. He saw the Tennessee Valley Authority, the New Deal program for damming the Tennessee River to harness hydroelectric power for distribution throughout the region, as an administrative model and means for channeling urban growth into discrete, park-surrounded cities.

Perhaps the most effective contribution of the RPAA—in addition to the body of literature Mumford produced—was the demonstration of new principles for community planning by the City Housing Corporation. The socially motivated real-estate developer and RPAA member Alexander Bing set up this limited-dividend company in order to build Sunnyside Gardens (1924) in the Borough of Queens, New York, and Radburn (1928) in the Borough of Fairlawn, New Jersey. In the absence of the government support that helped to underwrite later housing programs, the City Housing Corporation was a small, privately capitalized instrument designed to demonstrate the benefits of regional planning and the value of limited-dividend financing in returning a fixed profit to investors while also funding further community improvements.

However modest the scale of Sunnyside and Radburn, the entire RPAA fraternity applied assiduous attention and deep moral commitment to their design and building. Clarence Stein, planner and architect of these projects, collaborated with his partner, Henry Wright, as well as with Frederick Lee Ackerman, the architect of their houses. All three men were founding members of RPAA. Ackerman and Wright brought to bear their experience from Yorkship Village and other wartime emergency housing developments and with it their commitment to Clarence Perry's neighborhood unit as the fundamental community building block. As editor and writer, Whitaker and Mumford broadcast the philosophy of regional planning pioneered at Sunnyside and Radburn. Further, Mumford and his family took up residence in Sunnyside Gardens, remaining there for eleven years. MacKaye bolstered the other RPAA members' belief in technology as a powerful tool for social improvement and strengthened their commitment to natural areas preservation.

In 1924, on property Bing purchased from the Long Island Railroad to the east of Forest Hills in Sunnyside, Queens, Stein and Wright applied Perry's neighborhood-unit principles to the planning of Sunnyside Gardens. Ackerman served as architect for the blocks of houses, and Marjorie Sewell Cautley was hired as the project's landscape architect. Within the constraints of the preexisting grid, the design team developed a plan that maximized the amount of open space for private gardens, public greenery, and recreational commons, also providing an internal pedestrian circulation system for each block (fig. 12.23). Thus, their plan abandoned private property lot lines in favor of row houses with small individual backyards that faced a large communal parklike space where children could play. The Sunnyside commons were in time abandoned as land was sold to adjacent

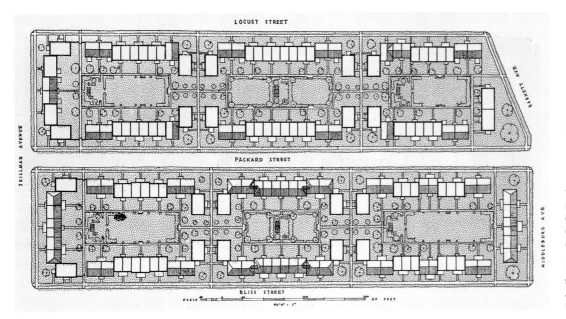

12.23. Plan of two blocks with inner courts, Sunnyside Gardens, Queens, New York, designed by Clarence Stein and Henry Wright. 1926

Below: 12.24. Plan of residential districts, Radburn, New Jersey, by Clarence Stein and Henry Wright. 1929

homeowners, who divided most of the once-shared landscape into individual parcels. But this early garden suburb was an important foundation for the work of Stein and Wright at Radburn, New Jersey, and for such later new towns as Reston, Virginia.

Radburn, undertaken as a successor to Sunnyside Gardens, carried the garden-city concept forward. The community was billed as a New Town for the Motor Age. As Stein explained in *Toward New Towns for America* (1957), "We believed thoroughly in green belts and towns of a limited size planned for work as well as living. We did not fully recognize that our main interest after our Sunnyside experience had been transferred to a more pressing need, that of a town in which people could live peacefully with the automobile — or rather in spite of it."[14] Traffic engineers soon became important professionals within the new fields of city planning and municipal administration.

The Radburn Idea was embodied in a layout that reduced the length of the roadway to the minimum necessary for automobile access, while providing abundant commonly held open space and a system of circulation routes modeled after the one developed by Olmsted and Vaux in Central Park (figs. 12.24, 12.25). To achieve this, Stein and Wright developed within the town's principal streets the superblock of 35 to 50 acres, a larger and more irregularly shaped area than that of a traditional city block. The savings associated with fewer linear feet of roadway made the provision of parkland cost-effective. Houses were turned so that their living rooms and bedrooms faced not the street but the green commons, which was continuous throughout the community.

Radburn was to have had a band of industrial development adjacent to the Erie Railroad lines and a new express highway. Then, in 1929, when the first families moved into Radburn, the nation was plunged into the Great Depression. Industry did not materialize, and home buying and home building everywhere came to a halt. Banks foreclosed the mortgages of some Radburn residents, and only two superblocks were completed. Still, Radburn as an idea lived on. In the United States it served as a direct model for the

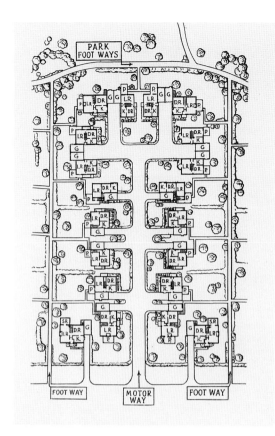

12.25. Plan of a single residential cul-de-sac, Radburn. The 18- to 20-foot-wide service road lead to the garages and service areas of fifteen to twenty homes. These face a commons, the green interior portion of a superblock. Foot ways connect residents to parks and athletic facilities.

Greenbelt Towns (Greenbelt, Maryland; Greenhills, Ohio; and Greendale, Wisconsin) built during President Franklin Roosevelt's New Deal administration under the economist Rexford Guy Tugwell (1891–1979), the ardent disciple of Ebenezer Howard and member of the U. S. president's "Brain Trust" who served as administrator of the Resettlement Administration.

The idea of rational planning by a diversified consortium of professional disciplines represented by the most skilled technical experts became something of an article of faith by the 1920s, even in the democratic United States with its free-market economy. The authoritarianism implicit in such planning was more acceptable than it would be today. The prevailing notion was that a new social order was being born and that modern technology in the service of democratic values could produce a more humane society and a higher standard of living for almost all classes. The United States was becoming a manufacturing titan, adding to its abundant natural resources unprecedented industrial wealth. Under these circumstances, people were optimistic that the solutions to social and physical problems could be found through financing and technical expertise, and they were willing to trust those in power to provide the benefits of modernity to society as a whole. The notion of an enlightened and beneficent mastermind arranging a total environment geared to the new working patterns and rising living standards of the times was an attractive one as people grappled with the rapid technological advances and complexity of modern society. In America as well as in Europe, certain architects were beginning to think of themselves as suited for this role, none more so than Frank Lloyd Wright, who well understood that the fundamental gift of the motor age was mobility.

FRANK LLOYD WRIGHT'S USONIAN VISION FOR BROADACRE CITY

The members of RPAA, Peter Kropotkin, and H. G. Wells had early intuited one of the most important aspects of modernity: ease of movement and the consequent liberation from being bound in place. Similarly, the architect Frank Lloyd Wright (1869–1959) saw decentralization as a positive force for improving the human condition. Unlike the RPAA group or the builders in the newly created Soviet Union, Wright did not promote a communal vision but one that celebrated individual freedom in the tradition of the transcendentalists Ralph Waldo Emerson, Henry David Thoreau, and Walt Whitman. He saw how mass automobile ownership, widespread communications enabled by radio, telegraph, and telephone, and easily distributed electric power could make possible a complete redistribution of population. At least in America with its abundance of developable land, it was now theoretically possible for people to live at very low densities, with each family occupying an entire acre. Wright also saw how standardization of industrial production creating inexpensive new building technologies and utilities construction could foster large-scale, low-density urbanization. According to his Usonian Vision, as he called his utopian scheme for Broadacre City, instead of living in a hive of nearly identical apartments or garden-city row houses, residents would occupy distinctive freestanding houses. Wright's anti-urban utopia was thus completely unlike that of Le Corbusier or the planners of Radburn except in its willing embrace of great systems of conveyance—distribution lines for power and utilities and transportation corridors for the movement of people and goods.

Publication of Wright's scheme for Broadacre City probably furthered his reputation as an architectural genius, but his proposal had little chance of being realized. In the United States, perhaps more than in other countries, the kind of civic leadership and initiative Tocqueville had observed a century earlier defied authoritarian visions and singular solutions. Planning, particularly on a regional scale, to be successful, necessitated close cooperation between the public and private sectors, and men such as Lewis Mumford and Frank Lloyd Wright were not temperamentally equipped to struggle and compromise within the political arena in order to advance a partial agenda. Nor were they willing to forsake an ideal premised upon low-density settlement in garden cities or on broad acres for one that served merely to guide the already forceful trend toward metropolitanism. Nowhere in the 1920s and 1930s were the implications of this dichotomy more evident than in the fast-growing counties surrounding New York City.

The Regional Plan for New York

In contrast to Mumford and his fellow members of the Regional Planning Association of America, the Regional Plan Association (RPA) proposed no radical agenda of garden-city decentralization. This group instead undertook the preparation of a plan to *guide* the growth of metropolitan New York City, which was rapidly spawning suburban development in several counties of the tri-state (New York, New Jersey, and Connecticut) region surrounding the five boroughs that constitute the incorporated city. Unlike the RPAA garden-city idealists who wished to retard metropolitan growth and foster discrete urban communities set well apart and separated by open space, the founders of the RPA recognized the momentum for cities to grow into massive regional complexes.[15] Planning, in their view, was essential to predict statistically, then guide rationally, not rearrange, this growth. Underlying the new urban scale they envisioned was a constant increase in automobile ownership, opening up the possibility of ever-expanding rings of residential settlement and the birth of the commuter society. Their metropolitan vision also implied increased density at the urban core with office skyscrapers thrusting ever higher into the air.

The Regional Plan Association, though not yet known by that name, had its beginning in 1921. That year Charles Dyer Norton (1871–1923), a trustee of the Russell Sage Foundation, the philanthropic fund that had sponsored Forest Hills Gardens, helped initiate the preparation of a privately financed plan for the rapidly growing region encompassing all of the counties of Long Island and those elsewhere within a two-hour rail commuting distance of New York City.[16] In some respects both independent, nongovernmental advocacy groups — RPAA and RPA — were like-minded. They addressed some of the same social issues, and RPA welcomed RPAA's Radburn Plan and other similarly innovative planning approaches, including the creation of the motor parkways that made MacKaye's vision of the "townless highway" a reality. But Norton was part of a business and philanthropic elite that maintained, when possible, a close working relationship with government. Understandably, RPA pragmatically focused on the physical, economic, social, and legal surveys that would guide political and corporate decision makers

and help direct existing market forces toward coherent, rational ends. Accepting as natural and inevitable the enlargement of the metropolis beyond the boundaries of the five-borough polity of Greater New York that had been created in 1898, RPA hoped to transform the city and its several surrounding counties into a better planned multigovernmental regional entity.

Although British garden-city planner Thomas Adams brought his professional experience in England to the Regional Plan Committee, the precursor of RPA, New York City's course of metropolitan regional growth was already set. Its destiny was to remain that of a commercial and entertainment core with vertically expanding skyscrapers and horizontally extending rings of commuter suburbs, none true garden cities. Unwin's Hampstead Gardens, which Norton had praised as "the best subdivision of suburban land ever I saw or heard of,"[17] was a leafy dormitory within the London metropolis, and it, rather than Letchworth, served as a paradigm for New York's expansion. Adams must have realized that the complexity and size of New York City and its environs, as well as the region's political fragmentation, militated against a British reformist approach to planning. In the United States, growth might be guided by infrastructure improvements and the reservation of certain lands for public use, but it would be practically impossible to mandate and locate new town construction within the context of a free-market real-estate economy.

Thomas Adams and Frederick Law Olmsted, Jr., a principal consultant on the plan, proposed that the task be addressed by individual team members taking responsibility for different geographical areas. Adams was chosen to chair and coordinate the activities of this Advisory Group as they tackled in their regional sectors problems of land use and population density; subdivision, land development, and housing; circulation and communication; and open spaces and recreation. Informing their inquiry was the work of the directors of the Economic, Legal, and Social Surveys. Olmsted was responsible for the important sector comprising all of beach-rich Long Island, and Adams made Westchester and Fairfield Counties his purview.

Adams tried to synthesize the many studies, a task made difficult by the application of each man's independent approach and individual set of planning values to his particular sector. Altogether, however, their reports set forth the need for regional zoning, including agricultural zoning; for circumferential roads rather than more radial transportation corridors; for centralization of some activities and decentralization of others according to their functional requirements; for increased parkland, especially along the waterfront; and for reservation of land for airport sites.

12.26. A proposal to increase street capacity, Advisory Committee of the Regional Plan Committee of Architects of the Regional Plan of New York and Its Environs. 1923. This drawing by Hugh Ferriss, a product of his collaboration with Harvey Wiley Corbett, is an affirmation of skyscraper modernity that weds the former's romantic urbanism with the latter's pragmatic belief in a multilevel city.

At this point, four committees of architects set to work sketching plans for various Manhattan projects, ranging in style from Beaux-Arts Neoclassicism to a visionary modernism emphasizing technology and movement (fig. 12.26). The drawings of Hugh Ferriss (1889–1962) and Harvey Wiley Corbett (1873–1954) made especially clear that, far from withering away as the city became more decentralized, the Manhattan core would become aggrandized as a transportation hub and commercial center.

Unfortunately, the planners studied traffic and transportation issues separately, and they therefore never achieved an integrated approach to the movement of people and goods by both highway and rail. Their proposals to integrate suburban rail and urban transit services also foundered because of political, administrative, and technical problems. Governmental fragmentation made it difficult to favor one jurisdiction over another. Private ownership of rail lines created rivalry for tax revenues and profits, rendering impossible any serious cooperation between companies. Furthermore, city transit officials refused to plan on an interstate regional basis. For these reasons, Adams oriented the Regional Plan toward the newer technology represented by the motor vehicle. It was simply easier to concentrate on building new highways to serve the anticipated growth in commuters and goods. Travel by automobile was also by now a form of recreation, as installment-plan financing made cars available to people of average means. Recreational parkways were therefore an important part of the Regional Plan. Here Adams followed a trend Olmsted, Sr., had begun and Olmsted, Jr., had followed in his work for the New York City Improvement Commission in 1907 when he proposed limited-access,

landscaped parkways linking the city's larger parks.

In 1929, the *Graphic Regional Plan* was published and presented to public officials with considerable fanfare. A document of overlays synthesizing several proposals, it was nevertheless without a unitary vision, clear objectives, or a set of strategies for implementation. To work toward the realization of the plan's carefully balanced and essentially pragmatic proposals, the Committee of the Regional Plan was reconstituted as the Regional Plan Association. With RPA's official birth as a permanent advocacy organization, the group now focused on publishing the eight volumes making up the Regional Survey and *The Building of the City* (1931), Adams's companion volume to the *Graphic Regional Plan*. It also worked to build broad regional support among civic leaders and elected officials.

In spite of harsh criticism from Mumford and other members of RPAA who harbored as their ideal a less market-oriented and less politically circumspect plan—one embodying their utopian vision of community at the scale of the town—and even though the organization was merely advisory and not legally constituted as a public authority with broad jurisdictional powers, the work of the RPA was influential. By 1933, the RPAA had disbanded; it had only been a loose consortium of like-minded visionaries unsupported by financial resources to staff a professional planning effort. But the RPA stayed in existence because its proposals were attuned to political circumstances and compatible with general market trends. The work of Adams and his colleagues lived on in the form of the official recognition of city planning as a profession. Harvard University expanded its landscape architecture department to include studies in this area and began offering a master's degree in planning in 1928; the Massachusetts Institute of Technology, Cornell University, and Columbia University established similar programs in the 1930s. In addition, in 1936, Mayor Fiorello LaGuardia created the New York City Planning Commission, and by 1937, 139 municipal planning boards had been established and 308 zoning ordinances adopted in the New York Region.

THE GREAT ERA OF PARK AND PARKWAY BUILDING

The greatest physical result of the 1929 Regional Plan was the creation of numerous state parks and regional parkways in New York and other states throughout the nation. Beginning in 1933, President Franklin Delano Roosevelt stimulated park and parkway building through the National Planning Board and federal public works programs. In making their recommendations for new regional parks and parkways in the New York Region, the RPA planners were in fact following a trend already in progress, giving it voice and rational shape through their studies.

As an outgrowth of Olmsted's 1907 report, the Bronx River Parkway, built between 1912 and 1923, had become America's first grade-separated highway. Unlike the intra-urban, boulevard-style parkways designed by Olmsted, Sr., and Vaux to provide a green framework for residential growth and to link several major parks within a city, the Bronx River Parkway was regional, rather than municipal in scale. More than a ribbon of tree-lined roadway with numerous intersections, it was planned as a landscape, an uninterrupted stretch of park scenery with widely spaced entrance points. The park-making motive was, in fact, initially paramount, and the road was the result of a secondary impulse. Only after the commissioners in charge of the project had launched it as an effort to clean the waters and beautify the banks of the Bronx River, as it flowed from the Kensico Dam in Westchester County to enter Bronx Park, did they decide that it should contain a roadway. The landscape architect, Hermann W. Merkel, and the principal engineer, Leslie G. Holleran, designed it for pleasure driving to various regional park destinations and to provide a dignified entrance into New York City from the north (fig. 12.27). They divided the roadway with a median of irregular width that accommodated grade changes and such topographical features as rock outcrops and particularly fine stands of trees. Construction, stopped during World War I, resumed after 1919, by which time more powerful automobile engines made greater speeds possible. This explains why the radii of the parkway's curves, designed for the pace of a carriage in its southern portion, become elongated as the road progressed northward. An ample right-of-way containing an entire "viewshed," its densely planted borders varying in width from 190 to 1,000 feet (57.9 to 304.8 meters), discouraged the erection of billboards at a time when there was no legislation banning them from adjacent properties. Landscape architect Gilmore D. Clarke (1892–1982) designed the individually distinctive bridge overpasses of rough-finished fieldstone.

So successful was this project as a work of landscape design and as a stimulant to nearby property values and taxes, that even before its completion a Westchester County Park Commission was set up in 1922. Its technical staff included Clarke and the engineer Jay Downer, who had also worked on the Bronx River Parkway. Over the next ten years these men collaborated on the construction of more than a dozen parks and several new parkways including the Saw Mill River and the Hutchinson River Parkways. In Putnam County, the Taconic State Park Commission was responsible for the extraordinarily inventive and beautiful Taconic State Parkway sweeping northward

12.27. Bronx River Parkway, New York State, landscape design by Hermann W. Merkel, roadway design by Leslie G. Holleran, principal engineer. 1912–23

Left: 12.28. Northern section, Taconic State Parkway, New York State, designed by Charles J. Baker of the New York State Department of Public Works. 1940–50

into Dutchess and Columbia Counties (fig. 12.28).

Although frequently dismissive of the work of Adams and his colleagues, Robert Moses (1888–1981) became responsible, more than any other individual, agency, or municipality, for transforming New York City into a regional entity by means of a 416-mile network of parkways.[18] Pragmatic and politically astute, Moses was adept at manipulating the media and encouraging the desires of the rising middle class for increased recreation facilities. Ruthless in the way he maneuvered his way to success, when it suited his ends, Moses co-opted the planning expertise of the Regional Plan Committee (later the Regional Plan Association). Many of the parkways and the related parks that Moses built were outlined in the Regional Plan. Nevertheless, he could also portray the group as protective of elitist class interests. Brooking no opposition, he amassed sufficient power to become a force equal to the elected officials whom he served, dominating government bureaucracies and often bending to his will business leaders, including the sponsors of the Regional Plan.

In 1924, Governor Alfred E. Smith appointed Moses chairman of the Long Island Park Commission and chairman of the New York State Council of Parks. In 1934, Governor Herbert H. Lehman named him commissioner of the New York City Department of Parks, which Moses immediately reorganized, con-

12.29. Jones Beach, Long Island, New York, built by Robert Moses. Completed 1929

solidating individual borough park administrations into a centralized citywide agency. Jones Beach, a palatial bathing and recreational complex built during the 1920s on Long Island's Great South Bay, is perhaps his most important landscape design achievement (fig. 12.29). Completed in 1929, the 2,245-acre oceanfront park had a 1-mile-long boardwalk, a 14-mile-long boat channel, archery ranges, an 18-hole golf course, pony tracks, bathhouses, wading and swimming pools, lawns, shrubbery, and sixty-four parking lots accommodating 12,000 automobiles. Moses thought of Jones Beach as an American Lido, a deluxe middle-class family resort, intentionally devoid of the honky-tonk concessions found at such beachside amusement parks as Coney Island. Here he converted a necessity into an icon, adopting Harvey Wiley Corbett's idea of turning the 200-foot (70-meter) water tower for pumping fresh water from 1,200 feet (366 meters) below sea level into a streamlined imitation of the campanile of Saint Mark's in Venice. Rising from the middle of a lavishly landscaped traffic circle containing reflecting pools with floral borders at the far end of the causeway linking the barrier beach with the mainland, this architectural beacon, washed by floodlights at night, could be seen from a distance of 25 miles away.

Moses was indifferent to the interests of the wealthy men who owned large estates and belonged to hunt clubs and country clubs. With the creation of numerous public parks, he substituted middle-class recreational ideals for the upper-class ones that had governed land use and shaped landscape design in the past. Not surprisingly, Jones Beach was an instant and huge public success. By 1936, Moses had built 100 miles of parkways on Long Island and in New York City, and by the end of the decade he had created 255 new city playgrounds, added several miles of urban beaches, given Central Park a major facelift, and renovated several other historic parks.

But Robert Moses did not single-handedly bring

the modern park and recreation era into being in New York State. Since the turn of the twentieth century, the old elite had made the general public the beneficiary of several enlightened philanthropic actions. J. Pierpont Morgan had saved the Palisades across the Hudson River from New York City from traprock mining, and in 1910 the Harriman family gave the state more than 40,000 additional acres along the Hudson River, a gift that included Bear Mountain State Park. William Letchworth donated his 1000-acre tract along the scenic Genesee River in western New York State, and the American Scenic and Historic Preservation Society successfully campaigned to have the state acquire the geologically fascinating Watkins Glen at the southern end of Seneca Lake.

While there was a great deal of sporadic action in other states at this time, only New York, Connecticut, Wisconsin, California, and Indiana had anything like an organized approach to acquiring and managing state parks. Nowhere was there a system of state parks until, in 1921, Stephen Mather, the director of the National Park Service, saw the need to protect the national parks from being overrun by automobile tourists. He sought to provide recreational opportunities in less spectacular settings closer to urban centers and set to work organizing the National Conference on State Parks. His efforts resulted in the creation of seventeen state park boards or commissions between 1921 and 1927.

During the Great Depression, the Civilian Conservation Corps (CCC) and the Works Progress Administration (WPA) provided vast numbers of workers to build parks and parkways all over the country. Building upon principles embodied in the National Park plan authored by Frederick Law Olmsted, Jr., in 1916, the National Park Service assumed increasing design responsibility, particularly after the Park, Parkway, and Recreational Study Act of 1936 authorized federal involvement in metropolitan and state park planning. Its own aesthetic, Government Rustic—an unpretentious style intended to harmonize with nature and to express an American pioneer ethos through the use of rough-hewn timbers, hatchet-cut stone, or boulders—offered an alternative to the stripped-down Beaux-Arts classicism characteristic of much park building design of the period (fig. 12.30).

By the 1920s, even where there were no parkways or state parks to serve them, Americans were taking to the road in increasing numbers.[19] Complaining about the confinement of the railroad—a confinement both temporal and spatial as one was a prisoner of both schedules and routes—they gamely coped with unmarked, often impassable dirt roads, cooked their meals over open fires, and slept under

the stars as their frontier forebears had done. They gave their Ford Model Ts names like Lizzie or Belle, and they identified these wonderful machines with the adventurous and leisurely stage coach. They called their style of travel "gypsying" and enjoyed the serendipitous companionship of fellow motorists with whom they formed an instantaneous fraternity as they passed on directions and assisted one another with mechanical and roadbed repairs. These hardy souls were the first to adopt the slogan "See America First" when World War I made European travel impossible. Even after the war, cultural chauvinism and pride in America's scenery promoted this new form of vacation, and the growing popularity of automobile touring increased the demand for national and state parks. As more and more Americans took to the road, it became necessary to set up municipal campsites. Soon entrepreneurs built roadside cabins to provide campers with basic amenities, and from this humble beginning, the motel industry was born.

The new regional mobility spelled the end of the Olmstedian ideal of the park as a pastoral refuge in the heart of the city as people with automobiles increasingly sought their bucolic pleasures in excursions to the new county and state parks, enjoying the drive there on landscaped parkways. Veblen's definition of the leisure class had been extended to a broad social spectrum, and *leisure* as a term was gaining common currency. Ball fields, golf courses, swimming pools, ice-skating rinks, bathing beaches, tennis courts, riding stables, and archery ranges assumed the status of public entitlements, accoutrements of the American way of life. This was the logical outcome of the movement that from the beginning of the twentieth century had placed playgrounds, along with housing, at the forefront of the social reformers' agenda.

Accurately reading the temper of the times, Robert Moses had a parks vision to match society's appetite for play. For him, transportation planning and park planning went hand in hand. During his thirty-year tenure as commissioner of the New York City Department of Parks and Recreation, he converted carriage drives into wider roadways for automobiles, turned meadows into ball fields, and built playgrounds and other recreational facilities.[20] Audaciously, he claimed that the nearly 3,000 acres of parkways and other transportation corridors he commissioned in New York City were really linear parks because of the addition of marginal playgrounds, foot and bicycle paths, and waterfront promenades within their rights-of-way. Moses' position as commissioner of parks, together with his chairmanship of the Long Island State Park Commission and the Triborough Bridge and Tunnel Authority, allowed him to reshape the New York metropolitan region according to an ethos of mass leisure.

JENS JENSEN AND THE PARKS OF CHICAGO

As the urban sociologist and American parks historian Galen Cranz points out in *The Politics of Park Design*, the factory system of industrial efficiency and Reform Era play, with its emphasis on physical exercise and sports, were contemporary phenomena, and both were organized in a highly regimented way.[21] Thus, increased recreational opportunities afforded by the shorter workweek, longer vacations, earlier retirement, and higher pay went hand in hand with highly structured play environments that were, ironically, as pragmatically focused and utilitarian as industrial factories—implicitly acknowledged as the dominant paradigm for the organization of modern life. Thanks to the efforts of early-twentieth-century reformers, the profession of recreational leader had been created. In the sphere of park administration as elsewhere, the basis for social reform shifted from reliance on sheer moral fervor and presumed class superiority to dependence on technical expertise and professional skill. Park departments hired recruits of upright character and instituted training programs for directors of playgrounds, as those parks emphasizing recreational activities were now called.

Chicago was the standard-bearer in the creation of Progressive Era playgrounds or neighborhood parks. Along with the branch library, the field house was an original Chicago recreational institution that also served as a neighborhood cultural and educational center. Social reformers saw it as an important instrument of civic improvement, and they vigorously sponsored the construction of both libraries and field houses in the city's poorest sections.

In Chicago's West Park District, where some of the city's least affluent residents lived, Jens Jensen (1860–1951), a Danish immigrant, served as chief landscape architect and general superintendent. Because of his agrarian background and education in Danish folk schools where teachers emphasized

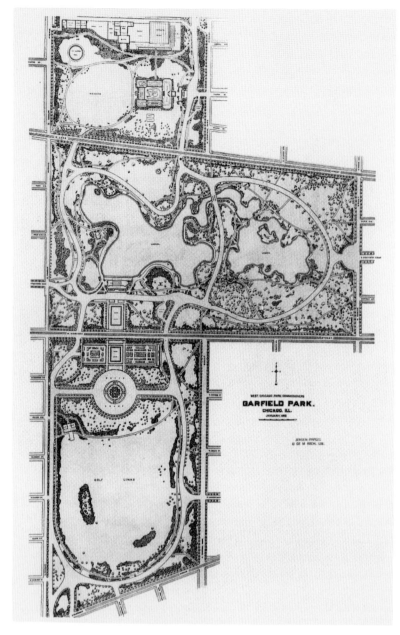

12.31. Plan for Garfield Park, Chicago, Illinois, designed by Jens Jensen. 1912

riors with circuit drives, and concealing park borders with densely planted vegetation (fig. 12.31).

Jensen also subscribed to the goals of the Regional Planning Association of America and adhered to the social reform ideas of Jane Addams. Inspired by Addams's use of pageantry as a means of fostering ethnic pride and inculcating democratic values, he borrowed this idea to promote conservation and spiritual bonds with nature. Anticipating the theories of Ian McHarg (1920–2001), author of *Design with Nature* (1969), he ardently promoted a naturalistic style of landscape design at a time when Beaux-Arts formality enjoyed favor nearly everywhere.

Although Jensen's refusal to accommodate the political machine that controlled park operational policy cost him this position in 1900, he continued to serve the Special Park Commission that had been established to develop plans for a metropolitan park system similar to the one Charles Eliot had envisioned for Boston (see Chapter Nine). Brought back into office as the head of the West Park District in 1905 by a reform administration, Jensen prepared new plans for Douglas, Garfield, and other partially built parks. In Garfield Park, he built what was then the world's largest conservatory, installing a naturalistic brook with water threading its way musically from one fern-embowered rocky ledge to another.

Jensen also designed the new small parks of the West Park District, all of which were under 8.5 acres in size, in a more informal manner than those of the South Park District. In the same vein, he urged William Carbys Zimmerman, the state architect and designer of the West Park District field houses, to consider the Chicago Prairie style that Wright and other architects were then developing as an expression compatible with the regional landscape. The Prairie style in architecture is characterized by broad, low, ground-hugging planes; a forthright expression of structure; and respect for native building materials.

Jensen's later work was often paired in exhibitions with that of such Prairie-style architects as George Grant Elmslie, William Purcell, and Wright, as well as with that of another likeminded landscape architect, Ossian Cole Simonds, who also favored open, naturalistic designs employing native plants. Along with Simonds, Jensen felt that the relatively featureless landscape of the Midwest held a particular subtle beauty. Its flatness was for him something to be celebrated, which he did with shelving planes of rocks beside winding stream courses and the horizontal branching patterns of hawthorns and crab apples (see fig. 12.33). He imitated natural plant communities in his choice and placement of these and other native species, and he sometimes attempted to achieve the appearance of plant succession, the

indigenous culture, Jensen had a natural sympathy for native scenery and local cultural mores. He deeply loved the Illinois prairie as an especially beautiful landscape. In his own work he developed plans that evoked prairie rivers and produced what he called "sun openings," small glades to serve as miniature prairies within parks. Although he integrated such geometrical elements as circular rose gardens into his park plans, and although in keeping with contemporary demand his meadows were designed for ball playing, golf, and tennis, Jensen subscribed to Olmsted's quintessentially American vision of landscape creation with its implicit transcendentalist objective of bringing city people into closer contact with nature. He employed some of the same design strategies as Olmsted—creating long views in which loosely arranged clumps of trees allow the eye to be beckoned from one landscape space to another, building large irregular lakes or lagoons, looping park inte-

sequential colonization by different species of a particular region until the species first there have given way to the region's natural climax situation, or ecological maturity. He also gave attention to effects of natural light, creating sun openings framed by groves of trees and planting in a way that made one's passage along gently winding roads an experience of alternating light and shade.

In 1916, near the city's western boundary and the town of Oak Park, Jensen designed Columbus Park, a square parcel comprising 144 acres. Characterized by his friend and follower Alfred Caldwell as "the finest and most complete of all the Jensen parks,"[22] it epitomized his original contribution toward developing a Prairie style in landscape architecture while still incorporating facilities for popular forms of recreation (fig. 12.32). Tennis courts, swimming pool, playground, and an athletic field are located between the park periphery and the interior circuit drive. Inside the drive is a large meadow—the prairie in miniature—designed to also serve as a golf course. Curving around its eastern edge is a lagoon, created when Jensen deepened a small watercourse, turning it into a "prairie river," which he bordered with wetland vegetation: irises, rose mallow, cordgrass, cattails, rushes, arrowheads, and water lilies. Around the source of this waterbody Jensen, who prided himself on his rockwork compositions, laid several irregular, horizontal layers of native limestone to give the appearance of a low, stratified prairie bluff (fig. 12.33). On a small hill near the lagoon, Jensen created a players' green—a clearing designed to serve as a performance area—orienting the position of the audience, who sat in the grass on the opposite side of one of the two brooks flowing into the lagoon, west toward the setting sun.

An admirer of the remaining traces of Native American occupancy in the natural landscape, Jensen used the Indian trail as inspiration in the design of his paths. He used rough-cut stone to build council rings, circular stone benches with a fire pit in the center. Council rings were gathering places where park visitors could converse, listen to stories, or participate in pageants. Players' greens—clearings designed to serve as settings for performances in nature—served a similar purpose.

In 1935, Jensen designed the Lincoln Memorial Garden in Springfield, Illinois. Here, on a gently sloping and undulating site that he helped select on the shore of Lake Springfield, he contrasted densely planted copses of native species—redbud, dogwood, hawthorn, crab apple, maple, cherry, sumac, birch, oak, ash, and locust—with open greens and broad grassy lanes leading to the water's edge in several places. In addition, he built eight council rings (four-

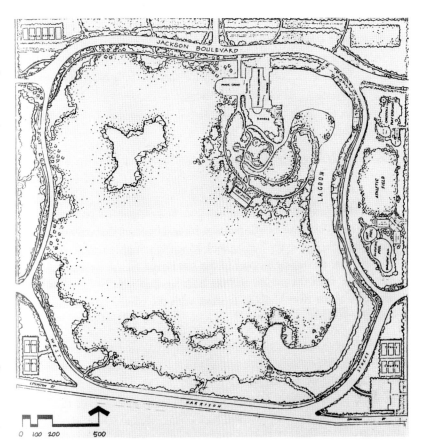

12.32. Plan for Columbus Park, Chicago, Illinois, designed by Jens Jensen. 1916

12.33. Spring in Columbus Park, Chicago, illustrating Jensen's stratified Prairie-style rockwork

teen were originally planned), including the Lincoln Council Ring set within a grove of white oaks overlooking the lake. Volunteers, especially schoolchildren and garden club members, were instrumental in collecting native plants not available in nurseries and in carrying out the details of Jensen's plan.

Jensen had long been an advocate of this kind of citizen participation in landscape stewardship. In

1913, to promote awareness of indigenous natural beauty, he had organized the Friends of Our Native Landscape, an early conservation group that led a citizen effort to have preserved in public ownership the Indiana Dunes along the southern shore of Lake Michigan and other portions of the natural heritage of the Midwest. Several state parks resulted from the staunch environmental commitment and protracted efforts of this group.

After the death of his wife in 1934, Jensen decided to leave Chicago to realize his cherished dream of founding a school similar to the Danish folk and agricultural schools of his youth. Its mission was to promote civic responsibility and environmental stewardship. At Ellison Bay, Wisconsin, where he had a vacation cabin, he established The Clearing, a non-degree-granting school in nature where students learn ecology and basic horticultural and landscape-design practices. Because he believed in a humanistic approach to education, his curriculum also included drawing, painting, sculpture, music, drama, poetry, and architecture.

URBAN PARKS IN TRANSITION

Increasingly, park designers were, as Jensen had been, employees of park agencies, rather than outside firms. But few held the Olmstedian ideals that Jensen did, and charged with retrofitting older parks with new facilities—notably ball fields and children's playgrounds—they displayed little of his sensitivity in harmonizing utilitarian and natural landscape elements. Once-broad park vistas were interrupted with fencing to restrain errant baseballs, protect the young, and serve as a barrier to intruding dogs. With the increased social emphasis on sports, playing fields rather than meadows, recreation facilities rather than views, and active rather than passive use became ever greater public priorities.

The multiplication of parks and recreational services in an effort to keep up with market forces in the manner of a commercial enterprise led "to an increased emphasis on the efficiency with which [park departments] could deliver services on demand, and this emphasis led to systems thinking and bureaucratization."[23] Greatly expanded in their scale of operations and no longer with any real sense of moral purpose, only efficient service delivery, as their raison d'être, parks agencies in New York and elsewhere fell behind in the budgetary competition with other city agencies, failing to attain sufficient funding to ensure necessary maintenance and programming. Working at a system scale rather than an individual park scale, agency designers sought economy through standardization, thereby making municipal parks conventional and stereotypical in appearance as they

minimized shrub plantings and other costly horticultural aspects of parks, paved paths with asphalt, and replaced grass with more apshalt in order to accommodate basketball, handball, shuffleboard, and other types of hard-surface, equipment-based recreation. Fences and regulatory signs proliferated as managers with constrained budgets substituted these for on-site supervision. It was no longer acceptable for parks to be merely tranquil; they had to be entertaining as well.

Landscape as entertainment had already been demonstrated at the several world's fairs that had taken place since the middle of the nineteenth century. Perhaps no other fair captured people's futuristic imagination or nourished their consumeristic hunger for the fruits of technology so successfully as the 1939 World's Fair in New York City. As with other earlier fairs, the sponsors of this one intended to leave behind a permanent park after its temporary structures and exhibitions had been dismantled. But now landscape design and the world's fair were merging in another way. More than a showcase of many cultures and new developments in industrial science and technology, this fair was billed as a visionary preview of the coming attractions of modern urbanism. It was called the World of Tomorrow.

THE WORLD OF TOMORROW: THE 1939 WORLD'S FAIR

The 1939 World's Fair held at New York City's Flushing Meadow–Corona Park presented Depression-ridden Americans with a consumerist vision of a future in which many electric gadgets and labor-saving household appliances would become commonplace. Moreover, there would be nearly universal automobile ownership, fast commuter highways, and single-family homes in leafy suburbs. Fairgoers thrilled to the possibilities of technological modernity as symbolically portrayed by Harrison & Fouilhoux's highly visible all-white Theme Center composed of the 610-foot-high (190-meter-high) Trylon and 180-foot-diameter (55-meter-diameter) Perisphere, embraced by the Helicline, a gently sloping, curving ramp almost a 1,000 feet (305 meters) long (fig. 12.34).[24]

George McAneny, head of the Regional Plan Association, Grover Whelan, business leader and former police commissioner, and Percy Straus, chief executive of Macy's department store, were the principal sponsors of the 1939 fair. They saw it as a means of stimulating the economy and promoting New York's leadership as a commercial capital. Parks Commissioner Robert Moses saw visitors' need to come to it by automobile as well as by subway as an opportunity to further his agenda of parkway building. He also saw the fair as a means of turning the destroyed Flushing Meadow salt marsh—described

12.34. Trylon and Perisphere, designed by Harrison & Fouilhoux, Flushing Meadow, New York City. 1939

by F. Scott Fitzgerald in *The Great Gatsby* as the "Valley of Ashes," a cindery wasteland where the city dumped its garbage—into "the Versailles of America" after the fair was over. He hired Gilmore D. Clarke to design the park in advance of the fair and then fit the fair's building program to its outlines.

Moses never fully realized his original dream of Versailles-in-Queens because World War II postponed the construction of parks and other public improvements. Estimated profits earmarked for the undertaking failed to materialize by the time a second fair on the same site, the World's Fair of 1964, closed in 1965. But the New York City Parks Department did build a park, minus some of its intended grandeur, within the retained footprint of the two fairs. Within its boundaries, a new science museum, botanical garden, zoo, ice-skating rink, boating lake, art museum, outdoor concert bowl, sports stadium, and several works of sculpture—all legacies from the two world's fairs—enriched the Borough of Queens. In design terms, the park bears the stamp of the Moses era when Beaux-Arts-trained landscape architects such as Clarke grappled with the influence of modernism, producing the type of stripped-down Neoclassical layout that still prevails in many of New York City's parks.

But it was not the design of the fairgrounds or the modernism of the architecture that created the almost breathless wonder that some people still remember experiencing at the 1939 fair. It was the exhibits. Visitors ascending the Helicline and entering the Perisphere found themselves to be giants overlooking a miniaturized 11,000-square-mile planned metropolis for 1.5 million people. Called Democracity and created by industrial designer Henry Dreyfuss with Wright's Broadacre City in mind, it segregated residential, commercial, and industrial activities into sectors linked by expressways. Here the commuters of the future saw satellite suburbs surrounding Centerton, the business, educational, and cultural hub of Democracity. Some of these suburbs were called Millvilles because, in the tradition of the garden-city movement, they were intended to contain sites for industry. Others, called Pleasantvilles, were purely residential and prefigured the suburbs that would blanket the agricultural fields of Long Island and other parts of the country after World War II.

An even more exciting exhibit at the fair was Norman Bel Geddes's Futurama housed in the General Motors Pavilion. Here was a 35,700-square-foot (10,880-square-meter) model of America in 1960, a technologically marvelous place crossed by seven-lane, continental-scale highways upon which low-cost, air-conditioned, diesel-powered, teardrop-shaped automobiles traveled at speeds up to 100 miles per hour. In a manner that suggested Frank Lloyd Wright and the metropolitan decentralists, there were self-sufficient farming and industrial communities. There were large cities, too, and these had tall skyscrapers set in an expanse of low-rise buildings with roof gardens. With its separate pedestrian and vehicular circulation systems, this was an urban scheme that Le Corbusier would have admired. Vast acres of nature were set aside in federally protected areas, and there were dams and mines built according to advanced engineering technology. The visitor to Futurama viewed this model of the imaginary new American landscape from a moving aerial "carry-go-round" with upholstered seats. It was almost like taking a cross-country ride in an airplane, certainly a rarity in 1939.

The 1939 World's Fair marked a pivotal moment in American life when the United States stood on the brink of World War II. Following the war, American business and industry led the nation to unparalleled prosperity, in the process rising to the status of powerful political entities within the national life as they allied with government to form what became known as the military-industrial complex. By the time the 1964 fair took place on the original fairgrounds at Flushing Meadow, the United States had already begun its fateful participation in the Vietnam War, following policies that would seriously undermine trust in government.

Not long before the popular will asserted itself nationally in protest against the war in Vietnam, there arose in New York a popular reaction to Robert Moses' authoritarian style of planning public works projects. Jane Jacobs, the magazine editor turned urban critic and theorist, saw the small-block scale and mixed residential and commercial uses in older neighborhoods as sources of irreplaceable human vitality. She organized her community to fight successfully against Moses's proposed Lower Manhattan Expressway, which would have destroyed much of the urban fabric of the West Village, where she lived, and the area of the city now known as SoHo. At the same time, she built the case against superblock urban renewal projects—the descendants of Le Corbusier's Radiant City—in her influential book *Death and Life of Great American Cities* (1961).

While Jacobs and others were calling for a revaluation of the American city, many middle-class residents were abandoning it, choosing the life of the commuter suburbs alluringly portrayed at the 1939 World of Tomorrow. Postwar affluence and the pent-up demand for material goods, delayed by the Great Depression and the prolonged national emergency, caused a fever of consumerism that idealistic social thinkers such as Mumford and Stein probably found appalling. Mumford's vision of the regionally planned future was evocatively portrayed in his contemporary documentary film *The City,* directed by

Pare Lorentz and with music by Aaron Copland. But forces other than planning ideals were at work, shaping the urban region. Government-sponsored loan programs designed for veterans and other qualified buyers abetted single-family home ownership. The federal interstate highway building program increased the commercial value of rural land, especially near expressway interchanges, and this had a powerful and broad-scale effect upon the entire American landscape. A new type of development, the shopping center, began to drain business vitality from the centers of cities and a new term, *suburbia,* was coined to denote the sprawling residential mass formed by the bedroom communities of the commuter generation. From the perspective of urban sprawl, as the most recent manifestation of this free-market trend is called, one may look back with admiration and some regret at the failed dreams of those who followed in Ebenezer Howard's footsteps.

After World War II, Americans became more receptive to European modernist architecture. Although popular eclectic taste still caused houses to be built in a variety of pseudohistorical idioms, there was a growing appreciation of the stylistic possibilities, construction economies, and functionalism of modern architecture in the United States as well as in Europe and South America. Landscape architects used garden design as an experimental laboratory to develop a style that was similarly emancipated from past tradition. Their efforts produced a new, if at times uncertain, direction for the profession. Whether they worked to create a regional idiom informed by local topology as did Jens Jensen, borrowed ideas from abstract art, or adhered to the architectural precepts of such exponents of European modernism as Le Corbusier and Gropius, these designers shared one characteristic: They were polemical. They would not warm their talents in the sunset glow of Beaux-Arts tradition as did the landscape architects who worked for Robert Moses. Modernism put a premium on iconoclasm, invention, and the new. It encouraged them to be original. They sought to address the needs of their time through rational, scientific problem solving. Contemporary lifestyle—especially the leisure-loving one being invented by culturally unfettered Californians—replaced past style as the modernist landscape designers' touchstone. Innovation, not tradition, became their watchword.

1. The Fabian Society derived its name from the Roman general Fabius Cunctator, who was known for his patient, nonconfrontational, and ultimately victorious strategies.

2. John Ruskin, "Of the Mystery of Life," *Sesame and Lilies: Three Lectures* (1871, Philadelphia: Henry Altemus, 1892), pp. 219–20.

3. In 1919, twenty years after its founding by Howard, the Garden City and Town Planning Association officially defined the subject of its advocacy as "a town designed for healthy living and industry: of a size that makes possible the full measure of social life but no larger: surrounded by a rural belt—all of the land being in public ownership or held in trust for the community."

4. A more pragmatic explanation for enclosing the development is given in Eusebio Güell's 1904 handwritten petition to the city of Barcelona for a building permit four years after work had begun. Here he declared, "Park conditions require special attention for maintenance and attention to the residents' security, given the fact that this is a city. For that purpose, it is necessary to surround the park with walls with large gates opening at convenient places and giving access to the main street leading to the park."

5. In his influential book, *Theory and Design in the First Machine Age* (New York: Praeger Publishers, 1960), Reyner Banham points out Gropius's pivotal and even ambivalent-seeming role in the transition from an Expressionist and crafts approach to a functionalist design method. Gropius continued to seek the expressive potential of architecture in abstract, holistic terms within a functionalist context. According to him, "the objective of all creative efforts in the visual arts is to give form to space . . . [in which] the laws of the physical world, the intellectual world and the world of the spirit function and are expressed simultaneously." See op. cit., p. 280. In a similar vein, the modernist Le Corbusier declared, "Architectural abstraction has this about it which is magnificently peculiar to itself, that while it is rooted in hard fact it spiritualizes it, because the naked fact is nothing more than the materialization of a possible idea." See Le Corbusier, *Towards a New Architecture* (London: The Architectural Press, 1946 ed.), p. 28.

6. Gropius's work before he assumed the directorship of the Bauhaus, notably the protomodern housing at Golzengüt and the Fagus Factory at Alfeld-an-der-Leine, Germany, which he designed in 1911 with Adolph Meyer (1881–1929), displays a thor-

ough command of various hallmarks of the International Style: mass production of housing; curtain walls of glass; unornamented, flat-roofed, cubic building blocks; and corners extending beyond the building's structural support system.

7. Le Corbusier, *Précisions*, pp. 234–36, as translated by and quoted in Norma Everson, *Le Corbusier: The Machine and the Grand Design* (New York: George Braziller, 1969), p. 26.

8. The term *International Style* was coined in 1932 by the architectural historian Henry-Russell Hitchcock (b. 1903) and the architect Philip Johnson (b. 1906) when they organized an exhibition of European modernist architecture at the Museum of Modern Art in New York City.

9. See Chapter Ten, footnote 4 for a brief discussion of Roland Barthes' essay, "The Eiffel Tower," which discusses the Tower's oneiric function as *sign,* a symbolic structure without utilitarian purpose other than that of providing visitors a panoramic view of Paris along with such quotidian commercial amenities as food and souvenirs.

10. Patrick Geddes, *Cities in Evolution* (London: Ernest Benn Limited, 1915), p. 13.

11. Ibid., p. 71.

12. Ibid., p. 73. Geddes, and Mumford after him, distinguished between "Utopia," translated as the idealistic "No Place," and "Eutopia," the good place in reality.

13. Ibid., p. 95.

14. Clarence S. Stein, *Toward New Towns for America* (New York: Reinhold Publishing Corporation, 1957), p. 37.

15. For the history of the Regional Plan of New York I am indebted to David A. Johnson, *Planning the Great Metropolis: The 1929 Regional Plan of New York and Its Environs* (London: E & FN Spon, An Imprint of Chapman & Hall, 1996), the source of much of the information in this section.

16. The area of the plan's purview comprised 5,528 square miles spread over three states and 436 local governmental jurisdictions.

17. Letter to Frederic Delano, August 21, 1922, Regional Plan Papers, as quoted in Johnson, *Planning the Great Metropolis: The 1929 Regional Plan of New York and Its Environs* (London: Chapman & Hall, 1996), p. 79.

18. Although the parkways built by Robert Moses had generously landscaped medians and margins, they were unlike the urban, boulevard-style parkways conceived by Olmsted and Vaux, being in effect MacKaye's "townless highways," with limited access points, no at-grade crossings,

and a regulatory ban on truck traffic. The Saw Mill River Parkway (1926); the Hutchinson River, Southern State, and Wantagh Parkways (1929); the Sunken Meadow, Meadowbrook, and Sagtikos Parkways linking a series of large parks and bathing beaches (1929–52); the Northern State Parkway (1931); the Henry Hudson Parkway (1933); the Grand Central, Interborough, and Laurelton Parkways (1936); and the Belt Parkway along the southern perimeter of Brooklyn and Queens (1938–40) were realized under Moses' authority.

19. For a good account of these automobile tourist "pioneers," see Warren James Belasco, *Americans on the Road: From Autocamp to Motel, 1910–1945* (Cambridge, Massachusetts: MIT Press, 1979).

20. In 1964, three decades after Moses became parks commissioner of New York, his chosen successor, Newbold Morris, could boast that "recreation facilities have increased sevenfold in these thirty years. . . . In 1934, there were 14,827 acres of park lands of which 928 acres represented land under water. Today there are 35,760 acres, of which 9,670 acres represent land under water reserved for wildlife and used for boating, bathing and fishing, and another 2,970 acres devoted to roadways in our parkway system. The total acreage represents approximately 17.5 per cent of the total area of the City of New York." This statistical emphasis reflected the agency's service attitude, one of keeping up with demand. Under the heading of "Golf," the 1964 Department of Parks reported that during the previous two years it had kept pace with demand: "The completion of the Verrazano-Narrows Bridge will enable Brooklynites to travel easily to Richmond's less congested golf facilities. Long-range plans have been made to provide an 18-hole golf course . . . in Idlewild Park and another is contemplated in Edgemere Park in Rockaway." But it was the 861 park playgrounds, some of which were built adjacent to schools and jointly operated with the Board of Education, that were the "hub of New York City's recreational system." Two recently constructed golf courses in Marine Park, Brooklyn, covered 210 acres of what had been "low salt marshlands, which were filled with sanitation refuse and covered with manufactured topsoil under our land reclamation program." The report further announced a contract "for the preparation of the site to receive sanitation fill in the area east of Shore Road in Eastchester Bay, in Pelham Bay Park [which] after completion of the

landfill, . . . will be developed as a park for recreational purposes." See *30 Years of Progress: 1934–1964,* Report to the Mayor and Board of Estimate (New York: New York Department of Parks, 1964), pp. 5-7, 69.

In 1964, altogether 1,466 acres of parkland had been, or were being, "created by landfill with refuse wastes." Here at the beginning of the environmental movement, the author participated in a battle led by the Parks Council, a civic association, to prevent this action and preserve the salt marsh in Pelham Bay Park. For the history and ecology of Pelham Bay Park, see Elizabeth Barlow, *The Forests and Wetlands of New York City* (Boston: Little, Brown and Company, 1971).

To understand how Moses fulfilled his vision and created a park system containing 14,000 acres of landscaped and natural parkland, 861 playgrounds, 17 swimming pools, 18 miles of public beaches, 12 golf courses, and 459 tennis courts, see Robert Caro, *The Power Broker* (New York: Alfred A. Knopf, 1974). Caro writes of the boldness and breadth of Moses' regional-scale vision, of which the New York City park system was merely the nucleus, and of how its implementation involved a complex nexus of appointments to offices that permitted him to weld transportation and recreation improvements into a unified construction program.

21. Galen Cranz, *The Politics of Park Design: A History of Urban Parks in America* (Cambridge, Massachusetts: MIT Press, 1982), pp. 98–99. This work of interdisciplinary scholarship by an architectural sociologist is an excellent study of the ways in which cultural values shape public space.

22. Dennis Domer, ed., *Alfred Caldwell: The Life and Work of a Prairie School Architect* (Baltimore: The Johns Hopkins Press, 1997), p. 183.

23. Cranz, *The Politics of Park Design,* p. 107.

24. For vivid accounts of the fair and and the impression the Trylon and Perisphere made on visitors, see E. L. Doctorow's autobiographical novel *World's Fair* (New York: Random House, 1985); Robert Rosenblum, "Remembrance of Fairs Past" in Rosemarie Haag Bletter, et al., *Remembering the Future: The New York World's Fair from 1939 to 1964* (New York: The Queens Museum/ Rizzoli, 1989); and David Gelernter, *1939: The Lost World of the Fair* (New York: Avon, 1995).

A NEW LANDSCAPE AESTHETIC:
THE MODERNIST GARDEN

Since the beginning of the nineteenth century, an eclectic application of past styles of landscape design had substituted for one expressing in a forthright, forceful, and original manner the tenets of contemporary Machine Age culture. Le Corbusier railed famously against "the Styles," and when architectural modernism at last found widespread acceptance, it became doctrinal in its radical break with tradition. No longer would architects camouflage the structural engineering systems of new buildings with the decor of previous eras as had been the case in modern nineteenth-century Paris, where carved masonry was applied as a veneer over industrial materials. In the same way that modern artists sought to abandon old formalist values including single-point perspective as the generally accepted convention of spatial representation, architects sought to express an entirely new aesthetic that was functionalist, democratic, and overtly expressive of machine technology. The avoidance of Neoclassical planning principles and handcrafted ornamentation became an article of faith for modern architects. Yet, while modern architecture overthrew eclecticism and developed its own radically functionalist aesthetic, landscape architecture lagged behind.

A somewhat debased version of Arts and Crafts garden style was well suited to the agenda of an expanding nursery industry with a broad array of plant materials and garden ornaments for sale. Moreover, the machinelike precision found in modernist architecture and a good deal of modern art was never wholly applicable to landscape design, because nature is biological and tectonic, not static. However hard-edged a ground plan may be, if it contains plants and soil and responds to the dynamics of natural ecosystems, its forms are inevitably subject to growth, decay, and the resulting organic transformation these processes involve. So argued those who sought to maintain a traditionalist approach to landscape design in the face of architectural modernism. In the United States, throughout the 1930s the Harvard's Graduate School of Design, the leading professional school for training in landscape architecture, remained firmly committed to a Beaux-Arts-based curriculum with its emphasis upon an Italianate stylistic vocabulary, even as Walter Gropius was transforming the school's architecture department into an outpost of the European avant-garde.

But as provincialism and reactionary taste succumbed to the establishment of modern art and as modern architecture gained status and began to seem less revolutionary, American professionals began at last to participate in the spirit of landscape design innovation that the French had pioneered at the 1925 Exposition Internationale des Arts Décoratifs et Industriels Modernes (International Exhibition of Modern Decorative and Industrial Arts). Unlike previous World's Fairs, which had emphasized technological progress, this one was distinguished by the impulse on the part of the French to establish cultural leadership in the design arts. Within the Fair's articulation of a vocabulary of design forms—now nostalgically recalled and revived as Art Moderne or Art Deco—existed several early experiments that attempted to ally landscape with modernism. But modernism had many faces besides the one of streamlined luxe known as Art Deco, including the machine aesthetic of the Bauhaus and of Le Corbusier, whose architecture was represented as one of the fair's pavilions. A Mediterranean spirit often informed it. Chinese and Japanese influences were present, too.

By the late 1930s, the carriers of modernism's several cultural crosscurrents included Mexican and South American landscape designers as well as European and American ones. Like architecture, landscape design became a regionally inflected international idiom. Although the United States still looked to Europe in cultural matters, the country's prosperity and the developments in industrial design as new consumer goods were produced following World War II created a climate that was congenial to innovation and the eventual assumption of a leadership role in the arts. This process was no doubt encouraged by the immigration to the United States from the 1930s onward of several European artists of rare genius. In addition, now, more than ever, travel abroad was seen as a valuable extension of the professional education of American designers along with the study of internationally circulated periodicals and books portraying the new. A stripped-down form of Beaux-Arts landscape design prevailed in a good deal of American public park design as late as the 1950s, as is evident from the parks built in New York City and under the administration of Robert Moses (see Chapter Twelve). Nevertheless, traditional landscape architecture based on Neoclassical planning principles had begun to seem anachronistic within the context of modernism's disavowal of historic styles and the premium it put on a certain shock value in the arts.

Moreover, within the context of a democratic society traditionalism was associated with a conservative elite. Progressive landscape architects needed to produce plans that were suitable for the construction budgets, lot sizes, and lives of middle-class homeowners. The emphasis modern people put on sports and physical recreation caused them to want houses and gardens that were more casual in appearance than those of former times, with open floor plans and informal ground plans that permitted the same unconstricted movement as did the relaxed clothing they now wore. This casual lifestyle, especially in California where a freewheeling cultural ethos prevailed overall, encouraged a fresh approach to landscape design. Here and in other warm-climate areas, outdoor entertaining and relaxation in and around a swimming pool were important elements in the landscape designer's program.

The spirit of radical innovation that characterized art and architecture of the modernist period gave license to the landscape designer to experiment with new forms and materials. New design concepts—the use of overlapping planes rather than axial alignment to provide spatial continuity, experimentation with both traditional and nontraditional materials, use of abstract biomorphic forms as emblems and expressions of organic fluidity, and an innovative application of the machine aesthetic to garden structures—furnished the modernist landscape with its own distinctive idiom as it addressed the age-old problem of exploiting visually the juxtaposition of the natural and the artificial.

Compensating for the elimination of applied ornament in Machine Age modern architecture was the new status given freestanding sculpture. The visual impact of the bronze nude by Georg Kolbe in the courtyard of the Barcelona Pavilion Mies van der Rohe built for that city's 1929 World's Fair is enhanced by the duty it performs, which is beyond all inherent aesthetic merit, as the only nonmachine form within the structure, demonstrating the power of a single art object to arrest and satisfy the eye as it completes its movement through the building's serenely impersonal overlapping spatial planes. So, too, as landscape architecture became more avowedly functional and abstract, several designers found that the perfectly placed piece by Jacques Lipchitz or Henry Moore gave compositional focus to their plans. Sculpture had, of course, been at home in the garden since ancient times, as we have amply discovered in this book, but with the advent of modernism it took up residence in the landscape devoid of the didactic or memorial intent of former times. In the modern garden sculpture was not intended as part of any allegorical program, nor was it meant to serve as commemoration; it was displayed simply as aesthetic object. The installation of outdoor sculpture according to the reputation of the artist rather than that of the subject depicted is a modernist contribution to landscape design. Corporations took a major role in this regard, and the same companies that commissioned prestigious modern architects to design their headquarters also installed major works of sculpture in adjacent plazas or surrounding industrial parks.

The challenges facing twentieth-century designers who sought to practice within the broader context of a rapidly transforming society with objectives that were more democratic in purpose than the provision of corporate prestige or idyllic retreats for the wealthy were considerable. As had been true in past ages, many of the patrons who commissioned modern gardens, corporate campuses, and high-style modern buildings with sculpture courts or plazas were indeed wealthy. Modernism's confidence in design as a primary means of addressing social problems now seems overweening and, in light of the record, often wrongheaded. This has promoted the current return to neo-traditional principles in urban planning that we will examine in Chapter Fifteen. But the landscape architects who came of age in the first half of the twentieth century shared the same optimism that we observed in the previous chapter as we studied the regional planners who sought to rationally guide metropolitan growth or the starry-eyed futurists who displayed their upbeat technologically oriented scenarios for the World of Tomorrow at the New York 1939 World's Fair. Especially in America, which was less scarred than Europe by the twentieth century's two World Wars, modernism held forth a sense of immense possibilities, and in an age that has become fetishistic about preserving and replicating the past, this optimism about the future may seem enviable to some.

I. TRANSITIONAL EXPERIMENTATION: DESIGN IDIOMS OF THE EARLY TWENTIETH CENTURY

13.1. Jardin d'Eau et de Lumière. Exposition Internationale des Arts Décoratifs et Industriels Modernes, Paris, designed by Gabriel Guévrékian. 1925

Below: 13.2. Garden view from lawn terrace, Villa Noailles, Hyères, France, designed by Gabriel Guévrékian. 1928

The 1925 Exposition Internationale des Arts Décoratifs et Industriels Modernes (International Exhibition of Modern Decorative and Industrial Arts) in Paris was guided by impulses different from those that stimulated the New York World's Fair of 1939. The New York fair was a demonstration of burgeoning American industrial might and the consumerist future. The 1925 Paris Exhibition was undertaken in large measure as a chauvinistic means of reasserting France's traditional hegemony as a stylistic trendsetter and unrivaled leader in the decorative arts.[1] Coming between the waning Arts and Crafts tradition and the rise of international modernism, the Paris fair represented not only a pivotal point in design history but also a definitive moment in the final stages of the cultural transition from an ethos of privilege to one of equality, which had been under way since the eighteenth century. Unlike the 1939 New York fair, which held out a clear vision of mass prosperity, the one in Paris, in spite of its declared intention to honor "art in life," nevertheless exuded an imagery of opulence and luxury, albeit in Machine Age terms and on a compact scale in keeping with the economic realities of the times.

THE FRENCH MODERNIST GARDEN

Jean-Claude Nicolas Forestier (1861–1930), the landscape architect who had had design responsibilities for several of the parks of Paris since 1887, was put in charge of all parks and gardens at the exhibition. Clearly evident was his own stylistic preference for Gallic formality softened by an Arts and Crafts horticultural palette and enlivened eclectically through the influence of Persia and southern Spain. Also evident was the influence of Cubism, Surrealism, and functionalism. The fair's purposeful endorsement of modernity was made somewhat superficial by the impulse to showcase design style, as implied by the word *décoratif* in the exposition's title. Several of the gardens of the fair were conceived as outdoor manifestations of Art Deco, the sleekly ornamental style found in the luxurious but spare furniture and architectural design of the period. A consensus that these modernistic gardens should be architectonic in character as well as architectural extensions of the house caused them to be more mineral than vegetal in character.

On a triangular site framed on two sides by glass walls, Gabriel Guévrékian (1900–1970) designed the Garden of Water and Light, the most avant-garde garden at the 1925 Paris Exposition (fig. 13.1). Forestier commissioned it, expecting Guévrékian to create a viewing garden, a *tableau-jardin* "in the modern spirit with elements from Persian decor."[2] Its triangular

shape announced the geometric motif contained in the small opaque pinkish panes of glass forming its screening walls, the zigzag pattern of flower beds arranged on an inclined plane, the subdivisions of its tiered pool, and some of the facets of an electrically illuminated, revolving, polyhedral sphere in its center. As a modernistic garden designer, Guévrékian did not consider plants interesting in their own right but deployed them simply as bedded masses of bold shapes and striking colors.

Charles de Noailles, an enthusiastic collector of modern art, was so impressed with Guévrékian's creation at the fair that he commissioned him to design a garden in Hyères where the architect Robert Mallet-Stevens was building a villa for him and his wife Marie-Laure. Here, in 1927, Guévrékian created a garden in a space that appeared like the bow of a beached ship (fig. 13.2). Divorced from the surrounding landscape by stark white converging walls forming an elongated isosceles triangle, the sharp geometries of

rectangular flower beds, mosaic paving panels, and pool set within these uncompromising boundaries assert a mathematical, antinatural angularity. Though often called a Cubist garden, it is unavoidably three-dimensional because it is an architectural space and cannot therefore have the elusive, tensile interplay between picture surface and picture space of a Cubist painting.[3] The Noailles garden did have, however, one element that linked it with the modern abstract art movement, a revolving sculpture by Jacques Lipchitz (1891–1973) called *La Joie de vivre (The Joy of Life)*. Guévrékian gave this pride of place at the apex of the isosceles triangle, the "prow" of the Noailles garden "ship." As modern garden design increasingly assumed a minimalist approach to horticulture, designers frequently placed large-scale works of sculpture like this Lipchitz piece in their landscape compositions simply for aesthetic effect. This quite naturally gave rise in time to gardens where the designers' primary goal was to arrange an outdoor setting for the display of works of art. Notable later examples in the New York metropolitan area include the sculpture garden of the Museum of Modern Art in New York City, Storm King Art Center in Mountainville, and the Isamu Noguchi Garden Museum in Long Island City.

At the time of the 1925 exposition, Charles and Marie-Laure de Noailles commissioned a second modernist essay in garden design on the 5,000-square-foot (1,524-square-meter) triangle of land adjacent to their nineteenth-century *hôtel* in Paris (fig. 13.3). Like their garden by Guévrékian in Noailles, the Parisian garden by André Vera (1881–1971) and his brother Paul Vera (1882–1957), a decorative artist, in collaboration with their friend Jean-Charles Moreau (1889–1956) was primarily a viewing garden, its vegetation being limited to low shrub masses and ground covers set within a ground plane of paving stones, pebbles, and gravel. A lattice-topped wall of light-catching mirrors reflected back upon the garden images of itself and the *hôtel*.

These and other avant-garde expressions of possible new directions in landscape design pioneered in France in the 1920s were to influence the approach of a new generation of landscape architects in America, notably Fletcher Steele and Thomas Church. Steele's work on the East Coast and Church's in California were pivotal in bringing a modernist sensibility to American landscape architecture.

FLETCHER STEELE AND THE TRANSITIONAL MODERNIST GARDEN

Avid study of the gardens of the 1925 Paris exposition by the American critic and landscape architect Fletcher Steele (1885–1971) demonstrated to him the

13.3. Noailles Garden, Place des États-Unis, Paris, designed by André and Paul Vera with Jean-Charles Moreau. c. 1926

"real impetus [of the French] to gardening in the new manner."[4] Steele, a native of Rochester, New York, graduated in 1907 from Williams College in western Massachusetts where he developed an appreciation of the rolling Berkshire landscape and American Colonial architecture. Harvard had just initiated the country's first graduate program in landscape architecture, and there Steele studied for a year with Frederick Law Olmsted, Jr., and Arthur Shurtleff, another member of the Olmsted firm. Their design approach was that of the prevailing Beaux-Arts system with its respect for axial planning and architectural integration of building and site. The arduous curriculum combined these planning principles with studies in art history, architecture, surveying, hydrology, road and wall construction, geology, meteorology, physiography, botany, horticulture, plant identification, planting design, mathematics, languages, and contracts and specifications.

Rather than return to Harvard the following year, Steele accepted the offer made by Warren Henry Manning (1860–1938), a landscape architect trained by Olmsted Sr., to serve as his personal assistant and supervisor of planting for the firm. The son of a well-established nurseryman and the author of much of the planting plan for the Biltmore estate, Manning was an acknowledged plantsman. Having designed the park system for Harrisburg, Pennsylvania, he was also a city planner, as well as busy professional with many important private commissions. Steele's apprenticeship with Manning lasted six years. It gave the aspiring young landscape architect a practical education that he valued above Harvard's academic one. His experience in Manning's Boston firm, combined with his intelligence, gift with words, and social skills, enabled Steele to begin an independent practice after returning from an extended study tour of European gardens in 1913. In this new phase of his career he absorbed the ideas of his friend, the Gothic Revival architect Ralph Adams Cram (1863–1942), as well as ideas gleaned from frequent travels abroad. After service as a photographer in World War I, he resumed his practice and gained a reputation as an outspoken shaper of opinion, engaging lecturer, and frequent contributor to professional and popular periodicals such as *Landscape Architecture, House Beautiful,* and *Garden Club of America Bulletin.*

The 1920s were mostly prosperous years up until the Great Depression, and Steele's practice flourished as wealthy clients called upon his services. But his interests in landscape design went beyond estate design. In Steele's view, the middle-class suburban garden should be a place of privacy with hedges or tall shrubbery screening it from passersby, a place for family life, friendship, and daydreaming. Modern psychology, with its emphasis upon the facets of individual personality and the importance of dreams, was a significant ingredient in his approach to garden design. Increasingly, Steele intended his gardens to serve as quasi-magical private realms where landscape art encouraged relaxation into a state of reverie and fantasy, spaces in which their owners would find freedom from the conventions that governed their daily lives.

In 1924, he published *Design in the Little Garden.* Here he argued for functional domestic arrangements, advising home builders to eliminate useless front lawns, place kitchen, garage, and laundry yard on the street side for convenience, and screen them from public view with shrubbery. If this were done, "our living-rooms should open on the old despised back-yards now turned into gardens and terraces, no matter how small. . . . With such a scheme we may be content that not a foot of room has been wasted; that everything is where use and common sense would have it; and that finally we have cleared the old back-yard to make ready for a proper setting for our out-of-door life."[5]

In his writing Steele was bold enough to criticize the Olympian serenity of Le Nôtre, suggesting that in landscape design rationality should be tempered with sensuality and a degree of poetic mystery. But French culture exerted a powerful hold upon his imagination, and he kept abreast of the published works of Forestier and André Vera and returned from the Paris exposition of 1925 filled with both positive and negative opinions on all that he had seen. He was excited by modernism's design potential for the creative landscape architect, and on subsequent trips to France he continued to study such gardens as the one Guévrékian created for the Noailles in Hyères. His article, "New Pioneering in Garden Design," published in *Landscape Architecture* in 1930, praises Tony Garnier for giving the garden "a marked vibration" by modifying symmetrical axial planning in a way that

"the axis is broken again and again, although rarely entirely lost."[6]

Steele's enthusiasm for abstract, nonassociational design concepts was transmitted to a new generation of young landscape architects, among them Garrett Eckbo, James Rose, and Daniel Urban Kiley (like Steele, an apprentice in Warren Manning's firm). This group of American modernist landscape designers also learned from Steele how to take into account their clients' twentieth-century lifestyle, with its more casual domesticity, fewer servants, and increased appreciation for the outdoors. They perceived rightly that Steele was both a link with the Beaux-Arts tradition and, because of his openness to experiment and innovation, the profession's foremost modernist influence in America.

Steele's masterpiece, Naumkeag, the estate of Mabel Choate in Stockbridge, Massachusetts, begun in 1926, bears witness to the synthesis of his Beaux-Arts training and deep appreciation of historic examples with his delight in modernism's abstract shaping of space and exploration of bold new materials, forms, and color. To this synthesis he added his own desire to design individualized garden spaces that were highly experiential outdoor rooms. Steele found the garden already there to be satisfactory in many respects. It had been designed by Nathan Barrett of Boston, the author of two early land-planning developments—the industrial community of Pullman, Illinois, and the residential suburb of Tuxedo Park, New York—after Joseph Choate had chosen to ignore Frederick Law Olmsted's advice to situate the house half-way down the hillside near a particularly fine oak tree, preferring instead the top of Prospect Hill.

Here Steele set about doing the thing he liked best, shaping landscape space, analyzing existing and desirable conditions in order to determine the outlines of Mabel Choate's proposed new terrace, or Afternoon Garden: its relationship to the house (a location was chosen next to the library), a wall to screen the entrance drive, the inclusion of a large elm

13.4. Afternoon Garden, Naumkeag, Stockbridge, Massachusetts, designed by Fletcher Steele. 1926–35. Steele explained, "We can bring the sky to our feet in a mirror. We can use plants with silver foliage and bright flowers: we can bring merry jets of water, the more the better. . . ."

tree within its embrace, a means of framing the view (fig. 13.4). Ingeniously, he decided to have an Italian sculptor carve old oak pilings from Boston harbor in a bold "Norwegian" manner. The masts were nevertheless meant to evoke the posts used for tying up gondolas in the canals of Venice, and their flaring finial-crowned, multicolored tops were painted to resemble "medieval trappings." These imaginative uprights framed the splendid view of the rolling Berkshires, and nothing more was needed to give the terrace a sense of spatial enclosure than a swag of rope festooned with clematis and Virginia creeper running between the vertical posts. A sculpture, *Boy with Heron,* by Frederick MacMonnies (1863–1937), was taken from inside the house and placed, not on the terrace as one might expect, but at the perimeter, where it could act as a foreground foil to the landscape beyond.

Steele then enlivened the ground plane with "four little fountains, memories of the Generalife" gardens in Granada (see fig. 3.9). Their scalloped edges set in motion a series of curves that, like "an old French knot," consisted of an edging of miniature box within which blue lobelia mulched with coal, yellow santolina, and pink crushed marble provided color, while a small black-glass-lined pool reflected the sky. Irregular brown flagstones surrounded the "giddy carpet" Steele had thus flung down, and on this paving with its green cushions of arenaria squeezing through the crevices and on the rustic masonry retaining walls of the terrace he now placed pots filled with fuchsias, calla lilies, agapanthus, and bamboo like those he had seen in the quiet patios of Seville or Córdoba. Beds of ferns and lilies in the corners, a quietly dripping wall fountain, and "thrones" with matching footstools of pink concrete completed the evocative picture.[7]

Steele's growing originality as a designer was manifested in a second campaign to improve the landscape at Naumkeag between 1929 and 1935. Now more than ever, he saw his art not only as one of shaping space, but also as one of making foreground and background enter into a design dialogue similar to that found in the Japanese garden when borrowed scenery is a compositional element. Together client and landscape architect discussed the problem of the South Lawn and its relationship to the spectacular view. The collaborators' stroke of genius was the creation of what Robin Karson, Steele's biographer, calls "the first modern earthwork in this country," a bold curve sculpted of landfill Miss Choate appropriated from a nearby excavation for a new house foundation. The line of its sloping ridge and the sweeping arc it traced on the ground provided a harmonious foreground echo of the view toward Bear Mountain that had been revealed by tree pruning. As Steele later

13.5. America's "first modern earthwork," a curving berm at Naumkeag

Below: 13.6. Blue Steps, Naumkeag

commented, "The only resource was to create an abstract form in the manner of modern sculpture, with swinging curves and slopes which would aim to make their impression directly, without calling on the help of associated ideas, whether in nature or art."[8] A line of locust trees with globular heads emphasize this form in the landscape (fig. 13.5). Steele and Choate then fashioned an original bit of *chinoiserie* out of recycled ornamental cast iron, which they placed at the terminus of the South Lawn, later setting within it a Chinese-scholar garden rock on a Ming pedestal.

Steele designed the Blue Steps, the most celebrated feature of the Naumkeag landscape, for the purely functional purpose of enabling Choate to descend the hillside to her greenhouse and cutting garden more comfortably and safely. Here four shallow arched grottoes, painted bright blue, flanked by four paired staircases, give a modernist twist to a design tradition dating to the Italian Renaissance (fig. 13.6). The motion of descent is fluidly expressed in the handrails, which Steele fashioned from white-painted tubular steel. As an inspired afterthought,

13.7. Rose Garden, Naumkeag

prompted by the presence of native birches elsewhere on the property, Steele planted a dense grove of these trees in the intervening spaces between the four sets of stairs. The tonal correspondence of the white trunks and the white railings, together with the juxtaposition of the stylishly crafted industrial material and the poetic evocation of nature, have made this scene the emblem of Steele's creative genius.

In 1952, Steele and Choate laid out a rose garden *parterre* south of Naumkeag's *allée* of tall arborvitae trees (fig. 13.7). Drawing once more upon a Chinese motif, a curvilinear imperial scepter, Steele delineated three sinuous, rhythmically repeating paths of pink crushed stone punctuated with small scalloped rose beds. The gently sloping square lawn in which the rose *parterre* was set lay several feet below the terrace that formed its eastern edge, and a spill of semicircular steps fanned out in the angle of its northeast corner.

Mabel Choate's will turned over her thirty-year garden-building project to the Trustees of Reservations, the Massachusetts organization that served as a model for the National Trust of England. Steele had counseled his client to do so, being convinced that regionally based, privately controlled organizations like the Trustees of Reservations are "most efficient, enthusiastic and understanding when it comes to the conservation and administration of local landmarks of natural beauty and historic interest."[9] He well knew that the future of his profession lay not with wealthy clients such as Mabel Choate, but with the government agencies that were responsible for the national, state, and municipal parks and parkways. He probably counted himself lucky to have been able to work at a high professional level for such a long time purely on the basis of his own talent for amusing himself and others, a gift for warm friendship, and the creative intelligence of a true artist.

INNISFREE: AN AMERICAN GARDEN INSPIRED BY CHINESE PAINTING

Included in the small and vanishing circle of monied Americans who could indulge a passion for landscape design on their private estates than could Mabel Choate were Walter Beck (1864–1954) and his wife, Marion Burt Stone Beck (1876–1959). On the 950-acre property she owned in Millbrook, New York, when they married in 1922, the couple set out to create an English-style landscape surrounding their newly completed Queen Anne-style house, which was modeled on Wisley, the experimental plant headquarters of the Royal Horticultural Society in England.[10] Beck was an artist with a deep appreciation of Chinese landscape painting. Around 1930, after having studied descriptions and images of the famous garden of Wang Wei, the Tang dynasty official who was a poet, painter, and garden builder (see Chapter Eight), he became convinced that Chinese design principles, rather than English ones, should govern Innisfree, as the couple called their garden after the poem of that title by William Butler Yeats.

Paintings after Wang Wei's original painting of his Wangchuan Villa garden consist of twenty scenes, compositional groupings of pines and other trees with various small structures set beside a broad river, which is cradled by softly rounded mountains. The bowl-like character of this landscape of rising forms rimming the river basin, as well as the gently cupped aspects of the individual scenes within it, appealed to Beck, who began to create around the lake in Millbrook a series of highly poetic "cup gardens" using weathered stones in carefully balanced compositions. With a work crew of twenty, Beck mined promising parts of the estate where boulders with the fine sculptural qualities prized by Chinese garden-builders lay partially buried in the knobby glacial till. He then ordered these excavated treasures to be transported to the sites where he wished to compose his cup gardens. One of these gardens might take the form of a rock- and vegetation-rimmed hollow. Another might appear as an overturned teacup, thereby resembling one of the softly rounded, mist-wreathed mountains in a painting of Wang Wei's garden. Beck took exquisite care in placing his rocks, using well-concealed cement to anchor them after achieving an intuitively "just right," often precarious, balance. He also took pains to find the appropriate compositional "dialogue" between

13.8. "Rock dialogue," Innisfree, Millbrook, New York, garden design by Walter Beck and Lester Collins. Begun 1930

Below: 13.9. Terrace, Innisfree, designed by Walter Beck

landscape and rocks and among the various individual rocks (fig. 13.8). Having invested the carefully selected stones with pictorial character, he then gave them names—Tiptoe Rock, Dragon Rock, Owl Rock, and Turtle Rock.

A comprehensive treatment of the entire landscape surrounding the lake on the Becks' Millbrook property had to await the integrative vision supplied by Lester Collins (1914–1993), a Harvard-trained landscape architect who had spent two years in China followed by a year in Kyoto. The Becks met Collins during his student days; he became instrumental in the garden's creation, and at Marion Beck's invitation after her husband's death in 1954, its principal creative force and the author of the plan transforming it from a private Elysium into a garden for public visitation. Collins took over Innisfree's design in 1960 where Beck had left off, arranging the several cup gardens into an integrated composition threaded with paths to link them. He made the overall landscape kinetically experiential. A knowledgeable horticulturist, as was Marion Beck who also contributed ideas, Collins enhanced some of Beck's cup gardens with vegetation and created special effects of his own. He also constructed several earthen berms, recontouring the land in order to frame views, direct movement, or develop a topographical profile that would either terminate a vista or else stimulate interest in what lay beyond. He designed the garden's wood bridges and the eighty wooden chairs in which visitors can now repose. Collins compared the Innisfree garden with its many individual scenes connected by paths and bridges with the Yuan Ming Yuan, the famous garden begun by the Yongzheng emperor and completed by the Qianlong emperor in the eighteenth-century Qing dynasty (see Chapter Eight).

In scale, the Millbrook garden is analogous to this imperial garden, and its studied tranquility evokes the mood of the broad river-valley scenery depicted in paintings of Wang Wei's garden; these, not the miniaturized landscapes of the Suzhou scholar-gardens, were the exemplars for Beck and Collins at Innisfree. But while the designers may have had the Yuan Ming Yuan most clearly in mind, Innisfree can also be compared with two other cupped lake-gardens examined in Chapters Seven and Eight: Henry Hoare's Stourhead and Shugakuin Rikyu, the lifework of the retired Japanese emperor Go-Mizunoo. Like these, Innisfree is a highly personal aesthetic statement, an exercise in garden poetics. Beck and Collins merely applied Chinese landscape design principles and rock vocabulary toward this end; they had no intention of replicating a Chinese garden in any more exact sense. Beck's inventiveness and training as an artist are evident not only in his Chinese-inspired rock arrangements but also in his retaining walls and stair steps. His technical ability as both an artist and a craftsman is especially apparent in the patterned brick-and-slate terrace he designed, with a dragon panel incised by him (fig. 13.9).

Collins's year in Japan resulted in his translation of the *Sensai Hisho* or *Secret Garden Book*. Its principles, particularly those concerning the construction of waterfalls, proved instructive as he and Beck worked together to achieve some of Innisfree's most beautiful effects.[11] Few drawings of the gardens at Innisfree exist, although Collins was a practicing landscape architect and an academic dean. All was created on the site, using Beck's own work crew. Garden hoses outlined a future shoreline or path, and stakes or a human figure stood in the landscape to help determine the position of a boulder. Patient experiment was needed to engineer a waterfall in such a way that it produced a cloud of mist, the merest trickle over a rock lip, a fluid sheet glossing a surface of schist or granite, a pluming jet, or a silvery runnel (fig. 13.10). Engineering expertise conducted this water into the ground where a carefully constructed drainage system carries it to the water table or the lake.

Collins's disciplined partnership with nature, which includes the application of modern engineering in the form of concealed pumps and electrical lines as well as the harvesting of algae from the lake, is the

13.10. Rock lip waterfall, Innisfree, engineered by Walter Beck. 1938

unromantic secret of Innisfree's continuing evolution from an ordinary second-growth woodland and glacial pond into a poetic landscape. Thus, unlike many modernist gardens, which openly exploit the design potential of industrial materials and express new methods of spatial composition, Innisfree conceals its technological apparatus beneath an Arts and Crafts aesthetic informed by Chinese art and organizes space in the manner of a traditional stroll garden. Collins's ability to effect a synthesis between art and nature through design and technology helped transform Innisfree from a private dreamworld into a publicly accessible one. He gave due consideration to visitor interest, comfort, and safety; at the same time he cut staff in order to work within the budget of the Innisfree Foundation, which owns and operates the garden.

II. Abstract Art and the Functional Landscape: Gardens for Modern Living

Personal Elysiums like Naumkeag and Innisfree, throwbacks to an earlier tradition of great estate landscapes, illustrate the growing influence of East Asian ideals on Western gardens. Like the Edwardian gardens we have studied, their fundamental purpose was to serve as idyllic retreats from the Machine Age. In England, in the 1930s, the long-lingering aesthetic of the Picturesque, the mellowing hand of the Arts and Crafts Movement, the energies of plant hybridizers, and a vigorous nursery trade still actively informed public taste, perpetuating this conservative landscape tradition. At the same time, however, a committed modernist dared to voice the grounds for radical change and to examine how the planning principles of the Japanese garden might stimulate a new approach to landscape design.

Christopher Tunnard's Influential Book

Christopher Tunnard (1910–1979) was a Canadian-born landscape architect who worked in England and then took up permanent residence in the United States where he became a professor of city planning first at Harvard and then at Yale.[12] No one who knew him in America, where he was a strong advocate of historic preservation, would have guessed that he had been an early firebrand in the cause of landscape modernism while still a young man living in England. But Tunnard, like Fletcher Steele, had taken note of Guévrékian's bold departure from tradition, and other new landscape design developments in France and elsewhere in Europe. A member of the Modern Architectural Research Group (MARS), the British affiliate of the Congrès Internationaux d'Architecture Moderne (CIAM), Tunnard was impressed with the polemical rhetoric and the work of Adolf Loos (1870–1933) and Le Corbusier.

Tunnard was also familiar with landscape design history and English gardening tradition. Without considering the relationship between older landscape idioms and cultural values, in *Gardens in the Modern Landscape* (1938), a loosely woven collection of revised essays on the subject, he adopted the radical stance then current among modern architects of debunking past styles. Having set up this foil of discredited history, Tunnard was ready to study how "as an element inseparable from the problems of housing, and urban and rural development, garden planning can, with the least opposition, achieve its modern form." Quoting Loos ("To find beauty in form instead of making it depend on ornament is the goal to which humanity is aspiring") and Le Corbusier ("The styles are a lie"), he set forth his own doctrine: "The functional garden," he wrote, "avoids the extremes both of the sentimental expressionism of the wild garden and the intellectual classicism of the 'formal' garden; it embodies rather a spirit of rationalism and through an aesthetic and practical ordering of its units provides a friendly and hospitable milieu for rest and recreation. It is, in effect, the social conception of the garden."[13]

He declared that "China's symbolical landscape gardens with their islands of eternal youth and happiness—scenes which provoked a century of Nature-copyism in the West—hold little for us." But in Japanese gardens he found a congenial minimalism, integration of indoor and outdoor space, and the compositional principle he called "occult balance," whereby counterpoise was achieved through an asymmetrical arrangement of parts in equilibrium along a diagonal axis. The Japanese editorial hand that pruned away unnecessary vegetation and carefully arranged those plants that remained for subtle but maximum effect was in keeping with modernism's movement away from a "barbaric massing of color" toward "an acceptance of form, line and economy of material as being of first importance."[14]

Tunnard allied himself with such modern architects as Le Corbusier and Frank Lloyd Wright. The former's country villas, raised from the ground by pilotis, were dissociated from nature but nevertheless presided over broad views that were an important aspect of their architectural planning and expressed a pastoral tradition harking back to Virgil.[15] The houses of the latter, on the other hand, sometimes grasped raw nature in an intimate embrace, as is particularly evident in Fallingwater of 1937, Wright's most famous work, poised above Bear Run, in western Pennsylvania. Both of these modernists created architecture that corresponded with what Tunnard called the "empathic" approach to landscape planning whereby "nature is not to be regarded as a refuge from life, but as an invigorator of it and a stimulus to body and mind."[16] If one of the unstated motives of such Picturesque theorists as Uvedale Price and Richard Payne Knight had been to make untamed nature more agreeable by considering it as art, that was now no longer an issue. By the mid-twentieth century, much of nature had been tamed, and it needed no apologists; it was simply there in the form of sunlight, fresh air, and good views to be actively, *functionally* enjoyed. Included in the empathic, functionalist layout were outdoor dining areas, decks, swimming pools, tennis courts, and other accoutrements of modern life with its orientation to leisure and recreation. Tunnard's later follower, Garrett Eckbo, called this a "landscape for living." (These aspects of design did not engage the imaginations of either Le Corbusier or Wright, who were more romantic than functionalist in their approach to nature.)

Further, Tunnard urged the collaboration of modern artists in the landscape design process; architects were already working with sculptors and painters. Mies van der Rohe's Barcelona Pavilion of 1929 was a notable recent example of the symbiosis of Machine Age architectural form and materials and a single perfectly placed work of sculpture. The Noailles garden in Hyères showed how effective the sculpture by Lipchitz was as an element in the landscape.

Tunnard's own career as a landscape architect

was brief, and he later retreated from radical modernist advocacy. But the work he presented in *Gardens in the Modern Landscape,* enhanced by the drawings of Gordon Cullen, illustrates how in the 1930s at Bentley Wood in Halland, East Sussex, the home of the architect Serge Chermayeff (1900–1996), and in his own house at St. Ann's Hill, Chertsey (fig.13.11), Tunnard practiced the landscape modernism he preached.

The Chermayeff house of steel-framed, weatherboarded construction, with expansive south walls of glass opening toward a distant rural view, had a terrace sheltered by a plate-glass screen away from the house. For a year before the house was built, he carefully removed trees in a second-growth woodland to open a view toward the distant horizon. He attempted no planting except for a mass of naturalized daffodils, a few carefully grouped trees and shrubs near the house, and some narrow flower beds along the terrace edge and its sheltering wall. Near the far open corner of this protected sundeck, there was a sculpture of a reclining female by Henry Moore (1898–1986), carefully positioned according to Tunnard's principle of occult balance.

In prescribing a modern landscape style, Tunnard expressed his own fundamental love of plants and scenery. Stripped of sentimental association, these were to be enjoyed, like abstract art, in terms of color, form, texture, and compositional balance. Whereas functionalist architects and planners usually paid little attention to horticulture, Tunnard urged that "[we] not let the humanism of the gardener's philosophy depart from us." At the same time, he saw the modern landscape as a space to be enjoyed collectively, not "the hedged, personal, half-acre of today, but a unit of the broad green landscape itself, controlled for the benefit of all."[17]

The last chapter of Tunnard's *Gardens in the*

13.11. Christopher Tunnard's house at St. Ann's Hill, Chertsey, Surrey. The drawing by Gordon Cullen shows Tunnard's functional, empathic, and artistic approach to landscape design. Humans and nature meet on friendly, equal terms, and, according to Tunnard's caption in *Gardens in the Modern Landscape,* this is "an architectural garden, part axial, part asymmetrical," in which "screen walls frame distant views. A sheltered position allows many half-hardy subjects to be grown, including cordylines and the chamaerops palm. The sculpture on the right of the sketch is by Willi Soukop." Particular attention has been given to the framing of distant views.

Modern Landscape is devoted to "the wider planning [of] civic landscape architecture."[18] Here he called for a new regional idiom linking society and nature, city planning and landscape architecture, the garden and the large-scale recreational park. Tunnard wished to promote egalitarian land planning synthesizing the talents of the engineer—"whose activities are perhaps the greatest contribution made to the landscape in the last one hundred years"[19]—the landscape architect, and the architect. His planning philosophy celebrating the builders of roadways and bridges as well as the makers of gardens and the designers of recreational facilities was similar in spirit to that of Robert Moses. At this hopeful moment in the 1930s it was possible to dream of a future of well-organized urban growth in which decision-making power was vested in planners capable of rationally premising their work on functionality and human needs as they wedded technology and nature into a grand design.

It is remarkable just how principled was the spirit of early modernism with its frank avowal of machine-made materials and its honest and optimistic search for an aesthetic that served and expressed a new social order. Although later shorn of its youthful idealism, the exploration of the problem raised by modernism with regard to landscape design continued in the belief that scientifically rational planning combined with an aesthetic of pure form and new spatial concepts could serve as expressive ends in themselves, replacing older cultural values emanating from cosmology, religion, and philosophy. And, much as the Becks had suspected when they saw the work of Le Corbusier and his followers as being more appropriately situated in South America than in Millbrook, New York, it was in Brazil, where a significant spark—the São Paulo Modern Art Week of 1922—had ignited a remarkable cultural and aesthetic revolution, that the modernist landscape in collaboration with modern architecture found one of its most creative exponents.

ROBERTO BURLE MARX AND THE GARDEN AS ABSTRACT ART

Roberto Burle Marx (1909–1994) was a protean artist—painter, sculptor, muralist, and craftsman—with an affinity for nature and the baroque morphology of the tropical vegetation of his native Brazil. Given the opportunity to collaborate with architects who were modernist innovators, he found his most expressive métier as a landscape designer. His approach to landscape paralleled his approach to painting; he employed a graphic style that treated the ground plane in the same abstract manner as Le Nôtre or Capability Brown had but with a modernist sensibility sympathetic to the undulating lines and biomorphic shapes found in the art of Jean Arp, Joan Miró, and Alexander Calder. The strong curvilinear forms of the Brazilian coastal landscape around Rio de Janeiro coincidentally echoed the biomorphic forms found in their work, and this native scenery had an obvious effect on Burle Marx as a designer. With a scientist's curiosity and an unrivaled botanical collection from his own expeditions in the Brazilian hinterlands, he confidently deployed luxuriant, vividly colored tropical plants, some with highly architectonic forms, in visually strong compositions that evoked and often directly echoed the local landscape, drawing it into the garden in the manner of Japanese "borrowed" scenery. This style effectively complemented and enriched the austere lines of functionalist buildings.

In 1934, at the inviation of Lima Cavalcanti, the governor of the state of Pernambuco, Burle Marx accepted a job in Recife redesigning and restoring the public gardens of that faded provincial capital. During his two-year sojourn in Recife, Burle Marx became an active member of the city's intellectual community, making friends and establishing lasting relationships among a group of young poets, painters, writers, and musicians. He developed his graphic approach to garden design as he prepared India ink perspectives of several public squares and parks, including the Euclides da Cunha Square (1935), which he envisioned as a cactus garden (fig. 13.12). For this project he went into the dry northeastern region of Brazil called the *caatinga* to collect various kinds of succulents, which he then arranged and installed.

Burle Marx's participation in a coterie with leftist views caused him to fall into disfavor with the mayor, prompting his resignation and return to Rio in 1937. There he set up an atelier and resumed contact with his friends from the School of Fine Arts. The architect Lúcio Costa (b. 1902) had invited Le Corbusier to come to Rio to advise on the design of a new building for the Ministry of Education and Public Health, a controversial early modernist structure where Burle Marx assisted the well-known artist Cândido Portinari (1903–1962) in painting a large mural

13.12. Euclides da Cunha Square, Recife, Pernambuco, Brazil, designed by Roberto Burle Marx. 1935

representing the economic cycles of Brazil. Probably at Costa's suggestion, Burle Marx was asked to also participate on the architectural design team, which included, in addition to Costa, Oscar Niemeyer and several other young Brazilian modernists. Burle Marx was put in charge of designing the ground-level plaza, the minister's office terrace garden, and a roof garden. This last occupied the top of the low-rise section of the building and therefore functioned as an old-fashioned *parterre,* being designed for viewing from above, in this case from the windows of the raised slab housing the offices of the ministry.

The gardens for the Ministry of Education and Public Health demonstrated Burle Marx's method of treating the garden plane in a manner analogous to a painter's canvas. Upon the roof garden, for instance, he "drew" curvilinear abstract forms reminiscent of aerial views of Brazilian rivers. Texture and color played important roles. There were spiky bird-of-paradise plants and other plants—agaves, dracaenas, and palms—laid out as sculptural accents or single masses of color. His approach to landscape design as aestheticized nature was essentially the same as his approach to painting. "My message is purely pictorial," he once declared, "it revolves around color, rhythm, and form, trying to abstain from the anecdotal, believing that pictorial language begins when the word loses the reason for being."[20]

Burle Marx's vision of the modernist garden as pure visual experience unencumbered by textual meaning can be appreciated in both the gouache plan and the realized landscape of the Odette Monteiro Garden (now the Luiz Cezar Fernandes Garden) in Correas in the state of Rio de Janeiro (1948) (figs. 13.13, 13.14, 13.15). Although he often worked in close collaboration with modern architects, he was unlike the garden formalists who followed Reginald Blomfield's prescription for integrating house and garden in a unified, axially coordinated scheme, or such landscape modernists as Tunnard, who wished to do the same thing in an asymmetrical manner. Instead, he

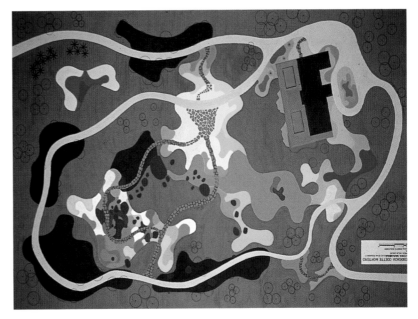

saw garden design as a generally independent, nonarchitectural, *contrapuntal,* and primarily artistic endeavor. On the Monteiro estate, he virtually ignored the house by Wladimir Alves Souza. His aim here was to reiterate in certain ground plane forms the profile of the surrounding mountainscape.

By the time Burle Marx designed the Odette Monteiro Garden, the landscape design and construction business he was running with his brother Siegfried had grown. In addition, he wanted space for his expanding botanical collection and the nursery where the brothers propagated and grew plants for the firm's projects. In 1949, they were able to purchase a former coffee plantation, Sítio Santo Antônio da Bica (Saint Anthony of the Spring), in Campo Grande, nineteen miles south of Rio. On this hilly site offering a series of microclimates, he installed his collection of tropical plants, which was becoming one of outstanding scientific merit, thanks to his friendship and collaboration with Henrique Llahmeyer de Mello Barreto, a botanist and the head of Rio's zoological garden, with whom he undertook several phytogeographical excursions into the Brazilian interior. At the

13.13. Plan of the Luiz Cezar Fernandes Garden (formerly the Odette Monteiro Garden), Correas, Rio de Janeiro, designed by Burle Marx. 1948

Left: 13.14. Luiz Cezar Fernandes Garden (formerly the Odette Monteiro Garden)

Below: 13.15. Luiz Cezar Fernandes Garden (formerly the Odette Monteiro Garden)

13.16. Pond Garden with architectural fragments from demolished Rio buildings, Sítio Santo Antônio da Bica, Campo Grande, Brazil, designed by Roberto Burle Marx. From 1949

Below: 13.17. Copacabana Beach, Rio de Janeiro, designed by Roberto Burle Marx. 1970

Sítio—now his weekend home, painting studio, and horticultural laboratory—he grew bromeliads, calatheas, philodendrons, anthuriums, and heliconia in shade houses. On higher ground, above the remodeled plantation house where he lived and entertained his many friends and visitors, he grew cactus, orchids, palms, and more bromeliads.

Although a knowledgeable plantsman and committed environmentalist concerned about the protection of the rain forest, art was for Burle Marx a more fundamental interest than science, for it was as an artist that he sought to use individually interesting plant species as a means of establishing accents, filling the biomorphic outlines of his planting beds, and shaping space. It was as an artist, too, that he salvaged bits of old architectural fabric from buildings that were being torn down as Rio's modernization rushed forward, and these he recomposed within the gardens of the Sítio (fig. 13.16). Here, where the slightly menacing air of tropical fecundity is interwoven with these enigmatic and melancholy-seeming fragments, one senses Burle Marx's affinity for Surrealism.[21]

The same spirit of improvisational protean creativity that characterized life at the Sítio also pervaded Burle Marx's office in Rio where he presided like a Renaissance *capo di bottega* over an artisans' workshop. From here flowed floral decorations for receptions, sculptures, murals, jewelry, textile designs, and stage sets as well as more than 2,000 plans for various landscapes and cityscapes. Although he achieved some of his finest results as a collaborator with modern architects such as Rino Levi with whom he designed the estate of the industrialist Olivo Gomes, in São José dos Campos, São Paulo, he remained as interested as he had been as a young park designer in Recife in applying his modernist landscape approach to public spaces. In 1954, he received a commission for the 289-acre Flamengo Park on landfill adjacent to Guanabara Bay near the heart of Rio. Like the recreational facilities that were built in conjunction with the waterfront parkways of Robert Moses, Flamengo Park was undertaken as part of a coastal highway project designed to relieve the city's growing automobile congestion. Burle Marx executed his plan with charac-

teristic boldness, engendering a visual dialogue between the park and the baroque landforms that rim the city and its bay.

In 1970, in a second landfill project, he extended his work along Rio's coastline with his design for the promenades and parkways along Copacabana Beach (fig. 13.17). Here, for the palm-tree-edged promenade, he employed a traditional Portuguese paving technique (*pedra portuguesa*) to create a black, white, and red mosaic that echoes the undulating line of the nearby surf. In contrast, he designed the roadbed median and sidewalk along the building edge as a series of individually conceived abstract panels with green planting pockets set at irregular intervals within them. The entire strip, including the sandy bathing beach, was thus transformed into a vibrant linear *parterre* for viewing from the windows of the contiguous skyscraper hotels and apartment buildings.

In 1956, the planning of Brazil's new capital, Brasília, began. Many were dismayed that for political reasons officials did not consult Burle Marx during the initial planning of this exercise in modernist urban design. Finally, in 1965, he received a commission to work with the architect Oscar Niemeyer on designs for the gardens of the Ministries of the Army, Justice, and Foreign Affairs. Here as elsewhere he exploited the reflective qualities of pools of water and his own fertile imagination to good effect. At the Ministry of Foreign Affairs, for instance, he reached beyond images derived from Brazil's colonial past to

ones from the Roman colonial past of its mother country, Portugal, drawing upon the gardens of an excavated Roman house in Conimbriga as inspiration for his floating planting beds (figs. 13.18, 13.19).

Luis Barragán and the Landscape of Surrealist Expressionism

Burle Marx developed a visually dynamic style that was an abstract, organic counterpoint to the modern architecture within or adjacent to it, a style only slightly tinged with Surrealism. His contemporary, the Mexican architect Luis Barragán (1902–1988), with starker Surrealist affinities and more influenced by American regionalist modernism as represented by Frank Lloyd Wright and certain Californian architects, forged an expressive style that wedded domestic space with raw, even violent, nature.

Trained in his native Guadalajara, Barragán traveled for a year and a half in Europe and then left his home city to establish himself in the capital in 1936. He carried with him remembered images from his sojourn in Europe—Surrealist paintings, Islamic patios in Spain, and the idyllic Mediterranean gardens of the writer, caricaturist, and illustrator Ferdinand Bac (1859–1952) at Les Colombières in Menton, France. At Les Colombières on the Côte d'Azure, Bac had employed a pastiche of vaguely allusive Mediterranean forms in which an Arts and Crafts approach and an Italianate stylistic sensibility were mingled to create a garden of memory and meditation.[22] Barragán, in a similar manner, gave his gardens a certain dreamlike character, imbuing them with memories of vernacular Mexican architecture and the rural landscape he had known as a child on his family's ranch near the village of Mazamitla. Working in a climate similar to Bac's Mediterranean, he created an architecture that completely fused interior and exterior spatial planning. Thoroughly abreast of modernist developments in his profession, Barragán forged an indigenous style devoid of stylistic specificity, a spare, stripped-down version of his native architecture that owed a strong debt to the influence of the Bauhaus and Le Corbusier. He particularly wished to avoid designing in the popular "California Colonial" idiom of ornate stucco and red tiles that some affluent Mexicans had begun to favor.

The practice he established in Mexico City was as a designer-developer, and he built about thirty, mostly speculative houses and small apartment buildings during his first four years there. With profits from these, he purchased and remodeled for himself a house in the Tacubaya district, for which he created a garden. He also created behind high buttressed, red-earth-colored walls a strange and enigmatic garden of "aestheticized desolation and decay"[23] in San Angel on a property called El Cabrío at the edge of the Pedregal, the lava field south of Mexico City. Before the volcanic eruption of Xictli around 100 C.E., this was the site of the Aztec ceremonial centers of Cuicuilco and Copilco. Because of its contorted topography, peculiar plant life, and the eerie legends associated with its weird basaltic landscape, the Pedregal was considered by respectable people as a place to be avoided. But Barragán's taste for the surreal attracted him to explore and then, beginning in 1944, to buy 865 acres (later increased to 1,250) of this inexpensive wasteland where he had decided to create a unique modernist garden suburb for prosperous middle-class Mexicans.

With lots one-acre minimum in size, houses occupying no more than 10 percent of the entire area of the subdivision, lava rock and indigenous plant life

13.18. Central Peristyle, House of the Fountains, Conimbriga, Portugal. 3rd century c.e.

13.19. Gardens of the Ministry of Foreign Affairs, Brasília, designed by Roberto Burle Marx. 1965

13.20. House at 140 Fuentes, San Angel Gardens, El Cabrio, El Pedregal, Mexico, designed by Luis Barragán and Max Cetto. 1951

Below: 13.21. Edgar J. Kaufmann House, Palm Springs, California, designed by Richard Neutra. 1946

protected from removal, and roads laid out to conform with the terrain, the San Angel Gardens of the Pedregal were to constitute a Surrealistic celebration of the violent inhuman forces that reside in the larger Mexican landscape. Asserting possession of this landscape, which bore no trace of colonial occupation but evoked a pre-catastrophe Aztec empire, was also symbolically important at a time when Mexican intellectuals, artists, and political leaders were concerned with issues of national identity. To choose a site such as this for domestic purposes was, like Wright's choice of a cantilevered platform over Bear Run for Edgar J. Kaufmann's Fallingwater, to state a modernist's confidence in technology, even in the face of nature's turbulence. It affirmed the idea that humans had reached a point where nature had become a subject of desire and personal dominion rather than an object of awe or admiration. Landscape in this sense meant an intimate coupling of architecture and nature. There would be no transition from the artificial to the natural environment through an intermediate zone in which the traditional skills of garden design and horticulture played a significant part.[24]

Although the winding streets of El Pedregal were similar to those of nineteenth- and twentieth-century suburbs in the United States, the continuous front lawns of the typical North American suburb were replaced, in conformity with a Mediterranean-derived Latin American tradition, by high walls at the line of the street or sidewalk. For Barragán these walls offered opportunities to create slightly mysterious "garden-streets" with "sex appeal."[25] The houses behind these walls, however, were rational, functionalist essays in modernism. In their cubic massing, flat roofs, concrete construction, expansive picture windows, open floor plans, and interpenetration of indoors and outdoors, they echoed current architectural modernism in Europe, the United States, Japan, and other parts of Latin America. Instead of enclosing a landscaped patio in the manner of countless Mediterranean-style exemplars, these houses were made simply to emerge out of the rugged landscape

(fig. 13.20). In discussing their design of one of the Pedregal properties, Barragán's collaborator, Max Cetto, spoke of the lava ridge that partially defined the edge of the swimming pool and all but dove into the living room as "the master key" that "made the house click."[26] Here, instead of the house's extending into the landscape by means of axial relationships, the landscape appears to be extending itself into the house.

Cetto was a German emigré modernist, and the style of functionalist architecture that he and Barragán professed, with its smooth, unadorned, white, planar surfaces, contrasted powerfully with the tortuous dark-gray basalt. The same mixture of spare, open-plan modernism and dramatic siting can be found in the work of the Austrian-born American architect Richard Neutra (1892–1970), especially in the house he designed in 1946 for Edgar J. Kaufmann in Palm Springs, California (fig. 13.21). Barragán knew of the developments in modern architecture in California and had established a personal friendship with Neutra. Californian landscape architects such as Thomas Church and Garrett Eckbo were forging a regional modernism that drew upon factors similar to those in Mexico: Hispanic cultural heritage, starkly beautiful natural scenery, and a climate that fostered luxuriant vegetation. Barragán's residential landscapes were meant to be, like theirs, private realms in which modernism was informed by vernacular traditions, places where garden and house merged to accommodate an informal lifestyle, and spaces of refuge and retreat from the turmoil of modern life.

This is eloquently evident at San Cristobal, an estate on the outskirts of Mexico City where Thoroughbred horses are raised and trained (fig. 13.22). Barragán's only remaining legacy that has not been severely altered, this complex of house, swimming pool, stable, and horse pool is a poetic meditation on his childhood memories of the rural village of Mazamitla, as well as an abstract composition of great sophistication and refinement in which color plays a role similar to that in the works of Color Field

painters such as Mark Rothko (1903–1970). Here as elsewhere the architect gave his austere, unornamented architecture warmth and animation as well as a Surrealist intensity by his use brilliant pinks and fuchsias against which the complementary green tones of the landscape act as a foil.

In terms of physical climate and a cultural climate hospitable to bold gestures and innovation, Mexico and southern California are closely related. Both places are conducive to the use of a Mediterranean plant palette and the interweaving of indoor and outdoor space found in Mediterranean lands. The patio of Spain, with its debt to Islamic models, and the loggia and casino of Italy, where villa owners had pioneered the art of open-air dining and entertaining, were forerunners of the paved, well-furnished garden court and terrace with pool and adjacent lanai.

In California, in the altered economic and social structure of the post–Great Depression years, an informal way of life stressing low maintenance requirements, casual dress, easy hospitality on the part of hosts without servants, and a proclivity for home-centered recreation contributed to the development of the modernist garden in California. *Sunset,* an early lifestyle magazine published in Menlo Park, California, and directed to western homeowners, promoted this agreeable mode of living and the flow between indoors and outdoors that it implied. It found a ready audience among the eastern and midwestern migrants pouring into the rapidly growing state. As David Streatfield, an authority on California's gardens, remarks, "The new garden designs united indoor and outdoor space to create a setting for a relaxed, often hedonistic way of living [in which] gardens were fully used as outdoor rooms."[27] It was a Beaux-Arts-trained landscape architect open to experimentation who was able to make the creative leap from stylistic imitation and reinterpretation of Spanish and Italian models, which we examined in Chapter Eleven, to the innovation of this new, in turn influential, landscape design idiom.

THOMAS CHURCH'S GARDENS FOR PEOPLE

Thomas Church (1902–1978) grew up in southern California. He earned a landscape architecture degree from the University of California at Berkeley in 1922, pursued further studies at the Harvard Graduate School of Design, and traveled extensively, studying Spanish and Italian garden design on a six-month fellowship in 1927. Thus trained in the prevailing Beaux-Arts curriculum, he began a long and successful practice centered primarily upon residential landscapes, receiving commissions in both the Bay Area and southern California. Florence Yoch (1890–1972) had begun to transform her style of eclectic originality into one that was more abstract and informal with the design in 1936 of a poolside garden for the film director George Cukor. Church, like Yoch, was capable of making traditional-style gardens that were aesthetically pleasing and functionally satisfying, which is what he did for a growing roster of clients throughout the 1930s. Like Yoch, he realized that a landscape designer could make a virtue of a small lot by ignoring the tenets of his training and adopting the aesthetic principles being pioneered by modern architects and artists. On a second visit to Europe in 1937 he saw the work of Le Corbusier and Alvar Aalto (1898–1976) as well as that of many modern painters and sculptors.

Beginning in the late 1930s, Church began to employ line, color, and texture in a bold and original manner. His use of shifting, asymmetrical axes rather than the balanced, geometrically oriented ones of Neoclassical design gave him the freedom to organize space in new ways. He became a master at harmonizing the angular geometries of architectural design with flowing, curvilinear forms. A beach garden in Aptos, California, shows clearly his understanding of ground-plane line as a means of defining space in a manner that energizes both the delineated, contained area and the more natural surrounding terrain (fig. 13.23). At this Pacific Coast beach house designed by Hervey Parke Clark, Church merged interior and exterior space so skillfully that he earned a reputation among architects as an ideal collaborator on site planning. As attentive to the lives and desires of his clients as to the conditions of the site, he conceived plans that were both functional and artistic. The pattern and texture of paving or decking and the manner in which the texture, scale, and structure of plants unite hard and soft surfaces is the hallmark of a Church landscape.

Church's first book, *Gardens Are for People* (1955), adopts the tone of a professional offering common-sense advice to homeowners. It gives excellent instruction on how to appreciate visually the natural assets of a property and how to make the most of it by orienting the plan to desirable sun angles and wind expo-

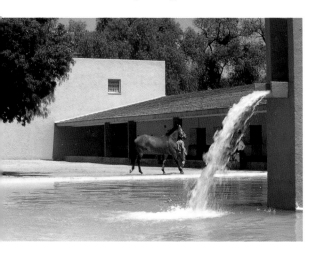

13.22. Water tank with water-feeding trough, Egerstrom House and Stables, San Cristobal, Los Clubes, Mexico City, designed by Luis Barragán. 1967–69

13.23. Beach Garden for Mr. and Mrs. Charles O. Martin, Aptos, California, house designed by Hervey Parke Clark, garden designed by Thomas Church. 1948. At this Pacific Coast beach house, Church extended the living space outdoors by means of redwood decking that complements the rectilinear planes of the house while assuming, in the raised perimeter seating, an assertive angularity that acts as a foil to the curvaceous line defining the rest of the edge of a "pool" of beach sand, the centerpiece of this low-maintenance garden.

Below: 13.24. Plan of Donnell Garden pool area, designed by Thomas Church, Sonoma, California, 1948

Below right: 13.25. Donnell Garden, Sonoma, California, designed by Thomas Church. 1948

sures, while considering scenic view lines, topography, and existing vegetation. Church pointed out how things had changed within a single generation: Garages had been absorbed into the house; drinks on the terrace had replaced tea in the parlor; modest attire had given way to bikini sunbathing; the circular carriage-turnaround entry court had been replaced by the automobile driveway; a service area for propagating and potting plants and composting weeds had become a requirement in an era of do-it-yourself gardeners; gunite and plastic swimming pools had made a former luxury commonplace; and plant-filled nurs-

eries and a scientific horticultural industry had grown up to serve the average homeowner. The prescriptions he offered stress the means of integrating house and garden so that they constitute a unified living space. They continually directed attention to the functional requirements of the entire family and its guests.

With the increasing popularity of home entertainment, Church sought to dramatize the point of arrival even in modest houses, stressing the role of attractive forecourt paving and planting as a means of welcoming guests. He also believed that a generous scale for the vestibule would signal the hospitality visitors were to receive as they proceeded into the the house and its garden. Increasing the house's ambience of cordiality sometimes involved removing heavy foundation plantings to give it a cleaner, more inviting appearance. Conscious of maintenance requirements in an era of rising labor costs, Church configured gardens with open centers and broad strips of grass that could be easily mowed.

California's climate made the swimming pool an especially appealing garden amenity and its surrounding paved area a center for family life and entertaining friends outdoors. Church's best known work, the Donnell Garden in Sonoma, which he designed in 1948, contains a kidney-shaped swimming pool. Resembling also one of the biomorphic images in a painting by Jean Arp (1887–1966) or Joan Miró (1893–1983), it has assumed the role of an icon in the California modernist garden movement (figs. 13.24, 13.25).

Modern sculpture, like modern painting, served as an inspiration for early modernist landscape architects like Church, who were seeking a new vocabulary of forms. They also employed modern sculpture as ornament. Ever pragmatic and people-oriented in his approach, Church made the sculptural feature he placed in the Donnell Garden swimming pool appear to be an afterthought. "The first idea was to use one of the big boulders from the site as a play island in the pool," Church explained. "This was changed (the rock would have torn the swimmers to pieces) into an

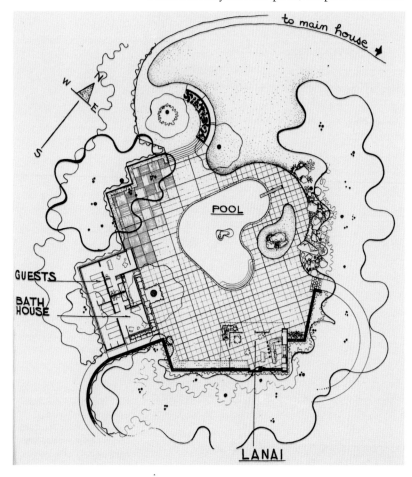

island of concrete designed by sculptor Adaline Kent."[28] This biomorphic form invited swimmers to sunbathe in its curvaceous embrace.

Church remained stylistically versatile, always taking his cues from the client, considering his or her preferences, personal and family requirements, and the conditions of the site. He never entirely abandoned his Beaux-Arts training, employing past styles or motifs as he deemed appropriate and in response to his clients' tastes. For some of his Bay Area clients living in town houses as well as those in Santa Barbara where there was a strong Italianate and Spanish Colonial design tradition, he drew upon his knowledge of historic landscape idioms (fig. 13.26). Though destined, like Fletcher Steele, by the culture and education of his time to straddle two design eras, he nevertheless transformed himself into a modernist of conviction, sharing many of the ideas of a slightly younger generation of landscape architects that included fellow Californian Garrett Eckbo.

GARRETT ECKBO'S LANDSCAPES FOR LIVING

Garret Eckbo (1910–2000) grew up in a town on Alameda Island in San Francisco Bay. He studied landscape architecture at the University of California in Berkeley and Harvard's School of Graduate Design. At Harvard he met Daniel Urban Kiley and James Rose, classmates who were, like him, sufficiently progressive in their social attitudes to sense that the program they were being offered was designed to serve the demands of a dwindling elite and did not deal with the needs of an industrialized, democratic society. Joseph Hudnut, the dean of the school, had recently brought Walter Gropius (1883–1969) to head the architecture department, and with him the teaching agenda of the Bauhaus, with its emphasis upon

large social issues and the abandonment of historic styles for functionalist design and industrial materials. However, the landscape architecture department at Harvard retained its Beaux-Arts curriculum, which Henry Hubbard and Theodora Kimball's textbook, *An Introduction to the Study of Landscape Design* had codified in 1917.[29] As Reuben Rainey points out, Hubbard and Kimball's method united several approaches. It called for Beaux-Arts, or formal, planning as a means of uniting house and garden along continuing axes, then recommended an Olmstedian naturalistic, or informal, design for the remainder of the property, often as a means of melding it with the larger landscape. A transitional lawn was proposed to mediate the stylistic contrast between these zones.

Eckbo was inspired by his own sense of possibilities derived from living and working in a less tradition-bound atmosphere than the Atlantic seaboard and by the current Zeitgeist—a heady mixture of jazz, film, fashion, industrial design, New Deal social progressiveness, the recently arrived automobile culture, and the growing acceptance of European modern art and architecture in America. Like his friends Rose and Kiley, he worked diligently while chafing at the limitations of Harvard's conservative approach to landscape architecture. The three probably read with keen interest the articles of the well-traveled Fletcher Steele, whose descriptions of modernist French gardens opened a window upon innovative alternatives to their program of study. They formed a receptive audience for Christopher Tunnard's *Gardens in the Modern Landscape* when it appeared in 1938.

Eckbo saw the potential of landscape design for serving a middle-class clientele. He thought of the modest row house and the suburban subdivision with its small front yards and backyards as interesting challenges, and he was skilled at manipulating spatial organization to maximize the visual interest and pleasurable use of an entire property. He explored these possibilities while still at Harvard in a student project comprising a city block of eighteen equal-size townhouse lots in which he demonstrated a synthesis of curvilinearity and angularity similar to the one found in Church's Aptos beach house. Landscape historian Marc Treib draws an instructive parallel between Eckbo's compositions and the work of the modern painters Wassily Kandinsky (1866–1944), Kasimir Malevich (1878–1935), and László Moholy-Nagy (1895–1946).[30] The cheerful, Jazz Age rhythms and explosive visual energy set up by the counterplay of geometric and "organic" lines and shapes in their paintings could inspire someone who wanted to substitute the shaping of space as a central compositional principle for the arrangement of views along static, single-perspective axes. In borrowing the free-flowing lines of abstract painting for his plans Eckbo found a means of creating a sense of mobile dynamism in the landscape, which had been impossible within the confines of Beaux-Arts spatial composition.

At the same time, the inspiration of architecture as derived from Mies van der Rohe's Barcelona Pavilion remained influential in Eckbo's work.[31] With its grid of eight cruciform columns set on a raised terrace, the Barcelona Pavilion organizes space in a way that is clear and yet ambiguous. Here, Mies established a modular system that performed the functions of framing the structure and supporting the roof, giving underlying mathematical order to the building, and at the same time freely modulating the interior space by positioning non-load-bearing walls as freestanding screens, articulating occupational zones without defining them precisely. The spatial continuum thus created gives an impression of uninterrupted flow. This type of construction also made possible the curtain wall composed of panels of glass or a combination of glass and opaque cladding hung in front of a steel frame. Because space is contained but not defined within these glass walls, there is no unequivocal separation between indoors and outdoors and no single point within the building that can be called its center.

Eckbo returned to California to establish his practice, and at Menlo Park, where he designed a garden in 1940, he acknowledged his debt to Mies, placing straight and curvilinear hedges in a manner he termed "a kind of de Stijl-van der Rohe planning," which served as a means of "baffling of garden space . . . to increase sense of volume" (fig. 13.27).[32] As in Mies's Barcelona Pavilion, the garden has an ordering geometric grid—the pear orchard into which it was set—and well-emphasized rectangular boundaries.

Above all, like Church, Eckbo wanted to focus on domestic human needs and the humanized landscape that was expanding with the population growth of California. He called his first book *Landscape for Liv-*

13.27. Garden in an existing pear orchard, Menlo Park, California, designed by Garrett Eckbo. 1940

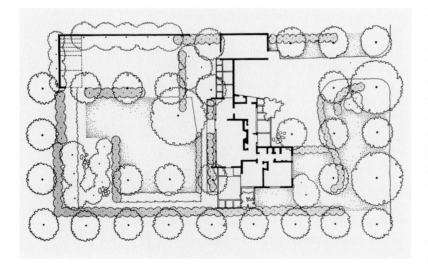

ing. Published in 1950 when his reputation was well established and illustrated with the work of his office, it implied the role of human beings as partners with nature, realizing their legitimate needs through science and technology rather than basing their spatial arrangements upon historic styles reflecting the aspirations and needs of people in other times and places.

After returning to California and before setting up a private practice, Eckbo had worked for more than four years for the Farm Security Administration designing fifty landscape plans for camps built to house 225 to 350 families of migrant and permanent agricultural workers. His concern for ordinary humanity was expressed in this context in the interesting spatial arrangements and varied palette of vegetation he provided, which probably offered some greater sense of place and therefore an element of psychological comfort to the populations living in the otherwise unremarkable surroundings of the camps of trailers and spartan temporary housing. *Landscape for Living* illustrates his plans for several of these camps along with some of his designs for single-family residences, campuses, parks, and tract-housing, selected from a portfolio that amounted to more than a thousand commissions during his years of practice.

As subsequently developed by Ian McHarg and the landscape planners he trained at the University of Pennsylvania, one approach to landscape architecture was through environmental science (see Chapter Fifteen). For Eckbo and other landscape functionalists of his generation, science was more a matter of professional perspective, a questioning approach to design problems, the discipline of asking the theoretical "why" as well as the practical "how." Wishing to advocate no style and to be an heir to all historic styles, Eckbo created his own design vocabulary to express the dynamic aspect of modernity, his preference for areal over axial design, and his commitment to democratic values. Even in such structures as garden pavilions, his emphasis was upon space, not mass. He saw plants as upthrusting verticals, sculptural objects, and vegetative texture, and for him they were a means of defining space, not an end in themselves. By contrast, he saw rocks as being pulled by gravity toward the center of the earth, and he sometimes used groupings of these to anchor and stabilize parts of his design. Like Church and other landscape architects in California, he designed many pools in the shape of amoebas, kidneys, and boomerangs. In his designs the pool became "a positive space-organizing element which controls physical movement."[33]

In 1956, when the Aluminum Corporation of America (Alcoa) asked Eckbo to develop a landscape plan promoting the use of this modern metal in the garden, he decided to create the Aluminum Garden on his own property in Wonderland Park, a subdivision in the Hollywood Hills above Laurel Canyon. The subdivision was situated on a steeply terraced slope, and Eckbo's contribution to its planning resulted in successive layers of vegetation along the side of the canyon and a unified appearance rather than the fragmented look characteristic of other suburban developments. Until his death in 2000, Eckbo remained a fierce and opinionated advocate of the "social-cultural-natural approach" to landscape design.

Daniel Urban Kiley's Synthesis of French Influence and Miesian Modernism

In contrast to Eckbo, whose experimental approach to landscape architecture was fostered by the innovative, freewheeling culture of California and by his commitment to low-cost housing for the mass society, Daniel Urban Kiley (b. 1912) became increasingly drawn to André Le Nôtre's principles of French seventeenth-century garden design. This was apparent after 1955 when Mr. and Mrs. J. Irwin Miller chose him to work in collaboration with architect Eero Saarinen (1910–1961) on the design of their house and garden in Columbus, Indiana (fig. 13.28). Posted overseas in 1945 during his military duty, Kiley was able to tour European gardens for the first time, and his exposure to the masterpieces of Le Nôtre made a lasting impression upon him. At the same time, he shared with his former classmates Eckbo and Rose a reverential fascination with the Barcelona Pavilion.

In 1955, when hired by the Millers to work with his friend Saarinen, Kiley had already been practicing for nineteen years, using a vocabulary of multiple, shifting axes and free-form, nonorthogonal, areal definitions similar to that of Eckbo and Rose. Now, having discovered his affinity for Le Nôtre and being given the opportunity to work with an architect who shared his appreciation of Mies van der Rohe's asymmetrical but rhythmically balanced way of organizing space by means of freestanding walls set in overlapping planes within a modular grid, he changed course.[34] Henceforth, he practiced a form of modern landscape architecture that married the classical geometrical planning principles of the French master with the dynamically ambiguous yet elegantly ordered spatial concepts of the German architect. In Mies's work architectural space had the appearance of being no longer contained. Space for Mies was an infinity-implying continuum similar to that of Le Nôtre's gardens, whose axes were metaphors for Descartes's principle of *res extensa,* or the indefinite extension of the universe (see Chapter Five). As landscape architect Gregg Bleam points out, "Perhaps more than any other architect of his time, Mies represented a synthesis of what would

seem to be the conflicting conceptions of neoclassicism and modernism."[35] Kiley, like Frank Lloyd Wright and Christopher Tunnard, found inspiration in Japanese design, where a similar underlying asymmetrical compositional balance and continuous, interpenetrating spatial organization are achieved.

Organized as a series of separate but overlapping zones, Kiley's functional and ornamental garden spaces carry the centrifugal movement of Saarinen's plan for the house into the surrounding landscape. The house, placed within a large square of their combined grid plan, is defined on three sides by clipped arborvitae hedges planted in a staggered pattern rather than as a single continuous line. Around the house are

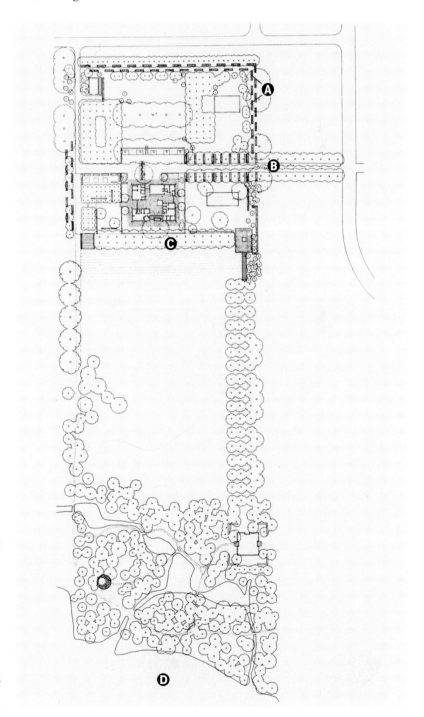

13.28. Plan of J. Irwin Miller Garden, Columbus, Indiana, designed by Daniel Urban Kiley. 1955
Ⓐ Staggered Hedges
Ⓑ Horsechestnut *Allée*
Ⓒ Locust *Allée*
Ⓓ Flatrock River

13.29. Locust *allée*, J. Irwin Miller Garden, with sculpture by Henry Moore

Below: 13.30. Fountain Place, Allied Bank Tower, Dallas, Texas, designed by Daniel Urban Kiley

a series of geometrically ordered gardens reminiscent of the *bosquets* and *allées* of Le Nôtre, but they do not employ Le Nôtre's axial symmetries. Freely arranged within their own grid in a manner that complements Saarinen's pinwheel disposition of the elements of the house, these geometrical garden spaces flow fluidly and expand outward. To define the remaining side of the square Kiley placed a honey locust *allée* adjacent to the house, with a platform terrace at either end for the display of sculpture (fig. 13.29).

For the platform terrace at the north end the Millers chose a reclining female figure in bronze by Henry Moore. At the other end of this *allée,* they installed a sculpture by Jacques Lipchitz. Stairs lead down to a lawn that slopes toward the floodplain beside the Flatrock River. Trees planted both in regular configurations and naturalistic clumps form walls on either side of the lawn. Some of the Miller garden's finest effects are due to the clients' horticultural knowledge, original plant selections, and intelligent replanting over the years. These include the entrance drive planted as an *allée* of horse chestnuts to remind Miller of the chestnut *allées* he had admired in French gardens when he was a graduate student in the 1930s; the weeping beeches in the front entry and on the terrace on the western side of the living room where they serve the function of exterior draperies; the planting of a glen of redbud trees outside the dining room; the substitution of red maples for the row of sycamores in the *allée* leading to the river; and the installation of willows, in the meadow near the water.

Kiley's cool reinterpretation of the Beaux-Arts French Neoclassical heritage along lines suggested by the architecture of Mies van der Rohe made him a logical partner for the high-style modern architects who received commissions to build prestigious buildings that served as corporate status symbols. His important contributions in this area in the later years of his career illustrate the growing importance of corporations in shaping both the urban and suburban landscape and their financial ability to supersede local governments as providers of attractive public spaces. From General Motors to Pepsico to Disney to Exxon and Time-Life, big companies have played an increasingly large role both directly and indirectly in the devel-

opment of the American landscape. Large institutions such as the Ford Foundation and Lincoln Center, both clients of Kiley's, have adopted the same understated Olympian grandeur as corporations in creating an image through architecture and landscape design

Within the discipline of an abstract geometrical order, Kiley seeks the sensuously grand gesture. Like his contemporary, Lawrence Halprin (see Chapter Fifteen), he is interested in extending the expressive potential of both still and animated water in reflecting pools, fountains, and cascades. His architectural imagination and ability to think boldly in terms of scale and spatial arrangement are qualities that have made him a congenial collaborator with some of the most eminent architects of the twentieth century, including Louis Kahn, Eero Saarinen, I. M. Pei, and Kevin Roche. In Dallas, Texas, he worked with Peter Ker Walker in designing Fountain Place, a large water garden built in conjunction with the Pei firm's Allied Bank Tower (fig. 13.30). Here, he planted bald cypress trees in circular concrete tubs set according to a grid within a broadly stepped cascade, which is further animated by 263 bubbler fountains placed in staggered rows between the trees. The cooling effect and pleasant roar of the sparkling, tree-shaded water, together with a grid of fountain jets that play according to various computer-programmed patterns, have made this corporate gift of public space a much-appreciated popular attraction.

JAMES ROSE'S FUNCTIONALIST AND ZEN APPROACH

James Rose (1910–1991) used a caustic pen and an original and deliberately unconventional eye to challenge established taste and convention. He found a forum for his ideas in the magazine *Pencil Points* (later *Progressive Architecture*) where he coauthored three articles with Kiley and Eckbo and also submitted pieces of his own. The freshness of his opinionated prose and perspective on landscape design won him an instant sympathetic readership, especially among architects. Rose's mission throughout his career was to create an intimate relationship between human

beings, nature, and architecture. This aspiration drew him into a close friendship with Christopher Tunnard. Like the architect Richard Neutra, Rose considered the separation between indoors and outdoors as a series of transparent planes, and his interlocking of exterior and interior forms promoted spatial fusion.

Rose compartmentalized garden space, always with a light hand to allow it visual flow. He did this sometimes with screens of modular wood-framed panels containing a plastic-impregnated wire mesh, sometimes with translucent plastic Japanese shoji screens, sometimes minimally with vertical strings of nylon parachute cord strung along a plane at intervals, sometimes with panels of twisted, slatted bamboo, or sometimes with the slender trunks of white birch trees (fig. 13.31). These screens filtered light and enriched the garden with their own pattern and that of silhouetted tree branches. Overhead, Rose's trellises carried modular grid patterns into the garden, supporting vines and framing the sky. Sometimes these extended horizontal roof lines; at others they acted as freestanding open-air awnings, which were often canted skyward, giving the garden a jaunty angularity. His ground-plane patterns and plant forms combined with those of the vertical and horizontal planes above to create a three-dimensional composition with a combination of spatial definition and ambiguity.

Rose had a craftsman's aesthetic sensibility and a spiritual bent, which he nourished by frequent trips to Japan, and at home, by the practice of Zen Buddhism. The garden was, for him, both a functional space and a place for reverie. For this reason the private garden, not the large-scale landscape, was his chosen métier. With a less extensive practice than either Kiley or Eckbo, Rose's method of approaching each commission was a highly personal one and involved his presence on the site much more than at a drafting table. He liked to shape his landscapes improvisationally, and he often participated in their long-term maintenance. No other modern landscape designer gave as much attention to ground-plane texture as Rose did, and his compositions in gravel, river-worn rocks, flagstones, ground covers, and shrubs are masterful essays in landscape craftsmanship (fig. 13.32).

In 1952, Rose designed his own small house in Ridgewood, New Jersey. He used it as a protest against the subsidiary role the landscape architect was usually assigned by the architect and subdivision developer. In his house, according to Rose, "The landscape is of the house instead of attached to it, and the space is one."[36] We can only speculate on what the appearance of the American suburb might be today if the prescriptions of Rose and Eckbo for site planning and the integration of architecture and landscape in a single design process had been broadly influential.

13.31. Depicted in *Creative Gardens,* this James Rose Tea Garden is captioned as follows: "This fabric of natural and man-made materials, woven in three dimensions, gives one the sense of being within something while still out of doors. Surface: a pattern of brick perforated with grass, pachysandra, day lilies and baby's breath. Sides: translucent shoji in removable panels, white birch stems, and the common grape vine. Ceiling: the trellis, overhanging branches, and the sky."

Below: 13.32. Garden by James Rose, Ridgewood, New Jersey

Society is influenced, but rarely led, by visionaries. The urge to regulate, systematize, and follow is too strong. Legislation creates town building codes, and banks and federally sponsored loan programs create requirements for mortgage financing that stifle deviation from standardized norms. With some exceptions such as James Rouse (1915–1996), the developers who shaped America in the second half of the twentieth century proved to be much less socially minded than the regional planners and landscape architects of the first half, who believed in rational science as a *modus operandi* and industrial technology as a positive force for raising the living standards of society through good engineering and design. The dreams of these idealists were soon deflated by the arrival of a future much less agreeable than the one they had imagined. The media, perhaps the most culturally influential area of corporate power, became a growing influence, urging people toward consumption, and popular entertainment became a mass industry affecting every corner of society. The manufacturers of the private automobile, the vanguard of consumer marketing, proved particularly adept at influencing government decision-making and the authorization of funding for highways. In the late twentieth century, private property as commodity, leisure as lifestyle, and the automobile as the dominant mode of transportation had a profound effect upon landscape, especially in America.

1. For an excellent discussion of the social, political, economic, and cultural forces underlying the 1925 Paris International Exhibition of Modern Decorative and Industrial Arts, see Dorothée Imbert, *The Modernist Garden in France* (New Haven: Yale University Press, 1993), chap. 3. I am indebted to this author for her analysis of the exposition and of the work of several forceful and original French landscape designers of the 1920s and 1930s who honored tradition and simultaneously attempted a radical break with the past.

2. Jean-Claude-Nicolas Forestier, "Les jardins à l'exposition des arts décoratifs," 12 September 1925, p. 526, as quoted in Imbert, op. cit., p. 128.

3. For perceptual differences between painting—a medium that allows the eye to experience optical shifts between the plane of the canvas and a series of ambiguous illusions of depth—and sculpture, architecture, and landscape design—arts in which three-dimensionality is objective—see Imbert, op. cit., pp. 63–68.

4. Fletcher Steele, "New Pioneering in Landscape Design," *Landscape Architecture Quarterly* 20, no. 3 (April 1930), p. 165, as quoted in Imbert, op. cit., p. 27. For Steele's life and career, which I have summarized below, see Robin Karson, *Fletcher Steele, Landscape Architect: An Account of the Gardenmaker's Life, 1885–1971* (New York: Harry N. Abrams, Inc./Sagapress, Inc., 1989).

5. Fletcher Steele, *Design in the Little Garden* (Boston: The Atlantic Monthly Press, 1924), pp. 17–18.

6. *Landscape Architecture* 20 (April 1930): 163–64, as cited in Karson, *Fletcher Steele, Landscape Architect,* p. 159.

7. The quotations in this paragraph are derived from Steele's own descriptions of the Naumkeag Garden as cited in Karson, op. cit., pp. 116–17.

8. "Naumkeag Gardens Develop" (Essay, Library of Congress, May 1947), p. 8, as cited in Karson, op. cit., p. 135.

9. Fletcher Steele letter dated March 27, 1948, Library of Congress, as cited in Karson, op. cit., p. 267.

10. The Becks interviewed Le Corbusier in Paris with the idea of commissioning him to design their house, but they decided that his work was better suited for South America than Millbrook, New York. See Lester Collins, *Innisfree: An American Garden* (New York: Sagapress/Harry N. Abrams, Inc., 1994), p. 3. This book, published posthumously a year after Collins's death, provides an excellent understanding of how two Western collaborators applied East Asian principles of landscape aesthetics to the creation of an American landscape.

11. See Collins, op. cit., pp. 17–20.

12. According to Lance Neckar, "At Harvard he [Tunnard] had the extraordinary opportunity to shape some of the ideas of the principal progenitors of modern design in the postwar era, including his friends Garrett Eckbo, Dan Kiley, and James Rose and his students Lawrence Halprin, Philip Johnson, and Edward Larrabee Barnes." See "Christopher Tunnard: The Garden in the Modern Landscape," *Modern Landscape Architecture: A Critical Review,* ed. Marc Treib (Cambridge, Mass.: MIT Press, 1993), p. 154.

13. *Gardens in the Modern Landscape* (London: The Architectural Press, 1938), p. 81.

14. Ibid., p. 92

15. Tunnard included an illustration of Le Corbusier's Villa Savoye at Poissy in *Gardens in the Modern Landscape* with this quote from the architect: "I shall place this house on columns in a beautiful corner of the countryside; we shall have twenty houses rising above the long grass of a meadow where cattle will continue to graze. Instead of the superfluous and detestable clothing of garden city roads and byways, the effect of which is always to destroy the site, we shall establish a fine arterial system running in concrete through the grass itself, and in the open country. Grass will border the roads; nothing will be disturbed—neither the trees, the flowers, nor the flocks and herds. The dwellers in these houses, drawn hence through love of the life of the countryside, will be able to see it maintained intact from their hanging gardens or from their ample windows. Their domestic lives will be set within a Virgilian dream."

Here Le Corbusier does not consider who will maintain this Virgilian dream or how, as Tunnard is quick to point out, the larger landscape can be organized in relationship with the house to accommodate the functional needs of human beings. Dryly, he wrote, "Few people want to be condemned to languish at a window and exercise exclusively on a roof garden." See Tunnard, op. cit., p. 79.

16. Ibid., p. 107.

17. Ibid., p. 137.

18. Ibid., p. 159.

19. Ibid., p. 161.

20. Soria Cals, *Roberto Burle Marx: Uma fotobiografia* (Rio de Janeiro: Sindicato Nacional dos Editores de Livros, RJ, 1995), p. 157 (translation of Portuguese text accompanying photograph on p. 29).

21. See Walker and Simo, *Invisible Gardens: The Search for Modernism in the American Landscape* (Cambridge, Mass.: The MIT Press, 1994), pp. 64–65 for a discussion of the Surrealist aspect of Burle Marx's work, derived from the recomposition of found objects into haunting compositions.

22. See Lawrence Joseph, "The Garden of Ulysses: Ferdinand Bac, modernism and the afterlife of muth," *Studies in the History of Gardens & Designed Landscapes,* 20:1 (January–March 2000), pp.6–24.

23. Keith Eggener, "Postwar Modernism in Mexico: Luis Barragán's Jardines del Pedregal and the International Discourse on Architecture and Place" in *Journal of the Society of Architectural Historians* 58:2 (June 1999): 125.

24. Joseph Hudnut, dean of the Harvard Graduate School of Design, understandably took exception to such complete reliance on the dramatic potential of site planning as was practiced by Wright. In an essay, "Space and the Modern Garden," reprinted in Christopher Tunnard's *Gardens in the Modern Landscape* (London: The Architectural Press, 1938), he reasoned: "Certainly a harmony between the modern house and its site is more evident when the site, like the house, has escaped both romance and an oppressive formality; but a deep or persuasive unity cannot be attained when one and the other has submitted to a conscious control of form. Therefore I do not despair of gardens which are, like houses, *designed.*"

25. From the text of a 1951 speech by Barragán, "Gardens for Environment: Jardines del Pedregal," printed in *Journal of the A.I.A.* 17 (April 1952), p. 170, as referenced in Eggener, op. cit., p. 127 (note 31). The architectural historian Keith Eggener argues that, in addition to the social convention of walled streets and domestic privacy inherited from Mediterranean antiquity, "El Pedregal's walls and gates, and the guards and guardhouses often placed beside them, evince both a substantial concern for security and a measure of ostentatiousness. Walls, gates, and guards not only protect property but also assert its value, its need for protection. Indeed, the security and exclusiveness of this gated, guarded community were among its major selling points; Barragán's advertising campaign for El Pedregal placed considerable emphasis on these issues and on those design features that addressed them."

26. As quoted in Eggener, op. cit., p. 131

27. *California Gardens: Creating a New Eden* (New York: Abbeville Press, 1994), p. 194.

28. Thomas Church, *Gardens Are for People* (New York: Reinhold Publishing Company, 1955), p. 231.

29. For an excellent description of the tenets of Beaux-Arts landscape style as presented in Hubbard and Kimball's book and Eckbo's opposition as articulated in his book, *Landscape for Living,* see Reuben Rainey, "'Organic Form in the Humanized landscape': Garrett Eckbo's *Landscape for Living*" in *Modern Landscape Architecture: A Critical Review,* ed. Marc Treib (Cambridge, Mass.: The MIT Press, 1993), pp. 180–205.

30. *Garrett Eckbo: Modern Landscapes for Living* (F. W. Dodge Corporation: An Architectural Record Book with Duell, Sloan, & Pearce, 1950), pp. 59–69, 87.

31. Marc Treib characterizes the Barcelona Pavilion as "the true archetype of modern spatial composition." See "Axioms for a Modern Landscape Architecture" in *Modern Landscape Architecture: A Critical Review,* p. 43. Reconstructed because of its significance in the history of modern architecture at the time of the 1992 Olympics held in Barcelona, the original Pavilion stood for a mere six months. However, the inclusion of it in plan and photographs in the Museum of Modern Art's exhibition on *The International Style* organized by Henry-Russell Hitchcock and Philip Johnson in 1932 made it a seminal and widely studied work of modernism.

32. *Landscape for Living* (1950), p. 137.

33. Conversation with Marc Treib anf Dorothée Imbert, as quoted in Treib and Imbert, *Garrett Eckbo: Modern Landscapes for Living,* p. 73.

34. Mies van der Rohe's concept of space was one of a modularly organized continuum of overlapping geometrical planes, which fused Frank Lloyd Wright planning theories with the spatial concepts of the De Stijl painters in Holland, especially Theo van Doesburg and Piet Mondrian. For a sound analysis of such asymmetrical compositional balance, see Gregg Bleam, "The Work of Dan Kiley" in *Modern Landscape Architecture: A Critical Review,* ed. Marc Treib, pp. 230–37. Both Kiley and Eckbo were influenced by Mies's brand of architectural modernism.

35. Gregg Bleam, op. cit., p. 234. As cited by Bleam, this conclusion is supported by Kenneth Frampton, "Notes on Classical and Modern Themes in the Architecture of Mies van der Rohe and Auguste Perret," in *Classical Tradition and the Modern Movement* (Helsinki: Finnish Association of Architects, Museum of Finnish Architecture, Alvar Aalto Museum, 1985), p. 22.

36. Ibid., p. 108.

CHAPTER FOURTEEN

HOME, COMMERCE, AND ENTERTAINMENT: LANDSCAPES OF CONSUMERISM

Consumption, or material self-gratification, is the engine that fuels many modern industrial economies. Consumerism directs much of the course of landscape design today. In addition, the notion of the nuclear family as the primary social unit for child rearing, replacing the extended family, the clan, the tribe, and the state, has resulted in the elevation to new status of the individual home and the plot of land upon which it sits. Indeed, no previous societies have ever focused so attentively as present Western ones upon defining a dedicated spatial realm for families and children. The culture of childhood and the realm of juvenile fantasy have increasingly informed our subject area during the past half century. Jean Piaget (1896–1980) and other child psychologists brought new social awareness of the value and purposes of play in the formation of human personality. This is manifested in the home yard with its swing set and wading pool and in numerous neighborhood parks and playgrounds.

The realization of the American dream of home ownership and the fulfillment of a pioneer spirit that had long been ingrained in the national temperament by settling a new urban frontier, the original Western one having vanished, brought real psychic rewards to millions of citizens. In transforming the middle landscape advocated by Downing and Olmsted in the nineteenth century as an ideal combination of civilization and nature into suburbia—a place replete with both urban amenities and pastoral greenery but increasingly autonomous and independent of the metropolis to which it is only loosely tied—they created a new kind of urbanism that theorists are still attempting to define. The patterns woven by the first weavers of the suburban fabric were far from exemplary as environmentalists, sociologists, and urban planners soon discovered. But for the young families in America at the end of World War II the suburban subdivision was an attractive ready-made cloth, which they gladly bought and soon cut to fit.

If democratic capitalism and the consumer society furthered the American ideal of a suburban realm, this middle landscape was enabled by the automobile. By the second half of the twentieth century, automobile and road engineering interests had been successful in enlarging the scale of the city as a physical entity, while retrofitting old urban streets as arteries for cars and trucks—a detriment to their former function as sociable public space—causing land use patterns to be rearranged in ways that left most people almost completely dependent on motor vehicular transportation. The automobile made it possible for the city to spread beyond all previously urbanized land as new areas became accessible and interconnected by arterial roads and the entire metropolitan mass looped by a circumferential highway. The much shorter journey to work that was accomplished on foot when the city was still a series of multiple-use districts, with commerce and residence side by side, had become extended for middle-class breadwinners in the early twentieth century with the development of streetcar suburbs. Now, new residential neighborhoods spread into the spaces between the radial rail lines as well as into the rural fringe, and old center-city neighborhoods in the United States were abandoned to the poorest members of society. The progressive outward migration related to increasing levels in income, with the wealthiest citizens of the city living farthest from the urban core, is a primarily American phenomenon. In continental European cities, by contrast, prestige still adheres to the urban center.

The great highway building period that ensued in the United States following the Highway Act of 1956 was rationalized as a boon to motorist safety, business accessibility, and civilian security, for with the escalation of the Cold War, government transportation officials made a priority of planning for troop movement and urban evacuation in the event of a nuclear attack. The biggest financial beneficiaries were the developers who bought land and constructed mass-market housing on tracts of real estate close to the new highways and those who financed, built, and rented to com-

14.1. Las Vegas

mercial tenants space in a new kind of retail facility, the suburban shopping center. The success of this new type of retail conglomeration, which led to the development of the shopping mall, was highly instrumental in the disaggregation of the city and the replacement of its old single-core form with the multinucleated regional model with which Americans are familiar today.

In the consumer society, the objects of dream and desire and the objects of industrial manufacture are often the same. Shopping malls are consumerist landscapes by definition, and their developers have been extremely inventive in creating recreational environments for commerce. These challenge older forms of urban design while providing a highly popular type of quasi-public space. In combining recreation with commerce, shopping malls have come increasingly to resemble another landscape form, the theme park.

Disneyland and its successors demonstrate the degree to which theater—a venerable component of garden design—has been subsumed by the fast-growing entertainment industry and how this industry, in turn, has affected landscape design. The popularity of the theme park as a participatory experience in which consumers and "cast members" intermingle in a theatrical setting carefully contrived by "imagineers"—the designers who create landscapes of association based on fairy tales, children's stories, animated cartoons, foreign countries, and heritage ideals—is a twentieth-century cultural phenomenon to ponder. Phenomenal is the degree to which the themes and characters of theme parks have influenced the general public's attitude toward animals, plants, exotic lands, famous sights, and the women and men of history. In this we see the power of the media, another outgrowth of consumer capitalism, for televised images and advertising implant these visions in the minds of old and young, no matter how they trivialize the art and realities that inspired them in the first place. These pervasive images of consumer culture have become as significant perhaps to the present generation as the gods and heroes in the Homeric epics and the tales of Ovid were in other centuries is a cause for wonder.

Yet, verisimilitude compels our admiration. The wizardry of the stage-set environments in theme parks, with their elaborate invisible technological infrastructures, has been augmented with imagery derived from the camera, a machine that has been exerting a profound influence upon the experience of place for a century and a half. That some people prefer theme-park replications to the original models is due in no small part to the large role that various forms of photography have come to have in our lives. We trust the camera as a recorder of "reality," and we easily transfer emotional responses from the actual world around us to the subjects and scenes in photographs.

Photography's role with regard to landscape has several dimensions. A nineteenth-century invention, the stereopticon camera, created three-dimensional "magic lantern" views of famous landscapes for armchair tourists. Then, in the hands of actual tourists, cameras became a means of recording visited landscapes. But today, photography is more than another method for imaging reality. In consumerist democracies of the West, the forces of cinematic narrative appealing to popular sentiment and taste actually propel landscape design. The relationship between theme parks and the movie industry is familial; the art of the Hollywood studio and the movie-set construction technology of the Hollywood back lot fostered Disneyland and its successors. Because of its popularity and commercial success, the thematic landscape is a growing phenomenon, especially in the United States.[1] Now, blurring the distinction between the real and the virtual, entire cities and towns are being "themed." Las Vegas, which markets itself as a family vacation resort as well as the casino capital of the world, is the most conspicuous representative of this trend, having turned its famous strip into a fantastic mélange of other times and other places, both fictional and real—Monte Carlo, Treasure Island, ancient Egypt, imperial Rome, modern New York City (fig. 14.1). Some may find it appropriate that the nation that invented Hollywood should be reinvented by Hollywood in turn.

I. A Home for the Family: The Landscape of Suburbia

The full potential of the automobile to transform life in the United States and other industrial nations in ways that even the visitors to the Futurama exhibit at the 1939 New York World's Fair would not have grasped only began to be realized with the passage by Congress of the 1956 Highway Act. This legislation contributed to the home-building explosion that accounts for suburbia, the wide ring of converging developer subdivisions surrounding major cities that succeeded the carefully planned garden suburbs of the 1920s and the New Deal Greenbelt Towns of the 1930s. The Highway Act authorized a federal Highway Trust Fund with revenues derived from taxes on fuel, tires, and new vehicles of all kinds, as well as a use tax on commercial trucks. The funds were to pay 90 percent of the cost of creating an interstate highway system, with the states paying the remaining 10 percent. The logic behind this extraordinary legislation was as simple as the consequences were far-reaching.

The Landscape of Suburbia: The Early Postwar Years

In the United States, the powers of the federal government were extended during the Great Depression and following World War II in order to stimulate new housing construction and large-scale suburban development by means of two important loan insurance programs—that of the Federal Housing Authority (FHA) and the Veterans Administration (VA). These proved a boon to developers and homeowners alike. The bias in America toward home ownership is still enshrined in the income tax laws by the allowable deduction from gross income of mortgage interest and real estate taxes. Because banks as lenders must assess the financial reliability of mortgage loan applicants, credit qualification is a frequent obstacle to home ownership. The New Dealers who created the Federal Housing Authority in 1934 during the Great Depression did so in order to encourage investment of private capital in the construction industry and thereby stimulate employment within the building trades. Ten years later, the Servicemen's Readjustment Act, or GI Bill as it is popularly known, created the Veterans Administration to ease the transition of military men to civilian society. Because both of these programs made possible minimum down payments of 10 percent or less on the purchase price, young Americans starting their families in the years immediately following World War II flocked to inspect the model homes and thereupon to sign up for purchase in the first tract housing suburbs. They sprang up in metropolitan fringes across the country, from Levittown on Long Island, to Lakewood in California (fig.

14.2. An early photograph of Levittown, Long Island

14.2).[2] Increased affluence combined with widespread status seeking, television's portrayal of suburban middle-class life, and the absence of household servants all stimulated the desire for mechanical conveniences, which had been pent up during the war. This occasioned the birth of the consumer society, and developers were quick to see that furnishing their small, cheaply constructed houses with new household appliances was an important sales asset.

Writing about Lakewood, which was built near the Douglas Aircraft Company and where he still lives in the house his parents bought in 1946, D. J. Waldie describes the sales process:

> The salesmen did not encourage buyers to linger. Husbands and wives selected a floor plan, signed a sales contract, looked at a map of the tract, and accepted the house they were assigned. The salesman got a thirty-five-dollar commission on each sale. In the office, among displays showing construction photographs and sales brochures, the houses may have retreated slightly. If the buyers hesitated, astonished at what they were about to do, the salesman looked past them to the line of other husbands and wives watching their children in the bright light.[3]

The economies of scale, factory methods of construction, relaxation of local building-code standards, small and uniform lot sizes, and simplification of house designs to a few variants upon a basic pattern made possible cheap offering prices for new homes. For developers who agreed to adhere to the FHA standards, the federal programs acted as a tremendous incentive, since the federal mortgage

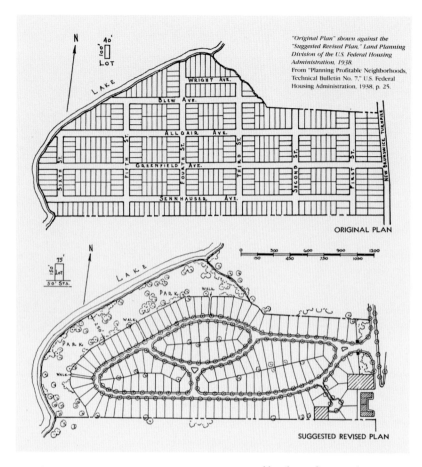

14.3. "Original Plan" and "Suggested Revised Plan," as illustrated in "Planning Profitable Neighborhoods, Technical Bulletin No. 7" by the Land Planning Division of the U.S. Housing Administration, 1938

guarantees encouraged banks to finance their entire costs: acquiring land, installing streets and utilities, and constructing houses. The programs even recommended prototypical subdivision layouts (fig. 14.3). These things accounted for the cookie-cutter look that critics soon began to castigate. The equally harsh judgment that from the air the typical plan of curving streets with their cul-de-sac offshoots resembled a can of worms did not acknowledge that it was derived from highly respected earlier new town planning models. One was Clarence Perry's 1929 hierarchical community-based network of winding local streets, feeder roads, and connecting arterials (see Chapter Twelve). The curvilinear streets were also much simplified versions of nineteenth-century Picturesque principles, which put a premium upon surprise by eliminating corridor views and withholding from sight what was around the bend. At eye level, this strategy may have mitigated the bland sameness of the new houses built on uniform lots, 50 to 60 feet wide and 100 to 120 feet deep with uniform setbacks along blocks 600 to 1300 feet long by 200 to 300 feet wide. A less artificial picturesqueness accrued as trees matured and homeowners set about enclosing garages, building additions to their houses, planting gardens, and otherwise improving their individual piece of the American Dream.

Although developers, in naming their subdivisions, usually included singly or in combination the words *park, wood, valley, hills, lake,* or *meadow,* thereby promoting the concept that the entire community was a park, they did not follow the builders of Radburn in making a green spine the armature of their plan. Such hills and valleys as existed were on the still-rural fringe of the new subdivision or in scraps of natural terrain within it that had been left vacant because they were topographically unsuited for house lots. These were the small paradises in which children played. Waldie remembers the 10-foot-deep, open drainage ditches between Lakewood's neighborhoods as filled with cattails and tadpoles in the spring. He writes, "The ditches attracted boys in packs of four or five, as did any empty lot where there was enough room to dig."[4]

Alfred Levitt, who was trained as an architect, laid out the lots of the Long Island Levittown with their near-identical Cape Cod Colonial houses around a series of "Village Greens," which contained neighborhood shops, a playground, and a swimming pool. But a more plentiful green space was to be found in the continuous lawn strip composed of contiguous front yards, the individual public face each neighboring family presents. Unfenced, these essential emblems for American homeowners of proprietorship, domesticity, and lingering rural values form a greensward that serves as a collectively maintained park. "When I walk to work," writes Waldie, "I walk through a vista that is almost one continuous garden and lawn, broken every fifty feet by a concrete driveway."[5] But the premium put on private space over this community space is evident in the fact that many subdivisions do not have sidewalks. The front porch no longer exists and has been replaced by a patio or deck in back. The phrase "right in your own backyard" denotes proximity, convenience, and the premium put on space dedicated to private family interests. Here, in addition to the swing sets and wading pools that equip innumerable family-scale playgrounds are to be found barbecue grills and various pieces of lawn furniture as well as accoutrements for pets.

Joseph Eichler (1900–1974), a developer from New York who took up residence in the Bay Area in 1940, brought architectural attention to the design of the California version of the suburban dream house. After having rented for three years a house designed by Frank Lloyd Wright in Hillsborough, California, Eichler decided to bring some of Wright's modernist principles to bear on tract house design. He hired Robert Anshen, a young architect, to work for him. The result, as the architectural historian Gwendolyn Wright explains, was that "American residential design crossbred a modernist pedigree with everyday vernacular 'livability.'"[6] The two-car garage is the most prominent feature of the front of an Eichler house, and the small landscaped entry courtyard has floor-to-ceiling, sliding glass doors, which increase its sense of airy openness (fig. 14.4). The open floor plan gave importance to the kitchen with its modern appliances, allowing eye contact between this area and the multipurpose family room, a postwar innovation where children could play indoors, teenagers could listen to phonograph records, and everyone could watch television. Becoming more than shelter, in the postwar years the American home had simultaneously shrunk in interior size and been transformed, climate permitting, into the locus of outdoor living.

Connecting the street with the carport or garage—no longer an ancillary structure in the backyard but now firmly attached to the house—the driveway assumed prominence as a recreational space, being an ideal surface for learning to ride a bicycle or toss a basketball. Cynthia Girling and Kenneth Helphand call this the "most representative of American open spaces" because, "[t]he driveway sits at that juncture between . . . the traditional stability of home, neighborhood, and community, and the modern mobility of the automobile, speed, and travel."[7] Not surprisingly, in Herbert Gans's pioneering study of Levittown, for adolescents, "the commonest gripe is

14.4. Single-family suburban house, California, designed by Joseph Eichler

the shortage of ready transportation, which makes not only facilities but, more important, other teenagers inaccessible."[8] This observation merely underlines the fact that the postwar suburb, being the creature of the automobile and the highway, reinforces the primacy of the automobile as the dominant mode of transportation and maroons its residents if they cannot drive. Because its existence made possible the development of certain new landscape types, it is the indispensable means of access to these places, as is also obvious in an examination of two closely related phenomena: the shopping mall and the theme park.

II. Commerce and Entertainment: Shopping Malls and Theme Parks

The image of the city as a coherent mass with a unitary center—a village green, main plaza, or courthouse square—has been superseded by that of the multinodal metropolis. This urban reconfiguration has been spearheaded by retailing. Indeed, the development of the highway-related shopping *center* was the first step in a process of urban disaggregation and reformation according to a texture that, though more loosely woven, nevertheless has knots of commercial density, retail and entertainment nuclei that serve many of the functions formerly accommodated in the city centers Americans have long referred to as "downtown." Developers with the ability to seize the opportunity presented by the new suburban market —its *auto-mobility* and continually expanding desire for consumer goods of all kinds and in all price ranges, as well as the growing distance to downtown and the heightened parking congestion there—were the primary shapers of this new urban landscape.

From Shopping Center to Shopping Mall

The Levitts soon realized that the convenience stores in their Village Greens on Long Island were losing money to a new regional shopping center on the high-

way, and when they developed the next Levittown in New Jersey, they built a related regional shopping center to draw business from beyond their property's own boundaries. The developers of the postwar shopping centers did not invent this form of retailing clustering but relied on a growing body of experience dating from the 1920s.[9] The pioneer of the first large-scale suburban shopping center, a 250-store shopping village as this type of new development became known, was J. C. Nichols, who developed the Country Club Plaza in Kansas City, Missouri, beginning in 1922 (fig. 14.5). Previously, commercial real estate developers assessed the potential markets implied by areas of suburban population, acquired land for shopping strips, and sold individual properties to businesses. These establishments competed for the driver's attention with boldly scaled frontage signs. Nichols realized that an increasing number of women residing in the affluent Country Club district of Kansas City now drove cars. To attract their business, he created within several contiguous conventional street blocks designed for local traffic an architecturally homogeneous, domestically accented environment with ample parking. Shoppers left their cars in free, landscaped, off-street lots and at the curbside adjacent

14.5. Country Club Plaza, Kansas City, Missouri, the first large-scale shopping center in the United States. 1922

to stores whose tenants were selected on the basis of careful market analysis. Because it was an integrated building complex under a single management, the Country Club Plaza could be built with a unified appearance, and its agreeable neoSpanish Colonial architecture and carefully controlled signs broadcast the message that shopping was enjoyable, even a pleasant recreational pastime.

Other successful early shopping centers included Shaker Square, serving the exclusive Shaker Heights suburb of Cleveland, Ohio. Though catering to the automobile, it was linked by public transit with the major downtown shopping and business complex at Terminal Tower. In contrast to the Tower's skyscraper modernity, the square's neo-Georgian architecture declared the symbiosis between shopping village and upscale residential suburb and defined the center's image as a gateway to genteel domesticity.

Hugh Prather, the developer of Highland Park Village, serving the 1,400-acre, prosperous Highland Park suburb of Dallas, based his plan on the county courthouse square prevalent in Texas, substituting for the traditional edifice of justice a central cluster of shops surrounded by plenty of convenient parking. In focusing inward, Highland Park Village became the first shopping center to turn its back to the street. Seeking architectural distinction, Prather took his designers to California and Spain to gain inspiration for "one of the more sophisticated adaptations of the Spanish Colonial Revival mode for commercial purposes."[10] The ideal of architectural theming as a means of crafting a highly distinctive, if borrowed, sense of place was thus well established in this early shopping center. Although the merchandising goals of Prather's selectively chosen commercial tenants were ambitious, the specialty items they offered did not compete seriously with the array of goods in downtown stores.

Suburban Square in Ardmore, Pennsylvania, on Philadelphia's Main Line began to alter the picture. Developed adjacent to Ardmore's existing commercial area and situated centrally rather than in relation to a specific residential enclave, Suburban Square did not seek a suburban image. Instead of fostering identity in architecturally revivalist, domestically oriented, low-rise stores, it proclaimed its status as an important business center by attracting the first major department store branch to anchor a shopping center. The syndicate of Philadelphia businessmen who planned and developed Suburban Square reserved land from the start for ample off-street parking. They also encouraged the nascent trend of medical and other professionals opening offices close to their patients and clients by including in the Times Building, home of the *Main Line Times,* seven stories of space accommodating fifty offices.

Stymied from widespread multiplication by the Great Depression and World War II, these suburban shopping centers remained the prominent predecessors of the ones that began to proliferate along with the new subdivisions after the war. With less need to focus upon attracting the upper-middle-class patron by then, developers could adopt a more pragmatic and less costly architectural approach. With profitability assured as the suburban exodus mounted, they no longer felt they had to create what Richard Longstreth calls "distinct signifiers of place."[11] Gone was the passing parade of downtown pedestrians. Window dressing, which older department stores had carried to an art form, was no longer considered important because parking lots had replaced urban sidewalks. By the 1950s, when the regional shopping mall—an important centrifugal force in the growth of what is now termed "spread city"—came into being, some of the earlier shopping villages declined. Today, however, in an atmosphere of revaluation of the city and its older suburbs, several have been revitalized.[12]

Planned to serve regional markets rather than specific suburbs, the shopping mall is frequently located at a highway interchange near the metropolitan periphery. Products, like much of suburbia, of the federal highway building program and federal tax laws that assisted developers in depreciating their investments, the malls were often the advance guard of suburbanization. The suburban house, socially focused on the private realm of indoors and backyard, with automobile functions—garage and driveway—prominently assigned to the front where no sidewalks or other signs of accommodation to public life exist, is a domestic form of the shopping mall. The mall's distinguishing feature is a vast perimeter parking area, or several parking areas, ringed by an exterior circu-

14.6. Ice rink, Houston Galleria, Houston, Texas, designed by Hellmuth, Obata and Kassabaum of St. Louis

lation road. Like the the house's little-used front yard, this exterior zone is often landscaped with planting islands of trees and other greenery.

The focus of the mall is its central, auto-free zone of stores. Here, the suburban shopper becomes separated from the necessary conveyance for arrival, a pedestrian like the urban shopper of former times. Pioneered by architect-planner Victor Gruen (1903–1980) in the early 1950s, mall layout soon became formulaic: a "dumbbell" plan consisting of two *magnet stores,* one—usually a high-end-retail department store branch—placed so as to be seen from the highway at one end—and the other—often a national franchise operation selling useful products for the home and garden as well as less expensive items—at the opposite end. In between, on either side of a pedestrian open space meant to evoke the historic New England village green, were small shops selling gifts, books, recordings, cosmetics, and other items that visitors to the magnet stores might purchase on an impulse as they walked by.

During the 1960s, the suburban mall became an enclosed pedestrian space. It also became much more commercial and urban in appearance. Its center no longer harked back to the New England township but instead to the high, glass-vaulted shopping arcades, or *gallerias,* in London, Milan, Paris, and other European cities.[13] In 1956, at Southdale, near Minneapolis, Gruen perfected as a development form what mall trade organizations call EMACs—Enclosed Malls Air-Conditioned. In the enclosed mall's pseudo-urban environment, shoppers presumably needed visual relief from the density of detail where such an abun-

dance of merchandise was on display. Gruen therefore created a central atrium—at Southdale called the Garden Court of Perpetual Spring—a ground-to-roof navelike space filled with light, greenery, flowers, and fountains. Well maintained, such naturalistic oases enhanced the image of the mall as an uplifting place to visit, while also serving the ancillary function of channeling shoppers into side aisles next to the chapel-like shops.

The mall in this new enclosed form became increasingly a place for recreation. Like its European predecessor, the EMAC has three or four levels of shopping ranged around a skylit central court (fig. 14.6). Park benches invite its use as a quasi-public space, and many mall visitors come not necessarily to shop but because they are seeking an attractive, comfortable, safe, yet lively and sociable place where they can pass time. Early-bird mall walkers find security and pleasure in congregating in the morning to jog for fitness along the interior "streets" of many enclosed malls.

Often the mall in its asphalt sea of parking appears as a blight upon the local scenery. But some mall operators have tried to stitch their centers together with the adjacent urban fabric. The Houston Galleria, for instance, was instrumental in creating a business improvement district in the Post Oak district, and this public-private corporation has sponsored new street furniture and public art along the mall's periphery in an effort to acknowledge the Galleria's status as a second downtown, the city's most visited tourist attraction, and the location of its greatest concentration of retail and hotel space and high-

14.7. Streetscape, Post Oak Boulevard, Houston, Texas. The sleek, architect-designed street furniture and scattered elements of public art are gestures that recognize the area's importance as a second downtown.

rise apartment units as well as the site of several office buildings, including the Transco Tower skyscraper (fig. 14.7).

Recreation and entertainment are becoming principal commodities for mall retailers and developers. A symbiotic profitability has been discovered between games, rides, and other theme-park activities and old-fashioned shopping. Retailers call this "adjacent attraction." Like the planners of Rockefeller Center in New York City, the creators of Houston's Galleria placed an ice-skating rink at its center. The 5.3-million-square-foot (1.58-million-square-meter) West Edmondton Mall in Alberta, Canada—the world's largest when it was built between 1981 and 1985—contains 11 department stores, more than 800 small retail shops, 110 restaurants, 13 nightclubs, a 360-room hotel with theme-park decor, 20 movie theaters, a 500,000-square-foot (46,450-square-meter) water park, and other similar-size amusement areas. Scattered throughout this immense bulky tourist destination are many recreational experiences, including a roller coaster, a golf course, and a replica of Christopher Columbus's *Santa Maria*.

West Edmonton Mall's kaleidoscopic juxtaposition of highly dissimilar images exemplifies the extent to which techniques of cinematic montage in the service of consumer psychology now govern design. The same principles account for the current renaissance of the downtown areas in many major American cities where old-fashioned department stores are being replaced by urban malls. The artful blending of stagecraft and retailing also explains the successes of James Rouse, the mall developer who transformed such historic districts as Boston's Quincy Market, New York's South Street Seaport, and Baltimore's Harborplace into "festival markets" for recreational shoppers and tourists. Old town centers from Santa Fe, New Mexico, to Prague and Budapest in Eastern Europe have been similarly reborn as commodified representations of their former states. Cultural institutions, in turn, are becoming more mall-like in the manner in which they present art and science as well as in the way they create museum shops for the display and sale of commercial products associated with their collections and exhibits. To understand the underlying relationships among theme parks, shopping centers, cultural institutions, and historic districts and the trend toward increasing similarity in their market-driven design and management is to understand how the commodification of leisure has become a driving force in the economy and culture of Western societies and, as a consequence, the extent to which much contemporary landscape design has become a combination of entertainment-based narrative and commerce.[14]

THE THEME PARK AS A COMMERCIAL INSTITUTION AND DEFINER OF PLACE

The motion picture industry proved that the visual consumption of stories was a marketable commodity. By making them experiential, too, Walter Elias ("Walt") Disney (1901–1966) pioneered the art of theming, which now pervades much of the built environment and the approach of many professional designers.

The relationship between the theater and the garden has always been strong. The garden as a place of fantasy and spectacle is an old notion. Le Nôtre planned seventeenth-century French gardens as sequences of theatrical spaces, with Molière staging actual plays at Vaux-le-Vicomte and Versailles. Eighteenth-century British aristocrats designed the grounds of their country estates as places of association where scenery and monuments stimulated reflection and reverie in which narrative played a role. But Disney invented the concept of the garden-as-entertainment, a stage set in which the visitor could participate in the action of an already scripted plot.

Disneyland and its successors epitomize the values of twentieth-century media-driven consumer culture and the growing influence of large corporations in American life. They also stand within the tradition of visionary idealism that includes the attempts by nineteenth-century park builders and twentieth-century planners of new towns to improve the industrial city or provide an alternative model to overcome its perceived ills. Disney wished to offer a highly positive and didactic experience that would influence human behavior and engender human happiness. His innovative genius lay in realizing that a fantasy-infused simulated landscape could carry this mission and be successfully mass-marketed in alliance with the emerging medium of television.

Disney understood well the value of market analysis, so in 1953, he hired the Stanford Research Institute to study siting options for a family entertainment park that, like the animated films that he produced, would be "a world of people past and present seen through the eyes of my imagination, a place of warmth and nostalgia, of illusion and color and delight."[15] With the Santa Ana Expressway being planned to connect Los Angles and Burbank with Orange County, his site-selection research team suggested Anaheim, California. There Disney purchased 160 acres of orange groves. Although he knew professional architects in Los Angeles, he was soon convinced that the vision he had—an amalgamation of storybook settings, the locales in the animated movies he produced, and his boyhood hometown of Marceline, Missouri—could only be carried out by people with experience in set design and cinematic scripting techniques. This meant the employees in the Burbank studios of the Walt Disney Company: Herbert Dickens Ryman (1910–1988), the Disney artist and animator who drew the perspective sketches that became the basis upon which the project received the $17 million needed to finance it.

Although Disneyland would have exhilarating rides, it rigorously eschewed association with Coney Island and other beachside amusement parks. The world's fairs of the previous hundred years were instead its close cousins, the expositions where people gathered in large numbers in an atmosphere of pristine cleanliness to view exhibitions that introduced them to new industrial technologies, new products to improve the conditions of contemporary life, and the folkways and crafts of other cultures. Disney's visionary agenda stressed the rosy themes of applied science without negative environmental consequences, history without shame, and human diversity without conflict.

Disney wanted to distract his park's visitors from the problems of the everyday world by giving them a good time and by carrying them backward to his own golden-age vision of the American small town of around 1900, when he was a boy. He also wanted to carry them forward imaginatively to the technologically improved future. His park would therefore be both a period piece and an optimistic scenario of the progressive perfection enabled by modern engineering. Disney *imagineers*—the title he coined for the members of his creative design team—would recapture for the public in Disneyland his delight in model trains and scale models of stage sets nostalgically evoking the vigor and wholesomeness of America's frontier-, rural-, and early-industrial-era past. Today, part of a global corporation, Walt Disney Imagineering, the division that develops the architectural programs and plans the company's theme parks, has a studio team of 1,200 planners, designers, architects, landscape architects, engineers, computer scientists, and construction managers.

Disney, like the developers of shopping malls, understood the value of a manageable, human-scale, auto-free environment that was friendly to pedestrians. His careful segregation of cars and people and the use of tramways and other technologically advanced modes of mass transportation distinguished his approach to planning. The Santa Ana Freeway would carry visitors to Disneyland but not into the area beyond the berm, the tree-planted, miniature-railway-encircled cordon sanitaire that sequestered the park from the parking lot. This berm defining the park's outer periphery also served as a metaphor that was often evoked to distinguish between the "real" world inside—Disney insisted, "Imagination is the model from which reality is created"[16]—and the chaotic, frustrating world outside where social and personal problems could not be banished by imagineering.

Superficially, the plan that originated in Disney's imagination and on Ryman's drawing board was not very different from that of the New York World's Fair of 1939 (fig. 14.8; see figs. 12.35, 12.36). Using a conventional landscape formula combining Beaux-Arts and Picturesque planning principles, Ryman created a strong main axis, a promenade leading to a central hub beyond which rose a focal structure, or "weenie"—slang for "wiener" or hot dog—the spicy if inelegant term coined by Disney to denote the park's visual magnet. From the hub radiated various zones that became progressively more naturalistic in style. Near the berm, some contained irregularly configured lakes. Animators by training, with some background in art and architecture, the imagineers working under Ryman conceived the park as they would a movie, as a series of *cinematic* shots. Led by Disney, they were obsessive about exact replication of detail but cavalier with scale, knowing that optical effects were all-important. As set designers they were familiar with forced perspective—the illusion of height gained by a progressive foreshortening of the vertical dimensions of a facade as it rises from ground level, so that the scale of the second floor is five-eighths that of the first, and so on—a technique they exploited ingeniously at Disneyland.

Perhaps because they were producing the movie

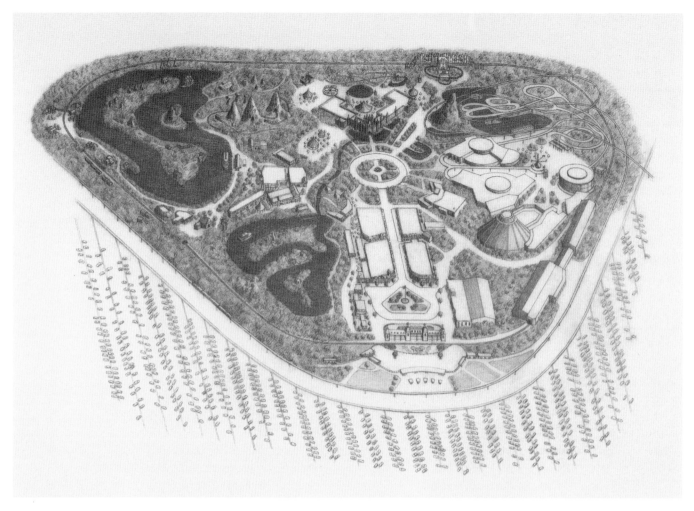

14.8. Disneyland, Anaheim, California, the original theme park designed and developed by Walt Disney, in collaboration with Herb Ryman, John Hench, and the staff of Walt Disney Imagineering. 1954

Sleeping Beauty at the time but also because it seemed to strike just the right note of magic, Disney and his designers chose for their "weenie" Sleeping Beauty's Castle. Forced perspective gives it the illusion of rising in the air, a soaring symbol of the fairy-tale quality they wanted to pervade the park. Forced perspective was also an important design tool in the creation of Main Street, an evocation of Disney's hometown of Marceline, Missouri,[17] with Victorian period architectural detailing derived from Fort Collins, Colorado, because Harper Goff, one of Disney's original imagineers had grown up there. This same effect was later repeated at Walt Disney World, near Orlando, Florida (fig. 14.9). The Western flavor of Main Street is intentional; big city urbanism and the tawdry seediness of Coney Island—Disney had a strong antipathy for both—were associated with the East. "Scene One," as the designers called Main Street, is a mélange of comforting impressions, which are reinforced by Disney's selectively recruited, highly trained employees, referred to as Cast Members. These personnel are encouraged to perfect a cheerful civility modeled on the perceived friendliness of Western small-town folk in bygone days.

Encouraged by Morgan "Bill" Evans, a nurseryman's son and landscape architect whom he hired to work for the company, Disney realized the capability of the California climate to support a widely diverse horticulture—tropical, subtropical, and temperate-climate plants. He also saw how this broad array of plant material might creatively serve as thematic background and how a specimen tree might even assume a starring role in one of his three-dimensional stories where guests and Cast Members mingle in a setting of enhanced nature. Working in collaboration with studio artists, the staff of landscape architects at the Imagineering headquarters in Glendale, California, pay close attention to color (fig. 14.10). In Fantasyland a palette of clear pinks, mauves, and lavender is echoed in the choice of floral and leaf tone. In Adventureland legumes and other plants keyed to a less dreamy, more action-oriented emotional pitch add splashes of vibrant red, flaming orange, and bright yellow to the scene. Disney horticulturists provide plantings with the same high level of maintenance as would a botanical garden because the sight of healthy vegetation serves the company's upbeat happy-ending storytelling mission. This meticulousness is part of a general operational strategy. Instantaneous repair and cleanliness were from the beginning hallmarks of the Disney management style, and the upkeep of its simulated historic places goes far beyond anything the real ones ever enjoyed.

Adept at editing film sequences so that nothing is disjointed and everything flows seamlessly, Disney's imagineers carefully orchestrated the transitions between the park's zones or "lands"—Frontierland, Adventureland, Fantasyland, and Tomorrowland. Everything, even the numerous litter receptacles, is styled in each "land's" particular flavor of place and period. Modernistic streamlining prevails in Tomorrowland; Cambodian, Polynesian, and African motifs in Adventureland; nineteenth-century Western vernacular in Frontierland; and the reigning idioms of fairy tales—Bavarian Picturesque and Old English—in Fantasyland. Yet so skillfully did the designers mediate among these styles that some interfacing buildings, such as the Plaza Pavilion restaurant, display on their opposing facades entirely different architectural detailing. Throughout the park, costumed personnel interact with *guests*—the term the Disney organization prefers to *visitor* or *customer*—entertaining those in line and further blurring the distinction between reality and fantasy. Disney's planners so perfected the art of crowd management that waiting in line became a form of entertainment in the guest-holding areas, where vendors also congregate and where souvenir shops abound. Disneyland's atmosphere of corporate friendliness also makes visitors more susceptible to the messages of industrial sponsors, and several of its original exhibits were financed by major companies. The Disney Company's own image as a kindly corporate wizard is in turn imparted to the corporations allied with it.

Unlike the eighteenth-century English garden with its merely suggestive agenda of poetical association in the landscape, Disneyland and its successors are tightly scripted. To achieve this objective, the original orange groves and all other preexisting features of the Disney property were removed when construction began in 1954. Instead of eliciting "the genius of *the place*" as did the creators of England's great estate parks, Disney imagineers ingeniously replicate *other places*. In order to add some valuable foreign currency to their bank of intellectual capital the company sends them to faraway locales where they absorb impressions and take notes and photographs. But Disney horticulturists do not, for obvious climatic reasons, adhere completely to the vegetative palette of those other environments but instead blend species native to many different countries to gain their desired effects.

Disneyland represents a new kind of American landscape. Built on the premise that an expanding population of automobile-owning families would pay to experience a richly storied environment at once nostalgic and future-oriented, where reality and imag-

ination, fact and fiction, nature and technology were seamlessly blended and enhanced through entertainment, it launched the concept of the park as a commercial venture, something quite different from the park as a public trust, free to all. In this it was, as we have already remarked, akin to world's fairs, which were also built with corporate participation as thematic, commercial ventures that aimed to entertain and uplift a mass audience.

If the theme park is seen as a hybrid landscape derived from the world's fair, a nineteenth-century creation, and cinema and television, which have exerted a profound influence on all facets of culture since the second half of the twentieth century, it can also be viewed as influential in its own right. The treatment of history as narrative capable of stage-set explication is a theme-park strategy that has been carried over into the preservation of historic towns and old urban centers. In 1856, with prescient horror John Ruskin wrote in *Modern Painters, Volume IV* of the transformation he foresaw at Lucerne, Switzerland:

14.9. Main Street, Magic Kingdom, Walt Disney World, Orlando, Florida, designed by Walt Disney Imagineering as a replication of Main Street at Disneyland, Anaheim, California

14.10. Flower beds, EPCOT, Walt Disney World, Orlando, Florida

"Lucerne consisting of a row of symmetrical hotels around the foot of the lake, its old bridges destroyed, an iron one built over the Reuss, and an acacia promenade carried along the lake-shore, with a German band playing under a Chinese temple at the end of it, and the enlightened travelers, representatives of European civilization, performing before the Alps, in each afternoon summer sunlight, in their modern manner, the Dance of Death."[18] One shudders to imagine what Ruskin might write about Lucerne today along with many other quaint old European towns whose natural picturesqueness has been self-consciously deployed in the interest of mass tourism, a strategy attended by advertising and marketing techniques he certainly never dreamed of.

In 1921, in "The Second Coming," the Irish poet William Butler Yeats lamented, "Things fall apart; the centre cannot hold; / Mere anarchy is loosed upon the world."[19] In a terrible century when old certainties about the existence of a God-ordained world order were challenged and Romantic intimations of Nature's inherent divinity waned, it is perhaps understandable that the seat of moral philosophy as cultural matrix would be superseded by mere storytelling, a theatrics of past and place in the interest of identity and present pleasure. Without denying that mass tourism and the theming of historic places has certain social and educational benefits, we should also recognize that narrative place-making is part of a pro-

foundly unsettling cultural pattern in which concepts of highly localized, particularized place are being replaced by a sense of universalized, instantaneously accessible, placeless "placeness." Thus, place is treated patronizingly as something easily replicable and fungible, and the unique qualities of particular places are curiously devalued even as they are being celebrated. This cultural bias away from place-making based upon ideological representation is symptomatic of the present Western world-view in which historical phenomena, especially those related to ethnicity and ethnic heritage, are signifiers of a multicultural perspective that has become a cultural value in its own right.

In pointing out the trend toward landscape "theming," we must not overlook the fact that preservationism also embraces a genuine reverence for important relics of the past that lies deeper than the exploitation of history as thematic entertainment, commercial asset, or political statement. Allied with the desire to preserve authentic landmarks is the awareness that the conservation of natural areas is vital both to planetary health and human happiness. In the face of the ease of mimesis in the new Information Age and the specter of increased wholesale destruction of "first nature" in the continuing Machine Age, we must now attempt to understand what landscape designers and artists have done in recent years as preservationists, conservationists, and creators of metaphorically meaningful Earthworks.

1. It will be recalled (see Chap. 4, note 10) that a given landscape can belong to one or more of three realms: first nature (wilderness), second nature (cultivated fields), and third nature (the garden as nature perfected and the representation through art of certain cultural ideas and ideals). We might provisionally term "fourth nature" a concept that recognizes the machine not as an alien intruder in the garden ("third nature") but rather as a commonplace adjunct to all nature, an often integral and expressive part of its fabric and, with the advent of Internet technology, the means of creating a new spatial realm independent of the material, physical world. Whether one takes a critical or neutral position about this, technology's penetration of the humanized landscape, which now encompasses even remote parts of the earth, is deep and irreversible.

Machinery in the form of automata and other kinds of operational infrastructure has long been at home in the garden, agriculture in the industrialized countries is almost wholly dependent upon mechanization, and even wilderness is impinged upon at every turn by technology. But the notion posited here of a "fourth nature" encompasses a partnership that recognizes more fully the position that the machine and technology have come to occupy within the human psyche, and their role in animating landscape design.

2. A body of sociological and historical literature has grown up documenting the three Levittowns in New York, New Jersey, and Pennsylvania. The instant popularity of the $7,000, 750-square-foot, four-room Cape Cod houses — predecessor to the "Rancher" and "Country Clubber" lines — the manner in which Abraham Levitt and his sons William and Alfred introduced factory management techniques and technological innovations to the construction industry, and the ways in which homeown-

ers modified their homes to meet their changing personal circumstances have been treated by Barbara Kelly in *Expanding the American Dream: Building and Rebuilding Levittown* (1993). The sociologist and city planner Herbert Gans lived in Levittown, New Jersey, for two years at its inception in 1958, and he chronicled the life and politics of that community in *The Levittowners; Ways of Life and Politics in a New Suburban Community* (New York: Pantheon Books, 1969). Kenneth Jackson's *Crabgrass Frontier: the Suburbanization of the United States* (New York: Oxford University Press, 1985) has a section on Levittown as does *Yard, Street, Park: The Design of Suburban Open Space* by Cynthia L. Girling and Kenneth I. Helphand. Lakewood, an early and less famous working-class suburb built on a grid plan, rather than the FHA-recommended curvilinear layout, has been rendered as an historical phenomenon and place resonant with human memory by Donald J. Waldie, a lifelong resident and the author of *Holy Land* (New York: W. W. Norton & Company, 1996).

3. *Holy Land,* pp. 36–37.

4. Ibid., p. 40.

5. Ibid., p. 59.

6. Gwendolyn Wright, *New York Times,* Sunday, February 7, 1999, Section 2, p. 37.

7. Cynthia L. Girling and Kenneth I. Helphand, *Yard, Street, Park,* p. 30.

8. Herbert Gans, *The Levittowners* (1967), p. 207.

9. See Richard Longstreth, "The Diffusion of the Community Shopping Center Concept during the Interwar Decades," *Journal of the Society of Architectural Historians,* September 1997, pp. 268–93.

10. Ibid., p. 278.

11. Ibid., p. 289.

12. For a good discussion of the evolution of the pedestrian mall and other American "retail realms," see Peter G. Rowe, *Making*

a Middle Landscape (Cambridge, Mass.: MIT Press, 1991), chap. 4, pp. 109–47.

13. See Walter Benjamin, *The Arcades Project (Das Passagen-Werk,* ed. Rolf Tiedemann, 1982), trans. Howard Eiland and Kevin McLaughlin (Cambridge, Mass.: The Belknap Press of Harvard University Press, 1999) for a discussion of the nineteenth-century French arcades, progenitors of the department store, which the author uses as a metaphorical device in developing his observations on modernity.

14. For the mall as an all-pervasive contemporary cultural phenomenon, see Margaret Crawford, "The World in a Shopping Mall," *Variations on a Theme Park,* ed. Michael Sorkin (New York: The Noonday Press, 1992).

15. As quoted in Beth Dunlop, *Building the Dream: The Art of Disney Architecture* (New York: Harry N. Abrams, Inc., 1996), p. 25.

16. Ibid., p. 14.

17. According to a *New York Times* article of October 15, 1998, "locals [in Marceline] still point out the garbage dump — a former slag pit outside Disney's bedroom window that he commemorated as Magic Mountain," one of Disneyland's themed roller-coaster rides.

18. Quoted within the caption text for "Lucerne from the Lake" (1845), by Joseph Mallord William Turner (1775–1851), in the exhibition "Ruskin's Italy, Ruskin's England" at the Pierpont Morgan Library, September 28, 2000–January 7, 2001. Ruskin had commissioned this watercolor but sold it in 1865, probably in part because he wanted to be no longer reminded of the Swiss Alpine village's alteration since he had first encountered it as a young man.

19. William Butler Yeats, "The Second Coming," *Michael Roberts and the Dancer* in *The Collected Works of W. B. Yeats: Volume I, The Poems,* rev. ed. (New York: Macmillan Publishing Company, 1983), p. 187.

CHAPTER FIFTEEN

HOLDING ON AND LETTING GROW: LANDSCAPE AS PRESERVATION, CONSERVATION, ART, SPORT, AND THEORY

The rapidity of change in the designed landscape is an important by-product of modernity. The accelerating powers of the Late Machine Age and the new Information Age have gained tremendous force as the fast-paced and continually evolving alliance of science and technology has assumed a position of extraordinary cultural dominance in contemporary society. This has caused the meaning of space and time to simultaneously expand and contract. Even as we contemplate travel to the outer reaches of our universe, contemporary cosmology offers only the most contingent explanation of our place within its framework. Because of these things, everything appears to be mutable. Increasingly, place appears to be in flux.

Just as modern physics has unseated old cosmological verities, proving that outer space is an indeterminate galactic sprawl, so too have the centrifugal forces that once constellated suburbs within the orbit of major urban centers been superseded by newer technologies that make even so-called Edge Cities edgeless, part of a patterning of amorphous human settlement never before seen. Like a mutating organism, this kind of sprawling urbanism is part of the unending process of landscape transformation.

Industrial technology has created within the span of a single century an entirely new landscape of electric power grids, continent-spanning highways, and skyscraper cities that would seem unbelievable to a visitor from the not-too-distant past. The modern regional city—a loose-knit urban agglomerate containing airports, expressways, a vast network of streets and corresponding pattern of lights and neon signs, and air-conditioned high-rise commercial buildings set in a sea of suburban homes and shopping centers—is still a recent phenomenon. The passenger elevator, water mains, and pipes for the delivery of hot and cold running water, the flush toilet—all these developments that we now take for granted are minor when compared with the way technology has revolutionized agriculture and gathered up entire populations from

the land and enfolded them into the city. Urbanism has so pervaded the rural landscape that the metaphor of "the machine in the garden," as analyzed by Leo Marx from a literary perspective in his book of that title, can now be inverted; the quintessential *rus in urbe,* Central Park, could be called "the garden in the machine" that is New York City, the heart of the Atlantic seaboard megalopolis, which extends from Boston to Washington, D.C.

Even where suburbanization has not occurred, farming as an economic mainstay and means of individual family livelihood has all but disappeared as industrial technology has transformed food production and efficient transportation systems have enabled national and global shipments of perishable commodities. Rural land, much of it reverting to second growth, is valued more as scenery than as cropland or pasture. Local farming, where it still exists, has become either marginal or a specialized enterprise catering to an upscale market. A rural residence no longer implies an agrarian occupation or outlook as increasingly for many people residential location is becoming a matter of personal choice.

Corporate franchises have assisted suburban developers in the colonization of regional space. Everywhere the forces of global capitalism are at work. Powered by mass marketing and advertising, they are creating a universal culture, making national and regional identities less distinctive even as growing numbers of tourists travel to remote places in search of *local* color.

Centripetal as well as centrifugal forces are at work. As cities in America and elsewhere begin to reverse their recent decades of decline with renewed capital investment in their core areas and the residential return of retirement couples and young professionals, their attractiveness as places to live as well as their role as tourist destinations and entertainment centers is increasing. Thus we see at the beginning of the twenty-first century a transformation of the city not by governmental planning, such as was sought by visionaries at the beginning of the previous century, but rather by free enterprise. No longer centers of manufacturing and trade, some cities are promoting themselves in terms of the service economy and a more vibrant lifestyle than can be found in the suburbs. Many are reconfiguring industrial waterfronts as promenades lined with restaurants, sports facilities, and outdoor festival spaces; retrofitting commercial real estate with mall-style stores and theaters; turning industrial buildings into loft apartments, shops, artists' studios and galleries; and reclaiming abandoned rail and canal rights-of-way as jogging and bike trails. Cultural centers, entertainment complexes, and arenas for spectator sports are high on almost every contemporary urban agenda. These things, together with electronic-game arcades, health clubs, tennis centers, and other fitness and recreational facilities, are making cities places that are increasingly dedicated to personal gratification.

In addition, with a sense of entitlement to recreational benefits implicit in the democratic values of Western industrial countries and Japan, leisure continues to give rise to new land uses and landscape designs, as evidenced by the construction of golf courses in many countries and climates, even desert ones, because of the phenomenal latter-day popularity of an obscure sport that originated on the links lands of estuarial Scotland in the fifteenth century. Thus, ironically, in accommodating new forms of pleasure, the metropolis, which has so urbanized its surrounding rural landscape that its natural environs have all but disappeared, is itself becoming more parklike in character.

Photography's relationship to landscape, discussed in the previous chapter, grows apace. As a genre, landscape photography stimulates an appreciation of the poetics of place and builds archives that register the appearance and uses of places through time. Today historical photographs of landscapes and cityscapes provide a valuable record of their former appearance, assisting preservationists and educating the public. Aerial photography is an important tool for the cultural geographer's reading of the vernacular landscape. It has made commonplace the *synoptic* vision that Patrick Geddes advocated from his Outlook Tower—that is, seeing cities and their regional landscapes entire in a single panoramic bird's-eye view that reveals overall structure while eliminating from sight close-range detail and disorder. Further, photography is the indispensable means whereby artists of Earthworks or Conceptual pieces of a temporary nature document and gain recognition of their work.

In addition, photography has altered the way in which we read the city. Film has made us comfortable with *montage,* choosing relevant fragments from a plethora of visual stimuli and reassembling them into a coherent personal imagery and narrative that is both sensory and symbolic. Urbanites are all film editors to a degree; understanding the metropolis and feeling at home in its impersonal immensity would be difficult without this strategy of composite conceptualization. An important means of distraction from everyday life, film has become a contemporary form of *flânerie,* the voyeuristic pursuit of the everyday dramas of the metropolis. Mental mapping of the city is, as urban design analyst Kevin Lynch taught, a means of parsing it through a process of personal landmarking.[1] Notable architecture and important public places—as well as the locations of establishments that cater to our personal needs—become geographies of the mind. As cities grow increasingly vast and diffuse, this imagistic form of perception is the only way in which we are able to make sense of our surroundings. Urban public space has, like films and photomontage, become for deconstructivist philosophers such as Jacques Derrida (b. 1930) an impersonal vessel for multiple, simultaneous, and sequential personal meanings.

The incomprehensibility of the modern city and its suburbs is mitigated by networks of communication and transportation—newspapers, radio and television broadcasting, bus and subway routes. We grasp the city in terms of these lines of movement and channels of information, media for a miscellany of messages as well as the means of navigating the metropolis. Photography in the form of advertising saturates these networks just as it dominates prominent public spaces where there is a large flow of traffic. We have become comfortable with our dichotomous existence, at home physically in front of the television set and at the same time mentally in Bangladesh where disaster has struck or at the scene of a crime in another part of our own city, courtesy of the news services' roving video crews.[2] We swim in a sea of visual stimuli, and increasingly what we focus upon most intently is not our visible surroundings but the mental images evoked by representations of another reality elsewhere.

With the commodification of urban life and culture, photography has played a significant role in eroticizing the public environment. Libidinal stimuli proliferate as ads on bus shelters, billboards, and movie marquees. With its rivers of rippling neon and moving car lights, the spatially ambiguous nocturnal city can assume a fantastic, surreal aspect catering to the dreams and desires that photography has projected so alluringly on the movie screen and on the street. By both night and day, shop windows proclaim the sexualization of the urban environment as well as the increasingly public face of pornography. Former cityscapes of stone and brick and steel and glass are being transformed into the scenery of signs as virtuality overwhelms reality.

The city as an arena of human endeavor, community, and pleasure persists in spite of ugliness, suburban sprawl, and the ravaging effect of the automobile upon its physical fabric and the experience of place within it. Shopping as a form of entertainment is a hallmark of the consumer society, and even in the face of electronic commerce and catalogue merchandising, people still gravitate to Fifth Avenue, Wilshire Boulevard, and Michigan Avenue as well as the mall. Today the city of smokestack factories has given way to the city of commingled commerce and recreation.

And yet there is a sense of malaise and loss. The commodification of space and the ease with which nature and the built environment can be altered with heavy earthmoving and construction equipment have made the human bond with nature appear tenuous and the tie with the past seem fragile. Just as many of the mighty monuments intended for the ages now lie in ruins, so, too, are the architectural wonders of one generation torn down by the next. The commitment to create public places that express the values of society has waned. Municipal governments in the United States are no longer able to sustain the parks they built only a century ago and must depend upon varying degrees of private citizen initiative to restore and help maintain them. Clearly, the notion that buildings and landscapes have any real permanence other than what we provide through repeated acts of maintenance and preservation is wishful thinking.

Many people fear that the Faustian forces that have propelled modernity may be careening out of control. Humanity's relationship with nature has been thoroughly inverted. Having gained the technological power Goethe foretold in *Faust, Part II* and behaving no longer as nature's subjects, humans have acted ruthlessly, poisoned air and water, destroyed forests and wetlands, and caused many wild species to decline or become extinct. Because of this, contemporary society can now look back with a degree of horror on the nineteenth- and twentieth-century belief in environmental engineering solely for human ends. Gone is the optimism and belief in technology as a worthy partner of nature as expressed by proponents of modernism such as Benton MacKaye, Christopher Tunnard, and Garrett Eckbo (see Chapters Twelve and Thirteen). Instead, the environmental movement, with its wide-ranging and sometimes intently focused mission of of planetary damage control, has gathered broad support within industrial nations since the 1970s.

Like wilderness, historic landscapes exist on sufferance; some are protected by legislation but remain vulnerable to encroachment and destruction by economic and political forces. Especially in America, where the citizenry has profligately exploited land and a mobile road culture has been a forceful determinant of land use, many once-handsome towns are both rammed through and rimmed by highways fringed with gas stations, fast-food franchise establishments, and other commercial operations with signs aggressively sized and illuminated to catch the eye of the rapidly moving motorist.

This willful eradication of much historic fabric in the twentieth century by transportation engineers and "urban renewal" planners has brutalized cities to a far greater degree than Haussmann did nineteenth-century Paris. Modernism's radical, intentional disregard for history created a palpable discontinuity with the past. In reaction, there arose a well-supported belief that traditional forms of architecture and urbanism are endangered. This helps account for the high regard in which landmark designation and preservation are held today.

But just as environmental stewardship inevitably turns nature into the worthy ward of humanity, preservation of the built environment, an entirely laudable and overdue effort, has come to a similarly patronizing position. Formerly, we created monuments as symbols honoring a moral contract that present and future generations hold with the values represented by past heroes. This has succumbed to a fascination with history as a means of experiencing through architecture and artifacts the social and economic practices and lost craft skills of pretechnological times. While dependent upon automobile transportation and the modern technological service infrastructure that makes tourism possible, Colonial Williamsburg and its counterparts ably serve this purpose. Guides provide interpretive narratives that satisfy people's desire to sample vicariously a comfortable facsimile of life in bygone days. Theme parks also simulate past environments for the same reasons, and today some historic small towns and urban centers are distinguished from these

only by virtue of occupying an authentically historic site.

Reaction to the architecturally bland, commercially ingratiating, diffuse, and chaotic landscape of late-twentieth-century America, coupled with a profound questioning of the established order of society and the discrediting of the symbolical value of traditional monuments, provided the context for a Conceptual art that engaged viewers in considerations of entropy. Unlike theme-park developers who create a familiar product aimed at the mass consumer, the artists who create a novel poetics of place with large-scale transformations of the landscape do so in reaction to the values of the consumer society and what they perceive as the commodification of art. Implicit in their art is an attitude toward time in which "both past and future are placed into an objective present."[3] The Earthworks movement pioneered by Robert Smithson and a group of fellow artists, who positioned themselves in opposition to traditional modes of artistic expression and the institutional framework for displaying art, created a new kind of anti-monumental, monumental art that was "not built for the ages, but rather against the ages."[4] Within the context of a consumer society surfeited with banal products, Smithson and other Earthworks artists, like an earlier generation of Surrealist artists, saw denatured and dehumanized emptiness—"a 'City of the Future' made of null structures and surfaces, [which] performs no natural function [but] simply exists between mind and matter, detached from both, representing neither"[5]—as a metaphorically appropriate expression. In their work they fostered the spirit found in the literature of Latin American Magic Realists such as Jorge Luis Borges. They often sought sites for their projects in desert environments where, using heavy earthmoving equipment, they constructed, on a similar scale and often with the same cosmological relationship between earth and sky, forms like the mounds and other earthworks found in prehistoric ritual centers.

Today, we find an orientation toward the psychological and the empirical in contemporary Western thought and life. Intellectual focus is upon exegesis and fact collection. Contemporary Western culture, lacking an overarching, society-embracing religious or ideological construct, is obsessed with history and historical revisionism. It places emphasis upon personal experience, individual rights, and the self. Along with diaspora populations attempting to replicate old folkways and familiar environments, indigenous groups threatened by the rapid transformation of the familiar into the strange cling to traditional forms as a means of maintaining self-recognition and personal esteem. As cultural geographer David Lowenthal posits, because the contemporary world is beset with many ills and uncertainties, people "revert to ancestral legacies. As hopes of progress fade, heritage consoles us with tradition."[6] Our challenge today is to safeguard the future by turning our understanding of the ephemeral nature of place to positive account, making good new spaces by preserving some good old places while daring to trust our capacity to create anew. Our success will depend upon our skill and luck in achieving environments that incorporate in their design a more perfect understanding of ecological processes and the rightful role of history and nature in human life than is now the case.

I. Preserving the Past: Place as Heritage, Identity, Tourist Landscape, and New Urbanist Community

Landscape preservation is the process of investing certain portions of environment, both designed spaces and vernacular places, with historical meaning, aesthetic value, and symbolical intent. Because all built things and created artifacts alter and deteriorate over time, preservation almost invariably implies restoration. If what is preserved and restored embodies sufficient significance, beauty, and mythic value to serve as cultural heritage in a more universal sense, broadscale reproduction and replication of the original historic forms in other contexts commonly occurs.

Preservation as Cultural Heritage

The Pennsylvania State Building at the World's Columbian Exposition of 1893 in Chicago was a facsimile of Independence Hall in Philadelphia, or rather an evocation of it, the replica being altered in scale and architectural program. Along with several other state buildings erected at the fair honoring (one year late) the four-hundredth anniversary of Columbus's landfall in America and, by association the Founders of the republic, it helped further the Colonial Revival that had been sparked by the Centennial Exposition of 1876 in Philadelphia. The Colonial Revival style was subsequently disseminated in tandem with the Neoclassical Beaux-Arts style, which was prominently featured in the monumental white buildings around Daniel Burnham's Court of Honor (see fig. 9.56). The iconic and narrative value of landmark reproductions of Independence Hall and the entire design vocabulary of the Colonial Revival is obvious; the relatively brief history of the United States is attractively grounded in the myth it embodies of the simple refinement of an industrious, freedom-loving people. It is not surprising therefore to find many echoes of Independence Hall, Mount Vernon, and other shrines of liberty and national foundation in the pseudohistoric architecture of the present. It is abundantly clear, too, why in Disney's Magic Kingdom, where the energetic wholesomeness of America and its people is the paramount message of the entire theme park, that there should be a mint-condition reproduction of Independence Hall (fig. 15.1).

Historic preservation's role in signaling present values helps account for the persistence of "the styles" in spite of Modernism's polemic against them. Like the view into an endlessly self-reflecting set of mirrors, these imitations of the past are often imitations of other earlier imitations of the past, and so on, a chainlike process in which old forms are continually reinvested with new meaning as present ideals are associated with past eras. Purged of political rancor and ordinary misery, the landscapes that project the mystique of former ages—whether ancient Greece or colonial America—retain their hold on the human imagination, becoming totems of both status and ideology.

But heritage icons do not tap the more personal reservoirs of memory. Kevin Lynch (1918–1984), an influential teacher, environmental design theorist, and thoughtful writer on the subject of place has suggested that "we might begin to commemorate the histories of ordinary people in ordinary places [inasmuch as] local, intimate time has a much more powerful meaning for us than the illustrious time of national monuments."[7] Lynch was interested in transcending stasis, the "preserved-in-amber" quality of so much historic preservation. A more dynamic model of preservation that included the evidence of time—the ebb and flow of events across a particular space—would encode into cherished spaces notations of change; it would commemorate death and demise as well as birth and creation. Lynch's radical-sounding idea was "to conserve *and* to destroy the physical environment so as to support and to enrich the sense of time held by the very people that use it."[8]

Dolores Hayden, professor of Architecture, Urbanism, and American Studies at Yale University, shares Lynch's concern to discover strategies for investing ordinary places with commemorative value as a means of connecting the lives of ordinary people to their immediate surroundings. Hayden worked

15.1. Independence Hall, Magic Kingdom, Walt Disney World, Orlando Florida

over a period of eight years "to situate women's history and ethnic history in downtown [Los Angeles], in public places, through experimental, collaborative projects by historians, designers, and artists."[9] The efforts of Hayden and others have been helped by a changing cultural climate that seeks, however imperfectly at times, to respect equally the contributions to society of both sexes and to honor the heroines and heroes of many different ethnic backgrounds. The stubborn fact remains that much preservation sentiment adheres especially to those outstanding individual buildings, cityscapes, and landscapes where substantial past investment of money and design talent was made by people who were prominent in their time. In addition, despite a contemporary disinclination toward heroic sentiment and religious and patriotic public monuments, some of the ideals and values of the past that are expressed in historically preserved landscapes often continue to hold important symbolical meaning for people today.

Closely allied with preservation as a means of assigning commemorative value to the built environment, conservation is the protection of natural areas from despoliation by human activity that harms essential qualities of place and the habitats of other species. Both preservation and conservation emerged as important causes in the second part of the nineteenth century. Since the 1960s—a period of widespread social and political change fostering populism and democratic empowerment—recognition of tremendous population growth and the dire consequences of rampant development and unchecked industrial pollution have given impetus to organized movements that continue to advance the related causes of preservation and conservation.

Although conservation groups often have an anti-urban bias and are therefore indifferent to issues regarding the design of cities, both forces—preservation and conservation—are essential to a landscape ethic that values the environment as a continuum in which nature is rightly perceived as being everywhere, in the densest urban neighborhoods as well as in the wilderness. To achieve a viable landscape ethic based on this integrated perspective it is also necessary to accept and help shape new industrial development, the mainstay of most modern economies and the means of sustaining decent living standards among the masses. There is hope that the reportorial power of new global information systems and the management capabilities made possible by computer technology and the Internet will assist in creating this necessary ethic of responsible total planetary stewardship. Our task here is to advocate that outcome as we examine how preservation and conservation have affected landscape as a place-making enterprise.

PRESERVATION AS CULTURAL IDENTITY

Cultures in transition are pulled in two directions, enthusiastically toward the future and nostalgically toward the past. Especially in times of great technological change, economic stress, and social dislocation, people entertain fantasies of recovering the past, a time when they imagine that life was simpler and more rewarding, craftskills were honest, people were prosperous, and communities lived in harmony. Although this is a thoroughly edited version of history, the trappings of the past provide useful symbols for the present. The artifacts, architecture, and landscapes of a bygone era are invested with value and meaning, becoming the delight of historians and connoisseurs as well as the icons of embattled gentility. There is a moral dimension and educative element to this process, which seeks to make reverence for ancestral forms and older lifeways a rallying point around which values of nation and community can cohere.

The New England town, whose origins we examined in Chapter Six, reached its apogee between 1780 and 1830, during America's early industrial age.[10] Nestled in hilly and mountainous terrain, most New England towns were subsequently bypassed by economic development, becoming depopulated backwaters as railroads sought more accessible routes and extended farther west, causing emigration to larger industrial centers and richer agricultural lands. But by the middle of the nineteenth century, wealthy people from New York and Boston began to establish themselves in summer colonies in Stockbridge, Massachusetts, and other towns of the Berkshires as well as elsewhere. These affluent part-time citizens helped form Village Improvement Societies for the purpose of planting trees along the towns' principal thoroughfares and transforming into grassy, parklike picturesqueness their central commons, which had been pastures in Puritan times and remained mostly barren, utilitarian, workaday spaces until this landscaping was undertaken.

During his brief but influential career, Andrew Jackson Downing was an early proselytizer for the beautification of towns and villages in this way. In Downing's time, the mid-nineteenth century, houses were adorned with brackets and painted in then-fashionable russet browns and other earth-tone colors. But following the Centennial of 1876, as the country began its race toward large-scale industrialization, the early preservationists who were tastemakers within these venerable communities—an alliance of summer residents and well-to-do natives who shared the same Anglo-Saxon ethnic origins—sought to connect themselves ideologically and symbolically with the nation's beginnings by adopting a more chaste, though elegant, architecture style harking back to the colonial and federal periods. In Litchfield, Connecticut, for instance, residents reproduced Colonial-style houses, which they painted white, although the original models were mostly unpainted, with shutters and trim of handsomely contrasting black or dark green. Outbuildings, barns, and other unprepossessing rural paraphernalia that had once surrounded the actual colonial houses were edited out of the restoration program. To commemorate the nation's Centennial, Litchfield's Village Improvement Society planted regularly spaced elm trees, whose overarching branches soon canopied the main street. In this way, Litchfield, along with Sharon, Stockbridge, and other early examples of gentrification throughout New England projected a composite image of an earlier America, a place that was gracious, green, white, and steepled.

There was an escapist element in this kind of historic preservation, a flight from the problems of the swelling industrial cities with their diverse immigrant populations. There was an element of snobbery, too; the Colonial theme expressed the assertion of primacy on the part of the old guard, a means of securing status and respect within the rapidly changing society. Beneath its veneer of republican virtue and communal decorum, inevitable tensions arose between those mostly well-to-do residents with incomes often derived from industrial enterprises elsewhere and local townspeople who valued historical ambiance less than economic development.

The re-created New England town assumed iconic status in the imaginations of many Americans, becoming a symbol of the prosperous, homogeneous, nuclear community of individuals living in a state of friendly symbiosis. Its architectural forms served as a common vocabulary employed by developers of early malls and subdivisions, as we have seen in our discussion of Levittown with its Cape Cod Colonial houses built around a series of "Village Greens." Appropriated by hotel chains and corporate franchises, the Colonial Revival style became a ubiquitous language, a means of fostering consumer trust by linking particular commercial corporations with patriotic sentiment.

The same forces that stimulated the preservation movement in New England promoted citizen efforts to save historic landscapes in the Old South and other parts of the country. Often these were led by women, many of whom belonged to genealogically oriented organizations such as the Colonial Dames or the Daughters of the Texas Republic (preservers and custodians of the Alamo). In 1931, Charleston, South Carolina, passed the first permanent design-review ordinance, mandating that private property owners within the designated historic area submit proposed alteration schemes for approval.

Enthusiasm for colonial heritage extended to other than its Anglo-Saxon Protestant forms. In California, New Mexico, Texas, and Florida, Anglo-Americans appropriated a Spanish Colonial design idiom, which they romanticized as the Mission Style, while residents in Louisiana looked appreciatively toward the residue of a French Colonial past. By the mid-1950s, about ten American cities, including Santa Barbara and New Orleans, had historic districts. This kind of preservation, like the yet-to-be-conceived theme park, treated landscape as historical narrative, with emphasis upon those parts of the story that were most attractive and laudable, omitting those, such as slavery, that caused embarrassment.

Restoration along approved lines in historic districts has led to wide replication of historic forms. In some places, this process has also become an exercise in genteel mythmaking in which restrictive covenants and a stringent building-approval process have codified design, resulting in the wholesale manufacture of regional cultural identity by architects and builders through the creation of a romanticized landscape of the past. Notable in this regard, Santa Fe, New Mexico, is a place where people of Anglo-Saxon stock dwell in adobe houses that are commodious versions of older Hispanic models, which in turn were derived from the architecture and building materials of Native American pueblos.[11] Few people seem to mind the faux-adobe gas stations and shopping centers on the highway, but some Hispanics and Native Americans understandably resent the hegemonic appropriation of cultural heritage and landscape by non-natives who wear the city's much-transformed design tradition like a colorful shawl while often considering its living representatives to be an underclass. But there is a candy coating, economically speaking, on outsider-financed, highly interpretive historic preservation: Cities such as Santa Fe that have cultivated their historic image in this way are tourist magnets. Having denied themselves the opportunity to transform their cultural landscape, they grow prosperous from the trade of visitors.

PRESERVATION AS CULTURAL TOURISM

In the same way that Disneyland pioneered the concept of the theme park, Colonial Williamsburg pioneered the historically preserved landscape as tourist attraction. Like Walt Disney, John D. Rockefeller, Jr., the philanthropic sponsor of the transformation of Williamsburg, Virginia, from a sleepy southern town into a bustling sightseers' mecca, had a dream that proved extremely popular. Beginning in 1926, he created Colonial Williamsburg by restoring 82 eighteenth-century buildings, removing 720 built subsequently, and reconstructing 341 colonial structures

15.3. Celebration, Florida. A pattern book developed by Robert A. M. Stern and other Disney architects is the source of Celebration's intended southern-accented eclecticism.

Below: 15.2. Garden of the Governor's Mansion, Colonial Williamsburg, designed by Arthur Shurcliff. c. 1930

according to the best available, but often sketchy, evidence. Black residents were relocated, power lines buried, and automobiles banned from the Historic Area. Rockefeller's intention was to make it possible, with the aid of costumed guides, for visitors to Williamsburg to experience another century with the same educational interest a curious tourist might bring to travel in another land.[12]

One may remark on the beauty of Williamsburg's gardens with the certainty that none much like them existed when Virginia was still a colony (see fig. 6.50). Garden archaeology here was scarcely rigorous or scientific, and Arthur A. Shurcliff (1870–1957), the landscape-architect member of Rockefeller's Colonial Williamsburg planning team, developed his restoration designs in a highly interpretive manner.[13] The wife of Williamsburg's mayor described his vigorous revision of the local scenery in this diary entry:

> May 22, 1931. Mr. Shurcliff came down like a wolf on the fold again today. He rushed in and out several times with charts and plans for all sorts of alarming "landscapes" in our yard. He has boxwood on the brain. . . . Mr. Shurcliff is hurt and grieved by our lack of appreciation when we declare that we don't want more boxwood mazes and hedges all over our yard![14]

Nevertheless, she found all the transplanting and laying out of trim brick walks a fascinating spectacle. With a substantial budget for maintenance, Colonial Williamsburg's re-created gardens have enjoyed a showcase level of seasonal display and year-round degree of neatness that would have been impossible in the case of the originals (fig. 15.2).[15]

The tendency to embellish the physical evidence of the past in the act of preservation and restoration reflects the homage we pay to the memories or myths it embodies. The impulse to suffuse with the golden light of a romantically recalled yesteryear the restored or re-created landscapes of today accounts for the glossy, picture-perfect quality of Disney's theme parks and Colonial Williamsburg. It also accounts for the setlike quality of Celebration, Florida, the new town that was financed, built, and marketed by the Disney Company, a symbolic landscape where every day is yesterday, or rather the same yesteryear of nostalgically recalled time (fig. 15.3). Celebration's neotraditional postmodern planners took their cue from the predominant period-and-place theme of Disneyland's Main Street, the imaginary golden-age paradise of the Midwestern small town as it was from the end of the nineteenth century through the first four decades of the twentieth century. As with the impulse toward nostalgia we have observed in the Arts and Crafts Movement, this kind of architectural eclecticism reflects a denial of the powerful prevailing forces of the industrial age and the yearning for an earlier, simpler time when, so it is presumed, neighbors were neighborly and people led lives rich in the commonplace pleasures of community. Governmentally controlled by its parent corporation, Celebration is a well-publicized and highly contested example of the historically flavored lifestyle communities that other developers are also offering to home buyers under the planning rubric of New Urbanism. More than cosmetic in intent, these communities are the most recent experiments in applying to the now vastly distended amorphous metropolitan realm some of the practical principles underlying workable, livable cities that were articulated by Jane Jacobs and other critics of American planning practice in the late 1950s and early 1960s.

Preservation and the New Urbanism

While the urge to validate our present lives by linking them to past tradition is necessary to our psychological well-being, preservationism is more than architectural appreciation, ancestral piety, or simple nostalgia. The polemic that Jane Jacobs (b. 1916) hurled against urban renewal in her classic *Death and Life of Great American Cities* (1961) was the cry of a preservationist who prized traditional urbanism not because of aesthetics or any particular regard for history *per se*. Her preservationism was not the same as that of the gentility-seeking social striver or the gentrifying homeowner in a reviving slum neighborhood.

As we observed in Chapter Twelve, Jacobs promoted the street patterns and land use of the old nineteenth-century city, with its sidewalks and ground-floor businesses where people were in continual visual communication. The resulting environment was safer and more socially vibrant than the one of single-use zoning, large-scale superblocks, and superhighways that authoritarian master planners were imposing on the cities of America. The segregation of land uses by zoning districts had become common practice after streetcar- and, later, automobile-served suburbs made it possible for people to live and work in widely separated locations. By the late 1950s, mass automobile ownership and the federal highway building program had accelerated suburban expansion, and commuting had become commonplace in metropolitan America. Middle-class, in-city living virtually disappeared except in a few culturally rich older cities such as New York and Boston.

Jacobs's thesis flew in the face of the conventional wisdom that had created these landscapes. With a journalist's keen eye for detail and practical common sense, she concluded that a mix of uses created good neighborhoods such as the one where she and her family lived in Greenwich Village. She held that effectively recycled old housing stock made better homes for the poor than high-rise projects where public space was green but grim, being generally unsafe. One could learn lessons from the structure of the historic tenement street despite the evils of unsanitary crowding in tenement houses.

Jacobs's words, unappreciated in planning circles at the time, have taken on an increasingly resonant ring of useful truth. Having fought the battle to save Soho, the warehouse district in Lower Manhattan, from destruction by Robert Moses's planned Lower Manhattan Expressway, she became the progenitor of its renaissance, which sparked the conversion of semi-abandoned industrial districts in other cities into zones of yeasty enterprise, filled with art galleries, boutiques, restaurants, and loft apartments.

Today, practitioners of the New Urbanism adhere to planning principles based largely on Jacobs's ideas as they seek to apply pedestrian-oriented, mixed-use planning principles in rectifying the flaws they perceive in the current monotonous, sprawling suburban landscape and deteriorated parts of older cities where opportunities exist to recycle real estate and replan neighborhoods. Andres Duany (b. 1950) and Elizabeth Plater-Zyberk (b. 1950), who head the architectural firm DPZ, and Peter Calthorpe (b. 1949) of Calthorpe Associates are prominent apostles of the New Urbanism. Their overriding goal is to re-create lost opportunities for community by disciplining the automobile and establishing the primacy of the public realm. For New Urbanists, streets are both the communal rooms and the passages of the city. By dethroning "King Car" as the ruler of surburbia and disavowing the conventional approach of transportation planners whose primary motive is to move automobile traffic efficiently, they have revalued the street as an important public space for people. To accomplish this, they have revived the street's historic appendage, the sidewalk, a fixture of older cities and their streetcar suburbs. They plan neighborhoods that organize building sites and traffic on a hierarchical network of streets. These are made as narrow as possible as a means of slowing down automobile traffic. Curbside parking replaces large off-site parking lots, and trees shade cars and make them less conspicuous.

New Urbanist plans are compact in scale, with higher densities per acre than conventional suburbs, so that schools and shops are within comfortable walking distances, one-quarter-mile—a "five-minute walk"—being the radius DPZ considers appropriate for development extension in any direction from the neighborhood center. Families therefore do not have to maintain more than one car, children do not have to be chauffeured or bused to school, and elderly people who no longer drive do not have to move away but can still lead independent lives.

Public space in New Urbanist communities also takes the form of village greens, the long-lasting legacies of the New England town commons. Like sidewalks, these promote face-to-face encounters, thereby stimulating the spirit of community. Unlike traditional modern suburbs where parks, if they exist at all, are randomly sited on residual pieces of land not suitable for residential development, these greens are central elements within the plan, nuclei for surrounding development. They become identifiable town centers, well defined architecturally by their surrounding buildings. These may consist of the local school, the town hall, the retail center, town houses, apartments, and offices, usually in combination since mixed use is a cardinal rule in New Urbanist planning.

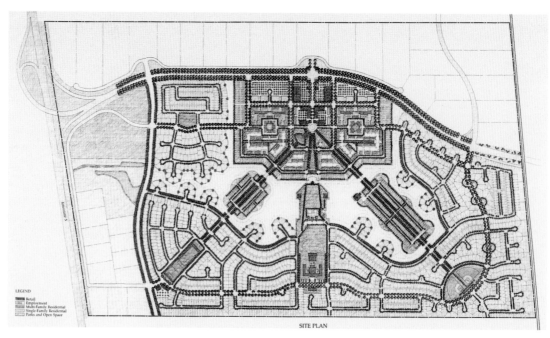

LEGEND

Retail
Employment
Multi-Family Residential
Single-Family Residential
Parks and Open Space

SITE PLAN

15.4. Plan of Laguna West, Sacramento County, California, designed by Calthorpe Associates. 1990

Mixed use means that there is more demographic diversity and more mutual interaction among population groups within a New Urbanist community than in a typical suburb. The pedestrian-oriented town center is a lively place because its ground-floor shops, restaurants, and services attract patrons from the entire community.

Perimeter parks, or at least natural borders, are also important in the New Urbanist developments. Edges that define and contain districts and the town itself are as important as the town center in overcoming the perception that has caused critics of conventional suburbs to echo Gertrude Stein's characterization of Oakland, California, as having "no 'there,' there." In Calthorpe's thinking especially, a regional planning perspective predominates. It is akin to the perspective of Benton MacKaye, the Regional Planning Association of America's advocate of directing metropolitan growth into a series of greenbelt-surrounded new towns modeled on the historic ones of New England (see Chapter Twelve). The Regional Plan Association (RPA), which has sought to guide New York's metropolitan growth since the 1920s, now subscribes to the New Urbanist notion of nodal urbanism. Calthorpe and the current leadership of RPA see the revival of the light-rail transit systems that were competitively dismantled by the automobile and highway interests after World War II as essential to overcoming suburban sprawl and preserving regional nature in any significant way.

New Urbanist planners maintain that design is meant to ensure a public realm, not to revive styles. But older models inspire much of their work, and they demonstrate a strong interest in design detail. Finding the results of Modernist planning bleak and dehumanizing and individualistic works of high-art

architecture to be posturing, they seek to reproduce the highly textured building fabric characteristic of older cities, adopting as well the more contextual, consensual approach of premodern architects. Duany and Plater-Zyberk label their method "TND," for *traditional neighborhood development,* and Calthorpe calls his "TOD," or *transit-oriented development,* because of its emphasis on a building density capable of supporting capital investment in transit infrastructure. Both produce results that are informed by ideas derived from Beaux-Arts Neoclassicism and the vernacular architecture of streetcar suburbs.

This community design for Laguna West, Sacramento County, California, is based on TOD (transit-oriented development) principles (fig. 15.4). Here, planner Peter Calthorpe has applied the *patte d'oie,* or goosefoot, pattern of avenue radials derived from seventeenth-century French garden design and subsequently appropriated by eighteenth-, nineteenth-, and early twentieth-century city planners to reinforce the centrality of the hub—the 100-acre town center with its cluster of shops, offices, apartments, and cultural and recreational facilities. Although light-rail transit does not yet exist at Laguna West, Calthorpe's plan presupposes its arrival by creating sufficient urban density to support this kind of transportation system. It also caters to the still-existing large market for more traditional suburban-style homes with a broad outer residential band platted according to the pattern of gently curving streets ending in cul-de-sacs, which has been typical of American subdivisions built since World War II.

Although it is only a small resort community occupying 80 acres of land on the Gulf Coast of Florida, Seaside, the town planned by Duany and Plater-Zyberk and developed by an especially sym-

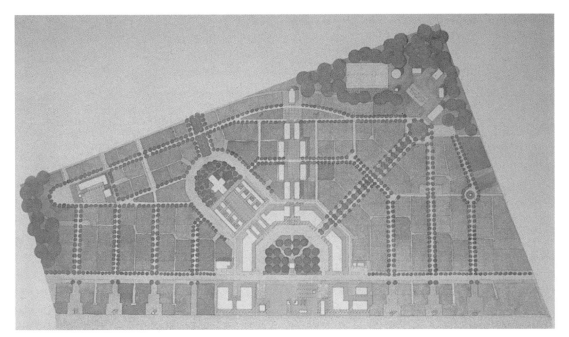

15.5. Plan of Seaside, Walton County, Florida, designed by Andres Duany and Elizabeth Plater-Zyberk. 1981

Below: 15.6. View of the commonly accessible beachfront, Seaside, Florida

pathetic client, Robert Davis, who also participated in its design, has garnered media attention as a leading example of New Urbanism (fig. 15.5). The three observed the beach cottages in Seagrove Beach, Florida, and other Gulf coastal summer colonies and traveled to suburbs in Southern cities where they studied residential architecture types. They sharpened their appreciation of traditional and vernacular styles, noting, for instance, how Charleston's distinctive historic house type with its long side porches on two floors is an architecturally pleasing adaptation to climate. The old-fashioned veranda, which had disappeared with the advent of air-conditioning and newer suburban house types, also drew their admiration. Influential in their revaluation of these past plans and building types was the teaching of Leon Krier (b. 1946), the Luxembourg-born architect who has led the crusade in London and elsewhere to revive neoclassical and vernacular approaches to community development.

The town plan, the Seaside Urban Code, and the Construction Regulations are simultaneously specific and flexible architectural directives that ensure compatibility among neighboring building types by giving guidelines for eight categories of construction and by specifying how structures are positioned on the lot and with regard to the street. Prescribed building types range from arcaded, party-wall, three-to-five-story buildings for stores and apartments in the Downtown Commercial Square to single-family "Classic-Romantic urban villas" on Seaside Avenue to southern bungalows and side-yard single houses on the residential streets elsewhere. The code encourages the construction of "carriage houses"—free-standing garages with living quarters above—as small apartments for elderly relatives, house guests, or rental

tenants. The regulations further control specific building materials and practices; they mandate, for instance, metal roofing, wood siding, exposed rafter ends, and operable wood-framed windows.

Seaside's prime real estate, a high dune bluff directly fronting on a magnificent stretch of white sand and the azure water of the Gulf of Mexico, could have been profitably exploited by the developer if he had chosen to sell the entire strip as individual high-priced large lots. Instead, holding the value—economic as well as social—of the entire project as paramount, Davis and DPZ made the beachfront property into a shared amenity. On the Gulf side of the highway that runs through Seaside they provided access points, which they marked with gazebos where stepped causeways begin their staged descent across the vegetated dune landscape leading to the beach (fig. 15.6). These have seating, another means of fostering the community's atmosphere of low-key sociability.

15.7. View of streetscape, with sandy footpath leading to the beach, Seaside, Florida

Running like a leitmotif throughout Seaside is a unifying vocabulary of white-painted wooden elements—picket fences, porch and balcony railings, lattices, gazebos, and window and door frames (fig. 15.7). The ground plane is a well-crafted mix of textures; there are brick-paved principal streets with crushed-shell margins for parked cars and sandy midblock footpaths leading to the beach. Designed by different architects—some of whom may bend the rules to express their personal visions—and by general contractors who simply follow the code and regulations, Seaside's compactly clustered mass of structures, often derided as "cute," are above all congenial. Although neotraditional, their design is the result of a somewhat more flexible approach than is the case at Celebration, where Disney's architects have provided a pattern book for builders to follow in order to achieve the look of pre-World War II suburbs with their mix of Neoclassical and vernacular styles (see fig. 15.3). One of Seaside's most important results in addition to stressing the values of community is its sense of containment. By setting appropriate limits to size and by thinking about centers and edges, Duany and Plater-Zyberk have made preservation of traditional community values and preservation of the natural environment complementary. Their critics maintain that the New Urbanism is merely a palliative that has not yet addressed the fundamental and politically complicated issues of reforming the real-estate financing practices and other factors that encourage suburban sprawl and foster urban blight.

It is doubtful that Jane Jacobs envisioned anything resembling Seaside when she wrote *Death and Life of Great American Cities.* The New Urbanism may be showing middle-class America the way back to the future, but as a movement it is still tentative. Davis's bet on community-oriented planning is paying off handsomely in terms of Seaside's real estate market,

which is geared to the buyers of second homes, but pockets of genteel affluence, however community-oriented in their physical structure, do not create the real social diversity Jacobs observed in cities. New Urbanist projects are achieving some impressive results in older cities such as Providence, Rhode Island; nevertheless, many of the people who need it most—for instance, the underfunded community groups who are waging battles to preserve urban fabric and community spirit in New York City's South Bronx—are struggling to find the private capital or government support to produce tangible results where they live.

For Jacobs, "projects" and "big money" were antithetical to the ideal community, in which social vibrancy and energetic consensus are achieved because numerous individual investments of time and money define the character of the urban space. "The cities of human beings are as natural, being a product of one form of nature, as are the colonies of prairie dogs or the beds of oysters."[16] Thus wrote Jane Jacobs in 1961 a year before Rachel Carson published *Silent Spring,* which heralded the environmental movement in the United States. Earth Day, often considered its official beginning, was still nine years away. Most of the national organizations that grew out of grassroots efforts to push government to enact legislation and set regulations to save threatened wilderness and reform the air- and water-polluting practices of industry did not yet exist. Because of the alarming dimensions of the problems that Industrial Age society was inflicting upon the planet, when environmental organizations came into being in the 1970s it was often with agendas that portrayed humankind as nature's enemy. Feeding this bias was the persistent strain of anti-urbanism that runs deep within American culture. Many people still believe the densely built-up older city cherished by Jacobs and others to be an inimical, inhuman environment that exists apart from nature. But, as Jacobs pointed out, "Human beings are, of course, a part of nature, as much so as grizzly bears or bees."[17] The suburban movement that spawned the current urban sprawl that she foresaw is based upon a false premise as well as a false promise: the sentimentalization and domestication of rural and wild nature through the development of a vast, undifferentiated, highway-dominated, ubiquitous suburban landscape of tract housing, commercial strips, and shopping malls. In this increasingly expansive metropolitan landscape, nature is residual, saved by political action but not promoted or planned through public policy.

By comprehending that the dinosaur of development will wantonly roam the land as long as there is population growth and economic prosperity and by wanting to guide that growth and prosperity by planning more livable suburbs, revitalizing old in-city neighborhoods, and saving natural areas as greenbelts, the New Urbanists appear to understand that the human environment and the natural environment are fundamentally one—an inextricable alliance of art, technology, and nature. The question remains: can we in fact build better cities, ones that do not oblit- erate but rather incorporate nature for our sake as well as for its own intrinsic, noneconomic worth? And can we accomplish this within the context of better regional planning, revitalizing historic cities as well as building better suburban towns? This is the true chal- lenge for the New Urbanism or whatever else we may choose to call it.

II. Conserving Nature: Landscape Design as Environmental Science and Art

The roots of today's environmental consciousness lie in nineteenth-century earth science. In 1863, the British geologist Charles Lyell (1797–1875) published *Geological Evidences of the Antiquity of Man*. Charles Darwin (1809–1882) was aware of Lyell's work, which promoted and helped confirm his theory of evolu- tionary biology as in *Origin of Species* (1859). The observations recorded by the German naturalist and explorer Alexander von Humboldt (1769–1859) dur- ing his voyages to South America, Cuba, and Mexico advanced the nascent field of ecology. Early geogra- phers such as the German Karl Ritter (1779–1859) and the Swiss-born Arnold Henry Guyot (1807–1884) studied the earth in relation to human activity. But it was an American, George Perkins Marsh (1801–1882), who attempted to show the extent to which human intervention was altering climate, topography, vege- tation patterns, soil, and the habitats of species, often with consequences inimical for future generations. In his landmark book *Man and Nature* (1864) Marsh, who claimed no scientific expertise but a great deal of prac- tical experience as a farmer, industrial investor, and diplomatic traveler, set out to show "that whereas Rit- ter and Guyot think that the earth made man, man in fact made the earth."[18]

A native of Vermont, Marsh saw firsthand how clear-cutting of forested slopes had promoted erosion and how these actions had caused the silting of for- mer wetlands and decimated many animal species. In biblical cadences, Marsh described how man the destroyer of nature

> has felled forests whose network of fibrous roots bound the mould to the rocky skeleton of the earth, . . . has broken up the mountain reser- voirs, the percolation of whose waters through unseen channels supplied the fountains that refreshed his cattle and fertilized his fields, . . . has torn the thin glebe which confined the light earth of extensive plains, and has destroyed the fringe of semi-aquatic plants which skirted the coast and checked the drifting of sea sand, . . . has warred on all the tribes of animated nature

whose spoil he could not convert to his own uses, and . . . not protected the birds which prey on the insects most destructive to his own har- vests.[19]

Fluent in several foreign languages, both ancient and modern, he read extensively and, as an ambassa- dor first to Turkey and then Italy, he was able to ana- lyze the Mediterranean basin at close range and to surmise why certain areas that had once supported extensive human settlement were now rocky, treeless, arid wastes, inhospitable to human life. By under- standing how the exploitation of the land's resources in the Old World, without any thought of husbandry beyond the immediate term, had reduced such sig- nificant portions of the ancient Roman empire to this condition, Marsh hoped to encourage his country- men to reconsider their heedless scramble for wealth at the expense of nature and to develop an ethos of land stewardship. The challenge that he put forth was to take his empirical observations in *Man and Nature* as warning signs and to assemble the necessary sci- entific data to understand "the action and reaction between humanity and the material world around it." Only by so doing would humanity be able to deter- mine at last "the great question, whether man is of nature or above her."[20]

Marsh fully approved of canals, dikes, river embankments, and other means of engineering that channeled the forces of nature toward human ends. But he believed that such controls could be produc- tive in the long term only if nature's regenerative forces were encouraged, not stymied. His book was influential in begetting awareness of the environment as an organic system in which all the parts were inter- dependent. Motives of overweening human greed persisted in his day as they do in ours, and in an aside, he railed against "the decay of commercial morality" and "unprincipled corporations, which not only defy the legislative power, but have, too often, corrupted even the administration of justice."[21] Although his urgent message sowed the seeds of forestry and land management practices that eventually became part of government, only in recent years have the dire effects that Marsh predicted—multiplied by pressures of population growth and forces of industrial mechanization that he could hardly have imagined—prompted political protest and legislative actions leading to pollution controls and some positive steps toward the responsible regeneration of degraded natural environments.

As we have seen, inherent in modernism was a celebratory attitude toward feats of engineering and little regard for their environmental consequences. Although modernist landscape architects following Christopher Tunnard intended and usually inflicted no serious environmental harm, their objectives were essentially aesthetic as they wished to bring their profession in line with the exciting new developments in architecture, painting, and sculpture. In terms of planning, the urban-rural balance that Lewis Mumford preached in opposition to metropolitanism, with greenbelt communities scattered throughout a region, went generally unheeded. Only since the 1970s has a belated awareness of the need to reconcile human objectives with the operation of natural ecosystems become general and influential upon the practice of landscape design. It was at the University of Pennsylvania where Mumford taught for a period in the early 1960s that the ground was laid for a landscape architecture that conjoined the regionalism of the 1920s with the emerging environmental consciousness.

LANDSCAPE AS ENVIRONMENTAL SCIENCE

"We need nature as much in the city as in the countryside," wrote Ian L. McHarg (b. 1920) in 1969 in his now-classic book, *Design with Nature.*[22] In the wake of Rachel Carson's eloquent call to environmental conscience in *Silent Spring* (1962), McHarg articulated with similar fervor a conservation strategy that sought to unseat the mind-set condoned by the Judeo-Christian biblical injunction encouraging humanity to subdue the earth. He enjoined planners, developers, and landscape architects to view Earth not as an exploitable resource but as the very source of life, the terrestrial miracle in space, an intricate organism of which humanity is an inseparable part. A gifted teacher, as chairman of the Department of Landscape Architecture and Regional Planning at the University of Pennsylvania from 1964 until 1986, McHarg became a leading exponent of an enlightened land-planning strategy that sought to make the constraints and opportunities presented by natural ecosystems an integral part of design and development. Informing his philosophy is his personal experience of the contrast of countryside to industrial city, of wartime landscape devastation to great landscape beauty, and

of post-World War II convalescence in both grim and exhilarating environments.

As a landscape architect, McHarg came to feel that it was not enough to simply ameliorate the conditions found in the Glasgow slums of his youth. Practicing in Philadelphia in the firm he founded in 1963, he recognized that "providing a decorative background for human play"[23] did not address the larger environmental threat posed by rings of suburbs encroaching upon rural and wild landscapes and the increasing divorce of human beings from wild nature. Further, the environment as a whole was being made toxic with pesticides and industrial wastes, and by then humans had sown the dire seeds of massive planetary devastation by producing the atomic bomb. He believes that urban planners and landscape architects can significantly alter this supremely dangerous course of science and technology and stem the harmful forces within industrial capitalist society.

As we have seen, other landscape architects—notably Charles Eliot and Jens Jensen—had preceded McHarg in advancing the cause of nature preserves in metropolitan areas, in studying native plant ecologies, and in forging a design idiom that expressed the simple beauties of regional locality. Stanley White (1891–1979) and Hideo Sasaki (b. 1919), both gifted teachers of landscape architecture, were instrumental in bringing environmental science into the student curriculum. For instance, Sasaki had his Harvard students study a site in terms of its soil conditions, drainage patterns, and vegetation character and ground-plane coverage. These then became the determinants in locating development and assigning preservation value. To this analytical approach based on principles of ecological determinism, McHarg added an intuitive methodology incorporating personal values that evinced his affinity for Japanese culture and the metaphysics expressed in the Zen garden as well as his respect for the architecture of Louis Kahn (1901–1974), who taught architecture at the University of Pennsylvania when McHarg led the landscape architecture program there. McHarg appreciated Kahn's notion of design as a poetic expression of space and light and of the essential, inherent qualities of material and site.

In an age of scientific rationalism that puts a premium on nonsubjective measures, McHarg felt compelled to further a science-based approach to designing with nature. He made the natural sciences an essential foundation for his department's curriculum at the University of Pennsylvania, with courses in plant ecology and geology. In his geophysical and environmental approach to landscape design, McHarg developed a coordinated mapping system with overlays to render analyses of ecological, cli-

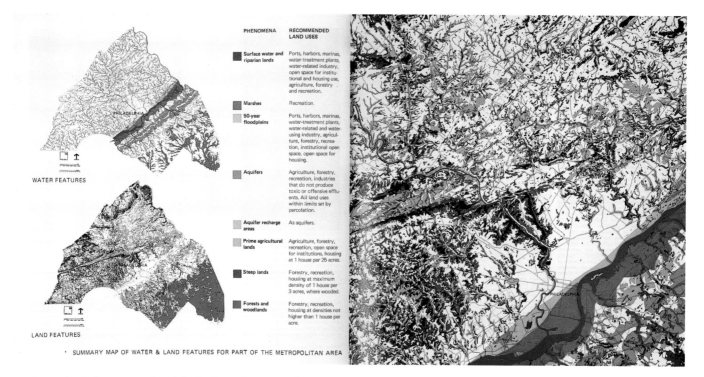

PHENOMENA | RECOMMENDED LAND USES

Surface water and riparian lands — Ports, harbors, marinas, water-treatment plants, water-related industry, open space for institutional and housing use, agriculture, forestry and recreation.

Marshes — Recreation.

50-year floodplains — Ports, harbors, marinas, water-treatment plants, water-related and water-using industry, agriculture, forestry, recreation, institutional open space, open space for housing.

Aquifers — Agriculture, forestry, recreation, industries that do not produce toxic or offensive effluents. All land uses within limits set by percolation.

Aquifer recharge areas — As aquifers.

Prime agricultural lands — Agriculture, forestry, recreation, open space for institutions, housing at 1 house per 25 acres.

Steep lands — Forestry, recreation, housing at maximum density of 1 house per 3 acres, where wooded.

Forests and woodlands — Forestry, recreation, housing at densities not higher than 1 house per acre.

WATER FEATURES

LAND FEATURES

· SUMMARY MAP OF WATER & LAND FEATURES FOR PART OF THE METROPOLITAN AREA

matic, geological, topographical, hydrological, economic, natural, scenic, and historical features (fig. 15.8). Assigning categories of social value to these, he has been able to chart optimum development paths and preservation zones according to the carrying capacity of the land and its fitness for specific uses. Put as simply as possible, a McHarg plan, such as the ones he prepared for the Philadelphia Metropolitan Area, the Baltimore Region, the Potomac River Basin, and for relocating the highway planned through the Staten Island Greenbelt, assigns levels of density and development and categories of land use based upon suitability. Flood and hurricane vulnerability and water conservation are paramount considerations. Overlay analysis shows invariably that valleys with their biologically and hydrologically important river basins and wetlands should be preserved, development on slopes should be minimized to allow groundwater to drain properly and recharge the subsurface aquifer, and uplands where settlement is least damaging allowed to become the zones of most intense occupation. Between 1970 and 1974, McHarg's firm, Wallace McHarg Roberts and Todd, applied this planning methodology to the development of Woodlands, an 18,000-acre new town built by developer George Mitchell north of Houston, Texas.

Sustainability is a new word in the lexicon of planners and designers. Woodlands, where the homes are clustered in a natural woodland setting rather than on conventionally landscaped lots, demonstrates McHarg's synthesis of human ecology and natural ecology in an economically viable plan that measures social and environmental costs together with dollar costs is hardly widespread in America. But to date,

the incentives to build similar communities are not widespread. Government's role in terms of environmental improvement remains principally regulatory. To plan on a large regional scale in the manner McHarg and others have suggested requires governmental effectiveness and creativity backed by elected officials and policy makers at all levels.

Without such environmental planning, social and economic demands—for jobs, for public access, for equity—result in higher political value being assigned to individual and class interests than to those of society at large. Yet elsewhere sustainable communities are being promoted however imperfectly, particularly in northern European countries such as the Netherlands, Sweden, and Germany where there is a stronger ethic and more ingrained politics of responsible land use and urban husbandry than in America.[24] Directing the policies of contemporary industrial capitalism and the consumer society toward this end in all countries is one of the most important challenges of the twenty-first century.

Landscape Design as Environmental Art

McHarg has been the most eloquent academic exponent of ecological landscape design in America, and Lawrence Halprin (b. 1916) has been one of its most active. Whereas McHarg has felt the need to put environmental planning within a rational natural-science framework, Halprin has honored the values of environment more in the manner of an artist, celebrating human creativity and community life within the context of nature and using environmental motifs metaphorically in his designs, which include several

15.8. Partial plan for the Philadelphia Metropolitan Area, showing land and water features, designed with nature by Ian McHarg. c. 1960

15.10. Freeway Park, Seattle, Washington, designed by Lawrence Halprin & Associates; Angela Danadijeva, project designer; Edward McCleod & Associates, associate landscape architects. 1970–76. Here a dramatically naturalistic space evokes the wilderness of the Pacific Northwest while masking the sounds of the freeway.

Above right: **15.9.** Lovejoy Plaza, Portland, Oregon, designed by Lawrence Halprin & Associates and Charles Moore, with Moore/Lyndon/ Turnbull/Whitaker, Architects. 1961–68

powerful evocations of nature in downtown public places (figs. 15.9, 15.10).

Halprin's long and productive career has been nourished by degrees in plant sciences and horticulture from Cornell and the University of Wisconsin, Madison, study at Harvard with his adopted mentor Christopher Tunnard after discovering Tunnard's *Gardens in the Modern Landscape,* and employment in the San Francisco office of Thomas Church where he worked on the Donnell Garden (see figs. 13.24, 13.25). Important to Halprin's work has been his understanding of landscape design as process rather than unchanging product. He calls this process "scoring," a musical metaphor implying his intention to create spatial frameworks that allow for change over time

and within which others can play participatory riffs. His legacy includes, besides his landscape designs, books that elucidate his design approach, including *The R.S.V.P. Cycles: Creative Processes in the Human Environment* (1969).

Between 1962 and 1965, Halprin was responsible for making San Francisco's Ghiradelli Square, an early effort at urban revitalization, into a vibrant public space animated by fountains, outdoor lighting, and landscaping, where people come for alfresco eating, shopping, socializing, and participating in performances, which are often impromptu. His "Take Part" design workshops elicit citizen collaboration in shaping a project's final program. Even as several other prominent landscape architects such as Hideo Sasaki and Peter Walker (b. 1932) have adopted the corporate-management style of successful large architectural firms, Halprin—like Roberto Burle Marx or Halprin's former employer, Thomas Church—has maintained his practice using an earlier model, that of the studio, because he finds the creative synergy of its collaborative atmosphere especially congenial.

With a strong interest in making landscape architecture transcend the functional and social to attain a spiritual dimension, Halprin has studied Jungian psychology in search of symbols and archetypes that hold universal meaning. Echoing Olmsted's notion of the fundamental benefit of parks as an uplifting of the spirit through the senses, Halprin has said, "What we are after is a sense of poetry in the landscape, a magnificent lift which will enrich the lives of the people who are moving about in the landscape."[25] He has nourished his own spiritual roots by maintaining a strong connection over the years with

Israel, where he spent some time after high school living on a kibbutz. His most notable project in that country is the Walter and Elise Haas Promenade built in the mid-1980s in Jerusalem on a hill overlooking the Old City.

In the United States, Halprin designed the 7.5-acre Franklin Delano Roosevelt Memorial located in West Potomac Park, a 66-acre peninsula beside the Tidal Basin in Washington, D.C. (fig. 15.11). Dedicated on May 2, 1997, the memorial to the thirty-second president of the United States consists of a richly planted 1,200-foot-long (365.8-meter-long) sequence of four interconnected garden spaces with narrative sculpture and fountains.[26] With his strong sense of landscape as theatrical performance and employing the storyboard technique used by filmmakers to plot what he called "Roosevelt's journey of life," Halprin scripted a sequence of 21 quotations,

brief texts from famous speeches by Roosevelt, which are incised into the memorial's walls of rusticated pink and red granite. He combined these inscriptions with sculptures by Tom Hardy, Neil Estern, Leonard Baskin, George Segal, and Robert Graham in a chronological narrative of Roosevelt's presidency and leadership during two of the nation's gravest ordeals, the Great Depression and World War II. The memorial also contains hope for world peace as symbolized by the inclusion of a statue of Eleanor Roosevelt as a delegate to the United Nations.

Halprin's connection with McHarg's approach to environmental planning is perhaps most evident in his "ecoscore" for Sea Ranch, a planned community of weekend and vacation homes and condominiums developed in the mid-1960s by Oceanic Properties on property occupying a 10-mile stretch of northern California coastline, which was once used for sheep grazing. Halprin conceived the plan for the first 1,800 acres to be developed of the original 5,300-acre parcel in collaboration with MLTW, the architectural firm of Charles Moore, Donlyn Lyndon, William Turnbull, and Richard Whitaker (figs. 15.12, 15.13). As was later true of Seaside's plan, Halprin's plan for Sea Ranch put a premium upon communal spaces, and only about 50 percent of the land was sold to private owners.

By clustering the sites for houses and condominiums adjacent to existing cypress hedgerows, Halprin was able to leave the former sheep pastures as open meadows with views to the ocean across the

15.11. Franklin Delano Roosevelt Memorial, Washington, D.C., designed by Lawrence Halprin. 1997. sculpture by Neil Estern

Below: 15.12. Plan of Sea Ranch, California, designed by Lawrence Halprin & Associates, Landscape Architects, Moore/Lyndon/Turnbull/Whitaker, and Joseph Esherick, Architects. 1967

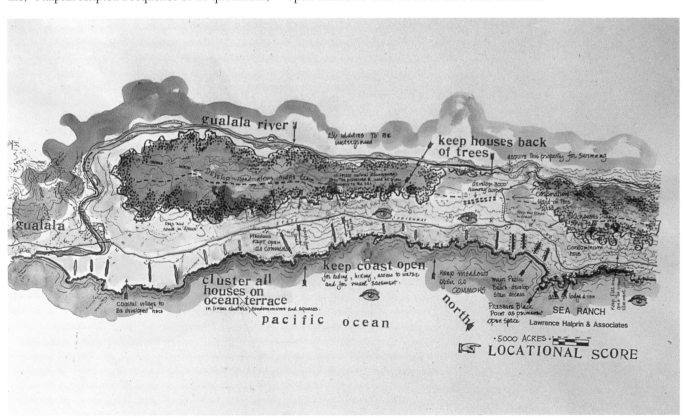

15.13. Sea Ranch

beach bluffs. Trails throughout enable residents to experience the landscape as a totality. The meadows are held as commons and their maintenance made a community responsibility. Unlike Seaside, where low picket fences manifest an ambience of yard-to-yard neighborliness, at Sea Ranch owners' rules specify that properties be kept unfenced. The clustered houses without visible property lines or landscaping appear to merge with their natural setting. This intention is furthered by Sea Ranch's rustic architectural vocabulary—unpainted redwood or cedar siding and eaveless shed roofs of shingle or sod, which are positioned to deflect the Pacific winds.

As an innovative effort in environmentally harmonious place making and an expression of the 1960s idealism that motivated the careers of both McHarg and Halprin, Sea Ranch deserves a place in the history of landscape design. Both of these landscape architects have seen city and country as a continuum, and their influence in furthering a new moral imperative by bringing ecological considerations to the fore has been influential within their profession.

As much of the aging industrial infrastructure of cities falls into disuse because of new transportation and manufacturing technologies, landscape architects have been engaged in the reclamation of *brownfields,* former factory sites and decaying waterfronts.

Notable among those who have attempted to poeticize the industrial past through landscape design is Richard Haag (b. 1923), an early Postmodern contextualist whose Gasworks Park (1970–78) on the shores of Lake Union in Seattle, Washington, and Bloedel Reserve, Bainbridge Island, Puget Sound, Washington (1985–), demonstrate concern for environmental healing through bioremediation.

Although contemporary landscape architects have not entirely abandoned the principles of the Picturesque, Arts and Crafts, Neoclassical, and Modernist design traditions that have constituted their training during the past century, and although they still rely on some of the principles of these design styles as well as upon McHargian environmentalism to inform their work, several are adopting an approach that seeks the same kind of creative freedom granted to Conceptual artists. Thus, they look to their own imaginative resources as they manipulate stones, earth, and water to produce land art, forms in and of the landscape. At the same time, Earthworks artists share some of the same concerns as environmentalists, and they work in a similar manner and at the same scale as landscape architects. As they, too, seek to manifest beauty within a brownfields context, the distinction between art and landscape design tends to dissolve.

III. EARTHWORKS, GOLF COURSES, PHILOSOPHICAL MODELS, AND POETIC METAPHORS: LANDSCAPE AS ART FORM, SPORT, DECONSTRUCTIVISM, AND PHENOMENOLOGY

Industrial technology has produced the machines that can manipulate landscapes with an ease previously undreamed of; without it Earthworks, or Land art, would probably not exist. There are certain ironies, both intended and not, in the creation of these monumental and often beautiful projects. Many evoke in scale and cosmological intent the primary earthworks of prehistoric peoples, yet they are not expressions of widely shared and deeply held cosmologically oriented religious belief as were the great earthworks created at Newark, Ohio, or Cahokia, Illinois, which we examined in Chapter One. Rather they are the heroic creations of artists who, often through the agency of bulldozers and other earthmoving equipment, have accomplished with relatively small work crews and within their own lifetimes landscape transformations on a scale rivaling that of these original earthworks, the building of which employed battalions of workers over a period of many decades or even centuries. Frequently placed by choice or necessity in remote and inaccessible locations, often the deserts of the American West, modern Earthworks exist primarily for the appreciation of tourists who are willing, usually by means of a four-wheel-drive vehicle, to experience them firsthand and for other followers of contemporary art who are content to view aerial photographs of them.

Indeed, the camera is their handmaiden, for rarely if ever are these sometimes ephemeral projects undocumented. Still and moving images are as important to the artists as the Earthworks themselves, and some artists such as Andy Goldsworthy (b. 1956), whose delicate and poetic constructions are exceedingly transitory, have become photographers of professional stature in the service of their art (fig. 15.14). Aerial photography, which also allows us to comprehend better the configuration of such prehistoric earthworks as the Nazca lines in Peru (see fig. 1.35) or Serpent Mound in Ohio (see fig. 1.37), is similarly important in making many modern Earthworks legible.

The space they occupy makes a territorial claim to the sublime that substitutes for the inherent divinity that prehistoric and ancient societies ascribed to their sacred places. Unlike the acts of cosmological centering performed by these early people, however, the creators of contemporary Earthworks must locate them through a necessarily mundane process involving negotiation of property leases or the purchase of real estate. In the case of some Earthworks

15.14. *Red River,* Jemez, New Mexico, by Andy Goldsworthy. July 28, 1999

artists, especially Christo (b. 1935), who for this reason perhaps chooses important and conspicuous urban areas for some of his projects, the process of obtaining permits is as important as the realization of the art itself.

Being explicitly identified with specific artists, contemporary Earthworks have an importance within the context of our celebrity-conscious culture more often linked to the name of the artist than to the concepts they are intended to manifest. This is

15.15. *Spiral Jetty,* Great Salt Lake, Utah, designed by Robert Smithson. 1970

15.15. *Spiral Jetty,* Great Salt Lake, Utah, designed by Robert Smithson. 1970

Below: 15.16. *Observatory,* Oostelijk (East) Flevoland, the Netherlands, designed by Robert Morris. 1971, reconstructed 1977. Influenced by archaeology and by the phenomenology of French philosopher Maurice Merleau-Ponty, Morris emphasized the experiential participation of the viewer who comprehends different scales of time through walking in and around this 300-foot-diameter (91.4-meter-diameter) Earthwork of concentric mounds, embankments, and canals. These different scales of time include the actual time spent on the site, prehistoric time as symbolized by its archaeological form, and cosmological time as referenced by Morris's solar solstice sight lines.

unfortunate because many were intended as a critique of art-world values as well as of Industrial Age environmental degradation. Although Earthworks have a materiality that transcends a strict definition of Conceptual art, the Earthworks movement is nevertheless contemporary with, and part of, the Conceptual art movement. Both Land art and Conceptual art are latter-day links in early-twentieth-century Modernism's break with tradition and expansion of the definition of what is art. Both are part of the same late 1960s gestalt of protest against the established norms for viewing and thinking about art. Both eschew style in favor of idea and form.

EARTHWORKS AS ART FORM AND LANDSCAPE

Robert Smithson (1938–1973), Robert Morris (b. 1931), Charles Ross (b. 1937), Nancy Holt (b. 1938), and James Turrell (b. 1941) are nontraditional American artists whose chosen medium is the land itself—soil, rocks, water, existing geological and topographical structures—as well as light and sky (figs. 15.15–15.21). Smithson, a prolific writer and the most articulate champion of the Earthworks movement before his premature death, made it clear that his concerns were with cosmic space and time rather than with historical space and time. He aligned his own intentions with those of fellow artists of his generation who were also concerned with "inactive history" that brought "to mind the Ice Age rather than the Golden Age."[27] Further, in the late 1960s, Smithson was in the vanguard of artists who wished to abandon the notion of art as object. Their polemic was directed against the current status of art as a marketable commodity.

Smithson was in a sense an environmentalist, a man acutely aware of the degradation of natural landscapes by twentieth-century industry. However, with the idea that even industrial wastelands have an intrinsic beauty that can be given form and expression through art, he actively sought as sites for his work abandoned quarries, strip mines, polluted lakes, and other disfigured portions of the landscape. His brand of environmentalism was devoid of sympathy for protesters who thought of industrialization as essentially evil, a catastrophe humanity had visited upon nature. His perception of time in "Ice Age" or geologic terms gave him the ability to think within the context of planetary, rather than human, dialectics. He brought to his art the perspective of earth science gained from frequent trips as a child to the American Museum of Natural History and on car trips with his family to the American West. From his boyhood interest in natural history and his impressions of the immensity and grandeur of Western scenery as contrasted with the densely suburbanized and heavily industrialized landscape around Passaic, New Jersey, where he grew up, Smithson extracted a worldview that considered modern Machine Age humanity as part of nature and environmental remediation through art as an interesting opportunity for artists like himself.

His explorations of desolate and deteriorating industrial landscapes resulted in an exhibition of a new kind of sculpture he called Non-Sites. His work as an artist-consultant to an architectural team competing for the contract to expand Dallas–Fort Worth Regional Airport helped him to conceptualize how he could independently make Land art on an airport scale. This led him to abandon the symbiotic relationship between artist and gallery, and in 1968, he traveled through the deserts of California, Nevada, and Utah in search of a suitable location for a large Earthwork. He was particularly attracted to the reddish-violet color of salt lakes, and in 1970, further search in the West led him and fellow artist Nancy Holt, also his wife, to a portion of the Great Salt Lake in Utah "which resembled an impassive faint violet sheet held captive in a stoney matrix, upon which the sun poured down its crushing light."[28] In Smithson's eyes, the peculiar beauty of the desolate site was

augmented by the industrial wastes and abandoned machinery he found there, rusting derricks that recorded past attempts to extract oil from tar deposits. The color of the water was the result of the presence of a microorganism. According to Smithson, the site "reverberated out to the horizons only to suggest an immobile cyclone while flickering light made the entire landscape appear to quake. . . . This site was a rotary that enclosed itself in an immense roundness. From that gyrating space emerged the possibility of the Spiral Jetty."[29]

Using heavy machinery like that which had scarred the site, Smithson deposited black basalt rocks and earth, creating a spiraling form 1,500-feet (457.2-meters) long in the purplish-pink water. Underlying

15.17. *Star Axis,* located in the desert east of Albuquerque, New Mexico, designed by Charles Ross. Begun 1974. *Star Axis* is a monumental demonstration of the relationship of Earth's axis and Polaris, the North Star.

Below: 15.18. *Roden Crater Project,* near Flagstaff, Arizona, designed by James Turrell. Begun 1970s. Turrell, who sees natural light as his primary medium, has created within the cone of an extinct volcano spaces in which to experience the ambiences created by the sun and moon at various times of day and year.

15.19 and 15.20. Interior and exterior views of *Up and Under,* Nokia, Finland, designed by Nancy Holt, 1998. Built in an abandoned quarry, this Earthwork is composed of sand, concrete, grass, and water. © Nancy Holt/licensed by VAGA, New York, NY

the sun at the time of the summer and winter solstices. Perforations in the pipes admit light in patterns that evoke various star constellations. More attuned to evoking ancient cosmological expressions in the landscape than modern physics, Holt's subsequent Earthworks include *30 Below* (1980) for the Winter Olympics in Lake Placid, New York; *Star Crossed* (1980) at Miami University, Oxford, Ohio; and *Dark Star Park* (1984) in Arlington, Virginia. Her most recent Earthwork, *Up and Under* (1998), located in an abandoned sand quarry in the village of Pinsiö near Nokia, Finland, consists of seven horizontal concrete tunnels, four of which are aligned on an east-west axis, while three are oriented with Polaris, the North Star (figs. 15.19, 15.20). The tunnels protrude from a 630-foot-long (192-meter-long) snakelike mound ending in a roughly circular mound that is approximately 230 feet (70 meters) in diameter and 26 feet (7.9 meters) high.

Smithson's dialectical vision of industrialist and artist engaged in exploitation and reclamation of the earth is the concept of the law of thermodynamics, modern physicists' notion of the universe as being in a state of entropy to which the artist grafted his contemporary perspective of the natural environment as being debased by human activity but capable nonetheless of poetic expressiveness.

Shortly after working with Smithson to document the creation of *Spiral Jetty,* Nancy Holt undertook to create *Sun Tunnels,* an earthwork in Lucin, Utah (1973–76). Set within a vast desert landscape, these 9-foot-diameter (2.7-meter-diameter), 18-foot-long (5.9-meter-long) industrial concrete pipes are positioned in alignment with the rising and setting of

Like ancient cosmological landscapes, *Up and Under* has an "axis mundi" in the form of a large vertical tunnel placed at the crossing of four tunnels beneath the round mound. It brings a circle of sky with clouds, stars, and sometimes the moon into the perception of the viewer within the tunnel. Reinforcing the cosmological idea of centering space, Holt took samples of soil from villages all over Finland and buried this mixture beneath the vertical tunnel. In addition, she placed three circular sky-reflecting pools, which are fed by an ancient spring, in the quarry floor adjacent to the mounds, whose slopes are covered with grass. The pools, which vary in diameter from 22 feet (6.7 meters) to 30 feet (9.1 meters) to 40 feet (12.2 meters), also mirror the Earthwork. It is meant,

15.21. Lower Portrack, Dumfriesshire, Scotland. Designed by the owners Charles Jencks and Maggie Keswick. 1990–2000. Characterized by Jencks as "a garden of cosmic speculation," it contains a terrace of polished aluminum and astroturf, which is arranged in a warped pattern suggesting the physical configuration of space caused by a "black hole" in the universe.

as its title suggests, to be viewed from above, along a path that follows the crescent-shaped cliffs created by the operation of the former quarry, and from underneath the earth, inside the tunnels. It can also be experienced by following the path at the top of the winding mound or by moving around the forms on the quarry floor. According to Holt, "Each changing visual experience leads to a questioning of perception itself—near and far, whole and detail, reflection and reality, aerial and ground."[30]

Charles Jencks (b. 1939), with his late wife, Maggie Keswick (1941–1995), a student of the Chinese garden and *feng shui* principles of landscape design, created a garden in Dumfriesshire, Scotland (figs. 15.21–15.23). Its modeled terrain bears a superficial resemblance to archaeologically inspired Earthworks in the United States. Jencks and Keswick, however, were not interested in evoking prehistory. An architectural theorist and popularizer of Postmodernism as well as the author of *The Architecture of the Jumping Universe,* Jencks is fascinated with forms that relate to a new theory of cosmogenesis, which claims that the universe continually jumps to new levels of organization. The "garden of cosmic speculation" in Scotland seeks to represent with elegance and wit Jencks's idea that "the new sciences of complexity, of which chaos is just one of twenty, show the omnipresence of these sudden leaps at all scales."[31] Among other things, he wanted the garden to represent the structure of space-time and quantum physics as envisioned by contemporary cosmologists. Different from Ptolemaic and Cartesian space, it portrays, according to

Jencks, a universe that is "curved, warped, undulating, jagged, zigzagged and sometimes beautifully crinkly."[32] For Keswick, their garden was a means to express in a twentieth-century Western context *qi,* the "breath," or inherent energy, possessed by all phenomena, an essential ingredient of Chinese painting and also sought by Chinese garden designers, as we observed in Chapter Eight.

Within a concave section of the Giant Dragon Ha Ha, lies the Symmetry Break Terrace, which is meant to represent the four basic jumps—energy, matter, life, consciousness—that have taken place since the creation of our universe. Another terrace designed as a curving recessive checkerboard of Astroturf and polished aluminum is meant to diagram the way black holes are thought to warp space-time (fig. 15.21). A Physics Garden (an intended pun upon the Physic Garden for medicinal herbs) displays gatepost finials that are metal spheres representing various models of the universe based upon the Gaia, Ptolemaic, armillary, constellational, and atomic hypotheses.[33] The climax of the garden is the 55-foot (16.8-meter) spiral mound and 400-foot (121.9-meter) double-wave Earthwork created with dredged spoil from the marsh that formerly occupied a part of the property (fig. 15.23). Here the designers' intentions were to represent in interlocking sculptural patterns of grass and water the Chinese concept of *qi* and the geomantic principles of *feng shui* together with the dynamics of complexity science and chaos theory. Thus, Jencks's spiral mound, dubbed the Snail, was created by piling the excavated material from the

15.22. Lower Portrack, kitchen garden with sculpture of polished aluminum representing a double-helix

15.23. Lower Portrack, spiral mound and double-wave Earthwork

marsh to an angle of repose just preceding that which will cause a landslide—"phase transition" as this point is called in the theory of complexity that physicists have developed to explain the creative patterning of matter that occurs on the border between chaos and order. The reversing curve implies the smooth transition observed in the manner in which unlike things are enfolded into a spatial continuum. As a result,

Keswick's serpentine ponds assume the form of fractals, the endlessly recurring paisley shapes observed in nature, while also serving as metaphors for the energy-charged calm that resides in pools throughout the universe.

Like the creators of Earthworks, golf-course designers are concerned with sculpting the land, although not to express conceptual meaning but

rather for strategic purposes that are intrinsic to the game. Yet because of the sport's venerable history, its impact on land and water resources, and its importance as an expression of contemporary cultural values, their work deserves discussion here.

Landscape as Sport: The Golf Course

Course architecture is such a basic element of golf that the characteristics of each course account for the degree of challenge it presents to players.[34] In a great global family tree of golf courses all the branches can be traced to Scotland where the game grew out of the landscape, the sandy, alluvial terrain called links. Natural links are found in estuarine areas where rivers deposit sediment on their way to the sea. Golf originated as a game along the estuaries of the rivers Eden, Tay, and Forth. The first golf course, St. Andrews, dating from the early fifteenth century, was in its earliest form completely natural, a treeless stretch of wind-swept, rolling dunes with soil pockets supporting native bent grasses and some fescue.

The original game involved batting a "featherie," a small leather-bound, feather-stuffed ball, along a route improvised from the grass-covered links, avoiding the natural hazards of the gorse-encrusted dunes and eroded sandy hollows. Tees, clearly defined fairways, and well-manicured putting greens were unknown. Players simply wandered across this hillocky, treeless landscape, aiming their shots at whatever small holes served as cups. Although a series of such holes became institutionalized through repeated play, the number of cups on different Scottish links varied.

In the mid-eighteenth century, golfers' clubs were formed to organize the play. The Society of St. Andrews Golfers instituted turf maintenance for the putting areas, or greens and, in 1764, set eighteen as the official circuit of holes that was later followed elsewhere. Golf-course architecture had its inception as the members of St. Andrews started to manipulate their natural golfing terrain by cutting double cups into enlarged greens—one for matches heading "out," the other for those heading "in," widening the grassy playing strip by substituting turf for heather, and adding artificial hazards. "Penal" design is represented by the Old Course as it originally existed, where it was necessary to clear many natural hazards; the alternative is "strategic" design, which allows the player the option of taking a slightly longer but safer route at the cost of additional strokes. From these basic principles, golf course architecture evolved.

Adopted in England and after 1779 in America, golf was played on rudimentary courses often lacking the characteristics of linksland terrain. But the popularity of the game grew, particularly when in 1848 the low-cost, durable ball made from the natural latex of the tropical gutta-percha plant was invented. This also made possible the use of revolutionary iron-headed golf clubs. As the demand for new courses grew with the gradual spread of the game, the first course designers were Scots and then Englishmen with professional qualifications derived from greenskeeping, not landscape design. They worked almost entirely on the ground, not from drawn plans, paying attention to the practicalities of the game rather than to any picturesque qualities inherent in the landscape. They did little to alter their sites, incorporating existing turf and other features or simply modifying courses, making them safer for the growing population of golfers or extending the length of holes to take into account the longer flight of the new gutta-percha balls.

In the second half of the nineteenth century, innovations in the routing of the course introduced variability in wind direction as a challenge for players. New machinery for mowing and new means of cutting and lining holes with metal cups improved the quality of the greens. Discovery through trial and error proved that the heathlands southwest of London were ideal inland golfing country when cleared of certain vegetation.

By 1900, nearly a thousand courses had been built in the United States. With their distant views across rolling meadowlike greenswards fringed with trees, many of these golf courses offer scenery similar to that found in "Capability" Brown's Grecian Valley at Stowe or Olmsted and Vaux's Long Meadow in Prospect Park (see Chapters Seven and Nine). But this is simply coincidence, because on golf courses the designer's primary consideration is not the scenery but rather the lie—the position of the golf ball as it ceases rolling and comes to a stop. Bodies of water, however scenic, are intended as hazards for the player, not aesthetic features. Near the putting greens, fairways are punctuated with bunkers, shallow sand-filled depressions, also intended as strategically positioned hazards. To provide a final challenge as the player reaches the hole, designers have greens graded with almost imperceptibly undulating surfaces.

The 1920s was a golden era for golf course construction in the United States, with an average of six hundred constructed each year between 1923 and 1929, boosting the national total from 1,903 to 5,648. Many of these were laid out by local greenskeepers, who were often emigrants from Great Britain, and amateur golfers whose primary intent was to shape the landscape to suit the objectives of the game. Given an extraordinary site on California's Monterey Peninsula, two regional tournament champions, John Francis Neville (1895–1978) and Douglas S. Grant

(1887–1981), designed the breathtaking Pebble Beach Golf Links in 1918. Built on a high bluff overlooking the Pacific Ocean, Pebble Beach does not occupy true linksland, but its sandy, hummocky, windswept terrain and magnificent views of Carmel Bay make it appear to fit its name.

Equally endowed, Cypress Point, adjacent to Pebble Beach, was laid out ten years later by Alister Mackensie (1870–1934), a British physician turned golf-course designer. Mackensie, who built courses in England, Scotland, Ireland, Canada, Australia, New Zealand, and South America as well as the United States, is considered one of the most eminent course designers in golf history, a reputation bolstered by his publication in 1920 of *Golf Architecture,* codifying thirteen key principles guiding course layout. These included—in addition to those directed at enhancing the strategic interest of the game, the comfort and convenience of players, and the year-round playability of the course—one that advised blending the course's artificial and natural features so that the two appeared indistinguishable.

By the mid-1930s, following the worst years of the Great Depression, course construction began to accelerate in the United States with the creation of the federal Works Progress Administration (WPA) to provide work for the unemployed. Municipal golf courses began to appear in cities across the country. The WPA crews moved earth and sculpted terrain using wheelbarrows and hand tools rather than heavy machinery, but after World War II when private golf course construction again boomed and massive unemployment was no longer a problem, modern earthmoving equipment was used. This greatly abbreviated the time it took to build a golf course. In addition, with petroleum no longer scarce, fuel for mowing machinery became readily available, which also stimulated course construction.

During this period Robert Trent Jones (b. 1906) rose to preeminence as America's foremost golf-course architect, and by 1990 his firm's portfolio contained 450 courses in forty-two states. Trent blended the "penal" and "strategic" types of design with the creation of a style he called "heroic." His "heroic" courses eschewed the elaborate bunkering of penal-type design, substituting a single, formidable, diagonally placed hazard such as a pond that the golfer had to clear with a long drive of more than 500 feet (152.4 meters). At the same time, the golfer was allowed to choose an alternative, less risky route to the green. Trent's particular gift as a designer lay in employing penal, strategic, and heroic design techniques according to the nature of play a course was expected to receive, taking into account whether it was municipal operation for the general public, a resort for paying guests, a country club for members, a private layout for an owner and friends, or a tournament venue for professional golfers.

In the 1960s, professional golfers were becoming celebrities, thanks especially to televised sports matches. The popularity of golf, particularly among the growing number of active retired people, was responsible for a new land-planning phenomenon: the residential community built around a golf course. However, by the mid-1970s, the escalating cost of course construction, the energy crisis, tight money, new environmental regulations in the United States, and land-use restrictions in Japan curtailed the rate of

15.24. Emerald Dunes Golf Course, West Palm Beach, Florida, designed by Thomas Fazio. 1990

golf-course building. Then, during the prosperous 1980s, the pace of course construction revived. George Fazio (1912–1986), working with his nephews, Thomas Joseph Fazio (b. 1945) and Vincent James Fazio (b. 1942) built and revised courses, including several for clubs hosting major tournaments. The view from Hole 18, known as Super Dune, on the Emerald Dunes Golf Course in West Palm Beach, Florida, shows how, in 1990, Tom Fazio sculpted artificial water bodies, sweeping fairways, and contoured greens to create a scenic panorama out of former scrub land covered with palmetto thickets (fig. 15.24).

In 1974, eminent professional golfer Jack Nicklaus (b. 1940) organized his own firm. In Scottsdale, Arizona, his Desert Highlands Golf Club (1984) demonstrated how a grass-demanding sport could be successfully integrated into a naturally arid landscape. Restricted in the amount of irrigation he could use, Nicklaus created wide swaths of playable sand between fairly narrow turfy fairways and the pebbles and coarse rock of the surrounding desert. Nevertheless, Nicklaus, who seeks a deluxe finish to his courses, insists upon velvety bent grass for all his greens no matter the climate. In addition, he typically builds cascades for his water hazards, installs elaborate irrigation systems, and specifies the use of state-of-the-art mowing equipment.

Perhaps Thorstein Veblen's theory of conspicuous consumption, or nonproductive leisure as a means of displaying wealth, discussed in Chapter Twelve, is nowhere more manifest than in the game of golf, especially if this assessment takes into account the difficult issue of water rights in dry climates. In spite of conservationists' protests, the popularity of the game is such that it is politically difficult to stem the tide of course construction, even in arid communities where water reservoirs run dangerously low and capacity cannot be expanded. The fact that golfing has become almost an obligatory ritual among corporate businesspeople who routinely meet clients on the links exacerbates this difficult and continuing ecological and societal problem.

Although contemporary enthusiasm for golf may be capricious, the story we have briefly traced of its evolution from the seaside links of Scotland to the inland desert around Scottsdale, from a sport whose objectives and rules were shaped by landscape to one that employs a high degree of artifice and mechanization in manipulating the landscape to create new challenges for players, is an entirely pragmatic one. At the opposite end of the spectrum is the landscape that is highly theoretical in its design intent, one that takes shape not from the land or the requirements of sport or other user demands. Such a landscape is Parc de la Villette in Paris.

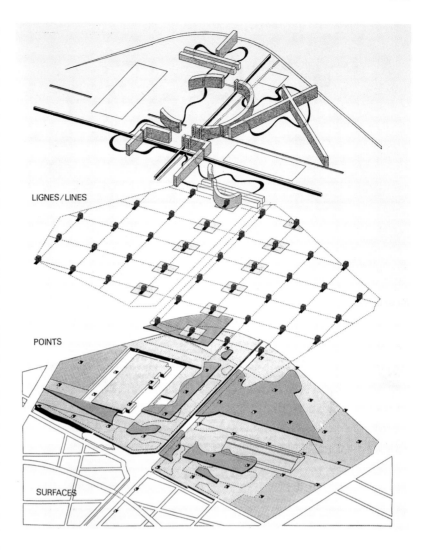

LIGNES / LINES

POINTS

SURFACES

LANDSCAPE AS DECONSTRUCTIVIST THEORY: PARC DE LA VILLETTE

Architect Bernard Tschumi (b. 1944) designed Parc de la Villette on the eastern rim of Paris as a deconstructivist exercise informed by the concepts of dissociation developed by philosopher Jacques Derrida (b. 1930) (figs. 15.25, 15.26). Whereas Earthworks artists such as Smithson sought metaphysical representation in their work, the deconstructivist Tschumi believes as did Derrida that "in architecture we find something that contradicts the metaphysics of representation and thus everything linked to representation."[35] Like Smithson, Tschumi starts from the same Postmodern position that chaos rules, but instead of creating as did Smithson an art that represents entropy, he subscribes to Derrida's concept of architecture in which "the strongest reference [is] to absence."[36]

Tschumi was one of 471 entrants in the design competition for the new 175-acre park that was to rise between 1984 and 1989 on the site of the old Parisian cattle market and slaughterhouses. The competition guidelines called for an innovative park that would be superior to the nineteenth-century Picturesque parks designed by Alphand (see Chapter Ten). A prolific the-

15.25. Plan of Parc de la Villette, designed by Bernard Tschumi. 1984–89

15.26. Sunday in the Parc de la Villette. The recreational experiences enjoyed by visitors within Tschumi's essay in park architecture as deconstructivist philosophy are more diverse and active than the ones Sunday parkgoers have in nineteenth-century Parisian parks.

Below right: 15.27. Parc André Citröen, designed by two teams of competition entrants: Alain Provost, Jean-Paul Viguier, and Jean-François Jodry and Patrick Berger and Gilles Clément. 1985–92

Below: 15.28. Parc André Citröen

orist who practices architecture from a highly intellectual perspective, Tschumi saw Parc de la Villette's design as an opportunity to manifest textual deconstructivism in terms of landscape. After his design was selected by a twenty-one-person jury chaired by Roberto Burle Marx, Tschumi invited architect Peter Eisenman and Derrida to participate with him by developing a small area within the park. To the commission of designing a space within Parc de la Villette Derrida brought his interest in Plato's *Timaeus* and its definition of space as *chora,* the virgin receptacle of place, or the spacing that is the condition for everything to take place, the necessary means of providing a web for places.

Tschumi's self-imposed challenge was to give spatial expression to a philosophical idea that rejects unitary meaning in favor of spontaneous multiple occurrences, or "event-texts" in the language of deconstructivism. His method was to create a fluid, nonspecific, uncentered, unconfined space — a theoretically boundaryless receptacle devoid of any rep-

resentational associations, a blank textbook in which anyone can inscribe whatever meaning they choose.

Although in Tschumi's theoretical view it has no boundaries, Parc de la Villette is anchored by a science museum on its southwest end and by a music conservatory and performance hall on its northeast perimeter. These large cultural institutions, also the result of design competitions, were built at approximately the same time as the park. In addition, the industrial structures that once served as slaughterhouses have been reused as event centers. The park in between and surrounding these buildings is an open grassy plain designed as an imaginary grid punctuated by *folies,* a series of bright red, cubelike buildings, which appear as large abstract geometric sculptures set at regular intervals upon the greensward. Tschumi intended his green platform with red *folies* placed at grid intersections as "a surface of multireferential anchoring points for things or people which leads to a partial coherence."[37] Though without specified uses at the time of construction, these now function like structures in conventional parks; some are snack bars, one is a children's play structure, another a first-aid station, and so forth. A curvilinear, below-grade Bamboo Garden designed by Alexandre Chemetoff (b. 1950) provides a counterpoint to the strict geometry of Tschumi's theoretically endless spatial grid. At grade, a similarly serpentine path also plays against the regularity of the overall plan.

This highly intellectualized approach to landscape creation is the province of design competitions and the product of an avant-garde cultural establishment. The French have historically been especially hospitable to innovation and cerebral forms of artistic expression. However, other new Parisian essays in landscape creation, notably the new parks of Bercy and André Citroën, do not pursue the deconstructivist course charted at Parc de la Villette. These other new parks project the kind of meaning and symbolic structure of older gardens where representation — the *re-presentation* of ideas, as opposed to the presen-

tation of an implicitly endless grid as an intentionally *meaning*-less space in which visitors find whatever "event-text" or momentary significance they may wish—aims to create poetical *place,* not merely value-neutral *space* (figs. 15.27, 15.28).

LANDSCAPE AS CONCRETE AND METAPHYSICAL POETRY

Poet and visual artist Ian Hamilton Finlay (b. 1925) established his reputation in the 1960s as a pioneer of concrete poetry, the arrangement of individual words on a page, often accompanied by pictorial images, in ways that gives them psychological resonance and heightened meaning. His garden near Lanark, Scotland, which he calls Little Sparta, with its textual elements—graphically beautiful incised stones and wood—explores the gap between language and sign, indulging a subtle interplay of word and form, within the context of landscape (figs. 15.29, 15.30). As a garden of association, Little Sparta is reminiscent of such eighteenth-century creations as William Shenstone's Leasowes or Henry Hoare's Stourhead, which also abound in evocations of antiquity.[38] As we saw in Chapter Seven, the Leasowes was a *ferme ornée,* and Stourhead, with its themes from the *Aeneid,* is a highly poetic landscape manifesting Virgil's epic narration of the founding of Rome. Like these eighteenth-century predecessors, Little Sparta consciously recalls the Arcadian paintings of the seventeenth-century artist Claude Lorrain and the nostalgic echoes of a Golden Age found in Virgil's *Eclogues,* the series of pastoral poems composed by the Latin poet between

42 and 37 C.E. Situated in the rolling Pentland Hills of southern Scotland where sheep graze, the garden effectively implies these earlier depictions of a bucolic landscape studded with a few antique ruins. In such Claudian or Virgilian scenes human action occurs within the rhythms of a timeless agrarian round as shepherds and flocks move in sunlit meadows and rest beside shady groves and softly gliding streams. At Little Sparta, the themes of water and land, waves and hills, boats and huts predominate, although the garden also contains references to the French Revolution and warfare, especially World War II, and symbolically hints at the shadow of destructive nuclear power under which we live today. With such memorials to our losses of innocence as the fallen "Arcadia" column

15.29. Prostrate column with the inscription "Arcadia, a Place in Sparta's Neighborhood," Little Sparta

Below: **15.30. Little Sparta, Stonypath, Dunsyre, near Lanark, Scotland, garden designed by Ian Hamilton Finlay. Begun 1966. Inscription on rough-hewn stones: "The Present Order is the Disorder of the Future—Saint Just."**

and "Nuclear Sail," a smoothly rounded, silkily finished, matte gray "gravestone," Little Sparta's improbable and ironic dialogue with the tranquil Scottish borderland may perhaps be best characterized as an elegant and elegiac meditation on postindustrial as well as postpastoral civilization.

Maya Ying Lin (b. 1959) is an artist who works in the conceptual zone between landscape design and sculpture, and, like Finlay, she understands the combined power of words and visual imagery. Often classified with Earthworks artists, she is less concerned with creating large-scale works of cosmological reference in remote locations than with imaging a metaphysical poetry in environments that are readily accessible and where her art gains significance from the opportunities presented by the site. For these reasons, Lin's work is not abstractly philosophical. Instead, it is informed by psychology and phenomenology. Unlike the awesome and somewhat intimidating works of some artists, Lin's con- structions are intimate and inviting, while serving an essentially poetic purpose. Water and stone and images of time and movement are important elements in her art, and she employs these in sensory as well as symbolical ways. Psychology is evident in her use of other forms of sensory stimulation besides the visual: her work is tactile and aural, encouraging one to touch, be still, and listen. She is more concerned with investing

places with universal human significance than with creating spaces like Parc de la Villette that are intended to serve as abstract architectural demonstrations of philosophical theory.

Lin sprang to prominence in 1981 as a Yale undergraduate when she won the design competition for the Vietnam Veterans Memorial (fig. 15.31). A requirement of the Vietnam Veterans Memorial Fund, sponsors of the competition, was that the memorial contain the names of the more than 57,000 servicemen who died or are missing in action in that tragic conflict. Conceived as two retaining walls of black polished granite holding a grassy bank at an angle of 132 degrees, this sober, tactile, meditation upon death and war leads the visitor along an inclined path past the inscribed necrology that begins and ends at the apex of the triangular incision in the earth.

Begun as a studio project in an architecture class, Lin's competition entry drew inspiration indirectly from a memorial that was formally quite different: Sir Edwin Lutyens's monument to the missing soldiers of the World War I Battle of the Somme in Thiepval, France, an immense archway upon which 100,000 names are inscribed. "To walk past those names and realize those lost lives—the effect of that is the strength of the design," Lin has written. Her approach was similarly "apolitical, harmonious with the site, and conciliatory." Lin wished to produce a monument

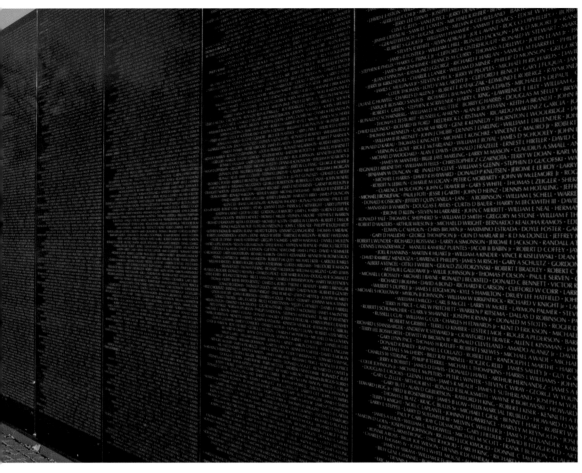

15.31. Vietnam Veterans Memorial, Constitution Gardens, Washington, D.C., designed by Maya Lin. 1982

that was lacking in histrionic content but capable of serving as a necessary cathartic vehicle for mourning the tragedy of the war, a means for veterans and other visitors to come to terms with the soldiers' deaths. About the design, she says, "I imagined taking a knife and cutting into the earth, opening it up, an initial violence and pain that in time would heal. The grass would grow back, but the initial cut would remain a pure flat surface in the earth with a polished, mirrored surface, much like the surface on a geode when you cut it and polish the edge. The need for the names to be on the memorial would become the memorial; there was no need to embellish the design further. The people and their names would allow everyone to respond and remember. . . . I always wanted the names to be chronological, to make it so that those who served and returned from the war could find their place in the memorial."[39]

One side of the Vietnam Memorial's wide sunken V points to the Washington Monument, which is reflected in the somber granite's mirror finish; the other is directed toward the Lincoln Memorial. The openness, darkness, and below-grade horizontality of the Vietnam Veterans Memorial subtly oppose the self-containment, whiteness, and verticality of those structures. "By linking these two strong symbols for the country, I wanted to create a unity between the nation's past and present," says Lin.

The mirror finish also reflects the visitors' images and the surrounding park, "creating two worlds, one we are a part of and one we cannot enter."[40] The stillness and emotion are palpable as visitors descend to experience the wide V's sober embrace, some of their fingers tracing over the letters of the names. Few overtly heroic monuments command this degree of respectful attention. Fresh flowers, recently written notes, and other newly deposited tokens of respect and love bespeak the continuing bond between the living and the dead.

In enjoining artists "to portray a more interesting, beautiful, dynamic, and tragic universe,"[41] Charles Jencks is thinking of the deeper cosmological consciousness produced by twentieth-century science. Along with Jencks, Lin is interested in giving landscape expression to the new concepts of the universe that are emerging through advanced science and technology. By coincidence, she was born and grew up in Athens, Ohio, near the Hopewell Mounds, and while these ancient relics probably hold the same fascination for her as for archaeologists and other cosmologically oriented artists of Earthworks, her primary objective is to discern and express what we are here suggesting as "fourth nature," a state that integrates the three preexisting categories of nature—wilderness, cultivated land, and the garden—with science and technology. This dimension of her work

15.32. *The Wave Field,*
François-Xavier Bagnoud
Aerospace Engineering Build-
ing, University of Michigan,
Ann Arbor, Michigan, designed
by Maya Lin. 1995

derives inspiration from the optical and photographic instruments—microscopes, telescopes, and satellite cameras—that make us perceive the world and universe in new ways.

To create *The Wave Field* (1995), a 100-foot-square (30.5-meter-square) earth and grass memorial commissioned for the François-Xavier Bagnoud Aerospace Engineering Building at the University of Michigan in Ann Arbor, Lin studied the fluid dynamics associated with the physics of flight (fig.15.32). The image that gave substance to the fluidity, indeterminacy, and unending repetitiousness of the movement of air currents essential to flight was for her a photograph of ocean waves in a turbulent sea. Here she evokes both her notion of the indeterminate character of the endless advancing and receding ocean and the oceanic appearance of the waving prairie that was once the American Midwest. Each of the earthen waves, which vary slightly in breadth and height, is a cozy shell in which students come to sit and read. As Michael Brenson explains:

> In *The Wave Field,* indeterminacy becomes place. Lin grounds it, makes it available to actual people. She also gives it a moral purpose, even an urgency, that would be inconceivable in many hymns to indeterminacy. *The Wave Field* makes a case for art's ability to encourage people to gather in an environment where they will be comfortable with one another and able to trust what they have not yet recognized and what they cannot measure or control; an environ-

ment in which children feel safe and inspired by the pleasure that can come from experiencing the world in terms of discovery, play, interconnectedness, and flow.[42]

Place as indeterminacy and experience as discovery, play, interconnectedness, and flow are concepts of the twentieth and twenty-first centuries. Earthworks and other forms of Conceptual art bear witness to the entropic character of contemporary civilization, engage our imaginations in new cosmological perspectives on the meaning of time and space, and provide metaphorical expression for our otherwise inexpressible sorrows or joys. At the same time, our everyday lives proceed in diurnal time and real space. Our understanding of contemporary place must therefore accommodate the accelerated change, motion, and communication that characterizes the new Postindustrial Age. We must seek to comprehend a geography that is both temporal and spatial, one of flows, instantaneousness, and virtuality. Place is, in the last analysis, experiential, as much a state of mind as an earthly reality. It is, according to contemporary thought, grounded within us, within our physical bodies as well as within our psyches. This is true whether we are stationary—*in place*—or traveling. It is important to understand that movement itself is part of the experience of place and that we are all in a sense weavers of landscape. It is with this notion of place-making as weaving and the reading of the world as a loom of landscape, a cultural geography, that we will conclude.

1. See Kevin Lynch, *The Image of the City,* Cambridge, Mass.: The M.I.T. Press, 1960. Lynch's small influential classic volume on reading the city develops the concept of nodes—topographic features, landmark structures, prominent or eccentric buildings, public open spaces—as easily visualized reference points in the mental maps that act like circuit boards of place within our brains.

2. These words are being written on January 1, 2000, after watching the millennial fireworks bursting in the night sky over New York City while also viewing a television broadcast of filmed New Year's celebrations in every part of the world. One saw the collapsing of time and space in the present century's intensely globalizing culture and observed iconic structures of place—the Eiffel Tower in Paris and many other world monuments—now presented as intensely illuminated spectacles, serving as talismans in a time of seemingly momentous transition as well as the foci of mass gatherings of humanity. New York City's Times Square, whose design character is—appropriately in an age of media power—distinguished more by highly technological visual display of information and photographic imagery than by any easily recognizable architectural character, was the self-proclaimed epicenter of this global party.

3. Robert Smithson, "Entropy and the New Monuments" (1966), *Robert Smithson: The Collected Writings,* ed. Jack Flam (Berkeley: University of California Press, 1996), p. 11.

4. Ibid. According to Smithson, "The slurbs, urban sprawl, and the infinite number of housing developments of the postwar boom have contributed to the architecture of entropy." op. cit., p. 13.

5. Ibid., p. 14.

6. David Lowenthal, *The Heritage Crusade and the Spoils of History* (Cambridge: Cambridge University Press, 1998), p. xiii.

7. Kevin Lynch, "Time and Place in Environmental Design," *City Sense and City Design: Writings and Projects of Kevin Lynch,* ed. Tridib Banerjee and Michael Southworth (Cambridge, Mass.: MIT Press, 1996), p. 630.

8. Ibid., pp. 629–30.

9. Delores Hayden, *The Power of Place: Urban Landscapes as Public History* (Cambridge, Mass.: MIT Press, 1995), p. xi.

10. For a good discussion of the changing meanings assigned the New England town, see William Butler, "Another City upon a Hill: Litchfield, Connecticut, and the Colonial Revival," in *The Colonial Revival in America* (New York: W. W. Norton & Company, 1985), pp. 15–51.

11. See Chris Wilson, *The Myth of Santa Fe: Creating a Modern Regional Tradition* (Albuquerque: University of New Mexico Press, 1997).

12. For a good interpretation of the motives, often unconscious, underlying the re-creation of historical narratives through landscape preservation and restoration, see David Lowenthal, *The Past Is a Foreign Country* (Cambridge: Cambridge University Press, 1985). According to Lowenthal, "We are often innocent of conscious intent to change what we mean simply to conserve or celebrate. . . . We can now see how pedagogic and patriotic commitments shaped Henry Ford's Greenfield and John D. Rockefeller's Williamsburg. But we cannot detect our own preconceptions, which warp the past no less than Ford's or Rockefeller's." See op. cit., pp. 325–26.

13. See Charles B. Hosmer, Jr., "The Colonial Revival in the Public Eye: Williamsburg and Early Garden Restoration," *The Colonial Revival in America,* pp. 52–70.

14. Mary Haldane Begg Coleman, "The Reminiscences of Mrs. George P. Coleman," transcript of interview, February 22, 1956 (Colonial Williamsburg Foundation Archives: Oral History Collection), p. 62. As quoted in Charles B. Hosmer, Jr., "The Colonial Revival in the Public Eye: Williamsburg and Early Garden Restoration," *The Colonial Revival in America,* pp. 61–62.

15. The impulse to make Williamsburg's faded past, which may have been "a little bit thin," nevertheless very pretty and in keeping with contemporary aesthetics as influenced by Industrial Age manufacturing standards and maintenance practices extends well beyond Shurcliff's gardens. For instance, "In restored Colonial Williamsburg, paints and fabrics brighter than colonists ever had were justified on the ground that eighteenth-century folk would surely have used such colours if they could have found and afforded them." See Lowenthal, *The Past Is a Foreign Country,* p. 329.

16. Jane Jacobs, *Death and Life of Great American Cities* (New York: Random House, 1961), pp. 443–44.

17. Ibid.

18. See David Lowenthal, *George Perkins Marsh: Prophet of Conservation* (Seattle: University of Washington Press, 2000), p. 267, note 1.

19. George Parkins Marsh, *Man and Nature, Or, Physical Geography as Modified by Human Action* (1864), ed. David Lowenthal (Cambridge, Massachusetts: The Belknap Press of Harvard University Press, 1965), pp. 38–9.

20. Ibid., p. 465.

21. Ibid., p. 51, note 53.

22. Ian McHarg, *Design With Nature,* 25th Anniversary edition (New York: John Wiley & Sons, Inc., 1992), p. 5.

23. Ibid, p. 19.

24. See Anne Whiston Spirn, *The Granite Garden: Urban Nature and Human Design* (New York: Basic Books, 1984). See also Timothy Beatley, *Green Urbanism: Learning from European Cities* (Washington, D.C.: Island Press, 2000). For a good discussion of the term *urban husbandry* as a means of revitalizing cities as places to live, see Roberta Gratz and Norman Mintz, *Cities Back from the Edge: New Life for Downtown* (New York: Preservation Press, John Wiley & Sons, Inc., 1998).

25. Harlow Whittemore, in *Proceedings of the National Conference on Instruction in Landscape Architecture,* Asilomar, Pacific Grove, California, July 5–7, 1957, p. 30. As quoted in Peter Walker and Melanie Simo, *Invisible Gardens: The Search for Modernism in the American Landscape* (Cambridge, Mass.: MIT Press, 1994), pp. 258–59.

26. For the history of the Franklin Delano Roosevelt Memorial, I am indebted to Reuben M. Rainey, "The Garden as Narrative: Lawrence Halprin's Franklin Delano Roosevelt Memorial," unpublished manuscript, 1995.

27. Robert Smithson, "Entropy and the New Monuments" (1966), *Robert Smithson: The Collected Writings,* ed. Jack Flam (Berkeley: University of California Press, 1996), p. 11.

28. Robert Smithson, "Spiral Jetty" (1972), *Robert Smithson: The Collected Writings,* p. 145.

29. Ibid, p. 146.

30. Interview with the author, July 27, 2000.

31. Charles Jencks, as quoted in Cooper and Taylor, *Paradise Transformed: The Private Garden for the Twenty-first Century,* p. 67.

32. As quoted by Julie V. Iovine, "Sermon on the Mound," *New York Times Magazine,* February 4, 1996, p. 44.

33. See Cooper and Taylor, op. cit., p. 72.

34. For my knowledge of the history of golf course design as outlined below I am indebted to Geoffrey S. Cornish and Ronald E. Whitten, *The Architects of Golf,* rev. ed. (New York: HarperCollins, Publishers, 1993).

35. Transcript of meeting in New York, September 17, 1985, in *Chora L Works* by Jacques Derrida and Peter Eisenman, edited by Jeffrey Kipnis and Thomas Leeser New York: The Monacelli Press, 1997), p. 8.

36. Ibid.

37. Bernard Tschumi, *Cinégramme Folie: Le Parc de la Villette* (Princeton, N.J.: Princeton Architectural Press, 1987), p. 24.

38. According to John Dixon Hunt, "Finlay is undoubtedly a special case in modern landscape architecture. He is special not because he is different but because his radical invocation of basic devices from the history of place-making makes more of those traditions than most other designers." See John Dixon Hunt, *Greater Perfections* (Philadelphia: University of Pennsylvania Press, 2000), p. 117.

39. Maya Lin, "Making the Memorial," *The New York Review of Books:* XLVII:17 (November 2, 2000), pp. 33–34.

40. Ibid.

41. "Landscape of Waves," *Prospect Magazine* (Winter, 1996): 2-5, as quoted in Beardsley, *Earthworks and Beyond,* p. 197.

42. "Maya Lin's Time," in *Maya Lin: Topologies* (Winston-Salem: Southeastern Center for Contemporary Art, 1998), p. 41.

THE WEAVING OF PLACE
AND THE GEOGRAPHY OF FLOWS:
LANDSCAPE AS BODILY EXPERIENCE
AND VERNACULAR EXPRESSION

The cultural background shaping contemporary attitudes toward landscape and place can be discerned in philosophy, which toward the end of the nineteenth century found its domain in alliance with psychology. During this period, confidence in Western society's progressive ideology began to erode as science and philosophy split ever further apart, and the restless search for truth became a matter of continually shifting premises. As revolutionary scientific discoveries overthrew former religious belief about the creation of the universe, they substituted no reasonable new cosmology, only the exhilarating yet sometimes disquieting intellectual voyage into the unknown that continues still.

The implications of evolutionary biology in *The Origin of Species,* which Charles Darwin (1809–1882) published in 1859, made it clear that humankind could no longer be viewed as separate from the rest of the animal kingdom. Furthermore, the field of scientific geology developed by Sir Charles Lyell (1797–1875), from whose fossil record Darwin drew many of his conclusions, undermined completely the notion that Earth's topography—the context and medium of landscape design—could have been modeled by mythological gods or a Divine Craftsman, rather than by the natural forces of crustal upthrust and erosion by wind and water.

At the same time that geologists learned that the shape of Earth's surface is the product of many eons of flux, physicists unsettled established verities regarding the stability and timelessness of the universe. At the beginning of the twentieth century, the formulation of the second law of thermodynamics, which foretells the disintegration of the universe as it moves toward a state of entropy, undermined the Enlightenment's confident, rational Cartesian-Newtonian cosmology. Albert Einstein (1879–1955) further eroded the principles of Enlightenment science with the theory of relativity, and thus the independent and absolute nature of space and time. Quantum mechanics further unseated accepted truths.

The Enlightenment concept of a heliocentric universe was relegated to the dustbin of science. In recent years, the theory of a Big Bang has gained general acceptance as the generative power behind a multigalactic universe composed of many hundreds of billions of solar masses. Telescopic space probes of heretofore unimaginable depth are revealing ever more remote galaxies. Today universal space is understood to be curved, even malleable, rather than as extending in a straight plane as René Descartes had logically supposed in the seventeenth century.

Seen thus in the light of biology, geology, and physics, belief in a stable, unchanging, God-created world and belief in the human being's extraordinary, semidivine status within it were severely shaken. Religion thus proved capable of providing personal conviction and moral guidance only for the individual rather than serving as a metaphysical structure of belief for society at large. Friedrich Nietzsche (1844–1900) laid down the premise for existentialism with his declaration of "the death of God." Nietzsche believed that, liberated from the concept of an objective reality based upon rationality, humans could realize their potential through the heroic enterprise of self-invention—the creation of an individual Truth. In Nietzsche's supremely Romantic vision of the unshackled self, art acquired the status formerly accorded religion, and the poet assumed the seat of the philosopher, whose function was now generally confined to the area of linguistics, logical positivism, and other noncosmological subjects.

Psychology began to preempt the role of philosophy in informing human thought and providing cultural context. Sigmund Freud (1856–1939) analyzed the human psyche by interpreting the experiences of childhood and the symbolical messages divulged in dreams. He posited that the unconscious mind and powerful biological instincts are the operative forces beneath civilization's veneer of rationality and ethical religion, accounting for its darker, chthonic impulses. To Freud's psychology Carl Jung (1875–1961) added his concept of the collective unconscious grounded in, and structured by, archetypal principles. Jung's theories provide insight into the universality of psychological experience and the persistence of myth as a cultural phenomenon and metaphorical instrument for shaping intellectual perception and making art.

The weakening of collective religious belief bolstered by Nietzsche's vision of the autonomous creative self and by psychology's focus on the interior lives of persons promoted individualism — belief in the primacy of the individual and the rights of individuals within the larger framework of society. To some extent, statism — belief in the supremacy of the state as the provider of a value system and social and economic structures capable of sustaining citizens both spiritually and physically — attempted to fill the vacuum left by religion's diminishing role in people's lives. But, as Nietzsche intuited, the liberating notion of humanity's essential freedom and ability to rationally fashion a society of its own choosing has a dark side. People during an increasingly troubled and complex twentieth century came to understand this as divisiveness, enmity, racism, and revolt flourished along with our propensity for exploitation and cruelty. Unpersuaded by the rhetoric of evil demagogues or inept political leaders of the state's supremacy and viability as a substitute for God, many thinking people found themselves in a condition of existential despair. Yet if humankind is its own ultimate resource, then philosophy must necessarily focus upon the individual as an instrument of action as well as cognition.

Phenomenology and existentialism offered new philosophical perspectives in this regard. The German philosopher Edmund Husserl (1859–1938) sought to overcome the dualism inherent in Enlightenment philosophy following Descartes's separation of the field of inquiry into an objective material universe and a subjective cognitive self. Husserl gave primacy to the experience of everyday life, *Lebenswelt*, or "life-world" as the basis of reality. Phenomenology, the investigation of the data of consciousness — moods, values, desires — and the things of the material world, including mathematics and the concept of space, constituted the philosophical basis for reforming spiritual life. Within this framework, psychology was more than a social science; it validated intuition and subjective awareness as means for understanding the world.

With the publication of *Being and Time* (1927), Martin Heidegger (1889–1976), Husserl's successor as professor of philosophy at the University of Freiburg, extended Husserl's phenomenological investigations and attempt to rescue humanity's understanding of itself from the confines of rational science. Implicit in the philosophical concept he called *Dasein* — meaning "attunement," or "being *there,* inhabiting and dwelling in the world" — is the cherishing of place as the intimate infrastructure of everyday experience. As the urban historian Sam Bass Warner, Jr., reminds us, Heidegger traced the verb *to dwell,* which is fundamental to his concept of *Dasein* to its original meaning: to build *and* to cultivate land.[1]

In his major work, *Phénoménologie de la perception* (Phenomenology of Perception, 1945), the French philosopher Maurice Merleau-Ponty (1908–1961) also countered the existential angst and the nihilism fostered by the spiritual crisis of modern life by focusing upon "sense experience." For Merleau-Ponty, "Sense experience is that vital communication with the world which makes it present as a familiar setting of our life."[2] The body anchors the individual in the world, connecting consciousness with the empirical and giving coherent structure to perception and behavior. In this light, we are not passive subjects registering by means of cognition the spectacle of the world but agents of its transformation, projecting significance upon both our personal and collective histories through real and symbolic actions, thereby giving life form.

In relation to our subject, landscape, Merleau-Ponty's discourse on the phenomenological aspect of space is instructive. He maintains that our need to feel stable, *in place,* not vertiginously adrift but anchored *somewhere,* proceeds from our bodily constitution, our innate sensation of up and down, which is our primary apprehension of space and of being in the world. The affirmation of this basic truth and Merleau-Ponty's poetic regard for personal experience puts him in league with another French philosopher, Gaston Bachelard (1884–1962). Bachelard used the combined approach of psychology and phenomenology to articulate in *The Poetics of Space* (1957) a concept of "topoanalysis" in which poetic reverie encourages the individual to spiritually reinhabit the intimate spaces of memory where he finds images "which are all light and shimmer," proving that "houses that were lost forever continue to live on in us."[3] According to Bachelard, through daydreams time is enfolded into psychic spatiality, as intimate places, particularly the places of childhood, abide in memory and dreams.

Bachelard's philosophical musing upon the poetics of place constitute an examination of "the quite simple images of *felicitous space.*"[4] His topophilia, or fond remembrance of place, however, has its counterpart. Instead of examining space, as did Bachelard, in terms of imaginative poetics and phenomenology resonant with Jungian archetypes and individual psychology, Michel Foucault (1926–1984) studied it as a historical, non-absolute, impermanent phenomenon, with widely differing interpretations from era to era and from culture to culture. Foucault posited a "heterotopology" of "countersites" that challenges Bachelard's order of intimate psychical place with an analysis of such politicized, historicized spaces as prisons, cemeteries, and parks.

In addition, in *Les Mots et les choses* (1966: translated into English as *The Order of Things: An Archaeology of the Human Sciences,* 1970) Foucault provides an analysis of the function of representation, which, as landscape historian John Dixon Hunt extrapolates, can be usefully applied to a new and needed historiography of the garden. That account would suppress recitation of a narrative of styles in favor of an analysis (such as has been attempted in this book) of landscape as a combination of nature and art manifesting historically relevant cultural values.[5] With these intellectual premises in mind, we will conclude our history of landscape design with a meditation on how all of us act as place-making agents as our moving bodies claim space and as we create forms and inscribe patterns upon the landscapes of the world, which are forever part of nature whatever our particular cultural values may be.

I. Body and Space: The Weaving of Place

Within the span of an individual life, it is especially difficult to grasp the fundamental truth that everything, including the architecture of nature—mountains, plains, rivers, seas—is forever changing. Imposing order on nature and believing that the spaces we shape have permanence seem to be necessary imperatives for maintaining our bearings psychologically. Even when space is outside of our personal influence in terms of structure, we appropriate it by the movements of our bodies.

Following Bachelard, we may think of our dwellings as nests of personal space and our craniums as the repositories in which are stored many remembered places, even, or especially, places erased by time. But we should not think of place as stationary. From the window of the moving automobile or, more sensationally, from the windswept, unprotected motorcyclist's perspective, place is fluid, the streaming scenery of the highway.[6] What is important to understand is that whether we are in fast or slow motion, we are claiming space with the sensations experienced by our moving bodies while internalizing meanings of place through the impressions stored in our minds. Space can be thus likened to a loom, and our shuttling motion as we traverse familiar habitats or explore unknown ones makes us weavers of place as we create a fabric of the mind with which to cloak our naked psyches and attach ourselves to the world.

We may observe that our feet trace and retrace habitual steps. In this way we weave and reweave the fabric of physical and psychological space, making ourselves at home in the world. Our weaving capability is such that, like birds, some of us can live transient lives and over their course borrow or build many nests that we call home. Thus adaptable, we are like other biological creatures, also weavers of space, place-making animals. To visualize this activity metaphorically we may think of strings with knots, or better, because it is a more maplike and therefore a more placelike image, intersecting lines in a field with dots. The strings or lines represent the routes we traverse and the knots or dots the stationary points where we settle for awhile.

Claiming Space

The theoretical reweaving of unraveled place constitutes the work of archaeological anthropologists who attempt to understand the role of movement—ritual processions, ceremonial dancing, pilgrimage to nature shrines, and so forth—in the place-making activities and hence the landscape designs of Paleolithic and Neolithic peoples. The Walbiri people in Australia, a society of contemporary hunter-gatherers, demonstrate how habitual passage over traditional lines of movement invests landscape with significance and mythic content. The Walbiri have imposed on their territory a sacred web of tracks called songlines linking stations that are associated with totemic beings, or dreamings. These dreaming sites are elements in a mnemonic system employed by the nomadic Walbiri, who must memorize the features of an arid locale where the scarcity of rainfall makes knowledge of potential water holes essential.[7]

Walbiri dreaming sites, the locus of religious ceremonies, serve as landmarks within an otherwise indistinguishable desert landscape.[8] The totems of the Walbiri consist of various animals, astronomical features, the elements—wind, rain, and fire—and even some important human artifacts such as spears or digging sticks. Cultural heroes wandered along the established songlines in the mythic period known as dreamtime, which is conceived as both a long-ago and continuing category of existence.[9] In dreamtime, these creative figures assumed human form, shaped topography, gave the landscape its features, and deposited their totemic essences in the places where they halted in their journeys before transforming themselves into animal or plant form and returning into the earth at a spot, usually of some topographical distinction, that served as their memorial and principal shrine. Dreamtime continues as an alternative to historical time, and the impregnation of the ordinary world with its spiritual essences and the corresponding impregnation of human fetuses with the dreamings of their place of conception shape the identity of individual members of the society and affect their mutual relationships. By performing rituals at the dreaming sites, Walbiri men may enter dreamtime for a brief period, becoming the heroes they impersonate. The care of the dreaming sites and custodial responsibility for the rituals and songs belonging to them are assigned to individual lodges associated with each location. At Ngama Cave, located near Yuendumu in a valley with abundant game and where three songlines converge, one lodge continues to maintain the totemic wall paintings depicting snake, dingo, and wallaby.

As we saw in Chapter Two, the ancient Greeks wove their colonial cities *per stringas,* as bands of north-south and east-west streets forming a Hippodamian grid, and then wove a looser net of territorial claims by extending pilgrimage routes to the shrines located near the limits of the *chora.* By moving along processional routes into the countryside to the temple shrines as well as by walking the streets of the *polis,* people activated this fabric of space and internalized it as place.[10] So, too, do we fashion from the patterns of our movement our notions of place. Thus place, which is coterminous with our own selves, is the claim our moving bodies make upon regional space, which, in accommodating our comings and goings, gains familiarity and accrues meaning. As philosophy historian Edward Casey reminds us, *"Bodies build places . . . through inhabiting and even by traveling between already built places."*[11] Seen in this way, place is something that is sequenced like the Walbiri songlines by movement along routes that are punctuated with landmarks in which we have invested significance, if only the significance of customary sight. In the highly commercial capitalist societies of the West, the rituals of shopping and eating out are important components in our contemporary concept of *chora*, the regional receptacle of place.

Place is therefore kinetic, a pattern of habitual movements through remembered space. Where our intuitive directional system based upon familiarity and repetition of experience breaks down, as when large numbers of strangers are in transit, passing through airports or train and bus stations, we substitute for our mental maps of place well-developed graphic systems containing conventional international symbols. As highways, automobiles, and trucks have put more and more people on the move and made mass marketing and distribution systems commonplace, society's impulse has been to delocalize place by creating ubiquitous and predictable cultural geographies. Retail and hotel chains and other instantly recognizable commercial franchise operations such as service stations and fast-food restaurants thus become the denominators of the placeless place where anyone can presumably feel at home.

As we saw in Chapter One, Puebloan people in the Southwest have woven place by establishing a flow of energy that also guides the people's footsteps between the pueblo and the inconspicuously stone-marked mountain shrines that establish the cosmological paradigm within the landscape. Like the *agora* of the Greek *polis*, the *bupingeh*, or central plaza, constitutes the civic and social heart of the pueblo, and the *nansipu*, the small stone-encircled depression within the *bupingeh*, marks the cosmological axis mundi and the centerpoint of the spatial tapestry that extends from the pueblo in four directions to the encircling mountains that rim the horizon. But although the pueblo sacralizes space, it is not itself considered to be a sacred, immutable form, being simply the temporary center of a people who may move to another location someday, allowing their adobe walls to melt back into the earth. The fixity of the pueblos as we know them today is a product of an Euro-American cultural construct that perceived nature in nonreligious terms as a commodity. The newcomers granted land by law as property or territory with established boundary lines. By contrast, the migration of Pre-Columbian Native Americans is found in the archaeological record, particularly in the ruins of long-abandoned pueblos dotted across the Southwest.

Ironically, at the same time that post-Columbian Americans began to restrict the movements of Native Americans, they set themselves in motion, weaving a new American *chora* of continental dimensions as they moved west to colonize the land. The warp and woof of Jefferson's national grid became a loom of spatial weaving such as the world had never seen before. Within the mile-square, 640-acre sections described by its orthogonal lines, fields and the smaller-scale grids of cities were established. But the actual roads that followed the engineers' surveys that mapped the national grid were not created until much later. Depressions in the prairie grass where the Great Plains end near Fort Union in eastern New Mexico mark the ruts of the wagon wheels that formed the Santa Fe Trail. Frederick Law Olmsted, traveling in the antebellum South, found himself continually slowed down by the miry, rutted roads. With tolls but no federal taxes to support their establishment or upkeep, the roads of America were all local for more than a century and a half of the republic's existence, making each region insular and all long-distance highway travel an arduous adventure.

In Chapter Twelve we examined how this situation changed as the automobile became a popular and increasingly dominant mode of transportation. The limited-access "townless highway" conceived by Benton MacKaye and the first motor parkways on Long Island and in Westchester County, New York, were thought of as regional arteries and their purpose as primarily recreational, bringing newly mobilized city-dwellers nearer to nature. But following World War II, a powerful congressional lobby supporting motor transportation interests fostered the creation of interstate highways, and the United States became laced with expressways—multilane arteries for trucks as well as cars. This national network supplanted the earlier regional one featuring parkways. The journey was no longer its own reward; speed and absence of traffic congestion replaced motorized recreation as the engineer's primary goals. As parkway construction waned, landscape architects were rarely employed on roadway design projects, as was the case in the early twentieth century when the Bronx River, Taconic, Merritt, and other parkways in the New York metropolitan region were built.

In the global, technology-oriented culture of the twenty-first century, images of local and historical

16.1. A "geography of flows." Freeway, Seattle

place have become universalized through endless replications, and we have become infinitely more mobilized than participants in prior civilizations. Time and space are experienced differently, and the world has become a geography of flows: of people, of goods, and of information (fig. 16.1). The result is a multicultural landscape pastiche, a transcultural scenery of borrowed design motifs and symbols. We may lament the frenetic pace of contemporary life and long to get back to nature, but the journey cannot be accomplished without connection to the technology of transportation flows.

Lawrence Halprin understood this. In his 1966 essay on freeways he wrote:

> Freeways out in the countryside, with their graceful, sinuous, curvilinear patterns, are like great free-flowing paintings in which, through participation, the sensations of motion through space are experienced. In cities the great overhead concrete structures with their haunches tied to the ground and the vast flowing cantilevers rippling above the local streets stand like enormous sculptures marching through the architectonic caverns. These vast and beautiful works of engineering speak to us in the language of a new scale, a new attitude in which high-speed motion and the qualities of change are not mere abstract conceptions but a vital part of our everyday experiences.[12]

Followers of Jane Jacobs would caution against romanticizing the beauty of engineering and panoramic skyline vistas from freeways. These exhil-

arating Faustian experiences of human power are all too often at the expense of existing neighborhoods, irremediably disrupting people's lives and social bonds. But that does not mean that all highway construction is inimical, especially were politicians and planners to heed the finest lesson offered by the Disney Company's theme-park planners: a system of multiple, integrated transportation technologies aimed at creating neighborhood-sized, car-free environments. This goal would force careful consideration of exterior access and parking needs along with the interior infrastructure necessary to facilitate pedestrian and light-rail transit flows.

An ethos of intelligent stewardship of Earth's biological and human environments and good frameworks for political decision-making are fundamental if we are to successfully address with scientific, technical, and artistic means the global challenges that confront us. In Europe especially, regional planners have begun to think of conservation in terms of the transportation costs associated with the environmental footprints of cities—that is, the amount of far-flung hinterland necessary to sustain them with food, water, and energy—and to mass buildings and preserve green space with stronger regard for the natural channels of air and water flowing through them.

The flows of images and information via satellite technology and the Internet provide new means of advancing global stewardship and promoting integrated international environmental management systems. To succeed fully, this stewardship must encompass a psychological and phenomenological attachment to place. We must therefore learn to value the qualities that constitute place and understand what it means to be a body that moves through space, a corporeal self at rest and in motion, a being that is capable of place making within the context of home, nature, and community.

Because mind and body cannot be divorced and because it is the mind that insists on organizing—imposing order on—space, place is, in fact, wherever we are physically. By being emplaced in space we ineluctably claim space as place. When the astronaut Neil Armstrong set his foot on the moon in 1969, claiming a giant stride for humankind, the moon became a place as well as a heavenly body.

Movement is pleasure and often spiritual reward. Curious by nature, we are explorers, claiming place by venturing forth to look and learn, even if we have no intention of settling. Scaling the mountain summit or diving below the ocean's surface imprints us with experience of place. Standing on the mesa or the open plain and watching the sun plunge beneath the horizon or, away from city lights, gazing into the dark immensity of the night sky at the Milky Way and the myriad stars produces in us the same sensation of cosmological awe that prehistoric peoples converted into religious myth and calendrical calculation.

It is important to distinguish between mind-body space and abstract, intellectualized space. Alone among sentient creatures, human beings are capable of conceptualizing space in both real and abstract terms, as lived experience on the one hand and as cartography, mathematical model, or cosmological diagram on the other. We have imposed a system of spatial coordinates—longitude and latitude—upon our planet as a universally agreed-upon aid to navigation. Satellites programmed to pinpoint position now beam information that can be captured by computers, giving drivers of automobiles or hikers in the wilderness accurate information about their current location and directions to their destinations. Surveyors have made possible the mapping of virtually the entire surface of the globe with great precision and at a fine scale. To this base of topographical information, geographers and natural scientists, as well as demographers, economists, and political scientists, have added much useful information regarding climate, geology, vegetation, wildlife habitat, the boundaries of cities, states, and nations, and human road systems and settlement patterns. Map reading enables us to picture accurately places we have never seen, and cinematic and still photography at both aerial and ground level increases our ability to visualize remote places. Nevertheless, the *experience* of space as place remains personal.

CAMPING

To go camping is to internalize spatial experience most vividly and to comprehend human place making in its most elemental form. Through availing themselves of all manner of technical aids, such as warm clothing made of industrially manufactured synthetic fibers, good topographical maps, or perhaps a handheld computer with satellite-beamed compass orientation, exact location, and directional information, the backcountry camper claims wilderness (first

16.2. Hikers on Crater Lake Trail, Crater Lake National Park, Oregon

nature) as an experience of place by following trails. Blazed by the original explorers of wilderness, trails are tracks made by the feet of horses, cattle, and humans who have gone ahead (fig. 16.2). Each hiker who threads a way along these paths or bushwhacks with stream courses and sun position for guidance weaves out of spatial distance a personal experience of place. This takes the form of a composite of sensory impressions: the resinous pungency of pine, the low rumble from the thundercloud over the mountain; the darkness and cool of the forest with its carpet of leaf litter, moss, ferns, and mushrooms; the picnic on a sun-warmed rock in the meadow of breeze-blown grasses and nodding wildflowers. If we are journalists, we may make of these experiences a string of words, for narrative is an important adjunct to place making, and even an illiterate camper will have his or her story of the Way.

Yet no story of a journey is without its caesuras, and no trek is without its pauses, breaks for rest and sleep. The camper, like the wayfarer seeking an inn for the night, must tie a knot in the string of space he or she is weaving, by selecting a temporary nest or den, the spot where a tent makes a home, the place where, cocooned in a sleeping bag and covered by a fragile shell of fabric, one sets forth on a voyage of nocturnal dreams. Or, dispensing with the insubstantial house that the tent represents, the camper joins those prehistoric ancestors who governed their lives through myth and celestial observation, studying the rotational movements of the bright lights overhead, still amazed, if not as wondering as they, about the cosmological meaning of those lights' majestic march across the heavens through the hours of darkness.

This exhilarating venture into nature, our first home, sharpens our senses, but we must not imagine that, even as campers relearning ancient skills, we can recover in wilderness the perspective of prehistoric humankind. We may only imagine it from our own cultural vantage point. The vapor trail of the jet overhead and the distant roar of its engine as it courses along its prescribed skyway join the flight and cry of the jay, reminding us that we live in a world that is increasingly of our own making. Yet even our technologically derived environments are part of nature and must submit to nature's laws: this is the lesson of camping in those reserves of "first nature" that remain on a crowded planet.

BODILY PLACE

Finally, *we* are place. The axis mundi of cosmology is imbedded in our unconscious because we walk upright. Because we walk upright we traverse space, making place through movement. If we are women, we have wombs, the primordial image of place as medium and matrix. In us abides the cave, prenatal paradise, and protected sanctuary. If we are men, we produce semen, the procreative male seed that fertilizes the female egg residing in the uterus. As men we stand for the potency represented by storm clouds and mountain peaks; as women we symbolize the earth's fertile valleys and hidden recesses, holding, containing, embracing life within our wombs and in our arms. Together women and men shape space and make place by virtue of our movements and our decisions.

To deconstruct space is to immediately reorganize it intellectually, for the ordering principle of our brain is much stronger than our will to acquiesce to formless, spatial chaos. To feel at sea, uncentered, adrift in undifferentiated, essentially placeless space, is to experience an unbearable sense of disorder and confusion, like the oppressive weight of darkness and silence in a sealed tomb or airless dungeon. Even in these dire circumstances, however, as long as we are aware of our spatial anxiety, experiencing our palpitating heart and dry-mouthed, wet-palmed fear, we are in place, being, so to speak, in body.

Settlements, especially cities, accrue meaning over time, although this meaning is always changing. Within cities, the more numerous and significant sacred spaces are, the greater the city. Because cities are fabrics of space dense with buildings, sometimes their most sacred spaces are their unbuilt places: the agora, the monumental plaza or square, the public park. These are the amply filled-in blanks within the metropolitan spatial continuum. In fact, parks and parklike open spaces are sometimes the most powerful definers of place, important markers in the mental geography of every resident beyond the age of early childhood when the concept of space is still limited, not yet expanded beyond mother, home, yard, and immediate neighborhood. One senses with special force, and sometimes poignance, the vitality and persistence of the human urge to interact with nature and to create satisfying places in the community garden, a provisional landscape occupying temporarily vacant urban land. The community garden contradicts facile assumptions regarding urban dwellers' indifference to nature and predictions about the death of public space. Within these and other superficially insignificant, often marginal spaces can be found expressions of ethnic identity, spiritual fulfillment, and economic improvement.

COMMUNITY GARDENS

With the alteration of the social landscape of America following World War II, the inner urban ring became less dense and more racially mixed as both migrants and immigrants took up residence. The drop in real estate values that made rents in these areas affordable for newcomers also gave landlords less incentive to maintain their properties. With the advent of the civil rights movement in the 1960s and the riots sparked by police confrontation with those demanding racial equality, some of these neighborhoods experienced wanton destruction. In the wake of the rioting, many landlords simply deserted their destroyed properties and already deteriorated buildings. With no utility or maintenance services, these sites were also abandoned by their tenants. Eventually many buildings were torn down and their sites left as rubble-strewn open space. With no remittance of the taxes due on them, municipal real estate departments were forced to claim these properties.

But still there were people who called the neighborhoods surrounding these lots home, and as Sam Bass Warner, Jr., points out, "today's American urban community garden is the child of new politics and abandoned city land."[13] Some of these gardens have become showcases of ornamental horticulture as well as green retreats, recreational centers in which to relax and socialize (fig. 16.3).

In spite of the community gardens' popularity, many public officials believe that they are not the best use of random parcels of city-owned land when measured against the need for housing and their desire to generate revenues from taxes and land sales to developers. Those who turn open spaces into green places through the investment of their creativity, time, and labor—gaining for themselves a sense of place in the process—are confronted by those with superior power over land because of ownership and the ability to regulate its use. This power stems from a value system in which land is considered a commodity and place as something fungible. In Boston, Philadelphia, Chicago, and Seattle, however, a new ethic that attempts to balance green space with the need for housing and municipal revenues is emerging, and governmentally sponsored redevelopment programs in these American cities are being undertaken within the context of neighborhood-based city planning.

Whether gardens are urban or suburban, of our own making or ones we create with the help of professional designers, they are personal paradises where we find soul space, our places for dreaming, family life, play, and entertaining friends. But these are not the only cherished landscapes. For some, Central Park or the city of Paris are homes for the heart even more valued than their own abodes, place being as much as anything a state of mind. As our bodies and minds claim space and live place, everywhere can be utopia, which literally means *nowhere,* but which we are able by our acts of imagination and will to convert into our own visionary *somewhere.* We ourselves *are* place, but we are also forever *in* place, whether moving or

16.3. Clinton Community Garden, New York City

at rest. To feel connected and centered in the world is to know how to find our way, to navigate ourselves spatially and locate ourselves in the small temporary centers we call home. Because we live in communities, not in isolation, our decisions and those of others affect the nature of place both individually and collectively with regard to the societal arrangements we create to structure the allocation and use of space and the examples and standards we set forth with regard to landscape design.

Our journey through landscape design history has enabled us to see that populism is ascendant in our time and that, although often vulnerable to superior economic forces, landscapes like community gardens are important expressions of culture and individual aspiration. When we look at the entire built landscape we see that it is a fabric woven by countless individuals. The term *vernacular* is often applied to landscapes that manifest place-making by ordinary people. To make generalized observations about this type of human landscape, it is necessary to adopt the analytic approach of the cultural geographer.

II. Cultural Geography: The Loom of Landscape

Histories have been written since ancient Greek times, and landscape inevitably figures in the narratives of battle scenes and descriptions of locales of human settlement. But like the landscapes found in Renaissance paintings, landscape description in historical writing most often functions as a backdrop for the tableau in the foreground where human action takes place. Novelists more than historians have proved capable of writing vivid prose descriptions integrating local landscape and human affairs. But even in novels, landscape as protagonist, the central subject of analysis and revelation, is absent. This is the province of the geographer turned cultural anthropologist.

Landscape as a Textbook of Human History and Daily Life

Cultural geography, the term describing the study of landscape in its broad dimensions as both nature and human artifact, is a recent subject of disciplined inquiry. More philosophical and intuitive than scientific and more eclectic in its approach than traditional geography, it is part of a trend we can trace to the nineteenth century when history, natural history, and art history emerged as fields of professional endeavor. At that time, when the pursuit of knowledge became increasingly specialized, geography evolved from its cartographic origins to become a combination of earth science and social science, with an emphasis upon the economic potential of natural resources. Not until the 1920s, however, did a group of French geographers attempt to project an intimate portrait of the settled regional countryside. As planned by Paul Vidal de la Blache and edited by Pierre Deffontaines, the *Géographie universelle* appeared between 1927 and 1948 as a series of monographs. As editor of the periodical *Revue de géographie humaine et d'ethnologie,* Deffontaines continued to relate landscape appearance to culture and the history of human occupation of the land.

William G. Hoskins (1908–1992), another pioneer in the field of cultural geography, published *The Making of the English Landscape* (1955), a portrait of his country from the perspective of the historical evolution of its landscape. By roaming the countryside on foot and bicycle and studying its surface features, vegetation patterns, transportation lines, and buildings, Hoskins made his readers aware that landscape could be read as a fascinating document, a morphological record of other times and other lives. Hoskins cherished the vestigial evidence of continuous human occupation over the centuries and the patina of ancient heritage he found in long-settled landscapes, and he was vociferously alarmed by the twentieth

century's highly mechanized, capitalist culture that disrupted these historic landscape patterns. Although his work was slow to win a popular audience, by the 1970s his academic post, a television series featuring Hoskins and the English countryside, and paperback republication of his remarkable book sparked considerable interest in landscape analysis from the perspective of cultural history in Great Britain and elsewhere.

John Brinckerhoff Jackson (1910–1996) took a related but very different stance from Hoskins.[14] Jackson's attention to landscape at a local scale, combined with an artist's eye for visual form and an appreciation of architecture, nurtured his interest in "reading" the landscape. He saw how he could apply the experience he had gained as an intelligence officer in wartime Europe to analyze the landscape of his adopted region, the American Southwest, and how the process of deciphering its cultural meanings could lead to a broader perspective on the relationship between humankind and nature. *Landscape,* the magazine that he began publishing three times a year in 1951, was his principal forum for the next seventeen years.

Like Patrick Geddes, Jackson was fascinated with aerial perspective as a means of interpreting human settlements, but he did not share Geddes's motives as a city planner. He wanted his readers simply to recognize and appreciate the social, economic, and cultural forces that had shaped "the compact Indian communities, perched on rocks overlooking the fields, the sprawling tree-grown checkerboard of the Anglo-American towns, the Spanish villages strung along a road or a stream; the huddle of filling stations and tourist courts at highway intersections in the desert."[15] In addition, there was the individual house, which Jackson viewed as a manifestation of culture as well as an expression of certain spiritual and biological needs.

The road, emblem of restless movement and the means of continental migration, resides within the American imagination as an important image. Jackson, who traversed the country many times by motorcycle, made the road an important, recurring subject in his work. Unlike the critics of urban and rural visual blight, he never deplored the effect of the automobile on the landscape (fig. 16.4). He saw speed as an exhilarating sensory stimulus, and he would not deny the abstract beauty of "the new landscape, seen at a rapid, sometimes even a terrifying pace."[16] The American highway was for him a collective work of industrial-age folk art, and he applied to the honky-tonk roadside strip of motels, gas stations, used-car lots, and fast-food franchises the same dispassionate

16.4. Highway commerce, Wichita, Kansas

perspective that allowed him to view side yards filled with rusting automobiles and other eyesores as evidence of people's means of gaining a livelihood. His article on "The Stranger's Path" describes the tawdry vitality of the route from the bus or train depot on the urban fringe to skid row, the business district, and civic center. He was interested in the ability of people at the bottom rung of society to find accommodation and even a sense of place within the landscape. Thus, landscape was for Jackson never something merely to look at, but to live in. From this attitude stemmed his aversion to modernism in architecture and city planning, even when architects and planners attempted to implement a thoroughly democratic agenda. He doubted that even intelligent suburban landscape design such as Garrett Eckbo's, whose book *Landscape for Living* Jackson criticized as too abstract, could serve as effectively as grassroots place-making.

Besides validating landscape studies as a field that included mobile homes and trailer courts, Jackson argued against the dichotomous attitude that sees nature and urbanity as polar opposites. In his unified vision, nature was all-pervasive, and he took pains to point out that the same forces of climate, topography, and vegetative growth that appear in the unbuilt countryside operate equally within the built city. Unlike Hoskins, who wished to arrest landscape change and ugly Machine Age incursions that bespoke contemporary people's increasing alienation from nature, Jackson stressed the inevitability of landscape's ever-changing character.

Jackson honed his iconoclastic perspective as a means of jolting conventional attitudes, especially the Romantic attitude toward nature promulgated by Jean-Jacques Rousseau and later Henry David Thoreau, but he never developed an analytical methodology, nor did he work in any programmatic way to bring about environmental improvement. His principal legacy lies in stimulating a more humanistic approach to looking at landscape.

Conclusion

As we have seen throughout this book, people have sought at certain times and places a correspondence between abstract, philosophical notions of space and designed manifestations of place. The builders of the cities of Ur, Knossos, and Teotihuacán centered their constructions in landscape space according to a cosmological diagram. At Vaux-le-Vicomte and Versailles there is a firm relationship between Cartesian cosmology and experiential space. The desire for a correspondence between philosophical and scientific concepts of space and landscape can be seen in our own day, as is evident from some of the Earthworks discussed in the previous chapter.

But the grounding of spatial abstractions in the landscape is only part of the story of place making. The force of history as inspiration for designing space has only increased during the last two hundred years. The cachet of history and historic places has never been more evident than now as civilization embarks upon its third millennium of the Common Era. The several styles prefaced with "neo–" attest to this. Beyond mere stylistic reiteration, history as a salvaging of the past and sometimes a literal replication and re-creation of place has garnered the momentum and resources of an international preservation movement. With the perceived endangerment of place, archaeological sites and landmarks are being protected from alteration. The consumption of history by tourists has become a powerful motive for the current reweaving of place. Old town centers, such as war-devastated Dresden, are being rebuilt, historic villages are being saved as exquisite corpses, their old functional lives now re*placed* by their new role as tourist destinations. Tourist accommodation necessarily alters the thus-valorized space. By way of example, the route leading to the sacred cave of Zeus on Mount Ida (see Chapter One) has been recently surfaced with asphalt paving to facilitate the arrival and parking of buses.

To value the vernacular landscape is to attest to the fundamental implausibility of master planning; no one can predict more than the basic functional needs of others, and human needs are neither universal nor static. While some regulation of land use is in the common interests of all who live together in a society, everyday environments are continually being improvised and reinvented within this spatial framework as the social circumstances of lives change, new economic opportunities arise out of new technologies, and new desires are born (fig. 16.5). And yet, in all the transactions that go on between human beings and nature, there is the impulse to arrest the fluidity of place, to save what is still held dear, and to renew the old as a representation of the desirable values that are believed to reside in certain bygone periods of history, even when the meaning of that period to contemporary people is undergoing change along with everything else.

Because of its use of industrial technology—

16.5. Mobile home with garden, Pecos, New Mexico. Contemporary vernacular landscapes created from commercially available products sometimes bespeak their debt to aristocratic tradition, as is evident from the symmetrical planning of this *parterre* with its Renaissance-style fountain.

exemplified by machine guns, fire bombs, gas chambers, rail transport to death camps, and other heinous applications—in the brutally efficient *displacement* of populations and eradication of spatial structure, the twentieth century witnessed more forced evacuation of place and destruction of spatial meaning than any other. In that century it became apparent that industrial technology is a power that can efficiently destroy the natural environment for short-term economic gain, impoverishing irreplaceable ecosystems, including the human ecosystem, and in some places destroying entire species with ferocious rapidity. But technology is not innately inimical, and it is also being used to improve the conditions and duration of human life, while environmental science is working to restore degraded ecosystems. In this light, place is the planet Earth, a collective human responsibility.

In our survey of cities, parks, and gardens we have examined landscapes as shaped space and defined place. In bringing our journey to an end, it is important to realize that the making and erasure of place are continuous processes, as is the philosophical conceptualization of space. These transactional activities between human beings and landscape will continue as long as there are minds to inquire about the cosmological meaning of space and to confer collective and personal meaning on place, and as long as there are hands, assisted by machines, to shape space in partnership with nature.

1. Sam Bass Warner, Jr., *To Dwell Is to Garden* (Boston: Northeastern University Press, 1987), p. xii.

2. Maurice Merleau-Ponty, *Phenomenology of Perception,* trans. Colin Smith (New York: Humanities Press, 1962), pp. 52–53.

3. Gaston Bachelard, *The Poetics of Space,* trans. Maria Jolas (Boston: Beacon Press, 1969), p. 33.

4. Gaston Bachelard, *The Poetics of Space,* p. xxxi.

5. Foucault's position is that "the coherence that existed, throughout the Classical age," which he assumes to be the seventeenth century, the period of the dawn of modern science, "between the theory of representation and the theories of language, or the natural orders, and of wealth and value" was shattered beginning in the nineteenth century. With this change, "the theory of representation disappears as the universal foundation of all possible orders; language as the spontaneous *tabula,* the primary grid of things, as an indispensable link between representation and things, is eclipsed in its turn; a profound historicity penetrates into the heart of things, isolates and defines them in their own coherence, imposes upon them the forms of order implied by the continuity of time; the analysis of exchange and money gives way to the study of production, that of the organism takes precedence over the search for taxonomic characteristics, and, above all, language loses its privileged position and becomes, in its turn, a historical form coherent with the density of its own past." See Michel Foucault, *The Order of Things* (New York: Vintage Books, 1994), p. xxiii.

For John Dixon Hunt's discussion of Foucault's exegesis on representation, see *Greater Perfections* (Philadelphia: University of Pennsylvania Press, 1999), pp. 78–80. Hunt's call for a revitalized historiography of landscape design and practice of landscape architecture can be found in *Greater Perfections,* chap. 8.

6. As D. W. Meinig points out, "the key landscape symbol in late twentieth century America is not the home but the highway, and community is not so much a discrete locality as a dispersed social network traced on the landscape by the moving automobile." See D. W. Meinig, "Symbolic Landscapes: Some Idealizations of American Communities," *The Interpretation of Ordinary Landscapes,* ed. D. W. Meinig (New York: Oxford University Press, 1979), p. 182.

7. See John E. Pfeiffer, *The Creative Explosion: An Inquiry into the Origins of Art and Religion* (New York: Harper & Row, Publishers, 1982), pp. 153–73.

8. See M. J. Meggitt, *Desert People: A Study of the Walbiri Aborigines of Central Australia* (Chicago: The University of Chicago Press, 1962), pp. 58–71.

9. According to David Abram, "Dreamtime—the *Jukurrpa,* or *Alcheringa*—that plays such a prominent part in the mythology of Aboriginal Australia . . . is a kind of time out of time, a time hidden beyond or even *within* the evident, manifest presence of the land, a magical temporality wherein the powers of the surrounding world first took up their current orientation with regard to one another, and hence acquired the evident shapes and forms by which we now know them. It is that time before the world itself was entirely awake (a time that still exists just below the surface of wakeful awareness)—that dawn when the totem Ancestors first emerged from their slumber beneath the ground and began to sing their way across the land in search of food, shelter, and companionship." See *The Spell of the Sensuous,* (New York: Pantheon Books, 1996), p. 164. See also Bruce Chatwin, *The Songlines* (New York: Penguin Books USA, 1987).

10. I am indebted to Indra Kagis McEwen, author of *Socrates' Ancestor: An Essay on Architectural Beginnings* (Cambridge, Mass.: MIT Press, 1993) for the description of "Weaving the Polis." See op. cit., pp. 80–93.

11. Edward Casey, *Getting Back into Place: Toward a Renewed Understanding of the Place-World* (Bloomington: Indiana University Press, 1993), p. 116. See also Casey's etymological deconstruction of the word *dwell,* which in modern usage means to reside or fasten close attention upon. Its Old Norse cognate *dvlja* denotes "to linger," "to tarry," or "to delay," while its Old English cognate *dwalde* signifies "to go astray," "to wander," or "to err." See op. cit., p. 114.

12. Lawrence Halprin, *Freeways* (New York: Reinhold Publishing Corporation, 1966), p. 15.

13. Sam Bass Warner, Jr., *To Dwell Is to Garden,* p. 20.

14. For a good comparative discussion of the work of Hoskins and Jackson, see D. W. Meinig, "Reading the Landscape: An Appreciation of W. G. Hoskins and J. B. Jackson," *The Interpretation of Ordinary Landscapes: Geographical Essays,* ed. D. W. Meinig (New York: Oxford University Press, 1979), pp. 195–244.

15. J. B. Jackson, *Landscape* 1, no. 1 (spring 1951).

16. J. B. Jackson, "The Abstract World of the Hot-Rodder," *Landscape* 7 (winter 1957–58): 22.

GLOSSARY

acropolis The fortified height of an ancient Greek city, a citadel sited upon a prominent elevation overlooking a surrounding plain and sometimes the sea.

agora In an ancient Greek city an important open public space around and in which important civic, commercial, and communication functions took place.

allée A tree- or hedge-bordered walk, usually of gravel or grass. *Allées* are a common component of French garden design where a desired geometrical layout is achieved by straight axes outlined by paths with perspective-reinforcing side elements such as *palissades, parterres de broiderie,* closely spaced trees, or compartments of lawn.

arbor A garden construction of open latticework or rustic work created to support climbing plants and provide shade.

arboretum A place where a collection of trees and other woody plants are arranged as botanical specimens for scientific study, educational instruction, and ornamental display.

archaeoastronomy The investigation of archaeological sites with the intent of discerning the relationship of certain features to summer and winter solstices, maximum and minimum moon set points, constellations, and other astronomical phenomena.

automata Mechanically propelled garden features, such as singing birds and various kinds of mobile statuary, which were sometimes built with waterworks in order to combine the movement of water with that of various sculptural parts.

avenue A tree-lined approach to a mansion or other important structure that is sufficiently wide to accommodate carriages.

axis-mundi An imaginary vertical axis running as a center pole from the zenith of the sky through the ground, uniting heaven, Earth, and the Underworld.

azulejos The Spanish term for glazed tiles, the production and use of which were derived from Islamic culture. *Azulejos* were incorporated into the ornamentation of Spanish and Portuguese buildings and gardens.

bagatelle The French term for a small, elegant house built in the eighteenth century to house a mistress.

balustrade A row of balusters topped with a continuous rail, usually of stone, employed to form a parapet on terraces and to encase stairs.

baradari An open-sided pavilion in a Mughal garden.

Baroque A term signifying art and architecture that is robust, boldly sumptuous, grandly ornamental, curvaceously plastic, and therefore full of movement and the play of light and shade. Baroque design forms originated in Italy at the end of the sixteenth century and flourished there and in Germany, Austira, and Spain during the seventeenth and early eighteenth centuries. A highly theatrical approach to design, the Baroque sensibility penetrated but never dominated the art and architecture of France or England.

bedding out The Victorian practice of arranging plants, usually brightly colored floral annuals, in either abstract designs or pictorial patterns.

belvedere A structure, usually elevated, designed for observing the surrounding landscape. The term is derived from the Italian *bel* (beautiful) and *vedere* (to see).

berceau An arched trellis for climbing plants similar to a pergola, also closely planted trees trained to form an arched foliage-covered walkway. This French term is derived from the word for cradle, probably because antique cradles have a similar deeply arched form.

bioremediation The human-assisted regeneration of natural ecosystems and their corresponding biological life.

borrowed scenery The design principle of taking into account scenic views beyond the confines of the garden and planning the garden with reference to them. Chinese garden designers frequently used borrowed scenery, *jie jing,* in their designs. Japanese gardeners imaginatively exploited the same design technique and term, which they pronounced as *shakkei,* and some Western landscape architects, such as the Brazilian Roberto Burle Marx, have adopted a similar approach, composing gardens that include within their visual frame natural scenery outside their boundaries.

boschetto Within an Italian garden a small compartment of trees, usually found near the house and often planted according to a regular plan.

bosco The Italian term for a wooded grove within a garden.

bosquet The French term for a wooded grove within a garden.

botanical garden A didactic garden in which families of plant specimens are arranged and labeled according to taxonomic categories of genus and species.

boulevard A French term that has been appropriated into English, signifying a landscaped roadway designed for promenading as well as for vehicular traffic. The word *boulevard* is derived from *boulevart,* meaning bastion fortification, the town walls upon which the first boulevards were built in the seventeenth century.

brownfields Former industrial sites that are candidates for ecological reconstitution and conversion into green fields, i.e., natural areas or recreational parkland, by means of bioremediation.

buffet d'eau A tablelike architectural arrangement of bowls, basins, and troughs set against a wall or placed in a niche in order to animate the flow of water in an ornamental manner.

bunker A sand-filled depression on a golf course intended as a hazard for the player, also referred to as a trap.

bupingeh In the Tewa language of some Puebloan peoples, the plaza around which the adobe dwellings of the Pueblo are centered.

cabinet The French term for a secluded compartment within a garden.

cabinet of curiosities A collection of specimens such as were sought when it was still believed possible to comprehensively assemble in a single room or garden representative samples of various forms of natural history.

carpet bedding The arrangement of low-growing foliage plants of the same height in intricate carpetlike patterns of contrasting leaf color or floral hue.

caryatid A supporting column in the form of a female figure.

casino, casina A term referring mostly to a small pavilion or lodge on the grounds of an Italian villa garden. Usually *casino* denotes a summerhouse for dining and refreshment some distance from the principal villa residence, but in cases where a villa might be used simply for a day's sojourn, it signifies the pleasure pavilion that serves as its principal architectural structure. The term was adopted by English-speaking people and used to denote certain ornamental pavilions and refreshment structures in gardens and parks in Britain and America. It is also used to signify a gaming hall where gambling and other forms of entertainment take place.

castellum The Latin term for castle or fortress; used also to denote a large architectural display fountain constructed as a rule to signal an aqueduct's formal point of entry into the city. Typically in Rome, where several such fountains were built, they commemorated the emperor or the pope who had commissioned the particular aqueduct marked by the *castellum.*

catena d'acqua The Italian term for water chain, an ornamental inclined channel designed to catch and animate the water falling from one shallow basin into another.

ceque A sight line emanating from Cuzco, the capital of the Inca emperors, like a sun ray and used as a path of pilgrimage.

chabutra A raised square stone dias in the center of the cross-axis of a *chahar bagh* designed to serve as a platform upon which pillows were arranged to accommodate one or two people who could enjoy from this central position the garden's water-cooled breezes and surrounding scenery.

chadar In Mughal gardens, an artificial cascade of masonry with ramplike surfaces carved in a faceted pattern in order to animate better the movement of water and reflective light.

chahar bagh The fourfold Timurid garden, which became the design paradigm for other Islamic gardens, *chahar* meaning "four," and *bagh* being the Turkish word for "garden." The variant spelling *char bagh* denotes the Mughal garden of India, whereas the spelling form *chahar bagh* is used in referring to the gardens of the Safavid rulers in Persia.

cha niwa Japanese tea garden where *cha no yu,* or tea ceremony, is performed.

cha no yu Japanese tea ceremony, an important cultural practice performed in settings that displayed an affinity for the aesthetic principles of Zen Buddhism, specifically that of rustic simplicity mellowed with age, called *sabi,* which were conducive to a mood of *wabi,* refined austerity.

château A magnificent establishment in the form of a castle or palatial manor house set in the French countryside, usually with attendant gardens.

chini kana One of a series of small recesses cut in the face of a terrace retaining wall in Mughal gardens to hold small oil lamps and flowers.

chinoiserie The European evocation of Chinese architecture and decorative arts that first appeared in the seventeenth century and assumed its full proportions in the eighteenth century, when the Rococo style was as its height and pagodas, "Chinese" bridges, and tea pavilions became popular features in Western gardens.

classicism Formal standards that honor as authoritative the principles governing the design arts and literature of ancient Greece and Rome.

conifer, coniferous A needle- or scale-leaved, cone-bearing, generally evergreen tree or shrub such as a pine, spruce, and fir. The adjective *coniferous* is used to describe plants of this category.

conservatory A building with heat and ample natural daylight, usually from south-facing windows, for the indoor protection and conservation of tender plants in the winter; a greenhouse or glass house. In the nineteenth century, although many conservatories were important, domed, freestanding glass structures large enough to accommodate the growth of tall palm trees, the term *conservatory* also came to denote a glass-covered extension of a house, accessible from a principal room, where exotic plants are displayed.

corso An Italian term signifying a principal thoroughfare, *corso* assumed new meaning as driving became a fashionable recreation in Rome and elsewhere after the appearance of spring-hung carriages in the early seventeenth century.

cours The French term for a wide thoroughfare capable of accommodating a daily parade of carriages.

deme A politically affiliated regional village or town within the territorial framework of an ancient Greek city-state, or *polis.*

espalier A fruit tree that is placed against a wall or other structure and trained, through pruning and manipulation of its branches, to grow in a flat plane, usually in a symmetrical fashion. The term *espalier* is derived from *spalla,* meaning shoulder in Italian.

exedra A semicircular bench with a high back, usually of stone, for placement in the landscape; also, in classical architecture, a semicircular portico with seats, which was used in Greek, Roman, and Renaissance times as a place for discussions; an apselike space formed by curving hedges in a garden.

eyecatcher A feature placed at a distant and usually elevated point in a garden or in a visible location outside its boundaries in order to accent the view, provide scenic interest, and draw one's gaze toward the horizon.

fabrique A Rococo garden structure closely allied with French Picturesque painting. *Fabriques* became popular in the eighteenth century when the *jardin anglais* and the *jardin anglo-chinois* appeared on the Continent. These *folies* assumed the form of Turkish tents constructed of wood, *chinoiserie* tea houses and bridges, "Gothic" towers, rustic huts, "Egyptian" pyramids, sham ruins, "hermitages," and other similar features intended to add visual interest to the garden and to evoke poetic associations with the past and with exotic locales.

faubourg The French term originally used for areas of urban development on the outskirts of the city; a suburb lying immediately outside the town walls. Today certain old Parisian *faubourgs* such as the Faubourg St. Germaine are fashionable city neighborhoods. Like a *faubourg,* formerly an outer-edge neighborhood, a *banlieue,* which in France is usually synonymous with an industrial, working-class area, is a zone of settlement on the urban fringe.

feng shui Translated from the Chinese as "wind and water," *feng shui* is the practice of professional geomancers who divine beneficial and malign influences within a particular location, thereby determining favorable sites and alignments for buildings and gardens while also neutralizing objectionable aspects of the landscape in question.

ferme ornée The French term for ornamental farm used by the English after Stephen Switzer appropriated it in *The Nobleman, Gentleman, and Gardener's Recreation* (1715) to promote the arrangement of agricultural estates as aesthetically pleasing compositions in which, typically, the hedgerows separating fields were enhanced with shrubs, vines, and flowers; an occasional monument was placed in a manner calculated to provoke poetic association; and a circuit drive was laid out to enable movement through the landscape.

folie The French term for folly, a garden structure intended as an evocation of past cultures or faraway places. *Folies,* which can be likened to theatrical scenery, were sometimes used to camouflage useful buildings, such as dairies, barns, or icehouses, but they often served no utilitarian purpose at all. They are usually associated with the *jardin anglais* and with the *jardin anglo-chinois.*

fontaniere A Renaissance hydraulic engineer capable of creating ingenious waterworks or automata.

Gardenesque style The term coined and design theory propounded by John Claudius Loudon beginning in 1832 to define and encourage a method of displaying plants to best advantage by granting them the appropriate horticultural conditions to develop into attractive individual botanical specimens.

geoglyph The term, which is compounded from the prefix *geo,* denoting Earth, and the term *glyph,* meaning an engraved or incised symbolic figure, signifies an Earthwork, such as those created by the Nazca of Peru, which is composed of an image pecked into the surface of a stony piece of ground.

giardino segreto The Italian term for a secret garden, a secluded and enclosed garden room commonly found in villa gardens of the Renaissance and seventeenth century.

giocchi d'acqua The Italian term for water games. *Giocchi d'acqua* were fountain effects designed by hydraulic engineers during the Renaissance to add an element of amusement to the garden experience as visitors, who unintentionally activated jets of water from hidden sources, were treated to surprise drenchings as a practical joke.

great house In England, the palatial mansion of an aristocratic country estate.

greenhouse A structure similar to a conservatory or an orangery in that it was originally conceived as a means of overwintering garden greenery that had been imported from warmer climates. With the increase of plant material by botanical discovery and the advance of horticultural science beginning in the eighteenth century, greenhouses were used for propagation as well as for the winter protection of tender plants. To promote indoor plant growth it was necessary to obtain a greater amount of sunlight than was admitted by orangeries and other masonry, windowed structures; in 1816, John Claudius Loudon invented a curvilinear sash bar of wrought iron, which led to the construction of greenhouses that admitted light from above. Because of its nearly all-glass construction, the greenhouse is sometimes referred to as a *glasshouse.* A greenhouse may be an independent, freestanding structure or attached to the side of a house.

grotto A natural cave, which has acquired human significance because of the spiritual forces presumed to inhabit it; also an architectural version of a cave, usually rustic in character and often containing water and sometimes sculptural representations of its presiding spirits. Grottoes that are identified with nymphs are often called *nymphaeums.*

ha-ha A fairly deep boundary ditch, invisible from a few feet away and serving the purpose of a fence separating the garden from the fields where cattle graze. The ha-ha was conceived in the eighteenth century

to give the illusion of continuity between the garden or residential park and the rural landscape beyond. John James's 1712 translation of Antoine-Joseph Dézallier d'Argenville's *Theory and Practice of Gardening* describes how the end of a "Terrass is terminated by an Opening, which the French call a *claire-voie,* or an Ah Ah, with a dry Ditch at the Foot of it." Horace Walpole said that the surprise experienced when one came upon this ditch caused one to exclaim, "Ha! Ha!"

hameau The French term for hamlet. In eighteenth-century French Picturesque garden design a *hameau* is a pretend-village, a group of farmlike buildings conceived as a piquant complement to the landscape and a means whereby aristocrats could make believe that they were rustics.

hedge Compactly planted shrubs or low-growing trees with dense foliage that is clipped so as to form a solid wall of greenery that acts as a boundary or a screen.

herm A male sculptural head mounted on masonry shaft. Originally displaying genitalia and conceived as representations of the god Hermes, herms were erected in antiquity as a series of boundary markers defining important public spaces, such as the agora. A single herm or pair of herms might mark the entrance to private property. In garden design from the Renaissance onward, the term has been used to signify any rectangular or tapering pedestal surmounted by a sculptural head.

hermitage A rustic garden structure built to resemble a rude hut such as might be inhabited by a hermit.

herradura The Spanish term for "horseshoe," also used to refer to an outdoor Native American shrine, usually a low, horseshoe-shaped enclosure, which is frequently located at a high point where there is a distant view.

hortus conclusus The Latin term signifying an enclosed, or walled, garden.

hôtel In France, an urban mansion originally built by families of the French nobility; after the Revolution, a building constructed on a scale and in a style of grandeur that followed this aristocratic model.

houri An Islamic term derived from the Persian *hūri,* meaning "gazelle-eyed," an attribute associated with the beautiful virgins who served as companions for the souls of the faithful in Paradise.

huaca In the Inca culture, a spirit-inhabited place in nature, which was located on a *ceque,* a sight line emanating from Cuzco like a sun ray, where offerings were made.

iwakura A sacred rock revered for its indwelling spirit in Japanese Shinto practice.

iwan A Persian structure consisting of large shallow-vaulted porch or hall with a pointed entrance arch. Fully developed under Sassanian rule, *iwans* are found in the ruins of the mid-sixth-century C.E. palace complex at Ctesiphon. They were later used as monumental entrances to mosques and as pavilions facing courtyards.

jardin anglais The French term for the English-style garden, which became popular in Europe in the eighteenth century. Conceived in reaction to the regularity of the geometrical French garden, it is often associated with *fabriques,* or *folies* in the form of garden pavilions and other Rococo features.

jardin anglais-chinois The French version of the Picturesque style of landscape design, which employed Rococo *chinoiserie* derived from William Chambers, whose books, *Designs of Chinese Buildings* (1757) and *Dissertation on Oriental Gardening* (1772), became popular on the Continent in the last quarter of the eighteenth century.

jie jing The Chinese technique of borrowing scenery by incorporating distant views into the garden's design.

kami Japanese gods and goddesses who sanctify certain places as their abodes.

kampaku Often translated as "chamberlain," a high governmental official in the Japanese court whose function was to mediate between the emperor and court officials in affairs of state.

kare sansui Dry landscape, a style of Japanese garden frequently associated with Zen temples. *Kare sansui* gardens are composed of carefully arranged rocks, moss, and gravel raked into lines that appear as rippling currents of water.

karikomi Meticulously clipped shrubs constituting an important element in Japanese gardens of the Edo Period (1603–1867) and beyond.

kirei sabi Beauty infused with a weathered rustic quality, a term used to describe certain Japanese gardens of the Edo Period (1603–1867), especially those designed by Kobori Enshu and his followers.

kiva In Native American Pueblo culture a subterranean circular structure descending from a *pit house* and serving as a room in which tribal rituals are conducted in secrecy.

knot garden A compartmentalized garden in which box or other low-growing compact shrubs or herbs such as rosemary, lavender, or thyme are planted in intricate designs resembling a looped and knotted rope, while the interstices are filled with colored gravel or ground-hugging flowers.

kokoro The Japanese term signifying "heart" or "center" and, by extended meaning, a heart-shaped lake. Japanese garden designers used the device of a bilobate waterbody to provide a middle ground within their landscape compositions.

lanai The Polynesian term borrowed from Hawaii by Californians and other mainland Americans to denote a breezeway, loggia, or roofed patio adjacent to a swimming pool.

limonaia Within an Italian garden, a walled garden filled with potted lemon trees.

locus amoenus The Latin term for a pleasant and delightful place; used in antiquity and the Renaissance to signify a rural or garden retreat of distinctive beauty.

loggia An open-sided covered arcade or gallery, usually attached to a building at ground- or upper-story level.

mall A tree-shaded promenade. The term originated in association with the Italian game *paglio maglio,* which became translated into English as *pall mall.* The game, similar to croquet, was played on an *allée* designed for the purpose. Since people promenaded there as well, the word *mall* eventually came to signify a dignified public space for outdoor exercise and social encounter. After the middle of the twentieth century, the term was commonly employed to denote a shopping center arranged as a series of stores lining a principal landscaped walkway. The first malls were outdoors, but later ones were enclosed, with tiers of stores rising above a broad, central open space serving as a place of respite and recreation.

mausoleum An elaborate architectural structure built as a tomb for one or more deceased persons.

maze A labyrinth in a garden that serves as a puzzle that must be navigated, avoiding blind alleys, if one is to reach the interior goal. Of ancient origins, mazes have been formed using various kinds of barrier material, but the hedge maze, popular since the seventeenth century, is the type commonly associated with gardens.

megalith An enormous stone, often used by prehistoric peoples as a monument or part of a landscape construction such as the circular arrangement of megaliths at Stonehenge.

Modernism The term signifying the early twentieth-century avant-garde approach to design based upon a functionalist and reformist aesthetic honoring the principles

of industrial manufacture and the tenets of the social welfare state.

nansipu In the tradition of Puebloan peoples of the southwestern United States, the earth navel on top of each sacred mountain. The term is also used to denote a small hole within the center of the pueblo's plaza, usually marked with a ring of stones and symbolizing the place from which the people emerged from the Underworld into the light.

naumachia A Renaissance garden feature consisting of a a flooded basin designed to function as a theater where mock naval battles were held.

Neoclassicism The late-eighteenth-century Enlightenment reaction to Baroque and Rococo art and architecture reflecting a return to the design principles of classicism, which were believed to reflect better the laws of nature and reason. Neoclassicism stimulated further interest in classical archaeology, which had been awakened during the Renaissance. Implicit in Neoclassicism is the belief in the purity of primitive and purely geometric forms. However, the term applies not only to architecture of a sober, non-ornamental nature such as that echoing Greek Doric forms but also to the more sumptuously ornamental Beaux-Arts style reflecting the historicizing tendencies fostered by the curriculum of the École des Beaux-Arts in Paris during the nineteenth- and early-twentieth-centuries.

niwa The Japanese word for "garden," which may also refer to a sanctified space in nature set apart for the worship of Shinto gods.

noria From the Arabic word *nūriy* meaning "shorter," also known as a *rehat,* this large river-current- or ox-driven wheel with attached buckets acting as pitchers was used for lifting water into an elevated canal or tank to irrigate Mughal gardens in India.

nymphaeum The Latin term signifying *grotto,* a cave or cavelike structure dedicated to nymphs and often containing fountains or other water features.

obelisk A monumental, rectangular, tapered masonry shaft with a pyramidal top, called a pyramidion. The obelisk as a form originated in ancient Egypt, where its pyramidion symbolized, like the large-scale pyramid, the life-giving, sun-blessed mound, the sacred *ben-ben,* revered in association with the worship of the Sun god Re. With its implicit promise of rebirth after death, the obelisk was appropriated in Western culture as a Christian symbol during the Renaissance when several toppled obelisks that had been garnered by the imperial Roman armies were surmounted by Christian

crosses and erected once more in public places in Rome. By the eighteenth century, because of its symbolic association with the afterlife, the obelisk had become a commonly accepted form for funerary and memorial monuments, and many miniature obelisks began to be used as grave markers, especially in the non-sectarian rural cemeteries built in the nineteenth century.

orangery A building designed with tall arched windows for admitting maximum sunlight and used for the winter protection of orange trees and other tender plants grown in boxes or tubs and placed in the garden in warm weather.

otium Denoting industrious leisure comprising worthwhile mental and physical pursuits away from the distractions of urban business, politics, and society. *Otium* as a concept originated with ancient Roman villa owners and was practiced by proprietors of rural estates in subsequent societies where civilized country life was equated with virtue and refinement.

palissade A tall, clipped, space-defining hedge in a French seventeenth-century-style garden.

parterre The French term for a ground plane composed of patterned garden beds. Compartmentalized and geometrical in the Renaissance following Italian example, *parterres* in France evolved into *parterres de broderie* in the seventeenth century.

parterre de broderie The French term signifying an embroiderylike ground-plane design in gravel and herbs, boxwood, or clipped grass, featuring decorative scrolls, palmettes, and arabesques, often with the addition of a monogram.

patte d'oie Three avenues radiating in the form of a goose foot from a central point.

pergola An open structure consisting of uprights and connecting joists or arches intended to support climbing plants, thereby creating a foliage-covered walkway similar to a *berceau.*

piazza The Italian term for a public square; in England the word is used to signify an arcaded passageway similar to the colonnades that often frame Italian *piazze.* In American English a piazza is a porch or verandah such as those advocated in the nineteenth century through the influence of domestic tastemaker Andrew Jackson Downing.

Picturesque The painting-influenced style enunciated by British landscape theorists William Gilpin, Richard Payne Knight, and Uvedale Price in the last quarter of the eighteenth century and practiced in England, on the Continent, and in America in variant forms until the end of the nineteenth century. Although the design of English landscape had been previously influenced by paintings, notably those of Claude Lorrain, it was the air of rugged wildness characteristic of the landscapes of Salvator Rosa that Picturesque landscape designers cultivated. Contemporary with the Rococo, the Picturesque style often incorporated Rococo effects, particularly in France, where Rococo taste originated. French Picturesque gardens also embodied the influence of Jean-Jacques Rousseau and thus express his sentimental view of nature and imply the virtues of life uncorrupted by society. The penchant for rusticity found in French Picturesque landscapes is also derived from an admiration of Dutch seventeenth-century landscape painting, as well as the works of French eighteenth-century artists Claude-Henri Watelet, François Boucher, and Hubert Robert.

pinetum An arboretum of specimen pines and other coniferous evergreen trees.

place In a general sense, space invested with use and meaning, a defined location. In a particular sense with regard to the urban landscape, place, which stems from the Latin *platea,* means a broad street, from which it became the French term for a public square.

plaisance A summerhouse or garden structure on the grounds of an estate. The term was also used as the name of a mall-like promenade that Frederick Law Olmsted and Calvert Vaux conceived to link Jackson Park and Washington Park in Chicago. Although designed for the South Park Commission in the 1870s, the Midway Plaisance, a linear band of lawns and shrubbery with a central canal, was not built until 1893 after Olmsted returned as a member of the design team of the World's Columbian Exposition.

pleasure garden In eighteenth-century England, a commercial establishment consisting of grounds with walks and groves of trees and offering food, drink, and music.

polis An ancient Greek city-state.

portico A porch or walkway with a roof supported by columns, often leading to the entrance of a building.

Postmodernism The term that gained currency in the 1970s to denote the reaction to the functionalist, anti-ornamental aesthetic of Modernism and signifying a late-twentieth-century architecture associated with vernacular elements as well as classical motifs.

potager The French term for a produce garden containing vegetables and fruit trees.

presidio A fortified military garrison established in Spanish colonial territories, especially in the American Southwest.

propylaia In ancient Greece, a large ceremonial gateway giving entry to an important ritual space.

pueblo A Spanish term meaning town, often used to denote a settlement on tribal lands in northern and western New Mexico and northeast Arizona, consisting of multilevel adobe or stone dwellings built by the descendants of indigenous prehistoric peoples.

pururuaca In the Inca culture, a large stone thought to be a transformed warrior and venerated as such.

pylon A monumental gateway composed of a pair of truncated pyramids marking the entrance to an Egyptian temple or some later important structure or space such as a nineteenth-century rural cemetery.

pyramid A monumental masonry structure with a rectangular base and four triangular faces rising to a common apex; in ancient Egypt during the Old Kingdom a tomb for a pharoah, or king.

quincunx A regular arrangement of five trees or other vertical elements, four of which comprise the angles of a square or rectangle, while the fifth serves to mark its center. The term often denotes a regular arrangement of trees set in a pattern composed of multiple units of five. When the quincunx form is thus used repetitively in the planting of a bosk, the resulting quincunx of trees appears as multiple rows set on a running diagonal when viewed at a 45-degree angle; read from a straight-on position, the rows assume a staggered pattern.

ragnaia In seventeenth-century Italian gardens, a series of parallel hedges to support the nets used to trap birds.

recinto A large enclosed parklike precinct within an Italian garden. *Recinti* might take the form of *boschetti,* informal groves of trees, or natural areas for hunting wild game.

rocaille A French term formed by conflating *rocher* (rock) and *coquille* (shell), which denotes the artistically rustic rockwork used to fashion grottoes and other rude-seeming garden structures.

Rococo A term derived from *rocaille* and used to characterize the final, eighteenth-century phase of Baroque art, architecture, and the decorative arts during which a curvaceous, asymmetrical, playful synthesis of abstract and naturalistic motifs developed in France and was universalized throughout the West. Rococo forms are delicate, elegant, lighthearted, and often amorous in spirit. In landscape design the term *Rococo* is associated with ornamental garden structures displaying a quirky elegance, fanciful exoticism, and ornamental exuberance, including especially representations of *chinoiserie.*

roji The path in a Japanese tea garden, *cha niwa,* that leads the visitor from the entry gate to the tea house, *cha no yu.* Visualized as a dewy path, it is composed of stones set in moss. Spatially, it usually consists of a narrow open corridor.

Romanticism The term denoting the late-eighteenth-century aesthetic movement fostered by the writing of Jean-Jacques Rousseau and Johann Wolfgang von Goethe. Derived from *romance,* the medieval genre of storytelling featuring chivalric heroes and adventurous exploits, Romanticism promotes emotion and feeling as modes of expression having as great a validity as those of reason and intellect. It is the counterpart of Classicism, and as such it values the individual and the subjective over the universal and the normative, holds the commonplace in high esteem, and does not look to Greece and Rome for inspiration, but rather to the landscapes of nature that are characterized as sublime, as well as in Picturesque scenery.

rond-point A circular area where a number of *allées* meet. Originally a clearing in the woods where converging paths brought huntsmen to a meeting place, the *rond-point* became prevalent in garden and urban design following its use by André Le Nôtre in the seventeenth century.

rural cemetery The result of religious and sanitary reform, the rural cemetery is a nineteenth-century landscape form harking back to ancient Greek burial practice and monumental commemoration outside the city walls.

rus in urbe Latin for "the country in the city," the term was used in advancing the case for public parks in the nineteenth century when people strongly believed in the therapeutic and spiritual benefit of creating rural scenery within the industrial metropolis. The expression "the lungs of the city" was also used at this time to urge the cause of the reservation of large open, green areas in rapidly growing, congested urban centers.

sabi The mellowness produced by weathered stone, mosses, and lichens. The quality of *sabi* is particularly characteristic of Japanese gardens dating from the Momoyama Period (1573–1603).

shakkei Japanese pronunciation of *jie jing,* the technique of visually incorporating into a garden's design borrowed scenery from beyond its borders.

shan shui Literally "mountains and water," the Chinese term for "landscape."

shin no mihashira The heart post of a deconstructed Shinto shrine, which marks the place next to an existing shrine where a new shrine will be built after a twenty-year interval.

shinden-zukuri A style of Japanese construction derived from Chinese norms of elegance, but austere in character. In Heian-period gardens, pavilions built in this fashion were placed at the edge of a lake.

shogun Often translated as "generalissimo," until 1867 the hereditary commander of the Japanese army, nominally in the service of the emperor, but exercising absolute authority in both civil as well as military affairs.

shoin zukuri A style of Japanese architecture comprising shoji-screen-divided rooms with proportions based upon the module of a tatami mat (approximately three by six feet).

sipapu In the cosmology of certain Puebloan cultures of the American Southwest, the mythical place where people emerged from the earth and the place where they return after death. The term is also used to denote the hole within the floor of a kiva, symbolizing this place of emergence from, and return to, the Underworld.

specimen An item such as a plant that is considered representative of an entire class, genus, or species; something that stands for an entirety. Botanical gardens and arboretums contain specimens that are planted to instruct observers in the characteristic appearance and growth habit of various plant species and their comparative aspects relative to other species within the same genus.

spoil Dredged material removed from an excavation.

stibadium A dining couch or divan, usually of carved stone, furnishing an ancient Roman *triclinium,* or dining area.

stroll garden A garden designed to be experienced sequentially as a series of scenes as the visitor walks along a prescribed route.

stucchi Stucco work in the form of low reliefs modeled wet in sand, cement, and lime and applied on the outside of a building. *Stucchi* for interiors are modeled in plaster.

style champêtre The French term for "rural style." The *style champêtre,* a component of the eighteenth-century French Picturesque style, implies the creation of *hameaux* and other rustic garden features suggesting country pleasures.

sublime In landscape terms, as analyzed by the philosopher Edmund Burke in his influential treatise *A Philosophical Enquiry into the Origin of Our Ideas of the Sublime and Beautiful,* the word *sublime* signifies majestic scenery or turbulent nature capable of stirring the human spirit, causing an emotion that can perhaps be characterized as fearful reverence or thrilled awe.

takamiya "Sacred precinct" in Japanese, often the sanctified area where a special object in nature is reverenced by practitioners of Shintoism.

tapis vert French for "green carpet," the term refers to a rectangular or other precisely shaped lawn.

temenos A precinct within the Greek landscape considered sacred to a particular indwelling deity. Marked off by stones or defined by walls, a *temenos* contained shrines, temples, and other sacred and symbolical structures, monuments, and natural forms.

tholos A circular temple, an architectural form developed in ancient Greece and often copied in Roman times as well as later when it was used extensively in Western gardens as an ornament within the landscape.

topia The Latin term for landscape paintings, used to denote frescoes of scenery in ancient Roman and Italian Renaissance gardens.

topos The notion of place as coterminous with contained and defined space, a concept derived from Aristotle.

treillage A piece of garden architecture composed of open latticework trellises used to support vines and train plants to assume a desired form.

trellis A structure of open latticework for supporting vines, often in the form of an arbor or arch.

trivio Three avenues radiating from a single point, called in French a *patte d'oie,* or goose foot.

vigna An Italian term denoting the type of suburban villa and rural retreat popular with wealthy aristocratic families during the Renaissance and later periods.

villa An Italian term denoting a country estate, originally an ancient Roman rural retreat with a substantial house. In the nineteenth century, English-speaking people used the word *villa* to signify a middle-class suburban dwelling.

villeggiatura A sojourn at a Renaissance villa, or country estate, usually occurring during the summer season.

volksgarten The public park, or people's garden, as developed in Germany according to the C.C.L. Hirschfeld's recommendation in *Theorie der Gardenkunst* (1779–85) for the creation of didactic landscapes in which monuments and inscriptions served to inculcate moral and patriotic sentiments, especially those promoting nationalism.

wabi Refined austerity, the pleasurable simplicity of poverty, a fundamental aesthetic principle of Japanese Zen Buddhism.

wilderness A wooded garden feature developed in England in the seventeenth century as a localized version of the contemporary French *bosquet.* Wilderness paths, which were originally straight *allées* arranged according to a geometrical plan, evolved from formal labyrinths into meandering byways as eighteenth-century designers attempted to induce in visitors within these secluded garden retreats greater sensations of adventure and surprise.

xian The immortals of Chinese myth, believed to inhabit, among other places, three enchanted islands upheld by giant tortoises.

yarimizu A Japanese riverbank garden.

yuniwa In Japan, a bare, gravel-covered, purified space associated with a Shinto shrine. The term may also be used to refer to the entry court of palaces and other monumental structures when these are empty or contain at most a pair of symbolic trees.

ziggurat A terraced pyramidal structure developed in ancient Mesopotamia by the Assyrians and the Babylonians to serve as a temple tower, an *axis-mundi* connecting earth and sky.

BIBLIOGRAPHY

Surveys and Reference Books

Ackerman, James S. *The Villa: Form and Ideology of Country Houses.* Princeton, N.J.: Princeton University Press, 1990.

Bazin, Germain. *Paradeisos.* Boston: Little, Brown & Co., 1990.

Birnbaum, Charles A. and Robin Karson. *Pioneers of American Landscape Design.* New York: McGraw-Hill, 2000.

Brown, Jane. *The Art and Architecture of English Gardens: Designs for the Garden from the Collection of the Royal Institute of British Architects 1609 to the Present Day.* New York: Rizzoli, 1989.

Clayton, Virginia Tuttle. *Gardens on Paper, Prints and Drawings, 1200–1900.* Washington, D. C.: National Gallery of Art, 1990; distributed by University of Pennsylvania Press.

Clifford, Derek. *A History of Garden Design.* New York: Praeger, 1966.

Fleming, John; Hugh Honour; and Nikolaus Pevsner. *The Penguin Dictionary of Architecture and Landscape Architecture.* 5th ed. London: Penguin Books, 1998.

Giedion, Sigfried. *Space, Time and Architecture.* Cambridge: Harvard University Press, 1967.

Gothein, Marie Luise. Translated by Mrs. Archer-Hind. *A History of Garden Art.* New York: E. P. Dutton, 1928.

Hall, Peter. *Cities in Civilization: The City as Cultural Crucible.* New York: Pantheon Books, 1998.

Hubbard, Henry Vincent, and Theodora Kimball. *An Introduction to the Study of Landscape Design.* New York: Macmillan, 1917.

Hunt, John Dixon. *Greater Perfections: The Practice of Garden Theory.* Philadelphia: University of Pennsylvania Press, 1999.

Hyams, Edward. *A History of Gardens and Gardening.* New York: Praeger, 1971.

Jellicoe, Geoffrey; Susan Jellicoe; Patrick Goode; and Michael Lancaster. *The Oxford Companion to Gardens.* Oxford: Oxford University Press, 1986.

Jellicoe, Geoffrey, and Susan Jellicoe. *The Landscape of Man.* 1975. Rev. ed. New York: Thames and Hudson, 1989.

Kostof, Spiro. *A History of Architecture: Settings and Rituals.* New York and Oxford: Oxford University Press, 1985.

———. *The City Assembled: The Elements of Urban Form Through History.* Boston: Little, Brown & Co., 1992.

———. *The City Shaped: Urban Patterns and Meanings Through History.* Boston: Little, Brown & Co., 1991.

Moore, Charles W.; William J Mitchell; and William Turnbull, Jr. *The Poetics of Gardens.* Cambridge: MIT Press, 1988.

Newton, Norman T. *Design on the Land: The Development of Landscape Architecture.* Cambridge: Harvard University Press, 1971.

Ross, Stephanie. *What Gardens Mean.* Chicago and London: University of Chicago Press, 1998.

Saudan, Michel, and Sylvia Saudan-Skira. *From Folly to Follies: Discovering the World of Gardens.* New York: Abbeville Press. 1988.

Schama, Simon. *Landscape and Memory.* New York: Alfred A. Knopf, 1995.

Scully, Vincent. *Architecture: The Natural and the Manmade.* New York: St. Martin's Press, 1991.

Thacker, Christopher. *The History of Gardens.* Berkeley and Los Angeles: University of California Press, 1979.

Torrance, Robert M., ed. *Encompassing Nature: A Sourcebook, Nature and Culture from Ancient Times to the Modern World.* Washington, D.C.: Counterpoint, 1998.

Studies in Cosmology, Philosophy, Psychology, and Phenomenology

Abram, David. *The Spell of the Sensuous: Perception and Language in a More-Than-Human World.* New York: Pantheon Books, 1996.

Bachelard, Gaston. *The Poetics of Space.* Translated by Maria Jolas. Boston: Beacon Press, 1969.

Barthes, Roland. *The Eiffel Tower and Other Mythologies.* Translated by Richard Howard. New York: Farrar, Straus and Giroux, 1979.

Berlin, Isaiah. *The Roots of Romanticism.* Edited by Henry Hardy. Princeton, N. J.: Princeton University Press, 1999.

Casey, Edward S. *Getting Back into Place: Toward a Renewed Understanding of the Place-World.* Bloomington: Indiana University Press, 1993.

———. *The Fate of Place: A Philosophical History.* Berkeley: University of California Press, 1997.

Deleuze, Gilles, and Félix Guattari. *A Thousand Plateaus: Capitalism and Schizophrenia.* Translated by Brian Massumi. Minneapolis: University of Minnesota Press, 1987.

Eliade, Mircea. *The Myth of the Eternal Return: Or, Cosmos and History.* Princeton, N.J.: Princeton University Press, 1954.

———. *Patterns in Comparative Religion.* Translated by Rosemary Sheed. Cleveland: Meridian Books, 1963.

Eisenberg, Evan. *The Ecology of Eden: Humans, Nature and Human Nature.* New York: Alfred A. Knopf, 1998.

Foucault, Michel. *The Order of Being: An Archaeology of the Human Sciences.* New York: Vintage Books, 1994. Originally published as *Les Mots et les choses* (Paris: Gallimard, 1966).

Harbison, Robert. *Eccentric Spaces.* Boston: David R. Godine, 1988.

Heidegger, Martin. *Being and Time (Sein und Zeit).* Translated by Joan Stambaugh. Albany: State University of New York, 1996.

Hetherington, Norriss S., ed. *Cosmology: Historical, Literary, Philosophical, Religious, and Scientific Perspectives.* New York and London: Garland Publishing, 1993.

Hiss, Tony. *The Experience of Place.* New York: Random House, 1991.

Jacobi, Jolande. *The Psychology of C. G. Jung.* New Haven: Yale University Press, 1973.

Lefebvre, Henri. *The Production of Space.* Translated by Donald Nicholson-Smith. Oxford, England, and Cambridge, Mass.: Blackwell, 1991.

Merleau-Ponty, Maurice. *Phenomenology of Perception.* Translated by Colin Smith. New York: Humanities Press, 1962.

———. *The Primacy of Perception.* Edited, with an Introduction by James M. Edie. Chicago: Northwestern University Press, 1964.

Miller, James E. *Rousseau: Dreamer of Democracy.* New Haven: Yale University Press, 1984.

———. *The Passion of Michel Foucault.* New York: Simon & Schuster, 1993.

Nancy, Jean-Luc. *Community: The Inoperative Community.* Edited by Peter Connor. Translated by Peter Connor, Lisa Garbus, Michael Holland, and Simona Sawhney. Minneapolis: University of Minnesota Press, 1991.

Stegner, Wallace. *Where the Bluebird Sings to the Lemonade Springs: Living and Writing in the West.* New York: Random House, 1992.

Tarnas, Richard. *The Passion of the Western Mind: Understanding the Ideas That Have Shaped Our World View.* New York: Harmony Books, 1991.

Weiss, Allen S. *Unnatural Horizons: Paradox and Contradiction in Landscape Architecture.* New York: Princeton Architectural Press, 1998.

WORLD PREHISTORIC AND ETHNOLOGICAL LANDSCAPES

Aveni, A. F., ed. *World Archaeoastronomy.* Cambridge: Cambridge University Press, 1989.

Bafna, Sonit. "On the Idea of the Mandala as a Governing Device in Indian Architectural Tradition." *Journal of the Society of Architectural Historians* 59:1 (March 2000): 26–49.

Burl, Aubrey. *Great Stone Circles.* New Haven: Yale University Press, 1999.

Chatwin, Bruce. *The Songlines.* Harmondsworth, England: Penguin, 1987.

Meggitt, M. J. *Desert People: A Study of the Walbiri Aborigines of Central Australia.* Chicago: University of Chicago Press, 1965.

Michell, George. *The Hindu Temple: An Introduction to Its Meaning and Forms.* Chicago: University of Chicago Press, 1977.

Millon, René; Bruce Drewitt; and George L. Cowgill. *The Teotihuacan Map.* Austin: University of Texas Press, 1973.

Mithen, Steven J. *Thoughtful Foragers: A Study of Prehistoric Decision Making.* Cambridge: Cambridge University Press, 1990.

Moctezuma, Eduardo Matos. *The Great Temple of the Aztecs: Treasures of Tenochtitlan.* London: Thames and Hudson, 1988.

Schafer, R. Murray. *The Tuning of the World.* Toronto: McClelland and Stewart, 1977.

EGYPTIAN AND MESOPOTAMIAN PREHISTORIC LANDSCAPES

Aldred, Cyril. *The Egyptians.* Rev. ed. London: Thames and Hudson, 1984.

Clayton, Peter A., and Martin J. Price. *The Seven Wonders of the Ancient World.* London: Routledge, 1988.

Ferry, David. *Gilgamesh: A New Rendering in English Verse.* New York: Farrar, Straus and Giroux, Noonday Press, 1992.

Frankfort, Henri. *The Birth of Civilization in the Near East.* Garden City, New York: Doubleday Anchor Books, 1956.

Grimal, Nicolas. *A History of Ancient Egypt.* Cambridge, Mass.: Blackwell, 1992.

Hawkes, Jacquetta. *The First Great Civilizations: Life in Mesopotamia, the Indus Valley, and Egypt.* New York: Alfred A. Knopf, 1973.

Lampl, Paul. *Cities and Planning in the Ancient Near East.* New York: George Braziller, 1968.

Saggs, H.W.F. *Civilization Before Greece and Rome.* New Haven: Yale University Press, 1989.

Starr, Chester G. *A History of the Ancient World.* New York: Oxford University Press, 1991.

CRETAN AND MYCENAEAN PREHISTORIC LANDSCAPES

Castleden, Rodney. *The Knossos Labyrinth.* London and New York: Routledge, 1990.

———. *Minoans: Life in Bronze Age Crete.* London and New York: Routledge, 1990.

Scully, Vincent. *The Earth, the Temple, and the Gods: Greek Sacred Architecture.* Rev. ed. New Haven and London: Yale University Press, 1979.

Taylour, William. *The Mycenaeans.* Rev. ed. London: Thames and Hudson, 1983.

PREHISTORIC AND HISTORIC LANDSCAPES OF THE ANCIENT AMERICAS

Berrin, Kathleen, and Esther Pasztory. *Teotihuacan: Art from the City of the Gods.* New York: Thames and Hudson, 1993.

Brody, J. J. *The Anasazi: Ancient Indian People of the American Southwest.* New York: Rizzoli, 1990.

Coe, Michael D. *The Maya.* 5th ed. New York: Thames and Hudson, 1993.

———. *Mexico: From the Olmecs to the Aztecs.* 4th ed. New York: Thames and Hudson, 1994.

Day, Jane S. *Aztec: The World of Moctezuma.* Denver: Denver Museum of Natural History and Roberts Rinehart Publishers, 1992.

Heth, Charlotte, ed. *Native American Dance: Ceremonies and Social Traditions.* Golden, Colo.: National Museum of the American Indian, Smithsonian Institution, 1992.

Hemming, John, and Edward Ranney (photographer). *Monuments of the Incas.* Boston: Little, Brown & Co., 1982.

Kosok, Paul. *Life, Land and Water in Ancient Peru.* New York: Long Island University Press, 1965.

Kubler, George. *The Art and Architecture of Ancient America.* New Haven: Yale University Press, 1962.

Lekson, Stephen H. *The Chaco Meridian: Centers of Political Power in the Ancient Southwest.* Walnut Creek, Calif.: Altamira Press, 1999.

Lekson, Stephen H., and Rina Swentzell. *Ancient Land, Ancestral Places: Paul Logsdon in the Pueblo Southwest.* Santa Fe: Museum of New Mexico Press, 1993.

Lekson, Stephen H.; John R. Stein; and Simon J. Ortiz. *Chaco Canyon: A Center and Its World.* Santa Fe: Museum of New Mexico, 1994.

Malville, J. McKim and Claudia Putnam. *Prehistoric Astronomy in the Southwest.* Rev. ed. Boulder, Colo.: Johnson Books, 1993.

Ortiz, Alfonso. *The Tewa World: Space, Time, Being, and Becoming in a Pueblo Society.* Chicago: University of Chicago Press, 1969.

Pasztory, Esther. *Teotihuacan: An Experiment in Living.* Norman: University of Oklahoma Press, 1997.

Pauketat, Timothy R., and Thomas E. Emerson, eds. *Cahokia: Domination and Ideology in the Mississippian World.* Lincoln: University of Nebraska Press, 1997.

Plog, Stephen. *Ancient Peoples of the American Southwest.* London: Thames and Hudson, 1997.

Sculy, Vincent. *Pueblo: Mountain, Village, Dance.* New York: Viking, 1975.

Skele, Mikels. *The Great Knob: Interpretations of Monks Mound.* Springfield: Illinois Historic Preservation Agency, 1988.

Sharer, Robert J. *The Ancient Maya.* 5th ed. Stanford: Stanford University Press,

Stierlin, Henri. *The Maya: Palaces and Pyramids of the Rainforest.* Cologne: Taschen, 1997.

Thomas, David Hurst. *Exploring Native America: An Archaeological Guide.* New York: Macmillan, 1994.

Townsend, Richard F. *The Aztecs.* London: Thames and Hudson, 1992.

———, ed. *The Ancient Americas: Art from Sacred Landscapes.* Chicago: The Art Institute of Chicago, 1992.

Ancient Greek and Roman Landscapes and Cityscapes

Camp, John M. *The Athenian Agora: Excavations in the Heart of Classical Athens.* London: Thames and Hudson, 1986.

Clarke, John R. *The Houses of Roman Italy, 100 B.C.–A.D. 250: Ritual, Space, and Decoration.* Berkeley: University of California Press, 1991.

Columella. *On Agriculture* (The Loeb Classical Library). Vol. 1. Translated by Harrison Boyd Ash. Cambridge: Harvard University Press, 1941.

———. *On Agriculture* (The Loeb Classical Library). Vols. 2–3. Translated by E. S. Forster and Edward H. Heffner. Rev. ed. Cambridge: Harvard University Press, 1968.

Crouch, Dora P. *Water Management in Ancient Greek Cities.* New York: Oxford, 1993.

de la Ruffinière du Prey, Pierre. *The Villas of Pliny: From Antiquity to Posterity.* Chicago: University of Chicago Press, 1994.

de Polignac, François. *Cults, Territory, and the Origins of the Greek City-State.* Translated by Janet Lloyd. Chicago and London: University of Chicago Press, 1995.

Doxiadis, C. A. *Architectural Space in Ancient Greece.* Translated and edited by Jacqueline Tyrwhitt. Cambridge: MIT Press, 1972.

Dupont, Florence. *Daily Life in Ancient Rome.* Translated by Christopher Woodall. Oxford, England, and Cambridge, Mass.: Blackwell Publishers, 1992.

Favro, Diane. *The Urban Image of Augustan Rome.* Cambridge and New York: Cambridge University Press, 1996.

Frazer, James George. *The Golden Bough: A Study in Magic and Religion.* 1922. Reprint, New York: Macmillan, Collier Books, 1963.

Geldard, Richard G. *The Traveler's Key to Ancient Greece: A Guide to the Sacred Places of Ancient Greece.* New York: Alfred A. Knopf, 1989.

Grimal, Pierre. *Les Jardins Romaines.* Paris: Presses Universitaires de France, 1969.

Homer. "The Homeric Hymns." In *Hesiod, The Homeric Hymns and Homerica* (Loeb Classical Library). Translated by Hugh G. Evelyn-White. Cambridge: Harvard University Press, 1914.

———. *The Odyssey.* Translated by Robert Fitzgerald. New York: Vintage Books, 1990.

Hurwit, Jeffrey M. *The Athenian Acropolis: History, Mythology, and Archaeology from the Neolithic Era to the Present.* Cambridge: Cambridge University Press, 1999.

Jashemski, Wilhelmina F. *The Gardens of Pompeii.* New Rochelle, N.Y.: Caratzas Brothers, 1979.

Lawrence, A. W. *Greek Architecture.* Rev. ed. Harmondsworth, England: Penguin Books, 1983.

MacDougall, Elizabeth Blair, ed. *Ancient Roman Villa Gardens.* Washington, D.C.: Dumbarton Oaks, 1987.

MacDougall, Elizabeth Blair, and Wilhelmina F. Jashemski, eds. *Ancient Roman Gardens.* Washington, D.C.: Dumbarton Oaks, 1981.

McEwen, Indra Kagis. *Socrates' Ancestor: An Essay on Architectural Beginnings.* Cambridge: MIT Press, 1993.

Meier, Christian. *Athens: A Portrait of the City in Its Golden Age.* Translated by Robert and Rita Kimber. New York: Henry Holt Company, Metropolitan Books, 1998.

Ovid. *Fasti.* Translated by James George Frazer. Cambridge: Harvard University Press, 1976.

Percival, John. *The Roman Villa.* Berkeley and Los Angeles: University of California Press, 1976.

Pliny the Younger. *Letters* (Loeb Classical Library). 2 vols. Translated by Betty Radice. Cambridge: Harvard University Press, 1969.

Rykwert, Joseph. *The Idea of a Town: The Anthropology of Urban Form in Rome, Italy and the Ancient World.* Cambridge: MIT Press, 1988.

Travlos, John. *Pictorial Dictionary of Ancient Athens.* New York: Praeger, 1971.

Virgil. *The Georgics.* Harmondsworth, England: Penguin, 1987.

Wallace-Hadrill, Andrew. *House and Society in Pompeii and Herculaneum.* Princeton, N.J.: Princeton University Press, 1994.

Ward-Perkins, J. B. *Cities of Ancient Greece and Italy: Planning in Classical Antiquity.* New York: George Braziller, 1974.

Yourcenar, Marguerite. *Memoirs of Hadrian.* New York: Farrar, Straus and Young, 1954.

Zanker, Paul. *Pompeii: Public and Private Life.* Cambridge: Harvard University Press, 1998.

Medieval Gardens

Boccaccio, G. *The Decameron.* Translated by Mark Musa and Peter Bondanella. New York: Norton, 1982.

Colvin, Howard. "Royal Gardens in Medieval England." In *Essays in English Architectural History.* New Haven: Yale University Press, 1999.

Giamatti, A. Bartlett. *The Earthly Paradise and the Renaissance Epic.* Princeton, N.J.: Princeton University Press, 1966.

Huizinga, Johan. Translated by Rodney J. Payton and Ulrich Mammitzsch. *The Autumn of the Middle Ages.* Chicago: University of Chicago Press, 1996.

MacDougall, Elizabeth Blair, ed. *Medieval Gardens,* Washington, D.C.: Dumbarton Oaks, 1986.

Prest, John. *The Garden of Eden: The Botanic Garden and the Recreation of Paradise.* New Haven and London: Yale University Press, 1981.

Persian and Islamic Gardens

Brookes, John. *Gardens of Paradise: The History and Design of the Great Islamic Gardens.* New York: New Amsterdam Books, 1987.

Crowe, Sylvia; Sheila Haywood; Susan Jellicoe; and Gordon Patterson. *The Gardens of Mughul India.* London: Thames and Hudson, 1972.

Gothein, Marie Louise. *Indische Gärten.* Munich: Drei Masken Verlag, 1926.

Grabar, Oleg. *The Alhambra.* Cambridge: Harvard University Press, 1978.

Khansari, Mehdi; M. Reza Moghtader; and Minouch Yavari. *The Persian Garden: Echoes of Paradise.* Washington, D.C.: Mage Publishers, 1998.

Koch, Ebba. *Mughal Architecture.* Munich: Prestel-Verlag, 1991.

Lehrman, Jonas. *Earthly Paradise: Garden and Courtyard in Islam.* Berkeley: University of California Press, 1980.

MacDougall, Elizabeth B., and Richard Ettinghausen, eds. *The Islamic Garden.* Washington, D.C: Dumbarton Oaks, 1976.

Moynihan, Elizabeth B. *Paradise as a Garden in Persia and Mughul India.* New York: George Braziller, 1979.

Nicipoglu, Gülru. *Architecture, Ceremonial, and Power: The Topkapi Palace in the Fifteenth and Sixteenth Centuries.* New York: The Architectural History Foundation, 1991.

Pope, Arthur Upham. *Persian Architecture.* New York: George Braziller, 1965.

Ruggles, D. Fairchild. *Gardens, Landscape, and Vision in the Palaces of Islamic Spain.* University Park: Pennsylvania State University Press, 2000.

Sackville-West, Vita. "The Persian Garden." In *Legacy of Persia.* Edited by A. J. Arberry. Oxford: Clarendon Press, 1952.

Valdéz Ozores, Beatrice; María Valdéz Ozores; and Micaela Valdéz Ozores. *Spanish Gardens.* Woodbridge, Suffolk, England: Antique Collectors' Club, 1987.

Wescoat, James L., Jr., and Joachim Wolschke-Bulmahn. *Mughal Gardens: Sources, Places, Representations, and Prospects.* Washington, D.C.: Dumbarton Oaks Research Library and Collection, 1996.

Wilber, Donald Newton. *Persian Gardens and Garden Pavilions.* Washington, D.C.: Dumbarton Oaks, 1979.

———. *Persian Gardens and Pavilions.* Rutland: Charles E. Tuttle, 1962.

Italian Renaissance Gardens

Ackerman, James S. *Palladio.* Harmondsworth, England: Penguin Books, 1966.

———. *Distant Points: Essays in Theory and Renaissance Art and Architecture.* Cambridge: MIT Press, 1991.

Acton, Harold. *The Villas of Tuscany.* 1973. Reprint, New York: Thames and Hudson, 1987.

Alberti, Leon Battista. *De Re Aedificatoria.* Translated by Joseph Rywert with Neil Leach and Robert Tavernor. Cambridge: MIT Press, 1988.

Barsali, Isa Belli. *Ville Di Roma*. 2nd ed. Milan: Rusconi, 1983.

Barsali, Isa Belli, and Maria Grazia Branchetti. *Ville Della Campagna Romana*. Milan: Rusconi, 1981.

Chatfield, Judith. *A Tour of Italian Gardens*. New York: Rizzoli, 1988.

Coffin, David R. *The Villa D'Este at Tivoli*. Princeton, N.J.: Princeton University Press, 1960.

————. *The Villa in the Life of Renaissance Rome*. Princeton, N.J.: Princeton University Press, 1979.

————. *Gardens and Gardening in Papal Rome*. Princeton, N.J.: Princeton University Press, 1991.

————, ed. *The Italian Garden*. Washington, D.C.: Dumbarton Oaks, 1972.

Colonna, Francesco. *Hypnerotomachia Poliphili: The Strife of Love in a Dream*. Translated by Joscelyn Godwin. New York: Thames and Hudson, 1999.

Constant, Caroline. *The Palladio Guide*. Princeton, N.J.: Princeton Architectural Press, 1985.

Cosgrove, Denis. *The Palladian Landscape*. University Park: Pennsylvania State Press, 1993.

Dewex, Guy. *Villa Madama: A Memoir Relating to Raphael's Project*. New York: Princeton Architectural Press, 1993.

Grafton, Anthony. *Leon Battista Alberti: Master Builder of the Renaissance*. New York: Farrar, Straus and Giroux (Hill and Wang), 2000.

Hunt, John Dixon, ed. *The Italian Garden: Art, Design and Culture*. Cambridge: Cambridge University Press, 1996.

Lazzaro, Claudia. *The Italian Renaissance Garden*. New Haven: Yale University Press, 1990.

MacDougall, Elizabeth B., ed. *Fons Sapientiae: Renaissance Garden Fountains*. Washington D.C.: Dumbarton Oaks, 1978.

Masson, Georgina. *Italian Gardens*. 1961. Rev. ed. Woodbridge, Suffolk, England: Antique Collectors' Club, 1987.

Platt, Charles A. *Italian Gardens*. Portland, Ore.: Sagapress/Timber Press, 1993.

Shepherd, J. C., and G. A. Jellicoe. *Italian Gardens of the Renaissance*. 1925. Rev. ed., Princeton, N.J.: Princeton Architectural Press, 1986.

Stewering, Roswitha. "Architectural Representations in the *Hypnnerotomachia Poliphili* (Aldus Manutius, 1499)." *Journal of the Society of Architectural Historians* 59:1 (March 2000): 6–25.

Triggs, H. Inigo. *The Art of Garden Design in Italy*. London: Longmans, Green & Co., 1906.

van der Ree, Paul; Gerrit Smienk; and Clemens Steenbergen. *Italian Villas and Gardens*. Amsterdam: Thoth Publishers, 1992.

Wharton, Edith. *Italian Villas and Their Gardens*. New York: Da Capo, 1976.

Wölfflin, Heinrich. "The Villa and the Garden." In *Renaissance and Baroque*. Translated by Kathrine Simon. Ithaca: Cornell University Press, 1966.

French Renaissance and Seventeenth-Century Garden Design and City Planning

Adams, William Howard. *Atget's Gardens*. Garden City, N.Y.: Doubleday, 1979.

————. *The French Garden 1500–1800*. New York: George Braziller, 1979.

Ballon, Hilary. *The Paris of Henri IV: Architecture and Urbanism*. Cambridge: MIT Press, 1991.

Berger, Robert W. *In the Garden of the Sun King: Studies on the Park of Versailles Under Louis XIV*. Washington, D.C.: Dumbarton Oaks, 1985.

Dezallier d'Argenville, Antoine-Joseph. *La Théorie et la practique du jardinage*. Paris: Charles-Antoine Jombert, 1760.

de Ganey, Ernest. *Les Jardins de France*. Paris: Editions d'Histoire et d'Art, 1949.

————. *André Le Nostre 1613–1700*. Paris: Éditions Vincent, Fréal & Cie., n.d.

Hazlehurst, F. Hamilton. *Jacques Boyceau and the French Formal Garden*. Athens: University of Georgia Press, 1966.

————. *Gardens of Illusion: The Genius of André Le Nôtre*. Nashville: Vanderbilt University Press, 1980.

Jeannel, Bernard. *Le Nôtre*. Paris: Fernand Hazan, 1985.

Lablaude, Pierre-André. *The Gardens of Versailles*. London: Zwemmer Publishers Limited, 1995.

Le Dantec, Denise, and Jean-Pierre Le Dantec. *Reading the French Garden: Story and History*. Cambridge: MIT Press, 1990.

MacDougall, Elizabeth B., and F. William Hazlehurst, eds. "The French Formal Garden." In *Dumbarton Oaks Colloquium on the History of Landscape Architecture*, Vol. 3. Cambridge: Harvard University Press, 1974.

Mariage, Thierry. *The World of André Le Nôtre*. Translated by Graham Larkin. Philadelphia: University of Pennsylvania Press, 1999.

Palissy, Bernard. *A Delectable Garden*. Translated by Helen Morgenthau Fox. Falls Village, Conn.: The Herb Grower Press, 1965.

Walton, Guy. *Louis XIV's Versailles*. Chicago: University of Chicago Press, 1986.

Weiss, Allen S. *Mirrors of Infinity: The French Formal Garden and 17th-Century Metaphysics*. New York: Princeton Architectural Press, 1995.

Woodbridge, Kenneth. *Princely Gardens: The Origins and Development of the French Formal Style*. New York: Rizzoli, 1986.

East Asian Gardens

Cao, Xuequin. *The Story of the Stone.* Vols. 1–3 translated by David Hawkes; vols. 4–5 translated by John Minford. Harmondsworth, England: Penguin, 1973–86.

Chan, Charis. *Imperial China.* San Francisco: Chronicle Books, 1992.

China Architecture and Building Press, Liu Dun-zhen. *Chinese Classical Gardens of Suzhou.* New York: McGraw-Hill, 1993.

Danby, Hope. *The Garden of Perfect Brightness.* London: Williams and Norgate, 1950.

Greenbie, Barrie B. *Space and Spirit in Modern Japan.* New Haven: Yale University Press, 1988.

Harada, Jiro. *The Gardens of Japan.* New York: A. and C. Boni, 1982.

Hay, John. *Kernels of Energy, Bones of Earth: The Rock in Chinese Art.* New York: China Institute in America, 1985.

Hayakama, Masao. *The Garden Art of Japan.* Vol. 28 of *The Heibonsha Survey of Japanese Art,* translated by Richard L. Gage. New York and Tokyo: Weatherhill/Heibonsha, 1973.

Hisamatsu, Shin'ichi. *Zen and the Fine Arts.* Translated by Gishin Tokiwa. Tokyo: Kodansha International, 1971.

Ito, Teiji. *The Japanese Garden: An Approach to Nature.* New Haven: Yale University Press, 1972.

Ji, Cheng. *The Craft of Gardens.* Translated by Alison Hardie. New Haven: Yale University Press, 1988.

Johnston, R. Stewart. *Scholar Gardens of China.* Cambridge: Cambridge University Press, 1991.

Keane, Marc P. *Japanese Garden Design.* Rutland: Charles E. Tuttle, 1996.

Keswick, Maggie. *The Chinese Garden: History, Art and Architecture.* New York: Rizzoli, 1978.

Kuck, Loraine. *The World of the Japanese Garden: From Chinese Origins to Modern Landscape Art.* New York: Weatherhill, 1968.

Laozi. *Tao-te ching: The Classic of the Way and Virtue.* As interpreted by Wang Bi. Translated by Richard John Lynn. New York: Columbia University Press, 1999.

Lip, Evelyn. *Chinese Geomancy.* Singapore: Times Books International, 1979.

Liu, Laurence G. *Chinese Architecture.* New York: Rizzoli, 1989.

Malone, Carroll Brown. "History of the Peking Summer Palaces Under the Ch'ing Dynasty." In *Illinois Studies in the Social Sciences,* vol. 19, nos. 1–2. Urbana: University of Illinois Press, 1934.

Mosher, Gouverneur. *Kyoto: A Contemplative Guide.* Rutland, Vt., and Tokyo, Japan: Charles E. Tuttle, 1964.

Murasaki Shikibu. *The Tale of Genji.* Translated by Edward G. Seidensticker. New York: Alfred A. Knopf, 1985.

Murck, Alfreda, and Wen Fong. *A Chinese Garden Court: The Astor Court at the Metropolitan Museum of Art.* New York: The Metropolitan Museum of Art, 1985.

Nishikawa, Takeshi, and Akira Naito. *Katsura: A Princely Retreat.* Tokyo, New York, London: Kodansha International, 1977.

Okakura Kakuzo. *The Book of Tea.* Rutland, Vt.: Charles E. Tuttle, 1956.

Rambach, Pierre, and Susan Rambach. *Gardens of Longevity in China and Japan: The Art of the Stone Raisers.* New York: Skira/Rizzoli, 1987.

Sirén, Osvald. *Gardens of China.* New York: Ronald Tree Press, 1949.

Siu, Victoria M. "China and Europe Intertwined: A New View of the European Sector of the Chang Chun Yuan." *Studies in the History of Gardens and Designed Landscapes,* 19:3/4 (July–December 1999): 376–93.

Strassberg, Richard E., trans. *Inscribed Landscapes: Travel Writing from Imperial China.* Berkeley: University of California Press, 1994.

Tregear, Mary. *Chinese Art.* London: Thames and Hudson, 1980.

Treib, Marc, and Ron Herman. *A Guide to the Gardens of Kyoto.* Tokyo: Shufunotomo, 1980.

Yoshida, Tetsuro. *Gardens of Japan.* New York: Praeger, 1957.

Sixteenth-, Seventeenth-, and Eighteenth-Century English Landscapes

Ballantyne, Andrew. *Architecture, Landscape and Liberty: Richard Payne Knight and the Picturesque.* Cambridge and New York: Cambridge University Press, 1997.

Batey, Mavis. "The High Phase of English Landscape Gardening." *Eighteenth Century Life* 8:2 (January 1983): 44–50.

Brewer, John. *The Pleasures of the Imagination: English Culture in the Eighteenth Century.* New York: Farrar, Straus, and Giroux, 1997.

Brownell, Morris R. *Alexander Pope and the Arts of Georgian England.* Oxford: Oxford University Press, 1978.

Burke, Edmund. *A Philosophical Enquiry into the Origin of Our Ideas of the Sublime and Beautiful.* 7th ed. London: J. Dodsley, 1773.

Gilpin, William. *Remarks on Forest Scenery and Other Woodland Views Relative Chiefly to Picturesque Beauty.* 3rd ed. London: T. Cadell and W. Davies, 1808.

———. *Practical Hints upon Landscape Gardening: With Some Remarks on Domestic Architecture as Connected with Scenery.* London: T. Cadell, 2nd ed., 1835.

Hoskins, W. G. *The Making of the English Landscape.* Harmondsworth, England: Penguin Books, 1955.

Hunt, John Dixon. *The Figure in the Landscape: Poetry, Painting, and Gardening during the Eighteenth Century.* Baltimore: Johns Hopkins University Press, 1976.

———. *Garden and Grove: The Italian Renaissance Garden in the English Imagination: 1600–1750*. Princeton, N. J.: Princeton University Press, 1986.

———. *William Kent: Landscape Garden Designer*. London: A. Zwemmer, 1987.

———. *Gardens and the Picturesque: Studies in the History of Landscape Design*. Cambridge: MIT Press, 1992.

Hunt, John Dixon, and Peter Willis, eds. *The Genius of the Place: The English Landscape Garden 1620–1820*. New York: Harper & Row, 1975.

Hyams, Edward. *Capability Brown and Humphrey Repton*. New York: Charles Scribner's Sons, 1971.

Hussey, Christopher. *The Picturesque*. 1927. Reprint. Hamdon, Conn.: Archon Books, 1967.

Jacques, David, and Arend Jan van der Horst. *The Gardens of William and Mary*. London: Christopher Helm, 1988.

Knight, Richard Payne. *An Analytical Inquiry into the Principles of Taste*. London: T. Payne and J. White, 1805.

Pevsner, Nikolaus, ed. "The Picturesque Garden and Its Influence Outside the British Isles." In *Dumbarton Oaks Colloquium on the History of Landscape Architecture*. Vol. 2. Washington, D.C.: Dumbarton Oaks Trustees for Harvard University, 1974.

Price, Sir Uvedale. *On the Picturesque*. Edited by Sir Thomas Dick Lauder. Edinburgh: Caldwell, Lloyd, & Co., 1842.

Shenstone, William. *The Works in Verse and Prose of William Shenstone, Esq*. London: R. & J. Dodsley, 1764.

Strong, Roy. *The Renaissance Garden in England*. London: Thames and Hudson, 1979 and 1998.

———. *Royal Gardens*. London: BBC Books / Conran Octopus, 1992.

Stroud, Dorothy. *Humphrey Repton*. London: Country Life, 1962.

Symes, Michael. "Nature as the Bride of Art: The Design and Structure of Painshill." *Eighteenth Century Life* 8:2 (January 1983): 65–83.

Templeman, William. *The Life and Work of William Gilpin (1724–1804): Master of the Picturesque*. Urbana: University of Illinois Press, 1939.

Thomson, James. *The Seasons*. 3rd ed. London: Longman, Brown, Green, and Longmans, 1852.

Turner, Roger. *Capability Brown and the Eighteenth Century English Landscape*. New York: Rizzoli, 1985.

Watkin, David. *The English Vision: The Picturesque in Architecture, Landscape and Garden Design*. New York: Harper & Row, 1982.

Whately, Thomas. *Observations on Modern Gardening*. London: T. Payne, 1770.

Woodbridge, Kenneth. *Landscape and Antiquity: Aspects of English Culture at Stourhead*. Oxford: Oxford University Press, 1970.

Wordsworth, Jonathan; Michael C. Jaye; and Robert Woof. *William Wordsworth and the Age of English Romanticism*. New Brunswick, N.J., and London: Rutgers University Press, 1987.

Wroth, Warwick. *The London Pleasure Gardens of the Eighteenth Century*. London: MacMillan and Co., 1896.

Sixteenth-, Seventeenth-, and Eighteenth-Century European Gardens

Bowe, Patrick. *Gardens of Portugal*. New York: M. T. Train/Scala Books, 1989.

———. *Gardens in Central Europe*. New York: M. T. Train/Sclala Books, 1991.

Carita, Heder. *Portuguese Gardens*. Wappingers Falls, New York: Antique Collectors' Club, 1990.

Casa Valdés. *Spanish Gardens*. Wappingers Falls, N.Y.: Antique Collectors' Club, 1987.

Correcher, Consuelo, and Michael George (photographer). *The Gardens of Spain*. New York: Harry N. Abrams, 1993.

Etlin, Richard A. *Symbolic Space: French Enlightenment Architecture and Its Legacy*. Chicago: University of Chicago Press, 1994.

Hunt, John Dixon. "Style and Idea in Anglo-Dutch Gardens." *Antiques* (December 1988).

Hunt, John Dixon, and Erik de Jong, eds. "The Anglo-Dutch Garden in the Age of William and Mary/De Gouden Eeuw van de Hollandse Tuinkunst." *Journal of Garden History* 8:2 and 3 (April–September 1988).

Kennett, Victor, and Audrey Kennett. *The Palaces of Leningrad*. London: Thames and Hudson, 1973.

Le Camus de Mézières, Nicolas. *The Genius of Architecture; or, The Analogy of That Art With Our Sensations*. Translated by David Britt. Santa Monica, Calif.: The Getty Center Publication Programs, 1992.

Morel, Jean Marie. *Théorie des Jardins*. Paris: Chez Pissot, 1776.

Rousseau, Jean-Jacques. *Julie ou la Nouvelle Héloïse (Julie or the New Heloise)*. Translated by Judith H. McDowell. University Park: Pennsylvania University Press, 1968.

Taylor-Leduc, Susan. "Luxury in the Garden: *La Nouvelle Héloïse* Reconsidered." *Studies in the History of Gardens and Designed Landscapes* 19:1 (January–March 1999): 74–85.

Thacker, Christopher. "The Volcano: Culmination of the Landscape Garden." *Eighteenth Century Life* 8:2 (January 1983): 74–83.

Wiebenson, Dora. *The Picturesque Garden in France*. Princeton, N. J.: Princeton University Press, 1978.

Botanical Gardens and Plant Hunters

Desmond, Ray. *Kew: The History of the Royal Botanic Gardens*. London: The Harvill Press, 1995.

———. *Sir Joseph Dalton Hooker: Traveler and Plant Collector.* Woodbridge, Suffolk, England: Antique Collectors' Club, 1999.

Prest, John. *The Garden of Eden: The Botanic Garden and the Re-Creation of Paradise.* New Haven and London: Yale University Press, 1981.

Reveal, James L. *Gentle Conquest: The Botanical Discovery of America With Illustrations from the Library of Congress.* Washington, D.C.: Starwood Publishing, 1992.

Spongberg, Stephen A. *A Reunion of Trees: The Discovery of Exotic Plants and Their Introduction into North American and European Landscapes.* Cambridge: Harvard University Press, 1990.

Università degli studi di Padova. *The Botanical Garden of Padua 1545–1995.* Edited by Alessandro Minelli. Venice: Marsilio Editori, 1995.

AMERICAN COLONIAL AND FEDERAL PERIOD CITIES AND GARDENS

Beiswanger, William. "The Temple in the Garden: Thomas Jefferson's Vision of the Monticello Landscape." *Eighteenth Century Life* 8:2 (January 1983): 170–88.

Boorstin, Daniel J. *The Lost Worlds of Thomas Jefferson.* Chicago: The University of Chicago Press, 1948.

Briggs, Loutrel W. *Charleston Gardens.* Columbia: University of South Carolina Press, 1951.

Brown, C. Allan. "Thomas Jefferson's Poplar Forest: The Mathematics of an Ideal Villa." *Journal of Garden History* 10:2 (1990): 117–39.

Chambers, S. Allen, Jr. *Poplar Forest and Thomas Jefferson.* Forest, Virginia: The Corporation for Jefferson's Poplar Forest, 1993.

Cothran, James R. *Gardens of Historic Charleston.* Columbia: University of South Carolina Press, 1995.

Conzen, Michael, ed. *The Making of the American Landscape.* Boston: Unwin Hyman, 1990.

Gasparini, Graziano. "The Law of the Indies: The Spanish-American Grid Plan, An Urban Bureaucratic Form." In *The New City.* Vol.1, *Foundations.* Coral Gables, Fl.: University of Miami School of Architecture, 1991.

Griswold, Mac. *Washington's Garden at Mount Vernon.* Boston: Houghton Mifflin, 1999.

Hatch, Peter J. *The Gardens of Thomas Jefferson's Monticello.* Charlottesville: Thomas Jefferson Memorial Foundation, 1992.

Hernandez, Jorge L. "Williamsburg: The Genesis of a Republican Civic Order from Under the Shadow of the Catalpas." In *The New City.* Vol.2, *The American City.* Coral Gables, Fl.: University of Miami School of Architecture, 1994.

Jefferson, Thomas. *Thomas Jefferson's Garden Book 1766–1824.* Edited by Edwin Morris Betts. Philadelphia: The American Philosophical Society, 1944.

Leighton, Ann. *American Gardens in the Eighteenth Century.* Boston: Houghton Mifflin, 1976.

Martin, Peter. *The Pleasure Gardens of Virginia.* Princeton, N.J.: Princeton University Press, 1991.

Nichols, Frederick Doveton, and Ralph E. Griswold. *Thomas Jefferson Landscape Architect.* Charlottesville: University Press of Virginia, 1978.

Peterson, Merrill D. *Thomas Jefferson and the New Nation.* London: Oxford University Press, 1970.

Reps, John W. *The Making of Urban America: A History of City Planning in the United States.* Princeton, N.J.: Princeton University Press, 1965.

Stilgoe, John R. *Common Landscape of America, 1580 to 1845.* New Haven: Yale University Press, 1982.

NINETEENTH- AND TWENTIETH-CENTURY RURAL CEMETERIES, PUBLIC PARKS, AND CITY PLANNING

Alex, William, and George B. Tatum (Introduction). *Calvert Vaux Architect and Planner.* New York: Ink, Inc., 1994.

Baxter, Sylvester, and Charles Eliot. *Report to the Board of the Metropolitan Park Commissioners.* Commonwealth of Massachusetts: House No. 150, January, 1893.

Barlow, Elizabeth. *Frederick Law Olmsted's New York.* New York: Whitney Museum-Praeger, 1972.

———, with Vernon Gray, Roger Pasquier, and Lewis Sharp. *The Central Park Book.* New York: Central Park Task Force, 1977.

———, with Marianne Cramer, Judith Heinz, Bruce Kelly, and Philip Winslow. Edited by John Berendt. *Rebuilding Central Park: A Management and Restoration Plan.* Cambridge: MIT Press, 1987.

Beveridge, Charles E., and Paul Rocheleau (photographer). *Frederick Law Olmsted: Designing the American Landscape.* New York: Rizzoli, 1995.

Bogart, Michele H. *Public Sculpture and the Civic Ideal in New York City 1890–1920.* Chicago: University of Chicago Press, 1989.

Boyer, Paul. *Urban Masses and Moral Order in America 1820–1920.* Cambridge: Harvard University Press, 1982.

Caro, Robert. *The Power Broker Robert Moses and the Fall of New York.* New York: Vintage, 1975.

Carr, Ethan. *Wilderness by Design: Landscape Architecture and the National Park Service.* Lincoln: University of Nebraska Press, 1998.

Chadwick, George F. *The Park and the Town: Public Landscape in the 19th and 20th Centuries.* New York: Praeger, 1966.

Conway, Hazel. *People's Parks: The Design and Development of Victorian Parks in Britain.* Cambridge: Cambridge University Press, 1991.

Cook, Clarence C. *A Description of the New York Central Park.* New York: F. J. Huntington and Co., 1869.

Cranz, Galen. *The Politics of Park Design: A History of Urban Parks in America*. Cambridge: MIT Press, 1982.

Cutler, Phoebe. *The Public Landscape of the New Deal*. New Haven: Yale University Press, 1985.

Downing, Andrew Jackson. *Rural Essays*. Edited by George William Curtis. New York: Leavitt & Allen, 1856.

————. *A Treatise on the Theory and Practice of Landscape Gardening*. 6th ed. With a supplement by Henry Winthrop Sargent. New York: A. O. Moore & Co., 1859.

Eliot, Charles William. *Charles Eliot, Landscape Architect*. Boston: Houghton, Mifflin & Company, 1902.

Elliott, Brent. *Victorian Gardens*. Portland, Ore.: Timber Press, 1986.

Etlin, Richard A. *The Architecture of Death*. Cambridge: MIT Press, 1984.

Evenson, Norma. *Paris: A Century of Change, 1879–1978*. New Haven and London: Yale University Press, 1979.

Fein, Albert, ed. *Landscape into Cityscape: Frederick Law Olmsted's Plans for a Greater New York City*. Ithaca: Cornell University Press, 1967.

Gloag, John. *Mr. Loudon's England*. Newcastle upon Tyne: Oriel Press, 1970.

Good, Albert H. *Park & Recreation Structures*. Boulder, Colo.: Graybooks, 1990.

Graff, M. M. *Central Park Prospect Park: A New Perspective*. New York: Greensward Foundation, 1985.

Hall, Lee. *Olmsted's America: An "Unpractical" Man and His Vision of Civilization*. Boston: Little, Brown & Co., 1995.

Herbert, Robert. *Impressionism: Art, Leisure and Parisian Society*. New Haven: Yale University Press, 1988.

Hines, Thomas S. *Burnham of Chicago: Architect and Planner*. Chicago: University of Chicago Press, 1979.

Huth, Hans. *Nature and the American: Three Centuries of Changing Attitudes*. Berkeley and London: University of California Press, 1957.

Irving, Robert Grant. *Indian Summer, Lutyens, Baker, and Imperial Delhi*. New Haven: Yale University Press, 1981.

Jackson, Kenneth T. and Camilo José Vergara. *Silent Cities: The Evolution of the American Cemetery*. New York: Princeton Architectural Press, 1989.

Jordan, David P. *Transforming Paris: The Life and Labors of Baron Haussmann*. New York: The Free Press, 1995.

Kelly, Bruce; Gail Travis Guillet; and Mary Ellen W. Hern. *Art of the Olmsted Landscape*. New York: New York City Landmarks Commission, 1981.

Kowsky, Francis R. *Country, Park and City: The Architecture and Life of Calvert Vaux*. New York and Oxford: Oxford University Press, 1998.

Lancaster, Clay. *Prospect Park Handbook*. New York: Greensward Foundation, 1967.

Lasdun, Susan. *The English Park: Royal, Private and Public*. New York: The Vendome Press, 1992.

Linden-Ward, Blanche. *Silent City on a Hill: Landscapes of Memory and Boston's Mount Auburn Cemetery*. Columbus: Ohio University Press, 1989.

Loudon, John Claudius. *An Encyclopaedia of Gardening*. London: Longman, Hurst, Rees, Orme, and Brown, 1822.

————. *The Villa Gardener*. 2nd ed. Edited by Mrs. Loudon. London: William S. Orr & Co., 1850.

————, ed. *Repton's Landscape Gardening and Landscape Architecture*. London: Longman & Co., 1840.

David Lowenthal. *George Perkins Marsh: Prophet of Conservation*. Seattle: University of Washington Press, 2000.

MacDougall, Elizabeth B., ed. "John Claudius Loudon and the Early Nineteenth Century in Great Britain." In *Dumbarton Oaks Colloquium on the History of Landscape Architecture*. Vol. 6. Washington, D.C.: Dumbarton Oaks Trustees for Harvard University, 1980.

Marsh, George Perkins. *Man and Nature: Or Physical Geography Modified by Human Action*. Edited by David Lowenthal. Cambridge: Harvard University Press, Belknap Press, 1965.

Marx, Leo. *The Machine in the Garden: Technology and the Pastoral Ideal in America*. New York: Oxford University Press, 1967.

McClelland, Linda Flint. *Building the National Parks: Historic Landscape Design and Construction*. Baltimore: Johns Hopkins University Press, 1998.

McLaughlin, Charles Capen, editor-in-chief, and Charles E. Beveridge, associate ed. *The Papers of Frederick Law Olmsted. Vol. 1, The Formative Years*. Baltimore: Johns Hopkins University Press, 1977.

McLaughlin, Charles Capen, editor-in-chief; Charles E. Beveridge and Charles Capen McLaughlin, eds.; and David Schuyler, associate ed. *The Papers of Frederick Law* Olmsted. Vol. 2, *Slavery and the South*. Baltimore: Johns Hopkins University Press, 1981.

McLaughlin, Charles Capen, editor-in-chief; Charles E. Beveridge, series ed.; and Charles E. Beveridge and David Schuyler, eds. *The Papers of Frederick Law Olmsted*. Vol. 3, *Creating Central Park*. Baltimore: Johns Hopkins University Press, 1983.

McLaughlin, Charles Capen, editor-in-chief; Charles E. Beveridge, series ed.; and Victoria Post Ranney, ed. *The Papers of Frederick Law Olmsted*. Vol. 5, *The California Frontier*. Baltimore: Johns Hopkins University Press, 1990.

McLaughlin, Charles Capen, editor-in-chief; Charles E. Beveridge, series ed.; David Schuyler and Jane Turner Censer, eds.; and Kenneth Hawkins, assistant ed. *The Papers of Frederick Law Olmsted*. Vol. 6, *The Years of Olmsted, Vaux and Company*. Baltimore: Johns Hopkins University Press, 1992.

Major, Judith K. *To Live in a New World: A. J. Downing and American Landscape Gardening*. Cambridge, Mass., and London: MIT Press, 1997.

Moody, Walter D. *Wacker's Manual of the Plan of Chicago.* Chicago: Auspices of Chicago Plan Commission, 1912.

Nash, Roderick. *Wilderness and the American Mind.* New Haven and London: Yale University Press, 1967.

New York City Parks Department. *30 Years of Progress: 1934–1964* (Report to the Mayor and Board of Estimate). New York: New York City Department of Parks, 1965.

Olmsted, Frederick Law. *Walks and Talks of an American Farmer in England.* New York: George P. Putnam, 1852.

———. *A Journey in the Seaboard Slave States.* New York: Dix, Edwards & Co., 1856.

———. *Journey Through Texas.* New York: Dix, Edwards & Co., 1857.

———. *A Journey in the Back Country.* New York: Mason Brothers, 1860.

Olmsted, Frederick Law, Jr., and Theodora Kimball, eds. *Forty Years of Landscape Architecture: Being the Professional Papers of Frederick Law Olmsted, Senior.* New York and London: G. P. Putnam's Sons, 1928.

Olsen, Donald J. *The City as a Work of Art: London Paris Vienna.* New Haven: Yale University Press, 1986.

Parsons, Mabel, ed. *Memories of Samuel Parsons.* New York and London: G. P. Putnam's Sons, 1926.

Parsons, Samuel. *Landscape Gardening Studies.* New York: John Lane Company, 1910.

———. *The Art of Landscape Architecture.* New York and London: G. P. Putnam's Sons, 1915.

Phillips, Sandra S., and Linda Weintraub, eds. *Charmed Places: Hudson River Artists and Their Houses, Studios, and Vistas.* New York: Harry N. Abrams, 1988.

Porter, Roy. *London: A Social History.* Cambridge: Harvard University Press, 1995.

Pückler-Muskau, Hermann Ludwig Heinrich, Prince von. *Tour in England, Ireland, and France, in the Years 1828, and 1829.* Philadelphia: Carey, Lea & Blanchard, 1833.

———. *Hints on Landscape Gardening.* Translated by Bernhard Sikert. Edited by Samuel Parsons. Boston: Houghton Mifflin, 1917.

Ranney, Victoria Post. *Olmsted in Chicago.* Chicago: R. R. Donnelley & Sons, 1972.

Reed, Henry Hope and Duckworth, Sophia. *Central Park: A History and a Guide.* 2nd ed. New York: Clarkson N. Potter, 1972.

Robinson, William. *The Parks, Promenades & Gardens of Paris.* London: John Murray, 1869.

Roberts, Ann Rockefeller. *Mr. Rockefeller's Roads: The Untold Story of Acadia's Carriage Roads and Their Creator.* Camden, Maine: Down East Books, 1990.

Roper, Laura Wood. *FLO: A Biography of Frederick Law Olmsted.* Baltimore: Johns Hopkins University Press, 1973.

Rosenzweig, Roy, and Elizabeth Blackmar. *The Park and the People:*

A History of Central Park. Ithaca and London: Cornell University Press, 1992.

Runte, Alfred. *National Parks: The American Experience.* Lincoln: University of Nebraska Press, 1979.

Russell, John. *Paris.* New York: Harry N. Abrams, 1983.

———. *London.* New York: Harry N. Abrams, 1994.

Rybczynski, Witold. *City Life: Urban Expectations in a New World.* New York: Scribner, 1995.

———. *A Clearing in the Distance: Frederick Law Olmsted and America in the Nineteenth Century.* New York: Scribner, 1999.

Scheper, George L. "The Reformist Vision of Frederick Law Olmsted and the Poetics of Park Design." *The New England Quarterly* 62:3 (September 1989): 369–402.

Schorske, Carl E. *Fin-de-Siècle Vienna: Politics and Culture.* New York: Alfred A. Knopf, 1980.

———. *Thinking with History: Explorations in the Passage to Modernism.* Princeton, N.J.: Princeton University Press, 1998.

Schuyler, David. *The New Urban Landscape: The Redefinition of City Form in Nineteenth Century America.* Baltimore: Johns Hopkins University Press, 1986.

———. *Apostle of Taste: Andrew Jackson Downing 1815–1852.* Baltimore and London: The Johns Hopkins University Press, 1996.

Sears, John F. *Sacred Places: American Tourist Attractions in the Nineteenth Century.* New York: Oxford University Press, 1989.

Simo, Melanie Louise. *Loudon and the Landscape: From Country Seat to Metropolis.* New Haven and London: Yale University Press, 1988.

Sitte, Camillo. *The Art of Building Cities.* Translated by Charles T. Stewart. New York: Reinhold Publishing Corporation, 1945.

Smillie, James, and Nehemiah Cleaveland. *Green-Wood Illustrated.* New York: R. Martin, 1847.

Smillie, James, and Cornelia W. Walter. *Mount Auburn Illustrated.* New York: R. Martin, 1851.

Stevenson, Elizabeth. *Park Maker: A Life of Frederick Law Olmsted.* New York: Macmillan, 1977.

Stilgoe, John R. *Borderland: Origins of the American Suburb 1820–1939.* Reprint, New Haven: Yale University Press, 1990.

Sutcliffe, Anthony. *Paris: An Architectural History.* New Haven and London: Yale University Press, 1993.

Tatum, George B., and Elizabeth Blair MacDougall, eds. *Prophet with Honor: The Career of Andrew Jackson Downing.* Washington, D.C.: Dumbarton Research Library and Collection, 1989.

Tishler, William, ed. *American Landscape Architecture: Designers and Places.* Washington, D.C.: Preservation Press, 1989.

Van Rensselaer, Mariana Griswold. *Accents as Well as Broad Effects: Writings on Architecture, Landscape, and the Environment, 1876–1925.* Edited by David Gebhard. Berkeley: University of California Press, 1996.

Van Zanten, David. *Building Paris: Architectural Institutions and the Transformation of the French Capital, 1830–1870.* Cambridge: Cambridge University Press, 1994.

Zeitzevsky, Cynthia. *Frederick Law Olmsted and the Boston Park System.* Cambridge: Harvard University Press, Belknap Press, 1982.

Nineteenth- and Twentieth-Century Gardens, Vernacular Landscapes, and Land Art

Adams, William Howard. *Grounds for Change: Major Gardens of the Twentieth Century.* Boston: Little, Brown & Co., 1993.

———. *Roberto Burle Marx: The Unnatural Art of the Garden.* New York: The Museum of Modern Art, 1991.

Aslet, Clive. *The American Country House.* New Haven and London: Yale University Press, 1990.

Axelrod, Alan, ed. *The Colonial Revival in America.* New York and London: W. W. Norton, 1985.

Balmori, Diana; Diana Kostial McGuire; and Eleanor McPeck. *Beatrix Farrand's American Landscapes: Her Gardens and Campuses.* Sagaponack, N.Y.: Sagapress, 1985.

Beardsley, John. *Earthworks and Beyond: Contemporary Art in the Landscape.* 3rd ed. New York: Abbeville Press, 1984.

———. *Gardens of Revelation: Environments by Visionary Artists.* New York: Abbeville Press, 1995.

Blomfield, Reginald. *The Formal Garden in England.* Illustrated by F. Inigo Thomas. London: Macmillan, 1892.

Brown, Jane. *Gardens of a Golden Afternoon. The Story of a Partnership: Edwin Lutyens and Gertrude Jekyll.* Harmondsworth, England: Penguin Books, 1985.

———. *Vita's Other World: A Gardening Biography of Vita Sackville-West.* New York: Viking, 1985.

———. *The English Garden in Our Time: From Gertrude Jekyll to Geoffrey Jellicoe.* Woodbridge, Suffolk, England: Antique Collectors' Club, 1986.

———. *Eminent Gardeners: Some People of Influence and Their Gardens 1880–1980.* New York: Viking, 1990.

———. *Beatrix: The Gardening Life of Beatrix Jones Farrand 1872–1959.* New York: Viking, 1995.

Cals, Soraia. *Roberto Burle Marx: Uma fotobiografia.* Rio de Janeiro: Sindicato Nacional dos Editores de Livros, RJ, 1995.

Caracciolo, Marella, and Giuppi Pietromarchi. *The Gardens of Ninfa.* Photographs by Marella Agnelli. Translated by Harriet Graham. Umberto Allemandi & C., n.d.

Church, Thomas. *Gardens Are for People.* New York: Reinhold Publishing Company, 1955.

———. *Your Private World: A Study of Intimate Gardens.* San Francisco: Chronicle Books, 1969.

Collins, Lester. *Innisfree: An American Garden.* New York: Sagapress/Harry N. Abrams, 1994.

Cooper, Guy and Gordon Taylor. *Paradise Transformed: The Private Garden in the Twentieth Century.* New York: Monacelli Press, 1996.

———. *Gardens for the Future: Gestures Against the Wild.* New York: Monacelli Press, 2000.

Dwight, Eleanor. *Edith Wharton: An Extraordinary Life.* New York: Harry N. Abrams, 1994.

Eckbo, Garrett. *Landscape for Living.* F. W. Dodge Corporation: An Architectural Record Book with Duell, Sloan, & Pearce, 1950.

———. *The Landscape We See.* New York: McGraw-Hill, 1969.

Eggener, Keith. "Postwar Modernism in Mexico: Luis Barragán's Jardines del Pedregal and the International Discourse on Architecture and Place." *Journal of the Society of Architectural Historians* 58:2 (June 1999): 122–45.

Elliott, Brent. *The Country House Garden: From the Archives of Country Life 1897–1939.* London: Mitchell Beazley, 1995.

Emmet, Alan. *So Fine a Prospect: Historic New England Gardens.* Hanover: University Press of New England, 1996.

Farrand, Beatrix. *The Bulletins of Reef Point Gardens.* Bar Harbor, Maine: The Island Foundation, 1997.

Festing, Sally. *Gertrude Jekyll.* New York: Viking, 1991.

Fraser, Valerie. "Cannibalizing Le Corbusier: The MES Gardens of Roberto Burle Marx." *Journal of the Society of Architectural Historians* 59:2 (June 2000), 180–93.

Griswold, Mac, and Eleanor Weller. *The Golden Age of American Gardens: Proud Owners, Private Estates, 1890–1940.* New York: Harry N. Abrams, 1991.

Hamerman, Conrad. "Roberto Burle Marx: The Last Interview." *The Journal of Decorative and Propaganda Arts* 21(1995): 157–79.

Hanson, A. E. *An Arcadian Landscape: The California Gardens of A. E. Hanson 1920–1932.* Edited by David Gebhard and Sheila Lynds. Los Angeles: Hennessey & Ingalls, 1985.

Hildebrand, Gary R. *The Miller Garden: Icon of Modernism.* Washington, D.C.: Spacemaker Press, 1999.

Hobhouse, Penelope, ed. *Gertrude Jekyll on Gardening.* Boston: David R. Godine, 1984.

Hunt, John Dixon, and Joachim Wolschke-Bulmahn, eds. *The Vernacular Garden.* Washington, D.C.: Dumbarton Oaks Research Library and Collection, 1993.

Hyams, Edward. *English Cottage Gardens.* Harmondsworth, England: Penguin Books, 1987.

Imbert, Dorothée. *The Modernist Garden in France.* New Haven: Yale University Press, 1993.

Jackson, John Brinckerhoff. *Landscapes.* Amherst: University of Massachusetts Press, 1970.

———. *The Necessity for Ruins*. Amherst: University of Massachusetts Press, 1980.

———. *Discovering the Vernacular Landscape*. New Haven: Yale University Press, 1984.

———. *Landscape in Sight: Looking at America*. Edited by Helen Lefkowitz Horowitz. New Haven: Yale University Press, 1997.

Jekyll, Gertrude. *Wood and Garden*. London: Longmans, Green, & Co., 1900.

———. *Wall and Water Gardens*. Covent Garden: Country Life, Ltd., 1901.

———. *Old West Surrey*. London: Longmans, Green, and Co., 1904.

———. *Children and Gardens*. London: Country Life, Ltd., 1908.

———. *Colour in the Flower Garden*. Covent Garden: Country Life, Ltd., 1908.

———. *Colour Schemes for the Flower Garden*. London: Country Life, Ltd., 1908. Reprint, Boston: Little, Brown & Co., 1988.

Jekyll, Gertrude and Lawrence Weaver. *Arts and Crafts Gardens*. London: Country Life, Ltd., 1912. Reprint, Woodbridge, Suffolk, England: Antique Collectors' Club, 1997.

Karson, Robin. *Fletcher Steele, Landscape Architect: An Account of the Gardenmaker's Life, 1885–1971*. New York: Harry N. Abrams / Sagapress, 1989.

———. *Masters of American Garden Design*. Vol. 3, *The Modern Garden in Europe and the United States*. Proceedings of the Garden Conservancy Symposium held March 12, 1993 at the Paine Webber Building in New York, New York. Cold Spring, N.Y.: The Garden Conservancy, 1994.

———. *Masters of American Garden Design*. Vol. 4, *Influences on American Garden Design: 1895 to 1940*. Proceedings of the Garden Conservancy Symposium held March 11, 1994 at the Paine Webber Building in New York, New York. Cold Spring, N.Y.: The Garden Conservancy, 1995.

———. *The Muses of Gwinn: Art and Nature in a Garden Designed by Warren H. Manning, Charles A. Olatt, & Ellen Biddle Shipman*. Sagaponack, N.Y.: Sagapress, 1995.

Kassler, Elizabeth B. *Modern Gardens and the Landscape*. New York: The Museum of Modern Art, 1964.

Mallet, Robert. *Rebirth of a Park / Renaissance d'Un Parc*. Varengeville-sur-Mer, France: Centre d'Art Floral, 1996.

Massingham, Betty. *Miss Jekyll: Portrait of a Great Gardener*. London: Country Life, 1966.

Mawson, Thomas H. *The Art and Craft of Garden Making*. London: B. T. Batsford, 1900.

McGuire, Diane Kostiel, and Lois Fern. "Beatrix Jones Farrand (1872–1959) Fifty Years of American Landscape Architecture." In *Dumbarton Oaks Colloquium on the History of Landscape Architecture*. Vol. 8. Washington, D.C.: Dumbarton Oaks Trustees for Harvard University, 1982.

Morgan, Keith N. *Charles A. Platt: The Artist as Architect*. Cambridge: MIT Press, 1985.

Ottewill, David. *The Edwardian Garden*. New Haven: Yale University Press, 1989.

Padilla, Victoria. *Southern California Gardens: An Illustrated History*. Santa Barbara, Calif.: Allen A. Knoll, 1994.

Power, Nancy Goslee, with Susan Heeger. Photographs by Mick Hales. *The Gardens of California: Four Centuries of Design from Mission to Modern*. New York: Clarkson Potter, 1995.

Prentice, Helaine Kaplan. Photographs by Melba Levick. *The Gardens of Southern California*. San Francisco: Chronicle Books, 1990.

Robinson, William. *The Wild Garden*. 5th ed. London: John Murray, 1895. Reprint, Portland, Ore.: Sagapress / Timber Press, 1994.

———. *Gravetye Manor*. London: John Murray, 1911.

———. *The English Flower Garden*. 15th ed. London: J. Murray, 1933. Reprint, New York: Amaryllis Press, 1984.

Rose, James. *Creative Gardens*. New York: Reinhold Publishing Corporation, 1958.

———. *The Heavenly Environment*. Hong Kong: New City Cultural Services Ltd., 1987.

Sackville-West, Vita. *A Joy of Gardening: A Selection for Americans*. Edited by Hermine I. Popper. New York: Harper & Row, 1958.

Saunders, William S., ed. *Daniel Urban Kiley*. New York: Princeton Architectural Press, 1999.

Sedding, John D. *Garden-Craft Old and New*. London: John Lane, 1902.

Shapiro, Gary. *Earthwards: Robert Smithson and Art after Babel*. Berkeley: University of California Press, 1995.

Shepheard, Peter. *Modern Gardens*. London: The Architectural Press, 1953.

Smithson, Robert. *Robert Smithson: The Collected Writings*. Edited by Jack Flam. Berkeley: University of California Press, 1996.

Southeastern Center for Contemporary Art. *Maya Lin: Topologies*. (Catalogue of exhibition organized by Jeff Fleming, with essays by Michael Brenson, Terri Dowell-Dennis, and Jeff Fleming). Winston-Salem, N.C.: Southeastern Center for Contemporary Art, 1998.

Steele, Fletcher. *Design in the Little Garden*. Boston: Atlantic Monthly Press, 1924.

Streatfield, David. *California Gardens: Creating a New Eden*. New York: Abbeville Press, 1994.

Tankard, Judith B. *The Gardens of Ellen Biddle Shipman*. Sagaponack, N.Y.: Sagapress, 1996.

Tankard, Judith B., and Michael R. VanValkenburgh. *Gertrude Jekyll: A Vision of Garden and Wood*. New York: Harry N. Abrams / Sagapress, 1989.

Thompson, Flora. *Lark Rise to Candleford: A Trilogy*. London: Oxford University Press, 1945.

Treib, Marc, and Dorothée Imbert. *Garrett Eckbo: Modern Landscapes for Living.* Berkeley: University of California Press, 1997.

Treib, Marc, ed. *Modern Landscape Architecture: A Critical Review.* Cambridge: MIT Press, 1993.

———, ed. "Thomas Dolliver Church, Landscape Architect." *Studies in the History of Gardens and Designed Landscapes* 20:2 (April–June 2000), 93–195.

Tunnard, Christopher. *Gardens in the Modern Landscape.* London: Architectural Press, 1938.

Vaccarino, Rossana. *Roberto Burle Marx: Landscapes Reflected.* New York: Princeton Architectural Press, 2000.

Walker, Peter, and Melanie Simo. *Invisible Gardens: The Search for Modernism in the American Landscape.* Cambridge: MIT Press, 1994.

Wolseley, Vicountess (Frances Garnet). *Gardens: Their Form and Design.* London: E. Arnold, 1919.

Wrede, Stuart, and William Howard Adams. *Denatured Visions: Landscape and Culture in the Twentieth Century.* New York: The Museum of Modern Art, 1991.

Twentieth- and Twenty-first-Century City and Park Planning

Banham, Reyner. *Theory and Design in the Machine Age.* 2nd ed. New York: Praeger Publishers, 1967.

Beatley, Timothy. *Green Urbanism: Learning from European Cities.* Washington, D.C.: Island Press, 2000.

Belasco, Warren James. *Americans on the Road: From Autocamp to Motel, 1910–1945.* Cambridge: MIT Press, 1979.

Bletter, Rosemarie Haag; Morris Dickstein; Helen A. Harrison; Marc H. Miller; Sheldon J. Reaven; and Ileen Sheppard, *Remembering the Future: The New York World's Fair From 1939 to 1964.* Introduction by Robert Rosenblum. New York: The Queens Museum/ Rizzoli, 1989.

Buisseret, David, ed. *Envisioning the City: Six Studies in Urban Cartography.* Chicago: University of Chicago Press, 1998.

Choay, Françoise. *The Modern City: Planning in the 19th Century.* New York: George Braziller, 1969.

Congress for the New Urbanism. *Charter of the New Urbanism.* Edited by Michael Leccese and Kathleen McCormick. New York: McGraw-Hill, 2000.

Davis, Timothy. "Rock Creek and Potomac Parkway, Washington, D.C.: The Evolution of a Contested Landscape." *Studies in the History of Gardens and Designed Landscapes* 19:2 (April–June 1999): 123–237.

Derrida, Jacques, and Peter Eisenman. *Chora L Works.* Edited by Jeffrey Kipnis and Thomas Leeser. New York: Monacelli Press, 1997.

Donald, James. *Imagining the Modern City.* London: Athlone Press, 1999.

Duany, Andres, Elizabeth Plater-Zyberk, and Jeff Speck. *Suburban Nation: The Rise of Sprawl and the Decline of the American Dream.* New York: Farrar, Straus and Giroux, North Point Press, 2000.

Dunlop, Beth. *The Art of Disney Architecture.* New York: Harry N. Abrams, 1996.

Evenson, Norma. *Le Corbusier: The Machine and the Grand Design.* New York: George Braziller, 1969.

Findlay, John M. *Magic Lands: Western Cities and American Culture after 1940.* Berkeley: University of California Press, 1992.

Francis, Mark; Lisa Cashdan; and Lynn Paxson. *Community Open Spaces: Greening Neighborhoods Through Community Action and Land Conservation.* Washington, D.C.: Island Press, 1984.

Galantay, Ervin Y. *New Towns: Antiquity to the Present.* New York: George Braziller, 1975.

Gans, Herbert. *The Levittowners: How People Live and Politic in Suburbia.* New York: Pantheon Books, 1967.

Garnier, Tony. *Une Cité Industrielle.* Translated by Andrew Ellis (with reproduction of the plates of the 1932 edition). New York: Rizzoli, 1990.

Gelernter, David. *1939: The Lost World of the Fair.* New York: Avon, 1995.

Girling, Cynthia L., and Kenneth I. Helphand. *Yard, Street, Park: The Design of Suburban Open Space.* New York: John Wiley & Sons, 1994.

Girouard, Mark. *Cities and People.* New Haven: Yale University Press, 1985.

Grese, Robert F. *Jens Jensen: Maker of Parks and Gardens.* Baltimore: Johns Hopkins University Press, 1992.

Groth, Paul, and Todd W. Bressi, eds. *Understanding Ordinary Landscapes.* New Haven: Yale University Press, 1997.

Halprin, Lawrence. *Cities.* New York: Reinhold Publishing Corporation, 1963.

———. *Freeways.* New York: Reinhold Publishing Company, 1966.

———. *The RSVP Cycles: Creative Processes in the Human Environment.* New York: George Braziller, 1969.

Hancock, John. "John Nolen: New Towns in Florida (1922–1929)." In *The New City.* Vol.1, *Foundations.* Coral Gables, Fl.: University of Miami School of Architecture, 1991.

Hayden, Dolores. *The Power of Place: Urban Landscapes as Public History.* Cambridge: MIT Press, 1995.

Howard, Ebenezer. *Garden Cities of To-Morrow.* London: Faber and Faber Ltd., 1946.

Horowitz, Helen Lefkowitz. *Culture and the City: Cultural Philanthropy in Chicago from the 1880s to 1917.* Chicago: University of Chicago Press, 1976.

Hynes, H. Patricia. *A Patch of Eden: America's Inner City Gardens.* White River Junction, Vt.: Chelsea Green Publishing, 1996.

Jackson, Kenneth. *Crabgrass Frontier: The Suburbanization of the United States.* New York: Oxford University Press, 1985.

Jacobs, Jane. *The Death and Life of Great American Cities.* New York: Random House, 1961.

Jensen, Jens. *"Siftings," The Major Portion of "The Clearing" and Collected Writings.* Chicago: Ralph Fletcher Seymour, 1956.

Johnson, David A. *Planning the Great Metropolis: The 1929 Regional Plan of New York and Its Environs.* London: E &FN Spon, an imprint of Chapman & Hall, 1996.

Jordon, David P. *Transforming Paris: The Life and Labors of Baron Haussmann.* New York: Free Press, 1995.

Katz, Peter. *The New Urbanism: Toward an Architecture of Community.* New York: McGraw-Hill, 1994.

Kelbaugh, Douglas. *Common Place: Toward Neighborhood and Regional Design.* Seattle: University of Washington Press, 1997.

Kelly, Barbara M. *Expanding the American Dream: Building and Rebuilding Levittown.* Albany: State University of New York Press, 1993.

Kent, Conrad, and Dennis Prindle. *Park Güell.* New York: Princeton Architectural Press, 1993.

Lee, Joseph. "Play as Landscape." *Charities and The Commons* 16:14 (July 7, 1906).

Lejeune, Jean-François. "Jean-Claude Nicolas Forestier: The City as Landscape." In *The New City.* Vol.1, *Foundations.* Coral Gables, Fl.: University of Miami School of Architecture, 1991.

Longstreth, Richard. *City Center to Regional Mall: Architecture, the Automobile, and Retailing in Los Angles, 1920–1950.* Cambridge: MIT Press, 1997.

Lubove, Roy. *The Urban Community: Housing and Planning in the Progressive Era.* Englewood Cliffs, N.J.: Prentice-Hall, 1967.

Malmberg, Melody. *The Making of Disney's Animal Kingdom Theme Park.* New York: Hyperion, 1998.

Marling, Karal Ann, ed. *Designing Disney's Theme Parks: The Architecture of Reassurance.* Paris: Flammarion, 1997.

McHarg, Ian L. *Design with Nature.* 25th Anniversary ed. New York: John Wiley & Sons, 1992.

Meacham, Standish. *Regaining Paradise: Englishness and the Early Garden City Movement.* New Haven: Yale University Press, 1999.

Moore, Charles, ed. *The Improvement of the Park System of the District of Columbia.* Washington, D.C.: Government Printing Office, 1902.

Osborn, F. J. *Green-Belt Cities: The British Contribution.* London: Faber and Faber, 1946.

Reps, John W. *Monumental Washington: The Planning and Development of the Capital Center.* Princeton, N.J.: Princeton University Press, 1967.

Robinson, Charles Mulford. *Modern Civic Art, or The City Made Beautiful.* 2nd ed. New York: G. P. Putnam's Sons, 1904.

Rowe, Peter G. *Making a Middle Landscape.* Cambridge: MIT Press, 1991.

Sexton, Richard. *Parallel Utopias: Sea Ranch, California, Seaside, Florida.* San Francisco: Chronicle Books, 1995.

Sies, Mary Corbin, and Christopher Silver, eds. *Planning the Twentieth-Century American City.* Baltimore: Johns Hopkins University Press, 1996.

Sniderman, Julia, and William W. Tippens. *A Breath of Fresh Air: Chicago's Neighborhood Parks of the Progressive Reform Era, 1900–1925.* Chicago: Special Collections Department, The Chicago Public Library, and the Chicago Park District, 1989.

Sorkin, Michael, ed. *Variations on a Theme Park: The New American City and the End of Public Space.* New York: The Noonday Press, 1992.

Spirn, Anne Whiston. *The Granite Garden: Urban Nature and Human Design.* New York: Basic Books, 1984.

Stein, Clarence. *Toward New Towns for America.* New York: Reinhold Publishing Corporation, 1957.

———. *The Writings of Clarence Stein.* Edited by Kermit Carlyle Parsons. Baltimore: Johns Hopkins University Press, 1998.

Stern, Robert A.M.; Gregory Gilmartin; and Thomas Mellins. *New York 1930: Architecture and Urbanism Between the Two World Wars.* New York: Rizzoli, 1987.

Triggs, H. Inigo. *Town Planning Past, Present and Possible.* London: Methuen & Co., 1909.

Tschumi, Bernard. *Cinégramme Folie: Le Parc de la Villette.* Princeton, N.J.: Princeton Architectural Press, 1987.

Tunnard, Christopher. *The City of Man.* New York: Charles Scribner's Sons, 1953.

———. *The Modern American City.* New York: Van Nostrand Reinhold Company, 1968.

Unwin, Raymond. *Town Planning in Practice.* 7th ed. London: Adelphi Terrace, 1920.

Venturi, Robert; Denise Scott Brown; and Steven Izenour. *Learning from Las Vegas: The Forgotten Symbolism of Architectural Form.* Rev. ed. Cambridge: MIT Press, 1977.

Waldie, Donald J. *Holy Land: A Suburban Memoir.* New York: W. W. Norton, 1996.

Warner, Sam Bass, Jr. *To Dwell Is to Garden.* Boston: Northeastern University Press, 1987.

Weimer, David R., ed. *City and Country in America.* New York: Appleton-Century-Crofts, 1962.

Wiebenson, Dora. *Tony Garnier: The Cité Industrielle.* New York: George Braziller, 1969.

Wojtowicz, Robert. *Lewis Mumford & American Modernism.* Cambridge: Cambridge University Press, 1996.

Zepp, Ira G. *The New Religious Image of Urban America: The Shopping Mall as Ceremonial Center.* Niwot: University Press of Colorado, 1986.

Zukin, Sharon. *Landscapes of Power: From Detroit to Disney World.* Berkeley: University of California Press, 1991.

INDEX

Note: Page numbers in italics refer to illustrations.

PHOTOGRAPH CREDITS